1996

CURRENT ISSUES AND ENDURING QUESTIONS

A Guide to Critical Thinking and Argument, with Readings

Fourth Edition

SYLVAN BARNET
Professor of English, Tufts University

HUGO BEDAU
Professor of Philosophy, Tufts University

Bedford Books *of* St. Martin's Press   BOSTON

For Bedford Books
President and Publisher: Charles H. Christensen
General Manager and Associate Publisher: Joan E. Feinberg
Managing Editor: Elizabeth M. Schaaf
Developmental Editor: Stephen A. Scipione
Editorial Assistant: Mark Reimold
Production Editor: Heidi Hood
Production Assistant: Pauline Chin
Copyeditor: Nancy Bell Scott
Cover Design: Diane Levy

Library of Congress Catalog Card Number: 95–76720

Manufactured in the United States of America.

0 9 8 7 6
f e d c b

For information, write: St. Martin's Press, Inc.
175 Fifth Avenue, New York, NY 10010

Editorial Offices: Bedford Books *of* St. Martin's Press
75 Arlington Street, Boston, MA 02116

ISBN: 0–312–11505–9

Acknowledgments
Floyd Abrams, "Save Free Speech," from the *New York Times*, November 23, 1993. Copyright © 1993 by the New York Times Company. Reprinted by permission.
Jonathan H. Adler, "Little Green Lies: The Environmental Miseducation of America's Children," from *Policy Review*, Summer 1992. Reprinted by permission.
Gar Alperovitz, "The U.S. Was Wrong," from the *New York Times*, August 8, 1985. Copyright © 1985 by the New York Times Company. Reprinted by permission.
W. H. Auden, "The Unknown Citizen," from *W. H. Auden: Collected Poems*, by W. H. Auden. Copyright © 1940 and renewed 1968 by W. H. Auden. Reprinted by permission of Random House, Inc. and Faber and Faber Ltd.
William J. Bennett, "Drug Policy and the Intellectuals," from *Drug Policy, 1989–1990: A Reformer's Catalogue Guide*, edited by Arnold S. Trebach and Kevin B. Zeese. Reprinted by permission of the Drug Policy Foundation, Washington, D.C.
Vivian Berger, "Rolling the Dice to Decide Who Dies," from the *New York State Bar Journal*, October 1988, vol. 60, no. 6. Reprinted by permission of the New York State Bar Association.
Derek Bok, "Protecting Freedom of Expression on the Campus" (editors' title), from "Protecting Freedom of Expression at Harvard," in the *Boston Globe*, May 25, 1991. Reprinted by permission of the author.

Preface

This book is a text—a book about reading other people's arguments and writing your own arguments—and it is also an anthology—a collection of more than a hundred essays, ranging from Plato to the present, with a strong emphasis on contemporary arguments. In a moment we will be a little more specific about what sorts of essays we include, but first we want to mention our chief assumptions about the aims of a course that might use *Current Issues and Enduring Questions: A Guide to Critical Thinking and Argument, with Readings.*

Probably most students and instructors would agree that, *as critical readers*, students should be able to

1. summarize accurately an argument they have read;
2. locate the thesis of an argument;
3. locate the assumptions, stated and unstated;
4. analyze and evaluate the strength of the evidence and the soundness of the reasoning offered in support of the thesis;
5. analyze, evaluate, and account for discrepancies among various readings on a topic (for example, explain why certain facts are used or not used, why two sources might differently interpret the same facts).

Probably, too, students and instructors would agree that, *as thoughtful writers*, students should be able to

1. imagine an audience, and write effectively for it (by such means as using the appropriate tone and providing the appropriate amount of detail);
2. present information in an orderly and coherent way;

3. incorporate sources into their own writing, not simply by quoting extensively or by paraphrasing, but also by having digested materials so that they can present it in their own words;

4. properly document all borrowings — not merely quotations and paraphrases but also borrowed ideas;

5. do all these things in the course of developing a thoughtful argument of their own.

Part One · In Part One (Chapters 1–6) we offer a short course in methods of thinking about arguments and in methods of writing arguments. By "thinking" we mean serious analytic thought; by "writing" we mean the use of effective, respectable techniques, not gimmicks such as the notorious note a politician scribbled in the margin of the text of his speech: "Argument weak; shout here." For a delightfully wry account of the use of gimmicks, we recommend that you consult "The Art of Controversy," in *The Will to Live,* by the nineteenth-century German philosopher Arthur Schopenhauer. Schopenhauer reminds his reader that a Greek or Latin quotation (however irrelevant) can be impressive to the uninformed, and that one can win almost any argument by loftily saying, "That's all very well in theory, but it won't do in practice."

We offer lots of advice about setting forth an argument, but we do not offer instruction in one-upmanship. Rather, we discuss responsible ways of arguing persuasively. We know, however, that before one can write a persuasive argument one must clarify one's own ideas — and that includes arguing with oneself — in order to find out what one really thinks about a problem. Therefore we devote Chapter 1 to critical thinking, Chapters 2 and 3 to critical reading, and Chapters 4, 5, and 6 to critical writing. These chapters are not all lecturing: They include twenty-two arguments (three are by students) for analysis and discussion.

All of the essays in the book are accompanied by questions. This is not surprising, given the emphasis we place on asking oneself questions in order to get ideas for writing. Among the chief questions that writers should ask, we suggest, are such matters as "What is X?" and "What is the value of X?" (pp. 1–9). By asking such questions — for instance (to look only at these two types of questions), "Is the fetus a person?" or "Is Arthur Miller a better playwright than Tennessee Williams?" — a writer probably will find ideas coming, at least after a few moments of head-scratching. The device of developing an argument by identifying issues is of course nothing new; indeed, it goes back to an ancient method of argument used by classical rhetoricians, who proceeded by identifying a *stasis* (an issue) and then asked questions about it: Did X do such-and-such? If so, was the action bad? If bad, how bad? And so on.

In keeping with our emphasis on writing as well as reading, we raise issues not only of what can roughly be called the "content" of the essays but also of what can (equally roughly) be called the "style" — that is, the ways in which the arguments are set forth. Content and style, of course, cannot finally be kept apart. As Cardinal Newman said, "Thought and meaning are inseparable from each other. . . . *Style is thinking out into language.*" In our questions we sometimes ask the student to evaluate the effectiveness of the opening paragraph, or to explain a shift in tone from one paragraph to the next, or to characterize the persona of the author as revealed in the whole essay. In short, the book is not designed as an introduction to some powerful ideas (though in fact it is that, too); it is designed as an aid to writing thoughtful, effective arguments on important political, social, scientific, ethical, and religious issues.

The essays reprinted in this book also illustrate different styles of argument that arise, at least in part, from the different disciplinary backgrounds of the various authors. Essays by journalists, lawyers, social scientists, policy analysts, philosophers, critics, activists, and other writers — including undergraduates — will be found in these pages. The authors develop and present their views in arguments that have distinctive features reflecting their special training and concerns. The differences in argumentative styles found in these essays foreshadow the differences students will encounter in the readings assigned in many of their other courses.

Part One, then, is a preliminary (but we hope substantial) discussion of such topics as *getting ideas, using sources, evaluating kinds of evidence,* and *organizing material,* as well as an introduction to some ways of thinking.

Part Two · Part Two, *Readings: Current Issues,* begins with one chapter that includes nine debates (pairs of opposing arguments) on such topics as bilingual education, gun control, and prayer in school. The bulk of the section is devoted to nine additional chapters, in each of which several voices speak, on such topics as AIDS, the legalization of drugs, the environment, immigration, multiculturalism, and sexual harassment. (In effect, these chapters, which range from three essays to seven essays, are mini-casebooks, suitable for controlled research papers.)

Part Three · Part Three, *Readings: Enduring Questions,* extends the arguments to such topics as "What Is the Ideal Society?" and "What Are the Grounds of Religious Faith?" Here the reader encounters classical writers such as St. Paul, Machiavelli, Jefferson, and Mill, as well as such contemporary writers as Irving Kristol, Ursula K. Le Guin, and Mitsuye Yamada.

Of the contemporary selections in the book (drawn chiefly from such sources as *Ms., The Nation, National Review,* the *New York Times*), many are very short — scarcely longer than the five-hundred-word essays that students are often asked to write.

Part Four · Part Four, *Further Perspectives,* begins with "A Literary Critic's View: Arguing about Literature." These pages should help students to see what sorts of things literary critics argue about and *how* they argue, so the students can then apply what they have learned to the literary readings that appear among the *Enduring Questions*, where we include three stories, seven poems, and a one-act play.

The second chapter in Part Four is a summary of the philosopher Stephen Toulmin's method for analyzing arguments. This summary will assist those who wish to apply Toulmin's methods to the readings in our book. The third chapter, a more rigorous analysis of deduction, induction, and fallacies than is usually found in textbooks designed for composition courses, reexamines from a logician's point of view material already treated briefly in Chapter 3. The fourth chapter, again on logic, is Max Shulman's amusing story, "Love Is a Fallacy." The fifth chapter, an essay by psychotherapist Carl R. Rogers, complements the discussion of audience, organization, and tone in Chapter 5.

The Instructor's Edition includes the appendix, "Resources for Teaching," containing detailed suggestions about ways in which the essays may be approached, and many additional suggestions for writing.

New to the Fourth Edition · In preparing the fourth edition we were greatly aided by suggestions from instructors who were using the third edition. In line with their recommendations, we have amplified the first chapter, a discussion of critical thinking, which examines the roles of imagination, analysis, and evaluation. Also new to Part One are nine of the twenty-two essays, including a new research paper on televising trials. Among the other new essays are "Just Take Away Their Guns" and "Five Myths about Immigration."

In Part Two we have included (in the nine paired debates) new essays on prayer in school and on sex education. In the chapters with more than two essays on a topic, we have added two new topics, "Immigration" and "Television Violence," and we have made many substitutions in the sections that we have retained from the previous edition.

In Part Three, *Readings: Enduring Questions,* we now include eleven works of literature.

In Part Four, "A Literary Critic's View: Arguing about Literature" is new.

There can be no argument about the urgency of the topics that we have added, but there can be lots of argument about the merits of the positions offered in the selections. That's where the users of the book, students and instructors alike, come in.

Note: For instructors who do not require a text with a large number of essays, a shorter edition of this book, *Critical Thinking, Reading, and Writing,* is also available. The shorter version contains the first six chapters of the present book (all of the material on critical thinking, reading, and writing) with twenty-eight essays, including three pairs of debates. It also contains five chapters of Part Four, with (1) material on arguing about literature; (2) the material on Toulmin; (3) additional material on deduction;

induction, and fallacies; (4) Max Shulman's "Love Is a Fallacy"; and (5) Carl R. Roger's essay on communication.

Acknowledgments • Finally, it is our pleasant duty to thank those who have strengthened the book by their advice: Roy M. Anker, Calvin College; Robert Baird, University of Illinois; Claudia Basha, Victor Valley College; Mark Bedau; Frank Beesley, University of Nebraska at Lincoln; Donavin Bennes, University of North Dakota; Laurie J. Bergamini, State University of New York at Plattsburgh; Jeffrey Berger, Community College of Philadelphia; B. J. Bowman, Radford University; Anthony Boyle, Fairleigh Dickinson University; Moana Boyle, Ricks College; Beverly M. Braud, Southwest Texas State University; Edward Brooks, Bergen Community College; Duane Bruce, University of Hartford; Jacintha Burke, King's College; Janet Carter, Bridgewater State College; Brandon Cesmat, Palomar College; Claire Chantell, University of Illinois at Urbana–Champaign; Jo Chern, University of Wisconsin at Green Bay; Barbara G. Clark, Adams State College; Denise Clark, Santa Clara University; James Clarke, Washington State University; Lorna Clymer, University of California at Santa Barbara; Sherill Cobb, Collin County Community College; Bobbie Cohen, Florida University; Paul Cohen, Southwest Texas State University; Minnie A. Collins, Seattle Central Community College; Marie Conte, California State University–Dominguez Hills; Genevieve Coogan, Houston Northwest Community College; Dr. Michael E. Cooley, Berry College; Susan Carolyn Cowan, University of Southern California; Linda Daigle, Houston Central Community College; Anne D'Arcy, California State University–Hayward; Fara Darland, Scottsdale Community College; Kent R. DeVault, Central Washington University; Robert Denham, Roanoke College; Allen DiWederburg, Clockamas Community College; Carl Dockery, Tri-County Community College; Paula Doctor, Muskegon Community College; Alberta M. Dougan, Southeast Missouri State University; Elizabeth Elclepp, Rancho Santiago Community College; Diane El-Rouaiheb, University of Louisville; Hal Enger, San Diego Mesa College; Dianne Fallon, State University of New York at Binghamton; Amy Farmer, University of Illinois; John Finnegan, West Liberty State College; Jane Fischer, Southwest State University; Anne Marie Frank, Elmhurst College; Amy Freed, Virginia Polytechnic Institute; Michael J. Galgano, James Madison University; Joseph E. Geist, Central Methodist College; Sheryl Gobble, San Diego City College; Stuart Goodman, Duke University; Mary Anne F. Grabarek, Durham Technical Community College; Tim Gracyk, Santa Clara University; Becky C. Graham, Livingston University; Rebecca Graham, University of Minnesota–Morris; Richard Grande, Pennsylvania State University; Mark A. Graves, Bowling Green State University; Verge Hagopian, Orange Coast College; Dennis R. Hall, University of Louisville; William M. Hamlin, Idaho State University; Donald Heidt, College of the Canyons; Charles Heimler, California State University at Hayward; Janet Ruth Heller, Grand Valley State University; John C. Herold, Elon College;

Edwin L. Hetfield, Jr., Onondaga Community College; Katherine Hoffman, Roanoke College; Pau-San Hoh, Marist College; Cathy Hope, Tarleton State University; Diane W. Howard, Valdosta State University; Barbara Hunter, Wright College; Joan Hutchison, Oakland Community College; Dr. Brian D. Ingraffia, Biola University; Shelly Jaffray, Rancho Santiago Community College; Alison Jasper, California Polytechnic State University; Janet Juhnke, Kansas Wesleyan University; Diane M. Kammeyer, Anoka-Ramsey Community College; Priscilla Kelly, Slippery Rock University; Mary Jane Kinnebrew, San Jacinto College Central; Geoffrey Klinger, University of Iowa; Bobbie Knable, Tufts University; Prudence Kohl, Baldwin–Wallace College; Elaine W. Kromhout, Indian River Community College; Brother Christopher Lambert, Quincy College; Richard L. Larson, Lehman College; John Lawing, Regent University; J. N. Lee, Portland State University; Charles Lefcourt, State University of New York at Buffalo; Elizabeth Lewis, Manhattanville College; L. M. Lewis, University of Texas at Brownsville; Alex Liddie, Trenton State College; Miriam Lilley, College of the Canyons; John Little, James Madison University; Martin Litz, Raymond Walters College; Warren H. Loveless, Indiana State University; Christopher Lukasik, University of Washington; Tom Lynch, California State University at Hayward; Carter Lyons, James Madison University; Marcia MacLennan, Kansas Wesleyan University; Kelli Maloy, West Virginia University; Ruth E. Manson, South Dakota State University; Diane Marlett, University of Wisconsin at Green Bay; Brian Massey, Winthrop College; Alice Maudsley, Cleveland State University; James May, Pennsylvania State University; Nelly McFeely, California State University and Merritt College; Ted McFerrin, Collin County Community College; Natalie McKnight, Boston University; Dan C. Miller, University of Northern Colorado; Peggy A. Moore, College of Siskiyous; Mary Munsil, University of Southern California; Cris Newport, New Hampshire Technical Institute; Melanie Ohler; Leonard Orr, Washington State University; Roswell Park, State University of New York at Buffalo; Scott Payne, University of Louisville; Robert Peltier, Trinity College; Nancy P. Pope, Washington University; Constance Putnam; Jan Rainbird, California State University at Fullerton; Sally Lynn Raines, West Virginia University; Elaine Reed, Kutztown University; M. Resnick, State University of New York at Farmingdale; Dan Richards; Susan Roberson, Auburn University; Helen M. Robinette, Glassboro State College; Linda Rosekraus, State University of New York, College at Cortland; Jennifer O. Rosti, Roanoke College; Julie H. Rubio, University of Southern California at Long Beach; Rebecca Sabounchi, University of Texas; Suzette Schlapkohl, Scottsdale Community College; Henry Schwarzschild; Andrew J. Smyth, St. Louis University; Lynn Steiner, Cuesta College; Skaidrite Stelzer, University of Toledo; Elisabeth Stephens, University of North Carolina at Greensboro; Ed Stieve, Nova College; Barbara W. Stewart, Long Beach City College; Suba Subbarao, Oakland Community College; Catherine Sutton, University of Louisville; Richard C. Taylor, East Carolina University; Diane Thompson,

Harrisburg Area Community College; Eve Thompson, College of the Siskiyons; Linda Toonen, University of Wisconsin at Green Bay; David Tumpleman, Monroe Community College; Pauline Uchmanowicz, University of Rhode Island; Lynn A. Walkiewicz, Cazenovia College; Kathleen Walsh, Central Oregon Community College; Nancy Weingart, John Carrol University; Stephen White; Phyllis C. Whitesoll, Franklin and Marshall College; Allen D. Widerburg, Clackamas Community College; Marilyn Wienk, Elmira College; Stephen Wilhoit, University of Dayton; Michelle L. Zath, Berry College; Bruce D. Zessin, University of Wisconsin at Waukesha.

We are also indebted to the people at Bedford Books, especially Charles H. Christensen, Joan E. Feinberg, Stephen A. Scipione, Elizabeth M. Schaaf, Heidi Hood, and Mark Reimold, who offered many valuable (and invaluable) suggestions. Intelligent, informed, firm yet courteous, they really know how to think, and how to argue.

Brief Contents

Contents

4 Critical Writing: Writing an Analysis of an Argument • 73

Part Three
READINGS: ENDURING QUESTIONS · 533

Part Four
FURTHER PERSPECTIVES ON ARGUMENT · 727

Part One

CRITICAL THINKING, READING, AND WRITING: A BRIEF GUIDE TO ARGUMENT

1

Critical Thinking

LEARNING FROM JACK BENNY

The comedian Jack Benny cultivated the stage personality of a penny-pincher. In one of his skits a stickup man thrusts a gun into Benny's ribs and says, "Your money or your life." Utter silence. The robber, getting no response, and completely baffled, repeats, "Your money or your life." Short pause, followed by Benny's exasperated reply: "I'm *thinking*, I'm *thinking!*"

Without making too much of this gag, we want to point out that Benny is using the word "thinking" in the sense that we use it in "critical thinking." "Thinking," by itself, can mean almost any sort of mental activity, from idle daydreaming ("During the chemistry lecture I kept thinking about how I'd like to go camping") to careful analysis ("I'm thinking about whether I can afford more than one week — say two weeks — of camping in the Rockies," or even "I'm thinking about *why* Benny's comment strikes me as funny," or, "I'm thinking about why you find Benny's comment funny and I don't").

In short, when we add the adjective "critical" to the noun "thinking," we pretty much eliminate reveries, just as we also eliminate snap judgments. We are talking about searching for hidden assumptions, noticing various facets, unraveling different strands, and evaluating what is most significant. (The word *critical* comes from a Greek word, *krinein*, meaning "to separate," "to choose"; it implies conscious, deliberate inquiry.)

THINKING ABOUT DRIVER'S LICENSES
AND SCHOOL ATTENDANCE:
IMAGINATION, ANALYSIS, EVALUATION

By way of illustration let's think critically about a law passed in West Virginia in 1989. The law provides that although students may drop out of school at the age of sixteen, no dropout younger than eighteen can hold a driver's license.

But what ought we to think of such a law? Is it fair? What is its purpose? Is it likely to accomplish its purpose? Might it unintentionally do some harm, and, if so, can we weigh the potential harm against the potential good? Suppose you had been a member of the West Virginia state legislature in 1989: How would you have voted?

In thinking critically about a topic, we try to see it from all sides before we come to our conclusion. We conduct an argument with ourselves, advancing and then questioning opinions. What can be said *for* the proposition, and what can be said *against* it? Our first reaction may be quite uncritical, quite unthinking: "What a good idea!" or "That's outrageous!" But critical thinking requires us to reflect further, trying to support our position *and also* trying to see the other side. One can almost say that the heart of critical thinking is a *willingness to face objections to one's own beliefs,* a willingness to adopt a skeptical attitude not only toward authority and toward views opposed to our own, but also toward common sense, that is, toward the views that seem obviously right to us. If we assume we have a monopoly on the truth and we dismiss as bigots those who oppose us, or if we say our opponents are acting merely out of self-interest, and we do not in fact analyze their views, we are being critical but we are not engaged in critical thinking.

Critical thinking requires us to use our *imagination,* seeing things from perspectives other than our own and envisioning the likely consequences of our position. (This sort of imaginative thinking—grasping a perspective other than our own, and considering the possible consequences of positions—is, as we have said, very different from daydreaming, an activity of unchecked fantasy.)

Thinking critically involves, along with imagination (so that we can see our own beliefs from another point of view), a twofold activity:

analysis, separating the parts of the problem, trying to see how things fit together; and

evaluation, judging the merit of our assumptions and the weight of the evidence in their favor.

If we engage in imaginative, analytic, and evaluative thought, we will have second and third ideas; almost to our surprise we may find ourselves adopting a position that we initially couldn't imagine we would hold. As we think about the West Virginia law, we might find ourselves coming up with a fairly wide variety of ideas, each triggered by the preceding idea but not necessarily carrying it a step further. For instance, we may think X, and then immediately think, "No, that's not quite right. In fact, come to think of it, the opposite to X is probably true." We haven't carried X further, but we have progressed in our thinking.

WRITING AS A WAY OF THINKING

In thinking about a problem, it's useful to jot down your ideas. Seeing your ideas on paper—even in the briefest form—will help bring other ideas to mind, and will also help you to evaluate them. For instance, after jotting down ideas as they come and responses to them,

1. you might go on to organize them into two lists, pro and con;
2. next, you might delete ideas that, when you come to think about them, strike you as simply wrong or irrelevant, and
3. then you might develop those ideas that strike you as pretty good.

You probably won't know where you stand until you have gone through some such process. It would be nice if we could make a quick decision and then immediately justify it with three excellent reasons, and could give three further reasons showing why the opposing view is inadequate. In fact, however, we almost never can come to a reasoned decision without a good deal of preliminary thinking.

Consider again the West Virginia law. Here is a kind of inner dialogue that you might engage in as you think critically about it.

The purpose is to give students an incentive to stay in school by making them pay a price if they choose to drop out.

Adolescents will get the message that education really is important.

But, come to think of it, *will* they? Maybe they will see this as just another example of adults bullying young people.

According to a newspaper article, the dropout rate in West Virginia decreased by 30 percent in the year after the bill was passed.

Well, that sounds good, but is there any reason to think that kids who are pressured into staying really learn anything? The *assumption* behind the bill is that if would-be dropouts stay in school, they—and society—will gain. But is the assumption sound? Maybe such students will become resentful, will not learn anything, and may even be so disruptive that they will interfere with the learning of other students.

Notice how part of the job is *analytic,* recognizing the elements or complexities of the whole, and part is *evaluative,* judging the adequacy of all of these ideas, one by one. Both tasks require *imagination.*

So far we have jotted down a few thoughts, and then immediately given some second thoughts contrary to the first. Of course, the counter-thoughts might not immediately come to mind. For instance, they might not occur until we reread the jottings, or try to explain the law to a friend, or until we sit down and begin drafting an essay aimed at supporting or undermining the law. Most likely, in fact, some good ideas won't occur until a second or third or fourth draft.

Here are some further thoughts on the West Virginia law. We list them more or less as they arose and as we typed them into a word processor — not sorted out neatly into two groups, pro and con, nor evaluated as you would want to do in further critical thinking of your own. And of course a later step would be to organize the material into some useful pattern. As you read, you might jot down your own responses in the margin.

Education is <u>not</u> optional, something left for the individual to take or not to take--like going to a concert, or jogging, or getting annual health checkups, or getting eight hours of sleep each night. Society has determined that it is <u>for the public good</u> that citizens have a substantial education, so we require education up to a certain age.

Come to think about it, maybe the criterion of age doesn't make much sense. If we want an educated citizenry, it would make more sense to require people to attend school until they demonstrated competence in certain matters, rather than until they reached a certain age. Exceptions of course would be made for mentally retarded persons, and perhaps for certain other groups.

What is needed is not legal pressure to keep teenagers in school, but schools that hold the interest of teenagers.

A sixteen-year-old usually is not mature enough to make a decision of this importance.

Still, a sixteen-year-old who finds school unsatisfying and who therefore drops out may become a perfectly useful citizen.

Denying a sixteen-year-old a driver's license may work in West Virginia, but it would scarcely work in a state with great urban areas, where most high school students rely on public transportation.

We earn a driver's license by demonstrating certain skills. The state has no right to take away such

a license unless we have demonstrated that we
are unsafe drivers.

To prevent a person of sixteen from having a driver's
license prevents that person from holding certain kinds of jobs, and that's unfair.

A law of this sort deceives adults into thinking that
they have really done something constructive for
teenage education, but it may work <u>against</u>
improving the schools. If we are really serious
about educating youngsters, we have to examine
the curriculum and the quality of our teachers.

Doubtless there is much that we haven't said, on both sides, but we hope
you will agree that the issue deserves thought. (A number of state legislatures are indeed thinking about bills resembling the West Virginia law.)
And if you were a member of the legislature of West Virginia in 1989 you
would have *had* to think about the issue.

One other point about this issue: *Today,* if you had to think about the
matter, you might also want to know whether the West Virginia legislation
of 1989 is considered a success, and on what basis. That is, you would want
to get answers to such questions as the following:

1. What sort of evidence tends to support the law or tends to suggest
   that the law is a poor idea?
2. Did the reduction in the dropout rate continue, or did the reduction occur only in the first year following the passage of the law?
3. If indeed students did not drop out, was their presence in school a
   good thing, both for them and for their classmates?
4. Have some people emerged as authorities on this topic? What
   makes them authorities, and what do they have to say?
5. Has the constitutionality of the bill been tested? With what results?

Some of these questions require you to do **research** on the topic. The
questions raise issues of fact, and some relevant evidence probably is available. If you are to arrive at a conclusion in which you can have confidence,
you will have to do some research to find out what the facts are.

Even without doing any research, however, you might want to look
over the ideas, pro and con, perhaps adding some totally new thoughts, or
perhaps modifying or even rejecting (for reasons that you can specify)
some of those already given. If you do think a bit further about this issue,
and we hope that you will, notice an interesting point about *your own*
thinking: It probably is not "linear" (moving in a straight line from A to B to
C) but "recursive," moving from A to C, back to B, or starting over at C and
then back to A and B. By zigging and zagging almost despite yourself, you'll
get to a conclusion that may finally seem correct. In retrospect it seems ob-

vious; *now* you can chart a nice line from A to B to C—but that was not at all evident to you at the start.

ASPECTS OF CRITICAL THINKING

Attitudes

Imaginative open-mindedness; intellectual curiosity

Willingness to examine one's own assumptions

Willingness to entertain new ideas—both those that you encounter while reading and those that come to mind while you are writing

Willingness to exert oneself, for instance to do research in order to acquire information and to evaluate evidence

Skills

Ability to summarize an argument accurately

Ability to evaluate assumptions, evidence, and inferences

Ability to effectively present one's ideas—e.g., ability to organize and to write in a manner appropriate to the imagined audience

---

EXAMINING ASSUMPTIONS

In Chapter 3 we will discuss **assumptions** (normally, unexamined beliefs) in some detail, but here we want to emphasize the importance of *examining* assumptions, both those that you encounter when you read and those that underlie your own essays.

Let's think a bit further about the West Virginia driver's license law. What assumptions did the legislature make in enacting this statute? We earlier mentioned one such assumption: If the law helped to keep teenagers from dropping out of school, then that was a good thing for them and for society in general. Perhaps the legislature made this assumption *explicit* and its advocate defended it on this ground. Perhaps not; maybe the legislature just took this point for granted, leaving this assumption *implicit* (or *tacit*) and unargued, believing that everyone *shared* the assumption. But of course everyone didn't share it, in particular many teenagers who wanted to drop out of school at sixteen and get their driver's license immediately.

The distinction between shared and unshared assumptions becomes critical when we consider their role in a partisan debate. (Below, we'll take a closer look at an actual debate of this sort.) As in the driver's license law, assumptions in debates can be either tacit or explicit. Further, in a debate assumptions can be either *shared* by both sides or *specific* to each side. Assumptions that you and your opponent share, especially if they are made explicit, play the important role of framing the debate. That is, they demark the outer edges of discussion, where both sides agree and so no argument over them need arise. The specific assumptions made by one side, however, are prime targets for criticism by the other side, especially if these assumptions have been left unstated. Any argument that relies on a tacit and perhaps dubious assumption is a prime candidate for refutation. Point out to your opponents that they have made — perhaps all unawares — tacit assumptions that can seriously weaken or even dissolve their argument.

Let's look at two essays that originally appeared in *Women's Sports & Fitness Magazine* (July/August 1990). The first is by an author who has written a book about competition; the second is an abridgement of an essay by an author who has written about sports.

Alfie Kohn

Competition Is Destructive

I learned my first game at a birthday party. You remember it: X players scramble for X-minus-one chairs each time the music stops. In every round a child is eliminated until at the end only one is left triumphantly seated while everyone else is standing on the sidelines, excluded from play, unhappy . . . losers.

This is how we learn to have a good time in America.

Several years ago I wrote a book called *No Contest,* which, based on the findings of several hundred studies, argued that competition undermines self-esteem, poisons relationships, and holds us back from doing our best. I was mostly interested in the win/lose arrangement that defines our workplaces and classrooms, but I found myself nagged by the following question: If competition is so destructive and counterproductive during the week, why do we take for granted that it suddenly becomes benign and even desirable on the weekend?

This is a particularly unsettling line of inquiry for athletes or parents. Most of us, after all, assume that competitive sports teach all sorts of useful lessons and, indeed, that games by definition must produce a winner and a loser. But I've come to believe that recreation at its best does not require people to try to triumph over others. Quite the contrary.

Terry Orlick, a sports psychologist at the University of Ottawa, took a   5 look at musical chairs and proposed that we keep the basic format of removing chairs but change the goal; the point becomes to fit everyone on a diminishing number of seats. At the end, a group of giggling children tries to figure out how to squish onto a single chair. Everybody plays to the end; everybody has a good time.

Orlick and others have devised or collected hundreds of such games for children and adults alike. The underlying theory is simple: All games involve achieving a goal despite the presence of an obstacle, but nowhere is it written that the obstacle has to be someone else. The idea can be for each person on the field to make a specified contribution to the goal, or for all the players to reach a certain score, or for everyone to work with her partners against a time limit.

Note the significance of an "opponent" becoming a "partner." The entire dynamic of the game shifts, and one's attitude toward the other players changes with it. Even the friendliest game of tennis can't help but be affected by the game's inherent structure, which demands that each person try to hit the ball where the other can't get to it. You may not be a malicious person, but to play tennis means that you try to make the other person fail.

I've become convinced that not a single one of the advantages attributed to sports actually requires competition. Running, climbing, biking, swimming, aerobics — all offer a fine workout without any need to try to outdo someone else. Some people point to the camaraderie that results from teamwork, but that's precisely the benefit of cooperative activity, whose very essence is that *everyone* on the field is working together for a common goal. By contrast, the distinguishing feature of team competition is that a given player works with and is encouraged to feel warmly toward only half of those present. Worse, a we-versus-they dynamic is set up, which George Orwell once called "war minus the shooting."

The dependence on sports to provide a sense of accomplishment or to test one's wits is similarly misplaced. One can aim instead at an objective standard (How far did I throw? How many miles did we cover?) or attempt to do better than last week. Such individual and group striving — like cooperative games — provides satisfaction and challenge without competition.

If large numbers of people insist that we can't do without win/lose activities, the first question to ask is whether they've ever tasted the alternative. When Orlick taught a group of children noncompetitive games, two-thirds of the boys and all of the girls preferred them to the kind that require opponents. If our culture's idea of fun requires beating someone else, it may just be because we don't know any other way. 10

It may also be because we overlook the psychological costs of competition. Most people lose in most competitive encounters, and it's obvious why that causes self-doubt. But even winning doesn't build character: It just lets us gloat temporarily. Studies have shown that feelings of self-worth become dependent on external sources of evaluation as a result of competition; your value is defined by what you've done and who you've beaten. The whole affair soon becomes a vicious circle: The more you compete, the more you *need* to compete to feel good about yourself. It's like drinking salt water when you're thirsty. This process is bad enough for us; it's a disaster for our children.

While this is going on, competition is having an equally toxic effect on our relationships. By definition, not everyone can win a contest. That means that each child inevitably comes to regard others as obstacles to his or her own success. Competition leads children to envy winners, to dismiss losers (there's no nastier epithet in our language than "Loser!"), and to be suspicious of just about everyone. Competition makes it difficult to regard others as potential friends or collaborators; even if you're not my rival today, you could be tomorrow.

This is not to say that competitors will always detest one another. But trying to outdo someone is not conducive to trust—indeed it would be irrational to trust a person who gains from your failure. At best, competition leads one to look at others through narrowed eyes; at worst, it invites outright aggression.

But no matter how many bad feelings erupt during competition, we have a marvelous talent for blaming the individuals rather than focusing on the structure of the game itself, a structure that makes my success depend on your failure. Cheating may just represent the logical conclusion of this arrangement rather than an aberration. And sportsmanship is nothing more than an artificial way to try to limit the damage of competition. If we weren't set against each other on the court or the track, we wouldn't need to keep urging people to be good sports; they might well be working *with* each other in the first place.

As radical or surprising as it may sound, the problem isn't just that we 15 compete the wrong way or that we push winning on our children too early. The problem is competition itself. What we need to be teaching our daughters and sons is that it's possible to have a good time—a better time—without turning the playing field into a battlefield.

Mariah Burton Nelson

At Its Best, Competition Is Not Divisive

Competition can damage self-esteem, create anxiety, and lead to cheating and hurt feelings. But so can romantic love. No one suggests we do away with love; rather, we must perfect our understanding of what love means.

So too with competition. "To compete" is derived from the Latin *competere,* meaning "to seek together." Women seem to understand this. Maybe it's because we sat on the sidelines for so long, watching. Maybe it's because we were raised to be kind and nurturing. I'm not sure why it is. But I've noticed that it's not women who greet each other with a ritualistic

"Who won?"; not women who memorize scores and statistics; not women who pride themselves on "killer instincts." Passionate though we are, women don't take competition that seriously.

We understand that trying to win is not tantamount to trying to belittle; that winning is not wonderful if the process of play is not challenging, fair, or fun; and that losing, though at times disappointing, does not connote failure. For women, if sports are power plays, they're not about power over (power as dominance) but power to (power as competence). Sports are not about domination and defeat but caring and cooperation. . . .

I think it's the responsibility of these women — and the men who remain unblinded by the seductive glow of victory — to share this vision with young players. Children, it seems to me, naturally enjoy comparing their skills: "How far can you throw the ball? Farther than I can? How did you do it? Will you show me?" It's only when adults ascribe undue importance to victory that losing becomes devastating and children get hurt.

Adults must show children that what matters is how one plays the game. It's important that we not just parrot that cliché, but demonstrate our commitment to fair, participatory competition by paying equal attention to skilled and unskilled children; by allowing all children to participate fully in games, regardless of the score; and by caring more about the process than results.

Some of my best friends are the men and women who share a court or pool or field with me. Together we take risks, make mistakes, laugh, push ourselves, and revel in the grace and beauty of sports. Who wins? Who cares? . . . At its best, competition is not divisive but unifying, not hateful but loving. Like other expressions of love, it should not be avoided simply because it has been misunderstood.

In the pair of essays reprinted here on competition in games, sports, and play, both writers tacitly assume that *competition is open to debate* and *competition is widespread in social life.* These are the main background assumptions of both essays and they explain in part why Kohn and Nelson give special attention to these recreational activities. The authors also share the view that *we take competition in sports pretty much for granted.* They also assume that *games are a desirable leisure activity.* Each author wants to rescue games from the dangers of harmful competition, but they propose to do this in different ways. Thus, these shared assumptions only lay a basis for their different remedies.

Kohn assumes that *it is possible to engage in games and play without competition at all;* this is the basis for his argument that it is feasible and desirable to replace harmful competition with healthy cooperation. He also assumes that *we can weigh, more or less, the harms of competition against its benefits.* Nelson does not directly challenge these assumptions; instead, she builds her argument on the assumptions that *women are more coopera-*

tive than men and that *men can learn to be as cooperative as women, despite their more aggressive nature.*

As you read critically, think about the assumptions the writer is making. Ask yourself:

- Are these assumptions necessary? Plausible?
- Does the writer give any evidence of even being aware of the hidden assumptions of his or her argument?
- Are these assumptions important to the author's argument, or only incidental?
- Would a critic be likely to share them — or are these assumptions exactly what a critic would challenge?
- Are you willing to grant the assumptions in question? If not, why not?

Remember, also, to ask these questions (except the last) when you are reading your own drafts. And remember to ask yourself why some people may *not* grant *your* assumptions.

Exercises

1. Think further about the West Virginia law, jotting down pros and cons, and then write a balanced dialogue between two imagined speakers who hold opposing views on the merits of the law. You'll doubtless have to revise your dialogue several times, and in revising your drafts you will find that further ideas come to you. Present *both* sides as strongly as possible. (You may want to give the two speakers distinct characters; for instance, one may be a student who has dropped out and the other a concerned teacher, or one a parent — who perhaps argues that he or she needs the youngster to work full-time driving a delivery truck — and one a legislator. But do not feel that the speakers must present the arguments they might be expected to hold. A student might argue *for* the law, and a teacher *against* it.)

2. Take one of the following topics, and jot down all the pro and con arguments you can think of, in, say, ten minutes. Then, at least an hour or two later, return to your jottings and see whether you can add to them. Finally, as in Exercise 1, write a balanced dialogue, presenting each idea as strongly as possible. (If none of these topics interests you, talk with your instructor about the possibility of choosing a topic of your own.) Suggested topics:

    a. Colleges should not award athletic scholarships.
    b. Bicyclists and motorcyclists should be required by law to wear helmets.
    c. High school teachers should have the right to search students for drugs on school grounds.
    d. Smoking should be prohibited in all parts of all college buildings.
    e. College administrators should take no punitive action against students who use racist language or language that offends any minority.
    f. Students should have the right to drop out of school at any age.
    g. In rape trials the names of the alleged victims should not be released to the public.

   h. Schools should be permitted (in an effort to combat the spread of AIDS) to distribute free condoms to students who request them.

   i. Prayer should be allowed in public schools.

   j. Doctors should be required by law to be tested every six months to see if they are HIV positive.

3. Take one of your dialogues and turn it into an essay of 500 to 750 words arguing the position that you have come to believe is the soundest. Your essay will of course recognize the opposed view(s), but chiefly will offer reasons supporting the belief that you have come to hold.

(*Note:* Although your instructor may be your only reader, imagine your classmates as your audience.)

Much of the next three chapters will be devoted to the kinds of thinking that are necessary in order to write an effective argument, but at this point we suggest that you will probably be able to strengthen your essay if you adopt the following procedure. After you have written a draft and have reread it thoughtfully and revised it, ask a friend to read it also—with these questions in mind:

- Are crucial terms adequately defined?
- Is evidence offered to support assertions?
- Are opposing arguments adequately faced?
- Is the structure of the essay—especially the sequence of ideas and reasons that constitutes the overall arguments—based on the needs of a reader?

(On page 147 we give a much fuller list of questions that may be of help to a reader of a draft, but the four questions given here will serve for a start.)

2

Critical Reading:
Getting Started

Some books are to be tasted, others to be chewed, and some
few to be chewed and digested.
— FRANCIS BACON

ACTIVE READING

In the passage that we quote at the top of the page, Bacon makes at least two good points. One is that books are of varying worth; the second is that a taste of some books may be enough.

But even a book (or an essay) that you will chew and digest is one that you first may want to taste. How can you get a taste — that is, how can you get some sense of a piece of writing *before* you sit down to read it carefully?

Previewing

Even before you read the work you may have some ideas about it, perhaps because you already know something about the **author.** You know, for example, that a work by Martin Luther King, Jr., will probably deal with civil rights. You know, too, that it will be serious and eloquent. On the other hand, if you pick up an essay by Woody Allen you will probably expect it to be amusing. It may be serious — Allen has written earnestly about many topics, especially those concerned with the media — but it's your hunch that the essay will be at least somewhat entertaining and it probably will not be terribly difficult. In short, a reader who has some knowledge of the author probably has some idea of what the writing will be like, and so the reader reads it in a certain mood. Admittedly, most of the authors represented in this book are not widely known, but we give biographical notes that may provide you with some sense of what to expect.

The **place of publication** may also tell you something about the essay. For instance, *The National Review* (formerly edited by William F.

Buckley, Jr.) is a conservative journal. If you notice that an essay on affirmative action was published in *The National Review,* you are probably safe in tentatively assuming that the essay will not endorse affirmative action. On the other hand, *Ms.* is a liberal magazine for women, and an essay on affirmative action published in *Ms.* will probably be an endorsement.

The **title** of an essay, too, may give you an idea of what to expect. Of course a title may announce only the subject and not the author's thesis or point of view ("On Gun Control," "Should Drugs Be Legal?"), but fairly often it will indicate the thesis too, as in "Give Children the Vote" and "Gay Marriages: Make Them Legal." Knowing more or less what to expect, you can probably take in some of the major points even on a quick reading.

Skimming: Finding the Thesis

Although most of the material in this book is too closely argued to be fully understood by merely skimming, still, skimming can tell you a good deal. Read the first paragraph of an essay carefully, because it may announce the author's thesis (chief point, major claim), and it may give you some sense of how the argument for that thesis will be conducted. (What we call the thesis can also be called the main idea, or the point, or even the argument, but in this book we use *argument* to refer not only to the thesis statement but also to the entire development of the thesis in the essay.) Run your eye over the rest, looking for key expressions that indicate the author's conclusions, such as "It follows, then, that. . . ." Passages of this sort often occur as the first or last sentence in a paragraph. And of course pay attention to any headings within the text. Finally, pay special attention to the last paragraph because it probably will offer a summary and a brief restatement of the writer's thesis.

Having skimmed the work, you probably know the author's thesis, and you may detect the author's methods — for instance, whether the author supports the thesis chiefly by personal experience, or by statistics, or by ridicule of the opposition. You also have a clear idea of the length and some idea of the difficulty of the piece. You know, then, whether you can read it carefully now, before dinner, or whether you had better put off a careful reading until you have more time.

Reading with a Pencil:
Underlining, Highlighting, Annotating

Once you have a general idea of the work — not only an idea of its topic and thesis but also a sense of the way in which the thesis is argued — you can then go back and start reading it carefully.

As you read, **underline** or **highlight** key passages and make **annotations** in the margins (but not in library books, please). Because you are reading actively, or interacting with the text, you will not simply let your eye rove across the page. You will underline or highlight what seem to be the chief points, so that later when you review the essay you can easily locate the main passages. But don't overdo a good thing. If you find yourself underlining or highlighting most of a page, you are probably not thinking carefully enough about what the key points are. Similarly, your marginal annotations should be brief and selective. Probably they will consist of hints or clues, things like "really?," "doesn't follow," "!!!," "???," "good," "compare with Jones," and "check this." In short, in a paragraph you might underline or highlight a key definition, and in the margin you might write "good" or, on the other hand, "?," if you think the definition is fuzzy or wrong. You are interacting with the text, and laying the groundwork for eventually writing your own essay on what you have read.

What you annotate will depend largely on your **purpose.** If you are reading an essay in order to see the ways in which the writer organizes an argument, you will annotate one sort of thing. If you are reading in order to challenge the thesis, you will annotate other things. Here is a passage from an essay entitled "On Racist Speech," with a student's rather skeptical, even aggressive annotations. But notice that at least one of the annotations— "Definition of 'fighting words' " —apparently was made chiefly in order to remind the reader of where an important term appears in the essay. The essay, printed in full on page 27, is by Charles R. Lawrence III, a professor of law at Stanford University. It originally appeared in *The Chronicle of Higher Education* (October 25, 1989), a publication read chiefly by college and university faculty members and administrators.

example of such a policy?

University officials who have formulated <u>policies</u> to respond to incidents of racial harassment have been characterized in the press as "thought police," but such policies generally do nothing more than impose (<u>sanctions</u>) against intentional face-to-face insults. When <u>racist</u> speech takes the form of <u>face-to-face insults,</u> catcalls, or other assaultive speech aimed at an individual or small group of persons, it falls directly within the <u>"fighting words"</u> exception to First Amendment protection. The Supreme Court has held that words which <u>"by their very utterance inflict injury</u> or tend to incite an immediate breach of the peace" are not protected by the First Amendment.

What about sexist speech?

Definition of "fighting words"

?

example?

If the purpose of the First Amendment is to foster the greatest amount of speech, racial insults disserve that purpose. Assaultive racist speech functions as a preemptive strike. <u>The invective is experienced as a blow, not as a proffered idea,</u> and once the blow is struck, it is unlikely that a dialogue will follow. Racial insults are particularly undeserving of First Amendment protection because the perpetrator's <u>intention is not to discover truth</u> or initiate dialogue but to injure the victim. <u>In most situations,</u> members of minority groups realize that they are likely to lose if they respond to epithets by fighting and are forced to remain silent and submissive.

Really? Probably depends on the individual

Why must speech always seek "to discover truth"

How does he know?

This, Therefore That

In order to arrive at a coherent thought, or a coherent series of thoughts that will lead to a reasonable conclusion, a writer has to go through a good deal of preliminary effort; and if the writer is to convince the reader that the conclusion is sound, the reasoning that led to the conclusion must be set forth in detail, with a good deal of "This, therefore that," and "If this, then that." The arguments in this book require more comment than President Calvin Coolidge provided when his wife, who hadn't been able to go to church on a Sunday, asked him what the preacher's sermon was about. "Sin," he said. His wife persisted: "What did the preacher say about it?" Coolidge's response: "He was against it."

But, again, our saying that most of the arguments in this book are presented at length and require careful reading does not mean that they are obscure; it means, rather, that the reader has to take the sentences one by one. And speaking of one by one, we are reminded of an episode in Lewis Carroll's *Through the Looking-Glass:*

> "Can you do Addition?" the White Queen asked. "What's one and one and one and one and one and one and one and one and one and one?"
> "I don't know," said Alice. "I lost count."
> "She can't do Addition," the Red Queen said.

It's easy enough to add one and one and one and so on, and Alice can, of course, do addition, but not at the pace that the White Queen sets. Fortunately, you can set your own pace in reading the cumulative thinking set forth in the essays we reprint. Skimming won't work, but slow reading — and thinking about what you are reading — will.

When you first pick up an essay, you may indeed want to skim it, for some of the reasons mentioned on page 16, but sooner or later you have to settle down to read it, and to think about it. The effort will be worthwhile. John Locke, the seventeenth-century English philosopher, said,

> *Reading* furnishes the mind with materials of knowledge; it is *thinking* [that] makes what we read ours. We are of the ruminating kind, and it is not enough to cram ourselves with a great load of collections; unless we chew them over again they will not give us strength and nourishment.

First, Second, and Third Thoughts

Suppose you are reading an argument about pornographic pictures. For the present purpose, it doesn't matter whether the argument favors or opposes censorship. As you read the argument, ask yourself whether "pornography" has been adequately defined. Has the writer taken the trouble to make sure that the reader and the writer are thinking about the same thing? If not, the very topic under discussion has not been adequately fixed, and therefore further debate over the issue may well be so unclear as to be futile. How, then, ought a topic such as this be fixed for effective critical thinking?

It goes without saying that pornography can't be defined simply as pictures of nude figures, or even of nude figures copulating, for such a definition would include not only photographs taken for medical, sociological, and scientific purposes but also some of the world's great art. Nobody seriously thinks pornography includes such things.

Is it enough, then, to say that pornography "stirs lustful thoughts" or "appeals to prurient interests"? No, because pictures of shoes probably stir lustful thoughts in shoe fetishists, and pictures of children in ads for underwear probably stir lustful thoughts in pedophiles. Perhaps, then, the definition must be amended to "material that stirs lustful thoughts in the average person." But will this restatement do? First, it may be hard to agree on the characteristics of "the average person." True, in other matters the law often assumes that there is such a creature as "the reasonable person," and most people would agree that in a given situation, there might be a reasonable response — for almost everyone. But we cannot be so sure that the same is true about the emotional responses of this "average person." In any case, far from stimulating sexual impulses, sadomasochistic pictures of booted men wielding whips on naked women probably turn off "the average person," yet this is the sort of material that most people would agree is pornographic.

Something must be wrong, then, with the definition that pornography is material that "stirs lustful thoughts in the average person." We began with a definition that was too broad ("pictures of nude figures"), but now we have a definition that is too narrow. We must go back to the drawing board. This is not nitpicking. The label "average person" was found to be inadequate in a pornography case argued before the Supreme Court; because the materials in question were aimed at a homosexual audience, it was agreed that the average person would not find them sexually stimulating.

One difficulty has been that pornography is often defined according to its effect on the viewer ("genital commotion," Father Harold Gardiner, S.J., called it, in *Catholic Viewpoint on Censorship*), but different people, we know, may respond differently. In the first half of the twentieth century, in an effort to distinguish between pornography and art — after all, most people don't want to regard Botticelli's *Venus* or Michelangelo's *David* as "dirty" — it was commonly said that a true work of art does not stimulate in the spectator ideas or desires that the real object might stimulate. But in 1956 Kenneth Clark, probably the most influential English-speaking art critic of our century, changed all that; in a book called *The Nude* he announced that "no nude, however abstract, should fail to arouse in the spectator some vestige of erotic feeling."

SUMMARIZING

Perhaps the best thing to do with a fairly difficult essay is, after a first reading, to reread it and simultaneously to take notes on a sheet of paper, perhaps summarizing each paragraph in a sentence or two. Writing a summary will help you

- to understand the contents, and
- to see the strengths and weaknesses of the piece.

Don't confuse a summary with a paraphrase; a **paraphrase** is a word-by-word or phrase-by-phrase rewording of a text, a sort of translation of the author's language into your own. A paraphrase is therefore as long as the original, or even longer; a **summary** is much shorter. Paraphrasing can be useful in helping you to grasp difficult passages; summarizing is useful in helping you to get the gist of the entire essay. (Caution: Do *not* incorporate a summary or a paraphrase into your own essay without acknowledging your source and stating that you are summarizing or paraphrasing.)

Summarizing each paragraph, or each group of closely related paragraphs, will help you to follow the thread of the discourse, and, when you are finished, will provide you with a useful map of the essay. Then, when you reread the essay yet again, you may want to underline passages that you now understand are the author's key ideas — for instance, definitions, generalizations, summaries — and you may want to jot notes in the margins, questioning the logic or expressing your uncertainty or calling attention to other writers who see the matter differently.

Here is a paragraph from a 1973 decision of the U.S. Supreme Court, written by Chief Justice Warren Burger, setting forth reasons why the government may censor obscene material. We follow it with a sample summary.

> If we accept the unprovable assumption that a complete education requires the reading of certain books, and the well-nigh universal belief that good books, plays, and art lift the spirit, improve the mind, enrich the human personality, and develop character, can we then say that a state legislature may not act on the corollary assumption that commerce in obscene books, or public exhibitions focused on obscene conduct, have a tendency to exert a corrupting and debasing impact leading to antisocial behavior? The sum of experience, including that of the past two decades, affords an ample basis for legislatures to conclude that a sensitive, key relationship of human existence, central to family life, community welfare, and the development of human personality, can be debased and distorted by crass commercial exploitation of sex. Nothing in the Constitution prohibits a State from reaching such a conclusion and acting on it legislatively simply because there is no conclusive empirical data.

Now for a student's summary. Notice that the summary does *not* include the reader's evaluation or any other sort of comment on the original;

it is simply an attempt to condense the original. Notice too that, because its purpose is merely to assist the reader to grasp the ideas of the original by focusing on them, it is written in a sort of shorthand (not every sentence is a complete sentence), though of course if this summary were being presented in an essay it would have to be grammatical.

```
    Unprovable but acceptable assumption that good books
etc. shape character, so that legislature can assume
obscene works debase character. Experience lets one
conclude that exploitation of sex debases the indi-
vidual, family, and community. Though no conclusive evi-
dence for this view, Constitution lets states act on it
legislatively.
```

The first sentence of the original, some eighty words, is reduced in the summary to eighteen words. Of course the summary loses much of the detail and flavor of the original: "Good books etc." is not the same as "good books, plays, and art"; and "shape character" is not the same as "lift the spirit, improve the mind, enrich the human personality, and develop character." But the statement in the summary will do as a rough approximation, useful for a quick review. More important, of course, the act of writing a summary forces the reader to go slowly and to think about each sentence of the original. Such thinking may help the reader-writer to see the complexity — or the hollowness — of the original.

The sample summary in the paragraph above was just that, a summary; but when writing your summaries, it is often useful to inject your own thoughts ("seems far-fetched," "strong point," "I don't get it"), enclosing them within square brackets, [   ], or in some other way keeping these responses distinct from your summary of the writer's argument. Remember, however, that if your instructor asks you to hand in a summary, it should not contain ideas other than those found in the original piece. You can rearrange these, add transitions as needed, and so forth, but the summary should give the reader nothing but a sense of the original piece.

We don't want to nag you, but we do want to emphasize the need to read with a pencil in hand. If you read slowly and take notes, you will find that what you read will give you the strength and nourishment that Locke spoke of.

Having insisted that although skimming is a useful early step, the essays in this book need to be read slowly because the writers build one reason upon another, we will now seem to contradict ourselves by presenting an essay that can *almost* be skimmed. Susan Jacoby's essay originally appeared in the *New York Times,* a thoroughly respectable journal but not one that requires its readers to linger over every sentence. Still, compared with most of the news accounts, Jacoby's essay requires close reading. When you read the essay you will notice that it zigs and zags, not because

Jacoby is careless or wants to befuddle her readers but because she wants to build a strong case to support her point of view, and she must therefore look at some widely held views that she does *not* accept; she must set these forth, and must then give her reasons for rejecting them.

Susan Jacoby

A First Amendment Junkie

It is no news that many women are defecting from the ranks of civil libertarians on the issue of obscenity. The conviction of Larry Flynt, publisher of *Hustler* magazine — before his metamorphosis into a born-again Christian — was greeted with unabashed feminist approval. Harry Reems, the unknown actor who was convicted by a Memphis jury for conspiring to distribute the movie *Deep Throat,* has carried on his legal battles with almost no support from women who ordinarily regard themselves as supporters of the First Amendment. Feminist writers and scholars have even discussed the possibility of making common cause against pornography with adversaries of the women's movement — including opponents of the equal rights amendment and "right-to-life" forces.

All of this is deeply disturbing to a woman writer who believes, as I always have and still do, in an absolute interpretation of the First Amendment. Nothing in Larry Flynt's garbage convinces me that the late Justice Hugo L. Black was wrong in his opinion that "the Federal Government is without any power whatsoever under the Constitution to put any type of burden on free speech and expression of ideas of any kind (as distinguished from conduct)." Many women I like and respect tell me I am wrong; I cannot remember having become involved in so many heated discussions of a public issue since the end of the Vietnam War. A feminist writer described my views as those of a "First Amendment junkie."

Many feminist arguments for controls on pornography carry the implicit conviction that porn books, magazines, and movies pose a greater threat to women than similarly repulsive exercises of free speech pose to other offended groups. This conviction has, of course, been shared by everyone — regardless of race, creed, or sex — who has ever argued in favor of abridging the First Amendment. It is the argument used by some Jews who have withdrawn their support from the American Civil Liberties Union because it has defended the right of American Nazis to march

Susan Jacoby (b. 1946), a journalist since the age of seventeen, is well known for her feminist writings. "A First Amendment Junkie" (our title) appeared in a "Hers" column in the New York Times *in 1978.*

through a community inhabited by survivors of Hitler's concentration camps.

If feminists want to argue that the protection of the Constitution should not be extended to *any* particularly odious or threatening form of speech, they have a reasonable argument (although I don't agree with it). But it is ridiculous to suggest that the porn shops on 42nd Street are more disgusting to women than a march of neo-Nazis is to survivors of the extermination camps.

The arguments over pornography also blur the vital distinction be-   5 tween expression of ideas and conduct. When I say I believe unreservedly in the First Amendment, someone always comes back at me with the issue of "kiddie porn." But kiddie porn is not a First Amendment issue. It is an issue of the abuse of power — the power adults have over children — and not of obscenity. Parents and promoters have no more right to use their children to make porn movies than they do to send them to work in coal mines. The responsible adults should be prosecuted, just as adults who use children for back-breaking farm labor should be prosecuted.

Susan Brownmiller, in *Against Our Will: Men, Women and Rape*, has described pornography as "the undiluted essence of antifemale propaganda." I think this is a fair description of some types of pornography, especially of the brutish subspecies that equates sex with death and portrays women primarily as objects of violence.

The equation of sex and violence, personified by some glossy rock record album covers as well as by *Hustler*, has fed the illusion that censorship of pornography can be conducted on a more rational basis than other types of censorship. Are all pictures of naked women obscene? Clearly not, says a friend. A Renoir nude is art, she says, and *Hustler* is trash. "Any reasonable person" knows that.

But what about something between art and trash — something, say, along the lines of *Playboy* or *Penthouse* magazines? I asked five women for their reactions to one picture in Penthouse and got responses that ranged from "lovely" and "sensuous" to "revolting" and "demeaning." Feminists, like everyone else, seldom have rational reasons for their preferences in erotica. Like members of juries, they tend to disagree when confronted with something that falls short of 100 percent vulgarity.

In any case, feminists will not be the arbiters of good taste if it becomes easier to harass, prosecute, and convict people on obscenity charges. Most of the people who want to censor girlie magazines are equally opposed to open discussion of issues that are of vital concern to women: rape, abortion, menstruation, contraception, lesbianism — in fact, the entire range of sexual experience from a women's viewpoint.

Feminist writers and editors and filmmakers have limited financial re-   10 sources: Confronted by a determined prosecutor, Hugh Hefner[1] will fare better than Susan Brownmiller. Would the Memphis jurors who convicted

---

[1]**Hugh Hefner** Founder and longtime publisher of *Playboy* magazine. [Editors' note.]

Harry Reems for his role in *Deep Throat* be inclined to take a more posi-tive view of paintings of the female genitalia done by sensitive feminist artists? *Ms.* magazine has printed color reproductions of some of those art works; *Ms.* is already banned from a number of high school libraries be-cause someone considers it threatening and/or obscene.

Feminists who want to censor what they regard as harmful pornogra-phy have essentially the same motivation as other would-be censors: They want to use the power of the state to accomplish what they have been un-able to achieve in the marketplace of ideas and images. The impulse to censor places no faith in the possibilities of democratic persuasion.

It isn't easy to persuade certain men that they have better uses for $1.95 each month than to spend it on a copy of *Hustler*? Well, then, give the men no choice in the matter.

I believe there is also a connection between the impulse toward cen-sorship on the part of people who used to consider themselves civil liber-tarians and a more general desire to shift responsibility from individuals to institutions. When I saw the movie *Looking for Mr. Goodbar*, I was stunned by its series of visual images equating sex and violence, coupled with what seems to me the mindless message (a distortion of the fine Ju-dith Rossner novel) that casual sex equals death. When I came out of the movie, I was even more shocked to see parents standing in line with chil-dren between the ages of ten and fourteen.

I simply don't know why a parent would take a child to see such a movie, any more than I understand why people feel they can't turn off a television set their child is watching. Whenever I say that, my friends tell me I don't know how it is because I don't have children. True, but I do have parents. When I was a child, they did turn off the TV. They didn't ex-pect the Federal Communications Commission to do their job for them.

I am a First Amendment junkie. You can't OD on the First Amend-   15
ment, because free speech is its own best antidote.

Suppose we want to make a rough summary, more or less paragraph by paragraph, of Jacoby's essay. Such a summary might look something like this. (The numbers refer to Jacoby's paragraphs.)

1. Although feminists usually support the First Amendment, when it comes to pornography many feminists take pretty much the posi-tion of those who oppose ERA and abortion and other causes of the women's movement.

2. Larry Flynt produces garbage, but I think his conviction repre-sents an unconstitutional limitation of freedom of speech.

3, 4. Feminists who want to control (censor) pornography argue that it poses a greater threat to women than similar repulsive speech poses to other groups. If feminists want to say that all offensive speech should be restricted they can make a case, but it is absurd to say that pornography is a "greater threat" to women than a march of neo-Nazis is to survivors of concentration camps.

5. Trust in the First Amendment is not refuted by kiddie porn; kiddie porn is not a First Amendment issue but an issue of child abuse.

6, 7, 8. Some feminists think censorship of pornography can be more "rational" than other kinds of censorship, but a picture of a nude woman strikes some women as base and others as "lovely." There is no unanimity.

9, 10. If feminists censor girlie magazines, they will find that they are unwittingly helping opponents of the women's movement to censor discussions of rape, abortion, and so on. Some of the art in the feminist magazine *Ms.* would doubtless be censored.

11, 12. Like other would-be censors, feminists want to use the power of the state to achieve what they have not achieved in "the marketplace of ideas." They display a lack of faith in "democratic persuasion."

13, 14. This attempt at censorship reveals a desire to "shift responsibility from individuals to institutions." The responsibility — for instance, to keep young people from equating sex with violence — is properly the parents'.

15. We can't have too much of the First Amendment.

Jacoby's **thesis,** or major claim, or chief proposition — that any form of censorship is wrong — is clear enough, even as early as the end of her first paragraph, but it gets its life or its force from the **reasons** offered throughout the essay. If we want to reduce our summary even further, we might say that Jacoby supports her thesis by arguing several subsidiary points. We will merely assert them briefly, but Jacoby **argues** them — that is, she gives reasons.

a. Pornography can scarcely be thought of as more offensive than Nazism.

b. Women disagree about which pictures are pornographic.

c. Feminists who want to censor pornography will find that they help antifeminists to censor discussions of issues advocated by the women's movement.

d. Feminist advocates are in effect turning to the government to achieve what they haven't achieved in the free marketplace.

e. One sees this abdication of responsibility in the fact that parents allow their children to watch unsuitable movies and television programs.

If we want to present a brief summary in the form of one coherent paragraph — perhaps as part of our own essay, in order to show the view we are arguing in behalf of or against — we might write something like this summary. (The summary would, of course, be prefaced by a **lead-in** along these lines: "Susan Jacoby, writing in the *New York Times,* offered a forceful argument against censorship of pornography. Jacoby's view, briefly, is . . .")

> When it comes to censorship of pornography, some feminists take a position shared by opponents of the feminist movement. They argue that pornography poses a greater threat to women than other forms of offensive speech offer to other groups, but this interpretation is simply a mistake. Pointing to kiddie porn is also a mistake, for kiddie porn is an issue involving not the First Amendment but child abuse. Feminists who support censorship of pornography will inadvertently aid those who wish to censor discussions of abortion and rape, or art that is published in magazines such as <u>Ms</u>. The solution is not for individuals to turn to institutions (i.e., for the government to limit the First Amendment) but for individuals to accept the responsibility for teaching young people not to equate sex with violence.

Whether we agree or disagree with Jacoby's thesis, we must admit that the reasons she sets forth to support it are worth thinking about. Only a reader who closely follows the reasoning with which Jacoby buttresses her thesis is in a position to accept or reject it.

Topics for Critical Thinking and Writing

1. What does Jacoby mean when she says she is a "First Amendment junkie"?

2. The essay is primarily an argument against the desire of some feminists to try to censor pornography of the sort that appeals to some heterosexual adult males, but the next-to-last paragraph is about television and children. Is the paragraph connected to Jacoby's overall argument? If so, how?

3. Evaluate the final paragraph as a final paragraph. (Effective final paragraphs are not, of course, all of one sort. Some, for example, round off the essay by echoing something from the opening; others suggest that the reader, having now seen the problem, should think further about it or even act on it. But a good final paragraph, whatever else it does, should make the reader feel that the essay has come to an end, not just broken off.)

4. This essay originally appeared in the *New York Times*. If you are unfamiliar with this newspaper, consult an issue or two in your library. Next, in a paragraph, try to characterize the readers of the paper—that is, Jacoby's audience.

5. Jacoby claims that she believes in an "absolute interpretation of the First Amendment." What does such an interpretation involve? Would it permit shouting "Fire!" in a crowded theater even though the shouter knows there is no

fire? Would it permit shouting racist insults at blacks or immigrant Vietnamese? Spreading untruths about someone's past? If the "absolutist" interpretation of the First Amendment does permit these statements, does that argument show that nothing is morally wrong with uttering them? (*Does* the First Amendment, as actually interpreted by the Supreme Court today, permit any or all of these claims? Consult your reference librarian for help in answering this question.)

6. Jacoby implies that permitting prosecution of persons on obscenity charges will lead eventually to censorship of "open discussion" of important issues such as "rape, abortion, menstruation, lesbianism." Do you find her fears convincing? Does she give any evidence to support her claim?

Next we present an essay that is somewhat longer and, we think, somewhat more difficult than Jacoby's. We suggest that you read it straight through, to get its gist, and then read it a second time, jotting down after each paragraph a sentence or two summarizing the paragraph.

Charles R. Lawrence III

On Racist Speech

I have spent the better part of my life as a dissenter. As a high school student, I was threatened with suspension for my refusal to participate in a civil defense drill, and I have been a conspicuous consumer of my First Amendment liberties ever since. There are very strong reasons for protecting even racist speech. Perhaps the most important of these is that such protection reinforces our society's commitment to tolerance as a value, and that by protecting bad speech from government regulation, we will be forced to combat it as a community.

But I also have a deeply felt apprehension about the resurgence of racial violence and the corresponding rise in the incidence of verbal and symbolic assault and harassment to which blacks and other traditionally subjugated and excluded groups are subjected. I am troubled by the way the debate has been framed in response to the recent surge of racist incidents on college and university campuses and in response to some universities' attempts to regulate harassing speech. The problem has been framed as one in which the liberty of free speech is in conflict with the elimination of racism. I believe this has placed the bigot on the moral high ground and fanned the rising flames of racism.

Charles R. Lawrence III (b. 1943), author of numerous articles in law journals and coauthor of The Bakke Case: The Politics of Inequality *(1979), teaches law at Stanford University. This essay originally appeared in* The Chronicle of Higher Education *(October 25, 1989), a publication read chiefly by faculty and administrators at colleges and universities. An amplified version of the essay appeared in* Duke Law Journal, *February 1990.*

Above all, I am troubled that we have not listened to the real victims, that we have shown so little understanding of their injury, and that we have abandoned those whose race, gender, or sexual preference continues to make them second-class citizens. It seems to me a very sad irony that the first instinct of civil libertarians has been to challenge even the smallest, most narrowly framed efforts by universities to provide black and other minority students with the protection the Constitution guarantees them.

The landmark case of *Brown v. Board of Education* is not a case that we normally think of as a case about speech. But *Brown* can be broadly read as articulating the principle of equal citizenship. *Brown* held that segregated schools were inherently unequal because of the *message* that segregation conveyed—that black children were an untouchable caste, unfit to go to school with white children. If we understand the necessity of eliminating the system of signs and symbols that signal the inferiority of blacks, then we should hesitate before proclaiming that all racist speech that stops short of physical violence must be defended.

University officials who have formulated policies to respond to incidents of racial harassment have been characterized in the press as "thought police," but such policies generally do nothing more than impose sanctions against intentional face-to-face insults. When racist speech takes the form of face-to-face insults, catcalls, or other assaultive speech aimed at an individual or small group of persons, it falls directly within the "fighting words" exception to First Amendment protection. The Supreme Court has held that words which "by their very utterance inflict injury or tend to incite an immediate breach of the peace" are not protected by the First Amendment.

If the purpose of the First Amendment is to foster the greatest amount of speech, racial insults disserve that purpose. Assaultive racist speech functions as a preemptive strike. The invective is experienced as a blow, not as a proffered idea, and once the blow is struck, it is unlikely that a dialogue will follow. Racial insults are particularly undeserving of First Amendment protection because the perpetrator's intention is not to discover truth or initiate dialogue but to injure the victim. In most situations, members of minority groups realize that they are likely to lose if they respond to epithets by fighting and are forced to remain silent and submissive.

Courts have held that offensive speech may not be regulated in public forums such as streets where the listener may avoid the speech by moving on, but the regulation of otherwise protected speech has been permitted when the speech invades the privacy of the unwilling listener's home or when the unwilling listener cannot avoid the speech. Racist posters, fliers, and graffiti in dormitories, bathrooms, and other common living spaces would seem to clearly fall within the reasoning of these cases. Minority students should not be required to remain in their rooms in order to avoid racial assault. Minimally, they should find a safe haven in their dorms and in all other common rooms that are a part of their daily routine.

I would also argue that the university's responsibility for ensuring that these students receive an equal educational opportunity provides a compelling justification for regulations that ensure them safe passage in all common areas. A minority student should not have to risk becoming the target of racially assaulting speech every time he or she chooses to walk across campus. Regulating vilifying speech that cannot be anticipated or avoided would not preclude announced speeches and rallies — situations that would give minority-group members and their allies the chance to organize counterdemonstrations or avoid the speech altogether.

The most commonly advanced argument against the regulation of racist speech proceeds something like this: We recognize that minority groups suffer pain and injury as the result of racist speech, but we must allow this hate mongering for the benefit of society as a whole. Freedom of speech is the lifeblood of our democratic system. It is especially important for minorities because often it is their only vehicle for rallying support for the redress of their grievances. It will be impossible to formulate a prohibition so precise that it will prevent the racist speech you want to suppress without catching in the same net all kinds of speech that it would be unconscionable for a democratic society to suppress.

Whenever we make such arguments, we are striking a balance on the 10 one hand between our concern for the continued free flow of ideas and the democratic process dependent on that flow, and, on the other, our desire to further the cause of equality. There can be no meaningful discussion of how we should reconcile our commitment to equality and our commitment to free speech until it is acknowledged that there is real harm inflicted by racist speech and that this harm is far from trivial.

To engage in a debate about the First Amendment and racist speech without a full understanding of the nature and extent of that harm is to risk making the First Amendment an instrument of domination rather than a vehicle of liberation. We have not known the experience of victimization by racist, misogynist, and homophobic speech, nor do we equally share the burden of the societal harm it inflicts. We are often quick to say that we have heard the cry of the victims when we have not.

The *Brown* case is again instructive because it speaks directly to the psychic injury inflicted by racist speech by noting that the symbolic message of segregation affected "the hearts and minds" of Negro children "in a way unlikely ever to be undone." Racial epithets and harassment often cause deep emotional scarring and feelings of anxiety and fear that pervade every aspect of a victim's life.

Brown also recognized that black children did not have an equal opportunity to learn and participate in the school community if they bore the additional burden of being subjected to the humiliation and psychic assault contained in the message of segregation. University students bear an analogous burden when they are forced to live and work in an environment where at any moment they may be subjected to denigrating verbal harassment and assault. The same injury was addressed by the Supreme Court when it held that sexual harassment that creates a hostile or abusive work environment violates the ban on sex discrimination in employment of Title VII of the Civil Rights Act of 1964.

Carefully drafted university regulations would bar the use of words as assault weapons and leave unregulated even the most heinous of ideas when those ideas are presented at times and places and in manners that provide an opportunity for reasoned rebuttal or escape from immediate injury. The history of the development of the right to free speech has been one of carefully evaluating the importance of free expression and its effects on other important societal interests. We have drawn the line between protected and unprotected speech before without dire results. (Courts have, for example, exempted from the protection of the First Amendment obscene speech and speech that disseminates official secrets, that defames or libels another person, or that is used to form a conspiracy or monopoly.)

Blacks and other people of color are skeptical about the argument that   15 even the most injurious speech must remain unregulated because, in an unregulated marketplace of ideas, the best ones will rise to the top and gain acceptance. Our experience tells us quite the opposite. We have seen too many good liberal politicians shy away from the issues that might brand them as being too closely allied with us.

Whenever we decide that racist speech must be tolerated because of the importance of maintaining societal tolerance for all unpopular speech, we are asking blacks and other subordinated groups to bear the burden for the good of all. We must be careful that the ease with which we strike the balance against the regulation of racist speech is in no way influenced by the fact that the cost will be borne by others. We must be certain that those who will pay that price are fairly represented in our deliberations and that they are heard.

At the core of the argument that we should resist all government regulation of speech is the ideal that the best cure for bad speech is good, that ideas that affirm equality and the worth of all individuals will ultimately prevail. This is an empty ideal unless those of us who would fight racism are vigilant and unequivocal in that fight. We must look for ways to offer assistance and support to students whose speech and political participation are chilled in a climate of racial harassment.

Civil rights lawyers might consider suing on behalf of blacks whose right to an equal education is denied by a university's failure to ensure a nondiscriminatory educational climate or conditions of employment. We must embark upon the development of a First Amendment jurisprudence grounded in the reality of our history and our contemporary experience. We must think hard about how best to launch legal attacks against the most indefensible forms of hate speech. Good lawyers can create exceptions and narrow interpretations that limit the harm of hate speech without opening the floodgates of censorship.

Everyone concerned with these issues must find ways to engage actively in actions that resist and counter the racist ideas that we would have the First Amendment protect. If we fail in this, the victims of hate speech must rightly assume that we are on the oppressors' side.

Topics for Critical Thinking and Writing

1. Summarize Lawrence's essay in a paragraph. (You may find it useful first to summarize each paragraph in a sentence, and then to revise these summary sentences into a paragraph.)

2. In a sentence state Lawrence's thesis (his main point).

3. Why do you suppose Lawrence included his first paragraph? What does it contribute to his argument?

4. Paragraph 7 argues that "minority students" should not have to endure "racist posters, fliers, and graffiti in dormitories, bathrooms, and other common living spaces." Do you think that Lawrence would also argue that straight white men should not have to endure posters, fliers, or graffiti that speak of "honkies" or "rednecks"? On what do you base your answer?

5. In paragraph 8 Lawrence speaks of "racially assaulting speech" and of "vilifying speech." It is easy to think of words that fit these descriptions, but what about other words? Is "Uncle Tom," used by an African American about another African American who is eager to please whites, an example? Or take the word "gay." Surely this word is acceptable because it is widely used by homosexuals, but what about "queer" (used by some homosexuals, but usually derogatory when used by heterosexuals)? A third example: There can be little doubt that women are demeaned when males speak of them as "chicks" or "babes," but are these terms "assaulting" and "vilifying"?

6. Find out if your college or university has a code governing hate speech. If it does, evaluate it. If your college has no such code, imagine that you are Lawrence, and draft one of about 250 words. (See especially his paras. 5, 7, and 14.)

Finally, here is an essay by Derek Bok, written while he was president of Harvard. The essay, first published in the *Boston Globe* in 1991, was prompted by the display of Confederate flags hung from a window of a Harvard dormitory.

Derek Bok

Protecting Freedom of Expression on the Campus

For several years, universities have been struggling with the problem of trying to reconcile the rights of free speech with the desire to avoid racial tension. In recent weeks, such a controversy has sprung up at Harvard. Two students hung Confederate flags in public view, upsetting stu-

---

Derek Bok was born in 1930 in Bryn Mawr, Pennsylvania, and educated at Stanford University and Harvard University, where he received a law degree. From 1971 to 1991 he served as president of Harvard University.

dents who equate the Confederacy with slavery. A third student tried to protest the flags by displaying a swastika.

These incidents have provoked much discussion and disagreement. Some students have urged that Harvard require the removal of symbols that offend many members of the community. Others reply that such symbols are a form of free speech and should be protected.

Different universities have resolved similar conflicts in different ways. Some have enacted codes to protect their communities from forms of speech that are deemed to be insensitive to the feelings of other groups. Some have refused to impose such restrictions.

It is important to distinguish between the appropriateness of such communications and their status under the First Amendment. The fact that speech is protected by the First Amendment does not necessarily mean that it is right, proper, or civil. I am sure that the vast majority of Harvard students believe that hanging a Confederate flag in public view— or displaying a swastika in response—is insensitive and unwise because any satisfaction it gives to the students who display these symbols is far outweighed by the discomfort it causes to many others.

I share this view and regret that the students involved saw fit to be- 5 have in this fashion. Whether or not they merely wished to manifest their pride in the South—or to demonstrate the insensitivity of hanging Confederate flags, by mounting another offensive symbol in return—they must have known that they would upset many fellow students and ignore the decent regard for the feelings of others so essential to building and preserving a strong and harmonious community.

To disapprove of a particular form of communication, however, is not enough to justify prohibiting it. We are faced with a clear example of the conflict between our commitment to free speech and our desire to foster a community founded on mutual respect. Our society has wrestled with this problem for many years. Interpreting the First Amendment, the Supreme Court has clearly struck the balance in favor of free speech.

While communities do have the right to regulate speech in order to uphold aesthetic standards (avoiding defacement of buildings) or to protect the public from disturbing noise, rules of this kind must be applied across the board and cannot be enforced selectively to prohibit certain kinds of messages but not others.

Under the Supreme Court's rulings, as I read them, the display of swastikas or Confederate flags clearly falls within the protection of the free-speech clause of the First Amendment and cannot be forbidden simply because it offends the feelings of many members of the community. These rulings apply to all agencies of government, including public universities.

Although it is unclear to what extent the First Amendment is enforceable against private institutions, I have difficulty understanding why a university such as Harvard should have less free speech than the surrounding society—or than a public university.

One reason why the power of censorship is so dangerous is that it is 10 extremely difficult to decide when a particular communication is offensive enough to warrant prohibition or to weigh the degree of offensiveness against the potential value of the communication. If we begin to forbid flags, it is only a short step to prohibiting offensive speakers.

I suspect that no community will become humane and caring by restricting what its members can say. The worst offenders will simply find other ways to irritate and insult.

In addition, once we start to declare certain things "offensive," with all the excitement and attention that will follow, I fear that much ingenuity will be exerted trying to test the limits, much time will be expended trying to draw tenuous distinctions, and the resulting publicity will eventually attract more attention to the offensive material than would ever have occurred otherwise.

Rather than prohibit such communications, with all the resulting risks, it would be better to ignore them, since students would then have little reason to create such displays and would soon abandon them. If this response is not possible — and one can understand why — the wisest course is to speak with those who perform insensitive acts and try to help them understand the effects of their actions on others.

Appropriate officials and faculty members should take the lead, as the Harvard House Masters have already done in this case. In talking with students, they should seek to educate and persuade, rather than resort to ridicule or intimidation, recognizing that only persuasion is likely to produce a lasting, beneficial effect. Through such effects, I believe that we act in the manner most consistent with our ideals as an educational institution and most calculated to help us create a truly understanding, supportive community.

Topics for Critical Thinking and Writing

1. Bok sketches the following argument (paras. 8 and 9): The First Amendment protects free speech in public universities and colleges; Harvard is not a public university; therefore Harvard does not enjoy the protection of the First Amendment. This argument is plainly valid. But Bok clearly rejects this conclusion ("I have difficulty understanding why . . . Harvard should have less free speech . . . than a public university"). Therefore, he must reject at least one of the premises. But which one? And why?

2. Bok objects to censorship in order to prevent students from being "offended." He would not object to the campus police preventing students from being harmed. In an essay of 100 words, explain the difference between conduct that is *harmful* and conduct that is (merely?) *offensive*.

3. Bok advises campus officials (and students) simply to "ignore" offensive words, flags, and so forth (para. 13). Do you agree with this advice? Or do you favor a different kind of response? Write a 250-word essay on the theme "How We Ought to Respond to the Offensive Misconduct of Others."

3

Critical Reading: Getting Deeper into Arguments

He that wrestles with us strengthens our nerves, and sharpens our skill. Our antagonist is our helper.
— EDMUND BURKE

PERSUASION, ARGUMENT, DISPUTE

When we think seriously about an argument (not name calling or mere rationalization), not only do we hear ideas that may be unfamiliar, but we are also forced to examine closely our own cherished opinions, and perhaps for the first time we really come to see the strengths and weaknesses of what we believe. As John Stuart Mill put it, "He who knows only his own side of the case knows little."

It is customary, and useful, to distinguish between persuasion and argument. **Persuasion** has the broader meaning. To persuade is to win over— whether by giving reasons (that is, by argument) or by appealing to the emotions, or, for that matter, by using torture. **Argument,** one form of persuasion, relies on reason; it offers statements as reasons for other statements.

Notice that an argument, in this sense, does not require two speakers or writers who represent opposed positions. The Declaration of Independence is an argument, setting forth the colonists' reasons for declaring their independence. In practice, of course, someone's argument usually advances reasons in opposition to someone else's position or belief. But even if one is writing only for oneself, trying to clarify one's thinking by setting forth reasons, the result is an argument. In a **dispute,** however, two or more people express views that are at odds.

Most of this book is about argument in the sense of the presentation of reasons, but of course reason is not the whole story. If an argument is to be effective, it must be presented persuasively. For instance, the writer's **tone** (attitude toward self, topic, and audience) must be appropriate if the discourse is to persuade the reader. The careful presentation of the self is not something disreputable, nor is it something that publicity agents or advertising agencies invented. Aristotle (384–322 B.C.) emphasized the importance of impressing upon the audience that the speaker is a person of good sense and high moral character. We will talk at length about tone, along with other matters such as the organization of an argument, in Chapter 5, but here we deal with some of the chief devices used in reasoning.

We should note at once, however, that an argument presupposes a fixed **topic.** Suppose we are arguing about Jefferson's assertion, in the Declaration of Independence, that "all men are created equal." Jones subscribes to this statement, but Smith says it is nonsense, and argues that one has only to look around to see that some people are brighter than others, or healthier, or better coordinated, or whatever. Jones and Smith, if they intend to argue the point, will do well to examine what Jefferson actually wrote.

> We hold these truths to be self-evident, that all men are created equal:
> that they are endowed by their Creator with certain unalienable rights;
> and that among these are life, liberty, and the pursuit of happiness.

There is room for debate over what Jefferson really meant, and about whether he is right, but clearly he was talking about *equality of rights,* and if Smith and Jones wish to argue about Jefferson's view of equality — that is, if they wish to offer their reasons for accepting, rejecting, or modifying it — they will do well first to agree on what Jefferson said or what he probably meant to say. Jones and Smith may still hold different views; they may continue to disagree on whether Jefferson was right, and proceed to offer arguments and counterarguments to settle the point. But only if they can agree on *what* they disagree about will their dispute get somewhere.

REASON VERSUS RATIONALIZATION

Reason may not be our only way of finding the truth, but it is a way we often rely on. The subway ran yesterday at 6:00 A.M. and the day before at 6:00 A.M. and the day before, and so I infer from this evidence that it is also running today at 6:00 A.M. (a form of reasoning known as **induction**). Or: Bus drivers require would-be passengers to present the exact change; I do not have the exact change; therefore I infer I cannot ride on the bus (**deduction**). (The terms *induction* and *deduction* will be discussed shortly.)

We also know that, if we set our minds to a problem, we can often find reasons (not necessarily sound ones, but reasons nevertheless) for almost anything we want to justify. Here is an entertaining example from Benjamin Franklin's *Autobiography:*

> I believe I have omitted mentioning that in my first voyage from Boston, being becalmed off Block Island, our people set about catching cod and hauled up a great many. Hitherto I had stuck to my resolution of not eat-

ing animal food, and on this occasion, I considered with my master Tryon the taking of every fish as a kind of unprovoked murder, since none of them had or ever could do us any injury that might justify the slaughter. All this seemed very reasonable. But I had formerly been a great lover of fish, and when this came hot out of the frying pan, it smelt admirably well. I balanced some time between principle and inclination, till I recollected that when the fish were opened I saw smaller fish taken out of their stomachs. Then thought I, if you eat one another, I don't see why we mayn't eat you. So I dined upon cod very heartily and continued to eat with other people, returning only now and then occasionally to a vegetable diet. So convenient a thing it is to be a *reasonable creature*, since it enables one to find or make a reason for everything one has a mind to do.

Franklin of course is being playful; he is *not* engaging in critical think-ing. He tells us that he loved fish, that this fish "smelt admirably well," and so we are prepared for him to find a reason (here one as weak as "Fish eat fish, so people may eat fish") to abandon his vegetarianism. (But think: Fish also eat their own young. May we therefore eat ours?) Still, Franklin touches on a truth: If necessary, we can find reasons to justify whatever we want. That is, instead of reasoning we may *rationalize* (devise a self-serving but dishonest reason), like the fox in Aesop's fables who, finding the grapes he desired were out of his reach, consoled himself with the thought they were probably sour.

Probably we can never be certain that we are not rationalizing, but— except when, like Franklin, we are being playful—we can seek to think critically about our own beliefs, scrutinizing our assumptions, looking for counterevidence, and wondering if different conclusions can reasonably be drawn.

SOME PROCEDURES IN ARGUMENT

Definition

We have already glanced at an argument over the proposition that "all men are created equal," and we saw that the words needed clarification. *Equal* meant, in the context, not physically or mentally equal but some-thing like "equal in rights," equal politically and legally. (And of course "men" meant "men and women.") Words do not always mean exactly what they seem to: There is no lead in a lead pencil, and a standard 2-by-4 is $1\frac{5}{8}$ inches in thickness and $3\frac{3}{8}$ inches in width.

Definition by Synonym • Let's return, for a moment, to *por-nography*, a word that, we saw, is not easily defined. One way to define a word is to offer a *synonym*. Thus, pornography can be defined, at least roughly, as "obscenity" (something indecent). But definition by synonym is usually only a start, because we find that we will have to define the synonym and, besides, very few words have exact synonyms. (In fact, *pornography* and *obscenity* are not exact synonyms.)

Definition by Example • A second way to define something is to point to an example (this is often called **ostensive definition,** from the Latin *ostendere,* "to show"). This method can be very helpful, ensuring that both writer and reader are talking about the same thing, but it also has its limitations. A few decades ago many people pointed to James Joyce's *Ulysses* and D. H. Lawrence's *Lady Chatterley's Lover* as examples of obscene novels, but today these books are regarded as literary masterpieces. Possibly they can be obscene and also be literary masterpieces. (Joyce's wife is reported to have said of her husband, "He may have been a great writer, but . . . he had a very dirty mind.")

One of the difficulties of using an example, however, is that the example is richer, more complex than the term it is being used to define, and this richness and complexity get in the way of achieving a clear definition. Thus, if one cites Lawrence's *Lady Chatterley's Lover* as an example of pornography, a listener may erroneously think that pornography has something to do with British novels or with heterosexual relationships outside of marriage. Yet neither of these ideas is part of the concept of pornography.

We are not trying here to formulate a satisfactory definition of *pornography;* our object is to say that an argument will be most fruitful if the participants first agree on what they are talking about, and that one way to secure such agreement is to define the topic ostensively. Choosing the right example, one that has all the central or typical characteristics, can make a topic not only clear but vivid.

Stipulative Definition • In arguing, you can legitimately **stipulate** a definition, saying, perhaps, that by *Native American* you mean any person with any Native American blood; or you can say that you mean any person who has at least one grandparent of pure Native American blood. Or you can stipulate that by *Native American* you mean someone who has at least one great-grandparent of pure Native American blood. A stipulative definition is appropriate where no fixed or standard definition is available and where some arbitrary specification is necessary in order to fix the meaning of a key term in the argument. Not everyone may be willing to accept your definition, and alternatives to your stipulations can probably be defended. In any case, when you stipulate a definition, your audience knows what *you* mean by it.

Of course it would *not* be reasonable to stipulate that by "Native American" you mean anyone with a deep interest in North American aborigines. That's just too idiosyncratic to be useful. Similarly, an essay on Jews in America will have to rely on some definition of the key idea. Perhaps the writer will stipulate the definition used in Israel: A Jew is any person with a Jewish mother, or, if not born of a Jewish mother, a person who has formally adopted the Jewish faith. Or perhaps the writer will stipulate another meaning: Jews are people who consider themselves to be Jews. Some sort of reasonable definition must be offered.

To stipulate, however, that by Jews you mean persons who believe that the area formerly called Palestine rightfully belongs to the Jews would hopelessly confuse matters. Remember the old riddle and the answer: If you call a dog's tail a leg, how many legs does a dog have? Answer: Four. Calling a tail a leg doesn't make it a leg.

Suppose someone says she means by a *Communist* "anyone who opposes the president, does not go to church, and favors a more nearly equal distribution of wealth and property." A dictionary or encyclopedia will tell us that a person is a Communist who accepts the main doctrines of Karl Marx (or perhaps of Marxism-Leninism). For many purposes, we may think of Communists as persons who belong to some Communist political party, by analogy with Democrats and Republicans. Or we may even think of a Communist as someone who supports what is common to the constitutions and governments currently in power in China and Cuba. But what is the point of the misleading stipulative definition of *Communist* given at the beginning of this paragraph, except to cast disapproval on everyone whose views bring them within the definition?

There is no good reason for offering this definition, and there are two goods reasons against it. The first is that we already have perfectly adequate definitions of *Communist,* and one should learn them and rely on them until the need to revise and improve them occurs. The second reason for refraining from using a misleading stipulative definition is that it is unfair to tar with a dirty and sticky brush nonchurchgoers and the rest by calling them derogatory names they do not deserve. Even if it is true that Communists favor more egalitarian distribution of wealth and property, the converse is *not* true: Not all egalitarians are Communists. Furthermore, if something is economically unsound or morally objectionable about such egalitarianism, the only responsible way to make that point is to argue against it.

A stipulation may be helpful and legitimate. Here is the opening paragraph of an essay by Richard B. Brandt titled "The Morality and Rationality of Suicide." Notice that the author first stipulates a definition and then, aware that the definition may strike some readers as too broad and therefore unreasonable or odd, he offers a reason on behalf of his definition:

> "Suicide" is conveniently defined, for our purposes, as doing something which results in one's death, either from the intention of ending one's life or the intention to bring about some other state of affairs (such as relief from pain) which one thinks it certain or highly probable can be achieved only by means of death or will produce death. It may seem odd to classify an act of heroic self-sacrifice on the part of a soldier as suicide. It is simpler, however, not to try to define "suicide" so that an act of suicide is always irrational or immoral in some way; if we adopt a neutral definition like the above we can still proceed to ask when an act of sui-

cide in that sense is rational, morally justifiable, and so on, so that all evaluations anyone might wish to make can still be made. — (*A Handbook for the Study of Suicide,* ed. Seymour Perlin)

Sometimes a definition that at first seems extremely odd can be made acceptable, if strong reasons are offered in its support. Sometimes, in fact, an odd definition marks a great intellectual step forward. For instance, recently the Supreme Court recognized that "speech" includes symbolic nonverbal expression such as protesting against a war by wearing armbands or by flying the American flag upside down. Such actions, because they express ideas or emotions, are now protected by the First Amendment. Few people today would disagree that *speech* should include symbolic gestures. (We include an example of controversy over precisely this issue, in Derek Bok's "Protecting Freedom of Expression on the Campus," in Chapter 2.)

An example that seems notably eccentric to many readers and thus far has not gained much support is from page 94 of *Practical Ethics,* in which Peter Singer suggests that a nonhuman being can be a *person.* He admits that "it sounds odd to call an animal a person," but says that it seems so only because of our bad habit of sharply separating ourselves from other species. For Singer, "persons" are "rational and self-conscious beings, aware of themselves as distinct entities with a past and a future." Thus, although a newborn infant is a human being, it is not a person; on the other hand, an adult chimpanzee is not a human being but probably is a person. You don't have to agree with Singer to know exactly what he means and where he stands. Moreover, if you read his essay you may even find that his reasons are plausible and that by means of his unusual definition he has enlarged your thinking.

The Importance of Definitions • Trying to decide on the best way to define a key idea or a central concept is often difficult as well as controversial. *Death,* for example, has been redefined in recent years. Traditionally, a person was dead when there was no longer any heartbeat. But with advancing medical technology, the medical profession has persuaded legislatures to redefine *death* by reference to cessation of cerebral and cortical functions — so-called "brain death." Recently, some scholars have hoped to bring clarity into the abortion debate by redefining *life.*

Traditionally, human life begins at birth, or perhaps at viability (the capacity of a fetus to live independently of the uterine environment). Now, however, some are proposing a "brain birth" definition, in the hope of resolving the abortion controversy. A *New York Times* story of November 8, 1990 reported that these thinkers want abortion to be prohibited by law at the point where "integrated brain functioning begins to emerge — about 70 days after conception." Whatever the merits of such a redefinition, the debate is convincing evidence of just how important the definition of certain terms can be.

Last Words about Definition • Since Plato's time, in the fourth century B.C., it has often been argued that the best way to give a definition is to state the *essence* of the thing being defined. Thus, the classic example defines *man* as "a rational animal." (Today, to avoid sexist implications, instead of *man* we would say *human being* or *person.*) That is, the property of *rational animality* is taken to be the essence of every human creature, and so it must be mentioned in the definition of *man*. This statement guarantees that the definition is neither too broad nor too narrow. But philosophers have long criticized this alleged ideal type of definition, on several grounds, one of which is that no one can propose such definitions without assuming that the thing being defined has an essence in the first place — an assumption that is not necessary. Thus, we may want to define *causality,* or *explanation,* or even *definition* itself, but it is doubtful whether it is sound to assume that any of these things has an essence.

A much better way to provide a definition is to offer a set of **sufficient and necessary conditions.** Suppose we want to define the word *circle* and are conscious of the need to keep circles distinct from other geometrical figures such as rectangles and spheres. We might express our definition by citing sufficient and necessary conditions as follows: "Anything is a circle *if and only if* it is a closed plane figure, all points on the circumference of which are equidistant from the center." Using the connective "if and only" (called the *biconditional*) between the definition and what is being defined helps to force into our consciousness the need to make the definition neither too exclusive (too narrow) nor too inclusive (too broad). Of course, for most ordinary purposes we don't require such a formally precise and explicit definition. Nevertheless, perhaps the best criterion to keep in mind when assessing a proposed definition is whether it can be stated in the "if and only if" form, and whether, if it is so stated, it is true; that is, if it truly specifies *all and only* the things covered by the word being defined.

Definitions can be given by

- synonym,
- example,
- stipulation,
- mentioning the essence, and
- stating necessary and sufficient conditions.

Assumptions

In Chapter 1 we discussed the **assumptions** made by the authors of two essays on competitive sports. But we have more to say about assumptions. We have already said that in the form of discourse known as argument, certain statements are offered as reasons for other statements. But even the longest and most complex chain of reasoning or proof is fastened to assumptions, one or more *unexamined beliefs*. (Even if such a belief is shared by writer and reader, it is no less an assumption.) Benjamin Franklin argued against paying salaries to the holders of executive offices in the federal government on the grounds that men are moved by ambition and by avarice (love of power and of money), and that powerful positions confering wealth incite men to do their worst. These assumptions he stated, though he felt no need to argue them at length because he assumed that his readers shared them.

An assumption may be unstated. The writer, painstakingly arguing specific points, may choose to keep one or more of the assumptions tacit. Or the writer may be as unaware of some underlying assumption as of the surrounding air. For example, Franklin didn't even bother to state another assumption. He assumed that persons of wealth who accept an unpaying job (after all, only persons of wealth could afford to hold unpaid government jobs) will have at heart the interests of all classes of people, not only the interests of their own class. If you think critically about this assumption, you may find reasons to doubt it. Surely one reason we pay our legislators is to make certain that the legislature does not consist only of people whose incomes may give them an inadequate view of the needs of others.

An Example: Assumptions in the Argument Permitting Abortion

1. Ours is a pluralistic society, in which we believe that the religious beliefs of one group should not be imposed on others.
2. Personal privacy is a right, and a woman's body is hers, not to be violated by laws that tell her she cannot do certain things to her body.

But these (and other) arguments *assume* that a fetus is not — or not yet — a person, and therefore is not entitled to the same protection against assaults that we are. Virtually all of us assume that it is usually wrong to kill a human being. Granted, we may find instances in which we believe it is acceptable to take a human life, such as self-defense against a would-be murderer. But even here we find a shared assumption, that persons are ordinarily entitled not to be killed.

The argument about abortion, then, usually depends on opposed assumptions: For one group, the fetus is a human being and a potential person — and this potentiality is decisive. But for the other group it is not. Persons arguing one side or the other of the abortion issue ought to be aware that opponents may not share their assumptions.

Premises and Syllogisms

Premises are stated assumptions used as reasons in an argument. The joining of two premises — two statements or propositions taken to be true —

to produce a conclusion, a third statement, is called a **syllogism** (Greek, for "a reckoning together"). The classic example is this:

Major Premise: All human beings are mortal.

Minor Premise: Socrates is a human being.

Conclusion: Socrates is mortal.

Deduction

The mental process of moving from one statement ("All human beings are mortal") through another ("Socrates is a human being") to yet a further statement ("Socrates is mortal") is called **deduction,** from Latin "lead down from." In this sense, deductive reasoning does not give us any new knowledge, although it is easy to construct examples that have so many premises, or premises that are so complex, that the conclusion really does come as news to most who examine the argument. Thus, the great detective Sherlock Holmes was credited by his admiring colleague, Dr. Watson, with unusual powers of deduction. Watson meant in part that Holmes could see the logical consequences of apparently disconnected reasons, the number and complexity of which left others at a loss. What is common in all cases of deduction is that the reasons or premises offered are supposed to contain within themselves, so to speak, the conclusion extracted from them.

Often a syllogism is abbreviated. Martin Luther King, Jr., defending a protest march, wrote, in "Letter from Birmingham Jail":

You assert that our actions, even though peaceful, must be condemned because they precipitate violence.

Fully expressed, the argument that King attributes to his critics would be stated thus:

We must condemn actions (even if peaceful) that precipitate violence.

This action (though peaceful) will precipitate violence.

Therefore we must condemn this action.

An incomplete or abbreviated syllogism, in which one of the premises is left unstated, of the sort found in King's original quotation, is called an **enthymeme** (Greek: "in the mind").

Here is another, more whimsical example of an enthymeme, in which both a premise and the conclusion are left implicit. Henry David Thoreau is said to have remarked that "Circumstantial evidence can be very strong, as when you find a trout in the milk." The joke, perhaps intelligible only to people born before 1930 or so, depends on the fact that milk used to be sold "in bulk"; that is, ladled out of a big can directly to the customer by the farmer or grocer. This practice was finally prohibited in the 1930s because for centuries the sellers, in order to increase their profit, were known to dilute the milk with water. Thoreau's enthymeme can be fully expressed thus:

> Trout live only in water.
>
> This milk has a trout in it.
>
> Therefore this milk has water in it.

Sound Arguments

The purpose of a syllogism is to *prove* its conclusion from its premises. This is done by making sure that the argument satisfies both of two independent criteria:

> First, all of the premises must be *true.*
>
> Second, the syllogism must be *valid.*

Once these criteria are satisfied, the conclusion of the syllogism is guaranteed. Any such argument is said to prove its conclusion, or, to use another term, is said to be **sound.** Here's an example of a sound argument, a syllogism that proves its conclusion:

> No city in Nevada has a population over 200,000.
>
> Denver has a population over 200,000.
>
> Therefore Denver is not a city in Nevada.

Each premise is true, and the syllogism is **valid,** so it proves its conclusion.

But how do we tell in any given case that an argument is sound? We perform two different tests, one for the truth of each of the premises and another for the validity of the argument.

The basic test for the **truth** of a premise is to determine whether what it asserts corresponds with reality; if it does, then it is true, and if it doesn't then it is false. Everything depends on the content of the premise—what it asserts—and the evidence for it. (In the preceding syllogism, the truth of the premises can be tested by checking population statistics in a recent almanac.)

The test for validity is quite different. We define a valid argument as one in which the conclusion follows from the premises, so that if all the premises are true then the conclusion *must* be true, too. The general test for validity, then, is this: If one grants the premises, one must also grant the conclusion. Or to put it another way, if one grants the premises but denies the conclusion, is one caught in a self-contradiction? If so, the argument is valid; if not, the argument is invalid.

The preceding syllogism obviously passes this test. If you grant the population information given in the premises but deny the conclusion, you have contradicted yourself. Even if the population information were in error, the conclusion in this syllogism would still follow from the premises—the hallmark of a valid argument! This is because the validity of an argument is a purely formal matter concerning the *relation* between premises and conclusion given what they mean.

One can see this more clearly by examining an argument that is valid but that does *not* prove its conclusion. Here is an example of such a syllogism:

> The whale is a large fish.
>
> All large fish have scales.
>
> Therefore, whales have scales.

We know that the premises and the conclusion are false: Whales are mammals, not fish, and not all large fish have scales (sharks have no scales, for instance). But where the issue is the validity of the argument, the truth of the premises and the conclusion is beside the point. Just a little reflection assures us that *if* both of these premises were true, then the conclusion would have to be true as well. That is, anyone who grants the premises of this syllogism and yet denies the conclusion has contradicted herself. So the validity of an argument does not in any way depend on the truth of the premises or the conclusion.

A sound argument, as we said, is an argument that passes both the test of true premises and the test of valid inference. To put it another way, a sound argument is one that passes the test of *content* (the premises are true, as a matter of fact) and the test of *form* (its premises and conclusion, by virtue of their very meanings, are so related that it is impossible for the premises to be true and the conclusion false).

Accordingly, an unsound argument, an argument that fails to prove its conclusion, suffers from one or both of two defects. First, not all of the premises are true. Second, the argument is invalid. Usually it is one or both of these defects that we have in mind when we object to someone's argument as "illogical." In evaluating someone's deductive argument, therefore, you must always ask: Is it vulnerable to criticism on the ground that one (or more) of its premises is false? Or is the inference itself vulnerable, because whether or not all the premises are all true, even if they were the conclusion still wouldn't follow?

A deductive argument *proves* its conclusion if and only if *two conditions* are satisfied: (1) All the premises are *true;* (2) it would be *inconsistent to assert the premises and deny the conclusions.*

A Word about False Premises · Suppose that one or more of the premises of a syllogism is false, but the syllogism itself is valid. What does that tell us about the truth of the conclusion? Consider this example:

> All Americans prefer vanilla ice cream to other flavors.
>
> Martina Navratilova is an American.
>
> Therefore Martina Navratilova prefers vanilla ice cream to other flavors.

The first (or major) premise in this syllogism is false. Yet the argument passes our formal test for validity; it is clear that if one grants both premises, one must accept the conclusion. So we can say that the conclusion *follows from* its premises, even though the premises *do not prove* the conclusion. This is not as paradoxical as it may sound. For all we know, the conclusion of this argument may in fact be true; Martina Navratilova may indeed prefer vanilla ice cream, and the odds are that she does, since consumption statistics show that *most* (even if not all) Americans prefer vanilla. Nevertheless, if the conclusion in this syllogism is true, it is not because this argument proved it.

A Word about Invalid Syllogisms · Usually, one can detect a false premise in an argument, especially when the suspect premise appears in someone else's argument. A trickier business is the invalid syllogism. Consider this argument:

All crows are black.

This bird is black.

Therefore this bird is a crow.

Let's assume that both of the premises are true. What does this tell us about the truth of the conclusion? Nothing, because the argument is invalid. The *form* of the reasoning, the structure of the argument, is such that its premises (whether true or false) do not guarantee the conclusion. Even if both the premises were true, the conclusion might still be false.

In the syllogism above, the conclusion may well be true. It could be that the bird referred to in the second (minor) premise is a crow. But the conclusion might be false, because not only crows are black; ravens and blackbirds are also black. If the minor premise is asserted on the strength of observing a blackbird, then the conclusion surely is false: *This* bird is *not* a crow. So the argument is invalid, since as it stands it would lead us from true premises to accept a false conclusion.

How do we tell, in general and in particular cases, whether a syllogism is valid? As you know, chemists use litmus paper to enable them to tell instantly whether the liquid in a test tube is an acid or a base. Unfortunately, logic has no litmus test to tell us instantly whether an argument is valid or invalid. Logicians beginning with Aristotle have developed techniques that enable them to test any given argument, no matter how complex or subtle, to determine its validity. But the results of their labors cannot be expressed in a paragraph or even a few pages; not for nothing are semester-long courses devoted to teaching formal deductive logic. Apart from advising you to consult the chapter on these matters ("A Logician's View"), all we can do here is repeat two basic points.

First, validity of deductive arguments is a matter of their *form* or *structure*. Even syllogisms like the one on page 43 come in a large variety of forms (256 different ones, to be precise), and only some of these forms are valid. Second, all valid deductive arguments (and only such arguments) pass this test: If one accepts all the premises, then one must accept the conclusion as well. Hence, if it is possible to accept the premises but reject the conclusion (without self-contradiction, of course), then the argument is invalid.

Let us exit from further discussion of this important but difficult subject on a lighter note. Many illogical arguments masquerade as logical. Consider this example: If it takes a horse and carriage four hours to go from Pinsk to Chelm, does it follow that if you have a carriage with two horses you will get there in two hours? In the chapter titled "A Logician's View," we discuss at some length other kinds of deductive arguments, as well as **fallacies,** which are kinds of invalid reasoning.

Induction

Whereas the purpose of deduction is to extract the hidden consequences of our beliefs and assumptions, the purpose of **induction** is to use information about observed cases in order to reach a conclusion about unobserved cases. (The word comes from Latin *in ducere,* "to lead into," or "to lead up to.") If we observe that the bite of a certain snake is poisonous, we may conclude on this evidence that another snake of the same general type is also poisonous. Our inference might be even broader. If we observe that snake after snake of a certain type has a poisonous bite, and that these snakes are all rattlesnakes, we are tempted to **generalize** that all rattlesnakes are poisonous.

Unlike deduction, induction gives us conclusions that go beyond the information contained in the premises used in their support. Not surprisingly, the conclusions of inductive reasoning are not always true, even when all the premises are true. Earlier we gave as an example the belief that the subway runs at 6:00 A.M. every day, based on our observation that on previous days it ran at 6:00 A.M. Suppose, following this reasoning, one arrives at the subway platform just before 6:00 A.M. on a given day only to discover after an hour of waiting that there still is no train. What inference should we draw to explain this? Possibly today is Sunday, and the subway doesn't run before 7:00 A.M. Or possibly there was a breakdown earlier this morning. Whatever the explanation, we relied on a sample that was not large enough (a larger sample might have included some early morning breakdowns), or not representative enough (a more representative sample would have included the later starts on holidays).

A Word about Samples • When we reason inductively, much depends on the size and the quality of the sample. We may interview five members of Alpha Tau Omega and find that all five are Republicans, yet we cannot legitimately conclude that all members of ATO are Republicans. The problem is not always one of failing to interview large numbers. A poll of ten thousand college students tells us very little about "college students" if all ten thousand are white males at the University of Texas. Such a sam-

ple, because it leaves out women and minority males, obviously is not sufficiently *representative* of "college students" as a group. Further, though not
all of the students at the University of Texas are from Texas, or even from
the Southwest, it is quite likely that the student body is not fully representative (for instance, in race and in income) of American college students. If
this conjecture is correct, even a truly representative sample of University
of Texas students would not allow one to draw firm conclusions about
American college students.

In short: An argument that uses samples ought to tell the reader how
the samples were chosen. If it does not provide this information, it may
rightly be treated with suspicion.

Evidence

Induction is obviously of use in arguing. If, for example, one is arguing
that handguns should be controlled, one will point to specific cases in
which handguns caused accidents, or were used to commit crimes. If one is
arguing that abortion has a traumatic effect on women, one will point to
women who testify to that effect. Each instance constitutes **evidence** for
the relevant generalization.

In a courtroom, evidence bearing on the guilt of the accused is introduced by the prosecution, and evidence to the contrary is introduced by
the defense. Not all evidence is admissible (hearsay, for one, is not, even if
it is true), and the law of evidence is a highly developed subject in jurisprudence. In the forum of daily life, the sources of evidence are less disci-
plined. Daily experience, a particularly memorable observation, an unusual
event we witnessed—any or all of these may be used as evidence for (or
against) some belief, theory, hypothesis, or explanation. The systematic
study of what experience can yield is what science does, and one of the
most distinctive features of the evidence that scientists can marshal on behalf of their claims is that it is the result of **experimentation.** Experiments
are deliberately contrived situations, often quite complex in their technology, designed to yield particular observations. What the ordinary person
does with unaided eye and ear, the scientist does, much more carefully and
thoroughly, with the help of laboratory instruments.

The variety, extent, and reliability of the evidence obtained in daily life
and in the laboratory are quite different. It is hardly a surprise that in our
civilization, much more weight is attached to the "findings" of scientists
than to the corroborative (much less the contrary) experiences of the ordinary person. No one today would seriously argue that the sun really does
go around the earth, just because it looks that way; nor would we argue
that because viruses are invisible to the naked eye they cannot cause symptoms such as swellings and fevers, which are quite plainly visible.

Examples

One form of evidence is the **example.** Suppose that we argue that a
candidate is untrustworthy and should not be elected to public office. We

point to episodes in his career — his misuse of funds in 1990, and the false charges he made against an opponent in 1994 — as examples of his untrustworthiness. Or, if we are arguing that Truman ordered the atom bomb dropped to save American (and, for that matter, Japanese) lives that otherwise would have been lost in a hard-fought invasion of Japan, we point to the stubbornness of the Japanese defenders in battles on the islands of Saipan, Iwo Jima, and Okinawa, where the Japanese fought to the death rather than surrender.

These examples, we say, show us that the Japanese defenders of the main islands would have fought to the end, even though they knew they would be defeated. Or, if we take a different view of Truman's action, and argue that the war in effect was already won and that Truman had no justification for dropping the bomb, we can cite examples of the Japanese willingness to end the war, such as secret negotiations in which they sent out peace feelers.

An example is a sample; the two words come from the same Old French word, *essample,* from the Latin *exemplum,* which means "something taken out"; that is, a selection from the group. A Yiddish proverb shrewdly says that "'For example' is no proof," but the evidence of well-chosen examples can go a long way toward helping a writer to convince an audience.

In arguments, three sorts of examples are especially common:

1. real events,
2. invented instances (artificial or hypothetical cases), and
3. analogies.

We will treat each of these briefly.

Real Events • In referring to Truman's decision to drop the atom bomb, we have already touched on examples drawn from real events, the battles at Saipan and elsewhere. And we have also seen Ben Franklin pointing to an allegedly real happening, a fish that had consumed a smaller fish. The advantage of an example drawn from real life, whether a great historical event or a local incident, is that its reality gives it weight. It can't simply be brushed off.

On the other hand, an example drawn from reality may not provide as clear-cut an instance as could be wished for. Suppose, for instance, that someone cites the Japanese army's behavior on Saipan and on Iwo Jima as evidence that the Japanese later would have fought to the death in an American invasion of Japan, and would therefore have inflicted terrible losses on themselves and on the Americans. This example is open to the response that in August 1945, when Truman dropped the bomb, the situation was very different. In June and July 1945, Japanese diplomats had already sent out secret peace feelers; Emperor Hirohito probably wanted peace by then; and so on.

Similarly, in support of the argument that nations will not resort to atomic weapons, some people have offered as evidence the fact that since World War I the great powers have not used poison gas. But the argument needs more support than this fact provides. Poison gas was not decisive or even highly effective in World War I. Moreover, the invention of gas masks made it obsolete.

In short, any *real* event is, so to speak, so entangled in its historical circumstances that one may question whether indeed it is adequate or even relevant evidence in the case being argued. In using a real event as an example (and real events certainly can be used), the writer ordinarily must demonstrate that the event can be taken out of its historical context so to speak, and used in the new context of argument. Thus, in an argument against any further use in warfare of atomic weapons, one might point to the example of the many deaths and horrible injuries inflicted on the Japanese at Hiroshima and Nagasaki, in the confident belief that these effects of nuclear weapons will invariably occur and did not depend on any special circumstances of their use in Japan in 1945.

Invented Instances • **Artificial** or **hypothetical cases, invented instances,** have the great advantage of being protected from objections of the sort just given. Recall Thoreau's trout in the milk; that was a colorful hypothetical case that nicely illustrated his point. An invented instance ("Let's assume that a burglar promises not to shoot a householder if the householder swears not to identify him. Is the householder bound by the oath?") is something like a drawing of a flower in a botany textbook, or a diagram of the folds of a mountain in a geology textbook. It is admittedly false, but by virtue of its simplifications it sets forth the relevant details very clearly. Thus, in a discussion of rights, the philosopher Charles Frankel says:

> Strictly speaking, when we assert a right for X, we assert that Y has a duty. Strictly speaking, that Y has such a duty presupposes that Y has the capacity to perform this duty. It would be nonsense to say, for example, that a nonswimmer has a moral duty to swim to the help of a drowning man.

This invented example is admirably clear, and it is immune to charges that might muddy the issue if Frankel, instead of referring to a wholly abstract person, Y, talked about some real person, Jones, who did not rescue a drowning man. For then he would get bogged down over arguing about whether Jones *really* couldn't swim well enough to help, and so on.

Yet invented cases have their drawbacks. First and foremost, they cannot be used as evidence. A purely hypothetical example can illustrate a point or provoke reconsideration of a generalization, but it cannot substitute for actual events as evidence supporting an inductive inference. Sometimes such examples are so fanciful, so remote from life that they fail to carry conviction with the reader. Thus the philosopher Judith Jarvis Thomson, in the course of an argument entitled "A Defense of Abortion," asks us to imagine that we wake up one day and find that against our will a celebrated violinist whose body is not adequately functioning has been hooked up into our body, for life-support. Do we have the right to unplug the violinist? Readers of the essays in this book will have to decide for themselves whether the invented cases proposed by various authors are helpful or whether they are so remote that they hinder thought. Readers will have to decide, too, about when they can use invented cases to advance their own arguments.

But we add one point: Even a highly fanciful invented case can have the valuable effect of forcing us to see where we stand. We may say that we are, in all circumstances, against vivisection. But what would we say if we thought that an experiment on one mouse would save the life of someone whom we love? Or, conversely, if one approves of vivisection, would one also approve of sacrificing the last giant panda in order to save the life of a senile stranger, a person who in any case probably would not live longer than another year? Artificial cases of this sort can help us to see that, well, no, we didn't really mean to say such-and-such when we said so-and-so.

Analogies • The third sort of example, **analogy,** is a kind of comparison. Strictly, an analogy is an extended comparison in which different things are shown to be similar in several ways. Thus, if one wants to argue that a head of state should have extraordinary power during wartime, one can argue that the state at such a time is like a ship in a storm: The crew is needed to lend its help, but the decisions are best left to the captain. (Notice that an analogy compares things that are relatively *unlike*. Comparing the plight of one ship to another, or of one government to another, is not an analogy; it is an inductive inference from one case of the same sort to another such case.) Or take another analogy: We have already glanced at Judith Thomson's hypothetical case in which the reader wakes up to find himself or herself hooked up to a violinist. Thomson uses this situation as an analogy in an argument about abortion. The reader stands for the mother, the violinist for the unwanted fetus. Whether this analogy is close enough to pregnancy to help illuminate our thinking about abortion is something that you may want to think about.

The problem with argument by analogy is this: Two admittedly different things are agreed to be similar in several ways, and the arguer goes on to assert or imply that they are also similar in the point that is being argued. (That is why Thomson argues that if something is true of the reader-hooked-up-to-a-violinist, it is also true of the pregnant mother-hooked-up-to-a-fetus.) But of course despite some similarities, the two things which are said to be analogous and which are indeed similar in characteristics A, B, and C, are also different, let's say in characteristics D and E. As Bishop Butler said, about two hundred fifty years ago, "Everything is what it is, and not another thing."

Analogies can be convincing, especially because they can make complex issues simple ("Don't change horses in midstream" of course is not a statement about riding horses across a river, but about choosing leaders in critical times). Still, in the end, analogies can prove nothing. What may be true about riding horses across a stream need not be true about choosing leaders in troubled times, or not true about a given change of leadership. Riding horses across a stream and choosing leaders are, at bottom, different things, and however much these activities may be said to resemble one another, they remain different, and what is true for one need not be true for the other.

Analogies can be helpful in developing our thoughts. It is sometimes argued, for instance—on the analogy of the doctor-patient or the lawyer-client or the priest-penitent relationship—that newspaper and television reporters should not be required to reveal their confidential sources. That is worth thinking about: Do the similarities run deep enough, or are there fundamental differences? Or take another example: Some writers who support abortion argue that the fetus is not a person any more than the acorn is an oak. That is also worth thinking about. But one should also think about this response: A fetus is not a person, just as an acorn is not an oak, but an acorn is a potential oak, and a fetus is a potential person, a potential adult human being. Children, even newborn infants, have rights, and one way to explain this claim is to call attention to their potentiality to become mature adults. And so some people argue that the fetus, by analogy, has the rights of an infant, for the fetus, like the infant, is a potential adult.

While we're on this subject let's consider a very brief comparison made by Jill Knight, a member of the British Parliament, speaking about abortion:

> Babies are not like bad teeth, to be jerked out because they cause suffering.

Her point is effectively put; it remains for the reader to decide whether or not fetuses are *babies;* and, second, if a fetus is not a baby, *why* it can or can't be treated like a bad tooth. And yet a further bit of analogical reasoning, again about abortion: Thomas Sowell, an economist at the Hoover Institute, grants that women have a legal right to abortion, but he objects to the government's paying for abortions:

> Because the courts have ruled that women have a legal right to an abortion, some people have jumped to the conclusion that the government has to pay for it. You have a constitutional right to privacy, but the government has no obligation to pay for your window shades. . . . (*Pink and Brown People*, p. 57)

We leave it to the reader to decide if the analogy is compelling—that is, if the points of resemblance are sufficiently significant to allow one to conclude that what is true of people wanting window shades should be true of people wanting abortions.

Authoritative Testimony

Another form of evidence is **testimony,** the citation or quotation of authorities. In daily life we rely heavily on authorities of all sorts: We get a doctor's opinion about our health, we read a book because an intelligent friend recommends it, we see a movie because a critic gave it a good review, and we pay at least a little attention to the weather forecaster.

In setting forth an argument, one often tries to show that one's view is supported by notable figures, perhaps Jefferson, Lincoln, and Martin Luther King, Jr., or scientists who won the Nobel Prize. You may recall that in the second chapter, in talking about definitions of pornography, we referred to Kenneth Clark. To make certain that you were impressed by his testimony even if you had never heard of him, we described him as "probably the most influential English-speaking art critic of our century." But heed some words of caution:

- Be sure that the authority, however notable, is an authority on the topic in question. A well-known biologist on vitamins, yes, but not on the justice of a war.

- Be sure the authority is not biased. A chemist employed by the tobacco industry isn't likely to admit that smoking may be harmful, and a "director of publications" (that means a press agent) for a hockey team isn't likely to admit that watching or even playing ice hockey stimulates violence.

- Beware of nameless authorities: "a thousand doctors," "leading educators," "researchers at a major medical school."

- Be careful in using authorities who indeed were great authorities in their day but who now may be out of date (Adam Smith on economics, Julius Caesar on the art of war, Pasteur on medicine).

- Cite authorities whose opinions your readers will value. William F. Buckley's opinion means a good deal to readers of The National Review but not to most feminists. Gloria Steinem's opinion carries weight with many feminists but not much with persons who support traditional family values. If you are writing for the general reader, your usual audience, cite authorities who are likely to be accepted by the general reader.

One other point: *You* may be an authority. You probably aren't nationally known, but on some topics you perhaps can speak with authority, the authority of personal experience. You may have been injured on a motorcycle while riding without wearing a helmet, or you may have escaped injury because you wore a helmet; you may have dropped out of school and then returned; you may have tutored a student whose native language is not English, or you may be such a student and you may have received tutoring. You may have attended a school with a bilingual education program. Your personal testimony on topics relating to these issues may be invaluable, and a reader will probably consider it seriously.

Statistics

The last sort of evidence we will discuss here is quantitative or statistical. The maxim More Is Better captures a basic idea of quantitative evidence. Because we know that 90 percent is greater than 75 percent, we are usually ready to grant that any claim supported by experience in 90 percent of the cases is more likely to be true than an alternative claim supported by experience only 75 percent of the time. The greater the difference, the greater our confidence. Consider an example. Honors at graduation from college are often computed on a student's cumulative grade-point average (GPA). The undisputed assumption is that the nearer a student's GPA is to a perfect record (4.0), the better scholar he or she is, and therefore the more deserving of highest honors. Consequently, a student with a GPA of 3.9 at the end of her senior year is a stronger candidate for graduation summa cum laude than another student with a GPA of 3.6. When faculty members on the honors committee argue over the relative academic merits of graduating seniors, we know that these quantitative, statistical differences in student GPAs will be the basic (even if not the only) kind of evidence under discussion.

Graphs, Tables, Numbers · Statistical information can be marshaled and presented in many forms, but it tends to fall into two main types: the graphic and the numerical. Graphs, tables, and pie charts are familiar ways of presenting quantitative data in an eye-catching manner. To prepare the graphics, however, one first has to get the numbers themselves under control, and for many purposes (such as writing argumentative essays) it is probably more convenient simply to stick with the numbers themselves.

But should the numbers be presented in percentages, or in fractions? Should one report, say, that the federal budget underwent a twofold increase over the decade, or that it increased by 100 percent, or that it doubled, or that the budget at the beginning of the decade was one-half what it was at the end? Taken strictly, these are equivalent ways of saying the same thing. Choice among them, therefore, in an example like this perhaps will rest on whether one's aim is to dramatize the increase (a 100 percent increase looks larger than a doubling) or to play down the size of the increase.

Thinking about Statistical Evidence · Statistics often get a bad name because it is so easy to misuse them, unintentionally or not, and so difficult to be sure that they have been correctly gathered in the first place. (We remind you of the old saw "There are lies, damned lies, and statistics.") Every branch of social science and natural science needs statistical information, and countless decisions in public and private life are based on quantitative data in statistical form. It is extremely important, therefore, to be sensitive to the sources and reliability of the statistics, and to develop a healthy skepticism when confronted with statistics whose parentage is not fully explained.

Consider, for instance, a statistic that kept popping up during the baseball strike of 1994. The owners of the clubs kept saying that the average salary of a major league player was $1.2 million. (The **average** in this case is the result of dividing the total number of salary dollars by the number of players.) The players' union, however, did not talk about the average; rather, the union talked about the **median,** which was less than half of the average, a mere $500,000. (The *median* is the middle value in a distribution. Thus, of the 746 players, 363 earned less than $500,000, 361 earned more, and 22 earned exactly $500,000.) The union kept saying, correctly, that *most* players earned a good deal less than the $1.2 million figure that the owners kept citing; but the $1.2 million average sounded more impressive to the general public, and that is the figure that the guy in the street mentioned when asked for an opinion about the strike.

Here is a more complicated example of the difficulty of interpreting statistics. Violent crime increased in the 1960s and early 1970s, then leveled off, and began to decline in 1981. Did America become more violent for a while, and then become more law-abiding? Bruce Jackson in *Law and Disorder* suggests that much of the rise in the 1960s was due to the baby boom of 1948 to 1952. Whereas in 1960 the United States had only about 11 million people aged twenty to twenty-four, by 1972 it had almost 18 million of them, and it is people in this age group who are most likely to commit violent crimes. The decline in the rate of violent crime in the 1980s was accompanied by a decline in the proportion of the population in this age group — though of course some politicians and law enforcement officers took credit for the reduction in violent crime.

One other example may help to indicate the difficulties of interpreting statistics. According to the San Francisco police department, in 1990 the city received 1,074 citizen complaints against the police. Los Angeles received only half as many complaints in the same period, and Los Angeles has five times the population of San Francisco. Does this mean that the police of San Francisco are much rougher than the police of Los Angeles? Possibly. But some specialists who have studied the statistics not only for these two cities but also for many other cities have concluded that a department with proportionately more complaints against it is not necessarily more abusive than a department with fewer complaints. According to these experts, the more confidence that the citizens have in their police force, the more the citizens will complain about police misconduct. The relatively small number of complaints against the Los Angeles police department thus may indicate that the citizens of Los Angeles are so intimidated and

A CHECKLIST FOR EVALUATING STATISTICAL EVIDENCE

Regard statistical evidence (like all other evidence) cautiously, and don't accept it until you have thought about these questions:

- Was it compiled by a disinterested source? Of course, the name of the source does not always reveal its particular angle (for example, People for the American Way), but sometimes the name lets you know what to expect (National Rifle Association, American Civil Liberties Union).

- Is it based on an adequate sample? (A study pointed out that criminals have an average IQ of 91 to 93, whereas the general population has an IQ of 100. The conclusion drawn was that criminals have a lower IQ than the general population. This reading may be accurate, but some doubts have been expressed. For instance, because the entire sample of criminals consisted only of *convicted* criminals, this sample may be biased; possibly the criminals with higher IQs have enough intelligence not to get caught. Or, if they are caught, they are smart enough to hire better lawyers.)

- Is the statistical evidence recent enough to be relevant?

- How many of the factors likely to be relevant were identified and measured?

- Are the figures open to a different and equally plausible interpretation? (Remember the decline in violent crime, for which law enforcement officers took credit.)

have so little confidence in the system that they do not bother to complain.

We are not suggesting, of course, that everyone who uses statistics is trying to deceive, or even that many who use statistics are unconsciously deceived by them. We mean only to suggest that statistics are open to widely different interpretations and that often those col... numbers, so precise with their decimal points, are in fact i... possibly even worthless because they may be based o... ased samples.

Quiz

What is wrong with the following statistical proof th... school?

One-third of the time they are sleeping (about 122 days);

One-eighth of the time they are eating (three hours a day, totaling 45 days);

One-fourth of the time is taken up by summer and other vacations (91 days);

Two-sevenths of the year is weekends (104 days).

Total: 362 days — so how can a kid have time for school?

SATIRE, IRONY, SARCASM

In talking about definition, deduction, and evidence, we have been talking about means of rational persuasion. But, as mentioned earlier, there are also other means of persuasion. Take force, for example. If X kicks Y, threatens to destroy Y's means of livelihood, or threatens Y's life, X may persuade Y to cooperate. As Al Capone noted, "You can get more out of people with a gun and a kind word than with just a kind word." One form of irrational but sometimes highly effective persuasion is **satire** — that is, witty ridicule. A cartoonist may persuade viewers that a politician's views are unsound by caricaturing (and thus ridiculing) the politician's appearance, or by presenting a grotesquely distorted (funny, but unfair) picture of the issue.

Satiric artists often use caricature; satiric writers, also seeking to persuade by means of ridicule, often use **verbal irony.** In irony of this sort there is a contrast between what is said and what is meant. For instance, words of praise may be meant to imply blame (when Shakespeare's Cassius says, "Brutus is an honorable man," he means his hearers to think that Brutus is dishonorable), and words of modesty may be meant to imply superiority ("Of course I'm too dumb to understand this problem"). Such language, when heavy-handed, is called **sarcasm** ("You're a great guy," said to someone who will not lend the speaker ten dollars). If it is witty — if the jeering is in some degree clever — it is called irony rather than sarcasm.

Although ridicule is not a form of argument (because it is not a form of reasoning), passages of ridicule, especially verbal irony, sometimes appear in essays that are arguments. These passages, like reasons, or for that matter like appeals to the emotions, are efforts to persuade the hearer to accept the speaker's point of view. For example, in Judy Brady's essay "I Want a Wife" (p. 70), the writer, a woman, cannot really mean that she wants a wife. The pretense that she wants a wife gives the essay a playful, joking quality; her words must mean something other than what they seem to mean. But that she is not merely joking (satire has been defined as "joking in earnest") is evident; she is seeking to persuade. She has a point, and could argue it straight, but that would produce a very different sort of

Finally, here is a checklist with suggestions and questions for analyzing text.

**A CHECKLIST FOR ANALYZING
AN ARGUMENT**

1. What is the writer's thesis? Ask yourself:
   a. What claim is being asserted?
   b. What assumptions are being made — and are they acceptable?
   c. Are important terms satisfactorily defined?
2. What support is offered on behalf of the claim? Ask yourself:
   a. Are the examples relevant, and are they convincing?
   b. Are the statistics (if there are any) relevant, accurate, and complete? Do they allow only the interpretation that is offered in the argument?
   c. If authorities are cited, are they indeed authorities on this topic, and can they be regarded as impartial?
   d. Is this logic — deductive and inductive — valid?
   e. If there is an appeal to emotion — for instance, if satire is used to ridicule the opposing view — is this appeal acceptable?
3. Does the writer seem to you to be fair? Ask yourself:
   a. Are counterarguments adequately considered?
   b. Is there any evidence of dishonesty or of a discreditable attempt to manipulate the reader?

ARGUMENTS FOR ANALYSIS

Thomas B. Stoddard

Gay Marriages: Make Them Legal

"In sickness and in health, 'til death do us part." With those familiar words, millions of people each year are married, a public affirmation of a private bond that both society and the newlyweds hope will endure. Yet for

---

Thomas B. Stoddard (b. 1948), a lawyer, is executive director of the Lambda Legal Defense and Education Fund, a gay rights organization. In 1995 New York University School of Law established a fellowship in Stoddard's name, honoring him for his work on behalf of gay and lesbian rights.

This article is from the Op-Ed section of the New York Times, *March 4, 1988.*

nearly four years, Karen Thompson was denied the company of the one person to whom she had pledged lifelong devotion. Her partner is a woman, Sharon Kowalski, and their home state of Minnesota, like every other jurisdiction in the United States, refuses to permit two individuals of the same sex to marry.

Karen Thompson and Sharon Kowalski are spouses in every respect except the legal. They exchanged vows and rings; they lived together until November 13, 1983 — when Ms. Kowalski was severely injured when her car was struck by a drunk driver. She lost the capacity to walk or to speak more than several words at a time, and needed constant care.

Ms. Thompson sought a court ruling granting her guardianship over her partner, but Ms. Kowalski's parents opposed the petition and obtained sole guardianship. They moved Ms. Kowalski to a nursing home three-hundred miles away from Ms. Thompson and forbade all visits between the two women. Last month, as part of a reevaluation of Ms. Kowalski's mental competency, Ms. Thompson was permitted to visit her partner again. But the prolonged injustice and anguish inflicted on both women hold a moral for everyone.

Marriage, the Supreme Court declared in 1967, is "one of the basic civil rights of man" (and, presumably, of woman as well). The freedom to marry, said the Court, is "essential to the orderly pursuit of happiness."

Marriage is not just a symbolic state. It can be the key to survival,   5 emotional and financial. Marriage triggers a universe of rights, privileges, and presumptions. A married person can share in a spouse's estate even when there is no will. She is typically entitled to the group insurance and pension programs offered by the spouse's employer, and she enjoys tax advantages. She cannot be compelled to testify against her spouse in legal proceedings.

The decision whether or not to marry belongs properly to individuals — not the government. Yet at present, all fifty states deny that choice to millions of gay and lesbian Americans. While marriage has historically required a male partner and a female partner, history alone cannot sanctify injustice. If tradition were the only measure, most states would still limit matrimony to partners of the same race.

As recently as 1967, before the Supreme Court declared miscegenation statutes unconstitutional, sixteen states still prohibited marriages between a white person and a black person. When all the excuses were stripped away, it was clear that the only purpose of those laws was, in the words of the Supreme Court, "to maintain white supremacy."

Those who argue against reforming the marriage statutes because they believe that same sex marriage would be "antifamily" overlook the obvious: Marriage creates families and promotes social stability. In an increasingly loveless world, those who wish to commit themselves to a relationship founded upon devotion should be encouraged, not scorned. Government has no legitimate interest in how that love is expressed.

And it can no longer be argued — if it ever could — that marriage is fundamentally a procreative unit. Otherwise, states would forbid marriage between those who, by reason of age or infertility, cannot have children, as well as those who elect not to.

As the case of Sharon Kowalski and Karen Thompson demonstrates, 10 sanctimonious illusions lead directly to the suffering of others. Denied the right to marry, these two women are left subject to the whims and prejudices of others, and of the law.

Depriving millions of gay American adults the marriages of their choice, and the rights that flow from marriage, denies equal protection of the law. They, their families and friends, together with fair-minded people everywhere, should demand an end to this monstrous injustice.

Topics for Critical Thinking and Writing

1. Study the essay as an example of ways to argue. What sorts of arguments does Stoddard offer? Obviously he does not offer statistics or cite authorities, but what *does* he do in an effort to convince the reader?

2. Stoddard draws an analogy between laws that used to prohibit marriage between persons of different races and laws that still prohibit marriage between persons of the same sex. Evaluate this analogy in an essay of 100 words.

3. Stoddard cites Karen Thompson and Sharon Kowalski. Presumably he could have found, if he had wished, a comparable example using two men rather than two women. Do you think the effect of his essay would be better, worse, or the same if his example used men rather than women? Why?

4. Do you find adequate Stoddard's response to the charge that "same sex marriage would be 'antifamily'"? Why?

5. One widespread assumption is that the family exists in order to produce children. Stoddard mentions this, but he does not mention that although gay couples cannot produce children they can (where legally permitted to do so) rear children, and thus fulfill a social need. (Further, if the couple is lesbian, one of the women can even be the natural mother.) Do you think he was wise to omit this argument in behalf of same sex marriages? Why?

6. Think about what principal claims one might make to contradict Stoddard's claims, and then write a 500-word essay defending this proposition: Lawful marriage should be limited to heterosexual couples. Or, if you believe that gay marriages should be legitimized, write an essay offering additional support to Stoddard's essay.

7. Stoddard's whole purpose is to break down the prejudice against same sex marriages, but he seems to take for granted the appropriateness of monogamy. Yet one might argue against Stoddard that if society opened the door to same sex marriages, it would be hard to keep the door closed to polygamy or polyandry. Write a 500-word essay exploring this question.

8. Would Stoddard's argument require him to allow marriage between a brother and a sister? A parent and a child? A human being and an animal? Why or why not?

Ronald Takaki

The Harmful Myth of Asian Superiority

Asian Americans have increasingly come to be viewed as a "model minority." But are they as successful as claimed? And for whom are they supposed to be a model?

Asian Americans have been described in the media as "excessively, even provocatively" successful in gaining admission to universities. Asian American shopkeepers have been congratulated, as well as criticized, for their ubiquity and entrepreneurial effectiveness.

If Asian Americans can make it, many politicians and pundits ask, why can't African Americans? Such comparisons pit minorities against each other and generate African American resentment toward Asian Americans. The victims are blamed for their plight, rather than racism and an economy that has made many young African American workers superfluous.

The celebration of Asian Americans has obscured reality. For example, figures on the high earnings of Asian Americans relative to Caucasians are misleading. Most Asian Americans live in California, Hawaii, and New York—states with higher incomes and higher costs of living than the national average.

Even Japanese Americans, often touted for their upward mobility, have not reached equality. While Japanese American men in California earned an average income comparable to Caucasian men in 1980, they did so only by acquiring more education and working more hours.   5

Comparing family incomes is even more deceptive. Some Asian American groups do have higher family incomes than Caucasians. But they have more workers per family.

The "model minority" image homogenizes Asian Americans and hides their differences. For example, while thousands of Vietnamese American young people attend universities, others are on the streets. They live in motels and hang out in pool halls in places like East Los Angeles; some join gangs.

Twenty-five percent of the people in New York City's Chinatown lived below the poverty level in 1980, compared with 17 percent of the city's population. Some 60 percent of the workers in the Chinatowns of Los Angeles and San Francisco are crowded into low-paying jobs in garment factories and restaurants.

Ronald Takaki, the grandson of agricultural laborers who had come from Japan, is professor of ethnic studies at the University of California, Berkeley. He is the editor of From Different Shores: Perspectives on Race and Ethnicity in America *(1987), and the author of (among other writings)* Strangers from a Different Shore: A History of Asian-Americans *(1989). The essay that we reprint appeared originally in the* New York Times, *June 16, 1990, p. 21.*

"Most immigrants coming into Chinatown with a language barrier cannot go outside this confined area into the mainstream of American industry," a Chinese immigrant said. "Before, I was a painter in Hong Kong, but I can't do it here. I got no license, no education. I want a living; so it's dishwasher, janitor, or cook."

Hmong and Mien refugees from Laos have unemployment rates that 10 reach as high as 80 percent. A 1987 California study showed that three out of ten Southeast Asian refugee families had been on welfare for four to ten years.

Although college-educated Asian Americans are entering the professions and earning good salaries, many hit the "glass ceiling"—the barrier through which high management positions can be seen but not reached. In 1988, only 8 percent of Asian Americans were "officials" and "managers," compared with 12 percent for all groups.

Finally, the triumph of Korean immigrants has been exaggerated. In 1988, Koreans in the New York metropolitan area earned only 68 percent of the median income of non-Asians. More than three-quarters of Korean greengrocers, those so-called paragons of bootstrap entrepreneurialism, came to America with a college education. Engineers, teachers, or administrators while in Korea, they became shopkeepers after their arrival. For many of them, the greengrocery represents dashed dreams, a step downward in status.

For all their hard work and long hours, most Korean shopkeepers do not actually earn very much: $17,000 to $35,000 a year, usually representing the income from the labor of an entire family.

But most Korean immigrants do not become shopkeepers. Instead, many find themselves trapped as clerks in grocery stores, service workers in restaurants, seamstresses in garment factories, and janitors in hotels.

Most Asian Americans know their "success" is largely a myth. They 15 also see how the celebration of Asian Americans as a "model minority" perpetuates their inequality and exacerbates relations between them and African Americans.

Topics for Critical Thinking and Writing

1. What is the thesis of Takaki's essay? What is the evidence he offers for its truth? Do you find his argument convincing? Explain your answers to these questions in an essay of 500 words.

2. Takaki several times uses statistics to make a point. Do some of the statistics seem more convincing than others? Explain.

3. Consider Takaki's title. To what group(s) is the myth of Asian superiority harmful?

4. Suppose you believed that Asian Americans are economically more successful in America today, relative to white Americans, than African Americans are. Does Takaki agree or disagree with you? What evidence, if any, does he cite to support or reject the belief?

5. Takaki attacks the "myth" of Asian American "success," and thus rejects the idea that they are a "model minority" (recall the opening and closing paragraphs). What do you think a genuine model minority would be like? Can you think of any racial or ethnic minority in the United States that can serve as a model? Explain why or why not in an essay of 500 words.

James Gorman

The Doctor Won't See You Now

In the confusion, hypocrisy, and animosity generated by the AIDS epidemic, finally we hear a voice of *sanity* — and from the medical profession at that. Thirty percent of doctors surveyed by the American Medical Association in November [1991] said they felt no ethical responsibility to treat AIDS patients.

And why should they? For too long, this country has faced rising medical costs and malpractice mania caused in large part by the mistaken notion that doctors are supposed to treat any slob who comes to them. This involves dealing with old people who are on the way out anyway, with all sorts of nasty sores and tumors, and now with AIDS patients, most of whom got sick because of some sort of disgusting behavior. Except, of course, hemophiliacs, the *good* AIDS patients.

No other profession faces such obligations. Does a stockbroker have to take on poor clients wanting to invest pathetically small amounts of money earned during years of wage slavery? No way. Do architects have to design your house if you are stupid and have no taste? Only if you are filthy rich. Do real estate developers have to build apartments for the homeless? Enough said.

Part of the medical profession is finally beginning to see that patients have a responsibility for their own health and that doctoring is no different from any other small business: When you run a convenience store, you want to keep the riffraff out. If doctors would only build on this insight and expand their notion of what constitutes riffraff, we'd be getting somewhere. We could cut down medical costs and stop a lot of disgusting habits as well.

Here are a few of the illnesses they should refuse to treat: coronary   5
artery disease — caused by the willful, piglike consumption of steak, butter, cream, and blintzes; skin cancer — the result of taking off your clothes and lying around, offending those of us with common sense, while soaking up ultraviolet radiation; lung cancer and cancer of the lip and throat and lar-

James Gorman, born in 1949, is a columnist for Discovery *magazine. Among his books are* Hazards to Your Health: The Problem of Environmental Disease *(1979),* Digging Dinosaurs *(1988), and* The Man with No Endorphins and Other Reflections on Science *(1988).*

ynx and tongue, all fostered by smoking and alcohol. Also, carpal tunnel syndrome in people who write a lot of trash about ethics and responsibility.

In fact, I don't think doctors need to specify diseases. A number of respondents to the AIDS survey said they didn't like treating drug addicts or homosexuals, period. Smart thinking. Let's also exclude smokers, drinkers, meat eaters, and anyone who has sex more often than I do.

I hope no one counters with the tired argument that doctors, because of the place they occupy in society, not to mention their incomes, should treat anybody who is sick. This plea is based on the long-discredited idea that doctoring is a profession, a calling, requiring commitment and integrity on the part of those who practice it. Really. How dumb can you get?

Topics for Critical Thinking and Writing

1. If Gorman's essay presents an argument, then it must have a thesis. Very well, what is Gorman's thesis?

2. What would you say is Gorman's chief method of persuasion?

3. What counterarguments can you offer to paragraph 3?

4. What function(s) do you think Gorman's last paragraph serves?

5. Lifeguards at the beach have a duty, for which they are trained, to rescue swimmers at risk, but not at the risk of their own lives. A lifeguard who risks her life to save a drowning swimmer acts above and beyond duty; she's a hero. Does Gorman think that doctors have a duty to risk their lives by serving AIDS patients? Do they have a duty to be heroes? Write a 500-word essay arguing for or against such a duty.

James Q. Wilson

Just Take Away Their Guns

The President wants still tougher gun control legislation and thinks it will work. The public supports more gun control laws but suspects they won't work. The public is right.

Legal restraints on the lawful purchase of guns will have little effect on the illegal use of guns. There are some 200 million guns in private ownership, about one-third of them handguns. Only about 2 percent of the latter are employed to commit crimes. It would take a Draconian, and

James Q. Wilson is a professor of management and public policy at the University of California, Los Angeles. Among his books are Thinking about Crime *(1975),* Bureaucracy *(1989), and* The Moral Sense *(1993). The essay that we reprint appeared originally in the* New York Times Magazine, *March 20, 1994.*

politically impossible, confiscation of legally purchased guns to make much of a difference in the number used by criminals. Moreover, only about one-sixth of the handguns used by serious criminals are purchased from a gun shop or pawnshop. Most of these handguns are stolen, borrowed, or obtained through private purchases that wouldn't be affected by gun laws.

What is worse, any successful effort to shrink the stock of legally purchased guns (or of ammunition) would reduce the capacity of law-abiding people to defend themselves. Gun control advocates scoff at the importance of self-defense, but they are wrong to do so. Based on a household survey, Gary Kleck, a criminologist at Florida State University, has estimated that every year, guns are used — that is, displayed or fired — for defensive purposes more than a million times, not counting their use by the police. If his estimate is correct, this means that the number of people who defend themselves with a gun exceeds the number of arrests for violent crimes and burglaries.

Our goal should not be the disarming of law-abiding citizens. It should be to reduce the number of people who carry guns unlawfully, especially in places — on streets, in taverns — where the mere presence of a gun can increase the hazards we all face. The most effective way to reduce illegal gun-carrying is to encourage the police to take guns away from people who carry them without a permit. This means encouraging the police to make street frisks.

The Fourth Amendment to the Constitution bans "unreasonable searches and seizures." In 1968 the Supreme Court decided (*Terry v. Ohio*) that a frisk — patting down a person's outer clothing — is proper if the officer has a "reasonable suspicion" that the person is armed and dangerous. If a pat-down reveals an object that might be a gun, the officer can enter the suspect's pocket to remove it. If the gun is being carried illegally, the suspect can be arrested.   5

The reasonable-suspicion test is much less stringent than the probable-cause standard the police must meet in order to make an arrest. A reasonable suspicion, however, is more than just a hunch; it must be supported by specific facts. The courts have held, not always consistently, that these facts include someone acting in a way that leads an experienced officer to conclude criminal activity may be afoot; someone fleeing at the approach of an officer; a person who fits a drug courier profile; a motorist stopped for a traffic violation who has a suspicious bulge in his pocket; a suspect identified by a reliable informant as carrying a gun. The Supreme Court has also upheld frisking people on probation or parole.

Some police departments frisk a lot of people, but usually the police frisk rather few, at least for the purpose of detecting illegal guns. In 1992 the police arrested about 240,000 people for illegally possessing or carrying a weapon. This is only about one-fourth as many as were arrested for public drunkenness. The average police officer will make *no* weapons arrests and confiscate *no* guns during any given year. Mark Moore, a professor of public policy at Harvard University, found that most weapons arrests were made because a citizen complained, not because the police were out looking for guns.

It is easy to see why. Many cities suffer from a shortage of officers, and even those with ample law-enforcement personnel worry about having their cases thrown out for constitutional reasons or being accused of police harassment. But the risk of violating the Constitution or engaging in actual, as opposed to perceived, harassment can be substantially reduced.

Each patrol officer can be given a list of people on probation or parole who live on that officer's beat and be rewarded for making frequent stops to insure that they are not carrying guns. Officers can be trained to recognize the kinds of actions that the Court will accept as providing the "reasonable suspicion" necessary for a stop and frisk. Membership in a gang known for assaults and drug dealing could be made the basis, by statute or Court precedent, for gun frisks.

The available evidence supports the claim that self-defense is a legiti- 10
mate form of deterrence. People who report to the National Crime Survey that they defended themselves with a weapon were less likely to lose property in a robbery or be injured in an assault than those who did not defend themselves. Statistics have shown that would-be burglars are threatened by gun-wielding victims about as many times a year as they are arrested (and much more often than they are sent to prison) and that the chances of a burglar being shot are about the same as his chances of going to jail. Criminals know these facts even if gun control advocates do not and so are less likely to burgle occupied homes in America than occupied ones in Europe, where the residents rarely have guns.

Some gun control advocates may concede these points but rejoin that the cost of self-defense is self-injury: Handgun owners are more likely to shoot themselves or their loved ones than a criminal. Not quite. Most gun accidents involve rifles and shotguns, not handguns. Moreover, the rate of fatal gun accidents has been declining while the level of gun ownership has been rising. There are fatal gun accidents just as there are fatal car accidents, but in fewer than 2 percent of the gun fatalities was the victim someone mistaken for an intruder.

Those who urge us to forbid or severely restrict the sale of guns ignore these facts. Worse, they adopt a position that is politically absurd. In effect, they say, "Your government, having failed to protect your person and your property from criminal assault, now intends to deprive you of the opportunity to protect yourself."

Opponents of gun control make a different mistake. The National Rifle Association and its allies tell us that "guns don't kill, people kill" and urge the Government to punish more severely people who use guns to commit crimes. Locking up criminals does protect society from future crimes, and the prospect of being locked up may deter criminals. But our experience with meting out tougher sentences is mixed. The tougher the prospective sentence the less likely it is to be imposed, or at least to be imposed swiftly. If the Legislature adds on time for crimes committed with a gun, prosecutors often bargain away the add-ons; even when they do not, the judges in many states are reluctant to impose add-ons.

Worse, the presence of a gun can contribute to the magnitude of the crime even on the part of those who worry about serving a long prison sentence. Many criminals carry guns not to rob stores but to protect themselves from other armed criminals. Gang violence has become more threatening to bystanders as gang members have begun to arm themselves. People may commit crimes, but guns make some crimes worse. Guns often convert spontaneous outbursts of anger into fatal encounters. When some people carry them on the streets, others will want to carry them to protect themselves, and an urban arms race will be underway.

And modern science can be enlisted to help. Metal detectors at air-   15
ports have reduced the number of airplane bombings and skyjackings to nearly zero. But these detectors only work at very close range. What is needed is a device that will enable the police to detect the presence of a large lump of metal in someone's pocket from a distance of ten or fifteen feet. Receiving such a signal could supply the officer with reasonable grounds for a pat-down. Underemployed nuclear physicists and electronics engineers in the post-cold-war era surely have the talents for designing a better gun detector.

Even if we do all these things, there will still be complaints. Innocent people will be stopped. Young black and Hispanic men will probably be stopped more often than older white Anglo males or women of any race. But if we are serious about reducing drive-by shootings, fatal gang wars and lethal quarrels in public places, we must get illegal guns off the street. We cannot do this by multiplying the forms one fills out at gun shops or by pretending that guns are not a problem until a criminal uses one.

Topics for Critical Thinking and Writing ══════════

1. If you had to single out one sentence in Wilson's essay as coming close to stating his thesis, what sentence would that be? Why do you think it states, better than any other sentence, the thesis of the essay?

2. In his third paragraph Wilson reviews some research by a criminologist purporting to show that guns are important for self-defense in American households. Does the research as reported show that displaying or firing guns in self-defense actually prevented crimes? Or wounded aggressors? Suppose you were also told that in households where guns may be used defensively, thousands of innocent people are injured, and hundreds are killed — for instance, children who find a loaded gun and play with it. Would you regard these injuries and deaths as a fair trade-off? Explain. What does the research presented by Wilson really show?

3. In paragraph 12 Wilson says that people who want to severely restrict the ownership of guns are in effect saying, "Your government, having failed to protect your person and your property from criminal assault, now intends to deprive you of the opportunity to protect yourself." What reply might an advocate of severe restrictions make? (Even if you strongly believe Wilson's summary is accu-

rate, try to put yourself in the shoes of an advocate of gun control, and come up with the best reply that you can.)

4. Wilson reports in paragraph 7 that the police arrest four times as many drunks on the streets as they do people carrying unlicensed firearms. Does this strike you as absurd, reasonable, or mysterious? Does Wilson explain it to your satisfaction?

5. In his final paragraph Wilson grants that his proposal entails a difficulty: "Innocent people will be stopped. Young black and Hispanic men will probably be stopped more often than older white Anglo males or women of any race." Assuming that his predictions are accurate, is Wilson's proposal therefore fatally flawed and worth no further thought, or (to take the other extreme view) do you think that innocent people who fall into certain classifications will just have to put up with frisking, for the public good?

6. In an essay of no more than 100 words, explain the difference between the "reasonable-suspicion test" and the "probable-cause standard" that the courts use in deciding whether a street frisk is lawful. (You may want to organize your essay into two paragraphs, one on each topic, or perhaps into three if you want to use a brief introductory paragraph.)

7. Wilson criticizes both gun control advocates and the National Rifle Association for their ill-advised views. In an essay of 500 words, state his criticisms of each side and explain whether and to what extent you agree.

Meg Greenfield

In Defense of the Animals

I might as well come right out with it. Contrary to some of my most cherished prejudices, the animal-rights people have begun to get to me. I think that in some part of what they say they are right.

I never thought it would come to this. As distinct from the old-style animal rescue, protection, and shelter organizations, the more aggressive newcomers, with their "liberation," of laboratory animals and periodic championship of the claims of animal well-being over human well-being when a choice must be made, have earned a reputation in the world I live in as fanatics and just plain kooks. And even with my own recently (relatively) raised consciousness, there remains a good deal in both their critique and their prescription for the virtuous life that I reject, being not just a practicing carnivore, a wearer of shoe leather, and so forth, but also a supporter of certain indisputably agonizing procedures visited upon innocent animals in the furtherance of human welfare, especially experiments undertaken to improve human health.

Meg Greenfield, born in Seattle in 1930, won a Pulitzer Prize in 1978 for her editorials in the Washington Post. *In addition to writing editorials for the newspaper, she writes a column for* Newsweek. *We reprint her column that appeared in* Newsweek, *April 17, 1989.*

So, viewed from the pure position, I am probably only marginally better than the worst of my kind, if that: I don't buy the complete "speciesist"[1] analysis or even the fundamental language of animal "rights" and continue to find a large part of what is done in the name of that cause harmful and extreme. But I also think, patronizing as it must sound, that the zealots are required early on in any movement if it is to succeed in altering the sensibility of the leaden masses, such as me. Eventually they get your attention. And eventually you at least feel obliged to weigh their arguments and think about whether there may not be something there.

It is true that this end has often been achieved—as in my case—by means of vivid, cringe-inducing photographs, not by an appeal to reason or values so much as by an assault on squeamishness. From the famous 1970s photo of the newly skinned baby seal to the videos of animals being raised in the most dark, miserable, stunting environment as they are readied for their life's sole fulfillment as frozen patties and cutlets, these sights have had their effect. But we live in a world where the animal protein we eat comes discreetly prebutchered and prepacked so the original beast and his slaughtering are remote from our consideration, just as our furs come on coat hangers in salons, not on their original proprietors; and I see nothing wrong with our having to contemplate the often unsettling reality of how we came by the animal products we make use of. Then we can choose what we want to do.

The objection to our being confronted with these dramatic, disturbing 5 pictures is first that they tend to provoke a misplaced, uncritical, and highly emotional concern for animal life at the direct expense of a more suitable concern for human suffering. What goes into the animals' account, the reasoning goes, necessarily comes out of ours. But I think it is possible to remain stalwart in your view that the human claim comes first and in your acceptance of the use of animals for human betterment and *still* to believe that there are some human interests that should not take precedence. For we have become far too self-indulgent, hardened, careless, and cruel in the pain we routinely inflict upon these creatures for the most frivolous, unworthy purposes. And I also think that the more justifiable purposes, such as medical research, are shamelessly used as cover for other activities that are wanton.

For instance, not all of the painful and crippling experimentation that is undertaken in the lab is being conducted for the sake of medical knowledge or other purposes related to basic human well-being and health. Much of it is being conducted for the sake of superrefinements in the cosmetic and other frill industries, the noble goal being to contrive yet another fragrance or hair tint or commercially competitive variation on all the daft, fizzy, multicolored "personal care" products for the medicine cabinet and dressing table, a firmer-holding hair spray, that sort of thing. In other

---

[1]**speciesist** A word formed as a sort of parallel to "racist"; speciesists are persons who believe that all and only members of the human species have a special moral status, and so are entitled to use other animals for whatever purposes they choose. [Editors' note.]

words, the conscripted, immobilized rabbits and other terrified creatures, who have been locked in boxes from the neck down, only their heads on view, are being sprayed in the eyes with different burning, stinging substances for the sake of adding to our already obscene store of luxuries and utterly superfluous vanity items.

Oddly, we tend to be very sentimental about animals in their idealized, fictional form and largely indifferent to them in realms where our lives actually touch. From time immemorial, humans have romantically attributed to animals their own sensibilities — from Balaam's biblical ass who providently could speak and who got his owner out of harm's way right down to Lassie and the other Hollywood pups who would invariably tip off the good guys that the bad guys were up to something. So we simulate phony cross-species kinship, pretty well drown in the cuteness of it all — Mickey and Minnie and Porky — and ignore, if we don't actually countenance, the brutish things done in the name of Almighty Hair Spray.

This strikes me as decadent. My problem is that it also causes me to reach a position that is, on its face, philosophically vulnerable, if not absurd — the muddled, middling, inconsistent place where finally you are saying it's all right to kill them for some purposes, but not to hurt them gratuitously in doing it or to make them suffer horribly for one's own trivial whims.

I would feel more humiliated to have fetched up on this exposed rock, if I didn't suspect I had so much company. When you see pictures of people laboriously trying to clean the Exxon gunk off of sea otters even knowing that they will only be able to help out a very few, you see this same outlook in action. And I think it *can* be defended. For to me the biggest cop-out is the one that says that if you don't buy the whole absolutist, extreme position it is pointless and even hypocritical to concern yourself with lesser mercies and ameliorations. The pressure of the animal-protection groups has already had some impact in improving the way various creatures are treated by researchers, trainers, and food producers. There is much more in this vein to be done. We are talking about rejecting wanton, pointless cruelty here. The position may be philosophically absurd, but the outcome is the right one.

Topics for Critical Thinking and Writing

1. Greenfield starts right out by admitting that she now thinks that "in some part what [animal-rights people] say" is true. List the points on which she agrees with them, and the points where she still disagrees. Can you think of some aspects of the animal-rights controversy she does not discuss?

2. In her fourth paragraph Greenfield mentions some "cringe-inducing photographs" — photographs that persuade "not by an appeal to reason or values so much as by an assault on squeamishness." Do you consider an appeal to reason somehow more respectable than an assault on "squeamishness"? If so, why? If not, why not?

3. In paragraphs 5 and 6 Greenfield argues that some human interests are too frivolous to warrant causing deliberate harm to experimental animals. Can you formulate a principle or criterion to cover all and only the uses of animals that she thinks are inappropriate or immoral?

4. Do you think that paragraph 6 is, or nearly is, an assault on "squeamishness"? Explain.

5. In her final paragraph Greenfield says that we should reject "wanton, pointless cruelty," something she thinks the cosmetic industry is guilty of. But suppose someone from the cosmetic industry said that its experiments are not pointless; they are aimed at producing a product, that is, at employing workers, making profits for investors, and (presumably) enhancing the lives of those who use the product. How acceptable is this reply? Explain.

6. Suppose someone said, "Animals are cruel to each other—think of a fox in a chicken coop, or a cat with a mouse—so why all this fuss about *us* not using them for our own purposes?" What would you say?

7. Evaluate carefully the closing sentence of Greenfield's essay. Has she convinced you that her position is "philosophically absurd" although the "outcome is the right one"?

Judy Brady

I Want a Wife

I belong to that classification of people known as wives. I am A Wife. And, not altogether incidentally, I am a mother.

Not too long ago a male friend of mine appeared on the scene fresh from a recent divorce. He had one child, who is, of course, with his ex-wife. He is looking for another wife. As I thought about him while I was ironing one evening, it suddenly occurred to me that I, too, would like to have a wife. Why do I want a wife?

I would like to go back to school so that I can become economically independent, support myself, and, if need be, support those dependent upon me. I want a wife who will work and send me to school. And while I am going to school I want a wife to take care of my children. I want a wife to keep track of the children's doctor and dentist appointments. And to keep track of mine, too. I want a wife to make sure my children eat properly and are kept clean. I want a wife who will wash the children's clothes and keep them mended. I want a wife who is a good nurturant attendant to my chil-

---

Born in San Francisco in 1937, Judy Brady married in 1960, and two years later earned a bachelor's degree in painting at the University of Iowa. Active in the women's movement and in other political causes, she has worked as an author, an editor, and a secretary. The essay reprinted here, written before she and her husband separated, appeared originally in the first issue of Ms. *in 1971.*

dren, who arranges for their schooling, makes sure that they have an adequate social life with their peers, takes them to the park, the zoo, etc. I want a wife who takes care of the children when they are sick, a wife who arranges to be around when the children need special care, because, of course, I cannot miss classes at school. My wife must arrange to lose time at work and not lose the job. It may mean a small cut in my wife's income from time to time, but I guess I can tolerate that. Needless to say, my wife will arrange and pay for the care of the children while my wife is working.

I want a wife who will take care of *my* physical needs. I want a wife who will keep my house clean. A wife who will pick up after my children, a wife who will pick up after me. I want a wife who will keep my clothes clean, ironed, mended, replaced when need be, and who will see to it that my personal things are kept in their proper place so that I can find what I need the minute I need it. I want a wife who cooks the meals, a wife who is a *good* cook. I want a wife who will plan the menus, do the necessary grocery shopping, prepare the meals, serve them pleasantly, and then do the cleaning up while I do my studying. I want a wife who will care for me when I am sick and sympathize with my pain and loss of time from school. I want a wife to go along when our family takes a vacation so that someone can continue to care for me and my children when I need a rest and change of scene.

I want a wife who will not bother me with rambling complaints about   5
a wife's duties. But I want a wife who will listen to me when I feel the need to explain a rather difficult point I have come across in my course of studies. And I want a wife who will type my papers for me when I have written them.

I want a wife who will take care of the details of my social life. When my wife and I are invited out by my friends, I want a wife who will take care of the babysitting arrangements. When I meet people at school that I like and want to entertain, I want a wife who will have the house clean, will prepare a special meal, serve it to me and my friends, and not interrupt when I talk about things that interest me and my friends. I want a wife who will have arranged that the children are fed and ready for bed before my guests arrive so that the children do not bother us. I want a wife who takes care of the needs of my guests so that they feel comfortable, who makes sure that they have an ashtray, that they are passed the hors d'oeuvres, that they are offered a second helping of the food, that their wine glasses are replenished when necessary, that their coffee is served to them as they like it. And I want a wife who knows that sometimes I need a night out by myself.

I want a wife who is sensitive to my sexual needs, a wife who makes love passionately and eagerly when I feel like it, a wife who makes sure that I am satisfied. And, of course, I want a wife who will not demand sexual attention when I am not in the mood for it. I want a wife who assumes the complete responsibility for birth control, because I do not want more children. I want a wife who will remain sexually faithful to me so that I do not have to clutter up my intellectual life with jealousies. And I want a wife who understands that *my* sexual needs may entail more than strict adherence to monogamy. I must, after all, be able to relate to people as fully as possible.

If, by chance, I find another person more suitable as a wife than the wife I already have, I want the liberty to replace my present wife with another one. Naturally, I will expect a fresh, new life; my wife will take the children and be solely responsible for them so that I am left free.

When I am through with school and have a job, I want my wife to quit working and remain at home so that my wife can more fully and completely take care of a wife's duties.

My God, who *wouldn't* want a wife? 10

Topics for Critical Thinking and Writing

1. If one were to summarize Brady's first paragraph, one might say it adds up to "I am a wife and a mother." But analyze it closely. Exactly what does the second sentence add to the first? And what does "not altogether incidentally" add to the third sentence?

2. Brady uses the word "wife" in sentences where one ordinarily would use "she" or "her." Why? And why does she begin paragraphs 4, 5, 6, and 7 with the same words, "I want a wife"?

3. In her second paragraph Brady says that the child of her divorced male friend "is, of course, with his ex-wife." In the context of the entire essay, what does this sentence mean?

4. Complete the following sentence by offering a definition: "According to Judy Brady, a wife is . . ."

5. Try to state the essential argument of Brady's essay in a simple syllogism. (*Hint:* Start by identifying the thesis or conclusion you think she is trying to establish, and then try to formulate two premises, based on what she has written, which would establish the conclusion.)

6. Drawing on your experience as observer of the world around you (and perhaps as husband, wife, or ex-spouse), do you think Brady's picture of a wife's role is grossly exaggerated? Or is it (allowing for some serious playfulness) fairly accurate, even though it was written in 1971? If grossly exaggerated, is the essay therefore meaningless? If fairly accurate, what attitudes and practices does it encourage you to support? Explain.

7. Whether or not you agree with Brady's vision of marriage in our society, write an essay (500 words) titled "I Want a Husband," imitating her style and approach. Write the best possible essay, and then decide which of the two essays — yours or hers — makes a fairer comment on current society. Or, if you believe Brady is utterly misleading, write an essay titled "I Want a Wife," seeing the matter in a different light.

8. If you feel that you have been pressed into an unappreciated, unreasonable role — built-in babysitter, listening post, or girl (or boy or man or woman) Friday — write an essay of 500 words that will help the reader to see both your plight and the injustice of the system. (*Hint:* A little humor will help to keep your essay from seeming to be a prolonged whine.)

4

Critical Writing: Writing an Analysis of an Argument

ANALYZING AN ARGUMENT

Examining the Author's Thesis

Most of your writing in other courses will require you to write an analysis of someone else's writing. In a course in political science you may have to analyze, say, an essay first published in *Foreign Affairs,* perhaps reprinted in your textbook, that argues against raising tariff barriers to foreign trade; or a course in sociology may require you to analyze a report on the correlation between fatal accidents and drunk drivers under the age of twenty-one. Much of your writing, in short, will set forth reasoned responses to your reading, as preparation for making an argument of your own.

Obviously you must understand an essay before you can analyze it thoughtfully. You must read it several times—not just skim it—and (the hard part) you must think about it. Again, you'll find that your thinking is stimulated if you take notes and if you ask yourself questions about the material. Notes will help you to keep track of the writer's thoughts and also of your own responses to the writer's thesis. The writer probably *does* have a thesis, a point, and if so, you must try to locate it. Perhaps the thesis is explicitly stated in the title or in a sentence or two near the beginning of the essay or in a concluding paragraph, but perhaps you will have to infer it from the essay as a whole.

Notice that we said the writer *probably* has a thesis. Much of what you read will indeed be primarily an argument; the writer explicitly or implicitly is trying to support some thesis and to convince you to agree with it. But some of what you read will be relatively neutral, with the argument just faintly discernible — or even with no argument at all. A work may, for instance, chiefly be a report: Here are the data, or here is what X, Y, and Z said; make of it what you will. A report might simply state how various ethnic groups voted in an election. In a report of this sort, of course the writer hopes to persuade readers that the facts are correct, but no thesis is advanced, at least not explicitly or perhaps even consciously; the writer is not evidently arguing a point and trying to change our minds. Such a document differs greatly from an essay by a political analyst who presents similar findings in order to persuade a candidate to sacrifice the votes of this ethnic bloc in order to get more votes from other blocs.

Examining the Author's Purpose

While reading an argument, try to form a clear idea of the author's purpose. Judging from the essay or the book, was the purpose to persuade, or was it to report? An analysis of a pure report (a work apparently without a thesis or argumentative angle) on ethnic voting will deal chiefly with the accuracy of the report. It will, for example, consider whether the sample poll was representative.

Much material that poses as a report really has a thesis built into it, consciously or unconsciously. The best evidence that the prose you are reading is argumentative is the presence of two kinds of key terms:

> **transitions that imply the drawing of a conclusion:** *therefore, because, for the reason that, consequently;*
>
> **verbs that imply proof:** *confirms, accounts for, implies, proves, disproves, is (in)consistent with, refutes, it follows that.*

Keep your eye out for such terms and scrutinize their precise role whenever they appear. If the essay does not advance a thesis, think of a thesis (a hypothesis) that it might support or some conventional belief that it might undermine.

Examining the Author's Methods

If the essay advances a thesis, you will want to analyze the strategies or methods of argument that allegedly support the thesis.

> Does the writer quote authorities? Are these authorities really competent in this field? Are equally competent authorities who take a different view ignored?
>
> If statistics are used, are they appropriate to the point being argued? Can they be interpreted differently?
>
> Does the writer build the argument by using examples, or analogies? Are they satisfactory?
>
> Are the writer's assumptions acceptable?
>
> Are all relevant factors considered? Has the author omitted some

points that you think should be discussed? For instance, should the author recognize certain opposing positions, and perhaps concede something to them?

Does the writer seek to persuade by means of ridicule? If so, is the ridicule fair — is it supported also by rational argument?

In writing your analysis, you will want to tell your reader something about the author's purpose and something about the author's **methods.** It is usually a good idea at the start of your analysis — if not in the first paragraph then in the second or third — to let the reader know the purpose (and thesis, if there is one) of the work you are analyzing, and then to summarize the work briefly.

Next you will probably find it useful (your reader will certainly find it helpful) to write out *your* thesis (your evaluation or judgment). You might say, for instance, that the essay is impressive but not conclusive, or is undermined by convincing contrary evidence, or relies too much on unsupported generalizations, or is wholly admirable, or whatever. Remember, because your paper is itself an argument, it needs its own thesis.

And then, of course, comes the job of setting forth your analysis and the support for your thesis. There is no one way of going about this work. If, say, your author gives four arguments (for example: an appeal to common sense, the testimony of authorities, the evidence of comparisons, an appeal to self-interest), you may want to take these four arguments up in sequence. Or you may want to begin by discussing the simplest of the four, and then go on to the more difficult ones. Or you may want first to discuss the author's two arguments that you think are sound and then turn to the two that you think are not. And, as you warm to your thesis, you may want to clinch your case by constructing a fifth argument, absent from the work under scrutiny but in your view highly important. In short, the organization of your analysis may or may not follow the organization of the work you are analyzing.

Examining the Author's Persona

You will probably also want to analyze something a bit more elusive than the author's explicit arguments: the author's self-presentation. Does the author seek to persuade readers partly by presenting himself or herself as conscientious, friendly, self-effacing, authoritative, tentative, or in some other light? Most writers do two things: They present evidence, and they present themselves (or, more precisely, they present the image of themselves that they wish us to behold). In some persuasive writing this persona or voice or presentation of the self may be no less important than the presentation of evidence.

In establishing a persona, writers adopt various rhetorical strategies, ranging from the use of characteristic words to the use of a particular form of organization. For instance, the writer who speaks of an opponent's "gimmicks" instead of "strategy" is trying to downgrade the opponent and also to convey the self-image of a streetwise person. On a larger scale, consider the way in which evidence is presented and the kind of evidence offered. One writer may first bombard the reader with facts and then spend relatively little time drawing conclusions. Another may rely chiefly on generalizations, waiting until the end of the essay to bring the thesis home with a few details. Another may begin with a few facts and spend most of the space reflecting on these. One writer may seem professorial or pedantic, offering examples of an academic sort; another, whose examples are drawn from ordinary life, may seem like a regular guy. All such devices deserve comment in your analysis.

The writer's persona, then, may color the thesis and help it develop in a distinctive way. If we accept the thesis, it is partly because the writer has won our goodwill.

The author of an essay may, for example, seem fair minded and open minded, treating the opposition with great courtesy and expressing interest in hearing other views. Such a tactic is, of course, itself a persuasive device. Or take an author who appears to rely on hard evidence such as statistics. This reliance on seemingly objective truths is itself a way of seeking to persuade — a rational way, to be sure, but a mode of persuasion nonetheless.

Especially in analyzing a work in which the author's persona and ideas are blended, you will want to spend some time commenting on the persona. Whether you discuss it near the beginning of your analysis or near the end will depend on your own sense of how you want to construct your essay, and this decision will partly depend on the work you are analyzing. For example, if the author's persona is kept in the background, and is thus relatively invisible, you may want to make that point fairly early, to get it out of the way, and then concentrate on more interesting matters. If, however, the persona is interesting — and perhaps seductive, whether because it seems so scrupulously objective or so engagingly subjective — you may want to hint at this quality early in your essay, and then develop the point while you consider the arguments.

Summary

In the last few pages we have tried to persuade you that, in writing an analysis of your reading, you must do the following:

1. Read and reread thoughtfully. Writing notes will help you to think about what you are reading.
2. Be aware of the purpose of the material to which you are responding.

We have also tried to point out these facts:

3. Most of the nonliterary material that you will read is designed to argue, or to report, or to do both.
4. Most of this material also presents the writer's personality, or voice,

SCOTT • SMOKERS GET A RAW DEAL **77**

and this voice usually merits attention in an analysis. An essay on, say, nuclear war, in a journal devoted to political science, may include a voice that moves from an objective tone to a mildly ironic tone to a hortatory tone, and this voice is worth commenting on.

Possibly all this explanation is obvious. There is yet another point, though, equally obvious but often neglected by students who begin by writing an analysis and end up by writing only a summary, a shortened version of the work they have read:

5. Although your essay is an analysis of someone else's writing, and you may have to include a summary of the work you are writing about, your essay is *your* essay. The thesis, the organization, and the tone are yours. Your thesis, for example, may be that although the author is convinced she has presented a strong case, her case is far from proved. Your organization may be deeply indebted to the work you are analyzing, but it need not be. The author may have begun with specific examples and then gone on to make generalizations and to draw conclusions, but you may begin with the conclusions. Similarly, your tone may resemble your subject's (let's say the voice is Courteous Academic), but it will nevertheless have its own ring, its own tone of (say) urgency, or caution, or coolness.

AN ARGUMENT, ITS ELEMENTS, AND A STUDENT'S ANALYSIS OF THE ARGUMENT

Stanley S. Scott

Smokers Get a Raw Deal

The Civil Rights Act, the Voting Rights Act, and a host of antidiscrimination laws notwithstanding, millions of Americans are still forced to sit in the back of planes, trains, and buses. Many more are subject to segregation in public places. Some are even denied housing and employment: victims of an alarming—yet socially acceptable—public hostility.

Stanley S. Scott (b. 1933) is vice president and director of corporate affairs of Philip Morris Companies Inc. This essay originally appeared on December 29, 1984, in the Op-Ed page of the New York Times.

This new form of discrimination is based on smoking behavior.

If you happen to enjoy a cigarette, you are the potential target of violent antismokers and overzealous public enforcers determined to force their beliefs on the rest of society.

Ever since people began smoking, smokers and nonsmokers have been able to live with one another using common courtesy and common sense. Not anymore. Today, smokers must put up with virtually unenforceable laws regulating when and where they can smoke — laws intended as much to discourage smoking itself as to protect the rights of nonsmokers. Much worse, supposedly responsible organizations devoted to the "public interest" are encouraging the harassment of those who smoke.

This year, for example, the American Cancer Society is promoting   5
programs that encourage people to attack smokers with canisters of gas, to blast them with horns, to squirt them with oversized water guns, and burn them in effigy.

Harmless fun? Not quite. Consider the incidents that are appearing on police blotters across America:

In a New York restaurant, a young man celebrating with friends was zapped in the face by a man with an aerosol spray can. His offense: lighting a cigarette. The aggressor was the head of a militant antismoker organization whose goal is to mobilize an army of two million zealots to spray smokers in the face.

In a suburban Seattle drugstore, a man puffing on a cigarette while he waited for a prescription to be filled was ordered to stop by an elderly customer who pulled a gun on him.

A 23-year-old lit up a cigarette on a Los Angeles bus. A passenger objected. When the smoker objected to the objection, he was fatally stabbed.

A transit policeman, using his reserve gun, shot and fatally wounded a man on a subway train in the Bronx in a shootout over smoking a cigarette.

The basic freedoms of more than 50 million American smokers are at risk today. Tomorrow, who knows what personal behavior will become socially unacceptable, subject to restrictive laws and public ridicule? Could travel by private car make the social engineers' hit list because it is less safe than public transit? Could ice cream, cake, and cookies become socially unacceptable because their consumption causes obesity? What about sky diving, mountain climbing, skiing, and contact sports? How far will we allow this to spread?

The question all Americans must ask themselves is: Can a nation that has struggled so valiantly to eliminate bias based on race, religion, and sex afford to allow a fresh set of categories to encourage new forms of hostility between large groups of citizens?

After all, discrimination is discrimination, no matter what it is based on.

_____

Let's examine Scott's essay with an eye to identifying those elements we mentioned earlier in this chapter (pp. 73–76) that deserve notice when examining *any* argument: the author's *thesis, purpose, methods,* and *persona.* And, while we're at it, let's also notice some other features of Scott's essay that will help us appreciate its effects and evaluate its strengths and weaknesses. All this will put us in a better position to write an evaluation or to write an argument of our own confirming, extending, or rebutting Scott's argument.

Title • Scott starts off with a bang—no one likes a "raw deal," and if that's what smokers are getting, then they probably deserve better. So, already in his title, Scott has made a plea for the reader's sympathy. He has also indicated something about his *topic* and his *thesis,* and (in the words "raw deal") something of his *persona;* he is a regular guy, someone who does not use fancy language but who calls a spade a spade.

Thesis • What is the basic *thesis* Scott is arguing? By the end of the second paragraph his readers have a good idea, and surely by paragraph 7, they can state his thesis explicitly, perhaps in these words: *Smokers today are victims of unfair discrimination.* Writers need not announce their thesis in so many words, but they ought to have a thesis, a point they want to make, and they ought to make it evident fairly soon—as Scott does.

Purpose • There's really no doubt that Scott's *purpose* in this essay is to *persuade* the reader to adopt his view of the plight of today's smokers. This amounts to trying to persuade us that his thesis (stated above) is *true.* Scott, however, does not show that his essay is argumentative or persuasive by using any of the key terms that normally mark argumentative prose. He doesn't call anything his "conclusion," none of his statements is labeled "my reasons" or "my premises," and he doesn't connect any clauses or sentences with a "therefore" or a "because."

But this doesn't matter. The argumentative nature of his essay is revealed by the *judgment* he states in paragraph 2: Smokers are experiencing undeserved discrimination. This is, after all, his thesis in brief form. Any author who has a thesis as obvious as Scott does is likely to want to persuade his readers to agree with it. To do that, he needs to try to *support* it; accordingly, the bulk of the rest of Scott's essay constitutes just such support.

Method • Scott's principal method of argument is to cite a series of *examples* (introduced by para. 6) in which the reader can see what Scott believes is actual discrimination against smokers. This is his *evidence* in support of his thesis. (Ought we to trust him here? He cites no sources for the events he reports. On the other hand, these examples sound plausible, and so we probably shouldn't demand documentation for them.) The nature of his thesis doesn't require experimental research or support from recognized authorities. All it requires is some *reported instances* that can properly be described as "harassment" (para. 4, end). Scott of course is relying here on an *assumption:* Harassment is unfair discrimination — but few would quarrel with that assumption.

Notice the *language* in which Scott characterizes the actions of the American Cancer Society ("blast," "squirt," "burn" — all in para. 5). He chose these verbs deliberately, to convey his disapproval of these actions and subtly to help the reader disapprove of them, too.

Another distinctive feature of Scott's method of argument is found in paragraph 7, after the examples. Here, he drives his point home by using the argumentative technique known as *the thin end of the wedge.* (We discuss it later at page 780. The gist of the idea is that just as the thin end of the wedge makes a small opening that will turn into a larger one, so a small step may lead to a large step. The idea is also expressed in the familiar phrase, "Give him an inch and he'll take a mile.") Scott here argues that tolerating discrimination today against a vulnerable minority (smokers) could lead to tolerating widespread discrimination against other minorities (mountain climbers) tomorrow — perhaps even a minority that includes the reader. (Does he exaggerate by overstating his case? Or are his examples well chosen and plausible?)

Notice, finally, the role that *rhetorical questions* play in Scott's argument. (A **rhetorical question,** such as Scott's "How far will we allow this to spread?" in para. 7, is a question to which no answer is expected, because only one answer can reasonably be made.) Writers who use a rhetorical question save themselves the trouble of offering further evidence to support their claims; the person asking the rhetorical question assumes the reader understands and agrees with the questioner's unstated answer.

Persona · Scott presents himself as a no-nonsense defender of the rights of a beleaguered minority. This may add little or nothing to the soundness of his argument, but it surely adds to its persuasive effect. By presenting himself as he does — plain-speaking but righteously indignant — Scott effectively jars the reader's complacency (surely, all the good guys *oppose* smoking — or do they?), and he cultivates at least the reader's grudging respect (we all like to see people stand up for their rights, and the more unpopular the cause the more we respect the sincere advocate).

Closing Paragraph · Scott ends with one of those seeming platitudes that tolerates no disagreement — "discrimination is discrimination," thus making one last effort to enlist the reader on his side. We say "seeming platitudes," because, when you come to think about it, of course not all discrimination is morally objectionable. After all, what's unfair with "discriminating" against criminals by punishing them?

Consider a parallel case, that popular maxim "Business is business." What is it, really, but a disguised claim to the effect that *in business, unfair practices must be tolerated or even admired.* But as soon as this sentiment is reformulated by removing its disguise as a tautology, its controversial character is immediately evident. So with Scott's "discrimination is discrimination"; it is designed to numb the reader into believing that all discrimination is *objectionable* discrimination. The critic might reply to Scott in the same vein: There is discrimination, and there is discrimination.

Let's turn now to a student's analysis of Scott's essay—and then to our analysis of the student's analysis.

Tom Wu
English 2B
Professor McCabe
March 13, 1995

Is All Discrimination Unfair?

Stanley S. Scott's "Smokers Get a Raw Deal," though a poor argument, is an extremely clever piece of writing. Scott writes clearly and he holds a reader's attention. Take his opening paragraph, which evokes the bad old days of Jim Crow segregation, when blacks were forced to ride at the back of the bus. Scott tells us, to our surprise, that there still are Americans who are forced to ride at the back of the bus. Who, we wonder, are the people who are treated so unfairly --or we would wonder, if the title of the essay hadn't let us make an easy guess. They are smokers. Of course most Americans detest segregation, and Scott thus hopes to tap our feelings of decency and fair play, so that we will recognize that smokers are people too, and they ought not to be subjected to the same evil that blacks were subjected to. He returns to this motif at the end of his essay, when he says, "After all, discrimination is discrimination, no matter what you call it." Scott is, so it seems, on the side of fair play.

But "discrimination" has two meanings. One is the ability to make accurate distinctions, as in "She can discriminate between instant coffee and freshly ground coffee." The second meaning is quite different: an act based on prejudice, as in "She does not discriminate against the handicapped," and of course this is Scott's meaning. Blacks were the victims of discrimination in this second sense when they were forced to sit at the back of the bus simply because they were black, not because they engaged in any action that might reasonably be perceived as offensive or harmful to others. That sort of segregation was the result of prejudice; it held people accountable for something (their color) over which they had no control. But smokers voluntarily engage in an action which can be annoying to others (like playing loud music on a radio at midnight, with the windows open), and which may have effects that can injure others. In pursuing their "right," smokers thus can interfere with the rights of others. In short, the "segregation" and "discrimination" against smokers is in no way comparable to the earlier treatment of blacks. Scott illegitimately--one might say outrageously--suggests that segregating smokers is as unjust, and as blindly prejudiced, as was the segregating of blacks.

Between his opening and his closing paragraphs, which present smokers as victims of "discrimination," he cites several instances of smokers who were subjected to violence, including two smokers who were killed. His point is, again, to show that smokers are being treated as blacks once were, and are in effect subjected to lynch law. The instances of violence that he cites are deplorable, but they scarcely prove that it is wrong to insist that people do not have the unrestricted right to smoke in public places. It is clearly wrong to assault smokers, but surely these assaults do not therefore make it right for smokers to subject others to smoke that annoys and may harm.

Scott's third chief argument, set forth in

Wu 3

the third paragraph from the end, is to claim that if today we infringe on "the basic freedoms of more than 50 million American smokers" we will perhaps tomorrow infringe on the freedom of yet other Americans. Here Scott makes an appeal to patriotism ("basic freedoms," "American") and at the same time warns the reader that the reader's innocent pleasures, such as eating ice cream or cake, are threatened. But this extension is preposterous: Smoking undoubtedly is greatly bothersome to many nonsmokers, and may even be unhealthy for them; eating ice cream cannot affect onlookers. If it was deceptive to classify smokers with blacks, it is equally deceptive to classify smoking with eating ice cream. Scott is trying to tell us that if we allow smokers to be isolated, we will wake up and find that <u>we</u> are the next who will be isolated by those who don't happen to like our habits, however innocent. The nation, he says, in his next-to-last paragraph, has "struggled valiantly [we are to pat ourselves on the back] to eliminate bias based on race, religion, and sex." Can we, he asks, afford to let a new bias divide us? The answer, of course, is that indeed we <u>should</u> discriminate, not in Scott's sense, but in the sense of making distinctions. We discriminate, entirely properly, between the selling of pure food and of tainted food, between law-abiding citizens and criminals, between licensed doctors and unlicensed ones, and so on. If smokers are a serious nuisance and a potential health hazard, it is scarcely un-American to protect the innocent from them. That's not discrimination (in Scott's sense) but is simply fair play.

AN ANALYSIS OF THE STUDENT'S ANALYSIS

Tom Wu's essay seems to us to be excellent, doubtless the product of a good deal of thoughtful revision. Of course he does not cover every possible aspect of Scott's essay—he concentrates on Scott's reasoning and he says very little about Scott's style—but we think that, given the limits of 500 to 750 words, he does a good job. What makes the student's essay effective? We can list the chief reasons:

- The essay has a title that is of at least a little interest, giving a hint of what is to follow. A title such as "An Analysis of an Argument" or "Scott on Smoking" would be acceptable, certainly better than no title at all, but in general it is a good idea to try to construct a more informative or a more interesting title that (like this one) arouses interest, perhaps by stirring the reader's curiosity.

- The author identifies his subject (he names the writer and the title of his essay) early.

- He reveals his thesis early. His topic is Scott's essay; his thesis or point is that it is clever but wrongheaded. Notice, by the way, that he looks closely at Scott's use of the word "discrimination," and that he defines this word carefully. Defining terms is often essential in argumentative essays. Of course Scott did *not* define the word, probably because he hoped his misuse of it would be overlooked.

- He takes up all of Scott's main points.

- He uses a few brief quotations, to let us hear Scott's voice and to assure us that he is staying close to Scott, but he does not pad his essay with long quotations.

- The essay has a sensible organization. The student begins with the beginning of Scott's essay, and then, because Scott uses the opening motif again at the end, touches on the end. The writer is not skipping around; he is taking a single point (a "new discrimination" is upon us) and following it through.

- He turns to Scott's next argument, that smokers are subjected to violence. He doesn't try to touch on each of Scott's four examples —he hasn't room, in an essay of 500 to 750 words—but he treats their gist fairly.

- He touches on Scott's next point, that no one will be safe from other forms of discrimination, and shows that it is both a gross exaggeration and, because it equates utterly unlike forms of behavior, a piece of faulty thinking.

- He concludes (without the stiffness of saying "in conclusion") with some general comments on discrimination, thus picking up a motif he introduced early in his essay. His essay, like Scott's, uses a sort of frame, or, changing the figure, it finishes off by tying a knot that was begun at the start. He even repeats the words "fair play," which he used at the end of his first paragraph, and neatly turns them to his advantage.

- Notice, finally, that he sticks closely to Scott's essay. He does not go off on a tangent and talk about the harm that smokers do to themselves. Because the assignment was to analyze Scott's essay (rather than to offer his own views on smoking) he confines himself to analyzing the essay.

Here is a checklist with some questions for an essay analyzing an argument.

Exercise ═══

Take one of the essays not yet discussed in class, or an essay assigned now by your instructor, and in an essay of 500 words analyze and evaluate it.

A CHECKLIST FOR AN ESSAY ANALYZING AN ARGUMENT

1. In your opening paragraph (or opening paragraphs) do you give the reader a good idea of what your essay will be doing? Do you identify the essay you will discuss, and introduce your subject?

2. Is your essay fair? Does it face all of the strengths (and weaknesses) of the argument?

3. Have you used occasional quotations, in order to let your reader hear the tone of the author, and in order to insure fairness?

4. Is your analysis effectively organized? Probably you can't move through the original essay paragraph by paragraph, but have you created a coherent structure for your own essay?

5. If the original essay relies partly on the writer's tone, have you sufficiently discussed this matter?

6. Is your own tone appropriate?

ARGUMENTS FOR ANALYSIS

Vita Wallace

Give Children the Vote

I first became interested in children's rights two years ago, when I learned that several states had passed laws prohibiting high school dropouts from getting driver's licenses. I was outraged, because I believe that children should not be forced to go to school or be penalized if they choose not to, a choice that is certainly the most sensible course for some people.

I am what is called a home schooler. I have never been to school, having always learned at home and in the world around me. Home schooling is absolutely legal, yet as a home schooler, I have had to defend what I consider to be my right to be educated in the ways that make the most sense to me, and so all along I have felt sympathy with people who insist on making choices about how they want to be educated, even if that means choosing not to finish high school. Now this choice is in jeopardy.

Since first learning about the discriminatory laws preventing high school dropouts from getting driver's licenses that have been passed by some state legislatures, I have done a lot of constitutional and historical research that has convinced me that children of all ages must be given the same power to elect their representatives that adults have, or they will continue to be unfairly treated and punished for exercising the few legal options they now have, such as dropping out of high school.

Most people, including children themselves, probably don't realize that children are the most regulated people in the United States. In addition to all the laws affecting adults, including tax laws, children must comply with school attendance laws, child labor laws, and alcohol and cigarette laws. They are denied driver's licenses because of their age, regardless of the dropout issue; they are victims of widespread child abuse; and they are blatantly discriminated against everywhere they go, in libraries, restaurants, and movie theaters. They have no way to protect themselves: Usually they cannot hire lawyers or bring cases to court without a guardian, and they are not allowed to vote.

The child labor and compulsory schooling laws were passed by well- 5 meaning people to protect children from exploitation. Child labor laws keep children from being forced to work, and compulsory schooling allows all children to get an education. But the abolition of slavery in 1865 didn't

---

Vita Wallace is a writer who lives in Philadelphia. This article originally appeared in a liberal publication, The Nation *(October 14, 1991).*

end the exploitation of black people. They needed the right to vote and the ability to bring lawsuits against their employers. Children need those rights too. Without them, laws that force children to go to school and generally do not allow them to work may be necessary to prevent exploitation, but they also take away children's rights as citizens to life, liberty, and the pursuit of happiness. In my case, the compulsory education laws severely limited my right to pursue the work that is important to me (which is surely what "the pursuit of happiness" referred to in the Declaration of Independence).

I am sixteen now, still not old enough to vote. Like all children, then, the only way I can fight for children's rights is by using my freedom of speech to try to convince adults to fight with me. While I am grateful that I have the right to speak my mind, I believe that it is a grave injustice to deny young people the most effective tool they could have to bring about change in a democracy. For this reason, I suggest that the right of citizens under 18 to vote not be denied or abridged on account of age.

Many people argue that it would be dangerous to let loose on society a large group of new voters who might not vote sensibly. They mean that children might not vote for the right candidates. The essence of democracy, however, is letting people vote for the wrong candidates. Democratic society has its risks, but we must gamble on the reasonableness of all our citizens, because it is less dangerous than gambling on the reasonableness of a few. That is why we chose to be a democracy instead of a dictatorship in the first place.

As it is, only 36 to 40 percent of adults who are eligible to vote actually vote in nonpresidential years, and about 25 percent of the population is under 18. As you can see, our representatives are elected by a very small percentage of our citizens. That means that although they are responsible *for* all of us, they are responsible *to* only a few of us. Politicians usually do all they can to keep that few happy, because both voters and politicians are selfish, and a politician's reelection depends on the well-being of the voters. Large segments of society that are not likely or not allowed to vote are either ignored or treated badly because of this system. It would be too much to expect the few always to vote in the interests of the many. Under these circumstances, surely the more people who vote the better, especially if they are of both sexes and of all races, classes, and ages.

People also claim that children are irresponsible. Most of the teenagers who act irresponsibly do so simply because they are not allowed to solve their problems in any way that would be considered responsible — through the courts or legislature. They fall back on sabotage of the system because they are not allowed to work within it.

Some people believe that children would vote the way their parents 10 tell them to, which would, in effect, give parents more votes. Similarly, when the Nineteenth Amendment was passed in 1920, giving women the vote, many people thought women would vote the way their husbands did. Now women are so independent that the idea of women voting on command seems absurd. The Nineteenth Amendment was a large part of the process that produced their independence. I think a similar and equally desirable result would follow if children were allowed to vote. They are naturally curious, and most are interested in the electoral process and the results of the elections even though they are not allowed to vote. Lacking world-weary cynicism, they see, perhaps even more clearly than their elders, what is going on in their neighborhoods and what is in the news.

Suffragist Belle Case La Follette's comment that if women were allowed to vote there would be a lot more dinner-table discussion of politics is as true of children today. More debate would take place not only in the home but among children and adults everywhere. Adults would also benefit if politics were talked about in libraries, churches, stores, laundromats, and other places where children gather.

People may argue that politicians would pander to children if they could vote, promising for instance that free ice cream would be distributed every day. But if kids were duped, they would not be duped for long. Children don't like to be treated condescendingly.

Even now, adults try to manipulate children all the time in glitzy TV ads or, for example, in the supposedly educational pamphlets that nuclear power advocates pass out in school science classes. Political candidates speak at schools, addressing auditoriums full of captive students. In fact, schools should be no more or less political than workplaces. Children are already exposed to many different opinions, and they would likely be exposed to even more if they could vote. The point is that with the vote, they would be better able to fight such manipulation, not only because they would have the power to do so but because they would have added reason to educate themselves on the issues.

What I suggest is that children be allowed to grow into their own right to vote at whatever rate suits them individually. They should not be forced to vote, as adults are not, but neither should they be hindered from voting if they believe themselves capable, as old people are not hindered.

As for the ability to read and write, that should never be used as a criterion for eligibility, since we have already learned from painful past experience that literacy tests can be manipulated to ensure discrimination. In any case, very few illiterate adults vote, and probably very few children would want to vote as long as they couldn't read or write. But I firmly believe that, whether they are literate or not, the vast majority of children would not attempt to vote before they are ready. Interest follows hand in hand with readiness, something that is easy to see as a home schooler but that is perhaps not so clear to many people in this society where, ironically, children are continually taught things when they are not ready, and so are not interested. Yet when they are interested, as in the case of voting, they're told they are not yet ready. I think I would not have voted until I was eight or nine, but perhaps if I had known I could vote I would have taken an interest sooner.

Legally, it would be possible to drop the voting-age requirements. In the Constitution, the states are given all powers to set qualifications for voters except as they defy the equal protection clause of the Fourteenth Amendment, in which case Congress has the power to enforce it. If it were proved that age requirements "abridge the privileges or immunities of citizens of the United States" (which in my opinion they do, since people born in the United States or to U.S. citizens are citizens from the moment they are born), and if the states could not come up with a "compelling interest" argument to justify a limit at a particular age, which Justices Potter Stewart, Warren Burger, and Harry Blackmun agreed they could not in *Oregon v. Mitchell* (the Supreme Court case challenging the 1970 amendment to the Voting Rights Act that gave 18-year-olds the vote), then age requirements would be unconstitutional. But it is not necessary that they be unconstitutional for the states to drop them. It is within the power of the states to do that, and I believe that we must start this movement at the state level. According to *Oregon v. Mitchell,* Congress cannot change the qualifications for voting in state elections except by constitutional amendment, which is why the Twenty-sixth Amendment setting the voting age at eighteen was necessary. It is very unlikely that an amendment would pass unless several states had tried eliminating the age requirement and had good results. The experience of Georgia and Kentucky, which lowered their age limits to eighteen, helped to pass the Twenty-sixth Amendment in 1971.

Already in our country's history several oppressed groups have been able to convince the unoppressed to free them. Children, who do not have the power to change their situation, must now convince the adults who do to allow them that power.

Topics for Critical Thinking and Writing

1. In a sentence or two, state the thesis of Wallace's essay. Then, in 500 words, state as succinctly as you can, her argument for that thesis.

2. In paragraph 4 Wallace says that children "are blatantly discriminated against everywhere they go, in libraries, restaurants, and movie theaters." Can you support this assertion by drawing on your own experience? Or can you cite an experience in which, you now believe, discrimination was entirely appropriate? Explain.

3. Wallace lists various objections to her position. In an essay of 500 to 750 words, set forth three of these objections, summarize Wallace's replies, and then evaluate the adequacy of her replies.

4. In paragraph 15 Wallace declares that she thinks she would not have voted (if she had had the right) "until [she] was eight or nine." Would you let a child of eight or nine drive a car on the public highways, decide how to spend the money she inherited from the premature death of her parents, choose medications for herself off the shelf of the local drugstore? If not, then why would you

let Wallace vote at such an early age? If you would permit all these things to a child of eight or nine, what would you *not* permit such a child to do? Discuss these matters in an essay of 750 words.

5. In paragraph 10 Wallace gives several reasons to support her view that children probably would not routinely vote the way their parents vote. List the reasons and evaluate each one.

6. On what grounds (if any) can compulsory education be justified?

Rita Kramer

Juvenile Justice Is Delinquent

Anyone who reads newspapers or watches TV is familiar with scenes of urban violence in which the faces of those who rob and rape, maim and kill get younger and younger. On the streets, in the subways, and even in the schools, juvenile crime has taken on a character unthinkable when the present justice system was set up to deal with it. That system, like so many of the ambitious social programs designed in the '60s, has had unintended results. Instead of solving society's ills, it has added to them.

The juvenile justice system now in place in most parts of the country is not very different from New York's Family Court. Originally conceived to protect children (defined by different states as those under age 16, 17, or 18) who ran afoul of the law, it was designed to function as a kind of wise parent providing rehabilitation.

The 1950s delinquent, who might have been a shoplifter, a truant or a car thief, would not be treated like an adult criminal. He was held to be, in the wording of the New York statute, "not criminally responsible . . . by reason of infancy." He would be given a hearing (not a trial) closed to the press and public and the disposition (not a sentence) would remain sealed, so the juvenile would not be stigmatized by youthful indiscretion. The optimistic belief was that under the guidance of social workers he would undergo a change of character.

It was a dream destined to become a nightmare. In the early 1960s, the character of juvenile court proceedings underwent a radical transformation. Due process was interpreted to grant youthful "respondents" (not defendants) not only the services of a lawyer, but also the protections the criminal justice system affords adults, who are liable to serious penalties if found guilty.

Rita Kramer, the author of At a Tender Age: Violent Youth and Juvenile Justice *(1988) and other books, published this article in the* Wall Street Journal *(May 27, 1992).*

In the hands of Legal Aid Society lawyers (and sometimes sympathetic   5
judges), the juvenile system focuses on the minutiae of procedural technicalities at the expense of fact-finding, in order to achieve the goal of
"getting the kid off." The questions is not whether a teenage boy has
beaten up a homeless old man, shot a storekeeper, or sodomized a little
girl. He may even admit the act. The question is whether his admission can
be invalidated because a police officer forgot to have him initial his responses to the Miranda warnings in the proper place or whether the arresting officer had probable cause to search him for the loaded gun that was
found on him.

It has become the lawyer's job not only to protect his young client
from punishment, but from any possibility of rehabilitation in the system's
various facilities. The best interests of the child or adolescent have been
reinterpreted to mean his legal rights, even when the two are in opposition.
He now has the right to continue the behavior that brought him into the
juvenile court, which he leaves with the knowledge that his behavior had
no real negative consequences to him.

Even when there are consequences, they are mild indeed, a fact not
lost on his peers. Eighteen months in a facility that usually has TV, a basketball court, and better food and medical care than at home is the worst
that all but the most violent repeat offenders have to fear in New York. The
system, based on a person's age and not his crimes, fails either to restrain
or retrain him.

As juvenile courts were changing, so were juvenile criminals. As recently as the early '70s, the majority of cases before children's and family
courts were misdemeanors. In New York City, the most common charge
was "jostling," pickpocketing without physical contact. By 1991, robbery —
a charge that involves violence against people — had outpaced drug-related
offenses as the largest category of crimes by juveniles. Between 1987 and
1991, the fastest-growing crime by juveniles was loaded gun possession,
and metal detectors and spot police checks had become routine in some
inner-city high schools.

Cases of violent group assault — "kids" causing serious physical injury
"for fun" — had increased dramatically. Predatory behavior was becoming
a form of entertainment for some of the urban young, white as well as
black and Hispanic. Last year, according to Peter Reinharz, chief of New
York City's Family Court Division, 85 percent of the young offenders
brought into Family Court were charged with felonies. "These are dangerous people," Mr. Reinharz says. "We hardly ever see the non-violent any
more."

Nationwide figures compiled by the FBI's Uniform Crime Reporting   10
Program in 1990 showed the highest number of arrests of youth for violent
offenses — homicide, armed robbery, rape, aggravated assault — in the
more than twenty-five years that the statistics have been compiled. Juvenile arrest rates, after rising steadily from the mid-1960s through the
1970s, remained relatively constant until the 1989–90 statistics revealed a

26 percent increase in the number of youths arrested for murder and non-negligent manslaughter, while arrests for robbery had increased by 16 percent, and those for aggravated assault by 17 percent.

But the system still defines juveniles as children rather than as criminals, a distinction that makes little sense to their victims or to the rest of the public. Family Court turns the worst juvenile offenders over to the adult system for trial, but they are still sentenced as juveniles.

When anything does happen it's usually so long after the event, so short in duration, and so ineffective that it's no wonder the young men who rob, maim, rape, and terrorize don't perceive those actions as having any serious consequences. Eighty percent of chronic juvenile offenders (five or more arrests) go on to adult criminal careers.

Is it possible to change these young criminals? And what should be done to protect the community from them?

The first necessity is legislation to open juvenile court proceedings to the public and the press. It makes no sense to protect the privacy of those who are a palpable menace to their neighbors or scruple about "stigmatizing" them. A repeat offender should know the authorities will make use of his past record in deciding what to do with him next time. At present, a young habitual criminal is born again with a virgin record when he reaches the age to be dealt with by the adult system.

Opening court records would also make it possible to undertake 15 follow-up studies to find out what works and what doesn't in the various detention facilities and alternative programs designed to rehabilitate. Taxpayers have a right to know what outcomes they are getting for the $85,000 a year it costs to keep a juvenile offender in a secure facility in New York state.

Intervention should occur early, while there is still time to try measures that might make a difference. First offenders should be required to make restitution to their victims or perform community service. A second arrest should be followed by stronger measures. For those who have families who undertake to be responsible for them, there should be intensive supervision by well-trained probation officers with manageable caseloads. For those who require placement out of the home, it should include intensive remedial schoolwork and practical training in some job-related skill. The youth should remain long enough for such efforts to have some hope of proving effective.

Sanctions should be swift and sure. Once arrested, a court appearance should follow without delay, preferably on the same day, so that there is a clear connection made between behavior and its consequences. Placement in appropriately secure institutions, locked away from the community for definite periods of time, should be the immediate and inevitable response to repeated acts of violence. And incarceration should involve some form of work that helps defray its cost to the community, not just a period of rest and recreation. Young criminals should know that is what they can expect.

A growing cadre of violent teenage boys are growing up with mothers who are children and no resident fathers. What they need most of all is structure and supervision. We may not be able to change attitudes, but we can change behavior. While there is no evidence that any form of therapy can really change a violent repeat offender into someone with empathy for others, it has been demonstrated that the one thing that can result in impulse control is the certainty of punishment.

The present system actually encourages the young to continue their criminal behavior by showing them that they can get away with it. No punishment means a second chance at the same crimes. A significant number of boys arrested for violent crimes were out on parole at the time of the arrest.

They think of the system as a game they can win. "They can't do noth- 20 ing to me, I ain't sixteen yet" is a repeated refrain in a system that breeds contempt for the law and for the other institutions of society. It is time to acknowledge its failure and restructure the system so that "juvenile justice" ceases to be an oxymoron. We owe it to the law-abiding citizens who share the streets and schools with the violent few to protect the rights of the community and not just those of its victimizers.

Topics for Critical Thinking and Writing

1. In her fifth paragraph Kramer indicates her distress with a system that allows a guilty juvenile to be released because the police failed to comply with some details. But the requirement that police comply with details was generated by police misconduct. If adults can be released because the police fail to act according to all of the standard procedures, why shouldn't juveniles also be released?

2. Kramer says (para. 6) that the current juvenile justice system has made it the defendant's lawyer's job "to protect his young client . . . from any possibility of rehabilitation. . . ." Explain her reasoning.

3. Kramer says (para. 7) that if a youthful offender is put away, it is "in a facility that usually has TV, a basketball court, and better food and medical care than at home." Let's assume she is right. Why do you suppose the government provides TV, a basketball court, and better food and medical care than the youth probably has at home? If you were running things, what would you change? Would you, for instance, do away with television sets, or provide medical care that is below the standard? Explain.

4. "But the system," Kramer says in paragraph 11, "still defines juveniles as children rather than as criminals, a distinction that makes little sense to their victims. . . ." Does she have a point here? Or might it also be said that of course the victims are distressed, but the feelings of the victims are irrelevant to a society that is trying to deal intelligently and humanely with youthful offenders? Explain.

5. In paragraph 18 Kramer says that "it has been demonstrated that the one thing that can result in impulse control is the certainty of punishment." She offers no

evidence. Do you take her statement on trust? Or because it seems self-evident? Or do you assume it is true because it is a principle that guides your own life? Or what? Explain.

6. Kramer says (para. 19) that "The present system actually encourages the young to continue their criminal behavior by showing them that they can get away with it." What evidence, if any, does she offer to support this sentence? If she does not support it, should she have, or is it self-evident?

7. In her final paragraph Kramer indicates that the reason we must reform the system is "to protect the rights of the community." Earlier in the essay, however, she also indicated the desirability of helping youthful offenders to reform their conduct. What do you make of the fact that she does not continue this point into her final paragraph?

8. Kramer reports a sudden increase (26 percent) in violent crimes by juveniles in the years 1989–90. If your library receives the FBI's annual *Uniform Crime Reports* or the *Sourcebook of Criminal Justice Statistics,* consult one of these sources and determine whether in the years since 1990 juvenile crime has continued to increase, has leveled off, or has decreased.

9. In paragraph 18 Kramer mentions the "growing cadre of violent teenage boys . . . growing up with . . . no resident fathers." She ends this paragraph insisting on the "certainty of punishment" for such boys. Why do you suppose she doesn't instead recommend measures to punish the fathers for neglecting their sons?

10. List the measures Kramer recommends to decrease juvenile crime. Does she cite any evidence to show that these reforms really would reduce such crime? Can you think of reasons to believe in or to doubt their efficacy?

Katha Pollitt

It Takes Two: A Modest Proposal for Holding Fathers Equally Accountable

"You start out with the philosophy that you can have as many babies as you want . . . if you don't ask the government to take care of them. But when you start asking the government to take care of them, the government ought to have some control over you. I would say, for people like that, if they want the government to take care of their children I would be for something like Norplant, mandatory Norplant."

What well-known politician made the above remarks? Newt Gingrich?

Katha Pollitt (b. 1949) often writes essays on literary, political, and social topics for The Nation, *a liberal journal that on January 30, 1995, published the essay that we reprint here. Some of Pollitt's essays have been collected and published in a volume called* Reasonable Creatures *(1994). Pollitt is also widely known as a poet; her first collection of poems,* Antarctic Traveller *(1982), won the National Book Critics Circle award for poetry.*

Jesse Helms? Dan Quayle? No, it was Marion Barry, newly installed Democratic mayor of our nation's capital, speaking last November to Sally Quinn of the *Washington Post*. The same Marion Barry whose swearing-in on January 2 featured a poetry reading by Maya Angelou, who, according to the *New York Times*, "drew thunderous applause when she pointed at Mr. Barry and crooned: 'Me and my baby, we gonna shine, shine!'" Ms. Angelou sure knows how to pick them.

One of my neighbors told me in the laundry room that it wasn't very nice of me to have mentioned Arianna Huffington's millions when we "debated" spirituality and school prayer on *Crossfire* the other day. So I won't belabor Mayor Barry's personal history[1] here. After all, the great thing about Christianity, of which Mayor Barry told Ms. Quinn he is now a fervent devotee, is that you can always declare yourself reformed, reborn, and redeemed. So maybe Mayor ("Bitch set me up") Barry really is the man to "bring integrity back into government," as he is promising to do.

But isn't it interesting that the male politicians who go all out for family values — the deadbeat dads, multiple divorcers, convicted felons, gropers, and philanderers who rule the land — always focus on women's behavior and always in a punitive way? You could, after all, see the plethora of women and children in poverty as the fruits of male fecklessness, callousness, selfishness, and sexual vanity. We hear an awful lot about pregnant teens, but what about the fact that 30 percent of fathers of babies born to girls under sixteen are men in their twenties or older? What about the fact that the condom is the only cheap, easy-to-use, effective, side-effectless nonprescription method of contraception — and it is the male partner who must choose to use it? What about the 50 percent of welfare mothers who are on the rolls because of divorce — i.e., the failure of judges to order, or husbands to pay, adequate child support?

Marion Barry's views on welfare are shared by millions: Women have   5
babies by parthenogenesis or cloning, and then perversely demand that the government "take care of them." Last time I looked, taking care of children meant feeding, bathing, and singing the Barney song, and mothers, not government bureaucrats, were performing those tasks. It is not the mother's care that welfare replaces, but the father's cash. Newt Gingrich's Personal Responsibility Act is directed against unmarried moms, but these women are actually assuming a responsibility that their babies' fathers have shirked. It's all very well to talk about orphanages, but what would happen to children if mothers abandoned them at the rate fathers do? A woman who leaves her newborn in the hospital and never returns for it still makes headlines. You'd need a list as thick as the New York City phone book to name the men who have no idea where or how or who their children are.

My point is not to demonize men, but fair's fair. If we've come so far down the road that we're talking about mandatory Norplant, about starving

---

[1]**Mayor Barry's personal history** Marion Barry served six months in prison for possessing drugs.

women into giving up their kids to orphanages (Republican version) or forcing young mothers to live in group homes (Democratic version); if *The Bell Curve* co-author Charles Murray elicits barely a peep when he suggests releasing men from financial obligations to out-of-wedlock children; and if divorced moms have to hire private detectives to get their exes to pay court-awarded child support, then it's time to ensure that the Personal Responsibility Act applies equally to both sexes. For example:

1. A man who fathers a child out of wedlock must pay $10,000 a year or 20 percent of his income, whichever is greater, in child support until the child reaches twenty-one. If he is unable to pay, the government will, in which case the father will be given a workfare (no wage) job and a dorm residence comparable to those provided homeless women and children— i.e., curfews, no visitors, and compulsory group-therapy sessions in which, along with other unwed fathers, he can learn to identify the patterns of irresponsibility that led him to impregnate a woman so thoughtlessly.

2. A man who fathers a second child out of wedlock must pay child support equal to that for the first; if he can't, or is already on workfare, he must have a vasectomy. A sample of his sperm will be preserved so he can father more children if he becomes able to support the ones he already has.

3. Married men who father children out of wedlock or in sequential marriages have the same obligations to all their children, whose living standards must be as close to equal as is humanly possible. This means that some older men will be financially unable to provide their much-younger trophy wives with the babies those women often crave. Too bad!

4. Given the important role played by fathers in everything from up- 10 ping their children's test scores to teaching them the meaning of terms like "wide receiver" and "throw weight," divorced or unwed fathers will be legally compelled to spend time with their children or face criminal charges of child neglect. Absentee dads, not overburdened single moms, will be legally liable for the crimes and misdemeanors of their minor children, and their paychecks will be docked if the kids are truant.

5. In view of the fact that men can father children unknowingly, all men will pay a special annual tax to provide support for children whose paternity is unknown. Men wishing to avoid the tax can undergo a vasectomy at state expense, with sperm to be frozen at personal expense (Republican version) or by government subsidy (Democratic version).

As I was saying, fair's fair.

Topics for Critical Thinking and Writing

1. In paragraph 5 Pollitt sums up what she says is a common view of welfare: "Women have babies by parthenogenesis or cloning, and then perversely demand that the government 'take care of them.'" What absurdity is she calling to our attention?

2. In paragraph 4 Pollitt cites three important facts for her argument pointing to "male . . . selfishness" as a chief cause of women on welfare. Consult some reliable source — a word with the reference librarian will probably help guide you to the right place — and verify at least one of these facts.

3. In paragraph 5 Pollitt mentions "Newt Gingrich's Personal Responsibility Act." With the assistance of your college's librarian, locate the text, or at least a summary, of this proposed law. Then look up the Republicans' *Contract with America*, edited by Ed Gillespie and Bob Schellhas (1994), and check out what is described there as the Family Reinforcement Act. How do these two proposed laws differ?

4. Reread the first five paragraphs. Do you think that Pollitt has helped you to think about a problem? Or has she muddied the waters? Explain.

5. Pollitt declares not only once but twice (paras. 6 and 12) that "fair's fair." People also sometimes say "business is business." Both expressions look like more tautologies (needless repetitions), explaining or justifying nothing — yet they aren't really tautologies at all. What do you think is the rhetorical or persuasive function of such expressions?

6. Do you think that any of Pollitt's five proposals might become law? If not, why not, and, further, what *is* her purpose in offering them?

7. If you have read Jonathan Swift's "A Modest Proposal" (p. 111), explain why Pollitt echoes Swift's title in her own title.

David Cole

Five Myths about Immigration

For a brief period in the mid-nineteenth century, a new political movement captured the passions of the American public. Fittingly labeled the "Know-Nothings," their unifying theme was nativism. They liked to call themselves "Native Americans," although they had no sympathy for people we call Native Americans today. And they pinned every problem in American society on immigrants. As one Know-Nothing wrote in 1856: "Four-fifths of the beggary and three-fifths of the crime spring from our foreign population; more than half the public charities, more than half the prisons and almshouses, more than half the police and the cost of administering criminal justice are for foreigners."

At the time, the greatest influx of immigrants was from Ireland, where the potato famine had struck, and Germany, which was in political and economic turmoil. Anti-alien and anti-Catholic sentiments were the order of the day, especially in New York and Massachusetts, which received the

David Cole, a professor at Georgetown University Law Center, is a volunteer staff attorney for the Center for Constitutional Rights. This essay originally appeared in The Nation *on October 17, 1994.*

brunt of the wave of immigrants, many of whom were dirt-poor and uneducated. Politicians were quick to exploit the sentiment: There's nothing like a scapegoat to forge an alliance.

I am especially sensitive to this history: My forebears were among those dirt-poor Irish Catholics who arrived in the 1860s. Fortunately for them, and me, the Know-Nothing movement fizzled within fifteen years. But its pilot light kept burning, and is turned up whenever the American public begins to feel vulnerable and in need of an enemy.

Although they go by different names today, the Know-Nothings have returned. As in the 1850s, the movement is strongest where immigrants are most concentrated: California and Florida. The objects of prejudice are of course no longer Irish Catholics and Germans; 140 years later, "they" have become "us." The new "they" — because it seems "we" must always have a "they" — are Latin Americans (most recently, Cubans), Haitians, and Arab-Americans, among others.

But just as in the 1850s, passion, misinformation and shortsighted fear   5 often substitute for reason, fairness, and human dignity in today's immigration debates. In the interest of advancing beyond know-nothingism, let's look at five current myths that distort public debate and government policy relating to immigrants.

America is being overrun with immigrants. In one sense, of course, this is true, but in that sense it has been true since Christopher Columbus arrived. Except for the real Native Americans, we are a nation of immigrants.

It is not true, however, that the first-generation immigrant share of our population is growing. As of 1990, foreign-born people made up only 8 percent of the population, as compared with a figure of about 15 percent from 1870 to 1920. Between 70 and 80 percent of those who immigrate every year are refugees or immediate relatives of U.S. citizens.

Much of the anti-immigrant fervor is directed against the undocumented, but they make up only 13 percent of all immigrants residing in the United States, and only 1 percent of the American population. Contrary to popular belief, most such aliens do not cross the border illegally but enter legally and remain after their student or visitor visa expires. Thus, building a wall at the border, no matter how high, will not solve the problem.

Immigrants take jobs from U.S. citizens. There is virtually no evidence to support this view, probably the most widespread misunderstanding about immigrants. As documented by a 1994 A.C.L.U. Immigrants' Rights Project report, numerous studies have found that immigrants actually *create* more jobs than they fill. The jobs immigrants take are of course easier to see, but immigrants are often highly productive, run their own businesses, and employ both immigrants and citizens. One study found that Mexican immigration to Los Angeles County between 1970 and 1980 was responsible for 78,000 new jobs. Governor Mario Cuomo reports that immigrants own more than 40,000 companies in New York, which provide thousands of jobs and $3.5 billion to the state's economy every year.

Immigrants are a drain on society's resources. This claim fuels many 10
of the recent efforts to cut off government benefits to immigrants. However, most studies have found that immigrants are a net benefit to the
economy because, as a 1994 Urban Institute report concludes, "immigrants
generate significantly more in taxes paid than they cost in services received." The Council of Economic Advisers similarly found in 1986 that
"immigrants have a favorable effect on the overall standard of living."

Anti-immigrant advocates often cite studies purportedly showing the
contrary, but these generally focus only on taxes and services at the local or
state level. What they fail to explain is that because most taxes go to the
federal government, such studies would also show a net loss when applied
to U.S. citizens. At most, such figures suggest that some redistribution of
federal and state monies may be appropriate; they say nothing unique
about the costs of immigrants.

Some subgroups of immigrants plainly impose a net cost in the short
run, principally those who have most recently arrived and have not yet
"made it." California, for example, bears substantial costs for its disproportionately large undocumented population, largely because it has on average
the poorest and least educated immigrants. But that has been true of every
wave of immigrants that has ever reached our shores; it was as true of the
Irish in the 1850s, for example, as it is of Salvadorans today. From a long-
term perspective, the economic advantages of immigration are undeniable.

Some have suggested that we might save money and diminish incentives to immigrate illegally if we denied undocumented aliens public services. In fact, undocumented immigrants are already ineligible for most social programs, with the exception of education for schoolchildren, which is
constitutionally required, and benefits directly related to health and safety,
such as emergency medical care and nutritional assistance to poor women,
infants, and children. To deny such basic care to people in need, apart
from being inhumanly callous, would probably cost us more in the long run
by exacerbating health problems that we would eventually have to address.

*Aliens refuse to assimilate, and are depriving us of our cultural and
political unity.* This claim has been made about every new group of immigrants to arrive on U.S. shores. Supreme Court Justice Stephen Field
wrote in 1884 that the Chinese "have remained among us a separate people, retaining their original peculiarities of dress, manners, habits, and
modes of living, which are as marked as their complexion and language."
Five years later, he upheld the racially based exclusion of Chinese immigrants. Similar claims have been made over different periods of our history
about Catholics, Jews, Italians, Eastern Europeans, and Latin Americans.

In most instances, such claims are simply not true; "American culture" 15
has been created, defined, and revised by persons who for the most part
are descended from immigrants once seen as anti-assimilationist. Descendants of the Irish Catholics, for example, a group once decried as separatist
and alien, have become Presidents, senators, and representatives (and all
of these in one family, in the case of the Kennedys). Our society exerts

tremendous pressure to conform, and cultural separatism rarely survives a generation. But more important, even if this claim were true, is this a legitimate rationale for limiting immigration in a society built on the values of pluralism and tolerance?

Noncitizen immigrants are not entitled to constitutional rights. Our government has long declined to treat immigrants as full human beings, and nowhere is that more clear than in the realm of constitutional rights. Although the Constitution literally extends the fundamental protections in the Bill of Rights to all people, limiting to citizens only the right to vote and run for federal office, the federal government acts as if this were not the case.

In 1893 the executive branch successfully defended a statute that required Chinese laborers to establish their prior residence here by the testimony of "at least one credible white witness." The Supreme Court ruled that this law was constitutional because it was reasonable for Congress to presume that nonwhite witnesses could not be trusted.

The federal government is not much more enlightened today. In a pending case I'm handling in the Court of Appeals for the Ninth Circuit, the Clinton Administration has argued that permanent resident aliens lawfully living here should be extended no more First Amendment rights than aliens applying for first-time admission from abroad—that is, none. Under this view, students at a public university who are citizens may express themselves freely, but students who are not citizens can be deported for saying exactly what their classmates are constitutionally entitled to say.

Growing up, I was always taught that we will be judged by how we treat others. If we are collectively judged by how we have treated immigrants—those who would appear today to be "other" but will in a generation be "us"—we are not in very good shape.

Topics for Critical Thinking and Writing

1. What are the "five current myths" about immigration that Cole identifies? Why does he describe them as "myths" (rather than "errors," "mistakes," or "falsehoods")?

2. In an encyclopedia or other reference work in your college library, look up the Know-Nothings. What, if anything, of interest do you learn about the movement that is not mentioned by Cole in his opening paragraphs (1 to 4)?

3. Cole attempts to show how insignificant the immigrant population really is (in paras. 7 and 13) because it is such a small fraction (8 percent in 1990) of the total population. Suppose someone said to him, "That's all very well, but 8 percent of the population is still 20 million people—far more than the 15 percent of the population during the years from 1870 to 1920." How might he reply?

4. Suppose Cole is right, that most illegal immigration results from overstaying visitor and student visas (para. 8). Why not pass laws prohibiting foreign students

from studying here, since so many abuse the privilege? Why not pass other laws forbidding foreign visitors?

5. Cole cites a study (para. 9) showing that Mexican immigration in Los Angeles County in the decade 1970–80 "was responsible for 78,000 new jobs." Suppose it were also true that this immigration was responsible for 78,000 other Mexican immigrants who joined criminal gangs or were otherwise not legally employed. How might Cole respond?

6. Cole admits (para. 12) that in California, the large population of undocumented immigrants imposes "substantial costs" on taxpayers. Does Cole offer any remedy for this problem? Should the federal government bear some or all of these extra costs that fall on California?

7. Cole thinks that "cultural separatism" among immigrants "rarely survives a generation" (para. 15). His evidence? Look at the Irish Catholics. But suppose someone argued that this is weak evidence: Today's immigrants are not Europeans, they are Asian and Hispanic; they will never assimilate to the degree that European immigrants did—their race, culture, religion, and the trend toward "multiculturalism" all block the way. How might Cole reply?

8. Do you think that immigrants who are not citizens and not applying for citizenship ought to be allowed to vote in state and local elections (the Constitution forbids them to vote in federal elections, as Cole points out in para. 16)? Why, or why not? How about illegal immigrants?

Janet Radcliffe Richards

Thinking Straight and Dying Well

Presumably you would not have invited me to give this lecture unless you had thought I was on your side; and this puts us from the start in a situation of intellectual and moral danger. People are inclined to be very tolerant of arguments that seem to support conclusions they already accept.

It is easy to think of this fact as just another symptom of the well-known irrationality of our species, but oddly enough, what appears as irrationality is often a sign of a deeper, underlying rationality. When people are careless about facts, or play fast and loose with logic, this is often because they are trying to make it seem (to themselves as well as others) as though various ideas to which they are strongly committed can be made to fit together. Think, for instance, of someone who refuses to give to a charity, asserting (without any investigation of the matter) that charities waste

Janet Radcliffe Richards is lecturer in philosophy in England on the central faculty of the Open University, where she specializes in ethics, philosophy of science, and applied philosophy. The essay reprinted here was published in the Newsletter of the Voluntary Euthanasia Society of Scotland *in September 1994.*

all the money given to them. Pretty obviously, the invented fact is there to allow the person to reach the desired conclusion (not giving money) without having to make an undesirable admission (not being generous).

This is a useful thing to bear in mind in any area where there are strong passions. They are breeding grounds for twisted arguments and invented facts, and identifying these not only clarifies the issues and sharpens political argument; it also offers important indications of what the real motivations are. This applies potentially as much to our own arguments as to our opponents', and provides a method of real progress in moral enquiry. But here I want to concentrate on arguments against euthanasia.

And the first thing to do is to qualify the little I have already said. I have referred to *sides* and *the euthanasia debate,* and *arguments against euthanasia.* But this is just where the trouble starts. A moment's thought shows that the word "euthanasia" is applied to a wide range of actions; not only the ones counted as voluntary euthanasia, but also such things as turning off life support machines, killing defective babies, and not trying to save the lives of people who are senile or badly damaged in accidents.

These are all different, and there is no reason to presume they must   5 be morally identical. Inevitably, however, whenever there is a single word people will tend to think of it as denoting a single thing, and this is always dangerous. In particular, people who think of themselves as against whatever it is will often pounce on arguments that seem to work against the most troubling cases, and wave them around as if they were objections to all.

The first thing to do, therefore, is to pull the issue out of the impressionistic blur produced by the word "euthanasia," and make sure that each issue is analyzed in its own right. We must make sure that the clearest cases are not weakened by spurious association with more difficult ones. And, of course, the other way round. We must not allow any relatively straightforward cases to disguise the difficulty of others.

Since this is a voluntary euthanasia society I shall keep to the range of issues that come up only under that heading. That will be more than enough to be going on with.

THE BASIC ISSUE: MAKING SUICIDE POSSIBLE

Slippery slopes. Two years ago there occurred the much-publicized case of Dr. Cox, who eventually gave in to the pleadings of a patient in desperate, terminal pain, and who wanted to die. This led to the usual rush of public alarm. Euthanasia must not be allowed, it was protested, because if we gave doctors the right to kill we should be off on a slippery slope, turning off life support machines, clearing geriatric wards, and moving inexorably towards Hitlerian extermination camps. Hitler is always the bogey at the bottom of the slope; an awful warning to anyone tempted to set out on it. Dr. Cox was forced, like Galileo, to recant.

But the issue brought up by this case has nothing to do with allowing doctors to decide whom to kill. It is, quite differently, that of whether people trapped by disability or institutions should be denied the freedom the rest of us have to commit suicide. Many people are simply not able to kill themselves; and it is, incidentally, a striking fact that the very helplessness which makes suicide impossible does itself provide some of the most rational grounds for wanting to die. The present law, which does not forbid suicide, nevertheless ensures that such people must stay alive, because no one else may help them to do what they cannot do alone.

But, say the objectors, at this point it ceases to be suicide and becomes 10 killing; and killing is wrong. But once again, it cannot be presumed that everything describable by a single word must fall into a single moral category.

Normally we regard it as charitable and generous when people put their own powers at the disposal of the powerless, to enable them to do what they otherwise could not, and we see this as morally quite different from doing the same things against their will. If your aunt whose fingers are crippled with arthritis cannot put the sugar in her tea, and you do it for her, we do not hesitate to distinguish it from malicious tea-sweetening (as from Cicely to Gwendolen in *The Importance of Being Earnest*). Why, then, if you get the pills she wants to make her escape from life, or manipulate the syringe because she cannot do it herself, should we put this in the same moral category as doing those things against her will? In any other case such a conflation would scream out its absurdity; and so it should in this one.

If assisting the suicide of the helpless is killing, we must insist that there are different kinds of killing, and that this kind bears no moral resemblance at all to murder, or even to justifiable forms of killing without consent.

When the matter is put this way, it provides an indication of what really lies behind the objections. When do we say that it is wrong to help other people to do what they want to do, but cannot? Only, surely, when what they want is itself wrong. You would not feel that kindness to your arthritic aunt should extend to putting poison on her behalf into her neighbor's tea. Surely, therefore, anyone who thinks it wrong to assist the suicide of the helpless must think suicide itself wrong. Conversely, if the law does not forbid suicide, it has no justification for its seeing the assisting of suicide as different from the assisting of anything else.

So we can start the clarification of the issues by resolutely detaching this most fundamental case — the desperate situation of people who want to die but cannot kill themselves — from anything else to which the label of euthanasia may have become attached. And when this is done, and (obviously most important) proper safeguards are in place to make sure that what is going on really is assisted suicide and not murder, the slippery-slope idea stands exposed for the irrelevance it is. There is no slope. Suicide is not a thing there is any danger of anyone's getting into a habit of.

Making life worth living. Needless to say, however, that will not be 15 the end of the argument, even when it is clear that the issue is the limited one of freedom to commit suicide. One of the commonest symptoms of deeply rooted attitudes, held not because of the arguments offered in their defense but for other, unstated, reasons, is the speed with which refuted arguments are replaced by others.

The next familiar line of argument is that euthanasia of this sort should not be necessary; that we should instead be making people's lives worth living, by controlling their pain and making them feel valued. And this argument is a good piece of strategy, because no one is going to rush in and deny that we should be doing these things. It also tends to divert supporters of euthanasia into arguments about the extent to which it is possible to control pain, when what they should really be doing is exposing this maneuver as a fudge of the first order, and a particularly dangerous one. To see this, all that is needed is a steady eye for the point at issue. It is claimed that we should make life worth living for the suffering, and *implied* that this is a reason for not allowing help with suicide. But how can a claim that something should not be needed be regarded as a reason for saying it should be forbidden? You might just as well say that because all children should learn to read at school, we should prohibit adult literacy classes.

If we could reliably make everyone's life worth living, no one would want to die, and laws preventing assistance would have no purpose. Conversely, to the extent that they have a purpose, *precisely* what they achieve is to force continuing life on people whose sufferings we have not managed to prevent. The claim that we should prevent suffering is being used to defend a law whose main effect is to perpetuate it.

This is a clear case of an argument so outrageously bad that it could not possibly be thought to work by anyone not already convinced of the conclusion on quite other grounds. It seems obvious, once again, that its proponents really disapprove of suicide altogether, but are unwilling to face the fact that this may mean forcing people to remain alive in agony.

To put the matter even more starkly, the prevention of suicide achieves nothing for the sufferers, but it does mean the rest of us can avoid having forced on our attention the knowledge of how many people there are who would rather be dead, and can more easily forget them. I do not think for a moment that that is the motive of the people who argue in this way, but it is the effect. Anyone who really wants to make people's lives worth living should be glad to allow suicide, as a reminder of the extent of failure.

The dangers of coercion. The final objection I want to consider 20 against allowing assistance with suicide is increasingly common, and widely accepted as conclusive. It is that if euthanasia were allowed, we could never be sure it was truly voluntary. Relatives and doctors might make people feel unwanted, or even (though I have not actually heard this suggested) leave them in more pain than necessary to coerce them into choosing death. And even if this did not happen, people might still feel burdensome and under an obligation to choose to go. We must therefore keep the option closed.

This issue is more complicated than the previous two, and there is no quick answer on the euthanasia side. But what can be shown is that the other side is even less entitled to its own quick answer.

It is necessary to get the form of the problem clear. We should not be thinking about wards full of old people and wondering what their relations would do if we decided to institute voluntary euthanasia. Rather the question is, for everyone in a democracy, about the kinds of institutions we should prefer to live by. Would we, individually, choose to live in a society which forbade voluntary euthanasia altogether, to protect ourselves from the risk of being put under pressure to choose it?

It is certainly true that making things impossible is one way to prevent our being coerced into doing them. This is a well understood maneuver (see, for instance, Thomas Schelling in *The Strategy of Conflict*). On the other hand, it is not one to be adopted lightly. Usually it is absurd to give up an option completely in order to avoid the chance of being put under pressure to use it in a particular way; you would hardly think of giving up the freedom to choose whom to marry in order to avoid the danger of being put under pressure to make the wrong choice. Such decisions can be made only through careful risk analysis, involving estimates of how bad the various possible outcomes are, and how likely they are to come about. How likely is it that our relatives would start putting pressure on us? Is it a severe enough danger to justify the sacrifice of the freedom to opt out if we are in terrible pain?

There is no algorithm for calculations of this sort, but a few comments may help to put the matter in perspective.

First, although this line of argument does not seem to be motivated by   25 a straightforward opposition to suicide, I think in fact it must be. Anyone who can see the anti-euthanasia conclusion as immediate and obvious, rather than as difficult and to be reached only after much agonizing, is willing to give up the suicide option to avoid any risk at all that anyone will be put under pressure to take it. No one who thought the option intrinsically valuable could give it up so quickly. And for anyone who would like to keep it, the case for giving it up need seem nothing like as strong.

For one thing, it is not at all obvious that allowing suicide will make it more likely that people are put under pressure to take that option. It could work quite the other way: Relatives and hospitals might become so afraid of being accused of driving anyone to euthanasia that they became assiduous in their attempts to prevent it. Until we try, we shall not know.

Furthermore, there is no reason to think of these probabilities, whatever they are, as fixed. We could try to influence them in various ways. Perhaps hospitals might deliberately develop a culture in which euthanasia was regarded as a failure, and patients were persuaded not to choose it. (Though that would, of course, create pressures the other way.)

And, finally, a most important point. If different people might have different preferences in this context, we should consider whether it might be possible to let people choose their own risks. Even if suicide were allowed, I do not see why people who did not want the risk of pressure could not (say) sign an anti-suicide pledge, and join societies and churches committed to the repudiation of this option.

That kind of possibility does, indeed, seem to me to settle the issue. But even if it does not, it still seems clear that we need not be bullied by what is widely regarded as a knock-down argument against euthanasia, but which, without the hidden presupposition that suicide is never morally acceptable, is nothing of the sort.

SECOND ISSUE: EASING DEATH

So far I have discussed only one part of the voluntary euthanasia issue, 30 that of making death possible for people who cannot choose to die, and considered three common arguments against it. But of course there are other issues, and a closely related one is that of making death pleasant. For many people suicide is not actually impossible, but can be achieved only by painful or distressing means. Many of us think everyone should have access to the means of dying painlessly.

The usual objection is that this makes suicide too easy, and people will do away with themselves during passing bouts of depression. That, however, confuses ease and pleasantness. Most of us probably think there should be a waiting time, perhaps longer for young people than old, and other safeguards. But that is quite compatible with making death painless for anyone who can show they really want it.

But still, it will be said, to make death less unpleasant is to make it more attractive, and more people will choose it than otherwise would have done. Surely we should keep death unattractive in order to discourage suicide?

If this sounds plausible, consider it in more detail. Think of life as measured against a scale of satisfaction, and each person as fixing a point on that scale at which life becomes not worth living. If we want to prevent people choosing suicide when they reach that point, there are two ways of doing it. One is to make life better, so that it rises again above the crisis point. The other is to make death so unpleasant that things have to get even worse before death becomes an attractive option. Either of these, therefore, would prevent suicides.

But why, exactly, do we want to prevent suicide? What is bad about it? Some people think it bad in itself, and probably as sinful; others think the ground for regret is that anyone's life should be not worth living. If you want to prevent suicide for this second reason, only the first way of proceeding—improving people's lives—makes any sense. Preventing suicide by making death unpleasant does not make anyone's life one scrap more worth living; it just gives them a reason to live with more misery.

In other words, the now-familiar background assumption appears 35 again, in yet another disguise. To oppose allowing people the means of painless suicide is to regard suicide as bad in itself, and to be discouraged whether life is worth living or not.

THIRD ISSUE: ADVANCE DIRECTIVES

Finally, many of us would like to be able to specify that if we became so ill or damaged that we could not make any wishes known, we should be actively killed. This is quite different from saying that everyone in a coma or irreversibly damaged by a stroke should be done away with; that is related, but it needs separate argument. Here the claim is only that we should be allowed to decide for ourselves. What reason could anyone offer for saying that we should not?

The usual line of argument here is that we can never be sure. We cannot be sure that the coma will not be emerged from, or that a new treatment will not be found. Furthermore, we cannot be sure about the state of mind of someone unable to communicate, and who may have undergone a change of mind since writing the directive.

All these arguments, however, make the same presuppositions. They all presuppose that in case of doubt we should err on the side of caution, and that caution means not killing unless we are absolutely certain. Since we can never be certain, we should never risk killing.

But this is another case where risk analysis is needed, and many of us would assess the situation in quite the opposite way. The worst imaginable outcome is not being killed when we might (conceivably) have changed our minds but be unable to say so; far worse than that would be the *unutterable horror* of being trapped for years in a dreadful, degrading existence, unable even to communicate a wish to escape. The same applies to the risk of dying when a cure might be found, as compared with that of being kept alive and its not being found.

This seems to me so clear that it seems also relevant to the involuntary 40 euthanasia issue: Surely in any case of doubt it would be better to risk killing quickly someone who might not want to die than to leave in such an appalling existence someone who might want to. But the voluntary case seems quite unanswerable, because this is not a matter that needs to be settled for everybody or nobody. It is something that people can choose for themselves, and it seems quite outrageous that they should not be allowed to.

Once again, the opposition to this kind of euthanasia clearly has nothing to do with respect for choices and fears about mistakes. It must arise from a general conviction that no one should be able to choose to die; or at least, to have anyone else's assistance in doing so.

So it seems to me that all the standard arguments against the different forms of voluntary euthanasia are not only seriously mistaken, but mistaken in ways that could not deceive anyone in neutral contexts. The situation seems to be the one I described at the outset. Deep feelings that these things are wrong accompany a wish to justify them (at least in public) in terms that seem more humane and enlightened than a simple opposition to suicide, and the arguments are a valiant attempt to reconcile the irreconcilable. If this were better understood, I think it might be much easier to overcome the continuing resistance to voluntary euthanasia.

DOCTORS AND DYING

Finally, one note on a rather different matter. Advocates of euthanasia often seem to take for granted the idea that it can be justified only by terminal illness and intolerable pain. But this is odd, because there could be innumerable good reasons for wanting to die. Hopeless disability, simple old age that made impossible all the things that gave life purpose, or just not wanting to waste on a nursing home the money you hoped to leave to your children or VESS,[1] might make it perfectly rational to wish to die. Why should we think some reasons, but not others, adequate for euthanasia?

My suspicion is that the idea of confining voluntary euthanasia to cases of terminal illness arises partly from political realism, but even more from assumptions about where doctors fit into all this.

A common line of argument against euthanasia is that doctors should be committed to preserving life. Other people say that their duty of care should be understood more broadly than this, and that there is a duty to end suffering, even by death, when life is declining and has nothing more to offer. But even these people rarely go so far as to say that doctors should help anyone who simply wants to die.

Obviously any society needs to decide the use its doctors may make of their powers. However, there is no reason why their role, whatever it is, should define the boundaries of euthanasia. There are two aspects to being a doctor: technical knowledge, and a set of commitments about the use that may be made of it. But these two are separable; and even though we might agree that there were certain things doctors should not do, that would not be a reason for saying that no one else should do it either. The means of suicide could be available elsewhere.

If this possibility is widely overlooked, that may be another consequence of the way the euthanasia issue has been seen as the question of what doctors should be allowed to do to people. Voluntary euthanasia is anyway not about allowing doctors to decide when anyone shall die, but about the permissibility of providing technical help for people who are not adequately equipped themselves. But if technical help is the issue, it need not come from doctors at all, and voluntary euthanasia need not be limited to cases of pain and imminent death.

We can see the issue for what it is: the idea that an essential element of a good life is the freedom to leave it in peace and with dignity.

---

[1]**VESS** Voluntary Euthanasia Society of Scotland. [Editors' note.]

Topics for Critical Thinking and Writing

1. Write a 250-word summary of the main points of Richards's essay.

2. Richards mentions what she calls "the invented fact" (para. 2). What, if any, invented facts about euthanasia does she identify in the course of her essay?

3. Richards mentions having discussed "three common arguments against" voluntary euthanasia (para. 30). What are these three arguments?

4. Formulate as precisely as you can the "slippery-slope" argument to which Richards alludes (para. 8). What is her view about this argument as applied to euthanasia? Richards says (para. 14), "Suicide is not a thing there is any danger of anyone's getting into a habit of." But does this show that *assisting* another to suicide is not something that an unscrupulous doctor might get into the habit of doing?

5. Richards reasons (para. 13) that "if the law does not forbid suicide, it has no justification for [making illegal] the assisting of suicide." Suppose someone objected, saying, "Well, if we were to abolish laws against prostitution, that doesn't mean we have to abolish laws against pimping and keeping a brothel." How might Richards reply?

6. Evaluate Richards's analogy in paragraph 16: Prohibiting euthanasia because it isn't needed is like prohibiting adult literacy classes because children ought to learn to read in school.

7. Richards refers (in para. 20) to worries over whether suicide is ever "truly voluntary." What do you think is required for an act to be truly voluntary?

8. Richards says (para. 24), "There is no algorithm for calculations of this sort." What is an "algorithm," and why do you think she asserts there is none of the required sort?

9. Richards refers (in para. 33) to an imaginary scale to measure the value or worth one attaches to going on living, and supposes that each of us might fix a point on that scale when our own "life becomes not worth living." In fifty words, write out what for you would make you conclude that your life was no longer "worth living."

10. Richards seems (in para. 35) to think that suicide is *not* "bad in itself," although it might be quite bad if unnecessary, or bad for other reasons. Can you think of any reasons why one might disagree with her, believing that suicide indeed is bad in itself?

11. In your library, look up (in *Facts on File* or some other source) the activities during the early 1990s of Dr. Jack Kevorkian, famous for his role in making physician-assisted suicide a headline issue. Would Richards approve of what Kevorkian has done? Why, or why not?

Jonathan Swift

A Modest Proposal

For Preventing the Children of Poor People in Ireland from Being a Burden to Their Parents or Country, and for Making Them Beneficial to the Public

It is a melancholy object to those who walk through this great town or travel in the country, when they see the streets, the roads, and cabin doors, crowded with beggars of the female sex, followed by three, four, or six children, all in rags and importuning every passenger for an alms. These mothers, instead of being able to work for their honest livelihood, are forced to employ all their time in strolling to beg sustenance for their helpless infants: who as they grow up either turn thieves for want of work, or leave their dear native country to fight for the Pretender in Spain, or sell themselves to the Barbadoes.

I think it is agreed by all parties that this prodigious number of children in the arms, or on the backs, or at the heels of their mothers, and frequently of their fathers, is in the present deplorable state of the kingdom a very great additional grievance; and, therefore, whoever could find out a fair, cheap, and easy method of making these children sound, useful members of the commonwealth, would deserve so well of the public as to have his statue set up for a preserver of the nation.

But my intention is very far from being confined to provide only for the children of professed beggars; it is of a much greater extent, and shall take in the whole number of infants at a certain age who are born of parents in effect as little able to support them as those who demand our charity in the streets.

As to my own part, having turned my thoughts for many years upon this important subject, and maturely weighed the several schemes of our projectors,[1] I have always found them grossly mistaken in their computation. It is true, a child just dropped from its dam may be supported by her milk for a solar year, with little other nourishment; at most not above the value of 2s.,[2] which the mother may certainly get, or the value in scraps, by

[1] **projectors** Persons who devise plans. [All notes are the editors'.]
[2] **2s.** Two shillings. In para. 7, "£" is an abbreviation for pounds sterling and "d" for pence.

Swift (1667–1745) was born in Ireland of English stock. An Anglican clergyman, he became Dean of St. Patrick's in Dublin in 1723, but the post he really wanted, that of high office in England, was never given to him. A prolific pamphleteer on religious and political issues, Swift today is known not as a churchman but as a satirist. His best known works are Gulliver's Travels *(1726, a serious satire but now popularly thought of as a children's book) and "A Modest Proposal" (1729). In "A Modest Proposal," which was published anonymously, Swift addresses the great suffering that the Irish endured under the British.*

her lawful occupation of begging; and it is exactly at one year old that I propose to provide for them in such a manner as instead of being a charge upon their parents or the parish, or wanting food and raiment for the rest of their lives, they shall on the contrary contribute to the feeding, and partly to the clothing, of many thousands.

There is likewise another great advantage in my scheme, that it will 5 prevent those voluntary abortions, and that horrid practice of women murdering their bastard children, alas! too frequent among us! sacrificing the poor innocent babes I doubt more to avoid the expense than the shame, which would move tears and pity in the most savage and inhuman breast.

The number of souls in this kingdom being usually reckoned one million and a half, of these I calculate there may be about 200,000 couple whose wives are breeders; from which number I subtract 30,000 couple who are able to maintain their own children (although I apprehend there cannot be so many, under the present distress of the kingdom); but this being granted, there will remain 170,000 breeders. I again subtract 50,000 for those women who miscarry, or whose children die by accident or disease within the year. There only remain 120,000 children of poor parents annually born. The question therefore is, how this number shall be reared and provided for? which, as I have already said, under the present situation of affairs, is utterly impossible by all the methods hitherto proposed. For we can neither employ them in handicraft or agriculture; we neither build houses (I mean in the country) nor cultivate land; they can very seldom pick up a livelihood by stealing, till they arrive at six years old, except where they are of towardly parts; although I confess they learn the rudiments much earlier; during which time they can, however, be properly looked upon only as probationers; as I have been informed by a principal gentleman in the county of Cavan, who protested to me that he never knew above one or two instances under the age of six, even in a part of the kingdom so renowned for the quickest proficiency in that art.

I am assured by our merchants, that a boy or a girl before twelve years old is no salable commodity; and even when they come to this age they will not yield above 3£. or 3£. 2s. 6d. at most on the exchange; which cannot turn to account either to the parents or kingdom, the charge of nutriment and rags having been at least four times that value.

I shall now therefore humbly propose my own thoughts, which I hope will not be liable to the least objection.

I have been assured by a very knowing American of my acquaintance in London, that a young healthy child well nursed is at a year old a most delicious, nourishing, and wholesome food, whether stewed, roasted, baked, or broiled; and I make no doubt that it will equally serve in a fricassee or a ragout.

I do therefore humbly offer it to public consideration that of the 10 120,000 children already computed, 20,000 may be reserved for breed, whereof only one-fourth part to be males; which is more than we allow to sheep, black cattle, or swine; and my reason is, that these children are seldom the fruits of marriage, a circumstance not much regarded by our savages; therefore one male will be sufficient to serve four females. That the remaining 100,000 may, at a year old, be offered in sale to the persons of quality and fortune through the kingdom; always advising the mother to let them suck plentifully in the last month, so as to render them plump and fat for a good table. A child will make two dishes at an entertainment for friends; and when the family dines alone, the fore or hind quarter will make a reasonable dish, and seasoned with a little pepper or salt will be very good boiled on the fourth day, especially in winter.

I have reckoned upon a medium that a child just born will weigh 12 pounds, and in a solar year, if tolerably nursed, will increase to 28 pounds.

I grant this food will be somewhat dear, and therefore very proper for landlords, who, as they have already devoured most of the parents, seem to have the best title to the children.

Infant's flesh will be in season throughout the year, but more plentiful in March, and a little before and after: for we are told by a grave author, an eminent French physician, that fish being a prolific diet, there are more children born in Roman Catholic countries about nine months after Lent than at any other season; therefore, reckoning a year after Lent, the markets will be more glutted than usual, because the number of popish infants is at least three to one in this kingdom: and therefore it will have one other collateral advantage, by lessening the number of papists among us.

I have already computed the charge of nursing a beggar's child (in which list I reckon all cottagers, laborers, and four-fifths of the farmers) to be about 2s. per annum, rags included; and I believe no gentleman would repine to give 10s. for the carcass of a good fat child, which, as I have said, will make four dishes of excellent nutritive meat, when he has only some particular friend or his own family to dine with him. Thus the squire will learn to be a good landlord, and grow popular among the tenants; the mother will have 8s. net profit, and be fit for work till she produces another child.

Those who are more thrifty (as I must confess the times require) may 15 flay the carcass; the skin of which artificially dressed will make admirable gloves for ladies, and summer boots for fine gentlemen.

As to our city of Dublin, shambles[3] may be appointed for this purpose in the most convenient parts of it, and butchers we may be assured will not be wanting: although I rather recommend buying the children alive, and dressing them hot from the knife as we do roasting pigs.

A very worthy person, a true lover of his country, and whose virtues I highly esteem, was lately pleased in discoursing on this matter to offer a refinement upon my scheme. He said that many gentlemen of this kingdom, having of late destroyed their deer, he conceived that the want of venison might be well supplied by the bodies of young lads and maidens, not exceeding fourteen years of age nor under twelve; so great a number of both

---

[3]**shambles** Slaughterhouses.

sexes in every country being now ready to starve for want of work and service; and these to be disposed of by their parents, if alive, or otherwise by
their nearest relations. But with due deference to so excellent a friend and
so deserving a patriot, I cannot be altogether in his sentiments; for as to the
males, my American acquaintance assured me from frequent experience
that their flesh was generally tough and lean, like that of our schoolboys by
continual exercise, and their taste disagreeable; and to fatten them would
not answer the charge. Then as to the females, it would, I think, with humble submission be a loss to the public, because they soon would become
breeders themselves: and besides, it is not improbable that some scrupulous people might be apt to censure such a practice (although indeed very
unjustly), as a little bordering upon cruelty; which, I confess, has always
been with me the strongest objection against any project, how well soever
intended.

But in order to justify my friend, he confessed that this expedient was
put into his head by the famous Psalmanazar[4] a native of the island Formosa, who came from thence to London about twenty years ago: and in
conversation told my friend, that in his country when any young person
happened to be put to death, the executioner sold the carcass to persons of
quality as a prime dainty; and that in his time the body of a plump girl of
fifteen, who was crucified for an attempt to poison the emperor, was sold
to his imperial majesty's prime minister of state, and other great mandarins
of the court, in joints from the gibbet, at 400 crowns. Neither indeed can I
deny, that if the same use were made of several plump young girls in this
town, who without one single groat to their fortunes cannot stir abroad
without a chair, and appear at the playhouse and assemblies in foreign
fineries which they never will pay for, the kingdom would not be the worse.

Some persons of a depending spirit are in great concern about the vast
number of poor people, who are aged, diseased, or maimed, and I have
been desired to employ my thoughts what course may be taken to ease the
nation of so grievous an encumbrance. But I am not in the least pain upon
that matter, because it is very well known that they are every day dying and
rotting by cold and famine, and filth and vermin, as fast as can be reasonably expected. And as to the young laborers, they are now in as hopeful a
condition: They cannot get work, and consequently pine away for want of
nourishment, to a degree that if at any time they are accidentally hired to
common labor, they have not strength to perform it; and thus the country
and themselves are happily delivered from the evils to come.

I have too long digressed, and therefore shall return to my subject. I 20
think the advantages by the proposal which I have made are obvious and
many, as well as of the highest importance.

For first, as I have already observed, it would greatly lessen the num-

---

[4]**Psalmanazar** George Psalmanazar (c. 1679–1763), a Frenchman who claimed to be from Formosa (now Taiwan); wrote *An Historical and Geographical Description of Formosa* (1704). The
hoax was exposed soon after publication.

ber of papists, with whom we are yearly overrun, being the principal breeders of the nation as well as our most dangerous enemies; and who stay at home on purpose to deliver the kingdom to the Pretender, hoping to take their advantage by the absence of so many good Protestants, who have chosen rather to leave their country than stay at home and pay tithes against their conscience to an Episcopal curate.

Secondly, The poor tenants will have something valuable of their own, which by law may be made liable to distress and help to pay their landlord's rent, their corn and cattle being already seized, and money a thing unknown.

Thirdly, Whereas the maintenance of 100,000 children from two years old and upward, cannot be computed at less than 10s. a-piece per annum, the nation's stock will be thereby increased £50,000 per annum, beside the profit of a new dish introduced to the tables of all gentlemen of fortune in the kingdom who have any refinement in taste. And the money will circulate among ourselves, the goods being entirely of our own growth and manufacture.

Fourthly, The constant breeders beside the gain of 8s. sterling per annum by the sale of their children, will be rid of the charge of maintaining them after the first year.

Fifthly, This food would likewise bring great custom to taverns, where 25 the vintners will certainly be so prudent as to procure the best receipts for dressing it to perfection, and consequently have their houses frequented by all the fine gentlemen, who justly value themselves upon their knowledge in good eating; and a skilful cook who understands how to oblige his guests, will contrive to make it as expensive as they please.

Sixthly, This would be a great inducement to marriage, which all wise nations have either encouraged by rewards or enforced by laws and penalties. It would increase the care and tenderness of mothers toward their children, when they were sure of a settlement for life to the poor babes, provided in some sort by the public, to their annual profit instead of expense. We should see an honest emulation among the married women, which of them would bring the fattest child to the market. Men would become as fond of their wives during the time of their pregnancy as they are now of their mares in foal, their cows in calf, their sows when they are ready to farrow; nor offer to beat or kick them (as is too frequent a practice) for fear of a miscarriage.

Many other advantages might be enumerated. For instance, the addition of some thousand carcasses in our exportation of barreled beef, the propagation of swine's flesh, and improvement in the art of making good bacon, so much wanted among us by the great destruction of pigs, too frequent at our table; which are no way comparable in taste or magnificence to a well-grown, fat, yearling child, which roasted whole will make a considerable figure at a lord mayor's feast or any other public entertainment. But this and many others I omit, being studious of brevity.

Supposing that 1,000 families in this city would be constant customers for infants' flesh, besides others who might have it at merry-meetings, particularly at weddings and christenings, I compute that Dublin would take off annually about 20,000 carcasses; and the rest of the kingdom (where probably they will be sold somewhat cheaper) the remaining 80,000.

I can think of no one objection that will possibly be raised against this proposal, unless it should be urged that the number of people will be thereby much lessened in the kingdom. This I freely own, and it was indeed one principal design in offering it to the world. I desire the reader will observe, that I calculate my remedy for this one individual kingdom of Ireland and for no other that ever was, is, or I think ever can be upon earth. Therefore let no man talk to me of other expedients: of taxing our absentees at 5s. a pound; of using neither clothes nor household furniture except what is of our own growth and manufacture; of utterly rejecting the materials and instruments that promote foreign luxury; of curing the expensiveness of pride, vanity, idleness, and gaming in our women; of introducing a vein of parsimony, prudence, and temperance; of learning to love our country, in the want of which we differ even from Laplanders and the inhabitants of Topinamboo; of quitting our animosities and factions, nor acting any longer like the Jews, who were murdering one another at the very moment their city was taken; of being a little cautious not to sell our country and conscience for nothing; of teaching landlords to have at least one degree of mercy toward their tenants; lastly, of putting a spirit of honesty, industry, and skill into our shopkeepers; who, if a resolution could now be taken to buy only our native goods, would immediately unite to cheat and exact upon us in the price the measure, and the goodness, nor could ever yet be brought to make one fair proposal of just dealing, though often and earnestly invited to it.

Therefore I repeat, let no man talk to me of these and the like expedi- 30 ents, till he has at least some glimpse of hope that there will be ever some hearty and sincere attempt to put them in practice.

But as to myself, having been wearied out for many years with offering vain, idle, visionary thoughts, and at length utterly despairing of success, I fortunately fell upon this proposal; which, as it is wholly new, so it has something solid and real, of no expense and little trouble, full in our own power, and whereby we can incur no danger in disobliging England. For this kind of commodity will not bear exportation, the flesh being of too tender a consistence to admit a long continuance in salt, although perhaps I could name a country which would be glad to eat up our whole nation without it.

After all, I am not so violently bent upon my own opinion as to reject any offer proposed by wise men, which shall be found equally innocent, cheap, easy, and effectual. But before something of that kind shall be advanced in contradiction to my scheme, and offering a better, I desire the author or authors will be pleased maturely to consider two points. First, as things now stand, how they will be able to find food and raiment for 100,000 useless mouths and backs. And secondly, there being a round million of creatures in human figure throughout this kingdom, whose subsistence put into a common stock would leave them in debt 2,000,000£. sterling, adding those who are beggars by profession to the bulk of farmers, cottagers, and laborers, with the wives and children who are beggars in effect; I desire those politicians who dislike my overture, and may perhaps be so bold as to attempt an answer, that they will first ask the parents of these mortals, whether they would not at this day think it a great happiness to have been sold for food at a year old in the manner I prescribe, and thereby have avoided such a perpetual scene of misfortunes as they have since gone through by the oppression of landlords, the impossibility of paying rent without money or trade, the want of common sustenance, with neither house nor clothes to cover them from the inclemencies of the weather, and the most inevitable prospect of entailing the like or greater miseries upon their breed for ever.

I profess, in the sincerity of my heart, that I have not the least personal interest in endeavoring to promote this necessary work, having no other motive than the public good of my country, by advancing our trade, providing for infants, relieving the poor, and giving some pleasure to the rich. I have no children by which I can propose to get a single penny; the youngest being nine years old, and my wife past childbearing.

Topics for Critical Thinking and Writing ════════

1. In paragraph 4 the speaker of the essay mentions proposals set forth by "projectors"; that is, by advocates of other proposals or projects. On the basis of the first two paragraphs of "A Modest Proposal," how would you characterize *this* projector, the speaker of the essay? Write your characterization in one paragraph. Then, in a second paragraph, characterize the projector as you understand him, having read the entire essay. In your second paragraph, indicate what *he thinks he is*, and also what the reader sees he really is.

2. The speaker or persona of "A Modest Proposal" is confident that selling children "for a good table" is a better idea than any of the then current methods of disposing of unwanted children, including abortion and infanticide. Can you think of any argument that might favor abortion or infanticide for parents in dire straits, rather than the projector's scheme?

3. In paragraph 29 the speaker considers, but dismisses out of hand, several other solutions to the wretched plight of the Irish poor. Write a 500-word essay in which you explain each of these ideas and their combined merits as an alternative solution to the one he favors.

4. What does the projector imply are the causes of the Irish poverty he deplores? Are there possible causes he has omitted? (If so, what are they?)

5. Imagine yourself as one of the poor parents to whom Swift refers, and write a 250-word essay explaining why you prefer not to sell your infant to the local butcher.

6. The modern version of the problem to which the proposal is addressed is called

"population policy." How would you describe our nation's current population policy? Do we have a population policy, in fact? If not, what would you propose? If we do have one, would you propose any changes in it? Why, or why not?

7. It is sometimes suggested that just as persons need to get a license to drive a car, to hunt with a gun, or to marry, a husband and wife ought to be required to get a license to have a child. Would you favor this idea, assuming that it applied to you as a possible parent? Would Swift? Explain your answers in an essay of 500 words.

8. Consider the six arguments advanced in paragraphs 21–26, and write a 1,000-word essay criticizing all of them. Or, if you find that one or more of the arguments is really unanswerable, explain why you find it so compelling.

Plato

Myth of the Cave

"I want you to go on to picture the enlightenment or ignorance of our human condition somewhat as follows. Imagine an underground chamber like a cave, with a long entrance open to the daylight and as wide as the cave. In this chamber are men who have been prisoners there since they

---

Plato (427–347 B.C.), an Athenian aristocrat by birth, was the student of one great philosopher (Socrates) and the teacher of another (Aristotle). His legacy of more than two dozen dialogues — imaginary discussions between Socrates and one or more other speakers, usually young Athenians — has been of such influence that the whole of Western philosophy can be characterized, A. N. Whitehead wrote, as "a series of footnotes to Plato." Plato's interests encompassed the full range of topics in philosophy: ethics, politics, logic, metaphysics, epistemology, aesthetics, psychology, and education.

Plato's dialogue, from Republic, *has for its ostensible topic the nature of justice. But the reader soon learns that Socrates (who speaks for Plato) believes we cannot understand what justice is until we first understand the truth about human nature; as he explains to Glaucon, because justice can be achieved only in an ideal state, the ideal state must be constructed from a correct account of human nature. To make these issues clear, we are led into many fundamental problems of philosophy.* Republic *is thus read not only for Plato's views on education, politics, and ethics, but also for his logical, metaphysical, and psychological theories.*

At the very center of the dialogue is an examination of epistemology; that is, the nature of human knowledge. Plato's strategy is to begin by contrasting knowledge with both ignorance and belief (or opinion, doxa in Greek). The excerpt here, the "Myth [or Allegory] of the Cave," relies on the reader's having a grasp of the relations among these fundamental concepts.

The distinction among knowledge, belief, and ignorance is not peculiar to Plato, of course. We, too, need to keep clearly in mind what it is to have one or more beliefs *about something, and what it is to* know *something. So long as we can deal with these concepts abstractly, it may not be too difficult to keep them distinct.*

were children, their legs and necks being so fastened that they can only look straight ahead of them and cannot turn their heads. Some way off, behind and higher up, a fire is burning, and between the fire and the prisoners and above them runs a road, in front of which a curtain-wall has been built, like the screen at puppet shows between the operators and their audience, above which they show their puppets."

"I see."

"Imagine further that there are men carrying all sorts of gear along behind the curtain-wall, projecting above it and including figures of men and animals made of wood and stone and all sorts of other materials, and that some of these men, as you would expect, are talking and some not."

"An odd picture and an odd sort of prisoner."

"They are drawn from life," I replied. "For, tell me, do you think our   5

If pressed, we can define belief and knowledge so that they will not be confused. But as soon as we confront one of our own beliefs, and ask whether we are correct in believing it—that is, whether the belief or opinion is true, and whether we have adequate reasons or evidence for it—then it is no longer so easy at all. (How, for example, do you tell whether you know or only believe that the earth is round, or that $3 \times 5 = \frac{30?}{2?}$)

In an earlier passage in Republic *(not reprinted here), Plato explained these concepts by correlating them with their proper objects. The object of knowledge is Reality, and the object of ignorance is Nothing, whereas the object of belief (the most troublesome of the three) is somewhere between, the shifting and unstable world of Appearances. And so belief is sometimes true but often false. As the Myth shows, Plato believes the Good is the most important part of Reality. His account of the blinding vision of the Good—seeing the Truth and seeing it whole—vouchsafed to that rare person (the true philosopher) who succeeds in escaping the cave, has inspired later writers to see in it a foreshadowing of the mystic's vision of God. (The sun, with its blinding light, has often been used as a metaphor for divine radiance.)*

The Myth of the Cave *has more to teach us than a lesson in epistemology. Plato's aim is to show the nature of our lives when we fail to realize our true ignorance, and also to show the terrible price of successfully breaking free from the mental prison of mistaken belief. As the Myth shows, we become irritable and even dangerous when challenged to examine our beliefs and way of life. The Myth invites us to reevaluate our lives from beginning to end, because (if the Myth can be trusted) right now most of us dwell in darkness, unaware of our true plight. Throughout our lives we have been and probably will continue to be deceived unwittingly into thinking we really "know" the nature of reality, when in fact we don't; we foolishly "believe" we know.*

A few words need to be said about the physical setting of Plato's cave. Imagine a darkened theater in which the audience is seated facing a screen. Behind the audience other persons parade back and forth with every variety of object carried on their heads. At the rear of the theater a spotlight is cleverly fixed so that it casts the shadows of these objects (but not of those carrying them) onto the screen. The shadow-show goes on endlessly, and shadows are all the audience ever sees, for they are strapped rigidly into their seats. The viewers take these shadows (mere "appearance") for "reality."

prisoners could see anything of themselves or their fellows except the shadows thrown by the fire on the wall of the cave opposite them?"

"How could they see anything else if they were prevented from moving their heads all their lives?"

"And would they see anything more of the objects carried along the
road?"

"Of course not."

"Then if they were able to talk to each other, would they not assume
that the shadows they saw were the real things?"

"Inevitably."   10

"And if the wall of their prison opposite them reflected sound, don't
you think that they would suppose, whenever one of the passers-by on the
road spoke, that the voice belonged to the shadow passing before them?"

"They would be bound to think so."

"And so in every way they would believe that the shadows of the objects we mentioned were the whole truth."

"Yes, inevitably."

"Then think what would naturally happen to them if they were re-   15
leased from their bonds and cured of their delusions. Suppose one of them
were let loose, and suddenly compelled to stand up and turn his head and
look and walk toward the fire; all these actions would be painful and he
would be too dazzled to see properly the objects of which he used to see
the shadows. What do you think he would say if he was told that what he
used to see was so much empty nonsense and that he was now nearer reality and seeing more correctly, because he was turned toward objects that
were more real, and if on top of that he were compelled to say what each of
the passing objects was when it was pointed out to him? Don't you think he
would be at a loss, and think that what he used to see was far truer than the
objects now being pointed out to him?"

"Yes, far truer."

"And if he were made to look directly at the light of the fire, it would
hurt his eyes and he would turn back and retreat to the things which he
could see properly, which he would think really clearer than the things
being shown him."

"Yes."

"And if," I went on, "he were forcibly dragged up the steep and
rugged ascent and not let go till he had been dragged out into the sunlight,
the process would be a painful one, to which he would much object, and
when he emerged into the light his eyes would be so dazzled by the glare
of it that he wouldn't be able to see a single one of the things he was now
told were real."

"Certainly not at first," he agreed.   20

"Because, of course, he would need to grow accustomed to the light
before he could see things in the upper world outside the cave. First he
would find it easiest to look at shadows, next at the reflections of men and

other objects in water, and later on at the objects themselves. After that he would find it easier to observe the heavenly bodies and the sky itself at night, and to look at the light of the moon and stars rather than at the sun and its light by day."

"Of course."

"The thing he would be able to do last would be to look directly at the sun itself, and gaze at it without using reflections in water or any other medium but as it is in itself."

"That must come last."

"Later on he would come to the conclusion that it is the sun that pro- 25 duces the changing seasons and years and controls everything in the visible world, and is in a sense responsible for everything that he and his fellow-prisoners used to see."

"That is the conclusion which he would obviously reach."

"And when he thought of his first home and what passed for wisdom there, and of his fellow-prisoners, don't you think he would congratulate himself on his good fortune and be sorry for them?"

"Very much so."

"There was probably a certain amount of honor and glory to be won among the prisoners, and prizes for keen-sightedness for those best able to remember the order of sequence among the passing shadows and so be best able to divine their future appearances. Will our released prisoner hanker after these prizes or envy this power or honor? Won't he be more likely to feel, as Homer says, that he would far rather be 'a serf in the house of some landless man,' or indeed anything else in the world, than hold the opinions and live the life that they do?"

"Yes," he replied, "he would prefer anything to a life like theirs." 30

"Then what do you think would happen," I asked, "if he went back to sit in his old seat in the cave? Wouldn't his eyes be blinded by the darkness, because he had come in suddenly out of the sunlight?"

"Certainly."

"And if he had to discriminate between the shadows, in competition with the other prisoners, while he was still blinded and before his eyes got used to the darkness — a process that would take some time — wouldn't he be likely to make a fool of himself? And they would say that his visit to the upper world had ruined his sight, and that the ascent was not worth even attempting. And if anyone tried to release them and lead them up, they would kill him if they could lay hands on him."

"They certainly would."

"Now, my dear Glaucon," I went on, "this simile must be connected 35 throughout with what preceded it. The realm revealed by sight corresponds to the prison, and the light of the fire in the prison to the power of the sun. And you won't go wrong if you connect the ascent into the upper world and the sight of the objects there with the upward progress of the mind into the intelligible region. That at any rate is my interpretation, which is what you are anxious to hear; the truth of the matter is, after all, known only to god. But in my opinion, for what it is worth, the final thing to be perceived in the intelligible region, and perceived only with difficulty, is the form of the good; once seen, it is inferred to be responsible for whatever is right and valuable in anything, producing in the visible region light and the source of light, and being in the intelligible region itself the controlling source of truth and intelligence. And anyone who is going to act rationally either in public or private life must have sight of it."

"I agree," he said, "so far as I am able to understand you."

"Then you will perhaps also agree with me that it won't be surprising if those who get so far are unwilling to involve themselves in human affairs, and if their minds long to remain in the realm above. That's what we should expect if our simile holds good again."

"Yes, that's to be expected."

"Nor will you think it strange that anyone who descends from contemplation of the divine to human life and its ills should blunder and make a fool of himself, if, while still blinded and unaccustomed to the surrounding darkness, he's forcibly put on trial in the law courts or elsewhere about the shadows of justice or the figures of which they are shadows, and made to dispute about the notions of them held by men who have never seen justice itself."

"There's nothing strange in that."   40

"But anyone with any sense," I said, "will remember that the eyes may be unsighted in two ways, by a transition either from light to darkness or from darkness to light, and will recognize that the same thing applies to the mind. So when he sees a mind confused and unable to see clearly he will not laugh without thinking, but will ask himself whether it has come from a clearer world and is confused by the unaccustomed darkness, or whether it is dazzled by the stronger light of the clearer world to which it has escaped from its previous ignorance. The first condition of life is a reason for congratulation, the second for sympathy, though if one wants to laugh at it one can do so with less absurdity than at the mind that has descended from the daylight of the upper world."

"You put it very reasonably."

"If this is true," I continued, "we must reject the conception of education professed by those who say that they can put into the mind knowledge that was not there before—rather as if they could put sight into blind eyes."

"It is a claim that is certainly made," he said.

"But our argument indicates that this is a capacity which is innate in   45 each man's mind, and that the organ by which he learns is like an eye which cannot be turned from darkness to light unless the whole body is turned; in the same way the mind as a whole must be turned away from the world of change until its eye can bear to look straight at reality, and at the brightest of all realities which is what we call the good. Isn't that so?"

"Yes."

"Then this turning around of the mind itself might be made a subject of professional skill, which would effect the conversion as easily and effectively as possible. It would not be concerned to implant sight, but to ensure that someone who had it already was not either turned in the wrong direction or looking the wrong way."

"That may well be so."

"The rest, therefore, of what are commonly called excellences of the mind perhaps resemble those of the body, in that they are not in fact innate, but are implanted by subsequent training and practice; but knowledge, it seems, must surely have a diviner quality, something which never loses its power, but whose effects are useful and salutary or again useless and harmful according to the direction in which it is turned. Have you never noticed how shrewd is the glance of the type of men commonly called bad but clever? They have small minds, but their sight is sharp and piercing enough in matters that concern them; it's not that their sight is weak, but that they are forced to serve evil, so that the keener their sight the more effective that evil is."

"That's true." 50

"But suppose," I said, "that such natures were cut loose, when they were still children, from all the dead weights natural to this world of change and fastened on them by sensual indulgences like gluttony, which twist their minds' vision to lower things, and suppose that when so freed they were turned toward the truth, then this same part of these same individuals would have as keen a vision of truth as it has of the objects on which it is at present turned."

"Very likely."

"And is it not also likely, and indeed a necessary consequence of what we have said, that society will never be properly governed either by the uneducated, who have no knowledge of the truth, or by those who are allowed to spend all their lives in purely intellectual pursuits? The uneducated have no single aim in life to which all their actions, public and private, are to be directed; the intellectuals will take no practical action of their own accord, fancying themselves to be out of this world in some kind of earthly paradise."

"True."

"Then our job as lawgivers is to compel the best minds to attain what 55 we have called the highest form of knowledge, and to ascend to the vision of the good as we have described, and when they have achieved this and see well enough, prevent them behaving as they are now allowed to."

"What do you mean by that?"

"Remaining in the upper world, and refusing to return again to the prisoners in the cave below and share their labors and rewards, whether trivial or serious."

"But surely," he protested, "that will not be fair. We shall be compelling them to live a poorer life than they might live."

"The object of our legislation," I reminded him again, "is not the special welfare of any particular class in our society, but of the society as a whole; and it uses persuasion or compulsion to unite all citizens and make them share together the benefits which each individually can confer on the community; and its purpose in fostering this attitude is not to leave everyone to please himself, but to make each man a link in the unity of the whole."

"You are right; I had forgotten," he said. 60

"You see, then, Glaucon," I went on, "we shan't be unfair to our philosophers, but shall be quite fair in what we say when we compel them to have some care and responsibility for others. We shall tell them that philosophers born in other states can reasonably refuse to take part in the hard work of politics; for society produces them quite involuntarily and unintentionally, and it is only just that anything that grows up on its own should feel it has nothing to repay for an upbringing which it owes to no one. 'But,' we shall say, 'we have bred you both for your own sake and that of the whole community to act as leaders and king bees in a hive; you are better and more fully educated than the rest and better qualified to combine the practice of philosophy and politics. You must therefore each descend in turn and live with your fellows in the cave and get used to seeing in the dark; once you get used to it you will see a thousand times better than they do and will distinguish the various shadows, and know what they are shadows of, because you have seen the truth about things admirable and just and good. And so our state and yours will be really awake, and not merely dreaming like most societies today, with their shadow battles and their struggles for political power, which they treat as some great prize. The truth is quite different: The state whose prospective rulers come to their duties with least enthusiasm is bound to have the best and most tranquil government, and the state whose rulers are eager to rule the worst.'"

"I quite agree."

"Then will our pupils, when they hear what we say, dissent and refuse to take their share of the hard work of government, even though spending the greater part of their time together in the pure air above?"

"They cannot refuse, for we are making a just demand of just men. But of course, unlike present rulers, they will approach the business of government as an unavoidable necessity."

"Yes, of course," I agreed. "The truth is that if you want a well- 65 governed state to be possible, you must find for your future rulers some way of life they like better than government; for only then will you have government by the truly rich, those, that is, whose riches consist not of gold, but of the true happiness of a good and rational life. If you get, in public affairs, men whose life is impoverished and destitute of personal satisfactions, but who hope to snatch some compensation for their own inadequacy from a political career, there can never be good government. They start fighting for power, and the consequent internal and domestic conflicts ruin both them and society."

"True indeed."

"Is there any life except that of true philosophy which looks down on positions of political power?"

"None whatever."

"But what we need is that the only men to get power should be men who do not love it, otherwise we shall have rivals' quarrels."

"That is certain."   70

"Who else, then, will you compel to undertake the responsibilities of Guardians of our state, if it is not to be those who know most about the principles of good government and who have other rewards and a better life than the politician's?"

"There is no one else."

Topics for Critical Thinking and Writing ══════════

1. Write an essay of 500 words in which you describe as vividly as possible, in your own language, the situation of the prisoners in the cave. You may find it helpful first to draw a rough picture of their situation as Plato describes it. Try to write your account as though you were an escaped prisoner returning to the cave.

2. Socrates claims (para. 45) that "our argument indicates that this is a capacity [i.e., for learning] which is innate in each man's mind." Explain this thesis, and state and evaluate the argument for it to which Socrates alludes.

3. The requirement that the philosophers should have to rule in the ideal state is, Glaucon suggests (para. 58), "not . . . fair." Why does he apparently think this demand is unfair, or unjust? To whom is it unjust? Evaluate Socrates' reply.

4. Socrates defends the idea (para. 61) that "the state whose prospective rulers come to their duties with least enthusiasm is bound to have the best and most tranquil government." Do you think this generalization is true? Can you think of arguments for and against it? How would you go about trying to prove or disprove it? How does Socrates argue for it?

5. Roughly midway through the essay, Socrates suggests (para. 33) that the prisoners "would kill" any of their own who escaped and returned. It is often said that in this passage Plato alludes to the historic fate of Socrates himself, who was executed under order of the Athenian government in 399 B.C. Read Plato's account of Socrates' trial in the dialogue called *Apology*, and write a 500-word essay in which you argue for or against this parallel.

5

Critical Writing: Developing an Argument of One's Own

PLANNING, DRAFTING, AND REVISING AN ARGUMENT

First, hear the wisdom of Mark Twain: "When the Lord finished the world, He pronounced it good. That is what I said about my first work, too. But Time, I tell you, Time takes the confidence out of these incautious early opinions."

All of us, teachers and students, have our moments of confidence, but for the most part we know that we have trouble writing clear, thoughtful prose. In a conversation we can cover ourselves with such expressions as "Well, I don't know, but I sort of think . . . ," and we can always revise our position ("Oh, well, I didn't mean it that way") but once we have handed in the final version of our writing we are helpless. We are (putting it strongly) naked to our enemies.

Getting Ideas

As the previous paragraph notes, we often improve our thoughts when we try to explain them to someone else. Partly, of course, we are responding to questions or objections raised by our companion in the conversation, but partly we are responding to ourselves; almost as soon as we hear what we have to say, we may find that it won't do, and, if we are lucky, we may find a better idea surfacing. One of the best ways of getting ideas is to talk things over.

The process of talking things over usually begins with the text that you are reading; your marginal notes, your summary, and your queries parenthetically incorporated within your summary are a kind of dialogue between you and the author you are reading. More obviously, when you talk with friends about your topic you are trying out and developing ideas. Finally, after reading, taking notes, and talking, you may feel that you now have clear ideas and you need only put them into writing. And so you take a sheet of blank paper, and perhaps a paralyzing thought suddenly strikes: "I have ideas but just can't put them into words."

Despite what many people believe, writing is not only a matter of putting one's ideas into words. Just as talking with others is a way of getting ideas, *writing is a way of getting and developing ideas.* Writing, in short, can be an important part of critical thinking. If fear of putting ourselves on record is one big reason we have trouble writing, another big reason is our fear that we have no ideas worth putting down. But by jotting down notes — or even free associations — and by writing a draft, however weak, we can help ourselves to think our way toward good ideas.

Freewriting · Writing for five or six minutes, nonstop, without censoring what you produce is one way of getting words down on paper that will help to lead to improved thoughts. Some people who write on a computer find it useful to dim the screen so they won't be tempted to look up and fiddle too soon with their words. Later they illuminate the screen, scroll back, and notice some key words or passages that can be used later in drafting a paper.

Listing · Jotting down items, just as you do when you make a shopping list, is another way of getting ideas. When you make a shopping list, you write *ketchup* and the act of writing it reminds you that you also need hamburger rolls — and *that* in turn reminds you (who knows how or why?) that you also need a can of tuna fish. Similarly, when you prepare a list of ideas for a paper, jotting down one item will generate another. Of course, when you look over the list you will probably drop some of these ideas — the dinner menu will change — but you are making progress.

Diagramming · Making some sort of visual representation of an essay is a kind of listing. Three methods of diagramming are especially common.

- *Clustering.* Write, in the middle of a sheet of paper, a word or phrase summarizing your topic (for instance, *health care*), circle it, and then write down and circle a related word (for example, *gov't-provided*). Perhaps this leads you to write *higher taxes,* and you then circle this phrase and connect it to *gov't-provided.* The next thing that occurs to you is *employer-provided* — and so you write this down and circle it. Obviously you will not connect this to *higher taxes,* but you will connect it to *health care,* since it is a sort of parallel to *gov't-provided.* The next thing that occurs to you is *unemployed people.* Obviously this category does not connect easily with *employer-provided,* so you won't connect these two terms with a line, but you probably will connect *unemployed people* with *health care,* and maybe also with *gov't-provided.* Keep going, jotting down ideas, and making connections where possible, indicating relationships.

• *Branching.* Some writers find it useful to build a tree, moving from the central topic to the main branches (chief ideas) and then to the twigs (aspects of the chief ideas).

• *Comparing in columns.* Draw a line down the middle of the page, and then set up oppositions. For instance, if you are concerned with health care, you might head one column *gov't-provided* and the other *employer-provided,* and you might then, under the first column, write *covers unemployed* and under the second column, write *omits unemployed.* You might go on to write, under the first column, *higher taxes,* and under the second, *higher prices*—or whatever else relevant comes to mind.

All of these methods can of course be executed with pen and paper, but if you write on a computer you may also be able to use them, depending on the capabilities of your program.

Whether one is using a computer or a pen, one puts down some words, and almost immediately sees that they need improvement, not simply a little polishing but a substantial overhaul. One writes, "Truman was justified in dropping the atom bomb for two reasons," and as soon as one writes these words, a third reason comes to mind. Or perhaps one of those "two reasons" no longer seems very good. As the little girl shrewdly replied when an adult told her to think before she spoke, "How do I know what I think before I hear what I say?" We have to see what we say, we have to get something down on paper, before we realize that we need to make it better.

Writing, then, is really **rewriting;** that is, revising, and a revision is a *re-vision,* a second look. The paper that you hand in should be clear and may even seem effortless to the reader, but in all likelihood the clarity and apparent ease are the result of a struggle with yourself, a struggle during which you greatly improved your first thoughts. One begins by putting down one's ideas, such as they are, perhaps even in the random order in which they occurred, but sooner or later comes the job of looking at them critically, developing what is useful in them and chucking out what is not. If you follow this procedure you will be in the company of Picasso, who said that he "advanced by means of destruction."

Whether you advance bit by bit (writing a sentence, revising it, writing the next, and so on) or whether you write an entire first draft and then revise it and revise it again and again is chiefly a matter of temperament. Probably most people combine both approaches, backing up occasionally but trying to get to the end fairly soon so that they can see rather quickly what they know, or think they know, and can then start the real work of thinking, of converting their initial ideas into something substantial.

Getting Ideas by Asking Questions • Getting ideas is mostly a matter of asking (and then thinking about) questions. We append questions to the end of each argumentative essay in this book, not in order to torment you but in order to help you to think about the arguments, for instance to turn your attention to especially important matters. If your instructor asks you to write an answer to one of these questions, you are lucky: Examining the question will stimulate your mind to work in a definite direction. But if a topic is not assigned, and you are asked to write an argument, you will find that some ideas (possibly poor ones, at this stage, but that doesn't matter because you will soon revise) will come to mind if you ask yourself questions. Here are five basic questions:

1. What is X?
2. What is the value of X?
3. What are the causes (or the consequences) of X?
4. What should (or ought or must) we do about X?
5. What is the evidence for my claims?

Let's spend a moment looking at each of these questions.

1. What is X? One can hardly argue about the number of people sentenced to death in the United States in 1995 — a glance at the appropriate government report will give the answer — but one can argue about whether or not capital punishment as administered in the United States is discriminatory. Does the evidence, one can ask, support the view that in the United States the death penalty is unfair? Similarly, one can ask whether a human fetus is a human being (in saying what something is, must we take account of its potentiality?), and, even if we agree that a fetus is a human being, we can further ask about whether it is a *person.* In *Roe v. Wade* the Supreme Court ruled that even the "viable" unborn human fetus is not a "person" as that term is used in the Fifth and Fourteenth Amendments. Here the question is this: Is the essential fact about the fetus that it is a person?

An argument of this sort makes a claim — that is, it takes a stand — but notice that it does not have to argue for an action. Thus, it may argue that the death penalty is administered unfairly — that's a big enough issue — but it need not therefore go on to argue that the death penalty should be abolished. After all, another possibility is that the death penalty should be administered fairly. The writer of the essay may be doing enough if he or she establishes the truth of the claim, and leaves to others the possible courses of action.

2. What is the value of X? No one can argue with you if you say you prefer the plays of Tennessee Williams to those of Arthur Miller. But as soon as you say that Williams is a better playwright than Miller, you have based your preference on implicit standards, and it is incumbent on you to support your preference by giving evidence about the relative skill, insight, and accomplishments of Williams and Miller. Your argument is an evaluation. The question now at issue is the merits of the two authors and the standards appropriate for such an appraisal. (For a discussion of literary evaluations, see pp. 732–35.)

In short, an essay offering an evaluation normally has two purposes: (a) to set forth an assessment, and (b) to convince the reader that the assessment is reasonable. In writing an evaluation you will have to establish criteria, and these will vary depending on your topic. For instance, if you are comparing the artistic merit of the plays of Miller and Williams, you may want to talk about the quality of the characterization, the significance of the theme, and so on. But if the topic is, Which playwright is more suitable to be taught in high school?, other criteria may be appropriate, such as the difficulty of the language, the presence of obscenity, and so on.

3. What are the causes (or the consequences) of X? Why did the rate of auto theft increase during a specific period? If we abolish the death penalty, will that cause the rate of murder to increase? Notice, by the way, that such problems may be complex. The phenomena that people usually argue about — say, such things as inflation, war, suicide, crime — have many causes, and it is therefore often a mistake to speak of *the* cause of X. A writer in *Time* mentioned that the life expectancy of an average American male is about sixty-seven years, a figure that compares unfavorably with the life expectancy of males in Japan and Israel. The *Time* writer suggested that an important cause of the relatively short life span is "the pressure to perform well in business." Perhaps. But the life expectancy of plumbers is no greater than that of managers and executives. Nutrition authority Jean Mayer, in an article in *Life*, attributed the relatively poor longevity of American males to a diet that is "rich in fat and poor in nutrients." Doubtless other authorities propose other causes, and in all likelihood no one cause accounts for the phenomenon.

4. What should (or ought or must) we do about X? Must we always obey the law? Should the law allow 18-year-olds to drink alcohol? Should 18-year-olds be drafted to do one year of social service? Should pornography be censored? Should steroid use by athletes be banned? Ought there to be "Good Samaritan" laws, making it a legal duty to intervene to save a person from death or great bodily harm, when one might do so with little or no risk to oneself? These questions involve conduct and policy; how we answer them will reveal our values and principles.

An essay of this sort usually begins by explaining what the issue is — and why the reader should care about it — and then offers the proposal, paying attention to the counterarguments.

5. What is the evidence for my claims? Critical reading, writing, and thinking depend essentially on identifying and evaluating the evidence for and against the claims one makes and encounters in the writings of others. It is not enough to have an *opinion* or belief one way or the other; you need to be able to support your opinions — the bare fact of your sincere belief in what you say or write is not itself any *evidence* that what you believe is true.

So what are good reasons for opinions, adequate evidence for one's beliefs? The answer, of course, depends on what kind of belief or opinion, assertion or hypothesis, claim or principle, you want to assert. For example, there is good evidence that President John F. Kennedy was assassinated on November 22, 1963, because this is the date for his death reported in standard almanacs. You could further substantiate the date by checking the back issues of the *New York Times.* But a different kind of evidence is needed to support the proposition that the chemical composition of water is H_2O; and you will need still other kinds of evidence to support your beliefs about the likelihood of rain tomorrow, whether the Red Sox will win the pennant this year, the twelfth digit in the decimal expansion of pi, the average cumulative grades of the graduating seniors over the past three years in your college, whether *Hamlet* is greater than *Death of a Salesman,* and whether sexual harassment is morally wrong. None of these issues is merely a matter of opinion; yet on some of them, educated and informed people may disagree over the reasons and the evidence and what they show. Your job as a critical thinker is to be alert to the relevant reasons and evidence, and to make the most of them as you present your views.

Again, an argument may take in two or more of these five issues. Someone who argues that pornography should (or should not) be censored will have to mark out the territory of the discussion by defining pornography (our first issue: What is X?). The argument probably will also need to examine the consequences of adopting the preferred policy (our third issue), and may even have to argue about its value—our second issue. (Some people maintain that pornography produces crime, but others maintain that it provides a harmless outlet for impulses that otherwise might vent themselves in criminal behavior.) Further, someone arguing about the wisdom of censoring pornography might have to face the objection that censorship, however desirable on account of some of its consequences, may be unconstitutional, and that even if censorship were constitutional it would (or might) have undesirable side effects, such as repressing freedom of political opinion. And one will always have to keep asking oneself the fifth question, What is the evidence for my claims?

Thinking about one or more of these questions may get you going. For instance, thinking about the first question, What is X?, will require you to produce a definition, and as you work at producing a satisfactory definition, you may find new ideas arising. If a question seems relevant, start writing, even if you write only a fragmentary sentence. You'll probably find that one word leads to another and that ideas begin to appear. Even if these ideas seem weak as you write them, don't be discouraged; you have put something on paper, and returning to these words, perhaps in five minutes or perhaps the next day, you will probably find that some are not at all bad, and that others will stimulate you to better ones.

It may be useful to record your ideas in a special notebook reserved for the purpose. Such a **journal** can be a valuable resource when it comes time to write your paper. Many students find it easier to focus their thoughts on writing if during the period of gestation they have been jotting down relevant ideas on something more substantial than slips of paper or loose sheets. The very act of designating a notebook as your journal for a course can be the first step in focusing your attention on the eventual need to write a paper.

If what we have just said does not sound convincing, and you know from experience that you often have trouble getting started with your writing, don't despair; first aid is at hand in a sure-fire method that we will now explain.

The Thesis

Let's assume that you are writing an argumentative essay—perhaps an evaluation of an argument in this book—and you have what seems to be a pretty good draft, or at least a bunch of notes that are the result of hard thinking. You really do have ideas now, and you want to present them effectively. How will you organize your essay? No one formula works best for every essayist and for every essay, but it is usually advisable to formulate a basic **thesis,** a central point, a chief position, and to state it early. Every essay that is any good, even a book-length one, has a thesis, a main point, which can be stated briefly. Remember Coolidge's remark on the preacher's sermon on sin: "He was against it." Don't confuse the **topic** (here it is sin) with the thesis (opposition to sin). The thesis is the argumentative theme, the author's primary claim or contention, the proposition that the rest of the essay will explain and defend. Of course the thesis may sound commonplace, but the book or essay or sermon ought to develop it interestingly and convincingly.

Here are some sample theses:

Smoking should be prohibited in all enclosed public places.

Smoking should be limited to specific parts of enclosed public places, and entirely prohibited in small spaces, such as elevators.

Proprietors of public places such as restaurants and sports arenas should be free to determine whether they wish to prohibit, limit, or impose no limitations on smokers.

Imagining an Audience

Of course the questions that you ask yourself, in order to stimulate your thoughts, will depend primarily on what you are writing about, but additional questions are always relevant:

- Who are my readers?
- What do they believe?
- How much common ground do we share?
- What do I want my readers to believe?
- What do they need to know?

These questions require a little comment. The literal answer to the first probably is "the teacher," but (unless you are given instructions to the contrary) you should not write specifically for the teacher; instead, you should write for an audience that is, generally speaking, like your classmates. In short, your imagined audience is literate, intelligent, and moderately well informed, but it does not know everything that you know, and it does not know your response to the problem that you are addressing.

The essays in this book are from many different sources, each with its own audience. An essay from the *New York Times* is addressed to the educated general reader; an essay from *Ms.* is addressed to readers sympathetic to the feminist movement. An essay from *Commonweal*, a Roman Catholic publication addressed to the nonspecialist, is likely to differ in point of view or tone from one in *Time*, even though both articles may advance approximately the same position. The writer of the article in *Commonweal* may, for example, effectively cite church fathers and distinguished Roman Catholic writers as authorities, whereas the writer of an article addressed largely to non-Catholic readers probably will cite few or even none of these figures because the audience might be unfamiliar with them or, even if familiar, might be unimpressed by their views.

The tone as well as the gist of the argument is in some degree shaped by the audience. For instance, popular journals, such as *The National Review* and *Ms.* are more likely to use ridicule than are journals chiefly addressed to, say, an academic audience.

The Audience as Collaborator

If you imagine an audience, and keep asking yourself what this audience needs to be told and what it doesn't need to be told, you will find that material comes to mind, just as it comes to mind when a friend asks you what a film was about, and who was in it, and how you liked it. Your readers do not have to be told that Thomas Jefferson was an American statesman in the early years of this country's history, but they do have to be told that Thomas Huxley was a late-nineteenth-century English advocate of Darwinism. You would identify Huxley because it's your hunch that your classmates never heard of him, or even if they may have heard the name, they can't quite identify it. But what if your class has been assigned an essay by Huxley? In that case your imagined reader knows Huxley's name and knows at least a little about him, so you don't have to identify Huxley as an Englishman of the nineteenth century. But you do still have to remind your reader about relevant aspects of his essay, and you do have to tell your reader about your responses to them.

After all, even if the instructor has assigned an essay by Huxley, you cannot assume that your classmates know the essay inside out. Obviously you can't say, "Huxley's third reason is also unconvincing," without reminding the reader, by means of a brief summary, of his third reason. Again, think of your classmates as your imagined readers; put yourself in their shoes, and be sure that your essay does not make unreasonable demands. If you ask yourself, "What do my readers need to know?" (and "What do I want them to believe?") you will find some answers arising, and you will start writing.

We have said that you should imagine your audience as your class-mates. But this is not the whole truth. In a sense, your argument is ad-dressed not simply to your classmates but to the world interested in ideas. Even if you can reasonably assume that your classmates have read only one work by Huxley, you will not begin your essay by writing "Huxley's essay is deceptively easy." You will have to name the work; it is possible that a reader has read some other work by Huxley. And by precisely identifying your subject you help to ease the reader into your essay.

Similarly, you won't begin by writing,

> The majority opinion in *Walker v. City of Birmingham* was that . . .

Rather, you'll write something like this:

> In *Walker v. City of Birmingham,* the Supreme Court ruled in 1966 that city authorities acted lawfully when they jailed Martin Luther King, Jr., and other clergymen in 1963 for marching in Birmingham without a per-mit. Justice Potter Stewart delivered the majority opinion, which held that . . .

By the way, if you think you suffer from a writing block, the mere act of writing out such obvious truths will help you to get started. You will find that putting a few words down on paper, perhaps merely copying the essay's title or an interesting quotation from the essay, will stimulate you to jot down thoughts that you didn't know you had in you.

Here, again, are the questions about audience. **If you write with a word processor,** consider putting these questions into a file. For each as-signment, copy (with the "copy" command) the questions into the file you are currently working on, and then, as a way of generating ideas, *enter your responses, indented, under each question.*

- Who are my readers?
- What do they believe?
- How much common ground do we share?
- What do I want my readers to believe?
- What do they need to know?

Thinking about your audience can help you to put some words on paper; even more important, it can help you to get ideas. Our second and third questions about the audience ("What do they believe?" and "How much common ground do we share?") will usually help you get ideas flowing. Pre-sumably your imagined audience does not share your views, or at least does not fully share them. But why? How can these readers hold a position that to you seems unreasonable? If you try to put yourself into your readers' shoes, and if you think about what your audience knows or thinks it knows, you will find yourself getting ideas.

You do not believe (let's assume) that people should be allowed to smoke in enclosed public places, but you know that some people hold a different view. Why do they hold it? Try to state their view in a way that would be satisfactory to them. Having done so, you may come to perceive that your conclusions and theirs differ because they are based on different premises, perhaps different ideas about human rights. Examine the opposition's premises carefully, and explain, first to yourself and ultimately to your readers, why you find some premises unsound.

Possibly some facts are in dispute, such as whether nonsmokers may be harmed by exposure to tobacco. The thing to do, then, is to check the facts. If you find that harm to nonsmokers has not been proved, but you nevertheless believe that smoking should be prohibited in enclosed public places, of course you can't premise your argument on the wrongfulness of harming the innocent (in this case, the nonsmokers). You will have to develop arguments that take account of the facts, whatever they are.

Among the relevant facts there surely are some that your audience or your opponent will not dispute. The same is true of the values relevant to the discussion; the two of you are very likely to agree, if only you stop to think about it, that you share belief in some of the same values (such as the principle mentioned above, that it is wrong to harm the innocent). These areas of shared agreement are crucial to effective persuasion in argument. If you wish to persuade, you'll have to begin by finding *premises you can share with your audience.* Try to identify and isolate these areas of agreement. There are two good reasons for doing so:

1. There is no point in disputing facts or values on which you and your readers really agree, and
2. it usually helps to establish goodwill between you and your opponent when you can point to beliefs, assumptions, facts, and values that the two of you share.

In a few moments we will return to the need to share some of the opposition's ideas.

Recall that in writing college papers it is usually best to write for a general audience, an audience rather like your classmates but without the specific knowledge that they all share as students enrolled in one course. If the topic is smoking in public places, the audience presumably consists of smokers and nonsmokers. Thinking about our fifth question on page 134 — What do the readers need to know? — may prompt you to give statistics about the harmful effects of smoking. Or, if you are arguing on behalf of smokers, it may prompt you to cite studies claiming that no evidence conclusively demonstrates that cigarette smoking is harmful to nonsmokers. If indeed you are writing for a general audience, and you are not advancing a highly unfamiliar view, our second question (What does the audience believe?) is less important here, but if the audience is specialized, such as an antismoking group, or a group of restaurant owners who fear that anti-smoking regulations will interfere with their business, or a group of civil libertarians, obviously an effective essay will have to address their special beliefs.

In addressing their beliefs (let's assume that you do not share them, or do not share them fully), you must try to establish some common ground. If you advocate requiring restaurants to provide nonsmoking areas, you should at least recognize the possibility that this arrangement will result in inconvenience for the proprietor. But perhaps (the good news) it will regain some lost customers or will attract some new customers. This thought should prompt you to think of kinds of evidence, perhaps testimony or statistics.

When one formulates a thesis and asks questions about it, such as who the readers are, what do they believe, what do they know, and what do they need to know, one begins to get ideas about how to organize the material, or at least one begins to see that some sort of organization will have to be worked out. The thesis may be clear and simple, but the reasons (the argument) may take many pages. The thesis is the point; the argument sets forth the evidence that is offered to support the thesis.

The Title

It's not a bad idea to announce your thesis in your **title.** If you scan the table of contents of this book, you will notice that a fair number of essayists use the title to let the readers know, at least in a very general way, what position will be advocated. Here are a few examples:

Gay Marriages: Make Them Legal

Smokers Get a Raw Deal

Why Handguns Must Be Outlawed

True, these titles are not especially engaging, but the reader welcomes them because they give some information about the writer's thesis.

Some titles do not announce the thesis but they at least announce the topic:

Is All Discrimination Unfair?

On Racist Speech

Although not clever or witty, these titles are informative.

Some titles seek to attract attention or to stimulate the imagination:

A First Amendment Junkie

The Doctor Won't See You Now

A Crime of Compassion

All of these are effective, but a word of caution is appropriate here. In your effort to engage your reader's attention, be careful not to sound like a wise guy. You want to engage your readers, not turn them off.

Finally, be prepared to rethink your title *after* you have finished the last draft of your paper. A title somewhat different from your working title may be an improvement because the emphasis of your finished paper may have turned out to be rather different from what you expected when you first thought of a title.

The Opening Paragraphs

A good introduction arouses the reader's interest and helps prepare the reader for the rest of the paper. How? Opening paragraphs usually do at least one (and often all) of the following:

- attract the reader's interest (often with a bold statement of the thesis, or with an interesting statistic or quotation or anecdote);
- prepare the reader's mind by giving some idea of the topic, and often of the thesis;
- give the reader an idea of how the essay is organized;
- define a term.

You may not wish to announce your thesis in your title, but if you don't announce it there, you should set it forth very early in the argument, in your introductory paragraph or paragraphs. In her title "Human Rights and Foreign Policy," Jeane J. Kirkpatrick merely announces her topic (subject) as opposed to her thesis (point), but she begins to hint at the thesis in her first paragraph, by deprecating President Jimmy Carter's policy:

> In this paper I deal with three broad subjects: first, the content and consequences of the Carter administration's human rights policy; second, the prerequisites of a more adequate theory of human rights; and third, some characteristics of a more successful human rights policy.

Or consider this opening paragraph from Peter Singer's "Animal Liberation":

> We are familiar with Black Liberation, Gay Liberation, and a variety of other movements. With Women's Liberation some thought we had come to the end of the road. Discrimination on the basis of sex, it has been said, is the last form of discrimination that is universally accepted and practiced without pretense, even in those liberal circles which have long prided themselves on their freedom from racial discrimination. But one should always be wary of talking of "the last remaining form of discrimination." If we have learned anything from the liberation movements, we should have learned how difficult it is to be aware of the ways in which we discriminate until they are forcefully pointed out to us. A liberation movement demands an expansion of our moral horizons, so

that practices that were previously regarded as natural and inevitable are now seen as intolerable.

Although Singer's introductory paragraph nowhere mentions animal liberation, in conjunction with its title it gives us a good idea of what Singer is up to and where he is going. Singer knows that his audience will be skeptical, so he reminds them that many of us in previous years were skeptical of reforms that we now take for granted. He adopts a strategy used fairly often by writers who advance highly unconventional theses: Rather than beginning with a bold announcement of a thesis that may turn off some of his readers because it sounds offensive or absurd, Singer warms his audience up, gaining their interest by cautioning them politely that although they may at first be skeptical of animal liberation, if they stay with his essay they may come to feel that they have expanded their horizons.

Notice, too, that Singer begins by establishing common ground with his readers; he assumes, probably correctly, that they share his view that other forms of discrimination (now seen to be unjust) were once widely practiced and were assumed to be acceptable and natural. In this paragraph, then, Singer is not only showing himself to be fair-minded but is also letting us know that he will advance a daring idea. His opening wins our attention and our goodwill. A writer can hardly hope to do more. (In a few pages we will talk a little more about winning the audience.)

In your introductory paragraphs you may have to give some background informing or reminding your readers of material that they will have to be familiar with if they are to follow your essay. You may wish to define some terms, if the terms are unfamiliar or if you are using familiar terms in an unusual sense. In writing, or at least in revising these paragraphs, remember to keep in mind this question: What do my readers need to know? Remember, your aim throughout is to write *reader-friendly* prose, and keeping the needs and interests of your audience constantly in mind will help you achieve this goal.

After announcing the topic, giving the necessary background, and stating your position (and perhaps the opposition's) in as engaging a manner as possible, it is usually a good idea to give the reader an idea of how you will proceed. Look on the preceding page at Kirkpatrick's opening paragraph, for an obvious illustration. She tells us she will deal with three subjects, and she names them. Her approach in the paragraph is concise, obvious, and effective.

Similarly, you may, for instance, want to announce fairly early that there are four common objections to your thesis, and that you will take them up one by one, beginning with the weakest (or most widely held, or whatever) and moving to the strongest (or least familiar), after which you will advance your own view in greater detail. Of course not every argument begins with refuting the other side, though many arguments do. The point to remember is that you usually ought to tell your readers where you will be taking them and by what route.

Organizing and Revising the Body of the Essay

Most arguments more or less follow this organization:

1. Statement of the problem
2. Statement of the structure of the essay
3. Statement of alternative solutions
4. Arguments in support of the proposed solution
5. Arguments answering possible objections
6. A summary, resolution, or conclusion

Let's look at each of these six steps.

1. **Statement of the problem.** Whether the problem is stated briefly or at length depends on the nature of the problem and the writer's audience. If you haven't already defined unfamiliar terms or terms you use in a special way, probably now is the time to do so. In any case, it is advisable here to state the problem objectively (thereby gaining the trust of the reader) and to indicate why the reader should care about the issue.

2. **Statement of the structure of the essay.** After stating the problem at the appropriate length, the writer often briefly indicates the structure of the rest of the essay. The commonest structure is suggested below, in points 3 and 4.

3. **Statement of alternative solutions.** In addition to stating the alternatives fairly, the writer probably conveys willingness to recognize not only the integrity of the proposers but also the (partial) merit of at least some of the alternative solutions.

The point made in the previous sentence is important and worth amplifying. Because it is important to convey your goodwill — your sense of fairness — to the reader, it is advisable to let your reader see that you are familiar with the opposition, and that you recognize the integrity of those who hold that view. This you do by granting its merits as far as you can. (For more about this approach, see the essay by Carl Rogers on page 794.)

The next stage, which constitutes most of the body of the essay, usually is this:

4. **Arguments in support of the proposed solution.** The evidence offered will, of course, depend on the nature of the problem. Relevant statistics, authorities, examples, or analogies may or may not come to mind or be available. This is usually the longest part of the essay.

5. **Arguments answering possible objections.** These arguments may suggest that

   a. the proposal won't work (perhaps it is alleged to be too expensive, or to make unrealistic demands on human nature, or to fail to get to the heart of the problem);

b. the proposed solution will create problems greater than the difficulty to be resolved. (A good example of a proposal that produced dreadful unexpected results is the law mandating a prison term for anyone over eighteen in possession of an illegal drug. Heroin dealers then began to use children as runners, and cocaine importers followed the practice.)

6. **A summary, resolution, or conclusion.** Here the writer may seek to accommodate the views of the opposition as far as possible, but clearly suggests that the writer's own position makes good sense. The end of the essay may suggest that the ball is now in the reader's court; in any case some sense of closure must be provided.

Of course not every essay will follow this six-part pattern, but let's assume that in the introductory paragraphs you have sketched the topic (and have shown or nicely said, or implied, that the reader doubtless is interested in it), and have fairly and courteously set forth the opposition's view, recognizing its merits and indicating the degree to which you can share part of that view. You now want to set forth your arguments explaining why you differ on some essentials.

In setting forth your own position, you can begin either with your strongest reasons or your weakest. Each method of organization has advantages and disadvantages. If you begin with your strongest, the essay may seem to peter out; if you begin with the weakest, you build to a climax but your readers may not still be with you because they may have felt at the start that the essay was frivolous. The solution to this last possibility is to make sure that even your weakest argument is an argument of some strength. You can, moreover, assure your readers that stronger points will soon be offered and you offer this point first only because you want to show that you are aware of it, and that, slight though it is, it deserves some attention. The body of the essay, then, is devoted to arguing a position, which means not only offering supporting reasons but also offering refutations of possible objections to these reasons.

Doubtless you will sometimes be uncertain, as you draft your essay, whether to present a given point before or after another point. When you write, and certainly when you revise, try to put yourself into your reader's shoes: Which point do you think the reader needs to know first? Which point *leads to* which further point? Your argument should not be a mere list of points, of course; rather, it should clearly integrate one point with another in order to develop an idea. But in all likelihood you won't have a strong sense of the best organization until you have written a draft and have reread it. You are likely to find that the organization needs some revising in order to make your argument clear to a reader.

Checking Paragraphs · When you revise your draft, watch out also for short paragraphs. Although a paragraph of only two or three sentences (like some in this chapter) may occasionally be helpful as a transition between complicated points, most short paragraphs are undeveloped paragraphs. (Newspaper editors favor very short paragraphs because they can be read rapidly when printed in the narrow columns typical of newspapers. Many of the essays reprinted in this book originally were published in newspapers, hence their very short paragraphs. There is no reason for you to imitate this style in the argumentative essays you will be writing.)

In revising, when you find a paragraph of only a sentence or two or three, check first to see if it should be joined to the paragraph that precedes or follows. Second, if on rereading you are certain that a given paragraph should not be tied to what comes before or after, think about amplifying the paragraph with supporting detail (this is not the same as mere padding).

Checking Transitions • Make sure, too, in revising, that the reader can move easily from the beginning of a paragraph to the end, and from one paragraph to the next. Transitions help the reader to perceive the connections between the units of the argument. For example (that's a transition, of course), they may

> **illustrate:** *for example, for instance, consider this case;*
>
> **establish a sequence:** *a more important objection, a stronger example, the best reason;*
>
> **connect logically:** *thus, as a result, therefore, so, it follows;*
>
> **compare:** *similarly, in like manner, just as, analogously;*
>
> **contrast:** *on the other hand, in contrast, however, but;*
>
> **summarize:** *in short, briefly.*

Expressions such as these serve as guideposts that enable your reader to move easily through your essay.

When writers revise an early draft they chiefly

- unify the essay by eliminating irrelevancies;
- organize the essay by keeping in mind an imagined audience;
- clarify the essay by fleshing out thin paragraphs, by making certain that the transitions are adequate, and by making certain that generalizations are adequately supported by concrete details and examples.

We are not talking about polish or elegance; we are talking about fundamental matters. Be especially careful not to abuse the logical connectives ("thus," "as a result," etc.). If you write several sentences followed by "therefore" or a similar word or phrase, be sure that what you write after the "therefore" *really does follow* from what has gone before. Logical connectives are not mere transitional devices used to link disconnected bits of prose. They are supposed to mark a real movement of thought—the essence of an argument.

The Ending

What about concluding paragraphs, in which you try to summarize the main points and reaffirm your position? If you can look back over your essay and can add something that enriches it and at the same time wraps it up, fine, but don't feel compelled to say, "Thus, in conclusion, I have argued *X, Y,* and *Z,* and I have refuted Jones." After all, *conclusion* can have two meanings: (1) ending, or finish, as the ending of a joke or a novel; (2) judgment or decision reached after deliberation. Your essay should finish effectively (the first sense), but it need not announce a judgment (the second).

If the essay is fairly short, so that a reader can more or less keep the whole thing in mind, you may not need to restate your view. Just make sure that you have covered the ground, and that your last sentence is a good one. Notice that the essay printed later in this chapter does not end with a formal conclusion (p. 152), though it ends conclusively, with a note of finality.

By a note of finality we do *not* mean a triumphant crowing. It's usually far better to end with the suggestion that you hope you have by now indicated why those who hold a different view may want to modify it and accept yours.

If you study the essays in this book, or, for that matter, the editorials and Op-Ed pieces in a newspaper, you will notice that writers often provide a sense of closure by using one of the following devices:

- a return to something in the introduction;
- a glance at the wider implications of the issue (for example, if smoking is restricted, other liberties are threatened);
- an anecdote that engagingly illustrates the thesis;
- a brief summary (but this sort of ending may seem unnecessary and even tedious, especially if the paper is short and if the summary merely repeats what has already been said).

The Uses of an Outline

Some writers find it useful to sketch an **outline** as soon as they think they know what they want to say, even before they write a first draft; others write an outline after a draft that has given them additional ideas. These procedures can be helpful in planning a tentative organization, but remember that in revising a draft new ideas will arise, and the outline may have to be modified. A preliminary outline is chiefly useful as a means of getting going, not as a guide to the final essay.

The Outline as a Way of Checking a Draft · Whether or not you use a preliminary outline, we suggest that after you have written what you hope is your last draft, you make an outline of it; there is no better way of finding out whether the essay is well organized.

Go through the draft and jot down the chief points, in the order in which you make them. That is, prepare a table of contents — perhaps a phrase for each paragraph. Next, examine your jottings to see what kind of sequence they reveal in your paper:

1. Is the sequence reasonable? Can it be improved?
2. Are any passages irrelevant?
3. Does something important seem to be missing?

If no structure or sequence clearly appears in the outline, then the full prose version of your argument probably doesn't have any, either. Therefore, produce another draft, moving things around, adding or subtracting paragraphs — cutting and pasting into a new sequence, with transitions as needed — and then make another outline to see if the sequence now is satisfactory.

You are probably familiar with the structure known as a **formal outline.** A major point is indicated by I, and points within this major point are indicated by A, B, C, and so on. Divisions within A, B, C, are indicated by 1, 2, 3, and so on, thus:

I. Arguments for opening all Olympic sports to professionals
  A. Fairness
    1. some Olympic sports are already open to professionals
    2. some athletes who really are not professionals are classified as professionals
  B. Quality (achievements would be higher)

You may want to outline your draft according to this principle, or it may be enough if you simply jot down a phrase for each paragraph and indent the subdivisions. But keep this point in mind: It is not enough for the parts to be ordered reasonably; the order must be made clear to the reader, probably by means of transitions such as *for instance, on the other hand, we can now turn to an opposing view,* and so on.

Tone and the Writer's Persona

Although this book is chiefly about argument in the sense of rational discourse — the presentation of reasons in support of a thesis or conclusion — the appeal to reason is only one form of persuasion. Another form is the appeal to emotion — to pity, for example. Aristotle saw, in addition to the appeal to reason and the appeal to emotion, a third form of persuasion, the appeal to the character of the speaker. He called it the **ethical appeal.** The idea is that effective speakers convey the suggestion that they are persons of good sense, benevolence, and honesty. Their discourse, accordingly, inspires confidence in their listeners. It is, of course, a fact that when we read an argument we are often aware of the "person" or "voice" behind the words, and our assent to the argument depends partly on the extent to which we can share the speaker's assumptions, look at the matter from the speaker's point of view — in short *identify* with this speaker.

How can a writer inspire the confidence that lets readers identify themselves with the writer? To begin with, the writer should possess the virtues Aristotle specified: intelligence or good sense, honesty, and benevolence or goodwill. As the Roman proverb puts it, "No one gives what he does not have." Still, possession of these qualities is not a guarantee that you will convey them in your writing. Like all other writers, you will have to revise your drafts so that these qualities become apparent, or, stated more moderately, you will have to revise so that nothing in the essay causes a reader to doubt your intelligence, honesty, and goodwill. A blunder in logic, a misleading quotation, a snide remark — all such slips can cause readers to withdraw their sympathy from the writer.

But of course all good argumentative essays do not sound exactly alike; they do not all reveal the same speaker. Each writer develops his or her own voice or (as literary critics and teachers call it) **persona.** In fact, one writer will have several voices or personae, depending on the topic and the audience. The president of the United States delivering an address on the State of the Union has one persona; chatting with a reporter at his summer home he has another. This change is not a matter of hypocrisy. Different circumstances call for different language. As a French writer put it, there is a time to speak of "Paris," and a time to speak of "the capital of the nation." When Lincoln spoke at Gettysburg, he didn't say "Eighty-seven years ago," but "Four score and seven years ago." We might say that just as some occasions required him to be the folksy Honest Abe, the occasion of the dedication of hallowed ground required him to be formal and solemn, and so the president of the United States appropriately used biblical language. The election campaigns called for one persona, and this occasion called for a different persona.

When we talk about a writer's persona, we mean the way in which the writer presents his or her attitudes:

> the attitude toward *the self,*
> toward *the audience,* and
> toward *the subject.*

Thus, if a writer says,

> I have thought long and hard about this subject, and I can say with assurance that . . .

we may feel that we are listening to a self-satisfied ass who probably is simply mouthing other people's opinions. Certainly he is mouthing other people's clichés: "long and hard," "say with assurance."

Let's look at a slightly subtler example of an utterance that reveals an attitude. When we read that

> President Nixon was hounded out of office by journalists

we hear a respectful attitude toward Nixon ("President Nixon") and a hostile attitude toward the press (they are beasts, curs who "hounded" our elected leader). If the writer's attitudes were reversed, she might have said something like this:

> The press turned the searchlight on Tricky Dick's criminal shenanigans.

"Tricky Dick" and "criminal" are obvious enough, but notice that "shenanigans" also implies the writer's contempt for Nixon, and of course "turned the searchlight" suggests that the press is a source of illumination, a source of truth. The original version and the opposite version both say that the press was responsible for Nixon's resignation, but the original version ("President Nixon was hounded") conveys indignation toward journalists, whereas the revision conveys contempt for Nixon.

These two versions suggest two speakers who differ not only in their view of Nixon but also in their manner, including the seriousness with which they take themselves. Although the passage is very short, it seems to us that the first speaker conveys righteous indignation ("hounded"), whereas the second conveys amused contempt ("shenanigans"). To our ears the tone, as well as the point, differs in the two versions.

We are talking about **loaded words,** words that convey the writer's attitude and that by their connotations are meant to win the reader to the writer's side. Compare "freedom fighter" with "terrorist," "pro-choice" with "pro-abortion," or "pro-life" with "anti-abortion." "Freedom fighter," "pro-choice," and "pro-life" sound like good things; speakers who use these words are seeking to establish themselves as virtuous people who are supporting worthy causes. The **connotations** (associations, overtones) of these pairs of words differ, even though the **denotations** (explicit meanings, dictionary definitions) are the same, just as the connotations of "mother" and "female parent" differ, although the denotations are the same. Similarly, although "four score and seven" and "eighty-seven" both denote "thirteen less than one hundred," they differ in connotation.

Tone is not only a matter of connotations ("hounded out of office," versus, let's say, "compelled to resign," or "pro-choice" versus "pro-abortion"); it is also a matter of such things as the selection and type of examples. A writer who offers many examples, especially ones drawn from ordinary life, conveys a persona different from that of a writer who offers no examples, or only an occasional invented instance. The first of these probably is, one might say, friendlier, more down-to-earth.

Last Words on Tone • On the whole, in writing an argument it is advisable to be courteous, respectful of your topic, of your audience, and even of your opposition. It is rarely effective to regard as villains or fools persons who hold views different from yours, especially if some of them are in your audience. Keep in mind the story of the two strangers on a train who, striking up a conversation, found that both were clergymen, though of different faiths. Then one said to the other, "Well, why shouldn't we be friends? After all, we both serve God, you in your way and I in His."

Complacency is all right when telling jokes but not in arguments. Recognize the opposition, assume that the views are held in good faith, state the views fairly (if you don't, you do a disservice not only to the opposition but to your own position, because the perceptive reader will not take you seriously), and be temperate in arguing your own position: "If I understand their view correctly . . ."; "It seems reasonable to conclude that . . . "; "Perhaps, then, we can agree that . . ."

"We," "One," or "I"?

The use of "we" in the last sentence brings us to another point: May the first-person pronouns "I" and "we" be used? In this book, because two of us are writing, we often use "we" to mean the two authors. And we sometimes use "we" to mean the authors and the readers, as in phrases like the one that ends the previous paragraph. This shifting use of one word can be troublesome, but we hope (clearly the "we" here refers only to the authors) that we have avoided any ambiguity. But can, or should, or must, an individual use "we" instead of "I"? The short answer is no.

If you are simply speaking for yourself, use "I." Attempts to avoid the first person singular by saying things like "This writer thinks . . . ," and "It is thought that . . . ," and "One thinks that . . . ," are far more irritating (and wordy) than the use of "I." The so-called editorial "we" is as odd sounding in a student's argument as is the royal "we." Mark Twain said that the only ones who can appropriately say "we" are kings, editors, and people with a tapeworm. And because one "one" leads to another, making the sentence sound (James Thurber's words) "like a trombone solo," it's best to admit that you are the author, and to use "I." But of course there is no need to preface every sentence with "I think." The reader knows that the essay is yours; just write it, using "I" when you must, but not needlessly.

Avoiding Sexist Language

Courtesy (as well as common sense) requires that you respect the feelings of your readers. Many people today find offensive the implicit sexism in the use of male pronouns to denote not only men but also women ("As the reader follows the argument, he will find . . ."). And sometimes the use of the male pronoun to denote all people is ridiculous: "An individual, no matter what his sex, . . ."

In most contexts there is no need to use gender-specific nouns or pronouns. One way to avoid using "he" when you mean any person is to use "he or she" (or "she or he") instead of "he," but the result is sometimes a bit cumbersome—although it is superior to the overly conspicuous "he/she" and to "s/he."

Here are two simple ways to solve the problem:

1. *use the plural* ("As readers follow the argument, they will find . . ."), or
2. *recast the sentence* so that no pronoun is required ("Readers following the argument will find . . .").

Because *man* and *mankind* strike many readers as sexist when used in such expressions as "Man is a rational animal" and "Mankind has not yet solved this problem," consider using such words as *human being, person, people, humanity,* and *we. (Examples:* "Human beings are rational animals"; "We have not yet solved this problem.")

PEER REVIEW

Your instructor may suggest — or may even require — that you submit an early draft of your essay to a fellow student or small group of students for comment. Such a procedure benefits both author and readers: You get the responses of a reader, and the student-reader gets experience in thinking about the problems of developing an argument, especially in thinking about such matters as the degree of detail that a writer needs to offer to a reader, and the importance of keeping the organization evident to a reader.

Here is an example of a checklist with suggestions and questions for peer review.

A PEER REVIEW CHECKLIST FOR A DRAFT OF AN ARGUMENT

Read the draft through, quickly. Then read it again, with the following questions in mind.

1. Does the draft show promise of fulfilling the assignment?
2. Looking at the essay as a whole, what thesis (main idea) is advanced?
3. Are the needs of the audience kept in mind? For instance, do some words need to be defined? Is the evidence (for instance, the examples, and the testimony of authorities) clear and effective?
4. Is any obvious evidence (or counterevidence) overlooked?
5. Can you accept the assumptions? If not, why not?
6. If the writer is proposing a solution,
   a. Are other equally attractive solutions adequately examined?
   b. Has the writer overlooked some unattractive effects of the proposed solution?

---

7. Looking at each paragraph separately:

   a. What is the basic point?

   b. How does each paragraph relate to the essay's main idea or to the previous paragraph?

   c. Should some paragraphs be deleted? Be divided into two or more paragraphs? Be combined? Be put elsewhere? (If you outline the essay by jotting down the gist of each paragraph, you will get help in answering these questions.)

   d. Is each sentence clearly related to the sentence that precedes and to the sentence that follows?

   e. Is each paragraph adequately developed? Are there sufficient details, perhaps brief supporting quotations from the text?

   f. Are the introductory and concluding paragraphs effective?

8. What are the paper's chief strengths?

9. Make at least two specific suggestions that you think will assist the author to improve the paper.

A STUDENT'S ESSAY, FROM
ROUGH NOTES TO FINAL VERSION

While we were revising this textbook we asked the students in one of our classes to write a short essay (500–750 words) on some ethical problem that concerned them. Because this assignment was the first writing assignment in the course, we explained that a good way to get ideas is to ask oneself some questions, jot down responses, question those responses, and write freely for ten minutes or so, not worrying about contradictions. We invited our students to hand in their initial jottings along with the finished essay, so that we could get a sense of how they proceeded as writers. Not all of them chose to hand in their jottings, but we were greatly encouraged by those who did. What was encouraging was the confirmation of an old belief, the belief — we call it a fact — that students will hand in a thoughtful essay if before they prepare a final version they nag themselves, ask themselves *why* they think this or that, jot down their responses, and are not afraid to change their minds as they proceed.

Here are the first jottings of a student, Emily Andrews, who elected to write about whether to give money to street beggars. She simply put down ideas, one after the other.

```
Help the poor? Why do I (sometimes) do it?

I feel guilty, and think I should help them: poor,
    cold, hungry (but also some of them are thirsty
```

for liquor, and will spend the money on liquor,
not on food)

I also feel annoyed by them--most of them:

Where does the expression "the deserving poor" come
from?

And "poor but honest"? Actually, that sounds a bit
odd. Wouldn't "rich but honest" make more sense?

Why don't they work? Fellow with red beard, always by
bus stop in front of florist's shop, always
wants a handout. He is a regular, there all day
every day, so I guess he is in a way "reliable,"
so why doesn't he put the same time in on a job?

Or why don't they get help? Don't they know they need
it? They <u>must</u> know they need it.

Maybe that guy with the beard is just a con artist.
Maybe he makes more money by panhandling than he
would by working, and it's a lot easier!

Kinds of poor--how to classify??
    drunks, druggies, etc.
    mentally ill (maybe drunks belong here too)
    decent people who have had terrible luck

Why private charity?

Doesn't it makes sense to say we (fortunate individuals) should give something--an occasional hand-
out--to people who have had terrible luck? (I
suppose some people might say that there is no
need for any of us to give anything--the government takes care of the truly needy--but I <u>do</u>
believe in giving charity. A month ago a friend
of the family passed away, and the woman's
children suggested that people might want to
make a donation in her name, to a shelter for
battered women. I know my parents made a donation.)

BUT how can I tell who is who, which are which? Which
of these people asking for "spare change" really
need (deserve???) help, and which are phonies?
Impossible to tell.

Possibilities:
    Give to no one
    Give to no one but make an annual donation,
    maybe to United Way
    Give a dollar to each person who asks. This

> would probably not cost me even a dollar a day
> Occasionally do without something--maybe a CD--
> or a meal in a restaurant--and give the money I
> save to people who seem worthy

WORTHY? What am I saying? How can I, or anyone, tell?
The neat-looking guy who says he just lost his
job may be a phony, and the dirty bum--probably
a drunk--may desperately need food. (OK, so
what if he spends the money on liquor instead of
food? At least he'll get a little pleasure in
life. No! It's not all right if he spends it on
drink.)

Other possibilities:
Do some volunteer work?
To tell the truth, I don't want to put in the
time. I don't feel _that_ guilty.

So what's the problem?

Is it, How I can help the very poor (handouts, or
through an organization)? or

How I can feel less guilty about being lucky enough
to be able to go to college, and to have a
supportive family?

I can't quite bring myself to believe I should help
every beggar who approaches, but I also can't
bring myself to believe that I should do nothing, on the grounds that:

a. it's probably their fault

b. if they are deserving, they can get gov't
help. No, I just can't believe that. Maybe
some are too proud to look for government
help, or don't know that they are entitled to
it.

What to do?

On balance, it seems best to
a. give to United Way
b. maybe also give to an occasional individual,
if I happen to be moved, without worrying
about whether he or she is "deserving" (since
it's probably impossible to know)

A day after making these notes Emily reviewed them, added a few
points, and then made a very brief selection from them, to serve as an outline for her first draft.

```
Opening para.: "poor but honest"? Deserve "spare change"?
Charity: private or through organizations?
            pros and cons
            guy at bus
            it wouldn't cost me much, but . . . better to
                give through organizations
Concluding para: still feel guilty?
                maybe mention guy at bus again?
```

After writing and revising a draft, Emily Andrews submitted her essay to a fellow student for peer review. She then revised her work in light of the suggestions she received, and in light of her own further thinking.

On the next page we give the final essay. If after reading the final version you reread the early jottings, you will notice that some of the jottings never made it into the final version. But without the jottings, the essay probably could not have been as interesting as it is. When the writer made the jottings, she was not so much putting down her ideas as *finding* ideas by the process of writing.

Emily Andrews
Professor Barnet
English 102
January 13, 1995

Why I Don't Spare "Spare Change"

"Poor but honest." "The deserving poor." I
don't know the origin of these quotations, but
they always come to mind when I think of "the
poor." But I also think of people who, perhaps
through alcohol or drugs, have ruined not only
their own lives but also the lives of others in
order to indulge in their own pleasure. Perhaps
alcoholism and drug addiction really are "diseases," as many people say, but my own feeling--
based, of course, not on any serious study--is
that most alcoholics and drug addicts can be
classified with the "undeserving poor." And that
is largely why I don't distribute spare change to
panhandlers.

But surely among the street people there are
also some who can rightly be called "deserving."
Deserving what? My spare change? Or simply the
government's assistance? It happens that I have
been brought up to believe that it is appropriate
to make contributions to charity--let's say a
shelter for battered women--but if I give some
change to a panhandler, am I making a contribution
to charity and thereby helping someone, or, on the
contrary, am I perhaps simply encouraging someone
not to get help? Or, maybe even worse, am I supporting a con artist?

If one believes in the value of private
charity, one can either give to needy individuals

or to charitable organizations. In giving to a panhandler one may indeed be helping a person who badly needs help, but one cannot be certain that one is giving to a needy individual. In giving to an organization such as the United Way, on the other hand, one can feel that one's money is likely to be used wisely. True, confronted by a beggar one may feel that this particular unfortunate individual needs help at this moment--a cup of coffee, or a sandwich--and the need will not be met unless I put my hand in my pocket right now. But I have come to think that the beggars whom I encounter can get along without my spare change, and indeed perhaps they are actually better off for not having money to buy liquor or drugs.

It happens that in my neighborhood I encounter few panhandlers. There is one fellow who is always by the bus stop where I catch the bus to the college, and I never give him anything precisely because he is always there. He is such a regular that, I think, he ought to be able to hold a regular job. Putting him aside, I probably don't encounter more than three or four beggars in a week. (I'm not counting street musicians. These people seem quite able to work for a living. If they see their "work" as playing or singing, let persons who enjoy their performances pay them. I do not consider myself among their audience.) The truth of the matter is that, since I meet so few beggars, I could give each one a dollar and hardly feel the loss. At most, I might go without seeing a movie some week. But I know nothing about these people, and it's my impression--admittedly based on almost no evidence--that they simply prefer begging to working. I am not generalizing about street people, and certainly I am not talking about street people in the big urban centers. I am talking only about the people whom I actually encounter.

   That's why I usually do not give "spare change," and I don't think I will in the future. These people will get along without me. Someone else will come up with money for their coffee or their liquor, or, at worst, they will just have to do without. I will continue to contribute occasionally to a charitable organization, not simply (I hope) to salve my conscience but because I believe that these organizations actually do good work. But I will not attempt to be a mini-charitable organization, distributing (probably to the unworthy) spare change.

Finally, here are a few comments about the essay:

The title is informative, alerting the reader to the topic and the author's position. (By the way, the student told us that in her next-to-last draft the title was "Is It Right to Spare 'Spare Change'?" This title, like the revision, introduces the topic but not the author's position. The revised version seems to us to be more striking.)

The opening paragraph holds a reader's interest, partly by alluding to the familiar phrase, "the deserving poor," and partly by introducing the *un*familiar phrase, "the *un*deserving poor." Notice, too, that this opening paragraph ends by clearly asserting the author's thesis. Of course writers need not always announce their thesis early, but it is usually advisable to do so. Readers like to know where they are going.

The second paragraph begins by voicing what probably is the reader's somewhat uneasy—perhaps even negative—response to the first paragraph. That is, *the writer has a sense of her audience;* she knows how her reader feels, and she takes account of the feeling.

The third paragraph clearly sets forth the alternatives. A reader may disagree with the writer's attitude, but the alternatives seem to be stated fairly.

The last two paragraphs are more personal than the earlier paragraphs. The writer, more or less having stated what she takes to be the facts, now is entitled to offer a highly personal response to them.

The final paragraph nicely wraps things up by means of the words "spare change," which go back to the title and to the end of the first paragraph. The reader thus experiences a sensation of completeness. The essayist of course has not solved the problem for all of us for all times, but she presents a thoughtful argument and she ends the essay effectively.

Exercise

In an essay of 500 words state a claim and support it with evidence. Choose an issue in which you are genuinely interested and about which you already know something. You may want to interview a few experts, and you may want to do some reading, but don't try to write a highly researched paper. Sample topics:

1. Students in laboratory courses should not be required to participate in the dissection of animals.

2. Washington, D.C., should be granted statehood.

3. Puerto Rico should be granted statehood.

4. Women should, in wartime, be exempted from serving in combat.

5. The annual Miss America contest is an insult to women.

6. All Olympic sports should be open to professional competitors.

7. The government should not offer financial support to the arts

8. The chief fault of the curriculum in high school was. . . .

9. Grades should be abolished in college and university courses.

10. No specific courses should be required in colleges or universities.

6

Critical Writing: Using Sources

WHY USE SOURCES?

We have pointed out that one gets ideas by writing; in the exercise of writing a draft, ideas begin to form, and these ideas stimulate further ideas, especially when one questions—when one *thinks* about—what one has written. But of course in writing about complex, serious questions, nobody is expected to invent all the answers. On the contrary, a writer is expected to be familiar with the chief answers already produced by others, and to make use of them through selective incorporation and criticism. In short, writers are not expected to reinvent the wheel; rather, they are expected to make good use of it, and perhaps round it off a bit or replace a defective spoke. In order to think out your own views in writing, you are expected to do some preliminary research into the views of others.

We use the word "research" broadly. It need not require taking copious notes on everything written on your topic; rather, it can involve no more than familiarizing yourself with at least some of the chief responses to your topic. In one way or another, almost everyone does some research. If we are going to buy a car, we may read an issue or two of a magazine that rates cars, or we may talk to a few people who own models that we are thinking of buying, and then we visit a couple of dealers to find out who is offering the best price.

Research, in short, is not an activity conducted only by college professors or by students who visit the library in order to write research papers. It is an activity that all of us engage in to some degree. In writing a research paper, you will engage in it to a great degree. But doing research is not the whole of a research paper. The reader expects the writer to have *thought* about the research, and to develop an argument based on the findings.

Most businesses today devote an entire section to research and development. That's what is needed in writing, too. The reader wants not only a lot of facts but also a developed idea, a point to which the facts lead. Don't let your reader say of your paper what Gertrude Stein said of Oakland, California: "When you get there, there isn't any there there."

Even an argument on a topic on which we all may think we already have opinions, such as whether the Olympics should be open to professional athletes, will benefit from research. By reading books and articles, a writer can learn such relevant things as: (1) even in ancient Greece the athletes were subsidized, so that in effect they were professionals; (2) eligibility today varies from sport to sport. For instance, in tennis, professionals under age twenty-one can compete; in basketball, players who had until recently played in National Basketball Association games were ineligible, but anyone else could compete, including European professionals — or even Antoine Carr, an American who had played in the Italian Basketball League and supposedly earned $200,000. Soccer professionals can compete, except those who have played in World Cup matches for European or South American countries. Track events bar professionals — even if they have professionally competed only in some other sport. Thus, Ron Brown, a sprinter, was barred from the track events in 1984 because he had signed a professional football contract. Football is not an Olympic event, and Brown in fact had not played professional football — he had merely signed a contract — but he nevertheless was barred. Of course a writer can argue that professionals in any sport should (or should not) be allowed to compete in the Olympics, but the argument will scarcely compel assent if it takes no account of what is already being done, and why it is being done.

To take a related matter, consider arguments about whether athletes should be permitted to take anabolic steroids, drugs that supposedly build up muscle, restore energy, and enhance aggressiveness. A thoughtful argument on this subject will have to take account of information that the writer can gather only by doing some research. Do steroids really have the effects commonly attributed to them? And are they dangerous? If they are dangerous, how dangerous are they? (After all, competitive sports are inherently dangerous, some of them highly so. Many boxers, jockeys, and football players have suffered severe injury, even death, from competing. Does anyone believe that anabolic steroids are more dangerous than the contests themselves?) Obviously, again, a respectable argument about steroids will have to show awareness of what is known about them.

Or take this question: Why did President Truman order that atomic bombs be dropped on Hiroshima and Nagasaki? The most obvious answer is, to end the war, but some historians believe he had a very different purpose. In their view, Japan's defeat was ensured before the bombs were dropped, and the Japanese were ready to surrender; the bombs were dropped not to save American (or Japanese) lives, but to show Russia that we were not to be pushed around. Scholars who hold this view, such as Gar Alperovitz in *Atomic Diplomacy,* argue that Japanese civilians in Hiroshima and Nagasaki were incinerated not to save the lives of American soldiers who otherwise would have died in an invasion of Japan, but to teach Stalin a lesson. Dropping the bombs, it is argued, marked not the end of the Pacific War but the beginning of the cold war.

One must ask: What evidence supports this argument or claim or thesis, which assumes that Truman could not have thought the bomb was needed to defeat the Japanese because the Japanese knew they were defeated and would soon surrender without a hard-fought defense that would cost hundreds of thousands of lives? What about the momentum that had built up to use the bomb? After all, years of effort and two billion dollars had been expended to produce a weapon with the intention of using it to end the war against Germany. But Germany had been defeated without the use of the bomb. Meanwhile, the war in the Pacific continued unabated. If the argument we are considering is correct, all this background counted for little or nothing in Truman's decision, a decision purely diplomatic and coolly indifferent to human life. The task for the writer is to evaluate the evidence available, and then to argue for or against the view that Truman's purpose in dropping the bomb was to impress the Soviet government.

A student writing on the topic (whether arguing one view or the other) will certainly want to read the chief books on the subject (Alperovitz's, cited above, Martin Sherwin's *A World Destroyed,* and John Toland's *The Rising Sun*), and perhaps reviews of them, especially the reviews in journals devoted to political science. (Reading a searching review of a serious scholarly book is a good way to identify quickly some of the book's main contributions and controversial claims.) Truman's letters and statements, and books and articles about Truman, are also clearly relevant, and doubtless important articles are to be found in recent issues of scholarly journals. In fact, even an essay on such a topic as whether Truman was morally justified in using the atomic bomb for *any* purpose will be a stronger essay if it is well informed about such matters as the estimated loss of life that an invasion would have cost, the international rules governing weapons, and Truman's own statements about the issue.

How does one go about finding the material needed to write a well-informed argument? We will provide help, but first we want to offer a few words about choosing a topic.

CHOOSING A TOPIC

We will be brief. If a topic is not assigned, choose one that

1. interests you, and that
2. can be researched with reasonable thoroughness in the allotted time.

Topics such as affirmative action, abortion, and bilingual education obviously impinge on our lives, and it may well be that one such topic is of especial interest to you.

As for the second point — a compassable topic — if the chief evidence for your tentative topic consists of a thousand unpublished letters a thousand miles away, or is in German and you don't read German, you will have to find something else to write on. Similarly, a topic such as the causes of World War II can hardly be mastered in a few weeks or argued in a ten-page paper. It is simply too big.

You can, however, write a solid paper analyzing, evaluating, and arguing for or against General Eisenhower's views on atomic warfare. What were they — and when did he hold them? (In his books of 1948 and 1963 Eisenhower says that he opposed the use of the bomb before Hiroshima, and that he argued with Secretary of War Henry Stimson against dropping it, but what evidence supports these claims? Was Eisenhower attempting to rewrite history in his books?) Eisenhower's own writings, and books on Eisenhower, will of course be the major sources for a paper on this topic, but you will also want to look at books and articles about Stimson, and at publications that contain information about the views of other generals, so that, for instance, you can compare Eisenhower's view with Marshall's or MacArthur's.

Your instructor understands that you are not going to spend a year writing a 200-page book, but you should understand that you must do more than consult the article on Eisenhower in one encyclopedia and the article on atomic energy in another encyclopedia.

FINDING MATERIAL

Your sources will of course depend on your topic. Some topics will require research in the library only, but others may require interviews. If you are writing about some aspect of AIDS, for instance, you probably will find it useful to consult your college health center.

For facts, you ought to try to consult experts — for instance, members of the faculty; for opinions and attitudes, you will usually consult interested laypersons. Remember, however, that experts have their biases, and that "ordinary" people may have knowledge that experts lack. When interviewing experts, keep in mind Picasso's comment: "You musn't always believe what I say. Questions tempt you to tell lies, particularly when there is no answer."

INTERVIEWING PEERS
AND LOCAL AUTHORITIES

If you are interviewing your peers, you will probably want to make an effort to get a representative sample. Of course, even within a group not all members share a single view — many African Americans favor affirmative action but not all do, and many gays favor legalizing gay marriage but, again, some don't. Make an effort to talk to a range of people who might be expected to offer varied opinions. You may learn some unexpected things.

Here we will concentrate, however, on interviews with experts.

1. Finding subjects for interviews. If you are looking for expert opinions, you may want to start with a faculty member on your campus. You may already know the instructor, or you may have to scan the catalog to see who teaches courses relevant to your topic. Department secretaries are good sources of information about the special interests of the faculty, and also about lecturers who will be visiting the campus.

2. Doing preliminary homework. (1) Know something about the person whom you will be interviewing. Biographical reference works such as *Who's Who in America, Who's Who Among Black Americans, Who's Who of American Women,* and *Directory of American Scholars* may include your interviewee, or, again, a departmental secretary may be able to provide a vita for a faculty member. (2) In requesting the interview, make evident your interest in the topic and in the person. (If you know something about the person, you will be able to indicate why you are asking him or her.) (3) Request the interview, preferably in writing, a week in advance, and ask for ample time—probably half an hour to an hour. Indicate whether or not the material will be confidential, and (if you want to use a recorder) ask if you may record the interview. (4) If the person accepts the invitation, ask if he or she recommends any preliminary reading, and establish a time and a suitable place, preferably not the cafeteria during lunchtime.

3. Preparing thoroughly. (1) If your interviewee recommended any reading, or has written on the topic, read the material. (2) Tentatively formulate some questions, keeping in mind that (unless you are simply gathering material for a survey of opinions) you want more than "yes" or "no" answers. Questions beginning with "Why" and "How" will usually require the interviewee to go beyond "yes" and "no."

Even if your subject has consented to let you bring a recorder, be prepared to take notes on points that strike you as especially significant; without written notes, you will have nothing if the recorder has malfunctioned. Further, by taking occasional notes you will give the interviewee some time to think, and perhaps to rephrase or to amplify a remark.

4. Conducting the interview. (1) Begin by engaging in brief conversation, without taking notes. If the interviewee has agreed to let you use a recorder, settle on the place where you will put the recorder. (2) Come prepared with an opening question or two, but as the interview proceeds don't hesitate to ask questions that you had not anticipated asking. (3) Near the end—you and your subject have probably agreed on the length of the interview—ask the subject if he or she wishes to add anything, perhaps by way of clarifying some earlier comment. (4) Conclude by thanking the interviewee, and by offering to provide a copy of the final version of your paper.

5. Writing up the interview. (1) As soon as possible—certainly within twenty-four hours after the interview—review your notes and clarify them. At this stage, you can still remember the meaning of your abbreviated notes and shorthand devices (maybe you have been using *n* to stand for *nurses* in clinics where abortions are performed), but if you wait even a whole day you may be puzzled by your own notes. If you have recorded the interview, you may want to transcribe all of it—the laboriousness of this task is one good reason why many interviewers do not use recorders—and you may then want to scan the whole and mark the parts that now strike you as especially significant. If you have taken notes by hand, type them up, along with your own observations, for example, "Jones was very tentative on this matter, but she said she was inclined to believe that . . ." (2) Be especially careful to indicate which words are direct quotations. If in doubt, check with the interviewer.

USING THE LIBRARY

Most topics, as we have said, will require research in the library. Notice that we have spoken of a topic, not of a thesis or even of a *hypothesis* (tentative thesis). Advanced students, because they are familiar with the rudiments of a subject (say, the origins of the cold war) usually have not only a topic but also a hypothesis or even a thesis in mind. Less experienced students are not always in this happy position: Before they can offer a hypothesis, they have to find a problem. Some instructors assign topics; others rely on students to find their own topics, based on readings in the course or in other courses.

When you have a *topic* ("Eisenhower and the atomic bomb"), and perhaps a *thesis* (an attitude toward the topic, a claim that you want to argue, such as "Eisenhower's disapproval of the bomb was the product of the gentleman-soldier code that he had learned at West Point"), it is often useful to scan a relevant book. You may already know of a relevant book, and it is likely in turn to cite others. If, however, you don't know of any book, you can find one by consulting the catalog (whether card or computerized) in the library, which lists books not only by author and by title but also by subject.

Of course if you are writing about Eisenhower, in the catalog you will find entries for books by him and about him listed under his name. But what if you are writing about the controversy over the use of steroids by athletes? If you look up "steroids" in the catalog, you will find an entry for steroids, directions to "see also" several other specified topics, some of which will doubtless be relevant to your topic, and entries for books the library has on steroids.

In fact, to learn what headings are included in the catalog, you don't even have to go to the catalog. You have only to look at a tome called *Subject Headings Used in the Dictionary Catalogs of the Library of Congress*, where you will find headings with cross-references indicated by *sa* ("see also"). Let's assume that you want to write about athletes' use of steroids. If you check *Subject Headings* for "steroids," you'll find an entry, and you'll also find a cross-reference to "anabolic steroids." If you look up "athletes" you'll find several cross-references; not all of these will, of course, be relevant, but you'll certainly want to follow up on the cross-references to "Athletic ability" and to "Medical examinations," and probably to "Sports medicine." After you have jotted down the headings that seem relevant, go to the catalog, look for the headings you have located, and you will find entries for books the library has on the topic. If your library has a computerized on-line catalog, the librarian will show you how to use it.

If there are many books on the topic, how do you choose just one? Choose first a fairly thin one, of fairly recent date, published by a reputable publisher. You may even want to jot down two or three titles and then check reviews of these books before choosing one book to skim. Five indexes enable you easily to locate book reviews in newspapers and periodicals:

> *Book Review Digest* (1905–)
>
> *Book Review Index* (1965–)
>
> *Humanities Index* (1974–)
>
> *Index to Book Reviews in the Humanities* (1960–)
>
> *Social Sciences Index* (1974–)

Book Review Digest includes brief extracts from the reviews, and so look there first, but its coverage is not as broad as the other indexes.

Scanning a recent book that has been favorably reviewed will give you an overview of your topic, from which you can formulate or reformulate a tentative thesis.

A very recent book may include notes or a bibliography that will put you on to most of the chief discussions of the problem, but unless the book came out yesterday, it is bound to be dated. And even if it came out yesterday it was probably written a year ago (it takes from six months to a year to turn a manuscript into a book), and so you will want to look for recent material, probably articles published in recent periodicals. The indexes with broadest coverage of periodicals are:

> *Humanities Index* (1974–)
>
> *Readers' Guide to Periodical Literature* (1900–)
>
> *Social Sciences Index* (1974–)

Readers' Guide is an index to more than a hundred serials, chiefly popular or semipopular publications such as *The Atlantic, Sports Illustrated,* and *Newsweek.* These publications have their uses, especially for papers dealing with current controversies, but for most topics one needs extended scholarly discussions published in learned journals, and for help in finding them one turns to the other two indexes.

Computer searches are available on most campuses, enabling you to see at a glance titles published during several years, whereas the printed indexes that we have just mentioned cover only one year in each volume.

INFOTRAC (or *InfoTrac*), for instance, is a CD-ROM system that searches publications of the last four years. The disc is preinstalled in a microcomputer that can be accessed from a computer terminal with a printer, and the instructions are easy to follow. INFOTRAC, which on many campuses has virtually replaced *Readers' Guide,* indexes authors and subjects in many popular and in some scholarly magazines and newspapers. It provides access to several database indexes, including

The *General Periodicals Index,* available in the Academic Library Edition (about 1,100 general and scholarly periodicals) and in the Public Library Edition (about 1,100 popular magazines).

The *Academic Index* (400 general-interest publications, all of which are also available in the Academic Library Edition of the *General Periodicals Index*).

The *Magazine Index Plus* (the four most recent years of the *New York Times,* the two most recent months of the *Wall Street Journal,* and 400 popular magazines, all of which are included in the Public Library Edition of the *General Periodicals Index*).

The National Newspaper (the four most recent years of the *New York Times,* the *Christian Science Monitor,* the *Washington Post,* and the *Los Angeles Times*).

For some specialized topics, however, you may still have to rely on print indexes. One widely used index is the *New York Times Index* (1851–), which lets you find articles published in the newspaper. Here are some valuable specialized indexes:

Applied Science and Technology Index (1958–)

Art Index (1929–)

Biological and Agricultural Index (1964–)

Biography Index (1947–)

Business Periodicals Index (1958–)

Chemical Abstracts (1907–)

Dramatic Index (1909–49)

Education Index (1929–)

Engineering Index Monthly and Author Index (1906–)

Film Literature Index (1973–)

Index to Legal Periodicals (1908–)

International Index to Film Periodicals (1972–)

MLA International Bibliography (1921–); an annual listing of books and articles on linguistics and on literature in modern languages

Monthly Catalog of United States Government Publications (1895–)

Music Index (1949–)

Philosopher's Index (1967–)

Poole's Index for Periodical Literature (1802–1907)

Public Affairs Information Service Bulletin (1915–)

United Nations Document Index (1950–)

Ordinarily it makes sense to begin with the most recent year, and to work one's way backward, collecting citations for material of the last four or five years. The recent material usually incorporates older findings, but occasionally you will have to consult an early piece, especially if the recent material suggests that it is still vital.

An enormous amount of computerized information, much of it updated daily, is also available through databases such as ERIC and DIALOG. Your reference librarian can tell you what services are available (and at what cost) at your institution.

READING AND TAKING NOTES

Most readers and writers have idiosyncratic ways of going about the business of doing research. Some can read only when their feet are on the desk, and others can take notes only when their feet are planted on the floor. The suggestions that follow are simply our way of doing research; we recommend it, but we know that others are quite successful using different methods.

When we have jotted down the citations to books and articles, and have actually obtained a work from the library, we usually scan it rather than read it, to get an idea of whether it is worth reading carefully, and, even more important, whether it is worth the labor of taking notes. For an article, look especially at the beginning. Sometimes an abstract gives the gist of the whole piece, but even if there is no abstract, the opening paragraph may announce the topic, the thesis, and the approach. And look at the end of the essay, where you may find a summary. If the article still seems worth reading, read it, perhaps without taking notes, and then (having got the sense of it) read it again, taking notes. For a book, scan the table of contents and the preface to see if it really is as relevant as the title suggests. If the book has an index, you may want to check the page references to some essential topic or term, to see how much relevant material really is in the book.

When it comes to taking notes, all researchers have their own habits that they swear by, and they can't imagine any other way of working. Possibly you already are fixed in your habits, but if not, you may want to borrow ours. We use 4-by-6-inch index cards. Smaller cards don't have space for enough notes, and larger cards have space for too much. We recommend the following techniques.

1. Write in ink (pencil gets smudgy).
2. Put only one idea on each card (though an idea may include several facts).
3. Write on only one side of the card (notes on the back usually get lost).
4. Summarize, for the most part, rather than quote at length.
5. Quote only passages in which the writing is especially effective, or passages that are in some way crucial.
6. Make sure that all quotations are exact. Enclose quoted words within quotation marks, indicate omissions by ellipses (three spaced periods: . . .), and enclose within square brackets ([ ]) any insertions or other additions you make.
7. *Never* copy a passage, changing an occasional word. *Either* copy it word for word, with punctuation intact, and enclose it within quotation marks, *or* summarize it drastically. If you copy a passage but change a word here and there, you may later make the mistake of using your note verbatim in your essay, and you will be guilty of plagiarism.
8. Give the page number of your source, whether you summarize or quote. If a quotation you have copied runs in the original from the bottom of page 210 to the top of page 211, in your notes put a diagonal line (/) after the last word on page 210, so that later, if in your paper you quote only the material from page 210, you will know that you must cite 210 and not 210–11.
9. Indicate the source. The author's last name is enough if you have consulted only one work by the author; but if you consult more than one work by an author, you need further identification, such as the author's name and a short title.
10. Don't hesitate to add your own comments about the substance of what you are recording. Such comments as "but contrast with Sherwin" or "seems illogical" or "evidence?" will ensure that you are thinking as well as writing, and will be of value when you come to transform your notes into a draft. Be sure, however, to enclose such notes within double diagonals (//), or to mark them in some other way, so that later you will know they are yours and not your source's.
11. Put a brief heading on the card, such as "Truman's last words on A-bomb."
12. Write a bibliographic card for each source, copying the author's name as it appears on the work (but last name first), the name of the translator if there is one, and (for a book) the title (taken from the title page, not from the cover), place of publication, publisher,

and date. For a journal, note (in addition to the author's name, which you record with the author's last name first) the title of the article, the title of the journal, the volume and year for scholarly journals, and the day, week, or month and the year for popular works such as *Time*, and the pages that the article encompasses.

A WORD ABOUT PLAGIARISM

Plagiarism is the unacknowledged use of someone else's work. The word comes from a Latin word for "kidnapping," and plagiarism is indeed the stealing of something engendered by someone else. We won't deliver a sermon on the dishonesty (and folly) of plagiarism; we intend only to help you understand exactly what plagiarism is, and the first thing to say is that plagiarism is not limited to the unacknowledged quotation of words.

A *paraphrase* is a sort of word-by-word or phrase-by-phrase translation of the author's language into your language. True, if you paraphrase you are using your own words, but you are also using someone else's ideas, and, equally important, you are using this other person's sequence of thoughts. Even if you change every third word in your source, and you do not give the author credit, you are plagiarizing. Here is an example of this sort of plagiarism, based on the previous sentence:

> Even if you alter every third or fourth word from your source, and you fail to give credit to the author, you will be guilty of plagiarism.

Even if the writer of this paraphrase had cited a source after it, the writer would still be guilty of plagiarism, because the passage borrows not only the idea but the shape of the presentation, the sentence structure. The writer of this passage hasn't really written anything; he or she has only adapted something. What the writer needs to do is to write something like this:

> Changing an occasional word does not free the writer from the obligation to cite a source.

And the source would still need to be cited, if the central idea were not a commonplace one.

You are plagiarizing if without giving credit you use someone else's ideas — even if you put these ideas entirely into your own words. When you use another's ideas, you must indicate your indebtedness by saying something like "Alperovitz points out that . . ." or "Secretary of War Stimson, as Martin Sherwin notes, never expressed himself on this point." Alperovitz and Sherwin pointed out something that you had not thought of, and so you must give them credit if you want to use their findings.

Again, even if after a paraphrase you cite your source, you are plagiarizing. How, you may wonder, can you be guilty of plagiarism if you cite a source? Easy. A reader assumes that the citation refers to information or an opinion, *not* to the presentation or development of the idea; and of course in a paraphrase you are not presenting or developing the material in your own way.

Now consider this question: *Why* paraphrase? Often there is no good answer. Since a paraphrase is as long as the original, you may as well quote the original, if you think that a passage of that length is worth quoting. Probably it is *not* worth quoting in full; probably you should *not* paraphrase but rather should drastically *summarize* most of it, and perhaps quote a particularly effective phrase or two.

Generally what you should do is to take the idea and put it entirely into your own words, perhaps reducing a paragraph of a hundred words to a sentence of ten words, but of course you must still give credit for the idea. If you believe that the original hundred words are so perfectly put that they cannot be transformed without great loss, you'll have to quote them, and cite your source. But clearly there is no point in paraphrasing the author's hundred words into a hundred of your own. Either quote or summarize, but cite the source.

Keep in mind, too, that almost all generalizations about human nature, no matter how common and familiar (e.g., "males are innately more aggressive than females") are not indisputable facts; they are at best hypotheses on which people differ and therefore should either not be asserted at all or should be supported by some cited source or authority. Similarly, because nearly all statistics (whether on the intelligence of criminals or the accuracy of lie detectors) are the result of some particular research and may well have been superseded or challenged by other investigators, it is advisable to cite a source for any statistics you use unless you are convinced they are indisputable, such as the number of registered voters in Memphis in 1988.

On the other hand, there is something called **common knowledge,** and the sources for such information need not be cited. The term does not, however, mean exactly what it seems to. It is common knowledge, of course, that Ronald Reagan was an American president (so you don't cite a source when you make that statement), and under the conventional interpretation of this doctrine, it is also common knowledge that he was born in 1911. In fact, of course, few people other than Reagan's wife and children know this date. Still, information that can be found in many places and that is indisputable belongs to all of us; therefore a writer need not cite her source when she says that Reagan was born in 1911. Probably she checked a dictionary or an encyclopedia for the date, but the source doesn't matter. Dozens of sources will give exactly the same information and, in fact, no reader wants to be bothered with a citation on such a point.

Some students have a little trouble developing a sense of what is and what is not common knowledge. Although, as we have just said, readers don't want to hear about the sources for information that is indisputable and can be documented in many places, if you are in doubt about whether to cite a source, cite it. Better risk boring the reader a bit than risk being accused of plagiarism.

WRITING THE PAPER

Organizing One's Notes

If you have read thoughtfully and taken careful (and, again, thoughtful) notes on your reading, and then (yet again) have thought about these notes, you are well on the way to writing a good paper. You have, in fact, already written some of it, in your notes. By now you should clearly have in mind the thesis you intend to argue. But of course you still have to organize the material, and, doubtless, even as you set about organizing it you will find points that will require you to do some additional research and much additional thinking.

Sort the index cards into packets, each packet devoted to one theme or point (for instance, one packet on the extent of use of steroids, another on evidence that steroids are harmful, yet another on arguments that even if harmful they should be permitted). Put aside all notes that—however interesting—you now see are irrelevant to your paper.

Next, arrange the packets into a tentative sequence. In effect, you are preparing a **working outline.** At its simplest, say, you will give three arguments on behalf of X, and then three counterarguments. (Or you might decide that it is better to alternate material from the two sets of three packets each, following each argument with an objection. At this stage, you can't be sure of the organization you will finally use, but make a tentative decision.)

The First Draft

Draft the essay, without worrying much about an elegant opening paragraph. Just write some sort of adequate opening that states the topic and your thesis. When you revise the whole later, you can put some effort into developing an effective opening. (Most experienced writers find that the opening paragraph in the final version is almost the last thing they write.)

If you handwrite or typewrite your draft, leave wide margins all around, so that later, when you reread it, you can add material. And try to use a separate sheet for each separable topic, such as each argument. This procedure lets you avoid cutting and pasting or recopying if you find, at a later stage, that you need to reorganize the essay. Even better is to compose on a word processor, which will let you effortlessly make additions anywhere.

In writing your draft, carefully copy into the draft all quotations that you plan to use. The mere act of copying the quotations will make you think about them. If you are faced with a long quotation, resist the temptation to write "see card" in your draft; copy the entire quotation, or paste the card (or a photocopy of it) on the page of your draft. (In the next section of this chapter we will talk briefly about leading into quotations, and about the form of quotations.) Include the citations, perhaps within double diagonals (///) in the draft, so that later if you need to check references in the library you don't have to go hunting through your index cards.

Later Drafts

Give the draft, and yourself, a rest, perhaps for a day or two, and then go back to it, read it over, make necessary revisions, and then **outline** it. That is, on a sheet of paper chart the organization and development, perhaps by jotting down a sentence summarizing each paragraph or each group of closely related paragraphs. Your outline or map may now show you that the paper obviously suffers from poor organization. For instance, it may reveal that you neglected to respond to one argument, or that one point is needlessly treated in two places. It may also help you to see that if you gave three arguments and then three counterarguments, you probably should instead have followed each argument with its rebuttal. Or, on the other hand, if you alternated arguments and objections, it may now seem better to use two main groups, all the arguments and then all the criticisms.

No one formula is always right. Much will depend on the complexity of the material. If the arguments are highly complex, it is better to respond to them one by one than to expect a reader to hold three complex arguments in mind before you get around to responding. If, however, the arguments can be stated briefly and clearly, it is effective to state all three, and then to go on to the responses. If you write on a word processor you will find it easy, even fun, to move passages of text around. If you write by hand, or on a typewriter, unless you put only one topic on each sheet you will have to use scissors and paste or transparent tape to produce your next draft — and your next. Allow enough time to produce several drafts.

A few more words about organization:

a. There is a difference between a paper that *has* an organization

and

b. a paper that *shows* what the organization is.

Write papers of the second sort, but (there is always a "but") take care not to belabor the obvious. Inexperienced writers sometimes either hide the organization so thoroughly that a reader cannot find it, or, on the other hand, they so ploddingly lay out the structure ("Eighth, I will show . . . ") that the reader becomes impatient. Yet it is better to be overly explicit than to be obscure.

The ideal, of course, is the middle route. Make the overall strategy of your organization evident by occasional explicit signs at the beginning of a paragraph ("We have seen . . . ," "It is time to consider the objections . . . ," "By far the most important . . . "); elsewhere make certain that the implicit structure is evident to the reader. When you reread your draft, if you try to imagine that you are one of your classmates, you will probably be able to sense exactly where explicit signs are needed, and where they are not needed.

Choosing a Tentative Title

By now a couple of tentative titles for your essay should have crossed your mind. If possible, choose a title that is both interesting and informative. Consider these three titles:

```
Are Steroids Harmful?
The Fuss over Steroids
Steroids: A Dangerous Game
```

"Are Steroids Harmful?" is faintly interesting, and it lets the reader know the gist of the subject, but it gives no clue about the writer's thesis, the writer's contention or argument. "The Fuss over Steroids" is somewhat better, for it gives information about the writer's position. "Steroids: A Dangerous Game" is still better; it announces the subject ("steroids") and the thesis ("dangerous"), and it also displays a touch of wit, because "game" glances at the world of athletics.

Don't try too hard, however; better a simple, direct, informative title than a strained, puzzling, or overly cute one. And remember to make sure that everything in your essay is relevant to your title. In fact, your title should help you to organize the essay and to delete irrelevant material.

The Final Draft

When at last you have a draft that is for the most part satisfactory, check to make sure that **transitions** from sentence to sentence and from paragraph to paragraph are clear ("Further evidence," "On the other hand," "A weakness, however, is apparent"), and then worry about your opening and your closing paragraphs. Your **opening paragraph** should be clear, interesting, and focused; if neither the title nor the first paragraph announces your thesis, the second paragraph probably should do so.

The **final paragraph** need not say, "In conclusion, I have shown that . . . " It should effectively end the essay, but it need not summarize your conclusions. We have already offered a few words about final paragraphs (p. 142), but the best way to learn how to write such paragraphs is to study the endings of some of the essays in this book, and to adopt the strategies that appeal to you.

Be sure that all indebtedness is properly acknowledged. We have talked about plagiarism; now we will turn to the business of introducing quotations effectively.

QUOTING FROM SOURCES

The Use and Abuse of Quotations

When is it necessary, or appropriate, to quote? Sometimes the reader must see the exact words of your source; the gist won't do. If you are arguing that Z's definition of "rights" is too inclusive, your readers have to know exactly how Z defined "rights." Your brief summary of the definition may be unfair to Z; in fact, you want to convince your readers that you are being fair, and so you quote Z's definition, word for word. Moreover, if the passage is only a sentence or two long, or even if it runs to a paragraph, it may be so compactly stated that it defies summary. And to attempt to paraphrase it — substituting "natural" for "inalienable," and so forth — saves no space and only introduces imprecision. There is nothing to do but to quote it, word for word.

Second, you may want to quote a passage which could be summarized but which is so effectively stated that you want your readers to have the pleasure of reading the original. Of course readers will not give you credit for writing these words, but they will give you credit for your taste, and for your effort to make especially pleasant the business of reading your paper.

In short, use (but don't overuse) quotations. Speaking roughly, quotations should occupy no more than 10 or 15 percent of your paper, and they may occupy much less. Most of your paper should set forth your ideas, not other people's ideas.

How to Quote

Long and Short Quotations • **Long quotations** (five or more lines of typed prose, or three or more lines of poetry) are set off from your text. To set off material, start on a new line, indent ten spaces from the left margin and type the quotation double-spaced. (Some style manuals call for triple-spacing before and after a long quotation, and for typing it single-spaced. Ask your instructors if they have a preference.) Do not enclose quotations within quotation marks if you are setting them off.

Short quotations are treated differently. They are embedded within the text; they are enclosed within quotation marks but otherwise they do not stand out.

All quotations, whether set off or embedded, must be exact. If you omit any words, you must indicate the ellipsis by substituting three spaced periods for the omission; if you insert any words or punctuation, you must indicate the addition by enclosing it within square brackets, not to be confused with parentheses.

Leading into a Quotation • Now for a less mechanical matter, the way in which a quotation is introduced. To say that it is "introduced" implies that one leads into it, though on rare occasions a quotation appears without an introduction, perhaps immediately after the title. Normally one leads into a quotation by giving the name of the author and (no less important) clues about the content of the quotation and the purpose it serves in the present essay. For example:

```
William James provides a clear answer to Huxley when he
says that ". . ."
```

The writer has been writing about Huxley, and now is signaling readers that they will be getting James's reply. The writer is also signaling (in "a clear answer") that the reply is satisfactory. If the writer believed that James's answer was not really acceptable, the lead-in might have run thus:

```
William James attempts to answer Huxley, but his re-
sponse does not really meet the difficulty Huxley calls
attention to. James writes, ". . ."
```

Or:

```
William James provided what he took to be an answer to
Huxley when he said that ". . ."
```

In this last example, clearly the words "what he took to be an answer" imply that the essayist will show, after the quotation from James, that the answer is in some degree inadequate. Or the essayist may wish to suggest the inadequacy even more strongly:

```
William James provided what he took to be an answer to
Huxley, but he used the word "religion" in a way that
Huxley would not have allowed. James argues that ". . ."
```

If after reading something by Huxley the writer had merely given us "William James says . . . ," we wouldn't know whether we were getting confirmation, refutation, or something else. The essayist would have put a needless burden on the readers. Generally speaking, the more difficult the quotation, the more important is the introductory or explanatory lead-in, but even the simplest quotation profits from some sort of brief lead-in, such as "James reaffirms this point when he says . . ."

DOCUMENTATION

In the course of your essay, you will probably quote or summarize material derived from a source. You must give credit, and although there is no one form of documentation to which all scholarly fields subscribe, two forms are widely followed. One, established by the Modern Language Association (MLA), is used chiefly in the humanities; the other, established by the American Psychological Association (APA), is used chiefly in the social sciences.

We include two papers that use sources. The first, "Why Trials Should Not Be Televised" (p. 193), uses the MLA format; the second, "Why Handguns Must Be Outlawed" (p. 277), uses the APA format. (You may notice that various styles are illustrated in other selections we have included.)

A Note on Footnotes (and Endnotes)

Before discussing these two formats a few words about footnotes are in order. Before the MLA and the APA developed their rules of style, citations commonly were given in footnotes. Although today footnotes are not so frequently used to give citations, they still may be useful for another purpose. (The MLA suggests endnotes rather than footnotes, and of course endnotes are easier to type, unless you use a word processing program, but all readers know that in fact footnotes are preferable to endnotes. After all, who wants to keep shifting from a page of text to a page of notes at the rear?) If you want to include some material that may seem intrusive in the body of the paper, you may relegate it to a footnote. For example, in a footnote you might translate a quotation given in a foreign language, or you might demote from text to footnote a paragraph explaining why you are not taking account of such-and-such a point. By putting the matter in a footnote you are signaling the reader that it is dispensable; it is something relevant but not essential, something extra that you are, so to speak, tossing in. Don't make a habit of writing this sort of note, but there are times when it is appropriate.

To indicate in the body of the text that you are adding a footnote, type a raised arabic numeral. Do *not* first hit the space bar; do *not* type a period after the numeral; do *not* enclose the numeral within parentheses. Usually the superior numeral is placed at the end of the sentence, but place it earlier if clarity requires. If the numeral is at the end of a sentence, hit the space bar twice before beginning the next sentence. If the numeral is within the sentence, hit the space bar once, and continue the sentence.

The note itself will go at the bottom of the page of text on which the footnote number appears. After the last line of text on the page, double-space twice, then indent five spaces, elevate the carriage half a line, type the numeral (again, without a period and without enclosing it within parentheses), lower the carriage, then hit the space bar once and type the note. If the note runs more than one line, type it double-spaced (unless your instructor tells you to the contrary), flush with the left margin. Double-space between notes, and begin each note with an indented raised numeral and then a capital letter. End each note with a period or, if the sentence calls for one, a question mark.

If you use a word processor, your software may do some of the job for you. It probably will automatically indent, elevate the footnote number, and print the note on the appropriate page.

MLA Format

This discussion is divided into two parts, a discussion of citations within the text of the essay, and a discussion of the list of references, called Works Cited, that is given at the end of the essay.

Citations within the Text · Brief citations within the body of the essay give credit, in a highly abbreviated way, to the sources for material you quote, summarize, or make use of in any other way. These "in-text citations" are made clear by a list of sources, titled Works Cited, appended to the essay. Thus, in your essay you may say something like this:

> Commenting on the relative costs of capital punishment
> and life imprisonment, Ernest van den Haag says that he
> doubts "that capital punishment really is more expen-
> sive" (33).

The **citation,** the number 33 in parentheses, means that the quoted words come from page 33 of a source (listed in Works Cited) written by van den Haag. Without Works Cited, a reader would have no way of knowing that you are quoting from page 33 of an article that appeared in the February 8, 1985, issue of *National Review.*

Usually the parenthetic citation appears at the end of a sentence, as in the example just given, but it can appear elsewhere; its position will depend chiefly on your ear, your eye, and the context. You might, for example, write the sentence thus:

> Ernest van den Haag doubts that "capital punishment
> really is more expensive" than life imprisonment (33),
> but other writers have presented figures that contradict
> him.

Five points must be made about these examples:

1. Quotation marks. The closing quotation mark appears after the last word of the quotation, *not* after the parenthetic citation. Since the citation is not part of the quotation, the citation is not included within the quotation marks.

2. Omission of words (ellipsis). If you are quoting a complete sentence or only a phrase, as in the examples given, you do not need to indicate (by three spaced periods) that you are omitting material before or after the quotation. But if for some reason you want to omit an interior part of the quotation, you must indicate the omission by inserting an *ellipsis,* the three spaced dots. To take a simple example, if you omit the word "really" from van den Haag's phrase, you must alert the reader to the omission:

```
Ernest van den Haag doubts that "capital punishment
. . . is more expensive" than life imprisonment (33).
```

Suppose you are quoting a sentence but wish to omit material from the end of the sentence. Suppose, also, that the quotation forms the end of your sentence. Write a lead-in phrase, then quote as much from your source as you need, then type three spaced periods for the omission, close the quotation, give the parenthetic citation, and finally type a fourth period to indicate the end of your sentence.

Here's an example. Suppose you want to quote the first part of a sentence that runs, "We could insist that the cost of capital punishment be reduced so as to diminish the differences." Your sentence would incorporate the desired extract as follows:

```
Van den Haag says, "We could insist that the cost of
capital punishment be reduced . . . " (33).
```

3. Punctuation with parenthetic citations. In the preceding examples, the punctuation (a period or a comma in the examples) *follows* the citation. If, however, the quotation ends with a question mark, include the question mark *within* the quotation, since it is part of the quotation, and put a period *after* the citation.

```
Van den Haag asks, "Isn't it better--more just and more
useful--that criminals, if they do not have the cer-
tainty of punishment, at least run the risk of suffering
it?" (35).
```

But if the question mark is your own, and not in the source, put it after the citation, thus:

```
What answer can be given to van den Haag's doubt that
"capital punishment really is more expensive" (33)?
```

4. Two or more works by an author. If your list of Works Cited includes two or more works by an author, you cannot, in your essay, simply cite a page number, since the reader will not know which of the works you are referring to. You must give additional information. You can give it in your lead-in, thus:

> In "New Arguments against Capital Punishment," van den
> Haag expresses doubt "that capital punishment really is
> more expensive" than life imprisonment (33).

Or you can give the title, in a shortened form, within the citation:

> Van den Haag expresses doubt that "capital punishment
> really is more expensive" than life imprisonment ("New
> Arguments" 33).

5. Citing even when you do not quote. Even if you don't quote a source directly, but use its point in a paraphrase or a summary, you will give a citation:

> Van den Haag thinks that life imprisonment costs more
> than capital punishment (33).

Note that in all of the previous examples, the author's name is given in the text (rather than within the parenthetic citation). But there are several other ways of giving the citation, and we shall look at them now. (We have already seen, in the example given under paragraph 4, that the title and the page number can be given within the citation.)

AUTHOR AND PAGE NUMBER IN PARENTHESES

> It has been argued that life imprisonment is more costly
> than capital punishment (van den Haag 33).

AUTHOR, TITLE, AND PAGE NUMBER IN PARENTHESES

We have seen that if Works Cited includes two or more works by an author, you will have to give the title of the work on which you are drawing, either in your lead-in phrase or within the parenthetic citation. Similarly, if you are citing someone who is listed more than once in Works Cited, and for some reason you do not mention the name of the author or the work in your lead-in, you must add the information in your citation:

> Doubt has been expressed that capital punishment is as
> costly as life imprisonment (van den Haag, "New Argu-
> ments" 33).

A GOVERNMENT DOCUMENT OR A WORK
OF CORPORATE AUTHORSHIP

Treat the issuing body as the author. Thus, you will probably write something like this:

```
The Commission on Food Control, in Food Resources Today,
concludes that there is no danger (37-38).
```

A WORK BY TWO OR MORE AUTHORS

If a work is by *two or three authors,* give the names of all authors, either in the parenthetic citation (the first example below) or in a lead-in (the second example below):

```
There is not a single example of the phenomenon (Smith,
Dale, and Jones 182-83).

Smith, Dale, and Jones insist there is not a single
example of the phenomenon (182-83).
```

If there are *more than three authors,* give the last name of the first author, followed by "et al." (an abbreviation for *et alii,* Latin for "and others"), thus:

```
Gittleman et al. argue (43) that . . .
```

Or:

```
On average, the cost is even higher (Gittleman et al.
43).
```

PARENTHETIC CITATION OF AN INDIRECT SOURCE (CITATION OF MATERIAL THAT ITSELF WAS QUOTED OR SUMMARIZED IN YOUR SOURCE)

Suppose you are reading a book by Jones, in which she quotes Smith, and you wish to use Smith's material. Your citation must refer the reader to Jones — the source you are using — but of course you cannot attribute the words to Jones. You will have to make it clear that you are quoting Smith, and so, after a lead-in phrase like "Smith says," followed by the quotation, you will give a parenthetic citation along these lines:

```
(qtd. in Jones 324-25).
```

PARENTHETIC CITATION OF TWO OR MORE WORKS

```
The costs are simply too high (Smith 301; Jones 28).
```

Notice that a semicolon, followed by a space, separates the two sources.

A WORK IN MORE THAN ONE VOLUME

This is a bit tricky. If you have used only one volume, in Works Cited you will specify the volume, and so in the parenthetic in-text citation you will not need to specify the volume. All that you need to include in the citation is a page number, as illustrated by most of the examples that we have given.

If you have used more than one volume, your parenthetic citation will have to specify the volume as well as the page, thus:

```
Jackson points out that fewer than one hundred fifty
people fit this description (2: 351).
```

The reference is to page 351 in volume 2 of a work by Jackson.

If, however, you are citing not a page but an entire volume — let's say volume 2 — your parenthetic citation will look like this:

```
Jackson exhaustively studies this problem (vol. 2).
```

Or:

```
Jackson (vol. 2) exhaustively studies this problem.
```

Notice the following points:

1. In citing a volume and page, the volume number, like the page number, is given in arabic (not roman) numerals, even if the original used roman numerals.
2. The volume number is followed by a colon, then a space, then the page number.
3. If you cite a volume number without a page number, as in the last example quoted, the abbreviation is "vol." Otherwise do *not* use such abbreviations as "vol." and "p." and "pg."

AN ANONYMOUS WORK

For an anonymous work, give the title in your lead-in, or give it in a shortened form in your parenthetic citation:

```
A Prisoner's View of Killing includes a poll taken of
the inmates on Death Row (32).
```

Or:

```
A poll is available (Prisoner's View 32).
```

AN INTERVIEW

Probably you won't need a parenthetic citation, because you'll say something like

```
Vivian Berger, in an interview, said . . .
```

or

```
According to Vivian Berger, in an interview . . .
```

and when your reader turns to Works Cited, he or she will see that Berger is listed, along with the date of the interview. But if you do not mention the source's name in the lead-in, you will have to give it in the parentheses, thus:

```
Contrary to popular belief, the death penalty is not
reserved for serial killers and depraved murderers
(Berger).
```

The List of Works Cited (MLA Format)

As the previous pages explain, parenthetic documentation consists of references that become clear when the reader consults the list titled Works Cited, given at the end of an essay.

The list of Works Cited continues the pagination of the essay; if the last page of text is 10, then Works Cited begins on page 11. Type the page number in the upper right corner, a half inch from the top of the sheet and flush with the right margin. Next, type the heading: Works Cited (*not* enclosed within quotation marks), centered, one inch from the top, then double-space and type the first entry.

An Overview • Here are some general guidelines.

FORM ON THE PAGE

1. Begin each entry flush with the left margin, but if an entry runs to more than one line, indent five spaces, or a half inch, for each succeeding line of the entry.
2. Double-space each entry, and double-space between entries.
3. Underline titles of works published independently—for instance, books, pamphlets, and journals. Enclose within quotation marks a work not published independently—for instance, an article in a journal, or a short story.
4. If you are citing a book that includes the title of another book, underline the main title but do *not* underline the title mentioned. Example:

<u>A Study of Mill's</u> On Liberty

5. In the sample entries below, pay attention to the use of commas, colons, and the space after punctuation.

ALPHABETIC ORDER

1. Arrange the list alphabetically by author, with the author's last name first.
2. For information about anonymous works, works with more than one author, and two or more works by one author, see below.

A Closer Look • Here is more detailed advice.

THE AUTHOR'S NAME • Notice that the last name is given first, but otherwise the name is given as on the title page. Do not substitute initials for names written out on the title page.

If your list includes two or more works by an author, do not repeat the author's name for the second title but represent it by three hyphens followed by a period. The sequence of the works is determined by the alphabetic order of the titles. Thus, Smith's book titled *Poverty* would be listed ahead of her book *Welfare*. See the example below, listing two works by Roger Brown.

For a book by more than one author, see page 181.

Anonymous works are listed under the first word of the title, or the second word if the first is *A, An,* or *The,* or a foreign equivalent. In a few moments we will discuss books by more than one author, government documents, and works of corporate authorship.

THE TITLE

After the period following the author's name, allow one space and then give the title. Take the title from the title page, not from the cover or the spine, but disregard any unusual typography such as the use of all capital letters or the use of the ampersand (&) for *and.* Underline the title and subtitle (separate them by a colon) with one continuous underline, to indicate italics, but do not underline the period that concludes this part of the entry.

Capitalize the first and the last word.

Capitalize all nouns, pronouns, verbs, adjectives, adverbs, and subordinating conjunctions (for example, *although, if, because*).

Do not capitalize (unless it's the first or last word of the title) articles (*a, an, the*), prepositions (for instance, *in, on, toward, under*), coordinating conjunctions (for instance, *and, but, or, for*), or the *to* in infinitives.

Examples:

The Death Penalty: A New View

On the Death Penalty: Toward a New View

On the Penalty of Death in a Democracy

PLACE OF PUBLICATION, PUBLISHER, AND DATE

For the place of publication, provide the name of the city; you can usually find it either on the title page or on the reverse of the title page. If a number of cities are listed, provide only the first. If the city is not likely to be known, or if it may be confused with another city of the same name (as is Cambridge, Massachusetts, with Cambridge, England), add the name of the state, abbreviated (use the newer two-letter postal code; NJ, not N.J.).

The name of the publisher is abbreviated. Usually the first word is enough (Random House becomes Random), but if the first word is a first name, such as in Alfred A. Knopf, the surname (Knopf) is used instead. University presses are abbreviated thus: Yale UP, U of Chicago P, State U of New York P.

The date of publication of a book is given when known; if no date appears on the book, write n.d. to indicate "no date."

SAMPLE ENTRIES • Here are some examples, illustrating the points we have covered thus far:

```
Douglas, Ann. The Feminization of American Culture. New
     York: Knopf, 1977.

Brown, Roger. Social Psychology. New York: Free, 1965.

---. Words and Things. Glencoe, IL: Free, 1958.

Hartman, Chester. The Transformation of San Francisco.
     Totowa, NJ: Rowman, 1984.

Kellerman, Barbara. The Political Presidency: Practice
     of Leadership from Kennedy through Reagan. New
     York: Oxford UP, 1984.
```

Notice that a period follows the author's name, and another period follows the title. If a subtitle is given, as it is for Kellerman's book, it is separated from the title by a colon and a space. A colon follows the place of publication, a comma follows the publisher, and a period follows the date.

A BOOK BY MORE THAN ONE AUTHOR

The book is alphabetized under the last name of the first author named on the title page. If there are *two or three authors,* the names of these are given (after the first author's name) in the normal order, *first name first.*

```
Gilbert, Sandra M., and Susan Gubar. The Madwoman in the
     Attic: The Woman Writer and the Nineteenth-Century
     Literary Imagination. New Haven, CT: Yale UP, 1979.
```

Notice, again, that although the first author's name is given *last name first,* the second author's name is given in the normal order, first name first. Notice, too, that a comma is put after the first name of the first author, separating the authors.

If there are *more than three authors,* give the name only of the first and then add (but *not* enclosed within quotation marks) "et al." (Latin for "and others").

Altshuler, Alan, et al. <u>The Future of the Automobile</u>.
    Cambridge, MA: MIT P, 1984.

GOVERNMENT DOCUMENTS

If the writer is not known, treat the government and the agency as the author. Most federal documents are issued by the Government Printing Office (abbreviated to GPO) in Washington, D.C.

United States Congress. Office of Technology Assessment.
    <u>Computerized Manufacturing Automation: Employment,</u>
    <u>Education, and the Workplace</u>. Washington: GPO,
    1984.

WORKS OF CORPORATE AUTHORSHIP

Begin the citation with the corporate author, even if the same body is also the publisher, as in the first example:

American Psychiatric Association. <u>Psychiatric Glossary</u>.
    Washington: American Psychiatric Association, 1984.

Carnegie Council on Policy Studies in Higher Education.
    <u>Giving Youth a Better Chance: Options for Educa-</u>
    <u>tion, Work, and Service</u>. San Francisco: Jossey,
    1980.

A REPRINT, FOR INSTANCE A PAPERBACK VERSION OF AN OLDER CLOTHBOUND BOOK

Gray, Francine du Plessix. Divine Disobedience: Profiles
    in Catholic Radicalism. 1970. New York: Vintage,
    1971.

After the title, give the date of original publication (it can usually be found on the reverse of the title page of the reprint you are using), then a period, and then the place, publisher, and date of the edition you are using. The example indicates that Gray's book was originally published in 1970 and that the student is using the Vintage reprint of 1971.

A BOOK IN SEVERAL VOLUMES

If you have used more than one volume, in a citation within your essay you will (as explained on pp. 177–78) indicate a reference to, say, page 250 of volume 3 thus: (3: 250).

If, however, you have used only one volume of the set — let's say volume 3 — in your entry in Works Cited, specify which volume you used, as in the next example:

>Friedel, Frank. <u>Franklin D. Roosevelt</u>. Vol. 3. Boston:
>   Little, 1973. 4 vols.

With such an entry in Works Cited, the parenthetic citation within your essay would be to the page only, not to the volume and page, since a reader who consults Works Cited will understand that you used only volume 3. In Works Cited, you may specify volume 3 and not give the total number of volumes, or you may add the total number of volumes, as in the example above.

ONE BOOK WITH A SEPARATE TITLE IN A SET OF VOLUMES

Sometimes a set with a title makes use also of a separate title for each book in the set. If you are listing such a book, use the following form:

>Churchill, Winston. <u>The Age of Revolution</u>. New York:
>   Dodd, 1957. Vol. 3 of <u>History of the English-
>   Speaking Peoples</u>. 4 vols. 1956-58.

A BOOK WITH AN AUTHOR AND AN EDITOR

>Kant, Immanuel. <u>The Philosophy of Kant: Immanuel Kant's
>   Moral and Political Writings</u>. Ed. Carl J.
>   Friedrich. New York: Modern, 1949.

>Churchill, Winston, and Franklin D. Roosevelt. <u>The
>   Complete Correspondence</u>. Ed. Warren F. Kimball. 3
>   vols. Princeton UP, 1985.

If the book has one editor, the abbreviation is "ed."; if two or more editors, "eds."

If you are making use of the editor's introduction or other editorial material rather than of the author's work, list the book under the name of the editor rather than of the author, as shown below under "An Introduction, Foreword, or Afterword."

A REVISED EDITION OF A BOOK

>Arendt, Hannah. <u>Eichmann in Jerusalem</u>. Rev. and enlarged
>   ed. New York: Viking, 1965.

>Honour, Hugh, and John Fleming. <u>The Visual Arts: A
>   History</u>. 2nd ed. Englewood Cliffs, NJ: Prentice,
>   1986.

A TRANSLATED BOOK

Franqui, Carlos. <u>Family Portrait with Fidel: A Memoir</u>.
    Trans. Alfred MacAdam. New York: Random, 1984.

AN INTRODUCTION, FOREWORD, OR AFTERWORD

Goldberg, Arthur J. Foreword. <u>An Eye for an Eye? The</u>
    <u>Morality of Punishing by Death</u>. By Stephen
    Nathanson. Totowa, NJ: Rowman, 1987. v-vi.

Usually a book with an introduction or some such comparable material is listed under the name of the author of the book (here Nathanson) rather than under the name of the writer of the introduction (here Goldberg), but if you are referring to the apparatus rather than to the book itself, use the form just given. The words *Introduction, Preface, Foreword,* and *Afterword* are neither enclosed within quotation marks nor underlined.

A BOOK WITH AN EDITOR BUT NO AUTHOR

Let's assume that you have used a book of essays written by various people but collected by an editor (or editors), whose name appears on the collection.

LaValley, Albert J., ed. <u>Focus on Hitchcock</u>. Englewood
    Cliffs, NJ: Prentice, 1972.

A WORK WITHIN A VOLUME OF WORKS BY ONE AUTHOR

The following entry indicates that a short work by Susan Sontag, an essay called "The Aesthetics of Silence," appears in a book by Sontag titled *Styles of Radical Will.* Notice that the inclusive page numbers of the short work are cited, not merely page numbers that you may happen to refer to but the page numbers of the entire piece.

Sontag, Susan. "The Aesthetics of Silence." In <u>Styles of</u>
    <u>Radical Will</u>. New York: Farrar, 1969. 3-34.

A BOOK REVIEW

Here is an example, citing Gerstein's review of Walker's book. Gerstein's review was published in a journal called *Ethics.*

Gerstein, Robert S. Rev. of <u>Punishment, Danger and</u>
    <u>Stigma: The Morality of Criminal Justice</u>, by Nigel
    Walker. <u>Ethics</u> 93 (1983): 408-10.

If the review has a title, give the title between the period following the reviewer's name and "Rev."

If a review is anonymous, list it under the first word of the title, or under the second word if the first word is *A*, *An*, or *The*. If an anonymous review has no title, begin the entry with "Rev. of" and then give the title of the work reviewed; alphabetize the entry under the title of the work reviewed.

AN ARTICLE OR ESSAY — NOT A REPRINT — IN A COLLECTION

A book may consist of a collection (edited by one or more persons) of new essays by several authors. Here is a reference to one essay in such a book. (The essay by Balmforth occupies pages 19–35 in a collection edited by Bevan.)

```
Balmforth, Henry. "Science and Religion." Steps to
     Christian Understanding. Ed. R. J. W. Bevan. Lon-
     don: Oxford UP, 1958. 19-35.
```

AN ARTICLE OR ESSAY REPRINTED IN A COLLECTION

The previous example (Balmforth's essay in Bevan's collection) was for an essay written for a collection. But some collections reprint earlier material, such as essays from journals or chapters from books. The following example cites an essay that was originally printed in a book called *The Cinema of Alfred Hitchcock*. This essay has been reprinted in a later collection of essays on Hitchcock, edited by Arthur J. LaValley, and it was LaValley's collection that the student used.

```
Bogdanovich, Peter. "Interviews with Alfred Hitchcock."
     The Cinema of Alfred Hitchcock. New York: Museum of
     Modern Art, 1963. 15-18. Rpt. in Focus on Hitch-
     cock. Ed. Albert J. LaValley. Englewood Cliffs, NJ:
     Prentice, 1972. 28-31.
```

The student has read Bogdanovich's essay or chapter, but not in Bogdanovich's book, where it occupied pages 15–18. The material was actually read on pages 28–31 in a collection of writings on Hitchcock, edited by LaValley. Details of the original publication — title, date, page numbers, and so forth — were found in LaValley's collection. Almost all editors will include this information, either on the copyright page or at the foot of the reprinted essay, but sometimes they do not give the original page numbers. In such a case, you need not include the original numbers in your entry.

Notice that the entry begins with the author and the title of the work you are citing (here, Bogdanovich's interviews), not with the name of the editor of the collection or the title of the collection.

AN ENCYCLOPEDIA OR OTHER ALPHABETICALLY ARRANGED REFERENCE WORK

The publisher, place of publication, volume number, and page number do *not* have to be given. For such works, list only the edition (if it is given) and the date.

For a *signed* article, begin with the author's last name. (If the article is signed with initials, check elsewhere in the volume for a list of abbreviations, which will inform you who the initials stand for, and use the following form.)

```
Williams, Donald C. "Free Will and Determinism." Ency-
    clopedia Americana. 1987 ed.
```

For an *unsigned article,* begin with the title of the article:

```
"Tobacco." Encyclopaedia Britannica: Macropaedia. 1988
    ed.

"Automation." The Business Reference Book. 1977 ed.
```

A TELEVISION OR RADIO PROGRAM

```
Sixty Minutes. CBS. 26 Feb. 1989.
```

AN ARTICLE IN A SCHOLARLY JOURNAL • The title of the article is enclosed within quotation marks, and the title of the journal is underlined to indicate italics.

Some journals are paginated consecutively; the pagination of the second issue begins where the first issue leaves off. Other journals begin each issue with page 1. The forms of the citations differ slightly. First, an article in

A JOURNAL THAT IS PAGINATED CONSECUTIVELY

```
Vilas, Carlos M. "Popular Insurgency and Social Revolu-
    tion in Central America." Latin American Perspec-
    tives 15 (1988): 55-77.
```

Vilas's article occupies pages 55–77 in volume 15, which was published in 1988. (Notice that the volume number is followed by a space, and then by the year, in parentheses, and then by a colon, a space, and the page numbers of the entire article.) Because the journal is paginated consecutively, the issue number does *not* need to be specified.

A JOURNAL THAT BEGINS EACH ISSUE WITH PAGE 1

If the journal is, for instance, a quarterly, there will be four page 1's each year, so the issue number must be given. After the volume number, type a period and (without hitting the space bar) the issue number, as in the next example:

```
Greenberg, Jack. "Civil Rights Enforcement Activity of
    the Department of Justice." The Black Law Journal
    8.1 (1983): 60-67.
```

Greenberg's article appeared in the first issue of volume 8 of *The Black Law Journal.*

AN ARTICLE IN A WEEKLY, BIWEEKLY, OR MONTHLY PUBLICATION

```
Lamar, Jacob V. "The Immigration Mess." Time 27 Feb.
     1989: 14-15.
```

AN ARTICLE IN A NEWSPAPER

Because a newspaper usually consists of several sections, a section number or a capital letter may precede the page number. The example indicates that an article begins on page 1 of section 2 and is continued on a later page.

```
Chu, Harry. "Art Thief Defends Action." New York Times 8
     Feb. 1989, sec. 2: 1+.
```

A DATABASE SOURCE

Treat material obtained from a computer service, such as Bibliographies Retrieval Service (BRS), like other printed material, but at the end of the entry add (if available) the title of the database (underlined), publication medium (*Online*), name of the computer service, and date of access.

```
Jackson, Morton. "A Look at Profits." Harvard Business
     Review 40 (1962): 106-13. Online. BRS. 23 Dec.
     1995.
```

Caution: Although we have covered the most usual kinds of sources, it is entirely possible that you will come across a source that does not fit any of the categories that we have discussed. For approximately two hundred pages of explanations of these matters, covering the proper way to cite all sorts of troublesome and unbelievable (but real) sources, see Joseph Gibaldi, *MLA Handbook for Writers of Research Papers,* Fourth Edition (New York: Modern Language Association of America, 1995).

APA Format

Your paper will conclude with a page headed "References," in which you list all of your sources. If the last page of your essay is numbered 10, number the first page of references 11.

Citations within the Text • The APA style emphasizes the date of publication; the date appears not only in the list of references at the end of the paper, but also in the paper itself, when you give a brief parenthetic citation of a source that you have quoted or summarized or in any other way used. Here is an example:

```
Statistics are readily available (Smith, 1989, p. 20).
```

The title of Smith's book or article will be given at the end of your paper, in the list titled "References." We will discuss the form of the material listed in References in a moment, but first we will look at some typical citations within the text of a student's essay.

A SUMMARY OF AN ENTIRE WORK

```
Smith (1988) holds the same view.
```

Or

```
Similar views are held widely (Smith, 1988; Jones &
Metz, 1990).
```

A REFERENCE TO A PAGE OR TO PAGES

```
Smith (1988, p. 17) argues that "the death penalty is a
lottery, and blacks usually are the losers."
```

A REFERENCE TO AN AUTHOR WHO IN THE LIST OF REFERENCES IS REPRESENTED BY MORE THAN ONE WORK

If in References you list two or more works that an author published in the same year, the works are listed in alphabetic order, by the first letter of the title. The first work is labeled *a*, the second *b*, and so on. Here is a reference to the second work that Smith published in 1989:

```
Florida presents "a fair example" of how the death
penalty is administered (Smith, 1989b).
```

References • Your brief parenthetic citations are made clear when the reader consults the list you give in References. Type this list on a separate page, continuing the pagination of your essay.

AN OVERVIEW • Here are some general guidelines.

FORM ON THE PAGE

1. Begin each entry flush with the left margin, but if an entry runs to more than one line, indent five spaces for each succeeding line of the entry.
2. Double-space each entry, and double-space between entries.

ALPHABETIC ORDER

1. Arrange the list alphabetically by author.
2. Give the author's last name first, then the initial of the first and of the middle name (if any).
3. If there is more than one author, name all of the authors, again in-

verting the name (last name first) and giving only initials for first and middle names. (But do not invert the editor's name when the entry begins with the name of an author who has written an article in an edited book.) When there are two or more authors, use an ampersand (&) before the name of the last author. Example (here, of an article in the tenth volume of a journal called *Developmental Psychology*):

Drabman, R. S., & Thomas, M. H. (1974). Does media violence increase children's tolerance of real-life aggression? <u>Developmental Psychology, 10,</u> 418–421.

4. If you list more than one work by an author, do so in the order of publication, the earliest first. If two works by an author were published in the same year, give them in alphabetic order by the first letter of the title, disregarding *A, An,* or *The,* and their foreign equivalent. Designate the first work as "a," the second as "b." Repeat the author's name at the start of each entry.

Donnerstein, E. (1980a). Aggressive erotica and violence against women. <u>Journal of Personality and Social Psychology, 39,</u> 269–277.

Donnerstein, E. (1980b). Pornography and violence against women. <u>Annals of the New York Academy of Sciences, 347,</u> 227–288.

Donnerstein, E. (1983). Erotica and human aggression. In R. Green and E. Donnerstein (Eds.), <u>Aggression: Theoretical and empirical reviews</u> (pp. 87–103). New York: Academic Press.

FORM OF TITLE

1. In references to books, capitalize only the first letter of the first word of the title (and of the subtitle, if any) and capitalize proper nouns. Underline the complete title.
2. In references to articles in periodicals or in edited books, capitalize only the first letter of the first word of the article's title (and subtitle, if any), and all proper nouns. Do not put the title within quotation marks. Type a period after the title of the article. For the title of the journal, and the volume and page numbers, see the next instruction.
3. In references to periodicals, give the volume number in arabic numerals, and underline it. Do *not* use *vol.* before the number, and do not use *p.* or *pg.* before the page numbers.

Sample References · Here are some samples to follow.

A BOOK BY ONE AUTHOR

Pavlov, I. P. (1927). <u>Conditioned reflexes</u> (G. V.
    Anrep, Trans.). London: Oxford University Press.

A BOOK BY MORE THAN ONE AUTHOR

Belenky, M. F., Clinchy, B. M., Goldberger, N. R., &
    Torule, J. M. (1986). <u>Women's ways of knowing: The
    development of self, voice, and mind</u>. New York:
    Basic Books.

A COLLECTION OF ESSAYS

Christ, C. P., & Plaskow, J. (Eds.). (1979). <u>Womanspirit
    rising: A feminist reader in religion</u>. New York:
    Harper & Row.

A WORK IN A COLLECTION OF ESSAYS

Fiorenza, E. (1979). Women in the early Christian move-
    ment. In C. P. Christ & J. Plaskow (Eds.), <u>Woman-
    spirit rising: A feminist reader in religion</u> (pp.
    84–92). New York: Harper & Row.

GOVERNMENT DOCUMENTS

If the writer is not known, treat the government and the agency as the
author. Most federal documents are issued by the Government Printing
Office in Washington, D.C. If a document number has been assigned, insert that number in parentheses between the title and the following period.

United States Congress. Office of Technology Assessment.
    (1984). <u>Computerized manufacturing automation:
    Employment, education, and the workplace.</u> Washing-
    ton, DC: U.S. Government Printing Office.

AN ARTICLE IN A JOURNAL WITH CONTINUOUS PAGINATION

Tversky, A., & Kahneman, D. (1981). The framing of
    decisions and the psychology of choice. <u>Science,
    211,</u> 453–458.

AN ARTICLE IN A JOURNAL THAT PAGINATES
EACH ISSUE SEPARATELY

Foot, R. J. (1988-89). Nuclear coercion and the ending
    of the Korean conflict. <u>International Security,
    13</u>(4), 92–112.

The reference informs us that the article appeared in issue number 4 of volume 13.

AN ARTICLE FROM A MONTHLY OR WEEKLY MAGAZINE

Maran, S. P. (1988, April). In our backyard, a star
     explodes. Smithsonian, 19, pp. 46-57.

Greenwald, J. (1989, February 27). Gimme shelter. Time,
     133, pp. 50-51.

AN ARTICLE IN A NEWSPAPER

Connell, R. (1989, February 6). Career concerns at heart
     of 1980s' campus protests. Los Angeles Times,
     pp. 1, 3.

(*Note:* If no author is given, simply begin with the title followed by the date in parentheses.)

A BOOK REVIEW

Daniels, N. (1984). Understanding physician power [Re-
     view of the book, The social transformation of
     American medicine]. Philosophy and Public Affairs,
     13, 347-356.

Daniels is the reviewer, not the author of the book. The book under review is called *The Social Transformation of American Medicine,* but the review, published in volume 13 of *Philosophy and Public Affairs,* had its own title, "Understanding Physician Power."

If the review does not have a title, retain the square brackets and use the material within as the title. Proceed as in the example just given.

For a full account of the APA method of dealing with all sorts of unusual citations, see the fourth edition (1994) of the APA manual, *Publication Manual of the American Psychological Association.*

A CHECKLIST FOR PAPERS USING SOURCES

1. All borrowed words and ideas credited?
2. Quotations and summaries not too long?
3. Quotations accurate?
4. Quotations provided with helpful lead-ins?
5. Documentation in proper form?

And of course you will also ask yourself the questions that you would ask of a paper that did not use sources, such as:

6. Topic sufficiently narrowed?

7. Thesis (to be advanced or refuted) stated early and clearly, perhaps even in title?

8. Audience kept in mind? Opposing views stated fairly and as sympathetically as possible? Controversial terms defined?

9. Assumptions likely to be shared by readers? If not, are they argued rather than merely asserted?

10. Focus clear (for example, evaluation, or recommendation of policy)?

11. Evidence (examples, testimony, statistics) adequate and sound?

12. Inferences valid?

13. Organization clear? (Effective opening, coherent sequence of arguments, unpretentious ending?)

14. All worthy opposition faced?

15. Tone appropriate?

16. Has the paper been carefully proofread?

17. Is the title effective?

18. Is the opening paragraph effective?

19. Is the structure reader-friendly?

20. Is the closing paragraph effective?

AN ANNOTATED STUDENT RESEARCH PAPER

The following argument makes good use of sources. Early in the semester the students were asked to choose one topic from a list of ten, and to write a documented argument of 750 to 1,250 words (three to five pages of double-spaced typing). The completed paper was due two weeks after the topics were distributed. The assignment, a prelude to working on a research paper of 2,500 to 3,000 words, was in part designed to give students practice in finding and in using sources.

The topic selected by this student was, as given in the list, "Write an argument about televising trials."

Citations are given in the MLA form. For an example of an essay using the APA form see Nan Desuka, "Why Handguns Must Be Outlawed" (p. 277).

The *MLA Handbook* does not insist on a title page and outline, but many instructors prefer them.

Title one-third down page.

} 1"

Why Trials Should Not Be Televised
By
Theresa Washington

Professor Wilson
English 102
April 17, 1995

All lines centered.

Washington i

Outline

Small roman
numerals for page
with outline.

Thesis: The televising of trials is a bad idea
because it has several negative effects on
the first amendment: it gives viewers a
deceptive view of particular trials and of
the judicial system in general, and it
degrades the quality of media reporting
outside the courtroom.

Roman numerals
for chief units (I,
II, etc.); capital
letters for chief
units within these
largest units; then,
for smaller and
smaller units,
arabic numerals
and lowercase
letters.

  I. Introduction
     A. Trend toward increasing trial coverage
     B. First amendment versus sixth amendment
 II. Effect of televising trials on first amend-
     ment
     A. Provides deceptive version of truth
        1. Confidence in verdicts misplaced
           a. Willie Smith trial
           b. Rodney King trial
        2. Nature of TV as a medium
           a. Distortion in sound bites
           b. Stereotyping trial participants
           c. Misleading camera angles
           d. Commentators and commercials
     B. Confuses viewers about judicial system
        1. Contradicts basic concept "innocent
           until proven guilty"
        2. Can't explain legal complexities
     C. Contributes to media circus outside of
        court
        1. Blurs truth and fiction
        2. Affects print media in negative ways
        3. Media makes itself the story
        4. Distracts viewers from other issues
III. Conclusion

Washington 1

Why Trials Should Not Be Televised

Although trials have been televised on and
off since the 1950s,[1] in the last few years the
availability of trials for a national audience has
increased dramatically.[2] Media critics, legal
scholars, social scientists, and journalists continue to debate the merits of this trend.

Proponents of cameras in the courtroom argue,
falsely, I believe, that confidence in the fairness of our institutions, including the judicial
system, depends on a free press, guaranteed by the
First Amendment. Keeping trials off television is
a form of censorship, they say. It limits the
public's ability to understand (1) what is happening in particular trials, and (2) how the judicial
system operates, which is often confusing to
laypeople. Opponents claim that televising trials
threatens the defendant's Sixth-Amendment rights
to a fair trial because it can alter the behavior
of the trial participants, including the jury
("Tale"; Thaler).

Regardless of its impact on due process of
law,[3] TV in court does not serve the First Amendment well. Consider the first claim, that particular trials are easier to understand when televised. But does watching trials on television
really allow the viewer to "see it like it is," to
get the full scope and breadth of a trial? Steven
Brill, founder of Court TV, would like us to
believe so. He points out that most high-profile
defendants in televised trials have been acquitted; he names William Kennedy Smith, Jimmy Hoffa,
John Connally, and John Delorean as examples

Title is focused
and announces the
thesis.

Double-space
between title and
first paragraph —
and throughout
the essay.

1" margin on each
side and at
bottom.

Summary of
opposing
positions.

Parenthetic
reference to an
anonymous source
and also to a
source with a
named author.

Superscript
numerals indicate
endnotes.

Parenthetic
reference to
author and page.

Parenthetic
reference to an
indirect source (a
borrowed
quotation).

(Clark 821). "Imagine if [Smith's trial] had not been shown and he got off. Millions of people would have said the Kennedys fixed the case" (Brill qtd. in "Tale" 29). Polls taken after the trial seem to confirm this claim, since they showed the public by and large agreed with the jury's decision to acquit (Quindlen).

However, Thaler points out that the public can just as easily disagree with the verdict as agree, and when this happens, the effects can be catastrophic. One example is the Rodney King case. Four white Los Angeles police officers were charged in 1991 with severely beating African American Rodney King, who, according to the officers, had been resisting arrest. At their first trial, all four officers were acquitted. This verdict outraged many African Americans throughout the country; they felt the evidence from watching the trial overwhelmingly showed the defendants to be guilty. The black community of south-central Los Angeles expressed its feelings by rioting for days (Thaler 50-51).

Clearly the black community did not experience the trial the same way the white community and the white jury did. Why? Marty Rosenbaum, an attorney with the New York State Defenders Association, points out that viewers cannot experience a trial the same way trial participants do. "What you see at home 'is not what jurors see'" (qtd. in Thaler 70). The trial process is slow, linear, and methodical, as the defense and prosecution each build their case, one piece of information at a time (Thaler 11). The process is intended to be

Although no
words are quoted,
the idea is
borrowed and so
the source is cited.

Washington 3

thoughtful and reflective, with the jury weighing all the evidence in light of the whole trial (Altheide 299-301). And it emphasizes words--both spoken and written--rather than images (Thaler 11).

In contrast, TV's general strength is in handling visual images that entertain or that provoke strong feelings. News editors and reporters choose footage for its assumed visual and emotional impact on viewers. Words are made to fit the images, not the other way around, and they tend to be short catchy phrases, easy to understand (Thaler 4, 7). As a result, the 15- to 30-second "sound bites" in nightly newscasts often present trial events out of context, emphasizing moments of drama rather than of legal importance (Thaler 7; Zoglin 62).

Furthermore, this emphasis on emotional visuals leads to stereotyping the participants, making larger-than-life symbols out of them, especially regarding social issues (Thaler 9): abused children (the Menendez brothers), the battered wife (Hedda Nussbaum), the abusing husband (Joel Steinberg, O. J. Simpson), the jealous lover (Amy Fisher), the serial killer (Jeffrey Dahmer), and date rapist (Willie Smith). It becomes difficult for viewers to see defendants as ordinary human beings.

One can argue, as Brill has done, that gavel-to-gavel coverage of trials counteracts the distortions in sound-bite journalism (Clark 821). Yet even here a number of editorial assumptions and decisions affect what viewers see. Camera angles

Clear transition ("In contrast").

Parenthetic citation of two sources.

Summary of an opposing view, then countered with a clear transition ("Yet").

Washington 4

and movements reinforce in the viewer differing
degrees of intimacy with the trial participant;
close-ups are often used for sympathetic witnesses, three-quarter shots for lawyers, and
profile shots for defendants (Entner 73-75).[4]

On-air commentators also shape the viewers'
experience. Several media critics have noted how
much commentators' remarks often have the play-by-
play tone of sportscasters informing viewers of
what each side (the defense and the prosecution)
needs in order to win (Cole 245; Thaler 71, 151).
Continual interruptions for commercials add to the
impression of watching a spectacle. "The CNN
coverage [of the Smith trial] isn't so much gavel-
to-gavel, actually, as gavel-to-commercial-to-
gavel, with former CNN Gulf War correspondent
Charles Jaco acting more as ringleader than reporter" (Bianculli 60). This encourages a sensa-
tionalistic tone to the proceedings that the jury
does not experience. In addition, breaking for ads
frequently occurs at important points in the trial
(Thaler 48).

In-court proponents also believe that watching televised trials will help viewers understand
the legal aspects of the judicial system. In June
1991, a month before Court TV went on the air,
Vincent Blasi, a law professor at Columbia University, told <u>Time</u> magazine, "Today most of us learn
about judicial proceedings from lawyers' sound
bites and artists' sketches. . . . Televised
proceedings [such as Court TV] ought to dispel
some of the myth and mystery that shroud our legal
system" (qtd. in Zoglin 62).

Marginal notes:

Author lets reader hear the opposition by means of a brief quotation.

Omitted material indicated by three periods, with a fourth to mark the end of a sentence.

Washington 5

But after several years of Court TV and CNN, we can now see this is not so. As a medium, TV is not good at educating the general public, either about concepts fundamental to our judicial system or about the complexities in particular cases.

For example, one basic concept--"innocent until proven guilty"--is contradicted in televised trials in numerous subtle ways: commentators sometimes make remarks about (or omit comment on) actions of the defense or prosecution that show a bias against the defendant.

Media critic Lewis Cole, watching the trial of Lorena Bobbitt on Court TV in 1994, observed:

> Court TV commentators rarely challenged
> the state's characterization of what it
> was doing, repeating without comment, for
> instance, the prosecution's claims about
> protecting the reputation of Lorena
> Bobbitt and concentrating on the prosecu-
> tion decision to pursue both cases as a
> tactical matter, rather than inquiring
> how the prosecution's view of the inci-
> dent as a "barroom brawl" had limited its
> approach to and understanding of the
> case. (245)

Quotation of more than four lines, indented 1" from left margin (ten spaces), double-spaced, paren-thetic reference set off from quotation.

Camera angles play a role also: watching the defendant day after day in profile, which makes him or her seem either vulnerable or remote, tends to reinforce his or her guilt (Entner 158).

Thaler points out that these editorial ef-fects arise because the goals of the media (print

as well as electronic) differ from the goals of
the judicial system. His argument runs as follows:
The court is interested in determining only
whether the defendant broke the law. The media
(especially TV) focus on acts in order to reinforce social values, whether they're codified into
law or not. This can lead viewers to conclude that
a defendant is guilty because pretrial publicity
or courtroom testimony reveals he or she has
transgressed against the community's moral code,
even when the legal system later acquits. This
happened in the case of Claus von Bulow, who
between 1982 and 1985 was tried and acquitted
twice for attempting to murder his wife, and who
clearly had behaved in reprehensible ways in the
eyes of the public (35). It also happened in the
case of Joel Steinberg, who was charged with
murdering his daughter. Extended televised testimony by his ex-partner, Hedda Nussbaum, helped
paint a portrait of "a monster" in the eyes of the
public (140-42). Yet the jury chose to convict him
on the lesser charge of manslaughter. When many
viewers wrote to the prosecutor, Peter Casolaro,
asking why the verdict was not first-degree murder, he had to conclude that TV does not effectively teach about due process of law (176).

In addition to being poor at handling basic
judicial concepts, television has difficulty
conveying more complex and technical aspects of
the law. Sometimes the legal nature of the case
makes for a poor translation to the screen. Brill
admitted that, despite attempts at hourly summaries, Court TV was unable to convey to its

Argument
supported by
specific examples.

Washington 7

viewers any meaningful understanding of the case
of Manuel Noriega (Thaler 61), the Panamanian
leader who was convicted by the United States in
1992 of drug trafficking and money laundering
("Former"). In other cases, like the Smith trial,
the "civics lesson" gets swamped by its sensational aspects (Thaler 45). In most cases print
media are better at exploring and explaining legal
issues than is TV (Thaler 4).

In addition to shaping the viewer's perceptions of trial reality directly, in-court TV also
negatively affects the quality of trial coverage
outside of court, which in turn limits the public's "right to know." Brill likes to claim that
Court TV helps to counteract the sensationalism of
such tabloid TV shows as A Current Affair and Hard
Copy, which pay trial participants to tell their
stories and publish leaks from the prosecution and
defense. "I think cameras in the courtroom is
[sic] the best antidote to that garbage" (Brill
qtd. in Clark 821). However, as founder and editor
of Court TV, he obviously has a vested interest in
affirming his network's social and legal worth.
There are several ways that in-court TV, rather
than supplying a sobering contrast, helps to feed
the media circus surrounding high-profile trials
(Thaler 43).

One way is by helping to blur the line between reality and fiction. This is an increasing
trend among all media, but is especially true of
TV, whose footage can be combined and recombined
in so many ways. An excellent example of this is
the trial of Amy Fisher, who pleaded guilty in

Transition (briefly
summarizes, then
moves to a new
point).

Author uses "[sic]"
(Latin for "thus")
to indicate that
the oddity is in the
source and is not
by the author of
the paper.

September 1992 to shooting her lover's wife, and
whose sentencing was televised by Court TV (Thaler
83). Three TV movies about this love triangle
appeared on network TV in the same week, just one
month after she had been sentenced to five to
fifteen years of jail (Thaler 82). Then Geraldo
Rivera, the syndicated TV talk-show host, held a
mock grand jury trial of her lover, Joey Buttafuoco; even though Buttafuoco had not at that
point been charged with a crime, Geraldo felt many
viewers thought he ought to have been (Thaler 83).
Then A Current Affair had a series that "tried"
Fisher for events and behaviors that never got
resolved in the actual trial. The announcer on the
program said, "When Ms. Fisher copped a plea and
went to jail she robbed the public of a trial,
leaving behind many unanswered questions. Tonight
we will try to . . . complete the unwritten chapter" ("Trial"). Buttafuoco's lawyer from the trial
served as a consultant on this program (Thaler
84). This is also a good example of how tabloid TV
reinforces people's beliefs and plays on people's
feelings. Had her trial not been televised, the
excitement surrounding her case would not have
been so high. Tabloid TV played off the audience's
expectation for what a televised trial should and
could reveal. Thus in-court television becomes one
more ingredient in the mix of docudramas, mock
trials, talk shows, and tabloid journalism. This
limits the public's "right to know" by making it
difficult to keep fact separate from storytelling.

In-court TV also affects the quality of print
journalism. Proponents like to claim that, "[f]rom

Useful analysis of
effect of TV.

Square brackets to
indicate author
has altered text
from capital to
lowercase letter.

Washington 9

the standpoint of the public's right to know,
there is no good reason why TV journalists should
be barred from trials while print reporters are
not" (Zoglin 62). But when TV is present, there is
no level playing field among the media. Because it
provides images, sound, and movement and a greater
sense of speed and immediacy, TV can easily out-
compete other media for audience attention and
thus for advertising dollars. In attempts to keep
pace, newspapers and magazines offer more and more
of the kinds of stories that once were beneath
their standards, such as elaborate focus both on
sensational aspects of the case and on "personali-
ties, analysis, and prediction" rather than news
(Thaler 45). While these attributes have always
been part of TV and the tabloid print press, this
trend is increasingly apparent in supposedly
reputable papers like the New York Times. During
the Smith trial, for example, the Times violated
previously accepted boundaries of propriety by not
only identifying the rape victim but also giving
lots of intimate details about her past (Thaler
45).

Because the media are, for the most part,
commercial, slow periods--and all trials have them
--must always be filled with some "story." One
such story is increasingly the media self-con-
sciously watching and analyzing itself, to see how
it is handling (or mishandling) coverage of the
trial (Thaler 43). At the Smith trial, for example, one group of reporters was covering the trial
while another group covered the other reporters

No citation
needed for a point
that can be
considered
common
knowledge, but
notice that point
in the second
sentence *is*
documented.

Washington 10

(44).[5] As bizarre as this "media watching" is, there would be no "story" if the trial itself had not been televised.

Last but not least, televising trials distracts viewers from other important issues. Some of these are abstract and thus hard to understand (like the savings-and-loan scandal in the mid-1980s or the causes of lingering unemployment in the 1990s), while others are painful to contemplate (like overseas wars and famines). Yet we have to stay aware of these issues if we are to function as active citizens in a democracy.

Altogether, televising trials is a bad idea. Not only does it provide deceptive impressions about what's happening in particular trials; it also doesn't reveal much about our judicial system. In addition, televising trials helps to lower the quality of trial coverage outside of court, thus increasingly depriving the public of neutral, fact-based reporting. A healthy free press depends on balance and knowing when to accept limits. Saturating viewers with extended media coverage of sensational trials oversteps those limits. In this case, more is not better.

Yet is is unlikely that TV coverage will be legally removed from the courtroom, now that it is here. Only one state (New York) has ever legislated a return to nontelevised trials (in 1991), and even it changed its mind in 1992 (Thaler 78). Perhaps the best we can do is to educate ourselves about the pitfalls of televising the judicial system, as we struggle to do so with the televised electoral process.

Useful summary of main points.

Realistic appraisal of the current situation and a suggestion of what the reader can do.

Washington 11

Double-space between heading and notes, and throughout notes.

Superscript number followed by one space.

Notes

[1] Useful discussions of this history can be found in Clark (829-32) and Thaler (19-31).

[2] Cable networks have been showing trial footage to national audiences since at least 1982, when Cable News Network (CNN) covered the trial of Claus von Bulow (Thaler 33). It continues to show trials. In the first week of February 1995, four to five million homes accounted for the top fifteen most-watched shows on cable TV; all were CNN segments of the O. J. Simpson trial ("Cable TV"). In July 1991, Steven Brill founded the Courtroom Television Network, or "Court TV" (Clark 821). Like CNN, it broadcasts around the clock, showing gavel-to-gavel coverage. It now claims over fourteen million cable subscribers (Clark 821) and, as of January 1994, had televised over 280 trials ("In Camera" 27).

[3] Thaler's study <u>The Watchful Eye</u> is a thoughtful examination of the subtle ways in which TV in court can affect trial participants, inhibiting witnesses from coming forward, provoking grandstanding in attorneys and judges, and pressuring juries to come up with verdicts acceptable to a national audience.

[4] Sometimes legal restrictions determine camera angles. For example, in the Steinberg trial (1988), the audience and the jury were not allowed to be televised by New York state law. This required placing the camera so that the judge and witnesses were seen in "full frontal view" (generally a more neutral or positive stance). The lawyers could only be seen from the rear when

Each note begins with ½" indent (five typewriter spaces), but subsequent notes of each line are flush left.

questioning witnesses, and the defendant was shot
in profile (Thaler 110-11). These camera angles,
though not chosen for dramatic effect, still
resulted in emotionally laden viewpoints not
experienced by the jury.

[5] At the Smith trial a journalist from one
German newspaper inadvertently filmed another
German reporter from a competing newspaper watching the Smith trial in the pressroom outside the
courtroom (Thaler 44).

1" $\frac{1}{2}$"

Washington 13

Works Cited

Altheide, David. "TV News and the Social Construc-
     tion of Justice." Justice and the Media:
     Issues and Research. Ed. Ray Surette. Spring-
     field, IL: Thomas, 1984. 292-304.

Bianculli, David. "Shame on You, CNN." New York
     Post 11 Dec. 1992: 60.

"Cable TV Squeezes High Numbers and Aces Competi-
     tion." All Things Considered. Natl. Public
     Radio. 9 Feb. 1994. Unedited transcript.
     Segment 12. NPR Audience Services. Washing-
     ton.

Clark, Charles S. "Courts and the Media." CQ
     Researcher 23 Sep. 1994: 817-40.

Cole, Lewis. "Court TV." Nation 21 Feb. 1994:
     243-45.

Entner, Roberta. "Encoding the Image of the Ameri-
     can Judiciary Institution: A Semiotic Analy-
     sis of Broadcast Trials to Ascertain Its
     Definition of the Court System." Diss. New
     York U, 1993.

"Former Panamanian Leader Noriega Sentence." Facts
     on File 16 July 1992: 526. Infotrac: Magazine
     Index Plus 1992-Feb. 1995. CD-ROM. Informa-
     tion Access. Feb. 1995.

"In Camera with Court TV." New Yorker 24 Jan.
     1994: 27-28.

Quindlen, Anna. "The Glass Eye." New York Times 18
     Dec. 1991: A29.

"A Tale of a Rug." Economist 15 Jan. 1994: 28-29.

Alphabetical by
author's last name.

Indent turnovers $\frac{1}{2}$"
(five typewriter
spaces).

Transcript of radio
program.

The title of an
unpublished work
is not italicized
but enclosed
within quotation
marks.

CD-ROM source.

Anonymous
source alphabet-
ized under first
word (or second if
first is *A*, *An*, or
The).

Washington 14

Thaler, Paul. <u>The Watchful Eye: American Justice
    in the Age of the Television Trial</u>. Westport:
    Praeger, 1994.

Television
program.

"The Trial That Had to Happen: The People versus
    Amy Fisher." <u>A Current Affair</u>. Fox. WFXT,
    Boston. 1-4 Feb. 1993.

Zoglin, Richard. "Justice Faces a Screen Test."
    <u>Time</u> 17 June 1991: 62.

Part Two

READINGS:
CURRENT ISSUES

7

Pro and Con: Nine Debates

In reading essays debating a given issue, keep in mind the questions given on page 57, "A Checklist for Analyzing an Argument." Here they are again, with a few additional points of special relevance to debates.

A CHECKLIST FOR ANALYZING A DEBATE

1. What is the writer's thesis?
   a. What claim is asserted?
   b. What assumptions are made?
   c. Are key terms defined satisfactorily?
2. What support is offered on behalf of the claim?
   a. Are examples relevant and convincing?
   b. Are statistics relevant, accurate, and convincing?
   c. Are the authorities appropriate?
   d. Is the logic — deductive and inductive — valid?
   e. If there is an appeal to emotion, is this appeal acceptable?
3. Does the writer seem fair?
   a. Are counterarguments considered?
   b. Is there any evidence of dishonesty?

Next, ask yourself the following additional questions:

4. Do the disputants differ in
   a. assumptions?
   b. interpretations of relevant facts?
   c. selection of and emphasis on these facts?
   d. definitions of key terms?
   e. values and norms?
5. What common ground do the disputants share?
6. Which disputant seems to you to have the better overall argument? Why?

ABORTION: WHOSE RIGHT TO LIFE IS IT ANYWAY?

Ellen Willis

Putting Women Back into the Abortion Debate

Some years ago I attended a New York Institute for the Humanities seminar on the new right. We were a fairly heterogeneous group of liberals and lefties, feminists and gay activists, but on one point nearly all of us agreed: The right-to-life movement was a dangerous antifeminist crusade. At one session I argued that the attack on abortion had significance far beyond itself, that it was the linchpin of the right's social agenda. I got a lot of supporting comments and approving nods. It was too much for Peter Steinfels, a liberal Catholic, author of *The Neoconservatives*, and executive editor of *Commonweal*. Right-to-lifers were not all right-wing fanatics, he protested. "You have to understand," he said plaintively, "that many of us

Ellen Willis (b. 1941) was educated at Barnard College and the University of California, Berkeley. She has been a freelance writer since 1966, publishing in such journals as The New Yorker, Rolling Stone, *and* The Village Voice, *where this essay first appeared on July 16, 1985.*

see abortion as a *human life issue.*" What I remember best was his air of frustrated isolation. I don't think he came back to the seminar after that.

Things are different now. I often feel isolated when I insist that abortion is, above all, a *feminist issue.* Once people took for granted that abortion was an issue of sexual politics and morality. Now, abortion is most often discussed as a question of "life" in the abstract. Public concern over abortion centers almost exclusively on fetuses; women and their bodies are merely the stage on which the drama of fetal life and death takes place. Debate about abortion — if not its reality — has become sexlessly scholastic. And the people most responsible for this turn of events are, like Peter Steinfels, on the left.

The left wing of the right-to-life movement is a small, seemingly eccentric minority in both "progressive" and antiabortion camps. Yet it has played a critical role in the movement: By arguing that opposition to abortion can be separated from the right's antifeminist program, it has given antiabortion sentiment legitimacy in left-symp and (putatively) profeminist circles. While left antiabortionists are hardly alone in emphasizing fetal life, their innovation has been to claim that a consistent "pro-life" stand involves opposing capital punishment, supporting disarmament, demanding government programs to end poverty, and so on. This is of course a leap the right is neither able nor willing to make. It's been liberals — from Garry Wills to the Catholic bishops — who have supplied the mass media with the idea that prohibiting abortion is part of a "seamless garment" of respect for human life.

Having invented this countercontext for the abortion controversy, left antiabortionists are trying to impose it as the only legitimate context for debate. Those of us who won't accept their terms and persist in seeing opposition to abortion, antifeminism, sexual repression, and religious sectarianism as the real seamless garment have been accused of obscuring the issue with demagoguery. Last year *Commonweal* — perhaps the most important current forum for left antiabortion opinion — ran an editorial demanding that we shape up: "Those who hold that abortion is immoral believe that the biological dividing lines of birth or viability should no more determine whether a developing member of the species is denied or accorded essential rights than should the biological dividing lines of sex or race or disability or old age. This argument is open to challenge. Perhaps the dividing lines are sufficiently different. Pro-choice advocates should state their reasons for believing so. They should meet the argument on its own grounds. . . ."

In other words, the only question we're allowed to debate — or the only one *Commonweal* is willing to entertain — is "Are fetuses the moral equivalent of born human beings?" And I can't meet the argument on its own grounds because I don't agree that this is the key question, whose answer determines whether one supports abortion or opposes it. I don't doubt that fetuses are alive, or that they're biologically human — what else would they be? I do consider the life of a fertilized egg less precious than the well-being of a woman with feelings, self-consciousness, a history, social ties; and I think fetuses get closer to being human in a moral sense as they come closer to birth. But to me these propositions are intuitively self-evident. I wouldn't know how to justify them to a "nonbeliever," nor do I see the point of trying.

I believe the debate has to start in a different place — with the recognition that fertilized eggs develop into infants inside the bodies of women. Pregnancy and birth are active processes in which a woman's body shelters, nourishes, and expels a new life; for nine months she is immersed in the most intimate possible relationship with another being. The growing fetus makes considerable demands on her physical and emotional resources, culminating in the cataclysmic experience of birth. And childbearing has unpredictable consequences; it always entails some risk of injury or death.

For me all this has a new concreteness: I had a baby last year. My much-desired and relatively easy pregnancy was full of what antiabortionists like to call "inconveniences." I was always tired, short of breath; my digestion was never right; for three months I endured a state of hormonal siege; later I had pains in my fingers, swelling feet, numb spots on my legs, the dread hemorrhoids. I had to think about everything I ate. I developed borderline glucose intolerance. I gained fifty pounds and am still overweight; my shape has changed in other ways that may well be permanent. Psychologically, my pregnancy consumed me — though I'd happily bought the seat on the roller coaster, I was still terrified to be so out of control of my normally tractable body. It was all bearable, even interesting — even, at times, transcendent — because I wanted a baby. Birth was painful, exhausting, and wonderful. If I hadn't wanted a baby it would only have been painful and exhausting — or worse. I can hardly imagine what it's like to have your body and mind taken over in this way when you not only don't look forward to the result, but positively dread it. The thought appalls me. So as I see it, the key question is "Can it be moral, under any circumstances, to make a woman bear a child against her will?"

From this vantage point, *Commonweal's* argument is irrelevant, for in a society that respects the individual, no "member of the species" in *any* stage of development has an "essential right" to make use of someone else's body, let alone in such all-encompassing fashion, without that person's consent. You can't make a case against abortion by applying a general principle about everybody's human rights; you have to show exactly the opposite — that the relationship between fetus and pregnant woman is an exception, one that justifies depriving women of their right to bodily integrity. And in fact all antiabortion ideology rests on the premise — acknowledged or simply assumed — that women's unique capacity to bring life into the world carries with it a unique obligation that women cannot be allowed to "play God" and launch only the lives they welcome.

Yet the alternative to allowing women this power is to make them impotent. Criminalizing abortion doesn't just harm individual women with unwanted pregnancies, it affects all women's sense of themselves. Without control of our fertility we can never envision ourselves as free, for our biology makes us constantly vulnerable. Simply because we are female our physical integrity can be violated, our lives disrupted and transformed, at any time. Our ability to act in the world is hopelessly compromised by our sexual being.

Ah, sex — it does have a way of coming up in these discussions, despite 10 all. When pressed, right-to-lifers of whatever political persuasion invariably point out that pregnancy doesn't happen by itself. The leftists often give patronizing lectures on contraception (though some find only "natural birth control" acceptable), but remain unmoved when reminded that contraceptives fail. Openly or implicitly they argue that people shouldn't have sex unless they're prepared to procreate. (They are quick to profess a single standard — men as well as women should be sexually "responsible." Yes, and the rich as well as the poor should be allowed to sleep under bridges.) Which amounts to saying that if women want to lead heterosexual lives they must give up any claim to self-determination, and that they have no right to sexual pleasure without fear.

Opposing abortion, then, means accepting that women must suffer sexual disempowerment and a radical loss of autonomy relative to men: If fetal life is sacred, the self-denial basic to women's oppression is also basic to the moral order. Opposing abortion means embracing a conservative sexual morality, one that subordinates pleasure to reproduction: If fetal life is sacred, there is no room for the view that sexual passion — or even sexual love — for its own sake is a human need and a human right. Opposing abortion means tolerating the inevitable double standard, by which men may accept or reject sexual restrictions in accordance with their beliefs, while women must bow to them out of fear ... or defy them at great risk. However much *Commonweal*'s editors and those of like mind want to believe their opposition to abortion is simply about saving lives, the truth is that in the real world they are shoring up a particular sexual culture, whose rules are stacked against women. I have yet to hear any left right-to-lifers take full responsibility for that fact or deal seriously with its political implications.

Unfortunately, their fuzziness has not lessened their appeal — if anything it's done the opposite. In increasing numbers liberals and leftists, while opposing antiabortion laws, have come to view abortion as an "agonizing moral issue" with some justice on both sides, rather than an issue — however emotionally complex — of freedom versus repression, or equality versus hierarchy, that affects their political self-definition. This above-the-battle stance is attractive to leftists who want to be feminist good guys but are uneasy or ambivalent about sexual issues, not to mention those who want to ally with "progressive" factions of the Catholic church on Central

America, nuclear disarmament, or populist economics without that sticky abortion question getting in the way.

Such neutrality is a way of avoiding the painful conflict over cultural issues that continually smolders on the left. It can also be a way of coping with the contradictions of personal life at a time when liberation is a dream deferred. To me the fight for abortion has always been the cutting edge of feminism, precisely because it denies that anatomy is destiny, that female biology dictates women's subordinate status. Yet recently I've found it hard to focus on the issue, let alone summon up the militance needed to stop the antiabortion tanks. In part that has to do with second-round weariness — do we really have to go through all these things twice? — in part with my life now.

Since my daughter's birth my feelings about abortion — not as a political demand but as a personal choice — have changed. In this society, the difference between the situation of a childless woman and of a mother is immense; the fear that having a child will dislodge one's tenuous hold on a nontraditional life is excruciating. This terror of being forced into the sea-change of motherhood gave a special edge to my convictions about abortion. Since I've made that plunge voluntarily, with consequences still unfolding, the terror is gone; I might not want another child, for all sorts of reasons, but I will never again feel that my identity is at stake. Different battles with the culture absorb my energy now. Besides, since I've experienced the primal, sensual passion of caring for an infant, there will always be part of me that does want another. If I had an abortion today, it would be with conflict and sadness unknown to me when I had an abortion a decade ago. And the antiabortionists' imagery of dead babies hits me with new force. Do many women — left, feminist women — have such feelings? Is this the sort of "ambivalence about abortion" that in the present atmosphere slides so easily into self-flagellating guilt?

Some left antiabortionists, mainly pacifists — Juli Loesch, Mary Meehan, and other "feminists for life"; Jim Wallis and various writers for Wallis's radical evangelical journal *Sojourners* — have tried to square their position with concern for women. They blame the prevalence of abortion on oppressive conditions — economic injustice, lack of child care and other social supports for mothers, the devaluation of childrearing, men's exploitative sexual behavior and refusal to take equal responsibility for children. They disagree on whether to criminalize abortion now (since murder is intolerable no matter what the cause) or to build a long-term moral consensus (since stopping abortion requires a general social transformation), but they all regard abortion as a desperate solution to desperate problems, and the women who resort to it as more sinned against than sinning.

This analysis grasps an essential feminist truth: that in a male-supremacist society no choice a woman makes is genuinely free or entirely in her interest. Certainly many women have had abortions they didn't want or wouldn't have wanted if they had any plausible means of caring for a child; and countless others wouldn't have gotten pregnant in the first place were it not for inadequate contraception, sexual confusion and guilt, male pressure, and other stigmata of female powerlessness. Yet forcing a woman to bear a child she doesn't want can only add injury to insult, while refusing to go through with such a pregnancy can be a woman's first step toward taking hold of her life. And many women who have abortions are "victims" only of ordinary human miscalculation, technological failure, or the vagaries of passion, all bound to exist in any society, however utopian. There will always be women who, at any given moment, want sex but don't want a child; some of these women will get pregnant; some of them will have abortions. Behind the victim theory of abortion is the implicit belief that women are always ready to be mothers, if only conditions are right, and that sex for pleasure rather than procreation is not only "irresponsible" (i.e., bad) but something men impose on women, never something women actively seek. Ironically, left right-to-lifers see abortion as always coerced (it's "exploitation" and "violence against women"), yet regard motherhood — which for most women throughout history has been inescapable, and is still our most socially approved role — as a positive choice. The analogy to the feminist antipornography movement goes beyond borrowed rhetoric: the antiporners, too, see active female lust as surrender to male domination and traditionally feminine sexual attitudes as expressions of women's true nature.

This Orwellian version of feminism, which glorifies "female values" and dismisses women's struggles for freedom — particularly sexual freedom — as a male plot, has become all too familiar in recent years. But its use in the abortion debate has been especially muddleheaded. Somehow we're supposed to leap from an oppressive patriarchal society to the egalitarian one that will supposedly make abortion obsolete without ever allowing women to see themselves as people entitled to control their reproductive function rather than be controlled by it. How women who have no power in this most personal of areas can effectively fight for power in the larger society is left to our imagination. A "New Zealand feminist" quoted by Mary Meehan in a 1980 article in *The Progressive* says, "Accepting short-term solutions like abortion only delays the implementation of real reforms like decent maternity and paternity leaves, job protection, high-quality child care, community responsibility for dependent people of all ages, and recognition of the economic contribution of childminders" — as if these causes were progressing nicely before legal abortion came along. On the contrary, the fight for reproductive freedom is the foundation of all the others, which is why antifeminists resist it so fiercely.

As "pro-life" pacifists have been particularly concerned with refuting charges of misogyny, the liberal Catholics at *Commonweal* are most exercised by the claim that antiabortion laws violate religious freedom.

The editorial quoted above hurled another challenge at the proabortion forces:

> It is time, finally, for the pro-choice advocates and editorial writers to abandon, once and for all, the argument that abortion [*sic*] is a religious "doctrine" of a single or several churches being imposed on those of other persuasions in violation of the First Amendment. . . . Catholics and their bishops are accused of imposing their "doctrine" on abortion, but not their "doctrine" on the needs of the poor, or their "doctrine" on the arms race, or their "doctrine" on human rights in Central America. . . .
>
> The briefest investigation into Catholic teaching would show that the church's case against abortion is utterly unlike, say, its belief in the Real Presence, known with the eyes of faith alone, or its insistence on a Sunday obligation, applicable only to the faithful. The church's moral teaching on abortion . . . is for the most part like its teaching on racism, warfare, and capital punishment, based on ordinary reasoning common to believers and nonbelievers. . . .

This is one more example of right-to-lifers' tendency to ignore the sexual ideology underlying their stand. Interesting, isn't it, how the editorial neglects to mention that the church's moral teaching on abortion jibes neatly with its teaching on birth control, sex, divorce, and the role of women. The traditional, patriarchal sexual morality common to these teachings is explicitly religious, and its chief defenders in modern times have been the more conservative churches. The Catholic and evangelical Christian churches are the backbone of the organized right-to-life movement and—a few Nathansons and Hentoffs notwithstanding—have provided most of the movement's activists and spokespeople.

Furthermore, the Catholic hierarchy has made opposition to abortion 20 a litmus test of loyalty to the church in a way it has done with no other political issue—witness Archbishop O'Connor's harassment of Geraldine Ferraro during her vice-presidential campaign. It's unthinkable that a Catholic bishop would publicly excoriate a Catholic officeholder or candidate for taking a hawkish position on the arms race or Central America or capital punishment. Nor do I notice anyone trying to read William F. Buckley out of the church for his views on welfare. The fact is there is no accepted Catholic "doctrine" on these matters comparable to the church's absolutist condemnation of abortion. While differing attitudes toward war, racism, and poverty cut across religious and secular lines, the sexual values that mandate opposition to abortion are the bedrock of the traditional religious world view, and the source of the most bitter conflict with secular and religious modernists. When churches devote their considerable political power, organizational resources, and money to translating those values into law, I call that imposing their religious beliefs on me—whether or not they're technically violating the First Amendment.

Statistical studies have repeatedly shown that people's views on abortion are best predicted by their opinions on sex and "family" issues, not on "life" issues like nuclear weapons or the death penalty. That's not because we're inconsistent but because we comprehend what's really at stake in the abortion fight. It's the antiabortion left that refuses to face the contradiction in its own position: you can't be wholeheartedly for "life"—or for such progressive aspirations as freedom, democracy, equality—and condone the subjugation of women. The seamless garment is full of holes.

Topics for Critical Thinking and Writing

1. What does Ellen Willis mean when she insists, in her second paragraph, that abortion is "a *feminist issue*"? Whether or not you agree, write a paragraph explaining her point. You may want to begin simply by saying, "When Ellen Willis says abortion is a *'feminist issue,'* she means . . . "

2. After describing the physical and psychological difficulties of pregnancy, Willis says (para. 8):

   > in a society that respects the individual, no "member of the species" in *any* stage of development has an "essential right" to make use of someone else's body, let alone in such all-encompassing fashion, without that person's consent. You can't make a case against abortion by applying a general principle about everybody's human rights; you have to show exactly the opposite—that the relationship between fetus and pregnant woman is an exception, one that justifies depriving women of their right to bodily integrity.

   Do you accept all of Willis's declarations? Any of them? Why, or why not? And (another topic) consider the expression, "without that person's consent." Suppose a woman takes no precautions against becoming pregnant—possibly she even wants to become pregnant—but at a late stage in pregnancy decides she does not wish to bear a child. Can she withdraw her "consent" at any time?

3. In the previous question we asked you to consider Willis's expression "without that person's consent." Here is a related problem: The relationship between fetus and pregnant woman is different from all other relationships, but is it relevant to point out that women are not alone in having their bodies possessed, so to speak, by others? In time of war, men—but not women—are drafted; the interruption of their normal career causes considerable hardship. At the very least, a draftee is required to give up months or even several years of his life, and to live in circumstances that severely interfere with his privacy and his autonomy. And of course he may in fact be required to yield his life.

4. Do you think (in contrast to Willis) that persons who are opposed to capital punishment and to increased military spending—persons who are, so to speak, "pro-life"—must, if they are to be consistent, also oppose abortion? Why, or why not?

Randall A. Terry

The Abortion Clinic Shootings: Why?

As the nation heard with sorrow the news of the deplorable shooting spree at abortion facilities in Brookline,[1] the question is asked: Why? Why this sudden rise of violence in this arena?

I have been intricately involved in the antiabortion movement for more than a decade. I have led thousands of people in peaceful antiabortion activism via Operation Rescue. Hence, I enjoy a perspective few have. So I submit these answers to the question "Why?"

Enemies of the babies and the antiabortion movement will argue that the conviction that abortion is murder, and the call to take nonviolent direct action to save children from death, inevitably leads to the use of lethal force. This argument is ludicrous — unless one is prepared to argue that Gandhi's nonviolent civil disobedience in India during the 1930s led to the murder of British officials; or that Dr. Martin Luther King's nonviolent civil disobedience led to the violent actions that accompanied the civil rights movement in the United States during the 1960s.

So why, then, this recent violent outburst? Law enforcement officials need look no further than *Roe v. Wade;* abortion providers need look no further than their own instruments of death; and Congress and the president need look no further than the Freedom of Access to Clinic Entrances Act to understand the roots of the shootings.

The Supreme Court's attempt to overthrow Law (capital "L") in order   5 to legalize and legitimize murder has led to the inevitable — a disregard of or contempt for law. I say the court's attempt, for the court can no more overturn Law and legalize murder than it can overturn the law of gravity. God's immutable commandment "Thou shalt not murder" has forever made murder illegal. The court's lawlessness is breeding lawlessness. The court cannot betray the foundation of law and civilization — the Ten Commandments — and then expect a people to act "lawful" and "civilized."

Let us look at the abortion industry itself. Abortion is murder. And just as segregation and the accompanying violence possess the seeds for further violence, likewise it appears that the Law of sowing and reaping is being visited upon the abortion industry. A society cannot expect to tear 35 million innocent babies from their mothers' wombs without reaping horrifying consequences. Was it perhaps inevitable that the violent abortion in-

---

[1]On December 30, 1994, a gunman opened fire at two abortion facilities in Brookline, Massachusetts, wounding several people, two of them fatally.

Randall A. Terry is the founder of the antiabortion organization Operation Rescue. This essay originally appeared in the Boston Globe, *January 9, 1995.*

dustry should itself reap a portion of what it has so flagrantly and callously sown?

Now to Congress and the judiciary. Similar to the civil rights activists, antiabortion activists have often been brutalized at the hands of police and then subjected to vulgar injustices in sundry courts of law. Add to this the Freedom of Access to Clinic Entrances Act, which turns peaceful antiabortion activists into federal felons and perhaps one can understand the frustration and anger that is growing in Americans.

The abortion industry can partly blame itself for the recent shootings. It clamored for harsh treatment of peaceful antiabortion activists, and it usually got it. Now it has to deal with an emerging violent fringe. John F. Kennedy stated, "Those who make peaceful revolution impossible will make violent revolution inevitable." One would think the prochoice crowd would belatedly heed the late president's warning, but they haven't. They're urging an all too political Justice Department to launch a witch hunt into the lives of peaceful antiabortion activists and leaders. Make no mistake — what the pro-choice people want is to pressure law enforcement and the courts to intimidate anyone who condemns abortion as murder. Their recent public relations scam is to blame all antiabortion people for the shootings. And they will not be content until they have crushed all dissent against abortion. We must not allow them to cause us to cower in silence.

To those who support the recent shootings or herald John Salvi as a hero, I ask you: Has God authorized one person to be policeman, judge, jury, and executioner? Is it logical to leap from nonviolent life-saving activities to lethal force? Read your history! Remember the principles of Calvin, Knox, and Cromwell concerning lower magistrates. Are you likening John Salvi and Co. to Knox or Cromwell? Are you calling for revolution? Please consider these questions before calling someone who walks into a clinic and starts randomly shooting people a hero.

So what can be done to curtail this trend? First, the Freedom of Access to Clinic Entrances Act should be repealed immediately. This oppressive law is an outrage. The crushing weight of the federal government punishing peaceful protesters is the kind of thing we would expect in Communist China against political dissidents.

Second, the courts must stop abusing antiabortion activists. We must be accorded the same tolerance and leniency that every politically correct protester receives nationwide, i.e., small fines, two days in jail, charges dismissed, etc.

Finally, and this is most urgent, child killing must be brought to an immediate end. Whether the Supreme Court declares the personhood and inalienable right to life of preborn children or the Constitution is amended or the president signs an emancipation proclamation for children or Congress outlaws abortion outright, we must bring a swift end to the murder of innocent children.

Topics for Critical Thinking and Writing

1. In his second paragraph, Terry draws a parallel between Operation Rescue and the nonviolent civil disobedience campaigns in India, led by Gandhi, and in the United States, led by Martin Luther King, Jr. Is the analogy a good one?

2. Does Terry think that the Supreme Court's decision in *Roe v. Wade* (upholding a woman's right to have an abortion) *causes* violent disruption of abortion clinics? Or that it *justifies* that violence? If so, spell out the details of this causation or justification. If not, what does he mean when he says in paragraph 4 that "Law enforcement officials need look no further than *Roe v. Wade*"?

3. Why does Terry think (see paras. 5 and 6) that "abortion is murder"?

4. In paragraph 8 Terry cites a remark of President Kennedy: "Those who make peaceful revolution impossible will make violent revolution inevitable." Evaluate the aptness of this quotation as an explanation of violent disruption of medical services at an abortion clinic.

5. What is the purpose and the effect of Terry's choice of words when he writes, in paragraph 8, of a "public relations scam," "crush[ing] all dissent," "not . . . cower[ing] in silence"?

6. In the library get some information about the Freedom of Access to Clinic Entrances Act (mentioned by Terry in paras. 7 and 10). Do you think its repeal, which Terry advocates, would help reduce violence at abortion clinics? Why, or why not? Why do you think this law was enacted by Congress in the first place?

7. Terry describes abortion as "child killing" (para. 12). Do you think that is a fair description? Why, or why not?

8. At the end of his essay (paras. 10–12), Terry proposes three things government ought to do to end the trend toward violence in the antiabortion movement. Do you think the pro-choice advocates can accept any of these policies? Why, or why not?

9. Terry asserts that "preborn children" have an "inalienable right to life" (para. 12). What does "inalienable" mean? Suppose a pregnant woman would die because of medical complications if she carried her unborn child to birth. Do you think Terry would favor the mother dying because we must respect "the inalienable right to life" of the unborn? Does the mother, too, have such a right? How do you think he ought to resolve this conflict of rights, and why?

AFFIRMATIVE ACTION: IS IT FAIR?

Ernest van den Haag

Affirmative Action and Campus Racism

Sufficient data are hard to come by, but it seems that racial incidents have increased recently, particularly in colleges. I should like to suggest two propositions about cause and cure. The first is that racial incidents are unavoidable in multiracial societies, though such incidents can be minimized by education, or by criminal prosecution when violence is involved. The second is that racial incidents in our colleges are likely to increase as the effects of affirmative action practices are felt, as colleges pursue policies ostensibly meant to promote the perceived interests of racial minorities, and as minorities are given privileges withheld from others. This second proposition will be my focus here.

Affirmative action asks educational institutions to give preference in admissions, and employers to give preference in employment, to minorities. Blacks (and Hispanics) must be admitted, employed, and promoted even when, according to relevant tests used for all applicants, others are more qualified.

When segregation prevailed, few racial incidents occurred, since educational institutions were racially nearly homogeneous. But segregation placed blacks at a disadvantage; some of the best colleges would not admit them, despite merit, and they often had to content themselves with an inferior education.

After the Second World War segregation declined, while racial incidents increased only moderately. But Congress and the judiciary, always eager to "solve" problems which are about to disappear without their intervention, invented affirmative action as a means to compensate contemporary minorities for injustices done to minorities in the past. Unfortunately, the minority individuals who suffered unwarranted disadvantages in the past are not the ones to whom compensatory advantages are granted. The compensatory advantage goes to persons who resemble past victims of discrimination or oppression, in skin color or minority status, but are not themselves identified as victims of discrimination. On the other hand, the

Ernest van den Haag (b. 1914) is a professor (retired) of jurisprudence at Fordham University Law School. He is the author of several books, including Punishing Criminals *(1975). His essay first appeared in the Summer 1989 issue of* Academic Questions.

persons at whose expense the compensatory advantages are granted—i.e., whites, who, though no less meritorious, are not admitted or promoted so as to give preference to blacks—are not the ones who caused the past discrimination, nor can they be shown to have directly or indirectly profited from it.

Whatever the original intent behind affirmative action, in its final   5 stage it has led educational institutions to admit a (disguised) quota of blacks who would not qualify by the criteria customarily applied to others.[1] Quotas are clearly inconsistent with the spirit of our educational institutions, which requires that there be no discrimination among members of actual or potential college populations, except on the basis of individual merit. This is what is meant by equality of opportunity or (originally) by nondiscrimination. The admission of blacks with lower qualifications than the whites they displace violates this spirit. It must unavoidably seem illegitimate to the majority.

To be sure, violations of equal opportunity have occurred in the past. But affirmative action institutionalizes a new discriminatory policy in the guise of compensating for a prior discriminatory policy. Whether favored blacks and Hispanics really benefit is dubious; it can be as harmful to be discriminated for as to be discriminated against. Many minority students feel uncomfortable in the majority environment, either because of background or insufficient qualifications. They tend to live together, apart from the rest of the college community. They take classes (e.g., black studies) that guarantee good grades without much effort. But, feeling uncomfortable, the black students tend to make demands for more black students, more black faculty, and a more black-oriented curriculum. Unwilling and unable to profit from the existing curriculum, they feel that courses of study should be adapted to minority demands. Often they are supported by guilt-ridden whites, particularly among the faculty. Indeed, it sometimes seems that demonstrations and occupations of college facilities by blacks constitute most of the campus "racial incidents" we are hearing about. Usually such demonstrations achieve concessions, however small the number of demonstrators, as well as impunity, however illegal the actions.

What is to be done? The admission of minority students less qualified than the majority students they replace cannot but increase friction within the student body. How could the preference extended to black students and faculty members not create bad blood and increase the number of racial incidents? The existence of numerous on-campus institutions to help minority students and dampen hostility to them will, if anything, increase

---

[1]Administrative agencies and the judiciary had no difficulty overcoming the congressional prohibition of quotas that had helped the original civil rights legislation pass. Once the Civil Rights Act of 1964 was on the books they simply acted as though it instituted quotas. Later congressional action countenanced this "interpretation," although it is clearly contrary to the words of the law and to the original intent of Congress. [van den Haag's note.]

the provocation. The minority is disliked not *qua* minority but *qua* preferred and privileged. The institutions that ostensibly exist to help minorities simply make the privileges more visible. The only way to diminish racial hostility, and thereby, the number of racial incidents in educational institutions, is to stop both discrimination against and preferment toward minorities, to treat all individuals equally regardless of race or sex, and to admit them solely on the basis of their individual merit.

Less formally, but quite as insistently, affirmative action is practiced by many universities in selecting and promoting black and Hispanic faculty members. The result is that black faculty members are often less qualified than white ones. Even well-qualified black degree holders suffer from the public perception that they got their degrees without meeting the same standards as whites. The perception, however unfair in some cases, does not help self-esteem, and those who are actually well qualified suffer. Among students, existing prejudices against blacks are confirmed when the students find that black faculty members are often less qualified than their white colleagues. Affirmative action has thus done as much injury to black scholars as to black students.

If colleges feel that blacks cannot meet ordinary admissions standards because they come from a deprived or disadvantaged environment—and surely this is true for some—the colleges can make suitable remedial efforts. They can tutor college-bound black high school students to help them meet admissions standards and to benefit from a college education, something only a few colleges now do. Tutoring efforts are economically unwise (returns are greater with the most rather than the least able) but politically wise: They may help produce proportional representation of blacks among the educated.

The greatest harm currently suffered by blacks is done by those who 10 want to favor them. Indeed, a vested bureaucratic interest in affirmative action has grown up, and unfortunately many black political leaders benefit from this policy. Schools and corporations have hired affirmative action officers to establish and hide employment quotas, as well as to provide and hide other privileges for minorities. These employees cling to their roles and for the most part are unemployable in any other. Leaders benefit from the advantages of being "spokesmen" and from being able to mobilize the guilt feeling of whites profitably, while telling their supporters that they can procure advantages without effort. In the long run blacks will have to pay for this demagogic leadership.

Since the foregoing remarks predictably will be called *racist* I should like to clarify the use of that term. I believe a person can properly be called a racist if he believes in the inferiority of one race to another, not in some activity or ability such as mathematics or baseball, but in a general sense; and further, if he believes that the "inferior" race should not be entitled to equal treatment, but subordinated to the "superior" one and discriminated against, i.e., deprived of advantages enjoyed by the superior race.

If this definition is accepted, I find nothing racist in my remarks or beliefs. On the contrary, I find affirmative action practices to be racist. Thus the racial incidents they inspire do not surprise me.

Topics for Critical Thinking and Writing

1. How does van den Haag define "affirmative action"? Read the accompanying essay by Thomas Nagel (p. 227), and decide whether Nagel and van den Haag agree precisely on what affirmative action is.

2. In paragraph 4, van den Haag describes "Congress and the judiciary" as "always eager to 'solve' problems which are about to disappear." How does this comment affect your view of the author's persona?

3. Do you agree with van den Haag that whites today cannot be shown "to have directly or indirectly profited" from past racial discrimination against blacks (para. 4)? Why, or why not?

4. Van den Haag claims that colleges have used a "(disguised) quota" to admit black students "who would not qualify by the criteria customarily applied to others" (para. 5). Interview your dean of admissions and find out whether, and to what extent, if any, this is true on your campus. If it is true, what argument does the dean offer in defense of this policy? Write an essay of 500 words in which you evaluate that argument.

5. Van den Haag describes affirmative action as a misguided device of "compensating" minorities for past injustices (paras. 4 and 6). But the accompanying essay by Thomas Nagel (p. 227) argues that affirmative action is not a technique of compensation, but of equality of opportunity — which is precisely what van den Haag denies (paras. 5 and 6). Write a 750-word essay in which you do two things: First, clarify these two different conceptions of affirmative action, and second, argue for or against affirmative action as you think it ought to be understood.

6. When van den Haag declares that the way to reduce racial conflict on campus is to admit students "solely on the basis of their individual merit" (para. 7), what do you think he means by "merit"? Measured IQ? High school academic record? College board admission scores? Degree of effort to overcome obstacles and handicaps to academic success? Ability to learn and thus profit from higher education? Some combination of these? Write a 500-word essay on the theme Who Merits College Admission, and Why?

7. Van den Haag suggests that college officials concerned about underrepresentation of blacks in the student body ought to undertake special tutorial programs to increase the number of qualified black college students (para. 9). But, a critic might argue, surely this is a form of affirmative action — that is, taking active, affirmative steps to ensure more racial diversity in the student body. So how can van den Haag support such a program? Or does he, really? In any case, could he do so without inconsistency?

8. Van den Haag anticipates that he will be called a "racist" because of the views

he expresses in this essay; but he denies that he deserves such a label (paras. 11 and 12). Do you agree? In an essay of 250 words, explain your views on what does and does not make a person a racist.

Thomas Nagel

A Defense of Affirmative Action

The term *affirmative action* has changed in meaning since it was first introduced. Originally it referred only to special efforts to ensure equal opportunity for members of groups that had been subject to discrimination. These efforts included public advertisement of positions to be filled, active recruitment of qualified applicants from the formerly excluded groups, and special training programs to help them meet the standards for admission or appointment. There was also close attention to procedures of appointment, and sometimes to the results, with a view to detecting continued discrimination, conscious or unconscious.

More recently the term has come to refer also to some degree of definite preference for members of these groups in determining access to positions from which they were formerly excluded. Such preference might be allowed to influence decisions only between candidates who are otherwise equally qualified, but usually it involves the selection of women or minority members over other candidates who are better qualified for the position.

Let me call the first sort of policy "weak affirmative action" and the second "strong affirmative action." It is important to distinguish them, because the distinction is sometimes blurred in practice. It is strong affirmative action — the policy of preference — that arouses controversy. Most people would agree that weak or precautionary affirmative action is a good thing, and worth its cost in time and energy. But this does not imply that strong affirmative action is also justified.

I shall claim that in the present state of things it is justified, most clearly with respect to blacks. But I also believe that a defender of the practice must acknowledge that there are serious arguments against it, and that it is defensible only because the arguments for it have great weight. Moral opinion in this country is sharply divided over the issue because significant values are involved on both sides. My own view is that while strong affirmative action is intrinsically undesirable, it is a legitimate and perhaps indispensable method of pursuing a goal so important to the national welfare that it can be justified as a temporary, though not short-term, policy

Thomas Nagel (b. 1937), professor of philosophy at New York University, is the author of several books, including The View from Nowhere (1986). *This essay appeared in the Fall 1981 issue of* QQ.

for both public and private institutions. In this respect it is like other policies that impose burdens on some for the public good.

THREE OBJECTIONS

I shall begin with the argument against. There are three objections to 5
strong affirmative action: that it is inefficient; that it is unfair; and that it
damages self-esteem.

The degree of inefficiency depends on how strong a role racial or sexual preference plays in the process of selection. Among candidates meeting
the basic qualifications for a position, those better qualified will on the average perform better, whether they are doctors, policemen, teachers, or
electricians. There may be some cases, as in preferential college admissions, where the immediate usefulness of making educational resources
available to an individual is thought to be greater because of the use to
which the education will be put or because of the internal effects on the institution itself. But by and large, policies of strong affirmative action must
reckon with the costs of some lowering in performance level: The stronger
the preference, the larger the cost to be justified. Since both the costs and
the value of the results will vary from case to case, this suggests that no one
policy of affirmative action is likely to be correct in all cases, and that the
cost of performance level should be taken into account in the design of a
legitimate policy.

The charge of unfairness arouses the deepest disagreements. To be
passed over because of membership in a group one was born into, where
this has nothing to do with one's individual qualifications for a position, can
arouse strong feelings of resentment. It is a departure from the ideal — one
of the values finally recognized in our society — that people should be
judged so far as possible on the basis of individual characteristics rather
than involuntary group membership.

This does not mean that strong affirmative action is morally repugnant
in the manner of racial or sexual discrimination. It is nothing like those
practices, for though like them it employs race and sex as criteria of selection, it does so for entirely different reasons. Racial and sexual discrimination are based on contempt or even loathing for the excluded group, a feeling that certain contacts with them are degrading to members of the
dominant group, that they are fit only for subordinate positions or menial
work. Strong affirmative action involves none of this: It is simply a means
of increasing the social and economic strength of formerly victimized
groups, and does not stigmatize others.

There is an element of individual unfairness here, but it is more like
the unfairness of conscription in wartime, or of property condemnation
under the right of eminent domain. Those who benefit or lose out because
of their race or sex cannot be said to deserve their good or bad fortune.

It might be said on the other side that the beneficiaries of affirmative 10 action deserve it as compensation for past discrimination, and that compensation is rightly exacted from the group that has benefited from discrimination in the past. But this is a bad argument, because as the practice usually works, no effort is made to give preference to those who have suffered most from discrimination, or to prefer them especially to those who have benefited most from it, or been guilty of it. Only candidates who in other qualifications fall on one or the other side of the margin of decision will directly benefit or lose from the policy, and these are not necessarily, or even probably, the ones who especially deserve it. Women or blacks who don't have the qualifications even to be considered are likely to have been handicapped more by the effects of discrimination than those who receive preference. And the marginal white male candidate who is turned down can evoke our sympathy if he asks, "Why me?" (A policy of explicitly *compensatory* preference, which took into account each individual's background of poverty and discrimination, would escape some of these objections, and it has its defenders, but it is not the policy I want to defend. Whatever its merits, it will not serve the same purpose as direct affirmative action.)

The third objection concerns self-esteem, and is particularly serious. While strong affirmative action is in effect, and generally known to be so, no one in an affirmative action category who gets a desirable job or is admitted to a selective university can be sure that he or she has not benefited from the policy. Even those who would have made it anyway fall under suspicion, from themselves and from others: It comes to be widely felt that success does not mean the same thing for women and minorities. This painful damage to esteem cannot be avoided. It should make any defender of strong affirmative action want the practice to end as soon as it has achieved its basic purpose.

JUSTIFYING AFFIRMATIVE ACTION

I have examined these three objections and tried to assess their weight, in order to decide how strong a countervailing reason is needed to justify such a policy. In my view, taken together they imply that strong affirmative action involving significant preference should be undertaken only if it will substantially further a social goal of the first importance. While this condition is not met by all programs of affirmative action now in effect, it is met by those which address the most deep-seated, stubborn, and radically unhealthy divisions in the society, divisions whose removal is a condition of basic justice and social cohesion.

The situation of black people in our country is unique in this respect. For almost a century after the abolition of slavery we had a rigid racial caste system of the ugliest kind, and it only began to break up twenty-five years ago. In the South it was enforced by law, and in the North, in a somewhat less severe form, by social convention. Whites were thought to be defiled by social or residential proximity to blacks, intermarriage was taboo, blacks were denied the same level of public goods — education and legal protection — as whites, were restricted to the most menial occupations, and were barred from any positions of authority over whites. The visceral feelings of black inferiority and untouchability that this system expressed were deeply ingrained in the members of both races, and they continue, not surprisingly, to have their effect. Blacks still form, to a considerable extent, a hereditary social and economic community characterized by widespread poverty, unemployment, and social alienation.

When this society finally got around to moving against the caste system, it might have done no more than to enforce straight equality of opportunity, perhaps with the help of weak affirmative action, and then wait a few hundred years while things gradually got better. Fortunately it decided instead to accelerate the process by both public and private institutional action, because there was wide recognition of the intractable character of the problem posed by this insular minority and its place in the nation's history and collective consciousness. This has not been going on very long, but the results are already impressive, especially in speeding the advancement of blacks into the middle class. Affirmative action has not done much to improve the position of poor and unskilled blacks. That is the most serious part of the problem, and it requires a more direct economic attack. But increased access to higher education and upper-level jobs is an essential part of what must be achieved to break the structure of drastic separation that was left largely undisturbed by the legal abolition of the caste system.

Changes of this kind require a generation or two. My guess is that 15 strong affirmative action for blacks will continue to be justified into the early decades of the next century, but that by then it will have accomplished what it can and will no longer be worth the costs. One point deserves special emphasis. The goal to be pursued is the reduction of a great social injustice, no proportional representation of the races in all institutions and professions. Proportional racial representation is of no value in itself. It is not a legitimate social goal, and it should certainly not be the aim of strong affirmative action, whose drawbacks make it worth adopting only against a serious and intractable social evil.

This implies that the justification for strong affirmative action is much weaker in the case of other racial and ethnic groups, and in the case of women. At least, the practice will be justified in a narrower range of circumstances and for a shorter span of time than it is for blacks. No other group has been treated quite like this, and no other group is in a comparable status. Hispanic-Americans occupy an intermediate position, but it seems to be frankly absurd to include persons of oriental descent as beneficiaries of affirmative action, strong or weak. They are not a severely deprived and excluded minority, and their eligibility serves only to swell the numbers that can be included on affirmative action reports. It also suggests that there is a drift in the policy toward adopting the goal of racial proportional representation for its own sake. This is a foolish mistake, and should be resisted. The only legitimate goal of the policy is to reduce egregious racial stratification.

With respect to women, I believe that except over the short term, and in professions or institutions from which their absence is particularly marked, strong affirmative action is not warranted and weak affirmative action is enough. This is based simply on the expectation that the social and economic situation of women will improve quite rapidly under conditions of full equality of opportunity. Recent progress provides some evidence for this. Women do not form a separate hereditary community, characteristically poor and uneducated, and their position is not likely to be self-perpetuating in the same way as that of an outcast race. The process requires less artificial acceleration, and any need for strong affirmative action for women can be expected to end sooner than it ends for blacks.

I said at the outset that there was a tendency to blur the distinction between weak and strong affirmative action. This occurs especially in the use of numerical quotas, a topic on which I want to comment briefly.

A quota may be a method of either weak or strong affirmative action, depending on the circumstances. It amounts to weak affirmative action — a safeguard against discrimination — if, and only if, there is independent evidence that average qualifications for the positions being filled are no lower in the group to which a minimum quota is being assigned than in the applicant group as a whole. This can be presumed true of unskilled jobs that most people can do, but it becomes less likely, and harder to establish, the greater the skill and education required for the position. At these levels, a quota proportional to population, or even to representation of the group in the applicant pool, is almost certain to amount to strong affirmative action. Moreover it is strong affirmative action of a particularly crude and indiscriminate kind, because it permits no variation in the degree of preference on the basis of costs in efficiency, depending on the qualification gap. For this reason I should defend quotas only where they serve the purpose of weak affirmative action. On the whole, strong affirmative action is better implemented by including group preference as one factor in appointment or admission decisions, and letting the results depend on its interaction with other factors.

I have tried to show that the arguments against strong affirmative action are clearly outweighed at present by the need for exceptional measures to remove the stubborn residues of racial caste. But advocates of the policy should acknowledge the reasons against it, which will ensure its termination when it is no longer necessary. Affirmative action is not an end in itself, but a means of dealing with a social situation that should be intolerable to us all. 20

Topics for Critical Thinking and Writing

1. Nagel distinguishes between "weak" and "strong" affirmative action (paras. 1–3). He does not bother to defend the weak variety. Do you think this kind of affirmative action is justified? Why, or why not? Read the article by van den Haag (p. 223) and decide whether he would agree.

2. Nagel's concept of "strong" affirmative action (para. 2) includes two different ideas: (a) breaking ties among equally qualified candidates by choosing non-whites or women over white males, and (b) preferring candidates who are non-white or women over white males regardless of their relative qualifications. Do you think it is easier to defend (a) than (b)? Why, or why not?

3. Nagel identifies three arguments against "strong" affirmative action. Read the essay by van den Haag (p. 223) and explain whether he advances any of these arguments. If he does, who— Nagel or van den Haag—has the better of the dispute? If he doesn't advance any of these three arguments, how do you think Nagel would respond to the arguments van den Haag does propose?

4. Nagel argues (paras. 7–10) against the claim that "strong" affirmative action is unfair. Does his argument try to show (a) that it is not unfair at all, or (b) that it is not as unfair as the discrimination it is intended to replace, or (c) does he advance some completely different argument? Write a 250-word essay explaining your answers.

5. Nagel thinks that even "strong" affirmative action will not remedy the plight of poor blacks, and so he advocates "a more direct economic attack" (para. 14). What sorts of programs do you think he has in mind? Write a 500-word essay identifying three such policies or programs, and explain why you think they would help.

6. Nagel mentions Hispanics and Asians but explicitly excludes the latter as undeserving of "strong" affirmative action programs (para. 16). What about American Indians? Do you think the claim of Native Americans on such programs is comparable to that of blacks? of Hispanics? of Asians? Explain your view in an essay of 250 words.

7. Presumably your college has some sort of affirmative action admissions program. Is it of the "weak" or "strong" variety, as Nagel defines those terms? Does it involve numerical quotas? Would Nagel defend them if it does? Would he advocate them if it doesn't? Write a 500-word essay on the topic, explaining your college program and defending or criticizing it.

ANIMAL RIGHTS: IS A HUMAN-CENTERED ETHICS JUST ANOTHER PREJUDICE?

Peter Singer

Animal Liberation

I

We are familiar with Black Liberation, Gay Liberation, and a variety of other movements. With Women's Liberation some thought we had come to the end of the road. Discrimination on the basis of sex, it has been said, is the last form of discrimination that is universally accepted and practiced without pretense, even in those liberal circles which have long prided themselves on their freedom from racial discrimination. But one should always be wary of talking of "the last remaining form of discrimination." If we have learned anything from the liberation movements, we should have learned how difficult it is to be aware of the ways in which we discriminate until they are forcefully pointed out to us. A liberation movement demands an expansion of our moral horizons, so that practices that were previously regarded as natural and inevitable are now seen as intolerable.

Animals, Men and Morals is a manifesto for an Animal Liberation movement. The contributors to the book may not all see the issue this way. They are a varied group. Philosophers, ranging from professors to graduate students, make up the largest contingent. There are five of them, including the three editors, and there is also an extract from the unjustly neglected German philosopher with an English name, Leonard Nelson, who died in 1927. There are essays by two novelist/critics, Brigid Brophy and Maureen Duffy, and another by Muriel the Lady Dowding, widow of Dowding of Battle of Britain fame and the founder of "Beauty without Cruelty," a movement that campaigns against the use of animals for furs and cosmet-

Educated at the University of Melbourne and at Oxford, Singer (b. 1946) has taught at Oxford and now teaches at Monash University in Australia. He has written on a variety of ethical issues, but he is especially known for caring about the welfare of animals.

This essay originally appeared in the New York Review of Books *(April 5, 1973), as a review of* Animals, Men and Morals, *edited by Stanley and Roslind Godlovitch and John Harris.*

ics. The other pieces are by a psychologist, a botanist, a sociologist, and Ruth Harrison, who is probably best described as a professional campaigner for animal welfare.

Whether or not these people, as individuals, would all agree that they are launching a liberation movement for animals, the book as a whole amounts to no less. It is a demand for a complete change in our attitudes to nonhumans. It is a demand that we cease to regard the exploitation of other species as natural and inevitable, and that, instead, we see it as a continuing moral outrage. Patrick Corbett, Professor of Philosophy at Sussex University, captures the spirit of the book in his closing words:

> We require now to extend the great principles of liberty, equality, and fraternity over the lives of animals. Let animal slavery join human slavery in the graveyard of the past.

The reader is likely to be skeptical. "Animal Liberation" sounds more like a parody of liberation movements than a serious objective. The reader may think: We support the claims of blacks and women for equality because blacks and women really are equal to whites and males—equal in intelligence and in abilities, capacity for leadership, rationality, and so on. Humans and nonhumans obviously are not equal in these respects. Since justice demands only that we treat equals equally, unequal treatment of humans and nonhumans cannot be an injustice.

This is a tempting reply, but a dangerous one. It commits the non- 5 racist and nonsexist to a dogmatic belief that blacks and women really are just as intelligent, able, etc., as whites and males—and no more. Quite possibly this happens to be the case. Certainly attempts to prove that racial or sexual differences in these respects have a genetic origin have not been conclusive. But do we really want to stake our demand for equality on the assumption that there are no genetic differences of this kind between the different races or sexes? Surely the appropriate response to those who claim to have found evidence for such genetic differences is not to stick to the belief that there are no differences, whatever the evidence to the contrary; rather one should be clear that the claim to equality does not depend on IQ. Moral equality is distinct from factual equality. Otherwise it would be nonsense to talk to the equality of human beings, since humans, as individuals, obviously differ in intelligence and almost any ability one cares to name. If possessing greater intelligence does not entitle one human to exploit another, why should it entitle humans to exploit nonhumans?

Jeremy Bentham expressed the essential basis of equality in his famous formula: "Each to count for one and none for more than one." In other words, the interests of every being that has interests are to be taken into account and treated equally with the like interests of any other being. Other moral philosophers, before and after Bentham, have made the same point in different ways. Our concern for others must not depend on whether they possess certain characteristics, though just what that concern involves may, of course, vary according to such characteristics.

Bentham, incidentally, was well aware that the logic of the demand for racial equality did not stop at the equality of humans. He wrote:

> The day *may* come when the rest of the animal creation may acquire those rights which never could have been withholden from them but by the hand of tyranny. The French have already discovered that the blackness of the skin is no reason why a human being should be abandoned without redress to the caprice of a tormentor. It may one day come to be recognized that the number of the legs, the villosity of the skin, or the termination of the *os sacrum,* are reasons equally insufficient for abandoning a sensitive being to the same fate. What else is it that should trace the insuperable line? Is it the faculty of reason, or perhaps the faculty of discourse? But a full-grown horse or dog is beyond comparison a more rational, as well as a more conversable animal, than an infant of a day, or a week, or even a month, old. But suppose they were otherwise, what would it avail? The question is not, Can they *reason?* nor Can they *talk?* but, Can they *suffer?*[1]

Surely Bentham was right. If a being suffers, there can be no moral justification for refusing to take that suffering into consideration, and, indeed, to count it equally with the like suffering (if rough comparisons can be made) of any other being.

So the only question is: Do animals other than man suffer? Most people agree unhesitatingly that animals like cats and dogs can and do suffer, and this seems also to be assumed by those laws that prohibit wanton cruelty to such animals. Personally, I have no doubt at all about this and find it hard to take seriously the doubts that a few people apparently do have. The editors and contributors of *Animals, Men and Morals* seem to feel the same way, for although the question is raised more than once, doubts are quickly dismissed each time. Nevertheless, because this is such a fundamental point, it is worth asking what grounds we have for attributing suffering to other animals.

It is best to begin by asking what grounds any individual human has for supposing that other humans feel pain. Since pain is a state of consciousness, a "mental event," it can never be directly observed. No observations, whether behavioral signs such as writhing or screaming or physiological or neurological recordings, are observations of pain itself. Pain is something one feels, and one can only infer that others are feeling it from various external indications. The fact that only philosophers are ever skeptical about whether other humans feel pain shows that we regard such inference as justifiable in the case of humans.

---

[1] *The Principles of Morals and Legislation.* ch. XVII, sec. 1, footnote to paragraph 4. [All notes are the author's unless otherwise specified.]

Is there any reason why the same inference should be unjustifiable for other animals? Nearly all the external signs which lead us to infer pain in other humans can be seen in other species, especially "higher" animals such as mammals and birds. Behavioral signs—writhing, yelping, or other forms of calling, attempts to avoid the source of pain, and many others—are present. We know, too, that these animals are biologically similar in the relevant respects, having nervous systems like ours which can be observed to function as ours do.

So the grounds for inferring that these animals can feel pain are nearly as good as the grounds for inferring other humans do. Only nearly, for there is one behavioral sign that humans have but nonhumans, with the exception of one or two specially raised chimpanzees, do not have. This, of course, is a developed language. As the quotation from Bentham indicates, this has long been regarded as an important distinction between man and other animals. Other animals may communicate with each other, but not in the way we do. Following Chomsky,[2] many people now mark this distinction by saying that only humans communicate in a form that is governed by rules of syntax. (For the purposes of this argument, linguists allow those chimpanzees who have learned a syntactic sign language to rank as honorary humans.) Nevertheless, as Bentham pointed out, this distinction is not relevant to the question of how animals ought to be treated, unless it can be linked to the issue of whether animals suffer.

This link may be attempted in two ways. First, there is a hazy line of philosophical thought, stemming perhaps from some doctrines associated with Wittgenstein, which maintains that we cannot meaningfully attribute states of consciousness to beings without language. I have not seen this argument made explicit in print, though I have come across it in conversation. This position seems to me very implausible, and I doubt that it would be held at all if it were not thought to be a consequence of a broader view of the significance of language. It may be that the use of a public, rule-governed language is a precondition of conceptual thought. It may even be, although personally I doubt it, that we cannot meaningfully speak of a creature having an intention unless that creature can use a language. But states like pain, surely, are more primitive than either of these, and seem to have nothing to do with language.

Indeed, as Jane Goodall points out in her study of chimpanzees, when it comes to the expression of feelings and emotions, humans tend to fall back on nonlinguistic modes of communication which are often found among apes, such as a cheering pat on the back, an exuberant embrace, a clasp of hands, and so on.[3] Michael Peters makes a similar point in his contribution to *Animals, Men and Morals* when he notes that the basic signals we use to convey pain, fear, sexual arousal, and so on are not specific to our

[2]**Chomsky** Noam Chomsky (b. 1928), a professor of linguistics and the author of (among other books) *Language and Mind* (1972). [Editors' note.]

[3]Jane van Lawick-Goodall, *In the Shadow of Man* (Houghton Mifflin, 1971), p. 225.

species. So there seems to be no reason at all to believe that a creature without language cannot suffer.

The second, and more easily appreciated way of linking language and the existence of pain is to say that the best evidence that we can have that another creature is in pain is when he tells us that he is. This is a distinct line of argument, for it is not being denied that a non-language-user conceivably could suffer, but only that we could know that he is suffering. Still, this line of argument seems to me to fail, and for reasons similar to those just given. "I am in pain" is not the best possible evidence that the speaker is in pain (he might be lying) and it is certainly not the only possible evidence. Behavioral signs and knowledge of the animal's biological similarity to ourselves together provide adequate evidence that animals do suffer. After all, we would not accept linguistic evidence if it contradicted the rest of the evidence. If a man was severely burned, and behaved as if he were in pain, writhing, groaning, being very careful not to let his burned skin touch anything, and so on, but later said he had not been in pain at all, we would be more likely to conclude that he was lying or suffering from amnesia than that he had not been in pain.

Even if there were stronger grounds for refusing to attribute pain to 15 those who do not have a language, the consequences of this refusal might lead us to examine these grounds unusually critically. Human infants, as well as some adults, are unable to use language. Are we to deny that a year-old infant can suffer? If not, how can language be crucial? Of course, most parents can understand the responses of even very young infants better than they understand the responses of other animals, and sometimes infant responses can be understood in the light of later development.

This, however, is just a fact about the relative knowledge we have of our own species and other species, and most of this knowledge is simply derived from closer contact. Those who have studied the behavior of other animals soon learn to understand their responses at least as well as we understand those of an infant. (I am not referring to Jane Goodall's and other well-known studies of apes. Consider, for example, the degree of understanding achieved by Tinbergen from watching herring gulls.[4]) Just as we can understand infant human behavior in the light of adult human behavior, so we can understand the behavior of other species in the light of our own behavior (and sometimes we can understand our own behavior better in the light of the behavior of other species).

The grounds we have for believing that other mammals and birds suffer are, then, closely analogous to the grounds we have for believing that other humans suffer. It remains to consider how far down the evolutionary scale this analogy holds. Obviously it becomes poorer when we get further away from man. To be more precise would require a detailed examination of all that we know about other forms of life. With fish, reptiles, and other vertebrates the analogy still seems strong, with molluscs like oysters it is

---

[4]N. Tinbergen, *The Herring Gull's World* (Basic Books, 1961).

much weaker. Insects are more difficult, and it may be that in our present state of knowledge we must be agnostic about whether they are capable of suffering.

If there is no moral justification for ignoring suffering when it occurs, and it does occur in other species, what are we to say of our attitudes toward these other species? Richard Ryder, one of the contributors to *Animals, Men and Morals*, uses the term "speciesism" to describe the belief that we are entitled to treat members of other species in a way in which it would be wrong to treat members of our own species. The term is not euphonious, but it neatly makes the analogy with racism. The nonracist would do well to bear the analogy in mind when he is inclined to defend human behavior toward nonhumans. "Shouldn't we worry about improving the lot of our own species before we concern ourselves with other species?" he may ask. If we substitute "race" for "species" we shall see that the question is better not asked. "Is a vegetarian diet nutritionally adequate?" resembles the slaveowner's claim that he and the whole economy of the South would be ruined without slave labor. There is even a parallel with skeptical doubts about whether animals suffer, for some defenders of slavery professed to doubt whether blacks really suffer in the way whites do.

I do not want to give the impression, however, that the case for Animal Liberation is based on the analogy with racism and no more. On the contrary, *Animals, Men and Morals* describes the various ways in which humans exploit nonhumans, and several contributors consider the defenses that have been offered, including the defense of meat-eating mentioned in the last paragraph. Sometimes the rebuttals are scornfully dismissive, rather than carefully designed to convince the detached critic. This may be a fault, but it is a fault that is inevitable, given the kind of book this is. The issue is not one on which one can remain detached. As the editors state in their Introduction:

> Once the full force of moral assessment has been made explicit there can be no rational excuse left for killing animals, be they killed for food, science, or sheer personal indulgence. We have not assembled this book to provide the reader with yet another manual on how to make brutalities less brutal. Compromise, in the traditional sense of the term, is simple unthinking weakness when one considers the actual reasons for our crude relationships with the other animals.

The point is that on this issue there are few critics who are genuinely 20 detached. People who eat pieces of slaughtered nonhumans every day find it hard to believe that they are doing wrong; and they also find it hard to imagine what else they could eat. So for those who do not place nonhumans beyond the pale of morality, there comes a stage when further argument seems pointless, a stage at which one can only accuse one's opponent of hypocrisy and reach for the sort of sociological account of our practices and the way we defend them that is attempted by David Wood in his contribution to his book. On the other hand, to those unconvinced by the arguments, and unable to accept that they are merely rationalizing their dietary preferences and their fear of being thought peculiar, such sociological explanations can only seem insultingly arrogant.

II

The logic of speciesism is most apparent in the practice of experimenting on nonhumans in order to benefit humans. This is because the issue is rarely obscured by allegations that nonhumans are so different from humans that we cannot know anything about whether they suffer. The defender of vivisection cannot use this argument because he needs to stress the similarities between man and other animals in order to justify the usefulness to the former of experiments on the latter. The researcher who makes rats choose between starvation and electric shocks to see if they develop ulcers (they do) does so because he knows that the rat has a nervous system very similar to man's, and presumably feels an electric shock in a similar way.

Richard Ryder's restrained account of experiments on animals made me angrier with my fellow men than anything else in this book. Ryder, a clinical psychologist by profession, himself experimented on animals before he came to hold the view he puts forward in his essay. Experimenting on animals is now a large industry, both academic and commercial. In 1969, more than 5 million experiments were performed in Britain, the vast majority without anesthetic (though how many of these involved pain is not known). There are no accurate U.S. figures, since there is no federal law on the subject, and in many cases no state law either. Estimates vary from 20 million to 200 million. Ryder suggests that 80 million may be the best guess. We tend to think that this is all for vital medical research, but of course it is not. Huge numbers of animals are used in university departments from Forestry to Psychology, and even more are used for commercial purposes, to test whether cosmetics can cause skin damage, or shampoos eye damage, or to test food additives or laxatives or sleeping pills or anything else.

A standard test for foodstuffs is the "LD50." The object of this test is to find the dosage level at which 50 percent of the test animals will die. This means that nearly all of them will become very sick before finally succumbing or surviving. When the substance is a harmless one, it may be necessary to force huge doses down the animals, until in some cases sheer volume or concentration causes death.

Ryder gives a selection of experiments, taken from recent scientific journals. I will quote two, not for the sake of indulging in gory details, but in order to give an idea of what normal researchers think they may legitimately do to other species. The point is not that the individual researchers are cruel men, but that they are behaving in a way that is allowed by our speciesist attitudes. As Ryder points out, even if only 1 percent of the experiments involve severe pain, that is 50,000 experiments in Britain each year, or nearly 150 every day (and about fifteen times as many in the United States, if Ryder's guess is right). Here then are two experiments:

> O. S. Ray and R. J. Barrett of Pittsburgh gave electric shocks to the feet of 1,042 mice. They then caused convulsions by giving more intense shocks through cup-shaped electrodes applied to the animals' eyes or through pressure spring clips attached to their ears. Unfortunately some of the mice who "successfully completed Day One training were found sick or dead prior to testing on Day Two." [*Journal of Comparative and Physiological Psychology*, 1969, vol. 67, pp. 110–116]
>
> At the National Institute for Medical Research, Mill Hill, London, W. Feldberg and S. L. Sherwood injected chemicals into the brains of cats — "with a number of widely different substances, recurrent patterns of reaction were obtained. Retching, vomiting, defecation, increased salivation and greatly accelerated respiration leading to panting were common features." . . .
>
> The injection into the brain of a large dose of Tubocuraine caused the cat to jump "from the table to the floor and then straight into its cage, where it started calling more and more noisily whilst moving about restlessly and jerkily . . . finally the cat fell with legs and neck flexed, jerking in rapid clonic movements, the condition being that of a major [epileptic] convulsion . . . within a few seconds the cat got up, ran for a few yards at high speed, and fell in another fit. The whole process was repeated several times within the next ten minutes, during which the cat lost faeces and foamed at the mouth."
>
> This animal finally died thirty-five minutes after the brain injection. [*Journal of Physiology*, 1954, vol. 123, pp. 148–167]

There is nothing secret about these experiments. One has only to open any recent volume of a learned journal, such as the *Journal of Comparative and Physiological Psychology*, to find full descriptions of experiments of this sort, together with the results obtained — results that are frequently trivial and obvious. The experiments are often supported by public funds.

It is a significant indication of the level of acceptability of these practices that, although these experiments are taking place at this moment on university campuses throughout the country, there has, so far as I know, not been the slightest protest from the student movement. Students have been rightly concerned that their universities should not discriminate on grounds of race or sex, and that they should not serve the purposes of the military or big business. Speciesism continues undisturbed, and many students participate in it. There may be a few qualms at first, but since everyone regards it as normal, and it may even be a required part of a course, the student soon becomes hardened and, dismissing his earlier feelings as "mere sentiment," comes to regard animals as statistics rather than sentient beings with interests that warrant consideration.

Argument about vivisection has often missed the point because it has been put in absolutist terms: Would the abolitionist be prepared to let thousands die if they could be saved by experimenting on a single animal? The way to reply to this purely hypothetical question is to pose another: Would the experimenter be prepared to experiment on a human orphan under six months old, if it were the only way to save many lives? (I say "orphan" to avoid the complication of parental feelings, although in doing so I am being overfair to the experimenter, since the nonhuman subjects of experiments are not orphans.) A negative answer to this question indicates that the experimenter's readiness to use nonhumans is simple discrimination, for adult apes, cats, mice, and other mammals are more conscious of what is happening to them, more self-directing, and, so far as we can tell, just as sensitive to pain as a human infant. There is no characteristic that human infants possess that adult mammals do not have to the same or a higher degree.

(It might be possible to hold that what makes it wrong to experiment on a human infant is that the infant will in time develop into more than the nonhuman, but one would then, to be consistent, have to oppose abortion, and perhaps contraception, too, for the fetus and the egg and sperm have the same potential as the infant. Moreover, one would still have no reason for experimenting on a nonhuman rather than a human with brain damage severe enough to make it impossible for him to rise above infant level.)

The experimenter, then, shows a bias for his own species whenever he carries out an experiment on a nonhuman for a purpose that he would not think justified him in using a human being at an equal or lower level of sentience, awareness, ability to be self-directing, etc. No one familiar with the kind of results yielded by these experiments can have the slightest doubt that if this bias were eliminated the number of experiments performed would be zero or very close to it.

III

If it is vivisection that shows the logic of speciesism most clearly, it is 30 the use of other species for food that is at the heart of our attitudes toward them. Most of *Animals, Men and Morals* is an attack on meat eating — an attack which is based solely on concern for nonhumans, without reference to arguments derived from consideration of ecology, macrobiotics, health, or religion.

The idea that nonhumans are utilities, means to our ends, pervades our thought. Even conservationists who are concerned about the slaughter of wildfowl but not about the vastly greater slaughter of chickens for our tables are thinking in this way — they are worried about what we would lose if there were less wildlife. Stanley Godlovitch, pursuing the Marxist idea that our thinking is formed by the activities we undertake in satisfying our needs, suggests that man's first classification of his environment was into Edibles and Inedibles. Most animals came into the first category, and there they have remained.

Man may always have killed other species for food, but he has never exploited them so ruthlessly as he does today. Farming has succumbed to business methods, the objective being to get the highest possible ratio of output (meat, eggs, milk) to input (fodder, labor costs, etc.). Ruth Harrison's essay "On Factory Farming" gives an account of some aspects of modern methods, and of the unsuccessful British campaigns for effective controls, a campaign which was sparked off by her *Animal Machines* (London: Stuart, 1964).

Her article is in no way a substitute for her earlier book. This is a pity since, as she says, "Farm produce is still associated with mental pictures of animals browsing in the fields . . . of hens having a last forage before going to roost. . . ." Yet neither in her article nor elsewhere in *Animals, Men and Morals* is this false image replaced by a clear idea of the nature and extent of factory farming. We learn of this only indirectly, when we hear of the code of reform proposed by an advisory committee set up by the British government.

Among the proposals, which the government refused to implement on the grounds that they were too idealistic, were: *"Any animal should at least have room to turn around freely."*

Factory farm animals need liberation in the most literal sense. Veal 35 calves are kept in stalls 5 feet by 2 feet. They are usually slaughtered when about four months old, and have been too big to turn in their stalls for at least a month. Intensive beef herds, kept in stalls only proportionately larger for much longer periods, account for a growing percentage of beef production. Sows are often similarly confined when pregnant, which, because of artificial methods of increasing fertility, can be most of the time. Animals confined in this way do not waste food by exercising, nor do they develop unpalatable muscle.

"A dry bedded area should be provided for all stock." Intensively kept animals usually have to stand and sleep in slatted floors without straw, because this makes cleaning easier.

"Palatable roughage must be readily available to all calves after one week of age." In order to produce the pale veal housewives are said to prefer, calves are fed on an all-liquid diet until slaughter, even though they are long past the age at which they would normally eat grass. They develop a craving for roughage, evidenced by attempts to gnaw wood from their stalls. (For the same reason, their diet is deficient in iron.)

"Battery cages for poultry should be large enough for a bird to be able to stretch one wing at a time." Under current British practice, a cage for four or five laying hens has a floor area of 20 inches by 18 inches, scarcely larger than a double page of the *New York Review of Books*. In this space, on a sloping wire floor (sloping so the eggs roll down, wire so the dung drips through) the birds live for a year or eighteen months while artificial lighting and temperature conditions combine with drugs in their food to squeeze the maximum number of eggs out of them. Table birds are also sometimes kept in cages. More often they are reared in sheds, no less crowded. Under these conditions all the birds' natural activities are frus-

trated, and they develop "vices" such as pecking each other to death. To prevent this, beaks are often cut off, and the sheds kept dark.

How many of those who support factory farming by buying its produce know anything about the way it is produced? How many have heard something about it, but are reluctant to check up for fear that it will make them uncomfortable? To nonspeciesists, the typical consumer's mixture of ignorance, reluctance to find out the truth, and vague belief that nothing really bad could be allowed seems analogous to the attitudes of "decent Germans" to the death camps.

There are, of course, some defenders of factory farming. Their argu- 40 ments are considered, though again rather sketchily, by John Harris. Among the most common: "Since they have never known anything else, they don't suffer." This argument will not be put by anyone who knows anything about animal behavior, since he will know that not all behavior has to be learned. Chickens attempt to stretch wings, walk around, scratch, and even dustbathe or build a nest, even though they have never lived under conditions that allowed these activities. Calves can suffer from maternal deprivation no matter at what age they were taken from their mothers. "We need these intensive methods to provide protein for a growing population." As ecologists and famine relief organizations know, we can produce far more protein per acre if we grow the right vegetable crop, soy beans for instance, than if we use the land to grow crops to be converted into protein by animals who use nearly 90 percent of the protein themselves, even when unable to exercise.

There will be many readers of this book who will agree that factory farming involves an unjustifiable degree of exploitation of sentient creatures, and yet will want to say that there is nothing wrong with rearing animals for food, provided it is done "humanely." These people are saying, in effect, that although we should not cause animals to suffer, there is nothing wrong with killing them.

There are two possible replies to this view. One is to attempt to show that this combination of attitudes is absurd. Roslind Godlovitch takes this course in her essay, which is an examination of some common attitudes to animals. She argues that from the combination of "animal suffering is to be avoided" and "there is nothing wrong with killing animals" it follows that all animal life ought to be exterminated (since all sentient creatures will suffer to some degree at some point in their lives). Euthanasia is a contentious issue only because we place some value on living. If we did not, the least amount of suffering would justify it. Accordingly, if we deny that we have a duty to exterminate all animal life, we must concede that we are placing some value on animal life.

This argument seems to me valid, although one could still reply that the value of animal life is to be derived from the pleasures that life can have for them, so that, provided their lives have a balance of pleasure over pain, we are justified in rearing them. But this would imply that we ought to produce animals and let them live as pleasantly as possible, without suffering.

At this point, one can make the second of the two possible replies to the view that rearing and killing animals for food is all right so long as it is done humanely. This second reply is that so long as we think that a nonhuman may be killed simply so that a human can satisfy his taste for meat, we are still thinking of nonhumans as means rather than as ends in themselves. The factory farm is nothing more than the application of technology to this concept. Even traditional methods involve castration, the separation of mothers and their young, the breaking up of herds, branding or earpunching, and of course transportation to the abattoirs and the final moments of terror when the animal smells blood and senses danger. If we were to try rearing animals so that they lived and died without suffering, we should find that to do so on anything like the scale of today's meat industry would be a sheer impossibility. Meat would become the prerogative of the rich.

I have been able to discuss only some of the contributions to this book, 45 saying nothing about, for instance, the essays on killing for furs and for sport. Nor have I considered all the detailed questions that need to be asked once we start thinking about other species in the radically different way presented by this book. What, for instance, are we to do about genuine conflicts of interest like rats biting slum children? I am not sure of the answer, but the essential point is just that we *do* see this as a conflict of interests, that we recognize that rats have interests too. Then we may begin to think about other ways of resolving the conflict — perhaps by leaving out rat baits that sterilize the rats instead of killing them.

I have not discussed such problems because they are side issues compared with the exploitation of other species for food and for experimental purposes. On these central matters, I hope that I have said enough to show that this book, despite its flaws, is a challenge to every human to recognize his attitudes to nonhumans as a form of prejudice no less objectionable than racism or sexism. It is a challenge that demands not just a change of attitudes, but a change in our way of life, for it requires us to become vegetarians.

Can a purely moral demand of this kind succeed? The odds are certainly against it. The book holds out no inducements. It does not tell us that we will become healthier, or enjoy life more, if we cease exploiting animals. Animal Liberation will require greater altruism on the part of mankind than any other liberation movement, since animals are incapable of demanding it for themselves, or of protesting against their exploitation by votes, demonstrations, or bombs. Is man capable of such genuine altruism? Who knows? If this book does have a significant effect, however, it will be a vindication of all those who have believed that man has within himself the potential for more than cruelty and selfishness.

Topics for Critical Thinking and Writing

1. In his fourth paragraph Singer formulates an argument on behalf of the skeptical reader. Examine that argument closely, restate it in your own words, and evaluate it. Which of its premises is most vulnerable to criticism? Why?

2. Singer quotes with approval (para. 7) Bentham's comment, "The question is not, Can they *reason?* nor Can they *talk?* but, Can they *suffer?*" Do you find this argument persuasive? Can you think of any effective challenge to it?

3. Singer allows that although developed linguistic capacity is not necessary for a creature to have pain, perhaps such a capacity is necessary for "having an intention" (para. 12). Do you think this concession is correct? Have you ever seen animal behavior that you would be willing to describe or explain as evidence that the animal has an intention to do something, despite knowing that the animal cannot talk?

4. Singer thinks that the readiness to experiment on animals cuts out the ground for believing that animals don't suffer pain (see para. 21). Do you agree with this reasoning?

5. Singer confesses (para. 22) to being made especially angry "with my fellow men" after reading the accounts of animal experimentation. What is it that aroused his anger? Do such feelings, and the acknowledgment that one has them, have any place in a sober discussion about the merits of animal experimentation? Why, or why not?

6. What is "factory farming" (paras. 32–40)? Why is Singer opposed to it?

7. To the claim that there is nothing wrong with "rearing and killing animals for food," provided it is done "humanely," Singer offers two replies (paras. 42–44). In an essay of 250 words summarize them briefly and then indicate whether either persuades you, and why or why not.

8. Suppose someone were to say to Singer: "You claim that capacity to suffer is the relevant factor in deciding whether a creature deserves to be treated as my moral equal. But you're wrong — the relevant factor is whether the creature is *alive.* Being alive is what matters, not being capable of feeling pain." In one or two paragraphs declare what you think would be Singer's reply.

9. Do you think it is worse to kill an animal for its fur than to kill, cook, and eat an animal? Is it worse to kill an animal for sport than to kill it for medical experimentation? What is Singer's view? Explain your view, making use of Singer's if you wish, in an essay of 500 words.

10. Are there any arguments, in your opinion, which show the immorality of eating human flesh (cannibalism) but which do not show a similar objection to eating animal flesh? Write a 500-word essay in which you discuss the issue.

Carl Cohen

The Case for the Use of Animals in Biomedical Research

Using animals as research subjects in medical investigations is widely condemned on two grounds: first, because it wrongly violates the *rights* of animals,[1] and second, because it wrongly imposes on sentient creatures much avoidable *suffering*.[2] Neither of these arguments is sound. The first relies on a mistaken understanding of rights; the second relies on a mistaken calculation of consequences. Both deserve definitive dismissal.

WHY ANIMALS HAVE NO RIGHTS

A right, properly understood, is a claim, or potential claim, that one party may exercise against another. The target against whom such a claim may be registered can be a single person, a group, a community, or (perhaps) all humankind. The content of rights claims also varies greatly: repayment of loans, nondiscrimination by employers, noninterference by the state, and so on. To comprehend any genuine right fully, therefore, we must know *who* holds the right, *against whom* it is held, and *to what* it is a right.

Alternative sources of rights add complexity. Some rights are grounded in constitution and law (e.g., the right of an accused to trial by jury); some rights are moral but give no legal claims (e.g., my right to your keeping the promise you gave me); and some rights (e.g., against theft or assault) are rooted both in morals and in law.

The different targets, contents, and sources of rights, and their inevitable conflict, together weave a tangled web. Notwithstanding all such complications, this much is clear about rights in general: They are in every case claims, or potential claims, within a community of moral agents. Rights arise, and can be intelligibly defended, only among beings who actually do, or can, make moral claims against one another. Whatever else rights may be, therefore, they are necessarily human; their possessors are persons, human beings.

The attributes of human beings from which this moral capability arises 5

[1]Regan T. The case for animal rights. Berkeley, Calif.: University of California Press, 1983. [All notes are the author's.]

[2]Singer P. Animal liberation. New York: Avon Books, 1977.

Carl Cohen (b. 1931) received his doctorate in philosophy from UCLA in 1955. A teacher at the University of Michigan, he is the author of many articles on social and political issues. The article that we reprint appeared originally in the New England Journal of Medicine in October 1986.

have been described variously by philosophers, both ancient and modern: the inner consciousness of a free will (Saint Augustine[3]); the grasp, by human reason, of the binding character of moral law (Saint Thomas[4]); the self-conscious participation of human beings in an objective ethical order (Hegel[5]); human membership in an organic moral community (Bradley[6]); the development of the human self through the consciousness of other moral selves (Mead[7]); and the underivative, intuitive cognition of the rightness of an action (Prichard[8]). Most influential has been Immanuel Kant's emphasis on the universal human possession of a uniquely moral will and the autonomy its use entails.[9] Humans confront choices that are purely moral; humans — but certainly not dogs or mice — lay down moral laws, for others and for themselves. Human beings are self-legislative, morally *auto-nomous*.

Animals (that is, nonhuman animals, the ordinary sense of that word) lack this capacity for free moral judgment. They are not beings of a kind capable of exercising or responding to moral claims. Animals therefore have no rights, and they can have none. This is the core of the argument about the alleged rights of animals. The holders of rights must have the capacity to comprehend rules of duty, governing all including themselves. In applying such rules, the holders of rights must recognize possible conflicts between what is in their own interest and what is just. Only in a community of beings capable of self-restricting moral judgments can the concept of a right be correctly invoked.

Humans have such moral capacities. They are in this sense self-legislative, are members of communities governed by moral rules, and do possess rights. Animals do not have such moral capacities. They are not morally self-legislative, cannot possibly be members of a truly moral community, and therefore cannot possess rights. In conducting research on animal subjects, therefore, we do not violate their rights, because they have none to violate.

To animate life, even in its simplest forms, we give a certain natural reverence. But the possession of rights presupposes a moral status not attained by the vast majority of living things. We must not infer, therefore, that a live being has, simply in being alive, a "right" to its life. The assertion

---

[3] St. Augustine. Confessions. Book Seven. 397 A.D. New York: Pocket Books, 1957:104–26.

[4] St. Thomas Aquinas. Summa theologica. 1273 A.D. Philosophic texts. New York. Oxford University Press, 1960:353–66.

[5] Hegel GWF. Philosophy of right. 1821. London: Oxford University Press, 1952:105–10.

[6] Bradley FH. Why should I be moral? 1876. In: Melden AI, ed. Ethical theories, New York: Prentice Hall, 1950:345–59.

[7] Mead GH. The genesis of the self and social control. 1925. In: Reck AJ, ed. Selected writings. Indianapolis: Bobbs-Merrill, 1964:264–93.

[8] Prichard HA. Does moral philosophy rest on a mistake? 1912. In: Sellars W, Hospers J, eds. Readings in ethical theory. New York: Appleton-Century-Crofts, 1952:149–63.

[9] Kant I. Fundamental principles of the metaphysic of morals. 1785. New York: Liberal Arts Press, 1949.

that all animals, only because they are alive and have interests, also possess the "right to life"[10] is an abuse of that phrase, and wholly without warrant.

It does not follow from this, however, that we are morally·free to do anything we please to animals. Certainly not. In our dealings with animals, as in our dealings with other human beings, we have obligations that do not arise from claims against us based on rights. Rights entail obligations, but many of the things one ought to do are in no way tied to another's entitlement. Rights and obligations are not reciprocals of one another, and it is a serious mistake to suppose that they are.

Illustrations are helpful. Obligations may arise from internal commit- 10 ments made: Physicians have obligations to their patients not grounded merely in their patients' rights. Teachers have such obligations to their students, shepherds to their dogs, and cowboys to their horses. Obligations may arise from differences of status: Adults owe special care when playing with young children, and children owe special care when playing with young pets. Obligations may arise from special relationships: The payment of my son's college tuition is something to which he may have no right, although it may be my obligation to bear the burden if I reasonably can; my dog has no right to daily exercise and veterinary care, but I do have the obligation to provide these things for her. Obligations may arise from particular acts or circumstances: One may be obliged to another for a special kindness done, or obliged to put an animal out of its misery in view of its condition — although neither the human benefactor nor the dying animal may have had a claim of right.

Plainly, the grounds of our obligations to humans and to animals are manifold and cannot be formulated simply. Some hold that there is a general obligation to do no gratuitous harm to sentient creatures (the principle of nonmaleficence); some hold that there is a general obligation to do good to sentient creatures when that is reasonably within one's power (the principle of beneficence). In our dealings with animals, few will deny that we are at least obliged to act humanely — that is, to treat them with the decency and concern that we owe, as sensitive human beings, to other sentient creatures. To treat animals humanely, however, is not to treat them as humans or as the holders of rights.

A common objection, which deserves a response, may be paraphrased as follows:

> If having rights requires being able to make moral claims, to grasp and apply moral laws, then many humans — the brain-damaged, the comatose, the senile — who plainly lack those capacities must be without rights. But that is absurd. This proves [the critic concludes] that rights do not depend on the presence of moral capacities.[1,10]

This objection fails; it mistakenly treats an essential feature of humanity as though it were a screen for sorting humans. The capacity for moral

[10]Rollin BE. Animal rights and human morality. New York: Prometheus Books, 1981.

judgment that distinguishes humans from animals is not a test to be administered to human beings one by one. Persons who are unable, because of some disability, to perform the full moral functions natural to human beings are certainly not for that reason ejected from the moral community. The issue is one of kind. Humans are of such a kind that they may be the subject of experiments only with their voluntary consent. The choices they make freely must be respected. Animals are of such a kind that it is impossible for them, in principle, to give or withhold voluntary consent or to make a moral choice. What humans retain when disabled, animals have never had.

A second objection, also often made, may be paraphrased as follows:

> Capacities will not succeed in distinguishing humans from the other animals. Animals also reason; animals also communicate with one another; animals also care passionately for their young; animals also exhibit desires and preferences.[11,12] Features of moral relevance — rationality, interdependence, and love — are not exhibited uniquely by human beings. Therefore [this critic concludes], there can be no solid moral distinction between humans and other animals.[10]

This criticism misses the central point. It is not the ability to commu- 15 nicate or to reason, or dependence on one another, or care for the young, or the exhibition of preference, or any such behavior that marks the critical divide. Analogies between human families and those of monkeys, or between human communities and those of wolves, and the like, are entirely beside the point. Patterns of conduct are not at issue. Animals do indeed exhibit remarkable behavior at times. Conditioning, fear, instinct, and intelligence all contribute to species survival. Membership in a community of moral agents nevertheless remains impossible for them. Actors subject to moral judgment must be capable of grasping the generality of an ethical premise in a practical syllogism. Humans act immorally often enough, but only they — never wolves or monkeys — can discern, by applying some moral rule to the facts of a case, that a given act ought or ought not to be performed. The moral restraints imposed by humans on themselves are thus highly abstract and are often in conflict with the self-interest of the agent. Communal behavior among animals, even when most intelligent and most endearing, does not approach autonomous morality in this fundamental sense.

Genuinely moral acts have an internal as well as an external dimension. Thus, in law, an act can be criminal only when the guilty deed, the *actus reus*, is done with a guilty mind, *mens rea*. No animal can ever commit a crime; bringing animals to criminal trial is the mark of primitive ignorance. The claims of moral right are similarly inapplicable to them. Does a

---

[11]Hoff C. Immoral and moral uses of animals. N Engl J Med 1980; 302:115–8.

[12]Jamieson D. Killing persons and other beings. In: Miller HB, Williams WH, eds. Ethics and animals. Clifton, N.J.: Humana Press, 1983:135–46.

lion have a right to eat a baby zebra? Does a baby zebra have a right not to be eaten? Such questions, mistakenly invoking the concept of right where it does not belong, do not make good sense. Those who condemn biomedical research because it violates "animal rights" commit the same blunder.

IN DEFENSE OF "SPECIESISM"

Abandoning reliance on animal rights, some critics resort instead to animal sentience — their feelings of pain and distress. We ought to desist from imposition of pain insofar as we can. Since all or nearly all experimentation on animals does impose pain and could be readily forgone, say these critics, it should be stopped. The ends sought may be worthy, but those ends do not justify imposing agonies on humans, and by animals the agonies are felt no less. The laboratory use of animals (these critics conclude) must therefore be ended — or at least very sharply curtailed.

Argument of this variety is essentially utilitarian, often expressly so;[13] it is based on the calculation of the net product, in pains and pleasures, resulting from experiments on animals. Jeremy Bentham, comparing horses and dogs with other sentient creatures, is thus commonly quoted: "The question is not, Can they reason? nor Can they talk? but, Can they suffer?"[14]

Animals certainly can suffer and surely ought not to be made to suffer needlessly. But in inferring, from these uncontroversial premises, that biomedical research causing animal distress is largely (or wholly) wrong, the critic commits two serious errors.

The first error is the assumption, often explicitly defended, that all sentient animals have equal moral standing. Between a dog and a human being, according to this view, there is no moral difference; hence the pains suffered by dogs must be weighed no differently from the pains suffered by humans. To deny such equality, according to this critic, is to give unjust preference to one species over another; it is "speciesism." The most influential statement of this moral equality of species was made by Peter Singer:

> The racist violates the principle of equality by giving greater weight to the interests of members of his own race when there is a clash between their interests and the interests of those of another race. The sexist violates the principle of equality by favoring the interests of his own sex. Similarly the speciesist allows the interests of his own species to override the greater interests of members of other species. The pattern is identical in each case.[2]

This argument is worse than unsound; it is atrocious. It draws an offensive moral conclusion from a deliberately devised verbal parallelism that

---

[13]Singer P. Ten years of animal liberation. New York Review of Books. 1985; 31:46–52.

[14]Bentham J. Introduction to the principles of morals and legislation. London: Athlone Press, 1970.

is utterly specious. Racism has no rational ground whatever. Differing degrees of respect or concern for humans for no other reason than that they are members of different races is an injustice totally without foundation in the nature of the races themselves. Racists, even if acting on the basis of mistaken factual beliefs, do grave moral wrong precisely because there is no morally relevant distinction among the races. The supposition of such differences has led to outright horror. The same is true of the sexes, neither sex being entitled by right to greater respect or concern than the other. No dispute here.

Between species of animate life, however — between (for example) humans on the one hand and cats or rats on the other — the morally relevant differences are enormous, and almost universally appreciated. Humans engage in moral reflection; humans are morally autonomous; humans are members of moral communities, recognizing just claims against their own interest. Human beings do have rights, theirs is a moral status very different from that of cats or rats.

I am a speciesist. Speciesism is not merely plausible; it is essential for right conduct, because those who will not make the morally relevant distinctions among species are almost certain, in consequence, to misapprehend their true obligations. The analogy between speciesism and racism is insidious. Every sensitive moral judgment requires that the differing natures of the beings to whom obligations are owed be considered. If all forms of animate life — or vertebrate animal life? — must be treated equally, and if therefore in evaluating a research program the pains of a rodent count equally with the pains of a human, we are forced to conclude (1) that neither humans nor rodents possess rights, or (2) that rodents possess all the rights that humans possess. Both alternatives are absurd. Yet one or the other must be swallowed if the moral equality of all species is to be defended.

Humans owe to other humans a degree of moral regard that cannot be owed to animals. Some humans take on the obligation to support and heal others, both humans and animals, as a principal duty in their lives; the fulfillment of that duty may require the sacrifice of many animals. If biomedical investigators abandon the effective pursuit of their professional objectives because they are convinced that they may not do to animals what the service of humans requires, they will fail, objectively, to do their duty. Refusing to recognize the moral differences among species is a sure path to calamity. (The largest animal rights group in the country is People for the Ethical Treatment of Animals; its codirector, Ingrid Newkirk, calls research using animal subjects "fascism" and "supremacism." "Animal liberationists do not separate out the *human* animal," she says, "so there is no rational basis for saying that a human being has special rights. A rat is a pig is a dog is a boy. They're all mammals."[15])

Those who claim to base their objection to the use of animals in bio- 25

---

[15]McCabe K. Who will live, who will die? Washingtonian Magazine. August 1986:115.

medical research on their reckoning of the net pleasures and pains produced make a second error, equally grave. Even if it were true — as it is surely not — that the pains of all animal beings must be counted equally, a cogent utilitarian calculation requires that we weigh all the consequences of the use, and of the nonuse, of animals in laboratory research. Critics relying (however mistakenly) on animal rights may claim to ignore the beneficial results of such research, rights being trump cards to which interest and advantage must give way. But an argument that is explicitly framed in terms of interest and benefit for all over the long run must attend also to the disadvantageous consequences of not using animals in research, and to all the achievements attained and attainable only through their use. The sum of the benefits of their use is utterly beyond quantification. The elimination of horrible disease, the increase of longevity, the avoidance of great pain, the saving of lives, and the improvement of the quality of lives (for humans and for animals) achieved through research using animals is so incalculably great that the argument of these critics, systematically pursued, establishes not their conclusion but its reverse: To refrain from using animals in biomedical research is, on utilitarian grounds, morally wrong.

When balancing the pleasures and pains resulting from the use of animals in research, we must not fail to place on the scales the terrible pains that would have resulted, would be suffered now, and would long continue had animals not been used. Every disease eliminated, every vaccine developed, every method of pain relief devised, every surgical procedure invented, every prosthetic device implanted — indeed, virtually every modern medical therapy is due, in part or in whole, to experimentation using animals. Nor may we ignore, in the balancing process, the predictable gains in human (and animal) well-being that are probably achievable in the future but that will not be achieved if the decision is made now to desist from such research or to curtail it.

Medical investigators are seldom insensitive to the distress their work may cause animal subjects. Opponents of research using animals are frequently insensitive to the cruelty of the results of the restrictions they would impose. Untold numbers of human beings — real persons, although not now identifiable — would suffer grievously as the consequence of this well-meaning but shortsighted tenderness. If the morally relevant differences between humans and animals are borne in mind, and if all relevant considerations are weighed, the calculation of long-term consequences must give overwhelming support for biomedical research using animals.

CONCLUDING REMARKS

Substitution. The humane treatment of animals requires that we desist from experimenting on them if we can accomplish the same result using alternative methods — in vitro experimentation, computer simulation, or others. Critics of some experiments using animals rightly make this point.

It would be a serious error to suppose, however, that alternative techniques could soon be used in most research now using live animal subjects. No other methods now on the horizon — or perhaps ever to be available — can fully replace the testing of a drug, a procedure, or a vaccine, in live organisms. The flood of new medical possibilities being opened by the successes of recombinant DNA technology will turn to a trickle if testing on live animals is forbidden. When initial trials entail great risks, there may be no forward movement whatever without the use of live animal subjects. In seeking knowledge that may prove critical in later clinical applications, the unavailability of animals for inquiry may spell complete stymie. In the United States, federal regulations require the testing of new drugs and other products on animals, for efficacy and safety, before human beings are exposed to them.[16,17] We would not want it otherwise.

Every new advance in medicine — every new drug, new operation, 30 new therapy of any kind — must sooner or later be tried on a living being for the first time. That trial, controlled or uncontrolled, will be an experiment. The subject of that experiment, if it is not an animal, will be a human being. Prohibiting the use of live animals in biomedical research, therefore, or sharply restricting it, must result either in the blockage of much valuable research or in the replacement of animal subjects with human subjects. These are the consequences — unacceptable to most reasonable persons — of not using animals in research.

Reduction. Should we not at least reduce the use of animals in biomedical research? No, we should increase it, to avoid when feasible the use of humans as experimental subjects. Medical investigations putting human subjects at some risk are numerous and greatly varied. The risks run in such experiments are usually unavoidable, and (thanks to earlier experiments on animals) most such risks are minimal or moderate. But some experimental risks are substantial.

When an experimental protocol that entails substantial risk to humans comes before an institutional review board, what response is appropriate? The investigation, we may suppose, is promising and deserves support, so long as its human subjects are protected against unnecessary dangers. May not the investigators be fairly asked, Have you done all that you can do to eliminate risk to humans by the extensive testing of that drug, that procedure, or that device on animals? To achieve maximal safety for humans we are right to require thorough experimentation on animal subjects before humans are involved.

Opportunities to increase human safety in this way are commonly missed; trials in which risks may be shifted from humans to animals are often not devised, sometimes not even considered. Why? For the investigator, the use of animals as subjects is often more expensive, in money and

---

[16]U.S. Code of Federal Regulations, Title 21, Sect. 505(i). Food, drug and cosmetic regulations.
[17]U.S. Code of Federal Regulations, Title 16, Sect. 1500.40–2. Consumer product regulations.

time, than the use of human subjects. Access to suitable human subjects is often quick and convenient, whereas access to appropriate animal subjects may be awkward, costly, and burdened with red tape. Physician-investigators have often had more experience working with human beings and know precisely where the needed pool of subjects is to be found and how they may be enlisted. Animals, and the procedures for their use, are often less familiar to these investigators. Moreover, the use of animals in place of humans is now more likely to be the target of zealous protests from without. The upshot is that humans are sometimes subjected to risks that animals could have borne, and should have borne, in their place. To maximize the protection of human subjects, I conclude, the wide and imaginative use of live animal subjects should be encouraged rather than discouraged. This enlargement in the use of animals is our obligation.

Consistency. Finally, inconsistency between the profession and the practice of many who oppose research using animals deserves comment. This frankly *ad hominem* observation aims chiefly to show that a coherent position rejecting the use of animals in medical research imposes costs so high as to be intolerable even to the critics themselves.

One cannot coherently object to the killing of animals in biomedical 35 investigations while continuing to eat them. Anesthetics and thoughtful animal husbandry render the level of actual animal distress in the laboratory generally lower than that in the abattoir. So long as death and discomfort do not substantially differ in the two contexts, the consistent objector must not only refrain from all eating of animals but also protest as vehemently against others eating them as against others experimenting on them. No less vigorously must the critic object to the wearing of animal hides in coats and shoes, to employment in any industrial enterprise that uses animal parts, and to any commercial development that will cause death or distress to animals.

Killing animals to meet human needs for food, clothing, and shelter is judged entirely reasonable by most persons. The ubiquity of these uses and the virtual universality of moral support for them confront the opponent of research using animals with an inescapable difficulty. How can the many common uses of animals be judged morally worthy, while their use in scientific investigation is judged unworthy?

The number of animals used in research is but the tiniest fraction of the total used to satisfy assorted human appetites. That these appetites, often base and satisfiable in other ways, morally justify the far larger consumption of animals, whereas the quest for improved human health and understanding cannot justify the far smaller, is wholly implausible. Aside from the numbers of animals involved, the distinction in terms of worthiness of use, drawn with regard to any single animal, is not defensible. A given sheep is surely no more justifiably used to put lamb chops on the supermarket counter than to serve in testing a new contraceptive or a new prosthetic device. The needless killing of animals is wrong; if the common killing of them for our food or convenience is right, the less common but more humane uses of animals in the service of medical science are certainly not less right.

Scrupulous vegetarianism, in matters of food, clothing, shelter, commerce, and recreation, and in all other spheres, is the only fully coherent position the critic may adopt. At great human cost, the lives of fish and crustaceans must also be protected, with equal vigor, if speciesism has been forsworn. A very few consistent critics adopt this position. It is the reductio ad absurdum of the rejection of moral distinctions between animals and human beings.

Opposition to the use of animals in research is based on arguments of two different kinds — those relying on the alleged rights of animals and those relying on the consequences for animals. I have argued that arguments of both kinds must fail. We surely do have obligations to animals, but they have, and can have, no rights against us on which research can infringe. In calculating the consequences of animal research, we must weigh all the long-term benefits of the results achieved — to animals and to humans — and in that calculation we must not assume the moral equality of all animate species.

Topics for Critical Thinking and Writing

1. Restate succinctly Cohen's argument to show that animals have no rights.

2. If, as Cohen argues, animals have no rights, why does he think we are not "morally free to do anything we please to animals" (para. 9)?

3. Cohen thinks it makes perfectly good sense to say, for example, "You have a right to eat lamb"; but he thinks it is false (or makes no sense? which is it?) to say, "The lion has a right to eat a baby zebra" (para. 16). What is his argument? Do you agree?

4. Cohen boasts, "I am a speciesist" (para. 23). What is a speciesist? (You may want to read the views of Peter Singer, who invented the concept, for further explanation; see p. 238.) Why does Cohen reject Singer's analogy between speciesism and racism? Write a 500-word essay in which you critically examine the arguments for and against speciesism.

5. Suppose someone were to criticize Cohen's position, arguing that animal experimentation causes far more pain and misery for animals than it causes benefits for humans. How would Cohen reply? (See especially paras. 25–27.)

6. What is the point about "substitution" (para. 28)? What is Cohen's position on this issue? Would you agree with him, or not? Why?

7. Do you think there is any morally relevant difference among the following common practices: (a) using animals for meat, (b) using animals in medical experiments, and (c) using animal hides for clothing? Do you think it is possible, without inconsistency, to reject one or two of these practices but approve of the

other(s)? (See Cohen's paras. 34–38.) In an essay of 500 words explain your position.

BILINGUAL EDUCATION: IS IT THE RIGHT APPROACH?

Angelo Gonzalez and Luis O. Reyes

The Key to Basic Skills

If we accept that a child cannot learn unless taught through the language he speaks and understands; that a child who does not speak or understand English must fall behind when English is the dominant medium of instruction; that one needs to learn English so as to be able to participate in an English-speaking society; that self-esteem and motivation are necessary for effective learning; that rejection of a child's native language and culture is detrimental to the learning process: then any necessary effective educational program for limited or no English-speaking ability must incorporate the following:

Language arts and comprehensive reading programs taught in the child's native language

Curriculum content areas taught in the native language to further comprehension and academic achievement

Intensive instruction in English

Use of materials sensitive to and reflecting the culture of children within the program

---

Angelo Gonzalez (b. 1943) received his bachelor's and master's degrees as an evening student at Hunter College while working during the day. He has held several posts in public service, and is now executive director of ASPIRA, a Hispanic civic organization.

Luis O. Reyes, born in Puerto Rico in 1944, grew up in New York City and was educated at Catholic University, Middlebury College, and Stanford University. He holds a Ph.D. in the sociology of education, and he has taught in high school, but he now works for ASPIRA, where he deals especially with bilingual education and with the rights and needs of minorities.

This essay was first published in the New York Times on November 10, 1985.

MOST IMPORTANT GOAL

The mastery of basic reading skills is the most important goal in primary education since reading is the basis for much of all subsequent learning. Ordinarily, these skills are learned at home. But where beginning reading is taught in English, only the English-speaking child profits from these early acquired skills that are prerequisites to successful reading development. Reading programs taught in English to children with Spanish as a first language waste their acquired linguistic attributes and also impede learning by forcing them to absorb skills of reading simultaneously with a new language.

Both local and national research data provide ample evidence for the efficacy of well-implemented programs. The New York City Board of Education Report on Bilingual Pupil Services for 1982–83 indicated that in all areas of the curriculum — English, Spanish, and mathematics — and at all grade levels, students demonstrated statistically significant gains in tests of reading in English and Spanish and in math. In all but two of the programs reviewed, the attendance rates of students in the program, ranging from 86 to 94 percent, were higher than those of the general school population. Similar higher attendance rates were found among students in high school bilingual programs.

At Yale University, Kenji Hakuta, a linguist, reported recently on a study of working-class Hispanic students in the New Haven bilingual program. He found that children who were the most bilingual, that is, who developed English without the loss of Spanish, were brighter in both verbal and nonverbal tests. Over time, there was an increasing correlation between English and Spanish — a finding that clearly contradicts the charge that teaching in the home language is detrimental to English. Rather, the two languages are interdependent within the bilingual child, reinforcing each other.

ESSENTIAL CONTRIBUTION

As Jim Cummins of the Ontario Institute for Studies in Education has argued, the use and development of the native language makes an essential contribution to the development of minority children's subject-matter knowledge and academic learning potential. In fact, at least three national data bases — the National Assessment of Educational Progress, National Center for Educational Statistics–High School and Beyond Studies, and the Survey of Income and Education — suggest that there are long-term positive effects among high school students who have participated in bilingual-education programs. These students are achieving higher scores on tests of verbal and mathematics skills.

These and similar findings buttress the argument stated persuasively in the recent joint recommendation of the Academy for Educational De-

velopment and the Hazen Foundation, namely, that America needs to become a more multilingual nation and children who speak a non-English
language are a national resource to be nurtured in school.

Unfortunately, the present [Reagan] administration's educational policies would seem to be leading us in the opposite direction. Under the guise
of protecting the common language of public life in the United States,
William J. Bennett, the Secretary of Education, unleashed a frontal attack
on bilingual education. In a major policy address, he engaged in rhetorical
distortions about the nature and effectiveness of bilingual programs, pointing only to unnamed negative research findings to justify the administration's retrenchment efforts.

Arguing for the need to give local school districts greater flexibility in determining appropriate methodologies in serving limited-English-
proficient students, Mr. Bennett fails to realize that, in fact, districts serving large numbers of language-minority students, as is the case in New
York City, do have that flexibility. Left to their own devices in implement-
ing legal mandates, many school districts have performed poorly at providing services to all entitled language-minority students.

A HARSH REALITY

The harsh reality in New York City for language-minority students was
documented comprehensively last month by the Educational Priorities
Panel. The panel's findings revealed that of the 113,831 students identified
as being limited in English proficiency, as many as 44,000 entitled students
are not receiving any bilingual services. The issue at hand is, therefore, not
one of choice but rather violation of the rights of almost 40 percent of
language-minority children to equal educational opportunity. In light of
these findings the Reagan administration's recent statements only serve to
exacerbate existing inequities in the American educational system for lin-
guistic-minority children. Rather than by adding fuel to a misguided debate, the administration would serve these children best by ensuring the
full funding of the 1984 Bilingual Education Reauthorization Act as passed
by the Congress.

Topics for Critical Thinking and Writing ═══════════

1. The opening sentence is unusually long. Is it comprehensible? Is it effective?
   Why?

2. The authors say that "ordinarily . . . [basic reading] skills are learned at home,"
   and that therefore "reading programs taught in English to children with Spanish
   as a first language waste their acquired linguistic attributes and also impede
   learning by forcing them to absorb skills of reading simultaneously with a new
   language" (para. 2). If your home language was not English, and if you did not

participate in a bilingual program, does your experience confirm Gonzalez's opinion? If your home language was English, assume for a moment that your parents were in the Foreign Service and you were brought up in Mexico. Do you think you would want to be plunged into an exclusively Spanish-speaking school, or would you prefer to receive at least some of your instruction in English? Why?

3. In paragraph 7, the authors refer to "a major policy address" delivered by William J. Bennett, the Secretary of Education. How would you go about finding the text of this address?

4. In the final paragraph the authors say that "the rights of almost 40 percent of language-minority children" are being violated. Exactly what are these "rights"?

Tina Bakka

Locking Students Out

Let's begin by defining "bilingual education." As commonly used today, the term does *not* mean teaching students a language other than English (almost everyone would agree that foreign-language instruction should be available, and that it is desirable for Americans to be fluent not only in English but also in some other language); nor does "bilingual education" mean offering courses in English as a second language to students whose native language is, for example, Chinese, or Spanish or Navajo or Aleut. (Again, almost everyone would agree that such instruction should be offered where economically possible.) Rather, it means offering instruction in such courses as mathematics, history, and science *in the student's native language,* while also offering courses in English as a second language. Programs vary in details, but the idea is that the non-native speaker should be spared the trauma of total immersion in English until he or she has completed several years of studying English as a second language. During this period, instruction in other subjects is given in the student's native language.

Proponents of bilingual education usually offer two not entirely consistent arguments: (1) it eases the youngster's transition into American culture, and (2) it preserves the youngster's cultural heritage. In the brief space available, I will argue against both of these positions.

First, despite the statistics commonly offered by proponents of bilingual education, there is no impartial evidence that such education in fact improves the academic work of students. Impartial investigators have consistently found that the results of the studies are uncertain. For example,

---

Born in Chicago in 1952 and educated in Arizona, Bakka has taught English as a second language in secondary school.

Iris Rothberg, writing in *Harvard Educational Review,* May 1982, says that the research findings are contradictory and inconclusive. Keith A. Baker and Adriane A. de Kanter, in "Effectiveness of Bilingual Education: A Review of the Literature" (an unpaginated document issued by the United States Department of Education in 1981), find that "The case for the effectiveness of transitional bilingual education is so weak that exclusive reliance on this instruction method is not justified. Too little is known about the problems of education language minorities to prescribe a specific remedy at the Federal level."

Why has the bilingual approach recently been invented, and why does it get so much attention? Part of the answer, of course, is that the U.S. Census for 1980 found that more than 10 percent of the United States' population spoke a language other than English at home. Of this 10 percent, half spoke Spanish. And since it is agreed that Hispanics were undercounted in the census, the actual figure of Spanish-speaking children is even higher than the official estimate. Although bilingual programs exist in many languages, Spanish is by far the most prominent, accounting for about 80 percent, and bilingual programs have been advocated most often, and most vigorously, for Spanish-speaking children. I will return to this point later, but first I want to speak more generally.

The two extreme solutions to the question of how to educate non-native speakers of English are these: (1) "immersion," in which the students hear and speak only English in school, and (2) bilingualism, in which students study major subjects in their native language and study English as a second language. The first approach — until recently the only approach — is based on the idea that America is a "melting pot" in which Russians, Germans, Italians, Chinese, and all others who come here should become "Americans." The method is sink or swim; the failure of the method cannot be calculated — we can hardly measure the psychological pain that some people endured — but the success can be. The history of the United States is, on the whole, a history of the success of immigrants. One has only to look at the names in a newspaper, or at the names in Congress, or at the names of teachers in any large school, to see a wide variety of ethnic backgrounds. Again, we cannot calculate the cost — the traumatic feelings undergone by countless non-native speakers of English who were baffled by what to them was an unintelligible language — but we do know that in the past the overwhelming majority coped and succeeded. This at least can be said for the total-immersion approach. (At this point perhaps I should mention that although I favor immersion, in most cases it should be complemented with instruction in English as a second language to assist students to do good work in their other courses.)

The second approach, bilingualism, usually requires a minimum of three years of instruction in English before instruction in other subjects is offered in English. (Many advocates argue for six years, and some even argue for twelve years.) Proponents base their view on two arguments: (1) Total immersion is traumatic, and (2) the "melting pot," in which ethnic identity is dissolved, has been discredited; the "salad bowl" or the "mosaic," in which ethnic identity is preserved, is said to be a much better outcome to aim for. The first of these arguments, about the psychological well-being of the child, is supported by claiming that a non-native speaker "can't learn English all day." But this is simply wrong; the child does not spend most of his or her day in school. There is plenty of time away from school for the child to speak the native language with friends and families, and even during school hours the child will inevitably speak the native language outside of the classroom, for instance in the hallways, the cafeteria, and at play. Further, young children are highly adaptive; they learn foreign languages relatively easily, and to postpone their entry into the English-speaking world is to make more difficult, ultimately, their learning of English. Bilingual programs, though originally intended to assist the student's transition into American culture, now for the most part impede the move by maintaining the child's home culture.

Moreover, although immersion may have adverse psychological effects on some children (again, these cannot be measured, and proponents of bilingualism have sometimes simply resorted to scare tactics), bilingual programs themselves may have adverse psychological effects, for they segregate children and make them feel that they are not part of mainstream America. Children in a bilingual program may come to believe that because they are in some sort of special program, they are judged unable to participate in the "regular" program. And the "Anglo" children may come to hold a similar view, seeing the Spanish-speaking child as an inferior who needs special help not only in learning English but in learning anything.

This brings us to the second argument advanced in favor of programs in bilingual education: They preserve ethnic identity. I have just suggested that this method, intended to preserve ethnic identity, can in fact lead to a sense of inferiority; the non-native speakers of English think they must have special help, and the native speakers think that the others can't cope. Both thoughts are destructive. And both are utterly false. Ethnic identity can be preserved even in a system of total immersion. If one looks around, one easily sees that even third- and fourth-generation Americans still value aspects of the culture of their ancestors. This is evident in countless ways, for instance in the religions they believe in, the foods they eat, the holidays they celebrate, and the jokes they tell. To some extent it is also evident in the jobs they enter.

But this gets to another, extremely important point. In America, jobs largely determine "class," since "class" is almost entirely a matter of money. Money largely depends on the kind of job one holds. It is a fact that most native speakers of Spanish in the United States belong to an economically disadvantaged class. Their disadvantage can be overcome only when they enter gringo society. I am speaking broadly, of course. There are many prosperous native speakers of Spanish, some active chiefly in Spanish-speaking communities; but on the whole, the better-paying jobs are in the gringo world, and the only way to get these jobs is to be at home in that world. To be at ease in that world requires fluency in the language, and an acceptance of the fact that English is the dominant language in this country.

In the past, severe discrimination operated against immigrants with 10
certain cultural backgrounds, including Hispanics. This discrimination has
not disappeared, but it is fading, and legal measures have been taken to reduce what remains. Discrimination, which in part meant keeping Hispanics out of better-paying jobs, surely was largely responsible for the lack of
interest in becoming American citizens that many Mexican immigrants displayed. The statistics are sad. John R. Garcia points out, in *International
Migration Review*, Winter 1981, that since 1920 the annual rate for naturalization of eligible Mexican-origin migrants varies between 3.89 and 5.88
percent. How does this figure compare with figures for other groups? "The
average rate of naturalization is one-tenth that of other immigrants' naturalization rates, and this pattern has not changed significantly over the
years." Why? Apparently because in most communities these persons of
Mexican origin were not led to feel they were part of America. In Garcia's
words, they do not feel much "social identity with being American" (p.
620). Because they were taught minimal English their options were severely limited. Segregating them reinforced their belief that they were outsiders, and prevented them from participating fully in the politics and
economy (and prosperity) of America.

I am arguing, then, that the proponents of bilingual education are
shortsighted; they talk of preserving ethnic culture, but they do not see that
their sort of preservation leads to a perpetuation of an economic disadvantage and to a sense of alienation. This in turn leads to a lack of full participation in the public life of America. Proponents of bilingualism see and
value ethnic identity, but they do not see that non-native speakers need
two identities if they are to thrive, a private (ethnic) identity and also a
public (economic, political) identity. All people living in this country must
be able not only to cherish their particular or private tradition but also to
claim a portion of the dominant culture — a portion of money and of political power. To do this, they must be at ease in the public (Anglo) as well as
in the private world. That may not be simple, but immersion (supple-
mented with instruction in English as a second language) is far more likely
to bring this about than is a pedagogical program that keeps young students from studying social sciences and physical and biological sciences in
English. Only when youngsters feel that these subjects are to be mastered
in English, however difficult the task, will we have youngsters who can
confidently aim at careers in those fields, and can confidently claim a place
(with the accompanying economic advantages) in society as a whole. Most
of the others will find themselves locked out.

Topics for Critical Thinking and Writing

1. Before you read Bakka's essay and the preceding one by Gonzalez and Reyes,
   did you have a clear idea of what "bilingual education" is? Is Bakka talking
   about the same thing as Gonzalez and Reyes? Why does Bakka go to some pains
   to define the topic early?

2. Do you find Bakka's definition clear and adequate? If so, write a paragraph accounting for the success of her definition (analyze her method of defining). If you don't find it clear and adequate, write a paragraph calling attention to the weaknesses.

3. Gonzalez and Reyes offer statistics to support their position, but Bakka, in her third paragraph, casts doubt on the statistical data collected so far. Do you think that statistical data can or should provide a decisive answer to the question of how non-native speakers should be educated?

4. Bakka argues that bilingual programs may make the students feel inferior, and may cause other students to regard those students as inferior. If you have any firsthand experience (on either side of the fence), write an essay of 250 to 500 words, supporting or countering her view on this matter.

5. In her ninth and tenth paragraphs Bakka argues that bilingual programs help to keep students in an economically disadvantaged class. In a paragraph indicate whether you think they do, and in a second paragraph indicate whether you think economic considerations are relevant in solving the problem.

EVOLUTIONARY THEORY: DOES DARWINISM REFUTE CREATIONISM?

Stephen Jay Gould

Evolution as Fact and Theory

Kirtley Mather, who died last year at age eighty-nine, was a pillar of both science and the Christian religion in America and one of my dearest friends. The difference of half a century in our ages evaporated before our common interests. The most curious thing we shared was a battle we each fought at the same age. For Kirtley had gone to Tennessee with Clarence Darrow to testify for evolution at the Scopes trial of 1925.[1] When I think

[1] In 1925 Tennessee made it a crime to teach evolution. In the "Monkey Trial," John Scopes was accused of teaching evolution in high school. He was defended by Clarence Darrow; the prosecution attorney was William Jennings Bryan. Scopes was convicted, and the law remained on the books until 1967, but the evolutionists considered that they had won a moral victory. [All notes are the editors'.]

A professor of geology at Harvard University, Gould (b. 1941) teaches paleontology, biology, and the history of science. Many of his essays have been collected in several highly readable books, one of which is Evolution as Fact and Theory *(1981). This essay originally appeared in* Discover, *May 1981.*

that we are enmeshed again in the same struggle for one of the best documented, most compelling and exciting concepts in all of science, I don't know whether to laugh or cry.

According to idealized principles of scientific discourse, the arousal of dormant issues should reflect fresh data that give renewed life to abandoned notions. Those outside the current debate may therefore be excused for suspecting that creationists have come up with something new, or that evolutionists have generated some serious internal trouble. But nothing has changed; the creationists have not a single new fact or argument. Darrow and Bryan were at least more entertaining than we lesser antagonists today. The rise of creationism is politics, pure and simple; it represents one issue (and by no means the major concern) of the resurgent evangelical right. Arguments that seemed kooky just a decade ago have reentered the mainstream.

CREATIONISM IS NOT SCIENCE

The basic attack of the creationists falls apart on two general counts before we even reach the supposed factual details of their complaints against evolution. First, they play upon a vernacular misunderstanding of the word "theory" to convey the false impression that we evolutionists are covering up the rotten core of our edifice. Second, they misuse a popular philosophy of science to argue that they are behaving scientifically in attacking evolution. Yet the same philosophy demonstrates that their own belief is not science, and that "scientific creationism" is therefore meaningless and self-contradictory, a superb example of what Orwell[2] called "newspeak."

In the American vernacular, "theory" often means "imperfect fact"— part of a hierarchy of confidence running downhill from fact to theory to hypothesis to guess. Thus the power of the creationist argument: Evolution is "only" a theory, and intense debate now rages about many aspects of the theory. If evolution is less than a fact, and scientists can't even make up their minds about the theory, then what confidence can we have in it? Indeed, President Reagan echoed this argument before an evangelical group in Dallas when he said (in what I devoutly hope was campaign rhetoric): "Well, it is a theory. It is a scientific theory only, and it has in recent years been challenged in the world of science — that is, not believed in the scientific community to be as infallible as it once was."

Well, evolution *is* a theory. It is also a fact. And facts and theories are   5
different things, not rungs in a hierarchy of increasing certainty. Facts are the world's data. Theories are structures of ideas that explain and interpret facts. Facts do not go away when scientists debate rival theories to explain

---

[2]**Orwell** George Orwell (1903–1950), English essayist and novelist. In Orwell's *1984*, the rulers have designed a language called *newspeak*, in which it is impossible to think independently.

them. Einstein's theory of gravitation replaced Newton's, but apples did not suspend themselves in midair pending the outcome. And human beings evolved from apelike ancestors whether they did so by Darwin's proposed mechanism or by some other, yet to be discovered.

Moreover, "fact" does not mean "absolute certainty." The final proofs of logic and mathematics flow deductively from stated premises and achieve certainty only because they are *not* about the empirical world. Evolutionists make no claim for perpetual truth, though creationists often do (and then attack us for a style of argument that they themselves favor). In science, "fact" can only mean "confirmed to such a degree that it would be perverse to withhold provisional assent." I suppose that apples might start to rise tomorrow, but the possibility does not merit equal time in physics classrooms.

Evolutionists have been clear about this distinction between fact and theory from the very beginning, if only because we have always acknowledged how far we are from completely understanding the mechanisms (theory) by which evolution (fact) occurred. Darwin continually emphasized the difference between his two great and separate accomplishments: establishing the fact of evolution, and proposing a theory—natural selection—to explain the mechanism of evolution. He wrote in *The Descent of Man:* "I had two distinct objects in view; firstly, to show that species had not been separately created, and secondly, that natural selection had been the chief agent of change. . . . Hence if I have erred in . . . having exaggerated in its [natural selection's] power . . . I have at least, as I hope, done good service in aiding to overthrow the dogma of separate creations."

Thus Darwin acknowledged the provisional nature of natural selection while affirming the fact of evolution. The fruitful theoretical debate that Darwin initiated has never ceased. From the 1940s through the 1960s, Darwin's own theory of natural selection did achieve a temporary hegemony that it never enjoyed in his lifetime. But renewed debate characterizes our decade, and, while no biologist questions the importance of natural selection, many now doubt its ubiquity. In particular, many evolutionists argue that substantial amounts of genetic change may not be subject to natural selection and may spread through populations at random. Others are challenging Darwin's linking of natural selection with gradual, imperceptible change through all intermediary degrees; they are arguing that most evolutionary events may occur far more rapidly than Darwin envisioned.

Scientists regard debates on fundamental issues of theory as a sign of intellectual health and a source of excitement. Science is—and how else can I say it?—most fun when it plays with interesting ideas, examines their implications, and recognizes that old information may be explained in surprisingly new ways. Evolutionary theory is now enjoying this uncommon vigor. Yet amidst all this turmoil no biologist has been led to doubt the fact that evolution occurred; we are debating *how* it happened. We are all trying to explain the same thing: the tree of evolutionary descent linking all organisms by ties of genealogy. Creationists pervert and caricature this debate by conveniently neglecting the common conviction that underlies it, and by falsely suggesting that we now doubt the very phenomenon we are struggling to understand.

Using another invalid argument, creationists claim that "the dogma of separate creations," as Darwin characterized it a century ago, is a scientific theory meriting equal time with evolution in high school biology curricula. But a prevailing viewpoint among philosophers of science belies this creationist argument. Philosopher Karl Popper has argued for decades that the primary criterion of science is the falsifiability of its theories. We can never prove absolutely, but we can falsify. A set of ideas that cannot, in principle, be falsified is not science.

The entire creationist argument involves little more than a rhetorical attempt to falsify evolution by presenting supposed contradictions among its supporters. Their brand of creationism, they claim, is "scientific" because it follows the Popperian model in trying to demolish evolution. Yet Popper's argument must apply in both directions. One does not become a scientist by the simple act of trying to falsify another scientific system; one has to present an alternative system that also meets Popper's criterion — it too must be falsifiable in principle.

"Scientific creationism" is a self-contradictory, nonsense phrase precisely because it cannot be falsified. I can envision observations and experiments that would disprove any evolutionary theory I know, but I cannot imagine what potential data could lead creationists to abandon their beliefs. Unbeatable systems are dogma, not science. Lest I seem harsh or rhetorical, I quote creationism's leading intellectual, Duane Gish, Ph.D., from his recent (1978) book *Evolution? The Fossils Say No!* "By creation we mean the bringing into being by a supernatural Creator of the basic kinds of plants and animals by the process of sudden, or fiat, creation. We do not know how the Creator created, what processes He used, *for He used processes which are not now operating anywhere in the natural universe* [Gish's italics]. This is why we refer to creation as special creation. We cannot discover by scientific investigations anything about the creative processes used by the Creator." Pray tell, Dr. Gish, in the light of your last sentence, what then is "scientific" creationism?

THE FACT OF EVOLUTION

Our confidence that evolution occurred centers upon three general arguments. First, we have abundant, direct, observational evidence of evolution in action, from both the field and the laboratory. It ranges from countless experiments on change in nearly everything about fruit flies subjected to artificial selection in the laboratory to the famous British moths that turned black when industrial soot darkened the trees upon which they rest. (The moths gain protection from sharp-sighted bird predators by blending into the background.) Creationists do not deny these observations; how could they? Creationists have tightened their act. They now argue that God only created "basic kinds," and allowed for limited evolutionary meandering within them. Thus toy poodles and Great Danes come from the dog kind and moths can change color, but nature cannot convert a dog to a cat or a monkey to a man.

The second and third arguments for evolution—the case for major changes—do not involve direct observation of evolution in action. They rest upon inference, but are no less secure for that reason. Major evolutionary change requires too much time for direct observation on the scale of recorded human history. All historical sciences rest upon inference, and evolution is no different from geology, cosmology, or human history in this respect. In principle, we cannot observe processes that operated in the past. We must infer them from results that still survive: living and fossil organisms for evolution, documents and artifacts for human history, strata and topography for geology.

The second argument—that the imperfection of nature reveals evolu-   15 tion—strikes many people as ironic, for they feel that evolution should be most elegantly displayed in the nearly perfect adaptation expressed by some organisms—the chamber of a gull's wing, or butterflies that cannot be seen in ground litter because they mimic leaves so precisely. But perfection could be imposed by a wise creator or evolved by natural selection. Perfection covers the tracks of past history. And past history—the evidence of descent—is our mark of evolution.

Evolution lies exposed in the *imperfections* that record a history of descent. Why should a rat run, a bat fly, a porpoise swim, and I type this essay with structures built of the same bones unless we all inherited them from a common ancestor? An engineer, starting from scratch, could design better limbs in each case. Why should all the large native mammals of Australia be marsupials, unless they descended from a common ancestor isolated on this island continent? Marsupials are not "better," or ideally suited for Australia; many have been wiped out by placental mammals imported by man from other continents. This principle of imperfection extends to all historical sciences. When we recognize the etymology of September, October, November, and December (seventh, eighth, ninth, and tenth, from the Latin), we know that two additional items (January and February) must have been added to an original calendar of ten months.

The third argument is more direct: Transitions are often found in the fossil record. Preserved transitions are not common—and should not be, according to our understanding of evolution (see next section)—but they are not entirely wanting, as creationists often claim. The lower jaw of reptiles contains several bones, that of mammals only one. The nonmammalian jawbones are reduced, step by step, in mammalian ancestors until they become tiny nubbins located at the back of the jaw. The "hammer" and "anvil" bones of the mammalian ear are descendants of these nubbins. How could such a transition be accomplished? the creationists ask. Surely a bone is either entirely in the jaw or in the ear. Yet paleontologists have discovered two transitional lineages or therapsids (the so-called mammal-like reptiles) with a double jaw joint—one composed of the old quadrate and articular bones (soon to become the hammer and anvil), the other of the squamosal and dentary bones (as in modern mammals). For that matter, what better transitional form could we desire than the oldest human, *Australopithecus afarensis,* with its apelike palate, its human upright stance, and a cranial capacity larger than any ape's of the same body size but a full 1,000 cubic centimeters below ours? If God made each of the half dozen human species discovered in ancient rocks, why did he create in an unbroken temporal sequence of progressively more modern features—increasing cranial capacity, reduced face and teeth, larger body size? Did he create to mimic evolution and test our faith thereby?

AN EXAMPLE OF CREATIONIST ARGUMENT

Faced with these facts of evolution and the philosophical bankruptcy of their own position, creationists rely upon distortion and innuendo to buttress their rhetorical claim. If I sound sharp or bitter, indeed I am—for I have become a major target of these practices.

I count myself among the evolutionists who argue for a jerky, or episodic, rather than a smoothly gradual, pace of change. In 1972 my colleague Niles Eldredge and I developed the theory of punctuated equilibrium [*Discover,* October]. We argued that two outstanding facts of the fossil record—geologically "sudden" origin of new species and failure to change thereafter (stasis)—reflect the predictions of evolutionary theory, not the imperfections of the fossil record. In most theories, small isolated populations are the source of new species, and the process of speciation takes thousands or tens of thousands of years. This amount of time, so long when measured against our lives, is a geological microsecond. It represents much less than 1 percent of the average life span for a fossil invertebrate species—more than 10 million years. Large, widespread, and well-established species, on the other hand, are not expected to change very much. We believe that the inertia of large populations explains the stasis of most fossil species over millions of years.

We proposed the theory of punctuated equilibrium largely to provide 20 a different explanation for pervasive trends in the fossil record. Trends, we argued, cannot be attributed to gradual transformation within lineages, but must arise from the differential success of certain kinds of species. A trend, we argued, is more like climbing a flight of stairs (punctuations and stasis) than rolling up an inclined plane.

Since we proposed punctuated equilibria to explain trends, it is infuriating to be quoted again and again by creationists—whether through design or stupidity, I do not know—as admitting that the fossil record includes no transitional forms. Transitional forms are generally lacking at the species level, but are abundant between larger groups. The evolution from reptiles to mammals, as mentioned earlier, is well documented. Yet a pamphlet entitled "Harvard Scientists Agree Evolution Is a Hoax" states: "The facts of punctuated equilibrium which Gould and Eldredge . . . are forcing Darwinists to swallow fit the picture that Bryan insisted on, and which God has revealed to us in the Bible."

Continuing the distortion, several creationists have equated the theory of punctuated equilibrium with a caricature of the beliefs of Richard Goldschmidt, a great early geneticist. Goldschmidt argued, in a famous book published in 1940, that new groups can arise all at once through major mutations. He referred to these suddenly transformed creatures as "hopeful monsters." (I am attracted to some aspects of the noncaricatured version, but Goldschmidt's theory still has nothing to do with punctuated equilibrium.) Creationist Luther Sunderland talks of the "punctuated equilibrium hopeful monster theory" and tells his hopeful readers that "it amounts to tacit admission that antievolutionists are correct in asserting there is no fossil evidence supporting the theory that all life is connected to a common ancestor." Duane Gish writes, "According to Goldschmidt, and now apparently according to Gould, a reptile laid an egg from which the first bird, feathers and all, was produced." Any evolutionist who believed such nonsense would rightly be laughed off the intellectual stage; yet the only theory that could ever envision such a scenario for the evolution of birds is creationism — God acts in the egg.

CONCLUSION

I am both angry at and amused by the creationists; but mostly I am deeply sad. Sad for many reasons. Sad because so many people who respond to creationist appeals are troubled for the right reason, but venting their anger at the wrong target. It is true that scientists have often been dogmatic and elitist. It is true that we have often allowed the white-coated, advertising image to represent us — "Scientists say that Brand X cures bunions ten times faster than . . ." We have not fought it adequately because we derive benefits from appearing as a new priesthood. It is also true that faceless bureaucratic state power intrudes more and more into our lives and removes choices that should belong to individuals and communities. I can understand that requiring that evolution be taught in the schools might be seen as one more insult on all these grounds. But the culprit is not, and cannot be, evolution or any other fact of the natural world. Identify and fight your legitimate enemies by all means, but we are not among them.

I am sad because the practical result of this brouhaha will not be expanded coverage to include creationism (that would also make me sad), but the reduction or excision of evolution from high school curricula. Evolution is one of the half dozen "great ideas" developed by science. It speaks to the profound issues of genealogy that fascinate all of us—the "roots" phenomenon writ large. Where did we come from? Where did life arise? How did it develop? How are organisms related? It forces us to think, ponder, and wonder. Shall we deprive millions of this knowledge and once again teach biology as a set of dull and unconnected facts, without the thread that weaves diverse material into a supple unity?

But most of all I am saddened by a trend I am just beginning to dis- 25 cern among my colleagues. I sense that some now wish to mute the healthy debate about theory that has brought new life to evolutionary biology. It provides grist for creationist mills, they say, even if only by distortion. Perhaps we should lie low and rally round the flag of strict Darwinism, at least for the moment—a kind of old-time religion on our part.

But we should borrow another metaphor and recognize that we too have to tread a straight and narrow path, surrounded by roads to perdition. For if we ever begin to suppress our search to understand nature, to quench our own intellectual excitement in a misguided effort to present a united front where it does not and should not exist, then we are truly lost.

Topics for Critical Thinking and Writing

1. What is the point of Gould's first sentence? Of his first paragraph? That is, what is he seeking to do in this paragraph?

2. In his second paragraph Gould says that "the rise of creationism is politics, pure and simple." When you first came across this sentence, did you believe it? By the end of the essay has Gould convinced you of its truth?

3. In paragraph 5 Gould says that evolution "is also a fact," and he goes on to say that "facts do not go away when scientists debate rival theories to explain them." He cites falling apples, and concludes the paragraph by saying, "And human beings evolved from apelike ancestors whether they did so by Darwin's proposed mechanism or by some other, yet to be discovered." Do you find his argument compelling? Why?

4. Gould says that evolution is a "theory" and is also a "fact," and he defines both words. Now, Gould is a "teacher" and he is also a "writer"; one thing can of course have two (or more) attributes. But does Gould's discussion make it entirely clear to you that something can be both a fact and a theory? If so, write a paragraph explaining the point to someone who finds Gould a bit unclear. If not, write a paragraph explaining why the matter is confusing.

5. Gould begins paragraph 12 by saying, " 'Scientific creationism' is a self-contradictory, nonsense phrase." A phrase or doctrine is self-contradictory if and only if it can be put into the form: p and not-p (where p is some sentence expressing the phrase or doctrine, and not-p denies p. For example: "This is a cat and is not a cat.") Can you restate the position of scientific creationism in this form? Do you believe that Gish (p. 271) would assert both parts of this contradiction, or not?

6. The first of Gould's three arguments for evolution is, he says, based on "abun-

dant, direct, observational evidence of evolution." Read the reply to Gould's essay by Gish (below) and answer these questions: Does Gish concede that these pieces of evidence do indeed exist? How does Gish think they bear on the controversy between the creationist and the evolutionist?

7. In his second argument Gould mentions "imperfections." What are they, exactly? In a paragraph explain why Gould concedes that this argument does not involve "direct observation of evolution in action" but instead "rest[s] upon inference."

8. Gould's third argument involves "transitional forms." Does he give any examples of such forms? Why are they important in the controversy over evolution? How does Gould apparently use his "theory of punctuated equilibrium" to account for the rarity of such forms?

9. In a paragraph analyze Gould's final paragraph. What makes it effective (or ineffective) as a final paragraph?

Duane T. Gish

A Reply to Gould

To the Editors:

In his essay "Evolution as Fact and Theory" [May 1981], Stephen Jay Gould states that creationists claim creation is a scientific theory. This is a false accusation. Creationists have repeatedly stated that neither creation nor evolution is a scientific theory (and each is equally religious). Gould in fact quotes from my book, *Evolution? The Fossils Say No!*, in which I state that both concepts of origins fail the criteria of a scientific theory.

Gould uses the argument of Sir Karl Popper that the primary criterion of a scientific theory is its potential falsifiability, and then uses this sword to strike down creation as a scientific theory. Fine. Gould surely realizes, however, that his is a two-edged sword. Sir Karl has used it to strike down evolution as a scientific theory, stating that Darwinism is not a testable scientific theory, but a metaphysical research program (*Unended Quest*, 1976).

Duane T. Gish (b. 1921) holds a Ph.D. in biochemistry from the University of California, Berkeley. He has carried out biochemical and biomedical research at Cornell University and at Berkeley, formerly served as Professor of Natural Science at Christian Heritage College in San Diego, and now is senior vice president of the Institute for Creation Research. An active lecturer and writer, his book titled Evolution? The Fossils Say No! *is widely regarded as a standard presentation of creationism.*

Reprinted here is a letter he wrote to the magazine Discover, *responding to an article by Stephen Jay Gould published in May 1981. (Gould's article precedes Gish's on p. 263.) The title of Gish's letter is ours.*

Another criterion that must apply to a scientific theory is the ability to repeatedly observe the events, processes, or properties used to support the theory. There were obviously no human witnesses to the origin of the universe, the origin of life, or in fact to the origin of a single living thing, and even if evolution were occurring today, the process would require far in excess of all recorded history to produce sufficient change to document evolution. Evolution has not and cannot be observed any more than creation.

Gould states, "Theories are structures of ideas that explain and interpret facts." Certainly, creation and evolution can both be used as theories in that sense. Furthermore, one or the other must be true, since ultimately they are the only two alternatives we have to explain origins.

Gould charges creationists with dogma. Please note, however, Gould's own dogmatism. His use of the term "fact of evolution" appears throughout his paper. Furthermore, Gould seems to have a strange view of the relationship of fact and theory. He says, "Facts do not go away when scientists debate rival theories to explain them. Einstein's theory of gravitation replaced Newton's, but apples did not suspend themselves in midair pending the outcome. And human beings evolved from apelike ancestors whether they did so by Darwin's proposed mechanism or by some other, yet to be discovered." Well, evolutionists believe indeed that both apes and hydrogen evolved into people (the latter just took longer), but neither has ever been observed. All of us, however, have seen apples fall off trees.

Gould's "fact of evolution" immediately deteriorates into "three general arguments," two of which quickly deteriorate further into mere inferences. Gould's only direct observational evidence for evolution (his first argument) is experiments on fruit flies and observations on peppered moths in Britain. Neither, of course, offers evidence for evolution, for from beginning to end fruit flies remain fruit flies and peppered moths remain peppered moths. The task of the evolutionist is to answer the question how moths came to be moths, tigers came to be tigers, and people came to be people. In fact, this type of evidence is what Gould himself has sought in recent years to discredit as an explanation for the origin of higher categories.

Gould's second argument is an inference based on *imperfections*. He mentions homologous structures as evidence for evolution from a common ancestor. Gould should know first that many, if not most, homologous structures are not even possessed by the assumed common ancestor and secondly that the actual evidence (particularly that from genetics) is so contradictory to what is predicted by evolution that Sir Gavin de Beer titled his Oxford biology reader (1971) on that subject *Homology, an Unsolved Problem*. Sir Gavin, along with S. C. Harland, felt compelled to suggest that organs, such as the eye, remain unchanged while the genes governing these structures become wholly altered during the evolutionary process! The whole Darwinian edifice collapses if that is true.

Gould's third argument is based on inferences drawn from the fossil record. The fossil record, with its "explosive appearance" (the term often used by geologists) of the highly complex creatures found in Cambrian rocks, for which no ancestors have been found, and the systematic absence of transitional forms between all higher categories of plants and animals, has proven an embarrassment to evolutionists ever since Darwin. Gould's argument, however, is that "transitions are often found in the fossil record." That is surprising indeed, since he seems intent in other publications to convey just the opposite opinion.

For example, in his 1977 *Natural History* essay "The Return of Hopeful Monsters," after recounting the derision meted out to Richard Goldschmidt for his hopeful-monster mechanism of evolution, Gould says, "I do, however, predict that during the next decade Goldschmidt will be largely vindicated in the world of evolutionary biology." Why? Among others, "The fossil record with its abrupt transitions offers no support for gradual change." A bit later: "All paleontologists know that the fossil record contains precious little in the way of intermediate forms; transitions between major groups are characteristically abrupt." Many similar statements by Gould and others could be cited.

Finally, Gould assails Sunderland and me for linking him to a hopeful-monster mechanism whereby a reptile laid an egg and a bird was hatched. He says an evolutionist who believed such nonsense would rightly be laughed off the intellectual stage. Let's see, then, what Goldschmidt really did say. In *The Material Basis of Evolution,* Goldschmidt says, "I need only quote Schindewolf (1936), the most progressive investigator known to me. He shows by examples from fossil material that the major evolutionary advances must have taken place in single large steps. . . . He shows that the many missing links in the paleontological record are sought for in vain because they have never existed: 'The first bird hatched from a reptilian egg.'" By Gould's own testimony, then, Goldschmidt, Gould's hero of the next decade, should be laughed off the intellectual stage. 10

Along with thousands of other creation scientists, in view of a wealth of evidence from thermodynamics, probability relationships, biology, molecular biology, paleontology, and cosmology, I have become convinced that evolution theory is scientifically untenable and that the concept of direct, special creation is a far more credible explanation.

Duane T. Gish
Vice President
Institute for Creation Research
El Cajon, California

Topics for Critical Thinking and Writing

1. In his opening paragraph, Gish claims that evolution is "religion." What do you think he means by this judgment? Do you agree with it? What evidence do you think Gish might cite to defend this claim? (Read the preceding essay by Gould before trying to answer this question.)

2. Gish describes Gould's explanation of evolution as an account that "immediately deteriorates" from "facts" to "arguments." What impression is this language intended to create in the reader's mind? Is it a fair impression of Gould's actual essay?

3. Both Gish and Gould appeal to "the criterion of demarcation" proposed by the philosopher Sir Karl Popper. According to this criterion, any theory, doctrine, or hypothesis is scientific (as opposed to nonscientific) if and only if it is possible that some experiment or other observational evidence could *dis*confirm or falsify the theory. Reexamine Gould's three arguments for evolution. Can you imagine any experiences or experiments that might disconfirm or falsify evolution as Gould presents it?

4. In his third paragraph Gish says, "Evolution has not and cannot be observed any more than creation." Judging from Gould's essay (p. 263), would Gould agree? Support your answer with evidence from Gould's essay.

5. In paragraph 4 Gish asserts that either evolution or creation "must be true." Why does he assert this judgment? Is he right?

6. In paragraph 8 Gish expresses surprise at Gould's assertion that "transitions are often found in the fossil record," because in some of Gould's other publications he emphasizes the enormous gaps in the fossil record. In his next paragraph Gish quotes Gould. Do the quotations seem to you hopelessly at odds with the opinions Gould expresses in the essay that we reprint? Why?

7. Reread Gish's closing paragraph. What effect is it intended to have on the reader?

8. We have called attention to Gish's statement, in his first paragraph, that creationists do not claim creationism is a scientific theory. Yet in his final paragraph Gish speaks of himself as one among "thousands" of "creation scientists." Is there a contradiction here?

GUN CONTROL: WOULD IT REALLY HELP?

J. Warren Cassidy

The Case for Firearms

The American people have a right "to keep and bear arms." This right is protected by the Second Amendment to the Constitution, just as the right to publish editorial comment in this magazine is protected by the First Amendment. Americans remain committed to the constitutional right to free speech even when their most powerful oracles have, at times, abused the First Amendment's inherent powers. Obviously the American people believe no democracy can survive without a free voice.

In the same light, the authors of the Bill of Rights knew that a democratic republic has a right — indeed, a need — to keep and bear arms. Millions of American citizens just as adamantly believe the Second Amendment is crucial to the maintenance of the democratic process. Many express this belief through membership in the National Rifle Association of America.

Our cause is neither trendy nor fashionable, but a basic American belief that spans generations. The NRA's strength has never originated in Washington but instead has reached outward and upward from Biloxi, Albuquerque, Concord, Tampa, Topeka — from every point on the compass and from communities large and small. Those who fail to grasp this widespread commitment will never understand the depth of political and philosophical dedication symbolized by the letters NRA.

Scholars who have devoted careers to the study of the Second Amendment agree in principle that the right to keep and bear arms is fundamental to our concept of democracy. No high-court decision has yet found grounds to challenge this basic freedom. Yet some who oppose this freedom want to waive the constitutionality of the "gun control" question for the sake of their particular — and sometimes peculiar — brand of social reform.

In doing so they seem ready, even eager, to disregard a constitutional   5
right exercised by at least 70 million Americans who own firearms. Contrary to current antigun evangelism, these gun owners are not bad people. They are hard working, law abiding, tax paying. They are safe, sane, and

---

When J. Warren Cassidy wrote this article, he was the National Rifle Association's executive vice president. The article was originally published in Time *(January 29, 1990).*

courteous in their use of guns. They have never been, nor will they ever be, a threat to law and order.

History repeatedly warns us that human character cannot be scrubbed free of its defects through vain attempts to regulate inanimate objects such as guns. What has worked in the past, and what we see working now, are tough, NRA-supported measures that punish the incorrigible minority who place themselves outside the law.

As a result of such measures, violent crimes with firearms, like assault and robbery, have stabilized or are actually declining. We see proof that levels of firearm ownership cannot be associated with levels of criminal violence, except for their deterrent value. On the other hand, tough laws designed to incarcerate violent offenders offer something gun control cannot: swift, sure justice meted out with no accompanying erosion of individual liberty.

Violent crime continues to rise in cities like New York and Washington even after severe firearm-control statutes were rushed into place. Criminals, understandably, have illegal ways of obtaining guns. Antigun laws — the waiting periods, background checks, handgun bans, et al. — only harass those who obey them. Why should an honest citizen be deprived of a firearm for sport or self-defense when, for a gangster, obtaining a gun is just a matter of showing up on the right street corner with enough money?

Antigun opinion steadfastly ignores these realities known to rank-and-file police officers — men and women who face crime firsthand, not police administrators who face mayors and editors. These law-enforcement professionals tell us that expecting firearm restrictions to act as crime-prevention measures is wishful thinking. They point out that proposed gun laws would not have stopped heinous crimes committed by the likes of John Hinckley, Jr., Patrick Purdy, Laurie Dann,[1] or mentally disturbed, usually addicted killers. How can such crimes be used as examples of what gun control could prevent?

There are better ways to advance our society than to excuse criminal 10 behavior. The NRA initiated the first hunter-safety program, which has trained millions of young hunters. We are the shooting sports' leading safety organization, with more than 26,000 certified instructors training 750,000 students and trainees last year alone. Through 1989 there were 9,818 NRA-certified law-enforcement instructors teaching marksmanship to thousands of peace officers.

Frankly, we would rather keep investing NRA resources in such worthwhile efforts instead of spending our time and members' money debunking the failed and flawed promises of gun prohibitionists.

If you agree, I invite you to join the NRA.

[1]**John Hinckley, Jr., Patrick Purdy, Laurie Dann** Hinckley attempted to assassinate President Ronald Reagan in Washington, D.C., in March 1981, wounding the president and three others. Purdy fired a hundred bullets from his AK-47 at children in a Stockton, California, schoolyard in January 1989. He killed five and then killed himself. Dann, firing three guns, shot six schoolchildren in a Chicago suburb in May 1988, killing one and herself as well. [Editors' note.]

Topics for Critical Thinking and Writing

1. Cassidy opens his essay by drawing a parallel between abuse of the First Amendment (speech that harms) and abuse of the Second Amendment (using guns to commit crimes), arguing that no sensible person would conclude that these abuses show the Bill of Rights ought to be revised. Do you agree? Is his parallel fair and instructive? Explain.

2. In his first paragraph Cassidy says, "The American people have a right 'to keep and bear arms.' This right is protected by the Second Amendment of the Constitution." The Second Amendment says this: "A well-regulated militia being necessary to the security of a free State, the right of the people to keep and bear arms shall not be infringed." Has Cassidy quoted a passage out of context? Support your answer.

3. In the second paragraph Cassidy says that there is not only a "right" but also a "need" in "a democratic republic . . . to keep and bear arms." Does he indicate what the need is? Or is it self-evident? Support your answer.

4. In paragraph 6 Cassidy says, "History repeatedly warns us that human character cannot be scrubbed free of its defects through vain attempts to regulate inanimate objects such as guns." He does not give examples. What examples can you offer to help make this generalization convincing? (If you cannot give any examples, do you think Cassidy should himself have provided them?)

5. Cassidy asserts (para. 7) that "violent crimes with firearms . . . have stabilized or are actually declining." Visit your college library, locate recent issues of *Uniform Crime Reports* (published annually by the FBI), and see whether you can verify Cassidy's claim.

6. Cassidy claims that "antigun laws," including "waiting periods [and] background checks," only "harass" law-abiding citizens (para. 8). Do you think it is unfair or futile to try to keep legally purchased guns out of the hands of ex-felons, or the mentally disturbed, by such laws? Explain your position in an essay of 250 words.

Nan Desuka

Why Handguns Must Be Outlawed

"Guns don't kill people—criminals do." That's a powerful slogan, much more powerful than its alternate version: "Guns don't kill people—people kill people." But this second version, though less effective, is much nearer to the whole truth. Although accurate statistics are hard to come by, and even harder to interpret, it seems indisputable that large numbers of

Nan Desuka (1957–1985) was born in Japan but at age two was brought by her parents to Los Angeles, where she was educated. Although she most often wrote about ecology, she occasionally wrote about other controversial topics.

people, not just criminals, kill, with a handgun, other people. Scarcely a day goes by without a newspaper in any large city reporting that a child has found a gun, kept by the child's parents for self-protection, and has, in playing with this new-found toy, killed himself or a playmate. Or we read of a storekeeper, trying to protect himself during a robbery, who inadvertently shoots an innocent customer. These killers are not, in any reasonable sense of the word, criminals. They are just people who happen to kill people. No wonder the gun lobby prefers the first version of the slogan, "Guns don't kill people — criminals do." This version suggests that the only problem is criminals, not you or me, or our children, and certainly not the members of the National Rifle Association.

Those of us who want strict control of handguns — for me that means the outlawing of handguns, except to the police and related service units — have not been able to come up with a slogan equal in power to "Guns don't kill people — criminals do." The best we have been able to come up with is a mildly amusing bumper sticker showing a teddy bear, with the words "Defend your right to arm bears." Humor can be a powerful weapon (even in writing *on behalf* of gun control, one slips into using the imagery of force), and our playful bumper sticker somehow deflates the self-righteousness of the gun lobby, but doesn't equal the power (again the imagery of force) of "Guns don't kill people — criminals do." For one thing, the effective alliteration of "*criminals*" and "*kill*" binds the two words, making everything so terribly simple. Criminals kill; when there are no criminals, there will be no deaths from guns.

But this notion won't do. Despite the uncertainty of some statistical evidence, everyone knows, or should know, that only about 30 percent of murders are committed by robbers or rapists (Kates, 1978). For the most part the victims of handguns know their assailants well. These victims are women killed by jealous husbands, or they are the women's lovers; or they are drinking buddies who get into a violent argument; or they are innocent people who get shot by disgruntled (and probably demented) employees or fellow workers who have (or imagine) a grudge. Or they are, as I've already said, bystanders at a robbery, killed by a storekeeper. Or they are children playing with their father's gun.

Of course this is not the whole story. Hardened criminals also have guns, and they use them. The murders committed by robbers and rapists are what give credence to Barry Goldwater's quip, "We have a crime problem in this country, not a gun problem" (1975, p. 186). But here again the half-truth of a slogan is used to mislead, used to direct attention away from a national tragedy. Different sources issue different statistics, but a conservative estimate is that handguns annually murder at least fifteen thousand Americans, accidentally kill at least another three thousand and wound at least another hundred thousand. Handguns are easily available, both to criminals and to decent people who believe they need a gun in order to protect themselves from criminals. The decent people, unfortunately, have good cause to believe they need protection. Many parts of many cities are utterly unsafe, and even the tiniest village may harbor a murderer. Senator Goldwater is right in saying there is a crime problem (that's the truth of his half-truth), but he is wrong in saying there is not also a gun problem.

Surely the homicide rate would markedly decrease if handguns were   5 outlawed. The FBI reports (Federal Bureau of Investigation, 1985) that more than 60 percent of all murders are caused by guns, and handguns are involved in more than 70 percent of these. Surely many, even most, of these handgun killings would not occur if the killer had to use a rifle, club, or knife. Of course violent lovers, angry drunks, and deranged employees would still flail out with knives or baseball bats, but some of their victims would be able to run away, with few or no injuries, and most of those who could not run away would nevertheless survive, badly injured but at least alive. But if handguns are outlawed, we are told, responsible citizens will have no way to protect themselves from criminals. First, one should re-member that at least 90 percent of America's burglaries are committed when no one is at home. The householder's gun, if he or she has one, is in a drawer of the bedside table, and the gun gets lifted along with the jewelry, adding one more gun to the estimated hundred thousand handguns annu-ally stolen from law-abiding citizens (Shields, 1981). Second, if the house-holder is at home, and attempts to use the gun, he or she is more likely to get killed or wounded than to kill or deter the intruder. Another way of looking at this last point is to recall that for every burglar who is halted by the sight of a handgun, four innocent people are killed by handgun acci-dents.

Because handguns are not accurate beyond ten or fifteen feet, they are not the weapons of sportsmen. Their sole purpose is to kill or at least to dis-able a person at close range. But only a minority of persons killed with these weapons are criminals. Since handguns chiefly destroy the innocent, they must be outlawed — not simply controlled more strictly, but outlawed — to all except to law-enforcement officials. Attempts to control handguns are costly and ineffective, but even if they were cheap and effective stricter controls would not take handguns out of circulation among criminals, be-cause licensed guns are stolen from homeowners and shopkeepers, and thus fall into criminal hands. According to Wright, Rossi, and Daly (1983, p. 181), about 40 percent of the handguns used in crimes are stolen, chiefly from homes that the guns were supposed to protect.

The National Rifle Association is fond of quoting a University of Wis-consin study that says, "gun control laws have no individual or collective ef-fect in reducing the rate of violent crime" (cited in Smith, 1981, p. 17). Agreed — but what if handguns were not available? What if the manufac-turer of handguns is severely regulated, and if the guns may be sold only to police officers? True, even if handguns are outlawed, some criminals will manage to get them, but surely fewer petty criminals will have guns. It is simply untrue for the gun lobby to assert that all criminals — since they are by definition lawbreakers — will find ways to get handguns. For the most part, if the sale of handguns is outlawed, guns won't be available, and fewer criminals will have guns. And if fewer criminals have guns, there is every reason to believe that violent crime will decline. A youth armed only with a knife is less likely to try to rob a store than if he is armed with a gun. This commonsense reasoning does not imply that if headguns are outlawed crime will suddenly disappear, or even that an especially repulsive crime such as rape will decrease markedly. A rapist armed with a knife probably has a sufficient weapon. But *some* violent crime will almost surely decrease. And the decrease will probably be significant if in addition to outlawing handguns, severe mandatory punishments are imposed on a person who is found to possess one, and even severer mandatory punishments are imposed on a person who uses one while committing a crime. Again, none of this activity will solve "the crime problem," but neither will anything else, including the "get tough with criminals" attitude of Senator Goldwater. And of course any attempt to reduce crime (one cannot realistically talk of "solving" the crime problem) will have to pay attention to our systems of bail, plea bargaining, and parole, but outlawing handguns will help.

What will the cost be? First, to take "cost" in its most literal sense, there will be the cost of reimbursing gun owners for the weapons they surrender. Every owner of a handgun ought to be paid the fair market value of the weapon. Since the number of handguns is estimated to be between 50 million and 90 million, the cost will be considerable, but it will be far less than the costs—both in money and in sorrow—that result from deaths due to handguns.

Second, one may well ask if there is another sort of cost, a cost to our liberty, to our constitutional rights. The issue is important, and persons who advocate abolition of handguns are blind or thoughtless if they simply brush it off. On the other hand, opponents of gun control do all of us a disservice by insisting over and over that the Constitution guarantees "the right to bear arms." The Second Amendment in the Bill of Rights says this: "A well-regulated militia being necessary to the security of a free State, the right of the people to keep and bear arms shall not be infringed." It is true that the founding fathers, mindful of the British attempt to disarm the colonists, viewed the presence of "a well-regulated militia" as a safeguard of democracy. Their intention is quite clear, even to one who has not read Stephen P. Halbrook's *That Every Man Be Armed,* an exhaustive argument in favor of the right to bear arms. There can be no doubt that the framers of the Constitution and the Bill of Rights believed that armed insurrection was a justifiable means of countering oppression and tyranny. The Second Amendment may be fairly paraphrased thus: "*Because* an organized militia is necessary to the security of the State, the people have the right to possess weapons." But the owners of handguns are not members of a well-regulated militia. Furthermore, nothing in the proposal to ban handguns would deprive citizens of their rifles or other long-arm guns. All handguns, however, even large ones, should be banned. "Let's face it," Guenther W. Bachmann (a vice president of Smith and Wesson) admits, "they are all concealable" (Kennedy, 1981, p. 6). In any case, it is a fact that when gun control laws have been tested in the courts, they have been found to be constitutional. The constitutional argument was worth making, but the question must now be regarded as settled, not only by the courts but by anyone who reads the Second Amendment.

Still, is it not true that "If guns are outlawed, only outlaws will have 10 guns"? This is yet another powerful slogan, but it is simply not true. First, we are talking not about "guns" but about handguns. Second, the police will have guns—handguns and others—and these trained professionals are the ones on whom we must rely for protection against criminals. Of course the police have not eradicated crime; and of course we must hope that in the future they will be more successful in protecting all citizens. But we must also recognize that the efforts of private citizens to protect themselves with handguns have chiefly taken the lives not of criminals but of innocent people.

REFERENCES

Goldwater, B. (1975, December). Why gun control laws don't work. *Reader's Digest, 107*, 183–188.

Halbrook, S. P. (1985). *That every man be armed: The evolution of a constitutional right.* Albuquerque: University of New Mexico Press.

Kates, D. B., Jr. (1978, September). Against civil disarming. *Harper's, 257*, 28–33.

Kennedy, E. (1981, October 5). Handguns: Preferred instruments of criminals. *Congressional Record.* Washington, DC: U.S. Government Printing Office.

Shields, P. (1981). *Guns don't die—people do.* New York: Arbor House.

Smith, A. (1981, April). Fifty million handguns. *Esquire, 96*, 16–18.

Federal Bureau of Investigation. (1985). *Uniform crime reports for the United States.* Washington, DC: U.S. Department of Justice.

Wright, J. D., Rossi, P. H., & Daly, K. (1983). *Under the gun.* New York: Aldine.

Topics for Critical Thinking and Writing

1. Reread the first and last paragraphs, and then in a sentence or two comment on the writer's strategy for opening and closing her essay.

2. On the whole, does the writer strike you as a person who is fair, or who at least is trying to be fair? Support your answer by citing specific passages that lead you to your opinion.

3. Many opponents of gun control argue that control of handguns will be only a

first move down the slippery slope that leads to laws prohibiting private ownership of any sort of gun. Even if you hold this view, state as best you can the arguments that one might offer against it. (Notice that you are asked to offer arguments, not merely an assertion that it won't happen.)

4. Do you agree with Desuka that a reasonable reading of the Second Amendment
   reveals that individuals do not have a constitutional right to own handguns, even
   though the founding fathers said that "the right of the people to keep and bear
   arms shall not be infringed"?

5. Write a 500-word analysis of Desuka's essay (for a sample analysis see p. 82), or
   write a 500-word reply to her essay, responding to her main points.

6. Do you think the prohibition of handguns is feasible? Could it be enforced?
   Would the effort to enforce it result in worse problems than we already have?
   Write a 500-word essay defending or attacking the feasibility of Desuka's pro-
   posal.

HIROSHIMA: WAS THE BOMBING IMMORAL?

John Connor

The U.S. Was Right

Forty years ago this week in Hiroshima: the dreadful flash, the wrist
watches fused forever at 8:16 A.M. The question still persists: Should we
have dropped the atomic bomb?

History seldom gives decisive answers, but recently declassified documents point to a clear judgment: Yes, it was necessary to drop the bomb. It
was needed to end the war. It saved countless American and Japanese
lives.

In the early summer of 1945, Japan, under tight control of the militarists, was an implacable, relentless adversary. The Japanese defended territory with a philosophy we had seldom encountered: Soldiers were taught
that surrender was worse than death. There was savage resistance to the
end in battle after battle.

---

*In August 1985, on the fortieth anniversary of the dropping of atomic bombs
on Japan, the* New York Times *invited two specialists to comment on the event.
Both of their essays are reprinted here. John Connor (b. 1930), professor of anthro-
pology at California State University, Sacramento, was attached to General
MacArthur's headquarters in Tokyo in 1949 and 1950.*

Of the 5,000-man Japanese force at Tarawa in November 1943, only seventeen remained alive when the island was taken. When Kwajalein was invaded in February 1944, Japanese officers slashed at American tanks with samurai swords; their men held grenades against the sides of tanks in an effort to disable them.

On Saipan, less than 1,000 of the 32,000 defending Japanese troops 5 survived. Casualties among the Japanese-ruled civilians on the island numbered 10,000. Parents bashed their babies' brains out on rocky cliff sides, then leaped to their deaths. Others cut each other's throats; children threw grenades at each other. America suffered 17,000 casualties.

Just 660 miles southeast of Tokyo, Iwo Jima's garrison was told to defend the island as if it were Tokyo itself. They did. In the first day of fighting, there were more American casualties than during D-Day in Normandy. At Okinawa—only 350 miles south of Kyushu—more than 110,000 Japanese soldiers and 100,000 civilians were killed. Kamikaze attacks cost the Navy alone some 10,000 casualties. The Army and Marines lost more than 50,000 men.

In the early summer of 1945, the invasion of Japan was imminent and everyone in the Pacific was apprehensive. The apprehension was justified, because our intelligence was good: With a system code-named "Magic," it had penetrated Japanese codes even before Pearl Harbor. "Magic" would play a crucial role in the closing days of the war.

Many have maintained that the bomb was unnecessary because in the closing days of the war intercepted Japanese diplomatic messages disclosed a passionate desire for peace. While that is true, it is irrelevant. The Japanese government remained in the hands of the militarists: *Their* messages indicated a willingness to fight to the death.

Japanese planes, gasoline, and ammunition had been hoarded for the coming invasion. More than 5,000 aircraft had been hidden everywhere to be used as suicide weapons, with only enough gas in their tanks for a one-way trip to the invasion beaches. More than two million men were moving into positions to defend the home islands.

The object was to inflict such appalling losses that the Americans 10 would agree to a treaty more favorable than unconditional surrender. The Army Chief of Staff, General George C. Marshall, estimated potential American casualties as high as a million.

The willingness of the Japanese to die was more than empty bravado. Several of my colleagues at Kyushu University told me that as boys of fourteen or fifteen, they were being trained to meet the Americans on the beaches with little more than sharpened bamboo spears. They had no illusions about their chances for survival.

The Potsdam declaration calling for unconditional surrender was beamed to Japan on July 27. On July 30, the Americans were informed that Japan would officially ignore the ultimatum. A week later, the bomb was dropped.

Could we not have warned the Japanese in advance, critics asked, and dropped a demonstration bomb? That alternative was vetoed on the grounds the bomb might not work, or that the plane carrying it might be shot down. Moreover, it is questionable how effective a demonstration bomb might have been. The militarists could have imposed a news black-out as complete as the one imposed after the disastrous battle of Midway and continued on their suicidal course. That is exactly what happened at Hiroshima. Within hours, the Japanese government sent in a team of scientists to investigate the damage. Their report was immediately suppressed and was not made public until many years after the war.

After midnight on August 10, a protracted debate took place in an air-raid shelter deep inside the Imperial Palace. The military insisted that Japan should hold out for terms far better than unconditional surrender. The peace faction favored accepting the Potsdam declaration, providing that the emperor would be retained. The two factions remained at an impasse. At 2 A.M., Prime Minister Kantaro Suzuki asked the emperor to decide. In a soft, deliberate voice, the emperor expressed his great longing for peace. The war had ended.

It was impossible, in August 1945, to predict the awesome shadow the 15 bomb would cast on humanity. The decision to drop it seemed both simple and obvious. Without it, the militarists might have prevailed, an invasion ordered. And the loss of both American and Japanese lives would have been awesome.

The atomic bomb accomplished what it had been designed to do. It ended the war.

Topics for Critical Thinking and Writing

1. What is Connor's thesis? Where do you first find it? Where else does he state it? Are these statements in effective positions? Explain.

2. Jot down the reasons Connor gives to justify dropping the atomic bomb on Hiroshima. In reading and rereading the essay, do you find his evidence persuasive, or do some questions and doubts come to mind? If questions and doubts arise, jot them down.

3. One might say that the essayist argues two points: America needed the bomb to win the war without enormous American casualties, and, second, dropping the bomb was right. Which of these two theses gets more attention? Does Connor assume that if we needed to win the war without further heavy losses, then using the bomb was morally right?

4. Connor concludes his essay by defending the bombing of Hiroshima in terms of its purpose and its effectiveness in achieving that purpose. Does this reasoning show that he implicitly takes the position that *any* weapon that our side could use to win the war was justifiable? Does his argument require him, in consistency, to condemn the massive aerial bombardment of Tokyo and Dresden earlier in 1945 because those raids did *not* "end the war"?

5. Connor mentions only one alternative to dropping the bomb on Hiroshima—

dropping instead "a demonstration bomb." Why does he think this alternative would have failed in its purpose? Were there other alternatives that he ignores? (In this connection, read the next essay, by Alperovitz.)

6. You may have been told to avoid (in general) writing short, choppy sentences and undeveloped paragraphs. Connor's final paragraph consists of only two sentences, one of them very short. Is the paragraph faulty? Explain.

7. Connor never mentions dropping the bomb on Nagasaki three days after the bomb on Hiroshima. Could he defend this act in exactly the same way as he defends the bombing of Hiroshima, or would he need to construct a somewhat different argument? Set forth your answer in one or two paragraphs.

Gar Alperovitz

The U.S. Was Wrong

Though it has not yet received broad public attention, there exists overwhelming historical evidence that President Harry S Truman knew he could almost certainly end World War II without using the atomic bomb: The United States had cracked the Japanese code, and a stream of documents released over the last forty years shows that Mr. Truman had two other options.

The first option was to clarify America's surrender terms to assure the Japanese we would not remove their emperor. The second was simply to await the expected Soviet declaration of war—which, United States intelligence advised, appeared likely to end the conflict on its own.

Instead, Hiroshima was bombed August 6, 1945, and Nagasaki on August 9. The planned date for the Soviet Union's entry into the war against Japan was August 8.

The big turning point was the emperor's continuing June-July decision to open surrender negotiations through Moscow. Top American officials—and, most critically, the president—understood the move was extraordinary: Mr. Truman's secret diaries, lost until 1978, call the key intercepted message "the telegram from Jap Emperor asking for peace."

Other documents—among them newly discovered secret memoran-   5
dums from William J. Donovan, director of the Office of Strategic Services—show that Mr. Truman was personally advised of Japanese peace

---

Gar Alperovitz was born in Racine, Wisconsin, in 1935 and educated at the University of Wisconsin, the University of California (Berkeley), and Cambridge University. He has served as a congressional assistant, a member of the U.S. Senate staff, and a special assistant to the Department of State. He has written several books, including Atomic Diplomacy: Hiroshima and Potsdam *(1965; revised edition, 1985) and* The Decision to Use the Atomic Bomb *(1995). This article first appeared in the* New York Times *on August 8, 1985.*

initiatives through Swiss and Portuguese channels as early as three months before Hiroshima. Moreover, Mr. Truman told several officials he had no objection in principle to Japan's keeping the emperor, which seemed the only sticking point.

American leaders were sure that if he so chose "the Mikado could stop the war with a royal word" — as one top presidential aide put it. Having decided to use the bomb, however, Mr. Truman was urged by Secretary of State James F. Byrnes not to give assurances to the emperor before the weapon had been demonstrated.

Additional official records, including minutes of top-level White House planning meetings, show the president was clearly advised of the importance of a Soviet declaration of war: It would pull the rug out from under Japanese military leaders who were desperately hoping the powerful Red Army would stay neutral.

General George C. Marshall in mid-June told Mr. Truman that "the impact of Russian entry on the already hopeless Japanese may well be the decisive action levering them into capitulation at that time or shortly thereafter if we land."

A month later, the American-British Combined Intelligence Staffs advised their chiefs of the critical importance of a Red Army attack. As the top British general, Sir Hastings Ismay, summarized the conclusions for Prime Minister Winston Churchill: "If and when Russia came into the war against Japan, the Japanese would probably wish to get out on almost any terms short of the dethronement of the Emperor."

Mr. Truman's private diaries also record his understanding of the sig- 10 nificance of this option. On July 17, 1945, when Stalin confirmed that the Red Army would march, Mr. Truman privately noted: "Fini Japs when that comes about."

There was plenty of time: The American invasion of Japan was not scheduled until the spring of 1946. Even a preliminary landing on the island of Kyushu was still three months in the future.

General Dwight D. Eisenhower, appalled that the bomb would be used in these circumstances, urged Mr. Truman and Secretary of War Henry L. Stimson not to drop it. In his memoirs, he observed that weeks before Hiroshima, Japan had been seeking a way to surrender. "It wasn't necessary," he said in a later interview, "to hit them with that awful thing."

The man who presided over the Joint Chiefs of Staff, Admiral William D. Leahy, was equally shocked: "The use of this barbarous weapon at Hiroshima and Nagasaki was of no material assistance in our war against Japan. The Japanese were already defeated and ready to surrender."

Why, then, was the bomb used?

American leaders rejected the most obvious option — simply waiting 15 for the Red Army attack — out of political, not military, concerns.

As the diary of one official put it, they wanted to end the war before Moscow got "in so much on the kill." Secretary of the Navy James V. Forrestal's diaries record that Mr. Byrnes "was most anxious to get the Japanese affair over with before the Russians got in."

United States leaders had also begun to think of the atomic bomb as what Secretary Stimson termed the "master card" of diplomacy. President Truman postponed his Potsdam meeting with Stalin until July 17, 1945 — one day after the first successful nuclear test — to be sure the atomic bomb would strengthen his hand before confronting the Soviet leader on the shape of a postwar settlement.

To this day, we do not know with absolute certainty Mr. Truman's personal attitudes on several key issues. Yet we do know that his most important adviser, Secretary of State Byrnes, was convinced that dropping the bomb would serve crucial long-range diplomatic purposes.

As one atomic scientist, Leo Szilard, observed: "Mr. Byrnes did not argue that it was necessary to use the bomb against the cities of Japan in order to win the war. Mr. Byrnes . . . view [was] that our possessing and demonstrating the bomb would make Russia more manageable."

Topics for Critical Thinking and Writing

1. In a few sentences summarize Alperovitz's essay.

2. If you have read Connor's essay (p. 282), do you find in it convincing (or at least substantial) evidence that Alperovitz ignores or distorts? If so, what is this evidence?

3. Suppose someone argued that although with hindsight we can now see that the bomb was not needed to end the war, President Truman could not have seen this fact in the summer of 1945. Does Alperovitz's evidence refute such an argument? Explain.

4. Alperovitz does not comment explicitly on Truman's character or morality, but, drawing on this essay, what do you think he thinks of Truman as a human being? Support your answer with evidence. Then consider another question: Does Alperovitz in this essay present evidence that supports what you take to be his view of Truman? Explain.

PRAYER IN SCHOOL: IS IT PERMISSIBLE?

Jay Alan Sekulow

Student-Led Prayers Should Be Permitted

Not only should student-led and student-initiated prayer be permitted at public high school graduations, it is a legally protected right.

In 1969, the Supreme Court ruled that student expression against the Vietnam War could not be quashed in public schools. The court ruled that neither "students [n]or teachers shed their constitutional rights to freedom of speech or expression at the schoolhouse gate."

It is now 1994, and once again there are those who seek to limit student speech. They claim that student-led prayers at graduation violate the Establishment Clause. That argument doesn't hold any water.

The First Amendment prohibits government from establishing religion. It leaves untouched private expression. In *Westside Community Schools v. Mergens* (1990), the Supreme Court said: "There is a crucial difference between government speech endorsing religion, which the Establishment Clause prohibits, and private speech, which the Free Speech and Free Exercise Clauses protect."

A student's right to free speech, including religious free speech, does   5 not end when he or she stands up at the graduation podium to accept a diploma.

Our organization sent nearly fifteen thousand bulletins to public school administrators nationwide last year, urging them to permit students to exercise free speech rights. The bulletins helped educate school officials and students by providing an accurate analysis of the law.

Last year, the Supreme Court decided not to hear *Jones v. Clear Creek Independent School District,* a case in which a federal appeals court permitted a student-led prayer in a Houston-area school. If the case posed a constitutional crisis, you can bet the court would have heard it.

All of this sends a powerful message: Student-initiated and student-led prayer at graduation is protected free speech.

Don't be confused over the need for a separation of church and state. No one is suggesting that one religion be given preference over another. No one is suggesting that a school endorse any kind of religious belief. But

Jay Alan Sekulow is chief counsel for the American Center for Law and Justice, a public interest law firm headed by televangelist Pat Robertson. This essay, paired with the next one, originally appeared in CQ Researcher *(February 18, 1994).*

religious speakers, even at school, must have equal access to the marketplace of ideas in America.

In 1969, when the Vietnam War controversy was raging, the Supreme 10
Court ruled that students' expression against the war could not be
squashed in public schools.

America survived those protests, some of which posed very real
threats to life and property. Should not student prayers, which pose no
threat to the Establishment Clause, also be permitted?

The answer has to be yes.

Topics for Critical Thinking and Writing

1. Sekulow sees no constitutional difference between permitting students to express antiwar sentiments in public schools and permitting students to pray in public schools. Yet the former is clearly a political issue, whereas the latter is clearly
   a religious issue. Do you attach any importance to this distinction? Explain.

2. Sekulow argues (para. 8) that "Student-initiated and student-led prayer at graduation is protected free speech." Suppose someone replied, "Of course students
   can pray, but organized prayer *at graduation,* even if student-initiated and student-led, takes place under the auspices of the school's administrators, who determine the graduation program, and such prayer therefore does not differ from
   prayer conducted by a member of the clergy who has been invited by the
   school's administration." What might Sekulow's reply be? What is *your* reply?

3. Many of those who advocate prayer at graduation say that schools have failed to
   stress moral and spiritual values, and prayer at graduation would be part of a
   program showing the school's commitment to such values. What is your reasoned response?

4. Advocates for prayer at graduation sometimes argue that belief in God is part of
   the country's "religious heritage." For instance, the day after passing the First
   Amendment ("Congress shall make no law respecting an establishment of religion, or prohibiting the free exercise thereof . . .") the House of Representatives of the First Congress called for a day of thanksgiving, and the first Thanksgiving Proclamation, signed by President Washington, asserts that "it is the duty
   of all nations to acknowledge the providence of almighty God." In 1954 Congress added "under God" to the Pledge of Allegiance, and in 1956 the motto "In
   God We Trust" was put on all coins and paper money. Can one therefore argue
   that indeed as a nation we believe in God, and therefore prayer at graduation
   ceremonies is entirely appropriate?

5. Rush Limbaugh writes, in *The Way Things Ought to Be* (1992), "People for
   whom belief in God is at best a charming superstition have managed to ban
   prayer from the public schools for the last thirty years. Is it only a coincidence
   that the quality of American education has declined ever since?" (page 275).
   What is your answer to Limbaugh's question? Explain.

6. No one disputes a student's right to pray silently in public school or vocally at
   home or in church. Why should religious Americans also want opportunities to

pray openly and vocally in public schools, especially at graduation ceremonies, knowing that there are or may be students present who cannot conscientiously share in such prayers? Respond in a 250-word essay.

Steven R. Shapiro

Student-Led Prayers Should Not Be Permitted

Last June, the Supreme Court decided not to review a Texas decision that allowed a student to deliver a nonsectarian and nonproselytizing invocation at high school graduation if that were the choice of a majority of the graduating seniors.

In the days and months following the Supreme Court's action, the radical right claimed that the court's action was an endorsement of student-initiated prayer and a vindication of the decision by the United States Court of Appeals for the Fifth Circuit in *Jones v. Clear Creek Independent School District*. In fact, the Supreme Court's action neither indicated approval, nor did it transform the Fifth Circuit's decision into a national precedent.

The Supreme Court agrees to review only a small percentage of the cases that are presented to it every year. As was true in the *Jones* case, the court rarely explains its decision to deny review. The court has consistently emphasized that a decision to deny review is not a decision on the merits.

Contrary to what some are claiming, therefore, the decision to deny review in *Jones* simply means that the law remains as it was when the Supreme Court last considered the issue of graduation prayer in *Lee v. Weisman* in 1992. And in *Weisman,* the court unambiguously held that even nonsectarian and nonproselytizing prayers at public school graduation ceremonies violate the Constitution's separation of church and state.

The fact that a majority of students may want the school district to 5 permit graduation prayer, even though it is prohibited by the Establishment Clause, is as irrelevant in this context as it would be if a majority of students asked the school district to violate the First Amendment by engaging in censorship or to violate the Fourth Amendment by engaging in an unreasonable search of a student's belongings.

The American Civil Liberties Union strongly believes that *Jones* was wrongly decided and is flatly inconsistent with the Supreme Court's ruling in *Weisman.*

Since *Jones v. Clear Creek,* the ACLU has been engaged in several

Steven R. Shapiro is legal director for the American Civil Liberties Union. This essay appeared paired with the preceding essay in CQ Researcher *(February 18, 1994).*

lawsuits over student-initiated prayers. In the most recent decision, federal Judge Albert V. Bryan in Virginia summed up the issue quite well when he wrote that "the notion that a person's constitutional rights may be subject to a majority vote is itself anathema."

"The graduating classes in Loudoun County certainly could not have voted to exclude from the ceremonies persons of a certain race," Judge Bryan said. "To be constructively excluded from graduation ceremonies because of one's religion or lack of religion is not a great deal different."

Topics for Critical Thinking and Writing

1. In his first paragraph Shapiro refers to "nonproselytizing" invocations and prayers. What would be examples of such things, and what would be examples of proselytizing invocations and prayers?

2. Do you think it makes a difference whether the prayer is initiated by the school administration or by a majority of the students? Do you agree with Shapiro, in paragraph 5, that the will of a majority of the students is irrelevant in this issue?

3. Judge Bryan (para. 8) draws a parallel between excluding persons from graduation ceremonies because of their race and "constructively" excluding persons from such ceremonies because of their religious or nonreligious beliefs. Do you think the two cases are parallel or not? Explain.

4. In *Wallace v. Jaffree* (1985) the Supreme Court held that an Alabama law requiring a moment of silence "for meditation or voluntary prayer" at the start of the school day improperly supports religion. The court left open, however, the possibility of sustaining "a moment of silence for meditation," if prayer is not mentioned. Putting aside the question of constitutionality, do you think "a moment of silence for meditation" would be a good or a bad thing to introduce into the schools? Why?

5. The American Civil Liberties Union thinks that what a majority of students want is irrelevant to what the Bill of Rights permits. Do you agree or not? Explain.

6. Putting aside the debated issue of prayer at graduation, do you think that religion was not adequately stressed when you were in secondary school? For instance, were you adequately informed that many of the early settlers of this country came here for religious reasons, or that religious groups played an important role in the abolitionist movement, or that African American churches played an important role in the civil rights movement? Construct an argument that in your secondary education more attention—or less—should have been paid to the roles of religion.

SEX EDUCATION: SHOULD CONDOMS BE DISTRIBUTED IN SCHOOLS?

Rush H. Limbaugh III

Condoms: The New Diploma

The logic and motivation behind this country's mad dash to distribute free condoms in our public schools is ridiculous and misguided. Worse, the message conveyed by mass condom distribution is a disservice and borders on being lethal. Condom distribution sanctions, even encourages, sexual activity, which in teen years tends to be promiscuous and relegates to secondary status the most important lesson to be taught: abstinence. An analysis of the entire condom distribution logic also provides a glimpse into just what is wrong with public education today.

First things first. Advocates of condom distribution say that kids are going to have sex, that try as we might we can't stop them. Therefore they need protection. Hence, condoms. Well, hold on a minute. Just whose notion is it that "kids are going to do it anyway, you can't stop them"? Why limit the application of that brilliant logic to sexual activity? Let's just admit that kids are going to do drugs and distribute safe, untainted drugs every morning in homeroom. Kids are going to smoke, too, we can't stop them, so let's provide packs of low-tar cigarettes to the students for their after-sex smoke. Kids are going to get guns and shoot them, you can't stop them, so let's make sure that teachers have bulletproof vests. I mean, come on! If we are really concerned about safe sex, why stop at condoms? Let's convert study halls to Safe Sex Centers where students can go to actually have sex on nice double beds with clean sheets under the watchful and approving eye of the school nurse, who will be on hand to demonstrate, along with the principal, just how to use a condom. Or even better: If kids are going to have sex, let's put disease-free hookers in these Safe Sex Centers. Hey, if safe sex is the objective, why compromise our standards?

There is something else very disturbing about all this. Let's say that Johnnie and Susie are on a date in Johnny's family sedan. Johnny pulls in to his town's designated Teen Parking Location hoping to score a little affection from Susie. They move to the backseat and it isn't long before Johnny, on the verge of bliss, whips out his trusty high school–distributed condom

---

Rush Limbaugh, born in Cape Girardeau, Missouri, became a Top 40 deejay in the 1960s, before becoming a radio talk show host in Sacramento. In 1988 his show went national. We reprint a passage from his book The Way Things Ought To Be *(1992).*

and urges Susie not to resist him. She is hesitant, being a nice girl and all, and says she doesn't think the time is right.

"Hey, everything is okay. Nothing will go wrong. Heck, the *school gave me this condom*, they know what they're doing. You'll be fine," coos the artful and suave Johnny.

Aside from what is obviously wrong here, there is something you prob- 5
ably haven't thought of which to me is profound. Not that long ago, school policy, including that on many college campuses, was designed to protect the girls from the natural and instinctive aggressive pursuit of young men. Chaperones, for example, were around to make sure the girls were not in any jeopardy. So much for that thinking now. The schools may just as well endorse and promote these backseat affairs. The kids are going to do it anyway.

Well, here's what's wrong. There have always been consequences to having sex. Always. Now, however, some of these consequences are severe: debilitating venereal diseases and AIDS. You can now die from having sex. It is that simple. If you look, the vast majority of adults in America have made adjustments in their sexual behavior in order to protect themselves from some of the dire consequences floating around out there. For the most part, the sexual revolution of the sixties is over, a miserable failure. Free love and rampant one-night stands are tougher to come by because people are aware of the risks. In short, we have modified our behavior. Now, would someone tell me what is so difficult about sharing this knowledge and experience with kids? The same stakes are involved. Isn't that our responsibility, for crying out loud, to teach them what's best for them? If we adults aren't responding to these new dangers by having condom-protected sex anytime, anywhere, why should such folly be taught to our kids?

Let me try the Magic Johnson example for you who remain unconvinced. Imagine that you are in the Los Angeles Lakers locker room after a game and you and Magic are getting ready to go hit the town. Outside the locker room are a bunch of young women, as there always are, and as Magic had freely admitted there always were, and that you know that the woman Magic is going to pick up and take back to the hotel has AIDS. You approach Magic and say, "Hey, Magic! Hold on! That girl you're going to take back to the hotel with you has AIDS. Here, don't worry about it. Take these condoms, you'll be fine."

Do you think Magic would have sex with that woman? Ask yourself: Would you knowingly have sex with *anyone* who has AIDS with only a condom to protect you from getting the disease? It doesn't take Einstein to answer that question. So, why do you think it's okay to send kids out into the world to do just that? Who is to know who carries the HIV virus, and on the chance your kid runs into someone who does have it, are you confident that a condom will provide all the protection he or she needs?

Doesn't it make sense to be honest with kids and tell them the best thing they can do to avoid AIDS or any of the other undesirable consequences is to abstain from sexual intercourse? It is the best way — in fact, it is the only surefire way — to guard against sexual transmission of AIDS, pregnancy, and venereal diseases. What's so terrible about saying so?

Yet, there are those who steadfastly oppose the teaching of abstinence, 10 and I think they should be removed from any position of authority where educating children is concerned. In New York, the City Board of Education *narrowly won* (4–3) the passage of a resolution requiring the inclusion of teaching abstinence in the AIDS education program in the spring of 1992. No one was trying to eliminate anything from the program, such as condom distribution or anal sex education (which does occur in New York public school sex education classes). All they wanted was that abstinence also be taught. Yet, the Schools Chancellor, Joseph Fernandez, vigorously fought the idea, saying it would do great damage to their existing program! Well, just how is that? The fact is that abstinence works every time it is tried. As this book went to press, the New York Civil Liberties Union was considering filing a lawsuit to stop this dangerous new addition to the curriculum. Now what in the name of God is going on here? This is tantamount to opposing a drug education program which instructs students not to use drugs because it would not be useful.

The Jacksonville, Florida, school board also decided that abstinence should be the centerpiece of their sexual education curriculum, and the liberals there were also outraged about this. What is so wrong with this? Whose agenda is being denied by teaching abstinence and just what is that agenda?

Jacksonville teachers are telling seventh-graders that "the only safe sex is no sex at all." Sex education classes provide some information about birth control and sexually transmitted diseases, but these areas are not the primary focus of the classes. Nancy Corwin, a member of the school board, admits the paradox when she says that the schools send a nonsensical message when they teach kids not to have sex but then give them condoms.

Instead of this twaddle, the Jacksonville school board has decided to teach real safe sex, which is abstinence. However, six families, along with Planned Parenthood and the ACLU, are suing the schools over this program. This bunch of curious citizens says that teaching abstinence puts the children at a greater risk of catching AIDS or other sexually transmitted diseases. Greater risk? !£#$£@! How can that be? What kind of contaminated thinking is this? The suit alleges that the schools are providing a "fear-based program that gives children incomplete, inaccurate, biased, and sectarian information." You want more? Try this: Linda Lanier of Planned Parenthood says, "It's not right to try to trick our students." Trick the students? #£&@£!? If anyone is trying to trick students, it's Planned Parenthood and this band of hedonists who try to tell kids that a condom will protect them from any consequences of sex.

Folks, here you have perhaps the best example of the culture war being waged in our country today. To say that "teaching abstinence is a trick" is absurd. Is Ms. Lanier having sex every night of the week? What adjustments has she made in her sex life because of AIDS? Does she think that a little sheath of latex will be enough to protect her?

This is terribly wrong. The Jacksonville public school system is at- 15 tempting to teach right from wrong, as opposed to teaching that sex does not have any consequences, which I believe is the selfish agenda these people hold dear. I have stated elsewhere in this book, and I state it again here, that there are many people who wish to go through life guilt-free and engage in behavior they know to be wrong and morally vacant. In order to assuage their guilt they attempt to construct and impose policies which not only allow them to engage in their chosen activities but encourage others to do so as well. There is, after all, strength in numbers.

Promiscuous and self-gratifying, of-the-moment sex is but one of these chosen lifestyles. Abortions on demand and condom distribution are but two of the policies and programs which, as far as these people are concerned, ensure there are no consequences. As one disgusted member of the Jacksonville school board said, "Every yahoo out there has a social program that they want to run through the school system. We are here for academic reasons and we cannot cure the social evils of the world."

The worst of all of this is the lie that condoms really protect against AIDS. The condom failure rate can be as high as 20 percent. Would you get on a plane — or put your children on a plane — if one in five passengers would be killed on the flight? Well, the statistic holds for condoms, folks.

Ah, but there is even more lunacy haunting the sacred halls of academe. According to the *Los Angeles Times,* administrators in the Los Angeles public schools have regretfully acknowledged that the sex education courses undertaken in the early 1970s "might" have a correlation to the rising teen pregnancy rates in their schools which can be traced to the same years. They have devised an enlightened and marvelous new approach to modernize and correct the sex education curriculum. It is called Outercourse. I am not making this up. Outercourse is, in essence, instruction in creative methods of masturbation.

"Hi, class, and welcome to Outercourse 101. I am your instructor, Mr. Reubens, from Florida, and I want to remind you that this is a hands-on course." We will know the graduates of Outercourse 101 in about forty years. They will be the people walking around with seeing-eye dogs.

Topics for Critical Thinking and Writing

1. In his second paragraph Limbaugh attempts to give a *reductio ad absurdum* of the proposal to distribute condoms in high school. (We discuss *reductio* on p. 764.) Do you think this tactic of criticism as used here is successful or not? Explain.

2. Limbaugh thinks that distributing condoms in high school will encourage sex among adolescents, as well as give premarital sex a stamp of approval by school authorities. Do you agree? Why, or why not?

3. In paragraph 17 Limbaugh says, "The condom failure rate can be as high as 20 percent." What do you take this statement to mean?

4. Limbaugh says that those who favor condom distribution "try to tell kids that a condom will protect them from *any* consequences of sex" (para. 13, emphasis added). Inquire at your campus health office to find out what current medical practice advises about the likelihood of condom failure, resulting in unwanted pregnancy or in acquiring a sexually transmitted disease.

5. Make a list of the *reasons* Limbaugh gives for opposing the distribution of condoms, and evaluate them.

6. Limbaugh quotes (para. 16) with evident approval the public school official who complained, "Every yahoo out there has a social program that they want to run through the school system. We are here for academic reasons." Yet elsewhere Limbaugh supports prayer in the public schools. Do you think this is inconsistent of him or not? Explain.

Anna Quindlen

A Pyrrhic Victory

Pop quiz: A 16-year-old is appropriately treated at a school clinic after he is advised that the reason it feels as if he is going to die when he urinates is because he has a sexually transmitted disease. Told that condoms could have protected him from infection, he asks for some. A nurse tells him to wait while she looks for his name on the list of students whose parents have confidentially requested that their sons and daughters not receive them.

The student replies: (a) "No problem"; (b) "Hmmm — an interesting way to balance the reproductive health of adolescents and the rights of parents"; (c) Nothing. He sidles out of the office and not long afterward gets a whopping case of chlamydia.

Condoms, condoms, condoms. As those who oppose condom distribution in the schools gloated over an appellate court decision that said the program violated parents' rights, Alwyn Cohall, the pediatrician who oversees several school-based clinics in New York, quoted Yogi Berra. "It's déjà vu all over again," said Dr. Cohall, who has to clean up the messes made when sexually active kids don't use condoms. And he wasn't smiling.

Over the last two years the Board of Education has wasted time better spent on instructional issues giving and receiving lectures on latex. The opt-out provision its members are now likely to adopt is the "let me see if

---

From 1986 to 1994, Anna Quindlen regularly wrote a column for the New York Times, *where this essay appeared on January 8, 1994.*

you're on the list, dear" scenario outlined above, and if you think it might have a chilling effect on a young man too self-conscious to ask for Trojans in a drugstore, then you get an A in adolescent psychology.

You get extra credit if you figure that being on the list will be scant 5 protection against disease if the young man has sex anyhow. "A victory for parents," some have called the provision. But is it Pyrrhic?

Dr. Cohall, a champion of condom distribution, agrees that it is best if teenagers abstain from sexual activity and talk to their parents about issues of sex, morality, and health. But he also notes that in 1992 his three high school clinics saw around 150 cases of sexually transmitted diseases like condyloma, chlamydia, and the better-known gonorrhea and syphilis.

He has a 16-year-old in the hospital right now who got AIDS from her second sexual partner. And he recalls a girl who broke her leg jumping out an apartment window because her mother found her birth control pills, seized her by the throat, and said, according to the kid, "I brought you into the world; I can take you out of it."

Don't you just love those little mother-daughter sex talks?

He also knows that at the heart of the balancing act between keeping kids healthy and keeping parents involved there has always been a covert place in which many opponents of condom distribution really settle. It's called Fantasyland.

You could see that in the response to the rather mild commercials on 10 condom use and abstinence that the Department of Health and Human Services unveiled this week. The general secretary of the National Conference of Catholic Bishops immediately said the ads "promote promiscuity" and the networks should reject them. At the same time ABC said it would not run the spots during its prime-time "family-oriented" programs.

So foolish. ABC's own *Roseanne* has been far more candid about sexuality than any of the new government public-service spots. And what could be a better way to foment conversation with the children of the video age than a television advertisement? Right there in your living room you have a goad to the kind of discussion that opponents of condom distribution have always argued is the purview of parents. And you put the ads on late at night? Do we really want to talk with our kids? Or do we just want to talk about talking to them?

The Board of Education could do a great good if it found ways to truly foster parent-child communication in all things, not just matters sexual. But instead its members argue about condoms. This isn't really about condoms, of course, but about control and the shock of adolescent sexuality and the difficulty parents have communicating with their kids and a deep and understandable yearning for simpler times.

While we yearn and argue, Dr. Cohall visits his 16-year-old AIDS patient. Her parents' involvement may someday consist of visiting the cemetery. Imagine how they'd feel if they put her on the no-condom list, then put her in the hospital, then put her in the ground. Some victory.

Topics for Critical Thinking and Writing

1. Exactly what is a Pyrrhic victory?

2. Quindlen offers three possible responses for her 16-year-old male student (para. 2). Write a fourth and (if possible) a fifth response.

3. As paragraph 3 indicates, some parents argue that the distribution of condoms violates parents' rights. What parental right is at stake in the dispute over whether high schools should distribute condoms to students who seek them? Or is there no such right, but instead a parental duty involved?

4. Quindlen mentions four sexually transmitted diseases. What are their names, their symptoms, and the cure in each case? (You will probably need to talk to a physician or nurse, or do some library research, to answer this question.)

5. Some people argue that any discussion of condoms, even in a context that advocates abstinence, in effect promotes promiscuity. Do you agree or disagree? Why?

6. Evaluate Quindlen's final paragraph as a piece of persuasive writing.

8

AIDS: What Is to Be Done?

**William E. Dannemeyer, Barbara C. Webb,
Sanford F. Kuvin, C. Everett Koop,
Peter Bayer, and Barbara Russell**

*Hearings before the Subcommittee on Health
and Environment, House of Representatives*

Prevention of HIV Transmission

CONGRESSMAN WILLIAM E. DANNEMEYER

This is another chapter in the unraveling of placing congressional scrutiny on the first politically protected disease in the history of this country. Mr. Waxman has observed that Kimberly Bergalis and the other four patients are unique.

In September 1991, the U.S. House of Representatives Subcommittee on Health and the Environment, under the chairmanship of Henry A. Waxman (D, California), held hearings on House Bill 2788, filed by William E. Dannemeyer (R, California) and cosponsored by other representatives. The bill would authorize mandatory testing for HIV+ at regular intervals for all health care personnel who use invasive procedures on their patients. The hearings occasioned national publicity because of the plight of Kimberly Bergalis, one of five patients known to have been infected with AIDS by their dentist, Dr. David Acer (who had died of AIDS some months earlier). Ms. Bergalis, nineteen, was quite ill and appeared briefly at the hearing. She died shortly after.

The CDC[1] has developed a computer model that tells us today that there are 128 Kimberly Bergalises in this country. This same computer study has indicated that there are 1,248 dentists in America infected with HIV, there are 336 surgeons.

We know for a fact that 6,436 health care professionals have been infected with AIDS, fully diagnosed with AIDS, and it has been estimated from reliable sources that approximately 40,000 health care workers in America today have HIV.

There has been a failure of leadership on the part of public health authorities in America to treat this as a public health issue. Unfortunately, too many of them have treated this as a civil rights issue, that somehow the civil rights of the infected take precedence over the civil rights of the uninfected. That is the unfortunate side.

The fortunate side is that the American people have not been fooled   5 by this failure of leadership of some in our public health profession and the medical profession in America, because a recent survey by an ABC news poll of 1,205 adults in America asked the following question: The government should require a test for all doctors performing surgery? Agree, 86 percent; disagree, 15.

The government should require that doctors and dentists who have AIDS notify their patients? Agree, 96 percent; disagree, 3. And the government should require that people who have AIDS notify their doctors and dentists? Agree, 96 percent; disagree, 4. A *Newsweek* poll published on July 1 found substantial confirming information for that assessment on the part of the American public.

I look forward to the testimony of these witnesses this morning because I think it will shed some light on some policy options this country will pursue, and I hope as a result of these hearings, our chairman will begin a markup session sooner rather than later for my bill, H.R. 2788, that will require that [persons] — or rather doctors and health care workers be tested by their medical associates, and those that are hepatitis B or HIV [positive], before they can perform invasive procedures, would be required to get the written consent of their patients.

And on the other side of the coin, those persons working in the health care system would have the right to test their patients if, in their judgment, it is called for whether or not they have hepatitis B or HIV.

I think health care workers have as much right to know the status of the patients they are dealing with as do the patients who come to doctors and dentists to be assured that when they go to a doctor and dentist, they are not going to come away with a fatal disease. . . .

---

[1]**CDC** Centers for Disease Control, a federal agency located in Atlanta, Georgia. [All notes are the editors'.]

PREPARED STATEMENT OF BARBARA C. WEBB

I, Barbara C. Webb of Palm City, Florida, have been invited by Rep- 10
resentatives Henry Waxman and William Dannemeyer to testify before the
Subcommittee on Health and the Environment. I wish to thank both these
gentlemen and the rest of the subcommittee members for giving me the
opportunity to share my experiences with you. Because I was infected with
HIV by my dentist, Dr. David Acer, I feel particularly strongly about the
subject of mandatory testing as proposed in Representative Dannemeyer's
bill, the Kimberly Bergalis Patient and Health Providers Protection Act.
This bill is now before you, and I urge you to put it before the entire
House of Representatives.

It is my firm belief that the volunteerism and universal precautions
propounded by the CDC, AMA, and ADA[2] are sufficient to safeguard individuals at risk from blood-to-blood contact. If we lived in a utopia where
every person at all times acted in the best interest of his fellow man, this
might be feasible. But we are human beings with human frailties; we make
mistakes. No matter how hard we try to avoid them, needle sticks and inadvertent cuts, which gloves will not stop, will occur. The shared knowledge
of HIV infection is absolutely vital for the mutual protection of health care
providers and patients involved in significant-risk procedures.

The argument that "testing negative today is no guaranty for tomorrow" is valid but, in the long run, meaningless. If testing were done once a
year, the vast majority of HIV+ individuals would be identified. Those who
were previously unaware of their status could start receiving treatment and
take the necessary steps to avoid infecting others. This would go a long way
toward slowing down an epidemic which is sweeping our country and terrifying our citizens.

The cost factor so highly emphasized by opponents to mandatory testing is invalid. If our United States Army, now known for its prudent use of
funds, can test and retest (when indicated) its soldiers for less than $4 per
person tested, certainly this feat can be accomplished elsewhere. Since the
cost of treating a single AIDS patient is over $85,000, eliminating risks
would be cost-effective.

Certainly our doctor-patient confidentiality practice has worked well
for centuries. I do not propose that it be violated, but I do find it difficult
to believe that so many caring individuals whose primary concern should
be the lives of their patients would put their personal right to privacy ahead
of their patients' right to continue to breathe. All of us have the right to live
our lives without being infected by this uniformly fatal disease. This is why
I wear an identification bracelet that says "HIV POSITIVE." I do not want
to end up unconscious in an emergency room and become another David
Acer to those caring for me.

---

[2]**AMA** and **ADA** American Medical Association, American Dental Association.

We have mandatory inoculations for children entering school, manda- 15
tory HIV testing for all blood donors, military personnel, and immigrants.
Why not expand this testing and treat this epidemic as a health threat, not a
political football? Why not test all who are at risk because of possible
blood-to-blood contact?

There is a need for people in the health field who test positive. Instructors, counselors, laboratory technicians, and AIDS clinicians will be
required in increasing numbers in the future. We need to enlighten the
American public, the world public, of the dangers associated with indiscriminate sex, needle sharing, and blood-to-blood infection. We need intelligent awareness to increase so that the fears which drove the Ray family[3]
from their home will not blind communities in the future. Certainly there
is enough caring, planning, and teaching to be done to occupy the lives of
those of us who test positive.

The groundswell of public support for mandatory testing is rapidly becoming a tidal wave. Please listen to what over 90 percent of the American
public wants; please be truly representative of their desires.

Do not let Kimberly Bergalis die in vain. Do not let Richard Driskill,
Lisa Shoemaker, John Yecs, and Barbara Webb join her in a meaningless
death. We are not the only ones in the world who have been infected; we
will not be the last. And the health community, which is far more vulnerable than any other, will come to accept the wisdom of mandatory two-way
testing. It will save their lives, too.

TESTIMONY OF SANFORD F. KUVIN

My name is Dr. Sanford Kuvin. I am chairman of the Kuvin Center
for Infectious and Tropical Diseases, vice chairman of the National Foundation for Infectious Diseases, and chairman of the Hepatitis B Action
Group. I want to thank you, Mr. Chairman, and all of the subcommittee
members for allowing me this opportunity to provide testimony on these
important public health issues.

For the very first time in medical history, health care providers who 20
are carriers of the human immunodeficiency virus (HIV) or hepatitis B are
being viewed as a risk group capable of transmitting lethal diseases to their
patients.

The guidelines of the Centers for Disease Control call for the voluntary testing of health care workers carrying out exposure-prone procedures, do not recommend mandatory patient testing to protect the health
care worker, and rely only on improved infection control and universal precautions. These guidelines fail to protect the patient and the health care

---

[3]**Ray family** In Florida in 1987, three hemophiliac children in the Ray family acquired AIDS
through contaminated blood. The family's house was burned down by local people, and the children were denied entry into the public schools. The family subsequently sued the schools and was
awarded a million dollars.

worker alike by not calling for mandatory testing for HIV and hepatitis B for health care workers and patients undergoing invasive procedures as called for in the H.R. 2788 Kimberly Bergalis Patient and Health Providers' Protection Act, which is pending before this Subcommittee.

The universal precautions called for by the CDC, including improved infection control, did not, do not, and will not provide for universal safety. Gloves leak, puncture, and rip, and the cognitive and motor skills of in- fected health care workers will always be subject to mistakes. In addition, approximately 30 to 40 percent of all patients with HIV develop clinically discernible neurologic symptoms at any stage of the infection and there- fore HIV-infected health care workers will develop AIDS dementia com- plex, which is characterized by motor disturbances and behavioral disor- ders. AIDS dementia complex causes mistakes of judgment and manual dexterity by the invasive health care worker leading to the additional spread of HIV and hepatitis B and other blood-borne diseases to patients.

Physicians and dentists have an absolute moral, ethical, professional, and legal obligation not to cause harm to a patient. Mandatory testing is necessary because every patient has the absolute right to know what harm can befall him or her from a health care worker, and conversely every health care worker has that same right to know. Blood is a two-way street and health care workers are in fact at much greater risk than patients and both need protection against each other not provided for in the CDC guidelines.

Voluntary testing called for by the CDC, the American Medical Asso- ciation, and the American Dental Association has failed. Failed volun- tarism is exactly what caused the five patients to be infected in Florida, and failed voluntarism has caused the almost weekly revelations about AIDS- infected dentists and physicians across this nation failing to voluntarily tell their patients they had AIDS or HIV.

There are over 6,000 health care workers with AIDS, about 50,000 25 with HIV, and thousands more with hepatitis B—and the epidemic is ex- panding. Will the thousands of health care workers who are carriers of HIV or hepatitis B voluntarily reveal their serological status to their patients or their peers? Will any member of this Subcommittee voluntarily send their spouse, their child, or their grandchild to an HIV or hepatitis B infected in- vasive health care worker? I think not!

Mandatory testing is already in place for all of our blood donors, all of our military, all our prisoners, our job corps, all immigrants, and all foreign service employees as well as our life insurance policies. Surely the Ameri- can people deserve that same kind of protection . . . [in] the health care setting where the majority of Americans face their only risk of contracting HIV or hepatitis B. This small but significant number of patients infected from their health care workers—just like Kimberly Bergalis—is totally unaware of their being infected with a lethal disease which is preventable. Liability insurers and hospital employers will demand mandatory testing in any event for malpractice coverage.

Seventy-six percent of HIV cases occur in twenty-two states where HIV is nonreportable. This is the first time in the history of our public health system that a lethal communicable disease is being treated as a secret disease. If you can't test for HIV, you can't trace it. And if you can't trace it, you can't treat it—and if you can't treat HIV/AIDS, you cannot prolong life. Confidentiality laws can and will be maintained. Our Public Health Service and our private medical sector have a 100-year proud tradition of maintaining confidentiality, and if necessary, additional laws can be made so punitive that confidentiality will be maintained.

Kimberly Bergalis is certainly not the *first* case of HIV transmission from health care worker to patient. Kimberly is the first *documented* case utilizing DNA high technology, which was never available before in medical history. This is the reason why this one cluster of cases is driving a change in public health policy. This is the reason why you do not wait for a second 747 to crash when you know the cause of the first one. And this is the reason why you test airline pilots and subway motormen once a year and on demand for alcohol and drugs. This same schedule of once-a-year and on-demand testing linked to professional licensure would remove over 95 percent of infected health care workers with HIV and hepatitis B as a reservoir of infection—which is basic public health. You do not treat a typhoid epidemic in a restaurant by cleaning the utensils. You remove "Typhoid Mary" from the kitchen. And you do not treat a malaria epidemic by putting mosquito netting around the beds—you eliminate the malaria-carrying mosquito. Public health and organized medical leadership has been medically anachronistic in medical logic concerning basic public health approaches to the expanding HIV epidemic. And if anyone says that the risk of HIV transmission is "remote" or "essentially nil" as articulated by Dr. C. Everett Koop[4]—then ask Kimberly Bergalis or Barbara Webb or Dr. Edward Rozar or any of the forty health care workers infected with AIDS—and hundreds more infected with HIV from patients. They will all tell you that their risk was 100 percent. And what about the paradigm of hepatitis B, which is of equal importance and an example of a blood-borne virus a hundred times more infectious with 7,000 health care workers last year alone getting hepatitis B from their patients and with almost 250 dying. The risk of HIV transmission is indeed small, but the results are definite, devastating, lethal, and entirely avoidable in the health care setting by simply removing the reservoir of infection—the infected invasive health care worker.

Testing is getting better, quicker, and cheaper all the time. Within one to two years there will be a rapid chairside saliva and urine test for HIV antibody and a rapid blood test for the virus itself. We are clearly in a decade of serious blood-borne diseases. The biotechnology of testing is far ahead of public health, and industry has ample profit motive to bring the cost of testing down. The Food and Drug Administration (FDA) should pursue the issue of licensing rapid diagnostics for HIV, which already exist, with as

---

[4]**Dr. C. Everett Koop** Koop served as Surgeon General in the Reagan administration.

much expediency as possible. Modern medicine demands that testing be done as a routine procedure to discover, prevent, and treat disease in all parameters of medicine. For example, in our own blood supply, mandatory testing is carried out for syphilis, HIV, HTLV I/II (human T cell lymphotropic virus—a leukemia-producing virus), hepatitis B, and hepatitis C. Mammograms, Pap smears, blood tests for diabetes, thyroid disorders, prostatic cancer, and a host of other tests are done regularly to discover, treat, and prevent disease. Are all people diagnosed with disease treated? Certainly not, but surely that is the very goal of medical discovery. It is not only bad medicine; it is bad public health to continue to single out and treat HIV as a secret disease in the health care worker and the patient, which prohibits the fundamental medical right to test for HIV for the purposes of discovery and which is necessary to prevent and treat this disease.

Legislation at the congressional and state levels and rule making at the regulatory level of the Occupational Safety and Health Administration (OSHA) are necessary to protect health care providers and patients against the risk of blood-borne pathogens. In addition, government and insurers have a responsibility to respond to the economic hardships that occupationally infected health care workers face when, by virtue of adhering to the CDC guidelines of no patient testing for HIV or hepatitis B, they are forced out of business after being infected from patients. Invasive health care workers including medical, dental, and nursing students, residents, house staff, and other health care workers should be covered with some form of economic indemnification for disability, workers compensation, life and health insurance, alternative job placement, and retraining programs as well as other mechanisms that compensate for the risk they face from infected patients with HIV and hepatitis B.

I know that you, Mr. Chairman, and all of the other subcommittee members will treat this issue with equanimity—not as a political civil rights issue, which it has become, but as a public health issue. Please allow Kimberly Bergalis's dying wish to be fulfilled, which is simply to give every member of the Congress an opportunity to vote on the Kimberly Bergalis Act.

The central principle of medicine is still "First do no harm." How can a physician or dentist know that he or she will do no harm when he or she is a carrier of HIV, hepatitis B, or any other blood-borne disease?

PREPARED STATEMENT OF DR. C. EVERETT KOOP[5]

The virus of AIDS is difficult to transmit.

Our scientific understanding of HIV and AIDS has not been changed by the report of apparent dentist-to-patient transfer of the virus. We still know that an HIV negative test is worthless because a positive serology does not turn positive for three to six months.

[5]See the footnote on page 304.

But time and attention directed to the HIV-infected health care worker 35 is time and attention away from the real issues of patient care and patient protection. All who seek to improve patient protection—be they in or out of the medical community—should be concentrating on better infection control.

Education in how to avoid exposure to HIV through sexual activity and needle sharing will protect tens of thousands from infection and death. It takes time and effort that should not be squandered on a theoretical danger that threatens few if any patients. Indeed the risk of a patient being infected through medical care from an HIV-infected physician is so remote that it may never be measured.

A concentrated effort to identify a case of physician-transmission to a patient of HIV infection has produced no such case. More than fifty ongoing programs to study patients of HIV-infected health care workers has not documented a single case of physician to patient transmission.

The case of patients being infected in a dentist's office with HIV seems to be a failure to follow infection control procedures. Specifically, failure to sterilize dental equipment adequately has been suggested. We may never know how the patients became infected in the dental office, but we do know that no model of dentist-to-patient transmission proposed fits this case. The Florida case is too bizarre to be helpful in determining policy.

We do have evidence the other way—patient to health care worker—where protection is ever so much more difficult because of unexpected and emergency situations. In ten years about forty transmissions have been reported at the bedside and in the laboratory, where the concentration of virus tends to be higher. The number of transmissions is only a small fraction of the number of misadventures occurring around HIV-infected patients, proving once again that it is not easy to transmit the HIV.

The emotional response to the HIV-infected health care worker ig- 40 nores experience, science, medical history, as well as the best interest of the patient and the health care worker. The emotional outcry is fed by the ignorance of some and the personal interest of others.

It is time to separate statesman-like behavior from political behavior; to separate those who serve the patient from those who use the patient, those who throw water on a fire from those who throw gasoline.

Because there is no scientific basis for the proposed restrictions on HIV-infected health care workers, there is disagreement in the medical community on how to proceed.

I am troubled because some are trying to manipulate us back into the dark era of this epidemic when a Ryan White could be shunned and kept out of school for a nonexistent threat. Or when the three Florida hemophilic boys had their house burned down because of unnatural and unfounded fear in the community. The day will come when those who support such a witch hunt will be ashamed they did.

I am a physician, but I appear before you as a patient advocate which I have always been.

So I say there is need for immediate action to improve patient protec- 45 tion: (1) There is a need for vigorous effort to assure adherence to infection control by health care workers; (2) there is a need to improve infection control procedures; (3) there is a need to review medical and dental equipment design to seek ways to improve infection control; (4) there is a need to educate the public about risks and benefits inherent in medical and dental care so they can be wise consumers; and (5) there is a need to educate all health care workers on the importance of infection control.

Then there is a need for more science on which to base decisions. (1) For example there is a need for scientifically conducted look back programs with regular reporting to the public of the number of patients tested for HIV and any documented case of transmission—if one ever occurs; (2) it would also be important to report on numbers of cases where HIV is transmitted from patient to health care workers—to emphasize the relative risk; (3) there is also a need for studies of the frequency of non-HIV transmission from health care worker to patient and patient to health care worker; and (4) there is a need for an independent reappraisal of the Florida in-dental office transmission to learn more about infection control and the investigation of such cases.

If the Congress wishes to get into this matter, I would suggest: (1) A public education campaign on the risks of HIV transmission to patients from health care workers; (2) a professional education campaign on proper infection control procedures, possibly with a certification process through states for physicians and dentists and appropriate coworkers; (3) a local committee to review and define the practice of each HIV positive physician with a monitoring function; and (4) revelation of the HIV positive status of a physician or dentist only when an HIV positive worker poses a significant risk to the patient.

These suggestions, Mr. Chairman, are based upon knowledge of the science of transmission, not on window dressing of unreliable information feeding the already unreasonable fear of the public.

I might add that last night I answered questions from the listening audience of a radio talk show. Every question on AIDS revealed a lack of understanding of the most basic science of HIV transmission. Some segments of the public are poorly informed.

People should be more concerned about their own risky behavior than 50 in the HIV status of their doctor, dentist, or nurse.

Enforced testing will give people a false sense of security. They will relax their guard against the one thing they can control—their behavior.

Who would do the testing of health care workers—a federal bureaucracy like the Post Office or Amtrak? And who would supervise them?

A certificate of HIV negativity is worthless unless you know the sexual behavior and drug abusing activity of the individual from six months before the test until the present.

Many people who are carrying the virus now test negative—and it is believed that they are most infectious before their test becomes positive.

One very plausible explanation of the Florida dental episode is trans- 55 mission of the HIV from patient to patient because of unacceptable technique with contaminated instruments. That means that an HIV negative dentist could pass AIDS from patient to patient, just by unsterile procedures.

If we have mandatory testing of health care workers we will eventually have mandatory testing of everyone — after all forty health care workers have contracted HIV through some misadventure in the course of treating an HIV positive patient.

Let's turn from this infinitesimally small risk and pay attention: (1) to unsafe sexual behavior, (2) to contaminated needles among drug abusers, (3) to guaranteeing a safe blood supply for transfusion, and (4) to scrupulous technique in health care.

Mr. Waxman: I want to ask you a question following from that point. Do you feel that the recommendations of the Centers for Disease Control are window dressing and not based on the best science? Do you feel those are guidelines that we ought to look to protect the public health?

Mr. Koop: I think they are guidelines that should be used to protect the public, and I noted, Mr. Chairman, in none of the previous hour was any mention made of the fact that whatever you put in to protect the patient also protects the health care worker. Whatever you do to protect the health care worker automatically protects the patient. So these are two interlocking sets of guidelines which double the concentration on protection of one from the other.

Mr. Waxman: The question we are always asked when we talk to people back home is why don't we just have all the doctors tested so the patients will know whether they are HIV infected, and that will protect the patients, and why don't we have all the patients tested to see if they are infected in order to protect the doctors and the health care workers.

Mr. Koop: As far as testing the doctors is concerned, sir, it would lead you to a very false sense of security because a negative test is worthless.

If you came to me as a patient today and said I want to know your HIV status, and I pulled out my paper and said I just got it back from the laboratory yesterday, you are perfectly safe with me, that is not reliable information. You would have had to live with me for at least six months, know my every behavior, sexual, drug abuse, whatever, in order to be sure that I had not had exposure to the virus.

So that is the chief basis on which this whole unreliable thing is concerned, and that is what I call window dressing. . . .

PREPARED STATEMENT OF PETER BAYER, ON BEHALF OF THE NATIONAL HEMOPHILIA FOUNDATION

Thank you Mr. Chairman. My name is Peter Bayer. I am a visiting professor of law at University of Miami. I testify today in my capacity as a hemophiliac infected with HIV and on behalf of the National Hemophilia

Foundation — the only national, voluntary health agency which works to improve the health and welfare of the twenty thousand persons in the United States with hemophilia, Von Willebrand disease, and other hereditary blood-clotting disorders.

I am grateful for this opportunity to address why mandatory HIV testing of health care workers and compelled disclosure of test results under penalty of imprisonment would not protect the health of the public but, rather, would generate terrible consequences including depriving hemophiliacs like me of vital medical treatment. . . .

If a system of mandatory testing and criminal penalties is enacted, doctors and other health care providers will not be willing to treat HIV-infected hemophiliacs and those who are perceived, rightly or wrongly, to be in that or any high-risk group. Although health care workers may be willing to run the exceedingly small risk of contracting HIV from a patient, many say — and I believe them — that the additional risk of disclosing their HIV status, losing their livelihoods, leaving their families destitute, and facing possible criminal and civil lawsuits is too much to bear.

Moreover, it is easy to foresee that mandatory testing of health care workers will just be a beginning. In addition to disclosing health care workers' HIV status, patients will demand to know if their doctors are treating or have ever treated HIV-infected individuals even though HIV-infected patients, like HIV-infected health care workers, pose no true threat so long as health care workers practice well-known sanitary procedures. Thus, to protect their livelihoods, health care workers will demand proof that patients are not HIV infected. At the very least, health care workers will refuse to treat persons actually infected with HIV and, very possibly, refuse treatment to persons perceived to be in high-risk groups.

I am very afraid that I might be turned away from a hospital emergency room, no matter how desperately I need medical attention, because the staff will no longer assume even the negligible risks associated with treating me. I, and other hemophiliacs, will be denied emergency treatment, needed operations, essential dental work, and other necessary medical care. A hemophiliac, bleeding and desperate after an accident, would be left to perish or may suffer irreparable damage before a doctor could be found willing to treat him.

These distressing fears do not begin to describe the potential harm mandatory testing can cause. As I mentioned a moment ago, the denial of medical care would not be limited to the large population of HIV-infected hemophiliacs. I worry that all hemophiliacs and their spouses will be refused adequate medical care because they are perceived as possible carriers of HIV.

And, it won't stop there. All persons with HIV, all persons in high-risk groups and all persons perceived rightly or wrongly as being in high-risk groups may be denied medical care by anxious doctors afraid that they will lose their practices if their other patients know or suspect that the doctors may have come into contact with HIV.

The denial of medical care to so many thousands of persons is too high a price to pay for a statute which will not reduce the already negligible risk of HIV transmission. The health of HIV-infected and non-HIV-infected hemophiliacs should not be sacrificed for a statute which fails to promote public health but, instead, indulges and fosters misconceptions and unreasoning, unfounded fears of how AIDS is transmitted.

In my *New York Times Magazine* [article], I describe AIDS as more than a disease. It is, as well, a sociological event. By that I mean, AIDS challenges more than our abilities as scientists and researchers, as important as those skills are. In addition, the advent of AIDS demands that our society and its lawmakers draw from its full measure of compassion and to overcome ignorance, fear, and prejudice.

I hope that this subcommittee will reject the misguided approach calling for mandatory testing of health care workers and disclosure of test results under penalty of imprisonment.

Thank you very much, Mr. Chairman and members of the subcommittee.

STATEMENT OF BARBARA RUSSELL, AMERICAN NURSES ASSOCIATION

Good morning. I am Barbara Russell, chair of the American Nurses 75 Association's (ANA) Task Force on AIDS. I appreciate the opportunity to testify today representing ANA and its fifty-three state and territorial nurses associations, on behalf of the nation's two million registered nurses. I am also representing the American Association of Critical-Care Nurses (AACN) and the Association of Operating Room Nurses (AORN). AACN's 70,000 nurse members provide care to critically ill patients and AORN's 47,000 registered nurse members provide care to patients in surgery. We commend the Committee for holding hearings on HIV disease, a worldwide public health problem.

Nurses are patient advocates who, since the early days of the HIV/AIDS epidemic, have been at the forefront of movements to provide comprehensive compassionate care to those with AIDS and HIV infection. Studies show that AIDS patients require almost double the amount of nursing time required by equally ill patients who do not have AIDS. Nurses have firsthand knowledge of the complexity and significance of the public health problem presented by the human immunodeficiency virus. We have been on the front lines providing care to patients in critical care units, in operating rooms, the community and wherever HIV patients receive care.

We are keenly aware of the widespread public anxiety generated by the AIDS epidemic and exacerbated by the tragic case of Kimberly Bergalis, a young woman who contracted AIDS during treatment in a Florida dentist's office. We have deep sympathy for Kimberly and her family and share their conviction that a patient has the right to protection against infection and disease. We believe strongly that both patients and health care workers have the right to protection against transmission of the HIV virus in all health care settings.

However, Mr. Chairman, we are deeply concerned by current legislative proposals which would require mandatory testing of patients or health care workers, or mandatory disclosure of HIV status with criminal penalties for noncompliance. Such approaches do nothing to provide the real public health protections that are critically needed.

Nursing, like other professions, is guided by standards of care including a code of ethics. Nurses uphold the values and tenets of the *Code for Nurses* in their daily practice. The *Code for Nurses* guides our response to the challenges presented by blood-borne diseases. These include that "the nurse participates in the profession's effort to protect the public from misinformation and misrepresentation and to maintain the integrity of nursing."

Nurses are considered a fundamental link in educating the public 80 about disease prevention and health promotion. That role has been critical in addressing the need for education about HIV to the health care worker and consumer. The challenge for our society and for the nursing profession is to reduce the risk of transmission of blood-borne diseases and to provide competent care to infected individuals.

Education and national standards are critical. As health care professionals, we understand that HIV transmission is halted by strict adherence to universal precautions and infection control practices as well as by intensive education of consumers and health care professionals.

All health care workers must follow universal precautions and established infection control procedures to reduce infection risks to patients and themselves. Appropriate use and disposal of needles and sharps is the most important risk reduction strategy. In addition, universal precautions include the use of gloves, masks, eye protection, and other barriers as needed for procedures that involve contact with blood and body fluids. Education of all health care workers about use of and enforcement of universal precautions in the workplace is critical to reducing the risk of transmission and must be ongoing.

ANA, AORN, and AACN have participated in the Occupational Safety and Health Administration (OSHA) rule making on employee exposures to blood-borne pathogens. We have undertaken educational programs on HIV and AIDS in the workplace setting and the OSHA standards for employee protection both nationally and with our individual state and regional bodies. We have pushed for better compliance and enforcement of CDC and OSHA standards.

The epidemiological data demonstrate that health care provided by HIV-infected health care workers does not pose a significant risk when established infection control procedures are enforced and complied with at all times. There have been no documented cases of HIV transmission from nurse to patient. Furthermore, there have been no cases identified of patients who contracted HIV disease from health care workers when those workers followed universal precautions.

ANA, AORN, and AACN support federal policies which would re- 85
quire annual education for all health care professionals to ensure that they are current on universal precautions.

We believe that consumers should expect health care workers to practice sound infection-control procedures and universal precautions. We encourage consumer education about these practices and recommend that patients question health care workers about these procedures.

ANA has developed a national consumer advisory statement outlining strict infection control procedures to be used by all health care providers and discussed individually with patients. It sets forth patients' rights in simple language and details the practices and procedures that provide protection against infection. We believe that health care consumers and patients have the right to quality health care without discrimination; answers to health-related questions; confidentiality; informed consent for procedures and tests. The advisory provides detailed information on the infection-control procedures required by law.

Our goal is to achieve the most widespread dissemination of the consumer advisory. It will be printed on a small card designed to fit in a wallet and on posters to be placed in medical offices, hospitals, clinics, etc. In addition, we will be placing the advisory in popular magazines and other publications for broader public access.

Policies must be based on epidemiological data.   We believe that policies and guidelines to address the transmission of blood-borne disease in the workplace—whether from patient to health care worker or health care worker to patient—must be based on epidemiological data from research on blood-borne disease transmission, risks associated with exposure-prone invasive procedures, and established infection prevention and control practices. As with other public, occupational, and environmental health hazards, public health officials and scientists are responsible for the assessment and determination of significant risk of transmission of blood-borne diseases. Therefore, we support the position outlined in the recently released Centers for Disease Control's (CDC) "Recommendations for Preventing Transmission of Human Immunodeficiency Virus and Hepatitis B Virus to Patients during Exposure-Prone Invasive Procedures." The CDC recommendations emphasize educating health care workers and patients about proper infection control procedures and government-established infection control standards. It must be noted that the CDC recommendations are explicit that mandatory testing is not the answer. The CDC notes that the cost of testing is not justified.

However, the CDC recommendations are just that—recommenda- 90
tions. They do not carry the force of law. Compliance is voluntary and the CDC has no enforcement power. Although the CDC recommendations

often become a standard of practice for professionals, we know that some do not believe voluntary compliance is enough. Therefore, we would support proposals for federal policy which mandate that the states implement policies consistent with the CDC guidelines in a timely fashion.

In addition, we support efforts to require the Department of Labor to issue the Occupational Safety and Health Administration (OSHA) Blood-borne Disease Standard as soon as possible. Enforcement of and compliance with the blood-borne standard is an effective response to the risk of HIV transmission in health care facilities. It requires employers to implement universal precautions, to educate and train workers, and to provide engineering controls and protective equipment to decrease employee risk of exposure to blood and body fluids and to injuries from needles and sharps.

The OSHA standard will cover 4.5 million health care workers and is designed to offer protection to workers and to patients against exposure to blood-borne diseases. Moreover, OSHA standards can be enforced through inspections, fines, and criminal penalties. Fines and penalties can go as high as $70,000 for each violation, and $7,000 for each day that a violation goes uncorrected.

We would urge Congress to ensure that the OSHA standard provides the most widespread coverage. The standard must cover all employers. Traditional exemptions of small employers of ten workers or less would mean that many medical and dental offices would not be subject to scheduled inspections. We believe that all patients have the right to expect and demand that health care providers follow established infection control guidelines to prevent the spread of disease.

Standards for those not included in OSHA. OSHA jurisdiction over employers and employees does not currently extend to professionals with clinical privileges such as doctors and students who are doing clinical learning experience. These two groups of health care practitioners may participate in procedures which have the risk of transmission of infection. Employee compliance with the OSHA standard must be ensured by employers. Compliance by nonemployee physicians with the infection control and universal precautions procedures outlined in the OSHA blood-borne disease standard can be ensured by utilizing the Department of Health and Human Services (DHHS) jurisdiction over conditions of participation for Medicare and Medicaid reimbursement. Likewise, student compliance can be ensured in the same manner. Additionally, health professional education is funded by HHS programs such as the Public Health Service (PHS), the Bureau of Health Professions, National Health Service Corps, and other PHS programs.

Cooperative efforts by OSHA, CDC, and DHHS to prevent the trans- 95 mission of blood-borne diseases in the health care setting are not new. HHS and the Department of Labor (DOL) issued a joint advisory statement in 1987 on the education and training of health care workers and universal precautions to prevent transmission of HIV and hepatitis B through exposures to blood and body fluids. The Occupational Safety and Health Act refers to the cooperative efforts of DOL and DHHS when necessary to ensure health and safety. It is important that this partnership must continue for effective compliance with infection control and universal precautions by all health care practitioners in all health care settings.

Mandatory testing is not sound policy. ANA, AACN, AORN, and other public health groups and the Centers for Disease Control do not believe mandatory universal testing is an efficient or a reliable means to protect against the transmission of and exposure to blood-borne diseases. Mandatory universal testing is not reliable because the incubation period and period of infectiousness for HIV infection is nonspecific. Someone who is HIV positive could test negative today and still be at risk of transmitting the virus. Studies of health care workers occupationally exposed to HIV demonstrate that the "window period" varies significantly.

It has been estimated that initial testing of a large group of patients to the age of sixty-five would cost over a billion dollars. And one-time testing would not suffice. Testing would have to be repeated over and over at various time intervals. We believe those dollars are needed to fund prevention, education, and treatment programs for all persons at risk of HIV infection.

We do support the availability of voluntary, anonymous, and confidential HIV testing with informed consent and appropriate counseling by qualified health care professionals. According to the *Code for Nurses*, "The nurse safeguards the client's right to privacy by judiciously protecting information of a confidential nature." This applies to all health care information. Knowledge of a patient's or a health care worker's HIV status does not protect others from transmission. Sound infection control procedures and universal precautions are effective in stopping transmission of the disease.

We believe that a nurse has an ethical responsibility to know his or her HIV status. According to the *Code for Nurses*, "The nurse acts to safeguard the client and public when health care and safety are affected. As an advocate for the client, the nurse must be alert to take appropriate action regarding any instance of incompetent, unethical, or illegal practice . . . that places the rights or best interests of the client in jeopardy."

The nurse has an ethical responsibility to report an incident in which 100 a nurse exposes him or herself or a patient to a risk of transmission of a blood-borne disease. Appropriate testing and confidential counseling should be provided to the patient and nurse to determine the risk of transmission of blood-borne disease with informed consent.

Conclusion. As you consider amendments designed to limit the risk of HIV infection in health care settings, we urge you to reject proposals that would mandate disclosure of HIV status or testing of health care providers or patients. We know that neither testing nor disclosure of HIV status will prevent the transmission of HIV disease. We know that strict adherence to universal precautions and infection control procedures will limit the risk of transmission. However, there is a need for continued research and data collection on HIV transmission in the health care setting.

ANA's position on HIV-infected workers was reaffirmed and adopted after much research and deliberation by its House of Delegates in June of this year. The AACN HIV Task Force, appointed in July 1991, will continue to address key HIV issues that affect critical care nurses and their patients. AORN has adopted the positions reflected in this testimony.

As patient advocates, public health and safety are both our priority and our responsibility. As nurses, we have relied on published public health epidemiological and/or research data to make decisions about contact with patients and to develop this position.

As we have met with members of Congress to discuss our position on this issue, we have occasionally been told that health care professionals are only concerned about their jobs. This is patently untrue. In the health care setting nurses are, first and foremost, patient advocates. Patients are our paramount concern. We are not only providers of care but we are also recipients of health care. We are patients, we are mothers and fathers, sisters and brothers, sons and daughters. The policies that we support to limit the risk of infection for our patients are the policies which will protect our mothers and our children and ourselves.

Only through clear thinking and positive prevention will we protect the public, our patients, and our families against AIDS and other infectious diseases. We urge Congress to ensure the health and safety of the American people through sound public policy based on scientific recommendations.   105

Topics for Critical Thinking and Writing ═══════════

1. Why does Dannemeyer describe AIDS as "the first politically protected disease in the history of this country" (para.1)? Do you agree that this is a fair description, or not? Why?

2. Webb, suffering from AIDS, wears an identification bracelet that announces "HIV POSITIVE" for all to see; her reason, she says, is "I do not want to end up unconscious in an emergency room and become another David Acer to those caring for me." If you were HIV positive, would you wear such a bracelet? Why, or why not?

3. Dr. Kuvin testified that "If you can't test for HIV, you can't trace it. And if you can't trace it, you can't treat it — and if you can't treat HIV/AIDS, you cannot prolong life." How might critics of mandatory testing respond to this argument?

4. Dr. Kuvin ends his testimony by reminding his audience of the central principle of medicine: "First do no harm." Suppose you were HIV positive and a health care professional, such as a plastic surgeon, in daily contact with the blood of your patients. Would this medical principle *require* you to inform any patient in advance of surgery that you were infected? Why, or why not?

5. Dr. Koop stresses the importance of "infection control procedures" as the way to prevent the spread of AIDS through the health care population. Why do you think he does not insist that these procedures become mandatory? Why do you think he does not stress voluntary testing for HIV positive among health care workers?

6. Dr. Koop stresses that "there is no scientific basis for the proposed restrictions on HIV-infected health care workers." What, in your judgment, would count as such a "scientific basis"? Read the accompanying testimony of Dr. Kuvin (p. 302); does he disagree with Dr. Koop on this issue?

7. Why does Bayer oppose mandatory testing for HIV? Are his reasons consistent with, identical with, or in conflict with those of Dr. Koop (p. 305) and Nurse Russell (p. 310)?

Albert B. Lowenfels and Gary Wormser

Risk of Transmission of HIV from Surgeon to Patient

To the Editor:

Using rates of operative injuries, one can estimate the risk of acquiring infection with the human immunodeficiency virus (HIV) as an occupational hazard for surgeons. Clearly, this issue is two-sided: Patients are concerned about acquiring HIV infection through an exchange of blood after an inadvertent injury during surgery. What is the chance of a patient seroconverting after a one-hour operation? The likelihood of such an event depends on three probabilities.

The first is the probability of a puncture injury during a surgical procedure. According to four reports from centers in the United States,[1–4] estimated rates of injuries to surgeons or their assistants ranged from 4 to 12

[1]Lowenfels AB, Wormser GP, Jain R. Frequency of puncture injuries in surgeons and estimated risk of HIV infection. Arch Surg 1989; 12:1284-6. [All notes are the authors'.]

[2]Gerberding JL, Littell C, Tarkington A, Brown A, Schecter WP. Risk of exposure of surgical personnel to patients' blood during surgery at San Francisco General Hospital. N Engl J Med 1990; 322:1788–93.

[3]Panlilio AL, Foy DR, Edwards JR, et al. Blood contacts during surgical procedures. JAMA 1991; 265:1533–7.

[4]Popejoy SL, Fry DE. Blood contact and exposure in the operating room. Surg Gynecol Obstet 1991; 172:480–3

This selection appeared as a letter in a professional journal, the New England Journal of Medicine *(September 19, 1991). The writers hold M.D. degrees and are affiliated with New York Medical College.*

per 1,000 hours, with a median of 8 per 1,000 (0.008) (upper and lower limits, 0.004 and 0.012).

The second is the probability that the surgeon is HIV positive. No estimates are available, but the lower and upper bounds of the prevalence among surgeons may fall between the estimate of 1.5 per 1,000 reported for Army recruits and the 7 per 1,000 reported to be the median HIV seroprevalence rate among patients at sentinel hospitals in this country.[5-6] A conservative estimate of this probability might be 0.004.

The third is the probability of the risk of transmission of HIV infection from surgeon to patient after a single puncture wound. Presumably, this risk would be lower than the recent estimate of 0.003, derived from reports of six seroconversions among 2,000 health care workers,[7] because the possibility of fluid exchange would be less.[8] If the overall risk were half as much, the probability would be 0.0015 (95 percent Poisson-based confidence limits, 0.0005 and 0.003).

Thus, when the HIV status of the operator is unknown, the overall probability of reverse transmission of HIV (i.e., from surgeon to patient) per hour of surgery can be estimated as the combined probability of the three independent events listed above:

$$0.008 \times 0.004 \times 0.0015 = 4.8 \times 10^{-8},$$

or 1 chance in 21 million per hour of surgery. The lower and upper bounds calculated from the highest and lowest individual probability values would be 1 in 333 million chances and 1 in 4 million chances.

If the surgeon was known to be HIV positive, the risk would still be low. According to the above data, the best estimate is approximately 1 chance in 83,000 per hour of surgery, with lower and upper bounds of 1 in 500,000 and 1 in 28,000. Other factors altering the risk might be the length of the procedure, the number of operators, and perhaps the type of operation, since some procedures appear to be associated with an increased frequency of injury.

These estimates give some perspective to the problem of transmission of HIV infection from surgeon to patient. We recognize that a decision about testing and disclosing the results of HIV status of a surgeon may involve more complex considerations than merely looking at probabilistic determinations. However, the risks are clearly low and might have about the

[5]Burke DS, Brundage JF, Herbold JR, et al. Human immunodeficiency virus infections among civilian applicants for United States military service, October 1985 to March 1986: demographic factors associated with seropositivity. N Engl J Med 1987; 317:131–6.

[6]St. Louis ME, Rauch KJ, Petersen LR, et al. Seroprevalence rates of human immunodeficiency virus infection at sentinel hospitals in the United States. N Engl J Med 1990; 323:213–8.

[7]Beekmann SE, Fahey BJ, Gerberding JL, Henderson DK. Risky business: using necessarily imprecise casualty counts to estimate occupational risks for HIV-1 infection. Infect Control Hosp Epidemiol 1990; 11:37–9.

[8]Recommendations for preventing transmission of human immunodeficiency virus and hepatitis B virus to patients during exposure-prone invasive procedures. MMWR 1991; 40(RR-8):4.

same magnitude as fatal injury to the patient en route to the hospital. The low risk of seroconversion in the patient should be balanced against the beneficial or detrimental effect of disclosure of the surgeon's HIV status and possible occupational restriction.

Topics for Critical Thinking and Writing

1. Are you troubled or reassured to learn that the risk of HIV infection from an infected surgeon is about the same as "fatal injury to the patient en route to the hospital" (para. 7)? Explain why.

2. Why is the probability of a patient's being infected with HIV from an infected surgeon so much higher if the surgeon is *known* to be infected (one chance in 83,000 hours of surgery, para. 6) than if the surgeon is *not known* to be infected (one chance in 21 million hours of surgery, para. 5)?

George F. Will

Family Intrusion

The Gadarene descent[1] of society was slightly reversed recently in an unlikely place, New York City. A state court struck down a particularly offensive facet of the city's condom crusade.

Some parents from Staten Island, the sensible borough that is trying to secede from the city, challenged the "condom availability" component of the school system's AIDS "education" program.

They objected not to AIDS education but to the fact that the program contained neither a requirement for prior parental consent, nor even a provision for parents to make their children ineligible for school-dispensed condoms.

The court sided with the parents. It said condom distribution is not a "health education" but a "health service" program, and hence under state law requires some parental consent. More importantly, the court held that the condom program without parental consent violates the parents' constitutional rights, specifically Fourteenth Amendment due process rights construed to concern the rearing of their children.

The court stressed that condoms are distributed not in clinics away   5

---

[1]**Gadarene descent** According to Mark 5:1–10, Jesus healed a demoniac by causing the demons to leave the afflicted man and to enter into a herd of pigs on a hillside at Gadara, near the Sea of Galilee. The pigs then "ran violently down a steep place into the sea." [Editors' note.]

George F. Will, born in Champaign, Illinois, in 1941, is a nationally known columnist. In 1977 he received the Pulitzer Prize for commentary. We reprint an article that appeared in more than four hundred fifty newspapers in 1994.

from schools, but in schools, where attendance is compulsory. There is, the court said, no compelling need for schools to act in loco parentis in this sensitive area, creating an environment where children "will be permitted, even encouraged" to obtain contraceptive devices, and advised about uses that may be contrary to their parents' fervent beliefs.

The court stressed that the parents' complaint was not just that their children were exposed to particular ideas, but that "the school offers the means for students to engage in sexual activity."

Condom distribution is the latest chapter in a long story of cultural clashes as old as American schooling. The Supreme Court recognized the liberty interests of parents in directing the rearing and education of their children in 1923, overturning a Nebraska statute prohibiting the teaching, even in private schools, of foreign languages to children before the ninth grade.

The desire of Nebraska and other states with comparable wartime laws, was to foster American homogeneity, especially by preventing the teaching of German. The court said this did not justify overriding more fundamental values.

In 1925 the court, saying that "the child is not the mere creature of the state," held that Oregon's law compelling children between ages eight and sixteen to attend public schools unreasonably interfered with parental discretion regarding private education.

What New York's court had no judicial occasion to say last month, but 10 what nonetheless needs saying, is suggested by something the court did note. It noted that when schools distribute condoms they are not making available items that are hard to come by, now that condoms are prominently displayed in drug and other stores and cost about as much as a slice of pizza. So what motives drive the condom crusade?

New York City's condom distribution program was instituted solely with reference to AIDS, rather than as a response to the epidemic of teenage pregnancies. The program is defended with reference to reports that although New York has only 3 percent of the nation's teenagers, they account for 20 percent of reported cases of adolescent AIDS.

However, those numbers do not reveal how much of this results from heterosexual intercourse and how much from needles shared during intravenous drug abuse, or other forms of transmission.

The transmission of AIDS through heterosexual intercourse is not nearly the primary means of transmission. That fact, and the fact that the condom crusade's rationale is exclusively about AIDS rather than illegitimacy, and the fact that the crusade radiates aggressive disdain for parental sovereignty, all this validates a suspicion: The condom distribution program, although justified solely with reference to disease prevention, actually is a tactic of ideological dissemination. It facilitates the campaign to "democratize" the public's perception of AIDS, a political program advanced behind such slogans as "AIDS does not discriminate" and "AIDS is an equal opportunity disease."

This campaign, misleading about the demographics and mechanics of the epidemic, has had the intended effect of making AIDS a spectacularly privileged disease. That is, AIDS receives a share of research resources disproportionate relative to the resources allocated to diseases more costly in lives and less optional, meaning less driven by behaviors known to be risky.

It is difficult to doubt that the public school condom crusade, imposed   15 without provisions for parental consent, appeals to some proponents precisely because it derogates parental authority and expands that of government. These are twin components of a political agenda.

The agenda is to assert equal legitimacy for all "lifestyles" or "preferences," and to reduce personal responsibility, under a therapeutic state, for the consequences of choices. In short, this is the 1960s coloring the 1990s.

Topics for Critical Thinking and Writing

1. Will reports (para. 3) that the Staten Island parents in question "objected not to AIDS education." Surely, they would not object to AIDS prevention. But since AIDS is overwhelmingly a sexually transmitted disease, and since the use of a condom can reduce the incidence of such transmission, do you think it was reasonable for the parents to oppose condom distribution to their teenagers by the public schools? Explain your answer in a 100-word essay.

2. The parents' complaint charged in part that by condom distribution, "the school offers the means for students to engage in sexual activity." Since it is obviously possible for adolescents to "engage in sexual activity" without ever going to high school, or ever obtaining and using condoms, what was the point of this part of the complaint? Do you agree with that point? Why, or why not?

3. Will reviews with evident approval the way the Supreme Court has struck down various state laws that violate "the liberty interests of parents" (para. 7). But the examples of such laws he gives all involved *compelling* students to do or not to do things. Since the condom distribution practice of the Staten Island schools did not *compel* students to take condoms, much less to use them, why are these cases cited by Will relevant?

4. Will thinks that AIDS is "a spectacularly privileged disease" (para. 14). What evidence does he give for this claim? As a research exercise, you might go to your college library and obtain a copy of *And the Band Played On*, by Randy Shilts, published in 1987, the best general survey of the first decade of the disease. After reading this book, are you inclined to agree or disagree with Will?

9

The Death Penalty: Can It Ever Be Justified?

Edward I. Koch

Death and Justice: How Capital Punishment Affirms Life

Last December a man named Robert Lee Willie, who had been convicted of raping and murdering an 18-year-old woman, was executed in the Louisiana state prison. In a statement issued several minutes before his death, Mr. Willie said: "Killing people is wrong. . . . It makes no difference whether it's citizens, countries, or governments. Killing is wrong." Two weeks later in South Carolina, an admitted killer named Joseph Carl Shaw was put to death for murdering two teenagers. In an appeal to the governor for clemency, Mr. Shaw wrote: "Killing is wrong when I did it. Killing is wrong when you do it. I hope you have the courage and moral strength to stop the killing."

It is a curiosity of modern life that we find ourselves being lectured on morality by cold-blooded killers. Mr. Willie previously had been convicted of aggravated rape, aggravated kidnapping, and the murders of a Louisiana deputy and a man from Missouri. Mr. Shaw committed another murder a week before the two for which he was executed, and admitted mutilating the body of the 14-year-old girl he killed. I can't help wondering what

Edward I. Koch (b. 1924), long active in Democratic politics, was mayor of New York from 1978 to 1989. This essay first appeared in The New Republic *on April 15, 1985.*

prompted these murderers to speak out against killing as they entered the deathhouse door. Did their newfound reverence for life stem from the realization that they were about to lose their own?

Life is indeed precious, and I believe the death penalty helps to affirm this fact. Had the death penalty been a real possibility in the minds of these murderers, they might well have stayed their hand. They might have shown moral awareness before their victims died, and not after. Consider the tragic death of Rosa Velez, who happened to be home when a man named Luis Vera burglarized her apartment in Brooklyn. "Yeah, I shot her," Vera admitted. "She knew me, and I knew I wouldn't go to the chair."

During my twenty-two years in public service, I have heard the pros and cons of capital punishment expressed with special intensity. As a district leader, councilman, congressman, and mayor, I have represented constituencies generally thought of as liberal. Because I support the death penalty for heinous crimes of murder, I have sometimes been the subject of emotional and outraged attacks by voters who find my position reprehensible or worse. I have listened to their ideas. I have weighed their objections carefully. I still support the death penalty. The reasons I maintain my position can be best understood by examining the arguments most frequently heard in opposition.

1. The death penalty is "barbaric." Sometimes opponents of capital punishment horrify with tales of lingering death on the gallows, of faulty electric chairs, or of agony in the gas chamber. Partly in response to such protests, several states such as North Carolina and Texas switched to execution by lethal injection. The condemned person is put to death painlessly, without ropes, voltage, bullets, or gas. Did this answer the objections of death penalty opponents? Of course not. On June 22, 1984, the New York Times published an editorial that sarcastically attacked the new "hygienic" method of death by injection, and stated that "execution can never be made humane through science." So it's not the method that really troubles opponents. It's the death itself they consider barbaric.

Admittedly, capital punishment is not a pleasant topic. However, one does not have to like the death penalty in order to support it any more than one must like radical surgery, radiation, or chemotherapy in order to find necessary these attempts at curing cancer. Ultimately we may learn how to cure cancer with a simple pill. Unfortunately, that day has not yet arrived. Today we are faced with the choice of letting the cancer spread or trying to cure it with the methods available, methods that one day will almost certainly be considered barbaric. But to give up and do nothing would be far more barbaric and would certainly delay the discovery of an eventual cure. The analogy between cancer and murder is imperfect, because murder is not the "disease" we are trying to cure. The disease is injustice. We may not like the death penalty, but it must be available to punish crimes of cold-blooded murder, cases in which any other form of punishment would be inadequate and, therefore, unjust. If we create a society in which injustice is not tolerated, incidents of murder — the most flagrant form of injustice — will diminish.

2. No other major democracy uses the death penalty. No other major democracy — in fact, few other countries of any description — are plagued by a murder rate such as that in the United States. Fewer and fewer Americans can remember the days when unlocked doors were the norm and murder was a rare and terrible offense. In America the murder rate climbed 122 percent between 1963 and 1980. During that same period, the murder rate in New York City increased by almost 400 percent, and the statistics are even worse in many other cities. A study at M.I.T. showed that based on 1970 homicide rates a person who lived in a large American city ran a greater risk of being murdered than an American soldier in World War II ran of being killed in combat. It is not surprising that the laws of each country differ according to differing conditions and traditions. If other countries had our murder problem, the cry for capital punishment would be just as loud as it is here. And I daresay that any other major democracy where 75 percent of the people supported the death penalty would soon enact it into law.

3. An innocent person might be executed by mistake. Consider the work of Hugo Adam Bedau, one of the most implacable foes of capital punishment in this country. According to Mr. Bedau, it is "false sentimentality to argue that the death penalty should be abolished because of the abstract possibility that an innocent person might be executed." He cites a study of the 7,000 executions in this country from 1892 to 1971, and concludes that the record fails to show that such cases occur. The main point, however, is this. If government functioned only when the possibility of error didn't exist, government wouldn't function at all. Human life deserves special protection, and one of the best ways to guarantee that protection is to assure that convicted murderers do not kill again. Only the death penalty can accomplish this end. In a recent case in New Jersey, a man named Richard Biegenwald was freed from prison after serving eighteen years for murder; since his release he has been convicted of committing four murders. A prisoner named Lemuel Smith, who, while serving four life sentences for murder (plus two life sentences for kidnapping and robbery) in New York's Green Haven Prison, lured a woman corrections officer into the chaplain's office and strangled her. He then mutilated and dismembered her body. An additional life sentence for Smith is meaningless. Because New York has no death penalty statute, Smith has effectively been given a license to kill.

But the problem of multiple murder is not confined to the nation's penitentiaries. In 1981, 91 police officers were killed in the line of duty in this country. Seven percent of those arrested in the cases that have been solved had a previous arrest for murder. In New York City in 1976 and 1977, 85 persons arrested for homicide had a previous arrest for murder.

Six of these individuals had two previous arrests for murder, and one had four previous murder arrests. During those two years the New York police were arresting for murder persons with a previous arrest for murder on the average of one every 8.5 days. This is not surprising when we learn that in 1975, for example, the median time served in Massachusetts for homicide was less than two and a half years. In 1976 a study sponsored by the Twentieth Century Fund found that the average time served in the United States for first-degree murder is ten years. The median time served may be considerably lower.

4. Capital punishment cheapens the value of human life. On 10 the contrary, it can be easily demonstrated that the death penalty strengthens the value of human life. If the penalty for rape were lowered, clearly it would signal a lessened regard for the victim's suffering, humiliation, and personal integrity. It would cheapen their horrible experience, and expose them to an increased danger of recurrence. When we lower the penalty for murder, it signals a lessened regard for the value of the victim's life. Some critics of capital punishment, such as columnist Jimmy Breslin, have suggested that a life sentence is actually a harsher penalty for murder than death. This is sophistic nonsense. A few killers may decide not to appeal a death sentence, but the overwhelming majority make every effort to stay alive. It is by exacting the highest penalty for the taking of human life that we affirm the highest value of human life.

5. The death penalty is applied in a discriminatory manner. This factor no longer seems to be the problem it once was. The appeals process for a condemned prisoner is lengthy and painstaking. Every effort is made to see that the verdict and sentence were fairly arrived at. However, assertions of discrimination are not an argument for ending the death penalty but for extending it. It is not justice to exclude everyone from the penalty of the law if a few are found to be so favored. Justice requires that the law be applied equally to all.

6. Thou Shalt Not Kill. The Bible is our greatest source of moral inspiration. Opponents of the death penalty frequently cite the sixth of the Ten Commandments in an attempt to prove that capital punishment is divinely proscribed. In the original Hebrew, however, the Sixth Commandment reads "Thou Shalt Not Commit Murder," and the Torah specifies capital punishment for a variety of offenses. The biblical viewpoint has been upheld by philosophers throughout history. The greatest thinkers of the nineteenth century — Kant, Locke, Hobbes, Rousseau, Montesquieu, and Mill — agreed that natural law properly authorizes the sovereign to take life in order to vindicate justice. Only Jeremy Bentham was ambivalent. Washington, Jefferson, and Franklin endorsed it. Abraham Lincoln authorized executions for deserters in wartime. Alexis de Tocqueville, who expressed profound respect for American institutions, believed that the death penalty was indispensable to the support of social order. The United States Constitution, widely admired as one of the seminal achievements in the history of humanity, condemns cruel and inhuman punishment, but does not condemn capital punishment.

   7. The death penalty is state-sanctioned murder. This is the defense with which Messrs. Willie and Shaw hoped to soften the resolve of those who sentenced them to death. By saying in effect, "You're no better than I am," the murderer seeks to bring his accusers down to his own level. It is also a popular argument among opponents of capital punishment, but a transparently false one. Simply put, the state has rights that the private individual does not. In a democracy, those rights are given to the state by the electorate. The execution of a lawfully condemned killer is no more an act of murder than is legal imprisonment an act of kidnapping. If an individual forces a neighbor to pay him money under threat of punishment, it's called extortion. If the state does it, it's called taxation. Rights and responsibilities surrendered by the individual are what give the state its power to govern. This contract is the foundation of civilization itself.

   Everyone wants his or her rights, and will defend them jealously. Not everyone, however, wants responsibilities, especially the painful responsibilities that come with law enforcement. Twenty-one years ago a woman named Kitty Genovese was assaulted and murdered on a street in New York. Dozens of neighbors heard her cries for help but did nothing to assist her. They didn't even call the police. In such a climate the criminal understandably grows bolder. In the presence of moral cowardice, he lectures us on our supposed failings and tries to equate his crimes with our quest for justice.

   The death of anyone — even a convicted killer — diminishes us all. But 15 we are diminished even more by a justice system that fails to function. It is an illusion to let ourselves believe that doing away with capital punishment removes the murderer's deed from our conscience. The rights of society are paramount. When we protect guilty lives, we give up innocent lives in exchange. When opponents of capital punishment say to the state, "I will not let you kill in my name," they are also saying to murderers: "You can kill in your *own* name as long as I have an excuse for not getting involved."

   It is hard to imagine anything worse than being murdered while neighbors do nothing. But something worse exists. When those same neighbors shrink back from justly punishing the murderer, the victim dies twice.

Topics for Critical Thinking and Writing

1. In paragraph 6 Koch draws an analogy between cancer and murder, and observes that imperfect as today's cures for cancer are, "to give up and do nothing would be far more barbaric." What is the relevance of this comment in the context of the analogy and the dispute over the death penalty?

2. In paragraph 8 Koch describes a convicted but unexecuted recidivist murderer as someone who "has effectively been given a license to kill." But a license to kill, as in a deer-hunter's license, entitles the holder to engage in lawful killing. (Think of the fictional hero James Bond — Agent 007 — who, we are told, had a real "license to kill.") What is the difference between really having a license and "effectively" having one? How might the opponent of the death penalty reply to Koch's position here?

3. Koch distinguishes between the "median" time served by persons convicted of murder but not sentenced to death, and the "average" time they serve, and he adds that the former "may be considerably longer" than the latter. Explain the difference between a "median" and an "average." Is knowing one of these more important for certain purposes than the other? Why?

4. Koch identifies seven arguments against the death penalty, and he rejects them all. Which of the seven arguments seems to you to be the strongest objection to the death penalty? Which the weakest? Why? Does Koch effectively refute the strongest argument? Can you think of any argument(s) against the death penalty that he neglects?

5. Koch says he supports the death penalty "for heinous crimes of murder." Does he imply that all murders are "heinous crimes," or only some? If the latter, what criteria seem to you to be the appropriate ones to distinguish the "heinous" murders from the rest? Why these criteria?

6. Koch asserts that the death penalty helps to "affirm" the idea that "life is indeed precious." Yet opponents of the death penalty often claim the reverse, arguing that capital punishment undermines the idea that human life is precious. Write an essay of 500 words in which you explain what it means to assert that life is precious, and why one of the two positions — support for or opposition to the death penalty — best supports (or is consistent with) this principle.

David Bruck

The Death Penalty

Mayor Ed Koch contends that the death penalty "affirms life." By failing to execute murderers, he says, we "signal a lessened regard for the value of the victim's life." Koch suggests that people who oppose the death penalty are like Kitty Genovese's neighbors, who heard her cries for help but did nothing while an attacker stabbed her to death.

This is the standard "moral" defense of death as punishment: Even if

---

David Bruck (b. 1949) graduated from Harvard College and received his law degree from the University of South Carolina. His practice is devoted almost entirely to the defense of persons under death sentence, through the South Carolina Office of Appellate Defense. The essay reprinted here originally appeared on May 20, 1985, in The New Republic *as a response to the essay by Edward I. Koch on p. 321.*

executions don't deter violent crime any more effectively than imprisonment, they are still required as the only means we have of doing justice in response to the worst of crimes.

Until recently, this "moral" argument had to be considered in the abstract, since no one was being executed in the United States. But the death penalty is back now, at least in the southern states, where every one of the more than thirty executions carried out over the last two years has taken place. Those of us who live in those states are getting to see the difference between the death penalty in theory, and what happens when you actually try to use it.

South Carolina resumed executing prisoners in January with the electrocution of Joseph Carl Shaw. Shaw was condemned to death for helping to murder two teenagers while he was serving as a military policeman at Fort Jackson, South Carolina. His crime, propelled by mental illness and PCP, was one of terrible brutality. It is Shaw's last words ("Killing was wrong when I did it. It is wrong when you do it. . . .") that so outraged Mayor Koch: He finds it "a curiosity of modern life that we are being lectured on morality by cold-blooded killers." And so it is.

But it was not "modern life" that brought this curiosity into being. It was 5 capital punishment. The electric chair was J. C. Shaw's platform. (The mayor mistakenly writes that Shaw's statement came in the form of a plea to the governor for clemency: Actually Shaw made it only seconds before his death, as he waited, shaved and strapped into the chair, for the switch to be thrown.) It was the chair that provided Shaw with celebrity and an opportunity to lecture us on right and wrong. What made this weird moral reversal even worse is that J. C. Shaw faced his own death with undeniable dignity and courage. And while Shaw died, the TV crews recorded another "curiosity" of the death penalty — the crowd gathered outside the death-house to cheer on the executioner. Whoops of elation greeted the announcement of Shaw's death. Waiting at the penitentiary gates for the appearance of the hearse bearing Shaw's remains, one demonstrator started yelling, "Where's the beef?"

For those who had to see the execution of J. C. Shaw, it wasn't easy to keep in mind that the purpose of the whole spectacle was to affirm life. It will be harder still when Florida executes a cop-killer named Alvin Ford. Ford has lost his mind during his years of death-row confinement, and now spends his days trembling, rocking back and forth, and muttering unintelligible prayers. This has led to litigation over whether Ford meets a centuries-old legal standard for mental competency. Since the Middle Ages, the Anglo-American legal system has generally prohibited the execution of anyone who is too mentally ill to understand what is about to be done to him and why. If Florida wins its case, it will have earned the right to electrocute Ford in his present condition. If it loses, he will not be executed until the state has first nursed him back to some semblance of mental health.[1]

[1]Florida lost its case to execute Ford. On June 26, 1986, the Supreme Court barred execution of convicted murderers who have become so insane that they do not know they are about to be executed nor the reason for it. If Ford regains his sanity, however, he can be executed. [Editors' note.]

We can at least be thankful that this demoralizing spectacle involves a prisoner who is actually guilty of murder. But this may not always be so. The ordeal of Lenell Jeter — the young black engineer who recently served more than a year of a life sentence for a Texas armed robbery that he didn't commit — should remind us that the system is quite capable of making the very worst sort of mistake. That Jeter was eventually cleared is a fluke. If the robbery had occurred at 7 P.M. rather than 3 P.M., he'd have had no alibi, and would still be in prison today. And if someone had been killed in that robbery, Jeter probably would have been sentenced to death. We'd have seen the usual execution-day interviews with state officials and the victim's relatives, all complaining that Jeter's appeals took too long. And Jeter's last words from the gurney would have taken their place among the growing literature of death-house oration that so irritates the mayor.

Koch quotes Hugo Adam Bedau, a prominent abolitionist, to the effect that the record fails to establish that innocent defendants have been executed in the past. But this doesn't mean, as Koch implies, that it hasn't happened. All Bedau was saying was that doubts concerning executed prisoners' guilt are almost never resolved. Bedau is at work now on an effort to determine how many wrongful death sentences may have been imposed: His list of murder convictions since 1900 in which the state eventually *admitted* error is some four hundred cases long. Of course, very few of these cases involved actual executions: The mistakes that Bedau documents were uncovered precisely because the prisoner was alive and able to fight for his vindication. The cases where someone is executed are the very cases in which we're least likely to learn that we got the wrong man.

I don't claim that executions of entirely innocent people will occur very often. But they will occur. And other sorts of mistakes already have. Roosevelt Green was executed in Georgia two days before J. C. Shaw. Green and an accomplice kidnapped a young woman. Green swore that his companion shot her to death after Green had left, and that he knew nothing about the murder. Green's claim was supported by a statement that his accomplice made to a witness after the crime. The jury never resolved whether Green was telling the truth, and when he tried to take a polygraph examination a few days before his scheduled execution, the State of Georgia refused to allow the examiner into the prison. As the pressure for symbolic retribution mounts, the courts, like the public, are losing patience with such details. Green was electrocuted on January 9, while members of the Ku Klux Klan rallied outside the prison.

Then there is another sort of arbitrariness that happens all the 10 time. Last October, Louisiana executed a man named Ernest Knighton. Knighton had killed a gas station owner during a robbery. Like any murder, this was a terrible crime. But it was not premeditated, and is the sort of crime that very rarely results in a death sentence. Why was Knighton electrocuted when almost everyone else who committed the same offense was not? Was it because he was black? Was it because his victim and all twelve members of the jury that sentenced him were white? Was it because Knighton's court-appointed lawyer presented no evidence on his behalf at his sentencing hearing? Or maybe there's no reason except bad luck. One thing is clear: Ernest Knighton was picked out to die the way a fisherman takes a cricket out of a bait jar. No one cares which cricket gets impaled on the hook.

Not every prisoner executed recently was chosen that randomly. But many were. And having selected these men so casually, so blindly, the death penalty system asks us to accept that the purpose of killing each of them is to affirm the sanctity of human life.

The death penalty states are also learning that the death penalty is easier to advocate than it is to administer. In Florida, where executions have become almost routine, the governor reports that nearly a third of his time is spent reviewing the clemency requests of condemned prisoners. The Florida Supreme Court is hopelessly backlogged with death cases. Some have taken five years to decide, and the rest of the Court's work waits in line behind the death appeals. Florida's death row currently holds more than 230 prisoners. State officials are reportedly considering building a special "death prison" devoted entirely to the isolation and electrocution of the condemned. The state is also considering the creation of a special public defender unit that will do nothing else but handle death penalty appeals. The death penalty, in short, is spawning death agencies.

And what is Florida getting for all of this? The state went through almost all of 1983 without executing anyone: Its rate of intentional homicide declined by 17 percent. Last year Florida executed eight people—the most of any state, and the sixth highest total for any year since Florida started electrocuting people back in 1924. Elsewhere in the United States last year, the homicide rate continued to decline. But in Florida, it actually rose by 5.1 percent.

But these are just the tiresome facts. The electric chair has been a centerpiece of each of Koch's recent political campaigns, and he knows better than anyone how little the facts have to do with the public's support for capital punishment. What really fuels the death penalty is the justifiable frustration and rage of people who see that the government is not coping with violent crime. So what if the death penalty doesn't work? At least it gives us the satisfaction of knowing that we got one or two of the sons of bitches.

Perhaps we want retribution on the flesh and bone of a handful of convicted murderers so badly that we're willing to close our eyes to all of the demoralization and danger that come with it. A lot of politicians think so, and they may be right. But if they are, then let's at least look honestly at what we're doing. This lottery of death both comes from and encourages an attitude toward human life that is not reverent, but reckless.

And that is why the mayor is dead wrong when he confuses such fury with justice. He suggests that we trivialize murder unless we kill murderers. By that logic, we also trivialize rape unless we sodomize rapists. The sin of Kitty Genovese's neighbors wasn't that they failed to stab her attacker to death. Justice does demand that murderers be punished. And common sense demands that society be protected from them. But neither justice nor self-preservation demands that we kill men whom we have already imprisoned.

The electric chair in which J. C. Shaw died earlier this year was built in 1912 at the suggestion of South Carolina's governor at the time, Cole Blease. Governor Blease's other criminal justice initiative was an impassioned crusade in favor of lynch law. Any lesser response, the governor insisted, trivialized the loathsome crimes of interracial rape and murder. In 1912, a lot of people agreed with Governor Blease that a proper regard for justice required both lynching and the electric chair. Eventually we are going to learn that justice requires neither.

Topics for Critical Thinking and Writing

1. After three introductory paragraphs, Bruck devotes two paragraphs to Shaw's execution. In a sentence or two, state the point he is making in his discussion of this execution. Then, in another sentence or two (or three) indicate the degree to which this point refutes Koch's argument.

2. In paragraph 7, Bruck refers to the case of Lenell Jeter, an innocent man who was condemned to a life sentence. Evaluate this point as a piece of evidence used to support an argument against the death penalty.

3. In paragraph 8, Bruck says that "the state eventually *admitted* error" in some four hundred cases. He goes on: "Of course, very few of these cases involved actual executions." How few is "very few"? Why do you suppose Bruck doesn't specify the number? If, say, it is only two, in your opinion does that affect Bruck's point?

4. Discussing the case of Roosevelt Green (para. 9), Bruck points out that Green offered to take a polygraph test but "the state of Georgia refused to allow the examiner into the prison." In a paragraph evaluate the state's position on this matter.

5. In paragraph 13 Bruck points out that although "last year" (1984) the state executed eight people, the homicide rate in Florida rose 5.1 percent, whereas elsewhere in the United States the homicide rate declined. What do you make of these figures? What do you think Koch would make of them?

6. In his next-to-last paragraph Bruck says that Koch "suggests that we trivialize murder unless we kill murderers. By that logic, we also trivialize rape unless we sodomize rapists." Do you agree that this statement brings out the absurdity of Koch's thinking?

7. Evaluate Bruck's final paragraph (a) as a concluding paragraph, and (b) as a piece of argumentation.

8. Bruck, writing early in 1985, stresses that all the "more than thirty" executions in the nation "in the last two years" have taken place in the South. Why does he

think this figure points to a vulnerability in Mayor Koch's argument? Would Bruck's argument here be spoiled if some executions were to occur outside of the South? (By the way, where exactly have most of the recent executions in the nation occurred?)

9. Bruck argues that the present death-penalty system — in practice even if not in theory — utterly fails to "affirm the sanctity of human life." Do you think Bruck would, or should, concede that at least in theory it is possible for a death-penalty system to be no more offensive to the value of human life than, say, a system of imprisonment is offensive to the value of human liberty, or a system of fines is offensive to the value of human property?

10. Can Bruck be criticized for implying that cases like those he cites — Shaw, Ford, Green, and Knightson in particular — are the rule, rather than the exception? Does either Bruck or Koch cite any evidence to help settle this question?

11. Write a paragraph explaining which of these events seems to you to be the more unseemly: a condemned prisoner, on the threshold of execution, lecturing the rest of us on the immorality of killing; or the crowd that bursts into cheers outside a prison when it learns that a scheduled execution has been carried out.

Robert H. Bork

An Outbreak of Judicial Civil Disobedience

The rule of law received a fresh body blow last week, this time from its sworn guardians. After thirteen years of procedural roadblocks, California was finally able to execute Robert Alton Harris. But only because the Supreme Court put an end to an excruciating series of last-minute stays issued by some judges on the U.S. Court of Appeals for the Ninth Circuit who were, apparently, determined to flout the law until Harris died of old age.

Press reaction was predictable, and wrong. Under the heading "The Court's Rush to Kill," the *New York Times* found the Supreme Court's performance "repugnant." London's *Daily Telegraph* said, "Yesterday's dreadful black farce on California's Death Row did no service to those who plead the cause of capital punishment."

Robert H. Bork (b. 1927) taught at Yale Law School, resigned to serve as Solicitor General of the United States, and was then appointed to the U.S. Circuit Court of Appeals. He is now a resident scholar at the American Enterprise Institute, Washington, D.C. The article reprinted here first appeared in the Wall Street Journal *(April 29, 1992).*

The *Daily Telegraph* had it backward. A "dreadful black farce" it certainly was, but it was not staged by the California authorities or the Supreme Court. It was caused by those so ardently opposed to capital punishment that they refuse to accept the decisions of the electorate and the jury. It is important to understand whose fault this was.

In 1978 Harris and his brother, wanting a car for a bank robbery, kidnapped two 16-year-old boys sitting in an automobile eating hamburgers, drove them to a deserted canyon and shot one. The other ran, screamed for help and tried to hide, but Harris pursued and killed him as well. The killer then got in the car, laughed, and finished the boys' hamburgers before proceeding to the bank. Most Americans think capital punishment is appropriate for such crimes. The jury agreed.

Harris appealed to the California Supreme Court that, under the guidance of Chief Justice Rose Bird, overturned sixty-four out of sixty-eight death sentences before Ms. Bird and her allies were voted out of office in 1986. Harris's was one of the four the Bird court let stand. His attorneys then got him three complete hearings on federal *habeas corpus* petitions and five more on state petitions. His case thus received nine separate reviews. Surely far more than enough, one would have thought. But then the case turned really bizarre. 5

Harris's execution was set for 12:01 A.M. PDT on April 21. Authorization for the execution would expire at 12:01 A.M. the next day. Delay beyond that time would require that the execution be reauthorized. On April 20, therefore, lawyers for Harris filed one state habeas petition, one federal habeas petition, and one federal court action claiming that execution in the gas chamber was cruel and unusual punishment under the Eighth Amendment. None of these ultimately went anywhere. An appeals court panel held that the habeas petition was an abuse of the writ and vacated the district court's temporary restraining order on the gas chamber question.

At this point another appeals court judge issued a stay of execution on the basis of the habeas petition, and ten judges put the restraining order back in place, although the court's rules provide for no such procedure. The state went to the U.S. Supreme Court in the middle of the night. Law clerks got their justices out of bed with telephone calls and the court— voting seven to two—lifted the stays.

Two more actions were filed immediately, one raising the cruel-and-unusual argument in a habeas petition and the other asking that the execution be videotaped as evidence that the punishment is in fact cruel and unusual. Meanwhile, Harris had actually been strapped into the chair in the gas chamber when a telephone call from a federal judge ordered the execution stayed.

Once more during the same all-night endurance contest, the Supreme Court—again by a seven-to-two vote—lifted the Ninth Circuit judges' stay and, fed up with the obduracy of those appeals court judges who continued to block the execution without justification, took the extraordinary, but necessary, step of ordering that no more stays be issued except by the Supreme Court. The Supreme Court noted that Harris had now filed four prior federal habeas petitions (not to mention five state petitions) and had no convincing explanation for his failure to raise the cruel-and-unusual punishment claim before.

"Equity must take into consideration the state's strong interest in pro- 10 ceeding with its judgment and Harris' obvious attempt at manipulation. . . . This claim could have been brought more than a decade ago. There is no good reason for this abusive delay, which has been compounded by last-minute efforts to manipulate the judicial process." Harris was executed.

It would be possible to dwell on the barbarity of a procedural system gone mad so that a man is held on death row for thirteen years of alternating hope and despair. It would be possible to dwell on the cruelty to the families who wait, seemingly endlessly, for justice to be done.

But perhaps the most dismaying thing is the display of civil disobedience within the federal judiciary. It is old news that the American Civil Liberties Union, whose lawyers orchestrated this debacle, will do almost anything to prevent duly enacted and imposed capital punishment from being carried out. Far from being devoted to the preservation of constitutional liberties, as it claims, the ACLU is instead devoted to using the courts to achieve political results that have lost at the polls and have nothing to do with the Constitution.

What is new, and exemplified by the legal disaster of the Harris case, is the resistance of lower-court judges both to law and to the Supreme Court. Those judges who, after years of judicial examination and re-examination of the conviction, repeatedly issued last-minute stays of execution evidently thought their personal opposition to capital punishment was reason enough to defy what law and their judicial superiors demanded.

But the more fanatical opponents of capital punishment insist on mis-understanding who is responsible for the degrading spectacle played out in the last hours of Harris's life. Amnesty International, apparently an international version of the ACLU, said, "The determination of the state authorities to gas their prisoner to death as soon as they possibly could with the backing of the U.S. Supreme Court ended in a sick battle against the clock."

The sick battle was that of attorneys and judges against the calendar. 15 Does Amnesty International or anybody else really suppose that Harris could ever have been executed, after however many hearings, without another battle against the clock? There would be last-minute petitions and stays forever. Those who have more respect for their own opinions than for the rule of law would see to that.

Topics for Critical Thinking and Writing ══════════

1. Bork complains of those who, opposing capital punishment, "refuse to accept the decisions of the electorate and the jury" (para. 3). How might he reply to this criticism: Since the electorate never convicted or sentenced Robert Harris, and since the jury that did might have been in error, what's wrong with defense counsel vigorously seeking to protect Harris's rights?

2. Bork describes the behavior of the judges in their handling of Harris's last-minute petitions as "civil disobedience within the federal judiciary" (para. 12). Do you think that Bork is objecting mainly to the idea of civil disobedience in general, or only to the idea of federal judges being civilly disobedient?

3. If, as Durfee claims in the next selection, there were "three crucial issues" in the Harris case that "no court . . . ever ruled on" (paras. 3–6), do you think that justified Harris's attorneys in desperately seeking last-minute stays of execution for their client? Why, or why not?

Glenn Durfee

Did Executions Kill Some of Our Rights?

In his April 29 Rule of Law column, "An Outbreak of Judicial Civil Disobedience" (op-ed page), Robert H. Bork excoriates the lower federal court judges whose stays temporarily halted the execution of Robert Alton Harris. He praises the seven justices of the U.S. Supreme Court who initially lifted those stays and who ultimately took the "extraordinary, but necessary, step of ordering that no more stays be issued." (Justices Stevens and Blackmun dissented.)

"Extraordinary" is too kind a word for that step. "Appalling" is better. The U.S. Supreme Court simply has no authority (constitutional, statutory, or other) to strip lower federal courts of jurisdiction in that way. Without the power to issue stays, lower federal courts can no longer rule on *habeas corpus* petitions that executions will moot.

That is not the only failing of the judicial system in the Harris case. Despite the seemingly interminable writs and appeals, no court (state or federal) ever ruled on three crucial issues:

- Whether fetal alcohol syndrome prevented Harris from forming the mental state necessary to justify the death penalty. (After hearing

---

Glenn Durfee, an attorney who practices in Davis, California, wrote the following letter in response to the preceding essay by Robert H. Bork. Durfee's piece, like Bork's, was published in the Wall Street Journal *(June 9, 1992).*

the evidence at the clemency hearing, Governor Pete Wilson acknowledged that Harris had fetal alcohol syndrome.)

- Whether poison gas causes suffering that constitutes cruel or unusual punishment. (Ever since the routine use of poison gas by Germany's Third Reich, civilized societies by and large have shied away from that practice.)

- Whether the authorities coerced false testimony about the killings from Harris's brother. (If his brother had to testify to a script, instead of to the truth, to keep his plea bargain, then the reliability of his testimony was gravely suspect.)

As despicable as the homicidal behavior of Robert Alton Harris was, the rights that he lost, we lost too. The public decries the anarchy in Los Angeles after the Rodney King verdict, but the lawlessness of the Supreme Court in the Harris case is equally frightening. Both pose grave risks to the survival of our society.

Mr. Bork argues that "perhaps the most dismaying thing is the display 5 of civil disobedience within the federal judiciary." He'd be right if he were speaking about the seven justices who, after a wakeful night lifting one stay after another, finally issued a despotic edict withdrawing lawful jurisdiction from lower federal courts.

Mr. Bork is right that the "rule of law received a fresh body blow" in the Harris case, but he is wrong about the identity of the assailant. To blame the lawyers, the American Civil Liberties Union and lower federal court judges is to engage in sophistry. The blame lies with the seven frustrated justices who disposed of Harris and his case, but who left us with the sorry spectacle of a judicial system that does an agonizingly slow job of imposing the death penalty and an even worse job of resolving crucial issues on which nothing less than human life depends.

Something we ask consistently of our judiciary, something for which there can be no waiver, is judicial temperament. In a society that operates on the rule of law, there can be no excuse for justices who, no matter how much they think others might have provoked them, retaliate in a way that disserves each and every one of us.

Topics for Critical Thinking and Writing

1. A century ago the U.S. Supreme Court judged that the electric chair was *not* a "cruel and unusual punishment" in the meaning of that phrase as it appears in the Eight Amendment to the U.S. Constitution. Do you think it is plausible that Harris's attorneys might have persuaded the Supreme Court that California's gas chamber was an unconstitutional "cruel and unusual" punishment? Why, or why not?

2. If you think the best answer to the preceding question is "No, the Supreme Court was very unlikely to rule on this issue by declaring the gas chamber un-

constitutional," then do you think Harris's attorneys should be accused of seeking delay just for delay's sake in raising the issue in the first place?

3. Both Bork and Durfee refer to "the rule of law," but neither defines the term and they evidently disagree over what it requires in death penalty cases. How would you define "the rule of law," and what do you think it requires in death penalty cases?

Ernest van den Haag

The Deterrent Effect of the Death Penalty

Crime is going to be with us as long as there is any social order articulated by laws. There is no point making laws that prohibit some action or other (e.g., murder or theft) unless there is some temptation to commit it. And however harsh the threats of the law, they will not restrain some people, whether because they discount the risk of punishment or because they are exposed to extraordinary temptation. They may hope for an immense profit; or be passionately angry or vindictive; or be in such misery that they feel they have nothing to lose. Thus, I repeat, the problem every society must attempt to solve (in part by means of punishment) is not eliminating crime but controlling it.

That threats will not deter everybody all the time must be expected. And it must also be expected that persons committed to criminal activity—career criminals—are not likely to be restrained by threats; nor are persons strongly under the influence of drugs or intoxicated by their own passions. However, if threats are not likely to deter habitual offenders, they are likely to help deter people from *becoming* habitual offenders.

People are not deterred by exactly calculating the size of the threat and the actual risk of suffering punishment against the likely benefit of the crime they consider committing. Few people calculate at all. Rather, the effect of threats is to lead most people to ignore criminal opportunities most of the time. One just does not consider them—any more than the ordinary person sitting down for lunch starts calculating whether he could have Beluga caviar and champagne instead of his usual hamburger and beer. He is not accustomed to caviar, and one reason he is not accustomed to it is that it costs too much. He does not have to calculate every time to know as much. Similarly, he is not accustomed to breaking the law, and one reason is that it costs too much. He does not need to calculate.

It is quite a different matter if one asks, not: "Do threats deter?" but

---

Ernest van den Haag (b. 1914) is a professor (retired) of jurisprudence at Fordham University Law School. He is the author of several books, including Punishing Criminals *(1975). His essay here is excerpted from* The Death Penalty Pro and Con: A Debate *(1983).*

rather: "How much does one threat deter compared to another?" Does the more severe threat deter significantly more? Does the added deterrence warrant the added severity? Thus, no one pondering the death penalty will contend that it does not deter. The question is: Does it deter more than alternative penalties proposed, such as life imprisonment or any lengthy term of imprisonment?

In the past many attempts were made to determine whether the death penalty deters the crimes for which it was threatened—capital crimes—more than other penalties, usually life imprisonment, mitigated by parole (and amounting therefore to something like ten years in prison in most cases). Most of these attempts led to ambiguous results, often rendered more ambiguous by faulty procedures and research methods. Frequently, contiguous states—one with and the other without the death penalty—were compared. Or states were compared before and after abolition. Usually these comparisons were based on the legal availability or unavailability of the death penalty rather than on the presence or absence of executions and on their frequency. But what matters is whether the death penalty is practiced, not whether theoretically it is available. Finally, nobody would assert that the death penalty—or any crime-control measure—is the only determinant of the frequency of the crime. The number of murders certainly depends as well on the proportion of young males in the population, on income distribution, on education, on the proportion of various races in the population, on local cultural traditions, on the legal definition of murder, and on other such factors.

Comparisons must take all of these matters into account if they are to evaluate the effect threatened penalties may have in deterring crimes. In contiguous states, influential factors other than the death penalty may differ; they may even differ in the same state before and after abolition. Hence, differences (or equalities) in capital crime frequencies cannot simply be ascribed to the presence or absence of the death penalty. Moreover, one does not know how soon a change in penalties will make a difference, if it ever does, or whether prospective murderers will know that the death penalty has been abolished in Maine and kept in Vermont. They certainly will know whether or not there is a death penalty in the United States. But in contiguous states? Or within a short time after abolition or reinstatement?

Theoretically, experiments to avoid all these difficulties are possible. But they face formidable obstacles in practice. If, for instance, the death penalty were threatened for murders committed on Monday, Wednesday, and Friday, and life imprisonment for murders committed on Tuesday, Thursday, and Saturday, we would soon see which days murderers prefer, i.e., how much the death penalty deters on Monday, Wednesday, and Friday over and above life imprisonment threatened for murders committed on the other days. If we find no difference, the abolitionist thesis that the death penalty adds no deterrence over and above the threat of life imprisonment would be confirmed.

In the absence of such experiments, none of the available studies seems conclusive. Recently such studies have acquired considerable mathematical sophistication, and some of the more sophisticated studies have concluded, contrary to what used to be accepted scholarly opinion, that the death penalty can be shown to deter over and above life imprisonment. Thus, Isaac Ehrlich, in a study published in the *American Economic Review* (June 1975), concluded that, over the period 1933–69, "an additional execution per year . . . may have resulted on the average in seven or eight fewer murders."

Other studies published since Ehrlich's contend that his results are due to the techniques and periods he selected, and that different techniques and periods yield different results. Despite a great deal of research on all sides, one cannot say that the statistical evidence is conclusive. Nobody has claimed to have *disproved* that the death penalty may deter more than life imprisonment. But one cannot claim, either, that it has been proved statistically in a conclusive manner that the death penalty does deter more than alternative penalties. This lack of proof does not amount to disproof. However, abolitionists insist that there ought to be proof positive.

Unfortunately, there is little proof of the sort sought by those who op-   10 pose the death penalty, for the deterrent effect of any sort of punishment. Nobody has statistically shown that four years in prison deter more than two, or twenty more than ten. We assume as much. But I know of no statistical proof. One may wonder why such proof is demanded for the death penalty but not for any other. To be sure, death is more serious a punishment than any other. But ten years in prison are not exactly trivial either. . . .

If it is difficult, perhaps impossible, to prove statistically — and just as hard to disprove — that the death penalty deters more from capital crimes than available alternative punishments do (such as life imprisonment), why do so many people believe so firmly that the death penalty is a more effective deterrent?

Some are persuaded by irrelevant arguments. They insist that the death penalty at least makes sure that the person who suffered it will not commit other crimes. True. Yet this confuses incapacitation with a specific way to bring it about: death. Death is the surest way to bring about the most total incapacitation, and it is irrevocable. But does incapacitation need to be that total? And is irrevocability necessarily an advantage? Obviously it makes correcting mistakes and rehabilitation impossible. What is the advantage of execution, then, over alternative ways of achieving the desired incapacitation?

More important, the argument for incapacitation confuses the elimination of one murderer (or of any number of murderers) with a reduction in the homicide rate. But the elimination of any specific number of actual or even of potential murderers — and there is some doubt that the actual murderers of the past are the most likely future (potential) murderers — will not affect the homicide rate, except through deterrence. There are enough potential murderers around to replace all those incapacitated. Deterrence may prevent the potential from becoming actual murderers. But incapacitation of some or all actual murderers is not likely to have much effect by itself. Let us then return to the question: Does capital punishment deter more than life imprisonment?

Science, logic, or statistics often have been unable to prove what common sense tells us to be true. Thus, the Greek philosopher Zeno some two thousand years ago found that he could not show that motion is possible; indeed, his famous paradoxes appear to show that motion is impossible. Though nobody believed them to be true, nobody succeeded in showing the fallacy of these paradoxes until the rise of mathematical logic less than a hundred years ago. But meanwhile, the world did not stand still. Indeed, nobody argued that motion should stop because it had not been shown to be logically possible. There is no more reason to abolish the death penalty than there was to abolish motion simply because the death penalty has not been, and perhaps cannot be, shown statistically to be a deterrent over and above other penalties. Indeed, there are two quite satisfactory, if nonstatistical, indications of the marginal deterrent effect of the death penalty.

In the first place, our experience shows that the greater the threatened penalty, the more it deters. Ceteris paribus, the threat of fifty lashes, deters more than the threat of five; a $1,000 fine deters more than a $10 fine; ten years in prison deter more than one year in prison — just as, conversely, the promise of a $1,000 reward is a greater incentive than the promise of a $10 reward, etc. There may be diminishing returns. Once a reward exceeds, say, $1 million, the additional attraction may diminish. Once a punishment exceeds, say, ten years in prison (net of parole), there may be little additional deterrence in threatening additional years. We know hardly anything about diminishing returns of penalties. It would still seem likely, however, that the threat of life in prison deters more than any other term of imprisonment. 15

The threat of death may deter still more. For it is a mistake to regard the death penalty as though it were of the same kind as other penalties. If it is not, then diminishing returns are unlikely to apply. And death differs significantly, in kind, from any other penalty. Life in prison is still life, however unpleasant. In contrast, the death penalty does not just threaten to make life unpleasant — it threatens to take life altogether. This difference is perceived by those affected. We find that when they have the choice between life in prison and execution, 99 percent of all prisoners under sentence of death prefer life in prison. By means of appeals, pleas for commutation, indeed by all means at their disposal, they indicate that they prefer life in prison to execution.

From this unquestioned fact a reasonable conclusion can be drawn in favor of the superior deterrent effect of the death penalty. Those who have the choice in practice, those whose choice has actual and immediate effects on their life and death, fear death more than they fear life in prison or any other available penalty. If they do, it follows that the threat of the death penalty, all other things equal, is likely to deter more than the threat of life in prison. One is most deterred by what one fears most. From which it follows that whatever statistics fail, or do not fail, to show, the death penalty is likely to be more deterrent than any other.

Suppose now one is not fully convinced of the superior deterrent effect of the death penalty. I believe I can show that even if one is genuinely uncertain as to whether the death penalty adds to deterrence, one should still favor it, from a purely deterrent viewpoint. For if we are not sure, we must choose either to (1) trade the certain death, by execution, of a convicted murderer for the probable survival of an indefinite number of murder victims whose future murder is less likely (whose survival is more likely) — if the convicted murderer's execution deters prospective murderers, as it might, or to (2) trade the certain survival of the convicted murderer for the probable loss of the lives of future murder victims more likely to be murdered because the convicted murderer's nonexecution might not deter prospective murderers, who could have been deterred by executing the convicted murderer.

To restate the matter: If we were quite ignorant about the marginal deterrent effects of execution, we would have to choose — like it or not — between the certainty of the convicted murderer's death by execution and the likelihood of the survival of future victims of other murderers on the one hand, and on the other his certain survival and the likelihood of the death of new victims. I'd rather execute a man convicted of having murdered others than to put the lives of innocents at risk. I find it hard to understand the opposite choice.

Topics for Critical Thinking and Writing

1. Van den Haag mentions (para. 5) several factors relevant to the volume of murder. Easy availability of handguns (not to mention automatic rifles) is not one of them. Read the essays by Cassidy (p. 275) and Desuka (p. 277) and explain in 100 words whether you think effective gun control would reduce the volume of murder in the United States.

2. Van den Haag proposes (para. 7) an ideal but impractical experiment that he thinks would settle the question whether the death penalty deters. Modifying his example, suppose there was conclusive evidence that the police were ineffective in catching murderers who commit their crimes on Mondays, Wednesdays, and Fridays, but were effective in arresting those who murder on Tuesdays, Thursdays, and Saturdays. If you planned to murder someone, which day(s) of the week would you choose for the crime, and why?

3. Van den Haag distinguishes (para. 13) between the death penalty as a *deterrent* and as *incapacitative*, and argues that in the latter role the death penalty cannot reduce the crime rate. What is his argument, and do you agree?

4. Van den Haag defends the death penalty as a deterrent, not because of strong evidence but by appeal to "common sense" (para. 14). How reliable are appeals to common sense, anyway? Suppose someone defended the proposition that the

sun moves around the earth, and not the earth around the sun, because it's obvious, common sense, as anyone can see. Why should we reject this appeal to common sense (if we should) and accept van den Haag's (if we should)?

5. Van den Haag implies (paras. 16–17) that because death row prisoners prefer to have their sentences commuted to life in prison, the threat of death in general may be a better deterrent than the threat of even a long prison sentence. Lay out this argument, step by step, and explain whether you think it is sound. On what assumptions does it rest? Are they vulnerable to criticism?

6. Van den Haag's final argument (para. 18) appears to assume that the convicted murderer whose execution is in question is really guilty. But suppose he's not, or that the evidence against him is not really conclusive. Do you think this affects the force of van den Haag's argument? Why, or why not?

Stephen Nathanson

What If the Death Penalty Did Save Lives?

I would not deny that if the death penalty prevented murders more successfully than other punishments, this would be a powerful argument in its favor. To grant this, however, is not the same as saying that deterrence is the only relevant factor or that it is by itself decisive. The morality of the death penalty, like the morality of many other acts and policies, depends on many diverse factors. For this reason, many different sorts of reasons bear on our assessment of it. We cannot deduce the moral rightness or wrongness of the death penalty from just one general principle, not even from a plausible principle like "protect innocent life whenever possible." Nonetheless, if the death penalty were a superior deterrent, that would introduce a very weighty moral consideration into the balance of reasons, and the greater its deterrent power (the more lives it could be credited with saving), the weightier that reason would be.

In spite of this, it is easy to see that evidence of superior deterrent power would not by itself show that the death penalty was morally legitimate. We can see this by imagining some punishment that it is plausible to believe would be an extremely effective deterrent and yet that we would regard as immoral in spite of the fact that it saved lives.

Imagine, for example, that we were to adopt a policy of punishing murderers by administering prolonged and extraordinarily painful forms of torture, to be followed by eventual execution. Instead of aiming for "humane" forms of execution, we would select the most awful forms of execution in the belief that the more awful the process, the more powerful the

---

Stephen Nathanson (b. 1943), a professor of philosophy at Northeastern University, is the author of The Ideal of Rationality *(1985). The following is excerpted from his book* An Eye for an Eye? The Morality of Punishing by Death *(1987).*

deterrent. It is certainly plausible to believe that this sort of policy would have greater deterrent power than the death penalty as now administered. (It might also stimulate violence, as the brutalization hypothesis suggests, but we can leave this possibility aside for the sake of our thought experiment.) Even if this form of punishment were remarkably successful as a deterrent, I doubt that we would think that it was morally permissible to impose it. Such a punishment would require extraordinary callousness to administer, and we would surely condemn it as barbaric.

Or, suppose we adopted the following punishment for murder. We would execute not only the person who committed the murder but also the three people in the world who were of greatest personal significance to the murderer. We could imagine a postconviction hearing in which a report was presented, assessing the murderer's relationship to other people and concluding with a judgment about which three people meant the most to the murderer. All of them would then be executed. If we were solely interested in making potential murderers "think twice," this policy would probably work much better than the death penalty as currently practiced. Yet, again, this particular practice would be truly abhorrent, and it would remain abhorrent, even if it saved more lives than other punishments.

What these examples show is that superior deterrent power is not the 5 only issue. A punishment may save more lives and yet involve society in such ghastly practices that we would reject it as immoral.

To establish in principle that a punishment with superior deterrent power may be immoral is a matter of considerable significance. Nonetheless, by itself, it does not show that the death penalty is sufficiently ghastly to merit rejection. The death penalty would qualify as sufficiently bad in itself to be rejected by the absolute pacifist, for whom all killing is immoral, or by the person who finds executions inherently barbaric. These reactions, however, are not widely shared. Most people believe that killing is morally permissible in some circumstances, and most people think that executions can be carried out in a way that is sufficiently humane to bring them within the bounds of civility. I am not sure that the second of these judgments is correct, but I see no effective way to argue against it.[1]

I will not then try to argue that executions are on a par with torture or with the practice of executing those whom murderers care about. Rather, having shown that superior deterrent power by itself would not guarantee the morality of punishing by death, I want to see whether there are other factors that would call into question the morality of executions, even if executions were the most effective way to save lives.

One of the most powerful objections to the death penalty arises from the possibility of executing innocent people. I take it that we would not *knowingly* execute innocent people even if this had a positive deterrent ef-

---

[1]For an attempt to show that executions are inhumane in the same way that torture is, see Jeffrey Reiman, "Justice, Civilization, and the Death Penalty," *Philosophy and Public Affairs* 14 (1985): 134–42. [All notes are the author's.]

fect on the homicide rate. If this is true, then we should be deeply disturbed if we could predict that, under a death penalty system, we would unintentionally execute innocent persons. If we could predict that among the effects of instituting the death penalty would be the execution of innocent persons, this would count heavily against the death penalty, even if we could predict that another effect would be a decrease in the homicide rate.

The problem of executing the innocent is, at a certain level, quite simple. Executing innocent people would be a dreadful effect of the death penalty, and it would not be a possible effect of long-term imprisonment, a possible alternative to executions. Hence, we could have a severe punishment that did not threaten to result in our killing innocent people. To maintain the death penalty is to be willing to risk innocent lives.

No one could dismiss the relevance or force of this argument, and no 10 one could deny that executing innocent persons is a terrible act. Nonetheless, this argument raises extraordinarily difficult issues of what has sometimes been called "moral arithmetic." There would be no problem, of course, if the number of innocent people executed were larger than the number of innocent lives saved. Nor, I take it, would there be a problem if the numbers were equal. But, the issue becomes much murkier in the situation in which more innocent lives are saved by deterrence than are lost through erroneous executions.

Suppose that there were a net gain in lives saved but that the number of lives saved was extremely small. Then, I think, we would reject the death penalty and forgo the added deterrence it provides. Our decision would be supported by the idea that it is worse for us actually to kill innocent people than it is for us to fail to prevent the deaths of innocent people. The moral significance of the distinction between the harms we cause and those we fail to prevent has been called into question by some recent thinkers.[2] Nonetheless, we generally do distinguish between failing to save a life (say, by not contributing to famine relief) and actually killing someone (by taking away his food, for example). While the failure to protect is morally bad, the active killing seems much worse. So, if innocents are to die, it is better that we not be the agents of their deaths.

If, however, the number of innocents likely to be executed by mistake is very small and the number of potential homicide victims whose lives can be saved is very large, then we might well conclude that morality requires us to execute murderers. If this were our judgment, we would then be under a great deal of pressure to try to specify what "very large" and "very small" mean in this context. How many lives must be saved by executions in order for us to be justified in accepting the death penalty, even though we know that some innocent people will be executed?

I fear that I have nothing very helpful to say about how to approach the "moral arithmetic" in this case.

---

[2]One noteworthy example is Peter Singer, *Practical Ethics* (Cambridge: Cambridge University Press, 1979), Ch. 8.

Nonetheless, I think we can reach several conclusions related to the problem of executing innocent people. First, if the death penalty is to be justified, we must have good reason to believe that our system is on the whole quite reliable and that very few innocent people will ever be executed. We must do our utmost to provide stringent safeguards that will make such executions highly unlikely — even if this means bearing extra legal costs, putting up with long delays, and sometimes seeing death sentences overturned for what appear to be merely "legal technicalities." Moreover, we must be confident that these safeguards will work.

Second, we must have reason to believe that the number of lives saved   15 is *substantial.* Superior deterrent power cannot mean simply that a few lives are likely to be saved. If we assume that some innocents will be executed and that it is worse for us actively to kill a person than it is for us to fail in our efforts to prevent someone's death, then executions can be justified only if they lead to substantial savings of lives.

Finally, it must be the case that there are no feasible, morally preferable alternatives to the death penalty, no policies that are available to us and that would be equally effective in saving these innocent lives. If there were other morally acceptable policies that did not involve the possibility of executing innocents and yet that were as effective in preventing murders, then we would be morally bound to try these alternatives. If it turned out, for example, that homicide rates could be lowered through greater controls on the availability of guns, or if homicide rates are related to unemployment rates so that lowering unemployment would (along with its other benefits) lower the homicide rate, then it would be our duty to adopt these alternatives to the death penalty. It would be immoral for us to adopt the death penalty if we could predict that some innocent people would be executed and if we knew that alternative policies could save lives equally well.

The problem of executing innocent people is not imaginary or purely hypothetical. The most thorough study available on the execution of innocents has recently been carried out by Hugo Bedau and Michael Radelet.[3] They claim to have found that for the period 1900 to 1980, about 350 people were wrongfully convicted of capital offenses. Of these, 139 were sentenced to death, and 23 were actually executed.

These figures may be reassuring to some. One might react by thinking that the number of errors is small and that most of those wrongfully convicted were not after all executed. Somehow, it might be thought, the system was able to correct these errors in time. A closer look is less reassuring, however, for the evidence that led to a particular person's escaping execution has usually appeared by chance or resulted from the efforts of people outside the legal process. Only in thirty-seven cases, about 10 percent of the cases, were errors discovered by officials. Moreover, as time passes and

---

[3]H. Bedau and M. Radelet, "Miscarriages of Justice in Potentially Capital Cases," *Stanford Law Review* 40 (1987).

with the death of those executed, further evidence regarding their cases becomes increasingly difficult to gather. It is plausible to suppose that unknown cases remain and that the number of innocent persons executed is larger than the twenty-three that Bedau and Radelet have verified. . . .

In a study of the death penalty in Georgia since the *Gregg* decision, Ursula Bentele reports on the case of Jerry Banks, a man who discovered two dead bodies while hunting.[4] Banks went to a road and stopped a car, asking the driver to report the deaths to the police. Banks waited for the police, and when they arrived, he led them to the bodies. One month later, Banks, a black man, was charged with the murder. He was tried, convicted, and sentenced to death, in spite of the fact that a neighbor testified that Banks had been at her home at the time when the shooting occurred. Moreover, the driver whom Banks had signaled and who phoned the police was never called as a witness, and a detective testified that he did not know his identity. In fact, this person, a Mr. Eberhardt, had left his name with the police, had made himself available to the grand jury, had spoken with the judge who conducted the trial, and had made a statement for the sheriff. The Supreme Court of Georgia, in ordering a new trial, specifically noted that the sheriff and other officers knew the identity of this witness but "either intentionally or inadvertently" kept it from Banks and his lawyer.

Banks was tried a second time and again convicted and sentenced to 20 death, apparently because of ineffective work by his lawyer. Only after this second death sentence did two new attorneys discover evidence that the murder weapon could not have been Banks's hunting rifle. They found witnesses who had reported hearing rapid fire shots that could not have come from Banks's shotgun. Others reported that they had seen two white men arguing shortly before the murder took place. Several of the witnesses had actually reported what they had seen to the police, but the reports were ignored and were not introduced at Banks's second trial.

In a second appeal, Banks again won a new trial. This time, after seven years of legal proceedings stretching from 1974 through 1981, all charges against him were dropped.

While this case may not be typical, the Bedau–Radelet study shows that it is far from unique. The occurrence of such cases is sufficient to call into question our confidence that the awesome responsibility of dealing with crimes that may lead to execution is treated with appropriate care by officials. In the Banks case, physical evidence and witnesses' reports were lost, neglected, or suppressed. If the new attorneys had not intervened on his behalf after the second trial, he would have been executed, and the error might never have come to light.

In considering the problem of executing innocent people, then, we are not dealing with a merely hypothetical problem. With the best will in the

---

[4]"The Death Penalty in Georgia: Still Arbitrary," *Washington University Law Quarterly* 62 (1985): 597–600.

world, our system will make mistakes. What Bentele's description of the Banks case and the Bedau–Radelet study clearly indicate is that we cannot count on the best will in the world being exercised by those involved in prosecuting and judging people accused of murder. This is a distressing but important fact about the criminal justice system.

A person can be wrongfully executed even if he or she actually did kill someone. As we have already seen, neither morality nor the law treats all killings as equally bad. In order to determine that a person has committed the type of killing for which the law sanctions execution, the crime must be distinguished from other killings that are not capital offenses. Finally, even after conviction for first degree murder, difficult issues concerning mitigating and aggravating circumstances must be considered. . . . [5]

[W]hen we are toting up the costs of the death penalty, we need to include not only the execution of those who were factually innocent of any crime whatever but also those cases in which the accused were guilty of a killing but nonetheless did not satisfy the legal criteria for execution. We need to recall as well the haziness of these criteria and the resulting fact that many who have been condemned to die would not strike most people as those who were most deserving of death.[6]   25

That wrongful executions of this sort occur is perhaps best revealed by the history of punishments for rape. While rape is a very serious crime, most people would not think that punishment by death is morally required for it. A similar judgment was reached by the Supreme Court in 1977. It ruled that execution is a disproportionately severe punishment for the crime of rape and thus constitutes a cruel and unusual punishment. Nonetheless, between 1930 and 1964, 455 people — 90 percent of whom were black — were executed for rape in the United States.[7]

Even in the case of killings, the facts are complicated, and leniency and severity in sentencing are the products of numerous factors, many of them irrelevant to the nature of the crime. There is no reason to believe that our system will cease to be arbitrary and discriminatory in these ways. Even a death penalty system that deterred murders and hence saved more lives than one that imposed imprisonment alone would continue to be flawed by uneven justice. As long as racial, class, religious, and economic bias continue to be important determinants of who is executed, the death penalty will both create and perpetuate injustice.

To recall an earlier example, imagine that one hundred executions per year save more lives than no executions at all. Imagine further that of all

[5]For a powerful and illuminating discussion of these issues, the reader is . . . referred to Charles Black, *Capital Punishment: The Inevitability of Caprice and Mistake*, 2nd ed. (New York: Norton, 1981).

[6]For some comparisons of cases, see U. Bentele, "The Death Penalty in Georgia: Still Arbitrary," *Washington University Law Quarterly* 62 (1985):585–91.

[7]H. Bedau, *The Death Penalty in America*, 3rd ed. (New York: Oxford University Press, 1982), Table 2–3–2.

those convicted of murder, the only ones who are executed have red hair. Consider how such people would regard the criminal justice system. Or, to bring home the point, imagine that instead of redheads, those executed are always members of some group (racial, ethnic, religious, or professional) to which *you* belong. Each of us would be deeply disturbed by such a pattern. We would feel strongly that members of our group were being treated unjustly, that our lives were not being treated as significant, that we alone were paying the price for added deterrence. Yet because of our increased exposure to executions, we would be gaining less from the decrease in homicide rates. Whatever the target group might be, this practice would be an expression of the strongest contempt and lack of regard for its members. The injustice would be obvious.

All of the defects of such an arbitrary system remain and continue to constitute a serious objection to the death penalty. Even if it were a more effective deterrent than imprisonment, an arbitrarily administered death penalty would be morally unjust, and it would be cruel and unusual in the sense affirmed by the Supreme Court in *Furman v. Georgia.*

Philosophers are especially fond of "what if?" questions. Such questions allow us to alter factual contingencies and are sometimes helpful in revealing the principles that underlie our judgments. So, let us ask, "What if the deterrent power of the death penalty were so great that it would be extremely difficult to deny its use?" 30

Suppose, for example, that every execution of a person for murder saved ten thousand lives. If that were the effect of the death penalty, it would be difficult for almost all of us to deny that it was justified, even if it possessed all the defects I have described. What does this show?

One might think that it shows that the death penalty is theoretically justifiable and hence that it offends no deep principles. If the world were a little different and the death penalty were more clearly a superior deterrent, then it would be morally permissible.

I think that this conclusion is mistaken. In this instance, the "what if?" question and the imaginary case of saving thousands by killing one are not helpful. They distort our thinking about the death penalty rather than helping to clarify it. We can see the distorting effects of the example by noting that we could construct a similar argument for the view that there is nothing deeply wrong with executing purely innocent people. Suppose that by executing a person who was totally innocent of any crime, we could get the same life-saving effects. Kill one innocent person — perhaps in a gruesome, torturous manner — and ten thousand others who would have been murder victims will be spared.

Even if we were to decide that executing an innocent person was the morally best thing to do *in this situation,* that would do nothing to show that knowingly executing innocent persons is not fundamentally wrong in our world. It would not show that if only things were a little different, executing innocent persons would be permissible. So, likewise, the fact that we can imagine the death penalty having extreme life-protecting powers does not show that it is not deeply defective in our world. It does not show that the only thing that matters is deterrence.

In this instance, stretching our imaginations may have the effect of 35 breaking down our ability to make a moral assessment. Our moral understanding breaks down here because we have a clash between the prohibition against performing a ghastly act, an act that is a paradigm of immorality, and the injunction that we perform an act that will result in the saving of many, many lives. Where the stakes are so high, the gains on one side so great, it may be that any moral rule or principle can be overwhelmed. Yet, this does nothing to show that in normal circumstances, we ought to treat these principles as if they had no moral importance.

Such examples are in the end totally irrelevant to our reflections about the death penalty.[8] In our world, the system of law and punishment does not operate in this way. No magical and extraordinary effects flow from the punishment of individual criminals. Rather, there are numerous actions that involve many different people, and it is the patterns formed by these actions that have overall social effects like the deterrence of homicide. It is the pattern of treatment of criminals that serves to deter. Likewise, it is the pattern of how we treat even those who violate the laws that reveals the extent to which concerns for justice and human dignity play a part in our lives.

It is highly unlikely that the death penalty will ever operate so effectively as to save many more lives than other, less severe punishments. Yet, given its defects, it would have to save many more lives in order for it to be a genuine candidate for moral legitimacy. If it had this positive effect, we would be faced with an anguished choice, just as we would be faced with an anguished choice if we found that executing innocent people saved many lives. Fortunately, all of this is merely hypothetical. We have no reason to believe that the death penalty does save more lives than other punishments, and so we need not actually confront this choice.

Topics for Critical Thinking and Writing

1. Nathanson believes (paras. 3–5) that some punishments are too "barbaric" to use even if they proved to be very effective deterrents. Later (para. 26) he cites the ruling of the Supreme Court in *Coker v. Georgia* (1977), holding that the death penalty for rape was a "cruel and unusual punishment" and therefore unconstitutional. Is this what Nathanson meant by a "barbaric" though effective punishment? Or did the Court really mean something else altogether? Go to your library and read the Court's reasoning in the *Coker* case, and write a 250-word essay on the topic.

---

[8]Charles Black argues against the relevance of several imaginary and hypothetical situations in *Capital Punishment: The Inevitability of Caprice and Mistake,* 2nd ed. (New York: Norton, 1981), 157–74.

2. Nathanson rejects "barbaric" punishments (paras. 3–5), but he does not object on this ground to life imprisonment. Yet why is this not barbaric, and no less barbaric than death? Or why is whipping (say, ten lashes) more barbaric, if it is, than a year in prison? If you were convicted of a serious crime, and could choose your sentence, which would you choose, prison or whipping? (Or, say, having your hand cut off instead of serving ten years in prison?) Defend your choice in an essay of 250 words.

3. In this century in the United States, executions have been carried out by firing squad, hanging, the electric chair, the gas chamber, and most recently by lethal injection. Which of these methods do you think is most humane, and why? The least humane? Write a 500-word essay explaining your views.

4. Suppose someone objected to Nathanson that he seems to expect the criminal justice system to be virtually infallible before he will allow any executions, whereas we know that no human institution is infallible. Certainly, parole boards are not, for they sometimes release convicted murderers who murder again. Nathanson's demands, therefore, are too strong. How might Nathanson reply?

5. Nathanson reflects on the problem of "moral arithmetic" (paras. 10–13) and concludes that he has "nothing very helpful to say" on it. But, surely, saving more lives rather than fewer is better. Consider the so-called trolley problem: You are at the control of a runaway streetcar, and all you can do is to throw the switch ahead. As you can see, if you go down the left track, you will surely hit and kill twenty innocent people, whereas if you go down the right track, you will hit and kill only one. You know nothing about any of these people, there is no way to warn them, etc. Surely, it is better to throw the switch so that you kill only the one, and not the twenty! Why might Nathanson argue that, true though this moral arithmetic is, it sheds little or no light on the trade-off between the murders prevented only by the death penalty (via deterrence of incapacitation, or both) and innocent persons executed?

Vivian Berger

Rolling the Dice to Decide Who Dies

Since 1984, when the Court of Appeals held unconstitutional the last vestige of the death penalty in New York State, New York has been one of fewer than a third of the states in this country that do not provide for capital punishment. In each of the past few years, however, our Legislature has passed bills reauthorizing death as the sanction for certain types of murder.

Vivian Berger (b. 1944), a professor of law at Columbia University in New York, is a founding member of the New York Lawyers against the Death Penalty. She wrote this article for the October 1988 issue of the New York State Bar Journal. *Footnotes, chiefly legal citations, have been omitted.*

Governor Cuomo, a committed opponent of capital punishment as was Governor Carey before him, has consistently vetoed these efforts. But sooner or later the governor will relinquish office. Surely, therefore, a time will come when the state acquires as chief executive someone who either supports execution or declines to counter the lawmakers' wishes. Then New Yorkers, acting through their elected officials, will have to regard the death penalty as more than a mere symbolic gesture — a banner to wave in the war against crime.

Because that point may be in the offing, the New York Bar, whose collective opinion should weigh heavily in the final decision whether we remain an abolitionist state, must begin to think seriously about the issues. I, like our governor, fervently oppose capital punishment; and I do so based on considerable experience with how it operates, not just with the rhetoric that surrounds it. I hope to persuade those of you who have no opinion on the subject and perhaps even some who currently favor reviving the death sentence in New York that such a course has nothing to commend it. To the contrary, reinstatement would amount to a giant step backward in this state's historical march toward a decent and efficient system of justice.

To plunge yourself right into the reality of capital punishment, imagine that you are sitting on a jury in Georgia or Florida or some other death-penalty state in the following cases. Your awesome task is to determine whether the defendant should receive life imprisonment or death. Even if you could in fact never sentence a person to die, you must try to envision that possibility — for the prosecution would have struck you for cause unless you had indicated on voir-dire that you would consider the option of death. Here are the five cases in cameo:

I. A 19-year-old man, John, and his companion stole a young woman's purse on the street, pushed her to the ground, and jumped into their nearby car. A taxi driver, observing the theft, sought to block their getaway with his cab. The defendant, John, shot and killed him. It was his first violent offense.

II. A 19-year-old man, Joe, tried to grab the purse of a 54-year-old 5 woman in a shopping center parking lot. She resisted and began screaming. They struggled for the purse and Joe shot her once in the side, killing her. He had prior misdemeanor convictions for shoplifting and simple battery as well as a felony conviction for theft.

III. A 21-year-old man, Robert, drove up to an all-night self-service station and filled his tank. He was paying for the gas with a "hot" credit card when the attendant, a college student, became suspicious that the card was stolen. Robert then shot the attendant once, killing him instantly, in order to avoid being arrested for the credit-card theft. Robert had previous convictions for an unarmed juvenile robbery and the burglary of a store.

IV. A 20-year-old man, Nickie, who was under the influence of drugs, broke into a neighbor's apartment and bludgeoned her and her 8-year-old daughter to death with a hammer. He said later that he had done it because he liked to see blood. Nickie had past convictions for robbery and attempted aggravated rape.

V. A 26-year-old man, Stephen, together with a 17-year-old friend, burglarized the home of an elderly widow for whom the friend had done yard work. They were planning to rob her. The woman ended by being raped, beaten, and strangled as well as robbed. The defendant, Stephen, admitted that the two of them had raped and robbed her. He insisted, however (and no witness supported or contradicted his story) that only the friend had killed the victim and that he, Stephen, had tried in vain to stop the murder. He had previously committed an unarmed "date rape."

Ask yourself which, if any, of these men you would have sentenced to life in prison and which to death. Next, try to guess how the actual jurors decided these cases. In fact, #1, John, the purse-snatcher who shot the cabbie, received life. #2, Joe, the other purse-snatcher who shot the 54-year-old woman, was sentenced to die. #3, Robert, the credit-card thief who shot the attendant at the gas service station, got death as well; he is one of my clients. #4, Nickie, the hammer-bludgeoner who liked to see blood, got life imprisonment. Finally, #5, Stephen, who robbed and raped and may (or may not) have strangled the widow, was sentenced to death; he is also my client.

Whether or not you called any of the cases correctly, you might want 10 to ask yourself: "Did the divergent results make sense?" If there was a pattern, I must say it eludes me. But for the moment, taking some liberties with the facts and treating my examples as hypothetical instead of the true accounts which they are, I want the reader to consider the possibility that jurors in a couple of the cases that ended in death might likelier have opted for life imprisonment if they had received some more information. For example, suppose the sentencing jurors had heard that Joe had been the incredibly abused child of a violent alcoholic father and a battered, helpless, incompetent mother? That the father had made a game of placing Joe and his siblings in a tight circle and throwing heavy objects like glass ashtrays into the air for the pleasure of seeing who would be hit? That Joe had at last run away from home at the age of twelve, camped for some months in a Dempsey dumpster, and then been taken in by a man who sheltered him in return for homosexual favors? That during his one, too-brief experience in foster care when he was nine, Joe responded with great affection and excellent behavior to the love and attention of his foster mother? Or, to take another example, suppose the jury had known that Stephen had an IQ in the high fifties or low sixties? That confronted once with a power mower that wasn't running, Stephen put water from a hose inside it because he had seen others fill the machine but never realized that not *any* type of liquid would do?

Of course, no one knows how real jurors would have reacted to the scenarios I described. But experts in capital defense work agree that no matter how appalling the crime, twelve not unduly sentimental jurors may well decide to spare a defendant when shown that he is a human being with some explanation if not excuse for his horrible acts. Yet while the jurors routinely hear the worst things about the defendant, including usually his criminal record, what is shocking is that in so many cases they hear *nothing* else about him that might be deemed relevant to sentence. (Why this occurs, and what it means for the operation of capital punishment, I will explore further shortly.) What they *do* necessarily learn is the race of both defendant and victim. If I had recounted some more examples of the type I asked you to judge as a juror and told you the race of the persons involved, or at least the victim's, you might have begun to detect a pattern that did not emerge from the *pertinent* data. To this topic, too, I will soon return. But what I hope I have done thus far is to give the reader a "slice of death." At the very least, by relating these sadly prosaic stories, I wanted to scotch the notion which so many people have that death is reserved for special cases: the serial killers, the depraved torturers, the Mafia hit men. In New York we deal with the Joes and Stephens each week by the hundreds.

A bit of history sheds some light on how Capital Punishment U.S.A. acquired its present salient features. The watershed came when the United States Supreme Court handed down the landmark *Furman v. Georgia* [decision] in 1972. *Furman* invalidated all existing death sentence statutes as violative of the Eighth Amendment's ban on cruel and unusual punishment and thus depopulated state death rows of their 629 occupants. Although there was no majority opinion and only Justices Brennan and Marshall would have held execution to be intrinsically cruel and unusual, Justice Stewart captured the essence of the centrist justices' view — that the death penalty *as actually applied* was unconstitutionally arbitrary — in his famous analogy between the imposition of a capital sentence and the freakishness of a strike of lightning. Being "struck" by a capital sentence was cruel and unusual in the same way as being hit by a lightning bolt: The event was utterly capricious and random.

But worse, if possible, than death sentences that are entirely arbitrary in the sense that a strike of lightning is freakish are those imposed on invidious grounds: where the lightning rod is race, religion, gender, or class. As Justice Douglas trenchantly remarked: "The Leopolds and Loebs are given prison terms, not sentenced to death." Blacks, however, were disproportionately sentenced to die, especially for the rape of white females. Indeed, the abolitionist campaign, which culminated in the *Furman* decision, had its genesis in the effort to eliminate capital punishment for rape. So perhaps, historically, the death penalty was really less "unusual" than "cruel": An invisible hand, and clearly a white one, was sorting out whites from blacks and thereby creating a pattern of results that many decent people abhorred.

Probably the justices hoped and believed that after *Furman* the death penalty in the United States would remain dead; if so, they were wrong.

Many legislatures simply determined to try until they got it right. And in 1976, in *Gregg v. Georgia* and its four companion cases, a majority of the Court upheld the post-*Furman* capital punishment statutes of Georgia, Florida, and Texas against a challenge to their facial validity, while simultaneously nullifying the revised laws of two other states. Those states had sought to resolve the randomness problem identified in *Furman* by ensuring that lightning would strike *all* persons convicted of murder in the first degree, rather than just a hapless few. In rejecting this tack, the Court noted that mandatory death sentence laws did not really resolve the problem but instead "simply papered [it] over" since juries responded by refusing to convict certain arbitrarily chosen defendants of first-degree murder.

More importantly, though, the justices ratified the so-called guided 15 discretion statutes at issue in three of the five cases. The Court specifically approved some features of the new statutes which it expected would reduce the capriciousness of capital punishment and at the same time further the goal of individualization in sentencing. Thus, to take Georgia's law as a sample, the *Gregg* majority endorsed its provision for separate trials on guilt and penalty and automatic appellate review of sentences of death. The bifurcated trial innovation permitted the admission of evidence relevant only to sentence (for instance, the defendant's prior convictions) in a way that would not prejudice the jury in deciding guilt or innocence. The Court also emphasized that, at the penalty trial, not only did the state have to prove some aggravating circumstances beyond the fact of the murder itself (for example, torture or a previous record of criminal violence) but also defendants had the opportunity to offer evidence in mitigation — brave-conduct medals, or thrown ashtrays and waterlogged mowers.

It is basically under these post-*Gregg* schemes that Capital Punishment U.S.A. has been operating for over a decade. Until recently, however, only a handful of executions occurred every year. But in the mid-1980s, in the wake of four adverse Supreme Court decisions — after a period in which the Court had overturned the capital sentence in fourteen out of fifteen cases, the engine of death acquired new steam. In 1984 alone, there were twenty-one executions (almost twice as many as in all of the years following *Gregg*); 1985 and 1986 saw eighteen apiece, and the body count continues to grow. Thus, *Furman II* is hardly on the horizon now. That being so, if our next governor permits the enactment of capital statutes, the Court will surely not "veto" them: Members of the Bar should understand that New York will have not dead-letter laws but dying defendants.

Why should New Yorkers oppose this result? Some believe that capital punishment inherently violates human dignity. But because many disagree with that view and my expertise is only lawyering, not moral philosophy, I leave it to others to debate the ultimate ethical issues. I take my stand with an eminent colleague, Professor Charles L. Black, Jr. Like me, refusing to resolve the basic clash of values, he reminds us wisely that there is "no abstract capital punishment." Asked how he would feel about the death penalty if only its administration were perfected, the professor replies:

"What would you do if an amoeba were taught to play the piano?" In other words, it's a silly question; capital punishment *is* as it *does.* Therefore, the often high-flown rhetoric bandied about by the pros and antis assumes, in my view, second place to the homely facts that make the American "legal system not good enough to choose people to die." I end with a few of the reasons why, which I hope that those who support or are open to reviving the death sentence in New York take deeply to heart.

Consider, first, the arbitrariness of the death penalty—how, in the real world, capital punishment must be forever married to caprice. From the initial decision to charge through the determination of sentence, the criminal justice system in general is rife with unreviewable discretion. The capital setting provides all of the same opportunities (and several more) for virtually unconstrained choice: The players roll the dice in a game where the stakes consist of life or death. Nonexhaustively, the prosecutor must decide such things as whether to charge capital murder instead of a lesser degree of homicide; whether to plea bargain with the accused or, in a mul- tidefendant case, whether to grant one of the defendants immunity or some other concession in return for cooperating with the state; and whether, if the defendant is convicted of a potentially capital charge, to move the case to the penalty phase and attempt to obtain a verdict of death. Many of those choices and especially the likelihood of plea bargain- ing will be dramatically affected by factors that have little or nothing to do with the nature of the crime or the strength of the evidence. These factors include geography (district attorneys have different policies on capital pun- ishment, not to speak of varying amounts of dollars to spend on costly capi- tal litigation); political concerns like the proximity of an election; the per- ceived acumen and aggressiveness of defense counsel; and the desires of the victim's family.

Other players than the prosecutor occupy key roles, too, of course. These include the judge and jury and, depending on local practice, the governor, administrative board, or both, who may be requested to grant clemency. Jurors, it is worth noting, not only possess the completely unre- viewable discretion to acquit or compromise on lesser charges; they are also asked, in penalty trials, to determine such intrinsically fuzzy questions as "Will the defendant kill again?" or "Was this murder especially heinous, atrocious, or cruel?" or "Do the aggravating circumstances outweigh the proof in mitigation?" The latter inquiry forces jurors to try to assess how, for instance, the fact that the murder occurred during the course of a rob- bery and was committed to eliminate a witness should be balanced against the facts that the defendant was high on crack, is a first offender, and has a wife and three children who love him. Could *you* meaningfully weigh such factors?

Consider, second, that these sources of arbitrariness are exacerbated   20 by extreme variations in the performance of defense counsel. Ineffective assistance of counsel completely permeates the penalty phase of capital tri- als in the post-*Gregg* era. With regard to cases like Stephen's and Joe's and the others with which I began this piece, I pointed out how often the jury hears nothing personal about the defendant even when substantial mitigating proof is readily available, yet I did not explain this phenomenon. The explanation is simply that many defense attorneys do little or nothing by way of investigation geared to sentencing issues and hence do not themselves learn what they should be spreading before the jury. Why do attorneys drop the ball at the penalty phase with such depressing regularity? Some lack the knowledge, experience, or will to assume the role demanded of them in the unique capital setting. Lawyers find it easier to hunt for what one whom I know called "eyeball witnesses" than to construct a psychodrama about a protagonist who is frequently hostile, uncommunicative, beset with mental or emotional problems, or all of the above—especially when to do so involves searching out potential witnesses (family, friends, neighbors, teachers) who, like the client, usually hail from a different racial or socioeconomic milieu from counsel. Others curtail their investigations on account of shockingly low compensation. Still others "throw in the towel" once the verdict of guilt is in. Whatever the causes of these derelictions, most or all can be expected both to cross jurisdictional lines and to continue into the future.

Consider, finally, the last but hardly the least point in my brief against the death penalty—racial discrimination in sentencing. In its modern guise, racial bias focuses primarily on the race of the *victim,* not the defendant. Sophisticated studies by social scientists have demonstrated that murderers of whites are much likelier to be sentenced to death than murderers of blacks. In Georgia, for instance, Professor David Baldus's prizewinning study revealed that, after one accounted for dozens of variables that might legitimately affect punishment, the killer of a white stood a *4.3 times* greater chance of receiving death than did a person who killed a black! The reason for these results is clear and as firmly rooted in our history as prejudice against the black defendant: White society places a premium upon white life. New Yorkers inclined to discount such division on grounds of race as a regional Southern phenomenon need only recall the tensions evoked by the Howard Beach and Goetz trials to see how very wrong they are. In any event, capital punishment only magnifies inequalities of race that persist in the criminal justice system and in American society generally.

Last term, the Supreme Court rejected a challenge, grounded on the damning Baldus statistics, to the death penalty as applied in Georgia. Assuming the validity of the study, the court nonetheless held 5–4 in *Mc-Cleskey v. Kemp* that unless a capital defendant could prove that some specific actor or actors purposely discriminated in his case, thereby causing his sentence of death, neither the Eight Amendment nor Equal Protection was offended. I hope, however, that New Yorkers will be offended by, and wary of, the prospect of even risking racially tainted sentencing where a person's life is at stake.

There is no good reason to take that risk. The death penalty has not been shown to deter murder. Administering it with even the minimum amount of decency will further increase the log jams in our crowded courts and will likely cost more in the end than the alternative of long-term imprisonment. At worst, some innocent men and women will be executed as time goes by. At best, the guilty we choose to kill will be morally indistinguishable from the rest whose lives we opt to spare. New York cannot — in any sense of the word — afford to resurrect such a bankrupt system. Thoughtful citizens should be proud that our last two governors have resisted the siren call of capital "justice." The Bar, therefore, should strongly support the principled and pragmatic stance of opposition to capital punishment.

Topics for Critical Thinking and Writing

1. Write a 100-word essay on the question whether a state governor should veto a death penalty law if he or she is personally opposed to capital punishment.

2. During the presidential campaign of 1988, the death penalty was frequently mentioned by then Vice President Bush, who was for it, and by his opponent, Governor Michael Dukakis of Massachusetts, who was against it. Do some research on the campaign and write a 100-word essay on the question whether the pro–capital punishment position of the Republicans was largely what Berger calls "a mere symbolic gesture" (para. 1).

3. Relying only on the information Berger gives in paragraphs 4–8 about those five cases, decide how you would sentence each defendant; then compare your results with those that actually occurred (para. 9). Write a 500-word essay defending your proposed sentences whether or not they agree with those the juries actually handed down.

4. Take into account the additional information Berger supplies in paragraph 10 about the five cases she discusses, and write a 250-word essay explaining why this additional evidence would or would not cause you to change your proposed sentences.

5. Defenders of the death penalty often arouse support for capital punishment by describing murderers as "savage beasts" or as "hopeless recidivists" and the like, whereas Berger (para. 11) arouses opposition to it by telling the reader "sadly prosaic stories" about "the Joes and the Stephens." To what extent do you think such techniques shed light on the morality of the death penalty? On the appropriate legal punishment for the crime of murder?

6. Berger quotes (para. 13) Justice Douglas's reference to Leopold and Loeb. Who were they, and why are their cases relevant to the death penalty controversy? Do some library research to find out, and write a 500-word essay on the lessons of the Leopold and Loeb case. (*Hint:* The case occurred in Chicago in the 1920s, and involved the famous defense attorney, Clarence Darrow.)

7. In response to Berger's point about the "arbitrariness" of the death penalty system (paras. 18–19), a death penalty advocate might reply: Since all murderers really deserve to die anyway, why make so much out of the arbitrary way in

which only some are actually sentenced to death and executed? What's so unfair about the good luck of all those who aren't executed even though they deserve to die? How might Berger reply?

8. In response to Berger's point about the "racial discrimination" in sentencing (para. 21), a defender of the death penalty might object: The solution to the problem of racial discrimination in death sentencing is not abolishing the death penalty; it is sentencing and executing more whites who kill blacks and more blacks who kill blacks. How might Berger reply?

10

Drugs: Should Their Sale and Use Be Legalized?

William J. Bennett

Drug Policy and the Intellectuals

. . . The issue I want to address is our national drug policy and the intellectuals. Unfortunately, the issue is a little one-sided. There is a very great deal to say about our national drug policy, but much less to say about the intellectuals — except that by and large, they're against it. Why they should be against it is an interesting question, perhaps more a social-psychological question than a properly intellectual one. But whatever the reasons, I'm sorry to say that on properly intellectual grounds the arguments mustered against our current drug policy by America's intellectuals make for very thin gruel indeed.

I should point out, however, that in the fields of medical and scientific research, there is indeed serious and valuable drug-related work going on. But in the great public policy debate over drugs, the academic and intellectual communities have by and large had little to contribute, and little of that has been genuinely useful or for that matter mentally distinguished.

The field of national drug policy is wide open for serious research and serious thinking on both the theoretical and the practical levels; treatment

---

William Bennett, born in Brooklyn in 1943, was educated at Williams College, the University of Texas, and Harvard Law School. Today he is most widely known as the author of an immensely popular book, The Book of Virtues: A Treasury of Great Moral Stories, *but he has also been a public servant, Secretary of Education, and a director of the National Drug Control Policy. In 1989, during his tenure as "drug czar," he delivered at Harvard the address that we reprint.*

and prevention; education; law enforcement and the criminal-justice system; the proper role of the federal government versus state and local jurisdictions; international diplomacy and foreign intelligence — these are only a few of the areas in which complex questions of policy and politics need to be addressed and resolved if our national drug strategy is to be successful. But apart from a handful of exceptions — including Mark Moore and Mark Kleiman here at the Kennedy School, and Harvard's own, or ex-own, James Q. Wilson — on most of these issues the country's major ideas factories have not just shut down, they've hardly even tooled up.

It's not that most intellectuals are indifferent to the drug issue, though there may be some of that, too. Rather, they seem complacent and incurious. They've made up their minds, and they don't want to be bothered with further information or analysis, further discussion or debate, especially when it comes from Washington. What I read in the opinion columns of my newspaper or in my monthly magazine or what I hear from the resident intellectual on my favorite television talk show is something like a developing intellectual consensus on the drug question. That consensus holds one or both of these propositions to be self-evident: (a) *that the drug problem in America is absurdly simple, and easily solved;* and (b) *that the drug problem in America is a lost cause.*

As it happens, each of these apparently contradictory propositions is 5 false. As it also happens, both are disputed by the *real* experts on drugs in the United States — and there are many such experts, though not the kind the media like to focus on. And both are disbelieved by the American people, whose experience tells them, emphatically, otherwise.

The consensus has a political dimension, which helps account for its seemingly divergent aspect. In some quarters of the far Right there is a tendency to assert that the drug problem is essentially a problem of the inner city, and therefore that what it calls for, essentially, is quarantine. "If those people want to kill themselves off with drugs, let them kill themselves off with drugs," would be a crude but not too inaccurate way of summarizing this position. But this position has relatively few adherents. On the Left, it is something else, something much more prevalent. There we see whole cadres of social scientists, abetted by whole armies of social workers, who seem to take it as catechism that the problem facing us isn't drugs at all, it's poverty, or racism, or some other equally large and intractable social phenomenon. If we want to eliminate the drug problem, these people say, we must first eliminate the "root causes" of drugs, a hopelessly daunting task at which, however, they also happen to make their living. Twenty-five years ago, no one would have suggested that we must first address the root causes of racism before fighting segregation. We fought it, quite correctly, by passing laws against unacceptable conduct. The causes of racism was an interesting question, but the moral imperative was to end it as soon as possible and by all reasonable means: education, prevention, the media and not least of all, the law. So too with drugs.

What unites these two views of the drug problem from opposite sides of the political spectrum is that they issue, inevitably, in a policy of neglect. To me that is a scandalous position, intellectually as well as morally scandalous. For I believe, along with those I have named as the real experts on drugs, and along with most Americans, that the drug problem is not easy but difficult—very difficult in some respects. But at the same time, and again along with those same experts and with the American people, I believe it is not a lost cause but a solvable one. I will return to this theme, but let me pause here to note one specific issue on which the Left/Right consensus has lately come to rest; a position around which it has been attempting to build national sentiment. That position is legalization.

It is indeed bizarre to see the likes of Anthony Lewis and William F. Buckley lining up on the same side of an issue; but such is the perversity that the so-called legalization debate engenders. To call it a "debate," though, suggests that the arguments in *favor* of drug legalization are rigorous, substantial, and serious. They are not. They are, at bottom, a series of superficial and even disingenuous ideas that more sober minds recognize as a recipe for a public policy disaster. Let me explain.

Most conversations about legalization begin with the notion of "taking the profit out of the drug business." But has anyone bothered to examine carefully how the drug business works? As a recent *New York Times* article vividly described, instances of drug dealers actually earning huge sums of money are relatively rare. There are some who do, of course, but most people in the crack business are the low-level "runners" who do not make much money at all. Many of them work as prostitutes or small-time criminals to supplement their drug earnings. True, a lot of naive kids are lured into the drug world by visions of a life filled with big money and fast cars. That's what they think the good life holds for them. But the reality is far different. Many dealers, in the long run, wind up smoking more crack than they sell. Their business becomes a form of slavery: long hours, dangerous work, small pay, and, as the *Times* pointed out, no health benefits either. In many cases, steady work at McDonald's over time would in fact be a step *up* the income scale for these kids. What does straighten them out, it seems, is not a higher minimum wage, or less stringent laws, but the dawning realization that dealing drugs invariably leads to murder or to prison. And that's exactly why we have drug laws—to make drug use a wholly unattractive choice.

Legalization, on the other hand, removes that incentive to stay away 10 from a life of drugs. Let's be honest—there are some people who are going to smoke crack whether it is legal or illegal. But by keeping it illegal, we maintain the criminal sanctions that persuade most people that the good life cannot be reached by dealing drugs.

The big lie behind every call for legalization is that making drugs legally available would "solve" the drug problem. But has anyone actually thought about what that kind of legalized regime would look like? Would crack be legal? How about PCP? Or smokable heroin? Or ice? Would they all be stocked at the local convenience store, perhaps just a few blocks from an elementary school? And how much would they cost? If we taxed drugs and made them expensive, we would still have the black market and crime problems that we have today; if we sold them cheap to eliminate the black market cocaine at, say, $10 a gram — then we would succeed in making a daily dose of cocaine well within the allowance budget of most sixth-graders. When pressed, the advocates of legalization like to sound courageous by proposing that we begin by legalizing marijuana. But they have absolutely nothing to say on the tough questions of controlling other, more powerful drugs, and how they would be regulated.

As far as marijuana is concerned, let me say this: I didn't have to become drug czar to be opposed to legalized marijuana. As Secretary of Education I realized that, given the state of American education, the last thing we needed was a policy that made widely available a substance that impairs memory, concentration, and attention span; why in God's name foster the use of a drug that makes you stupid?

Now what would happen if drugs were suddenly made legal? Legalization advocates deny that the amount of drug use would be affected. I would argue that if drugs are easier to obtain, drug use will soar. In fact, we have just undergone a kind of cruel national experiment in which drugs became cheap and widely available: That experiment is called the crack epidemic. When powder cocaine was expensive and hard to get, it was found almost exclusively in the circles of the rich, the famous, or the privileged. Only when cocaine was dumped into the country, and a $3 vial of crack could be bought on street corners did we see cocaine use skyrocket, this time largely among the poor and disadvantaged. The lesson is clear: If you're in favor of drugs being sold in stores like aspirin, you're in favor of boom times for drug users and drug addicts. With legalization, drug use will go up, way up.

When drug use rises, who benefits and who pays? Legalization advocates think that the cost of enforcing drug laws is too great. But the real question — the question they never ask — is what does it cost not to enforce those laws. The price that American society would have to pay for legalized drugs, I submit, would be intolerably high. We would have more drug-related accidents at work, on the highways, and in the airways. We would have even bigger losses in worker productivity. Our hospitals would be filled with drug emergencies. We would have more school kids on dope, and that means more dropouts. More pregnant women would buy legal cocaine, and then deliver tiny, premature infants. I've seen them in hospitals across the country. It's a horrid form of child abuse, and under a legalization scheme, we will have a lot more of it. For those women and those babies, crack has the same effect whether it's legal or not. Now, if you add to that the costs of treatment, social welfare, and insurance, you've got the price of legalization. So I ask you again, who benefits, who pays?

What about crime? To listen to legalization advocates, one might think 15 that street crime would disappear with the repeal of our drug laws. They haven't done their homework. Our best research indicates that most drug criminals were into crime well before they got into drugs. Making drugs legal would just be a way of subsidizing their habit. They would continue to rob and steal to pay for food, for clothes, for entertainment. And they would carry on with their drug trafficking by undercutting the legalized price of drugs and catering to teenagers, who, I assume, would be nominally restricted from buying drugs at the corner store.

All this should be old news to people who understand one clear lesson of prohibition. When we had laws against alcohol, there was less consumption of alcohol, less alcohol-related disease, fewer drunken brawls, and a lot less public drunkenness. And contrary to myth, there is no evidence that Prohibition caused big increases in crime. No one is suggesting that we go back to Prohibition. But at least we should admit that legalized alcohol, which is responsible for some 100,000 deaths a year, is hardly a model for drug policy. As Charles Krauthammer has pointed out, the question is not which is worse, alcohol or drugs. The question is can we accept both legalized alcohol *and* legalized drugs? The answer is no.

So it seems to me that on the merits of their arguments, the legalizers have no case at all. But there is another, crucial point I want to make on this subject, unrelated to costs or benefits. Drug use—especially heavy drug use—destroys human character. It destroys dignity and autonomy, it burns away the sense of responsibility, it subverts productivity, it makes a mockery of virtue. As our Founders would surely recognize, a citizenry that is perpetually in a drug-induced haze doesn't bode well for the future of self-government. Libertarians don't like to hear this, but it is a truth that everyone knows who has seen drug addiction up close. And don't listen to people who say drug users are only hurting themselves: They hurt parents, they destroy families, they ruin friendships. And let me remind this audience, here at a great university, that drugs are a threat to the life of the mind; anyone who values that life should have nothing but contempt for drugs. Learned institutions should regard drugs as the plague.

That's why I find the surrender of many of America's intellectuals to arguments for drug legalization so odd and so scandalous. For the past three months, I have been traveling the country, visiting drug-ridden neighborhoods, seeing treatment and prevention programs in action, talking to teachers, cops, parents, kids. These, it seems, are the real drug experts—they've witnessed the problem firsthand. But unlike some prominent residents of Princeton, Madison, Cambridge, or Palo Alto, they refuse to surrender. They are in the community, reclaiming their neighborhoods, working with police, setting up community activities, getting addicts into treatment, saving their children.

Too many American intellectuals don't know about this and seem not to want to know. Their hostility to the national war on drugs is, I think, partly rooted in a general hostility to law enforcement and criminal justice. That's why they take refuge in pseudosolutions like legalization, which stress only the treatment side of the problem. Whenever discussion turns to the need for more police and stronger penalties, they cry that our constitutional liberties are in jeopardy. Well, yes, they are in jeopardy, but not from drug *policy.* On this score, the guardians of our Constitution can sleep easy. Constitutional liberties are in jeopardy, instead, from drugs themselves, which every day scorch the earth of our common freedom. Yes, sometimes cops go too far, and when they do they should be held accountable. But these excursions from the law are the exception. Meanwhile drug dealers violate our rights everyday as a rule, as a norm, as their modus operandi. Why can't our civil libertarians see that?

When we are not being told by critics that law enforcement threatens 20 our liberties, we are being told that it won't work. Let me tell you that law enforcement does work and why it must work. Several weeks ago I was in Wichita, Kansas, talking to a teenage boy who was now in his fourth treatment program. Every time he had finished a previous round of treatment, he found himself back on the streets, surrounded by the same cheap dope and tough hustlers who had gotten him started in the first place. He was tempted, he was pressured, and he gave in. Virtually any expert on drug treatment will tell you that, for most people, no therapy in the world can fight temptation on that scale. As long as drugs are found on any street corner, no amount of treatment, no amount of education can finally stand against them. Yes, we need drug treatment and drug education. But drug treatment and drug education need law enforcement. And that's why our strategy calls for a bigger criminal justice system: as a form of drug *prevention.*

To the Americans who are waging the drug war in their own front yards every day, this is nothing new, nothing startling. In the San Jose section of Albuquerque, New Mexico, just two weeks ago, I spoke to Rudy Chavez and Jack Candelarla, and police chief Sam Baca. They had wanted to start a youth center that would keep their kids safe from the depredations of the street. Somehow it never worked — until together they set up a police station right in the heart of drug-dealing territory. Then it worked. Together with the cops, the law-abiding residents cleared the area, and made it safe for them and their children to walk outside their homes. The youth center began to thrive.

Scenes like this are being played out all across the country. I've seen them in Tulsa, Dallas, Tampa, Omaha, Des Moines, Seattle, New York. Americans — many of them poor, black, or Hispanic — have figured out what the armchair critics haven't. Drugs may threaten to destroy their neighborhoods, but *they* refuse to stand by and let it happen. *They* have discovered that it is possible not only to fight back, but to win. In some elite circles, the talk may be only of the sad state of the helpless and the hopeless, but while these circles talk on, the helpless and the hopeless themselves are carrying out a national drug policy. They are fighting back.

When I think of these scenes I'm reminded of what John Jacob, president of the Urban League, said recently: Drugs are destroying more black families than poverty ever did. And I'm thankful that many of these poor families have the courage to fight drugs now, rather than declaring themselves passive victims of root causes.

America's intellectuals—and here I think particularly of liberal intellectuals—have spent much of the last nine years decrying the social programs of two Republican administrations in the name of the defenseless poor. But today, on the one outstanding issue that disproportionately hurts the poor—that is wiping out many of the poor—where are the liberal intellectuals to be found? They are on the editorial and op-ed pages, and in magazines like this month's *Harper's*, telling us with an ignorant sneer that our drug policy won't work. Many universities, too, which have been quick to take on the challenges of sexism, racism, and ethnocentrism, seem content on the drug issue to wag a finger at us, or to point it mindlessly at American society in general. In public policy schools, there is no shortage of arms control scholars. Isn't it time we had more drug control scholars?

The current situation won't do. The failure to get serious about the 25 drug issue is, I think, a failure of civic courage—the kind of courage shown by many who have been among the main victims of the drug scourge. But it betokens as well a betrayal of the self-declared mission of intellectuals as the bearers of society's conscience. There may be reasons for this reluctance, this hostility, this failure. But I would remind you that not all crusades led by the U.S. government, enjoying broad popular support, are brutish, corrupt, and sinister. What is brutish, corrupt, and sinister is the murder and mayhem being committed in our cities' streets. One would think that a little more concern and serious thought would come from those who claim to care so deeply about America's problems.

So I stand here this afternoon with a simple message for America's pundits and academic cynics: Get serious about drug policy. We are grappling with complicated, stubborn policy issues, and I encourage you to join us. Tough work lies ahead, and we need serious minds to focus on how we should use the tools that we have in the most effective way.

I came to this job with realistic expectations. I am not promising a drug-free America by next week, or even by next year. But that doesn't mean that success is out of reach. Success will come—I've seen a lot of it already—in slow, careful steps. Its enemies are timidity, petulance, false expectations. But its three greatest foes remain surrender, despair, and neglect. So, for the sake of their fellow citizens, I invite America's deep thinkers to get with the program, or at the very least, to get in the game.

Topics for Critical Thinking and Writing

1. In paragraph 6, Bennett draws a parallel between racism and drug abuse, and suggests that society ought to fight the one (drug abuse) as it successfully fought the other (racism). What do you think of this parallel? Explain.

2. Bennett identifies two propositions on the issue of drug abuse that he believes are accepted by "consensus" thinking in America (para. 4). What are these propositions and what is Bennett's view of them? How does he try to convince the reader to agree with him?

3. What are Bennett's main objections to solving the problem of drug abuse by legalizing drugs?

4. At the time he gave this lecture, Bennett was a confirmed cigarette smoker trying to break the habit. Do you see any inconsistency in his opposing legalized marijuana and tolerating (and even using) legalized tobacco?

5. What measures besides stricter law enforcement does Bennett propose for wide-scale adoption, in the belief they will reduce drug abuse? Why does he object to relying only on such measures?

James Q. Wilson

Against the Legalization of Drugs

In 1972, the president appointed me chairman of the National Advisory Council for Drug Abuse Prevention. Created by Congress, the Council was charged with providing guidance on how best to coordinate the national war on drugs. (Yes, we called it a war then, too.) In those days, the drug we were chiefly concerned with was heroin. When I took office, heroin use had been increasing dramatically. Everybody was worried that this increase would continue. Such phrases as "heroin epidemic" were commonplace.

That same year, the eminent economist Milton Friedman published an essay in *Newsweek* in which he called for legalizing heroin. His argument was on two grounds: As a matter of ethics, the government has no right to tell people not to use heroin (or to drink or to commit suicide); as a matter of economics, the prohibition of drug use imposes costs on society that far exceed the benefits. Others, such as the psychoanalyst Thomas Szasz, made the same argument.

We did not take Friedman's advice. (Government commissions rarely do.) I do not recall that we even discussed legalizing heroin, though we did discuss (but did not take action on) legalizing a drug, cocaine, that many people then argued was benign. Our marching orders were to figure out how to win the war on heroin, not to run up the white flag of surrender.

That was 1972. Today, we have the same number of heroin addicts that we had then — half a million, give or take a few thousand. Having that many heroin addicts is no trivial matter; these people deserve our attention. But not having had an increase in that number for over fifteen years is

---

James Q. Wilson is Collins Professor of Management and Public Policy at the University of California, Los Angeles. He is the author of Thinking about Crime *(1975) and* Bureaucracy *(1989), and the coauthor of* Crime and Human Nature *(1985). The essay that we reprint appeared originally in February 1990 in* Commentary, *a conservative magazine.*

also something that deserves our attention. What happened to the "heroin epidemic" that many people once thought would overwhelm us?

The facts are clear: A more or less stable pool of heroin addicts has been getting older, with relatively few new recruits. In 1976 the average age of heroin users who appeared in hospital emergency rooms was about twenty-seven; ten years later it was thirty-two. More than two-thirds of all heroin users appearing in emergency rooms are now over the age of thirty. Back in the early 1970s, when heroin got onto the national political agenda, the typical heroin addict was much younger, often a teenager. Household surveys show the same thing—the rate of opiate use (which includes heroin) has been flat for the better part of two decades. More fine-grained studies of inner-city neighborhoods confirm this. John Boyle and Ann Brunswick found that the percentage of young blacks in Harlem who use heroin fell from 8 percent in 1970–71 to about 3 percent in 1975–76.

Why did heroin lose its appeal for young people? When the young blacks in Harlem were asked why they stopped, more than half mentioned "trouble with the law" or "high cost" (and high cost is, of course, directly the result of law enforcement). Two-thirds said that heroin hurt their health; nearly all said they had had a bad experience with it. We need not rely, however, simply on what they said. In New York City in 1973–75, the street price of heroin rose dramatically and its purity sharply declined, probably as a result of the heroin shortage caused by the success of the Turkish government in reducing the supply of opium base and of the French government in closing down heroin-processing laboratories located in and around Marseilles. These were short-lived gains for, just as Friedman predicted, alternative sources of supply—mostly in Mexico—quickly emerged. But the three-year heroin shortage interrupted the easy recruitment of new users.

Health and related problems were no doubt part of the reason for the reduced flow of recruits. Over the preceding years, Harlem youth had watched as more and more heroin users died of overdoses, were poisoned by adulterated doses, or acquired hepatitis from dirty needles. The word got around: Heroin can kill you. By 1974 new hepatitis cases and drug-overdose deaths had dropped to a fraction of what they had been in 1970.

Alas, treatment did not seem to explain much of the cessation in drug use. Treatment programs can and do help heroin addicts, but treatment did not explain the drop in the number of *new* users (who by definition had never been in treatment) nor even much of the reduction in the number of experienced users.

No one knows how much of the decline to attribute to personal observation as opposed to high prices or reduced supply. But other evidence suggests strongly that price and supply played a large role. In 1972 the National Advisory Council was especially worried by the prospect that U.S. servicemen returning to this country from Vietnam would bring their heroin habits with them. Fortunately, a brilliant study by Lee Robins of Washington University in St. Louis put that fear to rest. She measured drug use of Vietnam veterans shortly after they had returned home. Though many had used heroin regularly while in Southeast Asia, most gave up the habit when back in the United States. The reason: Here, heroin was less available and sanctions on its use were more pronounced. Of course, if a veteran had been willing to pay enough—which might have meant traveling to another city and would certainly have meant making an illegal contact with a disreputable dealer in a threatening neighborhood in order to acquire a (possibly) dangerous dose—he could have sustained his drug habit. Most veterans were unwilling to pay this price, and so their drug use declined or disappeared.

RELIVING THE PAST

Suppose we had taken Friedman's advice in 1972. What would have 10 happened? We cannot be entirely certain, but at a minimum we would have placed the young heroin addicts (and, above all, the prospective addicts) in a very different position from the one in which they actually found themselves. Heroin would have been legal. Its price would have been reduced by 95 percent (minus whatever we chose to recover in taxes). Now that it could be sold by the same people who make aspirin, its quality would have been assured—no poisons, no adulterants. Sterile hypodermic needles would have been readily available at the neighborhood drugstore, probably at the same counter where the heroin was sold. No need to travel to big cities or unfamiliar neighborhoods—heroin could have been purchased anywhere, perhaps by mail order.

There would no longer have been any financial or medical reason to avoid heroin use. Anybody could have afforded it. We might have tried to prevent children from buying it, but as we have learned from our efforts to prevent minors from buying alcohol and tobacco, young people have a way of penetrating markets theoretically reserved for adults. Returning Vietnam veterans would have discovered that Omaha and Raleigh had been converted into the pharmaceutical equivalent of Saigon.

Under these circumstances, can we doubt for a moment that heroin use would have grown exponentially? Or that a vastly larger supply of new users would have been recruited? Professor Friedman is a Nobel Prize–winning economist whose understanding of market forces is profound. What did he think would happen to consumption under his legalized regime? Here are his words: "Legalizing drugs might increase the number of addicts, but it is not clear that it would. Forbidden fruit is attractive, particularly to the young."

Really? I suppose that we should expect no increase in Porsche sales if we cut the price by 95 percent, no increase in whiskey sales if we cut the price by a comparable amount—because young people only want fast cars and strong liquor when they are "forbidden." Perhaps Friedman's uncharacteristic lapse from the obvious implications of price theory can be explained by a misunderstanding of how drug users are recruited. In his 1972 essay he said that "drug addicts are deliberately made by pushers, who give likely prospects their first few doses free." If drugs were legal it would not pay anybody to produce addicts, because everybody would buy from the cheapest source. But as every drug expert knows, pushers do not produce addicts. Friends or acquaintances do. In fact, pushers are usually reluctant to deal with nonusers because a nonuser could be an undercover cop. Drug use spreads in the same way any fad or fashion spreads: Somebody who is already a user urges his friends to try, or simply shows already-eager friends how to do it.

But we need not rely on speculation, however plausible, that lowered prices and more abundant supplies would have increased heroin usage. Great Britain once followed such a policy and with almost exactly those results. Until the mid-1960s, British physicians were allowed to prescribe heroin to certain classes of addicts. (Possessing these drugs without a doctor's prescription remained a criminal offense.) For many years this policy worked well enough because the addict patients were typically middle-class people who had become dependent on opiate painkillers while undergoing hospital treatment. There was no drug culture. The British system worked for many years, not because it prevented drug abuse but because there was no problem of drug abuse that would test the system.

All that changed in the 1960s. A few unscrupulous doctors began passing out heroin in wholesale amounts. One doctor prescribed almost six hundred thousand heroin tablets—that is, over thirteen pounds—in just one year. A youthful drug culture emerged with a demand for drugs far different from that of the older addicts. As a result, the British government required doctors to refer users to government-run clinics to receive their heroin.

But the shift to clinics did not curtail the growth in heroin use. Throughout the 1960s the number of addicts increased—the late John Kaplan of Stanford estimated by fivefold—in part as a result of the diversion of heroin from clinic patients to new users on the streets. An addict would bargain with the clinic doctor over how big a dose he would receive. The patient wanted as much as he could get, the doctor wanted to give as little as was needed. The patient had an advantage in this conflict because the doctor could not be certain how much was really needed. Many patients would use some of their "maintenance" dose and sell the remaining part to friends, thereby recruiting new addicts. As the clinics learned of this, they began to shift their treatment away from heroin and toward methadone, an addictive drug that, when taken orally, does not produce a "high" but will block the withdrawal pains associated with heroin abstinence.

Whether what happened in England in the 1960s was a miniepidemic or an epidemic depends on whether one looks at numbers or at rates of change. Compared to the United States, the numbers were small. In 1960 there were sixty-eight heroin addicts known to the British government; by 1968 there were two thousand in treatment and many more who refused treatment. (They would refuse in part because they did not want to get methadone at a clinic if they could get heroin on the street.) Richard Hartnoll estimates that the actual number of addicts in England is five times the number officially registered. At a minimum, the number of British addicts increased by thirtyfold in ten years; the actual increase may have been much larger.

In the early 1980s the numbers began to rise again, and this time nobody doubted that a real epidemic was at hand. The increase was estimated to be 40 percent a year. By 1982 there were thought to be twenty thousand heroin users in London alone. Geoffrey Pearson reports that many cities— Glasgow, Liverpool, Manchester, and Sheffield among them—were now experiencing a drug problem that once had been largely confined to London. The problem, again, was supply. The country was being flooded with cheap, high-quality heroin, first from Iran and then from Southeast Asia.

The United States began the 1960s with a much larger number of heroin addicts and probably a bigger at-risk population than was the case in Great Britain. Even though it would be foolhardy to suppose that the British system, if installed here, would have worked the same way or with the same results, it would be equally foolhardy to suppose that a combination of heroin available from leaky clinics and from street dealers who faced only minimal law-enforcement risks would not have produced a much greater increase in heroin use than we actually experienced. My guess is that if we had allowed either doctors or clinics to prescribe heroin, we would have had far worse results than were produced in Britain, if for no other reason than the vastly larger number of addicts with which we began. We would have had to find some way to police thousands (not scores) of physicians and hundreds (not dozens) of clinics. If the British civil service found it difficult to keep heroin in the hands of addicts and out of the hands of recruits when it was dealing with a few hundred people, how well would the American civil service have accomplished the same tasks when dealing with tens of thousands of people?

BACK TO THE FUTURE

Now cocaine, especially in its potent form, crack, is the focus of attention. Now as in 1972 the government is trying to reduce its use. Now as then some people are advocating legalization. Is there any more reason to yield to those arguments today than there was almost two decades ago?[1] 20

I think not. If we had yielded in 1972 we almost certainly would have had today a permanent population of several million, not several hundred thousand, heroin addicts. If we yield now we will have a far more serious problem with cocaine.

---

[1] I do not here take up the question of marijuana. For a variety of reasons—its widespread use and its lesser tendency to addict—it presents a different problem from cocaine or heroin. For a penetrating analysis, see Mark Kleiman, *Marijuana: Costs of Abuse, Costs of Control* (Greenwood Press, 217 pp.). [Wilson's note.]

Crack is worse than heroin by almost any measure. Heroin produces a pleasant drowsiness and, if hygienically administered, has only the physical side effects of constipation and sexual impotence. Regular heroin use incapacitates many users, especially poor ones, for any productive work or social responsibility. They will sit nodding on a street corner, helpless but at least harmless. By contrast, regular cocaine use leaves the user neither helpless nor harmless. When smoked (as with crack) or injected, cocaine produces instant, intense, and short-lived euphoria. The experience generates a powerful desire to repeat it. If the drug is readily available, repeat use will occur. Those people who progress to "bingeing" on cocaine become devoted to the drug and its effects to the exclusion of almost all other considerations—job, family, children, sleep, food, even sex. Dr. Frank Gawin at Yale and Dr. Everett Ellinwood at Duke report that a substantial percentage of all high-dose, binge users become uninhibited, impulsive, hypersexual, compulsive, irritable, and hyperactive. Their moods vacillate dramatically, leading at times to violence and homicide.

Women are much more likely to use crack than heroin, and if they are pregnant, the effects on their babies are tragic. Douglas Besharov, who has been following the effects of drugs on infants for twenty years, writes that nothing he learned about heroin prepared him for the devastation of cocaine. Cocaine harms the fetus and can lead to physical deformities or neurological damage. Some crack babies have for all practical purposes suffered a disabling stroke while still in the womb. The long-term consequences of this brain damage are lowered cognitive ability and the onset of mood disorders. Besharov estimates that about thirty thousand to fifty thousand such babies are born every year, about seven thousand in New York City alone. There may be ways to treat such infants, but from everything we now know the treatment will be long, difficult, and expensive. Worse, the mothers who are most likely to produce crack babies are precisely the ones who, because of poverty or temperament, are least able and willing to obtain such treatment. In fact, anecdotal evidence suggests the crack mothers are likely to abuse their infants.

The notion that abusing drugs such as cocaine is a "victimless crime" is not only absurd but dangerous. Even ignoring the fetal drug syndrome, crack-dependent people are, like heroin addicts, individuals who regularly victimize their children by neglect, their spouses by improvidence, their employers by lethargy, and their co-workers by carelessness. Society is not and could never be a collection of autonomous individuals. We all have a stake in ensuring that each of us displays a minimal level of dignity, responsibility, and empathy. We cannot, of course, coerce people into goodness, but we can and should insist that some standards must be met if society itself—on which the very existence of the human personality depends—is to persist. Drawing the line that defines those standards is difficult and contentious, but if crack and heroin use do not fall below it, what does?

The advocates of legalization will respond by suggesting that my pic- 25
ture is overdrawn. Ethan Nadelmann of Princeton argues that the risk of

legalization is less than most people suppose. Over twenty million Americans between the ages of eighteen and twenty-five have tried cocaine (according to a government survey), but only a quarter million use it daily. From this Nadelmann concludes that at most 3 percent of all young people who try cocaine develop a problem with it. The implication is clear: Make the drug legal and we only have to worry about 3 percent of our youth.

The implication rests on a logical fallacy and a factual error. The fallacy is this: The percentage of occasional cocaine users who become binge users *when the drug is illegal* (and thus expensive and hard to find) tells us nothing about the percentage who will become dependent when the drug is legal (and thus cheap and abundant). Drs. Gawin and Ellinwood report, in common with several other researchers, that controlled or occasional use of cocaine changes to compulsive and frequent use "when access to the drug increases" or when the user switches from snorting to smoking. More cocaine more potently administered alters, perhaps sharply, the proportion of "controlled" users who become heavy users.

The factual error is this: The federal survey Nadelmann quotes was done in 1985, *before* crack had become common. Thus the probability of becoming dependent on cocaine was derived from the responses of users who snorted the drug. The speed and potency of cocaine's action increases dramatically when it is smoked. We do not yet know how greatly the advent of crack increases the risk of dependency, but all the clinical evidence suggests that the increase is likely to be large.

It is possible that some people will not become heavy users even when the drug is readily available in its most potent form. So far there are no scientific grounds for predicting who will and who will not become dependent. Neither socioeconomic background nor personality traits differentiate between casual and intensive users. Thus, the only way to settle the question of who is correct about the effect of easy availability on drug use, Nadelmann or Gawin and Ellinwood, is to try it and see. But the social experiment is so risky as to be no experiment at all, for if cocaine is legalized and if the rate of its abusive use increases dramatically, there is no way to put the genie back in the bottle, and it is not a kindly genie.

HAVE WE LOST?

Many people who agree that there are risks in legalizing cocaine or heroin still favor it because, they think, we have lost the war on drugs. "Nothing we have done has worked" and the current federal policy is just "more of the same." Whatever the costs of greater drug use, surely they would be less than the costs of our present, failed efforts.

That is exactly what I was told in 1972 — and heroin is not quite as bad 30 a drug as cocaine. We did not surrender and we did not lose. We did not win, either. What the nation accomplished then was what most efforts to save people from themselves accomplish: The problem was contained and the number of victims minimized, all at a considerable cost in law enforcement and increased crime. Was the cost worth it? I think so, but others may disagree. What are the lives of would-be addicts worth? I recall some people saying to me then, "Let them kill themselves." I was appalled. Happily, such views did not prevail.

Have we lost today? Not at all. High-rate cocaine use is not commonplace. The National Institute of Drug Abuse (NIDA) reports that less than 5 percent of high-school seniors used cocaine within the last thirty days. Of course this survey misses young people who have dropped out of school and miscounts those who lie on the questionnaire, but even if we inflate the NIDA estimate by some plausible percentage, it is still not much above 5 percent. Medical examiners reported in 1987 that about 1,500 died from cocaine use; hospital emergency rooms reported about 30,000 admissions related to cocaine abuse.

These are not small numbers, but neither are they evidence of a nationwide plague that threatens to engulf us all. Moreover, cities vary greatly in the proportion of people who are involved with cocaine. To get city-level data we need to turn to drug tests carried out on arrested persons, who obviously are more likely to be drug users than the average citizen. The National Institute of Justice, through its Drug Use Forecasting (DUF) project, collects urinalysis data on arrestees in twenty-two cities. As we have already seen, opiate (chiefly heroin) use has been flat or declining in most of these cities over the last decade. Cocaine use has gone up sharply, but with great variation among cities. New York, Philadelphia, and Washington, D.C., all report that two-thirds or more of their arrestees tested positive for cocaine, but in Portland, San Antonio, and Indianapolis the percentage was one-third or less.

In some neighborhoods, of course, matters have reached crisis proportions. Gangs control the streets, shootings terrorize residents, and drug dealing occurs in plain view. The police seem barely able to contain matters. But in these neighborhoods — unlike at Palo Alto cocktail parties — the people are not calling for legalization, they are calling for help. And often not much help has come. Many cities are willing to do almost anything about the drug problem except spend more money on it. The federal government cannot change that; only local voters and politicians can. It is not clear that they will.

It took about ten years to contain heroin. We have had experience with crack for only about three or four years. Each year we spend perhaps $11 billion on law enforcement (and some of that goes to deal with marijuana) and perhaps $2 billion on treatment. Large sums, but not sums that should lead anyone to say, "We just can't afford this any more."

The illegality of drugs increases crime, partly because some users turn 35 to crime to pay for their habits, partly because some users are stimulated by certain drugs (such as crack or PCP) to act more violently or ruthlessly than they otherwise would, and partly because criminal organizations seeking to control drug supplies use force to manage their markets. These also are serious costs, but no one knows how much they would be reduced if drugs were legalized. Addicts would no longer steal to pay black-market prices for drugs, a real gain. But some, perhaps a great deal, of that gain would be offset by the great increase in the number of addicts. These people, nodding on heroin or living in the delusion-ridden high of cocaine, would hardly be ideal employees. Many would steal simply to support themselves, since snatch-and-grab, opportunistic crime can be managed even by people unable to hold a regular job or plan an elaborate crime. Those British addicts who get their supplies from government clinics are not models of law-abiding decency. Most are in crime, and though their per-capita rate of criminality may be lower thanks to the cheapness of their drugs, the total volume of crime they produce may be quite large. Of course, society could decide to support all unemployable addicts on welfare, but that would mean that gains from lowered rates of crime would have to be offset by large increases in welfare budgets.

Proponents of legalization claim that the costs of having more addicts around would be largely if not entirely offset by having more money available with which to treat and care for them. The money would come from taxes levied on the sale of heroin and cocaine.

To obtain this fiscal dividend, however, legalization's supporters must first solve an economic dilemma. If they want to raise a lot of money to pay for welfare and treatment, the tax rate on the drugs will have to be quite high. Even if they themselves do not want a high rate, the politicians' love of "sin taxes" would probably guarantee that it would be high anyway. But the higher the tax, the higher the price of the drug, and the higher the price the greater the likelihood that addicts will turn to crime to find the money for it and that criminal organizations will be formed to sell tax-free drugs at below-market rates. If we managed to keep taxes (and thus prices) low, we would get that much less money to pay for welfare and treatment and more people could afford to become addicts. There may be an optimal tax rate for drugs that maximizes revenue while minimizing crime, bootlegging, and the recruitment of new addicts, but our experience with alcohol does not suggest that we know how to find it.

THE BENEFITS OF ILLEGALITY

The advocates of legalization find nothing to be said in favor of the current system except, possibly, that it keeps the number of addicts smaller than it would otherwise be. In fact, the benefits are more substantial than that.

First, treatment. All the talk about providing "treatment on demand" implies that there is a demand for treatment. That is not quite right. There are some drug-dependent people who genuinely want treatment and will remain in it if offered; they should receive it. But there are far more who want only short-term help after a bad crash; once stabilized and bathed, they are back on the street again, hustling. And even many of the addicts who enroll in a program honestly wanting help drop out after a short while when they discover that help takes time and commitment. Drug-dependent people have very short time horizons and a weak capacity for commitment. These two groups — those looking for a quick fix and those unable to stick with a long-term fix — are not easily helped. Even if we increase the number of treatment slots — as we should — we would have to do something to make treatment more effective.

One thing that can often make it more effective is compulsion. 40 Douglas Anglin of UCLA, in common with many other researchers, has found that the longer one stays in a treatment program, the better the chances of a reduction in drug dependency. But he, again like most other researchers, has found that dropout rates are high. He has also found, however, that patients who enter treatment under legal compulsion stay in the program longer than those not subject to such pressure. His research on the California civil commitment program, for example, found that heroin users involved with its required drug-testing program had over the long term a lower rate of heroin use than similar addicts who were free of such constraints. If for many addicts compulsion is a useful component of treatment, it is not clear how compulsion could be achieved in a society in which purchasing, possessing, and using the drug were legal. It could be managed, I suppose, but I would not want to have to answer the challenge from the American Civil Liberties Union that it is wrong to compel a person to undergo treatment for consuming a legal commodity.

Next, education. We are now investing substantially in drug-education programs in the schools. Though we do not yet know for certain what will work, there are some promising leads. But I wonder how credible such programs would be if they were aimed at dissuading children from doing something perfectly legal. We could, of course, treat drug education like smoking education: Inhaling crack and inhaling tobacco are both legal, but you should not do it because it is bad for you. That tobacco is bad for you is easily shown; the Surgeon General has seen to that. But what do we say about crack? It is pleasurable, but devoting yourself to so much pleasure is not a good idea (though perfectly legal)? Unlike tobacco, cocaine will not give you cancer or emphysema, but it will lead you to neglect your duties to family, job, and neighborhood? Everybody is doing cocaine, but you should not?

Again, it might be possible under a legalized regime to have effective drug-prevention programs, but their effectiveness would depend heavily, I think, on first having decided that cocaine use, like tobacco use, is purely a matter of practical consequences; no fundamental moral significance attaches to either. But if we believe — as I do — that dependency on certain mind-altering drugs *is* a moral issue and that their illegality rests in part on their immorality, then legalizing them undercuts, if it does not eliminate altogether, the moral message.

That message is at the root of the distinction we now make between nicotine and cocaine. Both are highly addictive; both have harmful physical effects. But we treat the two drugs differently, not simply because nicotine is so widely used as to be beyond the reach of effective prohibition, but because its use does not destroy the user's essential humanity. Tobacco shortens one's life, cocaine debases it. Nicotine alters one's habits, cocaine alters one's soul. The heavy use of crack, unlike the heavy use of tobacco, corrodes those natural sentiments of sympathy and duty that constitute our human nature and make possible our social life. To say, as does Nadelmann, that distinguishing morally between tobacco and cocaine is "little more than a transient prejudice" is close to saying that morality itself is but a prejudice.

THE ALCOHOL PROBLEM

Now we have arrived where many arguments about legalizing drugs begin: Is there any reason to treat heroin and cocaine differently from the way we treat alcohol?

There is no easy answer to that question because, as with so many 45 human problems, one cannot decide simply on the basis either of moral principles or of individual consequences; one has to temper any policy by a commonsense judgment of what is possible. Alcohol, like heroin, cocaine, PCP, and marijuana, is a drug—that is, a mood-altering substance—and consumed to excess it certainly has harmful consequences: auto accidents, barroom fights, bedroom shootings. It is also, for some people, addictive. We cannot confidently compare the addictive powers of these drugs, but the best evidence suggests that crack and heroin are much more addictive than alcohol.

Many people, Nadelmann included, argue that since the health and financial costs of alcohol abuse are so much higher than those of cocaine or heroin abuse, it is hypocritical folly to devote our efforts to preventing cocaine or drug use. But as Mark Kleiman of Harvard has pointed out, this comparison is quite misleading. What Nadelmann is doing is showing that a *legalized* drug (alcohol) produces greater social harm than *illegal* ones (cocaine and heroin). But of course. Suppose that in the 1920s we had made heroin and cocaine legal and alcohol illegal. Can anyone doubt that Nadelmann would now be writing that it is folly to continue our ban on alcohol because cocaine and heroin are so much more harmful?

And let there be no doubt about it—widespread heroin and cocaine use are associated with all manner of ills. Thomas Bewley found that the mortality rate of British heroin addicts in 1968 was twenty-eight times as high as the death rate of the same age group of nonaddicts, even though in England at the time an addict could obtain free or low-cost heroin and clean needles from British clinics. Perform the following mental experiment: Suppose we legalized heroin and cocaine in this country. In what proportion of auto fatalities would the state police report that the driver was nodding off on heroin or recklessly driving on a coke high? In what proportion of spouse-assault and child-abuse cases would the local police report that crack was involved? In what proportion of industrial accidents would safety investigators report that the forklift or drill-press operator was in a drug-induced stupor or frenzy? We do not know exactly what the proportion would be, but anyone who asserts that it would not be much higher than it is now would have to believe that these drugs have little appeal except when they are illegal. And that is nonsense.

An advocate of legalization might concede that social harm — perhaps harm equivalent to that already produced by alcohol — would follow from making cocaine and heroin generally available. But at least, he might add, we would have the problem "out in the open" where it could be treated as a matter of "public health." That is well and good, *if* we knew how to treat — that is, cure — heroin and cocaine abuse. But we do not know how to do it for all the people who would need such help. We are having only limited success in coping with chronic alcoholics. Addictive behavior is immensely difficult to change, and the best methods for changing it — living in drug-free therapeutic communities, becoming faithful members of Alcoholics Anonymous or Narcotics Anonymous — require great personal commitment, a quality that is, alas, in short supply among the very persons — young people, disadvantaged people — who are often most at risk for addiction.

Suppose that today we had, not fifteen million alcohol abusers, but half a million. Suppose that we already knew what we have learned from our long experience with the widespread use of alcohol. Would we make whiskey legal? I do not know, but I suspect there would be a lively debate. The surgeon general would remind us of the risks alcohol poses to pregnant women. The National Highway Traffic Safety Administration would point to the likelihood of more highway fatalities caused by drunk drivers. The Food and Drug Administration might find that there is a nontrivial increase in cancer associated with alcohol consumption. At the same time the police would report great difficulty in keeping illegal whiskey out of our cities, officers being corrupted by bootleggers, and alcohol addicts often resorting to crime to feed their habit. Libertarians, for their part, would argue that every citizen has a right to drink anything he wishes and that drinking is, in any event, a "victimless crime."

However the debate might turn out, the central fact would be that the 50 problem was still, at that point, a small one. The government cannot legislate away the addictive tendencies in all of us, nor can it remove completely even the most dangerous addictive substances. But it can cope with harms when the harms are still manageable.

SCIENCE AND ADDICTION

One advantage of containing a problem while it is still containable is that it buys time for science to learn more about it and perhaps to discover a cure. Almost unnoticed in the current debate over legalizing drugs is that basic science has made rapid strides in identifying the underlying neurological processes involved in some forms of addiction. Stimulants such as cocaine and amphetamines alter the way certain brain cells communicate with one another. That alteration is complex and not entirely understood, but in simplified form it involves modifying the way in which a neurotransmitter called dopamine sends signals from one cell to another.

When dopamine crosses the synapse between two cells, it is in effect carrying a message from the first cell to activate the second one. In certain parts of the brain that message is experienced as pleasure. After the message is delivered, the dopamine returns to the first cell. Cocaine apparently blocks this return, or "reuptake," so that the excited cell and others nearby continue to send pleasure messages. When the exaggerated high produced by cocaine-influenced dopamine finally ends, the brain cells may (in ways that are still a matter of dispute) suffer from an extreme lack of dopamine, thereby making the individual unable to experience any pleasure at all. This would explain why cocaine users often feel so depressed after enjoying the drug. Stimulants may also affect the way in which other neurotransmitters, such as serotonin and noradrenaline, operate.

Whatever the exact mechanism may be, once it is identified it becomes possible to use drugs to block either the effect of cocaine or its tendency to produce dependency. There have already been experiments using desipramine, imipramine, bromocriptine, carbamazepine, and other chemicals. There are some promising results.

Tragically, we spend very little on such research, and the agencies funding it have not in the past occupied very influential or visible posts in the federal bureaucracy. If there is one aspect of the "war on drugs" metaphor that I dislike, it is its tendency to focus attention almost exclusively on the troops in the trenches, whether engaged in enforcement or treatment, and away from the research-and-development efforts back on the home front where the war may ultimately be decided.

I believe that the prospects of scientists in controlling addiction will be 55 strongly influenced by the size and character of the problem they face. If the problem is a few hundred thousand chronic, high-dose users of an illegal product, the chances of making a difference at a reasonable cost will be much greater than if the problem is a few million chronic users of legal substances. Once a drug is legal, not only will its use increase but many of those who then use it will prefer the drug to the treatment: They will want the pleasure, whatever the cost to themselves or their families, and they will resist — probably successfully — any effort to wean them away from experiencing the high that comes from inhaling a legal substance.

IF I AM WRONG . . .

No one can know what our society would be like if we changed the law to make access to cocaine, heroin, and PCP easier. I believe, for reasons given, that the result would be a sharp increase in use, a more widespread degradation of the human personality, and a greater rate of accidents and violence.

I may be wrong. If I am, then we will needlessly have incurred heavy costs in law enforcement and some forms of criminality. But if I am right, and the legalizers prevail anyway, then we will have consigned millions of people, hundreds of thousands of infants, and hundreds of neighborhoods to a life of oblivion and disease. To the lives and families destroyed by alcohol we will have added countless more destroyed by cocaine, heroin, PCP, and whatever else a basement scientist can invent.

Human character is formed by society; indeed, human character is inconceivable without society, and good character is less likely in a bad society. Will we, in the name of an abstract doctrine of radical individualism, and with the false comfort of suspect predictions, decide to take the chance that somehow individual decency can survive amid a more general level of degradation?

I think not. The American people are too wise for that, whatever the academic essayists and cocktail-party pundits may say. But if Americans today are less wise than I suppose, then Americans at some future time will look back on us now and wonder, what kind of people were they that they could have done such a thing?

Topics for Critical Thinking and Writing ===============

1. Wilson objects to the idea that drug abuse with cocaine is a "victimless crime" (para. 24; see also para. 49). A crime is said to be "victimless" when the offender consents to the act and those who do not consent are not harmed. Why does it matter to Wilson, do you think, whether drug abuse is a victimless crime?

2. Wilson accuses Nadelmann, an advocate of legalization, of committing "a logical fallacy and a factual error" (para. 26). What is the fallacy, and what is the error?

3. Wilson raises the question whether we "won" or "lost" the war on heroin in the 1970s, and whether we will do any better with the current war on cocaine (para. 30 and 31). What would you regard as convincing evidence that we are winning the war on drugs? Or losing it?

4. In his criticism of those who would legalize drugs, Wilson points to what he regards as an inescapable "economic dilemma" (para. 37). What is this dilemma? Do you see any way around it?

5. Economists tell us that we can control the use of some good or service either by controlling the cost (thus probably reducing the demand) or by ignoring the cost and controlling the supply, or by doing both. In the war on drugs, which of these three strategies does Wilson apparently favor, and why?

Kurt Schmoke

A War for the Surgeon General, Not the Attorney General

In the last ten years, the United States has become absolutely awash in illegal drugs. Tougher laws, greater efforts at interdiction, and stronger rhetoric at all levels of government and from both political parties have not and will not be able to stop the flow. That is why we must begin to consider what heretofore has been beyond the realm of consideration: decriminalization.

The violence brought about by the black market in drugs is attributable in large part to the fact that we have chosen to make criminals out of millions of people who have a disease. In the words of the American Medical Association, "It is clear that addiction is not simply the product of a failure of individual will-power. . . . It is properly viewed as a disease, and one that physicians can help many individuals control and overcome."

The nature of addiction is very important to the argument in favor of decriminalization. The sad truth is that heroin and morphine addiction is, for most users, a lifetime affliction that is impervious to any punishment that the criminal justice system could reasonably mete out.

Given the nature of addiction — whether to narcotics or cocaine — and the very large number of Americans using drugs (the National Institute on Drug Abuse estimates that one in six working Americans has a substance abuse problem), laws restricting their possession and sale have had predictable consequences — most of them bad.

Addicts commit crimes in order to pay for their drug habits. According   5
to the Justice Department, 90 percent of those who voluntarily seek treatment are turned away. In other words, on any given day, nine out of every ten addicts have no legal way to satisfy their addiction. And, failing to secure help, an untreated addict will commit a crime every other day to maintain his habit.

Whether one relies on studies, or on simple observation, it is indisputable that drug users are committing vast amounts of crime. Baltimore, the city with which I am most familiar, is no exception. According to James A. Inciardi, of the Division of Criminal Justice at the University of Delaware, a 1983 study of addicts in Baltimore showed that ". . . there were high rates of criminality among heroin users during those periods that

---

In 1987, after having served as Assistant U.S. Attorney and as State's Attorney for Baltimore, Kurt Schmoke was elected mayor of Baltimore, Maryland. The following essay, which appeared in New Perspectives Quarterly *in the summer of 1989, is based on testimony he gave before a congressional committee on September 29, 1988.*

they were addicted and markedly lower rates during times of nonaddiction." The study also showed that addicts committed crimes on a persistent day-to-day basis and over a long period of time. And the trends are getting worse. Thus, while the total number of arrests in Baltimore remained almost unchanged between 1983 and 1987, there was an approximately 40 percent increase in the number of drug-related arrests.

On the other hand, statistics recently compiled by the Maryland Drug and Alcohol Abuse Administration indicate that crime rates go down among addicts when treatment is available. Thus, for example, of the 6,910 Baltimore residents admitted to drug-abuse treatment in fiscal 1987, 4,386 or 63 percent had been arrested one or more times in the 24-month period prior to admission to treatment, whereas of the 6,698 Baltimore residents who were discharged from drug treatment in fiscal 1987, 6,152 or 91.8 percent were not arrested during the time of their treatment. These statistics tend to support the view that one way to greatly reduce drug-related crime is to assure addicts legal access to methadone or other drugs.

We cannot prosecute our way out of the drug problem. There are several reasons for this, but the most basic reason is that the criminal-justice system cannot — without sacrificing our civil liberties — handle the sheer volume of drug-related cases.

Nationwide last year, over 750,000 people were arrested for violating drug laws. Most of these arrests were for possession. In Baltimore, there were 13,037 drug-related arrests in 1987. Between January 1, 1988, and July 1, 1988, there were 7,981 drug-related arrests. Those numbers are large, but they hardly reflect the annual total number of drug violations committed in Baltimore. Should we, therefore, try to arrest still more? Yes — as long as the laws are on the books. But as a practical matter, we don't have any place to put the drug offenders we are now arresting. The population in the Baltimore City Jail is currently 2,900 inmates, even though its inmate capacity is only 2,700. This shortage of prison space has led to severe overcrowding, and Baltimore is now under court order to reduce its jail population.

Will more prisons help? Not in any significant way. We simply cannot 10 build enough of them to hold all of America's drug offenders — which number in the millions. And even if we could, the cost would far exceed what American taxpayers would be willing to pay.

Decriminalization is the single most effective step we could take to reduce prison overcrowding. And with less crowded prisons, there will be less pressure on prosecutors to plea bargain and far greater chance that nondrug criminals will go to jail — and stay in jail.

The unvarnished truth is that in our effort to prosecute and imprison our way out of the drug war, we have allowed the drug lords to put us exactly where they want us: wasting enormous resources — both in money and in personnel — attacking the fringes of the problem (the drug users and small-time pushers), while the heart of the problem—the traffickers and their profits—goes unsolved.

Not only can we not prosecute our way out of our drug morass, we cannot interdict our way out of it either. Lately, there have been calls for stepped-up border patrols, increased use of the military and greater pressure on foreign governments.

Assuming these measures would reduce the supply of illegal drugs, that reduction would not alleviate the chaos in our cities. According to statistics recently cited by the American Medical Association, Latin American countries produced between 162,000 and 211,400 metric tons of cocaine in 1987. That is five times the amount needed to supply the U.S. market. Moreover, we are probably only interdicting 10 to 15 percent of the cocaine entering this country. Thus, even if we quadrupled the amount of cocaine we interdict, the world supply of cocaine would still far outstrip U.S. demand.

If the drug laws in the United States simply didn't achieve their intent, 15 perhaps there would be insufficient reason to get rid of them. But these laws are doing more than not working—they are violating Hippocrates' famous admonition: First, do no harm.

The legal prohibition of narcotics, cocaine, and marijuana demonstrably increases the price of those drugs. For example, an importer can purchase a kilogram of heroin for $10,000. By the time that kilogram passes through the hands of several middlemen, its street value can reach $1,000,000. Such profits can't help but attract major criminal entrepreneurs willing to take any risk to keep their product coming to the American market.

Perhaps the most tragic victims of our drug laws are children. Many, for example, have been killed as innocent bystanders in gun battles among traffickers. Furthermore, while it is true that drug prohibition probably does keep some children from experimenting with drugs, almost any child who wants drugs can get them. Keeping drugs outlawed has not kept them out of children's hands.

Recent statistics in both Maryland and Baltimore prove the point: In a 1986–87 survey of Maryland adolescents, 13 percent of eighth graders, 18.5 percent of tenth graders, and 22.3 percent of twelfth graders report that they are currently using drugs. In Baltimore, the percentages are 16.6, 16.5, and 20.3, respectively. It should be noted that these numbers exclude alcohol and tobacco, and that current use means at least once a month. It should also be noted that these numbers show a decrease from earlier surveys in 1982 and 1984. Nevertheless, the fact remains that drugs are being widely used by students. Moreover, these numbers do not include the many young people who have left school or who failed to report their drug use.

A related problem is that many children, especially those living in the inner city, are frequently barraged with the message that selling drugs is an easy road to riches. In Baltimore, as in many other cities, small children are acting as lookouts and runners for drug pushers, just as they did for boot-leggers during Prohibition. Decriminalization and the destruction of the black market would end this most invidious form of child labor.

As for education, decriminalization will not end the *Just Say No* and 20 similar education campaigns. On the contrary, more money will be avail-able for such programs. Decriminalization will, however, end the compet-ing message of "easy money" that the drug dealers use to entice children. Furthermore, decriminalization will free up valuable criminal-justice re-sources that can be used to find, prosecute, and punish those who sell drugs to children.

This said, if there has been one problem with the current drug-reform debate, it has been the tendency to focus on narrow problems and narrow solutions. That is, we talk about the number of people arrested, the num-ber of tons of drugs entering our ports, the number of available treatment centers, and so on, but there is a bigger picture out there. We, as a nation, have not done nearly enough to battle the social and economic problems that make drug abuse an easy escape for the despairing, and drug traffick-ing an easy answer to a lack of education and joblessness.

Adolescents who take drugs are making a not-so-subtle statement about their confidence in the future. Children without hope are children who will take drugs. We need to give these children more than simple slo-gans. We need to give them a brighter tomorrow, a sense of purpose, a chance at economic opportunity. It is on that battlefield that the real war against drugs must be fought.

The 1980s have brought another major public health problem that is being made still worse because of our drug laws: AIDS. Contaminated in-travenous drug needles are now the principal means of transmission for the HIV infection. The users of drug needles infect not only those with whom they share needles, but also their sex partners and their unborn children.

One way to effectively slow this means of transmission would be to allow addicts to exchange their dirty needles for clean ones. However, in a political climate where all illicit drug use is condemned, and where posses-sion of a syringe can be a criminal offense, few jurisdictions have been will-ing to initiate a needle exchange program. This is a graphic example, along with our failure to give illegal drugs to cancer patients with intractable pain, of our blind pursuit of an irrational policy.

The case for the decriminalization of drugs becomes even stronger 25 when illegal drugs are looked at in the context of legal drugs.

It is estimated that over 350,000 people will die this year from tobacco-related diseases. Last year the number was equally large. And it will be again next year. Why do millions of people continue to engage in an activity which has been proven to cause cancer and heart disease? The answer is that smoking is more than just a bad habit. It is an addiction. In 1988, Surgeon General C. Everett Koop called nicotine as addictive as heroin and cocaine. And yet, with the exception of taxes and labeling, cigarettes are sold without restriction.

By every standard we apply to illicit drugs, tobacco should be a controlled substance. But it is not, and for good reason. Given that millions of people continue to smoke—many of whom would quit if they could—making cigarettes illegal would be an open invitation to a new black market.

The certain occurrence of a costly and dangerous illegal tobacco trade (if tobacco were outlawed) is well understood by Congress, the Bush Administration, and the criminal-justice community. No rationally thinking person would want to bring such a catastrophe down upon the United States—even if it would prevent some people from smoking.

Like tobacco, alcohol is a drug that kills thousands of Americans every year. It plays a part in more than half of all automobile fatalities; and is also frequently involved in suicides, nonautomobile accidents, domestic disputes, and crimes of violence. Millions of Americans are alcoholic, and alcohol costs the nation billions of dollars in health care and lost productivity. So why not ban alcohol? Because, as almost every American knows, we already tried that. Prohibition turned out to be one of the worst social experiments this country has ever undertaken.

I will not review the sorry history of Prohibition except to make two 30 important points. The first is that in repealing Prohibition, we made significant mistakes that should not be repeated in the event that drug use is decriminalized. Specifically, when alcohol was again made legal in 1934, we made no significant effort to educate people as to its dangers. There were no (and still are no) *Just Say No* campaigns against alcohol. We allowed alcohol to be advertised and have associated it with happiness, success, and social acceptability. We have also been far too lenient with drunk drivers.

The second point is that, notwithstanding claims to the contrary by critics of decriminalization, there are marked parallels between the era of Prohibition and our current policy of making drugs illegal, and important lessons to be learned from our attempts to ban the use and sale of alcohol.

During Prohibition, the government tried to keep alcohol out of the hands of millions of people who refused to give it up. As a result, our cities were overrun by criminal syndicates enriching themselves with the profits of bootleg liquor and terrorizing anyone who got in their way. We then looked to the criminal-justice system to solve the crime problems that Prohibition created. But the criminal-justice system—outmanned, outgunned, and often corrupted by enormous black market profits—was incapable of stopping the massive crime wave that Prohibition brought, just as it was incapable of stopping people from drinking.

As a person now publicly identified with the movement to reform our drug laws through the use of some form of decriminalization, I consider it very important to say that I am not soft on either drug use or drug dealers.

I am a soldier in the war against drugs. As Maryland's State Attorney, I spent years prosecuting and jailing drug traffickers, and had one of the highest rates of incarceration for drug convictions in the country. And if I were still State's Attorney, I would be enforcing the law as vigorously as ever. My experience as a prosecutor did not in any way alter my passionate dislike for drug dealers; it simply convinced me that the present system doesn't work and cannot be made to work.

During the Revolutionary War, the British insisted on wearing red coats and marching in formation. They looked very pretty. They also lost. A good general does not pursue a strategy in the face of overwhelming evidence of failure. Instead, a good general changes from a losing strategy to one that exploits his enemy's weakness, while exposing his own troops to only as much danger as is required to win. The drug war can be beaten and the public health of the United States can be improved if we are willing to substitute common sense for rhetoric, myth, and blind persistence, and to put the war in the hands of the Surgeon General, not the Attorney General.

Topics for Critical Thinking and Writing

1. Read paragraphs 39 and 40 in the accompanying article by James Q. Wilson (p. 365), and compare what Wilson says there about drug treatment with what Schmoke says about it in his paragraph 7. How do their views differ on the role of treatment in reducing drug abuse?

2. Schmoke says that the "heart of the [drug abuse] problem" is the "traffickers and their profits" (para. 12). Why does he think decriminalization of drug abuse would solve that problem? Do you agree? Why, or why not?

3. In paragraphs 25 to 29, Schmoke draws a parallel between two legal drugs, nicotine and alcohol, and a pair of illegal drugs, heroin and cocaine. He argues against making alcohol and tobacco illegal, despite the enormous harm caused by the abuse of these substances. What is his argument? Why does he think the parallel sheds light on whether to continue the legal ban on heroin and cocaine?

4. Explain and evaluate the phrase that Schmoke uses to title and close his article: "put the war [on drugs] in the hands of the Surgeon General, not the Attorney General."

Michael Tooley

Our Current Drug Legislation: Grounds for Reconsideration

Why is the American policy debate not focused more intensely on the relative merits or demerits of our current approach to drugs and of possible alternatives to it? The lack of discussion of this issue is rather striking, given that America has the most serious drug problem in the world, that alternatives to a prohibitionist approach are under serious consideration in other countries, and that the grounds for reconsidering our current approach are, I shall argue, so weighty.

One consideration that tells against our present approach to drugs is that prohibition simply does not work. For we have, after all, been pursuing this approach in the case of heroin since the Harrison Narcotic Act of 1914, and what has been the outcome? We have the worst heroin problem in the world. Our brief experiment in banning the consumption of what is undoubtedly our most harmful drug, alcohol, turned out to be an utter failure.

A second consideration, often noted, is the striking difference in our treatment of drugs such as alcohol and nicotine, on the one hand, and drugs such as marijuana, heroin, and LSD, on the other. This difference is so familiar that it may no longer seem strange. If so, it is worth asking the following question. If you were on a desert island, with a plentiful supply of both tobacco plants and opium poppies, and you knew that your son or daughter was going to wind up addicted either to nicotine or to heroin, which would you prefer? If your choice is nicotine, you have chosen the drug that, according to the testimony of most heroin addicts, is the more addictive of the two drugs. In addition, given access to heroin that has not been combined with dangerous chemicals, your son or daughter could be a lifelong addict without suffering serious organ damage. But a lifelong addiction to tobacco is often, of course, a very different story.

I want now to turn in detail to perhaps the two most important reasons for reconsidering our current drug policy: first, the difficulty of providing any adequate justification for the restrictions that prohibitive laws place on people's liberty; and second, the enormous social and personal costs associated with a prohibitionist approach.

JUSTIFYING LAWS

Under what conditions is a law justified? To answer this question, one   5
needs to determine what purposes may justifiably be pursued by means of

Michael Tooley, author of Abortion and Infanticide *(1983), is a professor of philosophy at the University of Colorado. The selection reprinted here first appeared in the Spring 1994 issue of the newsletter of the Center for Values and Social Policy, University of Colorado.*

legislation and what goals justify attaching penalties to certain actions. Particular laws can then be justified by reference to the relevant purpose or purposes—although one may also need to show that the costs associated with the law in question do not outweigh the relevant benefits. For the present, however, I shall defer discussion of costs, so that we can focus on what positive rationale might be offered for a prohibitionist approach to certain drugs.

What purpose, or purposes, then, may legislation justifiably serve? One very important answer—defended by John Stuart Mill in his *On Liberty*—is that the only actions that may be made illegal are actions that harm others against their will. (Philosophers of a less utilitarian sort would say that a law is justified if, and only if, it is necessary to protect people's rights.) If this answer were accepted, how would the case for prohibition stand? Not very well. For the laws in question prevent people from buying drugs that they want to consume from people who want to sell them those drugs, and provided that there is no misrepresentation, nor lack of relevant information—such as information about the potential for addiction—then no one is harmed against his or her will, and no one's rights are being violated. On a classical libertarian conception of the purpose of the law, then, prohibition cannot be justified.

Others have argued, however, that the law may serve other purposes beyond protecting the rights of individuals. Often, for example, it is suggested that an important function of the law is to enforce morality, thereby helping to ensure that people do not come to feel that, because certain actions do not violate anyone's rights, they are therefore morally acceptable. Such an appeal is often made, for example, to justify the laws against various types of noncoercive sexual activity which exist in most American states. For given that the behavior in question is voluntary, the laws in question could not be justified if the criterion was whether they were necessary to protect the rights of individuals. So if one is to justify such laws, one must be prepared to argue both that the actions in question are morally wrong, and that an appropriate function of the law is to enforce morality.

Would this view of the function of the law provide a justification of laws prohibiting the distribution and use of drugs? And if so, how?

Illegal drugs produce changes in one's state of consciousness, thereby providing interesting and/or pleasurable experiences. Might one argue, then, that it is morally wrong to consume substances that have such effects? Such a conclusion would be a very strong one, since many things that most people eat and drink produce interesting and/or pleasurable experiences. So unless one can show that illegal drugs are different in some important and morally relevant way, this line of argument will surely not be very plausible.

An alternative approach would be to argue, instead, that it is morally 10 wrong to become addicted to a drug. But this line of argument also seems problematic. First, caffeine and nicotine are addictive, and alcohol is addictive for some people, so the present line of thought would catch more than illegal drugs in its net: Tobacco products, alcoholic beverages, together with tea, coffee, and many soft drinks would also have to go. Second, many illegal drugs—including major hallucinogenic drugs, such as LSD, mescaline, and peyote—are not addicting, and so this line of argument would fail to justify a good deal of current legislation. And third, surely it is appropriate here to weigh pros and cons. Other things being equal, it is preferable not to be addicted to something. But if the substance to which one is addicted provides interesting or pleasurable experiences, might that not outweigh any disvalue associated with addiction? Are people who enjoy coffee, for example, really worse off for being addicted to caffeine?

A third purpose which people sometimes argue that legislation may legitimately serve is that of preventing people from harming themselves. Compulsory seat belt legislation, for example, is sometimes supported by an appeal to paternalistic considerations. But, aside from laws that are concerned with the well being of children, the idea that legislation can justifiably impose restrictions upon people so that they do not act contrary to their own interests is widely rejected. For consider the ways in which people can harm themselves: by being overweight; by not getting enough exercise; by eating diets that are high in fat, or low in fiber, or full of empty calories, etc. And even if one were prepared to embrace laws whose only justification is paternalistic, that would not serve to justify our current policies, since many illegal drugs are either not harmful or only marginally so.

SOME COSTS OF OUR CURRENT APPROACH

Setting justificatory questions aside, we must turn next to the significant costs associated with our present approach. Those costs can be divided into two categories: those borne by members of society as a whole and those that fall upon those who are addicted to, or who choose to use, illegal drugs.

Let us begin with the former. What are some of the ways in which a policy of prohibition affects all members of society, including those of us who do not use illegal drugs? One obvious first effect is increased crime and violence in society. When a drug is illegal, its cost may be one hundred times as great than the cost if it was legal. So many addicts need to steal to be able to buy drugs, generating many more crimes against property and against persons. In addition, the high cost of illegal drugs has the same effect that prohibition had for alcohol. Distribution of the illegal substance becomes an enormously profitable business, and violence is often necessary, both to discourage competitors from trying to take over one's markets, and to ward off interference by law enforcement agencies in one's business activities.

Second, the cost of enforcing drug laws is very great indeed. Detection is difficult, because we are dealing with crimes where there are no complaints, no victims to draw attention to the crimes in question. After arrests have been made, we must bear the substantial costs of prosecution, which slows down an already overloaded legal system still further. Then come the substantial costs associated with incarceration of convicted drug offenders, who often must serve lengthy mandatory sentences.

Third, given the heavy involvement of the criminal justice system in 15 enforcing drug legislation, a much smaller proportion of law enforcement effort can be given over to the prevention and solution of crimes that do involve victims. And because our prisons are crowded past their capacity with drug offenders, violent criminals are often released after strikingly short terms, free once again to inflict serious harm upon people.

What about the impact of a prohibitionist policy on those who use illegal drugs? One obvious consequence is that one may be convicted of using an illegal drug, thereby suffering a serious and extended loss of one's freedom. But bad as this is, other consequences may be much more serious. One, which results from the exorbitantly inflated costs of illegal drugs, is the degradation of addicts who are forced into a life of crime and/or prostitution in order to be able to purchase the drug that they need. Another arises from the fact that illegal drugs are not typically subject to quality control, and so may contain impurities and may vary dramatically in dose and concentration, and thus may lead to illness or premature death. Finally, the fact that a drug is illegal may encourage both the intravenous use of that drug and the sharing of needles. In a time of AIDS, and other serious diseases such as hepatitis B, the implications of this are ominous indeed, not only for those who use drugs, but for others as well. The rapid spread of AIDS into the heterosexual community, in this country, has been mainly via intravenous drug users.

CONCLUSION

It is difficult not to conclude that the costs of a prohibitionist approach are enormous — in terms of money, but even more so in terms of suffering and deaths. This, together with the difficulty, even ignoring those costs, of offering a satisfactory justification for our present drug legislation, strongly suggests that there are excellent reasons for thinking seriously about alternative approaches.

Topics for Critical Thinking and Writing

1. Tooley argues that "prohibition simply does not work" (para. 2). Despite the 1914 narcotic act that made heroin an illegal drug, he says we "have the worst heroin problem in the world." Suppose one were to reply, "So what? It would be much worse if we hadn't made it illegal in 1914." How do you think Tooley might reply?

2. Tooley cites two important objections to current drug policy. What are they? What is his argument in support of each of these objections?

3. Tooley concludes, "On a classical libertarian conception of the purpose of the law, . . . prohibition cannot be justified" (para. 6). What exactly is his argument for this conclusion?

4. Tooley thinks it is futile to argue against taking drugs such as heroin on the ground that the drug is addictive. What is his argument for this conclusion? Do you find it persuasive? Why, or why not?

5. Tooley concedes that "Other things being equal, it is preferable not to be addicted to something" (para. 10). But why? What do you think (Tooley thinks) is wrong with being addicted to something? If you liked coffee, say, but were not addicted to caffeine, do you think you'd be better off, worse off, or neither if you became addicted to it?

6. Construct an outline of Tooley's overall essay, making sure that each of his seventeen paragraphs is represented in the outline with its own number or letter, and that you sharply contrast his main from his subordinate points (for guidance on how to construct an outline, see pp. 142–43).

11

The Environment: Natural Resource or Raw Material?

Leila L. Kysar

A Logger's Lament

My father was a logger. My husband is a logger. My sons will not be loggers. Loggers are an endangered species, but the environmental groups, which so righteously protect endangered species in the animal kingdom, have no concern for their fellow human beings under siege. Loggers are a much misunderstood people, pictured as brutal rapists of our planet, out to denude it of trees and, as a result, of wildlife.

It is time to set the record straight. Loggers take great pride in the old-growth trees, the dinosaurs of the forests, and would be sorry to see them all cut. There are in the national forests in Washington and Oregon (not to mention other states) approximately 8.5 million acres of forested land, mostly old growth set aside, never to be used for timber production. In order to see it all, a man would have to spend every weekend and holiday for sixty years looking at timber at a rate of more than 1,000 acres per day. This does not include acreage to be set aside for spotted-owl protection.

In addition to this huge amount of forested land never to be logged, the State of Washington Forest Practices Act, established in 1973, specifies

Leila L. Kysar is the business manager of a tree-farm-management enterprise in the state of Washington. Her essay originally appeared as a "My Turn" column in Newsweek (October 22, 1990).

that all land that is clear-cut of trees must be replanted unless converted to some other use. As a tree farmer generally plants more trees per acre than he removes, more trees are being planted than are being cut. In the last twenty years in Clark County, Washington, alone, the Department of Natural Resources has overseen the planting of at least 15,000 acres of previously unforested private lands.

The term *logger* applies to the person harvesting trees. A tree farmer is the one who owns the land and determines what is to be done with it. To a tree farmer, clear-cutting is no more than the final harvest of that generation of trees. The next spring, he reforests the land. To the public, clear-cutting is a bad word. Does the public cry shame when a wheat farmer harvests his crop and leaves a field of stubble in place of the beautiful wheat?

In the Pacific Northwest, in five years, the newly planted trees will   5 grow taller than the farmer's head; in ten years, more than fifteen feet tall; and in twenty to thirty years, the trees will be ready for the first commercial harvest. The farmer then thins the trees to make room for better growth. In forty to fifty years, he will be ready to clear-cut his farm and replant again. Contrary to public opinion, it does *not* take three hundred to four hundred years to grow a Douglas fir tree to harvestable age.

Tree farming keeps us in wood products. We build with wood, write on paper, and even use the unmentionable in the bathroom. But in order to keep this flow of wood products available, we need to keep it economically feasible to grow trees. If we restrict the tree-farming practices because we do not like clear-cuts or because some animal might (and probably might not) become extinct, or we restrict markets for the timber by banning log exports or overtax the farmer, we are creating a situation where the farmer will no longer grow trees. If he cannot make money, he will not tree-farm. He will sell his tree farm so that it can grow houses. The *land* that grows trees is the natural resource; the *trees* are just a crop.

Legislation is constantly being introduced to take away the private-property rights of tree farmers. They are beleaguered by the public, who believe that any forest belongs to the public. Who, after all, buys the land and pays the taxes? Who invests money in property that will yield them an income only once every twenty to thirty years? Would John Q. Public picnic in a farmer's wheat field?

The tree farmer must have a diversified market. When there is a building slump in this country, it is vital to the industry to have an export market. Earlier recessions were devastating to tree farmers until markets were developed overseas. Some trees have little market value in the United States. The logs China and Korea bought in the late 1980s could not be sold here to cover the cost of delivery.

As to the wildlife becoming extinct, that is a joke that is not very funny. Animals thrive in clear-cuts better than in old-growth timber. Look at the Mount St. Helens blast area. Nature created an immense clearing and now deer, elk, and other wildlife are returning in numbers. Why? Because there is more food growing in an open area than under the tall trees. And as for the spotted owl, surely the 8.5 million acres set aside is enough to maintain quite a respectable owl population. Numerous recent observations show that the owl lives in second-growth timber as well as in old growth. In the Wenatchie National Forest there are more than two hundred fifty examples of spotted owls living in other than old-growth timber. The owl is a tool of the environmentalist groups to get what they want: the complete eradication of the species *Logger*.

BEAUTIFUL NEW TREES

Consider the scenic value of a preserved old-growth forest versus a 10
managed stand of timber. In Glacier National Park, Montana, for example, which is totally untouched, one sees the old trees, the dead and dying trees, the windfalls crisscrossing the forest. In a managed forest, one sees the older stands with the forest floor cleared of the dead windfalls, leaving a more parklike setting. In the younger stands, one sees the beautiful new trees with their brilliant greens thrusting their tops to the sky and, in the clear-cuts, before the new trees obscure the view, one sees the huckleberry bushes with their luscious-tasting berries, the bright pink of fireweed and deer and elk feeding. True environmentalists husband the land; they do not let the crops stagnate and rot. Tree farming regenerates the trees *and* utilizes the product.

A tree farmer from Sweden (where they are fined if they do *not* tree-farm their forests) asked me recently why we do not just explain these facts to the environmental groups so that they will work *with* us instead of *against* us. Well, do you know the difference between a terrorist and an environmentalist? It is easier to reason with the terrorist.

Topics for Critical Thinking and Writing ═══════════

1. In a few sentences summarize Kysar's essay.

2. What, exactly, is Kysar's thesis?

3. Kysar makes a comparison between the tree farmer clear-cutting his timber and the wheat farmer harvesting his crop (para. 4). Do you think this is a fair comparison? Why, or why not?

4. In the next-to-last paragraph, Kysar argues that national parks, with their "managed forest[s]," have more "scenic value" (as well as economic value) than untended natural forests. Can you think of any respects in which the reverse is true? Write a 500-word essay arguing for or against this proposition: All public natural forests in the United States ought to be turned into managed forests.

5. Kysar ends her essay by comparing "environmentalists" with "terrorists." What would it take to convince you that she was not exaggerating for rhetorical effect, but fairly describing the plight of the logger and tree farmer?

6. Kysar does not assert, but she does (through her silence) imply, that there are no adverse environmental effects from clear-cutting timber in part because as soon as the trees are cut, the tree farmer "reforests the land" (para. 4). Do some research in your college library on the practice of clear-cutting, and write a 500-word essay with the title "The Truth about Clear-Cutting for Timber."

Donella Meadows

Not Seeing the Forest for the Dollar Bills

The U.S. Fish and Wildlife Service has finally declared the spotted owl an endangered species. The decision will, if the administration enforces the law of the land, drastically cut back logging in the owl's habitat — old-growth forest in the Pacific Northwest.

The logging companies are fighting back. They will go to court to "dispute the science" behind the finding. Knowing that the science is not on their side, they have also leaned on the administration not to enforce the law. And they are trying to get the law changed.

The law in question is the Endangered Species Act. The companies want it to take into account economic considerations. If it did, they say over and over to the press, the politicians, and the public, we would never choose to sacrifice 28,000 jobs for an owl.

That is not the choice at all, of course. The choice is not between an owl and jobs, but between a forest and greed.

The spotted owl is, like every other species, the holder of a unique genetic code that is millions of years old and irreplaceable. Even more important, the owl is a canary, in the old miners' sense — a sign that all is well. It is an indicator species, a creature high up the food chain that depends upon a large area of healthy land for its livelihood.   5

Every thriving family of spotted owls means that 4,000 acres of forest are well. The trees are living their full lives and returning stored nutrients to the soil when they die. Two hundred other vertebrates that live in the forest are well, as are 1,500 insects and spiders and untold numbers of smaller creatures. The spongy soil under the trees is storing and filtering rain, controlling floods and droughts, keeping the streams clear and pure.

When old-growth is clear-cut, the trees and the owls disappear and so does everything else. Burned slash releases to the sky nutrients that have been sequestered and recycled by living things for 500 years. What's left of the soil bleeds downhill as from as open wound. Waters cloud and silt, flood and dry up. The temperature goes up, the humidity goes down. It

---

Donella Meadows is an adjunct professor of environmental studies at Dartmouth College in New Hampshire. *This essay originally appeared in* Valley News, *a regional newspaper, on June 30, 1990.*

will take hundreds of years to regather the nutrients, rebuild the soil, and restore the complex system of the intact forest, *if* there is still old-growth forest around to recolonize, and *if* the forest companies stay away.

They are unlikely to stay away. On their own land, they replant with a single, commercially valuable, fast-growing species and call it a forest. It bears as much resemblance to a 500-year-old natural forest as a suburb of identical ticky-tacky houses bears to a Renaissance cathedral. Ecologists call such plantations "cornfields." It's not at all certain how many cycles of these cornfields will be possible, given the loss of soil and nutrients when they are cut every fifty years or so.

In the past ten years, 13,000 forest-related jobs were lost in Oregon alone, though the annual cut increased. The jobs were lost to automation and to moving mills offshore, not to the Endangered Species Act.

The forest companies are interested not in jobs or forests, but in mul- 10 tiplying money. Old-growth forests yield higher profit than second-growth plantations. Therefore 85 percent of the old growth is already gone. The companies have stripped it from their own lands. Nearly all that remains is on federal land, owned by you and me. In Washington and Oregon, 2.4 million acres of old growth are left, of which 800,000 are protected in national parks. The rest, in national forests, is marked for cutting.

Our elected representatives are selling off old-growth logging rights in national forests at a rate of about 100,000 acres per year, and at a loss. Taxpayers are subsidizing this process. At the present cutting rate, all but the last protected bits will be gone in about twenty years. The owls will be on their way out — the 800,000 acres remaining will be too fragmented to sustain them. The jobs will be gone, not because of owls, but because of rapacious forestry.

If loggers and their communities cannot be sustained by second-growth cutting on private lands, then they were in trouble anyway. A compassionate nation would look for a dignified way to help them build a viable economy. It wouldn't sacrifice the biological treasure of an intact forest to keep them going twenty more years. That's the kind of behavior we are righteously telling the Brazilians to stop.

The Endangered Species Act should not take into account economic considerations. Economics doesn't know how to value a species or a forest. Its logic drives people to exploit resources to the point of extinction. The Endangered Species Act tells us that extinction is morally unacceptable. It was enacted by a Congress and president in a wise mood, to express a higher value than a bottom line. It should not be weakened. It should be enforced.

Topics for Critical Thinking and Writing

1. In a few sentences summarize Meadow's essay.

2. In a sentence or two state her thesis.

3. In paragraphs 3 and 13 Meadows refers to the Endangered Species Act. What,

exactly, does the act provide? Write a 250-word summary of the act. (You probably will want to consult with your college reference librarian in order to find
the text of this law and some details concerning its enactment by Congress.)

4. In paragraphs 3 and 4 Meadows says that the choice is not between 28,000 jobs
and an owl, but "between a forest and greed." Do you think she has properly
formulated the choice? Or do you think the choice *is* between the owl and jobs?
Or would you put the choice differently? Explain.

5. What do you think are Meadows's strongest points? Her weakest points?

6. In paragraph 5 Meadows says that the spotted owl is "the holder of a unique genetic code that is millions of years old and irreplaceable." In her final paragraph
she says that "extinction is morally unacceptable." Suppose someone were to
reply, "Extinction is nature's way. Countless species — all of the dinosaurs, for
instance — have become extinct." What reply might Meadows offer?

Sally Thane Christensen

Is a Tree Worth a Life?

For most of the last decade, federal timberlands in the West have
been held hostage in a bitter fight between environmental groups and the
timber industry. The environmentalists want to save the forests and their
wildlife occupants. The timber industry wants to cut trees and provide jobs
in a depressed economy. Caught in the middle is the United States Forest
Service, which must balance the conflicting concepts of sustained yield and
multiple use of national forest land.

The latest pawn in this environmental chess match is the Pacific yew
tree, a scrubby conifer found from southern Alaska to central California
and in Washington, Oregon, Idaho, and Montana. Historically the yew has
not been harvested for value but often has been treated as logging slash
and washed. Not any longer. An extract of the bark of the Pacific yew
known as taxol has been found to have cancer-fighting properties, particularly with ovarian cancer. As many as 30 percent of those treated with taxol
have shown significant responses. Some researchers call taxol the most significant new cancer drug to emerge in fifteen years.

For the first time, the environmental debate over the use of a natural
resource involves more than a question of the priority of the resource versus economic considerations. At stake is the value of a species of tree and
the habitat it provides for wildlife as opposed to the value of the greatest of
all natural resources, human life.

---

*Sally Thane Christensen was a 38-year-old resident of Missoula, Montana,
and a lawyer for the Forest Service when she published this essay in* Newsweek *on
October 22, 1990. She died in early 1992.*

When I was first diagnosed three years ago, no one had an inkling that I would become caught in the center of what may become the most significant environmental debate of my generation. Although as early as 1979 researchers had discovered that taxol killed cancer in a unique way, imprisoning malignant cells in a cage of scaffoldlike rods called microtubules, lab tests on animals were inconclusive. By 1985, however, a woman with terminal ovarian cancer was treated with taxol and had a dramatic response. Six years later, the once lowly yew tree is at the threshold of a controversy that challenges the fundamental precepts of even the most entrenched environmentalist.

MY FATE

It takes about three 100-year-old Pacific yew trees, or roughly 60   5
pounds of bark, to produce enough taxol to treat one patient. When the bark is removed, the tree dies. Environmental groups like the Oregon Natural Resources Council and the Audubon Society are concerned that the Pacific yew as a species may be decimated by the demand for taxol. But this year alone, twelve thousand women will die from ovarian cancer. Breast cancer will kill forty-five thousand women. Is preservation of the Pacific yew worth the price?

It is sublimely ironic that my fate hinges so directly on the Pacific yew. As a federal attorney representing the Forest Service, I have witnessed the environmental movement in the West from its embryonic stages. I have seen such diverse groups as the National Wildlife Federation and the Sierra Club challenge the Forest Service's ability to sell and harvest its trees. Win or lose, the forests are often locked up during the lengthy legal process.

The viability of the national forests does not rise or fall with the Pacific yew. But, unfortunately for cancer victims, the tree is most abundant on national-forest lands which are subject to environmental review by the public. Already challenges to the federal harvest of the yew have begun. In Montana, the Save the Yaak Committee has protested the Kootenai National Forest's intention to harvest yew trees and make them available for experimental use. The committee contends that the yew may be endangered by overharvesting.

I have news for the Save the Yaak Committee. I am endangered, too. I've had four major abdominal surgeries in two years. I've had the conventional chemotherapy for ovarian cancer, and it didn't work. Though I was in remission for almost a year, last August my cancer returned with a vengeance. Taxol may be my last hope.

Because of the scarcity of supply, taxol is not commercially available. It is available only in clinical trials at a number of institutions. Bristol-Myers, working with the National Cancer Institute in Bethesda, Maryland, asked the Forest Service to provide 750,000 pounds of bark for clinical studies this year.

The ultimate irony of my story is that I am one of the lucky ones. This 10 May I was accepted by the National Cancer Institute for one of its clinical trials. On May 8 I was infused with my first treatment of taxol. Hospitalized in intensive care at NCI, I watched the precious, clear fluid drip into my veins and prayed for it to kill the cancer that has ravaged my body. I thought about the thousands of women who will die of cancer this year, who will not have my opportunity.

Every effort should be made to ensure that the yew tree is made available for the continued research and development of taxol. Environmental groups, the timber industry, and the Forest Service must recognize that the most important value of the Pacific yew is as a treatment for cancer. At the same time, its harvest can be managed in a way that allows for the production of taxol without endangering the continued survival of the yew tree.

The yew may be prime habitat for spotted owls. It may be esthetically appealing. But certainly its most critical property is its ability to treat a fatal disease. Given a choice between trees or people, people must prevail. No resource can be more valuable or more important than a human life. Ask my husband. Ask my two sons. Ask me.

Topics for Critical Thinking and Writing

1. News reports early in 1992 informed the world that scientists were on the verge of synthesizing taxol. Assume that they succeed in doing so within the year. Does this success in creating synthetic taxol undermine Christensen's entire argument for harvesting the Pacific yew? Why, or why not?

2. Assume that taxol is, indeed, effective as a remedy for ovarian cancer. But assume also that the demand far exceeds the supply. How do you think it ought to be rationed to those who need it? By some form of random lottery? By raising the price so high that only a few can afford it? By some other method? Present your responses in an essay of 500 words.

3. Christensen says, "Given a choice between trees or people, people must prevail" (para. 12). Suppose all the yew trees were owned by private corporations who refused to sell to the highest bidder. Do you think Christensen ought to argue that, given a choice between someone's private property and someone else's life, human life must prevail? Why, or why not?

Sallie Tisdale

Save a Life, Kill a Tree?

Land wars are a constant in the West.

The latest battle concerns the Pacific yew tree, an unassuming conifer scattered throughout the Pacific Northwest. The yew's bark contains taxol, a chemical with potent anticancer effects. Taxol seems to work best against ovarian cancer, a devastating and often fatal disease.

No one knows how many yews there are here. Until last year loggers considered the humble Pacific yew a "trash tree." It was typically cut and burned with other logging debris. But suddenly it is invaluable.

In current taxol laboratory trials, it takes about 60 pounds of yew bark to treat one person. The National Cancer Institute expects to collect 750,000 pounds of yew bark this year, the bark of approximately thirty-eight thousand trees. And thus is the battle born: People versus Trees. Sally Thane Christensen, a cancer patient in a taxol trial, wrote recently in *Newsweek*, "Given a choice between trees or people, people must prevail."

Ms. Christensen is a lawyer for the Forest Service. She's used to argu-   5
ing against environmental protection lawsuits. She wants her drug now—
forget the future. But forgetting the future is exactly what uncontrolled yew harvesting will do.

The slow-growing yew requires shade. With rare exceptions, it lives its whole life in the understory, under the high canopy of Douglas fir and Western hemlock, which are themselves rapidly disappearing. The Forest Service, in response to the outcry of preservationists, has said that the nearly forty thousand yews killed this year for taxol had already been logged or were destined for logging anyway.

Perhaps I sound battle-weary. We've seen these same equations so many times before: people versus the old growth, people versus the spotted owl, people versus wild rivers, versus wetlands, the snail darter, caribou, wolves, salmon. But all of these battles are really just between us. There is one war and it is people versus people—a kind of civil war in which trees and rivers and owls are the innocent bystanders, taking stray bullets.

The real battle lies outside the few remaining forests. What does it mean that the Pacific yew was burned by the tens of thousands until last winter? Far from trash, the lowly yew is a beautiful hardwood. The prob-

---

Sallie Tisdale, a resident of Portland, Oregon, is a writer. Her most recent books are Stepping Westward: The Long Search for Home in the Pacific Northwest *(1991) and* Talk Dirty to Me: An Intimate Philosophy of Sex *(1994). The essay that we reprint originally appeared as an Op-Ed piece in the* New York Times *(October 26, 1991).*

lem is greed: The yew occurs too sparely in any given area to make logging it worthwhile. Its casual destruction in the course of more lucrative harvests was profiteering and nothing more.

Greed has gotten us here, to where one more loss is more than the forest can sustain. Loggers are desperate for work partly because we are running out of old-growth trees; we are running out of trees because the managers of the trees, including the Forest Service, hold a peculiarly narrow view of their job. They see the forest as a pile of goods first to be inventoried and then passed out. Loggers have a telling term for the commercial value of a forest stand: They call it "stumpage." You can't miss the results of that thinking. The clear-cuts crowd every road.

The worth of the Pacific yew is now dependent only on the demand 10 for taxol. Another product. If taxol were synthesized tomorrow, the Pacific yew would be back on the slash pile.

People versus people. The salmon are squeezed in the dams, between fishermen and the power companies. The spotted owl is driven from one shrinking island to another. The loggers are hurting, like the fishermen, like the cancer patients. My mother died of cancer a few years ago and both my sister and I are at risk for a death like hers. I would welcome almost any cure — but I reject the notion that our human future requires the sacrifice of the human habitat, the earth.

"People must prevail." Such comments degrade all we know of biology. God help us if people do finally prevail. Do we really think the undisturbed forest has nothing to offer the human race? Do we think we stand alone, separate, independent?

The forest, like any ecosystem, is an organism greater than the sum of its parts. Take away all the tall trees, or all the spotted owls, and it slowly bleeds to death. Whole, the forest makes and keeps great secrets: secrets like taxol, going up in smoke.

Topics for Critical Thinking and Writing ══════════

1. When Tisdale declares, "God help us if people do finally prevail" (para. 12), how is she interpreting the slogan "People must prevail"?

2. Suppose some environmentalist declared, "Human beings have never done anything good for the environment — and never will." Do you think Tisdale would agree? Why, or why not?

3. Tisdale seems unsympathetic to the plight of Christensen and others who suffer from a form of cancer that taxol from yew trees might cure. Do you think she really believes that it is better for Christensen to die of cancer than to cure her by cutting down yew trees to get taxol? If Tisdale doesn't believe this, what does she believe? What is your view? In an essay of 500 words, set forth what you take to be Tisdale's view in 100 to 200 words and your own view in the remainder of the essay.

Claudia Mills

Preserving Endangered Species: Why Should We Care?

When construction of the Tellico dam was temporarily halted because the project posed a threat to the endangered Tennessee snail darter, environmentalists were triumphant, economists relieved (the dam was an economic disaster in its own right). The general public seemed cheered by the triumph of such an improbable underdog, but uncertain that a lowly three-inch minnow was really worth the trouble of saving.

Surveys taken by Stephen Kellert of Yale University reflect this ambivalence in public attitudes toward species preservation. In a questionnaire modeled on the Tellico dam controversy, pitting an obscure fish species against various development projects, the fish species won out handily over recreational projects, tied with projects to divert water for industrial development, but was soundly defeated by projects to produce hydroelectric, agricultural, or drinking water improvements. As codified in the law of the land, the will of the people is expressed more strongly in favor of species preservation. The Endangered Species Act mandates stringent standards for protecting any plant or animal species that has been listed as threatened or endangered. However, the list of protected species is a short one, so the effect of the act is considerably weakened.

How much *should* we care about endangered species? Why, indeed, should we care at all? A first answer is that extinction is forever. It is irrevocable, the flung stone that cannot be called back. Still, we do irrevocable things all the time, sometimes half a dozen before breakfast. But our knowledge of the considerable benefits the human species has reaped from other species, together with our ignorance of what benefits we might someday glean from species currently threatened, make extinction particularly alarming. What if the *Penicillium* mold had gone extinct a century ago? Who knows what cure for cancer we would have discovered even a decade hence in some unknown species that went extinct yesterday? Thomas Lovejoy, executive vice president of the World Wildlife Fund, concludes, "Assuming that the biota contains ten million species, they then represent ten million successful sets of solutions to a series of biological problems, any one of which could be immensely valuable to us in a number of ways."

But this argument cannot bear a great deal of weight. It sounds too much like the reasoning of our old Aunt Tillie, who saves every bit of string or bottle cap on the off chance that it may someday come in useful. Clutter

---

Claudia Mills (b. 1954) is a member of the philosophy faculty at the University of Colorado in Boulder. This essay is taken from Values and Public Policy *(1992), a collection of essays she edited.*

mounts up exponentially, and someday never comes. After all, philosopher Elliott Sober observes, "There are so many species. How many geese that lay golden eggs are there apt to be in that number?" For Sober, an argument from ignorance is no argument at all: "If we literally do not know what consequences the extinction of this or that species may bring, then we should take seriously the possibility that extinction may be beneficial as well as the possibility that it may be deleterious. . . . Ignorance on a scale like this cannot provide the basis for any rational action."

If we can't appeal to the possible future usefulness of species, what 5 reasons do we have for preserving them? Put bluntly, what is it to us whether they live or die? But perhaps Aunt Tillie overlooked some benefits to preserving species. Do species have a value in their own right, independent of what value we place on them? Or can we, even within a human framework, find a noncommercial, nonscientific value to justify their preservation?

As Goes the Furbish Lousewort . . .

Let us concede that only relatively few species are likely to prove of direct commercial or scientific use. Does this mean that the rest are therefore useless — expendable in the face of competing resource needs? That conclusion would surely be a hasty one, given the sheer magnitude of the species currently threatened. Extinctions that might not be worrisome viewed one by one take on a new seriousness when multiplied many thousandfold.

Lovejoy reports that hundreds of thousands to more than a million extinctions are projected to take place by the end of the century. The estimates vary widely (nobody even knows how many species exist, let alone how many are endangered), but "what is important," in Lovejoy's view, "is that every effort to estimate extinction rates has produced a *large* number."

Of course, almost every species that has ever lived has gone extinct, so extinction itself is natural, normal, routine. Even extinctions caused by human practices such as hunting and habitat fragmentation cannot be called unnatural: Humans are part of nature, too, as much as any other predators. But they are predators of matchless efficiency, and while all creatures in one way or another transform their environments, humans are currently transforming theirs on an unprecedented scale. The current rate of extinctions is extraordinary and exceeds the rate of which new species are evolving. This means that the planet is in the throes of a process of biotic impoverishment.

How alarming is this? What is lost with biological diversity? Lovejoy points out that "natural aggregations of species (ecosystems) are more than a large collection of genetic material; they also are involved in ecological processes, often of immediate public service value." These include watershed protection and moderation of climatic, hydrological, and nutrient cycles. With diminished diversity comes loss of clean and reliable water supplies and of soil fertility. Biological impoverishment weakens nature's regenerative power to resist human exploitation.

Lovejoy recognizes that "in any immediate sense it is hard to see how 10 the loss of a single species will affect the day-to-day life of the average citizen who will probably not even know of the loss or that the species ever existed. Yet, when an ecosystem has been altered to the point that a public service benefit such as watershed protection is affected, it is not only quite obvious, but also, biological diversity will have by then suffered a significant reduction."

Lovejoy argues, in fact, that biological impoverishment may be directly responsible for human impoverishment. It is no accident, he suggests, that "those nations which are unsuccessful in maintaining their basic diversity of plant and animal life are also the ones least successful in protecting decent standards of living for their people." He blames heedless environmental policies in part for the fact that Haiti, the poorest nation in the Western Hemisphere, is in far more dire economic straits than its neighbor, the Dominican Republic, which has undertaken active initiatives to protect wildlife habitat.

Bryan Norton, an environmental ethicist, takes Lovejoy's argument to show that the preservationist does not need to document a specific present or anticipated commercial use for an individual species in order to justify saving it. Since "natural diversity, in and of itself, has utilitarian value," every species, as a unit of diversity, has prima facie utilitarian value as well. Rather than isolating a particular species and examining it for direct commercial or scientific potential, Norton views each species as a unit of diversity and looks at the total value we derive from living in a diverse world.

Granted, each species is only one tiny unit of the world's overall diversity, so perhaps Norton's argument leads in the end to our realizing that no one species matters very much. Speculations that the loss of any one species could trigger a chain reaction leading to some kind of environmental catastrophe are usually dismissed as fanciful. But if Lovejoy's and Norton's arguments do not support a heroic effort to preserve every threatened species, they provide a strong reason to preserve biological diversity generally, to protect the integrity of the natural world.

The objection can be raised, however, that the reasons given so far for preservation are the wrong kinds of reasons. We are doing what we can for other species because of what other species can do for us. We are taking a broader view of the benefits they provide, and a longer term view, but still a view from the same vantage point, of human needs and interests. Species here are still *commodities*.

INTRINSIC VALUE

Many environmentalists argue that species should be preserved, not 15 for our sakes, but for their own. They claim that species have intrinsic, not merely instrumental, value. They are valuable, not merely in virtue of what else they are good *for*, but because they are good in *themselves*.

While these claims have considerable rhetorical force—compared, say, to discussions of the role of species in tertiary waste treatment—they raise more questions than they answer. *Why* do we think species have intrinsic value? In what is it grounded? What is it about species that makes them valuable?

One way to address these questions is to look at a case where the answers are clearer. We can disagree about whether species as such have intrinsic value, but nobody doubts that individual human beings are intrinsically valuable, if anything is. So what is it about human beings that grounds their value? Are species valuable in the same way?

If human beings are intrinsically valuable because we can *think*, then no helpful parallel between humans and other creatures can be drawn. Rationality seems an attribute exclusively human. But if we count morally because we can *feel*, because we can experience pleasure and pain, then a case can be made that other sentient creatures count, too. This is one rationale behind the animal liberation movement. Plants do not suffer, however, nor do lower life forms, and so the argument cannot be generalized to include them in its sweep.

A thornier problem is that no argument modeled on the intrinsic value of individual human beings can justify attributions of intrinsic value to whole groups—that is, to species, whether human or otherwise. Sober explains, "What is special about environmentalism is that it values the preservation of species, communities, or ecosystems, rather than the individual organisms of which they are composed. 'Animal liberationists' have urged that we should take the suffering of sentient animals into account in ethical deliberation. . . . But trees, mountains, and salt marshes do not suffer. They do not experience pleasure and pain, because, evidently, they do not have experiences at all. The same is true of species." Individual animals have individual experiences, of course, but a species does not have a collective "experience."

A more promising approach may be to say that ethical status derives   20 not from having feelings or experiences, but from having needs or interests. A plant needs water, sunlight, and air, even if it does not consciously suffer from their deprivation. Likewise, we can say that a species needs to have its habitat protected, even if no conscious entity entertains such a want. Do "needs" of this sort have to be taken into account morally?

The problem, Sober points out, is that in this view of needs and interests almost nothing does not have moral standing. "If one does not require of an object that it have a mind for it to have wants or needs, what *is* required for the possession of these ethically relevant properties? Suppose one says that an object needs something if it will cease to exist if it does not get it. Then species . . . have needs, but only in the sense that automobiles, garbage dumps, and buildings do too. If everything has needs, the advice to take needs into account in ethical deliberation is empty." It is no help to the environmentalist if species turn out to be intrinsically valuable only in some sense in which just about *everything* is. We want a specific reason to value and preserve species, to hold their claims as counting for more than the claims—if any—of factories and junkyards.

It is more difficult than it might seem, then, to come up with a reason for granting intrinsic value to species that does not either piggyback illicitly on assignments of value to individuals or hand out attributions of value too indiscriminately. It looks as if the value of species is not intrinsic, but somehow dependent on the role species play in human lives and awareness.

TRANSFORMATIVE VALUE

If the value species have depends on the value they have *for us,* does this make them into commodities for human use, like so many widgits? There are at least two reasons why we might be reluctant to draw this conclusion. First of all, something makes us want to put species of living organisms in a class apart from other resources, even resources that serve basic human needs. We debate whether species have intrinsic value, but no one argues for the intrinsic value of, say, tractors or ball bearings. Second, if the value of other species rests only on their ability to fulfill human desires, this seems to give them no secure claim *against* human desires. But it is the voracious desires fueled by human civilization that endanger species in the first place.

Sober responds to the first of these worries by drawing an analogy between objects in nature and works of art. The two have important similarities. "For both natural objects and works of art," he maintains, "our values extend beyond the concerns we have for experiencing pleasure. . . . When we experience works of art, often what we value is not just the kind of experiences we have, but, in addition, the connections we usually have with certain real objects." We value the existence of Michelangelo's *Pietà* beyond any value we derive from just seeing what it looks like. We value the process by which it was created, its history, its authenticity. The same is true, he suggests, of objects in nature.

Yet we are willing to concede that artistic masterpieces are not valuable in themselves, completely apart from any human consciousness of them: "What is valuable [in a work of art] is the relation of a valuer to a valued object. . . . When valuers disappear, so does the possibility of aesthetic value." That art objects—and natural objects—are not intrinsically valuable does not mean that their value is not of a special kind.

Norton characterizes this deeper element of value in nature and art by saying that both not only fulfill human desires but also transform them. Whereas commodities satisfy existing human preferences whatever these are, taken as given, experiences of works of art and study of the natural world lead us to question our values, to criticize and reform them, to alter them altogether. Where environmentalists have gone wrong, he feels, is in accepting a dilemma between either giving free rein to human wants and desires, in their present materialistic form (endangering vast tracts of wild habitat in the process), or else insisting that other creatures, other species, and the ecosystems they inhabit must have some value independent of human wants and desires altogether. But the dilemma is a false one, because "it unnecessarily contracts the range of human values to those founded on demands for given preferences. . . . This is to ignore the role of other species and varied ecosystems in forming and transforming our values."

According to Norton, wild species and undisturbed ecosystems provide occasions for experiences that allow us to rethink our place in the natural order. We learn from other species about the forms and limits of survival on a fragile planet; we learn about sharing the destinies of our fellows in the biotic community. "Appeals to the transformative value of wild species and undisturbed ecosystems thereby provide the means to criticize and limit human demands that threaten to destroy those species and ecosystems while at the same time introducing an important value that humans should place on them."

CONCLUSION

Where does this leave the snail darter and the furbish lousewort, the whole host of lowly species that we may never encounter in our lifetime and would not recognize if we did? How do these enlighten and uplift us? What transformative value do they possess? The answer, in the end, may be "not very much." They doubtless have some role in maintaining the natural order that we do not understand, and the handful of scientists who do know and study them may take aesthetic pleasure in doing so. Is this enough to save them? At what cost?

Norton's conclusion is that this may be the wrong question to ask. To examine species one by one is always to miss the value — commercial, scientific, aesthetic, transformative — in their interaction, in the whole interlocking system of nature in which human beings play only one small part. The lesson of the environmental movement is that nature is not best understood and protected piecemeal. To focus on each individual scrap of creation may distract us from the magnificence — and vulnerability — of the whole. It is nature itself, in all its diversity, that uplifts and sustains us. This is what we are bound to preserve.

The views of Stephen Kellert, Thomas Lovejoy, and Elliott Sober are quoted from their essays in *The Preservation of Species,* ed. Bryan G. Norton (Princeton, N.J.: Princeton University Press, 1985). Bryan G. Norton's views are quoted from his chapter in *The Preservation of Species* and from his book *Why Preserve Natural Variety?* (Princeton, N.J.: Princeton University Press, 1987).

Topics for Critical Thinking and Writing

1. Mills, in paragraph 4, cites a philosopher who says that "an argument from ignorance is no argument at all." Is that true, or not? Explain.

2. Explain the idea that "biological impoverishment may be directly responsible for human impoverishment" (para. 11).

3. Mills contrasts the "intrinsic" value and the "instrumental" value of natural species (para. 15). Consider the lowly cockroach. Under what conditions (if any) could one say that the cockroach had instrumental value? Intrinsic value?

4. In paragraph 26, Mills refers to a certain "dilemma" faced by environmentalists. What, exactly, is this dilemma, and how does Mills think it can be avoided?

Jonathan H. Adler

Little Green Lies: The Environmental Miseducation of America's Children

Some have called it "Eco-Kid Power," while to others it is the "Newest Parental Nightmare." The latest craze sweeping this nation's youth is environmental consciousness, due in no small part to the spread of ecological issues into the classroom. This movement has reached almost every school district in the nation, as children are increasingly taught the importance of being green.

More Pennsylvania high school students are taking environmental education classes than physics. Even the federal government is actively involved. In 1990 President Bush signed the National Environmental Education Act, appropriating $65 million over five years to set up in the Environmental Protection Agency (EPA) an Office of Environmental Education that serves as a clearinghouse for green educational materials.

Most classroom environmental information, including most that is listed at the EPA clearinghouse, comes from literature and teaching guides drafted and distributed by the major environmental groups. These materials include everything from the World Wildlife Fund's "Vanishing Rain Forests Education Kit" and the Chesapeake Bay Foundation's "What I Can Do to Save the Bay," to the Acid Rain Foundation's curriculum, "Air Pollutants and Trees," and the Sierra Club educational newsletter, "Sierraecology." Similar material is targeted to children at home, including *50 Simple Things Kids Can Do to Save the Earth,* which has sold nearly a million copies, and TV's popular "Captain Planet and the Planeteers," not to mention the recent feature-length film *FernGully . . . The Last Rainforest.*

It is entirely appropriate for children to learn about the environment. Indeed, any comprehensive science program for primary and secondary schools ought to include discussions of the food chain, the life cycles of various species, and the fundamentals of meteorology. Using nature trails and

Jonathan H. Adler is an environmental policy analyst at the Competitive Enterprise Institute in Washington, D.C., and a contributor to the book Environmental Politics: Public Costs, Private Rewards *(1992). The essay reprinted here first appeared in the Summer 1992 issue of* Policy Review.

camping in the wilderness can be valuable educational experiences, particularly if children are taught to understand what they are seeing. Unfortunately, much of what is taught to children is simple-minded and inaccurate. Among the growing environmental disinformation spread through the classroom are ten myths that give children an incomplete understanding of environmental issues.

1. RECYCLING IS ALWAYS GOOD

The recycling craze has captured America's schools. From coast to 5 coast, children are organizing recycling programs in their schools and neighborhoods, separating their trash, and sending bottles, cans, newspapers, and yard waste to their local recycling centers. Various environmental groups, as well as the EPA through its "Recycle Today!" campaign, actively promote recycling as a means to "help stamp out the Garbage Gremlin." Animated characters such as Henry Cycle and Captain Planet sell the practice to elementary school children.

In one guide for parents and educators — *This Planet Is Mine* — Mary Metzger and Cynthia Whittaker claim that recycling is "by far the most commonsensible and energy-saving waste reduction technique." This sentiment is echoed in the EPA's *Let's Reduce and Recycle: Curriculum for Solid Waste Awareness,* where children in grades K–6 are told that recycling reduces pollution and saves natural resources, energy, money, and landfill space.

While recycling is often a sensible means of disposing solid waste, it is not so clear that recycling is always of benefit to the planet. Aluminum cans have been profitably recycled for years — indeed companies actually pay for used cans — because recycling aluminum costs less energy and money than does producing cans from virgin materials. Yet this may be the exception rather than the rule. Although recycled paper can be used for newsprint, ledger paper, and cardboard boxes, it is inappropriate for paper products that require the greater strength of unrecycled paper, as the fibers tend to deteriorate during the recycling process. The bleaching of recycled paper causes more water pollution than bleaching paper from virgin pulp. Even when materials are collected for recycling, they are often not used for that purpose. In Islip, New York, there are mountains of tinted glass from bottles collected for recycling, and in the nation's capital newspapers intended for recycling sit rotting in warehouses.

Children were told during a CBS "Schoolbreak Special" that "recycling paper saves trees," and that if all paper were recycled it would save five hundred thousand trees per week. However, 87 percent of all paper in the United States is produced from trees planted and grown for that purpose by the paper industry. Were there less of a market for unrecycled paper products, the incentive to plant more trees would likely shrink as well. Thus, is recycling really a policy that serves to save trees? Or, may it actually reverse the current trend of growth of America's forests? Roger

Sedjo of Resources for the Future, an environmental think tank, points out that there has been a steady increase in U.S. forestland for the past 40 years, and "profit-seeking firms are planting, growing, and harvesting forests on an unprecedented scale." The existence of vibrant markets for virgin wood materials has encouraged this growth.

What is more, it is not clear that recycling is always the *environmentally* preferable disposal option for solid waste. Cleaning cloth diapers, for example, may at first glance seem less wasteful than throwing out disposables, but collection and sterilization requires massive amounts of water, energy (for heat and transportation), and detergent, not to mention the additional time spent in cleaning. If recycling requires increased consumption of energy, it may not result in the net saving of resources that environmentalists desire.

2. PLASTIC IS BAD

Plastic has reached the top of the eco-kid enemies list. Among the "55 fun ways kids can make a difference" listed in Michael O'Brian's *I Helped Save the Earth* are: "Use paper, not plastic," "Don't buy drinks in plastic containers," and "Buy things packaged in cardboard, not plastic." *50 Simple Things Kids Can Do to Save the Earth* calls upon all children to "Stamp out Styrofoam" because "using Styrofoam means using up precious resources . . . and adding more garbage to our world." It further asserts that "plastic foam is often made with chemicals that make the ozone hole bigger!" One New York mother told the *New York Times* that her 12-year-old son's anti-plastic sentiments are so vehement that "If something is in plastic, I have to hide it if I want to use it." 10

This message has apparently had a significant effect. In Closter, New Jersey, the elementary-school group Kids Against Pollution (KAP) has been credited with successfully promoting a ban on foam containers in their community, and was very active in pressuring McDonald's to abandon its polystyrene "clamshell" containers.

One reason plastics are attacked is that they are often difficult to recycle. In addition, plastics are generally not biodegradable, and perhaps most important, rather than being "natural," are produced synthetically from man-made chemicals. Thus, the use of plastic is viewed as an inevitable source of pollution and an unnecessary contribution to the solid waste stream.

Because they are rarely recycled, most plastic products eventually find their way into a landfill. The greatest environmental concern raised by the use of landfills is the possibility that toxic wastes will seep into the local groundwater. Yet plastics are typically inert, and therefore they are certain not to decompose. The stable state of plastics—their nonbiodegradability —is a protection for human health when they are deposited in landfills.

Of course, many kids are upset by the notion that plastics placed by people in the earth today will remain there for centuries. But while plastic does not degrade in a landfill, rarely does anything else either. As the research of William Rathje at the University of Arizona has shown, in landfills, even newspapers fail to biodegrade for decades. What is held against plastic can be a criticism of paper as well.

Children uncomfortable with using plastic might want to ask why its 15 use is so common in contemporary society. Plastic packaging limits breakage and spoilage, and makes it possible to distribute foods and medicines over greater distances at significantly lower cost. Plastic can create strong but lightweight packaging for everything from candies and soft drinks to vitamins and vegetables that would otherwise require tremendous expenditures of natural resources. Do not these benefits offset, at least in part, the environmental concerns about disposal?

Consider aseptic packaging, the synthetic packaging for the "juice boxes" so many children bring to school with their lunch. One criticism of aseptic packaging is that it is nearly impossible to recycle, yet on almost every other count, aseptic packaging is environmentally preferable to the packaging alternatives. Not only do aseptic containers not require refrigeration to keep their contents from spoiling, but their manufacture requires less than one-tenth the energy of making glass bottles.

What is true for juice boxes is also true for other forms of synthetic packaging. The use of polystyrene, which is commonly (and mistakenly) referred to as "Styrofoam," can reduce food waste dramatically due to its insulating properties. (Thanks to these properties, polystyrene cups are much preferred over paper for that morning cup of coffee.) Polystyrene also requires significantly fewer resources to produce than its paper counterpart. As documented in *Science* magazine, a polystyrene cup can be produced with one-sixth the physical material, one-twelfth the steam, and one-thirty-sixth the electricity of its paper counterpart. It is no wonder that polystyrene cups are as much as 60 percent less expensive. It should also be noted that, contrary to popular perceptions, the production of polystyrene has not required the use of chlorofluorocarbons (CFCs) for years, and thus poses no threat to the ozone layer.

The environment benefits of plastic are demonstrated every day as over a million American students receive their milk from plastic, pillow-shaped pouches that require less material to produce than the conventional mini-milk carton and that create 70 percent less waste by volume. Indeed plastic is typically less bulky than other forms of packaging, and therefore reduces the amount of solid waste disposal.

Many environmental leaders now recognize that the plastic versus paper decision is not as clear-cut as they once supposed. As John Ruston of the Environmental Defense Fund acknowledged to the *New York Times*, "I don't think we have strong evidence that one is better than the other." Nonetheless, antiplastic messages are still pushed to many school-age children as part of environmental education.

3. THERE IS TOO MUCH GARBAGE

The popular children's book *50 Simple Things Kids Can Do to Save* 20 *the Earth* declares, "We are making so much garbage that in many places there is not enough room to bury it all." Another EarthWorks publication, *Kid Heroes of the Environment*, claims that "America faces a 'garbage crisis'; we're running out of places to dump our trash." A handbook produced by the Council for Solid Waste Solutions instructs children on how to establish school recycling programs because "overflowing landfills are threatening Mother Earth." In New Hampshire, a teacher's guide produced by the state for Earth Day 1990 calls for students to write to companies complaining about "excess packaging," and the EPA's solid waste curriculum even claims that the growing "garbage crisis" is a problem that "threatens to weaken our cities and consume valuable portions of our natural resource base." Many children's environmental concerns are based upon the underlying assumption that too much waste is being created and that there is no place to put it.

However, there is ample space in which to dispose of America's garbage through landfilling, should such an approach be desired. As the research of A. Clark Wiseman of Resources for the Future has demonstrated, all of the solid waste produced in America in the next thousand years could easily fit in a single landfill accounting for less than one-tenth of 1 percent of the United States. This landfill would be approximately forty-four miles on each side and only one hundred feet deep. If there is more than enough space to dispose of America's garbage, can we really say that there is too much trash? Given that landfilling is significantly less expensive than most other disposal options, advocating that landfilling not be used means that more money will be spent on waste disposal, and less will be available to spend on other things. Some communities have even discovered that modern landfills can be a welcome addition to the neighborhood, adding jobs and economic resources without producing the environmental hazards and aesthetic objections that accompanied the dumps of the past.

While landfilling remains an environmentally and economically viable option, other methods of waste disposal are continually being developed. One increasingly attractive approach is the development of "waste-to-energy" facilities, whereby garbage can be turned into a source of energy. As more communities begin to rely upon this approach to waste disposal, garbage will actually become an important commodity. What is more, should landfill space ever truly become scarce, the resulting increase in the costs of waste disposal would encourage individuals to reduce the amount of waste they produce and develop alternative waste disposal options.

It is important to remember that human activity has always involved the production of waste, and that efforts to reduce, or even eliminate, waste must ultimately come at the expense of much human activity. Product packaging may end up in the trash heap, but during its life it also serves important functions, such as the preservation and protection of perishable goods. As long as society has ample ability to dispose of the waste it produces, there seems to be little reason to worry children about a supposed garbage "crisis."

4. Pesticides Are Always Bad

ABC's for a Better Planet, a children's book featuring the immensely popular Teenage Mutant Ninja Turtles, recommends that children "get folks to buy fruits and vegetables that are grown organically — that is, without chemical pesticides. Organically grown stuff may not look as perfect, but it tastes great — and it's good for you." Linda Lowery's *Earth Day,* a book designed for children in grades K–4, asserts, "People don't need to use chemicals on their crops and lawns. There are safer, more natural ways to protect plants and help them grow."

To emphasize concern over pesticides even further, the National En- 25 vironmental Education Act requires that the EPA annually present a "Rachel Carson Award" in honor of the author who first brought fear of pesticides into the mainstream with her 1962 book *Silent Spring.* A biography of Carson is also one of the first in a new series of children's books published by Simon & Schuster's Silver Burdett Press.

While Carson deserves credit for raising awareness of the potentially damaging effects of DDT on eagle and osprey populations, many of the concerns she promoted, such as fear of the risks of pesticide residues on food, are greatly overblown. Metzger and Whittaker's *This Planet Is Mine* tells parents and eco-educators that pesticide use is killing millions of people, and that "children often receive greater pesticide exposure" than adults. However, the path-breaking work of Bruce Ames, a biochemist at the University of California at Berkeley, has demonstrated that pesticide residues on foods, such as fruits and vegetables, pose no significant health risk.

Notes Ames, "99.9 percent of all the pesticides we ingest, by weight, are natural, produced by the fruit and vegetable plants themselves as part of their protective mechanism." This can be seen in many common foods. While "everyone worries about minute amounts of dioxin," Ames has discovered that "there is a lot more of a dioxin-like compound naturally in broccoli than you will ever be exposed to through dioxin contamination in the environment." But, Ames points out, even the higher level of carcinogenic compounds naturally present in foods poses a negligible health risk.

As a result of the scare over Alar — a substance used to strengthen apple stems and prevent apples from falling off the tree prematurely — frightened mothers were calling the EPA to inquire if one could safely pour apple juice down the drain. Yet Alar residues posed no threat to their children. As Rutgers professor Joseph Rosen noted, Alar "has not been identified as the cause of a single childhood cancer." In fact, according to Dr. Sanford Miller, dean of the University of Texas Health Science Center's Graduate School of Biomedical Science, "The risk of pesticide residues to consumers is effectively zero." As he told the late columnist Warren Brookes, "This is what some fourteen scientific societies, representing over one hundred thousand microbiologists, toxicologists, and food scientists, said at the time of the ridiculous Alar scare. But we were ignored."

While pesticide residues pose no appreciable threat to human health, Ames has noted that the probable impact of efforts to limit pesticide use "will be to *raise* cancer risks, because it will cut consumption of the very foods most beneficial in preventing cancer." Pesticides, including those compounds used to fight insects, weeds, and fungi, increase agricultural productivity and help to prevent food spoilage. The result is that fruits and vegetables are more readily available to consumers at lower prices. And, pesticide-assisted increases in agricultural efficiency have enabled farmers to produce more food while devoting less land to agriculture. Fewer trees are cut down, and fewer wetlands are filled to meet increases in food demand.

5. ACID RAIN IS DESTROYING OUR FORESTS

The Teenage Mutant Ninja Turtles tell our children that "'acid rain' 30 pollutes rivers and kills fish and trees." *50 Simple Things* claims, "Acid rain is extremely harmful to plants, rivers, and lakes. . . . In some places it is killing forests. And it pollutes the water that animals and people need to drink." The EPA lists the Acid Rain Foundation as a source of educational materials in its booklet "Environmental Education Materials for Teachers and Young People (Grades K–12)." Materials provided include acid rain educational activities for grades 4–8 and a curriculum for grades 6–12 that repeat these charges time and time again.

Similar information is available from other sources as well. The children's comic book *Water In Your Hands,* published by the Soil and Water Conservation Society and distributed by the federal government, claims, "Acid precipitation can harm plants on land as well as plants and animals that live in streams and lakes thousands of miles from the source of pollution. Already there are many lakes in which only a few things can live because of high acid levels." The proposed solution is for people to use less energy. They should drive less and "use less electricity. The less you use, the less coal-burning power plants must produce. That may mean less acid precipitation."

The curricula state correctly that many trees are dying in the eastern United States, that northeastern lakes and streams have fewer trout and other sport fish than they did earlier this century, and that burning fossil fuels can make rain more acidic. But a $700-million study commissioned by Congress, the National Acid Precipitation Assessment Program (NAPAP), concluded that acid rain is not a major source of problems in eastern forests and fisheries.

On the contrary, the nitrogen contained in acid rain actually helps much of the eastern forest by providing a necessary nutrient. It also turns out that most acid lakes in the Northeast have been acidic for most of their history. Fish could live in them temporarily when the clearing of forests for farming and paper pulp made watersheds more alkaline; but the watersheds returned to their natural acidity when the farms and dairies became uneconomic and the forests grew back. NAPAP determined that little damage could be attributed to acid rain in the United States, and even then only at very high altitudes in a few small areas. (The minor effects of acid rain on this continent, and the history of lake acidity in the United States, were explained by soil scientist Edward C. Krug in "Fish Story" in the Spring 1990 issue of *Policy Review.*)

6. WE USE TOO MUCH

Last year the *New York Times* ran a story on the "Newest Parental Nightmare," the "eco-smart" child who constantly pesters his parents to use less and "conserve" energy, for one day we might run out. This pressure results in part from school materials such as the EPA children's activity books on water conservation, which proclaim, "We need to save water! This is also called 'conserving' water—not wasting it so we'll have enough for the future!" The TV special based upon *50 Simple Things* told children, "Turn down the heat and put on a sweater" because that is a more efficient use of resources. Muppets Kermit the Frog and Miss Piggy were enlisted to promote this message, appearing in a public service announcement for the National Wildlife Federation.

Children are taught to monitor the "wasteful" activities of their par- 35 ents. As Dee Kloss told the *Philadelphia Inquirer* about her 8-year-old-eco-conscious daughter, "She's harassing me, that child. If I leave the water on when I'm brushing my teeth, she yells at me. She says, 'Off, off, off. You're wasting that water.'" Ironically, some health groups actually recommend letting tap water run for a full minute before using due to concern over lead or other potentially toxic sediments.

Unfortunately, this effort to watchdog water use reflects a simplistic view of natural resources. Water in the United States will not "run out," although it may be misallocated. In almost all cases, water shortages have occurred as a result of political intervention; California's problems can be attributed, for example, to artificially low water prices for agricultural use. As for energy, oil and natural gas prices are at their lowest price in decades, a clear sign that fossil fuel supplies are abundant. The price of a resource rises when it becomes more scarce. But the prices for the vast majority of nonrenewable resources—from aluminum to zinc—have declined over the past century.

Even if a given resource were to become scarce, this would not be the end of the world. Its price would rise, and the economy would promote increased efficiency and the development of alternatives. Thus, it is understandable that 80 percent of the energy efficiency improvements in the

United States between 1973 and 1988 were the result of increases in energy prices. Fears of an impending coal shortage in England not only spurred the development of more efficient technologies, but also encouraged coal's eventual displacement by the use of petroleum. Similarly, when whale oil scarcity drove up prices, entrepreneurs were prompted to develop refined petroleum as a substitute for lighting and other uses.

In the case of energy, the goal should not be "conservation" in the sense of simply using less but "efficiency" — using less to accomplish more. Otherwise, reducing energy use would require sacrificing personal mobility, autonomy, and living standards. Any serious effort to reduce personal consumption would require giving up various human activities, from transportation of people and resources, to heating, lighting, and cooking. Driving to and from school or the office may burn fuel, but it often saves time that can then be devoted to other important activities. Almost all efforts to enhance energy efficiency involve trading capital expenditures in the present for potential energy savings in the future. These trade-offs are inherent in any serious effort to reduce the use of energy, and must always be considered. Nevertheless, they are rarely discussed in the classroom.

7. THERE ARE TOO MANY PEOPLE

As population continues to increase, so will the human impact on the natural environment. More people on the planet means that more people are engaged in activities that shape the world around them. As a result, children are taught, the earth faces dire ecological consequences, from resource depletion to famine and extinction. From the EPA's *Earth Notes* — sent to educators for grades K–6 — to the educational materials such as "For Earth's Sake" and "The Population Challenge" of Zero Population Growth, educational materials on population growth are becoming part and parcel of the environmental curriculum.

One educational guide, distributed in conjunction with Turner Broadcasting's "Save the Earth Season," provides a worksheet in which the students' "ultimate goal is protecting the environment through population control." A high-school text published by Addison-Wesley even talks of the "innovative" population measures developed in the People's Republic of China, a country known for coercive abortions and draconian laws limiting family size.

Some educational messages are more explicit in their advocacy of population control. *This Planet Is Mine* instructs educators to tell children that population growth will cause severe environmental problems "unless the use of birth control methods increases." In suggested activities, educators should "talk about what would happen to the planet if all the people in the world created large families generation after generation." Captain Planet and the Planeteers also tell children, "When it's your turn to have a family, keep it small. The more people there are the more pressure you put on our planet." The population message is summed up well by a "Green Tip" published in the daily Teenage Mutant Ninja Turtles comic strip: "The world grows by 95 million people each year; the U.S. by three million. We can help greatly by all having fewer children and considering adoption." The TBS children's special "One Child—One Voice" claims that population growth is causing the growth of the Sahara Desert in Africa, ignoring *Science* magazine's reports that the desert has actually been shrinking in recent years, and that its growth may have been more the result of climatic conditions than population-related pressures.

If population growth is such a dire threat, why are living standards worldwide increasing concurrently with increases in the world's population? Even in the Third World, increases in agricultural production typically outpace population growth. If it is true that a continually expanding population will overcome the limits of world food supply, why then is most of the world experiencing increases in agricultural productivity that far outpace the increases in people? There are indeed areas that continue to experience famine, but more often than not these areas are in the throes of civil war and violent unrest that disrupt the distribution of food. It should be no wonder that in nations with totalitarian regimes, such as that recently deposed in Ethiopia, there were also shortages of food. But these shortages were more the result of political problems than they were of a deficiency in the world supply of food.

Moreover, children are rarely taught that as societies become more prosperous, population growth eventually slows and resources are used more efficiently with less environmental damage.

8. THE AIR IS GETTING WORSE

A common refrain on air pollution in school materials is that "the problems are here and they are growing at an alarming rate" (*This Planet Is Mine*). *50 Simple Things* claims, "Today the air is so polluted in some places it's not always safe to breathe!" whereas "until about 150 years ago, the air was pure and clean." This sentiment is echoed in a Charlie Brown film produced for the American Lung Association with a grant from the EPA. In the film, the air is so polluted that Lucy cannot even see a baseball hit into the air due to a great cloud of smog.

There is little recognition in school curricula that, by most measure- 45
ments, air quality is actually improving. According to the EPA's own data, levels of ground-level ozone, the pollutant known as "smog," are declining significantly in most urban areas. Even were ozone levels not declining, there is little evidence that the moderate levels found in most cities are responsible for any long-term health effects.

The Virginia Department of Air Pollution Control's "Airy Canary" has trouble flying because of "Dastardly Dirt" created by increased industrial and commercial activity. Yet after initial industrialization, economic growth typically results in decreases of airborne particulates, the form of air pollution with the most significant health effects. Particulate concentrations in such cities as Tehran and Calcutta are almost ten times greater than those found in New York. As Resources for the Future vice president Paul Portney has noted, "It is important to remember that cities in the United States that are relatively polluted by our standards might be considered quite clean in other parts of the world." This is particularly true when compared with the cities of the former Soviet Union.

While children are taught to dislike automobiles, they are not told that not all cars pollute equally, or that in most cases the contributions of individual vehicle emissions are negligible. Much air pollution is the result of incomplete fuel combustion. As technology has improved over time, cars have naturally become more efficient and have thus polluted less. While many give full credit to federal laws for these gains, reductions in automobile emissions began well before the first national clean air legislation was enacted.

Another source of air pollution that is often overlooked is the natural environment. While air pollution is almost always blamed upon human activity, in some areas most of the pollution comes from natural sources. Particularly acute in some areas is the emission of methane and other volatile organic compounds—a primary component in the formation of smog—from plants and animals. In addition, the topography of some areas makes them natural air-pollution traps. As a result, cities located in valleys or depressions, such as Los Angeles, often suffer from greater pollution than those areas where there may actually be greater levels of emissions.

9. GLOBAL WARMING WILL KILL US ALL

Topping the list of environmental concerns these days is the threat of global warming. Increasing concentrations of carbon dioxide, methane, and other greenhouse gases, it is argued, will cause an irreversible change in the earth's climate by increasing average world temperatures by several degrees. Thus, it should be no surprise that discussions of global warming have become very prominent in the classroom. "Beat the Heat: The CO_2 Challenge," distributed to teachers by Scholastic, Inc., charges that "the world is hotter today than any time in recorded history," but fails to acknowledge that the "recorded history" of accurate temperatures barely extends back one hundred years.

In *The Greenhouse Effect: Life on a Warmer Planet*, an educational 50 text for grades 5 and up—praised by the *School Library Journal* as "a book that is especially noteworthy for its calm, balanced approach to a timely topic"—children are told:

> It's frightening to think about the world's food reserves dwindling away or entire islands disappearing under rising seas. Yet this is what scientists predict our world could be like in the next century if greenhouse gases continue to build up in the atmosphere.

Following the initial broadcast on PBS of *After the Warming*, the show's producer, Maryland Public Television, drafted a teachers' manual as if the program—which chronicled the "history" of environmental degradation to the year 2050—was based upon fact, rather than exaggerated assumptions and unfounded conjecture. The TBS children's special "One Child—One Voice" claimed that the greenhouse effect could increase temperatures by as much as 5 or 6 degrees. The American Museum of Natural History, in conjunction with the National Science Foundation and the Environmental Defense Fund, is promoting a series of educational activities and programs based upon its exhibit "Global Warming: Understanding the Forecast." Educational books like *50 Simple Things* tell children that with the greenhouse effect "places that are warm would become too hot to live in, and . . . the places that grow most of our food could get too hot to grow crops anymore." Simply put, global warming is portrayed in the classroom as a threat to all human civilization.

While these arguments are put forward as scientific fact in the classroom, various polls of climate scientists indicate little consensus on how the climate will change over the next century or the relationship between human activity and these changes. On the need for urgent action by the United States, there is even less agreement. In fact, one poll of climate scientists conducted by Greenpeace found that fewer scientists (45 percent) believed action was necessary to avert a "runaway greenhouse effect" than those who felt otherwise (47 percent).

Even if the world does warm up, the higher temperatures could well be beneficial. There is much research to show that plants would thrive in a carbon-dioxide enriched atmosphere, and that a slightly warmer climate would create a healthier planet. Agricultural experts point out that because carbon dioxide acts as a fertilizer for most plants, increasing concentrations of carbon dioxide will increase agricultural productivity. Also, most of the recorded temperature increases in recent years have occurred at night, meaning smaller swings between night and day temperatures, and thus, fewer killing frosts.

Any serious effort to reduce the claimed threat of warming through a massive reduction of greenhouse gas emissions would have drastic economic consequences. One recent study by the Department of Energy projects that reducing carbon dioxide emissions to only 20 percent below 1990 levels would cost as much as $95 billion each year—and for many environmental advocates, such reductions are only the first step. When massive expenditures are forcibly directed toward averting global warming, fewer resources are available for use in other sectors of the economy, from nutrition and education to health care and housing. As Richard Stroup of the Political Economy Research Center testified before Congress's Joint Economic Committee, "If 'insurance' against a particular risk, such as the threat of global warming, is bought at the cost of reduced economic growth, then a decline in the automatic insurance represented by wealth, and the social resilience it provides, is one of the costs borne by future generations." These costs of prevention are rarely accounted for in classroom calls for decisive action. Instead, children are exhorted to become politically involved.

For example, children were encouraged to write to President Bush to 55 attend the United Nations "Earth Summit" in Rio de Janeiro, where global climate change was at the top of the agenda. The TBS *Save the Earth* series, which included an episode of the popular cartoon "Captain Planet and the Planeteers" on the need to go to Rio, was in large part an effort to mobilize impressionable youth for this politically popular cause through the use of children's programming, "action packs," and educational materials.

10. THE OZONE LAYER IS GOING, AND SO ARE WE

The other global environmental threat that keeps children awake at night is the fear that human activity is destroying the ozone layer, exposing humans—and for that matter all types of flora and fauna—to hazardous levels of solar radiation. The Teenage Mutant Ninja Turtles tell children, "The ozone layer protects us from the sun's deadly radiation . . . but the ozone layer is getting thinner each year." According to *This Planet Is Mine,* ozone depletion will cause "DNA damage and resultant genetic defects." Moreover, "Ultraviolet rays also contribute to the dramatic increase we have seen in skin cancers, eye cataracts, . . . and impair the human immune system, reducing our ability to fight disease." In a recent debate on the Senate floor, Senator Albert Gore intoned, "We have to tell our children that they must redefine their relationship to the sky, and they must begin to think of the sky as a threatening part of their environment."

Children are rarely told that the ozone layer naturally thins and accretes every year in a seasonal cycle that is controlled by the sun. Manmade chlorofluorocarbons (CFCs) are blamed for ozone depletion, while natural sources of ozone-depleting substances (for example, the oceans and volcanos) are typically overlooked. Although chlorine molecules can contribute to ozone depletion, Linwood Callis of the National Aeronautics and Space Administration's Atmospheric Sciences Division charges that "73 percent of the global [ozone] declines between 1979 and 1985 are due to natural effects related to solar variability." While such claims are not universally accepted in the scientific community, it is clear that children are only getting a small part of a very complex story—a story that hardly justifies fears of an impending apocalypse.

Contrary to what is being taught, the marginal ozone depletion that may be caused by CFCs would only result in marginal increases in UV-B radiation. For example, if 10 percent (a common estimate of the maximum potential ozone decline) of the ozone layer above Washington, D.C., disappeared tomorrow, radiation levels would only increase to approximately those typically found in Richmond, Virginia, almost one hundred miles south. In fact, natural levels of UV-B rise rapidly as one approaches the equator or moves higher above sea level. Someone living in Denver receives significantly more UV-B exposure than a person in Minneapolis, but this is hardly cited as a reason not to move to the "mile-high city." It also must be noted that there is some inconclusive evidence that atmospheric ozone levels in the 1980s were higher than those in the 1950s.

The school materials also typically fail to explain the important human benefits that have resulted from the use of CFCs. For example, these chemicals have helped save millions of lives through making available to the peoples of the world inexpensive refrigeration for food and medicine. As with many environmental crusades, the drive to eliminate CFCs, even if potentially justified, involves trade-offs that children should be taught as well.

TOWARD A BETTER SHADE OF GREEN

While environmentalism is likely to be a mainstay of education in the 60 years to come, this does not mean that America's children are to be condemned to curricula of half-truths and political advocacy. Instead, children can, and should, be taught facts, not conjecture, and they should learn the whole story, including how an environmental concern fits into the greater ecological and economic context. Rather than impressing upon children the need for political advocacy, children should be encouraged to think of their own solutions after all the facts have been presented. If water use is an issue, a child should learn about the hydrological cycle; if the concern is solid waste, a child should learn where paper comes from and where it may eventually go. At that point it might be profitable for a schoolchild to hypothesize about how public or private action might address the concerns raised about a given issue. Children should not be told by their teachers that they should sign petitions, endorse political agendas, or write pleading letters to the president.

Children need to understand that modern activities do not cause only "negatives" and that all efforts to alleviate environmental impact are purely "positive." Children need to be taught that there are trade-offs implicit in every environmental issue. Recycling paper may reduce the logging of trees (although they are indeed a renewable resource), but it may increase the use of energy and water. Banning CFCs may theoretically affect the levels of stratospheric ozone, but it would restrict the availability of refrigeration needed to preserve food and medicine in the Third World.

Children also need to learn environmental issues in a balanced manner. If there is scientific uncertainty on the likelihood and probable impact of global climate change it is wholly inappropriate to scare children by telling them their parents are destroying the earth. Environmental regulations can often have significant impacts upon regional and national economies, yet wealthier societies are not only healthier, but also more likely to be concerned about the environment. This, too, should be an important consideration.

Environmental education can be a valuable addition to school curricula, but only if it is conducted in a careful, thoughtful, and nonideological manner. After all, schools are for education, not political indoctrination. If educators approach environmental issues in such a balanced fashion, our children might not turn out politically correct, but at least they will be much more "eco-smart."

Topics for Critical Thinking and Writing

1. Adler identifies ten "myths" about the environment that are now being taught to children in the schools. What are these ten myths? What efforts to save or improve the environment does Adler ignore—and, to that extent, does not treat as just another myth?

2. If, as Adler says, "mountains of tinted glass" await recycling in New York, and in Washington, D.C., old newspapers "sit rotting in warehouses" (para. 7), is this a reason for concluding that recycling is a bad idea? What alternative does Adler offer, or do you think he would favor, to recycling colored glass and old newspapers?

3. Adler asks, rhetorically (see para. 15), whether the benefits of plastic containers do not cancel out the costs associated with their use. How do you think a question of costs and benefits like this can be answered?

4. In his discussion of the garbage disposal problem (paras. 20–23), Adler omits any reference to compostable garbage—biodegradable coffee grounds, banana skins, and so on. Do you think he would regard recommendations to sort garbage and compost food waste as just another myth, not worth the effort? Why, or why not?

5. Adler reports scientific studies purporting to show that using pesticides in agriculture causes no harm to consumers (paras. 26–29). Can we trust this research? After all, research financed by the tobacco companies has never discovered any link between smoking and cancer. How would you regard the information Adler reports if you were to learn that the university laboratories in which the research was done were financed by a company like DuPont or Monsanto, manufacturers of the very pesticides in question?

6. In his discussion of acid rain, Adler implies that it probably is more beneficial than harmful to eastern forests (paras. 32–33). Is the same true elsewhere in the world? Ask your reference librarian for help in finding information about *Waldsterben*, literally "forest death," which has been a serious problem in Germany for a decade. Try to verify whether acid rain is the culprit.

7. In his discussion of myth 6, Adler concentrates on water resources and energy supplies and implies that, so far as those things are concerned, there is no reason to change our current habits of consumption and waste because that would interfere with our "personal mobility, autonomy, and living standards" (para. 38). How might one object to this line of reasoning?

8. Reread Adler's discussion of myth 7 and decide whether he believes (1) there is no limit to which human population can grow without causing problems for the environment; (2) there is such a limit, but unfortunately no one knows what it is or how to find it; or (3) whether or not there is such a limit, populations tend to stabilize as people become more affluent.

9. In paragraph 47 Adler says, "As technology has improved over time, cars have naturally become more efficient and have thus polluted less." Is "naturally" the right word? Might one argue that technology develops because of perceived needs, and if the new technology has produced cars that pollute less, it is because some people—we can call them environmentalists—pointed to the need for such technology? What are your views on this issue?

10. What, if anything, were you taught in elementary or secondary school about global warming and about the ozone layer? In the intervening years what, if anything, have you learned that has caused you to believe that the earlier teachings were faulty?

11. In paragraph 61 Adler says that "there are trade-offs implicit in every environmental issue." Consider one environmental program that you are familiar with, and discuss the trade-offs.

12

Euthanasia: Should Doctors Intervene at the End of Life?

Barbara Huttman

A Crime of Compassion

"Murderer," a man shouted. "God help patients who get *you* for a nurse."

"What gives you the right to play God?" another one asked.

It was the Phil Donahue show where the guest is a fatted calf and the audience a 200-strong flock of vultures hungering to pick up the bones. I had told them about Mac, one of my favorite cancer patients. "We resuscitated him fifty-two times in just one month. I refused to resuscitate him again. I simply sat there and held his hand while he died."

There wasn't time to explain that Mac was a young, witty, macho cop who walked into the hospital with thirty-two pounds of attack equipment, looking as if he could single-handedly protect the whole city, if not the entire state. "Can't get rid of this cough," he said. Otherwise, he felt great.

Before the day was over, tests confirmed that he had lung cancer. And before the year was over, I loved him, his wife, Maura, and their three kids as if they were my own. All the nurses loved him. And we all battled his disease for six months without ever giving death a thought. Six months isn't such a long time in the whole scheme of things, but it was long enough to

Barbara Huttman, born in Oakland, California, in 1935, earned nursing degrees in 1976 and 1978. She is the author of numerous articles and of several books, including Code Blue: A Nurse's True-Life Story (1982). The essay that we reprint originally appeared in Newsweek (August 8, 1983).

see him lose his youth, his wit, his macho, his hair, his bowel and bladder control, his sense of taste and smell, and his ability to do the slightest thing for himself. It was also long enough to watch Maura's transformation from a young woman into a haggard, beaten old lady.

When Mac had wasted away to a 60-pound skeleton kept alive by liquid food we poured down a tube, IV solutions we dripped into his veins, and oxygen we piped to a mask on his face, he begged us: "Mercy . . . for God's sake, please just let me go."

The first time he stopped breathing, the nurse pushed the button that calls a "code blue" throughout the hospital and sends a team rushing to resuscitate the patient. Each time he stopped breathing, sometimes two or three times in one day, the code team came again. The doctors and technicians worked their miracles and walked away. The nurses stayed to wipe the saliva that drooled from his mouth, irrigate the big craters of bedsores that covered his hips, suction the lung fluids that threatened to drown him, clean the feces that burned his skin like lye, pour the liquid food down the tube attached to his stomach, put pillows between his knees to ease the bone-on-bone pain, turn him every hour to keep the bedsores from getting worse, and change his gown and linen every two hours to keep him from being soaked in perspiration.

At night I went home and tried to scrub away the smell of decaying flesh that seemed woven into the fabric of my uniform. It was in my hair, the upholstery of my car—there was no washing it away. And every night I prayed that his agonized eyes would never again plead with me to let him die.

Every morning I asked the doctor for a "no code" order. Without that order, we had to resuscitate every patient who stopped breathing. His doctor was one of the several who believe we must extend life as long as we have the means and knowledge to do it. To not do it is to be liable for negligence, at least in the eyes of many people, including some nurses. I thought about what it would be like to stand before a judge, accused of murder, if Mac stopped breathing and I didn't call a code.

And after the fifty-second code, when Mac was still lucid enough to $_{10}$ beg for death again, and Maura was crumbled in my arms again, and when no amount of pain medication stilled his moaning and agony, I wondered about a spiritual judge. Was all this misery and suffering supposed to be building character or infusing us all with the sense of humility that comes from impotence?

Had we, the whole medical community, become so arrogant that we believed in the illusion of salvation through science? Had we become so self-righteous that we thought meddling in God's work was our duty, our moral imperative, and our legal obligation? Did we really believe that we had the right to force "life" on a suffering man who had begged for the right to die?

Such questions haunted me more than ever early one morning when Maura went home to change her clothes and I was bathing Mac. He had been still for so long, I thought he at last had the blessed relief of coma. Then he opened his eyes and moaned, "Pain . . . no more . . . Barbara . . . do something . . . God, let me go."

The desperation in the eyes and voice riddled me with guilt. "I'll stop," I told him as I injected the pain medication.

I sat on the bed and held Mac's hands in mine. He pressed his bony fingers against my hand and muttered, "Thanks." Then there was the one soft sigh and I felt his hands go cold in mine. "Mac?" I whispered, as I waited for his chest to rise and fall again.

A clutch of panic banded my chest, drew my finger to the code button, urged me to do something, anything . . . but sit there alone with death. I kept one finger on the button, without pressing it, as a waxen pallor slowly transformed his face from person to empty shell. Nothing I've ever done in my forty-seven years has taken so much effort as it took *not* to press that code button. 15

Eventually, when I was as sure as I could be that the code team would fail to bring him back, I entered the legal twilight zone and pushed the button. The team tried. And while they were trying, Maura walked in the room and shrieked, "No . . . don't let them do this to him . . . for God's sake . . . please, no more."

Cradling her in my arms was like cradling myself, Mac, and all those patients and nurses who had been in this place before who do the best they can in a death-denying society.

So a TV audience accused me of murder. Perhaps I am guilty. If a doctor had written a no-code order, which is the only *legal* alternative, would he have felt any less guilty? Until there is legislation making it a criminal act to code a patient who has requested the right to die, we will all of us risk the same fate as Mac. For whatever reason, we developed the means to prolong life, and now we are forced to use it. We do not have the right to die.

Topics for Critical Thinking and Writing

1. If you think that Huttman's title sounds somewhat familiar — if it seems to echo a familiar phrase — you are right. What does it echo, and how effective do you think the title is?

2. In order to advance a thesis Huttman narrates an experience. That is, she draws on her authority as a person who has undergone something. In a sentence or two state her thesis.

3. What persona does Huttman convey? How important is the persona to the argument?

4. Huttman's closing sentence is, "We do not have the right to die." Taking her words in the context of her essay, what do they mean?

5. Huttman obviously believes that euthanasia (mercy killing) is sometimes justi-

fied. Reflecting the argument of her essay, complete the following criterion: A person is justified in killing another person, as an act of mercy, if and only if . . ." Cite examples of three hypothetical cases of so-called mercy killing that this criterion would exclude—that is, that this criterion implies are *not* justified.

6. Huttman's patient, Mac, clearly wanted to die (see paras. 6 and 12). But suppose you do not know whether the patient wants to die, because, say, she arrives at the hospital in a coma, and is thus unable from the start to indicate to her family or the hospital staff whether she wants to be allowed to die. Write a 500- to 750-word essay exploring what you think Huttman would argue we ought to do in such a case.

7. As Huttman's final paragraph indicates, when she wrote her essay (1983) the only legal alternative to resuscitation was a physician's written no-code order. Today many states recognize "living wills," documents in which a person indicates his or her desires concerning resuscitation. Find out the legal status in your state of "living wills" expressing a "right to die." If such documents are recognized, study one and evaluate it.

Ellen Goodman

Who Lives? Who Dies? Who Decides?

Some have called it a Right to Die case. Others have labeled it a Right to Live case. One group of advocates has called for "death with dignity." Others have responded accusingly, "euthanasia."

At the center of the latest controversy about life and death, medicine and law, is a 78-year-old Massachusetts man whose existence hangs on a court order.

On one point, everyone agrees: Earle Spring is not the man he used to be. Once a strapping outdoorsman, he is now strapped to a wheelchair. Once a man with a keen mind, he is now called senile by many, and mentally incompetent by the courts. He is, at worst, a member of the living dead; at best, a shriveled version of his former self.

For more than two years, since his physical and then mental health began to deteriorate, Earle Spring has been kept alive by spending five hours on a kidney dialysis machine three times a week. Since January 1979, his family has pleaded to have him removed from the life-support system.

They believe deeply that the Earle Spring who was would not want to   5

Ellen Goodman, educated at Radcliffe College, worked as a reporter for Newsweek *and the* Detroit Free Press. *Since 1967 she has written for the* Boston Globe, *and since 1972 her column has been nationally syndicated. This column appeared in the* Boston Globe *in February 1980, the year she won a Pulitzer Prize for journalism.*

live as the Earle Spring who is. They believe they are advocates for the right to die in peace.

In the beginning, the courts agreed. Possibly for the first time, they ruled last month in favor of withdrawing medical care from an elderly patient whose mind had deteriorated. The dialysis was stopped.

But then, in a sudden intervention, an outside nurse and doctor visited Earle Spring and testified that he was alert enough to "make a weak expression of his desire to live." And so the treatments were resumed.

Now, while the courts are waiting for new and more thorough evidence about Spring's mental state, the controversy rages about legal procedures; no judge ever visited Spring, no psychiatrist ever testified. And even more important, we are again forced to determine one person's right to die or to live.

This case makes the Karen Ann Quinlan story seem simple in comparison. Quinlan today hangs onto her "life" long after her "plug was pulled." But when the New Jersey court heard that case, Quinlan had no will. She had suffered brain death by any definition.

The Spring story is different. He is neither competent nor comatose. 10 He lives in a gray area of consciousness. So the questions also range over the gray area of our consciences.

What should the relationship be between mental health and physical treatment? Should we treat the incompetent as aggressively as the competent? Should we order heart surgery for one senile citizen? Should we take another off a kidney machine? What is the mental line between a life worth saving and the living dead? Who is to decide?

Until recently, we didn't have the technology to keep an Earle Spring alive. Until recently, the life-and-death decisions about the senile elderly or the retarded or the institutionalized were made privately between families and medical people. Now, increasingly, in states like Massachusetts, they are made publicly and legally.

Clearly there are no absolutes in this case. No right to die. No right to live. We have to take into account many social as well as medical factors. How much of the resources of a society or a family should be allotted to a member who no longer recognizes it? How many sacrifices should the healthy and vital make for the terminally or permanently ill and disabled?

In England, where kidney dialysis machines are scarce, Earle Spring would never have remained on one. In America, one Earle Spring can decimate the energy and income of an entire family.

But the Spring case is a crucial, scary one that could affect all those 15 living under that dubious sentence "incompetent" or that shaky diagnosis "senile." So it seems to me that if there is one moment a week when the fog lifts and when this man wants to live, if there is any mental activity at all, then disconnecting him from life would be a dangerous precedent, far more dangerous than letting him continue.

The court ruled originally in favor of taking Spring off the machine. It ruled that this is what Earle Spring would have wanted. I have no doubt that his family believes it. I have no doubt of their affection or their pain.

But I remember, too, what my grandfather used to say: No one wants to live to be one hundred until you ask the man who is ninety-nine. Well, no one, including Earle Spring, wants to live to be senile. But once senile, he may well want to live. We simply have to give him the benefit of the doubt. Any doubt.

Topics for Critical Thinking and Writing

1. Suppose you were in the condition of Earle Spring, as described by Goodman (paras. 3, 4, and 10). Would you want to be kept alive, or not? In an essay of 250 words, explain why.

2. Goodman invites us to think about the relationship between "mental health and physical treatment" (para. 11). She concludes that we have to give everyone, no matter what mental condition he or she is in, "the benefit of the doubt" (para. 17). Does she give any argument for this conclusion? If so, what is it and what do you think of it? If not, invent an argument that you think she might accept.

3. Goodman declares, "Clearly there are no absolutes in this case. No right to die. No right to live" (para. 13). Why does she hold this view, do you think? Could there be a right to die (or to live) that is not "absolute"? What sort of right to die, or to live, do you think *you* have — if any? Explain your view in an essay of 500 words.

James Rachels

Active and Passive Euthanasia

The distinction between active and passive euthanasia is thought to be crucial for medical ethics. The idea is that it is permissible, at least in some cases, to withhold treatment and allow a patient to die, but it is never permissible to take any direct action designed to kill the patient. This doctrine seems to be accepted by most doctors, and it is endorsed in a statement adopted by the House of Delegates of the American Medical Association on December 4, 1973:

> The intentional termination of the life of one human being by another — mercy killing — is contrary to that for which the medical profession stands and is contrary to the policy of the American Medical Association.

James Rachels, professor of philosophy in the University of Alabama at Birmingham, is the author of several books, including The End of Life *and* Created from Animals: The Moral Implications of Darwinism. *The article reprinted here appeared in the* New England Journal of Medicine *in 1975.*

> The cessation of the employment of extraordinary means to prolong the life of the body when there is irrefutable evidence that biological death is imminent is the decision of the patient and/or his immediate family. The advice and judgment of the physician should be freely available to the patient and/or his immediate family.

However, a strong case can be made against this doctrine. In what follows I will set out some of the relevant arguments, and urge doctors to reconsider their views on this matter.

To begin with a familiar type of situation, a patient who is dying of incurable cancer of the throat is in terrible pain, which can no longer be satisfactorily alleviated. He is certain to die within a few days, even if present treatment is continued, but he does not want to go on living for those days since the pain is unbearable. So he asks the doctor for an end to it, and his family joins in the request.

Suppose the doctor agrees to withhold treatment, as the conventional doctrine says he may. The justification for his doing so is that the patient is in terrible agony, and since he is going to die anyway, it would be wrong to prolong his suffering needlessly. But now notice this. If one simply withholds treatment, it may take the patient longer to die, and so he may suffer more than he would if more direct action were taken and a lethal injection given. This fact provides strong reason for thinking that, once the initial decision not to prolong his agony has been made, active euthanasia is actually preferable to passive euthanasia, rather than the reverse. To say otherwise is to endorse the option that leads to more suffering rather than less, and is contrary to the humanitarian impulse that prompts the decision not to prolong his life in the first place.

Part of my point is that the process of being "allowed to die" can be relatively slow and painful, whereas being given a lethal injection is relatively quick and painless. Let me give a different sort of example. In the United States about one in six hundred babies is born with Down's syndrome. Most of these babies are otherwise healthy—that is, with only the usual pediatric care, they will proceed to an otherwise normal infancy. Some, however, are born with congenital defects such as intestinal obstructions that require operations if they are to live. Sometimes, the parents and the doctor will decide not to operate, and let the infant die. Anthony Shaw describes what happens then:

> When surgery is denied [the doctor] must try to keep the infant from suffering while natural forces sap the baby's life away. As a surgeon whose natural inclination is to use the scalpel to fight off death, standing by and watching a salvageable baby die is the most emotionally exhausting experience I know. It is easy at a conference, in a theoretical discussion to decide that such infants should be allowed to die. It is altogether different to stand by in the nursery and watch as dehydration and infection wither a tiny being over hours and days. This is a terrible ordeal for

me and the hospital staff—much more so than for the parents who never set foot in the nursery.[1]

I can understand why some people are opposed to all euthanasia, and insist that such infants must be allowed to live. I think I can also understand why other people favor destroying these babies quickly and painlessly. But why should anyone favor letting "dehydration and infection wither a tiny being over hours and days"? The doctrine that says that a baby may be allowed to dehydrate and wither, but may not be given an injection that would end its life without suffering, seems so patently cruel as to require no further refutation. The strong language is not intended to offend, but only to put the point in the clearest possible way.

My second argument is that the conventional doctrine leads to decisions concerning life and death made on irrelevant grounds.

Consider again the case of the infants with Down's syndrome who need operations for congenital defects unrelated to the syndrome to live. Sometimes, there is no operation, and the baby dies, but when there is no such defect, the baby lives on. Now, an operation such as that to remove an intestinal obstruction is not prohibitively difficult. The reason why such operations are not performed in these cases is, clearly, that the child has Down's syndrome and the parents and the doctor judge that because of that fact it is better for the child to die.

But notice that this situation is absurd, no matter what view one takes of the lives and potentials of such babies. If the life of such an infant is worth preserving, what does it matter if it needs a simple operation? Or, if one thinks it better that such a baby should not live on, what difference does it make that it happens to have an unobstructed intestinal tract? In either case, the matter of life and death is being decided on irrelevant grounds. It is the Down's syndrome, and not the intestines, that is the issue. The matter should be decided, if at all, on that basis, and not be allowed to depend on the essentially irrelevant question of whether the intestinal tract is blocked.

What makes this situation possible, of course, is the idea that when there is an intestinal blockage, one can "let the baby die," but when there is no such defect there is nothing that can be done, for one must not "kill" it. The fact that this idea leads to such results as deciding life or death on irrelevant grounds is another good reason why the doctrine would be rejected.

One reason why so many people think that there is an important moral difference between active and passive euthanasia is that they think killing someone is morally worse than letting someone die. But is it? Is killing, in itself, worse than letting die? To investigate this issue, two cases may be considered that are exactly alike except that one involves killing whereas the other involves letting someone die. Then, it can be asked whether this

5

[1]Anthony Shaw, "Doctor, Do We Have a Choice?" *New York Times Magazine*, January 30, 1972, p. 54. [Rachels's note.]

difference makes any difference to the moral assessments. It is important that the cases be exactly alike, except for this one difference, since otherwise one cannot be confident that it is this difference and not some other that accounts for any variation in the assessments of the two cases. So, let us consider this pair of cases:

In the first, Smith stands to gain a large inheritance if anything should happen to his six-year-old cousin. One evening while the child is taking his bath, Smith sneaks into the bathroom and drowns the child, and then arranges things so that it will look like an accident.

In the second, Jones also stands to gain if anything should happen to his 6-year-old cousin. Like Smith, Jones sneaks in planning to drown the child in his bath. However, just as he enters the bathroom Jones sees the child slip and hit his head, and fall face down in the water. Jones is delighted; he stands by, ready to push the child's head back under if it is necessary, but it is not necessary. With only a little thrashing about, the child drowns all by himself, "accidentally," as Jones watches and does nothing.

Now Smith killed the child, whereas Jones "merely" let the child die. That is the only difference between them. Did either man behave better, from a moral point of view? If the difference between killing and letting die were in itself a morally important matter, one should say that Jones's behavior was less reprehensible than Smith's. But does one really want to say that? I think not. In the first place, both men acted from the same motive, personal gain, and both had exactly the same end in view when they acted. It may be inferred from Smith's conduct that he is a bad man, although the judgment may be withdrawn or modified if certain further facts are learned about him — for example, that he is mentally deranged. But would not the very same thing be inferred about Jones from his conduct? And would not the same further considerations also be relevant to any modification of this judgment? Moreover, suppose Jones pleaded, in his own defense, "After all, I didn't do anything except just stand there and watch the child drown. I didn't kill him; I only let him die." Again, if letting die were in itself less bad than killing, this defense should have at least some weight. But it does not. Such a "defense" can only be regarded as a grotesque perversion of moral reasoning. Morally speaking, it is no defense at all.

Now, it may be pointed out, quite properly, that the cases of euthanasia with which doctors are concerned are not like this at all. They do not involve personal gain or the destruction of normal healthy children. Doctors are concerned only with cases in which the patient's life is of no further use to him, or in which the patient's life has become or will soon become a terrible burden. However, the point is the same in these cases: The bare difference between killing and letting die does not, in itself, make a moral difference. If a doctor lets a patient die, for humane reasons, he is in the same moral position as if he had given the patient a lethal injection for humane reasons. If his decision was wrong — if, for example, the patient's illness was in fact curable—the decision would be equally regrettable no matter which method was used to carry it out. And if the doctor's decision was the right one, the method used is not in itself important.

The AMA policy statement isolates the crucial issue very well; the crucial issue is "the intentional termination of the life of one human being by another." But after identifying this issue, and forbidding "mercy killing," the statement goes on to deny that the cessation of treatment is the intentional termination of life. This is where the mistake comes in, for what is the cessation of treatment, in these circumstances, if it is not "the intentional termination of the life of one human being by another?" Of course it is exactly that, and if it were not, there would be no point to it.

Many people will find this judgment hard to accept. One reason, I 15 think, is that it is very easy to conflate the question of whether killing is, in itself, worse than letting die, with the very different question of whether most actual cases of killing are more reprehensible than most actual cases of letting die. Most actual cases of killing are clearly terrible (think, for example, of all the murders reported in the newspapers), and one hears of such cases every day. On the other hand, one hardly ever hears of a case of letting die, except for the actions of doctors who are motivated by humanitarian reasons. So one learns to think of killing in a much worse light than of letting die. But this does not mean that there is something about killing that makes it in itself worse than letting die, for it is not the bare difference between killing and letting die that makes the difference in these cases. Rather, the other factors—the murderer's motive of personal gain, for example, contrasted with the doctor's humanitarian motivation—account for different reactions to the different cases.

I have argued that killing is not in itself any worse than letting die; if my contention is right, it follows that active euthanasia is not any worse than passive euthanasia. What arguments can be given on the other side? The most common, I believe, is the following:

> The important difference between active and passive euthanasia is that, in passive euthanasia, the doctor does not do anything to bring about the patient's death. The doctor does nothing, and the patient dies of whatever ills already afflict him. In active euthanasia, however, the doctor does something to bring about the patient's death: He kills him. The doctor who gives the patient with cancer a lethal injection has himself caused his patient's death; whereas if he merely ceases treatment, the cancer is the cause of the death.

A number of points need to be made here. This first is that it is not exactly correct to say that in passive euthanasia the doctor does nothing, for he does do one thing that is very important: He lets the patient die. "Letting someone die" is certainly different, in some respects, from other types of action—mainly in that it is a kind of action that one may perform by way of not performing certain other actions. For example, one may let a patient die by way of not giving medication, just as one may insult someone by way of not shaking his hand. But for any purpose of moral assessment, it is a type of action nonetheless. The decision to let a patient die is subject to moral appraisal in the same way that a decision to kill him would be subject to moral appraisal: It may be assessed as wise or unwise, compassionate or sadistic, right or wrong. If a doctor deliberately let a patient die who was suffering from a routinely curable illness, the doctor would certainly be to blame for what he had done, just as he would be to blame if he had needlessly killed the patient. Charges against him would then be appropriate. If so, it would be no defense at all for him to insist that he didn't "do anything." He would have done something very serious indeed, for he let his patient die.

Fixing the cause of death may be very important from a legal point of view, for it may determine whether criminal charges are brought against the doctor. But I do not think that this notion can be used to show a moral difference between active and passive euthanasia. The reason why it is considered bad to be the cause of someone's death is that death is regarded as a great evil—and so it is. However, if it has been decided that euthanasia—even passive euthanasia—is desirable in a given case, it has also been decided that in this instance death is not greater an evil than the patient's continued existence. And if this is true, the usual reason for not wanting to be the cause of someone's death simply does not apply.

Finally, doctors may think that all of this is only of academic interest—the sort of thing that philosophers may worry about but that has no practical bearing on their own work. After all, doctors must be concerned about the legal consequences of what they do, and active euthanasia is clearly forbidden by the law. But even so, doctors should also be concerned with the fact that the law is forcing upon them a moral doctrine that may be indefensible, and has a considerable effect on their practices. Of course, most doctors are not now in the position of being coerced in this matter, for they do not regard themselves as merely going along with what the law requires. Rather, in statements such as the AMA policy statement that I have quoted, they are endorsing this doctrine as a central point of medical ethics. In that statement, active euthanasia is condemned not merely as illegal but as "contrary to that for which the medical profession stands," whereas passive euthanasia is approved. However, the preceding considerations suggest that there is really no moral difference between the two, considered in themselves (there may be important moral differences in some cases in their *consequences*, but, as I pointed out, these differences may make active euthanasia, and not passive euthanasia, the morally preferable option). So, whereas doctors may have to discriminate between active and passive euthanasia to satisfy the law, they should not do any more than that. In particular, they should not give the distinction any added authority and weight by writing it into official statements of medical ethics.

Topics for Critical Thinking and Writing

1. Explain the distinction between "active" and "passive" euthanasia. Why do you think the American Medical Association attaches importance to the distinction?

2. Rachels argues that in certain cases, "active euthanasia is actually preferable to passive euthanasia" (para. 3). What is his argument? Do you think it ought to persuade a person who already favors "passive" euthanasia to perform "active" euthanasia in cases of the sort Rachels describes? Why, or why not?

3. What is Rachels's "second argument" (para. 5) and what is it supposed to prove? Do you think it succeeds, or not? Explain.

4. Rachels asks whether "killing" is worse, as many people think, than "letting die" (para. 9). He argues that it is not; what is his argument? Does it persuade you? Why, or why not?

5. Rachels opens his essay by discussing a genuine case of a newborn with Down's syndrome (in para. 4); but eventually he is forced to construct purely hypothetical cases (in paras. 10 and 11). Do you think that the persuasive power of his argument suffers when he shifts to hypothetical cases? Or does it improve? Or doesn't it matter whether he is discussing actual or only hypothetical cases? Explain.

6. The principal thesis of Rachels's essay is that "the bare difference between killing and letting die does not, in itself, make a moral difference" (para. 13). Summarize his argument for this thesis.

Timothy M. Quill

Death and Dignity: A Case of Individualized Decision Making

Diane was feeling tired and had a rash. A common scenario, though there was something subliminally worrisome that prompted me to check her blood count. Her hematocrit was 22, and the white-cell count was 4.3 with some metamyelocytes and unusual white cells. I wanted it to be viral, trying to deny what was staring me in the face. Perhaps in a repeated count it would disappear. I called Diane and told her it might be more serious

---

Timothy M. Quill, born in 1949, was educated at Amherst College and at the University of Rochester School of Medicine. He now teaches at the University of Rochester and is division head of internal medicine at the Genesee Hospital in Rochester, New York. The essay here first appeared on March 7, 1991, in the New England Journal of Medicine, *a publication read chiefly by physicians. Dr. Quill has recently expanded on the ideas in this essay, in a book entitled* Death and Dignity: Making Choices and Taking Charge (1993).

than I had initially thought—that the test needed to be repeated and that if she felt worse, we might have to move quickly. When she pressed for the possibilities, I reluctantly opened the door to leukemia. Hearing the word seemed to make it exist. "Oh, shit!" she said. "Don't tell me that." Oh, shit! I thought, I wish I didn't have to.

Diane was no ordinary person (although no one I have ever come to know has been really ordinary). She was raised in an alcoholic family and had felt alone for much of her life. She had vaginal cancer as a young woman. Through much of her adult life, she had struggled with depression and her own alcoholism. I had come to know, respect, and admire her over the previous eight years as she confronted these problems and gradually overcame them. She was an incredibly clear, at times brutally honest, thinker and communicator. As she took control of her life, she developed a strong sense of independence and confidence. In the previous three and a half years, her hard work had paid off. She was completely abstinent from alcohol, she had established much deeper connections with her husband, college-age son, and several friends, and her business and her artistic work were blossoming. She felt she was really living fully for the first time.

Not surprisingly, the repeated blood count was abnormal, and detailed examination of the peripheral-blood smear showed myelocytes. I advised her to come into the hospital, explaining that we needed to do a bone marrow biopsy and make some decisions relatively rapidly. She came to the hospital knowing what we would find. She was terrified, angry, and sad. Although we knew the odds, we both clung to the thread of possibility that it might be something else.

The bone marrow confirmed the worst: acute myelomonocytic leukemia. In the face of this tragedy, we looked for signs of hope. This is an area of medicine in which technological intervention has been successful, with cures 25 percent of the time—long-term cures. As I probed the costs of these cures, I heard about induction chemotherapy (three weeks in the hospital, prolonged neutropenia, probable infectious complications, and hair loss; 75 percent of patients respond, 25 percent do not). For the survivors, this is followed by consolidation chemotherapy (with similar side effects; another 25 percent die, for a net survival of 50 percent). Those still alive, to have a reasonable chance of long-term survival, then need bone marrow transplantation (hospitalization for two months and whole-body irradiation, with complete killing of the bone marrow, infectious complications, and the possibility for graft-versus-host disease—with a survival of approximately 50 percent, to 25 percent of the original group). Though hematologists may argue over the exact percentages, they don't argue about the outcome of no treatment—certain death in days, weeks, or at most a few months.

Believing that delay was dangerous, our oncologist broke the news to Diane and began making plans to insert a Hickman catheter and begin induction chemotherapy that afternoon. When I saw her shortly thereafter, she was enraged at his presumption that she would want treatment, and

5

devastated by the finality of the diagnosis. All she wanted to do was go home and be with her family. She had no further questions about treatment and in fact had decided that she wanted none. Together we lamented her tragedy and the unfairness of life. Before she left, I felt the need to be sure that she and her husband understood that there was some risk in delay, that the problem was not going to go away, and that we needed to keep considering the options over the next several days. We agreed to meet in two days.

She returned in two days with her husband and son. They had talked extensively about the problem and the options. She remained very clear about her wish not to undergo chemotherapy and to live whatever time she had left outside the hospital. As we explored her thinking further, it became clear that she was convinced she would die during the period of treatment and would suffer unspeakably in the process (from hospitalization, from lack of control over her body, from the side effects of chemotherapy, and from pain and anguish). Although I could offer support and my best effort to minimize her suffering if she chose treatment, there was no way I could say any of this would not occur. In fact, the last four patients with acute leukemia at our hospital had died very painful deaths in the hospital during various stages of treatment (a fact I did not share with her). Her family wished she would choose treatment but sadly accepted her decision. She articulated very clearly that it was she who would be experiencing all the side effects of treatment and that odds of 25 percent were not good enough for her to undergo so toxic a course of therapy, given her expectations of chemotherapy and hospitalization and the absence of a closely matched bone marrow donor. I had her repeat her understanding of the treatment, the odds, and what to expect if there were no treatment. I clarified a few misunderstandings, but she had a remarkable grasp of the options and implications.

I have been a long-time advocate of active, informed patient choice of treatment or nontreatment, and of a patient's right to die with as much control and dignity as possible. Yet there was something about her giving up a 25 percent chance of long-term survival in favor of almost certain death that disturbed me. I had seen Diane fight and use her considerable inner resources to overcome alcoholism and depression, and I half expected her to change her mind over the next week. Since the window of time in which effective treatment can be initiated is rather narrow, we met several times that week. We obtained a second hematology consultation and talked at length about the meaning and implications of treatment and nontreatment. She talked to a psychologist she had seen in the past. I gradually understood the decision from her perspective and became convinced that it was the right decision for her. We arranged for home hospice care (although at that time Diane felt reasonably well, was active, and looked healthy), left the door open for her to change her mind, and tried to anticipate how to keep her comfortable in the time she had left.

Just as I was adjusting to her decision, she opened up another area that would stretch me profoundly. It was extraordinarily important to Diane to maintain control of herself and her own dignity during the time remaining to her. When this was no longer possible, she clearly wanted to die. As a former director of a hospice program, I know how to use pain medicines to keep patients comfortable and lessen suffering. I explained the philosophy of comfort care, which I strongly believe in. Although Diane understood and appreciated this, she had known of people lingering in what was called relative comfort, and she wanted no part of it. When the time came, she wanted to take her life in the least painful way possible. Knowing of her desire for independence and her decision to stay in control, I thought this request made perfect sense. I acknowledged and explored this wish but also thought that it was out of the realm of currently accepted medical practice and that it was more than I could offer or promise. In our discussion, it became clear that preoccupation with her fear of a lingering death would interfere with Diane's getting the most out of the time she had left until she found a safe way to ensure her death. I feared the effects of a violent death on the family, the consequences of an ineffective suicide that would leave her lingering in precisely the state she dreaded so much, and the possibility that a family member would be forced to assist her, with all the legal and personal repercussions that would follow. She discussed this at length with her family. They believed that they should respect her choice. With this in mind, I told Diane that information was available from the Hemlock Society that might be helpful to her.

A week later she phoned me with a request for barbiturates for sleep. Since I knew that this was an essential ingredient in a Hemlock Society suicide, I asked her to come to the office to talk things over. She was more than willing to protect me by participating in a superficial conversation about her insomnia, but it was important to me to know how she planned to use the drugs and to be sure that she was not in despair or overwhelmed in a way that might color her judgment. In our discussion, it was apparent that she was having trouble sleeping, but it was also evident that the security of having enough barbiturates available to commit suicide when and if the time came would leave her secure enough to live fully and concentrate on the present. It was clear that she was not despondent and that in fact she was making deep, personal connections with her family and close friends. I made sure that she knew how to use the barbiturates for sleep, and also that she knew the amount needed to commit suicide. We agreed to meet regularly, and she promised to meet with me before taking her life, to ensure that all other avenues had been exhausted. I wrote the prescription with an uneasy feeling about the boundaries I was exploring — spiritual, legal, professional, and personal. Yet I also felt strongly that I was setting her free to get the most out of the time she had left and to maintain dignity and control on her own terms until her death.

The next several months were very intense and important for Diane. 10 Her son stayed home from college, and they were able to be with one another and say much that had not been said earlier. Her husband did his work at home so that he and Diane could spend more time together. She spent time with her closest friends. I had her come into the hospital for a conference with our residents, at which she illustrated in a most profound and personal way the importance of informed decision making, the right to refuse treatment, and the extraordinarily personal effects of illness and interaction with the medical system. There were emotional and physical hardships as well. She had periods of intense sadness and anger. Several times she became very weak, but she received transfusions as an outpatient and responded with marked improvement of symptoms. She had two serious infections that responded surprisingly well to empirical courses of oral antibiotics. After three tumultuous months, there were two weeks of relative calm and well-being, and fantasies of a miracle began to surface.

Unfortunately, we had no miracle. Bone pain, weakness, fatigue, and fevers began to dominate her life. Although the hospice workers, family members, and I tried our best to minimize the suffering and promote comfort, it was clear that the end was approaching. Diane's immediate future held what she feared the most — increasing discomfort, dependence, and hard choices between pain and sedation. She called up her closest friends and asked them to come over to say goodbye, telling them that she would be leaving soon. As we had agreed, she let me know as well. When we met, it was clear that she knew what she was doing, that she was sad and frightened to be leaving, but that she would be even more terrified to stay and suffer. In our tearful goodbye, she promised a reunion in the future at her favorite spot on the edge of Lake Geneva, with dragons swimming in the sunset.

Two days later her husband called to say that Diane had died. She had said her final goodbyes to her husband and son that morning and asked them to leave her alone for an hour. After an hour, which must have seemed an eternity, they found her on the couch, lying very still and covered by her favorite shawl. There was no sign of struggle. She seemed to be at peace. They called me for advice about how to proceed. When I arrived at their house, Diane indeed seemed peaceful. Her husband and son were quiet. We talked about what a remarkable person she had been. They seemed to have no doubts about the course she had chosen or about their cooperation, although the unfairness of her illness and the finality of her death were overwhelming to us all.

I called the medical examiner to inform him that a hospice patient had died. When asked about the cause of death, I said, "acute leukemia." He said that was fine and that we should call a funeral director. Although acute leukemia was the truth, it was not the whole story. Yet any mention of suicide would have given rise to a police investigation and probably brought the arrival of an ambulance crew for resuscitation. Diane would have become a "coroner's case," and the decision to perform an autopsy would have been made at the discretion of the medical examiner. The family or I could have been subject to criminal prosecution, and I to professional review, for our roles in support of Diane's choices. Although I truly believe that the family and I gave her the best care possible, allowing her to define her limits and directions as much as possible, I am not sure the law, society, or the medical profession would agree. So I said "acute leukemia" to protect all of us, to protect Diane from an invasion into her past and her body, and to continue to shield society from the knowledge of the degree of suffering that people often undergo in the process of dying. Suffering can be lessened to some extent, but in no way eliminated or made benign, by the careful intervention of a competent, caring physician, given current social constraints.

Diane taught me about the range of help I can provide if I know people well and if I allow them to say what they really want. She taught me about life, death, and honesty and about taking charge and facing tragedy squarely when it strikes. She taught me that I can take small risks for people that I really know and care about. Although I did not assist in her suicide directly, I helped indirectly to make it possible, successful, and relatively painless. Although I know we have measures to help control pain and lessen suffering, to think that people do not suffer in the process of dying is an illusion. Prolonged dying can occasionally be peaceful, but more often the role of the physician and family is limited to lessening but not eliminating severe suffering.

I wonder how many families and physicians secretly help patients over 15 the edge into death in the face of such severe suffering. I wonder how many severely ill or dying patients secretly take their lives, dying alone in despair. I wonder whether the image of Diane's final aloneness will persist in the minds of her family, or if they will remember more the intense, meaningful months they had together before she died. I wonder whether Diane struggled in that last hour, and whether the Hemlock Society's way of death by suicide is the most benign. I wonder why Diane, who gave so much to so many of us, had to be alone for the last hour of her life. I wonder whether I will see Diane again, on the shore of Lake Geneva at sunset, with dragons swimming on the horizon.

Topics for Critical Thinking and Writing

1. Do you think Diane's refusal to fight her leukemia (para. 5) shows — dare we say it? — that she was a coward in the face of death? When Dr. Quill says (para. 7) that her refusal "disturbed me," is he tacitly and evasively making just such a judgment? Or do his reservations have another source and meaning?

2. Dr. Quill refers to his belief that a patient has the "right to die with as much control and dignity as possible" (para. 7). How would you define human dignity? What do you think are appropriate criteria for dying with dignity? What is an undignified death — and how can it be avoided? Write an essay of 500 words explaining these ideas.

3. The reader is told that Diane wanted to "maintain control of herself and her own dignity during the time remaining to her" (para. 8; cf. para. 11, end). What

is the evidence that she succeeded or failed? Explain in an essay of 250 words whether you think she succeeded, or not.

4. Did Dr. Quill lie to the county medical examiner when he reported Diane's death as caused by "acute leukemia" (para. 13)? If not, why not? If he did, do you think the lie was justified? Why, or why not? Write an essay of 500 words in which you argue for your position on these questions.

Ronald Pies

Does Clinical Depression Undermine Physician-Assisted Suicide?

An article published this winter in the *Boston Globe* concerned an 88-year-old woman who attempted suicide. The essay was written by the woman's niece and, in essence, argued that her aunt's suicide attempt was an understandable, if not laudable, expression of personal autonomy. As the writer put it, her aunt "was simply striving to put the period at the end of a very run-on sentence." The author argued for what has come to be termed *physician-assisted suicide*, suggesting that those of us who wish to end our lives "when our bodies fail us" ought to have the benefit of a family physician's assistance. Curiously, the author's aunt *did not seem to have any severe or incapacitating physical illness*, other than arthritis. Rather, her aunt felt that she had "had enough," had "overstayed her welcome" and "wasn't contributing anything."

I found this essay disturbing on several levels. As a writer and physician, I objected to the misuse of a literary metaphor: A human life, even at age 88, is not a run-on sentence in need of terminal punctuation. As a psychiatrist specializing in mood disorders, I was distressed by the writer's apparent inability to recognize that her aunt may have been clinically depressed—she had shown some of the classic symptoms, and had been taking corticosteroids, a common organic cause of major depression. I also was uneasy with the notion that the medical profession should actively participate in ending the life of another human being—though I am not entirely opposed to "euthanasia" under certain carefully proscribed circumstances.

But first things first: Surely any discussion of physician-assisted suicide must be prefaced by the distinction between *treatable* and *untreatable* (more accurately, incurable) illness. Let us stipulate that patients who wish to end their lives during, say, the final stages of metastatic pancreatic carcinoma have an untreatable illness and might conceivably benefit from some

---

Ronald Pies, associate professor of psychiatry at Tufts University, is the author of a textbook on psychiatry. This essay appeared in the journal Tufts Medicine *(Spring 1994).*

form of assisted suicide. This is by no means the situation with respect to major depression—*a highly treatable* illness that often presents with *reversible* suicidal ideation. The recognition and aggressive treatment of major depression is the physician's first responsibility, long before any notion of "honoring" the patient's suicidal wishes.

Dr. James Jefferson of the University of Wisconsin Department of Psychiatry has spoken of the staggering human costs of depression—a condition he describes as "underdiagnosed, misdiagnosed, undertreated, and mistreated." Each year, major depression costs our economy nearly $30 billion in medical care and absenteeism. The Medical Outcomes Study (Wells and Burnam 1991) found that depression had more associated morbidity than any chronic medical condition except heart disease. Yet depression in primary care and nursing home settings often goes undetected and untreated. Why?

I believe that many physicians still are reluctant to give their patients a   5 "psychiatric" diagnosis, which is perceived as both stigmatizing and threatening—often as much to the physician as to the patient. Sometimes the well-meaning physician will overidentify with the patient, rationalizing away the signs of depression with the old saw "I'd be depressed, too, if I were in Mrs. Jones' shoes." This sort of fallacious reasoning often appears in nursing home settings, where it is expected that patients will be depressed. In reality, major depression is *less* prevalent among the elderly than among the middle-aged; when it shows up in an older person, it is not a normal development, but an illness. Clinical depression, of course, is different from unhappiness, of which there is no short supply in nursing homes, hospitals or anywhere else. But when that telltale cluster of signs and symptoms appears—*hopelessness, loss of pleasure, poor appetite, sleep disturbance, inappropriate guilt, social withdrawal, and suicidal ideation*—we must recognize it as major depression and begin vigorous treatment. More than 70 percent of patients will respond to adequate antidepressant medication, usually in combination with some form of psychotherapy. What seemed a hard-and-fast decision to die often melts into a renewed commitment to life. Incidentally, the elderly do benefit from psychotherapy, contrary to the unfortunate adage about "old dogs" and "new tricks."

But what about cases of untreatable or incurable illness, particularly when extreme pain or suffering is present? Should the physician then directly participate in a patient's wish to commit suicide? Easy answers don't leap to mind, but one thing seems clear to me: the one-man-army approach of Dr. Jack Kevorkian is not consonant with my understanding of medical ethics. (I often wonder how frequently Dr. Kevorkian seeks psychiatric consultation in order to rule out major depression in his suicidal patients.)

Recently, a Seattle-based group of physicians and clergy initiated an unusual service for those who wish to end their own lives. This group developed a strict set of guidelines for deciding whether to assist suicide, including a mandatory review of the case by a team of group members. Furthermore, patients must be able to obtain lethal drugs from their own doctor and be able to administer them. Group members will not do so. I find this sort of thoughtful, multidisciplinary approach infinitely more responsible than that of Dr. Kevorkian. But I still am not persuaded that physicians should be directly involved in assisted suicides. Perhaps we do need some segment of society to perform such a function, under scrupulous regulation, but I am not eager for physicians to step forward. We already have our hands full simply trying to detect and treat reversible illness — including that underdiagnosed and undertreated condition, depression.

Topics for Critical Thinking and Writing

1. Pies refers in his opening paragraph to "personal autonomy." How would you define this concept? Do a person's physical handicaps constitute an obstacle to personal autonomy? Why, or why not?

2. After reading Pies's essay, how would you define "clinical depression"—its symptoms, especially?

3. Pies explains the unwillingness of doctors to diagnose their patients as in need of "psychiatric" help on the ground that it is "stigmatizing and threatening" (para. 5). Would you agree? Why, or why not?

4. Pies obviously disapproves of "the one-man-army approach of Dr. Jack Kevorkian" (para. 6). What grounds does Pies give to persuade the reader to agree with this judgment? (You might check in the *New York Times Index* for newspaper articles on Kevorkian, and see whether such further information as you can obtain confirms or disconfirms your prior judgment.)

5. Read the essay by Dr. Timothy Quill (p. 433) and decide whether you agree with Pies in implicitly criticizing Quill for his failure to adopt a "thoughtful, multidisciplinary approach" (para. 7) to physician-assisted suicide.

Jeff Jacoby

Euthanasia: Barbarism Cloaked in Compassion

I will give no deadly medicine to anyone if asked, nor suggest any such counsel.
— FROM THE HIPPOCRATIC OATH

There is nothing new under the sun, not even the temptation to bring death to people whose lives become unbearable. Jack Kevorkian is not the first physician in Western history to cross the line from helping people live to helping people die, or the first to justify his actions in the name of mercy

---

Jeff Jacoby is a columnist for the Boston Globe. *The following essay appeared in the* Globe *on May 5, 1994.*

and dignity. The lure of euthanasia is ancient. That is why new doctors, for twenty-four hundred years, have taken an oath to resist it.

On Monday, a Michigan jury found Kevorkian not guilty of violating a law forbidding assisted suicide, even though he had described freely and candidly how he helped end the life of Thomas W. Hyde by hooking him up to a tank of carbon monoxide in the back of a Volkswagen van. Hyde was afflicted with amyotrophic lateral sclerosis, a dreadful, paralyzing disorder.

Gassing sick people to death in the back of German vehicles is not a new idea, either.

Who doesn't understand why a terminally ill person suffering uncontrollable pain might welcome the escape of death? When the alternative is lingering agony with no hope of a cure or a normal life, euthanasia seems neither criminal nor immoral. To many Kevorkian's crusade is admirable; the jurors in Detroit are not the only ones who believe, as one of them put it, that "he did this to relieve this man's pain and suffering."

But *is* that Kevorkian's motive? The twenty people who have died in   5 his mobile gas chamber were never patients of his. (Kevorkian is a retired pathologist, one of the few medical specializations that guarantee a physician never has to see a patient.) They had never been under his care, never received medical treatment from him. They came to him for the purpose of dying, and his only interest in them was in ending their lives — and winning publicity for his cause.

Kevorkian, *Newsweek* reported last year, has written about the "value for mankind" of the Nazis' horrific experiments on human beings during World War II. He recommends that our society, too, use prisoners for medical experimentation.

Maybe it is nothing more than a curiosity that the leading advocate of assisted suicide is such a morbid caricature of a doctor. But is it also irrelevant that half of Kevorkian's — what do we call them: patients? victims? subjects? — were *not* terminally ill and facing imminent death?

Concede the libertarian principle that a person has the right to end his life or to insist that it not be prolonged by artificial and invasive medical means. It does not follow that laws against facilitating the suicide of others are therefore irrational or inhumane. If we allow physician-assisted suicide, we signal agreement that certain lives aren't worth living. That is a fundamental departure from Western law and traditional morality and one that sets us on a dangerously slippery slope.

If an assisted exit is OK for those with terminal illnesses, how can we deny it to those facing years of prolonged and racking pain? Or to those in the early stages of AIDS or Alzheimer's who fear the misery and decay that lie ahead?

What about someone whose life-despairing pain is not physical but   10 emotional or psychic? The man crushed and humiliated by scandal, the woman whose husband and children die in a fire, the entrepreneur wiped out in a financial catastrophe — if they decide their lives have grown unbearable and wish to die, will we deprive them of assistance?

The twenty men and women who came to Kevorkian for death supposedly chose freely to do so. But who is to say they weren't talked into it by a well-meaning friend? Or pressured into it by a selfish relative? ("You can't imagine how terrible lung cancer is, Frank; the pain is unbearable and it will be torture on your family. You should let Kevorkian end it for you now.")

Consider how much more relentless such pressure will be in a society that abandons the ancient taboo against euthanasia. Already there are governors who talk about the old having a "duty to die" and university presidents who argue that when you've had a long life and you're ripe, then it's time to go.

From the idea that some of us should have the right to be helped into the grave it is one small step to the notion that some of us *ought* to be helped into the grave . . . and one step more to letting some of us be pushed into the grave.

In Holland, where assisted suicide is legal, many doctors don't wait to be asked. In 1991 alone, the Dutch government reports, more than one thousand patients who "had submitted no explicit request" to die were killed by their doctors.

Barbarism cloaked in compassion. Do we really intend to follow Jack   15 Kevorkian down that road?

Topics for Critical Thinking and Writing ══════════

1. If the facts are undisputed that show Dr. Kevorkian to have assisted the suicide of Thomas Hyde (see para. 2), why do you think the Michigan jury refused to find Kevorkian guilty under its new law forbidding assisted suicide? Do you think the jury did the right thing? Why, or why not?

2. When Jacoby says (para. 3) "Gassing sick people to death in the back of German vehicles is not a new idea, either," to what do you think he is referring?

3. Do you think there is any difference between assisted suicide and euthanasia? Explain.

4. Jacoby warns us that if we allow physician-assisted suicide, it "sets us on a dangerously slippery slope" (para. 8). Do you think his warning is correct, or not? Does he give any evidence in his essay in support of his prediction? Explain.

5. Do you agree with Jacoby that "it is one small step" from saying that we have the *right* to assisted suicide to saying that "some of us *ought* to be helped into the grave" (para. 13)? Can you think of other cases where you might be willing to insist that you or someone has a certain right but also that one ought *not* to act on it in the circumstances?

13

Immigration: How Wide Should We Open the Gates?

Thomas Fleming

The Real American Dilemma

America is a nation of immigrants. How often is that declaration trotted out to explain why it would be immoral to do something about controlling immigration, as if every country were not a nation of immigrants. If Britain ever had an indigenous population, it was overrun by Celts, Germans, Danes, and Normans — to say nothing of the Hollanders brought over and ennobled when Dutch William drove his father-in-law from the throne. Almost any country, excepting the poor benighted Scandinavians, could tell a similar story, and the present condition of Sweden is as good an argument as I can think of against a restricted gene pool. (It is also a total refutation of the hilarious idea of Nordic supremacy.)

It is conventional to speak of the great contributions made by immigrants and at the same time to deplore the unpleasant reception they were given by the WASP population. No one ever seems to carry the argument back to the reception the Indians usually tried to arrange for European settlers pushing into their territories. We are all, even the Indians, descended from immigrants, and it is hard to pick which group has contributed most to the fabric of our civilization.

In some sort of descending order one would have to include the various British stocks, the Germans and Dutch, the French (especially the

Thomas Fleming, trained as a classicist and the author of The Politics of Human Nature *(1987), is the editor of* Chronicles, *a magazine that covers all aspects of American culture. The essay we reprint here first appeared in* Chronicles *(March 1989).*

Huguenots), and the more recent arrivals from eastern and southern Europe. In addition, no account of American culture could leave out the strange and often strained relations between European Americans and the American blacks whose ancestors were brought here by force. Jazz, the blues, and rock music, all hybrids of the two stocks, could stand as a metaphor for our "peculiar" relationship.

In recent years, however, while the main focus in the polite media has remained on the contributions and sufferings of hyphenated Americans, ordinary Americans are more concerned with the problems caused by the virtual flood of arrivals from the Third World. For some years now, legal immigration has been at an average rate of over six hundred thousand per year, while the number of illegals in this country is anybody's guess. In 1985 Richard Lamm and Gary Imhoff (*The Immigration Time Bomb: The Fragmenting of America*) estimated eight and a half to eleven million, mostly from Latin America.

Immigration reform was the great issue of the Reagan years that never really took shape, and it will be up to Mr. Bush, the Congress, and above all to the opinion industry to settle the future of the United States. There was a debate, of course, and one celebrated bill that didn't make it (Simpson-Mazzoli) as well as the version that did, but most of the discussion was safely trivial: whether or not to tighten up the border controls and send back (temporarily) a certain number of illegals, and how merciful to be in granting amnesty. Ultimately — and this is a sign of how low we have fallen — most of the conversation was about money. Think of the jobs that need to be done, the fruit that needs to be picked, the houses cleaned. Think of the contributions to science and industry made by talented immigrants.

After we've done thinking about what's in it for agribusiness and electronics, we just might begin to wonder what is in store for the American people. Not too long ago, I had a chance to go over the whole ground with one of the brightest defenders of free trade and open borders in the country. He waxed eloquent over the family values of the Mexicans and the high intelligence of the Orientals. Finally, I asked him: Suppose we could set off neutron bombs all over the United States, wipe out the current citizen population and replace them with brilliant and hardworking Chinese. From his perspective, wouldn't that be a plus? I'm still waiting for an answer.

The trouble began with treating the nation as an abstraction: The land of the free and the home of the brave was turned into the land of opportunity for what the Statue of Liberty's plaque so quaintly calls "the wretched refuse" of the world. A real country, with its own history, its own particular set of virtues and vices, its own special institutions was reduced to cheap slogans and loyalty oaths. (I don't know which is worse: requiring children to mouth the Pledge of Allegiance or, once we have instituted such a form of petty fascism, refusing to require it. What an election.)

The truth is, we have to confine our discussion to abstractions, including that abstraction that serves as a metaphor for an entire way of life —

5

money, because what some Americans worry about cannot be spoken to the network reporters doing on-the-street interviews for the evening news. Despite the risks, some people are incautious enough to sign letters to the editor or call in to the radio talk shows that are increasingly the only form for free expression. What these simple folk are saying is that they do not care how smart the Chinese are or how religious the Mexicans are. If they're so smart, virtuous, and diligent, how come the countries they are leaving are in such a god-awful mess? The old question, "If you so smart, why ain't you rich?" applies to nations as well as individuals.

In his essay "Immigration and Liberal Taboos" (in *One Life at a Time, Please*), Edward Abbey sums up the situation with his customary restraint and discretion: "They come to stay and they stay to multiply. What of it? say the documented liberals; ours is a rich and generous nation, we have room for all, let them come. And let them stay, say the conservatives; a large, cheap, frightened, docile, surplus labor force is exactly what the economy needs. Put some fear into the unions: Tighten discipline, spur productivity, whip up the competition for jobs. The conservatives love their cheap labor; the liberals love their cheap cause."

Abbey concludes by asking, "How many of us, truthfully, would prefer   10 to be submerged in the Caribbean-Latin version of civilization?" Stripped of its anger, Abbey's question is worth asking. If we can judge from his novels, Abbey actually likes Mexico and its people. But for better or worse, he likes his own country more, and not necessarily because it is better (although he obviously thinks, as I do, that it is). But a nation, as the word implies (from *nascor*, be born) is a fictional extended family. Like members of a family, the citizens of a nation prefer each other's company and will sacrifice for the common good, not because they think their family or nation is superior to every other, but simply because it is theirs. The Germans may have better music, the English a clearer prose, the Russians a deeper spirituality, but Americans have, on occasion, been willing to shoot any of them in the defense or even the interest of the United States. And, it goes without saying, that all of these European people have displayed a marked capacity for becoming Americans.

There's the rub. Do Abbey's liberals and conservatives believe that there is anything particular about the American identity? After all, most of us don't blame the French for wanting to be French, and we all profess to sympathize with the desire of black Africans to rule their own countries and develop their own traditions without interference from white Europeans. Why is it only America that is denied an identity?

There is, after all, an American story that is primarily a saga of enterprising men and women who came here from Europe. The language and culture, as well as the legal and political systems, were derived from Britain. This way of life of ours is not the result of any general principle; it is the legacy of our forebears and a civilization that goes back to Greece and Rome. It is vastly creative and has shown an enormous capacity for transforming immigrants from somewhat differing cultures. This capacity is not infinite, and a United States dominated by Third World immigrants will be a very different nation in its cultural and its economic life.

Part of the problem is a question of numbers. Talented immigrants are, for the most part, highly assimilable, but mass migrations are disruptive and threaten social cohesion. Between 1976 and 1986, the number of immigrants from Africa doubled, while the numbers from Asia, Mexico, and Haiti all quadrupled. (Haiti, by the way, was on the low side for the Caribbean: Jamaica was up 700 percent.) The big winner, however was India, whose stock rose an impressive 2,000 percent.

Like most Americans since, Thomas Jefferson firmly believed that this country should provide a haven for talented and freedom-loving people. He was also aware of the risks. In his *Notes on the State of Virginia*, Jefferson pointed out that the American form of government was derived from "the freest principles of the English Constitution." It was diametrically opposed to the absolutisms that ruled over most of Europe. Emigrants from such countries, he warned, "will bring with them the principles of the governments they leave . . . or, if able to throw them off, it will be in exchange for an unbounded licentiousness, passing, as is usual, from one extreme to another."

What would have especially aroused Jefferson's fears is the current 15 reigning assumption that special arrangements have to be made for "refugees" from political oppression. Conservatives want to open the door· to Cubans and Nicaraguans, while leftists give shelter to Salvadorans and South African blacks. What both groups are saying, in essence, is that they would like the United States to turn into Nicaragua or Haiti. Of course, all humane people sympathize with the victims of political oppression; wherever possible we would like to do something for them. But we must never forget that immigration policy is the most significant means of determining the future of our nation, and we owe it to our children not to squander their birthright in spasms of imprudent charity.

One frightening dimension to American charity is the curious notion that aliens and immigrants have rights. Once upon a time, it was clearly understood that no one had anything like a "right" to enter the United States, and that aliens who were allowed in possessed only such benefits of the legal system as Congress and the various state governments chose to give them. Of course, illegal aliens could be routinely rounded up and interned pending their deportation, but even legal aliens were routinely denied state charity, government jobs, and even such government-licensed activities as commercial fishing and the operation of pool halls. These restrictions were routinely upheld by the Supreme Court.

After World War II, however, the federal courts have increasingly recognized—invented would be a better word—the rights of aliens. In a 1948 case (*Takashashi v. Fish and Game Commission*), the Supreme Court declared that California's restrictions on off-shore fishing were invalid, and in 1971 the Court declared that a state could not deny welfare to aliens, finding that aliens were a discriminated against minority deserving of special protection. In other words, they were to be given more rights than citizens.

One by one all the barriers have fallen, and legal aliens enjoy all the rights and privileges of citizenship, except for voting and holding office. Until recently, the one privilege the government did retain was the ability to detain and intern illegal aliens, but that too has come under fire. In late 1987 Cuban illegals staged a riot in two prisons where they were being held. The U.S. Court of Appeals in Atlanta did find — regretfully — that unadmitted aliens had no rights, but the effect of the riots was to blackmail the government into granting hearings on the rioters' cases. In the political debate that broke out, politicians and judges alike demanded a recognition of aliens' rights. Georgia Republican Pat Swindall — and I hope our Georgia readers will take note — argued that the Cubans actually had (not even ought to have) Fifth Amendment rights. Swindall is not entirely off the wall, since he has the support of Supreme Court Justice Thurgood Marshall, whose reverence for the Constitution is a matter of public record. In a number of dissenting opinions, Marshall has insisted that in criminal cases unadmitted aliens are entitled to all the protections of the Bill of Rights.

Of course, we could go on as we are doing, whittling away at our definition of citizenship, letting sovereignty slip through our fingers, but if we refuse to control immigration, our options are severely limited. The least unattractive solution would be to implement the federal principle on a state and regional level, recognizing Hispanics and Orientals, in states where they form a majority, as the dominant group — much as the French are given special status in Quebec. (We must not imitate the disastrous Canadian policy of nationwide bilingualism.) Descendants of the old settlers that fought and won the land from Mexico will be quite rightly indignant with what many Mexicans are already calling the Reconquest, and we shall probably have far more trouble than Canada in adjusting to a multicultural situation. Perhaps after a century or two we can evolve into a safely neutered society of consumers — like Switzerland. It is just as likely to be a bloodbath.

A far less attractive scenario than either Switzerland or tribal civil war 20 Nigerian style would be a forced Americanization on the grand scale. It didn't work all that well the last time we tried it, when Catholics were hectored and bullied out of the officially Protestant public schools, and considering the sort of people who run the federal bureaucracy today, we will in effect be writing the death sentence on republican self-government. Only an empire, with a vast machinery of manipulation (including some form of state religion) could succeed in creating order out of such a Babel, and the best we could hope for would be either a military *junta* or a fascist welfare state — Sweden with a führer.[1]

---

[1]**führer** German for *leader*, a term used by Hitler. [All notes are the editors'.]

What then, if anything, can be done? There are several obvious changes in immigration policy that need to be made. First of all, we need to put an end to the mass migrations to the United States. It was the Völkerwanderungen[2] of the Germans and Huns that brought the Roman Empire down, and we shall be even worse straits if we fail to control our Southern border and do not adopt a more hard-nosed approach to refugees fleeing the political turmoil, high population growth, and economic chaos of the Third World.

We also need to reexamine our priorities. From the '20s to the '50s, American immigration law made it very clear that we intended to be what we had always been: a European nation. The quota that took effect in 1929 was based on the ethnic background of the existing population of the United States and allotted 85 percent of the total to northern and western Europe and 12 percent to the rest of Europe.

The Immigration Act of 1952 did preserve the national origins quota (not abolished till 1965), but within the system a separate set of ordered priorities were established. Preference was given first to immigrants with desirable (i.e., marketable) skills, second to relatives of citizens and resident aliens. Along with the abolition of national quotas in 1965 came changes in the preference system. Now unmarried children of citizens come first, spouses of resident aliens second, and exceptional and talented immigrants third. Other relatives of citizens and resident aliens come fourth and fifth, while workers with needed skills come sixth.

The result is the all-too-familiar scams by which undesired aliens contrive to give birth on U.S. soil or arrange marriages of convenience. In either event, one unskilled alien can end up bringing "all his sisters and his cousins (whom he reckons up by dozens) and his aunts." The figures tell the story. Despite a total quota of only 270,000, the special categories have accelerated the rate of legal immigration to almost three times that. Ted Kennedy, by the way, is primarily responsible for the difference. In 1965, he served as floor manager of the legislation in the Senate, and in 1980 he sponsored amendments that removed the ceiling on admission, promising no more than 50,000 additional immigrants as a consequence.

What should come first is not the interest of the alien or even of U.S. businesses, but the interest of the historical population of the country. Family members must, as Lamm and Imhoff among others insist, be included under a comprehensive total. We should continue, as Jefferson wished, to open our doors to talented emigrants not because they will make money for IBM, but because bright and able people are a precious and scarce commodity. More fruit-pickers we do not need. Cut off the welfare payments and we shall be surprised at how many agricultural workers are living right now in Chicago and New York. The most pressing need, however, is the reestablishment of national quotas. These need not be

25

---

[2]**Völkerwanderungen** Migrations (German).

based on the formulas of the 1920s, but nonetheless should give first priority to the population base of the nation.

One doesn't wish to be unkind, but cultural pluralism is not the most attractive legacy we can leave to our children. As a nation, we have barely survived the existence of two separate populations, black and white, and we have a long way to go in working out better relations between those two groups. What shall we do when the whole of America becomes a multiracial Alexandria? As the Romans realized, citizenship implies certain very concrete rights and duties: the right to trade and make contracts, the obligation to serve in the army, the right to intermarry. While it is true that there are no laws restricting marriage between the races, such unions are very uncommon. According to census figures, less than two percent of existing marriages are of mixed race, and even projecting a modest rate of increase over the next few decades, it is highly unlikely that we shall realize anything approaching a homogeneous population in the near future.

The problem, if it is a problem, is not simply one more case of white intolerance. The pressures against mixed race dating and marriage are every bit as strong in the black and Oriental communities. This is not a question of *ought*, but a case of *is*, and the result will be a nation no longer stratified simply by class but by race as well. Europeans and Orientals will compete, as groups, for the top positions, while the other groups will nurse their resentment on the weekly welfare checks they receive from the other half. Perhaps such an arrangement can be worked out, but whatever emerges will not be a nation, certainly not the United States.

The situation is quite as serious as even the most frightened alarmists have suggested, but we cannot begin even to speak seriously about changes in the law until we are willing to violate the code of silence that the left has imposed upon the topic. There is a pressing need for plain speech and open discussion in which those who happen to agree with the overwhelming majority of Americans throughout our history are not stigmatized as xenophobes and racists. If the notion of aliens' rights really takes hold, we are in danger of losing the entire concept of American citizenship. Above all, we have to quit lying to ourselves about who we are and what we face. If sober and sensible people cannot solve the immigration problem through an orderly process of debate and legislation, then there are genuine crazies out there only waiting for the chance to use such an issue as a springboard to power.

Topics for Critical Thinking and Writing

1. Evaluate Fleming's opening paragraph as the beginning of an argumentative essay.

2. What answer would you give to the question that, according to the sixth paragraph, Fleming asked "one of the brightest defenders of free trade and open borders"?

3. In paragraph 7 Fleming characterizes as "petty fascism" our practice of "re-

quiring children to mouth the Pledge of Allegiance." Do you agree with him? And are you surprised that a writer who is clearly unhappy with our immigration policy takes this position? Explain.

4. In paragraph 13 Fleming reports several percentage increases in immigrants between 1976 and 1986. But how many people do these increases really amount to? After all, if only two immigrants from India arrived on these shores in 1976 and ten years later the immigration total increased by 2000 percent, that amounts to (only?) four thousand people. Visit your college library and look up immigration statistics for the decade in question in *The Statistical Abstract of the United States*, an annual volume published by the government; verify if you can the percentage increases Fleming cites and translate those percentages into actual numbers.

5. In paragraph 17 Fleming concludes that in 1971, thanks to the Supreme Court's (mis)interpretation of the Constitution, "[aliens] were to be given more rights than citizens." What are these additional rights to which Fleming refers? On what basis are they being denied to American citizens?

6. In paragraph 22 Fleming reports that our immigration policy of the 1920s was based on the assumption that "we intended to be what we had always been: a European nation." Review the evidence he relies on for this statement. Do you find it sufficient for his claim? Today, in the 1990s, do "we" no longer have that intention? What evidence would you cite either way? Or do you think the whole idea of what "we" want as an immigration policy is nonsense and undecidable? Explain.

7. In paragraph 21 Fleming says that the incursions of the Germans and the Huns "brought the Roman Empire down." One sometimes hears that the Roman Empire fell because it had become soft, decadent, overextended, and so forth—that is, that it fell because of its own inadequacies. What, if anything, were you taught about the fall of Rome? Does it have any relevance to what our immigration policies should be?

8. Why does Fleming say (para. 26) that "cultural pluralism is not the most attractive legacy we can leave to our children"? Suppose one were to reply, "Well, as of 1995, it's just too late to debate the issue: Cultural pluralism *is* the legacy we are leaving to our children, and it is impossible—as well as undesirable—to try to do anything about it." How might Fleming reply?

9. In paragraph 27 Fleming says, "The pressures against mixed race dating and marriage are every bit as strong in the black and Oriental communities [as in white communities]." Is it your impression that this is true? Or does it depend on region and on generation? For instance, is it your sense that although firsthand generation Asian Americans oppose "mixed race dating and marriage," their children do not? If you have firsthand experience, draw upon it. If not, you may want to interview people of Asian ancestry.

10. In his last paragraph Fleming speaks of a "code of silence that the left has imposed upon the topic." Were you aware of such a code? Has Fleming convinced you that such a code exists? If there is such a code, do you think it can be broken? Why, or why not?

11. Read the essay on immigration by Nathan Glazer (p. 457), and write a 500-word paper on the topic "Agreement and Disagreement on Immigration: Glazer versus Fleming."

Ron K. Unz

Value Added

This journal has performed a valuable service by clarifying the immigration debate. Rather than choosing the safe path of attacking only illegal immigration, *NR* has correctly pointed out that illegal immigration is dwarfed by legal immigration; that legal and illegal immigration share a wide range of important characteristics; and that most of the key arguments against the one apply to the other as well. Just as the debate about NAFTA[1] became a referendum on free trade in general, so the controversy over illegal immigration is a proxy for a critical reappraisal of post-1965 immigration policy.

With the underlying issue clear, reasoned debate should be possible on the pros and cons of immigration. And on those pros and cons I differ sharply with *NR*. The evidence shows that the immigration of the last thirty years has been a large net benefit for America, as well as an important source of strength for political parties espousing conservative principles.

Anyone walking the streets of our major cities sees that the majority of the shops are owned and operated by immigrant entrepreneurs — Korean grocery stores, Indian newsstands, Chinese restaurants. Most of these shops simply would not exist without immigrant families willing to put in long hours of poorly paid labor to maintain and expand them, in the process improving our cities. In Los Angeles, the vast majority of hotel and restaurant workers are hard-working Hispanic immigrants, most of them here illegally, and anyone who believes that these unpleasant jobs would otherwise be filled by natives (either black or white) is living in a fantasy world.

The same applies to nearly all the traditional lower-rung working-class jobs in Southern California, including the nannies and gardeners whose widespread employment occasionally embarrasses the Zoë Bairds[2] of this world (even as it facilitates their careers). The only means of making a job as a restaurant busboy even remotely attractive to a native American would be to raise the wage to $10 or $12 per hour, at which point the job would cease to exist.

Since most newcomers tend to be on the lower end of the wage scale,   5
and since many have children in the public schools, they do tend to cost

[1]**NAFTA** North American Free Trade Agreement. [All notes are the editors'.]
[2]**Zoë Baird** President Clinton nominated Ms. Baird for the position of Attorney General, but she withdrew after it was pointed out that she had failed to pay social security for a nanny whom she had employed.

Ron K. Unz, a Silicon Valley entrepreneur, received more than a third of the vote in his Republican primary challenge to Governor Pete Wilson of California in 1994. The following essay appeared in the November 7, 1994, issue of National Review, *a conservative journal that, as Unz mentions in his first paragraph, had published essays on both illegal and legal immigration.*

local governments more in services than they pay in sales and income taxes. (The same could probably be said for most members of the working class with young children.) This is the basis of California Governor Pete Wilson's lawsuit over the "costs" to California of illegal immigration. Yet the real culprit is our outrageously inefficient public-school system. Furthermore, because of their age profile, even working-class immigrants generally pay much more in federal taxes (primarily Social Security withholding) than they receive in federal benefits. So we might equally well say that immigrants are helping us balance the federal budget.

THE IMMIGRANT EDGE

Immigrants are crucial not just to industries that rely on cheap, low-skilled labor. Silicon Valley, which is home to my own software company, depends on immigrant professionals to maintain its technological edge. A third of all the engineers and chip designers here are foreign born, and if they left, America's computer industry would probably go with them. In fact, many of the most important technology companies of the 1980s, in California and elsewhere, were created by immigrants, including Sun Microsystems, AST, ALR, Applied Materials, Everex, and Gupta. Borland International, a software company worth hundreds of millions of dollars, was founded by Philippe Kahn, an illegal immigrant. These immigrant companies have generated hundreds of thousands of good jobs in California for native Americans and have provided billions of dollars in tax revenues. Without a continuing influx of immigrants, America's tremendous and growing dominance in sunrise industries would rapidly be lost.

If the above list of technology companies seems unfamiliar to *NR*'s writers, this highlights an important underlying reason for *NR*'s anti-immigrant stance. Most public-policy writers travel in narrow literary, political, or legal circles and have minimal contact with the worlds of science or technology (just as most technologists and entrepreneurs ignore politics). But the money and prestige of Silicon Valley will decisively turn against the Republican Party if it adopts an anti-immigrant stance, just as they would if it decided to oppose free trade.

While several of the most parasitic sectors of American society — politicians, government bureaucrats, lawyers — are almost entirely filled with native Americans, each year one-third to one-half of the student winners of the Westinghouse Science Talent Search (America's most prestigious high-school science competition) come from immigrant families, often quite impoverished. Many of America's elite universities have student bodies that are 20 percent Asian, with immigrants often accounting for half or more of the science and engineering students. *National Review* itself is not averse to seeking talent from abroad, notably including its leading anti-immigrant theorist (Peter Brimelow) and its editor (John O'Sullivan), both themselves recent immigrants, albeit from an Anglophone country.

So much for the purely economic side of the immigration ledger. The greater immigration concerns resonating among conservatives today are social and frankly racial: that the post-1965 immigrants, overwhelmingly Asian and Hispanic, contribute disproportionately to crime, welfare dependency, and social decay, and that their non-European origins will exacerbate America's growing ethnic strife, leading perhaps to separatist ethnic nationalisms.

If this scenario does not come to pass, it will not be for want of trying 10 by the government. State-sponsored affirmative action, bilingual education, and multiculturalism seem designed to promote ethnic conflict, while our welfare system breeds pathological levels of crime and dependency. But America's ethnic policies and welfare system would doom our future irrespective of immigration, and there is little evidence that the problems have any relation to immigrants, the overwhelming majority of whom are entrepreneurial and assimilationist.

A recent *NR* editorial made much of the statistic that 20 percent of California's prison inmates are immigrants. But this is hardly surprising in a state where 20 percent of the residents are immigrants. Contrast this with the truly alarming fact (unmentioned by *NR*) that blacks in California are incarcerated at nearly ten times the rate of the nonblack population. Similarly, *NR*'s emphasis on the welfare dependency rate among nonrefugee immigrants (7.8 percent, versus 7.4 percent for the general population — hardly a dramatic difference) seems like grasping at straws.

NR ignores the many countervailing indicators of immigrant advancement and assimilation. In California, for example, the ten most common names of recent home buyers include Martinez, Rodriguez, Garcia, Nguyen, Lee, and Wong, with the Nguyens outnumbering the Smiths 2 to 1 in affluent, conservative Orange County. Of California's Asians and Hispanics who were born in this country, nearly half marry into other ethnic groups, the strongest possible evidence of assimilation. These intermarriage rates are actually far higher than were those of Jews, Italians, or Poles as recently as the 1950s.

Or consider places in America where Peter Brimelow's deepest fears have already been realized, and white Americans of European origin ("Anglos") have become a minority of the population. San José, California, the eleventh largest city in the nation, is one example, having a white population of less than 50 percent, with the balance consisting mostly of Asian and Hispanic immigrants, including many illegal immigrants. San José has a flourishing economy, the lowest murder and robbery rates of any major city in America (less than one-fifth the rates in Dallas, for example), and virtually no significant ethnic conflict.

Similarly, El Paso, Texas, is the most heavily Hispanic (70 percent) of America's fifty largest cities, but it also has one of the lowest rates of serious crime, with a robbery rate just half that of Seattle, an overwhelmingly white city of similar size. The American state with the lowest share of whites in the population (about one-third) is Hawaii, hardly notorious as a boiling cauldron of ethnic conflict and racial hostility. And despite its heavy urbanization, Hawaii has among the lowest serious-crime rates of any state in the nation.

ALONG RACIAL LINES

The sad truth is that both crime and ethnic conflict today are almost entirely correlated with the presence of a black underclass, purely native and generally with American roots far deeper than most of *NR*'s staff or subscribers have. Confusing America's severe racial problems in this area with its comparatively minor immigrant tensions is as dishonest as it is politically unwise.

This dishonesty has been reinforced by the shameful deceit of the media in such matters. For example, the 1991 Mount Pleasant riot in a Hispanic neighborhood of D.C. has often been cited, not least in *NR*, as an example of Hispanic immigrant volatility, even though on-the-scene observers have pointed out that the rioters were primarily black. Similarly, during the Los Angeles riots the reluctance of the police to arrest black rioters and the attempt by the liberal media to portray the riots as a united multicultural uprising against the "system" blurred the fact that the rioters were almost all black, although Central American immigrants joined in some of the later looting. Heavily Hispanic East Los Angeles was one of the few parts of the city untouched by rioting or looting.

The political danger of an anti-immigrant position for Republicans is a consequence of demographics and voting strength. Today, 30 percent of California's population is Hispanic and 10 percent is Asian, with the vast majority being first- or second-generation Americans. Add in other immigrant groups classified as white, such as Iranians and Armenians, and the total comes to nearly half of California's population. Other large states, such as Texas and New York, have similar profiles.

Although immigrant voter registration is currently low—Asians and Hispanics account for just 10 percent of California's voters in most elections—this will change. Even if all immigration (both legal and illegal) ended tomorrow, immigrants and their children would soon dominate California politically. Furthermore, the economic success of many Asian immigrants should soon make them a major source of political funding.

This is potentially a very good thing for conservatives. Hispanics are classic blue-collar Reagan Democrats, much like Italians or Slavs, whose strong social conservatism should naturally move them toward the Republican Party. Asians can best be described as being like Jews without liberal guilt, and their small-business background and hostility to affirmative action make them natural Republicans as well.

This analysis is not mere wishful thinking. Although nearly all of California's prominent Asian and Hispanic political figures are liberal Democrats, ordinary Asians and Hispanics have regularly given the Republicans 40 to 50 percent of their vote, with Asians often voting more Republican than whites. Nearly every statewide Republican victory of the past decade depended on immigrant votes. So long as the Republican Party does not throw away its opportunity by turning anti-immigrant, these percentages should rise as immigrants grow in affluence and younger Asians and Hispanics rise through the ranks to become Republican leaders.

And since three of the most anti-immigrant constituencies in American society are blacks, union members, and environmentalists, it is likely that the Democratic Party will help push immigrants into the Republican camp. The virulently anti-immigrant leftist Senator Barbara Boxer (D, Calif.) is a notable example of this important trend. For the Republican Party to turn anti-immigrant would be a suicidal blunder.

Topics for Critical Thinking and Writing

1. State in one sentence in your own words what you believe to be Unz's main thesis. Explain why you believe this is the best way to formulate his thesis.

2. In paragraphs 2–4 Unz argues that many immigrants work as busboys, gardeners, nannies, clerks in small shops, and so on, thereby "improving our cities" (para. 3) and making life more pleasant for the middle-class people who use their services. What arguments, if any, can you set against this assertion?

3. While discussing the costs of educating immigrants, Unz speaks (para. 5) of "our outrageously inefficient public-school system." If possible, support or refute his evaluation of the system.

4. Unz cites (para. 6) the case of Philippe Kahn, an illegal immigrant. Does Unz favor unlimited immigration into the United States? If not, why does he cite this case?

5. Arguing against the idea that the new immigrants do not assimilate, in paragraph 12 Unz says that almost half of California's American-born Asians and Hispanics marry into other ethnic groups. Assuming the truth of the assertion, do you think this is a good thing, a bad thing, or something of no significance? Explain.

6. Unz cites the low incidence of crime in San José and El Paso (paras. 13–14). Try to verify his figures by checking them against the latest crime rates as reported in the FBI's *Uniform Crime Reports* or the *Sourcebook of Criminal Justice Statistics*. (Your reference librarian can help you to locate these materials.)

7. Unz describes Asians as "like Jews without liberal guilt" (para. 19). Explain what he means by this phrase.

8. In his final paragraph Unz claims that "three of the most anti-immigrant constituencies in American society are blacks, union members, and environmentalists." What evidence does he cite to support this claim? Do some research in the library and see what evidence, if any, you can find in support of this view.

9. Unz is writing in a conservative journal, presumably read chiefly by Republicans. Has he convinced you that immigrants form a natural Republican constituency, and that the Republicans should therefore not pursue an anti-immigrant policy? Explain.

Nathan Glazer

The Closing Door

Clearly we are at the beginning of a major debate on immigration. The issue has been raised most immediately in recent months by the immigrants, legal and illegal, now charged with the devastating bombing of the World Trade Center and with planning the bombing of other major New York buildings and New York transportation links; and by the interception of vessels carrying illegal Chinese immigrants approaching New York and California. But the issue is larger than how to control illegal immigration, difficult as this is. Despite the presence of a mass of laws, regulations, and court rulings controlling immigration, we are shaky as a polity on the largest questions that have to be answered in determining an immigration policy: What numbers should we admit, of what nations and races, on what basis should we make these decisions, how should we enforce them?

To answer these questions we will have to define our expectations about immigration, its effects on American society, economy, polity. It is a serious question whether the American political system is capable of giving any coherent response to these questions. Indeed, it could be argued that we have not been capable of a coherent response since the key decisions, now execrated in all quarters, of the 1920s.

I should say execrated in almost all quarters, for there are now bold voices, such as Thomas Fleming in the obscure journal *Chronicles* and Peter Brimelow in the not at all obscure *National Review*, that raise the question: What was wrong with the decisions of the 1920s, and do they not have something to teach us? Those decisions banned almost all immigration from Asia, and limited immigration from the eligible countries of the Eastern Hemisphere (almost all European) to 150,000 a year. Most of that was reserved for the British Isles and Germany: Southern and Eastern European countries—the source of most immigration at the time—were limited to tiny quotas. We see this act now as racist in its preference for whites and discriminatory in its preference for Protestant countries and its sharp restrictions on the countries from which Jewish immigrants then came. It was also considered anti-Catholic, although Catholics could come in under the ample quotas for Ireland and Germany.

But we can phrase the intentions of the 1924 act in quite another way: It said that what America was in 1920, in terms of ethnic and racial makeup, was in some way normative, and to be preferred to what it would

---

Nathan Glazer, born in 1923 in New York City, is a professor of education and sociology at Harvard University. He is the author of several books, including Ethnic Dilemmas *(1983), and the editor or coeditor of several books, including* Clamor at the Gates: The New American Immigration *(1985). We reprint an essay that originally appeared in* The New Republic *(December 27, 1993).*

become in the absence of immigration restriction; and it said that the United States was no longer to be a country of mass immigration. The 1924 law called for a remarkable scholarly exercise to determine the national origins of the white population: Each country would have a share in the quota of 150,000 proportional to its contribution to the makeup of the white population. That this system prevailed, with modifications, for forty years, suggests that the opposition to it, while impassioned, did not have much political power.

Despite the refugee crisis of the 1930s, the displaced persons crisis of   5 the post–World War II period, it survived: The McCarran-Walter Act of 1952 made little change in the overall pattern. The consensus of 1924 was finally swept away in 1965. The coalition that forced the abandonment of the arrangement of 1924 consisted of Jews, Catholics, and liberals, who had for years fought against the preferences for Northwestern Europe and the restrictions on Asia. The new immigration act abandoned all efforts to make distinctions among nations on grounds of race, size or historical connection. All would in principle be limited to a maximum of 20,000, under an overall cap of 290,000.

The dominating principles of the 1965 act were family connections and no discrimination on grounds of national origin. Italians, Poles, Greeks, or Jews would not be limited by highly restrictive quotas in their ability to enter the United States to join relatives; Asians would no longer be limited to minuscule quotas. But the government expected no great change in the volume or ethnic and racial character of immigration.

As it happens, there were not many Jews left in Europe who wanted to come or who could leave, even though Jewish organizations and members of Congress led the fight for a freer immigration policy. European prosperity soon reduced the number of Europeans who wanted to come; Communist rule restricted the number of Eastern Europeans who could come. Quite soon the composition of immigration changed from overwhelmingly European to overwhelmingly Asian, Latin American, and Caribbean. This was unintended and unexpected, but it was accepted. It played no role in the next great effort to fix immigration in the late 1970s. No one raised the question of why immigration to a country that had been settled by Europeans now included so few Europeans. The new immigration issue of the late 1970s was illegal immigration, primarily from Mexico.

A major immigration commission was set up in 1978. Its recommendations were incorporated into the Simpson-Mazzoli Immigration Reform Act of 1981, whose descendant finally became law as the Immigration Reform and Control Act of 1986. That act addressed the illegal immigration issue with a deal: those already here could apply, with restrictions, to legalize their status, but further numbers of illegal immigrants would be stanched by imposing penalties on employers who hired illegal immigrants.

In a few years further modifications were necessary. The new problem was that an immigration law oriented toward family preference meant preference for recent immigrants' relatives, those still linked by family connection to their emigrating relatives. This meant we would have few Europeans, who had immigrated a long time ago, and many Asians and Latin Americans. Congress tried to deal with this through lotteries. But the lotteries could not be for Europeans alone; they had to include a host of "underrepresented" nations.

Yet another issue that became evident under the settlement of 1965, and the changes of 1986, was that the numbers of immigrants who had family preference limited those who might enter with valuable skills in short supply in the United States, such as highly skilled machinists. And so the last major modification in the 1990 immigration law increased the number of those who could enter on the basis of needed skills. But it was not possible politically to reduce the number who came on the basis of family relationship, so the total number of allowable immigrants was raised. This is the kind of compromise that might surprise most Americans, if they knew about it. The total number of immigrants who can enter legally is now 700,000 (to which must be added 130,000 or so refugees, who come in under a separate allotment, and those seeking asylum).

So we move from crisis to crisis, or at least from problem to problem. The next crisis, already upon us, is the specific impact of large numbers of immigrants on the major cities that attract them: Los Angeles, New York, and Miami, preeminently. Here the issue is local costs, particularly for schools, hospitals, welfare services — costs that are inevitable when population rises. New York City reports that it added 65,000 immigrant children to its schools in 1992–93, and 46,000 in 1991–92.

This issue of immigration's cost is rather complicated. The immigrant population, despite the popular image, is not one of greater needs and lesser capacities than the American population. Rather, the immigrants are divided between those who come in with educational and work qualifications higher than those of the average American (most of the Asians) and those who come in with educational and work qualifications lower than those of the average American (mostly Hispanics and people from Caribbean countries).

And even within these large categories there are great differences by national origin. Some groups show a higher proportion on welfare than the American average (though almost none shows as high a proportion as American blacks and Puerto Ricans), some show a considerably lower proportion. Immigrants work and provide money to cities, states, and the federal government in taxes. Many work in hospitals as doctors and nurses and technicians, provide health services in underserved areas, do important research and teaching in universities and colleges. So how do we reckon up the balance? And is this the balance we should reckon?

In our efforts to determine just what kind of immigration policy we should have, we resort eagerly to the calculations of economists. But there is no clear guidance there. Julian Simon claims that people are always an economic asset: Increasing the number of people increases the numbers of consumers and producers. Other economists are doubtful that labor with poor qualifications is much of a benefit. Some point out that low-wage industries (garment manufacturing, for example) would go overseas in even greater proportion without low-paid immigrant labor. Others argue it should: Why is the most advanced economy in the world holding on to industries that have to compete with low-wage, developing countries? Some wonder who will provide service in restaurants and hotels, clean office buildings, take care of the children of high-paid professionals. Others point out that Japan manages to run hotels and restaurants with very few immigrants.

I have concluded that economics in general can give no large answer 15 as to what the immigration policy of a nation should be. At the margin, one would think, where the good effects clearly are evident, economic considerations must prevail. But I recall an Australian economist confidently pronouncing the end of the Japanese miracle in a talk in Tokyo in 1962. Why? Because Japan could not or would not, for reasons of culture or xenophobia, import labor, as Europe was then doing, and labor shortages would call a halt to Japanese economic growth. Clearly, he had it wrong. The Japanese did not import labor, but did manage to maintain phenomenal economic growth.

But if not economics, then what? Politics? Culture? Here we move on to murky and dangerous ground. Thinking of the economist's comments on Japan in the 1960s, and contrasting suspicious and closed Japan with open Europe, then recruiting Yugoslavs and Turks, one wonders whether Europeans would now agree that their course was better. Immigration and the fates of the workers recruited from distant cultures and their children have become a permanent part of Europe's politics, spawning an ugly nativism there similar to that which closed America's borders in the 1920s.

This is no argument for the United States in its thinking about immigration, one might say. We are used to greater differences than the more homogeneous countries of Europe. We are a nation based not on a common ethnic stock linked by mystic cords of memory, connection, kinship, but rather by common universal ideas. But I am not sure how deeply rooted this view is among Americans in general. We all know the power of the sense of kinship, real or mythical, in keeping people together — or in tearing them apart. (This possibility is exacerbated by our affirmative action policies, which, while designed to advance those American racial and ethnic groups that have suffered from and suffer still from discrimination, are not limited to citizens or legal residents.)

The present-day restrictionist movement deploys the economic arguments, but it is the others that really drive it. Much of its current modest strength comes from the heirs of the Zero Population Growth movement and from environmentalists who argue that there are already too many Americans. But an equally strong motivation of the movement comes from the sense that there was — is — an American culture that is threatened by too great diversity. It is harder to make this argument publicly, for obvious reasons, since the question comes up: How do you define this American culture? Should it be or remain Christian or white or European?

The two kinds of argument are closely related. There are many Americans who regret the loss of a less crowded country and a more homogeneous culture. We are too prone to label them racists. There are indeed racists, and bigots, and the restrictionist movement will undoubtedly attract them in number. Yet the motives I have pointed to among the current restrictionists, an attachment to a country more like what it once was, a preference for a less populated country, are not ignoble.

We go very far these days in testing motives for racism, if their effect 20 is to bear differentially on ethnic and racial groups. It is true that a lower level of immigration, more preference for those with needed skills, a spin in favor of the "underrepresented," would all mean more Europeans, fewer Hispanics and Caribbeans and Asians. But the effects of such policies are not an index to the motives of those who advocate them. Nor would I call a motive that would prefer an immigrant stream closer in racial and ethnic character to the present composition of the American population necessarily racist. In British immigration law there is a category of "partials" — persons born of British stock in other countries whose status is defined by ancestry, connection to Britain through parents or grandparents. In Germany, people of German origin, no matter how distant, have claims to immigration others do not. Israel has its "law of return"[1] — which was the ground on which the country was labeled "racist." I would not describe any of these policies as racist: There is a difference between recognizing those who are in some sense one's own, with links to a people and a culture, and a policy based on dislike, hostility, racial antagonism.

One other element should be mentioned as making up part of the immigration restriction movement. One finds in it children of immigrants, and immigrants themselves, who admire the ability of America to assimilate immigrants and their children, but who fear that the assimilatory powers of America have weakened, because of the legal support to bilingualism in education and voting, because of the power of multicultural trends in education. It is easy to accuse such people of wanting to pull up the drawbridge after they have gained entry. They would answer that they fear the United States is no longer capable of assimilating those now coming as it assimilated them.

Is this a fair argument, or have the aging immigrants of the last great European wave and their children who may be found active in immigration restriction simply adopted the nativist prejudices of those who tried to bar them? But it *is* a different country: less self-confident, less willing to im-

---

[1]**law of return** Any Jew may "return" to (i.e., emigrate to) Israel. [Editors' note.]

pose English and American customs and loyalty as simply the best in the world. We do not know whether this change in national mood and in educational philosophy and practice actually affects the rate at which immigrants assimilate, and much would depend on giving an answer as to what we mean by assimilation. Learning English? I do not think the new immigrants learn English at a slower rate than the older European immigrants. Taking up citizenship? This has always varied depending on the ethnic group. One sees the same variation among current immigrants, and if fewer become citizens one reason may be that there are now fewer advantages to citizenship as civil rights law spreads to protect aliens.

One even finds some anti-immigrant sentiment among the newest, post-1965 immigrants. This sentiment is directed primarily at illegal immigrants: It is exacerbated by the fact that there may be competition for jobs between older legal and newer illegal immigrants working at the same jobs. They may also share the same section of the city, and the older immigrants may see the new illegals contributing to neighborhood decline.

In time, American blacks may be numbered among the restrictionists. If there is indeed competition between immigrants, legal or illegal, and Americans, blacks are likely to be more affected than any other group. Up to now, the dream of the Rainbow Coalition has kept black members of Congress in the proimmigration camp. I doubt that this reflects the dominant view among blacks.

My sense is that the state of American public opinion is now modestly 25 restrictionist. The scale of immigration is larger than most people would choose, for a host of reasons: They don't think America should become a country of mass immigration again, and see no good reason, economic or other, for this. They ask why the stream of immigration should be so unrepresentative of the nation that already exists. They support the need to admit refugees. They are against illegal immigration, even though they may benefit from the services of such immigrants. They think immigration policies should reflect our compassion (refugees), our respect for human rights (asylum seekers), the desire of immigrant neighbors to bring in parents, children, and spouses, perhaps some brothers and sisters. They believe immigration policies should reflect our desire to improve the country — more of the kind of immigrants who become high-school class valedictorians and win science prizes.

That is about where I come out, too. There is no blueprint here, only a list of preferences that are not disreputable and should be respected. Whatever our policies are, however, I think our biggest problem will be to carry them out in a world in which so many see entry into the United States as a way of improving themselves.

How different would that be from what we have? When one considers present immigration policies, it seems we have insensibly reverted to mass immigration, without ever having made a decision to do so. Few Americans believe our population is too low, our land too lightly settled, our resources unexploited, our industries and commerce short of labor. But our policies, the result of various pressures operating within a framework of decent and generous ideals, end up looking as if we believe all this is true. The pressures consist of recent immigrants who want to bring in family members (no small group — there were 8 million immigrants in the 1980s), agricultural interests that want cheap labor, a Hispanic caucus that believes any immigration restriction demeans Hispanics, foreign policy interests that require us to take a substantial number of refugees, civil rights groups that expand the rights of illegal immigrants, refugees, and asylum seekers.

These interests are not necessarily distinguishable from ideals of generosity toward those in desperate need, compassion for those who simply seek a country with more opportunity, respect for a tradition, rather recently reminted, that asserts we are a nation of immigrants, should remain so and should be proud of it.

The fulfillment of these ideals does not, however, suggest that there are any moral and ethical imperatives that dictate we have no right to make the decision that the United States, as it stands, with all its faults, is what we prefer to the alternative that would be created by mass immigration. The United States can survive without large numbers of low-skilled workers, and would probably survive, if it was so inclined, without highly trained foreign engineers, doctors, scientists. At the level of the highest skills and talents we will undoubtedly always be happy to welcome immigrants — we did even in the restrictive 1930s and 1940s. In a world in which masses of people can move, or be moved, too easily beyond their native borders, we will always need policies to set limits as to what the responsibilities of this country are.

There is one kind of immigration restriction on which all (in theory) 30 agree, and that is control of illegal immigration. Much would be required to stem it, and the 1986 act did not. We would need identity documents more resistant to forgery, more Border Patrol officers, better qualified investigators of claims to asylum, and much more. The effort to control illegal immigration will be expensive if it is to be effective. We may be able to learn from the European countries now trying to stem illegal immigration. A stronger effort to reduce illegal immigration may serve as a prelude to a more effective immigration regime generally, and that will be task enough for the next few years. Or we may discover in the effort that such control requires measures that we simply don't want to live with. It will be valuable to learn that, too.

Topics for Critical Thinking and Writing

1. State as precisely as you can in one sentence Glazer's main thesis about immigration.

2. Why does Glazer express uncertainty (para. 2) about whether "the American

political system" is capable of having a "coherent" immigration policy? Are you inclined to agree or disagree? Why?

3. In paragraphs 9 and 10 Glazer touches on the three principles now governing the award of visas to applicants: (1) job skills, especially those that we need; (2) kinship to an American citizen or to a legal immigrant; (3) refugee status, either from war or from political persecution. Various arguments have been raised against all of these criteria. For instance, it has been said that even foreigners with unusual skills — let's say brain surgeons or professors of Swahili — rarely have skills that cannot be matched by Americans. Further, it has been said that we ought not help to impoverish certain foreign countries by accepting their most highly skilled citizens. For *each* of the three categories, list the best arguments pro *and* con that you can think of, and then write an essay of 250 to 500 words indicating why you would drop one or more of the criteria, or, if you prefer, why you would use a different criterion. Some people have, for instance, proposed a lottery, in which all applicants for visas, from wherever and with whatever skills, would have an equal chance at winning one of a fixed number of visas.

4. In paragraphs 12–14 Glazer touches on the difficulty of drawing conclusions about the costs of immigration. (Elsewhere in this chapter we include two opposing essays, one by Huddle and the other by Clark and Passel, that address themselves to the economics of immigration.) Do you think that the costs can be accurately calculated, and even if so, are the costs relevant to decisions about how many people to admit, and on what criteria?

5. In paragraph 19 Glazer suggests that a preference for a "more homogeneous culture," though sometimes said to be racist, is not in fact an "ignoble" preference. Reread the entire paragraph, and paragraph 20, and then indicate the degree to which you agree or disagree, and explain why.

6. Carefully reread Glazer's paragraph 25. With which of the things he asserts do you agree? With which do you disagree? Write a 500-word essay on the topic "Where I Agree and Disagree with Glazer's Position on Current Immigration Policy and Practice."

7. Glazer ends his essay by stating his chief worry: illegal immigration. However, he doesn't present any facts about the magnitude of the problem or what is being done to control it. Using the resources of your college library to explore these two issues, write a 500-word essay on the theme "Illegal Immigration into the United States: The Current Problem and What to Do about It."

8. Glazer does not touch on the fact that the United States grants citizenship to all people born in this country — including those born to illegal aliens. Most other countries determine citizenship on the basis of the citizenship of the parents. Construct the best argument you can on behalf of our present system, or against it.

Cathi Tactaquin

What Rights for the Undocumented?

Undocumented immigrants are perhaps the most powerless of any group of workers in this country — a permanent feature of the much talked about "underclass" of U.S. society. Over the last fifteen years, their rights have been under constant assault. Anti-immigrant hype, restrictive immigration legislation, broad attacks on civil rights, and the worsening conditions of the poor have all served to further isolate the undocumented.

At the same time, the undocumented have become increasingly adept at defending their rights both in the workplace and in the community at large. Numerous legal and political campaigns — waged by community groups, labor unions, immigrant and refugee rights advocates, civil rights and religious organizations, and even local governments — have managed to ameliorate some of the more repressive aspects of laws and policies pertaining to people without legal status. Occasionally, these battles have even resulted in an expansion of the limited rights of the undocumented.

Most current assessments place the number of undocumented in the United States at somewhere between 2.5 and 4 million. The number has always been hard to gauge, because this is a "shadow" population, often without the "official" recognition other residents take for granted. A great many undocumented are seasonal workers, here for a few months at a time; some come and go at the beginning and end of the workweek. While those wanting to restrict immigration often quote much higher figures, a number of experts agree that the undocumented population grows between two hundred thousand and three hundred thousand a year, about 40 percent of whom enter legally and overstay their visas. Among these are refugees from turbulent political situations and civil war who have not been granted official refugee status.

Current public concern over the influx of undocumented immigrants dates from the post–Vietnam War recession of the 1970s, when politicians launched appeals to save U.S. jobs for "Americans." The Immigration and Naturalization Service (INS) obligingly initiated massive raids on immigrant communities, deporting hundreds of thousands of undocumented Mexicans and provoking a heated response from immigrants and their advocates. In 1978, pledging to make a serious study of the immigration debate, President Carter created the Select Commission on Immigration and Refugee Policy.

The commission's report, "Immigration Policy and the National Interest," was released in 1981, after President Reagan had made his own ap- 5

Cathi Tactaquin is director of the National Network for Immigrant and Refugee Rights in Oakland, California. This essay originally appeared in July 1992 in Report on the Americas, *a journal devoted to matters of interest to immigrants.*

pointments to the commission. The report recommended a token amnesty program for long-residing undocumented immigrants, employer sanctions, and major funding increases for border enforcement and for the creation of immigrant detention centers. These elements formed the basis of sweeping immigration legislation introduced the following year by Republican Sen. Alan Simpson and Democratic Rep. Romano Mazzoli.

The fundamental premise that the undocumented were taking jobs away from U.S. workers continued to frame the immigration debate. An aggressive campaign by the Reagan Administration painted pictures of a "border out of control" and an invasion by "hordes of feet people" to prompt audiences once more to scapegoat "foreigners" for an unstable U.S. economy.

The Immigration Reform and Control Act (IRCA) became law in November 1986. Although it sparked a fairly wide-ranging movement for immigrant and refugee rights, IRCA's passage was widely recognized as a major blow not only to the immigrant communities, but also to labor and civil rights.

Many studies since have found that large numbers of employers fearing the "employer sanctions" provision of IRCA, which imposes civil and criminal penalties on those who continuously hire undocumented workers, will discriminate against those who appear or sound "foreign" to them—namely, racial minorities and the foreign born.

The impact of sanctions on the undocumented is even more severe. Prior to the passage of IRCA, entering or remaining in the United States without immigration papers was illegal, but working without papers was not a crime. Undocumented workers were considered employees with the same rights as other nonimmigrant workers, a definition which was upheld in court. The introduction of employer sanctions essentially redefined the labor rights of the undocumented, "criminalizing" workers without papers. A number of cases have been brought in which an employer challenged a worker's right to even file a claim because the worker was undocumented. While the courts seem to agree that claims may be filed, there is still considerable disagreement about whether reinstatement and/or back pay should be allowed as remedies in the case of an undocumented worker. . . .

The attacks on workplace rights due to IRCA have created an increased awareness in some parts of the labor movement about the importance and complexity of organizing immigrant workers. The California Immigrant Workers' Association (CIWA), launched as an associate member organization of the AFL-CIO in Los Angeles/Orange County, seeks to organize immigrant workers, many of whom are undocumented. With the assistance of CIWA, the International Association of Machinists persuaded workers to unionize at an auto-racing equipment factory in Los Angeles last year—the biggest manufacturing election victory since 1964. The workers at the plant were almost all Mexican and Salvadoran immigrants.

Many undocumented do not, however, have regular work, and are not affiliated with unions. "Street-corner" labor, in which immigrants and non-immigrants alike are hired by the day, is now commonplace in cities and towns across the United States. Particularly with the rise in unemployment, more and more citizens have joined the undocumented in search of any kind of work that offers a day's wage.

The passage of IRCA significantly increased the number of undocumented workers forced to stand on street corners advertising their services for the cheapest wage. In many cases, workers report that they are paid below the agreed-upon wage, or not at all. They are also often exposed to poor or hazardous working conditions. Because work-permit verification (required by IRCA of all employees hired after November 6, 1986) is not required for people who work "irregularly," "sporadically" or on an "intermittent basis," employers of day labor are generally not targets of employer-sanctions enforcement.

The response to the growing phenomenon of day labor has been mixed—in a number of cities, residents have organized to "get them out of the neighborhood," claiming the workers are a public nuisance. Others have responded more sympathetically, working with unions and cities to create day-labor hiring halls and programs that provide language training and "know-your-rights" outreach.

In San Francisco, the city-sponsored Day Labor Program has yielded another important outgrowth: the Asociación de Trabajadores Latinos — the Latino Workers Association. The member-run organization provides mutual assistance, organizes know-your-rights presentations, and has even agreed to seek a minimum wage of $6.25 an hour.

Another form of "organized" casual labor is the "cooperative," in 15 which members are essentially independent contractors, and do not have an employer/employee relationship with the person for whom they provide services. In the San Francisco Bay Area, there are a number of immigrant-based cooperatives, including "Heaven Sent," a housecleaning cooperative in East Palo Alto. Heaven Sent provides training and job referrals, and participants pay monthly dues.

Manos, in Alameda and Contra Costa counties, provides job placement for Latino immigrants. Initially organized through the Diocese of Oakland in the mid-1980s, it has helped to launch similar projects in other areas and has grown to include two job-referral collectives, and home-care and janitorial cooperatives. Employers contact the organizations for referrals, pay the workers directly, and make a donation to the organization for overhead costs.

Of course the impact of IRCA on undocumented rights also reaches beyond the workplace. For example, even though an estimated 70 percent of undocumented workers pay taxes, they are not eligible for most federal benefits. Because of IRCA, even access to those benefits and services for which they are eligible is constantly being challenged. For instance, immigrants have been denied access to housing because they were suspected of being undocumented. In some cities, the right of undocumented children to attend public schools has been questioned, even though this right was clearly established by the courts.

IRCA and employer sanctions have caused particular problems for undocumented immigrant women. Like other women, they may remain trapped in abusive relationships because they fear being unable to support themselves (and often their children). But they also fear deportation if they have no papers, or if their legal status is tied to remaining in a valid marriage for a minimum of two years. Advocates have fought for a "battered women waiver" to the 1986 Immigrant Marriage Fraud Act, in order to provide immigrant women in abusive relationships an opportunity to gain legal status if they leave their battering spouses.

Several organizations have sprung up around the country to address the particular needs of undocumented women. Mujeres Unidas y Activas in San Francisco, for example, conducts know-your-rights outreach, offers leadership training, language classes, and domestic violence counseling, and serves as a support network for immigrant women. La Mujer Obrera organizes immigrant women, including many who are undocumented, in the garment factories in El Paso. Their hunger strikes and organizing campaigns have gained national attention, since they target some of the country's leading manufacturers who contract with local sweatshops at poverty wages.

Hundreds of thousands of "unofficial" refugees are counted among 20 the undocumented. Largely from Central America and Haiti, these people have escaped conditions of political turmoil and civil war only to be rejected by the United States. Central Americans have found some safety from deportation through two programs. After seeking support for safe-haven measures in Congress for several years, in 1990 Salvadorans gained "Temporary Protected Status" or TPS. TPS provided an eighteen month period of protection from deportation (and work authorization) for Salvadoran refugees who registered with the INS. President George Bush announced that TPS participants would continue to enjoy that benefit for at least another year, although TPS is not being officially extended.

Guatemalans did not receive any deportation protection, but they, along with Salvadorans, also gained some relief through the settlement of a class action suit filed by the American Baptist Church in 1985. The "ABC" settlement resulted in readjudication for over 150,000 political asylum cases that had been denied Salvadoran and Guatemalan applicants. In the suit, the plaintiffs claimed that foreign-policy biases, instead of the merit of individual cases, had resulted in the overwhelming denial of political-asylum petitions. Ninety-seven percent had been denied; in contrast, 84 percent of 1987 asylum claims from anti-Sandinista Nicaraguans were approved. In the 1990 settlement, plaintiffs gained the right to have their cases reexamined under revised rules, and could get work authorization while their cases were pending.

IRCA seems to have given added license to the Border Patrol and to racist hate groups to commit crimes against undocumented immigrants. Throughout the U.S.–Mexico border area, harassment and physical violence have increased dramatically. Community activists and immigrant and refugee rights advocates are lobbying for a variety of measures to protect basic human rights. These measures include: local, state and federal investigation, monitoring, and prosecution of anti-immigrant activity; reform of INS regulations governing the use of deadly force and instituting some form of civilian review of Border Patrol practices; and an end to Border Patrol high-speed chases of suspected undocumented immigrants in the border area, which have resulted in numerous fatalities in recent years. They have also created an "Immigrant Rights Urgent Response Network" to coordinate efforts among local and national organizations to press for immediate action on critical issues of abuse.

A recent court settlement stipulates that undocumented immigrants in detention should be informed of their legal rights, and should have the opportunity to consult with a lawyer. The settlement stems from a case file fourteen years ago on behalf of a Mexican citizen, Rosa Melchor López, and several other immigrant workers who had been arrested in an INS raid at a Los Angeles shoe factory in 1978. They claimed they were not allowed to talk to a lawyer, were forced to sign a waiver of their rights, and were to be deported.

Expansion of undocumented rights has also been pursued in a number of other areas that are indicative of the integration of the undocumented into broader society. For example, in Takoma Park, Maryland, the "Share-the-Vote" campaign resulted in a successful nonbinding referendum providing noncitizens with the right to vote in local elections, and even to run for office. "This is really a civil rights challenge that's facing the next generation," George Leventhal, who headed the campaign, told the press. "When you broaden the electoral pool, everyone wins." The City Council is to follow up with a binding ordinance.

The issue sparked considerable controversy around the country. The 25 anti-immigrant Federation for American Immigration Reform (FAIR) argued that the proposed ordinance would "undermine the value of U.S. citizenship" and might create another "magnet" for unlawful immigration. Yet others favor the idea, citing numerous examples where noncitizens are permitted to vote in local elections (like New York's community school boards). They note that local voting by noncitizens was a common practice in the nineteenth century and into the twentieth.

Undocumented immigrants have also become part of the environmental movement, joining with other minority community activists to charge that "toxic racism" is responsible for an alarming rate of disabilities and fatalities from exposure to dangerous pesticides, waste dumps, and incinerators. Particularly in the Southwest, immigrant communities, including sizeable undocumented populations, have experienced "cancer clusters," babies born without brains or with other deformities, psychological changes, and fertility and reproduction problems which experts say can be largely traced to environmental hazards. Farmworkers are especially vulnerable to pesticides, as are their children, who must often accompany parents in the fields. In the small Latino town of Kettleman City, in south-central California, residents fought one of the country's largest waste disposal and treatment companies, Chemical Waste Management, to block construction of a toxic waste incinerator.

The number of local and national organizing efforts to protect and expand the rights of the undocumented have significantly increased over the last ten years. Nonetheless, community and other immigrant rights advocates feel their efforts have not kept pace with the impact of U.S. economic and foreign policies which continue to spur all types of immigration, and of domestic policies which lead to greater impoverishment and restriction of rights. Perhaps, as many now believe, nothing less than the repeal of employer sanctions will prevent further deterioration of rights.

Topics for Critical Thinking and Writing

1. Tactaquin speaks of "undocumented immigrants" (para. 1) and of "people without legal status" (para. 2), but never of "illegal immigrants." Is there a difference? If there is no difference, why does Tactaquin use only the first two of these terms?

2. In her title and in her second sentence Tactaquin assumes that undocumented immigrants have rights. In paragraph 9 she speaks of the rights of undocumented workers, and in paragraph 17 she says that the courts have upheld the rights of undocumented children to attend schools. In paragraph 18 she suggests that there should be a "battered women waiver" in order "to provide immigrant women in abusive relationships an opportunity to gain legal status if they leave their battering spouses." What rights (if any) do you think undocumented persons have, or should have, and why?

3. Tactaquin's tone suggests that she thinks there was something wrong being done when in the 1970s the INS returned to Mexico "hundreds of thousands of undocumented [Mexican immigrants]" (para. 4). What could possibly be wrong about enforcing the law in this or a similar case?

4. In paragraph 5 Tactaquin argues that the Select Commission on Immigration and Refugee Policy in 1981 recommended "a token amnesty program for long-residing undocumented immigrants." Using the resources of your college library, find out exactly what were the 1981 recommendations concerning amnesty for undocumented immigrants. Do you agree that they were "token"? Explain.

5. Do you think it is fair for undocumented workers to be required to pay taxes and yet to be ineligible for certain welfare benefits (see para. 17)? If so, which do you think is the better remedy: Allow them not to pay taxes, or extend to them the same benefits that other taxpayers receive? Why?

6. In paragraphs 24 and 25 Tactaquin mentions a nonbinding Maryland referendum giving noncitizens the right to vote in local elections, and even to run for office. What arguments can be offered on behalf of such an idea?

7. Tactaquin ends by implying that employer sanctions should be repealed—that

is, penalties should not be imposed on employers who hire undocumented workers. What reasons does she give for advancing this position? What are your responses? Is it relevant, by the way, that almost every nation in the developed world requires proof of work authorization, based on citizenship status?

Donald L. Huddle

A Growing Burden

In 1992, two major studies reported that immigrants used up a lot more public money—for education, medical care, welfare, and other social benefits—than they paid in taxes that year.

In a Los Angeles County government report, the gap for 2.3 million immigrants, both legal and illegal, was $808 million in county costs. A study of San Diego by the Auditor General of California found that the next cost of state and county services for two hundred thousand illegals was $145.9 million.

Both studies emphasized that while the county governments were bearing a large share of these costs, the Federal Government collected the lion's share of immigrants' tax revenues and returned little to the counties. State governments may be in a similar position. Last month, Gov. Pete Wilson of California said that illegal immigrants and their U.S.-born children (who are citizens) were costing the state $2.9 billion a year for only four services: welfare, education, health care, and—if it can be called a service—incarceration.

A study I conducted for the Carrying Capacity Network, a nonprofit educational organization, was the first comprehensive assessment of the costs of immigration at the Federal, state, and county levels. Do immigrants as a group contribute enough in Federal taxes to cancel out the burden they pose at the county and state levels? Or does government spending on immigrants outweigh their tax revenues? The answers have obvious implications for immigration policy.

Our nationwide study assessed the net costs to taxpayers of immi-   5
grants who have arrived since 1970 and projected spending on those expected to arrive from 1993 to 2002. It examined twenty-three categories of Federal, state, and local assistance, including county health and welfare services.

In three previous field studies, I found that for every one hundred unskilled immigrants who were working, twenty-five or more unskilled na-

---

Donald L. Huddle is professor emeritus of economics at Rice University. This essay originally appeared in the New York Times *(September 3, 1993) paired with the following essay by Rebecca L. Clark and Jeffrey S. Passel, under the heading "Immigrants: A Cost or a Benefit?"*

tive-born Americans were displaced or unable to get jobs. The Carrying Capacity Network study calculated the costs of public assistance for 2.1 million American workers displaced by immigrants, using the 25 percent displacement rate.

According to 1990 Census data, the poverty rate of immigrants is 42.8 percent higher than that of the native-born. On average, immigrant households receive 44.2 percent more public assistance dollars than do native households.

Public assistance costs in 1992 at the county, state, and national levels were $42.5 billion for the 19.3 million legal and illegal immigrants who have settled in the United States since 1970. These are net costs, after deducting the $20.2 billion in taxes paid by immigrants and including the $11.9 billion for public assistance for the 2.1 million displaced U.S.-born workers. The biggest expense was for primary and secondary public education, followed by Medicaid.

And these costs are projected to rise, assuming that laws and their enforcement don't change. Our estimate is that 11.1 million immigrants, legal and illegal, will enter the country in the next decade. The bill for supporting all immigrants and the American workers they displace for those 10 years will total $951.7 billion. We estimated that the immigrants will pay $283.2 billion in taxes.

Thus there will be a net cost to U.S. taxpayers of $668.5 billion over 10 the decade. Legal immigrants will account for almost three-quarters of the total cost; illegal aliens will account for $186.4 billion.

The costs over the next decade may increase if, as some project, the number of immigrants rises above the 11.1 million our study estimates. And the number may rise even more because spending is being increased for programs such as the earned-income tax credit and other services that act as magnets for potential immigrants.

The Clinton Administration's anticipated plan for universal health coverage would significantly raise medical costs for immigrants, a larger percentage of whom tend to be uninsured. Indeed, access to public health care alone might be enough to attract new immigrants, particularly those with difficult medical conditions.

How can the United States reduce this growing burden? It should not single out legal immigrants for cuts in entitlements because that would be discriminatory. But it should tighten financial responsibility requirements for families and other sponsors of immigrants.

A better way of cutting the costs would be to reduce immigration and select entrants more carefully.

Current law incorporates a preference for family reunification and for 15 political asylum seekers and refugees. Aliens who received amnesty under the 1986 immigration act are becoming eligible to bring in their families. World events could encourage an even greater number of refugees, most of whom will be low-skilled and dependent.

If the policies were changed, however, to accept only skilled or professional legal immigrants—38 percent of the current flow—we would avoid a projected cost of $171.8 billion, while netting a modest revenue gain of $13.7 billion by 2002.

Curbing illegal immigration could save $186 billion by 2002. Stricter control of the border, enforcement of sanctions against employers who hire illegals and better programs to screen immigrant welfare applications could help stem the flow.

Topics for Critical Thinking and Writing

1. Reread Huddle's essay and sort out into three categories the costs he cites that are incurred by immigrants: those he says arise from legal immigrants, those from illegal immigrants, and those he does not clearly describe either way. Are these annual costs, or are they incurred over longer periods of time? Which ones are projections, which actual expenditures?

2. List all the assumptions that Huddle makes that are relevant to the costs he predicts.

3. How, exactly, does Huddle think the nation ought to reduce the costs of immigration?

4. In paragraph 6 Huddle says that "for every one hundred unskilled immigrants who were working, twenty-five or more unskilled native-born Americans were displaced or unable to get jobs." In the following essay, by Clark and Passel, these statistics are disputed in paragraph 12; but putting aside the accuracy of the figures, do you accept the view, offered by Unz (p. 452, paras. 3–4) and others, that many unskilled immigrants are in jobs that other workers simply will not take, and that the jobs would not exist if it were not for the immigrants? Why do you hold the view that you do?

5. Suppose someone argued that one simply cannot talk only about dollars. One must also take account of services that immigrants—skilled and unskilled—provide: for example, as agricultural laborers and as research scientists. What is your view?

6. In paragraph 14 Huddle suggests that we should "select entrants more carefully." Most legal entrants are tourists, students, business people, or political refugees. Illegal immigrants are, roughly, of two sorts: people who entered legally with visas but who have overstayed their visas, or people who have crossed the borders without going through customs. Visas are normally issued to any foreigner whom the State Department's Bureau of Consular Affairs expects will return home—that is, to all applicants with jobs, property, or families in their own country. *How* might we "select entrants more carefully"?

Rebecca L. Clark and Jeffrey S. Passel

Studies Are Deceptive

The economy is dragging, and Americans are looking for scapegoats: Increasingly, they seem to find them in immigrants. But do immigrants cost more than they put into the economy, as has been reported in two recent studies? And is this the right question to ask?

According to the 1990 Census, there are 19.7 million immigrants living in the United States, or one in twelve Americans. Of these, 11 million entered the country before 1980; 2.6 million were granted amnesty under the 1986 immigration law. The Immigration and Naturalization Service recently estimated that there were 2.6 million illegal immigrants in 1990, and the number increased to 3.2 million in 1992.

Estimating the economic cost or benefit of legal and illegal immigrants — nationally or for local areas — is difficult. The necessary numbers are largely unavailable, so researchers must fill in gaps with assumptions.

Our intent is not to advocate higher or lower levels of immigration, but to provide guidance in assessing the assumptions — and thus plausibility — of the numbers used in the debate.

Most studies measure the costs of immigrants better than the benefits, 5 because social service expenses can be estimated from government data, whereas estimates of taxes paid require statistics on income and place of birth from a representative sample.

The net cost of immigrants can be estimated from the following:

Taxes paid. In our recent study of the impact of immigrants in Los Angeles County, we used Census survey data to estimate five Federal, state, and local taxes paid by immigrants. We found that adult immigrants who arrived after 1980 paid a total of $3,066 per person. This was almost twice as much as was estimated by a Los Angeles County government report.

The comparable figure for all immigrants, recent or not, is $4,264 a person, compared with $6,902 for natives. Long-term immigrants pay more than their proportionate share. They make up 15 percent of the Los Angeles County population and contribute 18 percent of the five taxes.

Jobs created and taxes paid by immigrant-owned or supported businesses. This major contribution to public coffers has not been quantified or included in any cost-benefit studies of immigrants.

Rebecca L. Clark and Jeffrey S. Passel are demographers at the Urban Institute, a research group in Washington, D.C. This essay originally appeared in the New York Times (September 3, 1993), paired with the preceding essay by Donald L. Huddle.

Cost of services. Despite a widespread belief that immigrants are at- 10 tracted to the United States by its social services, there are several reasons to expect immigrants' use of welfare to be relatively low.

Undocumented immigrants are barred from most public assistance programs. Recent legal immigrants are effectively prohibited from receiving most public assistance for three to five years after arrival. And a person with a history of receiving welfare finds it more difficult to bring relatives into the country.

The cost of services provided to recent legal immigrants in Los Angeles has been overestimated. For some social service programs, the Los Angeles County report mistakenly computed the costs for *recent* legal immigrants by using the costs for *all* legal immigrants. As a result, the report overestimated the costs of recent immigrants by one-third.

Displacement. Many studies find that the loss of jobs to immigrants is minimal to nonexistent. Yet, a recent well-publicized report by one research group, the Carrying Capacity Network, says that for every one hundred unskilled immigrant workers, twenty-five natives become permanently unemployed. But these figures were based on a very small sample of 378 unemployed Houston residents who were asked whether they would take an "illegal alien type unskilled" job "at $7 or less per hour." This approach rests on three unsupported assumptions: that such a job exists, that an illegal alien has it, and that the respondent would actually accept it.

In the end, the cost debate must address two questions: What is the cost of immigration to local governments? And what are the costs of keeping illegal immigrants out?

Most taxes that immigrants and natives pay go to the Federal and state 15 governments. But most of the costs of caring for, educating and sheltering people accrue at the local level.

The Los Angeles government report is probably correct in concluding that immigrants get more in services from the county than they contribute in county taxes. But this is also the case for natives. The study is incomplete because it fails to include all sources of revenue and omits indirect economic benefits from immigrants' consumer spending and businesses.

In order to keep illegal immigrants out, we spend three-quarters of a billion dollars a year, and would have to spend many times that amount to succeed in keeping them from crossing our borders.

Recent popular calls to reduce illegal immigration have focused on further limiting illegals' access to education and social programs and erecting barriers to entry. The proposals have not focused on jobs — the true incentive attracting immigrants. If the flow is to be significantly reduced, the U.S. Government may have to adopt stricter employer sanctions and tighter regulation of business hiring — actions that would not have widespread support.

Topics for Critical Thinking and Writing ═══════════

1. Read the essay by Donald L. Huddle (p. 471), and identify all the issues of fact that he and Clark and Passel mention but on which they take a different view. Do you find any basis to agree with one side rather than the other? Explain. What costs of immigration does Huddle mention that Clark and Passel ignore, and vice versa? Which of the two essays do you think gives a better overall picture of the costs of current immigration? Why?

2. In paragraph 13 Clark and Passel dispute the conclusion reached by Carrying Capacity Network to the effect that for every one hundred unskilled workers, twenty-five natives became unemployed. Do you agree that the figure seems unreliable? If so, what would be a better way of gaining information about the possible displacement of natives by immigrants?

3. In paragraph 15 Clark and Passel say—and most people would probably agree with them—that most of the taxes go to the federal and state governments, but most of the costs of "educating and sheltering people accrue at the local level." If this is true, what changes, if any, should be made?

4. Clark and Passel mention (para. 17) that the nation now spends $750 million a year to prevent illegal immigration. Do they imply that this money would be better spent elsewhere? If not, why do they cite this expenditure?

5. Think up three questions about the costs of immigration that Clark and Passel do not comment on but that you believe are important to answer if we really want to calculate the full costs of current immigration.

14

Multiculturalism: What Is It, and Is It Good or Bad?

Henry Louis Gates, Jr.

The Debate Has Been Miscast from the Start

What is multiculturalism and why are they saying such terrible things about it?

We've been told that it threatens to fragment American culture into a warren of ethnic enclaves, each separate and inviolate. We've been told that it menaces the Western tradition of literature and the arts. We've been told that it aims to politicize the school curriculum, replacing honest historical scholarship with a "feel-good" syllabus designed solely to bolster the self-esteem of minorities. The alarm has been sounded, and many scholars and educators—liberals as well as conservatives—have responded to it. After all, if multiculturalism is just a pretty name for ethnic chauvinism, who needs it?

But I don't think that's what multiculturalism is—at least, I don't think that's what it ought to be. And because the debate has been miscast from the beginning, it may be worth setting the main issues straight.

Henry Louis Gates, Jr., was born in West Virginia in 1950 and educated at Yale University, where he received his bachelor's degree summa cum laude in 1973. He earned his M.A. and Ph.D. degrees at Cambridge University. The author of several books, including Black Literature and Literary Theory *(1984),* Figures in Black *(1987), and* Loose Canons: Notes of the Culture Wars *(1992), Gates has taught at Yale, Cornell, and Duke, and now he is chairman of the Afro-American Studies Department and a professor of English at Harvard. The article reprinted here was first published in the* Boston Globe Magazine *(October 13, 1991), paired with the following essay by Kenneth T. Jackson.*

To both proponents and antagonists, multiculturalism represents—either refreshingly or frighteningly—a radical departure. Like most claims for cultural novelty, this one is more than a little exaggerated. For the challenges of cultural pluralism—and the varied forms of official resistance to it—go back to the very founding of our republic.

In the university today, it must be admitted, the challenge has taken 5 on a peculiar inflection. But the underlying questions are time-tested. What does it mean to be an American? Must academic inquiry be subordinated to the requirements of national identity? Should scholarship and education reflect our actual diversity, or should they, rather, forge a communal identity that may not yet have been achieved?

For answers, you can, of course, turn to the latest jeremiad on the subject from, say, George Will, Dinesh D'Souza, or Roger Kimball. But in fact these questions have always occasioned lively disagreement among American educators. In 1917, William Henry Hulme decried "the insidious introduction into our scholarly relations of the political propaganda of a wholly narrow, selfish, and vicious nationalism and false patriotism." His opponents were equally emphatic in their beliefs. "More and more clearly," Fred Lewis Pattee ventured in 1919, "is it seen now that the American soul, the American conception of democracy, Americanism, should be made prominent in our school curriculums, as a guard against the rising spirit of experimental lawlessness." Sound familiar?

Given the political nature of the debate over education and the national interest, the conservative penchant for changing the multiculturalists with "politics" is a little perplexing. For conservative critics, to their credit, have never hesitated to provide a political defense of what they consider to be the "traditional" curriculum: The future of the republic, they argue, depends on the inculcation of proper civic virtues. What these virtues are is a matter of vehement dispute. But to imagine a curriculum untouched by political concerns is to imagine—as no one does—that education can take place in a vacuum.

So where's the beef? Granted, multiculturalism is no panacea for our social ills. We're worried when Johnny can't read. We're worried when Johnny can't add. But shouldn't we be worried, too, when Johnny tramples gravestones in a Jewish cemetery or scrawls racial epithets on a dormitory wall? And it's because we've entrusted our schools with the fashioning of a democratic polity that education has never been exempt from the kind of debate that marks every other aspect of American political life.

Perhaps this isn't altogether a bad thing. As the political theorist Amy Gutmann has argued: "In a democracy, political disagreement is not something that we should generally seek to avoid. Political controversies over our educational problems are a particularly important source of social progress because they have the potential for educating so many citizens."

And while I'm sympathetic to what Robert Nisbet once dubbed the 10 "academic dogma"—the ideal of knowledge for its own sake—I also believe that truly humane learning, unblinkered by the constraints of narrow ethnocentrism, can't help but expand the limits of human understanding and social tolerance. Those who fear that "Balkanization" and social fragmentation lie this way have got it exactly backward. Ours is a world that already is fissured by nationality, ethnicity, race, and gender. And the only way to transcend those divisions — to forge, for once, a civic culture that respects both differences and commonalities — is through education that seeks to comprehend the diversity of human culture. Beyond the hype and the high-flown rhetoric is a pretty homely truth: There is no tolerance without respect — and no respect without knowledge.

The historical architects of the university always understood this. As Cardinal Newman wrote more than a century ago, the university should promote "the power of viewing many things at once as one whole, of referring them severally to their true place in the universal system, of understanding their respective values, and determining their mutual dependence." In just this vein, the critic Edward Said has recently suggested that "our model for academic freedom should therefore be the migrant or traveler: for if, in the real world outside the academy, we must needs be ourselves and only ourselves, inside the academy we should be able to discover and travel among other selves, other identities, other varieties of the human adventure. But, most essentially, in this joint discovery of self and other, it is the role of the academy to transform what might be conflict, or context, or assertion into reconciliation, mutuality, recognition, creative interaction."

But if multiculturalism represents the culmination of an age-old ideal — the dream known in the seventeenth century, as *mathesis universalis*[1] — why has it been the target of such ferocious attacks? On this point, I'm often reminded of a wonderfully wicked piece of nineteenth-century student doggerel about Benjamin Jowett, the great Victorian classicist and master of Balliol College, Oxford:

> Here stand I, my name is Jowett,
> If there's knowledge, then I know it;
> I am the master of this college,
> What I know not, is not knowledge.

Of course, the question of how we determine what is worth knowing is now being raised with uncomfortable persistence. So that in the most spirited attacks on multiculturalism in the academy today, there's a nostalgic whiff of the old sentiment: We are the masters of this college; what we know not is not knowledge.

I think this explains the conservative desire to cast the debate in terms of the West vs. the Rest. And yet that's the very opposition that the pluralist wants to challenge. Pluralism sees cultures as porous, dynamic, and interactive, rather than the fixed property of particular ethnic groups. Thus the idea of a monolithic, homogenous "West" itself comes into question

---

[1]*mathesis universalis* Knowledge of all things. [All notes are the editors'.]

(nothing new here: Literary historians have pointed out that the very concept of "Western culture" may date back only to the eighteenth century). But rather than mourning the loss of some putative ancestral purity, we can recognize what's valuable, resilient, even cohesive, in the hybrid and variegated nature of our modernity.

Genuine multiculturalism is not, of course, everyone's cup of tea. Vul- 15 gar cultural nationalists — like Allan Bloom or Leonard Jeffries[2] — correctly identify it as the enemy. These polemicists thrive on absolute partitions: between "civilization" and "barbarism," between "black" and "white," between a thousand versions of Us and Them. But they are whistling in the wind.

For whatever the outcome of the culture wars in the academy, the world we live in is multicultural already. Mixing and hybridity is the rule, not the exception. As a student of African American culture, of course, I've come to take this kind of cultural palimpsest for granted. Duke Ellington, Miles Davis, John Coltrane have influenced popular musicians the world over. Wynton Marsalis is as comfortable with Mozart as he is with jazz; Anthony Davis writes operas in a musical idiom that combines Bartok with the blues.

In dance, Judith Jamison, Alvin Ailey, Katherine Dunham all excelled at "Western" cultural forms, melding these with African American styles to produce performances that were neither, and both. In painting, Romare Bearden and Jacob Lawrence, Martin Puryear and Augusta Savage learned to paint and sculpt by studying Western masters, yet each has pioneered the construction of a distinctly African American visual art.

And in literature, of course, the most formally complex and compelling black writers — such as Jean Toomer, Sterling Brown, Langston Hughes, Zora Hurston, Richard Wright, Ralph Ellison, James Baldwin, and Gwendolyn Brooks — have always blended forms of Western literature with African American vernacular and written traditions. Then, again, even a vernacular form such as the spiritual took for its texts the King James version of the Old and New Testaments. Toni Morrison's master's thesis was on Virginia Woolf and Faulkner; Rita Dove is as comfortable with German literature as she is with the blues.

Indeed, the greatest African American art can be thought of as an exploration of that hyphenated space between the African and the American. As James Baldwin once reflected during his long European sojourn, "I would have to appropriate these white centuries, I would have to make them mine. I would have to accept my special attitude, my special place in this scheme, otherwise I would have no place in any scheme."

"Pluralism," the American philosopher John Dewey insisted early in 20 this century, "is the greatest philosophical idea of our times." But he recognized that it was also the greatest problem of our times: "How are we going

---

[2]**Allan Bloom . . . Leonard Jeffries** Bloom, a white professor at the University of Chicago, was known for his emphasis on the traditional Eurocentric curriculum; Jeffries, an African American professor at the City College of New York, is known for his belief that African Americans ("sun people") are superior to whites ("ice people").

to make the most of the new values we set on variety, difference, and individuality—how are we going to realize their possibilities in every field, and at the same time not sacrifice that plurality to the cooperation we need so much?" It has the feel of a scholastic conundrum: How can we negotiate between the one and the many?

Today, the mindless celebration of difference has proven as untenable as that bygone model of monochrome homogeneity. If there is an equilibrium to be struck, there's no guarantee we will ever arrive at it. The worst mistake we can make, however, is not to try.

Topics for Critical Thinking and Writing

1. How does Gates define "multiculturalism"? Does he use "cultural pluralism" as a synonym?

2. If before reading Gates's essay you had heard of "multiculturalism," in a few sentences explain what you took the word to mean. If Gates's "multiculturalism" differs from your earlier understanding, how do you account for the difference?

3. Gates says we must face anew the "time-tested" question "What does it mean to be an American" (para. 5). After reading Gates's essay, how would you answer this question? Set forth your answer in an essay of no more than 500 words.

4. In paragraph 7 Gates says that it is impossible "to imagine a curriculum untouched by political concerns" because it is impossible to imagine "that education can take place in a vacuum." Consider your experience in secondary school or in college, and set forth in 500 words evidence supporting or refuting Gates's assertion.

5. In his final paragraph Gates speaks of "the mindless celebration of difference." What does he mean? What examples might he (or you) cite?

Kenneth T. Jackson

Too Many Have Let Enthusiasm Outrun Reason

In June, after almost a year of deliberation, the New York State Social Studies Syllabus Review Committee released its report "One Nation, Many Peoples: A Declaration of Cultural Interdependence." In July, the state

Kenneth Terry Jackson was born in Memphis, Tennessee, in 1939 and educated at Memphis State University and the University of Chicago. Since 1968 he has taught history at Columbia University. Among his books is Crabgrass Frontier: The Suburbanization of the United States *(1985), which has won several prizes. This article first appeared in the* Boston Globe Magazine *(October 13, 1991), along with the selection by Henry Louis Gates, Jr., that appears on page 477.*

Board of Regents adopted the document as a blueprint for educational change in the schools.

The report occasioned a firestorm of controversy, perhaps because the committee recommended, among other things, that Christopher Columbus be viewed from the perspective of the natives already resident in North America, that Thanksgiving be understood as a day of mourning as well as of celebration, and that slaves be referred to as "enslaved persons." Most important, however, was the realization that "One Nation, Many Peoples" is about the purpose of social studies, the nature of community, and the meaning of the United States itself.

Along with Arthur Schlesinger and Paul A. Gagnon, I was one of three dissenters to the report. I agonized over my decision, in part because I have spent most of the past three decades, almost my entire adult life, studying the very topics that the committee suggests should receive more attention — ethnicity, racism, discrimination, inequality, and civil rights — and in part because I do believe that we should celebrate the cultural diversity that has made the United States unique among the world's nations. We should acknowledge the heterogeneity that has made this land rich and creative, and we should give our young people a varied and challenging multicultural education.

But too many of those who wave the flag for multiculturalism have let enthusiasm outrun reason. In particular, I believe four major issues deserve more debate and consideration before we embrace the brave new world of multicultural education.

First, we should not confuse moral judgment with historical judgment. 5 To study a subject is not necessarily to endorse it. As William Shakespeare reminded us in a line in *Henry IV*, there is history in all men's lives. Because we cannot study all men's lives, however, the curriculum should emphasize those people, places, and events that have disproportionately influenced the world in which we live. Thus, Europe should be an academic focus not because it has been morally good or even because it is the ancestral home of most Americans, but because, for the last five hundred years or so, it has been much more influential than any other place, and it has had a particularly heavy impact on the political, legal, and religious institutions of the United States.

This is a historical judgment, not a moral one. Quite simply, Europe has generated most of the political values which we hold dear, democracy and freedom prominent among them. It has also experienced more bloodletting, more intolerance, more terror, and more general nastiness than any other place. To analyze the Spanish Inquisition or the Thirty Years War or the Holocaust is not to wish we could have been there. Similarly, students need to know about Hitler because he may reasonably be held to account for 30 million or 40 million or 50 million deaths, not because anyone seeks to elevate the significance of Europe. Should the people of Africa, Asia, or South America feel historically slighted because they have not yet produced an approximation of Nazi Germany?

My second point is that in state after state across the country, a new social studies curriculum is already in place, and teachers have barely had time to familiarize themselves with the new guidelines. Why not give those revisions some time to percolate through the classrooms? In New York state, the focus of so much recent controversy, the entire social studies curriculum was revised just four years ago with the expressed purpose of making it more multicultural. The major consultants for the effort were Eric Foner, Hazel Hertzberg, and Christopher Lasch, three of the most respected historians in the United States. Their efforts to adjust classroom materials and objectives to the new social realities of our time were largely successful, and the current New York State curriculum in American history already reflects the latest social studies scholarship.

To hear multiculturalists talk, however, one would think that our teachers have changed not at all since the Eisenhower era. In fact, they are better prepared and more sophisticated than their critics allege, and most of them are already teaching a multicultural curriculum. In my quarter century of teaching, for example, I have encountered students who did not know whether Boston was northeast or southwest of New York City, whether the Soviet Union fought Germany in World War II, or whether Tammany Hall was a billiard parlor. But I have never met a person, of any age or circumstance, who thought that Columbus discovered an uninhabited world, or that the natives he encountered ultimately received a fair shake from the white invaders.

Meanwhile, the "Eurocentric" curriculum is itself a myth, largely because European history, so much reviled by multiculturalists, has practically disappeared from the nation's classrooms. Before 1970, the history of Western civilization was a standard part of the American educational experience. Since that time, its decline has been precipitous. A general trend has been to substitute an introductory course in world history for the traditional course in Western civilization. An even greater trend has been to substitute other social studies courses for history.

In 1987, for example, fewer than half of all American high school 10 graduates had taken a year of either European or world history. New York State again illustrates the trend. This year, under a curriculum presumed to be Eurocentric, students in New York spend no more time on Britain and Western Europe than they do on Africa, Asia, Latin America, or the Soviet Union. Equally important, they have little time to consider the history of any of the regions, whatever their location on the globe. Most students get around to Europe only in the last quarter of their sophomore year, and then the focus is on contemporary problems, not history. Only 1 percent of students take a year-long course in European history, and those are the kids in advanced placement classes. Everyone else must make do with an ahistorical concoction known as global studies.

My third reservation about multicultural education is the allegation of its supporters that a major purpose of the effort is to raise self-esteem, to make students feel good about themselves, and to make the curriculum reflect the demography of the classroom. These are questionable propositions that often lead to complications. One particularly dispiriting tendency is a willingness to teach controversial theories as facts. A favored theme of Afrocentrism at the moment is an insistence that ancient Egypt be regarded as a part of Africa, that many or most Egyptians were black or multiracial, and that residents of the Nile River Valley were largely responsible for the later glories of Greece and Rome in particular and of the West in general.

The specifics of the argument need not concern us here. The argument may indeed be correct. But this interpretation remains very much in dispute. Some distinguished scholars accept such claims; others ridicule them. Would it not be better to let the historians fight it out before we introduce such material in the classroom? Other, more generally accepted, examples could advance the argument that no one race, no one continent, and no one religion has a corner on human achievement. All students, for example, should know that Africa was once the home of many advanced civilizations, that Timbuktu, in what is now Mali, was a thriving center of learning and trade when Paris was a dump, and that Europe was a backwater for a thousand years while China was in its glory.

Another problem with the "feel-good" approach is that it can reduce history to a list of "firsts" by each ethnic or racial group. This type of teaching strategy is the main reason that students habitually list the social studies as the most boring and irrelevant of all their courses. Alternatively, the feel-good approach might simply replace one myth (e.g., slavery was a benign institution that actually benefited many of its victims) with another (slavery was a uniquely Western institution).

My final reservation is with the notion of cultural interdependence, the idea that all cultures are equal, and the proposition that no one tradition should have special status in the United States. I disagree. Every viable nation has to have a common culture to survive in peace. Precisely because we lack a common religion, a common race, and a common ethnicity, we need a common denominator of another sort. We can find it in our history, in our values, in our aspirations — in short, in our common culture. That common culture should be and has been ever changing. It began, in most Colonies, with the English language and with British legal and political institutions, but it has since metamorphosed over the centuries, and it is now an amalgam of every group that came here. Our food, our music, our holidays, our literature, our traditions, even our language, reflect this distinctive "American" culture.

This issue has special relevance in 1991, when ethnic, racial, religious, 15 and nationality fault lines are creating earthquakes around the world. Canada, Yugoslavia, the Soviet Union, India, and a dozen other places are examples of a powerful sentiment, which I regard as pernicious, that suggests that a country is a country only if it is ethnically pure. Citizenship thus becomes less a function of residence than of blood. Thus, the Baltic countries may deny the vote to Russians who have lived there for decades because they lack the proper pedigree. As more and more people begin to regard loyalty to group as more important than loyalty to country, we get a chilling preview of what the United States might be like if each of us maintains our own culture, if we reject mainstreaming and assimilation, and if in fact there is no mainstream.

Fortunately, the United States does not have the massive cultural divides that are bringing other nations to separation and even to civil war. But we are not immune to the problem. Too often today there is an ugliness associated with feelings of pride, the development of an "us vs. them" mentality. Across the United States, the concept of community, the idea of the melting pot, the feeling that we are all Americans — all seem quaintly out of date. The consensus-building institutions that once held us together, especially the big-city public systems, are in decline. Increasingly, Americans are retreating into private realms.

Nothing is wrong with being proud of one's family heritage, of wanting to remember and treasure the traditions handed down from parents. The United States has prospered and grown rich from its vibrant, vital, multiethnic and multiracial culture. But the maintenance of distinctive cultures should be the function of synagogues, churches, music festivals, ethnic celebrations, and, most especially, dinner tables. The public schools should emphasize common traditions and common values.

Topics for Critical Thinking and Writing

1. Jackson says (para. 3) that "we should celebrate the cultural diversity that has made the United States unique among the world's nations." Does he make clear, to your satisfaction, how he proposes to practice what he preaches? Do you think there are aspects of "cultural diversity" about which he is silent? Support your answer.

2. Jackson declares we must address "four major issues" before embracing "the brave new world of multicultural education" (para. 4). What are these four issues? Where does Jackson stand on each?

3. In paragraph 5 Jackson explains why, in his opinion, "Europe should be an academic focus." What response might someone who differs from Jackson make?

4. Jackson contrasts "historical" and "moral" judgments (paras. 5 and 6). Write a paragraph explaining the difference and giving an example of each kind of judgment.

5. In paragraph 9 Jackson says that "the 'Eurocentric' curriculum is itself a myth." Drawing on your experience in secondary school or college, indicate whether you think Jackson's assertion is true. Explain.

6. In paragraphs 11–13 Jackson attacks the idea that education should raise the self-esteem of students ("the 'feel-good' approach"). Do you share his reservations about this aspect of education? Explain.

7. In paragraph 15 Jackson looks at other countries, and he suggests that they offer

"a chilling preview of what the United States might be like if each of us maintains our own culture." Are you chilled? Why, or why not?

8. In his final sentence Jackson speaks of "common traditions and common values." What (if any) examples might he have given?

9. After rereading this essay by Jackson, (re)read carefully the essay by Gates (p. 477). On what (if anything) do these two writers seem to disagree? Agree?

Ronald Takaki

An Educated and Culturally Literate Person Must Study America's Multicultural Reality

In Palolo Valley, Hawaii, where I lived as a child, my neighbors were Japanese, Chinese, Portuguese, Filipino, and Hawaiian. I heard voices with different accents and I heard different languages. I played with children of different colors. Why, I wondered, were families representing such an array of nationalities living together in one little valley? My teachers and textbooks did not explain our diversity.

After graduation from high school, I attended a college on the mainland where students and even professors would ask me how long I had been in America and where I had learned to speak English. "In this country," I would reply. "I was born in America, and my family has been here for three generations."

Today, some twenty years later, Asian and also Afro-American, Chicano/Latino, and Native American students continue to find themselves perceived as strangers on college campuses. Moreover, they are encountering a new campus racism. The targets of ugly racial slurs and violence, they have begun to ask critical questions about why knowledge of their histories and communities is excluded from the curriculum. White students are also realizing the need to understand the cultural diversity of American society.

In response, colleges and universities across the country, from Brown to Berkeley, are currently considering requiring students to take courses designed to help them understand diverse cultures.

The debate is taking place within a general context framed by academic pundits like Allan Bloom and E. D. Hirsch. Both of them are asking: What is an educated, a culturally literate person?   5

I think Bloom is right when he says: "There are some things one must know about if one is to be educated. . . . The university should try to have a

---

For a biographical note on Ronald Takaki, professor of ethnic studies at the University of California at Berkeley, see page 60. This essay originally appeared on March 8, 1989, in the Chronicle of Higher Education, *a publication read chiefly by college and university teachers and administrators.*

vision of what an educated person is." I also agree with Hirsch when he insists that there is a body of cultural information that "every American needs to know."

But the question is: What should be the content of education and what does cultural literacy mean? The traditional curriculum reflects what Howard Swearer, former president of Brown University, has described as a "certain provincialism," an overly Eurocentric perspective. Concerned about this problem, a Brown University visiting committee recommended that the faculty consider requiring students to take an ethnic-studies course before they graduate. "The contemporary definition of an educated person," the committee said, "must include at least minimal awareness of multicultural reality."

This view now is widely shared. Says Donna Shalala, chancellor of the University of Wisconsin at Madison: "Every student needs to know much more about the origins and history of the particular cultures which, as Americans, we will encounter during our lives."

This need is especially felt in California, where racial minorities will constitute a majority of the population by 2000, and where a faculty committee at the University of California at Berkeley has proposed an "American-cultures requirement" to give students a deeper understanding of our nation's racial and cultural diversity. Faculty opposition is based mainly on a disdain for all requirements on principle, an unwillingness to add another requirement, an insistence on the centrality of Western civilization, and a fear that the history of European immigrant groups would be left out of the proposed course.

In fact, however, there are requirements everywhere in the curricu- 10 lum (for reading and composition, the major, a foreign language, breadth of knowledge, etc.). The American-cultures requirement would not be an additional course, for students would be permitted to use the course to satisfy one of their social-sciences or humanities requirements. Western civilization will continue to dominate the curriculum, and the proposed requirement would place the experiences of racial minorities within the broad context of American society. Faculty support for some kind of mandatory course is considerable, and a vote on the issue is scheduled this spring.

But the question often asked is: What would be the focus and content of such multicultural courses? Actually there is a wide range of possibilities. For many years I have been teaching a course on "Racial Inequality in America: a Comparative Historical Perspective." Who we are in this society and how we are perceived and treated have been conditioned by America's racial and ethnic diversity. My approach is captured in the phrase "from different shores." By "shores," I intend a double meaning. One is the shores that immigrants left to go to America—those in Europe, Africa, Latin America, and Asia. The second is the different and often conflicting shores or perspectives from which scholars have viewed the experiences of racial and ethnic groups.

In my course, students read Thomas Sowell's *Ethnic America: A History* along with my *Iron Cages: Race and Culture in 19th-Century America.* Readings also include Winthrop Jordan on the colonial origins of racism, John Higham on nativism, Mario Barrera on Chicanos, and William J. Wilson on the black underclass. By critically examining the different "shores," students are able to address complex comparative questions: How have the experiences of racial minorities such as blacks and Asians been similar to, and different from, one another? Is "race" the same as "ethnicity?" How have race relations been shaped by economic developments, as well as by culture? What impact have these forces had on moral values about how people should think and behave, beliefs about human nature and society, and images of the past as well as the future?

Other courses could examine racial diversity in relation to gender, immigration, urbanization, technology, or the labor market. Courses could also study specific topics such as Hollywood's racial images, ethnic music and art, novels by writers of color, the civil rights movement, or the Pacific Rim. Regardless of theme or topic, all of the courses should address the major theoretical issues concerning race and should focus on Afro-Americans, Asians, Chicanos/Latinos, and Native Americans.

Who would teach these courses? Responsibility could be located solely in ethnic-studies programs. But this would reduce them to service-course programs and also render even more remote the possibility of diversifying the traditional curriculum. The sheer logistics of meeting the demand generated by an institution-wide requirement would be overwhelming for any single department.

Clearly, faculty members in the social sciences and humanities will 15
have to be involved. There also are dangers in this approach, however. The diffusion of ethnic studies throughout the traditional disciplines could undermine the coherence and identity of ethnic studies as a field of teaching and scholarship. It could also lead to area-studies courses on Africa or Asia disguised as ethnic studies, to revised but essentially intact Western-civilization courses with a few "non-Western" readings tacked on, or to amorphous and bland "American studies" courses taught by instructors with little or no training in multicultural studies. Such courses, though well-intentioned, could result in the unwitting perpetuation of certain racial stereotypes and even to the transformation of texts by writers and scholars of color into "mistexts." This would only reproduce multicultural illiteracy.

But broad faculty participation in such a requirement can work if there is a sharply written statement or purpose, as well as clear criteria for courses on the racial and cultural diversity of American society. We also need interdisciplinary institutes to offer intellectual settings where faculty members from different fields can collaborate on new courses and where ethnic-studies scholars can share their expertise. More importantly, we need to develop and strengthen ethnic-studies programs and departments as academic foundations for this new multicultural curriculum. Such bases should bring together a critical mass of faculty members committed to, and trained in ethnic studies, and should help to preserve the alternative perspectives provided by this scholarly field.

In addition, research must generate knowledge for the new courses, and new faculty members must be trained for ethnic-studies teaching and scholarship. Berkeley already has a doctoral program in ethnic studies, but other graduate schools must also help prepare the next generation of faculty members. Universities will experience a tremendous turnover in teachers due to retirements, and this is a particularly urgent time to educate future scholars, especially from minority groups, for a multicultural curriculum.

The need to open the American mind to greater cultural diversity will not go away. We can resist it by ignoring the changing ethnic composition of our student bodies and the larger society, or we can realize how it offers colleges and universities a timely and exciting opportunity to revitalize the social sciences and humanities, giving both a new sense of purpose and a more inclusive definition of knowledge.

If concerted efforts are made, someday students of different racial backgrounds will be able to learn about one another in an informed and systematic way and will not graduate from our institutions or higher learning ignorant about how places like Palolo Valley fit into American society.

Topics for Critical Thinking and Writing

1. Takaki implies that higher education ought to address "cultural literacy" (para. 7). Can you tell from the context how Takaki would define this term? Write out your own definition in a sentence.

2. Takaki reports that, in the University of California at Berkeley, a new required course in "American cultures" was opposed by many faculty for four reasons (para. 9). Evaluate these reasons.

3. In paragraph 12 Takaki mentions six books that he uses in his course "Racial Inequality in America." In your library find one of these books, read it, and write a 500-word book review.

4. Speaking of an "American-cultures requirement," Takaki says (para. 13) that "all of the courses . . . should focus on Afro-Americans, Asians, Chicanos/Latinos, and Native Americans." What do you suppose he might say to someone who argued that it was equally important for an "American-cultures" course to focus on Protestantism, Catholicism, and Judaism?

5. In paragraph 16 Takaki says that a school with a multicultural requirement should set forth "a sharply written statement of purpose." In a paragraph or two write the best such statement that you can think of—even if you do not believe that there should be such a requirement.

6. Does Takaki favor having courses in non-Western culture taught only (or at least mainly) by faculty of non-European extraction? Why, or why not?

7. If your college or university has some sort of multicultural requirement, examine it in the light of Takaki's argument and then consider to what extent he would approve or disapprove of it.

Linda Chavez

Demystifying Multiculturalism

Multiculturalism is on the advance, everywhere from President Clinton's Cabinet to corporate boardrooms to public-school classrooms. If you believe the multiculturalists' propaganda, whites are on the verge of becoming a minority in the United States. The multiculturalists predict that this demographic shift will fundamentally change American culture — indeed destroy the very idea that America *has* a single, unified culture. They aren't taking any chances, however. They have enlisted the help of government, corporate leaders, the media, and the education establishment in waging a cultural revolution. But has America truly become a multicultural nation? And if not, will those who capitulate to these demands create a self-fulfilling prophecy?

At the heart of the argument is the assumption that the white population is rapidly declining in relation to the nonwhite population. A 1987 Hudson Institute report helped catapult this claim to national prominence. The study, *Workforce 2000,* estimated that by the turn of the century only 15 percent of new workers would be white males. The figure was widely interpreted to mean that whites were about to become a minority in the workplace — and in the country.

In fact, white males will still constitute about 45 percent — a plurality — of the workforce in the year 2000. The proportion of white men in the workforce *is* declining — it was nearly 51 percent in 1980 — but primarily because the proportion of white women is growing. They will make up 39 percent of the workforce within ten years, according to government projections, up from 36 percent in 1980. Together, white men and women will account for 84 percent of all workers by 2000 — hardly a minority share.

But the business world is behaving as if a demographic tidal wave is about to hit. A whole new industry of "diversity professionals" has emerged to help managers cope with the expected deluge of nonwhite workers. These consultants are paid as much as $10,000 a day to train managers to "value diversity," a term so ubiquitous that it has appeared in more than seven hundred articles in major newspapers in the last three years. According to Heather MacDonald in *The New Republic,* about half of

Linda Chavez, director of the Center for the New American Community, is John M. Olin Fellow at the Manhattan Institute and the author of Out of the Barrio *(1991). This essay first appeared in* National Review *(February 21, 1994).*

Fortune 500 corporations now employ someone responsible for "diversity."

What precisely does valuing diversity mean? The underlying assump- 5
tions seem to be that nonwhites are so different from whites that employers must make major changes to accommodate them, and that white workers will be naturally resistant to including nonwhites in their ranks.
Public-opinion polls don't bear out the latter. They show that support
among whites for equal job opportunity for blacks is extraordinarily high,
exceeding 90 percent as early as 1975. As for accommodating different cultures, the problem is not culture — or race, or ethnicity — but education.
Many young people, in particular, are poorly prepared for work, and the
problem is most severe among those who attended inner-city schools, most
of them blacks and Hispanics.

Nevertheless, multiculturalists insist on treating race and ethnicity as
if they were synonymous with culture. They presume that skin color and
national origin, which are immutable traits, determine values, mores, language, and other cultural attributes, which, of course, are learned. In the
multiculturalists' world view, African Americans, Puerto Ricans, or Chinese Americans living in New York City have more in common with persons of their ancestral group living in Lagos or San Juan or Hong Kong
than they do with other New Yorkers who are white. Culture becomes a
fixed entity, transmitted, as it were, in the genes, rather than through experience. Thus, "Afrocentricity," a variant of multiculturalism, is "a way of
being," its exponents claim. According to a leader of the Afrocentric education movement, Molefi Kete Asante, there is "one African Cultural System
manifested in diversities," whether one speaks of Afro-Brazilians, Cubans,
or Nigerians (or, presumably, African Americans). Exactly how this differs
from the traditional racist notion that all blacks (Jews, Mexicans, Chinese,
etc.) think alike is unclear. What is clear is that the multiculturalists have
abandoned the ideal that all persons should be judged by the content of
their character, not the color of their skin. Indeed, the multiculturalists
seem to believe that a person's character is *determined* by the color of his
skin and by his ancestry.

Such convictions lead multiculturalists to conclude that, again in the
words of Asante, "[T]here is no common American culture." The logic is
simple, but wrongheaded: Since Americans (or more often, their forebears) hail from many different places, each of which has its own specific
culture, the argument goes, America must be multicultural. And it is becoming more so every day as new immigrants bring their cultures with
them.

Indeed, multiculturalists hope to ride the immigrant wave to greater
power and influence. They have certainly done so in education. Some 2.3
million children who cannot speak English well now attend public school,
an increase of 1 million in the last seven years. Multicultural advocates cite
the presence of such children to demand bilingual education and other
multicultural services. The Los Angeles Unified School District alone currently offers instruction in Spanish, Armenian, Korean, Cantonese, Taga-

log, Russian, and Japanese. Federal and state governments now spend literally billions of dollars on these programs.

Ironically, the multiculturalists' emphasis on education undercuts their argument that culture is inextricable from race or national origin. They are acutely aware just how fragile cultural identification is; why else are they so adamant about reinforcing it? Multiculturalists insist on teaching immigrant children in their native language, instructing them in the history and customs of their native land and imbuing them with reverence for their ancestral heroes, lest these youngsters be seduced by American culture. Far from losing faith in the power of assimilation, they seem to believe that without a heavy dose of multicultural indoctrination, immigrants won't be able to resist it. And they're right, though it remains to be seen whether anything, including the multiculturalists' crude methods, will ultimately detour immigrants from the assimilation path.

The urge to assimilate has traditionally been overpowering in the   10 United States, especially among the children of immigrants. Only groups that maintain strict rules against intermarriage with persons outside the group, such as Orthodox Jews and the Amish, have ever succeeded in preserving distinct, full-blown cultures within American society. (It is interesting to note that religion seems to be a more effective deterrent to full assimilation than the secular elements of culture, including language.) Although many Americans worry that Hispanic immigrants, for example, are not learning English and will therefore fail to assimilate into the American mainstream, little evidence supports the case. By the third generation in the United States, a majority of Hispanics, like other ethnic groups, speak only English and are closer to other Americans on most measures of social and economic status than they are to Hispanic immigrants. On one of the most rigorous gauges of assimilation — intermarriage — Hispanics rank high. About one-third of young third-generation Hispanics marry non-Hispanic whites, a pattern similar to that of young Asians. Even for blacks, exogamy rates, which have been quite low historically, are going up; about 3 percent of blacks now marry outside their group.

The impetus for multiculturalism is not coming from immigrants, but from their more affluent and assimilated native-born counterparts. The proponents are most often the elite — the best educated and most successful members of their respective racial and ethnic groups. College campuses, where the most radical displays of multiculturalism take place, are fertile recruiting grounds. Last May, for example, a group of Mexican American students at UCLA, frustrated that the university would not elevate the school's 23-year-old Chicano studies program to full department status, stormed the faculty center, breaking windows and furniture and causing half a million dollars in damage. The same month, a group of Asian American students at UC Irvine went on a hunger strike to pressure administrators into hiring more professors of Asian American studies. These were not immigrants, or even, by and large, disadvantaged students, but middle-class beneficiaries of their parents' or grandparents' successful assimilation to the American mainstream.

The protestors' quest had almost nothing to do with any effort to maintain their ethnic identity. For the most part, such students probably never thought of themselves as anything but American before they entered college. A recent study of minority students at the University of California at Berkeley found that most Hispanic and Asian students "discovered" their ethnic identity after they arrived on campus—when they also discovered that they were victims of systematic discrimination. As one Mexican American freshman summed it up, she was "unaware of the things that have been going on with our people, all the injustice we've suffered, how the world really is. I thought racism didn't exist and here, you know, it just comes to light." The researchers added that "students of color" had difficulty pinpointing exactly what constituted this "subtle form of the new racism. . . . There was much talk about certain facial expressions, or the way people look, and how white students 'take over the class' and speak past you."

Whatever their new-found victim status, these students look amazingly like other Americans on most indices. For example, the median family income of Mexican American students at Berkeley in 1989 was $32,500, slightly above the national median for all Americans that year, $32,191; and 17 percent of those students came from families that earned more than $75,000 a year, even though they were admitted to the university under affirmative-action programs (presumably because they suffered some educational disadvantage attributed to their ethnicity).

Affirmative-action programs make less and less sense as discrimination diminishes in this society—which it indisputably has—and as minorities improve their economic status. Racial and ethnic identity, too, might wane if there weren't such aggressive efforts to ensure that this not happen. The multiculturalists know they risk losing their constituency if young blacks, Hispanics, Asians, and others don't maintain strong racial and ethnic affiliations. Younger generations must be *trained* to think of themselves as members of oppressed minority groups entitled to special treatment. And the government provides both the incentives and the money to ensure that this happens. Meanwhile, the main beneficiaries are the multicultural professionals, who often earn exorbitant incomes peddling identity.

One particularly egregious example occurred in the District of Columbia last fall. The school system paid $250,000 to a husband-and-wife consultant team to produce an Afrocentric study guide to be used in a single public elementary school. Controversy erupted after the two spent three years and produced only a five-page outline. Although the husband had previously taught at Howard University, the wife's chief credential was a master's degree from an unaccredited "university" which she and her husband had founded. When the *Washington Post* criticized the school superintendent for his handling of the affair, he called a press conference to defend the couple, who promptly claimed they were the victims of a racist vendetta.

D.C. students rank lowest in the nation in math and fourth-lowest in verbal achievement; one can only wonder what $250,000 in tutoring at one school might have done. Instead, the students were treated to bulletin boards in the classrooms proclaiming on their behalf: "We are the sons and daughters of The Most High. We are the princes and princesses of African kings and queens. We are the descendants of our black ancestors. We are black and we are proud." This incident is not unique. Thousands of consultants with little or no real expertise sell feel-good programs to school systems across the nation.

Multiculturalism is not a grassroots movement. It was created, nurtured, and expanded through government policy. Without the expenditure of vast sums of public money, it would wither away and die. That is not to say that ethnic communities would disappear from the American scene or that groups would not retain some attachment to their ancestral roots. American assimilation has always entailed some give and take, and American culture has been enriched by what individual groups brought to it. The distinguishing characteristic of American culture is its ability to incorporate so many disparate groups, creating a new whole from the many parts. What could be more American, for example, than jazz and film, two distinctive art forms created, respectively, by blacks and immigrant Jews but which all Americans think of as their own? But in the past, government — especially public schools — saw it as a duty to try to bring newcomers into the fold by teaching them English, by introducing them to the great American heroes as their own, by instilling respect for American institutions. Lately, we have nearly reversed course, treating each group, new and old, as if what is most important is to preserve its separate identity and space.

It is easy to blame the ideologues and radicals who are pushing the disuniting of America, to use Arthur Schlesinger's phrase, but the real culprits are those who provide multiculturalists the money and the access to press their cause. Without the acquiescence of policy-makers and ordinary citizens, multiculturalism would be no threat. Unfortunately, most major institutions have little stomach for resisting the multicultural impulse — and many seem eager to comply with whatever demands the multiculturalists make. Americans should have learned by now that policy matters. We have only to look at the failure of our welfare and crime policies to know that providing perverse incentives can change the way individuals behave — for the worse. Who is to say that if we pour enough money into dividing Americans we won't succeed?

Topics for Critical Thinking and Writing

1. In her first paragraph Chavez asks whether America has "truly become a multicultural nation." How would you define "multiculturalism," and what would you take as strong evidence that the nation is, or is about to become, or will not become, multicultural?

2. Chavez implies (para. 6) that it is a grave error to treat "race and ethnicity as if they were synonymous with culture." Can you define all three terms so that they are distinct? (Consulting an encyclopedia or unabridged dictionary might be of help.) Is there some overlap in the criteria for each?

3. Chavez introduces the idea of "assimilation" as the opposite of multiculturalism (see paras. 9–11 and 17) and implies that it was the traditional goal of all but a tiny minority of immigrant groups to this country. Does she indicate why this traditional goal is no longer so popular with recent immigrant groups? Does she (and can you) consider a third alternative to either assimilation and multiculturalism?

4. Chavez writes as if she believes there is a conspiracy afoot across the nation, fueled by "government policy" (para. 17), to impose multiculturalism on us whether we want it or not. She thinks that colleges and universities are among the worse offenders (see para. 11). Do some research on your own campus and write a 500-word essay on the subject "The Nature and Extent of Multiculturalism on Our Campus."

Nathan Glazer

In Defense of Multiculturalism

I served as a member of the committee appointed by New York's commissioner of education, Thomas Sobol, to review the social studies syllabi in the state's elementary and high schools. Our committee, composed of academics and teachers, was not particularly biased toward strong advocates of multiculturalism. It included critics of the multicultural trend — Arthur Schlesinger, Kenneth Jackson, Paul Gagnon, and myself. Nevertheless, the report that emerged, "One Nation, Many Peoples: A Declaration of Cultural Interdependence," called for further acknowledgment of American diversity, and was severely attacked by some members of the committee, and in many editorials (see "Mr. Sobol's Planet," *The New Republic,* July 15 and 22), for further dissolving the common bonds that make us a nation. I also appended critical remarks to the report, yet had reservations in joining in a frontal attack. The report needs its sharp critics (it was undoubtedly the criticism that subsequently led Mr. Sobol to make recommendations to the Regents of New York State that most critics of multiculturalism would agree with). But we also need to see why the demand for something called multiculturalism is now so widespread, and why American education will have to respond to it.

Nathan Glazer, born in 1923 in New York City, is a professor of education and sociology at Harvard University. He is the author of several books, including Ethnic Dilemmas (1983), *and the editor or coeditor of several books, including* Clamor at the Gates: The New American Immigration (1985). *This essay originally appeared on September 2, 1991 in* The New Republic.

Multiculturalism can mean many things, and no one argues with a curriculum that gives proper weight to the role of American Indians, blacks, Asians, and European immigrant and ethnic groups in American history. But as currently used, the word "multiculturalism" is something of a misnomer. It suggests a general desire or need for students to have something in the curriculum that relates to their own ethnic traits, if these exist, or to those of their parents or ancestors. I don't think this desire is particularly widespread among many ethnic groups. "We are all immigrants" is nice rhetoric, but in fact we are not all immigrants. Some of us came in the last decade, some of our parents came long before that, many millions of us have only the haziest idea of how many ancestors came from where. Since 1980 the Census has included a new question, "What is your ancestry?" The great majority of respondents report two, three, or more ancestries. Tens of millions simply insist on being "American," and nothing else.

Nor does multiculturalism reflect the increased immigration of recent decades, particularly to some of our largest cities, such as New York, Los Angeles, San Francisco, and Miami. It is not the new immigrants who are arguing for multiculturalism. Most of them would be content with the education provided to the previous waves of European immigrants, which paid not a whit of attention to their ethnic or racial background, or to their distinct culture or language. A product of that kind of education, I was also quite content with it.

But if it is not the new immigration that is driving the multicultural demands, what is? Multiculturalism in its present form derives basically from black educators. It is one of the longest settled elements in the American population that makes the sharpest case for multiculturalism. Asians, who make up half of current immigrants, are not much concerned. Nor are Spanish-speaking immigrants from Central and South America. Puerto Ricans and Mexican Americans do tend to support bilingual education and the maintenance of the Spanish language. But they are definitely junior partners in the fight for multiculturalism.

I'm convinced that were it not for the pattern of poor achievement   5 among blacks in the schools, the multicultural movement would lose much of its force. Even taking into account recent progress among blacks, shown in NAEP (National Assessment of Educational Progress) scores, SAT scores, and high school graduation rates, blacks still regularly score below whites, often below Hispanics and Native Americans, and far below Asians. Multiculturalism, and one of its variants, Afrocentrism, is presented to us by black educators and leaders as one of the means whereby this deficiency may be overcome.

It is not a new proposal, though it has achieved greater force and notoriety in the past few years. Many of us are simply not aware how far advanced our schools already are on the road to a black-oriented version of multiculturalism. The SATs, according to David Reich in the *New York Times,* are now thoroughly multicultural, the questions requiring knowledge of Zora Neale Hurston, Ralph Ellison, Richard Wright, Gwendolyn Brooks, Lorraine Hansberry, and Jackie Robinson (he comes up twice). The fiction reading is from Maya Angelou. Diane Ravitch and Chester Finn, in *What Do Our 17-Year-Olds Know?*, report that in a national sample of 17-year-olds more could identify Harriet Tubman than Winston Churchill or Joseph Stalin, more knew Tubman than knew that George Washington commanded the American Army during the Revolution, or that Lincoln wrote the Emancipation Proclamation.

The mass of materials that flowed in on us as we worked on our report showed how established multiculturalism was in New York State. One of the documents listed teachers' guides available from the State Education Department, in addition to the social studies syllabi. Of the seven publications available, four dealt with minorities and women. One of them, the most substantial, was a three-volume publication on the teaching of the Holocaust. A survey of in-service workshops completed by New York State teachers in 1990–91 showed that far more had taken workshops on African history, black studies, ethnic studies, multicultural education, and cultural diversity than on American and European history.

One of the reasons all this is so agitating to so many is historical. After all, when Jewish and Italian American students dominated the public schools of New York City, George Washington and Abraham Lincoln were still on the walls, not Herzl and Garibaldi, and students were told that the Anglo-American forefathers of the American commonwealth were their forefathers. The students and their parents did not object, and most embraced the new identity. This background dominates much of the argument over multiculturalism. "We didn't get it, why should they? We didn't need it, why do they? We didn't want it, why do they?" But things change. They—and by that I mean primarily American blacks—may need it. I say "may" because we don't know. Nor are we clear on how many want it, but there are certainly a good number.

Multiculturalism today is in the same class as the proposals for schools for black boys, another desperate try to help black high school achievement. Or vouchers to permit black students to attend private black schools. In view of the extensive failure among low-income blacks, it is not easy to stand four-square against these proposals, particularly when advanced by black advocates aiming to overcome black school failure.

I do not see how school systems with a majority of black and Latino 10 students, with black or Latino leadership at the top, as is true of almost all our big-city school systems, can stand firmly against the multicultural thrust. The new president of the New York City Board of Education, H. Carl McCall, is reported by the *New York Times* as saying he could support a school "focusing primarily, but not exclusively, on black male students" and that "an Afrocentric curriculum . . . can be positive." One could add other testimonials, from members of other big-city school boards, and from school superintendents. In the big cities, in many schools, an unbalanced, indeed distorted view of American and world history and culture is prevailing. We should fight its excesses. Yet when set against the reality of majorities of black and Latino students in these schools, the political dominance of black and Latino administrators, the weak preparation of teachers and administrators in history, and the responsiveness of textbook publishers to organized pressure, the weight of the truth of history, as determined by the best scholars, is reduced to only one interest.

This may appear shocking, but it is not an entirely new phenomenon. In the elementary and high schools, a properly nuanced historical truth based on the best available evidence has always been only one interest among many. History in the schools has always played a socializing, nationalizing function (sometimes a regional pride function, as in the Southern versions of some texts). That function was the inculcation of patriotism in immigrants, and their assimilation to a culture deriving from England, and the experience of English-speaking colonists.

Some recent trends, even without the pressure of multiculturalists, are already changing that pattern. The most important is the general challenge to an unquestioning, simple, and direct American patriotism. After the past twenty years, with the relative decline of American power and the doubts about an unblemished American virtue, we will not have the triumphalist history that prevailed until a few decades ago. Our little war in Iraq will not turn around this tendency to be skeptical about the American past and present. (The worst of all histories, except for all the others, we might say.)

What does one do in the face of these trends? One thing is to fight the errors, distortions, untruths, imbalances. Some of the comments attached to the report did that, and the report fortunately did not add further weight to the more extreme claims. But the sharper critics of the report, I believe, have failed to recognize that demographic and political pressures change the history that is to be taught. They direct us to look for things we could not have noticed before. Assertions that are at first glance fantastic may have to be given some modest acquiescence. Yes, it seems that there were some Egyptian pharaohs who were racially black. (What one makes of it is another matter.) Yes, it seems that some ancient Greeks believed that they got their gods, myths, mystical knowledge from ancient Egypt. Martin Bernal's *Black Athena* will eventually leave some deposit in textbook accounts. (It will be ironic if one consequence of Afrocentrism is that our students, who know nothing of ancient Greece and less of ancient Egypt, will now be forced to learn something in order to accommodate the argument of African influences!) Yes, there is another side to the story of the expansion of Europe and imperialism. Yes, it is possible that, as the economic historian Barbara Solow argues, the weight of slave-produced plantation products was much greater in shaping the economy of the American colonies than is generally understood. Yes, there is a Mexican perspective on the Mexican-American War, and when one deals with classes that are dominantly Latin American it would be best to know it. And so on.

Black and Hispanic advocates will call for these new perspectives; historians, attracted by new ideas, politicized by new trends, looking for new topics, will explore them, and their researches will over time change weight and nuance in the treatment of various issues in the textbooks. It's happened before; it will happen again.

Yet another development bears on the multicultural problem. This is   15 the push for more choice in the public school system. That effort, supported by conservatives today, was first introduced as a policy alternative in American education in the late 1960s by liberals and radicals. Choice bears upon this debate because it implies diversity of curricula, because there should be something to choose among. It implies that quite a range of emphases may be offered, from Afrocentrism to Eurocentrism—perhaps, some have noted in alarm, the spectrum will run all the way from black Muslims to white racists.

In Milwaukee today hundreds of low-income black students attend, with state grants, inner-city black private schools, some of which emphasize Afrocentrism or black nationalism in their curricula. This program, under strong attack by the local teachers' union and others, has been adopted less because Milwaukee black leaders want to promote Afrocentrism than because they are fed up with the poor education their children receive in the public schools and hope that private schools, whatever their orientation, will do better—a view bolstered by the researches of James Coleman, John Chubb, and Terry Moe.

The movement for choice means the acceptance of more diversity in school curricula. At the margin, this diversity can be limited, if public funds are to be provided to assist choice. But there seems to me a kind of contradiction in simultaneously insisting on a strong, common, assimilationist curriculum in the public schools and accepting a wide range of diversity in the nonpublic school system. The line between the two systems and the two functions will not be easily maintained.

Inevitably, the current debate is focused on high-profile reports, large statements. But much of it ignores the reality of what goes on in American schooling. While multiculturalism and Afrocentrism race ahead in some schools and systems, others may happily continue to be the schools many of us remember and approve of, with only some modest modifications to prepare students for tests with a surprisingly high content of questions dealing with blacks and women, and particularly black women. The New York State report is only one step in a process that is far from concluded. The syllabi we reviewed are not required or imposed. The specific curricula of the classrooms are developed by hundreds of school districts, thousands of schools, many thousands of administrators and teachers. The syllabi are themselves broad outlines with examples. Many schools in the state already do more in the way of "multiculturalism" than the syllabi call for, many do less, and this ragged pattern will continue.

Whatever the strength of the multicultural thrust, I believe that American history in its main lineaments will have to be what it has been, and will not become completely alien to those of us educated in another time. We will find the story of the settlement by the English, but students will also be told that the Spaniards got to New Mexico and Florida first. The description of colonial America will place more emphasis on blacks, slave and free. The War for Independence will still play a large role, but we will now certainly find the blacks who fought in the war, along with Pulaski, von Steuben, Lafayette, and Haym Solomon. The Constitution will maintain its centrality, but we will now emphasize the argument over slavery, the references to the Indians. The expansion westward will emphasize how nasty we were to the Indians and the Mexicans. The struggle over slavery leading to the Civil War will emphasize even more strongly the criminal failure of Reconstruction and the importance of the postwar amendments and their role. The story of industrialization and the rise of the city will include more about the immigrants and the black migration north. And so on.

The skeletal structure will remain, because we still live under the 20
polity established by the Constitution, and it is in that polity, under that Constitution, that radical and ethnic and minority groups and women seek to expand their rights. It will be quite a job to keep nonsense and exaggeration and mindless ethnic and racial celebration out of the schools, but the basic structure of instruction in history will survive.

In my own comments, attached to the report, I took issue with the attempt to turn the United States into a congeries of ethnic and racial groups, and nothing more. Assimilation is a reality; scores of millions of unhyphenated Americans, who owe no allegiance to any identity other than American, are evidence of that. And assimilation continues to work its way, through the processes of work and of entertainment, with less help from the schools than before.

In this respect, present-day immigrants will not be very different from previous immigrants. They will assimilate. But one group, because of its experience of cruel, centuries-long ill treatment, is not yet fully incorporated in this generally successful process of nation-building. Present-day multiculturalism is a product of that apartness. Most of those who embrace it, I believe, do so in the hope that it will overcome that apartness. They want, in some key respects, to become more like other Americans — for example, in educational achievement — not different from them, and believe that the way to becoming more like them is to take more account of difference, and yes, of ill-treatment, of past and current achievement, even if exaggerated.

That is where we stand, and while some parts of this phenomenon are alarming enough, the proper parallel is not with Serbia and Croatia, or even Quebec. It is with our own American past, and the varying ways over time in which people of different race, religion, and ethnic background have become one nation.

Topics for Critical Thinking and Writing

1. Glazer implicitly asks two questions: (a) Who really wants "multiculturalism" in the schools?, and (b) Why do they want it? What are his answers? From your experience in school and college, do you agree with him, or not — or does your experience so far provide no evidence one way or the other? Explain.

2. In paragraph 2 Glazer expresses his doubt that there is a widespread "desire or need for students to have something in the curriculum that relates to their own ethnic traits." Does your experience confirm or refute his doubt? Explain.

3. In paragraph 6 Glazer apparently accepts the view that the SATs are "thoroughly multicultural." If you are familiar with the SATs, indicate to what degree you share Glazer's belief on this point.

4. Glazer reports (para. 6) that more American 17-year-olds can identify Harriet Tubman than Winston Churchill or Joseph Stalin and that more know who Tubman was than know who wrote the Emancipation Proclamation. Does Glazer imply that this is regrettable? Do you think it is regrettable? Explain.

5. Glazer says (para. 11), "History in the schools has always played a socializing, nationalizing function. . . ." (Reread the entire paragraph to make sure you understand Glazer's point.) Does your experience (or, to your knowledge, the experience of your parents or grandparents) confirm Glazer's view? Explain.

Katha Pollitt

Canon to the Right of Me . . .

For the past couple of years we've all been witness to a furious debate about the literary canon. What books should be assigned to students? What books should critics discuss? What books should the rest of us read, and who are "we" anyway? Like everyone else, I've given these questions some thought, and when an invitation came my way, I leaped to produce my own manifesto. But to my surprise, when I sat down to write — in order to discover, as E. M. Forster once said, what I really think — I found that I agreed with all sides in the debate at once.

Katha Pollitt (b. 1949) often writes essays on literary, political, and social topics for The Nation, *a liberal journal, which on September 23, 1991, published the essay reprinted here. Some of Pollitt's essays have been collected and published in a volume titled* Reasonable Creatures *(1994). Pollitt is also widely known as a poet; her first collection of poems,* Antarctic Traveller *(1982), won the National Book Critics Circle award for poetry.*

The title of Pollitt's essay echoes a line from Tennyson's poem "The Charge of the Light Brigade," but for Tennyson's "cannon" ("Cannon to right of them") she substitutes "canon," meaning an authoritative list of books.

Take the conservatives. Now, this rather dour collection of scholars and diatribists — Allan Bloom, Hilton Kramer, John Silber, and so on — are not a particularly appealing group of people. They are arrogant, they are rude, they are gloomy, they do not suffer fools gladly, and everywhere they look, fools are what they see. All good reasons not to elect them to public office, as the voters of Massachusetts recently decided.[1] But what is so terrible, really, about what they are saying? I too believe that some books are more profound, more complex, more essential to an understanding of our culture than others; I too am appalled to think of students graduating from college not having read Homer, Plato, Virgil, Milton, Tolstoy — all writers, dead white Western men though they be, whose works have meant a great deal to me. As a teacher of literature and of writing, I too have seen at firsthand how ill-educated many students are, and how little aware they are of this important fact about themselves. Last year I taught a graduate seminar in the writing of poetry. None of my students had read more than a smattering of poems by anyone, male or female, published more than ten years ago. Robert Lowell was as far outside their frame of reference as Alexander Pope. When I gently suggested to one student that it might benefit her to read some poetry if she planned to spend her life writing it, she told me that yes, she knew she should read more but when she encountered a really good poem it only made her depressed. That contemporary writing has a history which it profits us to know in some depth, that we ourselves were not born yesterday, seems too obvious even to argue.

But ah, say the liberals, the canon exalted by the conservatives is itself an artifact of history. Sure, some books are more rewarding than others, but why can't we change our minds about which books those are? The canon itself was not always as we know it today: Until the 1920s, *Moby-Dick* was shelved with the boys' adventure stories. If T. S. Eliot[2] could single-handedly dethrone the Romantic poets in favor of the neglected Metaphysicals and place John Webster alongside Shakespeare, why can't we dip into the sea of stories and fish out Edith Wharton or Virginia Woolf? And this position too makes a great deal of sense to me. After all, alongside the many good reasons for a book to end up on the required-reading shelf are some rather suspect reasons for its exclusion: because it was written by a woman and therefore presumed to be too slight; because it was written by a black person and therefore presumed to be too unsophisticated or to reflect too special a case. By all means, say the liberals, let's have great books and a shared culture. But let's make sure that all the different kinds of greatness are represented and that the culture we share reflects the true range of human experience.

[1]**voters of Massachusetts** An allusion to John Silber's unsuccessful attempt to get elected as governor in 1990. [All notes are the editors'.]

[2]**T. S. Eliot** A highly influential poet and literary critic, Eliot (1888–1965) was cool about the Romantic poets (e.g., Percy Bysshe Shelley [1792–1822]) and enthusiastic about the Metaphysical poets (e.g., John Donne [1573–1631]).

If we leave the broadening of the canon up to the conservatives, this will never happen, because to them change only means defeat. Look at the recent fuss over the latest edition of the Great Books series published by Encyclopedia Britannica, headed by that old snake-oil salesman Mortimer Adler. Four women have now been added to the series: Virginia Woolf, Willa Cather, Jane Austen, and George Eliot. That's nice, I suppose, but really! Jane Austen has been a certified Great Writer for a hundred years! Lionel Trilling said so! There's something truly absurd about the conservatives earnestly sitting in judgment on the illustrious dead, as though up in Writers' Heaven Jane and George and Willa and Virginia were breathlessly waiting to hear if they'd finally made it into the club, while Henry Fielding, newly dropped from the list, howls in outer darkness and the Brontës, presumably, stamp their feet in frustration and hope for better luck in twenty years, when *Jane Eyre* and *Wuthering Heights* will suddenly turn out to have qualities of greatness never before detected in their pages. It's like Poets' Corner at Manhattan's Cathedral of St. John the Divine, where mortal men — and a woman or two — of letters actually vote on which immortals to honor with a plaque, a process no doubt complete with electoral campaigns, compromise candidates, and all the rest of the underside of the literary life. "No, I'm sorry, I just can't vote for Whitman. I'm a Washington Irving man myself."

Well, a liberal is not a very exciting thing to be, as *Nation* readers 5 know, and so we have the radicals, who attack the concepts of "greatness," "shared," "culture" and "lists." (I'm overlooking here the ultraradicals, who attack the "privileging" of "texts," as they insist on calling books, and think one might as well spend one's college years deconstructing *Leave It to Beaver.*) Who is to say, ask the radicals, what is a great book? What's so terrific about complexity, ambiguity, historical centrality, and high seriousness? If *The Color Purple,* say, gets students thinking about their own experience, maybe they ought to read it and forget about _____ and here you can fill in the name of whatever classic work you yourself found dry and tedious and never got around to finishing. For the radicals the notion of a shared culture is a lie, because it means presenting as universally meaningful and politically neutral books that reflect the interests and experiences and values of privileged white men at the expense of those of others — women, blacks, Latinos, Asians, the working class, whoever. Why not scrap the one-list-for-everyone idea and let people connect with books that are written by people like themselves about people like themselves? It will be a more accurate reflection of a multifaceted and conflict-ridden society, and will do wonders for everyone's self-esteem, except, of course, living white men — but they have too much self-esteem already.

Now, I have to say that I dislike the radicals' vision intensely. How foolish to argue that Chekhov has nothing to say to a black woman — or, for that matter, myself — merely because he is Russian, long dead, a man. The notion that one reads to increase one's self-esteem sounds to me like more snake oil. Literature is not an aerobics class or a session at the therapist's.

But then I think of myself as a child, leafing through anthologies of poetry for the names of women. I never would have admitted that I needed a role model, even if that awful term had existed back in the prehistory of which I speak, but why was I so excited to find a female name, even when, as was often the case, it was attached to a poem of no interest to me whatsoever? Anna Laetitia Barbauld, author of "Life! I know not what thou art / But know that thou and I must part!"; Lady Anne Lindsay, writer of languid ballads in incomprehensible Scots dialect; and the other minor female poets included by chivalrous Sir Arthur Quiller-Couch in the old *Oxford Book of English Verse:* I have to admit it, just by their presence in that august volume they did something for me. And although it had nothing to do with reading or writing, it was an important thing they did.

Now, what are we to make of this spluttering debate, in which charges of imperialism are met by equally passionate accusations of vandalism, in which each side hates the other, and yet each one seems to have its share of reason? Perhaps what we have here is one of those debates in which the opposing sides, unbeknownst to themselves, share a myopia that will turn out to be the most telling feature of the whole discussion: a debate, for instance, like that of our Founding Fathers over the nature of the franchise. Think of all the energy and passion spent pondering the question of property qualifications or direct versus legislative elections while all along, unmentioned and unimagined, was the fact—to us so central—that women and slaves were never considered for any kind of vote.

Something is being overlooked: the state of reading, and books, and literature in our country at this time. Why, ask yourself, is everyone so hot under the collar about what to put on the required-reading shelf? It is because while we have been arguing so fiercely about which books make the best medicine, the patient has been slipping deeper and deeper into a coma.

Let us imagine a country in which reading is a popular voluntary activity. There, parents read books for their own edification and pleasure, and are seen by their children at this silent and mysterious pastime. These parents also read to their children, give them books for presents, talk to them about books and underwrite, with their taxes, a public library system that is open all day, every day. In school—where an attractive library is invariably to be found—the children study certain books together but also have an active reading life of their own. Years later it may even be hard for them to remember if they read *Jane Eyre* at home and Judy Blume in class, or the other way around. In college young people continue to be assigned certain books, but far more important are the books they discover for themselves —browsing in the library, in bookstores, on the shelves of friends, one book leading to another, back and forth in history and across languages and cultures. After graduation they continue to read, and in the fullness of time produce a new generation of readers. Oh happy land! I wish we all lived there.

In that other country of real readers—voluntary, active, self-deter-   10 mined readers—a debate like the current one over the canon would not be taking place. Or if it did, it would be as a kind of parlor game: What books would *you* take to a desert island? Everyone would know that the top-ten list was merely a tiny fraction of the books one would read in a lifetime. It would not seem racist or sexist or hopelessly hidebound to put Hawthorne on the syllabus and not Toni Morrison. It would be more like putting oatmeal and not noodles on the breakfast menu—a choice part arbitrary, part a nod to the national past, part, dare one say it, a kind of reverse affirmative action: School might frankly be the place where one read the books that are a little off-putting, that have gone a little cold, that you might pass over because they do not address, in reader-friendly contemporary fashion, the issues most immediately at stake in modern life, but that, with a little study, turn out to have a great deal to say. Being on the list wouldn't mean so much. It might even add to a writer's cachet *not* to be on the list, to be in one way or another too heady, too daring, too exciting to be ground up into institutional fodder for teenagers. Generations of high school kids have been turned off to George Eliot by being forced to read *Silas Marner* at a tender age. One can imagine a whole new readership for her if grown-ups were left to approach *Middlemarch* and *Daniel Deronda* with open minds, at their leisure.

Of course, they rarely do. In America today the assumption underlying the canon debate is that the books on the list are the only books that are going to be read, and if the list is dropped no books are going to be read. Becoming a textbook is a book's only chance; all sides take that for granted. And so all agree not to mention certain things that they themselves, as highly educated people and, one assumes, devoted readers, know perfectly well. For example, that if you read only twenty-five, or fifty, or a hundred books, you can't understand them, however well chosen they are. And that if you don't have an independent reading life—and very few students do—you won't *like* reading the books on the list and will forget them the minute you finish them. And the books have, or should have, lives beyond the syllabus—thus, the totally misguided attempt to put current literature in the classroom. How strange to think that people need professorial help to read John Updike or Alice Walker, writers people actually do read for fun. But all sides agree, if it isn't taught, it doesn't count.

Let's look at the canon question from another angle. Instead of asking what books we want others to read, let's ask why we read books ourselves. I think the canon debaters are being a little disingenuous here, are suppressing, in the interest of their own agendas, their personal experience of reading. Sure, we read to understand our American culture and history, and we also read to recover neglected masterpieces, and to learn more about the accomplishments of our subgroup and thereby, as I've admitted about myself, increase our self-esteem. But what about reading for the aesthetic pleasures of language, form, image? What about reading to learn something new, to have a vicarious adventure, to follow the workings of an interesting, if possibly skewed, narrow, and ill-tempered mind? What about reading for the story? For an expanded sense of sheer human variety? There are a thousand reasons why a book might have a claim on our time and attention other than its canonization. I once infuriated an acquaintance by asserting that Trollope, although in many ways a lesser writer than Dickens, possessed some wonderful qualities Dickens lacked: a more realistic view of women, a more skeptical view of good intentions, a subtler sense of humor, a drier vision of life which I myself found congenial. You'd think I'd advocated throwing Dickens out and replacing him with a toaster. Because Dickens is a certified Great Writer, and Trollope is not.

Am I saying anything different from what Randall Jarrell said in his great 1953 essay "The Age of Criticism"? Not really, so I'll quote him. Speaking of the literary gatherings of the era, Jarrell wrote:

> If, at such parties, you wanted to talk about *Ulysses* or *The Castle* or *The Brothers Karamazov* or *The Great Gatsby* or Graham Greene's last novel — Important books — you were at the right place. (Though you weren't so well off if you wanted to talk about *Remembrance of Things Past*. Important, but too long.) But if you wanted to talk about Turgenev's novelettes, or *The House of the Dead*, or *Lavengro*, or *Life on the Mississippi*, or *The Old Wives' Tale*, or *The Golovlyov Family*, or Cunningham-Grahame's stories, or Saint-Simon's memoirs, or *Lost Illusions*, or *The Beggar's Opera*, or *Eugen Onegin*, or *Little Dorrit*, or the *Burnt Njal Saga*, or *Persuasion*, or *The Inspector-General*, or *Oblomov*, or *Peer Gynt*, or *Far from the Madding Crowd*, or *Out of Africa*, or the *Parallel Lives*, or *A Dreary Story*, or *Debits and Credits*, or *Arabia Deserta*, or *Elective Affinities*, or *Schweik*, or — any of a thousand good or interesting but Unimportant books, you couldn't expect a very ready knowledge or sympathy from most of the readers there. They had looked at the big sights, the current sights, hard, with guides and glasses; and those walks in the country, over unfrequented or thrice-familiar territory, all alone — those walks from which most of the joy and good of reading come — were walks that they hadn't gone on very often.

I suspect that most canon debaters have taken those solitary rambles, if only out of boredom — how many times, after all, can you reread the *Aeneid*, or *Mrs. Dalloway*, or *Cotton Comes to Harlem* (to pick one book from each column)? But those walks don't count, because of another assumption all sides hold in common, which is that the purpose of reading is none of the many varied and delicious satisfactions I've mentioned; it's medicinal. The chief end of reading is to produce a desirable kind of person and a desirable kind of society. A respectful, high-minded citizen of a unified society for the conservatives, an up-to-date and flexible sort for the liberals, subgroup-identified, robustly confident one for the radicals. How pragmatic, how moralistic, how American! The culture debaters turn out to share a secret suspicion of culture itself, as well as the antipornographer's belief that there is a simple, one-to-one correlation between books and behavior. Read the conservatives' list and produce a nation of sexists and racists — or a nation of philosopher kings. Read the liberals' list and produce a nation of spineless relativists — or a nation of open-minded world citizens. Read the radicals' list and produce a nation of psychobabblers and ancestor-worshipers — or a nation of stalwart proud-to-be-me pluralists.

But is there any list of a few dozen books that can have such a magical 15 effect, for good or for ill? Of course not. It's like arguing that a perfectly nutritional breakfast cereal is enough food for the whole day. And so the canon debate is really an argument about what books to cram down the resistant throats of a resentful captive populace of students; and the trick is never to mention the fact that, in such circumstances, one book is as good, or as bad, as another. Because, as the debaters know from their own experience as readers, books are not pills that produce health when ingested in measured doses. Books do not shape character in any simple way — if, indeed, they do so at all — or the most literate would be the most virtuous instead of just the ordinary run of humanity with larger vocabularies. Books cannot mold a common national purpose when, in fact, people are honestly divided about what kind of country they want — and are divided, moreover, for very good and practical reasons, as they always have been.

For these burly and energetic purposes, books are all but useless. The way books affect us is an altogether more subtle, delicate, wayward, and individual, not to say private, affair. And that reading is being made to bear such an inappropriate and simplistic burden speaks to the poverty both of culture and of frank political discussion in our time.

On his deathbed, Dr. Johnson — once canonical, now more admired than read — is supposed to have said to a friend who was energetically rearranging his bedclothes, "Thank you, this will do all that a pillow can do." One might say that the canon debaters are all asking of their handful of chosen books that they do a great deal more than any handful of books can do.

Topics for Critical Thinking and Writing

1. What does Pollitt mean (for instance in para. 3) by "the canon"?

2. In paragraphs 5 and 6 Pollitt glances at the argument that books by "privileged white men" may not mean much to others — "women, blacks, Latinos, Asians, the working class, whoever." If you have with considerable interest and enjoyment read a book (or even a short story) by a person who did not resemble you — for instance in sex, or in economic class, or in ethnic background — explain in 500 words *what* you especially liked about the work, and try to account for your response.

3. Pollitt mentions her pleasure (para. 6) at discovering a female poet in a famous anthology, and she notes that she "needed a role model." Does she believe that only a woman poet can be a role model for an aspiring woman poet? Do you? Must an aspiring black physicist find her role models only among black physicists? Among black women physicists? Why, or why not? Write a 500-word

essay on the role of race and gender in the idea of a role model. Draw on your own experience, if possible.

4. In paragraph 12 Pollitt talks about the reasons for reading on one's own. Which, if any, of her reasons correspond to your own experience? How much weight do you attach to this aspect of Pollitt's argument? Why?

5. Pollitt brings a light touch to her discussion of a topic that has often provoked acrimonious debate. Point to various passages where her sense of humor is evident. Is the overall effect of this feature of her style to trivialize the subject? To belittle those whom she criticizes? Or is there some other effect?

6. In paragraph 15 Pollitt declares that "the canon debate is really an argument about what books to cram down the resistant throats of a resentful captive populace of students." List five books or essays crammed down your resistant throat by teachers when you were a senior in high school and a freshman in college. List another five books or essays that you chose to read on your own during the same period. Why do you think none of those on the second list was required classroom reading? Do you think some or all of them ought to have been? Explain.

15

Sexual Harassment: Is There Any Doubt about What It Is?

Ellen Goodman

The Reasonable Woman Standard

Since the volatile mix of sex and harassment exploded under the Capitol dome, it hasn't just been senators scurrying for cover. The case of the professor and judge has left a gender gap that looks more like a crater.[1]

We have discovered that men and women see this issue differently. Stop the presses. Sweetheart, get me rewrite.

On the "Today" show, Bryant Gumbel asks something about a man's right to have a pinup on the wall and Katie Couric says what she thinks of that. On the normally sober "MacNeil/Lehrer" hour the usual panel of legal experts doesn't break down between left and right but between male and female.

On a hundred radio talk shows, women are sharing experiences and men are asking for proof. In ten thousand offices, the order of the day is the nervous joke. One boss asks his secretary if he can still say "good morning," or is that sexual harassment. Heh, heh. The women aren't laughing.

---

[1]Goodman is alluding to the charges that Professor Anita Hill, of the University of Oklahoma law school, made during the Senate hearings before confirmation of Justice Clarence Thomas to a seat on the Supreme Court. The hearings were televised nationally, and several senators on the Judiciary Committee were widely regarded as having treated Hill very badly. [Editors' note.]

Ellen Goodman, educated at Radcliffe College, worked as a reporter for Newsweek *and the* Detroit Free Press. *Since 1967 she has written for the* Boston Globe, *and since 1972 her column has been nationally syndicated. The essay that we reprint appeared in the* Boston Globe *in October 1991.*

Okay boys and girls, back to your corners. Can we talk? Can we hear?   5

The good news is that women have stopped rolling their eyes at each other and started speaking out. The bad news is that we may each assume the other gender not only doesn't understand but can't understand. "They don't get it" becomes "they can't get it."

Let's start with the fact that sexual harassment is a concept as new as date rape. Date rape, that should-be oxymoron, assumes a different perspective on the part of the man and the woman. His date, her rape. Sexual harassment comes with some of the same assumptions. What he labels sexual, she labels harassment.

This produces what many men tend to darkly call a "murky" area of the law. Murky however is a step in the right direction. When everything was clear, it was clearly biased. The old single standard was [a] male standard. The only options a working woman had were to grin, bear it, or quit.

Sexual harassment rules are based on the point of view of the victim, nearly always a woman. The rules ask, not just whether she has been physically assaulted, but whether the environment in which she works is intimidating or coercive. Whether she feels harassed. It says that her feelings matter.

This, of course, raises all sorts of hackles about women's *feelings*,   10 women's *sensitivity*. How can you judge the sensitivity level of every single woman you work with? What's a poor man to do?

But the law isn't psychiatry. It doesn't adapt to individual sensitivity levels. There is a standard emerging by which the courts can judge these cases and by which people can judge them as well. It's called "the reasonable woman standard." How would a reasonable woman interpret this? How would a reasonable woman behave?

This is not an entirely new idea, although perhaps the law's belief in the reasonableness of women is. There has long been a "reasonable man" in the law not to mention a "reasonable pilot," a "reasonable innkeeper," a "reasonable train operator."

Now the law is admitting that a reasonable woman may see these situations differently than a man. That truth — available in your senator's mailbag — is also apparent in research. We tend to see sexualized situations from our own gender's perspective. Kim Lane Scheppele, a political science and law professor at the University of Michigan, summarizes the miscues this way: "Men see the sex first and miss the coercion. Women see the coercion and miss the sex."

Does that mean that we are genetically doomed to our double vision? Scheppele is quick to say no. Our justice system rests on the belief that one person can get in another's head, walk in her shoes, see things from another perspective. And so does our hope for change.

If a jury of car drivers can understand how a "reasonable pilot" would   15 see one situation, a jury of men can see how a reasonable woman would see another event. The crucial ingredient is empathy.

Check it out in the office tomorrow. He's coming on, she's backing off, he keeps coming. Read the body language. There's a *Playboy* calendar on the wall and a PMS joke in the boardroom and the boss is just being friendly. How would a reasonable woman feel?

At this moment, when the air is crackling with hostility and consciousness-raising has the hair sticking up on the back of many necks, guess what? Men can "get it." Reasonable men.

Topics for Critical Thinking and Writing

1. Goodman is a journalist, which means in part that her writing is lively. Point to two or three sentences that you would not normally find in a textbook, and evaluate them. (Example: "Okay boys and girls, back to your corners," para. 5.) Are the sentences you have selected effective? Why, or why not?

2. Why does Goodman describe date rape as a "should-be oxymoron" (para. 7)?

3. In paragraphs 11 and 12 Goodman speaks of "the reasonable woman standard." In recent years several cases have come to the courts in which women have said that they are harassed by posters of nude women in the workplace. Such posters have been said to create an "intimidating, hostile, or offensive environment." (a) What do you think Goodman's opinion would be? (b) Imagine that you are a member of the jury deciding such a case. What is your verdict? Why?

4. According to Goodman's account of the law (paras. 8–13), the criterion for sexual harassment is whether the "reasonable woman" would regard the "environment" in which she works (or studies) as "intimidating" or "coercive," thus causing her to "feel harassed." In a 500-word essay describe three hypothetical cases, one of which you believe clearly involves sexual harassment, a second that clearly does not, and a third that is a borderline case.

5. Given what Goodman says about sexual harassment, can men be victims of sexual harassment? Why, or why not?

Catharine A. MacKinnon

Sex and Violence: A Perspective

I want to raise some questions about the concept of this panel's title, "Violence against Women," as a concept that may coopt us as we attempt to formulate our own truths. I want to speak specifically about four issues: rape, sexual harassment, pornography, and battery. I think one of the reasons we say that each of these issues is an example of violence against women is to reunify them. To say that aggression against women has this unity is to criticize the divisions that have been imposed on that aggression by the legal system. What I see to be the danger of the analysis, what makes it potentially cooptive, is formulating it — and it *is* formulated this way — these are issues of violence, *not* sex: Rape is a crime of violence, not sexuality; sexual harassment is an abuse of power, not sexuality; pornography is violence against women; it is not erotic. Although battering is not categorized so explicitly, it is usually treated as though there is nothing sexual about a man beating up a woman so long as it is with his fist. I'd like to raise some questions about that as well.

I hear in the formulation that these issues are violence against women, not sex, that we are in the shadow of Freud, intimidated at being called repressive Victorians. We're saying we're *op*pressed and they say we're *re*pressed. That is, when we say we're against rape, the immediate response is, "Does that mean you're against sex?" "Are you attempting to impose neo-Victorian prudery on sexual expression?" This comes up with sexual harassment as well. When we say we're against sexual harassment, the first thing people want to know is, "What's the difference between that and ordinary male-to-female sexual initiation?" That's a good question. . . . The same is also true of criticizing pornography. "You can't be against erotica?" It's the latest version of the accusation that feminists are antimale. To distinguish ourselves from this, and in reaction to it, we call these abuses violence. The attempt is to avoid the critique — we're not against sex — and at the same time retain our criticism of these practices. So we rename as violent those abuses that have been seen to be sexual, without saying that we have a very different perspective on violence and on sexuality and their relationship. I also think a reason we call these experiences violence is to avoid being called lesbians, which for some reason is equated with being

---

Catharine A. MacKinnon, a professor of law at the University of Michigan, is widely regarded as the nation's leading lawyer concerned with fighting sexual harassment and with outlawing pornography. The essay originally appeared in Aegis, *a magazine devoted to ending violence against women, and was later reprinted in MacKinnon's* Feminism Unmodified *(1987), where it was accompanied by this note: "This early synthesis was framed in part to respond to panel members' concerns with cooptation at the National Conference on Women and the Law, Boston, Massachusetts, April 5, 1981."*

against sex. In order to avoid that, yet retain our opposition to sexual violation, we put this neutral, objective, abstract word *violence* on it all.

To me this is an attempt to have our own perspective on these outrages without owning up to having one. To have our point of view but present it as *not* a particular point of view. Our problem has been to label something as rape, as sexual harassment, as pornography in the face of a suspicion that it might be intercourse, it might be ordinary sexual initiation, it might be erotic. To say that these purportedly sexual events violate us, to be against them, we call them not sexual. But the attempt to be objective and neutral avoids owning up to the fact that women do have a specific point of view on these events. It avoids saying that from women's point of view, intercourse, sex roles, and eroticism can be and at times are violent to us as women.

My approach would claim our perspective; we are not attempting to be objective about it, we're attempting to represent the point of view of women. The point of view of men up to this time, called objective, has been to distinguish sharply between rape on the one hand and intercourse on the other; sexual harassment on the one hand and normal, ordinary sexual initiation on the other; pornography or obscenity on the one hand and eroticism on the other. The male point of view defines them by distinction. What women experience does not so clearly distinguish the normal, everyday things from those abuses from which they have been defined by distinction. Not just "Now we're going to take what *you* say is rape and call it violence"; "Now we're going to take what *you* say is sexual harassment and call it violence"; "Now we're going to take what *you* say is pornography and call it violence." We have a deeper critique of what has been done to women's sexuality and who controls access to it. What we are saying is that sexuality in exactly these normal forms often *does* violate us. So long as we say that those things are abuses of violence, not sex, we fail to criticize what has been made of *sex*, what has been done to us *through* sex, because we leave the line between rape and intercourse, sexual harassment and sex roles, pornography and eroticism, right where it is.

I think it is useful to inquire how women and men (I don't use the   5 term *persons*, I guess, because I haven't seen many lately) live through the meaning of their experience with these issues. When we ask whether rape, sexual harassment, and pornography are questions of violence or questions of sexuality, it helps to ask, to whom? What is the perspective of those who are involved, whose experience it is—to rape or to have been raped, to consume pornography or to be consumed through it. As to what these things *mean* socially, it is important whether they are about sexuality to women and men or whether they are instead about "violence"—or whether violence and sexuality can be distinguished in that way, as they are lived out.

The crime of rape—this is a legal and observed, not a subjective, individual, or feminist definition—is defined around penetration. That seems to me a very male point of view on what it means to be sexually violated.

And it is exactly what heterosexuality as a social institution is fixated around, the penetration of the penis into the vagina. Rape is defined according to what men think violates women, and that is the same as what they think of as the sine qua non of sex. What women experience as degrading and defiling when we are raped includes as much that is distinctive to us as is our experience of sex. Someone once termed penetration a "peculiarly resented aspect" of rape — I don't know whether that meant it was peculiar that it was resented or that it was resented with heightened peculiarity. Women who have been raped often do resent having been penetrated. But that is not all there is to what was intrusive or expropriative of a woman's sexual wholeness.

I do think the crime of rape focuses more centrally on what men define as sexuality than on women's experience of our sexual being, hence its violation. A common experience of rape victims is to be unable to feel good about anything heterosexual thereafter — or anything sexual at all, or men at all. The minute they start to have sexual feelings or feel sexually touched by a man, or even a woman, they start to relive the rape. I had a client who came in with her husband. She was a rape victim, a woman we had represented as a witness. Her husband sat the whole time and sobbed. They couldn't have sex anymore because every time he started to touch her, she would flash to the rape scene and see his face change into the face of the man who had raped her. That, to me, is sexual. When a woman has been raped, and it is sex that she then cannot experience without connecting it to that, it was her sexuality that was violated.

Similarly, men who are in prison for rape think it's the dumbest thing that ever happened. . . . It isn't just a miscarriage of justice; they were put in jail for something very little different from what most men do most of the time and call it sex. The only difference is they got caught. That view is nonremorseful and not rehabilitative. It may also be true. It seems to me we have here a convergence between the rapist's view of what he has done and the victim's perspective on what was done to her. That is, for both, their ordinary experiences of heterosexual intercourse and the act of rape have something in common. Now this gets us into intense trouble, because that's exactly how judges and juries see it who refuse to convict men accused of rape. A rape victim has to prove that it was not intercourse. She has to show that there was force and she resisted, because if there was sex, consent is inferred. Finders of fact look for "more force than usual during the preliminaries." Rape is defined by distinction from intercourse — not nonviolence, intercourse. They ask, does this event look more like fucking or like rape? But what is their standard for sex, and is this question asked from the *woman's point of view?* The level of force is not adjudicated at her point of violation; it is adjudicated at the standard of the normal level of force. Who sets this standard?

In the criminal law, we can't put everybody in jail who does an ordinary act, right? Crime is supposed to be deviant, not normal. Women continue not to report rape, and a reason is that they believe, and they are right, that the legal system will not see it from their point of view. We get very low conviction rates for rape.[1] We also get many women who believe they have never been raped, although a lot of force was involved. They mean that they were not raped in a way that is legally provable. In other words, in all these situations, there was not *enough* violence against them to take it beyond the category of "sex"; they were not coerced enough. Maybe they were forced-fucked for years and put up with it, maybe they tried to get it over with, maybe they were coerced by something other than battery, something like economics, maybe even something like love.

What I am saying is that unless you make the point that there is much violence in intercourse, as a usual matter, none of that is changed. Also we continue to stigmatize the women who claim rape as having experienced a deviant violation and allow the rest of us to go through life feeling violated but thinking we've never been raped, when there were a great many times when we, too, have had sex and didn't want it. What this critique does that is different from the "violence, not sex" critique is ask a series of questions about normal, heterosexual intercourse and attempt to move the line between heterosexuality on the one hand—intercourse—and rape on the other, rather than allow it to stay where it is.   10

Having done that so extensively with rape, I can consider sexual harassment more briefly. The way the analysis of sexual harassment is sometimes expressed now (and it bothers me) is that it is an abuse of power, not sexuality. That does not allow us to pursue whether sexuality, as socially constructed in our society through gender roles, is *itself* a power structure. If you look at sexual harassment as power, not sex, what is power supposed to be? Power is employer/employee, not because courts are marxist but because this is a recognized hierarchy. Among men. Power is teacher/student, because courts recognize a hierarchy there. Power is on one side and sexuality on the other. Sexuality is ordinary affection, everyday flirtation. Only when ordinary, everyday affection and flirtation and "I was just trying to be friendly" come into the context of *another* hierarchy is it considered potentially an abuse of power. What is not considered to be hierarchy is women and men—men on top and women on the bottom. That is not considered to be a question of power or social hierarchy, legally or politically. A feminist perspective suggests that it is.

When we have examples of coequal sexual harassment (within these other hierarchies), worker to worker on the same level, involving women and men, we have a lot of very interesting, difficult questions about sex discrimination, which is supposed to be about gender difference, but does not

---

[1]Gerald D. Robin, "Forcible Rape: Institutionalized Sexism in the Criminal Justice System," *Crime and Delinquency* (April 1977), 136–53. "Forcible rape is unique among crimes in the manner in which its victims are dealt with by the criminal justice system. Raped women are subjected to an institutionalized sexism that begins with the treatment by the police, continues through a male-dominated criminal justice system influenced by pseudoscientific notions of victim precipitation, and ends with the systematic acquittal of many de facto rapists." Lorenne M. G. Clark and Debra Lewis, *Rape: The Price of Coercive Sexuality* 57 (1977). [All notes are the author's.]

conceive of gender as a social hierarchy. I think that implicit in race dis-crimination cases for a brief moment of light was the notion that there is a social hierarchy between blacks and whites. So that presumptively it's an exercise of power for a white person to do something egregious to a black person or for a white institution to do something egregious systematically to many black people. Situations of coequal power—among coworkers or students or teachers—are difficult to see as examples of sexual harassment unless you have a notion of male power. I think we lie to women when we call it not power when a woman is come onto by a man who is not her em-ployer, not her teacher. What do we labor under, what do we feel, when a man—any man—comes and hits on us? I think we require women to feel fine about turning down male-initiated sex so long as the man doesn't have some *other* form of power over us. Whenever—every and any time—a woman feels conflicted and wonders what's wrong with her that she can't decline although she has no inclination, and she feels open to male accusa-tions, whether they come from women or men, of "Why didn't you just tell him to buzz off?" we have sold her out, not named her experience. We are taught that we exist for men. We should be flattered or at least act as if we are—be careful about a man's ego because you never know what he can do to you. To flat out say to him, "You?" or "I don't want to" is not *in* most women's sex-role learning. To say it is, is bravado. And that's because he's a man, not just because you never know what he can do to you because he's your boss (that's two things—he's a man and he's the boss) or your teacher or in some other hierarchy. It seems to me that we haven't talked very much about gender *as* a hierarchy, as a division of power, in the way that's expressed and acted out, primarily I think sexually. And therefore we haven't expanded the definition according to women's experience of sexu-ality, including our own sexual intimidation, of what things are sexual in this world. So men have also defined what can be called sexual about us. They say, "I was just trying to be affectionate, flirtatious, and friendly," and we were just all felt up. We criticize the idea that rape comes down to her word against his—but it really *is* her perspective against his perspective, and the law has been written from *his* perspective. If he didn't mean it to be sexual, it's not sexual. If he didn't see it as forced, it wasn't forced.[2] Which is to say, only male sexual violations, that is, only male ideas of what sexually violates us as women, are illegal. We buy into this when we say our sexual violations are abuses of power, not sex.

Just as rape is supposed to have nothing against intercourse, just as sexual harassment is supposed to have nothing against normal sexual initia-tion (men initiate, women consent—that's mutual?), the idea that pornog-

[2]Examples are particularly clear in England, Canada, and California. Director of Public Prose-cutions v. Morgan, 2411 E.R.H.L. 347 (1975); Pappajohn v. The Queen, 11 D.L.R. 3d 1 (1980); People v. Mayberry, 15 Cal. 3d 143, 542 P. 2d 1337 (1975). But cf. People v. Barnes, 228 Cal. Rptr. 228 (Cal. 1986).

raphy is violence against women, not sex, seems to distinguish artistic creation on the one hand from what is degrading to women on the other. It is
candid and true but not enough to say of pornography, as Justice Stewart
said, "I know it when I see it."[3] *He* knows what he thinks it is when he sees
it—but is that what *I* know? Is that the same "it"? Is he going to know
what I know when I see it? I think pretty much not, given what's on the
newsstand, given what is not considered hard-core pornography. Sometimes I think what is obscene is what does *not* turn on the Supreme Court
—or what revolts them more. Which is uncommon, since revulsion is
eroticized. We have to admit that pornography turns men on; it is therefore
erotic. It is a lie to say that pornography is not erotic. When we say it is violence, not sex, we are saying, there is this degrading to women, over here,
and this erotic, over there, without saying to whom. It is overwhelmingly
disproportionately men to whom pornography is erotic. It is women, on the
whole, to whom it is violent, among other things. And this is not just a matter of perspective, but a matter of reality.

Pornography turns primarily men on. Certainly they are getting something out of it. They pay incredible amounts of money for it; it's one of the
largest industries in the country. If women got as much out of it as men do,
we would buy it instead of cosmetics. It's a massive industry, cosmetics. We
are poor but we have *some* money; we are some market. We spend our
money to set ourselves up as the objects that emulate those images that are
sold as erotic to men. What pornography says about us is that we enjoy
degradation, that we are sexually turned on by being degraded. For me
that obliterates the line, as a line at all, between pornography on one hand
and erotica on the other, if what turns men on, what men find beautiful, is
what degrades women. It is pervasively present in art, also, and advertising.
But it is definitely present in eroticism, if that is what it is. It makes me
think that women's sexuality as such is a stigma. We also sometimes have
an experience of sexuality authentic somehow in all this. We are not allowed to have it; we are not allowed to talk about it; we are not allowed to
speak of it or image it as from our own point of view. And, to the extent we
try to assert that we are beings equal with men, we have to be either asex-
ual or virgins.

To worry about cooptation is to realize that lies make bad politics. It is 15
ironic that cooptation often results from an attempt to be "credible," to be
strategically smart, to be "effective" on existing terms. Sometimes you become what you're fighting. Thinking about issues of sexual violation as issues of violence not sex could, if pursued legally, lead to opposing sexual
harassment and pornography through morals legislation and obscenity
laws. It is actually interesting that this theoretical stance has been widely
embraced but these legal strategies have not been. Perhaps women realize
that these legal approaches would not address the subordination of women

---

[3]Jacobellis v. Ohio, 378 U.S. 184, 197 (1964) (Stewart, J., concurring).

to men, specifically and substantively. These approaches are legally as abstract as the "violence not sex" critique is politically abstract. They are both not enough and too much of the wrong thing. They deflect us from criticizing everyday behavior that is pervasive and normal and concrete and fuses sexuality with gender in violation and it is not amenable to existing legal approaches. I think we need to think more radically in our legal work here.

Battering is called violence, rather than something sex-specific: This is done to women. I also think it is sexually done to women. Not only in where it is done — over half of the incidents are in the bedroom.[4] Or the surrounding events — precipitating sexual jealousy. But when violence against women is eroticized as it is in this culture, it is very difficult to say that there is a major distinction in the level of sex involved between being assaulted by a penis and being assaulted by a fist, especially when the perpetrator is a man. If women as gender female are defined as sexual beings, and violence is eroticized, then men violating women has a sexual component. I think men rape women because they get off on it in a way that fuses dominance with sexuality. (This is different in emphasis from what Susan Brownmiller says.[5]) I think that when men sexually harass women it expresses male control over sexual access to us. It doesn't mean they all want to fuck us, they just want to hurt us, dominate us, and control us, and that *is* fucking us. They want to be able to have that and to be able to say when they can have it, to *know* that. That is in itself erotic. The idea that opposing battering is about saving the family is, similarly, abstracted, gender-neutral. There are gender-neutral formulations of all these issues: law and order as opposed to derepression, Victorian morality as opposed to permissiveness, obscenity as opposed to art and freedom of expression. Gender-neutral, objective formulations like these avoid asking *whose* expression, from whose point of view? Whose law and whose order? It's not just a question of who is free to express ourselves; it's not just that there is almost no, if any, self-respecting women's eroticism. The fact is that what we do see, what we are allowed to experience, even in our own suffering, even in what we are to complain about, is overwhelmingly constructed from the male point of view. Laws against sexual violation express what men see and do when they engage in sex with women; laws against obscenity center on the display of women's bodies in ways that men are turned on by viewing. To me, it not only makes us cooptable to define such abuses in gender-neutral terms like violence; when we fail to assert that we are fighting for the affirmative definition and control of our own sexuality, of our own lives as women, and that these experiences violate *that*, we have already been bought.

---

[4]R. Emerson Dobash and Russell Dobash, *Violence against Wives* (1979) at 14–21.
[5]Susan Brownmiller, *Against Our Will: Men, Women and Rape* (1975).

Topics for Critical Thinking and Writing

1. Suppose a fellow student told you that he or she did not understand MacKinnon's first three paragraphs. In a few sentences summarize these paragraphs as clearly as possible.

2. In paragraph 4 MacKinnon sharply distinguishes between "the point of view of women" and "the point of view of men" concerning the experience of rape, sexual harassment, pornography, and battery. Do you agree that it is useful to make this clear-cut distinction? Support your answer.

3. In paragraph 14 MacKinnon notes that men far outnumber women as purchasers of pornography. How might you account for this fact?

4. MacKinnon's thesis might be formulated this way: Describing rape, sexual harassment, pornography, and battery as "violence against women," as distinct from *sexual* abuse, distorts the reality as experienced by women. (See especially MacKinnon's opening and closing paragraphs.) State as succinctly as you can what the reality is, and why "violence against women," distinguished from "sexual violence," distorts that reality.

5. Read the essay by Ellen Goodman on sexual harassment (p. 509), and write a 500-word essay explaining the similarities and differences between Goodman's view and MacKinnon's on this topic. Which view do you prefer? Why?

John Leo

Is Gossip Sexual Harassment?

The best story in the newspapers of July 20, 1990, was not the sentencing of Pete Rose, the opening of the Nixon Library, or the salvaging of the civil rights bill. It was Michelle Locke's wonderful AP story on the new sexual harassment code at Amherst-Pelham Regional High School in Massachusetts.

Here's how Ms. Locke began: "High schoolers who beam sexually charged stares at their classmates or exchange snippets of gossip in the halls could run afoul of new guidelines designed to curb sexual harassment among students." By the time the last line rolled by ("We're not Puritans," a school official said), I was convinced that Ms. Locke's piece and the Amherst code itself should go directly into a time capsule. This would give our baffled descendants an outside chance to comprehend some of the strange social obsessions of the 1990s.

John Leo, formerly a staff writer for Time *and for the* New York Times, *now writes a weekly column for* U.S. News & World Report *and for newspapers throughout the country. We reprint an essay from his book* Two Steps Ahead of the Thought Police *(1994).*

I phoned the superintendent of schools, Gus Sayer. Is there a serious harassment problem at the school? No, he said, we just thought these rules were a good idea. How much gazing or leering would it take to be brought up on sexual harassment charges? There is no time limit, he said, a single stare might do it. And what if a student told a friend, "I think Marcie and Allen have something going?" "That would qualify as sexual harassment," he replied.

This expansive view of harassment is in the air these days. Driven by feminist ideology, we have constantly extended the definition of what constitutes illicit male behavior. Very ambiguous incidents are now routinely flattened out into male predation and firmly listed under date rape. In a Swarthmore College's rape prevention pamphlet, "inappropriate innuendo" was actually listed as an example of acquaintance rape. At the University of Michigan, charges were filed against a male student who slipped the following joke under the door of a female student: "Q. How many men does it take to mop a floor? A. None, it's a woman's job."

Now this stern new femino-puritanism seems to be reaching down   5
into the high schools. Looking and talking can apparently be as career-threatening at Amherst-Pelham as mopping jokes at Michigan. The high school lists all the possible consequences of harassment: parent conference, apology to victim, detention, suspension, recommendation for expulsion, referral to police.

If I were in charge of a national program to ruin sex for the next generation, I would certainly want to include Amherst-Pelham's new rules. The code is a rich compost of antisex messages: Males are predatory; sex is so dangerous that chit-chat about it can get you brought up on charges; hormone-driven gazing at girls will bring the adult world down on your neck; women are victims — incapable of dismissing creeps by simply quipping "Buzz off, Bozo," they must be encouraged to run to the administration and say "Someone was looking at me" — and since hallway sex gossip is likely to get to authorities through the services of snitches, friends should probably not be trusted. Better to talk about the weather.

A small irony here is that gossip is the primary means by which an informal social group, such as a class or a student body, creates and maintains norms. Beneath the titillation of gossip, approval and disapproval are constantly being doled out, and behavior is being modified. A male who treats females badly is far more likely to be brought into line by peer-group gossip than by a huffy administration imposing rules from above.

There is another ominous aspect of the Amherst rules. In listing "the spreading of sex gossip" as a school offense, they impose, rather casually, what is apparently the first speech code at an American high school. At least I know of no other high school that censors or punishes private conversation. This too is smuggled in from the college level, where the new speech police have successfully imposed codes to defend the sensibilities of sexual, racial, and ethnic groups. The mopping joke was a violation of the University of Michigan code, since found unconstitutional. But many other colleges have installed these dubious programs, including the University of Wisconsin, the whole University of California system and (inevitably) Stanford. Now, I suppose, the yearning to solve problems by curbing speech will begin to hit the high schools.

The *Economist* featured an interesting lead editorial entitled "America's Decadent Puritans." Despite the tough headline, it was a friendly but very sober view of America's problems from "an unashamedly Americanophile" British publication. As it happens, most of the hallmarks of social decline mentioned in the piece are illustrated or strongly implied in the foolish Amherst harassment rules: the itch to censor; litigiousness and endless hearings over the problems of everyday life; the obsession with self-esteem and victimization; the constant truckling to pressure groups; the gradual assertion of a conformist and politically correct way of thinking; the expectation that the courts, the politicians, or somebody will supply us with a stress-free life ("I guess the people in our school, they're trying to make it a perfect world," an Amherst-Pelham student said to Ms. Locke).

That's why these rules are ideal for a time capsule. Let's just stuff 10 them there and skip the whole idea of imposing them on the unsuspecting young of Amherst-Pelham.

Topics for Critical Thinking and Writing ═══════════

1. Assuming the accuracy of Leo's report, do you think that the episode narrated in paragraphs 3 and 4 (staring, circulating a rumor, telling a joke about mopping the floor) require some sort of official action? Explain.

2. In paragraph 4 Leo points with evident derision at the Swarthmore rape-prevention pamphlet that treats "inappropriate innuendo" as "an example of acquaintance rape." What does "inappropriate innuendo" mean? Can you think of a couple of clear cases? Why does Leo imply that it is absurd to treat such innuendo as acquaintance rape? Do you agree? Why?

3. In paragraph 6 Leo says that the Amherst-Pelham code "is a rich compost of antisex messages." Do you agree that the code, as he describes it, is "antisex"? If you think it isn't, explain your position.

4. In his seventh paragraph Leo claims that gossip fulfills an important social function; it is the means by which "an informal social group . . . creates and maintains norms." Does your experience bear this out? In any case, does it matter whether such gossip is also harmful to "outsiders"? Whether it fosters a false sense of superiority among those in on the gossip? Do you think adolescents are bound to gossip, and especially about sexual behavior (real or imagined) of their friends and classmates, so that curbing such chatter is impossible? Explain.

5. In his next-to-last paragraph Leo suggests that the Amherst-Pelham code exemplifies several American shortcomings. Do you agree that the qualities he specifies in the paragraph are American shortcomings, and do you think that the code illustrates them? Explain.

6. If your high school or college has a code indicating what constitutes sexual harassment, give the most important provisions of the code and evaluate them.

7. In his last paragraph Leo takes the Amherst-Pelham code as evidence that schools should not formulate codes concerning sexual harassment. Do you agree or disagree? Why?

Sarah J. McCarthy

Cultural Fascism

On the same day that Ted Kennedy asked forgiveness for his personal "shortcomings," he advocated slapping lottery-size punitive damages on small-business owners who may be guilty of excessive flirting or whose employees may be guilty of talking dirty. Senator Kennedy expressed regrets that the new civil rights bill caps punitive damages for sexual harassment as high as $300,000 (depending on company size), and he promises to push for increases next year. Note that the senators have voted to exempt themselves from punitive damages.

I am the owner of a small restaurant/bar that employs approximately twenty young males whose role models range from Axl Rose to John Belushi. They work hard in a high-stress, fast-paced job in a hot kitchen and at times they are guilty of colorful language. They have also been overheard telling Pee-Wee Herman jokes and listening to obnoxious rock lyrics. They have discussed pornography and they have flirted with waitresses. One chef/manager has asked out a pretty blonde waitress probably a hundred times in three years. She seems to enjoy the game, but always says no. Everyone calls everyone else "Honey" — it's a ritual, a way of softening what sound like barked orders: "I need the medium-rare shish kebab *now!*"

"Honey" doesn't mean the same thing here as it does in women's studies departments or at the EEOC.[1] The auto body shop down the street has pinups. Perhaps under the vigilant eyes of the feminist political correctness gestapo we can reshape our employees' behavior so they act more like nerds from the Yale women's studies department. The gestapo will not lack for potential informers seeking punitive damages and instant riches.

With the Civil Rights Bill of 1991 we are witnessing the most organized and systematic assault on free speech and privacy since the McCarthy era. The vagueness of the sexual harassment law, combined with

[1]**EEOC** Equal Employment Opportunity Commission. [Editors' note.]

As Sarah J. McCarthy indicates in this essay, she is the owner of a small restaurant. The essay originally appeared in the December 9, 1991, issue of Forbes, *a business-oriented magazine.*

our current litigation explosion, is a frightening prospect for small businesses. We are now financially responsible for sexually offensive verbal behavior, even if we don't know it is occurring, under a law that provides no guidelines to define "offensive" and "harassment." This is a cultural fascism unmatched since the Chinese communists outlawed hand-holding, decorative clothing, and premarital sex.

This law is detrimental even to the women it professes to help. I am a 5 feminist, but the law has made me fearful of hiring women. If one of our cooks or managers — or my husband or sons — offends someone, it could cost us $100,000 in punitive damages and legal expenses. There will be no insurance fund or stockholders or taxpayers to pick up the tab.

When I was a feminist activist in the 1970s, we knew the dangers of a pedestal — it was said to be as confining as any other small place. As we were revolted and outraged by the woman-hatred in violent pornography, we reminded each other that education, not laws, was the solution to our problems. In Women Against Sexist Violence in Pornography and Media, in Pittsburgh, we were well aware of the dangers of encroaching on the First Amendment. Free speech was, perhaps more than anything else, what made our country grow into a land of enlightenment and diversity. The lesbians among us were aware that the same laws used to censor pornography could be used against them if their sexual expressions were deemed offensive.

We admired powerful women writers such as Marge Piercy and poets like Robin Morgan who swooped in from nowhere, writing break-your-chains poems about women swinging from crystal chandeliers like monkeys on vines and defecating in punch bowls. Are we allowed to talk about these poems in the current American workplace?

The lawyers — the prim women and men who went to the politically correct law schools — believe with sophomoric arrogance that the solution to all the world's problems is tort litigation. We now have eternally complicated questions of sexual politics judged by the shirting standards of the reasonable prude.

To the leadership of the women's movement: You do women a disservice. You ladies — and I use that term intentionally — have trivialized the women's movement. You have made us ladies again. You have not considered the unintended effects of your sexual harassment law. You are saying that too many things men say and do with each other are too rough-and-tumble for us. Wielding the power of your $300,000 lawsuits, you are frightening managers into hiring men over women. I know that I am so frightened. You have installed a double pane of glass on the glass ceiling with the help of your white knight and protector, Senator Kennedy.

You and your allies tried to lynch Clarence Thomas. You alienate your 10 natural allies. Men and women who wanted to work shoulder to shoulder with you are now looking over their shoulders. You have made women into china dolls that if broken come with a $300,000 price tag. The games, intrigue, nuances, and fun of flirting have been made into criminal activity.

We women are not as delicate and powerless as you think. We do not want victim status in the workplace. Don't try to foist it on us.

Topics for Critical Thinking and Writing

1. Reread McCarthy's opening paragraph. What is her point? How effective do you think this paragraph is as the opening of an argumentative essay?

2. In her third paragraph McCarthy speaks of "the feminist political correctness gestapo." What does she mean by this phrase, and why does she use it?

3. In paragraph 8 McCarthy refers to "tort litigation." Explain the phrase.

4. In her second paragraph McCarthy suggests that in "a high-stress, fast-paced" environment with young (and presumably not highly educated) males, "colorful language and dirty jokes" and "obnoxious rock lyrics" are to be expected. Would you agree that a women who takes a job in such an environment cannot reasonably complain that this sort of behavior constitutes sexual harassment? Explain.

5. How do you think McCarthy would define sexual harassment? That is, how according to her views should we complete the following sentence: Person A sexually harasses person B if and only if . . . ?

6. Read the essay by Ellen Goodman (p. 000) and explain in a brief essay of 100 words where she and Sarah J. McCarthy differ. With whom do you agree? Why?

16

Television Violence:
Are Regulations Necessary?

Leonard D. Eron

The Television Industry Must Police Itself

A recent summary of over two hundred studies, published in 1990, offers convincing evidence that the observation of violence, as seen in standard everyday television entertainment, does affect the aggressive behavior of the viewer. . . .

What can be done? As soon as the suggestion for action comes up, the TV industry raises the issue of censorship, violation of First Amendment rights, and abrogation of the Constitution. For many years now Western European countries have monitored TV and films and have not permitted the showing of excess violence, especially during child viewing hours. I have never heard of any complaints by citizens in those democratic countries that their rights have been violated. But in the United States, youth violence is a public health problem, so designated by the Centers for Disease Control [and Prevention]. . . . No one is claiming that TV violence is the sole cause of the epidemic. However, it is certainly *one* of the causes, and one which we at least can do something about. Is it too much to ask the industry to police itself? It has done so before with some success.

Leonard D. Eron, professor of psychology at the University of Michigan and a student of TV violence since 1957, is chair of the American Psychological Association's Commission on Violence and Youth. This essay originated in a panel discussion sponsored by the Harvard School of Public Health in 1992.

I don't favor censorship and I am jealous of my First Amendment rights. But I don't think some serious self-regulation and monitoring by the TV and film industry is a threat to our constitutional rights.

It would be appropriate for the FCC to require stations to document what they have done to lower the violence in their programming before their licenses are renewed. . . .

In the spring [of 1992] we had to face the implications of the uncon-   5
trolled violence in Los Angeles. TV cannot escape its share of the responsibility for this outburst. We know that children living in the inner city watch more TV than other children. Children living in the inner city are increasingly surrounded by violence — at home, in the neighborhood, on the way to and from school. They are constantly dodging bullets, cowering in hallways, hiding under tables, because the streets are so dangerous from drive-by shootings and other violence. They spend more and more time indoors watching TV.

And what do they see on TV? More violence. This validates what the children have seen in the neighborhood. It makes violence normative — everyone's doing it, not just in their neighborhood but all over. TV represents violence as an appropriate way to solve interpersonal problems, to get what you want out of life, avenge slights and insults and make up for perceived injustices.

Topics for Critical Thinking and Writing

1. In his first paragraph Eron asserts that a summary of studies shows "convincing evidence that the observation of violence . . . does affect the aggressive behavior of the viewer." Design a study that you think might show the effects of observing violence.

2. Eron says (para. 2) that censorship of violence on TV in Western European countries has led to no complaints "in those democratic countries that their rights have been violated." How might Eron respond if you pointed out to him that those countries do not have a First Amendment that guarantees their citizens "freedom of speech" and freedom of "the press"?

3. Eron thinks (para. 4) that TV stations ought to be required to show "what they have done to lower the violence" in their programs. How do you think the quantity or quality of violence ought to be measured?

4. If, as Eron admits [para. 5], inner-city children live in a world "surrounded by violence," why does he think that reducing fictional portrayals of violence on television will have a beneficial effect?

5. Violence on television is of many kinds — for instance, fictional stories of police, news images of war or murder, nature films of animals preying on other animals, and cartoons of animals knocking other animals around. Do you think episodes in cartoons such as *Bugs Bunny* and *Tom and Jerry* may stimulate children to act violently? Explain.

6. Get a copy of the week's *TV Guide*, turn on your television set, and devote twelve hours (from 10 A.M. to 10 P.M.) gathering your own data firsthand on TV violence. Then write an essay of 750 words explaining your methodology and your conclusions for or against this thesis: "There Is Too Much Violence Shown on Television during Prime-Time Viewing Hours."

Del Reisman

Additional Guidelines for Violence Are Not Called For

The only way to significantly reduce violence, or the threat of violence, in storytelling is for networks and cable to simply not order series or special films which are, virtually by definition, inherently violent, such as action-adventure, crime, futuristic melodrama, etc., and use instead the softer genres, such as we see on the networks now, shows such as *Homefront, Sisters, Northern Exposure,* and so on. Not a very realistic possibility, however.

Networks, as you know, follow. They do not lead. Networks react to social change and community standards. I *know.* I have served as a story editor on many weekly series. Story editors scan the headlines, searching for ways to paraphrase the truth and put it into fictional form. . . .

I believe that additional guidelines for violence should not be called for because they will simply reduce the actual sights of some violence but not the threatening storytelling that builds to it, and therefore such guidelines would be a crumb thrown to those who believe in a causal relationship.

I believe that writers should continue to tell the stories of our time. Abuse in the home toward children, or parents, or grandparents is out of the closest now, thanks to its dramatization on television. Child custody struggles, in which the losing parent literally kidnaps a child, at last is before the American public as the serious social problem that it is. Fictional television has seen this dramatized frequently. Gay bashing has found its way from the dark alleys of our cities to the films of both weekly series and movies-of-the-week. The violence on the home screen *follows* the violence in our lives.

We've lived with Broadcast Standards for forty years, fighting the departments frequently, losing most of the fights, but reacting positively as networks followed changes in community standards from the days of no "hells" and no "damns" to today's relatively explicit language, frank relationships, and open dramatizations of dysfunctional families. Writers want

5

Del Reisman is president of the Writers Guild of America, West. Like the preceding essay, this one originated in a panel discussion sponsored by the Harvard School of Public Health in 1992.

to involve audiences in our stories. Writers are family people, too. We're parents and children and siblings and grandparents and grandchildren. We are community-minded and we care deeply about the world around us. We are as shocked and concerned by what is happening on our streets, on our schoolyards, in our classrooms, and in our homes as any of you. We agree on very little but we do agree on fundamentals, such as freedom of expression and freedom from censorship, the official kind and the unofficial kind which induces self-censorship.

Topics for Critical Thinking and Writing

1. Reisman contrasts (para. 1) "inherently violent" TV films and series with those of "softer genres." Why does he think it is "not a very realistic possibility" that TV networks will shift from screening the former in favor of the latter?

2. Think further about the "inherently violent" genres, such as "action-adventure, crime, [and] futuristic melodrama." If we are convinced that watching such films does indeed make viewers more prone to acts of violence, should we not suppress these programs? Explain.

3. Reisman argues, in paragraph 4, that television tells "the stories of our time." How strong an argument against curbing depictions of violence do you find this? Explain.

4. In his closing paragraph Reisman reminds the reader that writers, too, are people ("parents and children and siblings and grandparents and grandchildren"). What does Reisman hope to accomplish by reminding us of this obvious fact?

Ernest F. Hollings

Save the Children

Imagine an intruder entering your home, seizing your children, and forcing them to watch 8,000 murders and 100,000 acts of violence. A monstrous crime? Yes. A crime that would do untold psychological harm to your children? No question about it.

Wake up, parents. Chances are that your child is the victim I just described. The statistics come from the American Psychological Association, which reported in 1992 that by the end of elementary school, the average American child has watched that many acts of violence on television. Satur-

Ernest F. Hollings, Democrat of South Carolina, is chairman of the Senate Commerce Committee. This essay was originally published in the New York Times *(November 23, 1993) as part of a dialogue called "TV Violence: Survival vs. Censorship," along with an essay by Floyd Abrams (p. 531).*

day morning children's programming leads the way in mayhem and gore, showing an average of thirty-two violent acts per hour.

Enough! It is time for decent Americans to rescue our children from this threat. To that end, I have co-sponsored with Senator Daniel K. Inouye the Children's Protection from Violent Programming Act of 1993, which would ban the broadcast or cable transmission of violent programming during hours when children make up a substantial share of the audience.

At a hearing before the committee in October, TV executives claimed that they have cleaned up their prime-time programming, created monitoring committees, and shown good faith. But we've heard these same hollow pledges for four decades.

Testifying, Attorney General Janet Reno remarked, "Don't things 5 seem upside-down when violent programming is turning television into one more obstacle that parents and teachers have to overcome in order to raise their children?"

First and foremost, the bill to fight TV violence is intended to benefit children — many of them unsupervised, all of them impressionable and vulnerable.

More than one thousand studies — including reports by the Surgeon General, the National Institute of Mental Health, and others — have demonstrated a direct link between exposure to violence in the media and aggressive, violent behavior.

Shamefully, Hollywood and the TV networks have thumbed their nose at this crisis. And they have mobilized to defeat the bill. Many media executives acknowledge the harmful effects of violent programming on children, but insist it isn't their responsibility. Their solution: parents should supervise children's viewing.

But what about the millions of kids whose viewing is unsupervised? A civic leader from South Central Los Angeles told the Commerce Committee that 80 percent of children in inner-city neighborhoods are latchkey kids — kids who return from school to parentless homes, where they spend four to five hours an afternoon, unsupervised, in front of the electronic baby sitter.

Some TV executives claim the bill infringes on their First Amendment 10 right to free speech. Not so, responded Attorney General Reno, testifying that the Supreme Court has upheld a "compelling state interest" in protecting the physical and psychological well-being of children. Under this principle, we have restricted sexual indecency on TV for decades. The same principle applies to violence.

Bear in mind that the legislation in no way seeks to control what adults watch. Premium cable channels such as HBO and Showtime are not covered. Networks and cable channels would remain free to broadcast violent programming during hours when children are not a substantial part of the audience.

For Hollywood, violence and sex translate into profits and market share. This is its corporate bottom line. But our society has a different bottom line. The proposed legislation gives concerned Americans a chance to fight back. If the TV and cable industries have no sense of shame, we must take it upon ourselves to stop licensing their violence-saturated programming.

Topics for Critical Thinking and Writing

1. In his first paragraph Hollings speaks of the 8,000 murders and the 100,000 acts of violence that children are likely to see by the time they complete elementary school. Drawing on your own experience, what sorts of people are treated violently on television?

2. Do you think that the murders and acts of violence you saw on television when you were young influenced your behavior? Often? Sometimes? Rarely? Never? Explain.

3. If you do not think you were influenced by seeing violence on television, do you think that other young people were? If so, why were they influenced but not you?

4. Some researchers argue that although televised violence may increase aggressiveness, it may also have other effects. For instance, it may increase fearfulness of becoming a victim, or it may increase callousness toward violence directed at others. Drawing on your own experience, can you support these views? Explain.

5. Hollings reports (para. 2) that a typical Saturday morning's worth of television for children shows "an average of thirty-two violent acts per hour." On a convenient Saturday morning, turn on your television and do some channel surfing between 8 A.M. and noon. How many "violent acts" did you see? What was your criterion of a "violent act"? Does your research incline you to agree or disagree with the data that Hollings reported?

6. If, as Hollings says in paragraph 9, "80 percent of children in inner-city neighborhoods are latchkey kids," and if we assume that many of their households have not only a TV set but also a VCR, and that children know how to operate a VCR, what's to keep these children from watching all the violence they want by the simple expedient of plugging in a suitable videocassette?

Floyd Abrams

Save Free Speech

As the Senate Commerce Committee's hearings on television violence drew to a close, two Senators argued about a movie.

Senator Conrad Burns had just seen *Rudy* in a theater. Although the movie was violent, he thought it was a "wonderful" and "delightful" story about a Notre Dame football player that the entire family should see on TV.

Senator Byron L. Dorgan disagreed. Seeing the movie in a theater was one thing, he said. Allowing it to come out of "a television box in the living room" was something else.

The exchange was illuminating. We cannot even agree on which violence children should not see. Should it include *Roots* and *Lonesome Dove? The War of the Roses* and *True Grit?* Or is the problem only "bad" violence, the sordid and frightening depiction, cited by Senator Paul Simon, of some fiend on the attack with a chainsaw?

Laws don't have vocabularies that distinguish between good and bad   5
violence. Adjectives help when we speak to each other — words like "sordid" and "frightening." Even a word like "bad." But these are not and cannot be the words of legislation.

If they were, we would need a constantly monitoring Federal Communications Commission deciding on matters of subjective taste and psychological reality: which violence is constructive, which gratuitous. We would, in short, need a national censorship board. But that is the world of the Ayatollah, not ours.

Even objective criteria would not help. How many bullets are too many? How much violence is too much? Does it matter if the movie is *Glory* or *Gettysburg?* Or the latest remake of *Nightmare on Elm Street?* Or if the characters are Tom or Jerry?

One proposal is that Congress should bar the showing of *any* act of violence on TV in the evening before, say, 11 P.M. That is the heart of the legislation proposed by Senators Ernest F. Hollings and Daniel K. Inouye.

No program or film with any violence, whatever its artistic value or potential social benefit, could thus be shown at a time when most adults and most children watch TV. Not *Rudy.* Not *A Streetcar Named Desire.* We could watch *Married With Children* but not *War and Remembrance,* *Star Search* but not *Star Wars.*

This is censorship, plain and simple. It is no less so because the legisla- 10

Floyd Abrams, a lawyer, has represented the New York Times, *other newspapers, and broadcasters. This essay was first published, along with the preceding essay by Senator Ernest F. Hollings (p. 528), in the* New York Times *(November 23, 1993), as part of a dialogue called "TV Violence: Survival vs. Censorship."*

tion is designed to protect children. As the Supreme Court Justice Felix Frankfurter put it in a 1957 opinion, we may not "reduce the adult population" to material "fit for children."

Justice Lewis Powell added a related conclusion in an opinion seventeen years later: "Speech that is neither obscene as to youths nor subject to some other legitimate prescription cannot be suppressed solely to protect the young from ideas or images that a legislative body thinks unsuitable for them."

That is precisely what all of the anti-violence legislation before Congress seeks to do. Much of it is justified on the ground that since Congress can regulate "indecency" on TV, it should be permitted to regulate violence as well.

But the depiction of violence, some of which is contained in the greatest works of literature and film, is hardly equivalent to that of "indecent material" — material that a much disputed 5–4 Supreme Court opinion in 1978 concluded "surely lies at the periphery of First Amendment concern."

Whatever the correctness of that ruling, there is nothing peripheral to the First Amendment of much of the TV programming that so many in Congress seek to regulate. Senator Burns was right: It is not for Congress to choose whether or when we see *Rudy* on TV. And he was right about something else. Legislation in this area cannot be passed "that would stay within the Constitution."

Topics for Critical Thinking and Writing

1. Abrams argues that reasonable people cannot agree on how to distinguish between "good and bad violence" (para. 5). Try to formulate a distinction — perhaps working with three or four of your classmates. Begin with examples that seem obvious and then work toward a grayer area but where you still think a line can be drawn. If you can think of an example that in your opinion could go on either side, briefly summarize the example and explain why you think it cannot be firmly classified.

2. Abrams argues that just because "Congress can regulate 'indecency,'" it doesn't follow that Congress can or ought to regulate violence (para. 12). How would Abrams reply to these objections: (1) Surely, depictions of violence can be far more harmful to the young than any depictions of indecency. (2) If publishers can comply with regulations against indecency, there is no good reason why movie and television producers cannot also comply with regulations against violence. (3) Censorship of violence is no more unreasonable than censorship of indecency — and since we have the latter, why not have the former, too?

3. How might Hollings reply to Abrams's point that under the Hollings-Inouye plan, families could not watch, say, *A Streetcar Named Desire* before 11 P.M.?

Part Three

READINGS: ENDURING QUESTIONS

17

What Is the Ideal Society?

Thomas More

From *Utopia*

[A DAY IN UTOPIA]

And now for their working conditions. Well, there's one job they all do, irrespective of sex, and that's farming. It's part of every child's education. They learn the principles of agriculture at school, and they're taken for regular outings into the fields near the town, where they not only watch farm work being done, but also do some themselves, as a form of exercise.

Besides farming which, as I say, is everybody's job, each person is taught a special trade of his own. He may be trained to process wool or flax, or he may become a stonemason, a blacksmith, or a carpenter. Those are the only trades that employ any considerable quantity of labor. They

The son of a prominent London lawyer, More (1478–1535) served as a page in the household of the Archbishop of Canterbury, went to Oxford, and then studied law in London. More's charm, brilliance, and gentle manner caused Erasmus, the great Dutch humanist who became his friend during a visit to London, to write to a friend: "Did nature ever create anything kinder, sweeter, or more harmonious than the character of Thomas More?"

More served in Parliament, became a diplomat, and after holding several important positions in the government of Henry VIII, rose to become Lord Chancellor. But when Henry married Anne Boleyn, broke from the Church of Rome, and

have no tailors or dressmakers, since everyone on the island wears the same sort of clothes—except that they vary slightly according to sex and marital status—and the fashion never changes. These clothes are quite pleasant to look at, they allow free movement of the limbs, they're equally suitable for hot and cold weather—and the great thing is, they're all home-made. So everybody learns one of the other trades I mentioned, and by everybody I mean the women as well as the men—though the weaker sex are given the lighter jobs, like spinning and weaving, while the men do the heavier ones.

Most children are brought up to do the same work as their parents, since they tend to have a natural feeling for it. But if a child fancies some other trade, he's adopted into a family that practices it. Of course, great care is taken, not only by the father, but also by the local authorities, to see that the foster father is a decent, respectable type. When you've learned one trade properly, you can, if you like, get permission to learn another—and when you're an expert in both, you can practice whichever you prefer, unless the other one is more essential to the public.

The chief business of the Stywards[1]—in fact, practically their only business—is to see that nobody sits around doing nothing, but that every-

---

[1]**Stywards** In Utopia, each group of thirty households elects a styward; each town has two hundred stywards, who elect the mayor. [All notes are the editors'.]

---

established himself as head of the Church of England, More refused to subscribe to the Act of Succession and Supremacy. Condemned to death as a traitor, he still refused to accept Henry as head of the church and so was executed in 1535, nominally for treason but really because he would not recognize the king rather than the pope as the head of his church. A moment before the ax fell, More displayed a bit of the whimsy for which he was known: When he put his head on the block, he brushed his beard aside, commenting that his beard had done no offense to the king. In 1886 the Roman Catholic Church beatified More, and in 1935, the four-hundredth anniversary of his death, it canonized him as St. Thomas More.

More wrote Utopia *(1514–1515) in Latin, the international language of the day. The book's name, however, is Greek for "no place" (ou topos), with a pun on "good place" (eu topos).* Utopia *owes something to Plato's* Republic, *and something to then-popular accounts of voyagers such as Amerigo Vespucci.* Utopia *purports to record an account given by a traveler named Hytholodaeus (Greek for "learned in nonsense"), who allegedly visited Utopia. The work is playful, but it is also serious. In truth, it is hard to know exactly where it is serious, and how serious it is. One inevitably wonders, for example, if More the devoted Roman Catholic could really have advocated euthanasia. And could More the persecutor of heretics really have approved of the religious tolerance practiced in Utopia? Is he perhaps in effect saying, "Let's see what reason, unaided by Christian revelation, can tell us about an ideal society"? But if so is he nevertheless also saying, very strongly, that Christian countries, though blessed with the revelation of Christ's teachings, are far behind these unenlightened pagans?* Utopia *has been widely praised by all sorts of readers—from Roman Catholics to communists—but for all sorts of reasons.*

The selection here is about one-twelfth of the book.

one gets on with his job. They don't wear people out, though, by keeping them hard at work from early morning till late at night, like cart horses. That's just slavery—and yet that's what life is like for the working classes nearly everywhere else in the world. In Utopia they have a six-hour working day—three hours in the morning, then lunch—then a two-hour break —then three more hours in the afternoon, followed by supper. They go to bed at 8 P.M., and sleep for eight hours. All the rest of the twenty-four they're free to do what they like—not to waste their time in idleness or self-indulgence, but to make good use of it in some congenial activity. Most people spend these free periods on further education, for there are public lectures first thing every morning. Attendance is quite voluntary, except for those picked out for academic training, but men and women of all classes go crowding in to hear them—I mean, different people go to different lectures, just as the spirit moves them. However, there's nothing to stop you from spending this extra time on your trade, if you want to. Lots of people do, if they haven't the capacity for intellectual work, and are much admired for such public-spirited behavior.

After supper they have an hour's recreation, either in the gardens or in   5 the communal dining-halls, according to the time of year. Some people practice music, others just talk. They've never heard of anything so silly and demoralizing as dice, but they have two games rather like chess. The first is a sort of arithmetical contest, in which certain numbers "take" others. The second is a pitched battle between virtues and vices, which illustrates most ingeniously how vices tend to conflict with one another, but to combine against virtues. It also shows which vices are opposed to which virtues, how much strength vices can muster for a direct assault, what indirect tactics they employ, what help virtues need to overcome vices, what are the best methods of evading their attacks, and what ultimately determines the victory of one side or the other.

But here's a point that requires special attention, or you're liable to get the wrong idea. Since they only work a six-hour day, you may think there must be a shortage of essential goods. On the contrary, those six hours are enough, and more than enough to produce plenty of everything that's needed for a comfortable life. And you'll understand why it is, if you reckon up how large a proportion of the population in other countries is totally unemployed. First you have practically all the women—that gives you nearly 50 percent for a start. And in countries where the women *do* work, the men tend to lounge about instead. Then there are all the priests, and members of so-called religious orders—how much work do they do? Add all the rich, especially the landowners, popularly known as nobles and gentlemen. Include their domestic staffs—I mean those gangs of armed ruffians that I mentioned before. Finally, throw in all the beggars who are perfectly hale and hearty, but pretend to be ill as an excuse for being lazy. When you've counted them up, you'll be surprised to find how few people actually produce what the human race consumes.

And now just think how few of these few people are doing essential work—for where money is the only standard of value, there are bound to be dozens of unnecessary trades carried on, which merely supply luxury goods or entertainment. Why, even if the existing labor force were distributed among the few trades really needed to make life reasonably comfortable, there'd be so much overproduction that prices would fall too low for the workers to earn a living. Whereas, if you took all those engaged in nonessential trades, and all who are too lazy to work—each of whom consumes twice as much of the products of other people's labor as any of the producers themselves—if you put the whole lot of them on to something useful, you'd soon see how few hours' work a day would be amply sufficient to supply all the necessities and comforts of life—to which you might add all real and natural forms of pleasure.

[THE HOUSEHOLD]

But let's get back to their social organization. Each household, as I said, comes under the authority of the oldest male. Wives are subordinate to their husbands, children to their parents, and younger people generally to their elders. Every town is divided into four districts of equal size, each with its own shopping center in the middle of it. There the products of every household are collected in warehouses, and then distributed according to type among various shops. When the head of a household needs anything for himself or his family, he just goes to one of these shops and asks for it. And whatever he asks for, he's allowed to take away without any sort of payment, either in money or in kind. After all, why shouldn't he? There's more than enough of everything to go round, so there's no risk of his asking for more than he needs—for why should anyone want to start hoarding, when he knows he'll never have to go short of anything? No living creature is naturally greedy, except from fear of want—or in the case of human beings, from vanity, the notion that you're better than people if you can display more superfluous property than they can. But there's no scope for that sort of thing in Utopia.

[UTOPIAN BELIEFS]

The Utopians fail to understand why anyone should be so fascinated by the dull gleam of a tiny bit of stone, when he has all the stars in the sky to look at—or how anyone can be silly enough to think himself better than other people, because his clothes are made of finer woollen thread than theirs. After all, those fine clothes were once worn by a sheep, and they never turned it into anything better than a sheep.

Nor can they understand why a totally useless substance like gold 10 should now, all over the world, be considered far more important than human beings, who gave it such value as it has, purely for their own convenience. The result is that a man with about as much mental agility as a lump of lead or a block of wood, a man whose utter stupidity is paralleled only by his immorality, can have lots of good, intelligent people at his beck and call, just because he happens to possess a large pile of gold coins. And if by some freak of fortune or trick of the law—two equally effective methods of turning things upside down—the said coins were suddenly transferred to the most worthless member of his domestic staff, you'd soon see the present owner trotting after his money, like an extra piece of currency, and becoming his own servant's servant. But what puzzles and disgusts the Utopians even more is the idiotic way some people have of practically worshipping a rich man, not because they owe him money or are otherwise in his power, but simply because he's rich—although they know perfectly well that he's far too mean to let a single penny come their way, so long as he's alive to stop it.

They get these ideas partly from being brought up under a social system which is directly opposed to that type of nonsense, and partly from their reading and education. Admittedly, no one's allowed to become a full-time student, except for the very few in each town who appear as children to possess unusual gifts, outstanding intelligence, and a special aptitude for academic research. But every child receives a primary education, and most men and women go on educating themselves all their lives during those free periods that I told you about. . . .

In ethics they discuss the same problems as we do. Having distinguished between three types of "good," psychological, physiological, and environmental, they proceed to ask whether the term is strictly applicable to all of them, or only to the first. They also argue about such things as virtue and pleasure. But their chief subject of dispute is the nature of human happiness—on what factor or factors does it depend? Here they seem rather too much inclined to take a hedonistic view, for according to them human happiness consists largely or wholly in pleasure. Surprisingly enough, they defend this self-indulgent doctrine by arguments drawn from religion—a thing normally associated with a more serious view of life, if not with gloomy asceticism. You see, in all their discussions of happiness they invoke certain religious principles to supplement the operations of reason, which they think otherwise ill-equipped to identify true happiness.

The first principle is that every soul is immortal, and was created by a kind God, Who meant it to be happy. The second is that we shall be rewarded or punished in the next world for our good or bad behavior in this one. Although these are religious principles, the Utopians find rational grounds for accepting them. For suppose you didn't accept them? In that case, they say, any fool could tell you what you ought to do. You should go all out for your own pleasure, irrespective of right and wrong. You'd merely have to make sure that minor pleasures didn't interfere with major ones, and avoid the type of pleasure that has painful aftereffects. For what's the sense of struggling to be virtuous, denying yourself the pleasant things of life, and deliberately making yourself uncomfortable, if there's nothing you hope to gain by it? And what *can* you hope to gain by it, if you receive no compensation after death for a thoroughly unpleasant, that is, a thoroughly miserable life?

Not that they identify happiness with every type of pleasure — only with the higher ones. Nor do they identify it with virtue — unless they belong to a quite different school of thought. According to the normal view, happiness is the *summum bonum*[2] toward which we're naturally impelled by virtue — which in their definition means following one's natural impulses, as God meant us to do. But this includes obeying the instinct to be reasonable in our likes and dislikes. And reason also teaches us, first to love and reverence Almighty God, to Whom we owe our existence and our potentiality for happiness, and secondly to get through life as comfortably and cheerfully as we can, and help all other members of our species to do so too.

The fact is, even the sternest ascetic tends to be slightly inconsistent in   15
his condemnation of pleasure. He may sentence *you* to a life of hard labor, inadequate sleep, and general discomfort, but he'll also tell you to do your best to ease the pains and privations of others. He'll regard all such attempts to improve the human situation as laudable acts of humanity — for obviously nothing could be more humane, or more natural for a human being, than to relieve other people's sufferings, put an end to their miseries, and restore their *joie de vivre*, that is, their capacity for pleasure. So why shouldn't it be equally natural to do the same thing for oneself?

Either it's a bad thing to enjoy life, in other words, to experience pleasure — in which case you shouldn't help anyone to do it, but should try to save the whole human race from such a frightful fate — or else, if it's good for other people, and you're not only allowed, but positively obliged to make it possible for them, why shouldn't charity begin at home? After all, you've a duty to yourself as well as to your neighbor, and, if Nature says you must be kind to others, she can't turn round the next moment and say you must be cruel to yourself. The Utopians therefore regard the enjoyment of life — that is, pleasure — as the natural object of all human efforts, and natural, as they define it, is synonymous with virtuous. However, Nature also wants us to help one another to enjoy life, for the very good reason that no human being has a monopoly of her affections. She's equally anxious for the welfare of every member of the species. So of course she tells us to make quite sure that we don't pursue our own interests at the expense of other people's.

On this principle they think it right to keep one's promises in private life, and also to obey public laws for regulating the distribution of "goods" — by which I mean the raw materials of pleasure — provided such laws have been properly made by a wise ruler, or passed by common consent of a whole population, which has not been subjected to any form of violence or deception. Within these limits they say it's sensible to consult one's own interests, and a moral duty to consult those of the community as

---

[2]*summum bonum* Latin for "the highest good."

well. It's wrong to deprive someone else of a pleasure so that you can enjoy one yourself, but to deprive yourself of a pleasure so that you can add to someone else's enjoyment is an act of humanity by which you always gain more than you lose. For one thing, such benefits are usually repaid in kind. For another, the mere sense of having done somebody a kindness, and so earned his affection and goodwill, produces a spiritual satisfaction which far outweighs the loss of a physical one. And lastly—a belief that comes easily to a religious mind—God will reward us for such small sacrifices of momentary pleasure, by giving us an eternity of perfect joy. Thus they argue that, in the final analysis, pleasure is the ultimate happiness which all human beings have in view, even when they're acting most virtuously.

Pleasure they define as any state or activity, physical or mental, which is naturally enjoyable. The operative word is *naturally*. According to them, we're impelled by reason as well as an instinct to enjoy ourselves in any natural way which doesn't hurt other people, interfere with greater pleasures, or cause unpleasant aftereffects. But human beings have entered into an idiotic conspiracy to call some things enjoyable which are naturally nothing of the kind—as though facts were as easily changed as definitions. Now the Utopians believe that, so far from contributing to happiness, this type of thing makes happiness impossible—because, once you get used to it, you lose all capacity for real pleasure, and are merely obsessed by illusory forms of it. Very often these have nothing pleasant about them at all— in fact, most of them are thoroughly disagreeable. But they appeal so strongly to perverted tastes that they come to be reckoned not only among the major pleasures of life, but even among the chief reasons for living.

In the category of illusory pleasure addicts they include the kind of person I mentioned before, who thinks himself better than other people because he's better dressed than they are. Actually he's just as wrong about his clothes as he is about himself. From a practical point of view, why is it better to be dressed in fine woollen thread than in coarse? But he's got it into his head that fine thread is naturally superior, and that wearing it somehow increases his own value. So he feels entitled to far more respect than he'd ever dare to hope for, if he were less expensively dressed, and is most indignant if he fails to get it.

Talking of respect, isn't it equally idiotic to attach such importance to 20 a lot of empty gestures which do nobody any good? For what real pleasure can you get out of the sight of a bared head or a bent knee? Will it cure the rheumatism in your own knee, or make you any less weak in the head? Of course, the great believers in this type of artificial pleasure are those who pride themselves on their "nobility." Nowadays that merely means that they happen to belong to a family which has been rich for several generations, preferably in landed property. And yet they feel every bit as "noble" even if they've failed to inherit any of the said property, or if they have inherited it and then frittered it all away.

Then there's another type of person I mentioned before, who has a passion for jewels, and feels practically superhuman if he manages to get hold of a rare one, especially if it's a kind that's considered particularly precious in his country and period—for the value of such things varies according to where and when you live. But he's so terrified of being taken in by appearances that he refuses to buy any jewel until he's stripped off all the gold and inspected it in the nude. And even then he won't buy it without a solemn assurance and a written guarantee from the jeweler that the stone is genuine. But my dear sir, why shouldn't a fake give you just as much pleasure, if you can't, with your own eyes, distinguish it from a real one? It makes no difference to you whether it's genuine or not—any more than it would to a blind man!

And now, what about those people who accumulate superfluous wealth, for no better purpose than to enjoy looking at it? Is their pleasure a real one, or merely a form of delusion? The opposite type of psychopath buries his gold, so that he'll never be able to use it, and may never even see it again. In fact, he deliberately loses it in his anxiety not to lose it—for what can you call it but lost, when it's put back into the earth, where it's no good to him, or probably to anyone else? And yet he's tremendously happy when he's got it stowed away. Now, apparently, he can stop worrying. But suppose the money is stolen, and ten years later he dies without ever knowing it has gone. Then for a whole ten years he has managed to survive his loss, and during that period what difference has it made to him whether the money was there or not? It was just as little use to him either way.

Among stupid pleasures they include not only gambling—a form of idiocy that they've heard about but never practiced—but also hunting and hawking. What on earth is the fun, they ask, of throwing dice onto a table? Besides, you've done it so often that, even if there was some fun in it at first, you must surely be sick of it by now. How can you possibly enjoy listening to anything so disagreeable as the barking and howling of dogs? And why is it more amusing to watch a dog chasing a hare than to watch one dog chasing another? In each case the essential activity is running—if running is what amuses you. But if it's really the thought of being in at the death, and seeing an animal torn to pieces before your eyes, wouldn't pity be a more appropriate reaction to the sight of a weak, timid, harmless little creature like a hare being devoured by something so much stronger and fiercer?

So the Utopians consider hunting below the dignity of free men, and leave it entirely to butchers, who are, as I told you, slaves. In their view hunting is the vilest department of butchery, compared with which all the others are relatively useful and honorable. An ordinary butcher slaughters livestock far more sparingly, and only because he has to, whereas a hunter kills and mutilates poor little creatures purely for his own amusement. They say you won't find that type of blood lust even among animals, unless they're particularly savage by nature, or have become so by constantly being used for this cruel sport.

There are hundreds of things like that, which are generally regarded 25 as pleasures, but everyone in Utopia is quite convinced that they've got nothing to do with real pleasure, because there's nothing naturally enjoyable about them. Nor is this conviction at all shaken by the argument that most people do actually enjoy them, which would seem to indicate an appreciable pleasure content. They say this is a purely subjective reaction caused by bad habits, which can make a person prefer unpleasant things to pleasant ones, just as pregnant women sometimes lose their sense of taste, and find suet or turpentine more delicious than honey. But however much one's judgment may be impaired by habit or ill health, the nature of pleasure, as of everything else, remains unchanged.

Real pleasures they divide into two categories, mental and physical. Mental pleasures include the satisfaction that one gets from understanding something, or from contemplating truth. They also include the memory of a well-spent life, and the confident expectation of good things to come. Physical pleasures are subdivided into two types. First there are those which fill the whole organism with a conscious sense of enjoyment. This may be the result of replacing physical substances which have been burnt up by the natural heat of the body, as when we eat or drink. Or else it may be caused by the discharge of some excess, as in excretion, sexual intercourse, or any relief of irritation by rubbing or scratching. However, there are also pleasures which satisfy no organic need, and relieve no previous discomfort. They merely act, in a mysterious but quite unmistakable way, directly on our senses, and monopolize their reactions. Such is the pleasure of music.

Their second type of physical pleasure arises from the calm and regular functioning of the body — that is, from a state of health undisturbed by any minor ailments. In the absence of mental discomfort, this gives one a good feeling, even without the help of external pleasures. Of course, it's less ostentatious, and forces itself less violently on one's attention than the cruder delights of eating and drinking, but even so it's often considered the greatest pleasure in life. Practically everyone in Utopia would agree that it's a very important one, because it's the basis of all the others. It's enough by itself to make you enjoy life, and unless you have it, no other pleasure is possible. However, mere freedom from pain, without positive health, they would call not pleasure but anesthesia.

Some thinkers used to maintain that a uniformly tranquil state of health couldn't properly be termed a pleasure since its presence could only be detected by contrast with its opposite — oh yes, they went very thoroughly into the whole question. But that theory was exploded long ago, and nowadays nearly everybody subscribes to the view that health is most definitely a pleasure. The argument goes like this — illness involves pain, which is the direct opposite of pleasure, and illness is the direct opposite of health, therefore health involves pleasure. They don't think it matters whether you say that illness *is* or merely *involves* pain. Either way it comes to the same thing. Similarly, whether health *is* a pleasure, or merely *produces* pleasure as inevitably as fire produces heat, it's equally logical to assume that where you have an uninterrupted state of health you cannot fail to have pleasure.

Besides, they say, when we eat something, what really happens is this. Our failing health starts fighting off the attacks of hunger, using the food as an ally. Gradually it begins to prevail, and, in this very process of winning back its normal strength, experiences the sense of enjoyment which we find so refreshing. Now, if health enjoys the actual battle, why shouldn't it also enjoy the victory? Or are we to suppose that when it has finally managed to regain its former vigor — the one thing that it has been fighting for all this time — it promptly falls into a coma, and fails to notice or take advantage of its success? As for the idea that one isn't conscious of health except through its opposite, they say that's quite untrue. Everyone's perfectly aware of feeling well, unless he's asleep or actually feeling ill. Even the most insensitive and apathetic sort of person will admit that it's delightful to be healthy — and what is delight, but a synonym for pleasure?

They're particularly fond of mental pleasures, which they consider of 30 primary importance, and attribute mostly to good behavior and a clear conscience. Their favorite physical pleasure is health. Of course, they believe in enjoying food, drink, and so forth, but purely in the interests of health, for they don't regard such things as very pleasant in themselves — only as methods of resisting the stealthy onset of disease. A sensible person, they say, prefers keeping well to taking medicine, and would rather feel cheerful than have people trying to comfort him. On the same principle it's better not to need this type of pleasure than to become addicted to it. For, if you think that sort of thing will make you happy, you'll have to admit that your idea of perfect felicity would be a life consisting entirely of hunger, thirst, itching, eating, drinking, rubbing, and scratching — which would obviously be most unpleasant as well as quite disgusting. Undoubtedly these pleasures should come right at the bottom of the list, because they're so impure. For instance, the pleasure of eating is invariably diluted with the pain of hunger, and not in equal proportions either — for the pain is both more intense and more prolonged. It starts before the pleasure, and doesn't stop until the pleasure has stopped too.

So they don't think much of pleasures like that, except insofar as they're necessary. But they enjoy them all the same, and feel most grateful to Mother Nature for encouraging her children to do things that have to be done so often, by making them so attractive. For just think how dreary life would be, if those chronic ailments, hunger and thirst, could only be cured by foul-tasting medicines, like the rarer types of disease!

They attach great value to special natural gifts such as beauty, strength, and agility. They're also keen on the pleasures of sight, hearing, and smell, which are peculiar to human beings — for no other species admires the beauty of the world, enjoys any sort of scent, except as a method of locating food, or can tell the difference between a harmony and a discord. They say these things give a sort of relish to life.

However, in all such matters they observe the rule that minor pleasures mustn't interfere with major ones, and that pleasure mustn't cause pain — which they think is bound to happen, if the pleasure is immoral.

But they'd never dream of despising their own beauty, overtaxing their strength, converting their agility into inertia, ruining their physique by going without food, damaging their health, or spurning any other of Nature's gifts, unless they were doing it for the benefit of other people or of society, in the hope of receiving some greater pleasure from God in return. For they think it's quite absurd to torment oneself in the name of an unreal virtue, which does nobody any good, or in order to steel oneself against disasters which may never occur. They say such behavior is merely self-destructive, and shows a most ungrateful attitude toward Nature—as if one refused all her favors, because one couldn't bear the thought of being indebted to her for anything.

Well, that's their ethical theory, and short of some divine revelation, they doubt if the human mind is capable of devising a better one. We've no time to discuss whether it's right or wrong—nor is it really necessary, for all I undertook was to describe their way of life, not to defend it.

[TREATMENT OF THE DYING]

As I told you, when people are ill, they're looked after most sympa- 35 thetically, and given everything in the way of medicine or special food that could possibly assist their recovery. In the case of permanent invalids, the nurses try to make them feel better by sitting and talking to them, and do all they can to relieve their symptoms. But if, besides being incurable, the disease also causes constant excruciating pain, some priests and government officials visit the person concerned, and say something like this:

"Let's face it, you'll never be able to live a normal life. You're just a nuisance to other people and a burden to yourself—in fact you're really leading a sort of posthumous existence. So why go on feeding germs? Since your life's a misery to you, why hesitate to die? You're imprisoned in a torture chamber—why don't you break out and escape to a better world? Or say the word, and we'll arrange for your release. It's only common sense to cut your losses. It's also an act of piety to take the advice of a priest, because he speaks for God."

If the patient finds these arguments convincing, he either starves himself to death, or is given a soporific and put painlessly out of his misery. But this is strictly voluntary, and, if he prefers to stay alive, everyone will go on treating him as kindly as ever.

[THE SUMMING UP]

Well, that's the most accurate account I can give you of the Utopian Republic. To my mind, it's not only the best country in the world, but the only one that has any right to call itself a republic. Elsewhere, people are always talking about the public interest, but all they really care about is private property. In Utopia, where's there's no private property, people take their duty to the public seriously. And both attitudes are perfectly reasonable. In other "republics" practically everyone knows that, if he doesn't look out for himself, he'll starve to death, however prosperous his country may be. He's therefore compelled to give his own interests priority over those of the public; that is, of other people. But in Utopia, where everything's under public ownership, no one has any fear of going short, as long as the public storehouses are full. Everyone gets a fair share, so there are never any poor men or beggars. Nobody owns anything, but everyone is rich — for what greater wealth can there be than cheerfulness, peace of mind, and freedom from anxiety? Instead of being worried about his food supply, upset by the plaintive demands of his wife, afraid of poverty for his son, and baffled by the problem of finding a dowry for his daughter, the Utopian can feel absolutely sure that he, his wife, his children, his grandchildren, his great-grandchildren, his great-great-grandchildren, and as long a line of descendants as the proudest peer could wish to look forward to, will always have enough to eat and enough to make them happy. There's also the further point that those who are too old to work are just as well provided for as those who are still working.

Now, will anyone venture to compare these fair arrangements in Utopia with the so-called justice of other countries? — in which I'm damned if I can see the slightest trace of justice or fairness. For what sort of justice do you call this? People like aristocrats, goldsmiths, or moneylenders, who either do no work at all, or do work that's really not essential, are rewarded for their laziness or their unnecessary activities by a splendid life of luxury. But laborers, coachmen, carpenters, and farmhands, who never stop working like cart horses, at jobs so essential that, if they *did* stop working, they'd bring any country to a standstill within twelve months — what happens to them? They get so little to eat, and have such a wretched time, that they'd be almost better off if they *were* cart horses. Then at least, they wouldn't work quite such long hours, their food wouldn't be very much worse, they'd enjoy it more, and they'd have no fears for the future. As it is, they're not only ground down by unrewarding toil in the present, but also worried to death by the prospect of a poverty-stricken old age — since their daily wages aren't enough to support them for one day, let alone leave anything over to be saved up when they're old.

Can you see any fairness or gratitude in a social system which lavishes 40 such great rewards on so-called noblemen, goldsmiths, and people like that, who are either totally unproductive or merely employed in producing luxury goods or entertainment, but makes no such kind provision for farmhands, coal heavers, laborers, carters, or carpenters, without whom society couldn't exist at all? And the climax of ingratitude comes when they're old and ill and completely destitute. Having taken advantage of them throughout the best years of their lives, society now forgets all the sleepless hours they've spent in its service, and repays them for all the vital work they've done, by letting them die in misery. What's more, the wretched earnings of the poor are daily whittled away by the rich, not only through private dishonesty, but through public legislation. As if it weren't unjust enough already that the man who contributes most to society should get the least in return, they make it even worse, and then arrange for injustice to be legally described as justice.

In fact, when I consider any social system that prevails in the modern world, I can't, so help me God, see it as anything but a conspiracy of the rich to advance their own interests under the pretext of organizing society. They think up all sorts of tricks and dodges, first for keeping safe their ill-gotten gains, and then for exploiting the poor by buying their labor as cheaply as possible. Once the rich have decided that these tricks and dodges shall be officially recognized by society — which includes the poor as well as the rich — they acquire the force of law. Thus an unscrupulous minority is led by its insatiable greed to monopolize what would have been enough to supply the needs of the whole population. And yet how much happier even these people would be in Utopia! There, with the simultaneous abolition of money and the passion for money, how many other social problems have been solved, how many crimes eradicated! For obviously the end of money means the end of all those types of criminal behavior which daily punishments are powerless to check: fraud, theft, burglary, brawls, riots, disputes, rebellion, murder, treason, and black magic. And the moment money goes, you can also say goodbye to fear, tension, anxiety, overwork, and sleepless nights. Why, even poverty itself, the one problem that has always seemed to need money for its solution, would promptly disappear if money ceased to exist.

Let me try to make this point clearer. Just think back to one of the years when the harvest was bad, and thousands of people died of starvation. Well, I bet if you'd inspected every rich man's barn at the end of that lean period you'd have found enough corn to have saved all the lives that were lost through malnutrition and disease, and prevented anyone from suffering any ill effects whatever from the meanness of the weather and the soil. Everyone could so easily get enough to eat, if it weren't for that blessed nuisance, money. There you have a brilliant invention which was designed to make food more readily available. Actually it's the only thing that makes it unobtainable.

I'm sure that even the rich are well aware of all this, and realize how much better it would be to have everything one needed, than lots of things one didn't need — to be evacuated altogether from the danger area, than to dig oneself in behind a barricade of enormous wealth. And I've no doubt that either self-interest, or the authority of our Savior Christ — Who was far too wise not to know what was best for us, and far too kind to recommend anything else — would have led the whole world to adopt the Utopian system long ago, if it weren't for that beastly root of all evils, pride. For pride's criterion of prosperity is not what you've got yourself, but what other people haven't got. Pride would refuse to set foot in paradise, if she thought there'd be no underprivileged classes there to gloat over and order about—nobody whose misery could serve as a foil to her own happiness, or whose poverty she could make harder to bear, by flaunting her own riches. Pride, like a hellish serpent gliding through human hearts—or shall we say, like a sucking-fish that clings to the ship of state?—is always dragging us back, and obstructing our progress toward a better way of life.

But as this fault is too deeply ingrained in human nature to be easily eradicated, I'm glad that at least one country has managed to develop a system which I'd like to see universally adopted. The Utopian way of life provides not only the happiest basis for a civilized community, but also one which, in all human probability, will last forever. They've eliminated the root causes of ambition, political conflict, and everything like that. There's therefore no danger of internal dissension, the one thing that has destroyed so many impregnable towns. And as long as there's unity and sound administration at home, no matter how envious neighboring kings may feel, they'll never be able to shake, let alone to shatter, the power of Utopia. They've tried to do so often enough in the past, but have always been beaten back.

Topics for Critical Thinking and Writing

1. More, writing early in the sixteenth century, of course was living in a primarily agricultural society. Laborers were needed on farms; but might More have had any other reason for insisting that all people should do some farming, and that farming should be part of "every child's education"? Do you think everyone should put in some time as a farmer? Why, or why not?

2. More indicates that in the England of his day many people loafed or engaged in unnecessary work (producing luxury goods, for one thing), putting an enormous burden on those who engaged in useful work. Is this condition, or any part of it, true of our society? Explain.

3. The Utopians cannot understand why the people of other nations value gems, gold, and fine clothes. If you value any of these, can you offer an explanation?

4. What arguments can you offer against the Utopians' treatment of persons who are incurably ill and in pain? (You may get some ideas from the essays by Goodman, p. 425; Pies, p. 439; and Jacoby, p. 441.)

5. Summarize More's report of the Utopians' idea of pleasure. (This summary will probably take three or four paragraphs.)

6. More's Utopians cannot understand why anyone takes pleasure in gambling or in hunting. If either activity gives you pleasure, in an essay of 500 words explain why, and offer an argument on behalf of your view.

7. As More makes clear in the part we entitle "The Summing Up," in Utopia there is no private property. In a sentence or two summarize the reasons he gives for this principle, and then in a paragraph evaluate them.

Niccolò Machiavelli

From *The Prince*

ON THOSE THINGS FOR WHICH MEN, AND PARTICULARLY PRINCES, ARE PRAISED OR BLAMED

Now there remains to be examined what should be the methods and procedures of a prince in dealing with his subjects and friends. And because I know that many have written about this, I am afraid that by writing about it again I shall be thought of as presumptuous, since in discussing this material I depart radically from the procedures of others. But since my intention is to write something useful for anyone who understands it, it seemed more suitable to me to search after the effectual truth of the matter rather than its imagined one. And many writers have imagined for themselves republics and principalities that have never been seen nor known to exist in reality; for there is such a gap between how one lives and how one ought to live that anyone who abandons what is done for what ought to be done learns his ruin rather than his preservation: for a man who wishes to make a vocation of being good at all times will come to ruin

---

Niccolò Machiavelli (1469–1527) was born in Florence at a time when Italy was divided into five major states: Venice, Milan, Florence, the Papal States, and Naples. Although these states often had belligerent relations with one another as well as with lesser Italian states, under the Medici family in Florence they achieved a precarious balance of power. In 1494, however, Lorenzo de' Medici, who had ruled from 1469 to 1492, died, and two years later Lorenzo's successor was exiled when the French army arrived in Florence. Italy became a field where Spain, France, and Germany competed for power. From 1498 to 1512 Machiavelli held a high post in the diplomatic service of the Florentine Republic, but when the French army reappeared and the Florentines in desperation recalled the Medici, Machiavelli lost his post, was imprisoned, tortured, and then exiled. Banished from Florence, he nevertheless lived in fair comfort on a small estate nearby, writing his major works and hoping to obtain an office from the Medici. In later years he was employed in a few minor diplomatic missions, but even after the collapse and expulsion of the Medici in 1527, and the restoration of the republic, he did not regain his old position of importance. He died shortly after the restoration.

Our selection comes from The Prince, *which Machiavelli wrote in 1513 during his banishment hoping that it would interest the Medici and thus restore him to favor; but the book was not published until 1532, five years after his death. In this book of twenty-six short chapters, Machiavelli begins by examining different kinds of states, but the work's enduring power resides in the discussions (in Chapters 15–18, reprinted here) of qualities necessary to a prince, that is, a head of state. Any such examination obviously is based in part on assumptions about the nature of the citizens of the realm.*

among so many who are not good. Hence it is necessary for a prince who wishes to maintain his position to learn how not to be good, and to use this knowledge or not to use it according to necessity.

Leaving aside, therefore, the imagined things concerning a prince, and taking into account those that are true, I say that all men, when they are spoken of, and particularly princes, since they are placed on a higher level, are judged by some of these qualities which bring them either blame or praise. And this is why one is considered generous, another miserly (to use a Tuscan word, since "avaricious" in our language is still used to mean one who wishes to acquire by means of theft; we call "miserly" one who excessively avoids using what he has); one is considered a giver, the other rapacious; one cruel, another merciful; one treacherous, another faithful; one effeminate and cowardly, another bold and courageous; one humane, another haughty; one lascivious, another chaste; one trustworthy, another cunning; one harsh, another lenient; one serious, another frivolous; one religious, another unbelieving; and the like. And I know that everyone will admit that it would be a very praiseworthy thing to find in a prince, of the qualities mentioned above, those that are held to be good; but since it is neither possible to have them nor to observe them all completely, because human nature does not permit it, a prince must be prudent enough to know how to escape the bad reputation of those vices that would lose the state for him, and must protect himself from those that will not lose it for him, if this is possible; but if he cannot, he need not concern himself unduly if he ignores these less serious vices. And, moreover, he need not worry about incurring the bad reputation of those vices without which it would be difficult to hold his state; since, carefully taking everything into account, one will discover that something which appears to be a virtue, if pursued, will end in his destruction; while some other thing which seems to be a vice, if pursued, will result in his safety and his well-being.

On Generosity and Miserliness

Beginning, therefore, with the first of the above-mentioned qualities, I say that it would be good to be considered generous; nevertheless, generosity used in such a manner as to give you a reputation for it will harm you; because if it is employed virtuously and as one should employ it, it will not be recognized and you will not avoid the reproach of its opposite. And so, if a prince wants to maintain his reputation for generosity among men, it is necessary for him not to neglect any possible means of lavish display; in so doing such a prince will always use up all his resources and he will be obliged, eventually, if he wishes to maintain his reputation for generosity, to burden the people with excessive taxes and to do everything possible to raise funds. This will begin to make him hateful to his subjects, and, becoming impoverished, he will not be much esteemed by anyone; so that, as a consequence of his generosity, having offended many and rewarded few, he will feel the effects of any slight unrest and will be ruined at the first sign of danger; recognizing this and wishing to alter his policies, he immediately runs the risk of being reproached as a miser.

A prince, therefore, unable to use this virtue of generosity in a manner which will not harm himself if he is known for it, should, if he is wise, not worry about being called a miser; for with time he will come to be considered more generous once it is evident that, as a result of his parsimony, his income is sufficient, he can defend himself from anyone who makes war against him, and he can undertake enterprises without overburdening his people, so that he comes to be generous with all those from whom he takes nothing, who are countless, and miserly with all those to whom he gives nothing, who are few. In our times we have not seen great deeds accomplished except by those who were considered miserly; all others were done away with. Pope Julius II, although he made use of his reputation for generosity in order to gain the papacy, then decided not to maintain it in order to be able to wage war; the present King of France has waged many wars without imposing extra taxes on his subjects, only because his habitual parsimony has provided for the additional expenditures; the present King of Spain, if he had been considered generous, would not have engaged in nor won so many campaigns.

Therefore, in order not to have to rob his subjects, to be able to defend himself, not to become poor and contemptible, and not to be forced to become rapacious, a prince must consider it of little importance if he incurs the name of miser, for this is one of those vices that permits him to rule. And if someone were to say: Caesar with his generosity came to rule the empire, and many others, because they were generous and known to be so, achieved very high positions; I reply: You are either already a prince or you are on the way to becoming one; in the first instance such generosity is damaging; in the second it is very necessary to be thought generous. And Caesar was one of those who wanted to gain the principality of Rome; but if, after obtaining this, he had lived and had not moderated his expenditures, he would have destroyed that empire. And if someone were to reply: There have existed many princes who have accomplished great deeds with their armies who have been reputed to be generous; I answer you: A prince either spends his own money and that of his subjects or that of others; in the first case he must be economical; in the second he must not restrain any part of his generosity. And for that prince who goes out with his soldiers and lives by looting, sacking, and ransoms, who controls the property of others, such generosity is necessary; otherwise he would not be followed by his troops. And with what does not belong to you or to your subjects you can be a more liberal giver, as were Cyrus, Caesar, and Alexander; for spending the wealth of others does not lessen your reputation but adds to it; only the spending of your own is what harms you. And there is nothing that uses itself up faster than generosity, for as you employ it you lose the means of employing it, and you become either poor or despised or, in order to escape poverty, rapacious and hated. And above all other things a prince must guard himself against being despised and hated; and generosity leads you to both one and the other. So it is wiser to live with the reputation of a miser, which produces reproach without hatred, than to be forced to incur the reputation of rapacity, which produces reproach along with hatred, because you want to be considered as generous.

ON CRUELTY AND MERCY AND WHETHER IT IS BETTER TO BE LOVED THAN TO BE FEARED OR THE CONTRARY

Proceeding to the other qualities mentioned above, I say that every prince must desire to be considered merciful and not cruel; nevertheless, he must take care not to misuse this mercy. Cesare Borgia[1] was considered cruel; nonetheless, his cruelty had brought order to Romagna, united it, restored it to peace and obedience. If we examine this carefully, we shall see that he was more merciful than the Florentine people, who, in order to avoid being considered cruel, allowed the destruction of Pistoia.[2] Therefore, a prince must not worry about the reproach of cruelty when it is a matter of keeping his subjects united and loyal; for with a very few examples of cruelty he will be more compassionate than those who, out of excessive mercy, permit disorders to continue, from which arise murders and plundering; for these usually harm the community at large, while the executions that come from the prince harm one individual in particular. And the new prince, above all other princes, cannot escape the reputation of being called cruel, since new states are full of dangers. And Virgil, through Dido, states: "My difficult condition and the newness of my rule make me act in such a manner, and to set guards over my land on all sides."[3]

Nevertheless, a prince must be cautious in believing and in acting, nor should he be afraid of his own shadow; and he should proceed in such a manner, tempered by prudence and humanity, so that too much trust may not render him imprudent nor too much distrust render him intolerable.

From this arises an argument: whether it is better to be loved than to be feared, or the contrary. I reply that one should like to be both one and the other; but since it is difficult to join them together, it is much safer to be feared than to be loved when one of the two must be lacking. For one can generally say this about men: that they are ungrateful, fickle, simulators and deceivers, avoiders of danger, greedy for gain; and while you work for their good they are completely yours, offering you their blood, their property, their lives, and their sons, as I said earlier, when danger is far

---

[1]**Cesare Borgia** The son of Pope Alexander VI, Cesare Borgia (1476–1507) was ruthlessly opportunistic. Encouraged by his father, in 1499 and 1500 he subdued the cities of **Romagna,** the region including Ferrara and Ravenna. [All notes are the editors' unless otherwise specified.]

[2]**Pistoia** A town near Florence; Machiavelli suggests that the Florentines failed to treat dissenting leaders with sufficient severity.

[3]In *Aeneid* I, 563–564, **Virgil** (70–19 B.C.) puts this line into the mouth of **Dido,** the woman ruler of Carthage.

away; but when it comes nearer to you they turn away. And that prince who bases his power entirely in their words, finding himself stripped of other preparations, comes to ruin; for friendships that are acquired by a price and not by greatness and nobility of character are purchased but are not owned, and at the proper moment they cannot be spent. And men are less hesitant about harming someone who makes himself loved than one who makes himself feared because love is held together by a chain of obligation which, since men are a sorry lot, is broken on every occasion in which their own self-interest is concerned; but fear is held together by a dread of punishment which will never abandon you.

A prince must nevertheless make himself feared in such a manner that he will avoid hatred, even if he does not acquire love; since to be feared and not to be hated can very well be combined; and this will always be so when he keeps his hands off the property and the women of his citizens and his subjects. And if he must take someone's life, he should do so when there is proper justification and manifest cause; but, above all, he should avoid the property of others; for men forget more quickly the death of their father than the loss of their patrimony. Moreover, the reasons for seizing their property are never lacking; and he who begins to live by stealing always finds a reason for taking what belongs to others; on the contrary, reasons for taking a life are rarer and disappear sooner.

But when the prince is with his armies and has under his command a multitude of troops, then it is absolutely necessary that he not worry about being considered cruel; for without that reputation he will never keep an army united or prepared for any combat. Among the praiseworthy deeds of Hannibal[4] is counted this: that, having a very large army, made up of all kinds of men, which he commanded in foreign lands, there never arose the slightest dissension, neither among themselves nor against their prince, both during his good and his bad fortune. This could not have arisen from anything other than his inhuman cruelty, which, along with his many other abilities, made him always respected and terrifying in the eyes of his soldiers; and without that, to attain the same effect, his other abilities would not have sufficed. And the writers of history, having considered this matter very little, on the one hand admire these deeds of his and on the other condemn the main cause of them.

And that it be true that his other abilities would not have been sufficient can be seen from the example of Scipio,[5] a most extraordinary man not only in his time but in all recorded history, whose armies in Spain rebelled against him; this came about from nothing other than his excessive compassion, which gave to his soldiers more liberty than military discipline allowed. For this he was censured in the senate by Fabius Maximus, who called him the corruptor of the Roman militia. The Locrians, having been

10

[4]**Hannibal** The Carthaginian general (247–183 B.C.) whose crossing of the Alps with elephants and full baggage train is one of the great feats of military history.

[5]**Scipio** Publius Cornelius Scipio Africanus the Elder (235–183 B.C.), the conqueror of Hannibal in the Punic Wars. The mutiny of which Machiavelli speaks took place in 206 B.C.

ruined by one of Scipio's officers, were not avenged by him, nor was the arrogance of that officer corrected, all because of his tolerant nature; so that someone in the senate who tried to apologize for him said that there were many men who knew how not to err better than they knew how to correct errors. Such a nature would have, in time, damaged Scipio's fame and glory if he had maintained it during the empire; but, living under the control of the senate, this harmful characteristic of his not only concealed itself but brought him fame.

I conclude, therefore, returning to the problem of being feared and loved, that since men love at their own pleasure and fear at the pleasure of the prince, a wise prince should build his foundation upon that which belongs to him, not upon that which belongs to others: He must strive only to avoid hatred, as has been said.

How a Prince Should Keep His Word

How praiseworthy it is for a prince to keep his word and to live by integrity and not by deceit everyone knows; nevertheless, one sees from the experience of our times that the princes who have accomplished great deeds are those who have cared little for keeping their promises and who have known how to manipulate the minds of men by shrewdness; and in the end they have surpassed those who laid their foundations upon honesty.

You must, therefore, know that there are two means of fighting: one according to the laws, the other with force; the first way is proper to man, the second to beasts; but because the first, in many cases, is not sufficient, it becomes necessary to have recourse to the second. Therefore, a prince must know how to use wisely the natures of the beast and the man. This policy was taught to princes allegorically by the ancient writers, who described how Achilles and many other ancient princes were given to Chiron[6] the Centaur to be raised and taught under his discipline. This can only mean that, having a half-beast and half-man as a teacher, a prince must know how to employ the nature of the one and the other; and the one without the other cannot endure.

Since, then, a prince must know how to make good use of the nature of the beast, he should choose from among the beasts the fox and the lion; for the lion cannot defend itself from traps and the fox cannot protect itself from wolves. It is therefore necessary to be a fox in order to recognize the traps and a lion in order to frighten the wolves. Those who play only the part of the lion do not understand matters. A wise ruler, therefore, cannot and should not keep his word when such an observance of faith would be to his disadvantage and when the reasons which made him promise are removed. And if men were all good, this rule would not be good; but since men are a sorry lot and will not keep their promises to you, you likewise need not keep yours to

15

[6]**Chiron** (Kī'ron) A centaur (half man, half horse), who was said in classical mythology to have been the teacher not only of Achilles but also of Theseus, Jason, Hercules, and other heroes.

them. A prince never lacks legitimate reasons to break his promises. Of this one could cite an endless number of modern examples to show how many pacts, how many promises have been made null and void because of the infidelity of princes; and he who has known best how to use the fox has come to a better end. But it is necessary to know how to disguise this nature well and to be a great hypocrite and a liar: and men are so simpleminded and so controlled by their present necessities that one who deceives will always find another who will allow himself to be deceived.

I do not wish to remain silent about one of these recent instances. Alexander VI[7] did nothing else, he thought about nothing else, except to deceive men, and he always found the occasion to do this. And there never was a man who had more forcefulness in his oaths, who affirmed a thing with more promises, and who honored his word less; nevertheless, his tricks always succeeded perfectly since he was well acquainted with this aspect of the world.

Therefore, it is not necessary for a prince to have all of the above-mentioned qualities, but it is very necessary for him to appear to have them. Furthermore, I shall be so bold as to assert this; that having them and practicing them at all times is harmful; and appearing to have them useful; for instance, to seem merciful, faithful, humane, forthright, religious, and to be so; but his mind should be disposed in such a way that should it become necessary not to be so, he will be able and know how to change to the contrary. And it is essential to understand this: that a prince, and especially a new prince, cannot observe all those things by which men are considered good, for in order to maintain the state he is often obliged to act against his promise, against charity, against humanity, and against religion. And therefore, it is necessary that he have a mind ready to turn itself according to the way the winds of Fortune and the changeability of affairs require him; and, as I said above, as long as it is possible, he should not stray from the good, but he should know how to enter into evil when necessity commands.

A prince, therefore, must be very careful never to let anything slip from his lips which is not full of the five qualities mentioned above: He should appear, upon seeing and hearing him, to be all mercy, all faithfulness, all integrity, all kindness, all religion. And there is nothing more necessary than to seem to possess this last quality. And men in general judge more by their eyes than their hands; for everyone can see but few can feel. Everyone sees what you seem to be, few perceive what you are, and those few do not dare to contradict the opinion of the many who have the majesty of the state to defend them; and in the actions of all men, and especially of princes, where there is no impartial arbiter, one must consider the final result.[8] Let a prince therefore act to seize and to maintain the

---

[7]**Alexander VI** Pope from 1492 to 1503; father of Cesare Borgia.

[8]The Italian original, *si guarda al fine,* has often been mistranslated as "the ends justify the means," something Machiavelli never wrote. [Translators' note.]

state; his methods will always be judged honorable and will be praised by all; for ordinary people are always deceived by appearances and by the outcome of a thing; and in the world there is nothing but ordinary people; and there is no room for the few, while the many have a place to lean on. A certain prince of the present day, whom I shall refrain from naming, preaches nothing but peace and faith, and to both one and the other he is entirely opposed; and both, if he had put them into practice, would have cost him many times over either his reputation or his state.

Topics for Critical Thinking and Writing

1. In the opening paragraph, Machiavelli claims that a ruler who wishes to keep in power must "learn how not to be good"—that is, must know where and when to ignore the demands of conventional morality. In the rest of the excerpt, does he give any convincing evidence to support this claim? Can you think of any recent political event in which a political leader violated the requirements of morality, as Machiavelli advises?

2. Machiavelli says in paragraph 1 that "a man who wishes to make a vocation of being good at all times will come to ruin among so many who are not good." (By the way, the passage is ambiguous. "At all times" is, in the original, a squinting modifier. It may look backward, to "being good," or forward, to "will come to ruin," but probably Machiavelli means, "A man who at all times wishes to make a vocation of being good will come to ruin among so many who are not good.") Is this view realistic or cynical? (What is the difference between these two?) Assume for the moment that the view is realistic. Does it follow that society requires a ruler who must act according to the principles Machiavelli sets forth?

3. In his second paragraph Machiavelli claims that it is impossible for a ruler to exhibit *all* the conventional virtues (trustworthiness, liberality, and so on). Why does he make this claim? Do you agree with it?

4. In paragraph 4 Machiavelli cites as examples Pope Julius II, the King of France, the King of Spain, and other rulers. Is he using these examples to illustrate his generalizations, or to provide evidence for them? If you think he is using them to provide evidence, how convincing do you find the evidence? (*Consider:* Could Machiavelli be arguing from a biased sample?)

5. In paragraphs 6–10 Machiavelli argues that it is sometimes necessary for a ruler to be cruel, and so he praises Cesare Borgia and Hannibal. What is it about human nature, according to Machiavelli, that explains this need to have recourse to cruelty? (By the way, how do you think "cruelty" should be defined here?)

6. Machiavelli says that Cesare Borgia's cruelty brought peace to Romagna, and that, on the other hand, the Florentines who sought to avoid being cruel in fact brought pain to Pistoia. Can you think of recent episodes supporting the view that cruelty can be beneficial to society? If so, restate Machiavelli's position, using these examples from recent history. Then go on to write two paragraphs,

arguing on behalf of your two examples. Or, if you believe that Machiavelli's point here is fundamentally wrong, explain why, again using current examples.

7. In *The Prince,* Machiavelli is writing about how to be a successful ruler. He explicitly says he is dealing with things as they are, not things as they should be. Do you think that in fact one can write usefully about statecraft without considering ethics? Explain. Or you may want to think about it in this way: The study of politics is often called "political science." Machiavelli can be seen as a sort of scientist, objectively analyzing the nature of governing—without offering any moral judgments. In an essay of 500 words argue for or against the view that the study of politics is rightly called "political science."

8. In paragraph 18 Machiavelli declares that "one must consider the final result." Taking account of the context, do you think the meaning is that (a) any end, goal, or purpose of anyone justifies using any means to reach it, or (b) the end of governing the state, nation, or country justifies using any means to achieve it? Or do you think Machiavelli means both, or something else entirely?

9. Take some important contemporary political figure and in 500 words argue that he or she does or does not act according to Machiavelli's principles.

10. If you have read the selection from More's *Utopia* (p. 535), write an essay of 500 words on one of these two topics: (1) Why More's book is or is not wiser than Machiavelli's, or (2) why one of the books is more interesting than the other.

11. More and Machiavelli wrote their books at almost exactly the same time. Write a dialogue of two or three double-spaced typed pages, in which the two men argue about the nature of the state. (During the argument, they will have to reveal their assumptions about the nature of human beings, and the role of government.)

Martin Luther King, Jr.

I Have a Dream

I am happy to join with you today in what will go down in history as the greatest demonstration for freedom in the history of our nation.

Five score years ago, a great American, in whose symbolic shadow we stand today, signed the Emancipation Proclamation. This momentous decree came as a great beacon light of hope to millions of Negro slaves who had been seared in the flames of withering injustice. It came as a joyous daybreak to end the long night of their captivity. But one hundred years later, the Negro still is not free. One hundred years later, the life of the Negro is still sadly crippled by the manacles of segregation and the chains of discrimination. One hundred years later, the Negro lives on a lonely island of poverty in the midst of a vast ocean of material prosperity. One hundred years later, the Negro is still anguished in the corners of American society and finds himself in exile in his own land. And so we have come here today to dramatize a shameful condition.

In a sense we have come to our nation's capital to cash a check. When the architects of our republic wrote the magnificent words of the Constitution and the Declaration of Independence, they were signing a promissory note to which every American was to fall heir. This note was the promise that all men—yes, Black men as well as white men—would be guaranteed the inalienable rights of life, liberty, and the pursuit of happiness.

It is obvious today that America has defaulted on this promissory note insofar as her citizens of color are concerned. Instead of honoring this sacred obligation, America has given the Negro people a bad check, a check which has come back marked "insufficient funds." But we refuse to believe that the bank of justice is bankrupt. We refuse to believe that there are insufficient funds in the great vaults of opportunity of this nation; and so we have come to cash this check, a check that will give us upon demand the riches of freedom and the security of justice.

We have also come to this hallowed spot to remind America of the 5

Martin Luther King, Jr. (1929–1968), was born in Atlanta and educated at Morehouse College, Crozer Theological Seminary, and Boston University. In 1954 he was called to serve as a Baptist minister in Montgomery, Alabama. During the next two years he achieved national fame when, using a policy of nonviolent resistance, he successfully led the boycott against segregated bus lines in Montgomery. He then organized the Southern Christian Leadership Conference, which furthered civil rights, first in the South and then nationwide. In 1964 he was awarded the Nobel Peace Prize. Four years later he was assassinated in Memphis, Tennessee, while supporting striking garbage workers.

"I Have a Dream" was delivered from the steps of the Lincoln Memorial, in Washington, D.C., in 1963, the hundredth anniversary of the Emancipation Proclamation. King's immediate audience consisted of more than two hundred thousand people who had come to demonstrate for civil rights.

fierce urgency of *now*. This is no time to engage in the luxury of cooling off or to take the tranquilizing drug of gradualism. *Now* is the time to make real promises of democracy. *Now* is the time to rise from the dark and desolate valley of segregation to the sunlit path of racial justice. *Now* is the time to lift our nation from the quicksands of racial injustice to the solid rock of brotherhood. *Now* is the time to make justice a reality for all of God's children.

It would be fatal for the nation to overlook the urgency of the moment. This sweltering summer of the Negro's legitimate discontent will not pass until there is an invigorating autumn of freedom and equality. Nineteen sixty-three is not an end, but a beginning. And those who hope that the Negro needed to blow off steam and will now be content will have a rude awakening if the nation returns to business as usual. There will be neither rest nor tranquility in America until the Negro is granted his citizenship rights. The whirlwinds of revolt will continue to shake the foundations of our nation until the bright day of justice emerges.

But there is something that I must say to my people who stand on the warm threshold which leads into the palace of justice. In the process of gaining our rightful place, we must not be guilty of wrongful deeds. Let us not seek to satisfy our thirst for freedom by drinking from the cup of bitterness and hatred. We must forever conduct our struggle on the high plane of dignity and discipline. We must not allow our creative protest to degenerate into physical violence. Again and again we must rise to the majestic heights of meeting physical force with soul force. And the marvelous new militancy which has engulfed the Negro community must not lead us to a distrust of all white people; for many of our white brothers, as evidenced by their presence here today, have come to realize that their destiny is tied up with our destiny, and they have come to realize that their freedom is inextricably bound to our freedom.

We cannot walk alone. And as we walk we must make the pledge that we shall always march ahead. We cannot turn back. There are those who are asking the devotees of civil rights, "When will you be satisfied?" We can never be satisfied as long as the Negro is the victim of the unspeakable horrors of police brutality. We can never be satisfied as long as our bodies, heavy with the fatigue of travel, cannot gain lodging in the motels of the highways and the hotels of the cities. We cannot be satisfied as long as the Negro's basic mobility is from a smaller ghetto to a larger one. We can never be satisfied as long as our children are stripped of their selfhood and robbed of their dignity by signs stating "For Whites Only." We cannot be satisfied as long as the Negro in Mississippi cannot vote and a Negro in New York believes he has nothing for which to vote. No, no, we are not satisfied, and we will not be satisfied until justice rolls down like waters and righteousness like a mighty stream.[1]

I am not unmindful that some of you have come here out of great tri-

---

[1] **justice . . . stream** A quotation from the Hebrew Bible: Amos 5:24. [All notes are the editors'.]

als and tribulations. Some of you have come fresh from narrow jail cells. Some of you have come from areas where your quest for freedom left you battered by the storms of persecution and staggered by the winds of police brutality. You have been the veterans of creative suffering. Continue to work with the faith that unearned suffering is redemptive.

Go back to Mississippi, and go back to Alabama. Go back to South 10 Carolina. Go back to Georgia. Go back to Louisiana. Go back to the slums and ghettos of our Northern cities, knowing that somehow this situation can and will be changed. Let us not wallow in the valley of despair.

I say to you today, my friends, even though we face the difficulties of today and tomorrow, I still have a dream. It is a dream deeply rooted in the American dream. I have a dream that one day this nation will rise up and live out the true meaning of its creed: "We hold these truths to be self-evident, that all men are created equal." I have a dream that one day, on the red hills of Georgia, sons of former slaves and the sons of former slave owners will be able to sit down together at the table of brotherhood. I have a dream that one day even the state of Mississippi, a state sweltering with the heat of injustice, sweltering with the heat of oppression, will be transformed into an oasis of freedom and justice. I have a dream that my four little children will one day live in a nation where they will not be judged by the color of their skin, but by the content of their character.

I have a dream today. I have a dream that one day down in Alabama—with its vicious racists, with its governor's lips dripping with the words of interposition and nullification—one day right there in Alabama, little Black boys and Black girls will be able to join hands with little white boys and white girls as sisters and brothers.

I have a dream today. I have a dream that one day every valley shall be exalted and every hill and mountain shall be made low, the rough places will be made plain and the crooked places will be made straight, and the glory of the Lord shall be revealed, and all flesh shall see it together.[2]

This is our hope. This is the faith that I go back to the South with. And with this faith we will be able to hew out of the mountain of despair a stone of hope. With this faith we will be able to transform the jangling discords of our nation into a beautiful symphony of brotherhood. With this faith we will be able to work together, to play together, to struggle together, to go to jail together, to stand up for freedom together, knowing that we will be free one day.

And this will be the day—this will be the day when all of God's chil- 15 dren will be able to sing with new meaning:

> My country, 'tis of thee,
> Sweet land of liberty,
>   Of thee I sing;
> Land where my fathers died,

---

[2]**every valley . . . see it together** Another quotation from the Hebrew Bible: Isaiah 40:4–5.

Land of the Pilgrim's pride,
From every mountainside
  Let freedom ring.

And if America is to be a great nation, this must become true.

And so let freedom ring from the prodigious hilltops of New Hampshire. Let freedom ring from the mighty mountains of New York. Let freedom ring from the heightening Alleghenies of Pennsylvania. Let freedom ring from the snow-capped Rockies of Colorado. Let freedom ring from the curvaceous slopes of California.

But not only that. Let freedom ring from Stone Mountain of Georgia. Let freedom ring from Lookout Mountain of Tennessee. Let freedom ring from every hill and molehill of Mississippi. "From every mountainside let freedom ring."

And when this happens — when we allow freedom to ring, when we let it ring from every village and every hamlet, from every state and every city — we will be able to speed up that day when all of God's children, Black men and white men, Jews and Gentiles, Protestants and Catholics, will be able to join hands and sing in the words of the old Negro spiritual: "Free at last! Free at last! Thank God Almighty. We are free at last!"

Topics for Critical Thinking and Writing

1. Analyze the rhetoric — the oratorical art — of the second paragraph. What, for instance, is gained by saying "Five score years ago" instead of "a hundred years ago"? By metaphorically calling the Emancipation Proclamation "a great beacon light?" By saying that "Negro slaves . . . had been seared in the flames of withering injustice"? And what of the metaphors "daybreak" and "the long night of captivity"?

2. Do the first two paragraphs make an effective opening? Why?

3. In the third and fourth paragraphs King uses the metaphor of a bad check. Rewrite the third paragraph *without* using any of King's metaphors, and then in a paragraph evaluate the difference between King's version and yours.

4. King's highly metaphoric speech of course appeals to emotions. But it also offers *reasons*. What reason(s), for instance, does King give to support his belief that blacks should not resort to physical violence?

5. When King delivered the speech, his audience at the Lincoln Memorial was primarily black. Do you think that the speech is also addressed to whites? Explain.

6. The speech can be divided into three parts: paragraphs 1 through 6; paragraphs 7 ("But there is") through 10; and paragraph 11 ("I say to you today, my friends") to the end. Summarize each of these three parts in a sentence or two, so that the basic organization is evident.

7. King says (para. 11) that his dream is "deeply rooted in the American dream." First, what is the American dream, as King seems to understand it? Second, how does King establish his point — that is, what evidence does he use to con-

vince us—that his dream is the American dream? (On this second issue, for a start one might point out that in the second paragraph King refers to the Emancipation Proclamation. What other relevant documents does he refer to?)

8. King delivered his speech in 1963, more than thirty years ago. In an essay of 500 words argue that the speech still is—or is not—relevant. Or write an essay of 500 words in which you state what you take to be the "American dream," and argue that it now is or is not readily available to blacks.

W. H. Auden

The Unknown Citizen

*(To JS/07/M/378
This Marble Monument
Is Erected by the State)*

He was found by the Bureau of Statistics to be
One against whom there was no official complaint,
And all the reports on his conduct agree
That, in the modern sense of an old-fashioned word, he was a saint,
For in everything he did he served the Greater Community.   5
Except for the War till the day he retired
He worked in a factory and never got fired,
But satisfied his employers, Fudge Motors Inc.
Yet he wasn't a scab or odd in his views,
For his Union reports that he paid his dues,   10
(Our report on his Union shows it was sound)
And our Social Psychology workers found
That he was popular with his mates and liked a drink.
The Press are convinced that he bought a paper every day
And that his reactions to advertisements were normal in every way.   15
Policies taken out in his name prove that he was fully insured,
And his Health-card shows he was once in hospital but left it cured.
Both Producers Research and High-Grade Living declare
He was fully sensible to the advantages of the Installment Plan
And had everything necessary to the Modern Man,   20
A phonograph, radio, a car and a frigidaire.
Our researches into Public Opinion are content

Wystan Hugh Auden (1907–1973) was born in York, England, and educated at Oxford. In the 1930s his left-wing poetry earned him wide acclaim as the leading poet of his generation. In 1939 he came to the United States, and in 1946 he became a citizen, although he returned to England for his last years. The poem reprinted here was originally published in 1940.

That he held the proper opinions for the time of year;
When there was peace, he was for peace; when there was war, he went.
He was married and added five children to the population,   25
Which our Eugenist says was the right number for a parent of his generation,
And our teachers report that he never interfered with their education.
Was he free? Was he happy? The question is absurd:
Had anything been wrong, we should certainly have heard.

Topics for Critical Thinking and Writing

1. Was he free? Was he happy?

2. In a paragraph or two, sketch the values of the speaker of the poem, and then sum them up in a sentence or two. Finally, in as much space as you feel you need, judge these values.

3. If you have read the selection from Thomas More's *Utopia* (p. 535), write an essay of 500 to 750 words — in More's voice — setting forth More's response to Auden's poem.

Ursula K. Le Guin

The Ones Who Walk Away from Omelas

With a clamor of bells that set the swallows soaring, the Festival of Summer came to the city Omelas, bright-towered by the sea. The rigging of the boats in harbor sparkled with flags. In the streets between houses with red roofs and painted walls, between old moss-grown gardens and under avenues of trees, past great parks and public buildings, processions

---

Ursula K. Le Guin was born in 1929 in Berkeley, California, the daughter of a distinguished mother (Theodora Kroeber, a folklorist) and father (Alfred L. Kroeber, an anthropologist). After graduating from Radcliffe College, she earned a master's degree at Columbia University; in 1952 she held a Fulbright Fellowship for study in Paris, where she met and married Charles Le Guin, a historian. She began writing in earnest while bringing up three children. Although her work is most widely known to buffs of science fiction, because it usually has larger moral or political dimensions it interests many other readers who normally do not care for sci-fi.

Le Guin has said that she was prompted to write the story by a remark she encountered in William James's "The Moral Philosopher and the Moral Life." James suggests here that if millions of people could be "kept permanently happy on the one simple condition that a certain lost soul on the far-off edge of things should lead a life of lonely torment," our moral sense "would make us immediately feel" it would be "hideous" to accept such a bargain.

moved. Some were decorous: old people in long stiff robes of mauve and gray, grave master workmen, quiet, merry women carrying their babies and chatting as they walked. In other streets the music beat faster, a shimmering of gong and tambourine, and the people went dancing, the procession was a dance. Children dodged in and out, their high calls rising like the swallows' crossing flights over the music and the singing. All the processions wound towards the north side of the city, where on the great watermeadow called the Green Fields boys and girls, naked in the bright air, with mudstained feet and ankles and long, lithe arms, exercised their restive horses before the race. The horses wore no gear at all but a halter without bit. Their manes were braided with streamers of silver, gold, and green. They flared their nostrils and pranced and boasted to one another; they were vastly excited, the horse being the only animal who has adopted our ceremonies as his own. Far off to the north and west the mountains stood up half encircling Omelas on her bay. The air of morning was so clear that the snow still crowning the Eighteen Peaks burned with white-gold fire across the miles of sunlit air, under the dark blue of the sky. There was just enough wind to make the banners that marked the racecourse snap and flutter now and then. In the silence of the broad green meadows one could hear the music winding through the city streets, farther and nearer and ever approaching, a cheerful faint sweetness of the air that from time to time trembled and gathered together and broke out into the great joyous clanging of the bells.

Joyous! How is one to tell about joy? How describe the citizens of Omelas?

They were not simple folk, you see, though they were happy. But we do not say the words of cheer much any more. All smiles have become archaic. Given a description such as this one tends to make certain assumptions. Given a description such as this one tends to look next for the King, mounted on a splendid stallion and surrounded by his noble knights, or perhaps in a golden litter borne by great-muscled slaves. But there was no king. They did not use swords, or keep slaves. They were not barbarians. I do not know the rules and laws of their society, but I suspect that they were singularly few. As they did without monarchy and slavery, so they also got on without the stock exchange, the advertisement, the secret police, and the bomb. Yet I repeat that these were not simple folk, not dulcet shepherds, noble savages, bland utopians. They were not less complex than us. The trouble is that we have a bad habit, encouraged by pedants and sophisticates, of considering happiness as something rather stupid. Only pain is intellectual, only evil interesting. This is the treason of the artist: a refusal to admit the banality of evil and the terrible boredom of pain. If you can't lick 'em, join 'em. If it hurts, repeat it. But to praise despair is to condemn delight, to embrace violence is to lose hold of everything else. We have almost lost hold, we can no longer describe a happy man, nor make any celebration of joy. How can I tell you about the people of Omelas? They were not naïve and happy children — though their children were, in fact, happy.

They were mature, intelligent, passionate adults whose lives were not wretched. O miracle! but I wish I could describe it better. I wish I could convince you. Omelas sounds in my words like a city in a fairy tale, long ago and far away, once upon a time. Perhaps it would be best if you imagined it as your own fancy bids, assuming it will rise to the occasion, for certainly I cannot suit you all. For instance, how about technology? I think that there would be no cars or helicopters in and above the streets; this follows from the fact that the people of Omelas are happy people. Happiness is based on a just discrimination of what is necessary, what is neither necessary nor destructive, and what is destructive. In the middle category, however—that of the unnecessary but undestructive, that of comfort, luxury, exuberance, etc.—they could perfectly well have central heating, subway trains, washing machines, and all kinds of marvelous devices not yet invented here, floating light-sources, fuelless power, a cure for the common cold. Or they could have none of that: it doesn't matter. As you like it. I incline to think that people from towns up and down the coast have been coming in to Omelas during the last days before the Festival on very fast little trains and double-decked trams, and that the train station of Omelas is actually the handsomest building in town, though plainer than the magnificent Farmers' Market. But even granted trains, I fear that Omelas so far strikes some of you as goody-goody. Smiles, bells, parades, horses, bleh. If so, please add an orgy. If an orgy would help, don't hesitate. Let us not, however, have temples from which issue beautiful nude priests and priestesses already half in ecstasy and ready to copulate with any man or woman, lover or stranger, who desires union with the deep godhead of the blood, although that was my first idea. But really it would be better not to have any temples in Omelas—at least, not manned temples. Religion yes, clergy no. Surely the beautiful nudes can just wander about, offering themselves like divine soufflés to the hunger of the needy and the rapture of the flesh. Let them join the processions. Let tambourines be struck above the copulations, and the glory of desire be proclaimed upon the gongs, and (a not unimportant point) let the offspring of these delightful rituals be beloved and looked after by all. One thing I know there is none of in Omelas is guilt. But what else should there be? I thought that first there were no drugs, but that is puritanical. For those who like it, the faint insistent sweetness of *drooz* may perfume the ways of the city, *drooz* which first brings a great lightness and brilliance to the mind and limbs, and then after some hours a dreamy languor, and wonderful visions at last of the very arcana and inmost secrets of the Universe, as well as exciting the pleasure of sex beyond all belief; and it is not habit-forming. For more modest tastes I think there ought to be beer. What else, what else belongs in the joyous city? The sense of victory, surely, the celebration of courage. But as we did without clergy, let us do without soldiers. The joy built upon successful slaughter is not the right kind of joy; it will not do; it is fearful and it is trivial. A boundless and generous contentment, a magnanimous triumph felt not against some outer enemy but in communion with the finest and fairest in the souls of all men everywhere and the splendor of the world's summer: this is what swells the hearts of the people of Omelas, and the victory they celebrate is that of life. I really don't think many of them need to take *drooz*.

Most of the processions have reached the Green Fields by now. A marvelous smell of cooking goes forth from the red and blue tents of the provisioners. The faces of small children are amiably sticky; in the benign grey beard of a man a couple of crumbs of rich pastry are entangled. The youths and girls have mounted their horses and are beginning to group around the starting line of the course. An old woman, small, fat, and laughing, is passing out flowers from a basket, and tall young men wear her flowers in their shining hair. A child of nine or ten sits at the edge of the crowd, alone, playing on a wooden flute. People pause to listen, and they smile, but they do not speak to him, for he never ceases playing and never sees them, his dark eyes wholly rapt in the sweet, thin magic of the tune.

He finishes, and slowly lowers his hands holding the wooden flute.   5

As if that little private silence were the signal, all at once a trumpet sounds from the pavilion near the starting line: imperious, melancholy, piercing. The horses rear on their slender legs, and some of them neigh in answer. Sober-faced, the young riders stroke the horses' necks and soothe them, whispering, "Quiet, quiet, there my beauty, my hope. . . ." They begin to form in rank along the starting line. The crowds along the race-course are like a field of grass and flowers in the wind. The Festival of Summer has begun.

Do you believe? Do you accept the festival, the city, the joy? No? Then let me describe one more thing.

In a basement under one of the beautiful public buildings of Omelas, or perhaps in the cellar of one of its spacious private homes, there is a room. It has one locked door, and no window. A little light seeps in dustily between cracks in the boards, secondhand from a cobwebbed window somewhere across the cellar. In one corner of the little room a couple of mops, with stiff, clotted, foul-smelling heads, stand near a rusty bucket. The floor is dirt, a little damp to the touch, as cellar dirt usually is. The room is about three paces long and two wide: a mere broom closet or dis-used tool room. In the room a child is sitting. It could be a boy or a girl. It looks about six, but actually is nearly ten. It is feeble-minded. Perhaps it was born defective, or perhaps it has become imbecile through fear, mal-nutrition, and neglect. It picks its nose and occasionally fumbles vaguely with its toes or genitals, as it sits hunched in the corner farthest from the bucket and the two mops. It is afraid of the mops. It finds them horrible. It shuts its eyes, but it knows the mops are still standing there; and the door is locked; and nobody will come. The door is always locked; and nobody ever comes, except that sometimes — the child has no understanding of time or interval — sometimes the door rattles terribly and opens, and a person, or several people, are there. One of them may come in and kick the child to make it stand up. The others never come close, but peer in at it with frightened, disgusted eyes. The food bowl and the water jug are hastily filled, the door is locked, the eyes disappear. The people at the door never say anything, but the child, who has not always lived in the tool room, and can remember sunlight and its mother's voice, sometimes speaks. "I will be good," it says. "Please let me out. I will be good!" They never answer. The child used to scream for help at night, and cry a good deal, but now it only makes a kind of whining, "eh-haa, eh-haa," and it speaks less and less often. It is so thin there are no calves to its legs; its belly protrudes; it lives on a half-bowl of corn meal and grease a day. It is naked. Its buttocks and thighs are a mass of festered sores, as it sits in its own excrement continually.

They all know it is there, all the people of Omelas. Some of them have come to see it, others are content merely to know it is there. They all know that it has to be there. Some of them understand why, and some do not, but they all understand that their happiness, the beauty of their city, the tenderness of their friendships, the health of their children, the wisdom of their scholars, the skill of their makers, even the abundance of their harvest and the kindly weathers of their skies, depend wholly on this child's abominable misery.

This is usually explained to children when they are between eight and 10 twelve, whenever they seem capable of understanding; and most of those who come to see the child are young people, though often enough an adult comes, or comes back, to see the child. No matter how well the matter has been explained to them, these young spectators are always shocked and sickened at the sight. They feel disgust, which they had thought themselves superior to. They feel anger, outrage, impotence, despite all the explanations. They would like to do something for the child. But there is nothing they can do. If the child were brought up into the sunlight out of that vile place, if it were cleaned and fed and comforted, that would be a good thing, indeed; but if it were done, in that day and hour all the prosperity and beauty and delight of Omelas would wither and be destroyed. Those are the terms. To exchange all the goodness and grace of every life in Omelas for that single, small improvement: to throw away the happiness of thousands for the chance of the happiness of one: that would be to let guilt within the walls indeed.

The terms are strict and absolute; there may not even be a kind word spoken to the child.

Often the young people go home in tears, or in a tearless rage, when they have seen the child and faced this terrible paradox. They may brood over it for weeks or years. But as time goes on they begin to realize that even if the child could be released, it would not get much good of its freedom: a little vague pleasure of warmth and food, no doubt, but little more. It is too degraded and imbecile to know any real joy. It has been afraid too long ever to be free of fear. Its habits are too uncouth for it to respond to humane treatment. Indeed, after so long it would probably be wretched without walls about it to protect it, and darkness for its eyes, and its own excrement to sit in. Their tears at the bitter injustice dry when they begin to perceive the terrible justice of reality, and to accept it. Yet it is their tears and anger, the trying of their generosity and the acceptance of their helplessness, which are perhaps the true source of the splendor of their lives. Theirs is no vapid, irresponsible happiness. They know that they, like the child, are not free. They know compassion. It is the existence of the child, and their knowledge of its existence, that makes possible the nobility of their architecture, the poignancy of their music, the profundity of their science. It is because of the child that they are so gentle with children. They know that if the wretched one were not there snivelling in the dark, the other one, the flute-player, could make no joyful music as the young riders line up in their beauty for the race in the sunlight of the first morning of summer.

Now do you believe in them? Are they not more credible? But there is one more thing to tell, and this is quite incredible.

At times one of the adolescent girls or boys who go to see the child does not go home to weep or rage, does not, in fact, go home at all. Sometimes also a man or woman much older falls silent for a day or two, and then leaves home. These people go out into the street, and walk down the street alone. They keep walking, and walk straight out of the city of Omelas, through the beautiful gates. They keep walking across the farmlands of Omelas. Each one goes alone, youth or girl, man or woman. Night falls; the traveler must pass down village streets, between the houses with yellow-lit windows, and on out into the darkness of the fields. Each alone, they go west or north, towards the mountains. They go on. They leave Omelas, they walk ahead into the darkness, and they do not come back. The place they go towards is a place even less imaginable to most of us than the city of happiness. I cannot describe it at all. It is possible that it does not exist. But they seem to know where they are going, the ones who walk away from Omelas.

Topics for Critical Thinking and Writing ══════════

1. Summarize the point of the story — not the plot, but what the story adds up to, what the author is getting at. Next, set forth what you would probably do (and why) if you were born in Omelas.

2. Consider the narrator's assertion that happiness "is based on a just discrimination of what is necessary."

3. Do you think the story implies a criticism of contemporary American society? Explain.

18

Are We Bound to Obey the State?

Plato

Crito

(Scene: A room in the State prison at Athens in the year 399 B.C. The time is half an hour before dawn, and the room would be almost dark but for the light of a little oil lamp. There is a pallet bed against the back wall. At the head of it a small table supports the lamp; near the foot of it Crito is sitting patiently on a stool. He is an old man, kindly, practical, simple-minded; at present he is suffering from acute emotional strain. On the bed lies Socrates asleep. He stirs, yawns, opens his eyes and sees Crito.)

Plato (427–347 B.C.), an Athenian aristocrat by birth, was the student of one great philosopher (Socrates) and the teacher of another (Aristotle). His legacy of more than two dozen dialogues — imaginary discussions between Socrates and one or more other speakers, usually young Athenians — has been of such influence that the whole of Western philosophy can be characterized, A. N. Whitehead wrote, as "a series of footnotes to Plato." Plato's interests encompassed the full range of topics in philosophy: ethics, politics, logic, metaphysics, epistemology, aesthetics, psychology, and education.

The selection reprinted here, Crito, is the third of four dialogues telling the story of the final days of Socrates (469–399 B.C.). The first in the sequence, Euthyphro, portrays Socrates in his typical role, questioning someone about his beliefs (in this case, the young aristocrat, Euthyphro). The discussion is focused on the nature of piety, but the conversation breaks off before a final answer is reached — perhaps none is possible — because Socrates is on his way to stand trial before the Athenian assembly. He has been charged with "preaching false gods" (heresy) and "corrupting the youth" by causing them to doubt or disregard the wisdom of their elders.

Socrates: Here already, Crito? Surely it is still early?

Crito: Indeed it is.

Socrates: About what time?

Crito: Just before dawn.

Socrates: I wonder that the warder paid any attention to you.   5

Crito: He is used to me now, Socrates, because I come here so often; besides, he is under some small obligation to me.

Socrates: Have you only just come, or have you been here for long?

Crito: Fairly long.

Socrates: Then why didn't you wake me at once, instead of sitting by my bed so quietly?

Crito: I wouldn't dream of such a thing, Socrates. I only wish I were   10 not so sleepless and depressed myself. I have been wondering at you, because I saw how comfortably you were sleeping; and I deliberately didn't wake you because I wanted you to go on being as comfortable as you could. I have often felt before in the course of my life how fortunate you are in your disposition, but I feel it more than ever now in your present misfortune when I see how easily and placidly you put up with it.

(How faithful to any actual event or discussion, Euthyphro *and Plato's other Socratic dialogues really are, scholars cannot say with assurance.)*

In Apology, *the second dialogue in the sequence, Plato (who remains entirely in the background, as he does in all the dialogues) recounts Socrates' public reply to the charges against him. During the speech, Socrates explains his life, reminding his fellow citizens that if he is (as the oracle had pronounced) "the wisest of men," then it is only because he knows that he doesn't know what others believe or pretend they do know. The dialogue ends with Socrates being found guilty and duly sentenced to death.*

The third in the series is Crito, *but we will postpone comment on it for a moment, and glance at the fourth dialogue,* Phaedo, *in which Plato portrays Socrates' final philosophical discussion. The topic, appropriately, is whether the soul is immortal. It ends with Socrates, in the company of his closest friends, bidding them a last farewell and drinking the fatal cup of hemlock.*

Crito, *the whole text of which is reprinted here, is the debate provoked by Crito, an old friend and admirer of Socrates. He visits Socrates in prison and urges him to escape while he still has the chance. After all, Crito argues, the guilty verdict was wrong and unfair, few Athenians really want to have Socrates put to death, his family and friends will be distraught, and so forth. Socrates will not have it. He patiently but firmly examines each of Crito's arguments and explains why it would be wrong to follow his advice.*

Plato's Crito *thus ranks with Sophocles' tragedy* Antigone *as one of the first explorations in Western literature of the perennial theme of our responsibility for obeying laws that challenge our conscientious moral convictions.* Antigone *concludes that she must disobey the law of Creon, tyrant of Thebes; Socrates concludes that he must obey the law of democratic Athens.*

In Crito, *we have not only a superb illustration of Socratic dialogue and argument, but also a portrait of a virtuous thinker at the end of a long life reflecting on its course and on the moral principles that have guided him. We see Socrates living "an examined life," the only life he thought was worth living.*

Socrates: Well, really, Crito, it would be hardly suitable for a man of my age to resent having to die.

Crito: Other people just as old as you are get involved in these misfortunes, Socrates, but their age doesn't keep them from resenting it when they find themselves in your position.

Socrates: Quite true. But tell me, why have you come so early?

Crito: Because I bring bad news, Socrates; not so bad from your point of view, I suppose, but it will be very hard to bear for me and your other friends, and I think that I shall find it hardest of all.

Socrates: Why, what is this news? Has the boat come in from Delos — 15 the boat which ends my reprieve when it arrives?[1]

Crito: It hasn't actually come in yet, but I expect that it will be here today, judging from the report of some people who have just arrived from Sunium and left it there. It's quite clear from their account that it will be here today; and so by tomorrow, Socrates, you will have to — to end your life.

Socrates: Well, Crito, I hope that it may be for the best; if the gods will it so, so be it. All the same, I don't think it will arrive today.

Crito: What makes you think that?

Socrates: I will try to explain. I think I am right in saying that I have to die on the day after the boat arrives?

Crito: That's what the authorities say, at any rate. 20

Socrates: Then I don't think it will arrive on this day that is just beginning, but on the day after. I am going by a dream that I had in the night, only a little while ago. It looks as though you were right not to wake me up.

Crito: Why, what was the dream about?

Socrates: I thought I saw a gloriously beautiful woman dressed in white robes, who came up to me and addressed me in these words: "Socrates, to the pleasant land of Phthia on the third day thou shalt come."

Crito: Your dream makes no sense, Socrates.

Socrates: To my mind, Crito, it is perfectly clear. 25

Crito: Too clear, apparently. But look here, Socrates, it is still not too late to take my advice and escape. Your death means a double calamity for me. I shall not only lose a friend whom I can never possibly replace, but besides a great many people who don't know you and me very well will be sure to think that I let you down, because I could have saved you if I had been willing to spend the money; and what could be more contemptible than to get a name for thinking more of money than of your friends? Most people will never believe that it was you who refused to leave this place although we tried our hardest to persuade you.

---

[1]**Delos . . . arrives** Ordinarily execution was immediately carried out, but the day before Socrates' trial was the first day of an annual ceremony that involved sending a ship to Delos. When the ship was absent — in this case for about a month — executions could not be performed. As Crito goes on to say, Socrates could easily escape, and indeed he could have left the country before being tried. [All notes are the editors'.]

Socrates: But my dear Crito, why should we pay so much attention to what "most people" think? The really reasonable people, who have more claim to be considered, will believe that the facts are exactly as they are.

Crito: You can see for yourself, Socrates, that one has to think of popular opinion as well. Your present position is quite enough to show that the capacity of ordinary people for causing trouble is not confined to petty annoyances, but has hardly any limits if you once get a bad name with them.

Socrates: I only wish that ordinary people *had* unlimited capacity for doing harm; then they might have an unlimited power for doing good; which would be a splendid thing, if it were so. Actually they have neither. They cannot make a man wise or stupid; they simply act at random.

Crito: Have it that way if you like; but tell me this, Socrates. I hope that you aren't worrying about the possible effects on me and the rest of your friends, and thinking that if you escape we shall have trouble with informers for having helped you to get away, and have to forfeit all our property or pay an enormous fine, or even incur some further punishment? If any idea like that is troubling you, you can dismiss it altogether. We are quite entitled to run that risk in saving you, and even worse, if necessary. Take my advice, and be reasonable.

Socrates: All that you say is very much in my mind, Crito, and a great deal more besides.

Crito: Very well, then, don't let it distress you. I know some people who are willing to rescue you from here and get you out of the country for quite a moderate sum. And then surely you realize how cheap these informers are to buy off; we shan't need much money to settle them; and I think you've got enough of my money for yourself already. And then even supposing that in your anxiety for my safety you feel that you oughtn't to spend my money, there are these foreign gentlemen staying in Athens who are quite willing to spend theirs. One of them, Simmias of Thebes, has actually brought the money with him for this very purpose; and Cebes and a number of others are quite ready to do the same. So as I say, you mustn't let any fears on these grounds make you slacken your efforts to escape; and you mustn't feel any misgivings about what you said at your trial, that you wouldn't know what to do with yourself if you left this country. Wherever you go, there are plenty of places where you will find a welcome; and if you choose to go to Thessaly, I have friends there who will make much of you and give you complete protection, so that no one in Thessaly can interfere with you.

Besides, Socrates, I don't even feel that it is right for you to try to do what you are doing, throwing away your life when you might save it. You are doing your best to treat yourself in exactly the same way as your enemies would, or rather did, when they wanted to ruin you. What is more, it seems to me that you are letting your sons down too. You have it in your power to finish their bringing up and education, and instead of that you are proposing to go off and desert them, and so far as you are concerned they will have to take their chance. And what sort of chance are they likely to get? The sort of thing that usually happens to orphans when they lose their parents. Either one ought not to have children at all, or one ought to see their upbringing and education through to the end. It strikes me that you are taking the line of least resistance, whereas you ought to make the choice of a good man and a brave one, considering that you profess to have made goodness your object all through life. Really, I am ashamed, both on your account and on ours your friends'; it will look as though we had played something like a coward's part all through this affair of yours. First, there was the way you came into court when it was quite unnecessary — that was the first act; than there was the conduct of the defense — that was the second; and finally, to complete the farce, we get this situation, which makes it appear that we have let you slip out of our hands through some lack of courage and enterprise on our part, because we didn't save you, and you didn't save yourself, when it would have been quite possible and practicable, if we had been any use at all.

There, Socrates; if you aren't careful, besides the suffering there will be all this disgrace for you and us to bear. Come, make up your mind. Really it's too late for that now; you ought to have it made up already. There is no alternative; the whole thing must be carried through during this coming night. If we lose any more time, it can't be done, it will be too late. I appeal to you, Socrates, on every ground; take my advice and please don't be unreasonable!

Socrates: My dear Crito, I appreciate your warm feelings very much 35 — that is, assuming that they have some justification; if not, the stronger they are, the harder they will be to deal with. Very well, then; we must consider whether we ought to follow your advice or not. You know that this is not a new idea of mine; it has always been my nature never to accept advice from any of my friends unless reflection shows that it is the best course that reason offers. I cannot abandon the principles which I used to hold in the past simply because this accident has happened to me; they seem to me to be much as they were, and I respect and regard the same principles now as before. So unless we can find better principles on this occasion, you can be quite sure that I shall not agree with you; not even if the power of the people conjures up fresh hordes of bogies to terrify our childish minds, by subjecting us to chains and executions and confiscations of our property.

Well, then, how can we consider the question most reasonably? Suppose that we begin by reverting to this view which you hold about people's opinions. Was it always right to argue that some opinions should be taken seriously but not others? Or was it always wrong? Perhaps it was right before the question of my death arose, but now we can see clearly that it was a mistaken persistence in a point of view which was really irresponsible nonsense. I should like very much to inquire into this problem, Crito, with your help, and to see whether the argument will appear in any different light to me now that I am in this position, or whether it will remain the same; and whether we shall dismiss it or accept it.

Serious thinkers, I believe, have always held some such view as the one which I mentioned just now: that some of the opinions which people entertain should be respected, and others should not. Now I ask you, Crito, don't you think that this is a sound principle?—You are safe from the prospect of dying tomorrow, in all human probability; and you are not likely to have your judgment upset by this impending calamity. Consider, then; don't you think that this is a sound enough principle, that one should not regard all the opinions that people hold, but only some and not others? What do you say? Isn't that a fair statement?

Crito: Yes, it is.

Socrates: In other words, one should regard the good ones and not the bad?

Crito: Yes.   40

Socrates: The opinions of the wise being good, and the opinions of the foolish bad?

Crito: Naturally.

Socrates: To pass on, then: What do you think of the sort of illustration that I used to employ? When a man is in training, and taking it seriously, does he pay attention to all praise and criticism and opinion indiscriminately, or only when it comes from the one qualified person, the actual doctor or trainer?

Crito: Only when it comes from the one qualified person.

Socrates: Then he should be afraid of the criticism and welcome the 45 praise of the one qualified person, but not those of the general public.

Crito: Obviously.

Socrates: So he ought to regulate his actions and exercises and eating and drinking by the judgment of his instructor, who has expert knowledge, rather than by the opinions of the rest of the public.

Crito: Yes, that is so.

Socrates: Very well. Now if he disobeys the one man and disregards his opinion and commendations, and pays attention to the advice of the many who have no expert knowledge, surely he will suffer some bad effect?

Crito: Certainly.   50

Socrates: And what is this bad effect? Where is it produced?—I mean, in what part of the disobedient person?

Crito: His body, obviously; that is what suffers.

Socrates: Very good. Well now, tell me, Crito—we don't want to go through all the examples one by one—does this apply as a general rule, and above all to the sort of actions which we are trying to decide about: just and unjust, honorable and dishonorable, good and bad? Ought we to be guided and intimidated by the opinion of the many or by that of the one— assuming that there is someone with expert knowledge? Is it true that we ought to respect and fear this person more than all the rest put together; and that if we do not follow his guidance we shall spoil and mutilate that part of us which, as we used to say, is improved by right conduct and destroyed by wrong? Or is this all nonsense?

Crito: No, I think it is true, Socrates.

Socrates: Then consider the next step. There is a part of us which is 55
improved by healthy actions and ruined by unhealthy ones. If we spoil it by
taking the advice of nonexperts, will life be worth living when this part is
once ruined? The part I mean is the body; do you accept this?

Crito: Yes.

Socrates: Well, is life worth living with a body which is worn out and
ruined by health?

Crito: Certainly not.

Socrates: What about the part of us which is mutilated by wrong actions and benefited by right ones? Is life worth living with this part ruined?
Or do we believe that this part of us, whatever it may be, in which right and
wrong operate, is of less importance than the body?

Crito: Certainly not. 60

Socrates: It is really more precious?

Crito: Much more.

Socrates: In that case, my dear fellow, what we ought to consider is
not so much what people in general will say about us but how we stand
with the expert in right and wrong, the one authority, who represents the
actual truth. So in the first place your proposition is not correct when you
say that we should consider popular opinion in questions of what is right
and honorable and good, or the opposite. Of course one might object "All
the same, the people have the power to put us to death."

Crito: No doubt about that! Quite true, Socrates; it is a possible objection.

Socrates: But so far as I can see, my dear fellow, the argument which 65
we have just been through is quite unaffected by it. At the same time I
should like you to consider whether we are still satisfied on this point: that
the really important thing is not to live, but to live well.

Crito: Why, yes.

Socrates: And that to live well means the same thing as to live honor-
ably or rightly?

Crito: Yes.

Socrates: Then in the light of this agreement we must consider
whether or not it is right for me to try to get away without an official discharge. If it turns out to be right, we must make the attempt; if not, we
must let it drop. As for the considerations you raise about expense and reputation and bringing up children, I am afraid, Crito, that they represent the
reflections of the ordinary public, who put people to death, and would
bring them back to life if they could, with equal indifference to reason. Our
real duty, I fancy, since the argument leads that way, is to consider one
question only, the one which we raised just now: Shall we be acting rightly
in paying money and showing gratitude to these people who are going to
rescue me, and in escaping or arranging the escape ourselves, or shall we
really be acting wrongly in doing all this? If it becomes clear that such conduct is wrong, I cannot help thinking that the question whether we are sure
to die, or to suffer any other ill effect for that matter, if we stand our

ground and take no action, ought not to weigh with us at all in comparison
with the risk of doing what is wrong.

Crito: I agree with what you say, Socrates; but I wish you would con- 70
sider what we ought to *do*.

Socrates: Let us look at it together, my dear fellow; and if you can
challenge any of my arguments, do so and I will listen to you; but if you
can't, be a good fellow and stop telling me over and over again that I ought
to leave this place without official permission. I am very anxious to obtain
your approval before I adopt the course which I have in mind; I don't want
to act against your convictions. Now give your attention to the starting
point of this inquiry — I hope that you will be satisfied with my way of stating it — and try to answer my questions to the best of your judgment.

Crito: Well, I will try.

Socrates: Do we say that one must never willingly do wrong, or does it
depend upon circumstance? Is it true, as we have often agreed before, that
there is no sense in which wrongdoing is good or honorable? Or have we
jettisoned all our former convictions in these last few days? Can you and I
at our age, Crito, have spent all these years in serious discussions without
realizing that we were no better than a pair of children? Surely the truth is
just what we have always said. Whatever the popular view is, and whether
the alternative is pleasanter than the present one or even harder to bear,
the fact remains that to do wrong is in every sense bad and dishonorable
for the person who does it. Is that our view, or not?

Crito: Yes, it is.

Socrates: Then in no circumstances must one do wrong. 75

Crito: No.

Socrates: In that case one must not even do wrong when one is
wronged, which most people regard as the natural course.

Crito: Apparently not.

Socrates: Tell me another thing, Crito: Ought one to do injuries or
not?

Crito: Surely not, Socrates. 80

Socrates: And tell me: Is it right to do an injury in retaliation, as most
people believe, or not?

Crito: No, never.

Socrates: Because, I suppose, there is no difference between injuring
people and wronging them.

Crito: Exactly.

Socrates: So one ought not to return a wrong or an injury to any per- 85
son, whatever the provocation is. Now be careful, Crito, that in making
these single admissions you do not end by admitting something contrary to
your real beliefs. I know that there are and always will be few people who
think like this; and consequently between those who do think so and those
who do not there can be no agreement on principle; they must always feel
contempt when they observe one another's decisions. I want even you to
consider very carefully whether you share my views and agree with me, and

whether we can proceed with our discussion from the established hypothesis that it is never right to do a wrong or return a wrong or defend one's self against injury by retaliation; or whether you dissociate yourself from any share in this view as a basis for discussion. I have held it for a long time, and still hold it; but if you have formed any other opinion, say so and tell me what it is. If, on the other hand, you stand by what we have said, listen to my next point.

Crito: Yes, I stand by it and agree with you. Go on.

Socrates: Well, here is my next point, or rather question. Ought one to fulfill all one's agreements, provided that they are right, or break them?

Crito: One ought to fulfill them.

Socrates: Then consider the logical consequence. If we leave this place without first persuading the State to let us go, are we or are we not doing an injury, and doing it in a quarter where it is least justifiable? Are we or are we not abiding by our just agreements?

Crito: I can't answer your question, Socrates; I am not clear in my 90 mind.

Socrates: Look at it in this way. Suppose that while we were preparing to run away from here (or however one should describe it) the Laws and Constitution of Athens were to come and confront us and ask this question: "Now, Socrates, what are you proposing to do? Can you deny that by this act which you are contemplating you intend, so far as you have the power, to destroy us, the Laws, and the whole State as well? Do you imagine that a city can continue to exist and not be turned upside down, if the legal judgments which are pronounced in it have no force but are nullified and destroyed by private persons?"—how shall we answer this question, Crito, and others of the same kind? There is much that could be said, especially by a professional advocate, to protest against the invalidation of this law which enacts that judgments once pronounced shall be binding. Shall we say "Yes, I do intend to destroy the laws, because the State wronged me by passing a faulty judgment at my trial"? Is this to be our answer, or what?

Crito: What you have just said, by all means, Socrates.

Socrates: Then what supposing the Laws say, "Was there provision for this in the agreement between you and us, Socrates? Or did you undertake to abide by whatever judgments the State pronounced?" If we expressed surprise at such language, they would probably say: "Never mind our language, Socrates, but answer our questions; after all, you are accustomed to the method of question and answer. Come now, what charge do you bring against us and the State, that you are trying to destroy us? Did we not give you life in the first place? Was it not through us that your father married your mother and begot you? Tell us, have you any complaint against those of us Laws that deal with marriage?" "No, none," I should say. "Well, have you any against the laws which deal with children's upbringing and education, such as you had yourself? Are you not grateful to those of us Laws which were instituted for this end, for requiring your father to give you a cultural and physical education?" "Yes," I should say. "Very good. Then since you have been born and brought up and educated, can you deny, in the first place, that you were our child and servant, both you and your ancestors? And if this is so, do you imagine that what is right for us is equally right for you, and that whatever we try to do to you, you are justified in retaliating? You did not have equality of rights with your father, or your employer (supposing that you had had one), to enable you to retaliate; you were not allowed to answer back when you were scolded or to hit back when you were beaten, or to do a great many other things of the same kind. Do you expect to have such license against your country and its laws that if we try to put you to death in the belief that it is right to do so, you on your part will try your hardest to destroy your country and us its Laws in return? And will you, the true devotee of goodness, claim that you are justified in doing so? Are you so wise as to have forgotten that compared with your mother and father and all the rest of your ancestors your country is something far more precious, more venerable, more sacred, and held in greater honor both among gods and among all reasonable men? Do you not realize that you are even more bound to respect and placate the anger of your country than your father's anger? That if you cannot persuade your country you must do whatever it orders, and patiently submit to any punishment that it imposes, whether it be flogging or imprisonment? And if it leads you out to war, to be wounded or killed, you must comply, and it is right that you should do so; you must not give way or retreat or abandon your position. Both in war and in the law courts and everywhere else you must do whatever your city and your country commands, or else persuade it in accordance with universal justice; but violence is a sin even against your parents, and it is a far greater sin against your country" — What shall we say to this, Crito? — that what the Laws say is true, or not?

Crito: Yes, I think so.

Socrates: "Consider, then, Socrates," the Laws would probably continue, "whether it is also true for us to say that what you are now trying to do to us is not right. Although we have brought you into the world and reared you and educated you, and given you and all your fellow citizens a share in all the good things at our disposal, nevertheless by the very fact of granting our permission we openly proclaim this principle: that any Athenian, on attaining to manhood and seeing for himself the political organization of the State and us its Laws, is permitted, if he is not satisfied with us, to take his property and go away wherever he likes. If any of you chooses to go to one of our colonies, supposing that he should not be satisfied with us and the State, or to emigrate to any other country, not one of us Laws hinders or prevents him from going away wherever he likes, without any loss of property. On the other hand, if any one of you stands his ground when he can see how we administer justice and the rest of our public organization, we hold that by so doing he has in fact undertaken to do anything that we tell him; and we maintain that anyone who disobeys is guilty of doing wrong on three separate counts: first because we are his parents, and secondly because we are his guardians; and thirdly because, after promising

obedience, he is neither obeying us nor persuading us to change our decision if we are at fault in any way; and although all our orders are in the
form of proposals, not of savage commands, and we give him the choice of
either persuading us or doing what we say, he is actually doing neither.
These are the charges, Socrates, to which we say that you will be liable if
you do what you are contemplating; and you will not be the least culpable
of your fellow countrymen, but one of the most guilty." If I said "Why do
you say that?" they would no doubt pounce upon me with perfect justice
and point out that there are very few people in Athens who have entered
into this agreement with them as explicitly as I have. They would say
"Socrates, we have substantial evidence that you are satisfied with us and
with the State. You would not have been so exceptionally reluctant to cross
the borders of your country if you had not been exceptionally attached to
it. You have never left the city to attend a festival or for any other purpose,
except on some military expedition; you have never traveled abroad as
other people do, and you have never felt the impulse to acquaint yourself
with another country or constitution; you have been content with us and
with our city. You have definitely chosen us, and undertaken to observe us
in all your activities as a citizen; and as the crowning proof that you are satisfied with our city, you have begotten children in it. Furthermore, even at
the time of your trial you could have proposed the penalty of banishment,
if you had chosen to do so; that is, you could have done then with the sanction of the State what you are now trying to do without it. But whereas at
that time you made a noble show of indifference if you had to die, and in
fact preferred death, as you said, to banishment, now you show no respect
for your earlier professions, and no regard for us, the Laws, whom you are
trying to destroy; you are behaving like the lowest type of menial, trying to
run away in spite of the contracts and undertakings by which you agreed to
live as a member of our State. Now first answer this question: Are we or
are we not speaking the truth when we say that you have undertaken, in
deed if not in word, to live your life as a citizen in obedience to us?" What
are we to say to that, Crito? Are we not bound to admit it?

Crito: We cannot help it, Socrates.

Socrates: "It is a fact, then," they would say, "that you are breaking
covenants and undertakings made with us, although you made them under
no compulsion or misunderstanding, and were not compelled to decide in a
limited time; you had seventy years in which you could have left the country,
if you were not satisfied with us or felt that the agreements were unfair. You
did not choose Sparta or Crete — your favorite models of good government
— or any other Greek or foreign state; you could not have absented yourself
from the city less if you had been lame or blind or decrepit in some other
way. It is quite obvious that you stand by yourself above all other Athenians
in your affection for this city and for us its Laws; — who would care for a city
without laws? And now, after all this, are you not going to stand by your
agreement? Yes, you are, Socrates, if you will take our advice; and then you
will at least escape being laughed at for leaving the city.

"We invite you to consider what good you will do to yourself or your friends if you commit this breach of faith and stain your conscience. It is fairly obvious that the risk of being banished and either losing their citizenship or having their property confiscated will extend to your friends as well. As for yourself, if you go to one of the neighboring states, such as Thebes or Megara, which are both well governed, you will enter them as an enemy to their constitution[2] and all good patriots will eye you with suspicion as a destroyer of law and order. Incidentally you will confirm the opinion of the jurors who tried you that they gave a correct verdict; a destroyer of laws might very well be supposed to have a destructive influence upon young and foolish human beings. Do you intend, then, to avoid well governed states and the higher forms of human society? And if you do, will life be worth living? Or will you approach these people and have the impudence to converse with them? What arguments will you use, Socrates? The same which you used here, that goodness and integrity, institutions and laws, are the most precious possessions of mankind? Do you not think that Socrates and everything about him will appear in a disreputable light? You certainly ought to think so. But perhaps you will retire from this part of the world and go to Crito's friends in Thessaly? That is the home of indiscipline and laxity, and no doubt they would enjoy hearing the amusing story of how you managed to run away from prison by arraying yourself in some costume or putting on a shepherd's smock or some other conventional runaway's disguise, and altering your personal appearance. And will no one comment on the fact that an old man of your age, probably with only a short time left to live, should dare to cling so greedily to life, at the price of violating the most stringent laws? Perhaps not, if you avoid irritating anyone. Otherwise, Socrates, you will hear a good many humiliating comments. So you will live as the toady and slave of all the populace, literally 'roistering in Thessaly,' as though you had left this country for Thessaly to attend a banquet there; and where will your discussions about goodness and uprightness be then, we should like to know? But of course you want to live for your children's sake, so that you may be able to bring them up and educate them. Indeed! by first taking them off to Thessaly and making foreigners of them, so that they may have that additional enjoyment? Or if that is not your intention, supposing that they are brought up here with you still alive, will they be better cared for and educated without you, because of course your friends will look after them? Will they look after your children if you go away to Thessaly, and not if you go away to the next world? Surely if those who profess to be your friends are worth anything, you must believe that they would care for them.

"No, Socrates; be advised by us your guardians, and do not think more of your children or of your life or of anything else than you think of what is right; so that when you enter the next world you may have all this to plead in your defense before the authorities there. It seems clear that if you do

---

[2]**as an enemy to their constitution** As a lawbreaker.

this thing, neither you nor any of your friends will be the better for it or be more upright or have a cleaner conscience here in this world, nor will it be better for you when you reach the next. As it is, you will leave this place, when you do, as the victim of a wrong done not by us, the Laws, but by your fellow men. But if you leave in that dishonorable way, returning wrong for wrong and evil for evil, breaking your agreements and covenants with us, and injuring those whom you least ought to injure — yourself, your friends, your country, and us — then you will have to face our anger in your lifetime, and in that place beyond when the laws of the other world know that you have tried, so far as you could, to destroy even us their brothers, they will not receive you with a kindly welcome. Do not take Crito's advice, but follow ours."

That, my dear friend Crito, I do assure you, is what I seem to hear 100 them saying, just as a mystic seems to hear the strains of music; and the sound of their arguments rings so loudly in my head that I cannot hear the other side. I warn you that, as my opinion stands at present, it will be useless to urge a different view. However, if you think that you will do any good by it, say what you like.

Crito: No, Socrates, I have nothing to say.

Socrates: Then give it up, Crito, and let us follow this course, since God points out the way.

Topics for Critical Thinking and Writing

1. State as precisely as you can all the arguments Crito uses to try to convince Socrates that he ought to escape. Which of these arguments seems to you to be the best? The worst? Why?

2. Socrates says to Crito, "I cannot abandon the principles which I used to hold in the past simply because this accident [the misfortune of being convicted by the Athenian assembly and then sentenced to death] has happened to me . . ." (para. 35). Does this remark strike you as self-righteous? Stubborn? Smug? Stupid? Explain.

3. Socrates declares that "serious thinkers" have always held the view that "some of the opinions which people entertain should be respected, and others should not" (para. 37). There are two main alternatives to this principle: (a) One should respect *all* the opinions that others hold, and (b) one should respect *none* of the opinions of others. Socrates attacks (a) but he ignores (b).What are his objections to (a)? Do you find them convincing? Can you think of any convincing arguments against (b)?

4. As Socrates shows in his reply to Crito, he seems ready to believe that there are "experts in right and wrong" — that is, persons with expert opinion or even authoritative knowledge on matters of right and wrong conduct — and that their advice should be sought and followed. Do you agree? Consider the thesis that there are no such experts, and write a 500-word essay defending or attacking it.

5. Socrates, as he comments to Crito, believes that "it is never right to do a wrong

or return a wrong or defend one's self against injury by retaliation" (para. 85). He does not offer any argument for this thesis in the dialogue (although he does elsewhere). It was a very strange doctrine in his day, and even now it is not generally accepted. Write a 1,000-word essay defending or attacking this thesis.

6. Socrates seems to argue: Because (a) no one ought to do wrong, and because (b) it would injure the state for someone in Socrates' position to escape, because (c) this act would break a "just agreement" between the citizen and his state, therefore (d) no one in Socrates' position should escape. Do you think this argument is valid? If not, what further assumptions would be needed to make it valid? Do you think the argument is sound (i.e., both valid and true in all its premises)? If not, explain. If you had to attack premise (b) or (c), which do you think is the more vulnerable, and why?

7. In the imaginary speech by the Laws of Athens to Socrates, especially in paragraph 93, the Laws convey a picture of the supremacy of the state over the individual — and Socrates seems to assent to this picture. Do you? Why, or why not?

8. The Laws (para. 95) claim that if Socrates were to escape, he would be "guilty of doing wrong on three separate counts." What are they? Do you agree with all or any? Why, or why not? Read the essay by Martin Luther King, Jr., "Letter from Birmingham Jail" (p. 593), and decide how King would have responded to the judgment of the Laws of Athens.

9. At the end of their peroration (para. 99), the Laws of Athens say to Socrates: Take your punishment as prescribed, and at your death "you will leave this place . . . as the victim of wrong done not by us, the Laws, but by your fellow men." To what wrong do the Laws allude? Do you agree that it is men and not laws who perpetrated this wrong? If you were in Socrates' position, would it matter to you if you were being wronged not by laws but only by men? Explain.

Thomas Jefferson

The Declaration of Independence

When in the course of human events, it becomes necessary for one people to dissolve the political bands which have connected them with another, and to assume among the Powers of the earth, the separate and equal station to which the Laws of Nature and of Nature's God entitle them, a decent respect to the opinions of mankind requires that they should declare the causes which impel them to the separation.

Thomas Jefferson (1743–1826) was a congressman, the governor of Virginia, the first Secretary of State, and the president of the United States, but he said he wished to be remembered for only three things: drafting the Declaration of Independence, writing the Virginia Statute for Religious Freedom, and founding the University of Virginia. All three were efforts to promote freedom.

We hold these truths to be self-evident, that all men are created equal, that they are endowed by their Creator with certain unalienable Rights, that among these are Life, Liberty and the pursuit of Happiness.

That to secure these rights, Governments are instituted among Men, deriving their just powers from the consent of the governed.

That whenever any Form of Government becomes destructive of these ends, it is the Right of the People to alter or to abolish it, and to institute a new Government, laying its foundation on such principles and organizing its powers in such form, as to them shall seem most likely to effect their Safety and Happiness. Prudence, indeed, will dictate that Governments long established should not be changed for light and transient causes; and accordingly all experience hath shown that mankind are more disposed to suffer, while evils are sufferable, than to right themselves by abolishing the forms to which they are accustomed. But when a long train of abuses and usurpations pursuing invariably the same Object evinces a design to reduce them under absolute Despotism, it is their right, it is their duty, to throw off such government, and to provide new Guards for their future security.

Such has been the patient sufferance of these Colonies; and such is now the necessity which constrains them to alter their former Systems of Government. The history of the present King of Great Britain is a history of repeated injuries and usurpations, all having in direct object the establishment of an absolute Tyranny over these States. To prove this, let Facts be submitted to a candid world. 5

He has refused his Assent to Laws, the most wholesome and necessary for the public good.

He has forbidden his Governors to pass Laws of immediate and pressing importance, unless suspended in their operation till his Assent should be obtained; and when so suspended, he has utterly neglected to attend to them.

He has refused to pass over Laws for the accommodation of large districts of people, unless those people would relinquish the right of Representation in the Legislature, a right inestimable to them and formidable to tyrants only.

He has called together legislative bodies at places unusual, uncomfortable, and distant from the depository of their Public Records, for the sole purpose of fatiguing them into compliance with his measures.

Jefferson was born in Virginia, and educated at William and Mary College in Williamsburg, Virginia. After graduating he studied law, was admitted to the bar, and in 1769 was elected to the Virginia House of Burgesses, his first political office. In 1776 he went to Philadelphia as a delegate to the second Continental Congress, where he was elected to a committee of five to write the Declaration of Independence. Jefferson drafted the document, which was than subjected to some changes by the other members of the committee and by the Congress. Although he was unhappy with the changes (especially with the deletion of a passage against slavery), his claim to have written the Declaration is just.

He has dissolved Representative Houses repeatedly, for opposing with 10 manly firmness his invasions on the rights of the people.

He has refused for a long time, after such dissolutions, to cause others to be elected; whereby the Legislative Powers, incapable of Annihilation, have returned to the People at large for their exercise; the State remaining in the mean time exposed to all the dangers of invasion from without, and convulsions within.

He has endeavored to prevent the population of these States, for that purpose obstructing the Laws of Naturalization of Foreigners; refusing to pass others to encourage their migration hither, and raising the conditions of new Appropriations of Lands.

He has obstructed the Administration of Justice, by refusing his Assent to Laws for establishing Judiciary Powers.

He has made Judges dependent on his Will alone, for the tenure of their offices, and the amount and payment of their salaries.

He has erected a multitude of New Offices, and sent hither swarms of 15 Officers to harass our People, and eat out their substance.

He has kept among us, in time of peace, Standing Armies without the consent of our Legislature.

He has affected to render the Military independent of and superior to the Civil Power.

He has combined with others to subject us to jurisdictions foreign to our constitution, and unacknowledged by our laws; giving his Assent to their acts of pretended Legislation:

For quartering large bodies of armed troops among us:

For protecting them, by a mock Trial, from Punishment for any Mur- 20 ders which they should commit on the Inhabitants of these States:

For cutting off our Trade with all parts of the world:

For imposing Taxes on us without our Consent:

For depriving us in many cases, of the benefits of Trial by Jury:

For transporting us beyond Seas to be tried for pretended offenses:

For abolishing the free System of English Laws in a Neighbouring 25 Province, establishing therein an Arbitrary government, and enlarging its boundaries so as to render it at once an example and fit instrument for introducing the same absolute rule into these Colonies:

For taking away our Charters, abolishing our most valuable Laws, and altering fundamentally the Forms of our Governments.

For suspending our own Legislatures, and declaring themselves invested with Power to legislate for us in all cases whatsoever.

He has abdicated Government here, by declaring us out of his Protection and waging War against us.

He has plundered our seas, ravaged our Coasts, burnt our towns and destroyed the Lives of our people.

He is at this time transporting large Armies of foreign Mercenaries to 30 compleat the works of death, desolation and tyranny, already begun with circumstances of Cruelty & perfidy scarcely paralleled in the most barbarous ages, and totally unworthy the Head of a civilized nation.

He has constrained our fellow Citizens taken Captive on the high Seas to bear Arms against their Country, to become the executioners of their friends and Brethren, or to fall themselves by their Hands.

He has excited domestic insurrections amongst us, and has endeavored to bring on the inhabitants of our frontiers, the merciless Indian Savages, whose known rule of warfare is an undistinguished destruction of all ages, sexes and conditions.

In every stage of these Oppressions We Have Petitioned for Redress in the most humble terms: Our repeated petitions have been answered only by repeated injury. A Prince, whose character is thus marked by every act which may define a Tyrant, is unfit to be the ruler of a free People.

Nor have We been wanting in attention to our British brethren. We have warned them from time to time of attempts by their legislature to extend an unwarrantable jurisdiction over us. We have reminded them of the circumstances of our emigration and settlement here. We have appealed to their native justice and magnanimity and we have conjured them by the ties of our common kindred to disavow these usurpations, which would inevitably interrupt our connections and correspondence. They too have been deaf to the voice of justice and of consanguinity. We must, therefore, acquiesce in the necessity, which denounces our Separation, and hold them, as we hold the rest of mankind, Enemies in War, in Peace Friends.

We, therefore, the Representatives of the United States of America, in 35 General Congress, Assembled, appealing to the Supreme Judge of the world of the rectitude of our intentions, do, in the Name, and by Authority of the good People of these Colonies, solemnly publish and declare, That these United Colonies are, and of Right ought to be, Free and Independent States; that they are Absolved from all Allegiance to the British Crown, and that all political connection between them and the State of Great Britain, is and ought to be totally dissolved; and that as Free and Independent States, they have full power to levy War, conclude Peace, contract Alliances, establish Commerce, and so all the other Acts and Things which Independent States may of right do. And for the support of this Declaration, with a firm reliance on the protection of Divine Providence, we mutually pledge to each other our lives, our Fortunes and our sacred Honor.

Topics for Critical Thinking and Writing

1. According to the first paragraph, for what audience was the Declaration written? What other audiences do you think the document was (in one way or another) addressed to?

2. The Declaration states that it is intended to "prove" that the acts of the govern-

ment of George III had as their "direct object the establishment of an absolute tyranny" in the American colonies. Write an essay of 500 to 750 words showing whether the evidence offered in the Declaration "proves" this claim to your satisfaction. (You will, of course, want to define "absolute tyranny.") If you think further evidence is needed to "prove" the colonists' point, indicate what this evidence might be.

3. Paying special attention to the paragraphs beginning "That whenever any Form of Government" (para. 4), "In every stage" (para. 33), and "Nor have We been wanting" (para. 34), in a sentence or two set forth the image of themselves that the colonists seek to convey.

4. In the Declaration of Independence it is argued that the colonists are entitled to certain things, and that under certain conditions they may behave in a certain way. Make explicit the syllogism that Jefferson is arguing.

5. What evidence does Jefferson offer to support his major premise? His minor premise?

6. The Declaration cites "certain unalienable Rights" and mentions three: "Life, Liberty and the pursuit of Happiness." What is an unalienable right? If someone has an unalienable (or inalienable) right, does that imply that he or she also has certain duties? If so, what are these duties? John Locke, a century earlier (1690), asserted that all men have a natural right to "life, liberty, and property." Do you think the decision to drop "property" from this list and substitute "pursuit of Happiness" made an improvement? Explain.

7. The Declaration ends thus: "We mutually pledge to each other our lives, our Fortunes and our sacred Honor." Is it surprising that Honor is put in the final, climactic position? Is this a better ending than "our Fortunes, our sacred Honor, and our lives," or than "our sacred Honor, our lives, and our fortunes?" Why?

8. King George III has asked you to reply, on his behalf, to the colonists, in 500 to 750 words. Write his reply. (*Caution:* A good reply will probably require you to do some reading about the period.)

9. Write a declaration of your own, setting forth in 500 to 750 words why some group is entitled to independence. You may want to argue that adolescents should not be compelled to attend school, or that animals should not be confined in zoos, or that persons who use drugs should be able to buy them legally. Begin with a premise, then set forth facts illustrating the unfairness of the present condition, and conclude by stating what the new condition will mean to society.

Elizabeth Cady Stanton

Declaration of Sentiments and Resolutions

When, in the course of human events, it becomes necessary for one portion of the family of man to assume among the people of the earth a position different from that which they have hitherto occupied, but one to which the laws of nature and of nature's God entitle them, a decent respect to the opinions of mankind requires that they should declare the causes that impel them to such a course.

We hold these truths to be self-evident: that all men and women are created equal; that they are endowed by their Creator with certain inalienable rights; that among these are life, liberty and the pursuit of happiness; that to secure these rights governments are instituted, deriving their just powers from the consent of the governed. Whenever any form of government becomes destructive of these ends, it is the right of those who suffer from it to refuse allegiance to it, and to insist upon the institution of a new government, laying its foundation on such principles, and organizing its powers in such form, as to them shall seem most likely to effect their safety and happiness. Prudence, indeed, will dictate that governments long established should not be changed for light and transient causes; and accordingly all experience hath shown that mankind are more disposed to suffer, while evils are sufferable, than to right themselves by abolishing the forms to which they were accustomed. But when a long train of abuses and usurpations, pursuing invariably the same object, evinces a design to reduce them under absolute despotism, it is their duty to throw off such government, and to provide new guards for their future security. Such has been the patient sufferance of the women under this government, and such is now the necessity which constrains them to demand the equal station to which they are entitled.

The history of mankind is a history of repeated injuries and usurpations on the part of man toward woman, having in direct object the establishment of an absolute tyranny over her. To prove this, let facts be submitted to a candid world.

He has never permitted her to exercise her inalienable right to the elective franchise.

He has compelled her to submit to laws, in the formation of which she   5
had no voice.

Elizabeth Cady Stanton (1815–1902), a lawyer's daughter and journalist's wife, proposed in 1848 a convention to address the "social, civil, and religious condition and rights of women." Responding to Stanton's call, women from all over the Northeast convened in the village of Seneca Falls, New York. Her Declaration, adopted by the Seneca Falls Convention — but only after vigorous debate and some amendments by others — became the platform for the women's movement in this country.

He has withheld from her rights which are given to the most ignorant and degraded men — both natives and foreigners.

Having deprived her of this first right of a citizen, the elective franchise, thereby leaving her without representation in the halls of legislation, he has oppressed her on all sides.

He has made her, if married, in the eye of the law, civilly dead.

He has taken from her all right in property, even to the wages she earns.

He has made her, morally, an irresponsible being, as she can commit 10 many crimes with impunity, provided they be done in the presence of her husband. In the covenant of marriage, she is compelled to promise obedience to her husband, he becoming to all intents and purposes, her master — the law giving him power to deprive her of her liberty, and to administer chastisement.

He has so framed the laws of divorce, as to what shall be the proper causes, and in case of separation, to whom the guardianship of the children shall be given, as to be wholly regardless of the happiness of women — the law, in all cases, going upon a false supposition of the supremacy of man, and giving all power into his hands.

After depriving her of all rights as a married woman, if single, and the owner of property, he has taxed her to support a government which recognizes her only when her property can be made profitable to it.

He has monopolized nearly all the profitable employments, and from those she is permitted to follow, she receives but a scanty remuneration. He closes against her all the avenues to wealth and distinction which he considers most honorable to himself. As a teacher of theology, medicine, or law, she is not known.

He has denied her the facilities for obtaining a thorough education, all colleges being closed against her.

He allows her in Church, as well as State, but a subordinate position, 15 claiming Apostolic authority for her exclusion from the ministry, and, with some exceptions, from any public participation in the affairs of the Church.

He has created a false public sentiment by giving to the world a different code of morals for men and women, by which moral delinquencies which exclude women from society, are not only tolerated, but deemed of little account in man.

He has usurped the prerogative of Jehovah himself, claiming it as his right to assign for her a sphere of action, when that belongs to her conscience and to her God.

He has endeavored, in every way that he could, to destroy her confidence in her own powers, to lessen her self-respect, and to make her willing to lead a dependent and abject life.

Now, in view of this entire disfranchisement of one-half the people of this country, their social and religious degradation — in view of the unjust laws above mentioned, and because women do feel themselves aggrieved, oppressed, and fraudulently deprived of their most sacred rights, we insist that they have immediate admission to all the rights and privileges which belong to them as citizens of the United States.

In entering upon the great work before us, we anticipate no small 20 amount of misconception, misrepresentation, and ridicule; but we shall use every instrumentality within our power to effect our object. We shall employ agents, circulate tracts, petition the State and National legislatures, and endeavor to enlist the pulpit and the press in our behalf. We hope this Convention will be followed by a series of Conventions embracing every part of the country.

[The following resolutions were discussed by Lucretia Mott, Thomas and Mary Ann McClintock, Amy Post, Catharine A. F. Stebbins, and others, and were adopted:]

Whereas, The great precept of nature is conceded to be, that "man shall pursue his own true and substantial happiness." Blackstone in his Commentaries remarks, that this law of Nature being coeval with mankind, and dictated by God himself, is of course superior in obligation to any other. It is binding over all the globe, in all countries, and at all times; no human laws are of any validity if contrary to this, and such of them as are valid, derive all their force, and all their validity, and all their authority, mediately and immediately, from this original; therefore,

Resolved, That such laws as conflict, in any way, with the true and substantial happiness of woman, are contrary to the great precept of nature and of no validity, for this is "superior in obligation to any other."

Resolved, That all laws which prevent woman from occupying such a station in society as her conscience shall dictate, or which place her in a position inferior to that of man, are contrary to the great precept of nature, and therefore of no force or authority.

Resolved, That woman is man's equal—was intended to be so by the Creator, and the highest good of the race demands that she should be recognized as such.

Resolved, That the women of this country ought to be enlightened in 25 regard to the laws under which they live, that they may no longer publish their degradation by declaring themselves satisfied with their present position, nor their ignorance, by asserting that they have all the rights they want.

Resolved, That inasmuch as man, while claiming for himself intellectual superiority, does accord to woman moral superiority, it is preeminently his duty to encourage her to speak and teach, as she has an opportunity, in all religious assemblies.

Resolved, That the same amount of virtue, delicacy, and refinement of behavior that is required of woman in the social state, should also be required of man, and the same transgressions should be visited with equal severity on both man and woman.

Resolved, That the objection of indelicacy and impropriety, which is so often brought against woman when she addresses a public audience, comes with a very ill-grace from those who encourage, by their attendance, her appearance on the stage, in the concert, or in feats of the circus.

Resolved, That woman has too long rested satisfied in the circumscribed limits which corrupt customs and a perverted application of the Scriptures have marked out for her, and that it is time she should move in the enlarged sphere which her great Creator has assigned her.

Resolved, That it is the duty of the women of this country to secure to 30 themselves their sacred right to the elective franchise.

Resolved, That the equality of human rights results necessarily from the fact of the identity of the race in capabilities and responsibilities.

Resolved, therefore, That, being invested by the Creator with the same capabilities, and the same consciousness of responsibility for their exercise, it is demonstrably the right and duty of woman, equally with man, to promote every righteous cause by every righteous means; and especially in regard to the great subjects of morals and religion, it is self-evidently her right to participate with her brother in teaching them, both in private and in public, by writing and by speaking, by any instrumentalities proper to be used, and in any assemblies proper to be held; and this being a self-evident truth growing out of the divinely implanted principles of human nature, any custom or authority adverse to it, whether modern or wearing the hoary sanction of antiquity, is to be regarded as a self-evident falsehood, and at war with mankind.

[At the last session Lucretia Mott offered and spoke to the following resolution:]

Resolved, That the speedy success of our cause depends upon the zealous and untiring efforts of both men and women, for the overthrow of the monopoly of the pulpit, and for the securing to woman an equal participation with men in the various trades, professions, and commerce.

Topics for Critical Thinking and Writing ══════

1. Stanton echoes the Declaration of Independence because she wishes to associate her ideas and the movement she supports with a document and a movement that her readers esteem. And of course she must have believed that if readers esteem the Declaration of Independence, they must grant the justice of her goals. Does her strategy work, or does it backfire by making her essay seem strained?

2. When Stanton insists that women have an "inalienable right to the elective franchise" (para. 4), what does she mean by inalienable?

3. Stanton complains that men have made women, "in the eye of the law, civilly dead" (para. 8). What does she mean by civilly dead? How is it possible for a person to be biologically alive yet civilly dead?

4. Stanton objects that women are "not known" as teachers of "theology, medicine, or law" (para. 13). Is this still true today? Do some research in your library, and then write three 100-word biographical sketches, one each on a well-known woman professor of theology, of medicine, and of law.

5. How might you go about proving (rather than merely asserting) that, as paragraph 24 says, "woman is man's equal—was intended to be so by the Creator"?

6. The Declaration claims that women have "the same capabilities" as men (para. 32). Yet in 1848 Stanton and the others at Seneca Falls knew, or should have known, that history recorded no example of an outstanding woman philosopher to compare with Plato or Kant, a great composer to compare with Beethoven or Chopin, a scientist to compare with Galileo or Newton, or a creative mathematician to compare with Euclid or Descartes. Do these facts contradict the Declaration's claim? If not, why not? How else but by different intellectual capabilities do you think such facts are to be explained?

7. Stanton's Declaration is almost 150 years old. Have all of the issues she raised been satisfactorily resolved? If not, which ones remain?

8. In our society, children have very few rights. For instance, a child cannot decide to drop out of elementary school or high school, and a child cannot decide to leave his or her parents in order to reside with some other family that he or she finds more compatible. Whatever your view of children's rights, compose the best Declaration of the Rights of Children that you can compose.

Martin Luther King, Jr.

Letter from Birmingham Jail

[In 1963 Dr. King was arrested in Birmingham, Alabama, for participating in a march for which no parade permit had been issued by the city officials. In jail he wrote a response to a letter that eight local clergymen had published in a newspaper. Their letter, titled "A Call for Unity," is printed here, followed by King's response.]

Martin Luther King, Jr., (1929–1968) was born in Atlanta and educated at Morehouse College, Crozer Theological Seminary, and Boston University. In 1954 he was called to serve as a Baptist minister in Montgomery, Alabama. During the next two years he achieved national fame when, using a policy of nonviolent resistance, he successfully led the boycott against segregated bus lines in Montgomery. He then organized the Southern Christian Leadership Conference, which furthered civil rights, first in the South and then nationwide. In 1964 he was awarded the Nobel Peace Prize. Four years later he was assassinated in Memphis, Tennessee, while supporting striking garbage workers.

A CALL FOR UNITY

April 12, 1963

We the undersigned clergymen are among those who, in January, issued "An Appeal for Law and Order and Common Sense," in dealing with racial problems in Alabama. We expressed understanding that honest convictions in racial matters could properly be pursued in the courts, but urged that decisions of those courts should in the meantime be peacefully obeyed.

Since that time there had been some evidence of increased forebearance and a willingness to face facts. Responsible citizens have undertaken to work on various problems which cause racial friction and unrest. In Birmingham, recent public events have given indication that we all have opportunity for a new constructive and realistic approach to racial problems.

However, we are now confronted by a series of demonstrations by some of our Negro citizens, directed and led in part by outsiders. We recognize the natural impatience of people who feel that their hopes are slow in being realized. But we are convinced that these demonstrations are unwise and untimely.

We agree rather with certain local Negro leadership which has called for honest and open negotiation of racial issues in our area. And we believe this kind of facing of issues can best be accomplished by citizens of our own metropolitan area, white and Negro, meeting with their knowledge and experience of the local situation. All of us need to face that responsibility and find proper channels for its accomplishment.

Just as we formerly pointed out that "hatred and violence have no   5
sanction in our religious and political traditions," we also point out that such actions as incite to hatred and violence, however technically peaceful those actions may be, have not contributed to the resolution of our local problems. We do not believe that these days of new hope are days when extreme measures are justified in Birmingham.

We commend the community as a whole, and the local news media and law enforcement officials in particular, on the calm manner in which these demonstrations have been handled. We urge the public to continue to show restraint should the demonstrations continue, and the law enforcement officials to remain calm and continue to protect our city from violence.

We further strongly urge our own Negro community to withdraw support from these demonstrations, and to unite locally in working peacefully for a better Birmingham. When rights are consistently denied, a cause should be pressed in the courts and in negotiations among local leaders, and not in the streets. We appeal to both our white and Negro citizenry to observe the principles of law and order and common sense.

C.C.J. Carpenter, D.D., L.L.D., Bishop of Alabama; Joseph A. Durick, D.D., Auxiliary Bishop, Diocese of Mobile-Birmingham; Rabbi

Milton L. Grafman, Temple Emanu-El, Birmingham, Alabama; Bishop Paul Hardin, Bishop of the Alabama–West Florida Conference of the Methodist Church; Bishop Nolan B. Harmon, Bishop of the North Alabama Conference of the Methodist Church; George M. Murray, D.D., L.L.D., Bishop Coadjutor, Episcopal Diocese of Alabama; Edward V. Ramage, Moderator, Synod of the Alabama Presbyterian Church in the United States; Earl Stallings, Pastor, First Baptist Church, Birmingham, Alabama.

LETTER FROM BIRMINGHAM JAIL

April 16, 1963

My Dear Fellow Clergyman:

While confined here in the Birmingham city jail, I came across your recent statement calling my present activities "unwise and untimely."[1] Seldom do I pause to answer criticism of my work and ideas. If I sought to answer all the criticisms that cross my desk, my secretaries would have little time for anything other than such correspondence in the course of the day, and I would have no time for constructive work. But since I feel that you are men of genuine good will and that your criticisms are sincerely set forth, I want to try to answer your statement in what I hope will be patient and reasonable terms.

I think I should indicate why I am here in Birmingham, since you have been influenced by the view which argues against "outsiders coming in." I have the honor of serving as president of the Southern Christian Leadership Conference, an organization operating in every southern state, with headquarters in Atlanta, Georgia. We have some eighty-five affiliated organizations across the South, and one of them is the Alabama Christian Movement for Human Rights. Frequently we share staff, educational, and financial resources with our affiliates. Several months ago the affiliate here in Birmingham asked us to be on call to engage in a nonviolent direct-action program if such were deemed necessary. We readily consented, and when the hour came we lived up to our promise. So I, along with several members of my staff, am here because I was invited here. I am here because I have organizational ties here.

But more basically, I am in Birmingham because injustice is here. Just as the prophets of the eighth century B.C. left their villages and carried their "thus saith the Lord" far beyond the boundaries of their home towns,

---

[1]This response to a published statement by eight fellow clergymen from Alabama (Bishop C.C.J. Carpenter, Bishop Joseph A. Durick, Rabbi Milton L. Grafman, Bishop Paul Hardin, Bishop Nolan B. Harmon, the Reverend George M. Murray, the Reverend Edward V. Ramage, and the Reverend Earl Stallings) was composed under somewhat constricting circumstances. Begun on the margins of the newspaper in which the statement appeared while I was in jail, the letter was continued on scraps of writing paper supplied by a friendly Negro trusty, and concluded on a pad my attorneys were eventually permitted to leave me. Although the text remains in substance unaltered, I have indulged in the author's prerogative of polishing it for publication. [King's note.]

and just as the Apostle Paul left his village of Tarsus and carried the gospel of Jesus Christ to the far corners of the Greco-Roman world, so am I compelled to carry the gospel of freedom beyond my own home town. Like Paul, I must constantly respond to the Macedonian call for aid.

Moreover, I am cognizant of the interrelatedness of all communities and states. I cannot sit idly by in Atlanta and not be concerned about what happens in Birmingham. Injustice anywhere is a threat to justice everywhere. We are caught in an inescapable network of mutuality; tied in a single garment of destiny. Whatever affects one directly, affects all indirectly. Never again can we afford to live with the narrow, provincial "outside agitator" idea. Anyone who lives inside the United States can never be considered an outsider anywhere within its bounds.

You deplore the demonstrations taking place in Birmingham. But your 5 statement, I am sorry to say, fails to express a similar concern for the conditions that brought about the demonstrations. I am sure that none of you would want to rest content with the superficial kind of social analysis that deals merely with effects and does not grapple with underlying causes. It is unfortunate that demonstrations are taking place in Birmingham, but it is even more unfortunate that the city's white power structure left the Negro community with no alternative.

In any nonviolent campaign there are four basic steps: collection of the facts to determine whether injustices exist; negotiation; self-purification; and direct action. We have gone through all these steps in Birmingham. There can be no gainsaying the fact that racial injustice engulfs this community. Birmingham is probably the most thoroughly segregated city in the United States. Its ugly record of brutality is widely known. Negroes have experienced grossly unjust treatment in the courts. There have been more unsolved bombings of Negro homes and churches in Birmingham than in any other city in the nation. These are the hard, brutal facts of the case. On the basis of these conditions, Negro leaders sought to negotiate with the city fathers. But the latter consistently refused to engage in good-faith negotiation.

Then, last September, came the opportunity to talk with leaders of Birmingham's economic community. In the course of the negotiations, certain promises were made by the merchants — for example, to remove the stores' humiliating racial signs. On the basis of these promises, the Reverend Fred Shuttlesworth and the leaders of the Alabama Christian Movement for Human Rights agreed to a moratorium on all demonstrations. As the weeks and months went by, we realized that we were the victims of a broken promise. A few signs, briefly removed, returned; the others remained.

As in so many past experiences, our hopes had been blasted, and the shadow of deep disappointment settled upon us. We had no alternative except to prepare for direct action, whereby we would present our very bodies as a means of laying our case before the conscience of the local and the national community. Mindful of the difficulties involved, we decided to undertake a process of self-purification. We began a series of workshops on nonviolence, and we repeatedly asked ourselves: "Are you able to accept blows without retaliating?" "Are you able to endure the ordeal of jail?" We decided to schedule our direct-action program for the Easter season, realizing that except for Christmas, this is the main shopping period of the year. Knowing that a strong economic-withdrawal program would be the by-product of direct action, we felt that this would be the best time to bring pressure to bear on the merchants for the needed change.

Then it occurred to us that Birmingham's mayoralty election was coming up in March, and we speedily decided to postpone action until after election day. When we discovered that the Commissioner of Public Safety, Eugene "Bull" Connor, had piled up enough votes to be in the run-off, we decided again to postpone action until the day after the run-off so that the demonstrations could not be used to cloud the issues. Like many others, we waited to see Mr. Connor defeated, and to this end we endured postponement after postponement. Having aided in this community need, we felt that our direct-action program could be delayed no longer.

You may well ask: "Why direct action? Why sit-ins, marches, and so 10 forth? Isn't negotiation a better path?" You are quite right in calling for negotiation. Indeed, this is the very purpose of direct action. Nonviolent direct action seeks to create such a crisis and foster such a tension that a community which has constantly refused to negotiate is forced to confront the issue. It seeks so to dramatize the issue that it can no longer be ignored. My citing the creation of tension as part of the work of the nonviolent-resister may sound rather shocking. But I must confess that I am not afraid of the word "tension." I have earnestly opposed violent tension, but there is a type of constructive, nonviolent tension which is necessary for growth. Just as Socrates felt that it was necessary to create a tension in the mind so that individuals could rise from the bondage of myths and half-truths to the unfettered realm of creative analysis and objective appraisal, so must we see the need for nonviolent gadflies to create the kind of tension in society that will help men rise from the dark depths of prejudice and racism to the majestic heights of understanding and brotherhood.

The purpose of our direct-action program is to create a situation so crisis-packed that it will inevitably open the door to negotiation. I therefore concur with you in your call for negotiation. Too long has our beloved Southland been bogged down in a tragic effort to live in monologue rather than dialogue.

One of the basic points in your statement is that the action that I and my associates have taken in Birmingham is untimely. Some have asked: "Why didn't you give the new city administration time to act?" The only answer that I can give to this query is that the new Birmingham administration must be prodded about as much as the outgoing one, before it will act. We are sadly mistaken if we feel that the election of Albert Boutwell as mayor will bring the millennium to Birmingham. While Mr. Boutwell is a much more gentle person than Mr. Connor, they are both segregationists, dedicated to maintenance of the status quo. I have hope that Mr. Boutwell will be reasonable enough to see the futility of massive resistance to desegregation. But he will not see this without pressure from devotees of civil rights. My friends, I must say to you that we have not made a single gain in civil rights without determined legal and nonviolent pressure. Lamentably, it is an historical fact that privileged groups seldom give up their privileges voluntarily. Individuals may see the moral light and voluntarily give up their unjust posture; but as Reinhold Niebuhr[2] has reminded us, groups tend to be more immoral than individuals.

We know through painful experience that freedom is never voluntarily given by the oppressor; it must be demanded by the oppressed. Frankly, I have yet to engage in a direct-action campaign that was "well timed" in the view of those who have not suffered unduly from the disease of segregation. For years now I have heard the word "Wait!" It rings in the ear of every Negro with piercing familiarity. This "Wait" has almost always meant "Never." We must come to see, with one of our distinguished jurists, that "justice too long delayed is justice denied."[3]

We have waited for more than 340 years for our constitutional and God-given rights. The nations of Asia and Africa are moving with jetlike speed toward gaining political independence, but we still creep at horse-and-buggy pace toward gaining a cup of coffee at a lunch counter. Perhaps it is easy for those who have never felt the stinging darts of segregation to say, "Wait." But when you have seen vicious mobs lynch your mothers and fathers at will and drown your sisters and brothers at whim; when you have seen hate-filled policemen curse, kick, and even kill your black brothers and sisters; when you see the vast majority of your twenty million Negro brothers smothering in an airtight cage of poverty in the midst of an affluent society; when you suddenly find your tongue twisted and your speech stammering as you seek to explain to your 6-year-old daughter why she can't go to the public amusement park that has just been advertised on television, and see tears welling up in her eyes when she is told that Funtown is closed to colored children, and see ominous clouds of inferiority beginning to form in her little mental sky, and see her beginning to distort her personality by developing an unconscious bitterness toward white people; when you have to concoct an answer for a 5-year-old son who is asking: "Daddy, why do white people treat colored people so mean?"; when you take a cross-country drive and find it necessary to sleep night after night in the uncomfortable corners of your automobile because no motel will accept you; when you are humiliated day in and day out by nagging signs reading "white" and "colored"; when your first name becomes "nig-

---

[2]**Reinhold Niebuhr** Niebuhr (1892–1971) was a minister, political activist, author, and professor of applied Christianity at Union Theological Seminary. [All notes are the editors' unless otherwise specified.]

[3]**justice . . . denied** A quotation attributed to William E. Gladstone (1809–1898), British statesman and prime minister.

ger," your middle name becomes "boy" (however old you are) and your last name becomes "John," and your wife and mother are never given the respected title "Mrs."; when you are harried by day and haunted by night by the fact that you are a Negro, living constantly at tiptoe stance, never quite knowing what to expect next, and are plagued with inner fears and outer resentments; when you are forever fighting a degenerating sense of "nobodiness"—then you will understand why we find it difficult to wait. There comes a time when the cup of endurance runs over, and men are no longer willing to be plunged into the abyss of despair. I hope, sirs, you can understand our legitimate and unavoidable impatience.

You express a great deal of anxiety over our willingness to break laws. 15 This is certainly a legitimate concern. Since we so diligently urge people to obey the Supreme Court's decision of 1954 outlawing segregation in the public schools, at first glance it may seem rather paradoxical for us consciously to break laws. One may well ask: "How can you advocate breaking some laws and obeying others?" The answer lies in the fact that there are two types of laws: just and unjust. I would be the first to advocate obeying just laws. One has not only a legal but a moral responsibility to obey just laws. Conversely, one has a moral responsibility to disobey unjust laws. I would agree with St. Augustine that "an unjust law is no law at all."

Now, what is the difference between the two? How does one determine whether a law is just or unjust? A just law is a man-made code that squares with the moral law or the law of God. An unjust law is a code that is out of harmony with the moral law. To put it in the terms of St. Thomas Aquinas: An unjust law is a human law that is not rooted in eternal law and natural law. Any law that uplifts human personality is just. Any law that degrades human personality is unjust. All segregation statutes are unjust because segregation distorts the soul and damages the personality. It gives the segregator a false sense of superiority and the segregated a false sense of inferiority. Segregation, to use the terminology of the Jewish philosopher Martin Buber, substitutes an "I-it" relationship for an "I-thou" relationship and ends up relegating persons to the status of things. Hence segregation is not only politically, economically, and sociologically unsound, it is morally wrong and sinful. Paul Tillich[4] has said that sin is separation. Is not segregation an existential expression of man's tragic separation, his awful estrangement, his terrible sinfulness? Thus it is that I can urge men to obey the 1954 decision of the Supreme Court, for it is morally right; and I can urge them to disobey segregation ordinances, for they are morally wrong.

Let us consider a more concrete example of just and unjust laws. An unjust law is a code that a numerical or power majority group compels a minority group to obey but does not make binding on itself. This is *differ-*

[4]**Paul Tillich** Tillich (1886–1965), born in Germany, taught theology at several German universities, but in 1933 he was dismissed from his post at the University of Frankfurt because of his opposition to the Nazi regime. At the invitation of Reinhold Niebuhr, he came to the United States and taught at Union Theological Seminary.

ence made legal. By the same token, a just law is a code that a majority compels a minority to follow and that it is willing to follow itself. This is *sameness* made legal.

Let me give another explanation. A law is unjust if it is inflicted on a minority that, as a result of being denied the right to vote, had no part in enacting or devising the law. Who can say that the legislature of Alabama which set up that state's segregation laws was democratically elected? Throughout Alabama all sorts of devious methods are used to prevent Negroes from becoming registered voters, and there are some counties in which, even though Negroes constitute a majority of the population, not a single Negro is registered. Can any law enacted under such circumstances be considered democratically structured?

Sometimes a law is just on its face and unjust in its application. For instance, I have been arrested on a charge of parading without a permit. Now, there is nothing wrong in having an ordinance which requires a permit for a parade. But such an ordinance becomes unjust when it is used to maintain segregation and to deny citizens the First Amendment privilege of peaceful assembly and protest.

I hope you are able to see the distinction I am trying to point out. In 20 no sense do I advocate evading or defying the law, as would the rabid segregationist. That would lead to anarchy. One who breaks an unjust law must do so openly, lovingly, and with a willingness to accept the penalty. I submit that an individual who breaks a law that conscience tells him is unjust, and who willingly accepts the penalty of imprisonment in order to arouse the conscience of the community over its injustice, is in reality expressing the highest respect for law.

Of course, there is nothing new about this kind of civil disobedience. It was evidenced sublimely in the refusal of Shadrach, Meshach, and Abednego to obey the laws of Nebuchadnezzar, on the ground that a higher moral law was at stake. It was practiced superbly by the early Christians, who were willing to face hungry lions and the excruciating pain of chopping blocks rather than submit to certain unjust laws of the Roman Empire. To a degree, academic freedom is a reality today because Socrates practiced civil disobedience. In our own nation, the Boston Tea Party represented a massive act of civil disobedience.

We should never forget that everything Adolf Hitler did in Germany was "legal" and everything the Hungarian freedom fighters did in Hungary was "illegal." It was "illegal" to aid and comfort a Jew in Hitler's Germany. Even so, I am sure that, had I lived in Germany at the time, I would have aided and comforted my Jewish brothers. If today I lived in a Communist country where certain principles dear to the Christian faith are suppressed, I would openly advocate disobeying that country's antireligious laws.

I must make two honest confessions to you, my Christian and Jewish brothers. First, I must confess that over the past few years I have been gravely disappointed with the white moderate. I have almost reached the regrettable conclusion that the Negro's great stumbling block in his stride toward freedom is not the White Citizen's Counciler or the Ku Klux Klanner, but the white moderate, who is more devoted to "order" than to justice; who prefers a negative peace which is the absence of tension to a positive peace which is the presence of justice; who constantly says: "I agree with you in the goal you seek, but I cannot agree with your methods or direct action"; who paternalistically believes he can set the timetable for another man's freedom; who lives by a mythical concept of time and who constantly advises the Negro to wait for a "more convenient season." Shallow understanding from people of good will is more frustrating than absolute misunderstanding from people of ill will. Lukewarm acceptance is much more bewildering than outright rejection.

I had hoped that the white moderate would understand that law and order exist for the purpose of establishing justice and that when they fail in this purpose they become the dangerously structured dams that block the flow of social progress. I had hoped that the white moderate would understand that the present tension in the South is a necessary phase of the transition from an obnoxious negative peace, in which the Negro passively accepted his unjust plight, to a substantive and positive peace, in which all men will respect the dignity and worth of human personality. Actually, we who engage in nonviolent direct action are not the creators of tension. We merely bring to the surface the hidden tension that is already alive. We bring it out in the open, where it can be seen and dealt with. Like a boil that can never be cured so long as it is covered up but must be opened with all its ugliness to the natural medicines of air and light, injustice must be exposed, with all the tension its exposure creates, to the light of human conscience and the air of national opinion before it can be cured.

In your statement you assert that our actions, even though peaceful, 25 must be condemned because they precipitate violence. But is this a logical assertion? Isn't this like condemning a robbed man because his possession of money precipitated the evil act of robbery? Isn't this like condemning Socrates because his unswerving commitment to truth and his philosophical inquiries precipitated the act by the misguided populace in which they made him drink hemlock? Isn't this like condemning Jesus because his unique God-consciousness and never-ceasing devotion to God's will precipitated the evil act of crucifixion? We must come to see that, as the federal courts have consistently affirmed, it is wrong to urge an individual to cease his efforts to gain his basic constitutional rights because the quest may precipitate violence. Society must protect the robbed and punish the robber.

I had also hoped that the white moderate would reject the myth concerning time in relation to the struggle for freedom. I have just received a letter from a white brother in Texas. He writes: "All Christians know that the colored people will receive equal rights eventually, but it is possible that you are in too great a religious hurry. It has taken Christianity almost two thousand years to accomplish what it has. The teachings of Christ take time to come to earth." Such an attitude stems from a tragic misconception of time, from the strangely irrational notion that there is something in the very flow of time that will inevitably cure all ills. Actually, time itself is neutral; it can be used either destructively or constructively. More and more I feel that the people of ill will have used time much more effectively than have the people of good will. We will have to repent in this generation not merely for the hateful words and actions of the bad people but for the appalling silence of the good people. Human progress never rolls in on wheels of inevitability; it comes through the tireless efforts of men willing to be co-workers with God, and without this hard work, time itself becomes an ally of the forces of social stagnation. We must use time creatively, in the knowledge that the time is always ripe to do right. Now is the time to make real the promise of democracy and transform our pending national elegy into a creative psalm of brotherhood. Now is the time to lift our national policy from the quicksand of racial injustice to the solid rock of human dignity.

You speak of our activity in Birmingham as extreme. At first I was rather disappointed that fellow clergymen would see my nonviolent efforts as those of an extremist. I began thinking about the fact that I stand in the middle of two opposing forces in the Negro community. One is a force of complacency, made up in part of Negroes who, as a result of long years of oppression, are so drained of self-respect and a sense of "somebodiness" that they have adjusted to segregation; and in part of a few middle-class Negroes who, because of a degree of academic and economic security and because in some ways they profit by segregation, have become insensitive to the problems of the masses. The other force is one of bitterness and hatred, and it comes perilously close to advocating violence. It is expressed in the various black nationalist groups that are springing up across the nation, the largest and best-known being Elijah Muhammad's Muslim movement. Nourished by the Negro's frustration over the continued existence of racial discrimination, this movement is made up of people who have lost faith in America, who have absolutely repudiated Christianity, and who have concluded that the white man is an incorrigible "devil."

I have tried to stand between these two forces, saying that we need emulate neither the "do-nothingism" of the complacent nor the hatred and despair of the black nationalist. For there is the more excellent way of love and nonviolent protest. I am grateful to God that, through the influence of the Negro church, the way of nonviolence became an integral part of our struggle.

If this philosophy had not emerged, by now many streets of the South should, I am convinced, be flowing with blood. And I am further convinced that if our white brothers dismiss as "rabble-rousers" and "outside agitators" those of us who employ nonviolent direct action, and if they refuse to support our nonviolent efforts, millions of Negroes will, out of frustration and despair, seek solace and security in black-nationalist ideologies—a development that would inevitably lead to a frightening racial nightmare.

Oppressed people cannot remain oppressed forever. The yearning for 30 freedom eventually manifests itself, and that is what has happened to the American Negro. Something within has reminded him of his birthright of freedom, and something without has reminded him that it can be gained. Consciously or unconsciously, he has been caught up by the *Zeitgeist*,[5] and with his black brothers of Africa and his brown and yellow brothers of Asia, South America, and the Caribbean, the United States Negro is moving with a sense of great urgency toward the promised land of racial justice. If one recognizes this vital urge that has engulfed the Negro community, one should readily understand why public demonstrations are taking place. The Negro has many pent-up resentments and latent frustrations, and he must release them. So let him march; let him make prayer pilgrimages to the city hall; let him go on freedom rides — and try to understand why he must do so. If his repressed emotions are not released in nonviolent ways, they will seek expression through violence; this is not a threat but a fact of history. So I have not said to my people: "Get rid of your discontent." Rather, I have tried to say that this normal and healthy discontent can be channeled into the creative outlet of nonviolent direct action. And now this approach is being termed extremist.

But though I was initially disappointed at being categorized as an extremist, as I continued to think about the matter I gradually gained a measure of satisfaction from the label. Was not Jesus an extremist for love: "Love your enemies, bless them that curse you, do good to them that hate you, and pray for them which despitefully use you, and persecute you." Was not Amos an extremist for justice: "Let justice roll down like waters and righteousness like an ever-flowing stream." Was not Paul an extremist for the Christian gospel: "I bear in my body the marks of the Lord Jesus." Was not Martin Luther an extremist: "Here I stand; I cannot do otherwise, so help me God." And John Bunyan: "I will stay in jail to the end of my days before I make a butchery of my conscience." And Abraham Lincoln: "This nation cannot survive half slave and half free." And Thomas Jefferson: "We hold these truths to be self-evident, that all men are created equal. . . ." So the question is not whether we will be extremists, but what kind of extremists we will be. Will we be extremists for hate or for love? Will we be extremists for the preservation of injustice or for the extension of justice? In that dramatic scene on Calvary's hill three men were crucified. We must never forget that all three were crucified for the same crime — the crime of extremism. Two were extremists for immorality, and thus fell below their environment. The other, Jesus Christ, was an extremist for love, truth, and goodness, and thereby rose above his environment. Perhaps the South, the nation, and the world are in dire need of creative extremists.

I had hoped that the white moderate would see this need. Perhaps I was too optimistic; perhaps I expected too much. I suppose I should have realized that few members of the oppressor race can understand the deep

---

[5]*Zeitgeist* German for "spirit of the age."

groans and passionate yearnings of the oppressed race, and still fewer have the vision to see that injustice must be rooted out by strong, persistent, and determined action. I am thankful, however, that some of our white brothers in the South have grasped the meaning of this social revolution and committed themselves to it. They are still all too few in quantity, but they are big in quality. Some — such as Ralph McGill, Lillian Smith, Harry Golden, James McBride Dabbs, Ann Braden, and Sarah Patton Boyle — have written about our struggle in eloquent and prophetic terms. Others have marched with us down nameless streets of the South. They have languished in filthy, roach-infested jails, suffering the abuse and brutality of policemen who view them as "dirty nigger-lovers." Unlike so many of their moderate brothers and sisters, they have recognized the urgency of the moment and sensed the need for powerful "action" antidotes to combat the disease of segregation.

Let me take note of my other major disappointment. I have been so greatly disappointed with the white church and its leadership. Of course, there are some notable exceptions. I am not unmindful of the fact that each of you has taken some significant stands on this issue. I commend you, Reverend Stallings, for your Christian stand on this past Sunday, in welcoming Negroes to your worship service on a nonsegregated basis. I commend the Catholic leaders of this state for integrating Spring Hill College several years ago.

But despite these notable exceptions, I must honestly reiterate that I have been disappointed with the church. I do not say this as one of those negative critics who can always find something wrong with the church. I say this as a minister of the gospel, who loves the church; who was nurtured in its bosom; who has been sustained by its spiritual blessings and who will remain true to it as long as the cord of life shall lengthen.

When I was suddenly catapulted into the leadership of the bus protest 35 in Montgomery, Alabama, a few years ago, I felt we would be supported by the white church. I felt that the white ministers, priests, and rabbis of the South would be among our strongest allies. Instead, some have been outright opponents, refusing to understand the freedom movement and misrepresenting its leaders; all too many others have been more cautious than courageous and have remained silent behind the anesthetizing security of stained-glass windows.

In spite of my shattered dreams, I came to Birmingham with the hope that the white religious leadership of this community would see the justice of our cause and, with deep moral concern, would serve as the channel through which our just grievances could reach the power structure. I had hoped that each of you would understand. But again I have been disappointed.

I have heard numerous southern religious leaders admonish their worshipers to comply with a desegregation decision because it is the law, but I have longed to hear white ministers declare: "Follow this decree because integration is morally right and because the Negro is your brother." In the midst of blatant injustices inflicted upon the Negro, I have watched white churchmen stand on the sideline and mouth pious irrelevancies and sanctimonious trivialities. In the midst of a mighty struggle to rid our nation of racial and economic injustice, I have heard many ministers say: "Those are social issues, with which the gospel has no real concern." And I have watched many churches commit themselves to a completely otherworldly religion which makes a strange, unbiblical distinction between body and soul, between the sacred and the secular.

I have traveled the length and breadth of Alabama, Mississippi, and all the other southern states. On sweltering summer days and crisp autumn mornings I have looked at the South's beautiful churches with their lofty spires pointing heavenward. I have beheld the impressive outlines of her massive religious-education buildings. Over and over I have found myself saying: "What kind of people worship here? Who is their God? Where were their voices when the lips of Governor Barnett dripped with words of interposition and nullification? Where were they when Governor Wallace gave a clarion call for defiance and hatred? Where were their voices of support when bruised and weary Negro men and women decided to rise from the dark dungeons of complacency to the bright hills of creative protest?"

Yes, these questions are still in my mind. In deep disappointment I have wept over the laxity of the church. But be assured that my tears have been tears of love. There can be no deep disappointment where there is not deep love. Yes, I love the church. How could I do otherwise? I am in the rather unique position of being the son, the grandson, and the great-grandson of preachers. Yes, I see the church as the body of Christ. But, Oh! How we have blemished and scarred that body through social neglect and through fear of being nonconformists.

There was a time when the church was very powerful—in the time 40 when the early Christians rejoiced at being deemed worthy to suffer for what they believed. In those days the church was not merely a thermometer that recorded the ideas and principles of popular opinion; it was a thermostat that transformed the mores of society. Whenever the early Christians entered a town, the people in power became disturbed and immediately sought to convict the Christians for being "disturbers of the peace" and "outside agitators." But the Christians pressed on, in the conviction that they were "a colony of heaven," called to obey God rather than man. Small in number, they were big in commitment. They were too God-intoxicated to be "astronomically intimidated." By their effort and example they brought an end to such ancient evils as infanticide and gladiatorial contests.

Things are different now. So often the contemporary church is a weak, ineffectual voice with an uncertain sound. So often it is an archdefender of the status quo. Far from being disturbed by the presence of the church, the power structure of the average community is consoled by the church's silent—and often even vocal—sanction of things as they are.

But the judgment of God is upon the church as never before. If today's church does not recapture the sacrificial spirit of the early church, it will lose its authenticity, forfeit the loyalty of millions, and be dismissed as an irrelevant social club with no meaning for the twentieth century. Every day I meet young people whose disappointment with the church has turned into outright disgust.

Perhaps I have once again been too optimistic. Is organized religion too inextricably bound to the status quo to save our nation and the world? Perhaps I must turn my faith to the inner spiritual church, the church within the church, as the true *ekklesia* and the hope of the world. But again I am thankful to God that some noble souls from the ranks of organized religion have broken loose from the paralyzing chains of conformity and joined us as active partners in the struggle for freedom. They have left their secure congregations and walked the streets of Albany, Georgia, with us. They have gone down the highways of the South on tortuous rides for freedom. Yes, they have gone to jail with us. Some have been dismissed from their churches, have lost the support of their bishops and fellow ministers. But they have acted in the faith that right defeated is stronger than evil triumphant. Their witness has been the spiritual salt that has preserved the true meaning of the gospel in these troubled times. They have carved a tunnel of hope through the dark mountain of disappointment.

I hope the church as a whole will meet the challenge of this decisive hour. But even if the church does not come to the aid of justice, I have no despair about the future. I have no fear about the outcome of our struggle in Birmingham, even if our motives are at present misunderstood. We will reach the goal of freedom in Birmingham and all over the nation, because the goal of America is freedom. Abused and scorned though we may be, our destiny is tied up with America's destiny. Before the pilgrims landed at Plymouth, we were here. Before the pen of Jefferson etched the majestic words of the Declaration of Independence across the pages of history, we were here. For more than two centuries our forebears labored in this country without wages; they made cotton king; they built the homes of their masters while suffering gross injustice and shameful humiliation — and yet out of a bottomless vitality they continue to thrive and develop. If the inexpressible cruelties of slavery could not stop us, the opposition we now face will surely fail. We will win our freedom because the sacred heritage of our nation and the eternal will of God are embodied in our echoing demands.

Before closing I feel impelled to mention one other point in your [45] statement that has troubled me profoundly. You warmly commended the Birmingham police force for keeping "order" and "preventing violence." I doubt that you would have so warmly commended the police force if you had seen its dogs sinking their teeth into unarmed, nonviolent Negroes. I doubt that you would so quickly commend the policemen if you were to observe their ugly and inhumane treatment of Negroes here in the city jail; if you were to watch them push and curse old Negro women and young Negro girls; if you were to see them slap and kick old Negro men and young boys; if you were to observe them, as they did on two occasions, refuse to give us food because we wanted to sing our grace together. I cannot join you in your praise of the Birmingham police department.

It is true that the police have exercised a degree of discipline in handling the demonstrators. In this sense they have conducted themselves rather "nonviolently" in public. But for what purpose? To preserve the evil system of segregation. Over the past few years I have consistently preached that nonviolence demands that the means we use must be as pure as the ends we seek. I have tried to make clear that it is wrong to use immoral means to attain moral ends. But now I must affirm that it is just as wrong, or perhaps even more so, to use moral means to preserve immoral ends. Perhaps Mr. Connor and his policemen have been rather nonviolent in public, as was Chief Pritchett in Albany, Georgia, but they used the moral means of nonviolence to maintain the immoral end of racial injustice. As T. S. Eliot has said: "The last temptation is the greatest treason: To do the right deed for the wrong reason."

I wish you had commended the Negro sit-inners and demonstrators of Birmingham for their sublime courage, their willingness to suffer, and their amazing discipline in the midst of great provocation. One day the South will recognize its real heroes. They will be the James Merediths, with the noble sense of purpose that enables them to face jeering and hostile mobs, and with the agonizing loneliness that characterizes the life of the pioneer. They will be old, oppressed, battered Negro women, symbolized in a 72-year-old woman in Montgomery, Alabama, who rose up with a sense of dignity and with her people decided not to ride segregated buses, and who responded with ungrammatical profundity to one who inquired about her weariness: "My feets is tired, but my soul is at rest." They will be the young high school and college students, the young ministers of the gospel and a host of their elders, courageously and nonviolently sitting in at lunch counters and willingly going to jail for conscience' sake. One day the South will know that when these disinherited children of God sat down at lunch counters, they were in reality standing up for what is best in the American dream and for the most sacred values in our Judaeo-Christian heritage, thereby bringing our nation back to those great wells of democracy which were dug deep by the founding fathers in their formulation of the Constitution and the Declaration of Independence.

Never before have I written so long a letter. I'm afraid it is much too long to take your precious time. I can assure you that it would have been much shorter if I had been writing from a comfortable desk, but what else can one do when he is alone in a narrow jail cell, other than write long letters, think long thoughts, and pray long prayers?

If I have said anything in this letter that overstates the truth and indicates an unreasonable impatience, I beg you to forgive me. If I have said anything that understates the truth and indicates my having a patience that allows me to settle for anything less than brotherhood, I beg God to forgive me.

I hope this letter finds you strong in the faith. I also hope that circum- 50 stances will soon make it possible for me to meet each of you, not as an integrationist or a civil-rights leader but as a fellow clergyman and a Christian brother. Let us all hope that the dark clouds of racial prejudice will soon pass away and the deep fog of misunderstanding will be lifted from our fear-drenched communities, and in some not too distant tomorrow the radiant stars of love and brotherhood will shine over our great nation with all their scintillating beauty.

Yours for the cause of Peace and Brotherhood,

Martin Luther King, Jr.

Topics for Critical Thinking and Writing

1. In his first five paragraphs, how does King assure his audience that he is not a meddlesome intruder but a man of good will?

2. In paragraph 3 King refers to Hebrew prophets and to the Apostle Paul, and later (para. 10) to Socrates. What is the point of these references?

3. In paragraph 11 what does King mean when he says that "our beloved Southland" has long tried to "live in monologue rather than dialogue"?

4. King begins paragraph 23 with "I must make two honest confessions to you, my Christian and Jewish brothers." What would have been gained or lost if he had used this paragraph as his opening?

5. King's last three paragraphs do not advance his argument. What do they do?

6. Why does King advocate breaking unjust laws "openly, lovingly" (para. 20)? What does he mean by these words? What other motives or attitudes do these words rule out?

7. Construct two definitions of "civil disobedience," and explain whether and to what extent it is easier (or harder) to justify civil disobedience, depending on how you have defined the expression.

8. If you feel that you wish to respond to King's letter on some point, write a letter nominally addressed to King. You may, if you wish, adopt the persona of one of the eight clergymen whom King initially addressed.

9. King writes (para. 46) that "nonviolence demands that the means we use must be as pure as the ends we seek." How do you think King would evaluate the following acts of civil disobedience: (a) occupying a college administration building in order to protest the administration's unsatisfactory response to a racial incident on campus, or in order to protest the failure of the administration to hire minority persons as staff and faculty; (b) sailing on a collision course with a whaling ship to protest against whaling; (c) trespassing on an abortion clinic to protest abortion? Set down your answer in an essay of 500 words.

Susan Glaspell

Trifles

(Scene: The kitchen in the now abandoned farmhouse of John Wright, a gloomy kitchen, and left without having been put in order—unwashed pans under the sink, a loaf of bread outside the breadbox, a dish towel on the table—other signs of incompleted work. At the rear the outer door opens, and the Sheriff comes in, followed by the County Attorney and Hale. The Sheriff and Hale are men in middle life, the County Attorney is a young man; all are much bundled up and go at once to the stove. They are followed by the two women—the Sheriff's Wife first; she is a slight wiry woman, a thin nervous face. Mrs. Hale is larger and would ordinarily be called more comfortable looking, but she is disturbed now and looks fearfully about as she enters. The women have come in slowly and stand close together near the door.)

County Attorney (rubbing his hands): This feels good. Come up to the fire, ladies.

Mrs. Peters (after taking a step forward): I'm not—cold.

Sheriff (unbuttoning his overcoat and stepping away from the stove as if to the beginning of official business): Now, Mr. Hale, before we move things about, you explain to Mr. Henderson just what you saw when you came here yesterday morning.

County Attorney: By the way, has anything been moved? Are things just as you left them yesterday?

Sheriff (looking about): It's just the same. When it dropped below   5 zero last night, I thought I'd better send Frank out this morning to make a fire for us—no use getting pneumonia with a big case on; but I told him not to touch anything except the stove—and you know Frank.

County Attorney: Somebody should have been left here yesterday.

Sheriff: Oh—yesterday. When I had to send Frank to Morris Center for that man who went crazy—I want you to know I had my hands full yesterday. I knew you could get back from Omaha by today, and as long as I went over everything here myself—

County Attorney: Well, Mr. Hale, tell just what happened when you came here yesterday morning.

Hale: Harry and I had started to town with a load of potatoes. We came along the road from my place; and as I got here, I said, "I'm going to

Susan Glaspell (1882–1948) was born in Davenport, Iowa, and educated at Drake University in Des Moines. In 1903 she married George Cram Cook and, with Cook and other writers, actors, and artists, in 1915 founded the Provincetown Players, a group that remained vital until 1929. Glaspell wrote Trifles (1916) for the Provincetown Players, but she also wrote stories, novels, and a biography of her husband. In 1931 she won the Pulitzer Prize for Alison's House, a play about the family of a deceased poet who in some ways resembles Emily Dickinson.

see if I can't get John Wright to go in with me on a party telephone." I
spoke to Wright about it once before, and he put me off, saying folks talked
too much anyway, and all he asked was peace and quiet—I guess you
know about how much he talked himself; but I thought maybe if I went to
the house and talked about it before his wife, though I said to Harry that I
didn't know as what his wife wanted made much difference to John—

County Attorney: Let's talk about that later, Mr. Hale. I do want to   10
talk about that, but tell now just what happened when you got to the house.

Hale: I didn't hear or see anything; I knocked at the door, and still it
was all quiet inside. I knew they must be up, it was past eight o'clock. So I
knocked again, and I thought I heard somebody say, "Come in." I wasn't
sure, I'm not sure yet, but I opened the door—this door *(indicating the
door by which the two women are still standing)*, and there in that rocker
—*(pointing to it)* sat Mrs. Wright. *(They all look at the rocker.)*

County Attorney: What—was she doing?

Hale: She was rockin' back and forth. She had her apron in her hand
and was kind of—pleating it.

County Attorney: And how did she—look?

Hale: Well, she looked queer.   15

County Attorney: How do you mean—queer?

Hale: Well, as if she didn't know what she was going to do next. And
kind of done up.

County Attorney: How did she seem to feel about your coming?

Hale: Why, I don't think she minded—one way or other. She didn't
pay much attention. I said, "How do, Mrs. Wright, it's cold, ain't it?" And
she said, "Is it?"—and went on kind of pleating at her apron. Well, I was
surprised; she didn't ask me to come up to the stove, or to set down, but
just sat there, not even looking at me, so I said, "I want to see John." And
then she—laughed. I guess you would call it a laugh. I thought of Harry
and the team outside, so I said a little sharp: "Can't I see John?" "No," she
says, kind o' dull like. "Ain't he home?" says I. "Yes," says she, "he's home."
"Then why can't I see him?" I asked her, out of patience. "'Cause he's
dead," says she. *"Dead?"* says I. She just nodded her head, not getting a bit
excited, but rockin' back and forth. "Why—where is he?" says I, not knowing what to say. She just pointed upstairs—like that *(himself pointing to
the room above)*. I got up, with the idea of going up there. I walked from
there to here—then I says, "Why, what did he die of?" "He died of a rope
around his neck," says she, and just went on pleatin' at her apron. Well, I
went out and called Harry. I thought I might—need help. We went upstairs, and there he was lyin'—

County Attorney: I think I'd rather have you go into that upstairs,   20
where you can point it all out. Just go on now with the rest of the story.

Hale: Well, my first thought was to get that rope off. I looked . . .
(Stops, his face twitches.) . . . but Harry, he went up to him, and he said,
"No, he's dead all right, and we'd better not touch anything." So we went
back downstairs. She was still sitting that same way. "Has anybody been no-

tified?" I asked. "No," says she, unconcerned. "Who did this, Mrs. Wright?" said Harry. He said it businesslike—and she stopped pleatin' of her apron. "I don't know," she says. "You don't *know*?" says Harry. "No," says she, "Weren't you sleepin' in the bed with him?" says Harry. "Yes," says she, "but I was on the inside." "Somebody slipped a rope round his neck and strangled him, and you didn't wake up?" says Harry. "I didn't wake up," she said after him. We must 'a looked as if we didn't see how that could be, for after a minute she said, "I sleep sound." Harry was going to ask her more questions, but I said maybe we ought to let her tell her story first to the coroner, or the sheriff, so Harry went fast as he could to Rivers' place, where there's a telephone.

County Attorney: And what did Mrs. Wright do when she knew that you had gone for the coroner?

Hale: She moved from that chair to this over here . . . (*Pointing to a small chair in the corner.*) . . . and just sat there with her hands held together and looking down. I got a feeling that I ought to make some conversation, so I said I had come in to see if John wanted to put in a telephone, and at that she started to laugh, and then she stopped and looked at me— scared. (*The County Attorney, who has had his notebook out, makes a note.*) I dunno, maybe it wasn't scared. I wouldn't like to say it was. Soon Harry got back, and then Dr. Lloyd came, and you, Mr. Peters, and so I guess that's all I know that you don't.

County Attorney (looking around): I guess we'll go upstairs first— and then out to the barn and around there. (*To the Sheriff.*) You're convinced that there was nothing important here—nothing that would point to any motive?

Sheriff: Nothing here but kitchen things. (*The County Attorney, after* 25 *again looking around the kitchen, opens the door of a cupboard closet. He gets up on a chair and looks on a shelf. Pulls his hand away, sticky.*)

County Attorney: Here's a nice mess. (*The women draw nearer.*)

Mrs. Peters (to the other woman): Oh, her fruit; it did freeze. (*To the Lawyer.*) She worried about that when it turned so cold. She said the fire'd go out and her jars would break.

Sheriff: Well, can you beat the women! Held for murder and worryin' about her preserves.

County Attorney: I guess before we're through she may have something more serious than preserves to worry about.

Hale: Well, women are used to worrying over trifles. (*The two women* 30 *move a little closer together.*)

County Attorney (with the gallantry of a young politician): And yet, for all their worries, what would we do without the ladies? (*The women do not unbend. He goes to the sink, takes a dipperful of water from the pail and, pouring it into a basin, washes his hands. Starts to wipe them on the roller towel, turns it for a cleaner place.*) Dirty towels! (*Kicks his foot against the pans under the sink.*) Not much of a housekeeper, would you say, ladies?

Mrs. Hale (stiffly): There's a great deal of work to be done on a farm.

County Attorney: To be sure. And yet . . . *(With a little bow to her.)* . . . I know there are some Dickson county farmhouses which do not have such roller towels. *(He gives it a pull to expose its full length again.)*

Mrs. Hale: Those towels get dirty awful quick. Men's hands aren't always as clean as they might be.

County Attorney: Ah, loyal to your sex. I see. But you and Mrs. 35 Wright were neighbors. I suppose you were friends, too.

Mrs. Hale (shaking her head): I've not seen much of her of late years. I've not been in this house — it's more than a year.

County Attorney: And why was that? You didn't like her?

Mrs. Hale: I liked her all well enough. Farmers' wives have their hands full, Mr. Henderson. And then —

County Attorney: Yes — ?

Mrs. Hale (looking about): It never seemed a very cheerful place.   40

County Attorney: No — it's not cheerful. I shouldn't say she had the homemaking instinct.

Mrs. Hale: Well, I don't know as Wright had, either.

County Attorney: You mean they didn't get on very well?

Mrs. Hale: No, I don't mean anything. But I don't think a place'd be any cheerfuller for John Wright's being in it.

County Attorney: I'd like to talk more of that a little later. I want to 45 get the lay of things upstairs now. *(He goes to the left, where three steps lead to a stair door.)*

Sheriff: I suppose anything Mrs. Peters does'll be all right. She was to take in some clothes for her, you know, and a few little things. We left in such a hurry yesterday.

County Attorney: Yes, but I would like to see what you take, Mrs. Peters, and keep an eye out for anything that might be of use to us.

Mrs. Peters: Yes, Mr. Henderson. *(The women listen to the men's steps on the stairs, then look about the kitchen.)*

Mrs. Hale: I'd hate to have men coming into my kitchen, snooping around and criticizing. *(She arranges the pans under sink which the Lawyer had shoved out of place.)*

Mrs. Peters: Of course it's no more than their duty.   50

Mrs. Hale: Duty's all right, but I guess that deputy sheriff that came out to make the fire might have got a little of this on. *(Gives the roller towel a pull.)* Wish I'd thought of that sooner. Seems mean to talk about her for not having things slicked up when she had to come away in such a hurry.

Mrs. Peters (who has gone to a small table in the left rear corner of the room, and lifted one end of a towel that covers a pan): She had bread set. *(Stands still.)*

Mrs. Hale (eyes fixed on a loaf of bread beside the breadbox, which is on a low shelf at the other side of the room. Moves slowly toward it): She was going to put this in there. *(Picks up loaf, then abruptly drops it. In a manner of returning to familiar things.)* It's a shame about her fruit. I won-der if it's all gone. *(Gets up on the chair and looks.)* I think there's some here that's all right, Mrs. Peters. Yes—here; *(Holding it toward the window.)* this is cherries, too. *(Looking again.)* I declare I believe that's the only one. *(Gets down, bottle in her hand. Goes to the sink and wipes it off on the outside.)* She'll feel awful bad after all her hard work in the hot weather. I remember the afternoon I put up my cherries last summer. *(She puts the bottle on the big kitchen table, center of the room. With a sigh, is about to sit down in the rocking chair. Before she is seated realizes what chair it is; with a slow look at it, steps back. The chair, which she has touched, rocks back and forth.)*

Mrs. Peters: Well, I must get those things from the front room closet. *(She goes to the door at the right, but after looking into the other room steps back.)* You coming with me, Mrs. Hale? You could help me carry them. *(They go into the other room; reappear, Mrs. Peters carrying a dress and skirt, Mrs. Hale following with a pair of shoes.)*

Mrs. Peters: My, it's cold in there. *(She puts the cloth on the big table, 55 and hurries to the stove.)*

Mrs. Hale (examining the skirt): Wright was close. I think maybe that's why she kept so much to herself. She didn't even belong to the Ladies' Aid. I suppose she felt she couldn't do her part, and then you don't enjoy things when you feel shabby. She used to wear pretty clothes and be lively, when she was Minnie Foster, one of the town girls singing in the choir. But that—oh, that was thirty years ago. This all you was to take in?

Mrs. Peters: She said she wanted an apron. Funny thing to want, for there isn't much to get you dirty in jail, goodness knows. But I suppose just to make her feel more natural. She said they was in the top drawer in this cupboard. Yes, here. And then her little shawl that always hung behind the door. *(Opens stair door and looks.)* Yes, here it is. *(Quickly shuts door leading upstairs.)*

Mrs. Hale (abruptly moving toward her): Mrs. Peters?

Mrs. Peters: Yes, Mrs. Hale?

Mrs. Hale: Do you think she did it? 60

Mrs. Peters (in a frightened voice): Oh, I don't know.

Mrs. Hale: Well, I don't think she did. Asking for an apron and her lit-tle shawl. Worrying about her fruit.

Mrs. Peters (starts to speak, glances up, where footsteps are heard in the room above. In a low voice): Mr. Peters says it looks bad for her. Mr. Henderson is awful sarcastic in speech, and he'll make fun of her sayin' she didn't wake up.

Mrs. Hale: Well, I guess John Wright didn't wake when they was slip-ping that rope under his neck.

Mrs. Peters: No, it's strange. It must have been done awful crafty and 65 still. They say it was such a—funny way to kill a man, rigging it all up like that.

Mrs. Hale: That's just what Mr. Hale said. There was a gun in the house. He says that's what he can't understand.

Mrs. Peters: Mr. Henderson said coming out that what was needed for the case was a motive; something to show anger or — sudden feeling.

Mrs. Hale (who is standing by the table): Well, I don't see any signs of anger around here. (*She puts her hand on the dish towel which lies on the table, stands looking down at the table, one half of which is clean, the other half messy.*) It's wiped here. (*Makes a move as if to finish work, then turns and looks at loaf of bread outside the breadbox. Drops towel. In that voice of coming back to familiar things.*) Wonder how they are finding things up-stairs? I hope she had it a little more red-up there. You know, it seems kind of *sneaking.* Locking her up in town and then coming out here and trying to get her own house to turn against her!

Mrs. Peters: But, Mrs. Hale, the law is the law.

Mrs. Hale: I s'pose 'tis. (*Unbuttoning her coat.*) Better loosen up your 70 things, Mrs. Peters. You won't feel them when you go out. (*Mrs. Peters takes off her fur tippet, goes to hang it on hook at the back of room, stands looking at the under part of the small corner table.*)

Mrs. Peters: She was piecing a quilt. (*She brings the large sewing basket, and they look at the bright pieces.*)

Mrs. Hale: It's log cabin pattern. Pretty, isn't it? I wonder if she was goin' to quilt or just knot it? (*Footsteps have been heard coming down the stairs. The Sheriff enters, followed by Hale and the County Attorney.*)

Sheriff: They wonder if she was going to quilt it or just knot it. (*The men laugh, the women look abashed.*)

County Attorney (rubbing his hands over the stove): Frank's fire didn't do much up there, did it? Well, let's go out to the barn and get that cleared up. (*The men go outside.*)

Mrs. Hale (resentfully): I don't know as there's anything so strange, 75 our takin' up our time with little things while we're waiting for them to get the evidence. (*She sits down at the big table, smoothing out a block with decision.*) I don't see as it's anything to laugh about.

Mrs. Peters (apologetically): Of course they've got awful important things on their minds. (*Pulls up a chair and joins Mrs. Hale at the table.*)

Mrs. Hale (examining another block): Mrs. Peters, look at this one. Here, this is the one she was working on, and look at the sewing! All the rest of it has been so nice and even. And look at this! It's all over the place! Why, it looks as if she didn't know what she was about! (*After she has said this, they look at each other, then start to glance back at the door. After an instant Mrs. Hale has pulled at a knot and ripped the sewing.*)

Mrs. Peters: Oh, what are you doing, Mrs. Hale?

Mrs. Hale (mildly): Just pulling out a stitch or two that's not sewed very good. (*Threading a needle.*) Bad sewing always made me fidgety.

Mrs. Peters (nervously): I don't think we ought to touch things. 80

Mrs. Hale: I'll just finish up this end. (*Suddenly stopping and leaning forward.*) Mrs. Peters?

Mrs. Peters: Yes, Mrs. Hale?

Mrs. Hale: What do you suppose she was so nervous about?

Mrs. Peters: Oh—I don't know. I don't know as she was nervous. I sometimes sew awful queer when I'm just tired. *(Mrs. Hale starts to say something, looks at Mrs. Peters, then goes on sewing.)* Well, I must get these things wrapped up. They may be through sooner than we think. *(Putting apron and other things together.)* I wonder where I can find a piece of paper, and string.

Mrs. Hale: In that cupboard, maybe.   85

Mrs. Peters (looking in cupboard): Why, here's a birdcage. *(Holds it up.)* Did she have a bird, Mrs. Hale?

Mrs. Hale: Why, I don't know whether she did or not—I've not been here for so long. There was a man around last year selling canaries cheap, but I don't know as she took one; maybe she did. She used to sing real pretty herself.

Mrs. Peters (glancing around): Seems funny to think of a bird here. But she must have had one, or why should she have a cage? I wonder what happened to it?

Mrs. Hale: I s'pose maybe the cat got it.

Mrs. Peters: No, she didn't have a cat. She's got that feeling some   90 people have about cats—being afraid of them. My cat got in her room, and she was real upset and asked me to take it out.

Mrs. Hale: My sister Bessie was like that. Queer, ain't it?

Mrs. Peters (examining the cage): Why, look at this door. It's broke. One hinge is pulled apart.

Mrs. Hale (looking, too): Looks as if someone must have been rough with it.

Mrs. Peters: Why, yes. *(She brings the cage forward and puts it on the table.)*

Mrs. Hale: I wish if they're going to find any evidence they'd be about   95 it. I don't like this place.

Mrs. Peters: But I'm awful glad you came with me, Mrs. Hale. It would be lonesome for me sitting here alone.

Mrs. Hale: It would, wouldn't it? *(Dropping her sewing.)* But I tell you what I do wish, Mrs. Peters. I wish I had come over sometimes when *she* was here. I—*(Looking around the room)*—wish I had.

Mrs. Peters: But of course you were awful busy, Mrs. Hale—your house and your children.

Mrs. Hale: I could've come. I stayed away because it weren't cheerful—and that's why I ought to have come. I—I've never liked this place. Maybe because it's down in a hollow, and you don't see the road. I dunno what it is, but it's a lonesome place and always was. I wish I had come over to see Minnie Foster sometimes. I can see now—*(Shakes her head.)*

Mrs. Peters: Well, you musn't reproach yourself, Mrs. Hale. Somehow 100 we just don't see how it is with other folks until—something comes up.

Mrs. Hale: Not having children makes less work—but it makes a quiet house, and Wright out to work all day, and no company when he did come in. Did you know John Wright, Mrs. Peters?

Mrs. Peters: Not to know him; I've seen him in town. They say he was a good man.

Mrs. Hale: Yes—good; he didn't drink, and kept his word as well as most, I guess, and paid his debts. But he was a hard man, Mrs. Peters. Just to pass the time of day with him. *(Shivers.)* Like a raw wind that gets to the bone. *(Pauses, her eye falling on the cage.)* I should think she would 'a' wanted a bird. But what do you suppose went with it?

Mrs. Peters: I don't know, unless it got sick and died. *(She reaches over and swings the broken door, swings it again; both women watch it.)*

Mrs. Hale: You weren't raised around here, were you? *(Mrs. Peters* 105 *shakes her head.)* You didn't know—her?

Mrs. Peters: Not till they brought her yesterday.

Mrs. Hale: She—come to think of it, she was kind of like a bird herself—real sweet and pretty, but kind of timid and—fluttery. How— she—did—change. *(Silence; then as if struck by a happy thought and relieved to get back to everyday things.)* Tell you what, Mrs. Peters, why don't you take the quilt in with you? It might take up her mind.

Mrs. Peters: Why, I think that's a real nice idea, Mrs. Hale. There couldn't possible be any objection to it, could there? Now, just what would I take? I wonder if her patches are in here—and her things. *(They look in the sewing basket.)*

Mrs. Hale: Here's some red. I expect this has got sewing things in it. *(Brings out a fancy box.)* What a pretty box. Looks like something somebody would give you. Maybe her scissors are in here. *(Opens box. Suddenly puts her hand to her nose.)* Why—*(Mrs. Peters bends nearer, then turns her face away.)* There's something wrapped up in this piece of silk.

Mrs. Peters: Why, this isn't her scissors.   110

Mrs. Hale (lifting the silk): Oh, Mrs. Peters—it's—*(Mrs. Peters bends closer.)*

Mrs. Peters: It's the bird.

Mrs. Hale (jumping up): But, Mrs. Peters—look at it. Its neck! Look at its neck! It's all—other side *to.*

Mrs. Peters: Somebody—wrung—its neck. *(Their eyes meet. A look of growing comprehension of horror. Steps are heard outside. Mrs. Hale slips box under quilt pieces, and sinks into her chain. Enter Sheriff and County Attorney, Mrs. Peters rises.)*

County Attorney (as one turning from serious things to little pleas- 115 *antries):* Well, ladies, have you decided whether she was going to quilt it or knot it?

Mrs. Peters: We think she was going to—knot it.

County Attorney: Well, that's interesting, I'm sure. *(Seeing the birdcage.)* Has the bird flown?

Mrs. Hale (putting more quilt pieces over the box): We think the— cat got it.

County Attorney (preoccupied): Is there a cat? *(Mrs. Hale glances in a quick covert way at Mrs. Peters.)*

Mrs. Peters: Well, not now. They're superstitious, you know. They 120 leave.

County Attorney (to Sheriff Peters, continuing an interrupted conversation): No sign at all of anyone having come from the outside. Their own rope. Now let's go up again and go over it piece by piece. *(They start upstairs.)* It would have to have been someone who knew just the — *(Mrs. Peters sits down. The two women sit there not looking at one another, but as if peering into something and at the same time holding back. When they talk now, it is the manner of feeling their way over strange ground, as if afraid of what they are saying, but as if they cannot help saying it.)*

Mrs. Hale: She liked the bird. She was going to bury it in that pretty box.

Mrs. Peters (in a whisper): When I was a girl — my kitten — there was a boy took a hatchet, and before my eyes — and before I could get there — *(Covers her face an instant.)* If they hadn't held me back, I would have — *(Catches herself, looks upstairs where steps are heard, falters weakly.)* — hurt him.

Mrs. Hale (with a slow look around her): I wonder how it would seem never to have had any children around. *(Pause.)* No, Wright wouldn't like the bird — a thing that sang. She used to sing. He killed that, too.

Mrs. Peters (moving uneasily): We don't know who killed the bird. 125

Mrs. Hale: I knew John Wright.

Mrs. Peters: It was an awful thing was done in this house that night, Mrs. Hale. Killing a man while he slept, slipping a rope around his neck that choked the life out of him.

Mrs. Hale: His neck. Choked the life out of him. *(Her hand goes and out and rests on the birdcage.)*

Mrs. Peters (with a rising voice): We don't know who killed him. We don't *know*.

Mrs. Hale (her own feeling not interrupted): If there'd been years and 130 years of nothing, then a bird to sing to you, it would be awful — still, after the bird was still.

Mrs. Peters (something within her speaking): I know what stillness is. When we homesteaded in Dakota, and my first baby died — after he was two years old, and me with no other then —

Mrs. Hale (moving): How soon do you suppose they'll be through, looking for evidence?

Mrs. Peters: I know what stillness is. *(Pulling herself back.)* The law has got to punish crime, Mrs. Hale.

Mrs. Hale (not as if answering that): I wish you'd seen Minnie Foster when she wore a white dress with blue ribbons and stood up there in the choir and sang. *(A look around the room.)* Oh, I *wish* I'd come over here once in a while! That was a crime! That was a crime! Who's going to punish that?

Mrs. Peters (looking upstairs): We mustn't — take on. 135

Mrs. Hale: I might have known she needed help! I know how things can be — for women. I tell you, it's queer, Mrs. Peters. We live close together and we live far apart. We all go through the same things — it's all just a different kind of the same thing. *(Brushes her eyes, noticing the bottle of fruit, reaches out for it.)* If I was you, I wouldn't tell her her fruit was gone. Tell her it *ain't*. Tell her it's all right. Take this in to prove it to her. She — she may never know whether it was broke or not.

Mrs. Peters (takes the bottle, looks about for something to wrap it in; takes petticoat from the clothes brought from the other room, very nervously begins winding this around the bottle. In a false voice): My, it's a good thing the men couldn't hear us. Wouldn't they just laugh! Getting all stirred up over a little thing like a — dead canary. As if that could have anything to with — with — wouldn't they *laugh!* (The men are heard coming downstairs.)

Mrs. Hale (under her breath): Maybe they would — maybe they wouldn't.

County Attorney: No, Peters, it's all perfectly clear except a reason for doing it. But you know juries when it comes to women. If there was some definite thing. Something to show—something to make a story about — a thing that would connect up with this strange way of doing it. *(The women's eyes meet for an instant. Enter Hale from outer door.)*

Hale: Well, I've got the team around. Pretty cold out there. 140

County Attorney: I'm going to stay here a while by myself. *(To the Sheriff.)* You can send Frank out for me, can't you? I want to go over everything. I'm not satisfied that we can't do better.

Sheriff: Do you want to see what Mrs. Peters is going to take in? *(The Lawyer goes to the table, picks up the apron, laughs.)*

County Attorney: Oh I guess they're not very dangerous things the ladies have picked up. *(Moves a few things about, disturbing the quilt pieces which cover the box. Steps back.)* No, Mrs. Peters doesn't need supervising. For that matter, a sheriff's wife is married to the law. Ever think of it that way, Mrs. Peters?

Mrs. Peters: Not — just that way.

Sheriff (chuckling): Married to the law. *(Moves toward the other* 145 *room.)* I just want you to come in here a minute, George. We ought to take a look at these windows.

County Attorney (scoffingly): Oh, windows!

Sheriff: We'll be right out, Mr. Hale.

(Hale goes outside. The Sheriff follows the County Attorney into the other room. Then Mrs. Hale rises, hands tight together, looking intensely at Mrs. Peters, whose eyes take a slow turn, finally meeting Mrs. Hale's. A moment Mrs. Hale holds her, then her own eyes point the way to where the box is concealed. Suddenly Mrs. Peters throws back quilt pieces and tries to put the box in the bag she is wearing. It is too big. She opens box, starts to take the bird out, cannot touch it, goes to pieces, stands there helpless.

Sound of a knob turning in the other room. Mrs. Hale snatches the box and puts it in the pocket of her big coat. Enter County Attorney and Sheriff.)

County Attorney (facetiously): Well, Henry, at least we found out that she was not going to quilt it. She was going to—what is it you call it, ladies?

Mrs. Hale (her hand against her pocket): We call it—knot it, Mr. Henderson.

Topics for Critical Thinking and Writing

1. Briefly describe the setting, indicating what it "says" and what atmosphere it evokes.

2. How would you characterize Mr. Henderson, the county attorney?

3. In paragraph 139, *"the women's eyes meet for an instant."* What do you think this bit of action "says"? What do you understand by the exchange of glances?

4. In paragraph 123, when Mrs. Peters tells of the boy who killed her cat, she says, "If they hadn't held me back, I would have—*(Catches herself, looks upstairs where steps are heard, falters weakly.)*—hurt him." What do you think she was about to say before she faltered? Why do you suppose Glaspell included this speech about Mrs. Peters's girlhood?

5. In paragraph 72, Mrs. Hale, looking at a quilt, wonders whether Mrs. Wright "was goin' to quilt or just knot it." The men are amused by the women's concern with this topic, and the last line of the play returns to the issue. What do you make of this emphasis on the matter?

6. We never see Mrs. Wright on stage. Nevertheless, by the end of *Trifles* we know a great deal about her. In an essay of 500 to 750 words explain both what we know about her—physical characteristics, habits, interests, personality, life before her marriage and after—and *how* we know these things.

7. Do you think the play is immoral? Explain.

8. Assume that the canary has been found, thereby revealing a possible motive, and that Minnie is indicted for murder. You are the defense attorney. In 500 words set forth your defense. (Take any position you wish. For instance, you may want to argue that she committed justifiable homicide or that—on the basis of her behavior as reported by Mr. Hale—she is innocent by reason of insanity.)

9. Assume that the canary had been found and Minnie Wright convicted. Compose the speech you think she might have delivered before the sentence was given.

Shirley Jackson

The Lottery

The morning of June 27th was clear and sunny, with the fresh warmth of a full-summer day; the flowers were blossoming profusely and the grass was richly green. The people of the village began to gather in the square, between the post office and the bank, around ten o'clock; in some towns there were so many people that the lottery took two days and had to be started on June 26th, but in this village, where there were only about three hundred people, the whole lottery took less than two hours, so it could begin at ten o'clock in the morning and still be through in time to allow the villagers to get home for noon dinner.

The children assembled first, of course. School was recently over for the summer, and the feeling of liberty sat uneasily on most of them; they tended to gather together quietly for a while before they broke into boisterous play, and their talk was still of the classroom and the teacher, of books and reprimands. Bobby Martin had already stuffed his pockets full of stones, and the other boys soon followed his example, selecting the smoothest and roundest stones; Bobby and Harry Jones and Dickie Delacroix—the villagers pronounced his name "Dellacroy"—eventually made a great pile of stones in one corner of the square and guarded it against the raids of the other boys. The girls stood aside, talking among themselves, looking over their shoulders at the boys, and the very small children rolled in the dust or clung to the hands of their older brothers or sisters.

Soon the men began to gather, surveying their own children, speaking of planting and rain, tractors and taxes. They stood together, away from the pile of stones in the corner, and their jokes were quiet and they smiled rather than laughed. The women, wearing faded house dresses and sweaters, came shortly after their menfolk. They greeted one another and exchanged bits of gossip as they went to join their husbands. Soon the women, standing by their husbands, began to call their children, and the children came reluctantly, having to be called four or five times. Bobby Martin ducked under his mother's grasping hand and ran, laughing, back to the pile of stones. His father spoke up sharply, and Bobby came quickly and took his place between his father and his oldest brother.

The lottery was conducted—as were the square dances, the teenage

---

Shirley Jackson (1919–1965) was born in San Francisco and went to college in New York, first at the University of Rochester and then at Syracuse University. Although one of her stories was published in The Best American Short Stories 1944, *she did not receive national attention until 1948, when* The New Yorker *published* "The Lottery." *Her first novel,* The Road Through the Wall, *was also published in 1948, and she went on to write other stories and novels, but "The Lottery" remains her best-known work.*

club, the Halloween program—by Mr. Summers, who had time and energy to devote to civic activities. He was a round-faced, jovial man and he ran the coal business, and people were sorry for him, because he had no children and his wife was a scold. When he arrived in the square, carrying the black wooden box, there was a murmur of conversation among the villagers and he waved and called, "Little late today, folks." The postmaster, Mr. Graves, followed him, carrying a three-legged stool, and the stool was put in the center of the square and Mr. Summers set the black box down on it. The villagers kept their distance, leaving a space between themselves and the stool, and when Mr. Summers said, "Some of you fellows want to give me a hand?" there was a hesitation before two men, Mr. Martin and his oldest son, Baxter, came forward to hold the box steady on the stool while Mr. Summers stirred up the papers inside it.

The original paraphernalia for the lottery had been lost long ago, and the black box now resting on the stool had been put into use even before Old Man Warner, the oldest man in town, was born. Mr. Summers spoke frequently to the villagers about making a new box, but no one liked to upset even as much tradition as was represented by the black box. There was a story that the present box had been made with some pieces of the box that had preceded it, the one that had been constructed when the first people settled down to make a village here. Every year, after the lottery, Mr. Summers began talking again about a new box, but every year the subject was allowed to fade off without anything's being done. The black box grew shabbier each year; by now it was no longer completely black but splintered badly along one side to show the original wood color, and in some places faded or stained. 5

Mr. Martin and his oldest son, Baxter, held the black box securely on the stool until Mr. Summers had stirred the papers thoroughly with his hand. Because so much of the ritual had been forgotten or discarded, Mr. Summers had been successful in having slips of paper substituted for the chips of wood that had been used for generations. Chips of wood, Mr. Summers had argued, had been all very well when the village was tiny, but now that the population was more than three hundred and likely to keep on growing, it was necessary to use something that would fit more easily into the black box. The night before the lottery, Mr. Summers and Mr. Graves made up the slips of paper and put them in the box, and it was then taken to the safe of Mr. Summers's coal company and locked up until Mr. Summers was ready to take it to the square next morning. The rest of the year, the box was put away, sometimes one place, sometimes another; it had spent one year in Mr. Graves's barn and another year underfoot in the post office, and sometimes it was set on a shelf in the Martin grocery and left there.

There was a great deal of fussing to be done before Mr. Summers declared the lottery open. There were lists to make up—of heads of families, heads of households in each family, members of each household in each family. There was the proper swearing-in of Mr. Summers by the postmaster, as the official of the lottery; at one time, some people remembered, there had been a recital of some sort, performed by the official of the lottery, a perfunctory, tuneless chant that had been rattled off duly each year; some people believed that the official of the lottery used to stand just so when he said or sang it, others believed that he was supposed to walk among the people, but years and years ago this part of the ritual had been allowed to lapse. There had been, also, a ritual salute, which the official of the lottery had had to use in addressing each person who came up to draw from the box, but this also had changed with time, until now it was felt necessary only for the official to speak to each person approaching. Mr. Summers was very good at all this; in his clean white shirt and blue jeans, with one hand resting carelessly on the black box, he seemed very proper and important as he talked interminably to Mr. Graves and the Martins.

Just as Mr. Summers finally left off talking and turned to the assembled villagers, Mrs. Hutchinson came hurriedly along the path to the square, her sweater thrown over her shoulders, and slid into place in the back of the crowd. "Clean forgot what day it was," she said to Mrs. Delacroix, who stood next to her, and they both laughed softly. "Thought my old man was out back stacking wood," Mrs. Hutchinson went on, "and then I looked out the window and the kids were gone, and then I remembered it was the twenty-seventh and came a-running." She dried her hands on her apron, and Mrs. Delacroix said, "You're in time, though. They're still talking away up there."

Mrs. Hutchinson craned her neck to see through the crowd and found her husband and children standing near the front. She tapped Mrs. Delacroix on the arm as a farewell and began to make her way through the crowd. The people separated goodhumoredly to let her through; two or three people said, in voices just loud enough to be heard across the crowd, "Here comes your Missus, Hutchinson," and "Bill, she made it after all." Mrs. Hutchinson reached her husband, and Mr. Summers, who had been waiting, said cheerfully, "Thought we were going to have to get on without you, Tessie." Mrs. Hutchinson said, grinning, "Wouldn't have me leave m'dishes in the sink, now would you, Joe?," and soft laughter ran through the crowd as the people stirred back into position after Mrs. Hutchinson's arrival.

"Well, now," Mr. Summers said soberly, "guess we better get started, 10 get this over with, so's we can go back to work. Anybody ain't here?"

"Dunbar," several people said. "Dunbar, Dunbar."

Mr. Summers consulted his list. "Clyde Dunbar," he said. "That's right. He's broke his leg, hasn't he? Who's drawing for him?"

"Me, I guess," a woman said, and Mr. Summers turned to look at her. "Wife draws for her husband," Mr. Summers said. "Don't you have a grown boy to do it for you, Janey?" Although Mr. Summers and everyone else in the village knew the answer perfectly well, it was the business of the official of the lottery to ask such questions formally. Mr. Summers waited with an expression of polite interest while Mrs. Dunbar answered.

"Horace's not but sixteen yet," Mrs. Dunbar said regretfully. "Guess I gotta fill in for the old man this year."

"Right," Mr. Summers said. He made a note on the list he was hold- 15 ing. Then he asked, "Watson boy drawing this year?"

A tall boy in the crowd raised his hand. "Here," he said. "I'm drawing for m'mother and me." He blinked his eyes nervously and ducked his head as several voices in the crowd said things like "Good fellow, Jack," and "Glad to see your mother's got a man to do it."

"Well," Mr. Summers said, "guess that's everyone. Old Man Warner make it?"

"Here," a voice said, and Mr. Summers nodded.

A sudden hush fell on the crowd as Mr. Summers cleared his throat and looked at the list. "All ready?" he called. "Now, I'll read the names— heads of families first—and the men come up and take a paper out of the box. Keep the paper folded in your hand without looking at it until everyone has had a turn. Everything clear?"

The people had done it so many times that they only half listened to 20 the directions, most of them were quiet, wetting their lips, not looking around. Then Mr. Summers raised one hand high and said, "Adams." A man disengaged himself from the crowd and came forward. "Hi, Steve," Mr. Summers said, and Mr. Adams said, "Hi, Joe." They grinned at one another humorlessly and nervously. Then Mr. Adams reached into the black box and took out a folded paper. He held it firmly by one corner as he turned and went hastily back to his place in the crowd, where he stood a little apart from his family, not looking down at his hand.

"Allen," Mr. Summers said. "Anderson . . . . Bentham."

"Seems like there's no time at all between lotteries any more," Mrs. Delacroix said to Mrs. Graves in the back row. "Seems like we got through with the last one only last week."

"Time sure goes fast," Mrs. Graves said.

"Clark . . . . Delacroix."

"There goes my old man," Mrs. Delacroix said. She held her breath 25 while her husband went forward.

"Dunbar," Mr. Summers said, and Mrs. Dunbar went steadily to the box while one of the women said, "Go on, Janey," and another said, "There she goes."

"We're next," Mrs. Graves said. She watched while Mr. Graves came around from the side of the box, greeted Mr. Summers gravely, and selected a slip of paper from the box. By now, all through the crowd there were men holding the small folded papers in their large hands, turning them over and over nervously. Mrs. Dunbar and her two sons stood together, Mrs. Dunbar holding the slip of paper.

"Harburt . . . . Hutchinson."

"Get up there, Bill," Mrs. Hutchinson said, and the people near her laughed.

"Jones."   30

"They do say," Mr. Adams said to Old Man Warner, who stood next to him, "that over in the north village they're talking of giving up the lottery."

Old Man Warner snorted, "Pack of crazy fools," he said. "Listening to the young folks, nothing's good enough for *them*. Next thing you know, they'll be wanting to go back to living in caves, nobody work any more, live *that* way for a while. Used to be a saying about 'Lottery in June, corn be heavy soon.' First thing you know, we'd all be eating stewed chickweed and acorns. There's *always* been a lottery," he added petulantly. "Bad enough to see young Joe Summers up there joking with everybody."

"Some places have already quit lotteries," Mrs. Adams said.

"Nothing but trouble in *that*," Old Man Warner said stoutly. "Pack of young fools."

"Martin." And Bobby Martin watched his father go forward. 35 "Overdyke . . . . Percy."

"I wish they'd hurry," Mrs. Dunbar said to her older son. "I wish they'd hurry."

"They're almost through," her son said.

"You get ready to run tell Dad," Mrs. Dunbar said.

Mr. Summers called his own name and then stepped forward precisely and selected a slip from the box. Then he called, "Warner."

"Seventy-seventh year I been in the lottery," Old Man Warner said as 40 he went through the crowd. "Seventy-seventh time."

"Watson." The tall boy came awkwardly through the crowd. Someone said, "Don't be nervous, Jack," and Mr. Summers said, "Take your time, son."

"Zanini."

After that, there was a long pause, a breathless pause, until Mr. Summers, holding his slip of paper in the air, said, "All right, fellows." For a minute, no one moved, and then all the slips of paper were opened. Suddenly, all women began to speak at once saying, "Who is it?," "Who's got it?," "Is it the Dunbars?," "Is it the Watsons?" Then the voices began to say, "It's Hutchinson. It's Bill." "Bill Hutchinson's got it."

"Go tell your father," Mrs. Dunbar said to her older son.

People began to look around to see the Hutchinsons. Bill Hutchinson 45 was standing quiet, staring down at the paper in his hand. Suddenly, Tessie Hutchinson shouted to Mr. Summers, "You didn't give him time enough to take any paper he wanted. I saw you. It wasn't fair!"

"Be a good sport, Tessie," Mrs. Delacroix called, and Mrs. Graves said, "All of us took the same chance."

"Shut up, Tessie," Bill Hutchinson said.

"Well, everyone," Mr. Summers said, "that was done pretty fast, and now we've got to be hurrying a little more to get done in time." He consulted his next list. "Bill," he said, "you draw for the Hutchinson family. You got any other households in the Hutchinsons?"

"There's Don and Eva," Mrs. Hutchinson yelled. "Make *them* take their chance!"

"Daughters draw with their husbands' families, Tessie," Mr. Summers 50 said gently. "You know that as well as anyone else."

"It wasn't fair," Tessie said.

"I guess not, Joe," Bill Hutchinson said regretfully. "My daughter draws with her husband's family, that's only fair. And I've got no other family except the kids."

"Then, as far as drawing for families is concerned, it's you," Mr. Summers said in explanation, "and as far as drawing for household is concerned, that's you, too. Right?"

"Right," Bill Hutchinson said.

"How many kids, Bill?" Mr. Summers asked formally. 55

"Three," Bill Hutchinson said, "There's Bill, Jr., and Nancy, and little Dave. And Tessie and me."

"All right, then," Mr. Summers said. "Harry, you got their tickets back?"

Mr. Graves nodded and held up the slips of paper. "Put them in the box, then," Mr. Summers directed. "Take Bill's and put it in."

"I think we ought to start over," Mrs. Hutchinson said, as quietly as she could. "I tell you it wasn't *fair*. You didn't give him time enough to choose. *Every*body saw that."

Mr. Graves had selected the five slips and put them in the box, and he 60 dropped all the papers but those onto the ground where the breeze caught them and lifted them off.

"Listen, everybody," Mrs. Hutchinson was saying to the people around her.

"Ready, Bill?" Mr. Summers asked and Bill Hutchinson, with one quick glance around at his wife and children, nodded.

"Remember," Mr. Summers said, "take the slips and keep them folded until each person has taken one. Harry, you help little Dave." Mr. Graves took the hand of the little boy, who came willingly with him up to the box. "Take a paper out of the box, Davy," Mr. Summers said. Davy put his hand into the box and laughed. "Take just *one* paper," Mr. Summers said. "Harry, you hold it for him." Mr. Graves took the child's hand and removed the folded paper from the tight fist and held it while little Dave stood next to him and looked up at him wonderingly.

"Nancy next," Mr. Summers said. Nancy was twelve, and her school friends breathed heavily as she went forward, switching her skirt, and took a slip daintily from the box. "Bill, Jr.," Mr. Summers said, and Billy, his face red and his feet over-large, nearly knocked the box over as he got a paper out. "Tessie," Mr. Summers said. She hesitated for a minute, looking around defiantly, and then set her lips and went up to the box. She snatched a paper out and held it behind her.

"Bill," Mr. Summers said, and Bill Hutchinson reached into the box 65 and felt around, bringing his hand out at last with the slip of paper in it.

The crowd was quiet. A girl whispered, "I hope it's not Nancy," and the sound of the whisper reached the edges of the crowd.

"It's not the way it used to be," Old Man Warner said clearly. "People ain't the way they used to be."

"All right," Mr. Summers said. "Open the papers. Harry, you open little Dave's."

Mr. Graves opened the slip of paper and there was a general sigh through the crowd as he held it up and everyone could see that it was blank. Nancy and Bill, Jr., opened theirs at the same time, and both beamed and laughed, turning around to the crowd and holding their slips of paper above their heads.

"Tessie," Mr. Summers said. There was a pause, and then Mr. Summers looked at Bill Hutchinson, and Bill unfolded his paper and showed it. It was blank. 70

"It's Tessie," Mr. Summers said, and his voice was hushed. "Show us her paper, Bill."

Bill Hutchinson went over to his wife and forced the slip of paper out of her hand. It had a black spot on it, the black spot Mr. Summers had made the night before with the heavy pencil in the coal-company office. Bill Hutchinson held it up, and there was a stir in the crowd.

"All right, folks," Mr. Summers said, "let's finish quickly." Although the villagers had forgotten the ritual and lost the original black box, they still remembered to use stones. The pile of stones the boys had made earlier was ready; there were stones on the ground with the blowing scraps of paper that had come out of the box. Mrs. Delacroix selected a stone so large she had to pick it up with both hands and turned to Mrs. Dunbar. "Come on," she said. "Hurry up."

Mrs. Dunbar had small stones in both hands, and she said, gasping for breath, "I can't run at all. You'll have to go ahead and I'll catch up with you."

The children had stones already, and someone give little Davy Hutchinson a few pebbles. 75

Tessie Hutchinson was in the center of a cleared space by now, and she held her hands out desperately as the villagers moved in on her. "It isn't fair," she said. A stone hit her on the side of the head.

Old Man Warner was saying, "Come on, come on, everyone." Steve Adams was in the front of the crowd of villagers, with Mrs. Graves beside him.

"It isn't fair, it isn't right," Mrs. Hutchinson screamed, and then they were upon her.

Topics for Critical Thinking and Writing

1. Is "The Lottery" more than a shocker?

2. Suppose someone claimed that the story is an attack on religious orthodoxy. What might be your response? (Whether you agree or disagree, set forth your reasons.)

3. Some years after writing the story Jackson said, "Explaining just what I had hoped the story to say is very difficult. I supposed, I hoped, by setting a particularly brutal ancient rite in the present and in my own village, to shock the story's readers with a graphic dramatization of the pointless violence and general inhumanity in their own lives." We have two questions: (1) Do you assume that because the author said the story concerns "pointless violence and general inhumanity," this indeed must be what the story is about? (2) Even if you agree that the story is about "pointless violence and general inhumanity," do you agree also that these qualities must be part of your own life?

Mitsuye Yamada

To the Lady

The one in San Francisco who asked:
Why did the Japanese Americans let
the government put them in
those camps without protest?

Come to think of it I   5
    should've run off to Canada
    should've hijacked a plane to Algeria
    should've pulled myself up from my
    bra straps
    and kicked'm in the groin   10
    should've bombed a bank
    should've tried self-immolation
    should've holed myself up in a
    woodframe house
    and let you watch me   15
    burn up on the six o'clock news
    should've run howling down the street
    naked and assaulted you at breakfast
    by AP wirephoto

Mitsuye Yamada, the daughter of Japanese immigrants to the United States, was born in Japan in 1923, during her mother's return visit to her native land. Yamada was raised in Seattle, but in 1942 she and her family were incarcerated and then relocated in a camp in Idaho, when Executive Order 9066 (signed by President Franklin D. Roosevelt in 1941) gave military authorities the right to remove any and all persons from "military areas." In 1954 she became an American citizen. A professor of English at Cypress Junior College in San Luis Obispo, California, Yamada is the author of poems and stories.

Yamada's poem concerns the compliant response to Executive Order 9066, which brought about the incarceration and relocation of the entire Japanese and

should've screamed bloody murder   20
like Kitty Genovese[1]

Then
YOU would've
come to my aid in shining armor
laid yourself across the railroad track   25
marched on Washington
tattooed a Star of David on your arm
written six million enraged
letters to Congress

But we didn't draw the line   30
anywhere
law and order Executive Order 9066
social order moral order internal order

YOU let'm
I let'm   35
All are punished.

Topics for Critical Thinking and Writing

1. Has the lady's question (lines 2–4) ever crossed your mind? If so, what answers
   did you think of?

2. What, in effect, is the speaker really saying in lines 5–21? And in lines 24–29?

3. What possible arguments can you offer for and against the removal of Japanese
   Americans in 1942?

4. Do you think the survivors of the relocation are entitled to some sort of redress?
   Why? And if you think they merit compensation, what should the compensation
   be?

---

[1]**Kitty Genovese** In 1964 Kitty Genovese of Kew Gardens, New York, was stabbed to death
when she left her car and walked toward her home. Thirty-eight persons heard her screams, but
no one came to her assistance. [Editors' note.]

---

*Japanese American population on the Pacific coast — about 112,000 people. More
than two-thirds of the people moved were native-born citizens of the United States.
(The 158,000 Japanese residents of the Territory of Hawaii were not affected.)
There was virtually no protest at the time, but in recent years the order has been
widely regarded as an outrageous infringement on liberty, and some younger
Japanese Americans cannot fathom why their parents and grandparents complied
with it.*

19

What Are the Bounds of Free Speech?

Plato

"The Greater Part of the Stories Current Today We Shall Have to Reject"

"What kind of education shall we give them then? We shall find it difficult to improve on the time-honored distinction between the physical training we give to the body and the education we give to the mind and character."

"True."

"And we shall begin by educating mind and character, shall we not?"

"Of course."

"In this education you would include stories, would you not?" 5

"Yes."

"These are of two kinds, true stories and fiction.[1] Our education must use both, and start with fiction."

---

[1] The Greek word *pseudos* and its corresponding verb meant not only "fiction" — stories, tales — but also "what is not true" and so, in suitable contexts, "lies": and this ambiguity should be borne in mind. [Editors' note: All footnotes are by the translator, but some have been omitted.]

Plato (427–347 B.C.), an Athenian aristocrat by birth, was the student of one great philosopher (Socrates) and the teacher of another (Aristotle). His legacy of more than two dozen dialogues — imaginary discussions between Socrates and one or more other speakers, usually young Athenians — has been of such influence that the whole of Western philosophy can be characterized, A. N. Whitehead wrote, as "a series of footnotes to Plato." Plato's interests encompassed the full range of topics in philosophy: ethics, politics, logic, metaphysics, epistemology, aesthetics, psychology, and education.

"I don't know what you mean."

"But you know that we begin by telling children stories. These are, in general, fiction, though they contain some truth. And we tell children stories before we start them on physical training."

"That is so."

"That is what I meant by saying that we must start to educate the mind before training the body."

"You are right," he said.

"And the first step, as you know, is always what matters most, particularly when we are dealing with those who are young and tender. That is the time when they are easily molded and when any impression we choose to make leaves a permanent mark."

"That is certainly true."

"Shall we therefore readily allow our children to listen to any stories made up by anyone, and to form opinions that are for the most part the opposite of those we think they should have when they grow up?"

"We certainly shall not."

"Then it seems that our first business is to supervise the production of stories, and choose only those we think suitable, and reject the rest. We shall persuade mothers and nurses to tell our chosen stories to their children, and by means of them to mold their minds and characters which are more important than their bodies. The greater part of the stories current today we shall have to reject."

"Which are you thinking of?"

"We can take some of the major legends as typical. For all, whether major or minor, should be cast in the same mold and have the same effect. Do you agree?"

"Yes: but I'm not sure which you refer to as major."

"The stories in Homer and Hesiod and the poets. For it is the poets who have always made up fictions and stories to tell to men."

"What sort of stories do you mean and what fault do you find in them?"

This selection from Plato's Republic, *one of his best known and longest dialogues, is about the education suitable for the rulers of an ideal society.* Republic *begins, typically, with an investigation into the nature of justice. Socrates (who speaks for Plato) convincingly explains to Glaucon that we cannot reasonably expect to achieve a just society unless we devote careful attention to the moral education of the young men who are scheduled in later life to become the rulers. (Here as elsewhere, Plato's elitism and aristocratic bias shows itself; as readers of* Republic *soon learn, Plato is no admirer of democracy or of a classless society.) Plato cares as much about what the educational curriculum should exclude as what it should include. His special target was the common practice in his day of using for pedagogy the Homeric tales and other stories about the gods. He readily embraces the principle of censorship, as the excerpt explains, because he thinks it is a necessary means to achieve the ideal society.*

"The worst fault possible," I replied, "especially if the fiction is an ugly one."

"And what is that?"

"Misrepresenting the nature of gods and heroes, like a portrait painter 25 whose portraits bear no resemblance to their originals."

"That is a fault which certainly deserves censure. But give me more details."

"Well, on the most important of subjects, there is first and foremost the foul story about Ouranos[2] and the things Hesiod says he did, and the revenge Cronos took on him. While the story of what Cronos did, and what he suffered at the hands of his son, is not fit as it is to be lightly repeated to the young and foolish, even if it were true; it would be best to say nothing about it, or if it must be told, tell it to a select few under oath of secrecy, at a rite which required, to restrict it still further, the sacrifice not of a mere pig but of something large and difficult to get."

"These certainly are awkward stories."

"And they shall not be repeated in our state, Adeimantus," I said. "Nor shall any young audience be told that anyone who commits horrible crimes, or punishes his father unmercifully, is doing nothing out of the ordinary but merely what the first and greatest of the gods have done before."

"I entirely agree," said Adeimantus, "that these stories are unsuitable." 30

"Nor can we permit stories of wars and plots and battles among the gods; they are quite untrue, and if we want our prospective guardians to believe that quarrelsomeness is one of the worst of evils, we must certainly not let them be told the story of the Battle of the Giants or embroider it on robes, or tell them other tales about many and various quarrels between gods and heroes and their friends and relations. On the contrary, if we are to persuade them that no citizen has ever quarrelled with any other, because it is sinful, our old men and women must tell children stories with this end in view from the first, and we must compel our poets to tell them similar stories when they grow up. But we can admit to our state no stories about Hera being tied up by her son, or Hephaestus being flung out of Heaven by his father for trying to help his mother when she was getting a beating, nor any of Homer's Battles of the Gods, whether their intention is allegorical or not. Children cannot distinguish between what is allegory and what isn't, and opinions formed at that age are usually difficult to eradicate or change; we should therefore surely regard it as of the utmost importance that the first stories they hear shall aim at encouraging the highest excellence of character."

"Your case is a good one," he agreed, "but if someone wanted details, and asked what stories we were thinking of, what should we say?"

---

[2]**Ouranos** (the sky), the original supreme god, was castrated by his son Cronos to separate him from Gaia (mother earth). Cronos was in turn deposed by Zeus in a struggle in which Zeus was helped by the Titans.

To which I replied, "My dear Adeimantus, you and I are not engaged on writing stories but on founding a state. And the founders of a state, though they must know the type of story the poet must produce, and reject any that do not conform to that type, need not write them themselves."

"True: but what are the lines on which our poets must work when they deal with the gods?"

"Roughly as follows," I said. "God must surely always be represented 35 as he really is, whether the poet is writing epic, lyric, or tragedy."

"He must."

"And in reality of course god is good, and he must be so described."

"Certainly."

"But nothing good is harmful, is it?"[3]

"I think not." 40

"Then can anything that is not harmful do harm?"

"No."

"And can what does no harm do evil?"

"No again."

"And can what does no evil be the cause of any evil?" 45

"How could it?"

"Well then; is the good beneficial?"

"Yes."

"So it must be the cause of well-being."

"Yes." 50

"So the good is not the cause of everything, but only of states of well-being and not of evil."

"Most certainly," he agreed.

"Then god, being good, cannot be responsible for everything, as is commonly said, but only for a small part of human life, for the greater part of which he has no responsibility. For we have a far smaller share of good than of evil, and while god must be held to be the sole cause of good, we must look for some factors other than god as cause of the evil."

"I think that's very true," he said.

"So we cannot allow Homer or any other poet to make such a stupid 55 mistake about the gods, as when he says that

> Zeus has two jars standing on the floor of his palace, full of fates, good in one and evil in the other

and that the man to whom Zeus allots a mixture of both has 'varying fortunes sometimes good and sometimes bad,' while the man to whom he al-

---

[3]The reader of the following passage should bear the following ambiguities in mind: (1) the Greek word for good (*agathos*) can mean (a) morally good, (b) beneficial or advantageous; (2) the Greek word for evil (*kakos*) can also mean harm or injury; (3) the adverb of *agathos* (*eu*-well) can imply either morally right or prosperous. The word translated "cause of" could equally well be rendered "responsible for."

lots unmixed evil is 'chased by ravening despair over the face of the earth.'[4] Nor can we allow references to Zeus as 'dispenser of good and evil.' And we cannot approve if it is said that Athene and Zeus prompted the breach of solemn treaty and oath by Pandarus, or that the strife and contentions of the gods were due to Themis and Zeus. Nor again can we let our children hear from Aeschylus that

> God implants a fault in man, when he wishes to destroy a house utterly.

No: We must forbid anyone who writes a play about the sufferings of Niobe (the subject of the play from which these last lines are quoted), or the house of Pelops, or the Trojan war, or any similar topic, to say they are acts of god; or if he does he must produce the sort of interpretation we are now demanding, and say that god's acts were good and just, and that the sufferers were benefited by being punished. What the poet must not be allowed to say is that those who were punished were made wretched through god's action. He may refer to the wicked as wretched because they needed punishment, provided he makes it clear that in punishing them god did them good. But if a state is to be run on the right lines, every possible step must be taken to prevent anyone, young or old, either saying or being told, whether in poetry or prose, that god, being good, can cause harm or evil to any man. To say so would be sinful, inexpedient, and inconsistent."

"I should approve of a law for this purpose and you have my vote for it," he said.

"Then of our laws laying down the principles which those who write or speak about the gods must follow, one would be this: *God is the cause, not of all things, but only of good.*"

"I am quite content with that," he said.

Topics for Critical Thinking and Writing

1. In the beginning of the dialogue Plato says that adults recite fictions to very young children, and that these fictions help to mold character. Think of some stories that you heard or read when young, such as "Snow White and the Seven Dwarfs" or "Ali Baba and the Forty Thieves." Try to think of a story that, in the final analysis, is not in accord with what you consider to be proper morality, such as a story in which a person triumphs through trickery, or a story in which evil actions — perhaps murders — are set forth without unfavorable comment. (Was it naughty of Jack to kill the giant?) Upon reflection, do you think children should not be told such stories? Why, or why not? Or think of the early film westerns, in which, on the whole, the Indians (except for an occasional Uncle Tonto) are depicted as bad guys and the whites (except for an occasional coward or rustler) are depicted as good guys. Many people who now have gray hair enjoyed such films in their childhood. Are you prepared to say that such films are not damaging? Or, on the other hand, are you prepared to say they are damaging and should be prohibited?

[4]Quotations from Homer are generally taken from the translations by Dr. Rieu in the Penguin series. At times (as here) the version quoted by Plato differs slightly from the accepted text.

2. It is often objected that censorship of reading matter and of television programs available to children underrates their ability to think for themselves and to discount the dangerous, obscene, and tawdry. Do you agree with this objection? Does Plato?

3. Plato says that allowing poets to say what they please about the gods in his ideal state would be "inconsistent." Explain what he means by this criticism, and then explain why you agree or disagree with it.

4. Do you believe that parents should censor the "fiction" their children encounter (literature, films, pictures, music), but that the community should not censor the "fiction" of adults? Write an essay of 500 words on one of these topics: "Censorship and Rock Lyrics"; "X-rated Films"; "Ethnic Jokes." (These topics are broadly worded; you can narrow one, and offer whatever thesis you wish.)

5. Were you taught that any of the founding fathers ever acted disreputably, or that any American hero had any serious moral flaw? Or that America ever acted immorally in its dealings with other nations? Do you think it appropriate for children to hear such things?

John Stuart Mill

From *On Liberty*

INTRODUCTORY

The object of this essay is to assert one very simple principle, as entitled to govern absolutely the dealings of society with the individual in the way of compulsion and control, whether the means used be physical force in the form of legal penalties or the moral coercion of public opinion. That principle is that the sole end for which mankind are warranted, individually or collectively, in interfering with the liberty of action of any of their number is self-protection. That the only purpose for which power can be right-

---

John Stuart Mill (1806–1873), one of England's most influential philosophers and essayists in the nineteenth century, was blessed with a precocious genius that enabled him to master foreign languages, mathematics, and other studies with equal ease. From his infancy he was raised by his formidable father, James Mill, for an arduous and ambitious career as a teacher, writer, editor, conversationalist, and public servant. (His Autobiography *[1873] tells the story of his youth with vivid detail.) For half a century he was active in the literary, cultural, and political life of London, but today even his major books — notably,* System of Logic *(1843) and* Principles of Political Economy *(1848) — are studied only by specialists. Several of his shorter pieces, however, continue to be widely read, including* Utilitarianism *(1863),* Subjection of Women *(1869), and the most influential of them all,* On Liberty *(1859), from which we reprint a substantial excerpt.*

fully exercised over any member of a civilized community, against his will, is to prevent harm to others. His own good, either physical or moral, is not a sufficient warrant. He cannot rightfully be compelled to do or forbear because it will be better for him to do so, because it will make him happier, because, in the opinions of others, to do so would be wise or even right. These are good reasons for remonstrating with him, or reasoning with him, or persuading him, or entreating him, but not for compelling him or visiting him with any evil in case he do otherwise. To justify that, the conduct from which it is desired to deter him must be calculated to produce evil to someone else. The only part of the conduct of anyone for which he is amenable to society is that which concerns others. In the part which merely concerns himself, his independence is, of right, absolute. Over himself, over his own body and mind, the individual is sovereign.

It is, perhaps, hardly necessary to say that this doctrine is meant to apply only to human beings in the maturity of their faculties. We are not speaking of children or of young persons below the age which the law may fix as that of manhood or womanhood. Those who are still in a state to require being taken care of by others must be protected against their own actions as well as against external injury. For the same reason we may leave out of consideration those backward states of society in which the race itself may be considered as in its nonage. The early difficulties in the way of spontaneous progress are so great that there is seldom any choice of means for overcoming them; and a ruler full of the spirit of improvement is warranted in the use of any expedients that will attain an end perhaps otherwise unattainable. Despotism is a legitimate mode of government in dealing with barbarians, provided the end be their improvement and the means justified by actually effecting that end. Liberty, as a principle, has no application to any state of things anterior to the time when mankind have become capable of being improved by free and equal discussion. Until then,

---

In this essay, Mill sets himself the task of stating a general principle that would appeal to his readers and serve to distinguish between the area of an individual's conduct that ought to be completely free from supervision and the area of conduct that is properly supervised, regulated, and even punished by government. Mill does not write for those with fascist or totalitarian sympathies, or for readers still in thrall to traditional (tribal, sectarian) ways of life. Such outlooks would grant to government an all-encompassing authority that Mill utterly rejects. He takes for granted an audience of sympathetic liberals, who prize freedom and individualism and yet recognize that these values are not absolutes without limit.

Mill is also a utilitarian; that is, he believes individual conduct or government policy is justified or condemned depending on whether (in Jeremy Bentham's famous phrase) it conduces to "the greatest good of the greatest number." Where a person's conduct has virtually no effect for good or ill on the interests of others, then the utilitarian criterion is equivalent to the ideal of enlightened self-interest. But because most of what we say and do does affect others, predicting and evaluating that influence can become crucial, as it is for Mill, in deciding whether speech or action ought to be tolerated rather than restricted.

there is nothing for them but implicit obedience to an Akbar or a Charlemagne,[1] if they are so fortunate as to find one. But as soon as mankind have attained the capacity of being guided to their own improvement by conviction or persuasion (a period long since reached in all nations with whom we need here concern ourselves), compulsion, either in the direct form or in that of pains and penalties for noncompliance, is no longer admissible as a means to their own good, and justifiable only for the security of others. . . .

There is a sphere of action in which society, as distinguished from the individual, has, if any, only an indirect interest: comprehending all that portion of a person's life and conduct which affects only himself or, if it also affects others, only with their free, voluntary, and undeceived consent and participation. When I say only himself, I mean directly and in the first instance; for whatever affects himself may affect others through himself; and the objection which may be grounded on this contingency will receive consideration in the sequel. This, then, is the appropriate region of human liberty. It comprises, first, the inward domain of consciousness, demanding liberty of conscience in the most comprehensive sense, liberty of thought and feeling, absolute freedom of opinion and sentiment on all subjects, practical or speculative, scientific, moral, or theological. The liberty of expressing and publishing opinions may seem to fall under a different principle, since it belongs to that part of the conduct of an individual which concerns other people, but, being almost of as much importance as the liberty of thought itself and resting in great part on the same reasons, is practically inseparable from it. Secondly, the principle requires liberty of tastes and pursuits, of framing the plan of our life to suit our own character, of doing as we like, subject to such consequences as may follow, without impediment from our fellow creatures, so long as what we do does not harm them, even though they should think our conduct foolish, perverse, or wrong. Thirdly, from this liberty of each individual follows the liberty, within the same limits, of combination among individuals; freedom to unite for any purpose not involving harm to others: the persons combining being supposed to be of full age and not forced or deceived.

No society in which these liberties are not, on the whole, respected is free, whatever may be its form of government; and none is completely free in which they do not exist absolute and unqualified. The only freedom which deserves the name is that of pursuing our own good in our own way, so long as we do not attempt to deprive others of theirs or impede their efforts to obtain it. Each is the proper guardian of his own health, whether bodily or mental and spiritual. Mankind are greater gainers by suffering each other to live as seems good to themselves than by compelling each to live as seems good to the rest. . . .

---

[1]**Akbar . . . Charlemagne** Akbar (1542–1605), Mogul Emperor of India; Charlemagne (742–815), King of the Franks, and later Emperor of the West. [All notes are the editors'.]

OF THE LIBERTY OF THOUGHT AND DISCUSSION

The time, it is to be hoped, is gone by when any defense would be necessary of the "liberty of the press" as one of the securities against corrupt or tyrannical government. No argument, we may suppose, can now be needed against permitting a legislature or an executive, not identified in interest with the people, to prescribe opinions to them and determine what doctrines or what arguments they shall be allowed to hear. This aspect of the question, besides, has been so often and so triumphantly enforced by preceding writers that it need not be specially insisted on in this place. Though the law of England, on the subject of the press, is as servile to this day as it was in the time of the Tudors,[2] there is little danger of its being actually put in force against political discussion except during some temporary panic when fear of insurrection drives ministers and judges from their propriety; and, speaking generally, it is not, in constitutional countries, to be apprehended that the government, whether completely responsible to the people or not, will often attempt to control the expression of opinion, except when in doing so it makes itself the organ of the general intolerance of the public. Let us suppose, therefore, that the government is entirely at one with the people, and never thinks of exerting any power of coercion unless in agreement with what it conceives to be their voice. But I deny the right of the people to exercise such coercion, either by themselves or by their government. The power itself is illegitimate. The best government has no more title to it than the worst. It is as noxious, or more noxious, when exerted in accordance with public opinion than when in opposition to it. If all mankind minus one were of one opinion, mankind would be no more justified in silencing that one person than he, if he had the power, would be justified in silencing mankind. Were an opinion a personal possession of no value except to the owner, if to be obstructed in the enjoyment of it were simply a private injury, it would make some difference whether the injury was inflicted only on a few persons or on many. But the peculiar evil of silencing the expression of an opinion is that it is robbing the human race, posterity as well as the existing generation — those who dissent from the opinion, still more than those who hold it. If the opinion is right, they are deprived of the opportunity of exchanging error for truth; if wrong, they lose, what is almost as great a benefit, the clearer perception and livelier impression of truth produced by its collision with error. . . .

We have now recognized the necessity to the mental well-being of mankind (on which all their other well-being depends) of freedom of opinion, and freedom of the expression of opinion, on four distinct grounds, which we will now briefly recapitulate:

---

[2]**the time of the Tudors** The period in England from the reign of Henry VII through the reign of Queen Elizabeth I; that is, 1485–1603.

First, if any opinion is compelled to silence, that opinion may, for aught we can certainly know, be true. To deny this is to assume our own infallibility.

Secondly, though the silenced opinion be an error, it may, and very commonly does, contain a portion of truth; and since the general or prevailing opinion on any subject is rarely or never the whole truth, it is only by the collision of adverse opinions that the remainder of the truth has any chance of being supplied.

Thirdly, even if the received opinion be not only true, but the whole truth; unless it is suffered to be, and actually is, vigorously and earnestly contested, it will, by most of those who receive it, be held in the manner of a prejudice, with little comprehension or feeling of its rational grounds. And not only this, but, fourthly, the meaning of the doctrine itself will be in danger of being lost or enfeebled, and deprived of its vital effect on the character and conduct: the dogma becoming a mere formal profession, inefficacious for good, but cumbering the ground and preventing the growth of any real and heartfelt conviction from reason or personal experience.

Before quitting the subject of freedom of opinion, it is fit to take some 10 notice of those who say that the free expression of all opinions should be permitted on condition that the manner be temperate, and do not pass the bounds of fair discussion. Much might be said on the impossibility of fixing where these supposed bounds are to be placed; for if the test be offense to those whose opinions are attacked, I think experience testifies that this offense is given whenever the attack is telling and powerful, and that every opponent who pushes them hard, and whom they find it difficult to answer, appears to them, if he shows any strong feeling on the subject, an intemperate opponent. But this, though an important consideration in a practical point of view, merges in a more fundamental objection. Undoubtedly, the manner of asserting an opinion, even though it be a true one, may be very objectionable and may justly incur severe censure. But the principal offenses of the kind are such as it is mostly impossible, unless by accidental self-betrayal, to bring home to conviction. The gravest of them is, to argue sophistically, to suppress facts or arguments, to misstate the elements of the case, or misrepresent the opposite opinion. But all this, even to the most aggravated degree, is so continually done in perfect good faith by persons who are not considered, and in many other respects may not deserve to be considered, ignorant or incompetent, that it is rarely possible, on adequate grounds, conscientiously to stamp the misrepresentation as morally culpable, and still less could law presume to interfere with this kind of controversial misconduct. With regard to what is commonly meant by intemperate discussion, namely invective, sarcasm, personality, and the like, the denunciation of these weapons would deserve more sympathy if it were ever proposed to interdict them equally to both sides; but it is only desired to restrain the employment of them against the prevailing opinion; against the unprevailing they may not only be used without general disapproval, but will be likely to obtain for him who uses them the praise of honest zeal and righteous indignation. Yet whatever mischief arises from their use is greatest when they are employed against the comparatively defenseless; and whatever unfair advantage can be derived by any opinion from this mode of asserting it accrues almost exclusively to received opinions. The worst offense of this kind which can be committed by a polemic is to stigmatize those who hold the contrary opinion as bad and immoral men. To calumny of this sort, those who hold any unpopular opinion are peculiarly exposed, because they are in general few and uninfluential, and nobody but themselves feels much interested in seeing justice done them; but this weapon is, from the nature of the case, denied to those who attack a prevailing opinion: They can neither use it with safety to themselves, nor, if they could, would it do anything but recoil on their own cause. In general, opinions contrary to those commonly received can only obtain a hearing by studied moderation of language and the most cautious avoidance of unnecessary offense, from which they hardly ever deviate even in a slight degree without losing ground, while unmeasured vituperation employed on the side of the prevailing opinion really does deter people from professing contrary opinions and from listening to those who profess them. For the interest, therefore, of truth and justice it is far more important to restrain this employment of vituperative language than the other; and, for example, if it were necessary to choose, there would be much more need to discourage offensive attacks on infidelity than on religion. It is, however, obvious that law and authority have no business with restraining either, while opinion ought, in every instance, to determine its verdict by the circumstances of the individual case—condemning everyone, on whichever side of the argument he places himself, in whose mode of advocacy either want of candor, or malignity, bigotry, or intolerance of feeling manifest themselves; but not inferring these vices from the side which a person takes, though it be the contrary side of the question to our own; and giving merited honor to everyone, whatever opinion he may hold, who has calmness to see and honesty to state what his opponents and their opinions really are, exaggerating nothing to their discredit, keeping nothing back which tells, or can be supposed to tell, in their favor. This is the real morality of public discussion; and if often violated, I am happy to think that there are many controversialists who to a great extent observe it, and a still greater number who conscientiously strive toward it.

OF THE LIMITS TO THE AUTHORITY OF SOCIETY OVER THE INDIVIDUAL

What, then, is the rightful limit to the sovereignty of the individual over himself? Where does the authority of society begin? How much of human life should be assigned to individuality, and how much to society?

Each will receive its proper share if each has that which more particularly concerns it. To individuality should belong the part of life in which it is chiefly the individual that is interested; to society, the part which chiefly interests society.

Though society is not founded on a contract, and though no good purpose is answered by inventing a contract in order to deduce social obligations from it, everyone who receives the protection of society owes a return for the benefit, and the fact of living in society renders it indispensable that each should be bound to observe a certain line of conduct toward the rest. This conduct consists, first, in not injuring the interests of one another, or rather certain interests which, either by express legal provision or by tacit understanding, ought to be considered as rights; and secondly, in each person's bearing his share (to be fixed on some equitable principle) of the labors and sacrifices incurred for defending the society or its members from injury and molestation. These conditions society is justified in enforcing at all costs to those who endeavor to withhold fulfillment. Nor is this all that society may do. The acts of an individual may be hurtful to others or wanting in due consideration for their welfare, without going to the length of violating any of their constituted rights. The offender may then be justly punished by opinion, though not by law. As soon as any part of a person's conduct affects prejudicially the interests of others, society has jurisdiction over it, and the question whether the general welfare will or will not be promoted by interfering with it becomes open to discussion. But there is no room for entertaining any such question when a person's conduct affects the interests of no persons besides himself, or needs not affect them unless they like (all the persons concerned being of full age and the ordinary amount of understanding). In all such cases, there should be perfect freedom, legal and social, to do the action and stand the consequences. . . .

The distinction here pointed out between the part of a person's life which concerns only himself and that which concerns others, many persons will refuse to admit. How (it may be asked) can any part of the conduct of a member of society be a matter of indifference to the other members? No person is an entirely isolated being; it is impossible for a person to do anything seriously or permanently hurtful to himself without mischief reaching at least to his near connections, and often far beyond them. If he injures his property, he does harm to those who directly or indirectly derived support from it, and usually diminishes, by a greater or less amount, the general resources of the community. If he deteriorates his bodily or mental faculties, he not only brings evil upon all who depended on him for any portion of their happiness, but disqualifies himself for rendering the services which he owes to his fellow creatures generally, perhaps becomes a burden on their affection or benevolence; and if such conduct were very frequent hardly any offense that is committed would detract more from the general sum of good. Finally, if by his vices or follies a person does not direct harm to others, he is nevertheless (it may be said) injurious by his example, and ought to be compelled to control himself for the sake of those whom the sight or knowledge of his conduct might corrupt or mislead.

And even (it will be added) if the consequences of misconduct could   15
be confined to the vicious or thoughtless individual, ought society to abandon to their own guidance those who are manifestly unfit for it? If protection against themselves is confessedly due to children and persons under
age, is not society equally bound to afford it to persons of mature years who
are equally incapable of self-government? If gambling, or drunkenness, or
incontinence, or idleness, or uncleanliness are as injurious to happiness,
and as great a hindrance to improvement, as many or most of the acts prohibited by law, why (it may be asked) should not law, so far as is consistent
with practicability and social convenience, endeavor to repress these also?
And as a supplement to the unavoidable imperfections of law, ought not
opinion at least to organize a powerful police against these vices and visit
rigidly with social penalties those who are known to practice them? There
is no question here (it may be said) about restricting individuality, or impeding the trial of new and original experiments in living. The only things it
is sought to prevent are things which have been tried and condemned from
the beginning of the world until now — things which experience has shown
not to be useful or suitable to any person's individuality. There must be
some length of time and amount of experience after which a moral or pru-
dential truth may be regarded as established; and it is merely desired to
prevent generation after generation from falling over the same precipice
which has been fatal to their predecessors.

I fully admit that the mischief which a person does to himself may seriously affect, both through their sympathies and their interests, those
nearly connected with him and, in a minor degree, society at large. When,
by conduct of this sort, a person is led to violate a distinct and assignable
obligation to any other person or persons, the case is taken out of the self-
regarding class and becomes amenable to moral disapprobation in the
proper sense of the term. If, for example, a man, through intemperance or
extravagance, becomes unable to pay his debts, or, having undertaken the
moral responsibility of a family, becomes from the same cause incapable of
supporting or educating them, he is deservedly reprobated and might be
justly punished; but it is for the breach of duty to his family or creditors,
not for the extravagance. If the resources which ought to have been devoted to them had been diverted from them for the most prudent invest-
ment, the moral culpability would have been the same. George Barnwell[3]
murdered his uncle to get money for his mistress, but if he had done it to
set himself up in business, he would equally have been hanged. Again, in
the frequent case of a man who causes grief to his family by addiction to
bad habits, he deserves reproach for his unkindness or ingratitude; but so
he may for cultivating habits not in themselves vicious, if they are painful to
those with whom he passes his life, or who from personal ties are dependent on him for their comfort. Whoever fails in the consideration generally

---

[3]**George Barnwell** An apprentice in a popular ballad and in George Lillo's play *The London Merchant* (1731).

due to the interests and feelings of others, not being compelled by some more imperative duty, or justified by allowable self-preference, is a subject of moral disapprobation for that failure, but not for the cause of it, nor for the errors, merely personal to himself, which may have remotely led to it. In like manner, when a person disables himself, by conduct purely self-regarding, from the performance of some definite duty incumbent on him to the public, he is guilty of a social offense. No person ought to be punished simply for being drunk; but a soldier or a policeman should be punished for being drunk on duty. Whenever, in short, there is a definite damage, or a definite risk of damage, either to an individual or to the public, the case is taken out of the province of liberty and placed in that of morality or law. . . .

But the strongest of all the arguments against the interference of the public with purely personal conduct is that, when it does interfere, the odds are that it interferes wrongly and in the wrong place. On questions of social morality, of duty to others, the opinion of the public, that is, of an overruling majority, though often wrong, is likely to be still oftener right, because on such questions they are only required to judge of their own interests, of the manner in which some mode of conduct, if allowed to be practiced, would affect themselves. But the opinion of a similar majority, imposed as a law on the minority, on questions of self-regarding conduct is quite as likely to be wrong as right, for in these cases public opinion means, at the best, some people's opinion of what is good or bad for other people, while very often it does not even mean that—the public, with the most perfect indifference, passing over the pleasure or convenience of those whose conduct they censure and considering only their own preference. There are many who consider as an injury to themselves any conduct which they have a distaste for, and resent it as an outrage to their feelings; as a religious bigot, when charged with disregarding the religious feelings of others, has been known to retort that they disregard his feelings by persisting in their abominable worship or creed. But there is no parity between the feeling of a person for his own opinion and the feeling of another who is offended at his holding it, no more than between the desire of a thief to take a purse and the desire of the right owner to keep it. And a person's taste is as much his own peculiar concern as his opinion or his purse. It is easy for anyone to imagine an ideal public which leaves the freedom and choice of individuals in all uncertain matters undisturbed and only requires them to abstain from modes of conduct which universal experience has condemned. But where has there been seen a public which set any such limit to its censorship? Or when does the public trouble itself about universal experience? In its interferences with personal conduct it is seldom thinking of anything but the enormity of acting or feeling differently from itself; and this standard of judgment, thinly disguised, is held up to mankind as the dictate of religion and philosophy by nine-tenths of all moralists and speculative writers. These teach that things are right because they are right; because we feel them to be so. They tell us to search in our own minds and hearts for laws of conduct binding on ourselves and on all others. What can the poor public do but apply these instructions and make their own personal feelings of good and evil, if they are tolerably unanimous in them, obligatory on all the world?

The evil here pointed out is not one which exists only in theory; and it may perhaps be expected that I should specify the instances in which the public of this age and country improperly invests its own preferences with the character of moral laws. I am not writing an essay on the aberrations of existing moral feeling. That is too weighty a subject to be discussed parenthetically, and by way of illustration. Yet examples are necessary to show that the principle I maintain is of serious and practical moment, and that I am not endeavoring to erect a barrier against imaginary evils. And it is not difficult to show, by abundant instances, that to extend the bounds of what may be called moral police until it encroaches on the most unquestionably legitimate liberty of the individual is one of the most universal of all human propensities. . . .

Without dwelling upon supposititious cases[4] there are, in our own day, gross usurpations upon the liberty of private life actually practiced, and still greater ones threatened with some expectation of success, and opinions propounded which assert an unlimited right in the public not only to prohibit by law everything which it thinks wrong, but, in order to get at what it thinks wrong, to prohibit a number of things which it admits to be innocent.

Under the name of preventing intemperance, the people of one English colony, and of nearly half the United States, have been interdicted by law[5] from making any use whatever of fermented drinks, except for medical purposes, for prohibition of their sale is in fact, as it is intended to be, prohibition of their use. And though the impracticability of executing the law has caused its repeal in several of the States which had adopted it, including the one from which it derives its name, an attempt has notwithstanding been commenced, and is prosecuted with considerable zeal by many of the professed philanthropists, to agitate for a similar law in this country. The association, or "Alliance," as it terms itself, which has been formed for this purpose, has acquired some notoriety through the publicity given to a correspondence between its secretary and one of the very few English public men who hold that a politician's opinions ought to be founded on principles. Lord Stanley's share in this correspondence is calculated to strengthen the hopes already built on him, by those who know how rare such qualities as are manifested in some of his public appearances unhappily are among those who figure in political life. The organ of the Alliance, who would "deeply deplore the recognition of any principle which could be wrested to justify bigotry and persecution," undertakes to point

20

---

[4]**supposititious cases** Cases depending on a supposition; hypothetical cases.
[5]**law** The Maine Liquor Law (1851) prohibited the manufacture, sale, and use of intoxicating drinks, with some exceptions.

out the "broad and impassable barrier" which divides such principles from those of the association. "All matters relating to thought, opinion, conscience, appear to me," he says, "to be without the sphere of legislation; all pertaining to social act, habit, relation, subject only to a discretionary power vested in the State itself, and not in the individual, to be within it." No mention is made of a third class, different from either of these, viz., acts and habits which are not social, but individual; although it is to this class, surely, that the act of drinking fermented liquors belongs. Selling fermented liquors, however, is trading, and trading is a social act. But the infringement complained of is not on the liberty of the seller, but on that of the buyer and consumer; since the State might just as well forbid him to drink wine as purposely make it impossible for him to obtain it. The secretary, however, says, "I claim, as a citizen, a right to legislate whenever my social rights are invaded by the social act of another." And now for the definition of these "social rights": "If anything invades my social rights, certainly the traffic in strong drink does. It destroys my primary right of security by constantly creating and stimulating social disorder. It invades my right of equality by deriving a profit from the creation of a misery I am taxed to support. It impedes my right to free moral and intellectual development by surrounding my path with dangers and by weakening and demoralizing society, from which I have a right to claim mutual aid and intercourse." A theory of "social rights" the like of which probably never before found its way into distinct language: being nothing short of this — that it is the absolute social right of every individual that every other individual shall act in every respect exactly as he ought; that whosoever fails thereof in the smallest particular violates my social right and entitles me to demand from the legislature the removal of the grievance. So monstrous a principle is far more dangerous than any single interference with liberty; there is no violation of liberty which it would not justify; it acknowledges no right to any freedom whatever, except perhaps to that of holding opinions in secret, without ever disclosing them; for the moment an opinion which I consider noxious passes anyone's lips, it invades all the "social rights" attributed to me by the Alliance. The doctrine ascribes to all mankind a vested interest in each other's moral, intellectual, and even physical perfection, to be defined by each claimant according to his own standard. . . .

Topics for Critical Thinking and Writing

1. Mill claims (para. 1) that the purpose of his essay is "to assert one very simple principle." Some critics have maintained that he asserts *two* principles. Who is right, Mill or these critics?

2. In his second paragraph, Mill grants two major exceptions to his principle barring state interference with personal conduct. What are these exceptions? Are you willing to agree with him? Explain why, preferably in two paragraphs.

3. In several places in his essay Mill describes what freedom (liberty) is, but he

never quite comes out and explicitly defines it. Try to help him out with an explicit definition of your own that faithfully expresses Mill's ideas.

4. Mill gives three main reasons against censorship of the press. One of them (as he later expresses it in para. 7) is that all silencing of discussion is an assumption of our own infallibility. Do you agree?

5. Would Mill agree that "Sticks and stones can break my bones, but words can never hurt me?" Do you agree? Explain.

6. How adequate is Mill's distinction (para. 13) between a person's conduct that affects the interests of others, and conduct that affects no one else? What objections to it does Mill himself anticipate? Can you think of troubling borderline cases that put the distinction in doubt?

7. Mill allows (para. 16) that a person who injures a pedestrian while driving "under the influence" (as we euphemistically say) may be punished—but so long as his drunkenness injures no one, or no one but himself, he may not be punished. Write an essay of 500 to 750 words either attacking or defending Mill's position. (By the way, do the laws on this matter currently in force in your state coincide with Mill's position, or not?)

8. Would Mill agree with Susan Brownmiller (p. 661) in defending legal regulation of obscene and pornographic materials, or would he agree with Susan Jacoby (p. 22) in leaving such publications unregulated? Explain.

9. Suppose you believed that cigarette manufacture, distribution, sale, use, and advertising should be made illegal, or that these should at least be severely regulated. Would you find an ally or a hostile critic in Mill? Explain.

John Marshall Harlan and Harry A. Blackmun

Paul Robert Cohen, Appellant, v. State of California

Justice Harlan delivered the opinion of the Court.

This case may seem at first blush too inconsequential to find its way into our books, but the issue it presents is of no small constitutional significance.

Appellant Paul Robert Cohen was convicted in the Los Angeles Mu-

---

During the 1960s, draft-age men often protested against the Selective Service System on grounds that it was administered unfairly and that it was being used to provide troops to fight an unjust war in Vietnam. Protest took varied forms, including civil disobedience and violent resistance. Peaceful objections were far more frequent, but in some cases it was hard to tell whether the protest was lawful or not. The conduct of Paul Robert Cohen is one of these borderline cases. Cohen was convicted in 1968 in Los Angeles of a misdemeanor for behaving in a manner that vio-

nicipal Court of violating that part of California Penal Code §415 which prohibits "maliciously and willfully disturb[ing] the peace or quiet of any neighborhood or person, . . . by . . . offensive conduct. . . ." He was given thirty days' imprisonment. The facts upon which his conviction rests are detailed in the opinion of the Court of Appeal of California, Second Appellate District, as follows:

> On April 26, 1968 the defendant was observed in the Los Angeles County Courthouse in the corridor outside of Division 20 of the Municipal Court wearing a jacket bearing the words "Fuck the Draft" which were plainly visible. There were women and children present in the corridor. The defendant was arrested. The defendant testified that he wore the jacket as a means of informing the public of the depth of his feelings against the Vietnam War and the draft.
>
> The defendant did not engage in, nor threaten to engage in, nor did anyone as the result of his conduct in fact commit or threaten to commit any act of violence. The defendant did not make any loud or unusual noise, nor was there any evidence that he uttered any sound prior to his arrest.

In affirming the conviction the Court of Appeal held that "offensive conduct" means "behavior which has a tendency to provoke *others* to acts of violence or to in turn disturb the peace," and that the State had proved this element because, on the facts of this case, "[i]t was certainly reasonably foreseeable that such conduct might cause others to rise up to commit a violent act against the person of the defendant or attempt to forcibly remove his jacket." The California Supreme Court declined review by a divided vote. We brought the case here, postponing the consideration of the question of our jurisdiction over this appeal to a hearing of the case on the merits. We now reverse.

The question of our jurisdiction need not detain us long. Throughout 5 the proceedings below, Cohen consistently claimed that, as construed to apply to the facts of this case, the statute infringed his rights to freedom of expression guaranteed by the First and Fourteenth Amendments of the Federal Constitution. That contention has been rejected by the highest California state court in which review could be had. Accordingly, we are

---

lated a California statute forbidding "tumultuous or offensive conduct." Cohen argued that his conduct was protected by the United States Constitution as an act of "free speech," but the California Court of Appeals disagreed and upheld his conviction. He appealed to the United States Supreme Court and won by a vote of six to three. Excerpted here is the majority opinion, written by Associate Justice John Marshall Harlan (1899–1971), one of the most respected jurists to sit on the Court during the past generation. The facts of the case are briefly set out by Harlan in his opening paragraphs. We also reprint the main argument of the brief dissenting opinion, written by Associate Justice Harry A. Blackmun (b. 1908). Legal citations have been omitted.

fully satisfied that Cohen has properly invoked our jurisdiction by this appeal.

I

In order to lay hands on the precise issue which this case involves, it is useful first to canvass various matters which this record does *not* present.

The conviction quite clearly rests upon the asserted offensiveness of the *words* Cohen used to convey his message to the public. The only "conduct" which the State sought to punish is the fact of communication. Thus, we deal here with a conviction resting solely upon "speech," not upon any separately identifiable conduct which allegedly was intended by Cohen to be perceived by others as expressive of particular views but which, on its face, does not necessarily convey any message and hence arguably could be regulated without effectively repressing Cohen's ability to express himself. Further, the State certainly lacks power to punish Cohen for the underlying content of the message the inscription conveyed. At least so long as there is no showing of an intent to incite disobedience to or disruption of the draft. Cohen could not, consistently with the First and Fourteenth Amendments, be punished for asserting the evident position on the inutility or immorality of the draft his jacket reflected.

Appellant's conviction, then, rests squarely upon his exercise of the "freedom of speech" protected from arbitrary governmental interference by the Constitution and can be justified, if at all, only as a valid regulation of the manner in which he exercised that freedom, not as a permissible prohibition on the substantive message it conveys. This does not end the inquiry, of course, for the First and Fourteenth Amendments have never been thought to give absolute protection to every individual to speak whenever or wherever he pleases, or to use any form of address in any circumstance that he chooses. In this vein, too, however, we think it important to note that several issues typically associated with such problems are not presented here.

In the first place, Cohen was tried under a statute applicable throughout the entire State. Any attempt to support this conviction on the ground that the statute seeks to preserve an appropriately decorous atmosphere in the courthouse where Cohen was arrested must fail in the absence of any language in the statute that would have put appellant on notice that certain kinds of otherwise permissible speech or conduct would nevertheless, under California law, not be tolerated in certain places. No fair reading of the phrase "offensive conduct" can be said sufficiently to inform the ordinary person that distinctions between certain locations are thereby created.[1]

---

[1] It is illuminating to note what transpired when Cohen entered a courtroom in the building. He removed his jacket and stood with it folded over his arm. Meanwhile, a policeman sent the presiding judge a note suggesting that Cohen be held in contempt of court. The judge declined to do so and Cohen was arrested by the officer only after he emerged from the courtroom. [All notes are the authors'.]

In the second place, as it comes to us, this case cannot be said to fall 10 within those relatively few categories of instances where prior decisions have established the power of government to deal more comprehensively with certain forms of individual expression simply upon a showing that such a form was employed. This is not, for example, an obscenity case. Whatever else may be necessary to give rise to the States' broader power to prohibit obscene expression, such expression must be, in some significant way, erotic. It cannot plausibly be maintained that this vulgar allusion to the Selective Service System would conjure up such psychic stimulation in anyone likely to be confronted with Cohen's crudely defaced jacket.

This Court has also held that the States are free to ban the simple use, without a demonstration of additional justifying circumstances, of so-called "fighting words," those personally abusive epithets which, when addressed to the ordinary citizen, are, as a matter of common knowledge, inherently likely to provoke violent reaction. While the four-letter word displayed by Cohen in relation to the draft is not uncommonly employed in a personally provocative fashion, in this instance it was clearly not "directed to the person of the hearer." No individual actually or likely to be present could reasonably have regarded the words on appellant's jacket as a direct personal insult. Nor do we have here an instance of the exercise of the State's police power to prevent a speaker from intentionally provoking a given group to hostile reaction. There is, as noted above, no showing that anyone who saw Cohen was in fact violently aroused or that appellant intended such a result.

Finally, in arguments before this Court much has been made of the claim that Cohen's distasteful mode of expression was thrust upon unwilling or unsuspecting viewers, and that the State might therefore legitimately act as it did in order to protect the sensitive from otherwise unavoidable exposure to appellant's crude form of protest. Of course, the mere presumed presence of unwitting listeners or viewers does not serve automatically to justify curtailing all speech capable of giving offense. While this Court has recognized that government may properly act in many situations to prohibit intrusion into the privacy of the home of unwelcome views and ideas which cannot be totally banned from the public dialogue, we have at the same time consistently stressed that "we are often 'captives' outside the sanctuary of the home and subject to objectionable speech." The ability of government, consonant with the Constitution, to shut off discourse solely to protect others from hearing it is, in other words, dependent upon a showing that substantial privacy interests are being invaded in an essentially intolerable manner. Any broader view of this authority would effectively empower a majority to silence dissidents simply as a matter of personal predilections.

In this regard, persons confronted with Cohen's jacket were in a quite different posture than, say, those subjected to the raucous emissions of sound trucks blaring outside their residences. Those in the Los Angeles courthouse could effectively avoid further bombardment of their sensibilities simply by averting their eyes. And, while it may be that one has a more substantial claim to a recognizable privacy interest when walking through a courthouse corridor than, for example, strolling through Central Park, surely it is nothing like the interest in being free from unwanted expression in the confines of one's own home. Given the subtlety and complexity of the factors involved, if Cohen's "speech" was otherwise entitled to constitutional protection, we do not think the fact that some unwilling "listeners" in a public building may have been briefly exposed to it can serve to justify this breach of the peace conviction where, as here, there was no evidence that persons powerless to avoid appellant's conduct did in fact object to it, and where that portion of the statute upon which Cohen's conviction rests evinces no concern, either on its face or as construed by the California courts, with the special plight of the captive auditor, but, instead, indiscriminately sweeps within its prohibitions all "offensive conduct" that disturbs "any neighborhood or person."[2]

II

Against this background, the issue flushed by this case stands out in bold relief. It is whether California can excise, as "offensive conduct," one particular scurrilous epithet from the public discourse, either upon the theory of the court below that its use is inherently likely to cause violent reaction or upon a more general assertion that the States, acting as guardians of public morality, may properly remove this offensive word from the public vocabulary.

The rationale of the California court is plainly untenable. At most it 15 reflects an "undifferentiated fear or apprehension of disturbance [which] is not enough to overcome the right to freedom of expression." We have been shown no evidence that substantial numbers of citizens are standing ready to strike out physically at whoever may assault their sensibilities with execrations like that uttered by Cohen. There may be some persons about with such lawless and violent proclivities, but that is an insufficient base upon which to erect, consistently with constitutional values, a governmental power to force persons who wish to ventilate their dissident views into avoiding particular forms of expression. The argument amounts to little more than the self-defeating proposition that to avoid physical censorship of one who has not sought to provoke such a response by a hypothetical co-

---

[2]In fact, other portions of the same statute do make some such distinctions. For example, the statute also prohibits disturbing "the peace or quiet . . . by loud or unusual noise" and using "vulgar, profane or indecent language within the presence or hearing of women or children, in a loud and boisterous manner." . . . This second quoted provision in particular serves to put the actor on much fairer notice as to what is prohibited. It also buttresses our view that the "offensive conduct" portion, as construed and applied in this case, cannot legitimately be justified in this Court as designed or intended to make fine distinctions between differently situated recipients.

terie of the violent and lawless, the States may more appropriately effectuate that censorship themselves.

Admittedly, it is not so obvious that the First and Fourteenth Amendments must be taken to disable the States from punishing public utterance of this unseemly expletive in order to maintain what they regard as a suitable level of discourse within the body politic. We think, however, that examination and reflection will reveal the shortcoming of a contrary viewpoint.

At the outset, we cannot overemphasize that, in our judgment, most situations where the State has a justifiable interest in regulating speech will fall within one or more of the various established exceptions, discussed above but not applicable here, to the usual rule that governmental bodies may not prescribe the form or content of individual expression. Equally important to our conclusion is the constitutional backdrop against which our decision must be made. The constitutional right of free expression is powerful medicine in a society as diverse and populous as ours. It is designed and intended to remove governmental restraints from the arena of public discussion, putting the decision as to what views shall be voiced largely into the hands of each of us, in the hope that use of such freedom will ultimately produce a more capable citizenry and more perfect polity and in the belief that no other approach would comport with the premise of individual dignity and choice upon which our political system rests.

To many, the immediate consequence of this freedom may often appear to be only verbal tumult, discord, and even offensive utterance. These are, however, within established limits, in truth necessary side effects of the broader enduring values which the process of open debate permits us to achieve. That the air may at times seem filled with verbal cacophony is, in this sense, not a sign of weakness but of strength. We cannot lose sight of the fact that, in what otherwise might seem a trifling and annoying instance of individual distasteful abuse of a privilege, these fundamental societal values are truly implicated. That is why "[w]holly neutral futilities . . . come under the protection of free speech as fully as do Keats's poems or Donne's sermons," and why "so long as the means are peaceful, the communication need not meet standards of acceptability."

Against this perception of the constitutional policies involved, we discern certain more particularized considerations that peculiarly call for reversal of this conviction. First, the principle contended for by the State seems inherently boundless. How is one to distinguish this from any other offensive word? Surely the State has no right to cleanse public debate to the point where it is grammatically palatable to the most squeamish among us. Yet no readily ascertainable general principle exists for stopping short of that result were we to affirm the judgment below. For, while the particular four-letter word being litigated here is perhaps more distasteful than most others of its genre, it is nevertheless often true that one man's vulgarity is another's lyric. Indeed, we think it is largely because governmental officials cannot make principled distinctions in this area that the Constitution leaves matters of taste and style so largely to the individual.

Additionally, we cannot overlook the fact, because it is well illustrated 20 by the episode involved here, that much linguistic expression serves a dual communicative function: It conveys not only ideas capable of relatively precise, detached explication, but otherwise inexpressible emotions as well. In fact, words are often chosen as much for their emotive as their cognitive force. We cannot sanction the view that the Constitution, while solicitous of the cognitive content of individual speech, has little or no regard for that emotive function which, practically speaking, may often be the more important element of the overall message sought to be communicated. Indeed, as Mr. Justice Frankfurter has said, "One of the prerogatives of American citizenship is the right to criticize public men and measures — and that means not only informed and responsible criticism but the freedom to speak foolishly and without moderation."

Finally, and in the same vein, we cannot indulge the facile assumption that one can forbid particular words without also running a substantial risk of suppressing ideas in the process. Indeed, governments might soon seize upon the censorship of particular words as a convenient guise for banning the expression of unpopular views. We have been able, as noted above, to discern little social benefit that might result from running the risk of opening the door to such grave results.

It is, in sum, our judgment that, absent a more particularized and compelling reason for its actions, the State may not, consistently with the First and Fourteenth Amendments, make the simple public display here involved of this single four-letter expletive a criminal offense. Because that is the only arguably sustainable rationale for the conviction here at issue, the judgment below must be

Reversed

Justice Blackmun, with whom the Chief Justice and Justice Black join. I dissent:

Cohen's absurd and immature antic, in my view, was mainly conduct 25 and little speech. The California Court of Appeal appears so to have described it, and I cannot characterize it otherwise. . . .

Topics for Critical Thinking and Writing ═══════════

1. After reading the facts of the case, do you agree with the dissenting opinion that what Cohen did was "mainly conduct and little speech"? Does it matter if this evaluation is correct?

2. State briefly and in your own words the several kinds of issues that, in the majority's opinion, the Cohen case does *not* involve. If the case doesn't involve them, why does the majority discuss them?

3. In Part II of the majority opinion, the Court gives its reasons for reversing

Cohen's conviction. State those reasons in your own words, perhaps in three or four sentences.

4. Suppose Cohen's behavior and arrest had occurred in a neighborhood office of the Selective Service System (a local draft board), rather than in the county court house. Do you think this circumstance might have affected the Court's judgment? Explain in an essay of 250 words.

5. Suppose, contrary to fact, there had been evidence that Cohen's conduct actually had provoked others to acts of violence or to disturb the peace (para. 4). In an essay of 250 to 500 words, explain whether you think this evidence should have led the majority to uphold his conviction, and why.

Irving Kristol

Pornography, Obscenity, and the Case for Censorship

I

Being frustrated is disagreeable, but the real disasters in life begin when you get what you want. For almost a century now, a great many intelligent, well-meaning and articulate people — of a kind generally called liberal or intellectual, or both — have argued eloquently against any kind of censorship of art and/or entertainment. And within the past ten years, the courts and the legislatures of most Western nations have found these arguments persuasive — so persuasive that hardly a man is now alive who clearly remembers what the answers to these arguments were. Today, in the United States and other democracies, censorship has to all intents and purposes ceased to exist.

Is there a sense of triumphant exhilaration in the land? Hardly. There is, on the contrary, a rapidly growing unease and disquiet. Somehow, things have not worked out as they were supposed to, and many notable civil libertarians have gone on record as saying this was not what they meant at all. They wanted a world in which *Desire under the Elms* could be produced,

---

Irving Kristol (b. 1920), a professor at New York University and coeditor of the journal The Public Interest, *describes himself as a "neoconservative." According to Kristol, in* Reflections of a Neoconservative *(1984), neoconservativism is "a current of thought emerging out of the academic-intellectual world and provoked by disillusionment with contemporary liberalism." In a sense, Kristol might call himself a neoliberal, for he says, in his collection of essays, that he wants "a return to the original sources of liberal vision and liberal energy so as to correct the warped version of liberalism that is today's orthodoxy." The following is excerpted from* On the Democratic Idea in America *(1972).*

or *Ulysses*[1] published, without interference by philistine busybodies holding public office. They have got that, of course; but they have also got a world in which homosexual rape takes place on the stage, in which the public flocks during lunch hours to witness varieties of professional fornication, in which Times Square has become little more than a hideous market for the sale and distribution of printed filth that panders to all known (and some fanciful) sexual perversions.

But disagreeable as this may be, does it really matter? Might not our unease and disquiet be merely a cultural hangover—a "hangup," as they say? What reason is there to think that anyone was ever corrupted by a book?

This last question, oddly enough, is asked by the very same people who seem convinced that advertisements in magazines or displays of violence on television do indeed have the power to corrupt. It is also asked, incredibly enough and in all sincerity, by people—e.g., university professors and schoolteachers—whose very lives provide all the answers one could want. After all, if you believe that no one was ever corrupted by a book, you have also to believe that no one was ever improved by a book (or a play or a movie). You have to believe, in other words, that all art is morally trivial and that, consequently, all education is morally irrelevant. No one, not even a university professor, really believes that.

To be sure, it is extremely difficult, as social scientists tell us, to trace   5
the effects of any single book (or play or movie) on an individual reader or any class of readers. But we all know, and social scientists know it too, that the ways in which we use our minds and imaginations do shape our characters and help define us as persons. That those who certainly know this are nevertheless moved to deny it merely indicates how a dogmatic resistance to the idea of censorship can—like most dogmatism — result in a mindless insistence on the absurd.

I have used these harsh terms—"dogmatism" and "mindless"—advisedly. I might also have added "hypocritical." For the plain fact is that none of us is a complete civil libertarian. We all believe that there is some point at which the public authorities ought to step in to limit the "self expression" of an individual or a group, even where this might be seriously intended as a form of artistic expression, and even where the artistic transaction is between consenting adults. A playwright or theatrical director might, in this crazy world of ours, find someone willing to commit suicide on the stage, as called for by the script. We would not allow that—any more than we would permit scenes of real physical torture on the stage, even if the victim were a willing masochist. And I know of no one, no matter how free in spirit, who argues that we ought to permit gladiatorial contests in Yankee Stadium, similar to those once performed in the Colosseum at Rome— even if only consenting adults were involved.

---

[1]***Desire under the Elms . . . Ulysses*** Respectively, a play by Eugene O'Neill (1888–1953) and a novel by James Joyce (1882–1941). [All notes are the editors' unless otherwise specified.]

The basic point that emerges is one that Professor Walter Berns has powerfully argued: No society can be utterly indifferent to the ways its citizens publicly entertain themselves.[2] Bearbaiting and cockfighting are prohibited only in part out of compassion for the suffering animals; the main reason they were abolished was because it was felt that they debased and brutalized the citizenry who flocked to witness such spectacles. And the question we face with regard to pornography and obscenity is whether, now that they have such strong legal protection from the Supreme Court, they can or will brutalize and debase our citizenry. We are, after all, not dealing with one passing incident — one book, or one play, or one movie. We are dealing with a general tendency that is suffusing our entire culture.

I say pornography *and* obscenity because, though they have different dictionary definitions and are frequently distinguishable as "artistic" genres, they are nevertheless in the end identical in effect. Pornography is not objectionable simply because it arouses sexual desire or lust or prurience in the mind of the reader or spectator; this is a silly Victorian notion. A great many nonpornographic works — including some parts of the Bible — excite sexual desire very successfully. What is distinctive about pornography is that, in the words of D. H. Lawrence, it attempts "to do dirt on [sex] . . . [It is an] insult to a vital human relationship."

In other words, pornography differs from erotic art in that its whole purpose is to treat human beings obscenely, to deprive human beings of their specifically human dimension. That is what obscenity is all about. It is light years removed from any kind of carefree sensuality — there is no continuum between Fielding's *Tom Jones* and the Marquis de Sade's *Justine*. These works have quite opposite intentions. To quote Susan Sontag: "What pornographic literature does is precisely to drive a wedge between one's existence as a full human being and one's existence as a sexual being — while in ordinary life a healthy person is one who prevents such a gap from opening up." This definition occurs in an essay *defending* pornography — Miss Sontag is a candid as well as gifted critic — so the definition, which I accept, is neither tendentious nor censorious.

Along these same lines, one can point out — as C. S. Lewis pointed   10 out some years back — that it is no accident that in the history of all literatures obscene words, the so-called "four-letter words," have always been the vocabulary of farce or vituperation. The reason is clear; they reduce men and women to some of their mere bodily functions — they reduce man to his animal component, and such a reduction is an essential purpose of farce or vituperation.

Similarly, Lewis also suggested that it is not an accident that we have no offhand, colloquial, neutral terms — not in any Western European language at any rate — for our most private parts. The words we do use are ei-

---

[2]This is as good a place as any to express my profound indebtedness to Walter Berns's superb essay, "Pornography vs. Democracy," in the Winter 1971 issue of *The Public Interest*. [Kristol's note.]

ther (a) nursery terms, (b) archaisms, (c) scientific terms, or (d) a term from the gutter (i.e., a demeaning term). Here I think the genius of language is telling us something important about man. It is telling us that man is an animal with a difference: He has a unique sense of privacy, and a unique capacity for shape when this privacy is violated. Our "private parts" are indeed private, and not merely because convention prescribes it. This particular convention is indigenous to the human race. In practically all primitive tribes, men and women cover their private parts; and in practically all primitive tribes, men and women do not copulate in public.

It may well be that Western society, in the latter half of the twentieth century, is experiencing a drastic change in sexual mores and sexual relationships. We have had many such "sexual revolutions" in the past — the bourgeois family and bourgeois ideas of sexual propriety were themselves established in the course of a revolution against eighteenth-century "licentiousness" — and we shall doubtless have others in the future. It is, however, highly improbable (to put it mildly) that what we are witnessing is the Final Revolution which will make sexual relations utterly unproblematic, permit us to dispense with any kind of ordered relationships between the sexes, and allow us freely to redefine the human condition. And so long as humanity has not reached that utopia, obscenity will remain a problem.

II

One of the reasons it will remain a problem is that obscenity is not merely about sex, any more than science fiction is about science. Science fiction, as every student of the genre knows, is a peculiar vision of power: what it is really about is politics. And obscenity is a peculiar vision of humanity: what it is really about is ethics and metaphysics.

Imagine a man — a well-known man, much in the public eye — in a hospital ward, dying an agonizing death. He is not in control of his bodily functions, so that his bladder and his bowels empty themselves of their own accord. His consciousness is overwhelmed and extinguished by pain, so that he cannot communicate with us, nor we with him. Now, it would be, technically, the easiest thing in the world to put a television camera in his hospital room and let the whole world witness this spectacle. We don't do it — at least we don't do it as yet — because we regard this as an *obscene* invasion of privacy. And what would make the spectacle obscene is that we would be witnessing the extinguishing of humanity in a human animal.

Incidentally, in the past our humanitarian crusaders against capital 15 punishment understood this point very well. The abolitionist literature goes into great physical detail about what happens to a man when he is hanged or electrocuted or gassed. And their argument was — and is — that what happens is shockingly obscene, and that no civilized society should be responsible for perpetrating such obscenities, particularly since in the nature of the case there must be spectators to ascertain that this horror was indeed being perpetrated in fulfillment of the law.

Sex — like death — is an activity that is both animal and human. There are human sentiments and human ideals involved in this animal activity. But when sex is public, the viewer does not see — cannot see — the sentiments and the ideals. He can only see the animal coupling. And that is why, when men and women make love, as we say, they prefer to be alone — because it is only when you are alone that you can make love, as distinct from merely copulating in an animal and casual way. And that, too, is why those who are voyeurs, if they are not irredeemably sick, also feel ashamed at what they are witnessing. When sex is a public spectacle, a human relationship has been debased into a mere animal connection.

It is also worth noting that this making of sex into an obscenity is not a mutual and equal transaction but rather an act of exploitation by one of the partners — the male partner. I do not wish to get into the complicated question as to what, if any, are the essential differences — as distinct from conventional and cultural differences — between male and female. I do not claim to know the answer to that. But I do know — and I take it as a sign that has meaning — that pornography is, and always has been, a man's work; that women rarely write pornography; and that women tend to be indifferent consumers of pornography.[3] My own guess, by way of explanation, is that a woman's sexual experience is ordinarily more suffused with human emotion than is man's, that men are more easily satisfied with auto-erotic activities, and that men can therefore more easily take a more "technocratic" view of sex and its pleasures. Perhaps this is not correct. But whatever the explanation, there can be no question that pornography is a form of "sexism," as the women's liberation movement calls it, and that the instinct of women's liberation has been unerring in perceiving that when pornography is perpetrated, it is perpetrated against them, as part of a conspiracy to deprive them of their full humanity.

But even if all this is granted, it might be said — and doubtless will be said — that I really ought not to be unduly concerned. Free competition in the cultural marketplace — it is argued by people who have never otherwise had a kind word to say for laissez-faire — will automatically dispose of the problem. The present fad for pornography and obscenity, it will be asserted, is just that, a fad. It will spend itself in the course of time; people will get bored with it, will be able to take it or leave it alone in a casual way, in a "mature way," and, in sum, I am being unnecessarily distressed about the whole business. The *New York Times*, in an editorial, concludes hopefully in this vein.

> In the end . . . the insensate pursuit of the urge to shock, carried from one excess to a more abysmal one, is bound to achieve its own antidote in total boredom. When there is no lower depth to descend to, ennui will erase the problem.

---

[3]There are, of course, a few exceptions. *L'Histoire d'O*, for instance, was written by a woman. It is unquestionably the most *melancholy* work of pornography ever written. And its theme is precisely the dehumanization accomplished by obscenity. [Kristol's note.]

I would like to be able to go along with this line of reasoning, but I cannot. I think it is false, and for two reasons, the first psychological, the second political.

The basic psychological fact about pornography and obscenity is that it [20] appeals to and provokes a kind of sexual regression. The sexual pleasure one gets from pornography and obscenity is autoerotic and infantile; put bluntly, it is masturbatory exercise of the imagination, when it is not masturbation pure and simple. Now, people who masturbate do not get bored with masturbation, just as sadists don't get bored with sadism, and voyeurs don't get bored with voyeurism.

In other words, infantile sexuality is not only a permanent temptation for the adolescent or even the adult — it can quite easily become a permanent, self-reinforcing neurosis. It is because of an awareness of this possibility of regression toward the infantile condition, a regression which is always open to us, that all the codes of sexual conduct ever devised by the human race take such a dim view of autoerotic activities and try to discourage autoerotic fantasies. Masturbation is indeed a perfectly natural autoerotic activity, as so many sexologists blandly assure us today. And it is precisely because it is so perfectly natural that it can be so dangerous to the mature or maturing person, if it is not controlled or sublimated in some way. That is the true meaning of Portnoy's complaint.[4] Portnoy, you will recall, grows up to be a man who is incapable of having an adult sexual relationship with a woman; his sexuality remains fixed in an infantile mode, the prisoner of his autoerotic fantasies. Inevitably, Portnoy comes to think, in a perfectly *infantile* way, that it was all his mother's fault.

It is true that, in our time, some quite brilliant minds have come to the conclusion that a reversion to infantile sexuality is the ultimate mission and secret destiny of the human race. I am thinking in particular of Norman O. Brown, for whose writings I have the deepest respect. One of the reasons I respect them so deeply is that Mr. Brown is a serious thinker who is unafraid to face up to the radical consequences of his radical theories. Thus, Mr. Brown knows and says that for his kind of salvation to be achieved, humanity must annul the civilization it has created — not merely the civilization we have today, but all civilization — so as to be able to make the long descent backward into animal innocence.

And that is the point. What is at stake is civilization and humanity, nothing less. The idea that "everything is permitted," as Nietzsche put it, rests on the premise of nihilism and has nihilistic implications. I will not pretend that the case against nihilism and for civilization is an easy one to make. We are here confronting the most fundamental of philosophical questions, on the deepest levels. In short, the matter of pornography and obscenity is not a trivial one, and only superficial minds can take a bland and untroubled view of it.

In this connection, I must also point out those who are primarily

---

[4]**Portnoy's complaint** Title of a novel (1969) by Philip Roth.

against censorship on liberal grounds tell us not to take pornography or obscenity seriously, while those who are for pornography and obscenity on radical grounds take it very seriously indeed. I believe the radicals — writers like Susan Sontag, Herbert Marcuse, Norman O. Brown, and even Jerry Rubin — are right, and the liberals are wrong. I also believe that those young radicals at Berkeley, some seven years ago, who provoked a major confrontation over the public use of obscene words, showed a brilliant political instinct. And once Mark Rudd could publicly ascribe to the president of Columbia a notoriously obscene relationship to his mother, without provoking any kind of reaction, the S.D.S.[5] has already won the day. The occupation of Columbia's buildings merely ratified their victory. Men who show themselves unwilling to defend civilization against nihilism are not going to be either resolute or effective in defending the university against anything.

III

I am already touching upon a political aspect of pornography when I   25 suggest that it is inherently and purposefully subversive of civilization and its institutions. But there is another and more specifically political aspect, which has to do with the relationship of pornography and/or obscenity to democracy, and especially to the quality of public life on which democratic government ultimately rests.

Though the phrase "the quality of life" trips easily from so many lips these days, it tends to be one of those clichés with many trivial meanings and no large, serious one. Sometimes it merely refers to such externals as the enjoyment of cleaner air, cleaner water, cleaner streets. At other times it refers to the merely private enjoyment of music, painting, or literature. Rarely does it have anything to do with the way the citizen in a democracy views himself — his obligations, his intentions, his ultimate self-definition.

Instead, what I would call the "managerial" conception of democracy is the predominant opinion among political scientists, sociologists, and economists, and has, through the untiring efforts of these scholars, become the conventional journalistic opinion as well. The root idea behind this "managerial" conception is that democracy is a "political system" (as they say) which can be adequately defined in terms of — can be fully reduced to — its mechanical arrangements. Democracy is then seen as a set of rules and procedures, and *nothing but* a set of rules and procedures, whereby majority rule and minority rights are reconciled into a state of equilibrium. If everyone follows these rules and procedures, then a democracy is in working order. I think this is a fair description of the democratic idea that currently prevails in academia. One can also fairly say that it is now the liberal idea of democracy par excellence.

I cannot help but feel that there is something ridiculous about being

[5]**S.D.S.** Students for a Democratic Society, a radical group active in the 1960s.

this kind of democrat, and I must further confess to having a sneaking sympathy for those of our young radicals who also find it ridiculous. The absurdity is the absurdity of idolatry, of taking the symbolic for the real, the means for the end. The purpose of democracy cannot possibly be the endless functioning of its own political machinery. The purpose of any political regime is to achieve some version of the good life and the good society. It is not at all difficult to imagine a perfectly functioning democracy which answers all questions except one—namely, why should anyone of intelligence and spirit care a fig for it?

There is, however, an older idea of democracy—one which was fairly common until about the beginning of this century—for which the conception of the quality of public life is absolutely crucial. This idea starts from the proposition that democracy is a form of self-government, and that if you want it to be a meritorious polity, you have to care about what kind of people govern it. Indeed, it puts the matter more strongly and declares that if you want self-government, you are only entitled to it if that "self" is worthy of governing. There is no inherent right to self-government if it means that such government is vicious, mean, squalid, and debased. Only a dogmatist and a fanatic, an idolater of democratic machinery, could approve a self-government under such conditions.

And because the desirability of self-government depends on the char-   30
acter of the people who govern, the older idea of democracy was very solicitous of the condition of this character. It was solicitous of the individual self, and felt an obligation to educate it into what used to be called "republican virtue." And it was solicitous of that collective self which we call public opinion and which, in a democracy, governs us collectively. Perhaps in some respects it was nervously oversolicitous—that would not be surprising. But the main thing is that it cared, cared not merely about the machinery of democracy but about the quality of life that this machinery might generate.

And because it cared, this older idea of democracy had no problem in principle with pornography and/or obscenity. It censored them—and it did so with a perfect clarity of mind and a perfectly clear conscience. It was not about to permit people capriciously to corrupt themselves. Or, to put it more precisely: In this version of democracy, the people took some care not to let themselves be governed by the more infantile and irrational parts of themselves.

I have, it may be noticed, uttered that dreadful word *censorship*. And I am not about to back away from it. If you think pornography and/or obscenity is a serious problem, you have to be for censorship. I will go even further and say that if you want to prevent pornography and/or obscenity from becoming a problem, you have to be for censorship. And lest there be any misunderstanding as to what I am saying, I will put it as bluntly as possible: If you care for the quality of life in our American democracy, then you have to be for censorship.

But can a liberal be for censorship? Unless one assumes that being a liberal *must* mean being indifferent to the quality of American life, then the answer has to be yes, a liberal can be for censorship—but he ought to favor a liberal form of censorship.

Is that a contradiction in terms? I do not think so. We have no problem in contrasting *repressive* laws governing alcohol and drugs and tobacco with laws *regulating* (i.e., discouraging the sale of) alcohol and drugs and tobacco. Laws encouraging temperance are not the same thing as laws that have as their goal prohibition or abolition. We have not made the smoking of cigarettes a criminal offense. We have, however, and with good liberal conscience, prohibited cigarette advertising on television, and may yet, again with good liberal conscience, prohibit it in newspapers and magazines. The idea of restricting individual freedom, in a liberal way, is not at all unfamiliar to us.

I therefore see no reason why we should not be able to distinguish re- 35 pressive censorship from liberal censorship of the written and spoken word. In Britain, until a few years ago, you could perform almost any play you wished, but certain plays, judged to be obscene, had to be performed in private theatrical clubs, which were deemed to have a "serious" interest in theater. In the United States, all of us who grew up using public libraries are familiar with the circumstances under which certain books could be circulated only to adults, while still other books had to be read in the library reading room, under the librarian's skeptical eye. In both cases, a small minority that was willing to make a serious effort to see an obscene play or read an obscene book could do so. But the impact of obscenity was circumscribed and the quality of public life was only marginally affected.[6]

I am not saying it is easy in practice to sustain a distinction between liberal and repressive censorship, especially in the public realm of a democracy, where popular opinion is so vulnerable to demagoguery. Moreover, an acceptable system of liberal censorship is likely to be exceedingly difficult to devise in the United States today, because our educated classes, upon whose judgment a liberal censorship must rest, are so convinced that there is no such thing as a problem of obscenity, or even that there is no such thing as obscenity at all. But, to counterbalance this, there is the further, fortunate truth that the tolerable margin for error is quite large, and single mistakes or single injustices are not all that important.

This possibility of error, of course, occasions much distress among artists and academics. It is a fact, one that cannot and should not be denied, that any system of censorship is bound, upon occasion, to treat unjustly a particular work of art—to find pornography where there is only gentle eroticism, to find obscenity where none really exists, or to find both where its existence ought to be tolerated because it serves a larger moral

---

[6]It is fairly predictable that someone is going to object that this point of view is "elitist"—that, under a system of liberal censorship, the rich will have privileged access to pornography and obscenity. Yes, of course, they will—just as, at present, the rich have privileged access to heroin if they want it. But one would have to be an egalitarian maniac to object to this state of affairs on the grounds of equality. [Kristol's note.]

purpose. Though most works of art are not obscene, and though most obscenity has nothing to do with art, there are some few works of art that are, at least in part, pornographic and/or obscene. There are also some few works of art that are in the special category of the comic-ironic "bawdy" (Boccaccio, Rabelais). It is such works of art that are likely to suffer at the hands of the censor. That is the price one has to be prepared to pay for censorship — even liberal censorship.

But just how high is this price? If you believe, as so many artists seem to believe today, that art is the only sacrosanct activity in our profane and vulgar world — that any man who designates himself an artist thereby acquires a sacred office — then obviously censorship is an intolerable form of sacrilege. But for those of us who do not subscribe to this religion of art, the costs of censorship do not seem so high at all.

If you look at the history of American or English literature, there is precious little damage you can point to as a consequence of the censorship that prevailed throughout most of that history. Very few works of literature — of real literary merit, I mean — ever were suppressed; and those that were, were not suppressed for long. Nor have I noticed, now that censorship of the written word has to all intents and purposes ceased in this country, that hitherto suppressed or repressed masterpieces are flooding the market. Yes, we can now read *Fanny Hill* and the Marquis de Sade. Or, to be more exact, we can now openly purchase them, since many people were able to read them even though they were publicly banned, which is as it should be under a liberal censorship. So how much have literature and the arts gained from the fact that we can all now buy them over the counter, that, indeed, we are all now encouraged to buy them over the counter? They have not gained much that I can see.

And one might also ask a question that is almost never raised: How much has literature lost from the fact that everything is now permitted? It has lost quite a bit, I should say. In a free market, Gresham's law can work for books or theater as efficiently as it does for coinage — driving out the good, establishing the debased. The cultural market in the United States today is being preempted by dirty books, dirty movies, dirty theater. A pornographic novel has a far better chance of being published today than a nonpornographic one, and quite a few pretty good novels are not being published at all simply because they are not pornographic, and are therefore less likely to sell. Our cultural condition has not improved as a result of the new freedom. American cultural life wasn't much to brag about twenty years ago; today one feels ashamed for it.

Just one last point which I dare not leave untouched. If we start censoring pornography or obscenity, shall we not inevitably end up censoring political opinion? A lot of people seem to think this would be the case — which only shows the power of doctrinaire thinking over reality. We had censorship of pornography and obscenity for 150 years, until almost yesterday, and I am not aware that freedom of opinion in this country was in any way diminished as a consequence of this fact. Fortunately for those of us who are liberal, freedom is not indivisible. If it were, the case for liberalism would be indistinguishable from the case for anarchy; and they are two very different things.

But I must repeat and emphasize: What kind of laws we pass governing pornography and obscenity, what kind of censorship — or, since we are still a federal nation, what kinds of censorship — we institute in our various localities may indeed be difficult matters to cope with; nevertheless the real issue is one of principle. I myself subscribe to a liberal view of the enforcement problem: I think that pornography should be illegal *and* available to anyone who wants it so badly as to make a pretty strenuous effort to get it. We have lived with under-the-counter pornography for centuries now, in a fairly comfortable way. But the issue of principle, of whether it should be over or under the counter, has to be settled before we can reflect on the advantages and disadvantages of alternative modes of censorship. I think the settlement we are living under now, in which obscenity and democracy are regarded as equals, is wrong; I believe it is inherently unstable; I think it will, in the long run, be incompatible with any authentic concern for the quality of life in our democracy.

Topics for Critical Thinking and Writing

1. If you find some of Kristol's sentences particularly effective as examples of persuasive writing, copy out two or three and then explain *why* they are effective.

2. In his second paragraph Kristol refers to Eugene O'Neill's *Desire under the Elms* (1924) and James Joyce's *Ulysses* (1922). If you have read either of these works, write a paragraph in which you explain why some members of an earlier generation might have wanted to censor them.

3. In his second paragraph Kristol implies that a play ought not to show such an act as a homosexual rape. Is it relevant to inquire about the context of the scene? That is, is it relevant to ask whether the rape is presented as acceptable, or is presented as abominable? Or is the presentation of homosexual rape inherently unacceptable?

4. In paragraph 4 Kristol says, "If you believe that no one was ever corrupted by a book, you have also to believe that no one was ever improved by a book (or a play or a movie). You have to believe, in other words, that all art is morally trivial and that, consequently, all education is morally irrelevant." If you think a reply can be made, make it, perhaps in an essay of 500 words.

5. In paragraph 6 Kristol says that as civil libertarians we are all hypocrites, and he cites our presumed intolerance of an exhibition in which someone would really commit suicide. Jot down the chief arguments you would use in arguing for or against allowing such an exhibition.

6. Is Kristol's distinction between pornography and erotic art clear to you? If so, rephrase it in your own words. If not, what makes it obscure, and how could it be made clearer?

7. In paragraphs 33 and 34, arguing for "a liberal form of censorship," Kristol makes a distinction between "*repressive* laws" and "laws *regulating* (i.e., discouraging the sale of) alcohol and drugs and tobacco." He points out that regulatory laws prohibit cigarette advertisements on television. What forms might laws "regulating" but not "repressing" pornography take? Would you favor such laws? Why? Write an essay of 500 to 750 words explaining how "liberal censorship" might work, and on what moral principles it is supposedly based.

8. Kristol admits (para. 37) that "any system of censorship is bound, upon occasion, to treat unjustly a particular work of art." But this, he says, "is the price one has to be prepared to pay." Are you prepared to pay it? Why?

9. In the eighteenth century the German writer and critic Gotthold Ephraim Lessing wrote: "The object of art is pleasure, and pleasure is not indispensable. What kind and what degree of pleasure shall be permitted may justly depend on the lawgiver." Taking this as your text, but drawing also on Kristol's essay, write an essay of 500 words, supporting or rebutting Lessing.

10. Look again at paragraph 38, and analyze Kristol's persuasive methods. How does his choice of words help to support his point?

Susan Brownmiller

Let's Put Pornography Back in the Closet

Free speech is one of the great foundations on which our democracy rests. I am old enough to remember the Hollywood Ten, the screenwriters who went to jail in the late 1940s because they refused to testify before a congressional committee about their political affiliations. They tried to use the First Amendment as a defense, but they went to jail because in those days there were few civil liberties lawyers around who cared to champion the First Amendment right to free speech, when the speech concerned the Communist party.

The Hollywood Ten were correct in claiming the First Amendment. Its high purpose is the protection of unpopular ideas and political dissent. In the dark, cold days of the 1950s, few civil libertarians were willing to declare themselves First Amendment absolutists. But in the brighter, though frantic, days of the 1960s, the principle of protecting unpopular political speech was gradually strengthened.

It is fair to say now that the battle has largely been won. Even the American Nazi party has found itself the beneficiary of the dedicated, tire-

---

Susan Brownmiller (b. 1935), a graduate of Cornell University, is the founder of Women against Pornography, *and the author of several books, including* Against Our Will: Men, Women, and Rape *(1975). The essay reprinted here is from* Take Back the Night *(1980), a collection of essays edited by Laura Lederer. The book has been called "the manifesto of antipornography feminism."*

less work of the American Civil Liberties Union. But—and please notice the quotation marks coming up—"To equate the free and robust exchange of ideas and political debate with commercial exploitation of obscene material demeans the grand conception of the First Amendment and its high purposes in the historic struggle for freedom. It is a misuse of the great guarantees of free speech and free press."

I didn't say that, although I wish I had, for I think the words are thrilling. Chief Justice Warren Burger said it in 1973, in the United States Supreme Court's majority opinion in *Miller v. California*. During the same decades that the right to political free speech was being strengthened in the courts, the nation's obscenity laws also were undergoing extensive revision.

It's amazing to recall that in 1934 the question of whether James 5 Joyce's *Ulysses* should be banned as pornographic actually went before the Court. The battle to protect *Ulysses* as a work of literature with redeeming social value was won. In later decades, Henry Miller's *Tropic* books, *Lady Chatterley's Lover*, and the *Memoirs of Fanny Hill* also were adjudged not obscene. These decisions have been important to me. As the author of *Against Our Will*, a study of the history of rape that does contain explicit sexual material, I shudder to think how my book would have fared if James Joyce, D. H. Lawrence, and Henry Miller hadn't gone before me.

I am not a fan of *Chatterley* or the *Tropic* books, I should quickly mention. They are not to my literary taste, nor do I think they represent female sexuality with any degree of accuracy. But I would hardly suggest that we ban them. Such a suggestion wouldn't get very far anyway. The battle to protect these books is ancient history. Time does march on, quite methodically. What, then, is unlawfully obscene, and what does the First Amendment have to do with it?

In the Miller case of 1973 (not Henry Miller, by the way, but a porn distributor who sent unsolicited stuff through the mails), the Court came up with new guidelines that it hoped would strengthen obscenity laws by giving more power to the states. What it did in actuality was throw everything into confusion. It set up a three-part test by which materials can be adjudged obscene. The materials are obscene if they depict patently offensive, hard-core sexual conduct; lack serious scientific, literary, artistic, or political value; and appeal to the prurient interest of an average person—as measured by contemporary community standards.

"Patently offensive," "prurient interest," and "hard-core" are indeed words to conjure with. "Contemporary community standards" are what we're trying to redefine. The feminist objection to pornography is not based on prurience, which the dictionary defines as lustful, itching desire. We are not opposed to sex and desire, with or without the itch, and we certainly believe that explicit sexual material has its place in literature, art, science, and education. Here we part company rather swiftly with old-line conservatives who don't want sex education in the high schools, for example.

No, the feminist objection to pornography is based on our belief that pornography represents hatred of women, that pornography's intent is to humiliate, degrade, and dehumanize the female body for the purpose of erotic stimulation and pleasure. We are unalterably opposed to the presentation of the female body being stripped, bound, raped, tortured, mutilated, and murdered in the name of commercial entertainment and free speech.

These images, which are standard pornographic fare, have nothing to 10 do with the hallowed right of political dissent. They have everything to do with the creation of a cultural climate in which a rapist feels he is merely giving in to a normal urge and a woman is encouraged to believe that sexual masochism is healthy, liberated fun. Justice Potter Stewart once said about hard-core pornography, "You know it when you see it," and that certainly used to be true. In the good old days, pornography looked awful. It was cheap and sleazy, and there was no mistaking it for art.

Nowadays, since the porn industry has become a multimillion dollar business, visual technology has been employed in its service. Pornographic movies are skillfully filmed and edited, pornographic still shots using the newest tenets of good design artfully grace the covers of *Hustler, Penthouse,* and *Playboy,* and the public — and the courts — are sadly confused.

The Supreme Court neglected to define "hard-core" in the Miller decision. This was a mistake. If "hard-core" refers only to explicit sexual intercourse, then that isn't good enough. When women or children or men — no matter how artfully — are shown tortured or terrorized in the service of sex, that's obscene. And "patently offensive," I would hope, to our "contemporary community standards."

Justice William O. Douglas wrote in his dissent to the Miller case that no one is "compelled to look." This is hardly true. To buy a paper at the corner newsstand is to subject oneself to a forcible immersion in pornography, to be demeaned by an array of dehumanized, chopped-up parts of the female anatomy, packaged like cuts of meat at the supermarket. I happen to like my body and I work hard at the gym to keep it in good shape, but I am embarrassed for my body and for the bodies of all women when I see the fragmented parts of us so frivolously, and so flagrantly, displayed.

Some constitutional theorists (Justice Douglas was one) have maintained that any obscenity law is a serious abridgement of free speech. Others (and Justice Earl Warren was one) have maintained that the First Amendment was never intended to protect obscenity. We live quite compatibly with a host of free-speech abridgements. There are restraints against false and misleading advertising or statements — shouting "fire" without cause in a crowded movie theater, etc. — that do not threaten, but strengthen, our societal values. Restrictions on the public display of pornography belong in this category.

The distinction between permission to publish and permission to dis- 15 play publicly is an essential one and one which I think consonant with First Amendment principles. Justice Burger's words which I quoted above support this without question. We are not saying "Smash the presses" or "Ban the bad ones," but simply "Get the stuff out of our sight." Let the legislatures decide — using realistic and humane contemporary community standards — what can be displayed and what cannot. The courts, after all, will be the final arbiters.

Topics for Critical Thinking and Writing

1. Objecting to Justice Douglas's remark that no one is "compelled to look" (para. 13), Brownmiller says, "This is hardly true. To buy a paper at the corner newsstand is to subject oneself to forcible immersion in pornography, to be demeaned by an array of dehumanized, chopped-up parts of the female anatomy, packaged like cuts of meat at the supermarket." Is this true at your local newsstand, or are the sex magazines kept in one place, relatively remote from the newspapers?

2. When Brownmiller attempts to restate the "three-part test" for obscenity established by the Supreme Court in *Miller v. California*, she writes (para. 7): "The materials are obscene if they depict . . ." and so on. She should have written: "The materials are obscene if and only if they depict . . ." and so on. Explain what is wrong here with her "if," and why "if and only if" is needed.

3. In her next-to-last paragraph, Brownmiller reminds us that we already live quite comfortably with some "free-speech abridgements." The examples she gives are that we may not falsely shout "fire" in a crowded theater, and we may not issue misleading advertisements. Do you think that these widely accepted restrictions are valid evidence in arguing in behalf of limiting the display of what Brownmiller considers pornography? Why?

4. Brownmiller insists that defenders of the First Amendment, who will surely oppose laws that interfere with the freedom to publish, need not go on to condemn laws that regulate the freedom to "display publicly" pornographic publications. Do you agree? Suppose a publisher insists he cannot sell his product at a profit unless he is permitted to display it to advantage, and so restriction on the latter amounts to interference with his freedom to publish. How might Brownmiller reply?

5. In her last paragraph Brownmiller says that "contemporary community standards" should be decisive. Can it be argued that, because standards vary from one community to another, and from time to time even in the same place, her recommendation subjects the rights of a minority to the whims of a majority? The Bill of Rights, after all, was supposed to safeguard constitutional rights from the possible tyranny of the majority.

6. How does Brownmiller's objection to pornography agree and disagree with the position taken by Irving Kristol in the preceding selection?

7. When Brownmiller accuses "the public . . . and the courts" of being "sadly confused" (para. 11), what does she think they are confused about? The definition of "pornography" or "obscenity"? The effects of such literature on men and women? Or is it something else?

20

What Are the Grounds of Religious Faith?

The Hebrew Bible

Psalm 19

The heavens declare the glory of God; and the firmament[1] sheweth his handywork.

2 Day unto day uttereth speech, and night unto night sheweth knowledge.

---

[1]**firmament** Dome of the sky. [All notes are the editors'.]

Among the books in the Hebrew Bible (usually called the Old Testament by Christians) is the Book of Psalms (psalm is from the Greek psalmoi, songs of praise), or the Psalter (Greek, psalterion, a stringed instrument). The Book of Psalms contains about 150 songs, prayers, and meditations. The number is a bit imprecise for several reasons: For instance, in the Hebrew Bible the numbering from Psalm 10 to Psalm 148 is one digit ahead of the numbering in Bibles used in the Christian church, which joins 9 and 10, and 114 and 115, but which divides both 116 and 147 into two.

The Hebrew text attributes seventy-three of the psalms to David, who reigned circa 1010–970 B.C.E. David is said to have been a musician (1 Samuel 16:23; Amos 6:5), but these attributions are no longer accepted by scholars, who point out that although some of the psalms may indeed go back to the tenth century B.C.E., some others may be as late as 200 B.C.E. The book in fact is a compilation of earlier collections from hundreds of years of Hebrew history.

The psalms are of various types, for instance lamentations, songs of thanksgiving, songs of sacred history, and songs of praise. Psalm 19 is a song of praise. We give it in the King James Version (1611); later translations are recognized as more accurate, but none is regarded as the literary equal of the King James Version.

3 There is no speech nor language, where their voice is not heard.

4 Their line is gone out through all the earth, and their words to the end of the world. In them hath he set a tabernacle for the sun,

5 Which is as a bridegroom coming out of his chamber, and rejoiceth as a strong man to run a race.

6 His going forth is from the end of the heaven, and his circuit unto the ends of it: and there is nothing hid from the heat thereof.

7 The law of the Lord is perfect, converting the soul: the testimony of the Lord is sure, making wise the simple.

8 The statutes of the Lord are right, rejoicing the heart: the commandment of the Lord is pure, enlightening the eyes.

9 The fear[2] of the Lord is clean, enduring for ever: the judgments of the Lord are true and righteous altogether.

10 More to be desired are they than gold, yea, than much fine gold: sweeter also than honey and the honeycomb.

11 Moreover by them is thy servant warned: and in keeping of them there is great reward.

12 Who can understand his errors? cleanse thou me from secret faults.[3]

13 Keep back thy servant also from presumptuous sins; let them not have dominion over me: then shall I be upright, and I shall be innocent from the great transgression.

14 Let the words of my mouth, and the meditation of my heart, be acceptable in thy sight, O Lord, my strength, and my redeemer.

Topics for Critical Thinking and Writing

1. In Psalm 19, probably most readers will agree about the structure of the poem: 1–6 are on nature, 7–11 are on the Law, and 12–14 are a prayer. How might you state the *argument* of lines 1–6? Of lines 7–11?

2. Do you think these three units cohere into a whole? For instance, does it make sense to say that the second unit is connected to the first by the idea that just as nothing is hidden from the heat of the sun (6), in like manner "the law of the Lord" is everywhere? Is such a reading appropriate, or is it strained? Explain.

---

[2]**fear** Often emended in later translations to *word*.
[3]**secret faults** Unconscious violations of God's will.

Paul

1 Corinthians 15

Moreover, brethren, I declare unto you the gospel which I preached unto you, which also ye have received, and wherein ye stand;

2 By which also ye are saved, if we keep in memory what I preached unto you, unless ye have believed in vain.

3 For I delivered unto you first of all that which I also received, how that Christ died for our sins according to the scriptures;

4 And that he was buried, and that he rose again the third day according to the scriptures:

Paul (A.D. 5?–67?), known as Saul before his conversion from Judaism to Christianity, was a native of Tarsus, a commercial town in the land that is now Turkey. Tarsus was part of the Roman Empire, and Saul, though a Jew, was a Roman citizen. After attending a rabbinical school in Jerusalem, Saul set out for Damascus in A.D. 33 or 34 to suppress Christianity there, but on the way he saw a blinding light, heard the voice of Jesus, and experienced a conversion, described in Acts of the Apostles 9:1–22. In later years he traveled widely, preaching Christianity to Jews and gentiles. In 59–61 he was imprisoned in Rome, and he may have been convicted and executed, but nothing certain is known about his death.

Paul seems to have been the first Christian missionary to Corinth, a Roman colony in Greece, a little to the west of Athens. After his initial visit, probably from 50 to 52, he is reported to have gone to Judea, Syria, Ephesus, and elsewhere. While at Ephesus, however, he heard reports of disorders in Corinth. His letter of response, probably written in about 54, was incorporated into the New Testament as 1 Corinthians, one of his two extant epistles addressed to the Christian community at Corinth. From this letter we reprint Chapter 15.

It is not entirely clear what doctrine(s) of resurrection Paul is opposing in this passage. Perhaps some members of the church did not believe in any form of life after death; perhaps others believed that the resurrection took place at baptism; and perhaps others debated the nature of the resurrection body.

The Interpreter's Bible, 10:12, outlines the fifty-eight verses of Chapter 15 thus:

A. The resurrection of Jesus (1–19)
 1. The tradition concerning the fact (1–11)
 2. The significancy of the resurrection (12–19)
B. The eschatological drama [i.e., concern with ultimate things, such as death and heaven] (20–34)
 1. The order of events (20–28)
 2. Ad hominem rebuttal (29–34)
C. The resurrection body (35–50)
 1. Various types of body (35–41)
 2. A spiritual body (42–50)
D. The Christian confidence (51–58)

The translation used here is the Authorized Version (1611), also known as the King James Version.

5 And that he was seen of Cephas, then of the twelve:

6 After that, he was seen of above five hundred brethren at once; of whom the greater part remain unto this present, but some are fallen asleep.

7 After that, he was seen of James; then of all the apostles.

8 And last of all he was seen of me also, as of one born out of due time.

9 For I am the least of the apostles, that am not meet to be called an apostle, because I persecuted the church of God.

10 But by the grace of God I am what I am: and his grace which was bestowed upon me was not in vain; but I laboured more abundantly than they all: yet not I, but the grace of God which was with me.

11 Therefore whether it were I or they, so we preach, and so ye believed.

12 Now if Christ be preached that he rose from the dead, how say some among you that there is no resurrection of the dead?

13 But if there be no resurrection of the dead, then is Christ not risen:

14 And if Christ be not risen, then is our preaching vain, and your faith is also vain.

15 Yea, and we are found false witnesses of God; because we have testified of God that he raised up Christ: whom he raised not up, if so be that the dead rise not.

16 For if the dead rise not, then is not Christ raised:

17 And if Christ be not raised, your faith is vain; ye are yet in your sins.

18 Then they also which are fallen asleep in Christ are perished.

19 If in this life only we have hope in Christ, we are of all men most miserable.

20 But now is Christ risen from the dead, and become the firstfruits of them that slept.

21 For since by man came death, by man came also the resurrection of the dead.

22 For as in Adam all die, even so in Christ shall all be made alive.

23 But every man in his own order: Christ the firstfruits; afterward they that are Christ's at his coming.

24 Then cometh the end, when he shall have delivered up the kingdom to God, even the Father; when he shall have put down all rule and all authority and power.

25 For he must reign, till he hath put all enemies under his feet.

26 The last enemy that shall be destroyed is death.

27 For he hath put all things under his feet. But when he saith all things are put under him, it is manifest that he is excepted, which did put all things under him.

28 And when all things shall be subdued unto him, then shall the Son

also himself be subject unto him that put all things under him, that God may be all in all.

29 Else what shall they do which are baptized for the dead, if the dead rise not at all? why are they then baptized for the dead?

30 And why stand we in jeopardy every hour?

31 I protest by your rejoicing which I have in Christ Jesus our Lord, I die daily.

32 If after the manner of men I have fought with beasts at Ephesus, what advantageth it me, if the dead rise not? let us eat and drink; for to-morrow we die.

33 Be not deceived: evil communications corrupt good manners.

34 Awake to righteousness, and sin not; for some have not the knowledge of God: I speak this to your shame.

35 But some man will say, How are the dead raised up? and with what body do they come?

36 Thou fool, that which thou sowest is not quickened, except it die:

37 And that which thou sowest, thou sowest not that body that shall be, but bare grain, it may chance of wheat, or of some other grain:

38 But God giveth it a body as it hath pleased him, and to every seed his own body.

39 All flesh is not the same flesh: but there is one kind of flesh of men, another flesh of beasts, another of fishes, and another of birds.

40 There are also celestial bodies, and bodies terrestrial: but the glory of the celestial is one, and the glory of the terrestrial is another.

41 There is one glory of the sun, and another glory of the moon, and another glory of the stars: for one star differeth from another star in glory.

42 So also is the resurrection of the dead. It is sown in corruption; it is raised in incorruption:

43 It is sown in dishonour; it is raised in glory: it is sown in weakness; it is raised in power:

44 It is sown a natural body; it is raised a spiritual body. There is a natural body, and there is a spiritual body.

45 And so it is written, The first man Adam was made a living soul; the last Adam was made a quickening spirit.

46 Howbeit that was not first which is spiritual, but that which is natural; and afterward that which is spiritual.

47 The first man is of the earth, earthy: the second man is the Lord from heaven.

48 As is the earthy, such are they also that are earthy: and as is the heavenly, such are they also that are heavenly.

49 And as we have borne the image of the earthy, we shall also bear the image of the heavenly.

50 Now this I say, brethren, that flesh and blood cannot inherit the kingdom of God; neither doth corruption inherit incorruption.

51 Behold, I shew you a mystery; We shall not all sleep, but we shall all be changed,

52 In a moment, in the twinkling of an eye, at the last trump: for the trumpet shall sound, and the dead shall be raised incorruptible, and we shall be changed.

53 For this corruptible must put on incorruption, and this mortal must put on immortality.

54 So when this corruptible shall have put on incorruption, and this mortal shall have put on immortality, then shall be brought to pass the saying that is written, Death is swallowed up in victory.

55 O death, where is thy sting? O grave, where is thy victory?

56 The sting of death is sin; and the strength of sin is the law.

57 But thanks be to God, which giveth us the victory through our Lord Jesus Christ.

58 Therefore, my beloved brethren, be ye stedfast, unmoveable, always abounding in the work of the Lord, forasmuch as ye know that your labour is not in vain in the Lord.

Topics for Critical Thinking and Writing

1. Why is belief in the Resurrection of Christ important to Paul? What evidence does he offer to support his belief in it?

2. What leads Paul to the conclusion that the dead are resurrected? What evidence does he offer to support this belief? What conclusion, according to Paul, follows if the dead are not resurrected?

3. In verse 22 Paul speaks of people who are "in Adam," and of others who are "in Christ." Explain the distinction to someone who finds it puzzling. (If you find it puzzling, check a guide to the Bible, such as *The Interpreter's Bible,* or *A New Catholic Commentary on Holy Scripture,* ed. Reginald C. Fuller et al.)

4. What mistaken belief, according to Paul, leads people to conclude that we should (as he says in verse 32) "eat and drink; for tomorrow we die"?

5. In verses 35–50 Paul insists again on bodily resurrection of human beings. In 35–44 he uses an analogy to explain that the body that dies and the body that is resurrected are continuous and yet also are different. Put his analogy into your own words. Do you think analogy is an effective way of making this point? Why? In verse 45 Paul uses a different argument, contrasting Adam ("the first man Adam") with Christ ("the last Adam"). Why do you think he drops the analogy and now offers this evidence? How in verses 46–47 does Paul bring the two points together?

6. In verse 55 Paul says, "O death, where is thy sting? O grave, where is thy victory?" In a paragraph summarize the beliefs (expressed in this selection) that lead Paul to the conclusion that death and the grave are conquered.

William James

From *The Will to Believe*

What then do we now mean by the religious hypothesis? Science says things are; morality says some things are better than other things; and religion says essentially two things.

First, she says that the best things are the more eternal things, the overlapping things, the things in the universe that throw the last stone, so to speak, and say the final word. "Perfection is eternal"—this phrase of Charles Secrétan—seems a good way of putting this first affirmation of religion, an affirmation which obviously cannot yet be verified scientifically at all.

The second affirmation of religion is that we are better off even now if we believe her first affirmation to be true.

Now, let us consider what the logical elements of this situation are *in case the religious hypothesis in both its branches be really true.* (Of course, we must admit that possibility at the outset. If we are to discuss the question at all, it must involve a living option. If for any of you religion be a hypothesis that cannot, by any living possibility, be true, then you need go no farther. I speak to the "saving remnant" alone.) So proceeding, we see, first, that religion offers itself as a *momentous* option. We are supposed to gain, even now, by our belief, and to lose by our nonbelief, a certain vital good. Secondly, religion is a *forced* option, so far as that good goes. We cannot escape the issue by remaining skeptical and waiting for more light, because, although we do avoid error in that way *if religion be untrue*, we

---

William James (1842–1910), brother of Alice James and of the novelist Henry James, was born into a wealthy family in New York City. He at first studied to be a painter, then turned to chemistry and biology, and took a degree in medicine. Although given to depression and hallucinations, it seems that he saved himself by an act of will or of faith: "My first act of free will," he said, "shall be to believe in free will." James accepted a position as instructor in physiology at Harvard, but, considering his uncertain health, he decided that he did not have the strength to do laboratory work, and he turned to philosophy and psychology. "I never had any philosophic instruction, the first lecture on psychology I ever heard being the first I ever gave." He published his first book, Principles of Psychology (1890), *when he was forty-eight.*

James developed his ideas partly under the influence of Darwin's writing, but he gave Darwinism a decidedly special twist. Impressed by Darwin's findings that "variations" assisted some creatures to survive in a changing environment, James saw the human mind as a potent force, not as a consciousness that merely receives external impressions. "Mental interests, hypotheses, postulates, so far as they are the basis for human action—action which to a great extent transforms the world—help to make the truth which they declare."

In 1897 James published a book of essays titled The Will to Believe. *Part of one essay is reprinted here.*

lose the good, *if it be true,* just as certainly as if we positively chose to dis-
believe. It is as if a man should hesitate indefinitely to ask a certain woman
to marry him because he was not perfectly sure that she would prove an
angel after he brought her home. Would he not cut himself off from that
particular angel-possibility as decisively as if he went and married someone
else? Skepticism, then, is not avoidance of option; it is option of a certain
particular kind of risk. *Better risk loss of truth than chance of error*—that
is your faith-vetoer's exact position. He is actively playing his stake as much
as the believer is; he is backing the field against the religious hypothesis,
just as the believer is backing the religious hypothesis against the field. To
preach skepticism to us as a duty until "sufficient evidence" for religion be
found, is tantamount therefore to telling us, when in presence of religious
hypothesis, that to yield to our fear of its being error is wiser and better
than to yield to our hope that it may be true. It is not intellect against all
passions, then; it is only intellect with one passion laying down its law. And
by what, forsooth, is the supreme wisdom of this passion warranted?
Dupery for dupery, what proof is there that dupery through hope is so
much worse than dupery through fear? I, for one, can see no proof; and I
simply refuse obedience to the scientist's command to imitate his kind of
option, in a case where my own stake is important enough to give me the
right to choose my own form of risk. If religion be true and the evidence
for it be still insufficient, I do not wish, by putting your extinguisher upon
my nature (which feels to me as if it had after all some business in this matter), to forfeit my sole chance in life of getting upon the winning side—
that chance depending, of course, on my willingness to run the risk of acting as if my passional need of taking the world religiously might be
prophetic and right.

All this is on the supposition that it really may be prophetic and right, 5
and that, even to us who are discussing the matter, religion is a live hypothesis which may be true. Now, to most of us religion comes in a still further
way that makes a veto on our active faith even more illogical. The more
perfect and more eternal aspect of the universe is represented in our religions as having personal form. The universe is no longer a mere *It* to us,
but a *Thou,* if we are religious; and any relation that may be possible from
person to person might be possible here. For instance, although in one
sense we are passive portions of the universe, in another we show a curious
autonomy, as if we were small active centers on our own account. We feel,
too, as if the appeal of religion to us were made to our own active goodwill,
as if evidence might be forever withheld from us unless we met the hypothesis halfway. To take a trivial illustration: Just as a man who in a company of gentlemen made no advances, asked a warrant for every concession, and believed no one's word without proof, would cut himself off by
such churlishness from all the social rewards that a more trusting spirit
would earn—so here, one who should shut himself up in snarling logicality
and try to make the gods extort his recognition willy-nilly, or not get it at
all, might cut himself off forever from his only opportunity of making the

gods' acquaintance. This feeling, forced on us we know not whence, that by obstinately believing that there are gods (although not to do so would be so easy both for our logic and our life) we are doing the universe the deepest service we can, seems part of the living essence of the religious hypothesis. If the hypothesis *were* true in all its parts, including this one, then pure intellectualism, with its veto on our making willing advances, would be an absurdity; and some participation of our sympathetic nature would be logically required. I, therefore, for one, cannot see my way to accepting the agnostic rules for truth-seeking, or willfully agree to keep my willing nature out of the game. I cannot do so for this plain reason, that *a rule of thinking which would absolutely prevent me from acknowledging certain kinds of truth if those kinds of truth were really there, would be an irrational rule.* That for me is the long and short of the formal logic of the situation, no matter what the kinds of truth might materially be.

I confess I do not see how this logic can be escaped. But sad experience makes me fear that some of you may still shrink from radically saying with me, *in abstracto,* that we have the right to believe at our own risk any hypothesis that is live enough to tempt our will. I suspect, however, that if this is so, it is because you have got away from the abstract logical point of view altogether, and are thinking (perhaps without realizing it) of some particular religious hypothesis which for you is dead. The freedom to "believe what we will" you apply to the case of some patent superstition; and the faith you think of is the faith defined by the schoolboy when he said, "Faith is when you believe something that you know ain't true." I can only repeat that this is misapprehension. *In concreto,* the freedom to believe can only cover living options which the intellect of the individual cannot by itself resolve; and living options never seem absurdities to him who has them to consider. When I look at the religious question as it really puts itself to concrete men, and when I think of all the possibilities which both practically and theoretically it involves, then this command that we shall put a stopper on our heart, instincts, and courage, and *wait* — acting of course meanwhile more or less as if religion were *not* true[1] — till doomsday, or till such time as our intellect and senses working together may have raked in evidence enough — this command, I say, seems to me the queerest idol ever manufactured in the philosophic cave.[2] Were we scholastic absolutists, there might be more excuse. If we had an infallible intellect with

---

[1]Since belief is measured by action, he who forbids us to believe religion to be true, necessarily also forbids us to act as we should if we did believe it to be true. The whole defense of religious faith hinges upon action. If the action required or inspired by the religious hypothesis is in no way different from that dictated by the naturalistic hypothesis, then religious faith is a pure superfluity, better pruned away, and controversy about its legitimacy is a piece of idle trifling, unworthy of serious minds. I myself believe, of course, that the religious hypothesis gives to the world an expression which specifically determines our reactions, and makes them in a large part unlike what they might be on a purely naturalistic scheme of belief. [James's note.]

[2]According to Francis Bacon (1561–1626), in *The Novum Organum,* "The Idols of the Cave are the idols of the individual man," whose judgment may go astray because of heredity, environment, or education. [Editors' note.]

its objective certitudes, we might feel ourselves disloyal to such a perfect organ of knowledge in not trusting to it exclusively, in not waiting for its releasing word. But if we are empiricists, if we believe that no bell in us tolls to let us know for certain when truth is in our grasp, then it seems a piece of idle fantasticality to preach so solemnly our duty of waiting for the bell. Indeed we *may* wait if we will — I hope you do not think that I am denying that — but if we do so, we do so at our peril as much as if we believed. In either case we *act*, taking our life in our hands. No one of us ought to issue vetoes to the other, nor should we bandy words of abuse. We ought, on the contrary, delicately and profoundly to respect one another's mental freedom: then only shall we bring about the intellectual republic; then only shall we have that spirit of inner tolerance without which all our outer tolerance is soulless, and which is empiricism's glory; then only shall we live and let live, in speculative as well as in practical things. . . .

Topics for Critical Thinking and Writing

1. In paragraph 4 James says that for the person who believes that "the religious hypothesis" may indeed be true, religion is a *"forced"* option." He goes on to clarify his point with the example of a man thinking about getting married. In your own words, and with an example of your own invention, in one or two paragraphs explain James's point to a reader who has not grasped it.

2. Normally a hypothesis is a proposition that (unlike 2 + 2 = 4) is not necessarily true but that can be tested — and either confirmed or disconfirmed. Moreover, a hypothesis should not be embraced in the absence of adequate evidence or in the face of strong counterevidence, and the truth of a hypothesis should in no way depend on the proposer's belief (or disbelief) in it. Is James's "religious hypothesis" a hypothesis in this sense? Does it have or lack other features crucial to its status as a hypothesis?

3. In paragraph 5 James says that "the universe is no longer a mere *It* to us, but a *Thou*, if we are religious." Explain his point in your own words.

4. Reduce the main argument in James's essay to a syllogism. Formulate his major premise, his minor premise, and his conclusion.

5. James is eager to defend "the religious hypothesis" as a "living option" against skeptical criticism. But what, exactly, is the content or meaning of this hypothesis for James? Is it, for example, such as to make someone who believes it a Christian? Why, or why not? (It may be useful to read the next essay, by C. S. Lewis, before answering this question.)

6. In an essay of 500 words explain whether, for you, Buddhism, Islam, Judaism, or Christianity — or none of them — is a "living option," as James uses that term (para. 4). Devote part of your essay to explaining what conditions enter into something's being a live option.

7. If you are unconvinced by James's argument, write a 500-word response. If you are convinced by his argument, write a 500-word analysis of his methods of arguing.

C. S. Lewis

What Christians Believe

1. THE RIVAL CONCEPTIONS OF GOD

I have been asked to tell you what Christians believe, and I am going to begin by telling you one thing that Christians do not need to believe. If you are a Christian you do not have to believe that all the other religions are simply wrong all through. If you are an atheist you do have to believe that the main point in all the religions of the whole world is simply one huge mistake. If you are a Christian, you are free to think that all these religions, even the queerest ones, contain at least some hint of the truth. When I was an atheist I had to try to persuade myself that most of the human race have always been wrong about the question that mattered to them most; when I became a Christian I was able to take a more liberal view. But, of course, being a Christian does mean thinking that where Christianity differs from other religions, Christianity is right and they are wrong. As in arithmetic—there is only one right answer to a sum, and all other answers are wrong: but some of the wrong answers are much nearer being right than others.

The first big division of humanity is into the majority, who believe in some kind of God or gods, and the minority who do not. On this point, Christianity lines up with the majority—lines up with ancient Greeks and Romans, modern savages, Stoics, Platonists, Hindus, Mohammedans, etc., against the modern Western European materialist.

Now I go on to the next big division. People who all believe in God can be divided according to the sort of God they believe in. There are two very different ideas on this subject. One of them is the idea that He is beyond good and evil. We humans call one thing good and another thing bad. But according to some people that is merely our human point of view. These people would say that the wiser you become the less you would want to call anything good or bad, and the more clearly you would see that everything is good in one way and bad in another, and that nothing could have been different. Consequently, these people think that long before you got anywhere near the divine point of view the distinction would have disappeared altogether. We call a cancer bad, they would say, because it kills a man; but you might just as well call a successful surgeon bad because he kills a cancer. It all depends on the point of view. The other and opposite

---

Clive Staples Lewis (1898–1963), a professor of English literature at Oxford and later at Cambridge, wrote several important books on literature, but he is most widely known for his writings on Christianity (he converted to Christianity from atheism) and for his children's stories. The material reprinted here was originally delivered to the British public in a series of radio addresses in the early 1940s.

idea is that God is quite definitely "good" or "righteous," a God who takes sides, who loves love and hates hatred, who wants us to behave in one way and not in another. The first of these views—the one that thinks God beyond good and evil—is called Pantheism. It was held by the great Prussian philosopher Hegel and, as far as I can understand them, by the Hindus. The other view is held by Jews, Mohammedans, and Christians.

And with this big difference between Pantheism and the Christian idea of God, there usually goes another. Pantheists usually believe that God, so to speak, animates the universe as you animate your body: that the universe almost *is* God, so that if it did not exist He would not exist either, and anything you find in the universe is a part of God. The Christian idea is quite different. They think God invented and made the universe—like a man making a picture or composing a tune. A painter is not a picture, and he does not die if his picture is destroyed. You may say, "He's put a lot of himself into it," but you only mean that all its beauty and interest has come out of his head. His skill is not in the picture in the same way that it is in his head, or even in his hands. I expect you see how this difference between Pantheists and Christians hangs together with the other one. If you do not take the distinction between good and bad very seriously, then it is easy to say that anything you find in this world is a part of God. But, of course, if you think some things really bad, and God really good, then you cannot talk like that. You must believe that God is separate from the world and that some of the things we see in it are contrary to His will. Confronted with a cancer or a slum the Pantheist can say, "If you could only see it from the divine point of view, you would realize that this also is God." The Christian replies, "Don't talk damned nonsense."[1] For Christianity is a fighting religion. It thinks God made the world—that space and time, heat and cold, and all the colors and tastes, and all the animals and vegetables, are things that God "made up out of His head" as a man makes up a story. But it also thinks that a great many things have gone wrong with the world that God made and that God insists, and insists very loudly, on our putting them right again.

And, of course, that raises a very big question. If a good God made the world why has it gone wrong? And for many years I simply refused to listen to the Christian answers to this question, because I kept on feeling "whatever you say, and however clever your arguments are, isn't it much simpler and easier to say that the world was not made by any intelligent power? Aren't all your arguments simply a complicated attempt to avoid the obvious?" But then that threw me back into another difficulty.

My argument against God was that the universe seemed so cruel and unjust. But how had I got this idea of *just* and *unjust?* A man does not call a line crooked unless he has some idea of a straight line. What was I com-

---

[1]One listener complained of the word *damned* as frivolous swearing. But I mean exactly what I say—nonsense that is *damned* is under God's curse, and will (apart from God's grace) lead those who believe it to eternal death. [Lewis's note.]

paring this universe with when I called it unjust? If the whole show was bad and senseless from A to Z, so to speak, why did I, who was supposed to be part of the show, find myself in such violent reaction against it? A man feels wet when he falls into water, because man is not a water animal: A fish would not feel wet. Of course I could have given up my idea of justice by saying it was nothing but a private idea of my own. But if I did that, then my argument against God collapsed too — for the argument depended on saying that the world was really unjust, not simply that it did not happen to please my private fancies. Thus in the very act of trying to prove that God did not exist — in other words, that the whole of reality was senseless — I found I was forced to assume that one part of reality — namely my idea of justice — was full of sense. Consequently atheism turns out to be too simple. If the whole universe has no meaning, we should never have found out that it has no meaning: Just as, if there were no light in the universe and therefore no creatures with eyes, we should never know it was dark. *Dark* would be without meaning.

2. THE INVASION

Very well then, atheism is too simple. And I will tell you another view that is also too simple. It is the view I call Christianity-and-water, the view which simply says there is a good God in Heaven and everything is all right — leaving out all the difficult and terrible doctrines about sin and hell and the devil, and the redemption. Both these are boys' philosophies.

It is no good asking for a simple religion. After all, real things are not simple. They look simple, but they are not. The table I am sitting at looks simple: But ask a scientist to tell you what it is really made of — all about the atoms and how the light waves rebound from them and hit my eye and what they do to the optic nerve and what it does to my brain — and, of course, you find that what we call "seeing a table" lands you in mysteries and complications which you can hardly get to the end of. A child saying a child's prayer looks simple. And if you are content to stop there, well and good. But if you are not — and the modern world usually is not — if you want to go on and ask what is really happening — then you must be prepared for something difficult. If we ask for something more than simplicity, it is silly then to complain that the something more is not simple.

Very often, however, this silly procedure is adopted by people who are not silly, but who, consciously or unconsciously, want to destroy Christianity. Such people put up a version of Christianity suitable for a child of six and make that the object of their attack. When you try to explain the Christian doctrine as it is really held by an instructed adult, they then complain that you are making their heads turn round and that it is all too complicated and that if there really were a God they are sure He would have made "religion" simple, because simplicity is so beautiful, etc. You must be on your guard against these people for they will change their ground every minute and only waste your time. Notice, too, their idea of God "making religion simple": as if "religion" were something God invented, and not His statement to us of certain quite unalterable facts about His own nature.

Besides being complicated, reality, in my experience, is usually odd. It is not neat, not obvious, not what you expect. For instance, when you have grasped that the earth and the other planets all go round the sun, you would naturally expect that all the planets were made to match—all at equal distances from each other, say, or distances that regularly increased, or all the same size, or else getting bigger or smaller as you go farther from the sun. In fact, you find no rhyme or reason (that we can see) about either the sizes or the distances; and some of them have one moon, one has four, one has two, some have none, and one has a ring.

Reality, in fact, is usually something you could not have guessed. That is one of the reasons I believe Christianity. It is a religion you could not have guessed. If it offered us just the kind of universe we had always expected, I should feel we were making it up. But, in fact, it is not the sort of thing anyone would have made up. It has just that queer twist about it that real things have. So let us leave behind all these boys' philosophies—these oversimple answers. The problem is not simple and the answer is not going to be simple either.

What is the problem? A universe that contains much that is obviously bad and apparently meaningless, but containing creatures like ourselves who know that it is bad and meaningless. There are only two views that face all the facts. One is the Christian view that this is a good world that has gone wrong, but still retains the memory of what it ought to have been. The other is the view called Dualism. Dualism means the belief that there are two equal and independent powers at the back of everything, one of them good and the other bad, and that this universe is the battlefield in which they fight out an endless war. I personally think that next to Christianity Dualism is the manliest and most sensible creed on the market. But it has a catch in it.

The two powers, or spirits, or gods—the good one and the bad one—are supposed to be quite independent. They both existed from all eternity. Neither of them made the other, neither of them has any more right than the other to call itself God. Each presumably thinks it is good and thinks the other bad. One of them likes hatred and cruelty, the other likes love and mercy, and each backs its own view. Now what do we mean when we call one of them the Good Power and the other the Bad Power? Either we are merely saying that we happen to prefer the one to the other—like preferring beer to cider—or else we are saying that, whatever the two powers think about it, and whichever we humans, at the moment, happen to like, one of them is actually wrong, actually mistaken, in regarding itself as good. Now if we mean merely that we happen to prefer the first, then we must give up talking about good and evil at all. For good means what you ought to prefer quite regardless of what you happen to like at any given moment. If "being good" meant simply joining the side you happened to fancy, for no real reason, then good would not deserve to be called good. So we must mean that one of the two powers is actually wrong and the other actually right.

But the moment you say that, you are putting into the universe a third thing in addition to the two Powers: some law or standard or rule of good which one of the powers conforms to and the other fails to conform to. But since the two powers are judged by this standard, then this standard, or the Being who made this standard, is farther back and higher up than either of them, and He will be the real God. In fact, what we meant by calling them good and bad turns out to be that one of them is in a right relation to the real ultimate God and the other in a wrong relation to Him.

The same point can be made in a different way. If Dualism is true, 15 then the bad Power must be a being who likes badness for its own sake. But in reality we have no experience of anyone liking badness just because it is bad. The nearest we can get to it is in cruelty. But in real life people are cruel for one of two reasons—either because they are sadists, that is, because they have a sexual perversion which makes cruelty a cause of sensual pleasure to them, or else for the sake of something they are going to get out of it—money, or power, or safety. But pleasure, money, power, and safety are all, as far as they go, good things. The badness consists in pursuing them by the wrong method, or in the wrong way, or too much. I do not mean, of course, that the people who do this are not desperately wicked. I do mean that wickedness, when you examine it, turns out to be the pursuit of some good in the wrong way. You can be good for the mere sake of goodness; you cannot be bad for the mere sake of badness. You can do a kind action when you are not feeling kind and when it gives you no pleasure, simply because kindness is right; but no one ever did a cruel action simply because cruelty is wrong—only because cruelty was pleasant or useful to him. In other words badness cannot succeed even in being bad in the same way in which goodness is good. Goodness is, so to speak, itself: Badness is only spoiled goodness. And there must be something good first before it can be spoiled. We called sadism a sexual perversion; but you must first have the idea of a normal sexuality before you can talk of its being perverted: and you can see which is the perversion, because you can explain the perverted from the normal, and cannot explain the normal from the perverted. It follows that this Bad Power, who is supposed to be on an equal footing with the Good Power, and to love badness in the same way as the Good Power loves goodness, is a mere bogy. In order to be bad he must have good things to want and then to pursue in the wrong way: He must have impulses which were originally good in order to be able to pervert them. But if he is bad he cannot supply himself either with good things to desire or with good impulses to pervert. He must be getting both from the Good Power. And if so, then he is not independent. He is part of the Good Power's world: He was made either by the Good Power or by some power above them both.

Put it more simply still. To be bad, he must exist and have intelligence and will. But existence, intelligence, and will are in themselves good.

Therefore he must be getting them from the Good Power: Even to be bad he must borrow or steal from his opponent. And do you now begin to see why Christianity has always said that the devil is a fallen angel? That is not a mere story for the children. It is a real recognition of the fact that evil is a parasite, not an original thing. The powers which enable evil to carry on are powers given it by goodness. All the things which enable a bad man to be effectively bad are in themselves good things—resolution, cleverness, good looks, existence itself. That is why Dualism, in a strict sense, will not work.

But I freely admit that real Christianity (as distinct from Christianity-and-water) goes much nearer to Dualism than people think. One of the things that surprised me when I first read the New Testament seriously was that it talked so much about a Dark Power in the universe—a mighty evil spirit who was held to be the Power behind death and disease, and sin. The difference is that Christianity thinks this Dark Power was created by God, and was good when he was created, and went wrong. Christianity agrees with Dualism that this universe is at war. But it does not think this is a war between independent powers. It thinks it is a civil war, a rebellion, and that we are living in a part of the universe occupied by the rebel.

Enemy-occupied territory—that is what this world is. Christianity is the story of how the rightful king has landed, you might say landed in disguise, and is calling us all to take part in a great campaign of sabotage. When you go to church you are really listening in to the secret wireless from our friends: That is why the enemy is so anxious to prevent us from going. He does it by playing on our conceit and laziness and intellectual snobbery. I know someone will ask me, "Do you really mean, at this time of day, to reintroduce our old friend the devil—hoofs and horns and all?" Well, what the time of day has to do with it I do not know. And I am not particular about the hoofs and horns. But in other respects my answer is "Yes, I do." I do not claim to know anything about his personal appearance. If anybody really wants to know him better I would say to that person, "Don't worry. If you really want to, you will. Whether you'll like it when you do is another question."

3. THE SHOCKING ALTERNATIVE

Christians, then, believe that an evil power has made himself for the present the Prince of this World. And, of course, that raises problems. Is this state of affairs in accordance with God's will or not? If it is, He is a strange God, you will say: And if it is not, how can anything happen contrary to the will of a being with absolute power?

But anyone who has been in authority knows how a thing can be in accordance with your will in one way and not in another. It may be quite sensible for a mother to say to the children, "I'm not going to go and make you tidy the schoolroom every night. You've got to learn to keep it tidy on your own." Then she goes up one night and finds the Teddy bear and the ink and the French Grammar all lying in the grate. That is against her will. She would prefer the children to be tidy. But on the other hand, it is her will which has left the children free to be untidy. The same thing arises in any regiment, or trade union, or school. You make a thing voluntary and then half the people do not do it. That is not what you willed, but your will has made it possible.

It is probably the same in the universe. God created things which had free will. That means creatures which can go either wrong or right. Some people think they can imagine a creature which was free but had no possibility of going wrong; I cannot. If a thing is free to be good it is also free to be bad. And free will is what has made evil possible. Why, then, did God give them free will? Because free will, though it makes evil possible, is also the only thing that makes possible any love or goodness or joy worth having. A world of automata—of creatures that worked like machines—would hardly be worth creating. The happiness which God designs for His higher creatures is the happiness of being freely, voluntarily united to Him and to each other in an ecstasy of love and delight compared with which the most rapturous love between a man and a woman on this earth is mere milk and water. And for that they must be free.

Of course God knew what would happen if they used their freedom the wrong way: Apparently He thought it worth the risk. Perhaps we feel inclined to disagree with him. But there is a difficulty about disagreeing with God. He is the source from which all your reasoning power comes: You could not be right and He wrong any more than a stream can rise higher than its own source. When you are arguing against Him you are arguing against the very power that makes you able to argue at all: It is like cutting off the branch you are sitting on. If God thinks this state of war in the universe a price worth paying for free will—that is, for making a live world in which creatures can do real good or harm and something of real importance can happen, instead of a toy world which only moves when He pulls the strings—then we may take it it is worth paying.

When we have understood about free will, we shall see how silly it is to ask, as somebody once asked me: "Why did God make a creature of such rotten stuff that it went wrong?" The better stuff a creature is made of—the cleverer and stronger and freer it is—then the better it will be if it goes right, but also the worse it will be if it goes wrong. A cow cannot be very good or very bad; a dog can be both better and worse; a child better and worse still; an ordinary man, still more so; a man of genius, still more so; a superhuman spirit best—or worst—of all.

How did the Dark Power go wrong? Here, no doubt, we ask a question to which human beings cannot give an answer with any certainty. A reasonable (and traditional) guess, based on our own experiences of going wrong, can, however, be offered. The moment you have a self at all, there is a possibility of putting yourself first—wanting to be the center—wanting to be God, in fact. That was the sin of Satan: And that was the sin he taught the human race. Some people think the fall of man had something to do with sex, but that is a mistake. (The story in the Book of Genesis rather suggests that some corruption in our sexual nature followed the fall and was its result, not its cause.) What Satan put into the heads of our remote ancestors was the idea that they could "be like gods"—could set up on their own as if they had created themselves—be their own masters—invent some sort of happiness for themselves outside God, apart from God. And out of that hopeless attempt has come nearly all that we call human history—money, poverty, ambition, war, prostitution, classes, empires, slavery—the long terrible story of man trying to find something other than God which will make him happy.

The reason why it can never succeed is this. God made us: invented us 25 as a man invents an engine. A car is made to run on gasoline, and it would not run properly on anything else. Now God designed the human machine to run on Himself. He Himself is the fuel our spirits were designed to burn, or the food our spirits were designed to feed on. There is no other. That is why it is just no good asking God to make us happy in our own way without bothering about religion. God cannot give us a happiness and peace apart from Himself, because it is not there. There is no such thing.

That is the key to history. Terrific energy is expended—civilizations are built up—excellent institutions devised; but each time something goes wrong. Some fatal flaw always brings the selfish and cruel people to the top and it all slides back into misery and ruin. In fact, the machine conks. It seems to start up all right and runs a few yards, and then it breaks down. They are trying to run it on the wrong juice. That is what Satan has done to us humans.

And what did God do? First of all He left us conscience, the sense of right and wrong: And all through history there have been people trying (some of them very hard) to obey it. None of them ever quite succeeded. Secondly, he sent the human race what I call good dreams: I mean those queer stories scattered all through the heathen religions about a god who dies and comes to life again and, by his death, has somehow given new life to men. Thirdly, He selected one particular people and spent several centuries hammering into their heads the sort of God He was—that there was only one of Him and that He cared about right conduct. Those people were the Jews, and the Old Testament gives an account of the hammering process.

Then comes the real shock. Among these Jews there suddenly turns up a man who goes about talking as if He was God. He claims to forgive sins. He says He has always existed. He says He is coming to judge the world at the end of time. Now let us get this clear. Among Pantheists, like the Indians, anyone might say that he was a part of God, or one with God: There would be nothing very odd about it. But this man, since He was a Jew, could not mean that kind of God. God, in their language, meant the Being outside the world Who had made it and was infinitely different from anything else. And when you have grasped that, you will see that what this man said was, quite simply, the most shocking thing that has ever been uttered by human lips.

LEWIS • WHAT CHRISTIANS BELIEVE   **683**

One part of the claim tends to slip past us unnoticed because we have heard it so often that we no longer see what it amounts to. I mean the claim to forgive sins: any sins. Now unless the speaker is God, this is really so preposterous as to be comic. We can all understand how a man forgives offenses against himself. You tread on my toe and I forgive you, you steal my money and I forgive you. But what should we make of a man, himself unrobbed and untrodden on, who announced that he forgave you for treading on other men's toes and stealing other men's money? Asinine fatuity is the kindest description we should give of his conduct. Yet this is what Jesus did. He told people that their sins were forgiven, and never waited to consult all the other people whom their sins had undoubtedly injured. He unhesitatingly behaved as if He was the party chiefly concerned, the person chiefly offended in all offenses. This makes sense only if He really was the God whose laws are broken and whose love is wounded in every sin. In the mouth of any speaker who is not God, these words would imply what I can only regard as a silliness and conceit unrivaled by any other character in history.

Yet (and this is the strange, significant thing) even His enemies, when they read the Gospels, do not usually get the impression of silliness and conceit. Still less do unprejudiced readers. Christ says that He is "humble and meek" and we believe Him; not noticing that, if He were merely a man, humility and meekness are the very last characteristics we could attribute to some of His sayings.

I am trying here to prevent anyone saying the really foolish thing that people often say about Him: "I'm ready to accept Jesus as a great moral teacher, but I don't accept His claim to be God." That is the one thing we must not say. A man who was merely a man and said the sort of things Jesus said would not be a great moral teacher. He would either be a lunatic — on a level with the man who says he is a poached egg — or else he would be the Devil of Hell. You must make your choice. Either this man was, and is, the Son of God: or else a madman or something worse. You can shut Him up for a fool, you can spit at Him and kill Him as a demon; or you can fall at His feet and call Him Lord and God. But let us not come with any patronizing nonsense about His being a great human teacher. He has not left that open to us. He did not intend to.

4. THE PERFECT PENITENT

We are faced, then, with a frightening alternative. This man we are talking about either was (and is) just what He said or else a lunatic, or something worse. Now it seems to me obvious that He was neither a lunatic nor a fiend: And consequently, however strange or terrifying or unlikely it may seem, I have to accept the view that he was and is God. God has landed on this enemy-occupied world in human form.

And now, what was the purpose of it all? What did He come to do? Well, to teach, of course; but as soon as you look into the New Testament or any other Christian writing you will find they are constantly talking about something different — about His death and His coming to life again. It is obvious that Christians think the chief point of the story lies here. They think the main thing He came to earth to do was to suffer and be killed.

Now before I became a Christian I was under the impression that the first thing Christians had to believe was one particular theory as to what the point of this dying was. According to that theory God wanted to punish men for having deserted and joined the Great Rebel, but Christ volunteered to be punished instead, and so God let us off. Now I admit that even this theory does not seem to me quite so immoral and so silly as it used to; but that is not the point I want to make. What I came to see later on was that neither this theory nor any other is Christianity. The central Christian belief is that Christ's death has somehow put us right with God and given us a fresh start. Theories as to how it did this are another matter. A good many different theories have been held as to how it works: What all Christians are agreed on is that it does work. I will tell you what I think it is like. All sensible people know that if you are tired and hungry a meal will do you good. But the modern theory of nourishment — all about the vitamins and proteins — is a different thing. People ate their dinners and felt better long before the theory of vitamins was ever heard of: And if the theory of vitamins is some day abandoned they will go on eating their dinners just the same. Theories about Christ's death are not Christianity: They are explanations about how it works. Christians would not all agree as to how important these theories are. My own church — the Church of England — does not lay down any one of them as the right one. The Church of Rome goes a bit further. But I think they will all agree that the thing itself is infinitely more important than any explanations that theologians have produced. I think they would probably admit that no explanation will ever be quite adequate to the reality. But as I said in the preface to this book, I am only a layman, and at this point we are getting into deep water. I can only tell you, for what it is worth, how I, personally, look at the matter.

On my view the theories are not themselves the thing you are asked to 35 accept. Many of you no doubt have read Jeans or Eddington. What they do when they want to explain the atom, or something of that sort, is to give you a description out of which you can make a mental picture. But then they warn you that this picture is not what the scientists actually believe. What the scientists believe is a mathematical formula. The pictures are there only to help you to understand the formula. They are not really true in the way the formula is; they do not give you the real thing but only something more or less like it. They are only meant to help, and if they do not help you can drop them. The thing itself cannot be pictured, it can only be expressed mathematically. We are in the same boat here. We believe that the death of Christ is just that point in history at which something absolutely unimaginable from outside shows through into our own world. And if we cannot picture even the atoms of which our own world is built, of course we are not going to be able to picture this. Indeed, if we found that we could fully understand it, that very fact would show it was not what it professes to be—the inconceivable, the uncreated, the thing from beyond nature, striking down into nature like lightning. You may ask what good will it be to us if we do not understand it. But that is easily answered. A man can eat his dinner without understanding exactly how food nourishes him. A man can accept what Christ has done without knowing how it works; indeed, he certainly would not know how it works until he has accepted it.

We are told that Christ was killed for us, that His death has washed out our sins, and that by dying He disabled death itself. That is the formula. That is Christianity. That is what has to believed. Any theories we build up as to how Christ's death did all this are, in my view, quite secondary: mere plans or diagrams to be left alone if they do not help us, and, even if they do help us, not to be confused with the thing itself. All the same, some of these theories are worth looking at.

The one most people have heard is the one I mentioned before—the one about our being let off because Christ had volunteered to bear a punishment instead of us. Now on the face of it that is a very silly theory. If God was prepared to let us off, why on earth did He not do so? And what possible point could there be in punishing an innocent person instead? None at all that I can see, if you are thinking of punishment in the police-court sense. On the other hand, if you think of a debt, there is plenty of point in a person who has some assets paying it on behalf of someone who has not. Or if you take "paying the penalty," not in the sense of being punished, but in the more general sense of "standing the racket" or "footing the bill," then, of course, it is a matter of common experience that, when one person has got himself into a hole, the trouble of getting him out usually falls on a kind friend.

Now what was the sort of "hole" man had got himself into? He had tried to set up on his own, to behave as if he belonged to himself. In other words, fallen man is not simply an imperfect creature who needs improvement: He is a rebel who must lay down his arms. Laying down your arms, surrendering, saying you are sorry, realizing that you have been on the wrong track and getting ready to start life over again from the ground floor —that is the only way out of a "hole." This process of surrender—this movement full speed astern—is what Christians call repentance. Now repentance is no fun at all. It is something much harder than merely eating humble pie. It means unlearning all the self-conceit and self-will that we have been training ourselves into for thousands of years. It means killing part of yourself, undergoing a kind of death. In fact, it needs a good man to repent. And here comes the catch. Only a bad person needs to repent: Only a good person can repent perfectly. The worse you are the more you need it and the less you can do it. The only person who could do it perfectly would be a perfect person—and he would not need it.

Remember, this repentance, this willing submission to humiliation and a kind of death, is not something God demands of you before He will take you back and which He could let you off if He chose: It is simply a description of what going back to Him is like. If you ask God to take you back without it, you are really asking Him to let you go back without going back. It cannot happen. Very well, then, we must go through with it. But the same badness which makes us need it, makes us unable to do it. Can we do it if God helps us? Yes, but what do we mean when we talk of God helping us? We mean God putting into us a bit of Himself, so to speak. He lends us a little of His reasoning powers and that is how we think: He puts a little of His love into us and that is how we love one another. When you teach a child writing, you hold its hand while it forms the letters: That is, it forms the letters because you are forming them. We love and reason because God loves and reasons and holds our hand while we do it. Now if we had not fallen, that would be all plain sailing. But unfortunately we now need God's help in order to do something which God, in His own nature, never does at all — to surrender, to suffer, to submit, to die. Nothing in God's nature corresponds to this process at all. So that the one road for which we now need God's leadership most of all is a road God, in His own nature, had never walked. God can share only what He has: This thing, in His own nature, He has not.

But supposing God became a man — suppose our human nature   40 which can suffer and die was amalgamated with God's nature in one person — then that person could help us. He could surrender His will, and suffer and die, because He was man; and He could do it perfectly because He was God. You and I can go through this process only if God does it in us; but God can do it only if He becomes man. Our attempts at this dying will succeed only if we men share in God's dying, just as our thinking can succeed only because it is a drop out of the ocean of His intelligence: But we cannot share God's dying unless God dies; and He cannot die except by being a man. That is the sense in which He pays our debt, and suffers for us what He Himself need not suffer at all.

I have heard some people complain that if Jesus was God as well as man, then His sufferings and death lose all value in their eyes, "because it must have been so easy for him." Others may (very rightly) rebuke the ingratitude and ungraciousness of this objection; what staggers me is the misunderstanding it betrays. In one sense, of course, those who make it are right. They have even understated their own case. The perfect submission, the perfect suffering, the perfect death were not only easier to Jesus because He was God, but were possible only because He was God. But surely that is a very odd reason for not accepting them? The teacher is able to form the letters for the child because the teacher is grown-up and knows how to write. That, of course, makes it easier for the teacher; and only because it is easier for him can he help the child. If it rejected him because "it's easy for grown-ups" and waited to learn writing from another child who could not write itself (and so had no "unfair" advantage), it would not get on very quickly. If I am drowning in a rapid river, a man who still has one foot on the bank may give me a hand which saves my life. Ought I to shout back (between my gasps) "No, it's not fair! You have an advantage! You're keeping one foot on the bank"? That advantage—call it "unfair" if you like—is the only reason why he can be of any use to me. To what will you look for help if you will not look to that which is stronger than yourself?

Such is my own way of looking at what Christians call the Atonement. But remember this is only one more picture. Do not mistake it for the thing itself: And if it does not help you, drop it.

5. THE PRACTICAL CONCLUSION

The perfect surrender and humiliation were undergone by Christ: perfect because He was God, surrender and humiliation because He was man. Now the Christian belief is that if we somehow share the humility and suffering of Christ we shall also share in His conquest of death and find a new life after we have died and in it become perfect, and perfectly happy, creatures. This means something much more than our trying to follow His teaching. People often ask when the next step in evolution—the step to something beyond man—will happen. But on the Christian view, it has happened already. In Christ a new kind of man appeared: And the new kind of life which began in Him is to be put into us.

How is this to be done? Now, please remember how we acquired the old, ordinary kind of life. We derived it from others, from our father and mother and all our ancestors, without our consent—and by a very curious process, involving pleasure, pain, and danger. A process you would never have guessed. Most of us spend a good many years in childhood trying to guess it: And some children, when they are first told, do not believe it—and I am not sure that I blame them, for it is very odd. Now the God who arranged that process is the same God who arranges how the new kind of life—the Christ life—is to spread. We must be prepared for it being odd too. He did not consult us when He invented sex: He has not consulted us either when He invented this.

There are three things that spread the Christ life to us: baptism, belief, and that mysterious action which different Christians call by different names—Holy Communion, the Mass, the Lord's Supper. At least, those are the three ordinary methods. I am not saying there may not be special cases where it is spread without one or more of these. I have not time to go into special cases, and I do not know enough. If you are trying in a few minutes to tell a man how to get to Edinburgh you will tell him the trains: He can, it is true, get there by boat or by a plane, but you will hardly bring that in. And I am not saying anything about which of these three things is the most essential. My Methodist friend would like me to say more about belief and less (in proportion) about the other two. But I am not going into that. Anyone who professes to teach you Christian doctrine will, in fact, tell you to use all three, and that is enough for our present purpose.

I cannot myself see why these things should be the conductors of the

45

new kind of life. But then, if one did not happen to know, I should never have seen any connection between a particular physical pleasure and the appearance of a new human being in the world. We have to take reality as it comes to us: There is no good jabbering about what it ought to be like or what we should have expected it to be like. But though I cannot see why it should be so, I can tell you why I believe it is so. I have explained why I have to believe that Jesus was (and is) God. And it seems plain as a matter of history that He taught His followers that the new life was communicated in this way. In other words, I believe it on His authority. Do not be scared by the word *authority*. Believing things on authority only means believing them because you have been told them by someone you think trustworthy. Ninety-nine percent of the things you believe are believed on authority. I believe there is such a place as New York. I have not seen it myself. I could not prove by abstract reasoning that there must be such a place. I believe it because reliable people have told me so. The ordinary man believes in the Solar System, atoms, evolution, and the circulation of the blood on authority—because the scientists say so. Every historical statement in the world is believed on authority. None of us has seen the Norman Conquest or the defeat of the Armada. None of us could prove them by pure logic as you prove a thing in mathematics. We believe them simply because people who did see them have left writings that tell us about them: in fact, on authority. A man who jibbed at authority in other things as some people do in religion would have to be content to know nothing all his life.

Do not think I am setting up baptism and belief and the Holy Communion as things that will do instead of your own attempts to copy Christ. Your natural life is derived from your parents; that does not mean it will stay there if you do nothing about it. You can lose it by neglect, or you can drive it away by committing suicide. You have to feed it and look after it: But always remember you are not making it, you are only keeping up a life you got from someone else. In the same way a Christian can lose the Christ-life which has been put into him, and he has to make efforts to keep it. But even the best Christian that ever lived is not acting on his own steam —he is only nourishing or protecting a life he could never have acquired by his own efforts. And that has practical consequences. As long as the natural life is in your body, it will do a lot toward repairing that body. Cut it, and up to a point it will heal, as a dead body would not. A live body is not one that never gets hurt, but one that can to some extent repair itself. In the same way a Christian is not a man who never goes wrong, but a man who is enabled to repent and pick himself up and begin over again after each stumble—because the Christ-life is inside him, repairing him all the time, enabling him to repeat (in some degree) the kind of voluntary death which Christ Himself carried out.

That is why the Christian is in a different position from other people who are trying to be good. They hope, by being good, to please God if there is one; or—if they think there is not—at least they hope to deserve approval from good men. But the Christian thinks any good he does comes from the Christ-life inside him. He does not think God will love us because we are good, but that God will make us good because He loves us; just as the roof of a greenhouse does not attract the sun because it is bright, but becomes bright because the sun shines on it.

And let me make it quite clear that when Christians say the Christ-life is in them, they do not mean simply something mental or moral. When they speak of being "in Christ" or of Christ being "in them," this is not simply a way of saying that they are thinking about Christ or copying Him. They mean that Christ is actually operating through them; that the whole mass of Christians are the physical organism through which Christ acts— that we are His fingers and muscles, the cells of His body. And perhaps that explains one or two things. It explains why this new life is spread not only by purely mental acts like belief, but by bodily acts like baptism and Holy Communion. It is not merely the spreading of the idea; it is more like evolution—a biological or superbiological fact. There is no good trying to be more spiritual than God. God never meant man to be a purely spiritual creature. That is why He uses material things like bread and wine to put the new life into us. We may think this rather crude and unspiritual. God does not: He invented eating. He likes matter. He invented it.

Here is another thing that used to puzzle me. Is it not frightfully un-   50 fair that this new life should be confined to people who have heard of Christ and been able to believe in Him? But the truth is God has not told us what His arrangements about the other people are. We do know that no man can be saved except through Christ; we do not know that only those who know Him can be saved through Him. But in the meantime, if you are worried about the people outside, the most unreasonable thing you can do is to remain outside yourself. Christians are Christ's body, the organism through which He works. Every addition to that body enables Him to do more. If you want to help those outside you must add your own little cell to the body of Christ who alone can help them. Cutting off a man's fingers would be an odd way of getting him to do more work.

Another possible objection is this. Why is God landing in this enemy-occupied world in disguise and starting a sort of secret society to undermine the devil? Why is He not landing in force, invading it? Is it that He is not strong enough? Well, Christians think He is going to land in force; we do not know when. But we can guess why He is delaying. He wants to give us the chance of joining His side freely. I do not suppose you and I would have thought much of a Frenchman who waited till the Allies were marching into Germany and then announced he was on our side. God will invade. But I wonder whether people who ask God to interfere openly and directly in our world quite realize what it will be like when He does. When that happens, it is the end of the world. When the author walks on to the stage the play is over. God is going to invade, all right: But what is the good of saying you are on His side then, when you see the whole natural universe melting away like a dream and something else—something it never entered your head to conceive—comes crashing in; something so beautiful to some of us and so terrible to others that none of us will have any choice left? For this time it will be God without disguise; something so overwhelming that it will strike either irresistible love or irresistible horror into every creature. It will be too late then to choose your side. There is no use saying you choose to lie down when it has become impossible to stand up. That will not be the time for choosing: It will be the time when we discover which side we really have chosen, whether we realized it before or not. Now, today, this moment, is our chance to choose the right side. God is holding back to give us that chance. It will not last forever. We must take it or leave it.

Topics for Critical Thinking and Writing

1. What is Lewis's argumentative strategy in his opening paragraph? Why does he bother to tell us about his atheistic days?

2. Lewis often seeks to clarify his points by giving rather simple examples—of a painter (para. 4), of straight and crooked lines (para. 6), of a fish (para. 6), and of a car (para. 25). Reread the paragraphs in which these examples are given, and see if you find the examples helpful—or do you find them too simple?

3. In paragraph 44 Lewis talks about sex. Exactly why does he introduce this point?

4. In part 3 of his essay, Lewis refers to "the Dark Power." Reflect on this metaphor: Why "dark"? Why "power"? How much power does Lewis allow that the Dark Power has over us?

5. Lewis accepts Jesus as God because he finds only three alternatives, and rejects all of them. What are these alternatives, and what is Lewis's argument for rejecting each? Do you find this a convincing argument—identifying four possible positions, rejecting three, and concluding that the remaining one must be true?

6. Put yourself in the shoes of Lewis's original audience—persons listening to a radio in the 1940s. Let's assume you were not a believer at the start, and you remained a nonbeliever at the finish. Do you think that you have learned anything —other than, of course, what Lewis believed? And, second, do you think, as a nonbeliever, that you have been addressed courteously and fairly?

7. Lewis says (para. 11) one of his reasons for believing Christianity is that "it is a religion you could not have guessed." In an essay of 500 words explain what he means by this comment, and discuss whether, in general, inability to guess something is a good reason for believing in it.

Bertrand Russell

Why I Am Not a Christian

As your Chairman has told you, the subject about which I am going to speak to you tonight is "Why I Am Not a Christian." Perhaps it would be as well, first of all, to try to make out what one means by the word *Christian*. It is used these days in a very loose sense by a great many people. Some people mean no more by it than a person who attempts to live a good life. In that sense I suppose there would be Christians in all sects and creeds; but I do not think that that is the proper sense of the word, if only because it would imply that all the people who are not Christians — all the Buddhists, Confucians, Mohammedans, and so on — are not trying to live a good life. I do not mean by a Christian any person who tries to live decently according to his lights. I think that you must have a certain amount of definite belief before you have a right to call yourself a Christian. The word does not have quite such a full-blooded meaning now as it had in the times of St. Augustine and St. Thomas Aquinas. In those days, if a man said that he was a Christian it was known what he meant. You accepted a whole collection of creeds which were set out with great precision, and every single syllable of those creeds you believed with the whole strength of your convictions.

WHAT IS A CHRISTIAN?

Nowadays it is not quite that. We have to be a little more vague in our meaning of Christianity. I think, however, that there are two different items which are quite essential to anybody calling himself a Christian. The first is one of a dogmatic nature — namely, that you must believe in God and immortality. If you do not believe in those two things, I do not think that you can properly call yourself a Christian. Then, further than that, as

Bertrand Russell (1872–1970), born in England, made his academic reputation as a mathematician and logician, but he won a popular reputation as a philosopher and social critic. Among his highly readable books are History of Western Philosophy *(1945) and* Why I Am Not a Christian *(1957).*

A pacifist during World War I, Russell was imprisoned in 1916 and deprived of his teaching position at Cambridge University. His unorthodox opinions continued to cause him personal difficulties. In 1938 he was offered a post at the City College of New York, but a judge refused to grant him a visa because of Russell's allegedly dangerous views on sex. During the last two decades of his life, Russell's criticism of American foreign policy made him an especially provocative figure in this country.

Reprinted here is one of his most famous essays on religion. An amusing note: On one occasion when he was imprisoned, the jailer asked him his religion. Russell replied that he was an atheist, a remark that puzzled the jailer, but the man, wishing to be friendly, replied, "Ah well, we all believe in the same God, don't we?"

the name implies, you must have some kind of belief about Christ. The Mohammedans, for instance, also believe in God and in immortality, and yet they would not call themselves Christians. I think you must have at the very lowest the belief that Christ was, if not divine, at least the best and wisest of men. If you are not going to believe that much about Christ, I do not think you have any right to call yourself a Christian. Of course, there is another sense, which you find in *Whitaker's Almanack* and in geography books, where the population of the world is said to be divided into Christians, Mohammedans, Buddhists, fetish worshipers, and so on; and in that sense we are all Christians. The geography books count us all in, but that is a purely geographical sense, which I suppose we can ignore. Therefore I take it that when I tell you why I am not a Christian I have to tell you two different things: first, why I do not believe in God and in immortality; and, secondly, why I do not think that Christ was the best and wisest of men, although I grant him a very high degree of moral goodness.

But for the successful efforts of unbelievers in the past, I could not take so elastic a definition of Christianity as that. As I said before, in olden days it had a much more full-blooded sense. For instance, it included the belief in hell. Belief in eternal hell-fire was an essential item of Christian belief until pretty recent times. In this country, as you know, it ceased to be an essential item because of a decision of the Privy Council, and from that decision the Archbishop of Canterbury and the Archbishop of York dissented; but in this country our religion is settled by Act of Parliament, and therefore the Privy Council was able to override their Graces and hell was no longer necessary to a Christian. Consequently I shall not insist that a Christian must believe in hell.

THE EXISTENCE OF GOD

To come to this question of the existence of God: It is a large and serious question, and if I were to attempt to deal with it in any adequate manner I should have to keep you here until Kingdom Come, so that you will have to excuse me if I deal with it in a somewhat summary fashion. You know, of course, that the Catholic Church has laid it down as a dogma that the existence of God can be proved by the unaided reason. That is a somewhat curious dogma, but it is one of their dogmas. They had to introduce it because at one time the freethinkers adopted the habit of saying that there were such and such arguments which mere reason might urge against the existence of God, but of course they knew as a matter of faith that God did exist. The arguments and the reasons were set out at great length, and the Catholic Church felt that they must stop it. Therefore they laid it down that the existence of God can be proved by the unaided reason and they had to set up what they considered were arguments to prove it. There are, of course, a number of them, but I shall take only a few.

THE FIRST CAUSE ARGUMENT

Perhaps the simplest and easiest to understand is the argument of the   5
First Cause. (It is maintained that everything we see in this world has a
cause, and as you go back in the chain of causes further and further you
must come to a First Cause, and to that First Cause you give the name of
God.) That argument, I suppose, does not carry very much weight nowadays, because, in the first place, cause is not quite what it used to be. The
philosophers and the men of science have got going on cause, and it has
not anything like the vitality it used to have; but, apart from that, you can
see that the argument that there must be a First Cause is one that cannot
have any validity. I may say that when I was a young man and was debating
these questions very seriously in my mind, I for a long time accepted the
argument of the First Cause, until one day, at the age of eighteen, I read
John Stuart Mill's *Autobiography,* and I there found this sentence: "My father taught me that the question 'Who made me?' cannot be answered,
since it immediately suggests the further question 'Who made God?'" That
very simple sentence showed me, as I still think, the fallacy in the argument of the First Cause. If everything must have a cause, then God must
have a cause. If there can be everything without a cause, it may just as well
be the world as God, so that there cannot be any validity in that argument.
It is exactly of the same nature as the Hindu's view that the world rested
upon an elephant and the elephant rested upon a tortoise; and when they
said, "How about the tortoise?" the Indian said, "Suppose we change the
subject." The argument is really no better than that. There is no reason
why the world could not have come into being without a cause; nor, on the
other hand, is there any reason why it should not have always existed.
There is no reason to suppose that the world had a beginning at all. The
idea that things must have a beginning is really due to the poverty of our
imagination. Therefore, perhaps, I need not waste any more time upon the
argument about the First Cause.

THE NATURAL LAW ARGUMENT

Then there is a very common argument from natural law. That was a
favorite argument all through the eighteenth century, especially under the
influence of Sir Isaac Newton and his cosmogony. People observed the
planets going around the sun according to the law of gravitation, and they
thought that God had given a behest to these planets to move in that particular fashion, and that was why they did so. That was, of course, a convenient and simple explanation that saved them the trouble of looking any
further for explanations of the law of gravitation. Nowadays we explain the
law of gravitation in a somewhat complicated fashion that Einstein has introduced. I do not propose to give you a lecture on the law of gravitation,
as interpreted by Einstein, because that again would take some time; at any

rate, you no longer have the sort of natural law that you had in the Newtonian system, where, for some reason that nobody could understand, nature behaved in a uniform fashion. We now find that a great many things we thought were natural laws are really human conventions. You know that even in the remotest depths of stellar space there are still three feet to a yard. That is, no doubt, a very remarkable fact, but you would hardly call it a law of nature. And a great many things that have been regarded as laws of nature are of that kind. On the other hand, where you can get down to any knowledge of what atoms actually do, you will find they are much less subject to law than people thought, and that the laws at which you arrive are statistical averages of just the sort that would emerge from chance. There is, as we all know, a law that if you throw dice you will get double sixes only about once in thirty-six times, and we do not regard that as evidence that the fall of the dice is regulated by design; on the contrary, if the double sixes came every time we should think that there was design. The laws of nature are of that sort as regards a great many of them. They are statistical averages such as would emerge from the laws of chance; and that makes this whole business of natural law much less impressive than it formerly was. Quite apart from that, which represents the momentary state of science that may change tomorrow, the whole idea that natural laws imply a lawgiver is due to a confusion between natural and human laws. Human laws are behests commanding you to behave a certain way, in which way you may choose to behave, or you may choose not to behave; but natural laws are a description of how things do in fact behave, and being a mere description of what they in fact do, you cannot argue that there must be somebody who told them to do that, because even supposing that there were, you are then faced with the question "Why did God issue just those natural laws and no others?" If you say that he did it simply from his own good pleasure, and without any reason, you then find that there is something which is not subject to law, and so your train of natural law is interrupted. If you say, as more orthodox theologians do, that in all the laws which God issues he had a reason for giving those laws rather than others —the reason, of course, being to create the best universe, although you would never think it to look at it—if there were a reason for the laws which God gave, then God himself was subject to law, and therefore you do not get any advantage by introducing God as an intermediary. You have really a law outside and anterior to the divine edicts, and God does not serve your purpose, because he is not the ultimate lawgiver. In short, this whole argument about natural law no longer has anything like the strength that it used to have. I am traveling on in time in my review of the arguments. The arguments that are used for the existence of God change their character as time goes on. They were at first hard intellectual arguments embodying certain quite definite fallacies. As we come to modern times they become less respectable intellectually and more and more affected by a kind of moralizing vagueness.

THE ARGUMENT FROM DESIGN

The next step in this process brings us to the argument from design. You all know the argument from design: Everything in the world is made just so that we can manage to live in the world, and if the world was ever so little different, we could not manage to live in it. That is the argument from design. It sometimes takes a rather curious form; for instance, it is argued that rabbits have white tails in order to be easy to shoot. I do not know how rabbits would view that application. It is an easy argument to parody. You all know Voltaire's remark, that obviously the nose was designed to be such as to fit spectacles. That sort of parody has turned out to be not nearly so wide of the mark as it might have seemed in the eighteenth century, because since the time of Darwin we understand much better why living creatures are adapted to their environment. It is not that their environment was made to be suitable to them but that they grew to be suitable to it, and that is the basis of adaptation. There is no evidence of design about it.

When you come to look into this argument from design, it is a most astonishing thing that people can believe that this world, with all the things that are in it, with all its defects, should be the best that omnipotence and omniscience have been able to produce in millions of years. I really cannot believe it. Do you think that, if you were granted omnipotence and omniscience and millions of years in which to perfect your world, you could produce nothing better than the Ku Klux Klan or the Fascists? Moreover, if you accept the ordinary laws of science, you have to suppose that human life and life in general on this planet will die out in due course: It is a stage in the decay of the solar system; at a certain stage of decay you get the sort of conditions of temperature and so forth which are suitable to protoplasm, and there is life for a short time in the life of the whole solar system. You see in the moon the sort of thing to which the earth is tending — something dead, cold, and lifeless.

I am told that that sort of view is depressing, and people will sometimes tell you that if they believed that, they would not be able to go on living. Do not believe it; it is all nonsense. Nobody really worries much about what is going to happen millions of years hence. Even if they think they are worrying much about that, they are really deceiving themselves. They are worried about something much more mundane, or it may merely be a bad digestion; but nobody is really seriously rendered unhappy by the thought of something that is going to happen to this world millions and millions of years hence. Therefore, although it is of course a gloomy view to suppose that life will die out — at least I suppose we may say so, although sometimes when I contemplate the things that people do with their lives I think it is almost a consolation — it is not such as to render life miserable. It merely makes you turn your attention to other things.

THE MORAL ARGUMENTS FOR DEITY

Now we reach one stage further in what I shall call the intellectual de- 10
scent that the Theists have made in their argumentations, and we come to
what are called the moral arguments for the existence of God. You all
know, of course, that there used to be in the old days three intellectual arguments for the existence of God, all of which were disposed of by Immanuel Kant in the *Critique of Pure Reason;* but no sooner had he disposed of those arguments than he invented a new one, a moral argument,
and that quite convinced him. He was like many people: In intellectual
matters he was skeptical, but in moral matters he believed implicitly in the
maxims that he had imbibed at his mother's knee. That illustrates what the
psychoanalysts so much emphasize — the immensely stronger hold upon us
that our very early associations have than those of later times.

Kant, as I say, invented a new moral argument for the existence of
God, and that in varying forms was extremely popular during the nineteenth century. It has all sorts of forms. One form is to say that there would
be no right or wrong unless God existed. I am not for the moment concerned with whether there is a difference between right and wrong, or
whether there is not: That is another question. The point I am concerned
with is that, if you are quite sure there is a difference between right and
wrong, you are then in this situation: Is that difference due to God's fiat or
is it not? If it is due to God's fiat, then for God himself there is no difference between right and wrong, and it is no longer a significant statement to
say that God is good. If you are going to say, as theologians do, that God is
good, you must then say that right and wrong have some meaning which is
independent of God's fiat, because God's fiats are good and not bad independently of the mere fact that he made them. If you are going to say that,
you will then have to say that it is not only through God that right and
wrong came into being, but that they are in their essence logically anterior
to God. You could, of course, if you liked, say that there was a superior
deity who gave orders to the God who made this world, or could take up
the line that some of the gnostics took up — a line which I often thought
was a very plausible one — that as a matter of fact this world that we know
was made by the devil at a moment when God was not looking. There is a
good deal to be said for that, and I am not concerned to refute it.

THE ARGUMENT FOR THE REMEDYING OF INJUSTICE

Then there is another very curious form of moral argument, which is
this: They say that the existence of God is required in order to bring justice
into the world. In the part of this universe that we know there is great injustice, and often the good suffer, and often the wicked prosper, and one
hardly knows which of those is the more annoying; but if you are going to
have justice in the universe as a whole you have to suppose a future life to
redress the balance of life here on earth. So they say that there must be a

God, and there must be heaven and hell in order that in the long run there may be justice. That is a very curious argument. If you looked at the matter from a scientific point of view, you would say, "After all, I know only this world. I do not know about the rest of the universe, but so far as one can argue at all on probabilities one would say that probably this world is a fair sample, and if there is injustice here the odds are that there is injustice elsewhere also." Supposing you got a crate of oranges that you opened, and you found all the top layer of oranges bad, you would not argue, "The underneath ones must be good, so as to redress the balance." You would say, "Probably the whole lot is a bad consignment"; and that is really what a scientific person would argue about the universe. He would say, "Here we find in this world a great deal of injustice, and so far as that goes that is a reason for supposing that justice does not rule in the world; and therefore so far as it goes it affords a moral argument against deity and not in favor of one." Of course I know that the sort of intellectual arguments that I have been talking to you about are not what really moves people. What really moves people to believe in God is not any intellectual argument at all. Most people believe in God because they have been taught from early infancy to do it, and that is the main reason.

Then I think that the next most powerful reason is the wish for safety, a sort of feeling that there is a big brother who will look after you. That plays a very profound part in influencing people's desire for a belief in God.

THE CHARACTER OF CHRIST

I now want to say a few words upon a topic which I often think is not quite sufficiently dealt with by Rationalists, and that is the question whether Christ was the best and the wisest of men. It is generally taken for granted that we should all agree that that was so. I do not myself. I think that there are a good many points upon which I agree with Christ a great deal more than the professing Christians do. I do not know that I could go with Him all the way, but I could go with Him much further than most professing Christians can. You will remember that He said, "Resist not evil: But whosoever shall smite thee on thy right cheek, turn to him the other also." That is not a new precept or a new principle. It was used by Lao-tse and Buddha some 500 or 600 years before Christ, but it is not a principle which as a matter of fact Christians accept. I have no doubt that the present Prime Minister,[1] for instance, is a most sincere Christian, but I should not advise any of you to go and smite him on one cheek. I think you might find that he thought this text was intended in a figurative sense.

Then there is another point which I consider excellent. You will re- 15
member that Christ said, "Judge not lest ye be judged." That principle I do not think you would find was popular in the law courts of Christian coun-

---

[1]Stanley Baldwin (1867–1947). [Editors' note.]

tries. I have known in my time quite a number of judges who were very earnest Christians, and none of them felt that they were acting contrary to Christian principles in what they did. Then Christ says, "Give to him that asketh of thee, and from him that would borrow of thee turn not thou away." That is a very good principle. Your Chairman has reminded you that we are not here to talk politics, but I cannot help observing that the last general election was fought on the question of how desirable it was to turn away from him that would borrow of thee, so that one must assume that the Liberals and Conservatives of this country are composed of people who do not agree with the teaching of Christ, because they certainly did very emphatically turn away on that occasion.

Then there is one other maxim of Christ which I think has a great deal in it, but I do not find that it is very popular among some of our Christian friends. He says, "If thou wilt be perfect, go and sell that which thou hast, and give to the poor." That is a very excellent maxim, but, as I say, it is not much practiced. All these, I think, are good maxims, although they are a little difficult to live up to. I do not profess to live up to them myself; but then, after all, it is not quite the same thing as for a Christian.

DEFECTS IN CHRIST'S TEACHING

Having granted the excellence of these maxims, I come to certain points in which I do not believe that one can grant either the superlative wisdom or the superlative goodness of Christ as depicted in the Gospels; and here I may say that one is not concerned with the historical question. Historically it is quite doubtful whether Christ ever existed at all, and if He did we do not know anything about Him, so that I am not concerned with the historical question, which is a very difficult one. I am concerned with Christ as He appears in the Gospels, taking the Gospel narrative as it stands, and there one does find some things that do not seem to be very wise. For one thing, He certainly thought that His second coming would occur in clouds of glory before the death of all the people who were living at that time. There are a great many texts that prove that. He says, for instance, "Ye shall not have gone over the cities of Israel till the Son of Man be come." Then He says, "There are some standing here which shall not taste death till the Son of Man comes into His kingdom"; and there are a lot of places where it is quite clear that He believed that His second coming would happen during the lifetime of many then living. That was the belief of His earlier followers, and it was the basis of a good deal of His moral teaching. When He said, "Take no thought for the morrow," and things of that sort, it was very largely because He thought that the second coming was going to be very soon, and that all ordinary mundane affairs did not count. I have, as a matter of fact, known some Christians who did believe that the second coming was imminent. I knew a parson who frightened his congregation terribly by telling them that the second coming was very imminent indeed, but they were much consoled when they found that he was planting trees in his garden. The early Christians did really believe it, and they did abstain from such things as planting trees in their gardens, because they did accept from Christ the belief that the second coming was imminent. In that respect, clearly He was not so wise as some other people have been, and He was certainly not superlatively wise.

THE MORAL PROBLEM

Then you come to moral questions. There is one very serious defect to my mind in Christ's moral character, and that is that He believed in hell. I do not myself feel that any person who is really profoundly humane can believe in everlasting punishment. Christ certainly as depicted in the Gospels did believe in everlasting punishment, and one does find repeatedly a vindictive fury against those people who would not listen to His preaching — an attitude which is not uncommon with preachers, but which does somewhat detract from superlative excellence. You do not, for instance, find that attitude in Socrates. You find him quite bland and urbane toward the people who would not listen to him; and it is, to my mind, far more worthy of a sage to take that line than to take the line of indignation. You probably all remember the sort of things that Socrates was saying when he was dying, and the sort of things that he generally did say to people who did not agree with him.

You will find that in the Gospels Christ said, "Ye serpents, ye generation of vipers, how can ye escape the damnation of hell." That was said to people who did not like His preaching. It is not really to my mind quite the best tone, and there are a great many of these things about hell. There is, of course, the familiar text about the sin against the Holy Ghost: "Whosoever speaketh against the Holy Ghost it shall not be forgiven him neither in this World nor in the world to come." That text has caused an unspeakable amount of misery in the world, for all sorts of people have imagined that they have committed the sin against the Holy Ghost, and thought that it would not be forgiven them either in this world or in the world to come. I really do not think that a person with a proper degree of kindliness in his nature would have put fears and terrors of that sort into the world.

Then Christ says, "The Son of Man shall send forth His angels, and they 20 shall gather out of His kingdom all things that offend, and them which do iniquity, and shall cast them into a furnace of fire; there shall be wailing and gnashing of teeth"; and He goes on about the wailing and gnashing of teeth. It comes in one verse after another, and it is quite manifest to the reader that there is a certain pleasure in contemplating wailing and gnashing of teeth, or else it would not occur so often. Then you all, of course, remember about the sheep and the goats; how at the second coming He is going to divide the sheep from the goats, and He is going to say to the goats, "Depart from me, ye cursed, into everlasting fire." He continues, "And these shall go away into everlasting fire." Then He says again, "If thy hand offend thee, cut it off; it is better for thee to enter into life maimed, than having two hands to go into hell, into the fire that never shall be quenched; where the worm dieth not and the fire is not quenched." He repeats that again and again also. I must say that I think all this doctrine, that hell-fire is a punishment for sin, is a doctrine of cruelty. It is a doctrine that put cruelty into the world and gave the world generations of cruel torture; and the Christ of the Gospels, if you could take Him as His chroniclers represent Him, would certainly have to be considered partly responsible for that.

There are other things of less importance. There is the instance of the Gadarene swine, where it certainly was not very kind to the pigs to put the devils into them and make them rush down the hill to the sea. You must remember that He was omnipotent, and He could have made the devils simply go away; but He chose to send them into the pigs. Then there is the curious story of the fig tree, which always rather puzzled me. You remember what happened about the fig tree. "He was hungry; and seeing a fig tree afar off having leaves, He came if haply He might find anything thereon; and when He came to it He found nothing but leaves, for the time of figs was not yet. And Jesus answered and said unto it: 'No man eat fruit of thee hereafter for ever' . . . and Peter . . . saith unto Him: 'Master, behold the fig tree which thou cursedst is withered away.'" This is a very curious story, because it was not the right time of year for figs, and you really could not blame the tree. I cannot myself feel that either in the matter of wisdom or in the matter of virtue Christ stands quite as high as some other people known to history. I think I should put Buddha and Socrates above Him in those respects.

THE EMOTIONAL FACTOR

As I said before, I do not think that the real reason why people accept religion has anything to do with argumentation. They accept religion on emotional grounds. One is often told that it is a very wrong thing to attack religion, because religion makes men virtuous. So I am told; I have not noticed it. You know, of course, the parody of that argument in Samuel Butler's book, *Erewhon Revisited*. You will remember that in *Erewhon* there is a certain Higgs who arrives in a remote country, and after spending some time there he escapes from that country in a balloon. Twenty years later he comes back to that country and finds a new religion in which he is worshipped under the name of the "Sun Child," and it is said that he ascended into heaven. He finds that the Feast of the Ascension is about to be celebrated, and he hears Professors Hanky and Panky say to each other that they never set eyes on the man Higgs, and they hope they never will; but they are the high priests of the religion of the Sun Child. He is very indignant, and he comes up to them, and he says, "I am going to expose all this humbug and tell the people of Erewhon that it was only I, the man Higgs, and I went up in a balloon." He was told, "You must not do that, because all the morals of this country are bound round this myth, and if they once

know that you did not ascend into heaven they will all become wicked";
and so he is persuaded of that and he goes quietly away.

That is the idea—that we should all be wicked if we did not hold to
the Christian religion. It seems to me that the people who have held to it
have been for the most part extremely wicked. You find this curious fact,
that the more intense has been the religion of any period and the more
profound has been the dogmatic belief, the greater has been the cruelty
and the worse has been the state of affairs. In the so-called ages of faith,
when men really did believe the Christian religion in all its completeness,
there was the Inquisition, with its tortures; there were millions of unfortunate women burned as witches; and there was every kind of cruelty practiced upon all sorts of people in the name of religion.

You find as you look around the world that every single bit of progress
in humane feeling, every improvement in the criminal law, every step toward the diminution of war, every step toward better treatment of the colored races, or every mitigation of slavery, every moral progress that there
has been in the world, has been consistently opposed by the organized
churches of the world. I say quite deliberately that the Christian religion,
as organized in its churches, has been and still is the principal enemy of
moral progress in the world.

HOW THE CHURCHES HAVE RETARDED PROGRESS

You may think that I am going too far when I say that that is still so. I 25
do not think that I am. Take one fact. You will bear with me if I mention it.
It is not a pleasant fact, but the churches compel one to mention facts that
are not pleasant. Supposing that in this world that we live in today an inexperienced girl is married to a syphilitic man; in that case the Catholic
Church says, "This is an indissoluble sacrament. You must endure celibacy
or stay together. And if you stay together, you must not use birth control to
prevent the birth of syphilitic children." Nobody whose natural sympathies
have not been warped by dogma, or whose moral nature was not absolutely
dead to all sense of suffering, could maintain that it is right and proper that
that state of things should continue.

That is only an example. There are a great many ways in which, at the
present moment, the church, by its insistence upon what it chooses to call
morality, inflicts upon all sorts of people undeserved and unnecessary suffering. And of course, as we know, it is in its major part an opponent still of
progress and of improvement in all the ways that diminish suffering in the
world, because it has chosen to label as morality a certain narrow set of
rules of conduct which have nothing to do with human happiness; and
when you say that this or that ought be done because it would make for
human happiness, they think that has nothing to do with the matter at all.
"What has human happiness to do with morals? The object of morals is not
to make people happy."

FEAR, THE FOUNDATION OF RELIGION

Religion is based, I think, primarily and mainly upon fear. It is partly the terror of the unknown and partly, as I have said, the wish to feel that you have a kind of elder brother who will stand by you in all your troubles and disputes. Fear is the basis of the whole thing—fear of the mysterious, fear of defeat, fear of death. Fear is the parent of cruelty, and therefore it is no wonder if cruelty and religion have gone hand in hand. It is because fear is at the basis of those two things. In this world we can now begin a little to understand things, and a little to master them by help of science, which has forced its way step by step against the Christian religion, against the churches, and against the opposition of all the old precepts. Science can help us to get over this craven fear in which mankind has lived for so many generations. Science can teach us, and I think our own hearts can teach us, no longer to look around for imaginary supports, no longer to invent allies in the sky, but rather to look to our own efforts here below to make this world a fit place to live in, instead of the sort of place that the churches in all these centuries have made it.

WHAT WE MUST DO

We want to stand upon our own feet and look fair and square at the world—its good facts, its bad facts, its beauties, and its ugliness; see the world as it is and be not afraid of it. Conquer the world by intelligence and not merely by being slavishly subdued by the terror that comes from it. The whole conception of God is a conception derived from the ancient Oriental despotisms. It is a conception quite unworthy of free men. When you hear people in church debasing themselves and saying that they are miserable sinners, and all the rest of it, it seems contemptible and not worthy of self-respecting human beings. We ought to stand up and look the world frankly in the face. We ought to make the best we can of the world, and if it is not so good as we wish, after all it will still be better than what these others have made of it in all these ages. A good world needs knowledge, kindliness, and courage; it does not need a regretful hankering after the past or a fettering of the free intelligence by the words uttered long ago by ignorant men. It needs a fearless outlook and a free intelligence. It needs hope for the future, not looking back all the time toward a past that is dead, which we trust will be far surpassed by the future that our intelligence can create.

Topics for Critical Thinking and Writing

1. Russell's talk was originally delivered to the National Secular Society. What sort of a group do you think this Society was? Do you imagine that the audience approved or disapproved of the talk? Do you think that to some extent

the talk was geared to the taste of this audience? What evidence can you offer for your view?

2. In a sentence summarize Russell's first paragraph, and in another sentence summarize his second paragraph. Finally, write a third sentence, this one describing and evaluating Russell's strategy in beginning his essay with these two paragraphs.

3. Read and reread Russell's third paragraph, about hell. In the last line of this paragraph, he says, "Consequently I shall not insist that a Christian must believe in hell." "Consequently," of course, suggests that what follows is logically derived from what precedes. State in your own words the reason that Russell offers for the conclusion here. What do you think Russell thought of that reason?

4. In paragraph 8 Russell wonders why an omnipotent and omniscient creator would "produce nothing better than the Ku Klux Klan or the Fascists." Even if you do not believe in an omnipotent and omniscient creator, try to write a one-paragraph response to this point.

5. Many Christians would say that they believe in God because Jesus believed in God. (This point is made by C. S. Lewis, in the preceding essay.) They would add that because historical evidence supports their belief that Jesus did indeed live and die and was resurrected, there can be no reason to doubt Jesus' teachings. Why, in your opinion, does Russell not comment on this argument?

6. Russell discusses the meaning of the term *Christian,* and offers his own definition. Look up in two unabridged dictionaries the definitions of this term, and explain whether Russell's definition agrees with all or any of those in the dictionaries. (By the way, do the dictionaries fully agree with each other?)

7. In paragraph 15 Russell says that many Christians do not practice certain teachings of Jesus. Suppose he is right; does this failing show that Jesus' teachings are wrong? Or that it is unreasonable to believe in Jesus? What, exactly, does Russell's argument prove?

8. In paragraph 21, setting forth what he takes to be some of Jesus' unpleasant teachings and doings, Russell refers to one episode in which exorcised devils entered into swine (Matthew 8:28–34; Mark 5:1–20) and another in which Jesus cursed a fig tree (Matthew 21:19; Mark 11:13–14). In the library examine several Christian commentaries on the Bible (for instance, D. E. Nineham's *The Gospel of St. Mark,* or even *The Interpreter's One-Volume Commentary on the Bible*) to see what explanations believers have offered. Do you find any of these explanations adequate? Why?

9. In paragraph 24 Russell asserts that "every single bit of progress in humane feeling . . . has been consistently opposed by the organized churches of the world." What evidence does he offer? What evidence can you offer to support or to refute this view?

10. Russell states and criticizes five arguments for God's existence. Whether or not you find any of these arguments wholly convincing, which of them seems to you to be the strongest or the most likely to be sound, and which the weakest? In an essay of 500 words explain your evaluation. Optional: If you believe in God's existence, does it matter to you whether any of these arguments survived Russell's criticisms? Explain.

11. In paragraph 27 Russell says that "fear" is the basis of religion. Many Christians would disagree and would insist that love is the basis of Christianity. On this issue, where do you stand? Why?

12. In his final paragraph Russell says that people who debase themselves and call themselves "miserable sinners" in fact are "contemptible." If you have done things of which you have been deeply ashamed, do you think your confession (even if only to yourself) is "contemptible"?

13. Putting aside your own views of Christianity, in an essay of 500 to 750 words assess the strengths and the weaknesses of Russell's essay as an argument.

Joseph Addison

Ode

The Spacious Firmament on high,
With all the blue Etherial Sky,
And spangled Heav'ns, a Shining Frame,
Their great Original proclaim:
Th'unwearied Sun, from Day to Day,   5
Does his Creator's Power display,
And publishes to every land
The Work of an Almighty Hand.

Soon as the Evening Shades prevail,
The Moon takes up the wondrous Tale,   10
And nightly to the listning Earth
Repeats the Story of her Birth:

---

*Joseph Addison (1672–1719), an English essayist and poet, was perhaps the most influential literary critic of his day. His essays, written chiefly for two newspapers (*The Tatler *and* The Spectator*), were immensely popular and they remain highly esteemed today, at least by teachers of English.*

In one issue of The Spectator *(#465, August 23, 1712) Addison published the poem that we reprint here, a version of Psalm 19. He called it simply "Ode." (An ode is a song of praise, specifically of an exalted subject such as heroism, or one's nation, or God.) In the essay he introduced the poem thus:*

> The Supream Being has made the best Arguments for his own Existence, in the Formation of the Heavens and the Earth, and these are Arguments which a Man of Sense cannot forbear attending to, who is out of the Noise and Hurry of Human Affairs. Aristotle says, that should a Man live under Ground, and there converse with Works of Art and Mechanism, and should afterwards be brought up into the open Day, and see the several Glories of the Heav'n and Earth, he would immediately pronounce them the Works of such a Being as we define God to be.

What Addison is here offering is his version of the Argument from Design, the argument that the world obviously is a designed thing, like, say, a watch, and therefore there must be a designer, God.

Whilst all the Stars that round her burn,
And all the Planets, in their turn,
Confirm the Tidings as they rowl,   15
And spread the truth from Pole to Pole.

What though, in solemn Silence, all
Move round the dark terrestrial Ball?
What tho' nor real Voice nor Sound
Amid their radiant Orbs be found?   20
In Reason's Ear they all rejoice,
And utter forth a glorious Voice,
For ever singing, as they shine,
"The Hand that made us is Divine."

Topics for Critical Thinking and Writing

1. In a sentence or two summarize Addison's argument for the existence of God.

2. In the biographical note we mention the Argument from Design — the idea that
   the universe is a complex, functioning thing and therefore it must have been
   made by a creator. Some Christian theologians argued that because the universe
   functions perfectly, we can infer the perfection of the creator. What objections, if
   any, can be offered against the basic argument, and against the amplified argument that we can infer the qualities of the creator from the creation?

Emily Dickinson

Papa above!

Papa above!
Regard a Mouse
O'erpowered by the Cat!
Reserve within thy kingdom
A "Mansion" for the Rat!   5

Emily Dickinson (1830–1886) was born into a proper New England family in
Amherst, Massachusetts. Although she spent her seventeenth year a few miles
away, at Mount Holyoke Seminary (now Mount Holyoke College), in the next
twenty years she left Amherst only five or six times, and in the following twenty
years she may never have left her house.

Dickinson's attitude toward religion seems to have been decidedly untradi-
tional. She apparently disliked the patriarch deity of the Hebrew Bible, whom she
calls "Burglar! Banker — Father!"; she mentioned to a correspondent that the
members of her family were all religious, except for her, and that they "address an
Eclipse every morning — whom they call their 'Father.'"

Snug in seraphic Cupboards
To nibble all the day,
While unsuspecting Cycles[1]
Wheel solemnly away!

Topics for Critical Thinking and Writing

1. In the Gospel according to St. John, 14:2, Jesus says, "In my Father's house are many mansions." What does this mean, and is it relevant to this poem?

2. Some readers take the poem to be a satire on religious faith. Do you agree? Explain.

Emily Dickinson

This World is not Conclusion

This World is not Conclusion.
A Species stands beyond—
Invisible, as Music—
But positive, as Sound—
It beckons, and it baffles—   5
Philosophy—don't know—
And through a Riddle, at the last—
Sagacity, must go—
To guess it, puzzles scholars—
To gain it, Men have borne   10
Contempt of Generations
And Crucifixion, shown—
Faith slips—and laughs, and rallies—
Blushes, if any see—
Plucks at a twig of Evidence—   15
And asks a Vane, the way—
Much Gesture, from the Pulpit—
Strong Hallelujahs roll—
Narcotics cannot still the Tooth
That nibbles at the soul—   20

Topics for Critical Thinking and Writing

1. Given the context of the first two lines, what do you think "Conclusion" means in the first line?

[1]**Cycles** Long periods, eons. [Editors' note.]

2. Although white spaces here are not used to divide the poem into stanzas, the poem seems to be constructed in units of four lines each. Summarize each four-line unit in a sentence or two.

3. Compare your summaries with those of a classmate. If you substantially disagree, reread the poem to see if, on reflection, one or the other of you seems in closer touch with the poem. Or does the poem (or some part of it) allow for two very different interpretations?

4. In the first four lines the speaker seems (to use a word from line 4) quite "positive." Do some or all of the following stanzas seem less positive? If so, which — and what makes you say so?

5. Would you agree with a reader who said that "Much Gesture, from the Pulpit" (line 17) suggests — by its vigorous action — *a lack* of deep conviction?

Emily Dickinson

Those — dying, then

Those — dying, then
Knew where they went
They went to God's Right Hand —
The Hand is amputated now
And God cannot be found —   5

The abdication of Belief
Makes the Behavior small —
Better an ignis fatuus
Than no illume at all —

Topics for Critical Thinking and Writing

1. In a sentence or two, state the point of the poem.

2. Is the image in line 4 in poor taste? Explain.

3. What is an *ignis fatuus?* In what ways does it connect visually with traditional images of hell and heaven?

Robert Frost

Design

I found a dimpled spider, fat and white,
On a white heal-all,[1] holding up a moth
Like a white piece of rigid satin cloth —
Assorted characters of death and blight
Mixed ready to begin the morning right,   5
Like the ingredients of a witches' broth —
A snow-drop spider, a flower like froth,
And dead wings carried like a paper kite.

What had that flower to do with being white,
The wayside blue and innocent heal-all?   10
What brought the kindred spider to that height,
Then steered the white moth thither in the night?
What but design of darkness to appall? —
If design govern in a thing so small.

Topics for Critical Thinking and Writing

1. The poem is a sonnet, divided into an octave (the first eight lines) and a sestet
   (the next six). How does the structure shape the thought?

2. What meanings of the word *design* come to your mind? Which of these meanings are relevant to the poem?

[1]**heal-all** A flower, which is normally blue. [Editors' note.]

*Robert Frost (1874–1963) studied for part of one term at Dartmouth College
in New Hampshire, then did odd jobs (including teaching), and from 1897 to 1899
was enrolled as a special student at Harvard. He then farmed in New Hampshire,
published a few poems in newspapers, did some more teaching, and in 1912 left for
England, where he hoped to achieve success as a writer. By 1915 he was known in
England, and he returned to the United States. By the time of his death he was the
unofficial poet laureate.*

Flannery O'Connor

Revelation

The doctor's waiting room, which was very small, was almost full when the Turpins entered and Mrs. Turpin, who was very large, made it look even smaller by her presence. She stood looming at the head of the magazine table set in the center of it, a living demonstration that the room was inadequate and ridiculous. Her little bright black eyes took in all the patients as she sized up the seating situation. There was one vacant chair and a place on a sofa occupied by a blond child in a dirty blue romper who should have been told to move over and make room for the lady. He was five or six, but Mrs. Turpin saw at once that no one was going to tell him to move over. He was slumped down in the seat, his arms idle at his sides and his eyes idle in his head; his nose ran unchecked.

Mrs. Turpin put a firm hand on Claud's shoulder and said in a voice that included anyone who wanted to listen, "Claud, you sit in that chair there," and gave him a push down into the vacant one. Claud was florid and bald and sturdy, somewhat shorter than Mrs. Turpin, but he sat down as if he were accustomed to doing what she told him to.

Mrs. Turpin remained standing. The only man in the room besides Claud was a lean stringy old fellow with a rusty hand spread out on each knee, whose eyes were closed as if he were asleep or dead or pretending to be so as not to get up and offer her his seat. Her gaze settled agreeably on a well-dressed grey-haired lady whose eyes met hers and whose expression said: If that child belonged to me, he would have some manners and move over—there's plenty of room there for you and him too.

Claud looked up with a sigh and made as if to rise.

"Sit down," Mrs. Turpin said. "You know you're not supposed to stand on that leg. He has an ulcer on his leg," she explained. 5

Claud lifted his foot onto the magazine table and rolled his trouser leg up to reveal a purple swelling on a plump marble-white calf.

"My!" the pleasant lady said. "How did you do that?"

Flannery O'Connor (1925–1964) was born in Savannah, Georgia, but she spent most of her life in Milledgeville, Georgia, where her family moved when she was twelve. She was educated at parochial schools and at the local college, and then went to the School for Writers at the University of Iowa, where she earned an M.F.A. in 1946. In 1951, when she was twenty-five, she discovered that she had lupus erythematosus, an incurable degenerative blood disease. She died at the age of thirty-nine.

A devout Roman Catholic, O'Connor summarized the relation between her belief and her writing:

I see from the standpoint of Christian orthodoxy. This means that for me the meaning of life is centered in our Redemption by Christ and what I see in the world I see in its relation to that.

"A cow kicked him," Mrs. Turpin said.

"Goodness!" said the lady.

Claud rolled his trouser leg down. 10

"Maybe the little boy would move over," the lady suggested, but the child did not stir.

"Somebody will be leaving in a minute," Mrs. Turpin said. She could not understand why a doctor — with as much money as they made charging five dollars a day to just stick their head in the hospital door and look at you — couldn't afford a decent-sized waiting room. This one was hardly bigger than a garage. The table was cluttered with limp-looking magazines and at one end of it there was a big green glass ash tray full of cigaret butts and cotton wads with little blood spots on them. If she had had anything to do with the running of the place, that would have been emptied every so often. There were no chairs against the wall at the head of the room. It had a rectangular-shaped panel in it that permitted a view of the office where the nurse came and went and the secretary listened to the radio. A plastic fern in a gold pot sat in the opening and trailed its fronds down almost to the floor. The radio was softly playing gospel music.

Just then the inner door opened and a nurse with the highest stack of yellow hair Mrs. Turpin had ever seen put her face in the crack and called for the next patient. The woman sitting beside Claud grasped the two arms of her chair and hoisted herself up; she pulled her dress free from her legs and lumbered through the door where the nurse had disappeared.

Mrs. Turpin eased into the vacant chair, which held her tight as a corset. "I wish I could reduce," she said, and rolled her eyes and gave a comic sigh.

"Oh, *you* aren't fat," the stylish lady said. 15

"Ooooo I am too," Mrs. Turpin said. "Claud he eats all he wants to and never weighs over one hundred and seventy-five pounds, but me I just look at something good to eat and I gain some weight," and her stomach and shoulders shook with laughter. "You can eat all you want to, can't you, Claud?" she asked, turning to him.

Claud only grinned.

"Well, as long as you have such a good disposition," the stylish lady said, "I don't think it makes a bit of difference what size you are. You just can't beat a good disposition."

Next to her was a fat girl of eighteen or nineteen, scowling into a thick blue book which Mrs. Turpin saw was entitled *Human Development*. The girl raised her head and directed her scowl at Mrs. Turpin as if she did not like her looks. She appeared annoyed that anyone should speak while she tried to read. The poor girl's face was blue with acne and Mrs. Turpin thought how pitiful it was to have a face like that at that age. She gave the girl a friendly smile but the girl only scowled the harder. Mrs. Turpin herself was fat but she had always had good skin, and, though she was forty-seven years old, there was not a wrinkle in her face except around her eyes from laughing too much.

Next to the ugly girl was the child, still in exactly the same position, 20
and next to him was a thin leathery old woman in a cotton print dress. She
and Claud had three sacks of chicken feed in their pump house that was in
the same print. She had seen from the first that the child belonged with the
old woman. She could tell by the way they sat — kind of vacant and white-
trashy, as if they would sit there until Doomsday if nobody called and told
them to get up. And at right angles but next to the well-dressed pleasant
lady was a lank-faced woman who was certainly the child's mother. She had
on a yellow sweat shirt and wine-colored slacks, both gritty-looking, and
the rims of her lips were stained with snuff. Her dirty yellow hair was tied
behind with a little piece of red paper ribbon. Worse than niggers any day,
Mrs. Turpin thought.

The gospel hymn playing was, "When I looked up and He looked
down," and Mrs. Turpin, who knew it, supplied the last line mentally, "And
wona these days I know I'll we-eara crown."

Without appearing to, Mrs. Turpin always noticed people's feet. The
well-dressed lady had on red and grey suede shoes to match her dress.
Mrs. Turpin had on her good black patent leather pumps. The ugly girl had
on Girl Scout shoes and heavy socks. The old woman had on tennis shoes
and the white-trashy mother had on what appeared to be bedroom slip-
pers, black straw with gold braid threaded through them — exactly what
you would have expected her to have on.

Sometimes at night when she couldn't go to sleep, Mrs. Turpin would
occupy herself with the question of who she would have chosen to be if she
couldn't have been herself. If Jesus had said to her before he made her,
"There's only two places available for you. You can either be a nigger or
white-trash," what would she have said? "Please, Jesus, please," she would
have said, "just let me wait until there's another place available," and he
would have said, "No, you have to go right now and I have only those two
places so make up your mind." She would have wiggled and squirmed and
begged and pleaded but it would have been no use and finally she would
have said, "All right, make me a nigger then — but that don't mean a trashy
one." And he would have made her a neat clean respectable Negro-
woman, herself but black.

Next to the child's mother was a red-headed youngish woman, reading
one of the magazines and working a piece of chewing gum, hell for leather,
as Claud would say. Mrs. Turpin could not see the woman's feet. She was
not white-trash, just common. Sometimes Mrs. Turpin occupied herself at
night naming the classes of people. On the bottom of the heap were most
colored people, not the kind she would have been if she had been one, but
most of them; then next to them — not above, just away from — were the
white-trash; then above them were the home-owners, and above them the
home-and-land owners, to which she and Claud belonged. Above she and
Claud were people with a lot of money and much bigger houses and much
more land. But here the complexity of it would begin to bear in on her, for
some of the people with a lot of money were common and ought to be

below she and Claud and some of the people who had good blood had lost their money and had to rent and then there were colored people who owned their homes and land as well. There was a colored dentist in town who had two red Lincolns and a swimming pool and a farm with registered white-face cattle on it. Usually by the time she had fallen asleep all the classes of people were moiling and roiling around in her head, and she would dream they were all crammed in together in a box car, being ridden off to be put in a gas oven.

"That's a beautiful clock," she said and nodded to her right. It was a big wall clock, the face encased in a brass sunburst. 25

"Yes, it's very pretty," the stylish lady said agreeably. "And right on the dot too," she added, glancing at her watch.

The ugly girl beside her cast an eye upward at the clock, smirked, then looked directly at Mrs. Turpin and smirked again. Then she returned her eyes to her book. She was obviously the lady's daughter because, although they didn't look anything alike as to disposition, they both had the same shape of face and the same blue eyes. On the lady they sparkled pleasantly but in the girl's seared face they appeared alternately to smolder and to blaze.

What if Jesus had said, "All right, you can be white-trash or a nigger or ugly"!

Mrs. Turpin felt an awful pity for the girl, though she thought it was one thing to be ugly and another to act ugly.

The woman with the snuff-stained lips turned around in her chair and looked up at the clock. Then she turned back and appeared to look a little to the side of Mrs. Turpin. There was a cast in one of her eyes. "You want to know wher you can get one of themther clocks?" she asked in a loud voice. 30

"No, I already have a nice clock," Mrs. Turpin said. Once somebody like her got a leg in the conversation, she would be all over it.

"You can get you one with green stamps," the woman said. "That's most likely wher he got hisn. Save you up enough, you can get you most anythang. I got me some joo'ry."

Ought to have got you a wash rag and some soap, Mrs. Turpin thought.

"I get contour sheets with mine," the pleasant lady said.

The daughter slammed her book shut. She looked straight in front of her, directly through Mrs. Turpin and on through the yellow curtain and the plate glass window which made the wall behind her. The girl's eyes seemed lit all of a sudden with a peculiar light, an unnatural light like night road signs give. Mrs. Turpin turned her head to see if there was anything going on outside that she should see, but she could not see anything. Figures passing cast only a pale shadow through the curtain. There was no reason the girl should single her out for her ugly looks. 35

"Miss Finley," the nurse said, cracking the door. The gum chewing woman got up and passed in front of her and Claud and went into the office. She had on red high-heeled shoes.

Directly across the table, the ugly girl's eyes were fixed on Mrs. Turpin as if she had some very special reason for disliking her.

"This is wonderful weather, isn't it?" the girl's mother said.

"It's good weather for cotton if you can get the niggers to pick it," Mrs. Turpin said, "but niggers don't want to pick cotton any more. You can't get the white folks to pick it and now you can't get the niggers—because they got to be right up there with the white folks."

"They gonna *try* anyways," the white-trash woman said, leaning forward. 40

"Do you have one of those cotton-picking machines?" the pleasant lady asked.

"No," Mrs. Turpin said, "they leave half the cotton in the field. We don't have much cotton anyway. If you want to make it farming now, you have to have a little of everything. We got a couple of acres of cotton and a few hogs and chickens and just enough white-face that Claud can look after them himself."

"One thang I don't want," the white-trash woman said, wiping her mouth with the back of her hand. "Hogs. Nasty stinking things, a-gruntin and a-rootin all over the place."

Mrs. Turpin gave her the merest edge of her attention. "Our hogs are not dirty and they don't stink," she said. "They're cleaner than some children I've seen. Their feet never touch the ground. We have a pig-parlor— that's where you raise them on concrete," she explained to the pleasant lady, "and Claud scoots them down with the hose every afternoon and washes off the floor." Cleaner by far than that child right there, she thought. Poor nasty little thing. He had not moved except to put the thumb of his dirty hand into his mouth.

The woman turned her face away from Mrs. Turpin. "I know I 45 wouldn't scoot down no hog with no hose," she said to the wall.

You wouldn't have no hog to scoot down, Mrs. Turpin said to herself.

"A-gruntin and a-rootin and a-groanin," the woman muttered.

"We got a little of everything," Mrs. Turpin said to the pleasant lady. "It's no use in having more than you can handle yourself with help like it is. We found enough niggers to pick our cotton this year but Claud he has to go after them and take them home again in the evening. They can't walk that half a mile. No they can't. I tell you," she said and laughed merrily, "I sure am tired of buttering up niggers, but you got to love em if you want em to work for you. When they come in the morning, I run out and I say, 'Hi yawl this morning?' and when Claud drives them off to the field I just wave to beat the band and they just wave back." And she waved her hand rapidly to illustrate.

"Like you read out of the same book," the lady said, showing she understood perfectly.

"Child, yes," Mrs. Turpin said. "And when they come in from the 50 field, I run out with a bucket of icewater. That's the way it's going to be from now on," she said. "You may as well face it."

"One thang I know," the white-trash woman said. "Two thangs I ain't going to do: love no niggers or scoot down no hog with no hose." And she let out a bark of contempt.

The look that Mrs. Turpin and the pleasant lady exchanged indicated they both understood that you had to *have* certain things before you could *know* certain things. But every time Mrs. Turpin exchanged a look with the lady, she was aware that the ugly girl's peculiar eyes were still on her, and she had trouble bringing her attention back to the conversation.

"When you got something," she said, "you got to look after it." And when you ain't got a thing but breath and britches, she added to herself, you can afford to come to town every morning and just sit on the Court House coping and spit.

A grotesque revolving shadow passed across the curtain behind her and was thrown palely on the opposite wall. Then a bicycle clattered down against the outside of the building. The door opened and a colored boy glided in with a tray from the drug store. It had two large red and white paper cups on it with tops on them. He was a tall, very black boy in discolored white pants and a green nylon shirt. He was chewing gum slowly, as if to music. He set the tray down in the office opening next to the fern and stuck his head through to look for the secretary. She was not in there. He rested his arms on the ledge and waited, his narrow bottom stuck out, swaying slowly to the left and right. He raised a hand over his head and scratched the base of his skull.

"You see that button there, boy?" Mrs. Turpin said. "You can punch 55 that and she'll come. She's probably in the back somewhere."

"Is that right?" the boy said agreeably, as if he had never seen the button before. He leaned to the right and put his finger on it. "She sometime out," he said and twisted around to face his audience, his elbows behind him on the counter. The nurse appeared and he twisted back again. She handed him a dollar and he rooted in his pocket and made the change and counted it out to her. She gave him fifteen cents for a tip and he went out with the empty tray. The heavy door swung to slowly and closed at length with the sound of suction. For a moment no one spoke.

"They ought to send all them niggers back to Africa," the white-trash woman said. "That's wher they come from in the first place."

"Oh, I couldn't do without my good colored friends," the pleasant lady said.

"There's a heap of things worse than a nigger," Mrs. Turpin agreed. "It's all kinds of them just like it's all kinds of us."

"Yes, and it takes all kinds to make the world go round," the lady said 60 in her musical voice.

As she said it, the raw-complexioned girl snapped her teeth together. Her lower lip turned downwards and inside out, revealing the pale pink inside of her mouth. After a second it rolled back up. It was the ugliest face Mrs. Turpin had ever seen anyone make and for a moment she was certain that the girl had made it at her. She was looking at her as if she had known and disliked her all her life — all of Mrs. Turpin's life, it seemed too, not just all the girl's life. Why, girl, I don't even know you, Mrs. Turpin said silently.

She forced her attention back to the discussion. "It wouldn't be practical to send them back to Africa," she said. "They wouldn't want to go. They got it too good here."

"Wouldn't be what they wanted — if I had anythang to do with it," the woman said.

"It wouldn't be a way in the world you could get all the niggers back over there," Mrs. Turpin said. "They'd be hiding out and lying down and turning sick on you and wailing and hollering and raring and pitching. It wouldn't be a way in the world to get them over there."

"They got over here," the trashy woman said. "Get back like they got 65 over."

"It wasn't so many of them then," Mrs. Turpin explained.

The woman looked at Mrs. Turpin as if here was an idiot indeed but Mrs. Turpin was not bothered by the look, considering where it came from.

"Nooo," she said, "they're going to stay here where they can go to New York and marry white folks and improve their color. That's what they all want to do, every one of them, improve their color."

"You know what comes of that, don't you?" Claud asked.

"No, Claud, what?" Mrs. Turpin said.   70

Claud's eyes twinkled. "White-faced niggers," he said with never a smile.

Everybody in the office laughed except the white-trash and the ugly girl. The girl gripped the book in her lap with white fingers. The trashy woman looked around her from face to face as if she thought they were all idiots. The old woman in the feed sack dress continued to gaze expressionless across the floor at the high-top shoes of the man opposite her, the one who had been pretending to be asleep when the Turpins came in. He was laughing heartily, his hands still spread out on his knees. The child had fallen to the side and was lying now almost face down in the old woman's lap.

While they recovered from their laughter, the nasal chorus on the radio kept the room from silence.

> You go to blank blank
> And I'll go to mine
> But we'll all blank along
> To-geth-ther,
> And all along the blank
> We'll hep each other out
> Smile-ling in any kind of
> Weath-ther!

Mrs. Turpin didn't catch every word but she caught enough to agree with the spirit of the song and it turned her thoughts sober. To help anybody out that needed it was her philosophy of life. She never spared herself when she found somebody in need, whether they were white or black, trash or decent. And of all she had to be thankful for, she was most thankful that this was so. If Jesus had said, "You can be high society and have all the money you want and be thin and svelte-like, but you can't be a good woman with it," she would have had to say, "Well don't make me that then. Make me a good woman and it don't matter what else, how fat or how ugly or how poor!" Her heart rose. He had not made her a nigger or white-trash or ugly! He had made her herself and given her a little of everything. Jesus, thank you! she said. Thank you thank you thank you! Whenever she counted her blessings she felt as buoyant as if she weighed one hundred and twenty-five pounds instead of one hundred and eighty.

"What's wrong with your little boy?" the pleasant lady asked the white- 75 trashy woman.

"He has a ulcer," the woman said proudly. "He ain't give me a minute's peace since he was born. Him and her are just alike," she said, nodding at the old woman, who was running her leathery fingers through the child's pale hair. "Look like I can't get nothing down them two but Co'-Cola and candy."

That's all you try to get down em, Mrs. Turpin said to herself. Too lazy to light the fire. There was nothing you could tell her about people like them that she didn't know already. And it was not just that they didn't have anything. Because if you gave them everything, in two weeks it would all be broken or filthy or they would have chopped it up for lightwood. She knew all this from her own experience. Help them you must, but help them you couldn't.

All at once the ugly girl turned her lips inside out again. Her eyes were fixed like two drills on Mrs. Turpin. This time there was no mistaking that there was something urgent behind them.

Girl, Mrs. Turpin exclaimed silently, I haven't done a thing to you! The girl might be confusing her with somebody else. There was no need to sit by and let herself be intimidated. "You must be in college," she said boldly, looking directly at the girl. "I see you reading a book there."

The girl continued to stare and pointedly did not answer. 80

Her mother blushed at this rudeness. "The lady asked you a question, Mary Grace," she said under her breath.

"I have ears," Mary Grace said.

The poor mother blushed again. "Mary Grace goes to Wellesley College," she explained. She twisted one of the buttons on her dress. "In Massachusetts," she added with a grimace. "And in the summer she just keeps right on studying. Just reads all the time, a real book worm. She's done real well at Wellesley; she's taking English and Math and History and Psychology and Social Studies," she rattled on, "and I think it's too much. I think she ought to get out and have fun."

The girl looked as if she would like to hurl them all through the plate glass window.

"Way up north," Mrs. Turpin murmured and thought, well, it hasn't 85 done much for her manners.

"I'd almost rather to have him sick," the white-trash woman said, wrenching the attention back to herself. "He's so mean when he ain't. Look like some children just take natural to meanness. It's some gets bad when they get sick but he was the opposite. Too sick and turned good. He don't give me no trouble now. It's me waitin to see the doctor," she said.

If I was going to send anybody back to Africa, Mrs. Turpin thought, it would be your kind, woman. "Yes, indeed," she said aloud, but looking up at the ceiling, "it's a heap of things worse than a nigger." And dirtier than a hog, she added to herself.

"I think people with bad dispositions are more to be pitied than anyone on earth," the pleasant lady said in a voice that was decidedly thin.

"I thank the Lord he has blessed me with a good one," Mrs. Turpin said. "The day has never dawned that I couldn't find something to laugh at."

"Not since she married me anyways," Claud said with a comical 90 straight face.

Everybody laughed except the girl and the white-trash.

Mrs. Turpin's stomach shook. "He's such a caution," she said, "that I can't help but laugh at him."

The girl made a loud ugly noise through her teeth.

Her mother's mouth grew thin and tight. "I think the worst thing in the world," she said, "is an ungrateful person. To have everything and not appreciate it. I know a girl," she said, "who has parents who would give her anything, a little brother who loves her dearly, who is getting a good education, who wears the best clothes, but who can never say a kind word to anyone, who never smiles, who just criticizes and complains all day long."

"Is she too old to paddle?" Claud asked. 95

The girl's face was almost purple.

"Yes," the lady said, "I'm afraid there's nothing to do but leave her to her folly. Some day she'll wake up and it'll be too late."

"It never hurt anyone to smile," Mrs. Turpin said. "It just makes you feel better all over."

"Of course," the lady said sadly, "but there are just some people you can't tell anything to. They can't take criticism."

"If it's one thing I am," Mrs. Turpin said with feeling, "it's grateful. 100 When I think who all I could have been besides myself and what all I got, a little of everything, and a good disposition besides, I just feel like shouting, 'Thank you, Jesus, for making everything the way it is!' It could have been different!" For one thing, somebody else could have got Claud. At the thought of this, she was flooded with gratitude and a terrible pang of joy ran through her. "Oh thank you, Jesus, Jesus, thank you!" she cried aloud.

The book struck her directly over her left eye. It struck almost at the same instant that she realized the girl was about to hurl it. Before she could utter a sound, the raw face came crashing across the table toward her, howling. The girl's fingers sank like clamps into the soft flesh of her neck. She heard the mother cry out and Claud shout, "Whoa!" There was an instant when she was certain that she was about to be in an earthquake.

All at once her vision narrowed and she saw everything as if it were happening in a small room far away, or as if she were looking at it through the wrong end of a telescope. Claud's face crumpled and fell out of sight. The nurse ran in, then out, then in again. Then the gangling figure of the doctor rushed out of the inner door. Magazines flew this way and that as the table turned over. The girl fell with a thud and Mrs. Turpin's vision suddenly reversed itself and she saw everything large instead of small. The eyes of the white-trashy woman were staring hugely at the floor. There the girl, held down on one side by the nurse and on the other by her mother, was wrenching and turning in their grasp. The doctor was kneeling astride her, trying to hold her arm down. He managed after a second to sink a long needle into it.

Mrs. Turpin felt entirely hollow except for her heart which swung from side to side as if it were agitated in a great empty drum of flesh.

"Somebody that's not busy call for the ambulance," the doctor said in the offhand voice young doctors adopt for terrible occasions.

Mrs. Turpin could not have moved a finger. The old man who had 105 been sitting next to her skipped nimbly into the office and made the call, for the secretary still seemed to be gone.

"Claud!" Mrs. Turpin called.

He was not in his chair. She knew she must jump up and find him but she felt like some one trying to catch a train in a dream, when everything moves in slow motion and the faster you try to run the slower you go.

"Here I am," a suffocated voice, very unlike Claud's, said.

He was doubled up in the corner on the floor, pale as paper, holding his leg. She wanted to get up and go to him but she could not move. Instead, her gaze was drawn slowly downward to the churning face on the floor, which she could see over the doctor's shoulder.

The girl's eyes stopped rolling and focused on her. They seemed a 110 much lighter blue than before, as if a door that had been tightly closed behind them was now open to admit light and air.

Mrs. Turpin's head cleared and her power of motion returned. She leaned forward until she was looking directly into the fierce brilliant eyes. There was no doubt in her mind that the girl did know her, knew her in some intense and personal way, beyond time and place and condition. "What you got to say to me?" she asked hoarsely and held her breath, waiting, as for a revelation.

The girl raised her head. Her gaze locked with Mrs. Turpin's. "Go back to hell where you came from, you old wart hog," she whispered. Her voice was low but clear. Her eyes burned for a moment as if she saw with pleasure that her message had struck its target.

Mrs. Turpin sank back in her chair.

After a moment the girl's eyes closed and she turned her head wearily to the side.

The doctor rose and handed the nurse the empty syringe. He leaned 115 over and put both hands for a moment on the mother's shoulders, which were shaking. She was sitting on the floor, her lips pressed together, holding Mary Grace's hand in her lap. The girl's fingers were gripped like a baby's around her thumb. "Go on to the hospital," he said. "I'll call and make the arrangements."

"Now let's see that neck," he said in a jovial voice to Mrs. Turpin. He began to inspect her neck with his first two fingers. Two little moon-shaped lines like pink fish bones were indented over her windpipe. There was the beginning of an angry red swelling above her eye. His fingers passed over this also.

"Lea' me be," she said thickly and shook him off. "See about Claud. She kicked him."

"I'll see about him in a minute," he said and felt her pulse. He was a thin grey-haired man, given to pleasantries. "Go home and have yourself a vacation the rest of the day," he said and patted her on the shoulder.

Quit your pattin me, Mrs. Turpin growled to herself.

"And put an ice pack over that eye," he said. Then he went and squat- 120 ted down beside Claud and looked at his leg. After a moment he pulled him up and Claud limped after him into the office.

Until the ambulance came, the only sounds in the room were the tremulous moans of the girl's mother, who continued to sit on the floor. The white-trash woman did not take her eyes off the girl. Mrs. Turpin looked straight ahead at nothing. Presently the ambulance drew up, a long dark shadow, behind the curtain. The attendants came in and set the stretcher down beside the girl and lifted her expertly onto it and carried her out. The nurse helped the mother gather up her things. The shadow of the ambulance moved silently away and the nurse came back in the office.

"That ther girl is going to be a lunatic, ain't she?" the white-trash woman asked the nurse, but the nurse kept on to the back and never answered her.

"Yes, she's going to be a lunatic," the white-trash woman said to the rest of them.

"Po' critter," the old woman murmured. The child's face was still in her lap. His eyes looked idly out over her knees. He had not moved during the disturbance except to draw one leg up under him.

"I thank Gawd," the white-trash woman said fervently, "I ain't a lu- 125 natic."

Claud came limping out and the Turpins went home.

As their pick-up truck turned into their own dirt road and made the crest of the hill, Mrs. Turpin gripped the window ledge and looked out suspiciously. The land sloped gracefully down through a field dotted with lavender weeds and at the start of the rise their small yellow frame house, with its little flower beds spread out around it like a fancy apron, sat primly in its accustomed place between two giant hickory trees. She would not have been startled to see a burnt wound between two blackened chimneys.

Neither of them felt like eating so they put on their house clothes and lowered the shade in the bedroom and lay down, Claud with his leg on a pillow and herself with a damp washcloth over her eye. The instant she was flat on her back, the image of a razor-backed hog with warts on its face and horns coming out behind its ears snorted into her head. She moaned, a low quiet moan.

"I am not," she said tearfully, "a wart hog. From hell." But the denial had no force. The girl's eyes and her words, even the tone of her voice, low but clear, directed only to her, brooked no repudiation. She had been singled out for the message, though there was trash in the room to whom it might justly have been applied. The full force of this fact struck her only now. There was a woman there who was neglecting her own child but she had been overlooked. The message had been given to Ruby Turpin, a respectable, hard-working, church-going woman. The tears dried. Her eyes began to burn instead with wrath.

She rose on her elbow and the washcloth fell into her hand. Claud was 130 lying on his back, snoring. She wanted to tell him what the girl had said. At the same time she did not wish to put the image of herself as a wart hog from hell into his mind.

"Hey, Claud," she muttered and pushed his shoulder.

Claud opened one pale baby blue eye.

She looked into it warily. He did not think about anything. He just went his way.

"Wha, whasit?" he said and closed the eye again.

"Nothing," she said. "Does your leg pain you?" 135

"Hurts like hell," Claud said.

"It'll quit terreckly," she said and lay back down. In a moment Claud was snoring again. For the rest of the afternoon they lay there. Claud slept. She scowled at the ceiling. Occasionally she raised her fist and made a small stabbing motion over her chest as if she was defending her innocence to invisible guests who were like the comforters of Job,[1] reasonable-seeming but wrong.

About five-thirty Claud stirred. "Got to go after those niggers," he sighed, not moving.

She was looking straight up as if there were unintelligible handwriting on the ceiling. The protuberance over her eye had turned a greenish-blue. "Listen here," she said.

"What?" 140

"Kiss me."

---

[1] In the Book of Job, in the Hebrew Bible, Job is afflicted terribly. Friends seek to comfort him, but they insist that he must have sinned and offended God. Job rejects their view, insisting on his sinlessness, but at the end, when God addresses him in a whirlwind, Job is humbled and he says, "I abhor myself, and repent in dust and ashes." [Editors' note.]

Claud leaned over and kissed her loudly on the mouth. He pinched her side and their hands interlocked. Her expression of ferocious concentration did not change. Claud got up, groaning and growling, and limped off. She continued to study the ceiling.

She did not get up until she heard the pick-up truck coming back with the Negroes. Then she rose and thrust her feet in her brown oxfords, which she did not bother to lace, and stumped out onto the back porch and got her red plastic bucket. She emptied a tray of ice cubes into it and filled it half full of water and went out into the back yard. Every afternoon after Claud brought the hands in, one of the boys helped him put out hay and the rest waited in the back of the truck until he was ready to take them home. The truck was parked in the shade under one of the hickory trees.

"Hi yawl this evening?" Mrs. Turpin asked grimly, appearing with the bucket and the dipper. There were three women and a boy in the truck.

"Us doin nicely," the oldest woman said. "Hi you doin?" and her gaze 145 stuck immediately on the dark lump on Mrs. Turpin's forehead. "You done fell down, ain't you?" she asked in a solicitous voice. The old woman was dark and almost toothless. She had on an old felt hat of Claud's set back on her head. The other two women were younger and lighter and they both had new bright green sun hats. One of them had hers on her head; the other had taken hers off and the boy was grinning beneath it.

Mrs. Turpin set the bucket down on the floor of the truck. "Yawl hep yourselves," she said. She looked around to make sure Claud had gone. "No. I didn't fall down," she said, folding her arms. "It was something worse than that."

"Ain't nothing bad happen to you!" the old woman said. She said it as if they all knew Mrs. Turpin was protected in some special way by Divine Providence. "You just had you a little fall."

"We were in town at the doctor's office for where the cow kicked Mr. Turpin," Mrs. Turpin said in a flat tone that indicated they could leave off their foolishness. "And there was this girl there. A big fat girl with her face all broke out. I could look at that girl and tell she was peculiar but I couldn't tell how. And me and her mamma were just talking and going along and all of a sudden WHAM! She throws this big book she was reading at me and . . ."

"Naw!" the old woman cried out.

"And then she jumps over the table and commences to choke me."   150

"Naw!" they all exclaimed, "naw!"

"Hi come she do that?" the old woman asked. "What ail her?"

Mrs. Turpin only glared in front of her.

"Somethin ail her," the old woman said.

"They carried her off in an ambulance," Mrs. Turpin continued, "but 155 before she went she was rolling on the floor and they were trying to hold her down to give her a shot and she said something to me." She paused. "You know what she said to me?"

"What she say?" they asked.

"She said," Mrs. Turpin began, and stopped, her face very dark and heavy. The sun was getting whiter and whiter, blanching the sky overhead so that the leaves of the hickory tree were black in the face of it. She could not bring forth the words. "Something real ugly," she muttered.

"She sho shouldn't said nothin ugly to you," the old woman said. "You so sweet. You the sweetest lady I know."

"She pretty too," the one with the hat on said.

"And stout," the other one said. "I never knowed no sweeter white 160 lady."

"That's the truth befo' Jesus," the old woman said. "Amen! You des as sweet and pretty as you can be."

Mrs. Turpin knew just exactly how much Negro flattery was worth and it added to her rage. "She said," she began again and finished this time with a fierce rush of breath, "that I was an old wart hog from hell."

There was an astounded silence.

"Where she at?" the youngest woman cried in a piercing voice.

"Lemme see her. I'll kill her!"   165

"I'll kill her with you!" the other one cried.

"She b'long in the sylum," the old woman said emphatically. "You the sweetest white lady I know."

"She pretty too," the other two said. "Stout as she can be and sweet. Jesus satisfied with her!"

"Deed he is," the old woman declared.

Idiots! Mrs. Turpin growled to herself. You could never say anything 170 intelligent to a nigger. You could talk at them but not with them. "Yawl ain't drunk your water," she said shortly. "Leave the bucket in the truck when you're finished with it. I got more to do than just stand around and pass the time of day," and she moved off and into the house.

She stood for a moment in the middle of the kitchen. The dark protuberance over her eye looked like a miniature tornado cloud which might any moment sweep across the horizon of her brow. Her lower lip protruded dangerously. She squared her massive shoulders. Then she marched into the front of the house and out the side door and started down the road to the pig parlor. She had the look of a woman going single-handed, weaponless, into battle.

The sun was a deep yellow now like a harvest moon and was riding westward very fast over the far tree line as if it meant to reach the hogs before she did. The road was rutted and she kicked several good-sized stones out of her path as she strode along. The pig parlor was on a little knoll at the end of a lane that ran off from the side of the barn. It was a square of concrete as large as a small room, with a board fence about four feet high around it. The concrete floor sloped slightly so that the hog wash could drain off into a trench where it was carried to the field for fertilizer. Claud was standing on the outside, on the edge of the concrete, hanging onto the top board, hosing down the floor inside. The hose was connected to the faucet of a water trough nearby.

Mrs. Turpin climbed up beside him and glowered down at the hogs inside. There were seven long-snouted bristly shoats in it — tan with liver-colored spots — and an old sow a few weeks off from farrowing. She was lying on her side grunting. The shoats were running about shaking themselves like idiot children, their little slit pig eyes searching the floor for anything left. She had read that pigs were the most intelligent animal. She doubted it. They were supposed to be smarter than dogs. There had even been a pig astronaut. He had performed his assignment perfectly but died of a heart attack afterwards because they left him in his electric suit, sitting upright throughout his examination when naturally a hog should be on all fours.

A-gruntin and a-rootin and a-groanin.

"Gimme that hose," she said, yanking it away from Claud. "Go on and 175 carry them niggers home and then get off that leg."

"You look like you might have swallowed a mad dog," Claud observed, but he got down and limped off. He paid no attention to her humors.

Until he was out of earshot, Mrs. Turpin stood on the side of the pen, holding the hose and pointing the stream of water at the hind quarter of any shoat that looked as if it might try to lie down. When he had had time to get over the hill, she turned her head slightly and her wrathful eyes scanned the path. He was nowhere in sight. She turned back again and seemed to gather herself up. Her shoulders rose and she drew in her breath.

"What do you send me a message like that for?" she said in a low fierce voice, barely above a whisper but with the force of a shout in its concentrated fury. "How am I a hog and me both? How am I saved and from hell too?" Her free fist was knotted and with the other she gripped the hose, blindly pointing the stream of water in and out of the eye of the old sow whose outraged squeal she did not hear.

The pig parlor commanded a view of the back pasture where their twenty beef cows were gathered around the hay-bales Claud and the boy had put out. The freshly cut pasture sloped down to the highway. Across it was their cotton field and beyond that a dark green dusty wood which they owned as well. The sun was behind the wood, very red, looking over the paling of trees like a farmer inspecting his own hogs.

"Why me?" she rumbled. "It's no trash around here, black or white, 180 that I haven't given to. And break my back to the bone every day working. And do for the church."

She appeared to be the right size woman to command the arena before her. "How am I a hog?" she demanded. "Exactly how am I like them?" and she jabbed the stream of water at the shoats. "There was plenty of trash there. It didn't have to be me."

"If you like trash better, go get yourself some trash then," she railed. "You could have made me trash. Or a nigger. If trash is what you wanted why didn't you make me trash?" She shook her fist with the hose in it and a watery snake appeared momentarily in the air. "I could quit working and take it easy and be filthy," she growled. "Lounge about the sidewalks all day drinking root beer. Dip snuff and spit in every puddle and have it all over my face. I could be nasty."

"Or you could have made me a nigger. It's too late for me to be a nigger," she said with deep sarcasm, "but I could act like one. Lay down in the middle of the road and stop traffic. Roll on the ground."

In the deepening light everything was taking on a mysterious hue. The pasture was growing a peculiar glassy green and the streak of highway had turned lavender. She braced herself for a final assault and this time her voice rolled out over the pasture. "Go on," she yelled, "call me a hog! Call me a hog again. From hell. Call me a wart hog from hell. Put that bottom rail on top. There'll still be a top and bottom!"

A garbled echo returned to her.   185

A final surge of fury shook her and she roared, "Who do you think you are?"

The color of everything, field and crimson sky, burned for a moment with a transparent intensity. The question carried over the pasture and across the highway and the cotton field and returned to her clearly like an answer from beyond the wood.

She opened her mouth but no sound came out of it.

A tiny truck, Claud's, appeared on the highway, heading rapidly out of sight. Its gears scraped thinly. It looked like a child's toy. At any moment a bigger truck might smash into it and scatter Claud's and the niggers' brains all over the road.

Mrs. Turpin stood there, her gaze fixed on the highway, all her mus- 190 cles rigid, until in five or six minutes the truck reappeared, returning. She waited until it had had time to turn into their own road. Then like a monumental statue coming to life, she bent her head slowly and gazed, as if through the very heart of the mystery, down into the pig parlor at the hogs. They had settled all in one corner around the old sow who was grunting softly. A red glow suffused them. They appeared to pant with a secret life.

Until the sun slipped finally behind the tree line, Mrs. Turpin remained there with her gaze bent to them as if she were absorbing some abysmal life-giving knowledge. At last she lifted her head. There was only a purple streak in the sky, cutting through a field of crimson and leading, like an extension of the highway, into the descending dusk. She raised her hands from the side of the pen in a gesture hieratic and profound. A visionary light settled in her eyes. She saw the streak as a vast swinging bridge extending upward from the earth through a field of living fire. Upon it a vast horde of souls were rumbling toward heaven. There were whole companies of white-trash, clean for the first time in their lives, and bands of black niggers in white robes, and battalions of freaks and lunatics shouting and clapping and leaping like frogs. And bringing up the end of the procession was a tribe of people whom she recognized at once as those who, like herself and Claud, had always had a little of everything and the God-given wit to use it right. She leaned forward to observe them closer. They were marching behind the others with great dignity, accountable as they had always been for good order and common sense and respectable behavior. They alone were on key. Yet she could see by their shocked and altered faces that even their virtues were being burned away. She lowered her hands and gripped the rail of the hog pen, her eyes small but fixed unblinkingly on what lay ahead. In a moment the vision faded but she remained where she was, immobile.

At length she got down and turned off the faucet and made her slow way on the darkening path to the house. In the woods around her the invisible cricket choruses had struck up, but what she heard were the voices of the souls climbing upward into the starry field and shouting hallelujah.

Topics for Critical Thinking and Writing

1. Characterize Mrs. Turpin before her revelation. Did your attitude toward her change at the end of the story?

2. The two chief settings are a doctor's waiting room and a "pig parlor." Can these settings reasonably be called "symbolic"? If so, symbolic of what?

3. When Mrs. Turpin goes toward the pig parlor, she has "the look of a woman going single-handed, weaponless, into battle." Once there, she dismisses Claud, uses the hose as a weapon against the pigs, and talks to herself "in a low fierce voice." What is she battling, besides the pigs?

4. If you were a high school teacher of literature, would you teach this story? Why?

Part Four

FURTHER
PERSPECTIVES
ON ARGUMENT

21

A Literary Critic's View:
Arguing about Literature

You might think that literature—fiction, poetry, drama—is meant only to be enjoyed, not to be argued about. Yet literature in fact is constantly the subject of argumentative writing—not all of it by teachers of English. For instance, if you glance at the current issue of *Time* or *Newsweek* you probably will find a review of a play, suggesting that the play is worth seeing or is not worth seeing. Or, in the same magazine, you may find an article reporting that a senator or member of Congress argued that the National Endowment for the Humanities wasted its grant money by funding research on such-and-such an author, or that the National Endowment for the Arts insulted taxpayers by making an award to a writer who defamed the American family.

Probably most writing about literature, whether done by college students, their professors, journalists, members of Congress, or whomever, does one or more of these five things: It *describes, analyzes, interprets, judges* (or *evaluates*), and *theorizes*. Let's look at each of these, drawing our examples chiefly from Shakespeare's *Macbeth*.

DESCRIBING

Perhaps the most obvious sort of description of a literary work is a summary. We have earlier talked about summarizing an argument (pp. 20–26); here we will talk about summarizing the plot of a story, poem, or play. There might seem to be very little room for argument about a summary, but just think of the varying accounts of two eyewitnesses to an accident, to say nothing of the wild differences between the summarizing statements to the jury from two opposing lawyers. Still, let's try to summarize, very briefly, *Macbeth*:

> *Macbeth* tells the story of a brave man who succumbs to the temptation
> to assassinate his king in order to become king. He suffers mental tor-
> ment, and eventually is killed by the rightful heir to the throne.

This summary, accurate in the sense that it doesn't say anything false, of
course leaves out a great deal. Every summary leaves out a great deal. And
of course the writer of a summary usually does not go on to argue on behalf
of the accuracy of the summary; the writer, doubtless concerned with other
things, offers the summary only as a helpful reminder to the reader. But a
summary nevertheless is a tiny veiled assertion claiming that the gist of the
work is such-and-such. A summary claims to give a brief version of what
happens, but the writer of a summary in effect selects the details on the
basis of an *interpretation*, and other summaries, based on other interpretations, are possible and perhaps are better. In his comic strip *Peanuts*
Charles M. Schultz gave an amusing example. Lucy, asked to summarize
Snow White, says,

> This Snow White has been having trouble sleeping, see? Well, she goes to
> this witch who gives her an apple to eat which puts her to sleep. Just as
> she's beginning to sleep real well . . . you know, for the first time in weeks
> . . . this stupid prince comes along and kisses her and wakes her up.

Linus offers a comment: "I admire the wonderful way you have of getting
the real meaning out of the story."
  Many readers or viewers of *Macbeth* would say that the summary we
gave of the play, a moment ago, is deficient because it makes no mention of
Macbeth's wife, who urges him to commit the crime. A summary, again,
makes an assertion and thus implicitly is an argument: The version given
above does not mention Lady Macbeth, because, presumably, the author of
the summary believed that, in the final analysis, the play is really about Macbeth and not about Lady Macbeth. This is an argument that needs to be supported with evidence. One piece of evidence might be this: If Shakespeare
had wanted us to think the play was about Lady Macbeth as well as about
Macbeth he would have called the play *Macbeth and Lady Macbeth*. After
all, he called one of his other tragedies *Romeo and Juliet*, and he called yet
another *Antony and Cleopatra*. (We are not saying that this evidence is compelling; we are saying only that one must offer evidence to support one's
views. In fact, the evidence is not at all compelling. What Shakespeare himself called the play is unknown, since *Macbeth* was not published with that
name until after his death. The same is true of *Antony and Cleopatra*.)
  Aside from the plot, described in a summary, what else can we describe in *Macbeth*? We might describe a character: "Lady Macbeth has the
following traits: A, B, C." We might describe two characters who resemble
each other, or two contrasting characters: "Lady Macbeth is A, B, and C,
whereas Lady Macduff is X, Y, and Z." Here each character helps, by resemblance or by contrast, to describe (sketch, delineate, outline) the other.
Or we might describe the language: "The play is largely in verse; in particu-

lar it is written in the kind of poetry that is called blank verse (unrhymed lines of ten syllables each, with—in a sort of textbook example—every second syllable stressed), but it includes a few lines that rhyme, and it also includes substantial passages of prose."

One other point: In describing a poem, in addition to giving a brief summary of what happens in the poem, we will probably specify the meter (see the preceding sentence) and the pattern of rhymes.

ANALYZING

The line between *describing* and *analyzing* cannot always be sharply drawn, and we may have crossed the line in the preceding paragraph. An analysis (as we have indicated in earlier chapters) sets forth the relationships of a part to other parts, or to the whole, or both. A detailed description of the verse and prose in *Macbeth* would tell us exactly what the proportions are, how they are related, and whether there is a pattern—for instance, it would tell us whether the prose is limited to certain speakers, or to certain kinds of scenes. Most people would agree that a description of this sort—a description that shows a mind thinking about relationships— is an analysis. This analysis might argue that the noble characters usually speak verse, whereas the socially lower characters (servants) speak prose— but when Lady Macbeth goes mad she speaks prose, indicating that her status has changed. There might, of course, be other passages of prose that must be accounted for; even more obviously than a description, an analysis at bottom is based on a particular view and thus is a sort of implicit argument, staking out a position that the writer should be able to support by pointing to evidence in the text.

An analysis of the uses of verse and prose in *Macbeth* probably would draw the reader's attention to the various parts—unrhymed poetry, rhymed poetry, prose (perhaps of various sorts, for instance highly colloquial prose versus formal prose, brief prose speeches versus long prose speeches, and so on). Similarly, a detailed, thoughtful description of Macbeth (What are his traits? Why does he act the way he does? Does he change during the play?) can be regarded as an analysis of Macbeth's character. And a study built on a comparison of Macbeth with his friend Banquo—whom Macbeth ultimately murders—would also be called an analysis: In what ways do the two men resemble each other? In what ways do they differ? If we ask "What does Banquo contribute to the play?" we are talking about an analysis that might well be titled "Banquo's Role in *Macbeth*."

INTERPRETING

Interpreting is a matter of setting forth the *meaning* or the meanings of a work. For some readers, a work has *a* meaning, the one intended by the writer, which we may or may not perceive. For most critics today, however, a work has many *meanings*, for instance the meaning it had for the writer, the meanings it has accumulated over time, and the meanings it has for each of today's readers. Take *Macbeth*, a play about a Scottish King, written soon after a Scot—James VI of Scotland—had been installed as James I, King of England. The play must have meant something special to the king—we know that it was presented at court—and something a little different to the ordinary English citizen. And surely it means something different to us. For instance, few if any people today believe in the divine right of kings, although James I certainly did; and few if any people today believe in malignant witches, although witches play an important role in the tragedy. What *we* see in the play must be rather different from what Shakespeare's audience saw in it.

Many interpretations of *Macbeth* have been offered. Let's take two fairly simple and clearly opposed views.

1. Macbeth is a villain who, by murdering his lawful king, offends God's rule, so he is overthrown by God's earthly instruments, Malcolm and Macduff. Macbeth is justly punished; the reader or spectator rejoices in his defeat.

One can offer a good deal of evidence—and if one is taking this position in an essay of course one must *argue* it—by giving supporting reasons rather than merely assert the position. Here is a second view.

2. Macbeth is a hero-villain, a man who commits terrible crimes, but who never completely loses the reader's sympathy; although he is justly punished, the reader feels that with the death of Macbeth the world has become a smaller place.

Again, one *must* offer evidence in an essay that presents this thesis, or indeed presents any interpretation. For instance, one might offer as evidence the fact that the survivors, especially Macduff and Malcolm, have not interested us nearly as much as Macbeth has. One might argue, too, that although Macbeth's villainy is undeniable, his conscience never deserts him—here one would point to specific passages, and would offer some brief quotations. His pained awareness of what he has done, it can be argued, enables the reader to sympathize with him continually.

Or consider an interpretation of Lady Macbeth. Is she simply evil through and through, or are there reasons for her actions? Might one argue, perhaps in a feminist interpretation, that despite her intelligence and courage she had no outlet for expression except through her husband? In order to make this argument, the writer might want to go beyond the text of the play, offering as evidence Elizabethan comments about the proper role of women.

JUDGING (OR EVALUATING)

Literary criticism is also concerned with such questions as these: Is *Macbeth* a great tragedy? Is *Macbeth* a greater tragedy than *Romeo and Juliet*? The writer offers an opinion about the worth of the literary work, but the opinion must be supported by an argument, expressed in sentences that offer supporting evidence.

Let's pause for a moment to think about evaluation in general. When we say "This is a great play," are we in effect saying only "I like this play"? That is, are we merely *expressing* our taste rather than *asserting* anything about something out there—something independent of our tastes and feelings? (The next few paragraphs will not answer this question, but they may start you thinking about your own answer.) Consider these three sentences.

1. It's raining outside.
2. I like vanilla.
3. This is a great book.

If you are indoors and you say that it is raining outside, a hearer may ask for verification. Why do you say what you say? "Because," you reply, "I'm looking out the window." Or "Because Jane just came in, and she is drenched." Or "Because I just heard a weather report." If, on the other hand, you say that you like vanilla, it's almost unthinkable that anyone would ask you why. No one expects you to justify—to support, to give a reason for—an expression of taste.

Now consider the third statement, "This is a great book." It is entirely reasonable, we think, for someone to ask you why you say that. And you reply, "Well, the characters are realistic, and the plot held my interest," or "It really gave me an insight into what life among the rich [or the poor] must be like," or some such thing. That is, statement 3 at least seems to be stating a fact, and it seems to be something we can discuss, even argue about, in a way that we cannot argue about a personal preference for vanilla. Almost everyone would agree that when we offer an aesthetic judgment we ought to be able to give reasons for it. At the very least, we might say, we hope to show *why* we evaluate the work as we do, and to suggest that if our readers try to see it from our point of view they may then accept our evaluation.

Evaluations are always based on assumptions, although these assumptions may be unstated, and in fact the writer may even be unaware of them. Some of these assumptions play the role of criteria; they control the sort of evidence the writer believes is relevant to the evaluation. What sorts of assumptions may underlie value judgments? We will mention a few, merely as examples. Other assumptions are possible, and all of these assumptions can themselves become topics of dispute:

1. A good work of art, although fictional, says something about real life.
2. A good work of art is complex yet also is unified.
3. A good work of art sets forth a wholesome view of life.
4. A good work of art is original.
5. A good work of art deals with an important subject.

Let's look briefly at these views, one by one.

1. *A good work of art, although fictional, says something about real life.* If you hold this view, that literature is connected to life, and you believe that human beings behave in fairly consistent ways, that is, that each of us has an enduring "character," you probably will judge as inferior a work in which the figures behave inconsistently or seem not to be adequately motivated. (The point must be made, however, that different literary forms or genres are governed by different rules. For instance, consistency of character is usually expected in tragedy but not in melodrama or in comedy, where last-minute reformations may be welcome and greeted with applause. The novelist Henry James said, "You will not write a good novel unless you possess the sense of reality." He is probably right — but does his view hold for the writer of farces?) In the case of *Macbeth* you might well find that the characters are consistent; although the play begins by showing Macbeth as a loyal defender of King Duncan, Macbeth's later treachery is understandable, given the temptation and the pressure. Similarly, Lady Macbeth's descent into madness, although it may come as a surprise, may strike you as entirely plausible; at the beginning of the play she is confident that she can become an accomplice to a murder, but she has overestimated herself (or, we might say, she has underestimated her own humanity, the power of her guilty conscience, which drives her to insanity).

2. *A good work of art is complex yet is also unified.* If Macbeth is only a "tyrant" (Macduff's word) or a "butcher" (Malcolm's word), he is a unified character but he may be too simple and too uninteresting a character to be the subject of a great play. But, one argument holds, he in fact is a complex character, not simply a villain but a hero-villain, and the play as a whole is complex. *Macbeth* is great, one might argue, partly because it shows us so many aspects of life (courage, fear, loyalty, treachery, for a start) through a richly varied language (the diction ranges from a grand passage in which Macbeth says that his bloody hands will "incarnadine" (make red) "the multitudinous seas" to colloquial passages such as the drunken porter's "Knock, knock." The play shows us the heroic Macbeth tragically destroying his own life, and it shows us the comic porter making coarse jokes about deceit and damnation, jokes that (although the porter doesn't know it) connect with Macbeth's crimes.

3. *A good work of art sets forth a wholesome view of life.* The idea that a work should be judged partly or largely on the moral view that it contains is widely held by the general public. Thus, a story that demeans women — perhaps one that takes a casual view of rape — would be given a low rating, and so would a play that treats a mass murderer as a hero. Implicit in this approach is what is called an *instrumentalist* view — the idea that a work of art is an instrument, a means, to some higher value. Thus, many people hold that reading great works of literature makes us better — or at least does not make us worse. In this view, a work that is pornographic or in some other way thought to be immoral will be given a low value. At the

time we are writing this chapter, a law requires the National Endowment for the Arts to take into account standards of decency when making awards. Moral judgments, it should be noted, do not come only from the conservative right; the liberal left has been quick to detect political incorrectness. In fact, except for those people who subscribe to the now unfashionable view that a work of art is an independent aesthetic object with little or no connection to the real world — something like a pretty floral arrangement, or a wordless melody — most people judge works of literature largely by their content, by what the works seem to say about life. Marxist critics, for instance, have customarily held that literature should make the reader aware of the political realities of life; feminist critics are likely to hold that literature should make us aware of gender relationships — for example, aware of patriarchal power and of female accomplishments. It is difficult to imagine a feminist critic who would give a high value to Shakespeare's *The Taming of the Shrew* — unless (and this position has in fact been taken) the play is interpreted as showing that Katherine, the shrew, is driven to shrewish behavior by an oppressive patriarchal society, and that she only *pretends* to yield her independence to her husband, and that she *really* is a thoroughly engaging woman who is much brighter than the men in the play.

4. *A good work of art is original.* This assumption puts special value on new techniques and new subject matter. Thus, the *first* playwright who introduces a new subject (say, AIDS) gets extra credit, so to speak. Or, to return to Shakespeare, one sign of his genius, it is held, is that he was so highly varied; none of his tragedies seems merely to duplicate another, each is a world of its own, a new kind of achievement. Compare, for instance, *Romeo and Juliet*, with its two youthful and innocent heroes, with *Macbeth*, with its deeply guilty hero. Both plays are tragedies, but we can hardly imagine two more different plays — even if a reader perversely argues that the young lovers are guilty of impetuosity and of disobeying appropriate authorities.

5. *A good work of art deals with an important subject.* Here we are concerned with theme: Great works deal with great themes. Love, death, patriotism, and God, say, are great themes; a work that deals with these may achieve a height, an excellence, that, say, a work describing a dog scratching for fleas may not. (Of course if the reader feels that the dog is a symbol of humanity plagued by invisible enemies, then the poem about the dog may reach the heights, but then, too, it is *not* a poem about a dog and fleas — it is really a poem about humanity and the invisible.)

The point: In writing an evaluation you must let your reader know *why* you value the work as you do. Obviously it is not enough just to keep saying that *this* work is great whereas *that* work is not so great; the reader wants to know *why* you offer the judgments that you do, which means that you will have to set forth your criteria and then offer evidence that is in accord with them.

THEORIZING

Some literary criticism is concerned with such theoretical questions as these:

What is tragedy?

Why do tragedies — works showing good or at least interesting people destroyed — give us pleasure?

Does a work of art — a play or a novel, say, a made-up world with imagined characters — offer anything that can be called "truth"? Do works of art affect our character?

Does a work of art have meaning in itself, or is the meaning simply whatever anyone wishes to say it is?

And, yet again, one hopes that anyone asserting a thesis concerned with any of these topics will offer evidence, will, indeed, *argue* rather than merely assert.

CHARACTERISTICS OF A PERSUASIVE ARGUMENT ABOUT LITERATURE

1. It offers evidence, usually from the text itself, but conceivably from other sources, such as a statement by the author, or a statement by a person regarded as an authority, or perhaps the evidence of comparable works.
2. The essay is inclusive. The more that it takes account of all details, the more convincing it will be.
3. The essay is focused. To say that it is "inclusive" is not to say that it includes everything the writer knows about the work—for instance, that it was made into a film, that it is widely taught in colleges, that the author died poor, and so on. It concentrates on offering a detailed, supported argument.

As with arguments on nonliterary topics, arguments about literature can rarely be airtight, utterly conclusive. But they can and ought to be *reasonable, coherent (consistent)*, and *inclusive*.

AN EXAMPLE: TWO STUDENTS INTERPRET ROBERT FROST'S "MENDING WALL"

Let's consider two competing interpretations of a poem, Frost's "Mending Wall." We say "competing" because these interpretations clash head-on. Differing interpretations need not, of course, be incompatible. For instance, an historical interpretation of *Macbeth*, arguing that an understanding of the context of English-Scottish politics around 1605 helps us to appreciate the play, need not be in any way incompatible with a psychoanalytic interpretation that tells us that Macbeth's murder of King Duncan is rooted in an Oedipus complex, the king being a father figure. Different approaches thus can illuminate different aspects of the work, just as they can emphasize or subordinate different elements in the plot or characters portrayed. But, again, in the next few pages we will deal with mutually incompatible interpretations of the meaning of Frost's poem — of what Frost's poem is about.

After reading the poem and the two interpretations written by students, spend a few minutes thinking about the questions that we raise after the second interpretation.

Robert Frost

Mending Wall

Something there is that doesn't love a wall,
That sends the frozen-ground-swell under it
And spills the upper boulders in the sun,
And makes gaps even two can pass abreast.
The work of hunters is another thing: 5
I have come after them and made repair
Where they have left not one stone on a stone,
But they would have the rabbit out of hiding,
To please the yelping dogs. The gaps I mean,
No one has seen them made or heard them made,   10
But at spring mending-time we find them there.
I let my neighbor know beyond the hill;
And on a day we meet to walk the line
And set the wall between us once again.
We keep the wall between us as we go.   15
To each the boulders that have fallen to each.
And some are loaves and some so nearly balls
We have to use a spell to make them balance:
"Stay where you are until our backs are turned!"
We wear our fingers rough with handling them.   20
Oh, just another kind of outdoor game,

Robert Frost (1874–1963) studied for part of one term at Dartmouth College in New Hampshire, then did odd jobs (including teaching), and from 1897 to 1899 was enrolled as a special student at Harvard. He then farmed in New Hampshire, published a few poems in newspapers, did some more teaching, and in 1912 left for England, where he hoped to achieve success as a writer. By 1915 he was known in England, and he returned to the United States. By the time of his death he was the nation's unofficial poet laureate.

One on a side. It comes to little more:
There where it is we do not need the wall:
He is all pine and I am apple orchard.
My apple trees will never get across   25
And eat the cones under his pines, I tell him
He only says, "Good fences make good neighbors."
Spring is the mischief in me, and I wonder
If I could put a notion in his head:
"*Why* do they make good neighbors? Isn't it   30
Where there are cows? But here there are no cows.
Before I built a wall I'd ask to know
What I was walling in or walling out,
And to whom I was like to give offense.
Something there is that doesn't love a wall,   35
That wants it down." I could say "Elves" to him,
But it's not elves exactly, and I'd rather
He said it for himself. I see him there,
Bringing a stone grasped firmly by the top
In each hand, like an old-stone savage armed.   40
He moves in darkness as it seems to me,
Not of woods only and the shade of trees.
He will not go behind his father's saying,
And he likes having thought of it so well
He says again, "Good fences make good neighbors."   45

Jonathan Deutsch

Professor Walton

English 102

March 3, 1995

The Deluded Speaker in Frost's "Mending Wall"

Our discussions of "Mending Wall" in high
school showed that most people think Frost is
saying that walls between people are a bad thing,
and that we should not try to separate ourselves
from each other unnecessarily. Perhaps the wall,
in this view, is a symbol for race prejudice or
religious differences, and Frost is suggesting
that these differences are minor and that they
should not keep us apart. In this common view, the
neighbor's words, "Good fences make good neighbors" (lines 27 and 45) show that the neighbor is
shortsighted. I disagree with this view, but first
I want to present the evidence that might be
offered for it, so that we can then see whether it
really is substantial.

First of all, someone might claim that in
lines 23 to 26 Frost offers a good argument
against walls:

> There where it is we do not need the wall:
> He is all pine and I am apple orchard.
> My apple trees will never get across
> and eat the cones under his pines, I tell him.

The neighbor does not offer a valid reply to this
argument; in fact, he doesn't offer any argument
at all but simply says, "Good fences make good
neighbors."

Another piece of evidence supposedly showing
that the neighbor is wrong, it is said, is found

Deutsch 2

in Frost's description of him as "an old-stone savage," and someone who "moves in darkness" (40, 41). And a third piece of evidence is said to be that the neighbor "will not go behind his father's saying" (43), but he merely repeats the saying.

There is, however, another way of looking at the poem. As I see it, the speaker is a very snide and condescending person. He is confident that he knows it all and that his neighbor is an ignorant savage; he is even willing to tease his supposedly ignorant neighbor. For instance, the speaker admits that "the mischief is in me" (28), and he is confident that he could tell the truth to the neighbor but he arrogantly thinks that it would be a more effective form of teaching if the neighbor "said it for himself" (38).

The speaker is not only unpleasantly mischievous and condescending toward his neighbor, but he is also shallow, for he does not see the great wisdom that there is in proverbs. The American Heritage Dictionary of the English Language, third edition, defines a proverb as "A short, pithy saying in frequent and widespread use that expresses a basic truth." Frost, or at least the man who speaks this poem, does not seem to realize that proverbs express truths. He just dismisses them, and he thinks the neighbor is wrong not to "go behind his father's saying" (43). But there is a great deal of wisdom in the sayings of our fathers. For instance, in the Bible (in the Old Testament) there is a whole book of proverbs, filled with wise sayings such as "Reprove not a scorner, lest he hate thee: rebuke a wise man, and

he will love thee" (9:8); "He that trusteth in his
riches shall fall" (11:28); "The way of a fool is
right in his own eyes" (12:15; this might be said
of the speaker of "Mending Wall"); "A soft answer
turneth away wrath" (15:1); and (to cut short what
could be a list many pages long), "Whoso diggeth a
pit shall fall therein" (26:27).

The speaker is confident that walls are unnecessary and probably bad, but he doesn't realize that even where there are no cattle, walls
serve the valuable purpose of clearly marking out
our territory. They help us to preserve our independence and our individuality. Walls--man-made
structures--are a sign of civilization. A wall
more or less says, "<u>This</u> is mine, but I respect
<u>that</u> as yours." Frost's speaker is so confident of
his shallow view that he makes fun of his neighbor
for repeating that "Good fences make good neighbors" (27, 45). But he himself repeats his own
saying, "Something there is that does not love a
wall" (1, 35). And at least the neighbor has age-
old tradition on his side, since the proverb is
the saying of his father. On the other hand, the
speaker has only his own opinion, and he can't
even say what the "something" is.

It may be that Frost meant for us to laugh at
the neighbor, and to take the side of the speaker,
but I think it is much more likely that he meant
for us to see that the speaker is mean-spirited
(or at least given to unpleasant teasing), too
self-confident, foolishly dismissing the wisdom of
the old times, and entirely unaware that he has
these unpleasant characteristics.

Felicia Alonso
Professor Walton
English 102
March 3, 1995

The Debate in Robert Frost's "Mending Wall"

I think the first thing to say about Frost's
"Mending Wall" is this: The poem is not about a
debate over whether good fences do or do not make
good neighbors. It is about two debaters: One of
the debaters is on the side of vitality, and the
other is on the side of an unchanging, fixed--
dead, we might say--tradition.

How can we characterize the speaker? For one
thing, he is neighborly. Interestingly, it is he,
and not the neighbor, who initiates the repairing
of the wall: "I let my neighbor know beyond the
hill" (line 12). This seems strange, since the
speaker doesn't see any point in this wall, whereas the neighbor is all in favor of walls. Can
we explain this apparent contradiction? Yes; the
speaker is a good neighbor, willing to do his
share of the work, and willing (perhaps in order
not to upset his neighbor) to maintain an old
tradition even though he doesn't see its importance. It may not be important, he thinks, but
it is really rather pleasant, "another kind of
outdoor game" (21). In fact, sometimes he even re-
pairs fences on his own, after hunters have destroyed them.

Second, we can say that the speaker is on the
side of nature. "Something there is that does not
love a wall," he says, and of course the "something" is nature itself. Nature "sends the frozen-

ground-swell" under the wall and "spills the upper
boulders in the sun, / And makes gaps even two can
pass abreast." Notice that nature itself makes the
gaps, and that "two can pass abreast," that is,
people can walk together in a companionable way.
It is hard to imagine the neighbor walking side by
side with anyone.

Third, we can say that the speaker has a
sense of humor. When he thinks of trying to get
his neighbor interested in the issue, he admits
that "the mischief is in [him]" (28), and he
amusingly attributes his playfulness to a natural
force, the spring. He playfully toys with the
obviously preposterous idea of suggesting to his
neighbor that elves caused the stones to fall, but
he stops short of making this amusing suggestion
to his very serious neighbor. Still, the mere
thought assures us that he has a playful, genial
nature, and the idea also again implies that not
only the speaker but also some sort of mysterious
natural force dislikes walls.

Finally, though of course he thinks he is
right and that his neighbor is mistaken, he at
least is cautious in his view. He does _not_ call
his neighbor "an old-stone savage"; rather, he
uses a simile ("like") and he then adds that this
is only his opinion, so the opinion is softened
quite a bit. Here is the description of the neighbor, with italics added in order to clarify my
point. The neighbor is

> _like_ an old-stone savage armed.
> He moves in darkness _as it seems to me_ . . . (40-41)

Of course the only things we know about the neighbor are those things that the speaker chooses to tell us, so it is not surprising that the speaker comes out ahead. He comes out ahead not because he is right about walls (real or symbolic) and his neighbor is wrong--that's an issue that is not settled in the poem. He comes out ahead because he is a more interesting figure, someone who is neighborly, thoughtful, playful. Yes, maybe he seems to us to feel superior to his neighbor, but we can be certain that he doesn't cause his neighbor any embarrassment. Take the very end of the poem. The speaker tells us that the neighbor

> . . . will not go behind his father's saying,
> And he likes having thought of it so well
> He says again, "Good fences make good
>   neighbors."

The speaker is telling <u>us</u> that the neighbor is utterly unoriginal and that the neighbor confuses <u>remembering</u> something with <u>thinking</u>. But the speaker doesn't get into an argument; he doesn't rudely challenge his neighbor and demand reasons, which might force the neighbor to see that he can't think for himself. And in fact we probably like the neighbor just as he is, and we don't want him to change his mind. The words that ring in our ears are not the speaker's but the neighbor's: "Good fences make good neighbors." The speaker of the poem is a good neighbor. After all, one can hardly be more neighborly than to let the neighbor have the last word.

Topics for Critical Thinking and Writing

1. State the thesis of each essay. Do you believe the theses are sufficiently clear and appear sufficiently early in the essays?

2. Consider the evidence that each essay offers by way of supporting its thesis. Do you find some of the evidence unconvincing? Explain.

3. Putting aside the question of which interpretation you prefer, comment on the organization of each essay. Is the organization clear? Do you want to propose some other pattern that you think might be more effective?

4. Consult the Peer Review Checklist on page 147, and offer comments on one of the two essays. Or: If you were the instructor in the course in which these two essays were submitted, what might be your final comments on each of them? Or: Write an analysis (250–500 words) of the strengths and weaknesses of either essay.

Exercises: Reading a Poem and Reading a Story

First, read the following poem.

A. E. Housman

Loveliest of Trees

Loveliest of trees, the cherry now
Is hung with bloom along the bough,
And stands about the woodland ride
Wearing white for Eastertide.

Now, of my threescore years and ten,   5
Twenty will not come again,
And take from seventy springs a score,
It only leaves me fifty more.

And since to look at things in bloom
Fifty springs are little room,   10
About the woodlands I will go
To see the cherry hung with snow.

Alfred Edward Housman (1859–1936) was born in rural Shropshire, England, and was educated in classics and philosophy at Oxford University. A professor of classics, he was known for his rigorous standards and, indeed, for the severity of his reviews of the work of other classicists. But he was also known for his rather romantic lyric poetry, most of which appeared in a volume called A Shropshire Lad *(1986).*

Now read the following assertions, and consider whether you agree or disagree, and why. For each assertion, draft a paragraph with your arguments.

1. In the first line, "Loveliest" is a fault. First of all, the word is colorless. Second, a poet should not tell us that something is "lovely"; he or she should describe it in such a way that *we* say it is lovely.

2. The idea that the cherry tree, when in bloom, is "wearing white for Eastertide" offers a fresh perception and makes us see (or think of) the blossoms on cherry trees in a fresh way, and this is what good literature does — makes us see things freshly.

3. When the poet tells us that the cherry trees are "wearing white for Eastertide" he is telling us that nature itself (like a priest wearing a white robe) is celebrating the resurrection of Jesus.

4. In the second stanza, the speaker must be some sort of nut, since at the age of twenty he is worried that he has "only" fifty more years to live.

5. Although the speaker dwells on the brevity of life, the references to Easter remind us of the resurrection and of immortality, and these are the true themes of the poem. Nature itself is reborn each spring, when vegetation that seems to have died in the winter is reborn. There is thus an ironic contrast between the naive speaker who thinks life is brief, and the scene itself, which suggests immortality.

6. In the first stanza the reference to Easter is a figure of speech, a metaphor. In fact, the season is winter, and the trees really are covered with snow, but the poet imaginatively describes the snow as cherry blossoms at Eastertime. This interpretation is confirmed by the last line of the poem, where the poet speaks directly of snow.

7. "Snow" in the last line is a figure of speech describing the blossoms, but it nevertheless introduces into this poem about spring and youth a note of winter and therefore of death.

8. The poem, in essence, says nothing beyond this: The cherry trees are blooming, so I'm going to go out and enjoy them.

9. The first stanza is about the cherry trees. The second is about the speaker. The third is about the speaker and the trees. This structure (A, B, A + B), in which the third stanza brings together material from the two earlier stanzas, is one of the things that makes the poem appealing.

10. The poem is very poor.

Read the following short story.

Kate Chopin

The Story of an Hour

Knowing that Mrs. Mallard was afflicted with a heart trouble, great care was taken to break to her as gently as possible the news of her husband's death.

It was her sister Josephine who told her, in broken sentences, veiled hints that revealed in half concealing. Her husband's friend Richards was there, too, near her. It was he who had been in the newspaper office when intelligence of the railroad disaster was received, with Brently Mallard's name leading the list of "killed." He had only taken the time to assure himself of its truth by a second telegram, and had hastened to forestall any less careful, less tender friend in bearing the sad message.

She did not hear the story as many women have heard the same, with a paralyzed inability to accept its significance. She wept at once, with sudden, wild abandonment, in her sister's arms. When the storm of grief had spent itself she went away to her room alone. She would have no one follow her.

There stood, facing the open window, a comfortable, roomy armchair. Into this she sank, pressed down by a physical exhaustion that haunted her body and seemed to reach into her soul.

She could see in the open square before her house the tops of trees 5 that were all aquiver with the new spring life. The delicious breath of rain was in the air. In the street below a peddler was crying his wares. The notes of a distant song which some one was singing reached her faintly, and countless sparrows were twittering in the eaves.

There were patches of blue sky showing here and there through the clouds that had met and piled one above the other in the west facing her window.

She sat with her head thrown back upon the cushion of the chair, quite motionless, except when a sob came up into her throat and shook her, as a child who has cried itself to sleep continues to sob in its dreams.

She was young, with a fair, calm face, whose lines bespoke repression and even a certain strength. But now there was a dull stare in her eyes, whose gaze was fixed away off yonder on one of those patches of blue sky. It was not a glance of reflection, but rather indicated a suspension of intelligent thought.

There was something coming to her and she was waiting for it, fear-

---

Kate Chopin (1851–1904) was born in St. Louis and named Katherine O'Flaherty. At the age of nineteen she married a cotton broker in New Orleans, Oscar Chopin (the name is pronounced something like "show pan"), who was descended from the early French settlers in Louisiana. After her husband's death in 1883, Kate Chopin turned to writing fiction.

fully. What was it? She did not know; it was too subtle and elusive to name. But she felt it, creeping out of the sky, reaching toward her through the sounds, the scents, the color that filled the air.

Now her bosom rose and fell tumultuously. She was beginning to rec- 10 ognize this thing that was approaching to possess her, and she was striving to beat it back with her will — as powerless as her two white slender hands would have been.

When she abandoned herself a little whispered word escaped her slightly parted lips. She said it over and over under her breath: "Free, free, free!" The vacant stare and the look of terror that had followed it went from her eyes. They stayed keen and bright. Her pulses beat fast, and the coursing blood warmed and relaxed every inch of her body.

She did not stop to ask if it were not a monstrous joy that held her. A clear and exalted perception enabled her to dismiss the suggestion as trivial.

She knew that she would weep again when she saw the kind, tender hands folded in death; the face that had never looked save with love upon her, fixed and gray and dead. But she saw beyond that bitter moment a long procession of years to come that would belong to her absolutely. And she opened and spread her arms out to them in welcome.

There would be no one to live for her during those coming years; she would live for herself. There would be no powerful will bending her in that blind persistence with which men and women believe they have a right to impose a private will upon a fellow creature. A kind intention or a cruel intention made the act seem no less a crime as she looked upon it in that brief moment of illumination.

And yet she had loved him — sometimes. Often she had not. What did 15 it matter! What could love, the unsolved mystery, count for in face of this possession of self-assertion which she suddenly recognized as the strongest impulse of her being.

"Free! Body and soul free!" she kept whispering.

Josephine was kneeling before the closed door with her lips to the keyhole, imploring for admission. "Louise, open the door! I beg; open the door — you will make yourself ill. What are you doing, Louise? For heaven's sake open the door."

"Go away. I am not making myself ill." No; she was drinking in a very elixir of life through that open window.

Her fancy was running riot along those days ahead of her. Spring days, and summer days, and all sorts of days that would be her own. She breathed a quick prayer that life might be long. It was only yesterday she had thought with a shudder that life might be long.

She arose at length and opened the door to her sister's importunities. 20 There was a feverish triumph in her eyes, and she carried herself unwittingly like a goddess of Victory. She clasped her sister's waist, and together they descended the stairs. Richards stood waiting for them at the bottom.

Some one was opening the front door with a latchkey. It was Brently

Mallard who entered, a little travel-stained, composedly carrying his grip-sack and umbrella. He had been far from the scene of accident, and did not even know there had been one. He stood amazed at Josephine's piercing cry; at Richards' quick motion to screen him from the view of his wife.

But Richards was too late.

When the doctors came they said she had died of heart disease — of joy that kills.

Now read the following assertions, and consider whether you agree or disagree, and why. For each assertion, draft a paragraph with your arguments.

1. The railroad accident is a symbol of the destructiveness of the industrial revolution.

2. The story claims that women rejoice in the deaths of their husbands.

3. Mrs. Mallard's death at the end is a just punishment for the joy she takes in her husband's death.

4. The story is rich in irony. Some examples: (1) The other characters think she is grieving, but she is rejoicing; (2) she prays for a long life, but she dies almost immediately; (3) the doctors say she died of "the joy that kills," but they think her joy was seeing her husband alive.

5. The story is excellent because it has a surprise ending.

22

A Philosopher's View:
The Toulmin Model

In Chapter 3, we explained the contrast between *deductive* and *inductive* arguments in order to focus on two ways in which we reason: either

making explicit something hidden in what we already accept (**deduction**)

or

going beyond what we know to assert or propose something new (**induction**).

Both types of reasoning share some structural features, as we also noticed. Thus, all reasoning is aimed at establishing some **thesis** (or conclusion) and does so by means of some **reasons.** These are two basic characteristics that any argument contains.

After a little scrutiny we can in fact point to several features shared by all arguments, deductive and inductive, good and bad alike. Using the vocabulary popularized by Stephen Toulmin in *An Introduction to Reasoning* (1979; second edition 1984), they are as follows:

THE CLAIM

Every argument has a purpose, goal, or aim, namely to establish a **claim** (*conclusion* or *thesis*). Suppose you were arguing in favor of equal rights for women. You might state your thesis or claim as follows:

    Men and women should have equal legal rights.

A more precise formulation of the claim might be

Equal legal rights should become part of the Constitution.

A still more precise formulation might be

Equal legal rights should become constitutional law by
amendment.

This is what the controversy in the 1970s over the Equal Rights Amendment was all about.

Consequently, in reading or analyzing someone else's argument, your first question should naturally be: What is the argument intended to prove or establish? *What claim is it making?* Has this claim been precisely formulated, so that it unambiguously asserts what its advocate means?

GROUNDS

Once we have the argument's purpose or point clearly in mind and thus know what the arguer is claiming to establish, then we can ask for the evidence, reasons, support, in short, for the **grounds** on which the claim is based. In a deductive argument these grounds are the premises from which the claim is derived; in an inductive argument the grounds are the evidence that makes the claim plausible or probable.

Obviously, not every kind of claim can be supported by every kind of ground, and conversely, not every kind of ground gives support for every kind of claim. Suppose I claim that half the students in the room are women. I can ground this claim in either of two ways.

(1) I can count all the women and all the men. Suppose the total equals fifty. If the number of women is twenty-five, and the number of men is twenty-five, I have vindicated my claim.

(2) I can count a sample of, say, ten students, and find that in the sample, five of the students are women, and thus have inductive — plausible but not conclusive — grounds for my claim.

So far, we have merely restated points about premises and conclusions covered in Chapter 3. But now we want to notice four additional features of all kinds of arguments, features we did not consider earlier.

WARRANTS

Once we have the claim or the point of an argument fixed in mind, and the evidence or reasons offered in its support, the next question to ask is *why* these reasons support this conclusion. What is the **warrant,** or guarantee, that the reasons proffered do support the claim or lead to the conclusion? In simple deductive arguments, the warrant takes different forms, as we shall see. In the simplest cases, we can point to the way in which the *meanings* of the key terms are really equivalent. Thus, if John is taller than Bill, then Bill must be shorter than John because of the meaning in English of "is shorter than" and "is taller than." In this case, the warrant is something we can state quite literally and explicitly.

In other cases, we may need to be more resourceful. A reliable tactic is to think up a simple *parallel argument* exactly parallel in form and structure to the argument we are trying to defend, and then point out that if one is ready to accept the simpler argument then in consistency one must accept the more controversial argument, because both arguments have exactly the same structure. For example, in her much-discussed essay of 1972 on the abortion controversy, "A Defense of Abortion," philosopher Judith Thomson argues that a pregnant woman has the right to an abortion to save her life, even if it involves the death of her unborn child. She anticipates that some readers may balk at her reasoning, and so she offers this parallel argument: Suppose you were locked in a tiny room with another human being, which through no fault of its own is growing uncontrollably, with the result that it is slowly crushing you to death. Of course it would be morally permissible to kill the other person to save your own life. With the reader's presumed agreement on that conclusion, the parallel argument concerning the abortion situation — so Thomson hopes — is obvious and convincing.

In simple inductive arguments, we are likely to point to the way in which observations or sets of data constitute a *representative sample* of a whole (unexamined) population. Here, the warrant is the representativeness of the sample. Or in plotting a line on a graph through a set of points, we defend one line over alternatives on the ground that it makes the smoothest fit through most of the points. In this case, the warrant is *simplicity*. Or in defending one explanation against competing explanations of a phenomenon, we appeal to the way in which the preferred explanation can be seen as a *special case* of generally accepted physical laws. Examples of such warrants for inductive reasoning will be offered in following pages (see "A Logician's View," p. 758).

Establishing the warrants for our reasoning — that is, explaining why our grounds really support our claims — can quickly become a highly technical and exacting procedure that goes far beyond what we can hope to explain in this book. Only a solid course or two in formal deductive logic and statistical methods can do justice to our current state of knowledge about these warrants. Developing a "feel" for why reasons or grounds are or are not relevant to what they are alleged to support is the most we can hope to do here without recourse to more rigorous techniques.

Even without formal training, however, one can sense that something is wrong with many bad arguments. Here is an example. British professor C. E. M. Joad found himself standing on a station platform, annoyed because he had just missed his train, when another train, making an unscheduled stop, pulled up to the platform in front of him. He decided to jump aboard, only to hear the porter say "I'm afraid you'll have to get off, sir. This train doesn't stop here." "In that case," replied Joad, "don't worry. I'm not on it."

BACKING

The kinds of reasons appropriate to support an amendment to the Constitution are completely different from the kinds appropriate to settle the question of what caused the defeat of Napoleon's invasion of Russia. Arguments for the amendment might be rooted in an appeal to fairness, whereas arguments about the military defeat might be rooted in newly discovered historical data. The canons of good argument in each case derive from appropriate ways in which the scholarly communities in law and history, respectively, have developed over the years to support, defend, challenge, and undermine a given kind of argument. Thus, the support or **backing** appropriate for one kind of argument might be quite inappropriate for another kind of argument.

Another way of stating this point is to recognize that once one has given reasons for a claim, one is then likely to be challenged to explain why these reasons are good reasons — why, that is, one should believe these reasons rather than regard them skeptically. Why (a simple example) should we accept the testimony of Dr. X when Dr. Y, equally renowned, supports the opposite side? Or: Why is it safe to rest a prediction on a small though admittedly carefully selected sample? Or: Why is it legitimate to argue that (a) if I dream I am the King of France then I must exist, whereas it is illegitimate to argue that (b) if I dream I am the King of France, then the King of France must exist? To answer these kinds of challenges is to *back up* one's reasoning, and no argument is any better than its backing.

MODAL QUALIFIERS

As we have seen, all arguments are made up of assertions or propositions, which can be sorted into three categories:

the **claim** (conclusion, thesis to be established),

the **grounds** (explicit reasons advanced), and

the **backing** (implicit assumptions)

All such propositions have an explicit or tacit **modality** in which they are asserted, indicating the scope and character with which they are believed to hold true. Is the claim, for instance, believed to be *necessary* — or only *probable?* Is the claim believed to be *plausible* or only *possible?* Indicating the modality with which an assertion is advanced is crucial to any argument for or against it.

Empirical generalizations are typically *contingent* on various factors, and it is important to indicate such contingencies to protect the generalization against obvious counterexamples. Thus, consider this empirical generalization:

Students do best on final examinations if they study hard for them.

Are we really to believe that students who study regularly throughout the whole course and so do not need to cram for the final will do less well than students who neglect regular work in favor of several all-nighters at the last minute? Probably not; what is really meant is that *all other things being equal* (in Latin, *caeteris paribus*), concentrated study just before an exam will yield good results. Alluding to the contingencies in this way shows that the writer is aware of possible exceptions and that they are conceded right from the start.

Assertions also have varying **scope,** and indicating their scope is equally crucial to the role that an assertion plays in argument. Thus, suppose you are arguing against smoking, and the ground for your claim is this:

> Heavy smokers cut short their life span.

Such an assertion will be clearer, as well as more likely to be true, if it is explicitly **quantified.** Here, there are three obvious alternative quantifications to choose among: *all* smokers cut short their life span, or *most* do, or only *some* do. Until the assertion is quantified in one of these ways, we really do not know what is being asserted — and so we do not know what degree and kind of evidence and counterevidence is relevant.

In sum, sensitivity to the quantifiers and qualifiers appropriate for each of our assertions, whatever their role in an argument, will help prevent you from asserting exaggerations and other misguided generalizations.

REBUTTALS

Very few arguments of any interest are beyond dispute, conclusively knockdown affairs, in which the claim of the argument is so rigidly tied to its grounds, warrants, and backing, and its quantifiers and qualifiers so precisely orchestrated that it really proves its conclusion beyond any possibility of doubt. On the contrary, most arguments have many counterarguments, and sometimes it is the counterargument that is the more convincing.

Suppose one has taken a sample that appears to be random — an interviewer on your campus accosts the first ten students whom she sees, and seven of them happen to be fraternity or sorority members. She is now ready to argue: Seven-tenths of the student body belong to Greek organizations.

You believe, however, that the Greeks are in the minority and point out that she happens to have conducted her interview around the corner from the Panhellenic Society's office just off Sorority Row. Her random sample is anything but. The ball is now back in her court as you await her response to your rebuttal.

As this example illustrates, it is safe to say that we do not understand our own arguments very well until we have tried to get a grip on the places in which they are vulnerable to criticism, counterattack, or refutation. Edmund Burke (quoted in Chapter 3 but worth repeating) said, "He that wrestles with us strengthens our nerves, and sharpens our skill. Our antagonist is our helper." Therefore, cultivating alertness to such weak spots, girding one's loins to defend at these places, always helps strengthen one's position.

A MODEL ANALYSIS USING THE TOULMIN METHOD

In order to see how the Toulmin method can be used, let's apply it to an argument in this book, Susan Jacoby's "A First Amendment Junkie," on page 22.

The Claim • Jacoby's central thesis or claim is this: Any form of *censorship* — including feminist censorship of pornography in particular — *is wrong.*

Grounds • Jacoby offers six main reasons or grounds for her claim, roughly in this sequence (but arguably not in this order of importance).

First, feminists exaggerate the harm caused by pornography because they confuse expression of offensive ideas with harmful conduct.

Second, letting the government censor the expression of ideas and attitudes is the wrong response to the failure of parents to control the printed materials that get into the hands of their children.

Third, there is no unanimity even among feminists over what is pornography and what isn't.

Fourth, permitting censorship of pornography, in order to please feminists, could well lead to censorship on many issues of concern to feminists ("rape, abortion, menstruation, lesbianism").

Fifth, censorship under law shows a lack of confidence in the democratic process.

Finally, censorship of words and pictures is suppression of self-expression; and that violates the First Amendment.

Warrants • The grounds Jacoby has offered provide support for her central claim in three ways, although Jacoby (like most writers) is not so didactic as to make these warrants explicit.

First, since the First Amendment protects speech in the broadest sense, the censorship that the feminist attack on pornography advocates is *inconsistent* with the First Amendment.

Second, if feminists want to be consistent, then they must advocate censorship of *all* offensive self-expression; but such a radical interference with free speech (amounting virtually to repeal of the First Amendment) is indefensible.

Third, feminists ought to see that *they risk losing more than they can hope to gain* if they succeed in censoring pornography, because antifeminists will have equal right to censor the things they find offensive but that many feminists seek to publish.

Backing • Why should the reader agree with Jacoby's grounds? She does not appeal to expert authority, the results of experimental tests or other statistical data, or the support of popular opinion. Instead, she relies principally on two things — but without saying so explicitly.

First, she assumes that the reader accepts the propositions that freedom of self-expression is valuable and that censoring it requires the strongest of reasons. If there is no fundamental agreement on these propositions, several of her reasons cease to support her claim.

Second, she relies on the reader's open-mindedness and willingness to evaluate commonsense (untechnical, ordinary, familiar) considerations at each step of the way. She relies also on the reader having had some personal experience with erotica, pornography, and art. Without that open-mindedness and experience, a reader is not likely to be persuaded by her replies to the feminist demand for censorship.

Modal Qualifiers • Jacoby defends what she calls an "absolute interpretation" of the First Amendment, that is, the view that *all* censorship of words, pictures, ideas, is not only inconsistent with the First Amendment, it is also politically unwise and morally objectionable. She allows that *some* pornography is highly offensive (it offends her, she insists); she allows that *some* pornography ("kiddie porn") may even be harmful to *some* viewers. But she also insists that *more* harm than good would result from the censorship of pornography. She points out that *some* paintings of nude women are art, not pornography; she implies that it is *impossible* to draw a sharp line between permissible erotic pornography and impermissible offensive pornography. She clearly believes that *all* Americans ought to understand and defend the First Amendment under the "absolute interpretation" she favors.

Rebuttals • Jacoby mentions several objections to her views, and perhaps the most effective aspect of her entire argument is her skill in identifying possible objections and meeting them effectively. (Notice the diversity of the objections and the various ways in which she replies.)

Objection: Some of her women friends tell her she is wrong.

Rebuttal: She admits she's a "First Amendment junkie" and she doesn't apologize for it.

Objection: "Kiddie porn" is harmful and deserves censorship.

Rebuttal: Such material is *not* protected by the First Amendment, because it is an "abuse of power" of adults over children.

Objection: Pornography is a form of violence against women, and therefore it is especially harmful.

Rebuttal: (a) No, it really isn't harmful, but it is disgusting and offensive. (b) In any case, it's surely not as harmful as allowing American neo-Nazis to parade in Jewish neighborhoods. (Jacoby is referring to the march in Skokie, Illinois, in 1977, upheld by the courts as permissible political expression despite its offensiveness to survivors of the Nazi concentration camps.)

Objection: Censoring pornography advances public respect for women.

Rebuttal: Censoring *Ms.* magazine, which antifeminists have already done, undermines women's freedom and self-expression.

Objection: Reasonable people can tell pornography when they see it, so censoring it poses no problems.

Rebuttal: Yes, there are clear cases of gross pornography; but there are lots of borderline cases, as women themselves prove when they disagree over whether a photo in *Penthouse* is offensively erotic or "lovely" and "sensuous."

23

A Logician's View: Deduction,
Induction, Fallacies

In Chapter 3 we introduced these terms. Now we will discuss them in
greater detail.

DEDUCTION

The basic aim of deductive reasoning is to start with some assumption
or premise, and extract from it consequences that are concealed but implicit in it. Thus, taking the simplest case, if I assert

(1) The cat is on the mat,

it is a matter of simple deduction to infer that

(2) The mat is under the cat.

Everyone would grant that (2) is entailed by, or follows from (1)—or, that
(2) can be validly deduced from (1)—because of the meaning of the key
connective concepts in each proposition. Anyone who understands English
knows that, whatever A and B are, if A is *on* B, then B must be *under* A.
Thus, in this and all other cases of valid deductive reasoning, we can say
not only that we are entitled to *infer* the conclusion from the premise—in
this case, infer (2) from (1)—but that the premise *implies* or entails the
conclusion. Remember, too, the inference of (2) from (1) does not depend
on the truth of (1). (2) follows from (1) whether or not (1) is true; consequently, if (1) is true then so is (2); but if (1) is false then (2) is false, also.
Let's take another example—more interesting, but comparably sim-
ple:

(3) President Truman was underrated by his critics.

Given (3), a claim amply verified by events of the 1950s, one is entitled to infer

(4) The critics underrated President Truman.

On what basis can we argue that (3) implies (4)? The two propositions are equivalent because a rule of English grammar assures us that we can convert the position of subject and predicate phrases in a sentence by shifting from the passive to the active voice (or vice versa); without any change in the conditions that make the proposition true (or false).

Both pairs of examples illustrate that in deductive reasoning, our aim is to transform, reformulate, or restate in our conclusion some (or, as in the two examples above, all) of the information contained in our premises.

Remember, even though a proposition or statement follows from a previous proposition or statement, the statements need not be true. We can see why if we consider another example. Suppose someone asserts or claims that

(5) The Hudson River is longer than the Mississippi.

As every student of American geography knows, (5) is false. But, false or not, we can validly deduce from it:

(6) The Mississippi is shorter than the Hudson.

This inference is valid (even though the conclusion is untrue) because the conclusion follows logically (more precisely, deductively) from (5): In English, as we know, the meaning of "A shorter than B," which appears in (6), is simply the converse of "B is longer than A," which appears in (5).

The deductive relation between (5) and (6) reminds us again that the idea of *validity*, which is so crucial to deduction, is not the same as the idea of *truth*. False propositions have implications—logical consequences— too, every bit as precisely as do true propositions.

In the three pairs of examples so far, what can we point to as the *warrant* for our claims? Well, look at the reasoning in each case; the arguments rely on rules of ordinary English. In the first and third pairs of examples, it is a rule of English semantics; in the second pair it is a rule of English syntax. Change those rules and the inferences will no longer be valid; fail to comply with those rules and one will not trust the inferences.

In many cases, of course, the deductive inference or pattern of reasoning is much more complex than that which we have seen in the examples so far. When we introduced the idea of deduction in Chapter 3, we gave as our primary example the syllogism. Here is another example:

(7) Texas is larger than California; California is larger than Arizona; therefore, Texas is larger than Arizona.

The conclusion in this syllogism is derivable from the two premises; that is, anyone who asserts the two premises is committed to accepting the conclusion as well, whether or not one thinks of it.

Notice again that the *truth* of the conclusion is not established merely by validity of the inference. The conclusion in this syllogism happens to be true. And the premises of this syllogism imply the conclusion. But the argument *proves* the conclusion only because both of the premises on which the conclusion depends are true. Even a Californian admits that Texas is larger than California, which in turn is larger than Arizona. In other words, argument (7) is a *sound* argument, because (as we explained in Chapter 3) it is valid and all its premises are true. All—and only—arguments that *prove* their conclusions have these two traits.

How might we present the warrant for the argument in (7)? Short of a crash course in formal logic, either of two strategies might suffice. One is to argue from the fact that the validity of the inference depends on the meaning of a key concept, *being larger than,* which has the property of *transitivity,* a property that many concepts share (for example, *is equal to, is to the right of, is smarter than*—all are transitive concepts). Consequently, whatever A, B, and C are, if A is larger than B, and B larger than C, then A will be larger than C. The final step is to substitute Texas, California, and Arizona for A, B, and C, respectively.

A second strategy is to think of representing Texas, California, and Arizona by concentric circles, with the largest for Texas, a smaller circle inside it for California, and a smaller one inside California for Arizona. (This is an adaptation of the technique used in elementary formal logic known as Venn diagrams.) In this manner one can give graphic display to the important fact that the conclusion follows from the premises, because one can literally *see* the conclusion represented by nothing more than a representation of the premises.

Both of these strategies bring out the fact that validity of deductive inference is a purely *formal* property of argument. Each strategy abstracts the form from the content of the propositions involved to show how the concepts in the premises are related to the concepts in the conclusion.

Not all deductive reasoning occurs in syllogisms, however, or at least not in syllogisms like the one in (7). (The term *syllogism* is sometimes used to refer to any deductive argument of whatever form, provided only that it has two premises.) In fact, syllogisms such as (7) are not the commonest form of our deductive reasoning at all. Nor are they the simplest (and of course not the most complex). For an argument that is even simpler, consider this:

(8) If the horses are loose, then the barn door was left unlocked. The horses are loose. Therefore, the barn door was left unlocked.

Here the pattern of reasoning is called **modus ponens,** which means positing or laying down the minor premise ("the horses are loose"). It is also called **hypothetical syllogism,** because its major premise ("if the horses are loose, then the barn door was left unlocked") is a hypothetical or conditional proposition. The argument has the form: If A then B; A; therefore B. Notice that the content of the assertions represented by A and B do not matter; any set of expressions having the same form or structure will do equally well, including assertions built out of meaningless terms, as in this example:

(9) If the slithy toves, then the gyres gimble. The slithy toves. Therefore the gyres gimble.

Argument (9) has exactly the same form as argument (8), and as a piece of deductive inference it is every bit as good. Unlike (8), however, (9) is of no interest to us because none of its assertions make any sense (unless you are a reader of Lewis Carroll's "Jabberwocky," and even then the sense of (9) is doubtful). You cannot, in short, use a valid deductive argument to prove anything unless the premises and the conclusion are *true*, but they can't be true unless they *mean* something in the first place.

This parallel between arguments (8) and (9) shows once again that deductive validity in an argument rests on the *form* or structure of the argument, and not on its content or meaning. If all one can say about an argument is that it is valid—that is, its conclusion follows from the premises— one has not given a sufficient reason for accepting the argument's conclusion. It has been said that the Devil can quote Scripture; similarly, an argument can be deductively valid and of no further interest or value whatever, because valid (but false) conclusions can be drawn from false or even meaningless assumptions. Nevertheless, although validity by itself is not enough, it is a necessary condition of any deductive argument that purports to *prove* its conclusion.

Now let us consider another argument with the same form as (8) and (9), only more interesting.

(10) If President Truman knew the Japanese were about to surrender, then it was immoral of him to order that atom bombs be dropped on Hiroshima and Nagasaki. Truman knew the Japanese were about to surrender. Therefore it was immoral of him to order dropping those bombs.

As in the two previous examples, anyone who assents to the premises in argument (10) must assent to the conclusion; the form of arguments (8), (9), and (10) is identical. But do the premises of argument (10) *prove* the conclusion? That depends on whether both premises are true. Well, are they? This turns on a number of considerations, and it is worthwhile pausing to examine this argument closely to illustrate the kinds of things that are involved in answering this question.

Let us begin by examining the second (minor) premise. Its truth is controversial even to this day. Autobiography, memoranda, other documentary evidence—all are needed to assemble the evidence to back up the grounds for the thesis or claim made in the conclusion of this valid argument. Evaluating this material effectively will probably involve not only further deductions, but inductive reasoning as well.

Now consider the first (major) premise in argument (10). Its truth doesn't depend on what history shows, but on the moral principles one accepts. The major premise has the form of a hypothetical proposition ("if . . . then . . ."), and asserts a connection between two very different kinds of things. The antecedent of the hypothetical (the clause following "if") mentions facts about Truman's *knowledge,* and the consequent of the hypothetical (the clause following "then") mentions facts about the *morality* of his conduct in light of such knowledge. The major premise as a whole can thus be seen as expressing a principle of *moral responsibility.*

Such principles can, of course, be controversial. In this case, for instance, is the principle peculiarly relevant to the knowledge and conduct of a president of the United States? Probably not; it is far more likely that this principle is merely a special case of a more general proposition about anyone's moral responsibility. (After all, we know a great deal more about the conditions of our own moral responsibility than we do about those of high government officials.) We might express this more general principle in this way: If we have knowledge that would make our violent conduct unnecessary, then we are immoral if we deliberately act violently anyway. Thus, accepting this general principle can serve as a basis for defending the major premise of argument (10).

We have examined this argument in some detail because it illustrates the kinds of considerations needed to test whether a given argument is not only valid but whether its premises are true — that is, whether its premises really prove the conclusion.

The great value of the form of argument known as hypothetical syllogism, exemplified by arguments (8), (9), and (10), is that the structure of the argument is so simple and so universally applicable in reasoning that it is often both easy and worthwhile to formulate one's claims so that they can be grounded by an argument of this sort.

Before leaving the subject of deductive inference, consider three other forms of argument, each of which can be found in actual use elsewhere in the readings in this volume. The simplest of these is **disjunctive syllogism,** so called because, again, it has two premises, and its major premise is a **disjunction.** That is, a disjunctive syllogism is a complex assertion built from two or more alternatives joined by the conjunction "or"; each of these alternatives is called a **disjunct.** For example,

(11) Either censorship of television shows is overdue, or our society is indifferent to the education of its youth. Our society is not indifferent to the education of its youth. Therefore, censorship of television is overdue.

Notice, by the way, that the validity of an argument, as in this case, does not turn on pedantic repetition of every word or phrase as the argument moves along; nonessential elements can be dropped, or equivalent expressions substituted for variety without adverse effect on the reasoning. Thus, in conversation, or in writing, the argument in (11) might actually be presented like this:

(12) Either censorship of television is overdue, or our society is indifferent to the education of its youth. But, of course, we aren't indifferent; it's censorship that's overdue.

The key feature of disjunctive syllogism, as example (12) suggests, is that the conclusion is whichever of the disjuncts is left over after the others have been negated in the minor premise. Thus, we could easily have a very complex disjunctive syllogism, with a dozen disjuncts in the major premise, and seven of them denied in the minor premise, leaving a conclusion of the remaining five. Usually, however, a disjunctive argument is formulated in this manner: Assert a disjunction with two or more disjuncts in the major premise; then *deny all but one* in the minor premise; and infer validly the remaining disjunct as the conclusion. That was the form of argument (12).

Another type of argument, especially favored by orators and rhetoricians, is the **dilemma**. Ordinarily we use the term "dilemma" in the sense of an awkward predicament, as when we say, "His dilemma was that he didn't have enough money to pay the waiter." But when logicians refer to a dilemma, they mean a forced choice between two or more equally unattractive alternatives. For example, the predicament of the United States government during the mid-1980s as it faced the crisis brought on by terrorist attacks on American civilian targets, which were believed, during that time, to be inspired and supported by the Libyan government, can be formulated in a dilemma:

(13) If the United States bombs targets in Libya, innocent people will be killed and the Arab world will be angered. If the United States doesn't bomb Libyan targets, then terrorists will go unpunished and the United States will lose respect among other governments. Either the United States bombs Libyan targets or it doesn't. Therefore, in either case unattractive consequences will follow: The innocent will be killed or terrorists will go unpunished.

Notice first the structure of the argument: two conditional propositions asserted as premises, followed by another premise that states a **necessary truth.** (The premise, "Either we bomb the Libyans or we don't," is a disjunction of two exhaustive alternatives, and so one of the two alternatives must be true. Such a statement is often called analytically true, or a *tautology.*) No doubt the conclusion of this dilemma follows from its premises.

But does the argument prove, as it purports to do, that whatever the United States government does, it will suffer undesirable consequences? If the two conditional premises failed to exhaust the possibilities, then one can escape from the dilemma by going "between the horns"; that is, by finding a third alternative. If (as in this case) that is not possible, one can still ask whether both of the main premises are true. (In this argument, it should be clear that neither of these main premises spells out all or even most of the consequences that could be foreseen.) Even so, in cases where both these conditional premises are true, it may be that the consequences of one alternative are nowhere nearly so bad as those of the other. If that is true, but our reasoning stops before evaluating that fact, we may be guilty of failing to distinguish between the greater and the lesser of two admitted evils. The logic of the dilemma itself cannot decide on this choice for us. Instead, we must bring to bear empirical inquiry and imagination to the evaluation of the grounds of the dilemma itself.

Finally, one of the most powerful and dramatic forms of argument is **reductio ad absurdum** (from the Latin, meaning "reduction to absurdity"). The idea of a reductio argument is to establish a conclusion by refuting its opposite, and it is an especially attractive tactic when you can use it to refute your opponent's position in order to prove your own. For example, in Plato's *Republic,* Socrates asks an old gentleman, Cephalus, to define what right conduct is. Cephalus says that it is paying your debts and keeping your word. Socrates rejects this answer by showing that it leads to a contradiction. He argues that Cephalus cannot have given the correct answer because if we assume that he did, we will be quickly led into contradictions; in some cases when you keep your word you will nonetheless be doing the wrong thing. For suppose, says Socrates, that you borrowed a weapon from a man, promising to return it when he asks for it. One day he comes to your door, demanding his weapon and swearing angrily that he intends to murder a neighbor. Keeping your word under those circumstances is absurd, Socrates implies; and the reader of the dialogue is left to infer that Cephalus' definition, which led to this result, is refuted.

Let's take a closer look at another example. Suppose you are opposed to any form of gun control, whereas I am in favor of gun control. I might try to refute your position by attacking it with a reductio argument. To do that, I start out by assuming the very opposite of what I believe or favor, and try to establish a contradiction that results from following out the consequences of this initial assumption. My argument might look like this:

> (14) Let's assume your position, namely, that there ought to be no legal restrictions whatever on the sale and ownership of guns. That means that you'd permit having every neighborhood hardware store sell pistols and rifles to whoever walks in the door. But that's not all. You apparently also would permit selling machine guns to children, antitank weapons to lunatics, small-bore cannons to the near-sighted, as well as guns and the ammunition to go with them to anyone with a criminal record. But this is utterly preposterous. No one could favor such a dangerous policy. So the only question worth debating is what *kind* of gun control is necessary.

Now in this example, my reductio of your position on gun control is not based on claiming to show that you have strictly contradicted yourself, for there is no purely logical contradiction in opposing all forms of gun control. Instead, what I have tried to do (just as Socrates did) is to show that there is a contradiction between what you profess—no gun controls whatever—and what you probably really believe, if only you will stop to think about it—no lunatic should be allowed to buy a loaded machine gun.

My refutation of your position rests on whether I succeed in establishing an inconsistency among your own beliefs. If it turns out that you really believe lunatics should be free to purchase guns and ammunition, then my attempted refutation fails.

In explaining reductio ad absurdum, we have had to rely on another idea fundamental to logic, that of **contradiction,** or inconsistency. (We used this idea, remember, to define validity in Chapter 3. A deductive argument is valid if and only if affirming the premises and denying the conclusion results in a contradiction.) The opposite of contradiction is **consistency,** a notion of hardly less importance to good reasoning than validity. These concepts deserve a few words of further explanation and illustration. Consider this pair of assertions:

(15) Abortion is homicide.
(16) Racism is unfair.

No one would plausibly claim that we can infer or deduce (16) from (15), or, for that matter, (15) from (16). This almost goes without saying, because there is no evident connection between (15) and (16). They are unrelated assertions; logically speaking, they are *independent* of each other. In such cases the two assertions are mutually consistent; that is, both could be true—or both could be false. But now consider another proposition:

(17) Euthanasia is not murder.

Could a person assert (15) *abortion is homicide* and also assert (17), and be consistent? This question is equivalent to asking whether one could assert the **conjunction** of these two propositions, namely,

(18) Abortion is homicide and euthanasia is not murder.

It is not so easy to say whether (18) is consistent or inconsistent. The kinds of moral scruples that might lead a person to assert one of these conjuncts (that is, one of the two initial propositions, *Abortion is homicide* and *Euthanasia is not murder*) might lead to the belief that the other one must be false, and thus to the conclusion that (18) is inconsistent. (Notice that if [15] were the assertion that *Abortion is murder,* instead of *Abortion is homicide,* the problem of asserting consistently both [15] and [17] would be more acute.) Yet, if we think again, we might imagine someone being convinced that there is no inconsistency in asserting that *Abortion is homicide,* say, and that *Euthanasia is not murder,* or even the reverse. (For instance, suppose you believed that the unborn deserve a chance to live, and that putting elderly persons to death in a painless manner and with their consent confers a benefit on them.)

Let us generalize: We can say of any set of propositions that they are *consistent* if and only if *all could be true together.* (Notice that it follows from this definition that propositions that mutually imply each other, as do *The cat is on the mat* and *The mat is under the cat,* are consistent.) Remember that, once again, the truth of the assertions in question does not matter. Propositions can be consistent or not, quite apart from whether they are true. Not so their falsehood: It follows from our definition of consistency that an *inconsistent* proposition must be *false.* (We have relied on this idea in explaining how a reductio ad absurdum works.)

Assertions or claims that are not consistent can take either of two forms. Suppose you assert proposition (15), that abortion is homicide, early in an essay you are writing, but after you say

(19) Abortion is harmless.

You have now asserted a position on abortion that is strictly **contrary** to the one with which you began; contrary in the sense that both assertions (15) and (19) cannot be true. It is simply not true that if an abortion involves killing a human being (which is what *homicide* strictly means) then it causes no one any harm (killing a person always causes harm — even if it is excusable, or justifiable, or not wrong, or the best thing to do in the circumstances, and so on). Notice that although (15) and (19) cannot both be true, they can both be false. In fact, many people who are perplexed about the morality of abortion believe precisely this. They concede that abortion does harm the fetus, so (19) must be false; but they also believe that abortion doesn't kill a person, so (15) must also be false.

Or consider another, simpler case. If you describe the glass as half empty and I describe it as half full, both of us can be right; the two assertions are consistent, even though they sound vaguely incompatible. (This is the reason that disputing over whether the glass is half full or half empty has become the popular paradigm of a futile, purely *verbal disagreement.*) But if I describe the glass as half empty whereas you insist that it is two-thirds empty, then we have a real disagreement; your description and mine are strictly contrary, in that both cannot be true — although both can be false. (Both are false if the glass is only one-quarter full.)

This, by the way, enables us to define the difference between a pair of contradictory propositions and a pair of contrary propositions. Two propositions are **contrary** if and only if both cannot be true (although both can be false); two propositions are **contradictory** if and only if one is true and the other is false.

Genuine contradiction, and not merely contrary assertion, is the situation we should expect to find in some disputes. Someone advances a thesis — such as the assertion in (15), *Abortion is homicide* — and someone else flatly contradicts it by the simple expedient of negating it, thus:

(20) Abortion is not homicide.

If we can trust public opinion polls, many of us are not sure whether to agree with (15) or with (20). But we should agree that whichever is true, *both* cannot be true, and *both* cannot be false. The two assertions, between them, exclude all other possibilities; they pose a forced choice for our belief. (Again, we have met this idea, too, in a reductio ad absurdum.)

Now it is one thing for Jack and Jill in a dispute or argument to contradict each other. It is quite another matter for Jack to contradict himself. One wants (or should want) to avoid self-contradiction because of the embarrassing position in which one then finds oneself. Once I have contradicted myself, what are others to believe I really believe? What, indeed, *do* I believe, for that matter?

It may be, as Emerson observed, that a "foolish consistency is the hobgoblin of little minds"—that is, it may be shortsighted to purchase a consistency in one's beliefs at the expense of flying in the face of common sense. But making an effort to avoid a foolish inconsistency is the hallmark of serious thinking.

INDUCTION

Deduction involves logical thinking that applies to any assertion or claim whatever—because every possible statement, true or false, has its deductive logical consequences. Induction is relevant to one kind of assertion only; namely, to **empirical** or *factual* claims. Other kinds of assertions (such as definitions, mathematical equations, and moral or legal norms) simply are not the product of inductive reasoning and cannot serve as a basis for further inductive thinking.

And so, in studying the methods of induction, we are exploring tactics and strategies useful in gathering and then using **evidence**—empirical, observational, experimental—in support of a belief as its ground. Modern scientific knowledge is the product of these methods, and they differ somewhat from one science to another because they depend on the theories and technology appropriate to each of the sciences. Here, all we can do is discuss generally the more abstract features common to inductive inquiry generally. For fuller details, you must eventually consult your local physicist, chemist, geologist, or their colleagues and counterparts in other scientific fields.

Observation and Inference

Let us begin with a simple example. Suppose we have evidence (actually we don't, but that will not matter for our purposes) in support of the claim that

(1) Two hundred and thirty persons observed in a sample of 500 smokers have cardiovascular disease.

The basis for asserting (1)—the evidence or ground—would be, presumably, straightforward physical examination of the 500 persons in the sample, one by one.

With this claim in hand, we can think of the purpose and methods of induction as being pointed in both of two opposite directions: toward establishing the basis or ground of the very empirical proposition with which we start, in this example the observation stated in (1); or toward understanding what that observation indicates or suggests as a more general, inclusive, or fundamental fact of nature.

In each case, we start from something we *do* know (or take for granted and treat as a sound starting point) — some fact of nature, perhaps a striking or commonplace event that we have observed and recorded — and then go on to something we do *not* fully know and perhaps cannot directly observe. In example (1), only the second of these two orientations is of any interest, and so let us concentrate exclusively on it. Let us also generously treat as a *method* of induction any regular pattern or style of nondeductive reasoning that we could use to support a claim such as that in (1).

Anyone truly interested in the observed fact that (1) *230 of 500 smokers have cardiovascular disease* is likely to start speculating about, and thus be interested in finding out, whether any or all of several other propositions are also true. For example, one might wonder whether

(2) *All* smokers have cardiovascular disease or will develop it during their lifetimes.

This claim is a straightforward generalization of the original observation as reported in claim (1). When we think inductively about the linkage between (1) and (2), we are reasoning from an observed sample (some smokers, that is, 230 of the 500 *observed*) to the entire membership of a more inclusive class (*all* smokers, whether observed or not). The fundamental question raised by reasoning from the narrower claim (1) to the broader claim (2) is whether we have any ground for believing that what is true of *some* members of a class is true of them *all*. So the difference between (1) and (2) is that of *quantity* or scope.

We can also think inductively about the *relation* between the factors mentioned in (1). Having observed data as reported in (1), we may be tempted to assert a different and profounder kind of claim:

(3) Smoking *causes* cardiovascular disease.

Here our interest is not merely in generalizing from a sample to a whole class; it is the far more important one of *explaining* the observation with which we began in claim (1). Certainly the preferred, even if not the only, mode of explanation for a natural phenomenon is a *causal* explanation. In proposition (3), we propose to explain the presence of one phenomenon (cardiovascular disease) by the prior occurrence of an independent phenomenon (smoking). The observation reported in (1) is now being used as evidence or support for this new conjecture stated in (3).

Our original claim in (1) asserted no causal relation between anything and anything else; whatever the cause of cardiovascular disease may be, that cause is not observed, mentioned, or assumed in assertion (1). Similarly, the observation asserted in claim (1) is consistent with many explanations. For example, the explanation of (1) might not be (3), but some other, undetected, carcinogenic factor unrelated to smoking, for instance, exposure to high levels of radon. The question one now faces is what can be added to (1), or teased out of it, in order to produce an adequate ground for claiming (3). (We shall return to this example for closer scrutiny.)

But there is a third way to go beyond (1). Instead of a straightforward generalization, as we had in (2), or a pronouncement on the cause of a phenomenon, as in (3), we might have a somewhat more complex and cautious further claim in mind, such as this:

(4) Smoking is a factor in the causation of cardiovascular disease in some persons.

This proposition, like (3), advances a claim about causation. But (4) is obviously a weaker claim than (3). That is, other observations, theories, or evidence that would require us to reject (3) might be consistent with (4); evidence that would support (4) could easily fail to be enough to support (3). Consequently, it is even possible that (4) is true although (3) is false, because (4) allows for other (unmentioned) factors in the causation of cardiovascular disease (genetic or dietary factors, for example) which may not be found in all smokers.

Propositions (2), (3), and (4) differ from proposition (1) in an important respect. We began by assuming that (1) states an empirical fact based on direct observation, whereas these others do not. Instead, they state empirical *hypotheses* or conjectures — tentative generalizations not fully confirmed — each of which goes beyond the observed facts asserted in (1). Each of (2), (3), and (4) can be regarded as an *inductive inference* from (1). We can also say that (2), (3), and (4) are hypotheses relative to (1), even if relative to some other starting point (such as all the information that scientists today really have about smoking and cardiovascular disease) they are not.

Probability

Another way of formulating the last point is to say that whereas proposition (1), a statement of observed fact, has a **probability** of 1.0 — that is, it is absolutely certain — the probability of each of the hypotheses stated in (2), (3), and (4), *relative* to (1) is smaller than 1.0. (We need not worry here about how much smaller than 1.0 the probabilities are, nor about how to calculate these probabilities precisely.) Relative to some starting point other than (1), however, the probability of these same three hypotheses might be quite different. Of course, it still would not be 1.0, absolute certainty. But it takes only a moment's reflection to realize that, whatever may be the probability of (2) or (3) or (4) relative to (1), those probabilities in each case will be quite different relative to different information, such as this:

> (5) Ten persons observed in a sample of 500 smokers have cardiovascular disease.

The idea that a given proposition can have different probabilities relative to different bases is fundamental to all inductive reasoning. It can be convincingly illustrated by the following example. Suppose we want to consider the probability of this proposition being true:

> (6) Susanne Smith will live to be eighty.

Taken as an abstract question of fact, we cannot even guess what the probability is with any assurance. But we can do better than guess; we can in fact even calculate the answer, if we are given some further information. Thus, suppose we are told that

> (7) Susanne Smith is seventy-nine.

Our original question then becomes one of determining the probability that (6) is true given (7); that is, relative to the evidence contained in proposition (7). No doubt, if Susanne Smith really is seventy-nine, then the probability that she will live to be eighty is greater than if we know only that

> (8) Susanne Smith is more than nine years old.

Obviously, a lot can happen to Susanne in the seventy years between nine and seventy-nine that is not very likely to happen to her in the one year between seventy-nine and eighty. And so, proposition (6) is more probable relative to proposition (7) than it is relative to proposition (8).

Let us disregard (7) and instead further suppose for the sake of the argument that the following is true:

> (9) Ninety percent of the women alive at seventy-nine live to be eighty.

Given this additional information, we now have a basis for answering our original question about proposition (6) with some precision. But suppose, in addition to (8), we are also told that

> (10) Susanne Smith is suffering from inoperable cancer.

and also that

> (11) The survival rate for women suffering from inoperable cancer is 0.6 years (that is, the average life span for women after a diagnosis of inoperable cancer is about seven months).

With this new information, the probability that (6) will be true has dropped significantly, all because we can now estimate the probability in relation to a new body of evidence.

The probability of an event, thus, is not a fixed number, but one that varies, because it is always relative to some evidence — and given different evidence, one and the same event can have different probabilities. In other words, the probability of any event is always relative to how much is known (assumed, believed), and because different persons may know different things about a given event, or the same person may know different things at different times, one and the same event can have two or more probabilities. This conclusion is not a paradox but a logical consequence of the concept of what it is for an event to have (that is, to be assigned) a probability.

If we shift to the *calculation* of probabilities, we find that generally we have two ways to calculate them. One way to proceed is by the method of **a priori** or **equal probabilities,** that is, by reference to the relevant possibilities taken abstractly and apart from any other information. Thus, in an election contest with only two candidates, A and B, each of the candidates has a fifty-fifty chance of winning (whereas in a three-candidate race, each candidate would have one chance in three of winning). Therefore the probability that candidate A will win is 0.5, and the probability that candidate B will win is also 0.5. (The sum of the probabilities of all possible independent outcomes must always equal 1.0, which is obvious enough if you think about it.)

But in politics the probabilities are not reasonably calculated so abstractly. We know that many empirical factors affect the outcome of an election, and that a calculation of probabilities in ignorance of those factors is likely to be drastically misleading. In our example of the two-candidate election, suppose candidate A has strong party support and is the incumbent, whereas candidate B represents a party long out of power and is further handicapped by being relatively unknown. No one who knows anything about electoral politics would give B the same chance of winning as A. The two events are not equiprobable in relation to all the information available.

Similarly, suppose hundreds of throws with a given pair of dice reveal that a pair of ones comes up not one-twelfth of the time, as would be expected if all possible combinations were equally possible, but only 1 time in 100. This information would immediately suggest that either the throws were rigged or the dice are loaded, and in any case that the probability of a pair of ones for these dice is not 0.08 (1 in 12) but much less, perhaps 0.01 (1 in 100). Probabilities calculated in this way are **relative frequencies;** that is, they are calculated in terms of the observed frequency with which a specified event actually occurs.

Both methods of calculating probabilities are legitimate; in each case the calculation is relative to observed circumstances. But, as the examples show, it is most reasonable to have recourse to the method of equiprobabilities only when few or no other factors affecting possible outcomes are known.

Mill's Methods

Let us return to our earlier discussion of smoking and cardiovascular disease, and consider in greater detail the question of a causal connection between the two phenomena. We began thus:

> (1) Two hundred and thirty of an observed sample of 500 smokers had cardiovascular disease.

We regarded (1) as an observed fact, though in truth, of course, it is mere supposition. Our question now is, how might we augment this information so as to strengthen our confidence that

> (3) Smoking causes cardiovascular disease.

or at least

> (4) Smoking is a factor in the causation of cardiovascular disease in some persons.

Suppose further examination showed that

> (12) In the sample of 230 smokers with cardiovascular disease, no other suspected factor (such as genetic predisposition, lack of physical exercise, age over fifty) was also observed.

Such an observation would encourage us to believe (3) or (4) is true. Why? We are encouraged to believe it because we are inclined to believe also that whatever the cause of a phenomenon is, it must *always* be present when its effect is present. Thus, the inference from (1) to (3) or (4) is supported by (12), using **Mill's Method of Agreement,** named after the British philosopher, John Stuart Mill (1806–1873), who first formulated it. It is called a method of agreement because of the way in which the inference relies on *agreement* among the observed phenomena where a presumed cause is thought to be *present.*

Let us now suppose that in our search for evidence to support (3) or (4) we conduct additional research, and discover:

> (13) In a sample of 500 nonsmokers, selected to be representative of both sexes, different ages, dietary habits, exercise patterns, and so on, none is observed to have cardiovascular disease.

This observation would further encourage us to believe that we had obtained significant additional confirmation of (3) or (4). Why? Because we now know that factors present (such as male sex, lack of exercise, family history of cardiovascular disease) in cases where the effect is absent (no cardiovascular disease observed) cannot be the cause. This is an example of **Mill's Method of Difference,** so called because the cause or causal factor of an effect must be *different* from whatever the factors are that are present when the effect is *absent.*

Suppose now that, increasingly confident we have found the cause of cardiovascular disease, we study our first sample of 230 smokers ill with the disease, and discover this:

> (14) Those who smoke two or more packs of cigarettes daily for ten or more years have cardiovascular disease either much younger or much more severely than those who smoke less.

This is an application of **Mill's Method of Concomitant Variation,** perhaps the most convincing of the three methods. Here we deal not merely with the presence of the conjectured cause (smoking) or the absence of the effect we are studying (cardiovascular disease), as we were previously, but with the more interesting and subtler matter of the *degree and regularity of the correlation* of the supposed cause and effect. According to the observations reported in (14), it strongly appears that the more we have of the "cause" (smoking) the sooner or the more intense the onset of the "effect" (cardiovascular disease).

Notice, however, what happens to our confirmation of (3) and (4) if, instead of the observation reported in (14), we had observed:

> (15) In a representative sample of 500 nonsmokers, cardiovascular disease was observed in 34 cases.

(Let us not pause here to explain what makes a sample more or less representative of a population, although the representativeness of samples is vital to all statistical reasoning.) Such an observation would lead us almost immediately to suspect some other or additional causal factor: Smoking might indeed be *a* factor in causing cardiovascular disease, but it can hardly be *the* cause, because (using Mill's Method of Difference) we cannot have the effect, as we do in the observed sample reported in (15), unless we also have the cause.

An observation such as the one in (15), however, is likely to lead us to think our hypothesis that *smoking causes cardiovascular disease* has been disconfirmed. But we have a fall-back position ready; we can still defend a weaker hypothesis, namely (4), *Smoking is a factor in the causation of cardiovascular diseases in some persons.* Even if (3) stumbles over the evidence in (15), (4) does not. It is still quite possible that smoking is a factor in causing this disease, even if it is not the *only* factor — and if it is, then (4) is true.

Confirmation, Mechanism, and Theory

Notice that in the discussion so far, we have spoken of the *confirmation* of a hypothesis, such as our causal claim in (4), but not of its *verification*. (Similarly, we have imagined very different evidence, such as that stated in [15], leading us to speak of the *disconfirmation* of [3], though not of its *falsification*.) Confirmation (getting some evidence for) is weaker than verification (getting sufficient evidence to regard as true); and our (imaginary) evidence so far in favor of (4) falls well short of conclusive support. Further research—the study of more representative or much larger samples, for example—might yield very different observations. It might lead us to conclude that although initial research had confirmed our hypothesis about smoking as the cause of cardiovascular disease, the additional information obtained subsequently disconfirmed the hypothesis. For most interesting hypotheses, both in detective stories and in modern science, there is both confirming and disconfirming evidence simultaneously. The challenge is to evaluate the hypothesis by considering such conflicting evidence.

As long as we confine our observations to *correlations* of the sort reported in our several (imaginary) observations, such as proposition (1), *230 smokers in a group of 500 have cardiovascular disease,* or (12), *230 smokers with the disease share no other suspected factors,* such as lack of exercise, any defense of a *causal* hypothesis such as claim (3), *Smoking causes cardiovascular disease,* or claim (4), *Smoking is a factor in causing the disease,* is not likely to convince the skeptic or lead those with beliefs alternative to (3) and (4) to abandon them and agree with us. Why is that? It is because a causal hypothesis without any account of the *underlying mechanism* by means of which the (alleged) cause produces the effect will seem superficial. Only when we can specify in detail *how* the (alleged) cause produces the effect will the causal hypothesis be convincing.

In other cases, in which no mechanism can be found, we seek instead to embed the causal hypothesis in a larger *theory,* one that rules out as incompatible any causal hypothesis except the favored one. (That is, we appeal to the test of consistency and thereby bring deductive reasoning to bear on our problem.) Thus, perhaps we cannot specify any mechanism—any underlying structure that generates a regular sequence of events, one of which is the effect we are studying—to explain why, for example, the gravitational mass of a body causes it to attract other bodies. But we can embed this claim in a larger body of physical theory that rules out as inconsistent any alternative causal explanation. To do that convincingly in regard to any given causal hypothesis, as this example suggests, requires detailed knowledge of the current state of the relevant body of scientific theory, something far beyond our aim or need to consider in further detail here.

FALLACIES

The straight road on which sound reasoning proceeds gives little latitude for cruising about. Irrationality, carelessness, passionate attachment to one's unexamined beliefs, and the sheer complexity of some issues, not to mention Original Sin, occasionally spoil the reasoning of even the best of us. Although in this book we reprint many varied voices and arguments, we hope we have reprinted no readings that exhibit the most flagrant errors or commit the graver abuses against the canons of good reasoning. Nevertheless, an inventory of those abuses and their close examination can be an instructive (as well as an amusing) exercise. Instructive, because the diagnosis and repair of error helps to fix more clearly the principles of sound reasoning on which such remedial labors depend. Amusing, because we are so constituted that our perception of the nonsense of others can stimulate our mind, warm our heart, and give us comforting feelings of superiority.

The discussion that follows, then, is a quick tour through the twisting lanes, mudflats, forests, and quicksands of the faults that one sometimes encounters in reading arguments that stray from the highway of clear thinking.

We can and do apply the term "fallacy" to many types of errors, mistakes, and confusions in oral and written discourse, in which our reasoning has gone awry. For convenience, we can group the fallacies by referring to the six aspects of reasoning identified in the Toulmin Method, described earlier (p. 755). Let us take up first those fallacies that spoil our *claims* or our *grounds* for them. These are errors in the meaning, clarity, or sense of a sentence, or of some word or phrase in a sentence, being used in the role of a claim or ground. They are thus not so much errors of *reasoning* as they are errors in *reasons* or in the *claims* that our reasons are intended to support or criticize.

Many Questions

The old saw, "Have you stopped beating your wife?" illustrates the **fallacy of many questions.** This question, as one can readily see, is unanswerable unless both of its implicit presuppositions are true. The questioner presupposes that (a) the addressee has or had a wife, and that (b) he used to beat her. If either of these presuppositions is false, then the question is pointless; it cannot be answered strictly and simply either with a yes or a no.

Ambiguity

Near the center of the town of Concord, Massachusetts, is an empty field with a sign reading "Old Calf Pasture." Hmm. A pasture in former times in which calves grazed? A pasture now in use for old calves? An erstwhile pasture for old calves? The error here is **ambiguity;** brevity in the sign has produced a group of words that give rise to more than one possible interpretation, confusing the reader and (presumably) frustrating the signwriter's intentions.

Consider a more complex example. Suppose someone asserts *People have equal rights* and also *Everyone has a right to property.* Many people believe both these claims, but their combination involves an ambiguity. On one interpretation, the two claims entail that everyone has an *equal right* to property. (That is, you and I each have an equal right to whatever property we have.) But the two claims can also be interpreted to mean that everyone has a *right to equal property.* (That is, whatever property you have a right to, I have a right to the same, or at least equivalent, property.) The latter interpretation is radically revolutionary, whereas the former is not. Arguments over equal rights often involve this ambiguity.

Death by a Thousand Qualifications

In a letter of recommendation, sent in support of an applicant for a job on your newspaper, you find this sentence: "Young Smith was the best student I've ever taught in an English course." Pretty strong endorsement, you think, except that you do not know, because you have not been told, the letter writer is a very junior faculty member, has been teaching for only two years, is an instructor in the history department, and taught a section of freshman English as a courtesy for a sick colleague, and only eight students were enrolled in the course. Thanks to these implicit qualifications, the letter writer did not lie or exaggerate in his praise; but the effect of his sentence on you, the unwitting reader, is quite misleading. The explicit claim in the letter, and its impact on you, is quite different from the tacitly qualified claim in the mind of the writer.

The **fallacy of death by a thousand qualifications** gets its name from the ancient torture of death by a thousand small cuts. Thus, a bold assertion can be virtually killed, its true content reduced to nothing, bit by bit, as all the appropriate or necessary qualifications are added to it. Consider another example. Suppose you hear a politician describing another country (let's call it Ruritania so as not to offend anyone) as a "democracy"—except it turns out that Ruritania doesn't have regular elections, lacks a written constitution, has no independent judiciary, prohibits religious worship except of the state-designated deity, and so forth. So what is left of the original claim that Ruritania is a democracy is little or nothing. The qualifications have taken all the content out of the original description.

Oversimplification

"Poverty causes crime," "taxation is unfair," "Truth is stranger than fiction"—these are examples of generalizations that exaggerate and therefore oversimplify the truth. Poverty as such can't be the sole cause of crime, because many poor people do not break the law. Some taxes may be unfairly high, others unfairly low—but there is no reason to believe that *every* tax is unfair to all those who have to pay it. Some true stories do amaze us as much or more than some fictional stories, but the reverse is true, too. (In the language of the Toulmin Method, **oversimplification** is the result of a failure to use suitable modal qualifiers in formulating one's claims or grounds or backing.)

Suppressed Alternatives

Sometimes oversimplification takes a more complex form, in which contrary possibilities are wrongly presented as though they were exhaustive and exclusive. "Either we get tough with drug users or we must surrender

and legalize all drugs." Really? What about doing neither, and instead offering education and counseling, detoxification programs and incentives to
"Say No"? A favorite of debaters, the either/or assertion always runs the
risk of ignoring a third (or fourth) possibility. Some disjunctions are indeed
exhaustive: "Either we get tough with drug users or we do not." This
proposition, though vague (what does "get tough" really mean?), is a tautology; it cannot be false, and there is no third alternative. But most disjunctions do not express a pair of *contradictory* alternatives — they offer only a
pair of *contrary* alternatives, and mere contraries do not exhaust the possibilities (recall our discussion of contraries vs. contradictories, at pp.
766–67).

Equivocation

In a delightful passage in *Alice in Wonderland,* the king asks his messenger, "Who did you pass on the road?" and the messenger replies, "Nobody." This prompts the king to observe, "Of course, nobody walks slower
than you," provoking the messenger's sullen response: "I do my best. I'm
sure nobody walks much faster than I do." At this the king remarks with
surprise, "He can't do that or else he'd have been here first!" (This, by the
way, is the classic predecessor of the famous comic dialogue, "Who's on
First?" between the comedians Bud Abbott and Lou Costello.) The king
and the messenger are equivocating on the term *nobody.* The messenger
uses it in the normal way as an indefinite pronoun equivalent to "not anyone." But the king uses the word as though it were a proper noun, *Nobody,*
the rather odd name of some person. No wonder the king and the messenger talk right past each other.

Equivocation (from the Latin for "equal voice," that is, giving utterance to two meanings at the same time in one word or phase) can ruin otherwise good reasoning, as in this example: *Euthanasia is a good death; one
dies a good death when one dies peacefully in old age; therefore euthanasia
is dying peacefully in old age.* The etymology of *euthanasia* is literally "a
good death," and so the first premise is true. And the second premise is
certainly plausible. But the conclusion of this syllogism is false. Euthanasia
cannot be defined as a peaceful death in one's old age, for two reasons.
First, euthanasia requires the intervention of another person who kills
someone (or lets the person die); second, even a very young person can be
given euthanasia. The problem arises because "a good death" is used in the
second premise in a manner that does not apply to euthanasia. Both meanings of "a good death" are legitimate, but when used together they constitute an equivocation that spoils the argument.

The fallacy of equivocation takes us from the discussion of confusions
in individual claims or ground to the more troublesome fallacies that infect
the linkages between the claims we make and the grounds (or reasons) for
them. These are the fallacies that occur in statements that, following the
vocabulary of the Toulmin Method, are called the *warrant* of reasoning.

Each fallacy is an example of reasoning that involves a **non sequitur** (Latin for "It does not follow"). That is, the *claim* (the conclusion) does not follow from the *grounds* (the premises).

For a start, here is an obvious *non sequitur:* "He went to the movies on three consecutive nights, so he must love movies." Why doesn't the claim ("he must love movies") follow from the grounds ("He went to the movies on three consecutive nights")? Perhaps the person was just fulfilling an assignment in a film course (maybe he even hated movies so much that he had postponed three assignments to see films, and now had to see them all in quick succession), or maybe he went with a girlfriend who was a movie buff, or maybe . . . , well, one can think of any number of other possible reasons.

Composition

Could an all-star team of professional basketball players beat the Boston Celtics in their heyday, say the team of 1985–1986? Perhaps in one game or two, but probably not in seven out of a dozen games in a row. As students of the game know, teamwork is an indispensable part of outstanding performance, and the 1985–1986 Celtics were famous for their self-sacrificing style of play.

The **fallacy of composition** can be convincingly illustrated, therefore, in this argument: *A team of five NBA all-stars is the best team in basketball if each of the five players is the best at his position.* The fallacy is called composition because the reasoning commits the error of arguing from the true premise that each member of a group has a certain property to the false conclusion that the group (the composition) itself has the property. (That is, because A is the best player at forward, B is the best center, and so on, therefore the team of A, B . . . is the best team.)

Division

In the Bible, we are told that the apostles of Jesus were twelve and that Matthew was an apostle. Does it follow that Matthew was twelve? No. To argue in this way from a property of a group to a property of a member of that group is to commit the **fallacy of division.** The example of the Apostles may not be a very tempting instance of this error; here is a classic version that is a bit more interesting. If it is true that the average American family has 1.8 children, does it follow that your brother and sister-in-law are likely to have 1.8 children? If you think it does, you have committed the fallacy of division.

Poisoning the Well

During the 1970s some critics of the Equal Rights Amendment (ERA) argued against it by pointing out that Marx and Engels, in their *Communist Manifesto,* favored equality of women and men — and therefore ERA is immoral, or undesirable, and perhaps even a communist plot. This kind of reasoning is an attempt to **poison the well;** that is, an attempt to shift attention from the merits of the argument—the validity of the reasoning, the truth of the claims—to the source or origin of the argument. Such criticism nicely deflects attention from the real issue; namely, whether the view in question is true and what the quality of evidence is in its support. The mere fact that Marx (or Hitler, for that matter) believed something does not show that the belief is false or immoral; just because some scoundrel believes the world is round, that is no reason for you to believe it is flat.

Ad Hominem

Closely allied to poisoning the well is another fallacy, **ad hominem** argument (from the Latin for "against the person"). Since arguments and theories are not natural occurrences but are the creative products of particular persons, a critic can easily yield to the temptation to attack an argument or theory by trying to impeach or undercut the credentials of its advocates.

The Genetic Fallacy

Another member of the family of related fallacies that includes poisoning the well and ad hominem is the **genetic fallacy.** Here the error takes the form of arguing against some claim by pointing out that its origin (genesis) is tainted or that it was invented by someone deserving our contempt. Thus, one might attack the ideas of the Declaration of Independence by pointing out that its principal author, Thomas Jefferson, was a slaveholder. Assuming that it is not anachronistic and inappropriate to criticize a public figure of two centuries ago for practicing slavery, and conceding that slavery is morally outrageous, it is nonetheless fallacious to attack the ideas or even the sincerity of the Declaration by attempting to impeach the credentials of its author. Jefferson's moral faults do not by themselves falsify, make improbable, or constitute counterevidence to the truth or other merits of the claims made in his writings. At most, one's faults cast doubt on one's integrity or sincerity if one makes claims at odds with one's practice.

The genetic fallacy can take other forms less closely allied to ad hominem argument. For example, an opponent of the death penalty might argue:

> Capital punishment arose in barbarous times; but we claim to be civilized; therefore we should discard this relic of the past.

Such reasoning shouldn't be persuasive, because the question of the death penalty for our society must be decided by the degree to which it serves our purposes—justice and defense against crime, presumably—to which its historic origins are irrelevant. The practices of beer- and wine-making are as old as human civilization, but their origin in antiquity is no reason to outlaw them in our time. The curious circumstances in which something originates usually play no role whatever in its validity. Anyone who would argue that nothing good could possibly come from molds and fungi is refuted by Sir Alexander Fleming's discovery of penicillin in 1928.

Appeal to Authority

The example of Jefferson can be turned around to illustrate another fallacy. One might easily imagine someone from the South in 1860 defending the slavocracy of that day by appealing to the fact that no less a person than Jefferson — a brilliant public figure, thinker, and leader by any measure — owned slaves. Or, today, one might defend capital punishment on the ground that Abraham Lincoln, surely one of the nation's greatest presidents, signed many death warrants during the Civil War, authorizing the execution of Union soldiers. No doubt the esteem in which such figures as Jefferson and Lincoln are deservedly held amounts to impressive endorsement for whatever acts and practices, policies and institutions, they supported. But the **authority** of these figures in itself is not *evidence* for the truth of their views, and so their authority cannot be a reason for anyone to agree with them. Obviously, Jefferson and Lincoln themselves could not support their beliefs by pointing to the fact that they held them. Because their own authority is no reason for them to believe what they believe, it is no reason for anyone else, either.

Sometimes the appeal to authority is fallacious because the authoritative person is not an expert on the issue in dispute. The fact that a high-energy physicist has won the Nobel Prize is no reason for attaching any special weight to her views on the causes of cancer, the reduction of traffic accidents, or the legalization of marijuana. On the other hand, one would be well advised to attend to her views on the advisability of ballistic missile-defense systems. For there may be a connection between the kind of research for which she received the prize and the defense research projects.

All of us depend heavily on the knowledge of various experts and authorities, and so it ill-behooves us to ignore their views. Conversely, we should resist the temptation to accord their views on diverse subjects the same respect that we grant them in the area of their expertise.

The Slippery Slope

One of the most familiar arguments against any type of government regulation is that if it is allowed, then it will be just the first step down the path that leads to ruinous interference, overregulation, and totalitarian control. Fairly often we encounter this mode of arguments in the public debates over handgun control, the censorship of pornography, and physician-assisted suicide. The argument is called the **slippery slope argument** (or the **wedge argument,** from the way we use the thin end of a wedge to split solid things apart; it is also called, rather colorfully, "letting the camel's nose under the tent"). The fallacy here is in implying that the first step necessarily leads to the second, and so on down the slope to disaster, when in fact there is no necessary slide from the first step to the second at all. (Would handgun registration lead to a police state? Well, it hasn't in Switzerland.) Sometimes the argument takes the form of claiming that a seemingly innocent or even attractive principle that is being applied in a given case (censorship of pornography, to avoid promoting sexual violence) requires one for the sake of consistency to apply the same principle in other cases, only with absurd and catastrophic results (censorship of everything in print, to avoid hurting anyone's feelings).

Here's an extreme example of this fallacy in action:

> Automobiles cause more deaths than handguns do. If you oppose handguns on the ground that doing so would save lives of the innocent, you'll soon find yourself wanting to outlaw the automobile.

Does opposition to handguns have this consequence? Not necessarily. Most people accept without dispute the right of society to regulate the operation of motor vehicles by requiring drivers to have a license, a greater restriction than many states impose on gun ownership. Besides, a gun is a lethal weapon designed to kill whereas an automobile or truck is a vehicle designed for transportation. Private ownership and use in both cases entail risks of death to the innocent. But there is no inconsistency in a society's refusal to tolerate this risk in the case of guns and its willingness to do so in the case of automobiles.

The Appeal to Ignorance

In the controversy over the death penalty, as the debate between Edward Koch (p. 321) and attorney David Bruck (p. 326) shows, the issues of deterrence and executing the innocent are bound to be raised. Because no one knows how many innocent persons have been convicted for murder and wrongfully executed, it is tempting for abolitionists to argue that the death penalty is too risky. It is equally tempting for the proponent of the death penalty to argue that since no one knows how many people have been deterred from murder by the threat of execution, we abolish it at our peril.

Each of these arguments suffers from the same flaw: the **fallacy of appeal to ignorance.** Each argument invites the audience to draw an inference from a premise that is unquestionably true — but what is that premise? It asserts that there is something "we don't know." But what we *don't* know cannot be *evidence* for (or against) anything. Our ignorance is no reason for believing anything, except perhaps that we ought to try to undertake an appropriate investigation in order to reduce our ignorance and replace it with reliable information.

Begging the Question

The argument we have just considered also illustrates another fallacy. From the fact that you were not murdered yesterday, we cannot infer that the death penalty was a deterrent. Yet it is tempting to make this inference, perhaps because—all unawares—we are relying on the **fallacy of begging the question.** If someone tacitly assumes from the start that the death penalty is an effective deterrent, then the fact that you weren't murdered yesterday certainly looks like evidence for the truth of that assumption. But it isn't, so long as there are competing but unexamined alternative explanations, as in this case. (The fallacy is called "begging the question," *petitio principii* in Latin, because the conclusion of the argument is hidden among its assumptions—and so the conclusion, not surprisingly, follows from the premises.)

Of course, the fact that you weren't murdered is *consistent* with the claim that the death penalty is an effective deterrent, just as someone else's being murdered is also consistent with that claim (for an effective deterrent need not be a *perfect* deterrent). In general, from the fact that two propositions are consistent with each other, we cannot infer that either is evidence for the other.

False Analogy

Argument by analogy, as we have pointed out in Chapter 3, and as many of the selections in this book show, is a familiar and even indispensable mode of argument. But it can be treacherous, because it runs the risk of the **fallacy of false analogy.** Unfortunately, we have no simple or foolproof way of distinguishing between the useful and legitimate analogies, and the others. The key question to ask yourself is this: Do the two things put into analogy differ in any essential and relevant respect, or are they different only in unimportant and irrelevant aspects?

In a famous example from his discussion in support of suicide, philosopher David Hume rhetorically asked: "It would be no crime in me to divert the Nile or Danube from its course, were I able to effect such purposes. Where then is the crime of turning a few ounces of blood from their natural channel?" This is a striking analogy, except that it rests on a false assumption. No one has the right to divert the Nile or the Danube or any other major international watercourse; it would be a catastrophic crime to do so without the full consent of people living in the region, their government, and so forth. Therefore, arguing by analogy, one might well say that no one has the right to take his or her own life, either. Thus, Hume's own analogy can be used to argue against his thesis that suicide is no crime. But let us ignore the way in which his example can be turned against him. The analogy is a terrible one in any case. Isn't it obvious that the Nile, whatever its exact course, would continue to nourish Egypt and the Sudan, whereas the blood flowing out of someone's veins will soon leave that person dead?

The fact that the blood is the same blood, whether in one's body or in a pool on the floor (just as the water of the Nile is the same body of water whatever path it follows to the sea) is, of course, irrelevant to the question of whether one has the right to commit suicide.

Let us look at a more complex example. During the 1960s, when the nation was convulsed over the purpose and scope of our military involvement in Southeast Asia, advocates of more vigorous United States military participation appealed to the so-called "domino effect," supposedly inspired by a passing remark from President Eisenhower in the 1950s. The analogy refers to the way in which a row of standing dominoes will collapse, one after the other, if the first one is pushed. If Vietnam turns communist, according to this analogy, so too will its neighbors, Laos and Cambodia, followed by Thailand and then Burma, until the whole region is as communist as China to the north. The domino analogy (or metaphor) provided, no doubt, a vivid illustration, and effectively portrayed the worry of many anticommunists. But did it really shed any light on the likely pattern of political and military developments in the region? The history of events there during the 1970s and 1980s did not bear out the domino analogy.

Post Hoc Ergo Propter Hoc

One of the most tempting errors in reasoning is to ground a claim about causation on an observed temporal sequence; that is, to argue "after this therefore because of this" (which is what the phrase **post hoc ergo propter hoc** means in Latin). About thirty-five years ago, when the medical community first announced that smoking tobacco caused lung cancer, advocates for the tobacco industry replied that the doctors were guilty of this fallacy.

These industry advocates argued the medical researchers had merely noticed that in some people, lung cancer developed *after* considerable smoking, indeed, years after; but (they insisted) this correlation was not at all the same as a causal relation between smoking and lung cancer. True enough. The claim that A *causes* B is not the same as the claim that B comes after A. After all, it was possible that smokers as a group had some other common trait and that this factor was the true cause of their cancer.

As the long controversy over the truth about the causation of lung cancer shows, to avoid the appearance of fallacious *post hoc* reasoning one needs to find some way to link the observed phenomena (the correlation of smoking and the onset of lung cancer). This step requires some further theory, and preferably some experimental evidence for the exact sequence or physical mechanism, in full detail, of how ingestion of tobacco smoke is a crucial factor—and is not merely an accidental or happenstance prior event—in the subsequent development of the cancer.

Protecting the Hypothesis

In Chapter 3, we contrast *reasoning* and *rationalization* (or the finding of bad reasons for what one intends to believe anyway). Rationalization can take subtle forms, as the following example indicates. Suppose you're standing with a friend on the shore or on a pier, and you watch as a ship heads out to sea. As it reaches the horizon, it slowly disappears—first the hull, then the upper decks, and finally the tip of the mast. Because the ship (you both assume) isn't sinking, it occurs to you that you have in this sequence of observations convincing evidence that the earth's surface is curved. Nonsense, says your companion. Light waves sag, or bend down, over distances of a few miles, and so a flat surface (such as the ocean) can intercept them. Hence the ship, which appears to be going "over" the horizon, really isn't—it's just moving steadily farther and farther away in a straight line. Your friend, you discover to your amazement, is a card-carrying member of the Flat Earth Society (yes, there really is such an organization). Now most of us would regard the idea that light rays bend down in the manner required by the Flat Earther's argument as a rationalization whose sole purpose is to protect the flat-earth doctrine against counterevidence. We would be convinced it was a rationalization, and not a very good one at that, if the Flat Earther held to it despite a patient and thorough explanation from a physicist that showed modern optical theory to be quite incompatible with the view that light waves sag.

This example illustrates two important points about the *backing* of arguments. First, it is always possible to protect a hypothesis by abandoning adjacent or connected hypotheses; this is the tactic our Flat Earth friend has used. This maneuver is possible, however, only because—and this is the second point—whenever we test a hypothesis, we do so by taking for granted (usually quite unconsciously) many other hypotheses as well. So the evidence for the hypothesis we think we are confirming is impossible to separate entirely from the adequacy of the connected hypotheses. As long as we have no reason to doubt that light rays travel in straight lines (at least over distances of a few miles), our Flat Earth friend's argument is unconvincing. But once that hypothesis is itself put in doubt, the idea that looked at first to be a pathetic rationalization takes on an even more troublesome character.

There are, then, not one but two fallacies exposed by this example. The first and perhaps graver is in rigging your hypothesis so that *no matter what* observations are brought against it, you will count nothing as falsifying it. The second and subtler is in thinking that as you test one hypothesis, all of your other background beliefs are left safely to one side, immaculate and uninvolved. On the contrary, our beliefs form a corporate structure, intertwined and connected to each other with great complexity, and no one of them can ever be singled out for unique and isolated application, confirmation, or disconfirmation, to the world around us.

24

A Humorist's View

Max Shulman

Love Is a Fallacy

Cool was I and logical. Keen, calculating, perspicacious, acute, and astute — I was all of these. My brain was as powerful as a dynamo, as precise as a chemist's scales, as penetrating as a scalpel. And — think of it! — I was only eighteen.

It is not often that one so young has such a giant intellect. Take, for example, Petey Bellows, my roommate at the university. Same age, same background, but dumb as an ox. A nice enough fellow, you understand, but nothing upstairs. Emotional type. Unstable. Impressionable. Worst of all, a faddist. Fads, I submit, are the very negation of reason. To be swept up in

---

Max Shulman (1919–1988) began his career as a writer when he was a journalism student at the University of Minnesota. Later he wrote humorous novels, stories, and plays. One of his novels, Barefoot Boy with Cheek *(1943), was made into a musical and another,* Rally Round the Flag, Boys! *(1957), was made into a film starring Paul Newman and Joanne Woodward.* The Tender Trap *(1954), a play which he wrote with Robert Paul Smith, still retains its popularity with theater groups.*

"Love Is a Fallacy" was first published in 1951, when demeaning stereotypes about women and minorities were widely accepted in the marketplace as well as the home. Thus, jokes about domineering mothers-in-law or about dumb blondes routinely met with no objection.

After you have finished reading "Love Is a Fallacy," you may want to write an argumentative essay of 500–750 words on one of the following topics: (1) the story, rightly understood, is not antiwoman; (2) if the story is antiwoman, it is equally antiman; (3) the story is antiwoman but nevertheless belongs in this book; or (4) the story is antiwoman and does not belong in the book.

every new craze that comes along, to surrender yourself to idiocy just because everybody else is doing it — this, to me, is the acme of mindlessness. Not, however, to Petey.

One afternoon I found Petey lying on his bed with an expression of such distress on his face that I immediately diagnosed appendicitis. "Don't move," I said. "Don't take a laxative. I'll call a doctor."

"Raccoon," he mumbled thickly.

"Raccoon?" I said, pausing in my flight.   5

"I want a raccoon coat," he wailed.

I perceived that his trouble was not physical, but mental. "Why do you want a raccoon coat?"

"I should have known it," he cried, pounding his temples. "I should have known they'd come back when the Charleston came back. Like a fool I spent all my money for textbooks, and now I can't get a raccoon coat."

"Can you mean," I said incredulously, "that people are actually wearing raccoon coats again?"

"All the Big Men on Campus are wearing them. Where've you been?"   10

"In the library," I said, naming a place not frequented by Big Men on Campus.

He leaped from the bed and paced the room. "I've got to have a raccoon coat," he said passionately. "I've got to!"

"Petey, why? Look at it rationally. Raccoon coats are unsanitary. They shed. They smell bad. They weigh too much. They're unsightly. They——"

"You don't understand," he interrupted impatiently. "It's the thing to do. Don't you want to be in the swim?"

"No," I said truthfully.   15

"Well, I do," he declared. "I'd give anything for a raccoon coat. Anything!"

My brain, that precision instrument, slipped into high gear. "Anything?" I asked, looking at him narrowly.

"Anything," he affirmed in ringing tones.

I stroked my chin thoughtfully. It so happened that I knew where to get my hands on a raccoon coat. My father had had one in his undergraduate days; it lay now in a trunk in the attic back home. It also happened that Petey had something I wanted. He didn't *have* it exactly, but at least he had first rights on it. I refer to his girl, Polly Espy.

I had long coveted Polly Espy. Let me emphasize that my desire for   20 this young woman was not emotional in nature. She was, to be sure, a girl who excited the emotions, but I was not one to let my heart rule my head. I wanted Polly for a shrewdly calculated, entirely cerebral reason.

I was a freshman in law school. In a few years I would be out in practice. I was well aware of the importance of the right kind of wife in furthering a lawyer's career. The successful lawyers I had observed were, almost without exception, married to beautiful, gracious, intelligent women. With one omission, Polly fitted these specifications perfectly.

Beautiful she was. She was not yet of pin-up proportions, but I felt sure that time would supply the lack. She already had the makings.

Gracious she was. By gracious I mean full of graces. She had an erectness of carriage, an ease of bearing, a poise that clearly indicated the best of breeding. At table her manners were exquisite. I had seen her at the Kozy Kampus Korner eating the specialty of the house — a sandwich that contained scraps of pot roast, gravy, chopped nuts, and a dipper of sauerkraut — without even getting her fingers moist.

Intelligent she was not. In fact, she veered in the opposite direction. But I believed that under my guidance she would smarten up. At any rate, it was worth a try. It is, after all, easier to make a beautiful dumb girl smart than to make an ugly smart girl beautiful.

"Petey," I said, "are you in love with Polly Espy?" 25

"I think she's a keen kid," he replied, "but I don't know if you'd call it love. Why?"

"Do you," I asked, "have any kind of formal arrangement with her? I mean are you going steady or anything like that?"

"No. We see each other quite a bit, but we both have other dates. Why?"

"Is there," I asked, "any other man for whom she has a particular fondness?"

"Not that I know of. Why?" 30

I nodded with satisfaction. "In other words, if you were out of the picture, the field would be open. Is that right?"

"I guess so. What are you getting at?"

"Nothing, nothing," I said innocently, and took my suitcase out of the closet.

"Where you going?" asked Petey.

"Home for the week end." I threw a few things into the bag. 35

"Listen," he said, clutching my arm eagerly, "while you're home, you couldn't get some money from your old man, could you, and lend it to me so I can buy a raccoon coat?"

"I may do better than that," I said with a mysterious wink and closed my bag and left.

"Look," I said to Petey when I got back Monday morning. I threw open the suitcase and revealed the huge, hairy, gamy object that my father had worn in his Stutz Bearcat in 1925.

"Holy Toledo!" said Petey reverently. He plunged his hands into the raccoon coat and then his face. "Holy Toledo!" he repeated fifteen or twenty times.

"Would you like it?" I asked. 40

"Oh yes!" he cried, clutching the greasy pelt to him. Then a canny look came into his eyes. "What do you want for it?"

"Your girl," I said, mincing no words.

"Polly?" he said in a horrified whisper. "You want Polly?"

"That's right."

He flung the coat from him. "Never," he said stoutly. 45

I shrugged. "Okay. If you don't want to be in the swim, I guess it's your business."

I sat down in a chair and pretended to read a book, but out of the corner of my eye I kept watching Petey. He was a torn man. First he looked at the coat with the expression of a waif at a bakery window. Then he turned away and set his jaw resolutely. Then he looked back at the coat, with even more longing in his face. Then he turned away, but with not so much resolution this time. Back and forth his head swiveled, desire waxing, resolution waning. Finally he didn't turn away at all; he just stood and stared with mad lust at the coat.

"It isn't as though I was in love with Polly," he said thickly. "Or going steady or anything like that."

"That's right," I murmured.

"What's Polly to me, or me to Polly?"   50

"Not a thing," said I.

"It's just been a casual kick — just a few laughs, that's all."

"Try on the coat," said I.

He complied. The coat bunched high over his ears and dropped all the way down to his shoe tops. He looked like a mound of dead raccoons. "Fits fine," he said happily.

I rose from my chair. "Is it a deal?" I asked, extending my hand.   55

He swallowed. "It's a deal," he said and shook my hand.

I had my first date with Polly the following evening. This was in the nature of a survey; I wanted to find out just how much work I had to do to get her mind up to the standard I required. I took her first to dinner. "Gee, that was a delish dinner," she said as we left the restaurant. Then I took her to a movie. "Gee, that was a marvy movie," she said as we left the theater. And then I took her home. "Gee, I had a sensaysh time," she said as she bade me good night.

I went back to my room with a heavy heart. I had gravely underestimated the size of my task. This girl's lack of information was terrifying. Nor would it be enough merely to supply her with information. First she had to be taught to *think*. This loomed as a project of no small dimensions, and at first I was tempted to give her back to Petey. But then I got to thinking about her abundant physical charms and about the way she entered a room and the way she handled a knife and fork, and I decided to make an effort.

I went about it, as in all things, systematically. I gave her a course in logic. It happened that I, as a law student, was taking a course in logic myself, so I had all the facts at my fingertips. "Polly," I said to her when I picked her up on our next date, "tonight we are going over to the Knoll and talk."

"Oo, terrif," she replied. One thing I will say for this girl: You would go   60
far to find another so agreeable.

We went to the Knoll, the campus trysting place, and we sat down under an old oak, and she looked at me expectantly: "What are we going to talk about?" she asked.

"Logic."

She thought this over for a minute and decided she liked it. "Magnif," she said.

"Logic," I said, clearing my throat, "is the science of thinking. Before we can think correctly, we must first learn to recognize the common fallacies of logic. These we will take up tonight."

"Wow-dow!" she cried, clapping her hands delightedly.   65

I winced, but went bravely on. "First let us examine the fallacy called Dicto Simpliciter."

"By all means," she urged, batting her lashes eagerly.

"Dicto Simpliciter means an argument based on an unqualified generalization. For example: Exercise is good. Therefore everybody should exercise."

"I agree," said Polly earnestly. "I mean exercise is wonderful. I mean it builds the body and everything."

"Polly," I said gently, "the argument is a fallacy. *Exercise is good* is an   70
unqualified generalization. For instance, if you have heart disease, exercise is bad, not good. Many people are ordered by their doctors *not* to exercise. You must *qualify* the generalization. You must say exercise is *usually* good, or exercise is good *for most people*. Otherwise you have committed a Dicto Simpliciter. Do you see?"

"No," she confessed. "But this is marvy. Do more! Do more!"

"It will be better if you stop tugging at my sleeve," I told her, and when she desisted, I continued. "Next we take up a fallacy called Hasty Generalization. Listen carefully: You can't speak French. I can't speak French. Petey Bellows can't speak French. I must therefore conclude that nobody at the University of Minnesota can speak French."

"Really?" said Polly, amazed. *"Nobody?"*

I hid my exasperation. "Polly, it's a fallacy. The generalization is reached too hastily. There are too few instances to support such a conclusion."

"Know any more fallacies?" she asked breathlessly. "This is more fun   75
than dancing even."

I fought off a wave of despair. I was getting nowhere with this girl, absolutely nowhere. Still, I am nothing if not persistent. I continued. "Next comes Post Hoc. Listen to this: Let's not take Bill on our picnic. Every time we take him out with us, it rains."

"I know somebody just like that," she exclaimed. "A girl back home — Eula Becker, her name is. It never fails. Every single time we take her on a picnic——"

"Polly," I said sharply, "it's a fallacy. Eula Becker doesn't *cause* the rain. She has no connection with the rain. You are guilty of Post Hoc if you blame Eula Becker."

"I'll never do it again," she promised contritely. "Are you mad at me?"

I sighed. "No, Polly, I'm not mad."   80

"Then tell me some more fallacies."

"All right. Let's try Contradictory Premises."

"Yes, let's," she chirped, blinking her eyes happily.

I frowned, but plunged ahead. "Here's an example of Contradictory Premises: If God can do anything, can He make a stone so heavy that He won't be able to lift it?"

"Of course," she replied promptly.

"But if He can do anything, He can lift the stone," I pointed out. 85

"Yeah," she said thoughtfully. "Well, then I guess He can't make the stone."

"But He can do anything," I reminded her.

She scratched her pretty, empty head. "I'm all confused," she admitted.

"Of course you are. Because when the premises of an argument con- 90 tradict each other, there can be no argument. If there is an irresistible force, there can be no immovable object. If there is an immovable object, there can be no irresistible force. Get it?"

"Tell me some more of this keen stuff," she said eagerly.

I consulted my watch. "I think we'd better call it a night. I'll take you home now, and you go over all the things you've learned. We'll have another session tomorrow night."

I deposited her at the girl's dormitory, where she assured me that she had had a perfectly terrif evening, and I went glumly home to my room. Petey lay snoring in his bed, the raccoon coat huddled like a great hairy beast at his feet. For a moment I considered waking him and telling him that he could have his girl back. It seemed clear that my project was doomed to failure. The girl simply had a logic-proof head.

But then I reconsidered. I had wasted one evening; I might as well waste another. Who knew? Maybe somewhere in the extinct crater of her mind a few embers still smoldered. Maybe somehow I could fan them into flame. Admittedly it was not a prospect fraught with hope, but I decided to give it one more try.

Seated under the oak the next evening I said, "Our first fallacy tonight 95 is called Ad Misericordiam."

She quivered with delight.

"Listen closely," I said. "A man applies for a job. When the boss asks him what his qualifications are, he replies that he has a wife and six children at home, the wife is a helpless cripple, the children have nothing to eat, no clothes to wear, no shoes on their feet, there are no beds in the house, no coal in the cellar, and winter is coming."

A tear rolled down each of Polly's pink cheeks. "Oh, this is awful, awful," she sobbed.

"Yes, it's awful," I agreed, "but it's no argument. The man never answered the boss's question about his qualifications. Instead he appealed to the boss's sympathy. He committed the fallacy of ad Misericordiam. Do you understand?"

"Have you got a handkerchief?" she blubbered. 100

I handed her a handkerchief and tried to keep from screaming while she wiped her eyes. "Next," I said in a carefully controlled tone, "we will discuss False Analogy. Here is an example: Students should be allowed to look at their textbooks during examinations. After all, surgeons have X rays to guide them during an operation, lawyers have briefs to guide them during a trial, carpenters have blueprints to guide them when they are building a house. Why, then, shouldn't students be allowed to look at their textbooks during an examination?"

"There now," she said enthusiastically, "is the most marvy idea I've heard in years."

"Polly," I said testily, "the argument is all wrong. Doctors, lawyers, and carpenters aren't taking a test to see how much they have learned, but students are. The situations are altogether different, and you can't make an analogy between them."

"I still think it's a good idea," said Polly.

"Nuts," I muttered. Doggedly I pressed on. "Next we'll try Hypothesis 105 Contrary to Fact."

"Sounds yummy," was Polly's reaction.

"Listen: If Madame Curie had not happened to leave a photographic plate in a drawer with a chunk of pitchblende, the world today would not know about radium."

"True, true," said Polly, nodding her head. "Did you see the movie? Oh, it just knocked me out. That Walter Pidgeon is so dreamy. I mean he fractures me."

"If you can forget Mr. Pidgeon for a moment," I said coldly, "I would like to point out that the statement is a fallacy. Maybe Madame Curie would have discovered radium at some later date. Maybe somebody else would have discovered it. Maybe any number of things would have happened. You can't start with a hypothesis that is not true and then draw any supportable conclusions from it."

"They ought to put Walter Pidgeon in more pictures," said Polly. "I 110 hardly ever see him any more."

One more chance, I decided. But just one more. There is a limit to what flesh and blood can bear. "The next fallacy is called Poisoning the Well."

"How cute!" she gurgled.

"Two men are having a debate. The first one gets up and says, 'My opponent is a notorious liar. You can't believe a word that he is going to say.' . . . Now, Polly, think. Think hard. What's wrong?"

I watched her closely as she knit her creamy brow in concentration. Suddenly a glimmer of intelligence — the first I had seen — came into her eyes. "It's not fair," she said with indignation. "It's not a bit fair. What chance has the second man got if the first man calls him a liar before he even begins talking?"

"Right!" I cried exultantly. "One hundred percent right. It's not fair. 115

The first man has *poisoned the well* before anybody could drink from it. He has hamstrung his opponent before he could even start. . . . Polly, I'm proud of you."

"Pshaw," she murmured, blushing with pleasure.

"You see, my dear, these things aren't so hard. All you have to do is concentrate. Think — examine — evaluate. Come now, let's review everything we have learned."

"Fire away," she said with an airy wave of her hand.

Heartened by the knowledge that Polly was not altogether a cretin, I began a long, patient review of all I had told her. Over and over and over again I cited instances, pointed out flaws, kept hammering away without letup. It was like digging a tunnel. At first everything was work, sweat, and darkness. I had no idea when I would reach the light, or even *if* I would. But I persisted. I pounded and clawed and scraped, and finally I was rewarded. I saw a chink of light. And then the chink got bigger and the sun came pouring in and all was bright.

Five grueling nights this took, but it was worth it. I had made a logi- 120 cian out of Polly; I had taught her to think. My job was done. She was worthy of me at last. She was a fit wife for me, a proper hostess for my many mansions, a suitable mother for my well-heeled children.

It must not be thought that I was without love for this girl. Quite the contrary. Just as Pygmalion loved the perfect woman he had fashioned, so I loved mine. I decided to acquaint her with my feelings at our very next meeting. The time had come to change our relationship from academic to romantic.

"Polly," I said when next we sat beneath our oak, "tonight we will not discuss fallacies."

"Aw, gee," she said, disappointed.

"My dear," I said, favoring her with a smile, "we have now spent five evenings together. We have gotten along splendidly. It is clear that we are well matched."

"Hasty Generalization," said Polly brightly. 125

"I beg your pardon," said I.

"Hasty Generalization," she repeated. "How can you say that we are well matched on the basis of only five dates?"

I chuckled with amusement. The dear child had learned her lessons well. "My dear," I said, patting her hand in a tolerant manner, "five dates is plenty. After all, you don't have to eat a whole cake to know that it's good."

"False Analogy," said Polly promptly. "I'm not a cake. I'm a girl."

I chuckled with somewhat less amusement. The dear child had 130 learned her lesson perhaps too well. I decided to change tactics. Obviously the best approach was a simple, strong, direct declaration of love. I paused for a moment while my massive brain chose the proper words. Then I began:

"Polly, I love you. You are the whole world to me, and the moon and the stars and the constellations of outer space. Please, my darling, say that you will go steady with me, for if you will not, life will be meaningless. I will languish. I will refuse my meals. I will wander the face of the earth, a shambling, hollow-eyed hulk."

There, I thought, folding my arms, that ought to do it.

"Ad Misericordiam," said Polly.

I ground my teeth. I was not Pygmalion; I was Frankenstein, and my monster had me by the throat. Frantically I fought back the tide of panic surging through me. At all costs I had to keep cool.

"Well, Polly," I said, forcing a smile, "you certainly have learned your 135 fallacies."

"You're darn right," she said with a vigorous nod.

"And who taught them to you, Polly?"

"You did."

"That's right. So you do owe me something, don't you, my dear? If I hadn't come along you never would have learned about fallacies."

"Hypothesis Contrary to Fact," she said instantly. 140

I dashed perspiration from my brow. "Polly," I croaked, "You mustn't take all these things so literally. I mean this is just classroom stuff. You know that the things you learn in school don't have anything to do with life."

"Dicto Simpliciter," she said, wagging her finger at me playfully.

That did it. I leaped to my feet, bellowing like a bull. "Will you or will you not go steady with me?"

"I will not," she replied.

"Why not?" I demanded. 145

"Because this afternoon I promised Petey Bellows that I would go steady with him."

I reeled back, overcome with the infamy of it. After he promised, after he made a deal, after he shook my hand! "That rat!" I shrieked, kicking up great chunks of turf. "You can't go with him, Polly. He's a liar. He's a cheat. He's a rat."

"Poisoning the Well," said Polly, "and stop shouting. I think shouting must be a fallacy too."

With an immense effort of will, I modulated my voice. "All right," I said. "You're a logician. Let's look at this thing logically. How could you choose Petey Bellows over me? Look at me — a brilliant student, a tremendous intellectual, a man with an assured future. Look at Petey — a knothead, a jitterbug, a guy who'll never know where his next meal is coming from. Can you give me one logical reason why you should go steady with Petey Bellows?"

"I certainly can," declared Polly. "He's got a raccoon coat." 150

25

A Psychologist's View: Rogerian Argument

Carl R. Rogers

Communication: Its Blocking and Its Facilitation

It may seem curious that a person whose whole professional effort is devoted to psychotherapy should be interested in problems of communication. What relationship is there between providing therapeutic help to individuals with emotional maladjustments and the concern of this

---

Carl R. Rogers (1902–1987), perhaps best known for his book entitled On Becoming a Person, *was a psychotherapist, not a teacher of writing. This short essay by Rogers has, however, exerted much influence on instructors who teach argument. Written in the 1950s, this essay reflects the political climate of the "Cold War" between the United States and the USSR, which dominated headlines for more than forty years (1947–1989). Several of Rogers's examples of bias and frustrated communication allude to the tensions of that era.*

On the surface, many arguments seem to show A arguing with B, presumably seeking to change B's mind; but A's argument is really directed not to B but to C. This attempt to persuade a nonparticipant is evident in the courtroom, where neither the prosecutor (A) nor the defense lawyer (B) is really trying to convince the opponent. Rather, both are trying to convince a third party, the jury (C). Prosecutors do not care whether they convince defense lawyers; they don't even mind infuriating defense lawyers, because their only real goal is to convince the jury. Similarly, the writer of a letter to a newspaper, taking issue with an editorial, does not expect to change the paper's policy. Rather, the writer hopes to convince a third party, the reader of the newspaper.

But suppose A really does want to bring B around to A's point of view. Suppose Mary really wants to persuade the teacher to allow her little lamb to

conference with obstacles to communication? Actually the relationship is very close indeed. The whole task of psychotherapy is the task of dealing with a failure in communication. The emotionally maladjusted person, the "neurotic," is in difficulty first because communication within himself has broken down, and second because as a result of this his communication

---

stay in the classroom. Rogers points out that when we engage in an argument, if we feel our integrity or our identity is threatened, we will stiffen our position. (The teacher may feel that his or her dignity is compromised by the presence of the lamb, and will scarcely attend to Mary's argument.) The sense of threat may be so great that we are unable to consider the alternative views being offered, and we therefore remain unpersuaded. Threatened, we may defend ourselves rather than our argument, and little communication takes place. Of course a third party might say that we or our opponent presented the more convincing case, but we, and perhaps the opponent, have scarcely listened to each other, and so the two of us remain apart.

Rogers suggests, therefore, that a writer who wishes to communicate with someone (as opposed to convincing a third party) needs to reduce the threat. In a sense, the participants in the argument need to become partners rather than adversaries. Rogers writes, "Mutual communication tends to be pointed toward solving a problem rather than toward attacking a person or group." Thus, an essay on whether schools should test students for use of drugs, need not—and probably should not—see the issue as black or white, either/or. Such an essay might indicate that testing is undesirable because it may have bad effects, but in some circumstances it may be acceptable. This qualification does not mean that one must compromise. Thus, the essayist might argue that the potential danger to liberty is so great that no circumstances justify testing students for drugs. But even such an essayist should recognize the merit (however limited) of the opposition, and should grant that the position being advanced itself entails great difficulties and dangers.

A writer who wishes to reduce the psychological threat to the opposition, and thus facilitate the partnership in the study of some issue, can do several things: One can show sympathetic understanding of the opposing argument; one can recognize what is valid in it; and one can recognize and demonstrate that those who take the other side are nonetheless persons of goodwill.

Thus a writer who takes Rogers seriously will, usually, in the first part of an argumentative essay

1. *State the problem,*
2. *Give the opponent's position, and*
3. *Grant whatever validity the writer finds in that position—for instance, will recognize the circumstances in which the position would indeed be acceptable. Next, the writer will, if possible,*
4. *Attempt to show how the opposing position will be improved if the writer's own position is accepted.*

Sometimes, of course, the differing positions may be so far apart that no reconciliation can be proposed, in which case the writer will probably seek to show how the problem can best be solved by adopting the writer's own position. We have discussed these matters in Chapter 5, but not from the point of view of a psychotherapist, and so we reprint Rogers's essay here.

with others has been damaged. If this sounds somewhat strange, then let me put it in other terms. In the "neurotic" individual, parts of himself which have been termed unconscious, or repressed, or denied to awareness, become blocked off so that they no longer communicate themselves to the conscious or managing part of himself. As long as this is true, there are distortions in the way he communicates himself to others, and so he suffers both within himself, and in his interpersonal relations. The task of psychotherapy is to help the person achieve, through a special relationship with a therapist, good communication within himself. Once this is achieved he can communicate more freely and more effectively with others. We may say then that psychotherapy is good communication, within and between men. We may also turn that statement around and it will still be true. Good communication, free communication, within or between men, is always therapeutic.

It is, then, from a background of experience with communication in counseling and psychotherapy that I want to present here two ideas. I wish to state what I believe is one of the major factors in blocking or impeding communication, and then I wish to present what in our experience has proven to be a very important way to improving or facilitating communication.

I would like to propose, as an hypothesis for consideration, that the major barrier to mutual interpersonal communication is our very natural tendency to judge, to evaluate, to approve or disapprove, the statement of the person, or the other group. Let me illustrate my meaning with some very simple examples. As you leave the meeting tonight, one of the statements you are likely to hear is, "I didn't like that man's talk." Now what do you respond? Almost invariably your reply will be either approval or disapproval of the attitude expressed. Either you respond, "I didn't either. I thought it was terrible," or else you tend to reply, "Oh, I thought it was really good." In other words, your primary reaction is to evaluate what has just been said to you, to evaluate it from *your* point of view, your own frame of reference.

Or take another example. Suppose I say with some feeling, "I think the Republicans are behaving in ways that show a lot of good sound sense these days," what is the response that arises in your mind as you listen? The overwhelming likelihood is that it will be evaluative. You will find yourself agreeing, or disagreeing, or making some judgment about me such as "He must be a conservative," or "He seems solid in his thinking." Or let us take an illustration from the international scene. Russia says vehemently, "The treaty with Japan is a war plot on the part of the United States." We rise as one person to say "That's a lie!"

This last illustration brings in another element connected with my hypothesis. Although the tendency to make evaluations is common in almost all interchange of language, it is very much heightened in those situations where feelings and emotions are deeply involved. So the stronger our feelings, the more likely it is that there will be no mutual element in the com- 5 munication. There will be just two ideas, two feelings, two judgments, missing each other in psychological space. I'm sure you recognize this from your own experience. When you have not been emotionally involved yourself, and have listened to a heated discussion, you often go away thinking, "Well, they actually weren't talking about the same thing." And they were not. Each was making a judgment, an evaluation, from his own frame of reference. There was really nothing which could be called communication in any genuine sense. This tendency to react to any emotionally meaningful statement by forming an evaluation of it from our own point of view, is, I repeat, the major barrier to interpersonal communication.

But is there any way of solving this problem, of avoiding this barrier? I feel that we are making exciting progress toward this goal and I would like to present it as simply as I can. Real communication occurs, and this evaluative tendency is avoided, when we listen with understanding. What does that mean? It means *to see the expressed idea and attitude from the other person's point of view, to sense how it feels to him, to achieve his frame of reference in regard to the thing he is talking about.*

Stated so briefly, this may sound absurdly simple, but it is not. It is an approach which we have found extremely potent in the field of psychotherapy. It is the most effective agent we know for altering the basic personality structure of an individual, and improving his relationships and his communications with others. If I can listen to what he can tell me, if I can understand how it seems to him, if I can see its personal meaning for him, if I can sense the emotional flavor which it has for him, then I will be releasing potent forces of change in him. If I can really understand how he hates his father, or hates the university, or hates communists — if I can catch the flavor of his fear of insanity, or his fear of atom bombs, or of Russia — it will be of the greatest help to him in altering those very hatreds and fears, and in establishing realistic and harmonious relationships with the very people and situations toward which he has felt hatred and fear. We know from our research that such empathic understanding — understanding *with* a person, not *about* him — is such an effective approach that it can bring about major changes in personality.

Some of you may be feeling that you listen well to people, and that you have never seen such results. The changes are very great indeed that your listening has not been of the type I have described. Fortunately I can suggest a little laboratory experiment which you can try to test the quality of your understanding. The next time you get into an argument with your wife, or your friend, or with a small group of friends, just stop the discussion for a moment and for an experiment, institute this rule. "Each person can speak up for himself only *after* he has first restated the ideas and feelings of the previous speaker accurately, and to that speaker's satisfaction." You see what this would mean. It would simply mean that before presenting your own point of view, it would be necessary for you to really achieve the other speaker's frame of reference — to understand his thoughts and feelings so well that you could summarize them for him. Sounds simple, doesn't it? But if you try it you will discover it one of the most difficult things you have ever tried to do. However, once you have been able to see the other's point of view, your own comments will have to be drastically revised. You will also find the emotion going out of the discussion, the differences being reduced, and those differences which remain being of a rational and understandable sort.

Can you imagine what this kind of an approach would mean if it were projected into larger areas? What would happen to a labor-management dispute if it was conducted in such a way that labor, without necessarily agreeing, could accurately state management's point of view in a way that management could accept; and management, without approving labor's stand, could state labor's case in a way that labor agreed was accurate? It would mean that real communication was established, and one could practically guarantee that some reasonable solution would be reached.

If then this way of approach is an effective avenue to good communication and good relationships, as I am quite sure you will agree if you try the experiment I have mentioned, why is it not more widely tried and used? I will try to list the difficulties which keep it from being utilized. 10

In the first place it takes courage, a quality which is not too widespread. I am indebted to Dr. S. I. Hayakawa, the semanticist, for pointing out that to carry on psychotherapy in this fashion is to take a very real risk, and that courage is required. If you really understand another person in this way, if you are willing to enter his private world and see the way life appears to him, without any attempt to make evaluative judgments, you run the risk of being changed yourself. You might see it his way, you might find yourself influenced in your attitudes or your personality. This risk of being changed is one of the most frightening prospects most of us can face. If I enter, as fully as I am able, into the private world of a neurotic or psychotic individual, isn't there a risk that I might become lost in that world? Most of us are afraid to take that risk. Or if we had a Russian communist speaker here tonight, or Senator Joe McCarthy, how many of us would dare to try to see the world from each of these points of view? The great majority of us could not *listen;* we would find ourselves compelled to *evaluate,* because listening would seem too dangerous. So the first requirement is courage, and we do not always have it.

But there is a second obstacle. It is just when emotions are strongest that it is most difficult to achieve the frame of reference of the other person or group. Yet it is the time the attitude is most needed, if communication is to be established. We have not found this to be an insuperable obstacle in our experience in psychotherapy. A third party, who is able to lay aside his own feelings and evaluations, can assist greatly by listening with understanding to each person or group and clarifying the views and attitudes each holds. We have found this very effective in small groups in which contradictory or antagonistic attitudes exist. When the parties to a dispute realize that they are being understood, that someone sees how the situation seems to them, the statements grow less exaggerated and less defensive, and it is no longer necessary to maintain the attitude, "I am 100 percent right and you are 100 percent wrong." The influence of such an understanding catalyst in the group permits the members to come closer and closer to the objective truth involved in the relationship. In this way mutual communication is established and some type of agreement becomes much more possible. So we may say that though heightened emotions make it much more difficult to understand *with* an opponent, our experience makes it clear that a neutral, understanding, catalyst type of leader or therapist can overcome this obstacle in a small group.

This last phrase, however, suggests another obstacle to utilizing the approach I have described. Thus far all our experience has been with small face-to-face groups—groups exhibiting industrial tensions, religious tensions, racial tensions, and therapy groups in which many personal tensions are present. In these small groups our experience, confirmed by a limited amount of research, shows that this basic approach leads to improved communication, to greater acceptance of others and by others, and to attitudes which are more positive and more problem-solving in nature. There is a decrease in defensiveness, in exaggerated statements, in evaluative and critical behavior. But these findings are from small groups. What about trying to achieve understanding between larger groups that are geographically remote? Or between face-to-face groups who are not speaking for themselves, but simply as representatives of others, like the delegates at Kaesong?[1] Frankly we do not know the answers to these questions. I believe the situation might be put this way. As social scientists we have a tentative test-tube solution of the problem of breakdown in communication. But to confirm the validity of this test-tube solution, and to adapt it to the enormous problems of communication breakdown between classes, groups, and nations, would involve additional funds, much more research, and creative thinking of a high order.

Even with our present limited knowledge we can see some steps which might be taken, even in large groups, to increase the amount of listening *with*, and to decrease the amount of evaluation *about*. To be imaginative for a moment, let us suppose that a therapeutically oriented international group went to the Russian leaders and said, "We want to achieve a genuine understanding of your views and even more important, of your attitudes and feelings, toward the United States. We will summarize and resummarize the views and feelings if necessary, until you agree that our description represents the situation as it seems to you." Then suppose they did the same thing with the leaders in our own country. If they then gave the widest possible distribution to these two views, with the feelings clearly described but not expressed in name-calling, might not the effect be very great? It would not guarantee the type of understanding I have been de-

---

[1]**the delegates at Kaesong** Representatives of North and South Korea met at the border town of Kaesong to arrange terms for an armistice to hostilities during the Korean War (1950–1953). [All notes are the editors'.]

scribing, but it would make it much more possible. We can understand the feelings of a person who hates us much more readily when his attitudes are accurately described to us by a neutral third party, than we can when he is shaking his fist at us.

But even to describe such a first step is to suggest another obstacle to 15 this approach of understanding. Our civilization does not yet have enough faith in the social sciences to utilize their findings. The opposite is true of the physical sciences. During the war[2] when a test-tube solution was found to the problem of synthetic rubber, millions of dollars and an army of talent was turned loose on the problem of using that finding. If synthetic rubber could be made in milligrams, it could and would be made in the thousands of tons. And it was. But in the social science realm, if a way is found of facilitating communication and mutual understanding in small groups, there is no guarantee that the finding will be utilized. It may be a generation or more before the money and the brains will be turned loose to exploit that finding.

In closing, I would like to summarize this small-scale solution to the problem of barriers in communication, and to point out certain of its characteristics.

I have said that our research and experience to date would make it appear that breakdowns in communication, and the evaluative tendency which is the major barrier to communication, can be avoided. The solution is provided by creating a situation in which each of the different parties come to understand the other from the *other's* point of view. This has been achieved, in practice, even when feelings run high, by the influence of a person who is willing to understand each point of view empathically, and who thus acts as a catalyst to precipitate further understanding.

This procedure has important characteristics. It can be initiated by one party, without waiting for the other to be ready. It can even be initiated by a neutral third person, providing he can gain a minimum of cooperation from one of the parties.

This procedure can deal with the insincerities, the defensive exaggerations, the lies, the "false fronts" which characterize almost every failure in communication. These defensive distortions drop away with astonishing speed as people find that the only intent is to understand, not judge.

This approach leads steadily and rapidly toward the discovery of the 20 truth, toward a realistic appraisal of the objective barriers to communication. The dropping of some defensiveness by one party leads to further dropping of defensiveness by the other party, and truth is thus approached.

This procedure gradually achieves mutual communication. Mutual communication tends to be pointed toward solving a problem rather than toward attacking a person or group. It leads to a situation in which I see how the problem appears to you, as well as to me, and you see how it appears to me, as well as to you. Thus accurately and realistically defined, the

[2]**the war** World War II.

problem is almost certain to yield to intelligent attack, or if it is in part in-soluble, it will be comfortably accepted as such.

This then appears to be a test-tube solution to the breakdown of com-munication as it occurs in small groups. Can we take this small-scale an-swer, investigate it further, refine it; develop it and apply it to the tragic and well-nigh fatal failures of communication which threaten the very exis-tence of our modern world? It seems to me that this is a possibility and a challenge which we should explore.

Acknowledgments continued from page ii

Robert H. Bork, "An Outbreak of Judicial Civil Disobedience," from the *Wall Street Journal*, April 29, 1992. Reprinted with permission of the author and of the *Wall Street Journal*, © 1992 by Dow Jones & Company, Inc. All rights reserved.

Judy Brady, "I Want a Wife." Reprinted by permission of the author.

Susan Brownmiller, "Let's Put Pornography Back in the Closet." First appeared in *Newsday*, 1979. Reprinted by permission of Susan Brownmiller.

David Bruck, "The Death Penalty," from *The New Republic*, May 20, 1985. Copyright © 1985, *The New Republic*, Inc. Reprinted by permission of *The New Republic*.

J. Warren Cassidy, "The Case for Firearms," from *Time*, January 29, 1990. Copyright © Time, Inc. Reprinted by permission.

Linda Chavez, "Demystifying Multiculturalism," from *National Review*, February 21, 1994. Copyright © 1994 by *National Review*, Inc., 150 East 35th Street, New York, NY 10016. Reprinted by permission.

Sally Thane Christensen, "Is a Tree Worth a Life?," from *Newsweek*, October 22, 1990. Reprinted by permission of Michael Christensen.

Rebecca L. Clark and Jeffrey S. Passel, "Studies are Deceptive," from the *New York Times*, September 3, 1993. Copyright © 1993 by the New York Times Company. Reprinted by permission.

Carl Cohen, "The Case for the Use of Animals in Biomedical Research," from *The New England Journal of Medicine*, vol. 315, pp. 865–887, October 1986. Copyright 1986. Massachusetts Medical Society. Reprinted by permission of *The New England Journal of Medicine*.

David Cole, "Five Myths about Immigration," from *The Nation*, October 17, 1994. Reprinted with permission from the *The Nation* magazine. Copyright © The Nation Company, L.P.

John Connor, "The U.S. Was Right," from the *New York Times*, August 4, 1985. Copyright © 1985 by the New York Times Company. Reprinted by permission.

Emily Dickinson, "Papa above!," "This World is not Conclusion," and "Those dying — then." Reprinted by permission of the publishers and the Trustees of Amherst College from *The Poems of Emily Dickinson*, Thomas H. Johnson, ed., Cambridge, MA: The Belknap Press of Harvard University Press. Copyright © 1951, 1955, 1979, 1983 by the President and Fellows of Harvard College.

Glenn Durfee, "Did Executions Kill Some of Our Rights?," from the *Wall Street Journal*, June 9, 1992. Reprinted by permission of the author.

Thomas Fleming, "The Real American Dilemma," from *Chronicles*, 13:3, March 1989, pp. 8–11. Reprinted by permission of the author.

Robert Frost, "Design" and "Mending Wall," from *The Poetry of Robert Frost*, edited by Edward Connery Lathem. Copyright © 1936 by Robert Frost. Copyright © 1964 by Lesley Frost Ballantine. Copyright © 1969 by Henry Holt and Co., Inc. Reprinted by permission of Henry Holt and Co., Inc.

Henry Louis Gates, Jr., "The Debate Has Been Miscast from the Start." First appeared in the *Boston Globe*, October 13, 1991. Copyright © 1991 Henry Louis Gates, Jr. Reprinted by permission of Brandt and Brandt Literary Agents, Inc.

Duane T. Gish, "A Reply to Gould." Courtesy of *Discover*, Copyright © 1981. Reprinted by permission of the author.

Susan Glaspell, *Trifles*, Copyright © 1951 by Walter H. Baker Co. is the sole property of the author and is fully protected under the copyright laws of the United States, the British Empire including the Dominion of Canada, and all other countries of the Copyright Union, and is subject to royalty. The play may not be acted by professionals or amateurs without formal permission in writing and the payment of royalty. All rights, including professional, amateur, stock, radio and television broadcasting, motion picture, recitation, lecturing, public reading and the rights of translation into foreign languages are reserved. All inquiries should be directed to Baker's Plays, 100 Chauncy Street, Boston, MA 02111.

Nathan Glazer, "In Defense of Multiculturalism," from the *New Republic*, September 2, 1991. "The Closing Door," from the *New Republic*, December 27, 1993. Copyright © 1991 and © 1993, The New Republic, Inc. Both essays reprinted by permission of the *New Republic*.

Angelo Gonzales and Luis O. Reyes, "The Key to Basic Skills," from the *New York Times*, November 10, 1985. Copyright © 1985 by the New York Times Company. Reprinted by permission.

Ellen Goodman, "Who Lives? Who Dies? Who Decides?," copyright © 1980, The Boston Globe Newspaper Co./Washington Post Writer's Group, "The Reasonable Woman Standard," copyright © 1991, The Boston Globe Newspaper Co./Washington Post Writer's Group. Both articles reprinted with permission.

James Gorman, "The Doctor Won't See You Now," from the *New York Times*, January 12, 1992. Copyright © 1992 by the New York Times Company. Reprinted by permission.

Stephen Jay Gould, "Evolution as Fact and Theory." Copyright © 1981 by Stephen J. Gould. First appeared in *Discover*. Reprinted by permission of the author.

Meg Greenfield, "In Defense of the Animals," from *Newsweek*, April 17, 1989. Copyright © 1989, Newsweek, Inc. All rights reserved. Reprinted by permission.

Ernest F. Hollings, "Save the Children," from the *New York Times*, November 23, 1993. Copyright © 1993 by the New York Times Company. Reprinted by permission.

A. E. Housman, "Loveliest of Trees." Reprinted with permission of the Society of Authors as the literary representative of the Estate of A. E. Houseman.

Donald L. Huddle, "A Growing Burden," from the *New York Times*, September 3, 1993. Copyright © 1993 by the New York Times Company. Reprinted by permission.

Barbara Huttman, "A Crime of Compassion," from *Newsweek*, August 8, 1983. Reprinted by permission of the author.

Kenneth T. Jackson, "Too Many Have Let Enthusiasm Outrun Reason," from the *Boston Globe*, October 13, 1991. Reprinted by permission of the author.

Shirley Jackson, "The Lottery," from *The Lottery* by Shirley Jackson. Copyright © 1948, 1949 by Shirley Jackson. Copyright renewed © 1976, 1977 by Laurence Hyman, Barry Hyman, Mrs. Sarah Webster and Mrs. Joanne Schnurer. Reprinted by permission of Farrar, Straus & Giroux, Inc.

Jeff Jacoby, "Euthanasia: Barbarism Cloaked in Compassion," from the *Boston Globe*, May 5, 1994. Reprinted courtesy of the *Boston Globe*.

Susan Jacoby, "A First Amendment Junkie," from the *New York Times*, January 26, 1978. Copyright © 1978 by Susan Jacoby. Reprinted by permission of Georges Borchardt, Inc.

Martin Luther King, Jr., "I Have a Dream." Copyright © 1963 by Martin Luther King, Jr., copyright renewed 1991 by Coretta Scott King. "Letter from Birmingham Jail," copyright © 1963, 1964 by Martin Luther King, Jr., copyright renewed 1991, 1992 by Coretta Scott King. Both selections reprinted by arrangement with the Heirs to the Estate of Martin Luther King, Jr., c/o Joan Daves Agency as the agent for the proprietor.

Edward I. Koch, "Death and Justice: How Capital Punishment Affirms Life," from *The New Republic*, April 15, 1985. Copyright © 1985, The New Republic, Inc. Reprinted by permission of *The New Republic*.

Alfie Kohn, "Competition Is Destructive," from *Women's Sports and Fitness*. Copyright © 1990 by Alfie Kohn. Adapted from Kohn's book, *No Contest: The Case Against Competition*, Houghton Mifflin, 1986. Reprinted by permission of the author.

Rita Kramer, "Juvenile Justice Is Delinquent," from the *Wall Street Journal*, May 27, 1992. Copyright © 1992 Dow Jones & Company, Inc. All rights reserved. Reprinted with permission of the Wall Street Journal.

Irving Kristol, "Pornography, Obscenity, and the Case for Censorship," from *On the Democratic Idea in America* by Irving Kristol. Copyright © 1972, pp. 31–47 by Harper & Row, Publishers. Reprinted by permission of the Public Interest.

Leila L. Kysar, "A Logger's Lament," from *Newsweek*, October 22, 1990. Reprinted by permission of the author.

Charles R. Lawrence III, "On Racist Speech," from the *Chronicle of Higher Education*, October 25, 1989. Copyright © 1989 by Charles R. Lawrence III. Reprinted by permission of the author.

Ursula K. Le Guin, "The Ones Who Walk Away from Omelas." Copyright © 1973 by Ursula Le Guin. First appeared in *New Dimensions 3*. Reprinted by permission of the author and the author's agent, Virginia Kidd.

John Leo, "Is Gossip Sexual Harassment?," from *Two Steps Ahead of the Thought Police*, pp. 235–237. Copyright © 1994 by Chloe Consulting Ltd. Reprinted by permission of Simon & Schuster, Inc.

C. S. Lewis, "What Christians Believe," from *Mere Christianity*, Book II, by C. S. Lewis. Used with permission from HarperCollins Publishers Ltd.

Rush H. Limbaugh, III, "Condoms: The New Diploma," from *The Way Things Ought to Be*. Copyright © 1992 by Rush Limbaugh. Reprinted by permission of Pocket Books, a division of Simon and Schuster, Inc.

Albert B. Lowenfels, et al., "Risk of Transmission of HIV from Surgeon to Patient," from *The New England Journal of Medicine,* vol. 325, 1991, pp. 888–889. Copyright © 1991 by Massachusetts Medical Society. Reprinted by permission of *The New England Journal of Medicine.*

Niccolò Machiavelli, excerpt from *The Prince,* from *The Portable Machiavelli,* edited by Peter Bondanella and Mark Musa. Copyright © 1979 by Viking Penguin, Inc. Reprinted by permission of Viking Penguin, a division of Penguin Books USA, Inc.

Sarah J. McCarthy, "Cultural Fascism," from *Forbes,* December 9, 1991. Copyright © Forbes Inc., 1991. Reprinted by permission of *Forbes* Magazine.

Catharine A. MacKinnon, "Sex and Violence: A Perspective," from *Feminism Unmodified* by Catharine MacKinnon. Copyright © 1987 by the President and Fellows of Harvard College. Reprinted by permission of Harvard University Press.

Donella Meadows, "Not Seeing the Forest for the Dollar Bills," from *Valley News* (White River Junction, VT), June 30, 1990. Reprinted by permission of the author.

Claudia Mills, "Preserving Endangered Species: Why Should We Care?," from *Report from the Institute for Philosophy and Public Policy*, vol. 6, no. 4, Fall 1985. Reprinted with the permission of the Institute for Philosophy and Public Policy, School of Public Affairs, University of Maryland.

Thomas More, excerpts from *Utopia*. Translated by Paul Turner (Penguin Classics 1961). Copyright © Paul Turner, 1961, pp. 75–77, 80, 89, 90–99, 102, 128–131. Reprinted by permission of Penguin Books Ltd.

Thomas Nagel, "A Defense of Affirmative Action," from *QQ: Report from the Center for Philosophy and Public Policy*, Fall 1986, pp. 6–9. Reprinted by permission.

Stephen Nathanson, "What If the Death Penalty Did Save Lives?," from *An Eye for an Eye? The Morality of Punishing by Death* by Stephen Nathanson, Rowman & Littlefield, 1987, pp. 120–129. Reprinted by permission of Rowman & Littlefield, Savage, MD.

Maria Burton Nelson, "At Its Best, Competition Is Not Divisive," from *Women's Sports and Fitness,* July/August 1990. Reprinted by permission of the author.

Flannery O'Connor, "Revelation," from *The Complete Stories of Flannery O'Connor.* Copyright © 1964, 1965 by the Estate of Mary Flannery O'Connor. Copyright renewed © 1993 by Regina O'Connor. Reprinted by permission of Farrar, Straus, & Giroux, Inc.

Ronald Pies, "Does Clinical Depression Undermine Physician-Assisted Suicide?" (editor's title), from "Undiagnosed Depression May Lurk in Requests for Doctor-

Assisted Suicides," in *Tufts Medicine,* Spring 1994. Reprinted with permission of *Tufts Medicine,* the alumni magazine of Tufts University School of Medicine.

Plato, "Crito," from *The Last Days of Socrates* by Plato, translated by Hugh Tredennick (Penguin Classics, Revised Edition, 1969), copyright © Hugh Tredennick, 1954, 1959, 1969. "The Greater Part of the Stories Current Today We Shall Have to Reject" and "Myth of the Cave," from *The Republic* by Plato, translated by Desmond Lee (Penguin Classics, Revised Edition, 1974), copyright © H. D. P. Lee, 1955, 1974. Reprinted by permission of Penguin Books Ltd.

Katha Pollitt, "Canon to the Right of Me . . . , from *The Nation,* September 23, 1991. Copyright © The Nation Company, L. P. "It Takes Two: A Modest Proposal for Holding Fathers Equally Accountable," from the *Boston Globe,* January 27, 1995. Also appeared as "Subject to Debate" column in *The Nation,* January 30, 1995. Copyright © The Nation Company, L. P. Both essays reprinted with permission from *The Nation* Magazine.

Timothy M. Quill, "Death and Dignity: A Case of Individualized Decision Making," from *The New England Journal of Medicine,* vol. 324, 1991, pp. 691–694. Copyright © 1991 by Massachusetts Medical Society. Reprinted by permission of *The New England Journal of Medicine.*

Anna Quindlen, "A Pyrrhic Victory," from the *New York Times,* January 8, 1994. Copyright © 1994 by the New York Times Company. Reprinted by permission.

James Rachels, "Active and Passive Euthanasia," from *The New England Journal of Medicine,* vol. 292, 1975, pp. 78–80. Copyright © 1975 by Massachusetts Medical Society. Reprinted by permission of *The New England Journal of Medicine.*

Janet Radcliffe Richards, "Thinking Straight and Dying Well," from *Newsletter of the Volunteer Euthanasia Society of Scotland,* September 1994. Reprinted by permission.

Carl R. Rogers, "Communication: Its Blocking and Its Facilitation." Reprinted by permission of Carl R. Rogers.

Bertrand Russell, excerpt from *Why I Am Not a Christian,* by Bertrand Russell. Copyright © 1957, 1985 by Allen & Unwin. Reprinted by permission of Simon & Schuster, Inc., and Allen & Unwin 1985.

Kurt Schmoke, "A War for the Surgeon General, Not the Attorney General," from *New Perspectives.* Reprinted by permission of the author.

Stanley S. Scott, "Smokers Get a Raw Deal," from the *New York Times,* December 29, 1984. Copyright © 1984 by the New York Times Company. Reprinted by permission.

Jay Alan Sekulow, "Student-Led Prayers Should Be Permitted," from *Congressional Quarterly Researcher,* February 18, 1994. Reprinted by permission.

Steven R. Shapiro, "Student-Led Prayers Should Not Be Permitted," from *Congressional Quarterly Researcher,* February 18, 1994. Reprinted by permission.

Max Shulman, "Love Is a Fallacy." Copyright © 1951, renewed 1979 by Max Shulman. Reprinted by permission of Harold Matson Co., Inc.

Peter Singer, "Animal Liberation," from the *New York Review of Books,* April 5, 1973. Reprinted by permission of the author.

Thomas B. Stoddard, "Gay Marriages: Make Them Legal," from the *New York Times,* March 4, 1989. Copyright © 1989 by the New York Times Company. Reprinted by permission.

Cathi Tactaquin, "What Rights for the Undocumented?," from *NACLA Report on the Americas,* vol. 26:1, pp. 25–28. Copyright © 1992 by the North American Congress on Latin America, 475 Riverside Dr., #454, New York, NY 10115–0122.

Ronald Takaki, "An Educated and Culturally Literate Person Must Study America's Multicultural Reality," from the *Chronicle of Higher Education,* March 8, 1989. Reprinted by permission of the author. "The Harmful Myth of Asian Superiority," from the *New York Times,* June 16, 1990. Copyright © 1990 by the New York Times Company. Reprinted by permission.

Randall Terry, "The Abortion Clinic Shootings: Why?," from the *Boston Globe*, January 9, 1995. Randall Terry is the Founder of Operation Rescue and the host of *Randall Terry Live*. Reprinted by permission of the author.

Sallie Tisdale, "Save a Life, Kill a Tree?," from the *New York Times*, October 26, 1991. Copyright © 1991 by the New York Times Company. Reprinted by permission.

Michael Tooley, "Our Current Drug Legislation: Grounds for Reconsideration," from *Newsletter of the Center for Values and Social Policy*, vol. 8, no. 1, Spring 1994.

Ron K. Unz, "Value Added," from *National Review*, November 7, 1994. Copyright © 1994 by *National Review*, Inc., 150 East 35th Street, New York, NY 10016. Reprinted by permission.

Ernest van den Haag, "Affirmative Action and Campus Racism," from *Academic Questions*, vol. 2, issue 3, copyright © 1989. Reprinted by permission of Transaction Publishers. All rights reserved. "The Deterrent Effect of the Death Penalty," from *The Death Penalty Pro and Con: A Debate* by Ernest van den Haag and John Conrad, Plennum Press, 1983. Reprinted by permission of Plennum Press and the author.

Vita Wallace, "Give Children the Vote," from *The Nation*, October 14, 1991. Copyright © The Nation Company, L.P. Reprinted with permission from *The Nation* magazine.

George Will, "Family Intrusion," copyright © 1994, Washington Post Writers Group. Reprinted with permission.

Ellen Willis, "Putting Women Back into the Abortion Debate," from *No More Nice Girls*. Copyright © 1992 by Ellen Willis, Wesleyan University Press. Reprinted by permission of University Press of New England.

James Q. Wilson, "Against the Legalization of Drugs," from *Commentary*, February 1990. Reprinted by permission; all rights reserved. "Just Take Away Their Guns," from the *New York Times*, March 20, 1994. Copyright © 1994 by the New York Times Company. Reprinted by permission.

Mitsuye Yamada, "To the Lady," from *Camp Notes and Other Poems*. Copyright © 1992 by Mitsuye Yamada. Reprinted by permission of the author and of Kitchen Table: Women of Color Press, Box 40-4920, Brooklyn, NY 11240–4920.

Index of Authors and Titles

Index of Terms